The
Radio 5 Live
Sports Yearbook
1995

Published in Great Britain by Oddball Publishing Ltd, 38 Lincoln Street, Brighton, East Sussex BN2 2UH

Cover design by Rob Kelland
Cover pictures by Allsport
Text design and layout by Oddball Publishing Ltd, Brighton
using QuarkXpress on Apple Mac computers
Repro by Image Setting, Brighton
Printed and bound in Great Britain by Redwood Books, Trowbridge, Wilts

A catalogue record for this book is available from the British Library

ISBN 0-9524044-0-0

Foreword

It was always going to be a crowded, dramatic sporting year, but no-one could have predicted the rollercoaster ride of laughter and tears, tragedy and triumph, disgrace and acclaim that was 1994.

Reflect for just a few moments and the memories come flooding back. Here are some of them:

- The death of the seemingly indestructible Ayrton Senna

- Roberto Baggio's World Cup Final penalty miss

- That incredible putt from Nick Price to set up his Open Championship victory

- The Mike Atherton ball tampering incident and Brian Lara's record-breaking year

- The peerless form of Sally Gunnell, Linford Christie and Colin Jackson week after week and the Diane Modahl affair which threatened to eclipse all their triumphs

- Martina Navratilova plucking a few blades of grass from the Centre Court as she left for the last time

The Radio 5 Live Sports team brought you all those moments and was there at every major event as the year unfolded and that's why we are delighted to be associated with the Yearbook

Thumbing through the pages will invoke memories of an amazing year for players, fans and commentators alike

Enjoy the experience.

Mike Lewis
Deputy Controller, 5 Live

Introduction

Welcome to the Radio 5 Live Sports Yearbook, the second edition of our Yearbook. We've kept to virtually the same format as last year, concentrating on covering as much statistical ground as possible, while lightening the load with lots of perky quotes (and you don't get much perkier than Graham Taylor's selection) and elegant prose (which may accidentally have slipped in). In a book like this, accuracy is everything and we've tried to be as accurate as possible. If you find an error and it's only a minor one (like a Chinese name back to front) please keep it to yourself. If it's a whopper (like Lara scoring 502), we would like to know. But don't shout at us. Sit us down quietly and tell us over a pint, 'cos we'll be just as upset as you are. In fact, even more so.

The list of thanks this year must begin with **Penny Dain, Andy Edwards, Betty Maitland, Pat Molineux, Chris Sainty, Brian Smith, David Smith, Iain Smith, Anna Wallace and Hugh Wallace** without whom the book wouldn't have got off the ground. We are delighted that this years edition should be associated with **BBC Radio 5 Live** as they are, quite comfortably, the best sports broadcasters in the business. Yes, I know we would say that anyway, but we mean it too, all right?

The federations have responded, generally with alacrity, to our many and various demands. Some have been almost devotional. Nicola at the IYRU faxed us 16 pages of priceless results when we gave her a last minute call; Amy at the US PGA Tour reckoned there was no information in the office they could supply because we had everything.

The Guardian, as well as being a delight to read, was the source for much material and the *Daily Telegraph* , because of its extensive coverage, was always useful for reference. Our only minor gripe is that they can't get a final edition to Brighton, so many match reports from the World Cup, for example, didn't appear at all. *L'Équipe* was as definitive as ever and we cannot praise it too highly. Thanks also to **Autosport, Baseball Briefing, Cycling Weekly, Raceform, Regatta, The Cricketer, The Polo Advertiser, Calude Abrahams at Boxing News, The Press Association, Ron Cox, Vic Batchelder, Mark Popham** and everyone else who helped us sort out the innumerable problems that occur with a book like this.

Finally, we must thank the correspondents who supplied the copy, **Katy Thompson** and **Rosa Weekes** who typed in the mountainous volume of results, **Michael Butcher**, who ran a final eye over the text, **Stuart Duff,** who scoured the copy for factual errors and was responsible for the office investments, usually on an animal that *started* the race lame. And to my assistant editor, **David Luckes**, who brought sanity to the whole enterprise.

Peter Nichols

Contents

Abbreviations

Times
Where a time is shown, the hours minutes and seconds are separated by a colon. A full point is used only as a decimal point for parts of a second. eg 3 hours 23 minutes and 7.5 seconds is shown as 3:23:7.5

Records
WR	World Record
ER	European Record
NR	National Record
BR	British Record
CR	Championship Record
J	Junior

Countries

ALB	Albania	ETH	Ethiopia	PER	Peru
ALG	Algeria	FIJ	Fiji	PHI	Philippines
ANG	Anguilla	FIN	Finland	POL	Poland
ANO	Angola	FRA	France	POR	Portugal
ANT	Antigua	GAB	Gabon	PRK	North Korea
ARG	Argentina	GAM	The Gambia	PUR	Puerto Rico
ARM	Armenia	GBR	Great Britain and N Ireland	QUT	Qatar
AUS	Australia	GEO	Georgia	ROM	Romania
AUT	Austria	GER	Germany	RSA	South Africa
AZE	Azerbaijan	GHA	Ghana	RUS	Russia
BAH	Bahamas	GRE	Greece	RWA	Rwanda
BAR	Barbados	GRN	Grenada	SAU	Saudi Arabia
BEL	Belgium	GUA	Guatemala	SCO	Scotland
BER	Bermuda	GUY	Guyana	SEN	Senegal
BHR	Bahrain	HKG	Hong Kong	SEY	Seychelles
BLS	Belarus	HOL	Holland	SIN	Singapore
BOS	Bosnia-Herzegovina	HON	Honduras	SLE	Sierra Leone
BRA	Brazil	HUN	Hungary	SLO	Slovenia
BUL	Bulgaria	INA	Indonesia	SOM	Somalia
BUR	Burundi	IND	India	SRI	Sri Lanka
CAN	Canada	IRL	Ireland	STL	St Lucia
CAY	Cayman Islands	IRN	Iran	SUD	Sudan
CGO	Congo	IRQ	Iraq	SUI	Switzerland
CHI	Chile	ISL	Iceland	SUR	Surinam
CHN	People's Republic of China	ISR	Israel	SWE	Sweden
CIV	Ivory Coast	ISV	US Virgin Islands	SYR	Syria
CMR	Cameroon	ITA	Italy	TAN	Tanzania
COL	Colombia	JAM	Jamaica	TCH	The Czech Republic
CRC	Costa Rica	JOR	Jordan	THA	Thailand
CRO	Croatia	JPN	Japan	TJK	Tadjikistan
CUB	Cuba	KZK	Kazakhstan	TKM	Turkmenistan
CYP	Cyprus	KEN	Kenya	TPE	Taiwan (Chinese Taipeh)
DEN	Denmark	KGZ	Kyrgyzstan	TRI	Trinidad & Tobago
DJI	Djibouti	KOR	Korea	TUN	Tunisia
DMN	Dominica	KUW	Kuwait	TUR	Turkey
DOM	Dominican Republic	KZK	Kazakhstan	UAE	United Arab Emirates
ECU	Equador	LAT	Latvia	UGA	Uganda
EGY	Egypt	LES	Lesotho	UKR	Ukraine
ENG	England	LIE	Liechenstein	URU	Uruguay
ESA	El Salvador	LTU	Lithuania	USA	United States
ESP	Spain	LUX	Luxembourg	UZB	Uzbekistan
EST	Estonia	MAD	Madagascar	VEN	Venezuela
		MAL	Malaysia	WAL	Wales
		MAR	Morocco	WSA	Western Samoa
		MEX	Mexico	YUG	Yugoslavia
		MLD	Moldova	ZAM	Zambia
		MOZ	Mozambique	ZIM	Zimbabwe
		MRI	Mauritius		
		MYA	Myanmar		
		NAM	Namibia		
		NAU	Nauru		
		NCA	Nicaragua		
		NGR	Nigeria		
		NGU	Papua New Guinea		
		NIR	Northern Ireland		
		NOR	Norway		
		NZL	New Zealand		
		OMA	Oman		
		PAK	Pakistan		
		PAN	Panama		
		PAR	Paraguay		

The Year in Brief

OCTOBER

1   A week after being awarded the Olympic Games of 2000, 80,000 people jam the streets of Sydney for a ticker-tape parade.

2   In the early hours at Cardiff, Lennox Lewis stops Frank Bruno in round seven to retain his WBC heavyweight title.

3   Nicola Fairbrother wins the world lightweight judo title in Hamilton, Canada. French trained Urban Sea wins the Prix de l'Arc de Triomphe.

6   Manchester United announce an end-of-year profit of £4.2m.
    Michael Jordan announces his retirement from basketball.

7   Liam Brady resigns after two years as Celtic manager.

9   Nigel Benn and Chris Eubank fight a draw for the WBC and WBO world super-middleweight titles in front of 42,000 fans at Old Trafford.

10 Zambia, the team which lost 18 players and officials in an air crash six months earlier, lose out to Morocco 1-0 and fail to qualify for the World Cup finals.
    Miami Dophins quarterback Dan Marino tears an achilles tendon and misses almost the entire NFL season.

12 Diego Maradona recalled to the Argentinian World Cup squad.

13 England are beaten 2-0 by Holland in Rotterdam and effectively eliminated from the World Cup, Wales beat Cyprus and keep hopes alive.
    Günther Parche, convicted of stabbing Monica Seles, receives a two year suspended sentence.

16 Great Britain beat New Zealand 17-0 at Wembley in the 1st Rugby League Test.

19 Norwich City beat Bayern Munich 2-1 in Germany in the UEFA Cup, 2nd round.

20 Manchester United draw 3-3 at home to Turkish champions Galatasaray in the European Cup and the club's share price drops 7.5%.

23 Steve Robinson beats Colin McMillan to retain his WBO featherweight title.
    Toronto Blue Jays win baseball's World Series 4-2 against the Philadelphia Phillies, thus retaining the title they won last year.

24 American Corey Pavin beats Nick Faldo in the final of the World Matchplay.
    Ayrton Senna punches Ulsterman Eddie Irvine following an incident-packed Japanese Grand Prix, won by Senna.

30 Michael Bentt, born in East Dulwich, beats Tommy Morrison to win the WBO heavyweight title
    Manchester United finish the month nine points clear in the Premier League.
    Great Britain rugby league team beats New Zealand 29-12 in the 2nd Test.
    Jonathan Callard is severely gashed playing for Redruth against the All-Black touring team. Callard's injury, across the eyelid, requires 15 stitches.

31 Nigel Mansell joins the line-up of a touring car race at Donington and crashes.
    Chinese women take the first four places in the World Marathon Cup, but break no records. Richard Nerurkar, of Britain, wins the men's race.

NOVEMBER

2 Ireland's Vintage Crop, ridden by Mick Kinane, wins the Melbourne Cup, the richest horse race in the southern hemisphere, with almost £600,000 prize money.

3 Eric Cantona is sent off as Manchester United draw 0-0 at home to Galatasaray and are eliminated from the European Cup.

6 Great Britain beat New Zealand in the 3rd rugby league Test, to complete a 3-0 series victory against the tourists.
British horses fail in all seven races on Breeders' Cup day in Santa Anita.
Evander Holyfield defeats Riddick Bowe for the WBA and IBF world heavyweight titles. James Miller parachutes into the ring in the seventh round.

7 Colin Montgomerie wins the Volvo Masters to take his 1993 European earnings to £613,682, placing him ahead of Nick Faldo.

11 Wales' rugby union team are defeated 26-24 by Canada in Cardiff.

13 David Gower announces his retirement from cricket. In 117 tests, Gower scored 8,231 runs at an average of 44.25 including 18 centuries.

14 United States win golf's World Cup in Florida.
Uta Pippig and Andres Espinosa triumph in the New York Marathon.

17 Welsh supporter John Hill is killed when a distress rocket is fired into the crowd at the Wales-Romania World Cup match.
San Marino score after nine seconds of the World Cup qualifier against England. England go on to win 7-1 but fail to reach the finals as Holland beat Poland.
All the home nations are eliminated, but Jack Charlton's Republic of Ireland team book their place with a 1-1 draw in Belfast.

18 Libel action brought by Pakistan fast bowler Sarfraz Nawaz against England's Allan Lamb ends when lawyers reach a deal following evidence from umpire Don Oslear that ball-tampering had occurred.

20 New Zealand's rugby union tourists beat Scotland 51-15 at Murrayfield.
Aintree tests its new starting procedures in the John Parrett Memorial Chase.

23 Graham Taylor resigns. During his three year and two month spell, Taylor selected 59 different players for his England teams.

24 Gary Mabbutt suffers a depressed fracture of the cheekbone following an onfield clash with Wimbledon's John Fashanu.

25 Damon Hill survives a high speed crash during a test session at Estoril in Portugal.

27 England beat New Zealand 15-9, for only their fourth victory against the All Blacks since 1905. Fullback Jonathan Callard kicks four penalties on his international debut.
Manchester United beat Coventry 1-0 and go 14 points clear in the title chase.
Ronnie O'Sullivan, at 17, becomes the youngest ever winner of a ranking tournament when he beats Stephen Hendry 10-6 to take the UK Championship.
Cogent wins the Hennessy Gold Cup for trainer Andrew Turnell.

28 At the Central American and Caribbean Games in Puerto Rico, 34 members of the Cuban team defect.

29 Peter Swales resigns as chairman of Manchester City after receiving death threats.

DECEMBER

3 Karen Pickering becomes Britain's first female World Champion by winning the 200m freestyle title at the World Short Course Championships at Palma, Majorca.

4 Nick Gillingham earns Britain's second gold at Palma when the 26 year old takes the 200m title.

Gareth Chilcott, the Bath and England prop, retires to pursue a career in the theatre.

5 At the World Short Course Championships, Mark Foster wins the 50m freestyle, taking Britain's gold tally to three.

Nick Price wins the Sun City Challenge by 12 strokes and pockets a cool $1 million. Price's earnings for 1993 reach a record $2.78m.

8 Internazionale defeat Norwich City 1-0, knocking Mike Walker's team out of the UEFA Cup.

9 Danny Blanchflower dies, aged 67. Blanchflower, who led Tottenham to the Double in 1961, was the most cultured footballer of his age.

11 Seven members of the England A team touring South Africa are struck down by gastro-enteritis. The start of play against Transvaal is delayed for almost three hours as only four members of the England team are fit to take the field.

12 Linford Christie wins the BBC Sports Personality of the Year award. The England rugby union squad win the team award and the overseas winner is Greg Norman.

14 Roberto Duran fights his 100th professional fight. Duran won his first world title, at lightweight, in 1972 and won further titles at welterweight and middleweight.

15 Brighton & Hove Albion FC, close to bankruptcy, appoint Liam Brady as manager.

18 John Crawley hits 286 for England A against Eastern Province, the highest score by an Englishman in a representative match abroad for 27 years.

19 Ireland drawn in Group E, with Italy, Mexico and Norway, for World Cup Finals.

20 Odds against Terry Venables becoming the next England manager drop to 5-2 with bookmakers William Hill.

21 'Dickie' Bird becomes the first umpire appointed to the new international panel.

23 Boris Becker claims drug taking is 'rife' in men's tennis.

27 Barton Bank, partnered by Adrian Maguire, wins the King George VI Chase at Kempton Park.

30 Gavin Hastings, captain of the British Lions touring team, receives an OBE in the Honours list. Footballer Gary Mabbutt and rugby union player Peter Winterbottom earn MBEs.

Nigeria join Wales and England in the hunt for the services of Terry Venables.

31 Manchester United end the year 16 points clear at the head of the FA Carling Premiership.

Miguel Induráin, who completed the Tour de France/Giro double, is named as the best world athlete of the year in a survey by *Gazzetta dello Sport*, the Italian sports newspaper. Krisztina Egerszegi, the Hungarian swimmer, tops the women's list.

JANUARY

2   Paul Gascoigne cracks a rib playing for Lazio against Sampdoria.

3   Grant Fox, the most prolific points scorer in NZ rugby union history, retires.

5   Brian Johnston, who commentated on cricket for BBC TV and radio for 48 years, dies from a heart attack in his 82nd year.
    Racing is called off at Worcester, where the river Severn floods the entire course.

6   South Africa beat Australia by five runs at Sydney in the 1st Test of the series.
    American skater Nancy Kerrigan is struck on the knee after leaving the ice at Cobo Hall, Detroit following practice for the US Figure Skating Championships.

7   Mike Walker joins Everton as manager amidst complaints of 'poaching' from Norwich chairman Robert Chase.
    Monica Seles confirms she will not start in the Australian Open.

8   Torvill and Dean take the British title at Sheffield with a full set of nine 6.0s for the Free Dance. It is their first appearance in the 'amateur' ranks since 1984.

10   Herbie Hide and Michael Bentt come to blows at a Kensington press conference to publicise their WBO heayweight title fight.

13   Tonya Harding is implicated in the attack on Nancy Kerrigan when three suspects are arrested, including her former husband and her bodyguard.
    The Sports Council is heavily criticised in a National Audit Office report.

15   The British Athletic Federation promises an inquiry into the affairs of Andy Norman after its promotions officer is implicated in the suicide of journalist Cliff Temple.
    Francesco Moser fails in an attempt to beat Chris Boardman's one-hour record.
    England's cricketers leave for the tour of the West Indies.
    The Five Nations Championship begins with wins for Wales against Scotland, 29-6, and France, over Ireland, 35-15.

19   A football international between England and Germany in Hamburg is cancelled. Officials are concerned that the date of the game, April 20th, was Hitler's birthday.

20   Sir Matt Busby, who led Manchester United to two FA Cup wins, five league titles and a European Cup triumph, dies aged 84.

21   Torvill and Dean win the European Ice Dance title by the narrowest of margins.

23   England all-rounder Chris Lewis shaves his head, leaves his hat off and gets sunstroke during the opening match of the West Indies tour.

28   Terry Venables is formally announced as the new England national coach.
    Graeme Souness tenders his resignation as manager of Liverpool.

29   Ulrike Maier, the former Super G world champion, dies after crashing against a timing post on the slopes of Garmisch-Partenkirchen.

30   The International Cycle Union bans the unconventional bike of Graeme Obree.
    Manchester United's defeat of Norwich in the FA Cup 5th round leads bookmakers to shorten their odds against the Treble to 5-1.
    Pete Sampras and Steffi Graf win the Australian Open titles.

31   Dallas Cowboys retain the Superbowl title with a 30-13 victory over Buffalo Bills. It is the Bills 4th successive defeat in the Superbowl.

FEBRUARY

1   Peter Radford, Olympic 100m bronze medallist in the 1960 Games and former world record holder at 200m, takes over as executive chairman of British Athletics.
     Terry Yorath threatens to sue the Welsh FA over his dismissal as manager of the national team.

2   Manchester, having lost the race for the 2000 Olympics, gain some consolation by winning the English nomination to host the 2002 Commonwealth Games.

5   Liverpool draw at Norwich in Roy Evans' first game as manager.
     Chris Eubank retains his WBO super-middleweight title by beating Graciano Rocchigiani in Berlin.
     England scrape home against Scotland 15-14, and Wales defeat Ireland 17-15 in the second weekend of the Five Nations Championship.

8   Kapil Dev becomes the leading wicket taker in Test history when he captures the wicket of Sri Lanka's Hashan Tillekeratne. Kapil's 432nd dismissal overtakes the previous record of Sir Richard Hadlee.

9   Bolton Wanderers knock holders Arsenal out of the FA Cup.

10   Liz McColgan withdraws from the NutraSweet London Marathon.

12   Lillehammer Winter Olympics opens.
     Colin Jackson, in Glasgow, equals the 60m hurdles indoor world record of 7.35 secs.

13   Tonya Harding is cleared by the US Olympic Committee to compete in Lillehammer.

16   England win the first one day international in Bridgetown, Barbados by 61 runs.

17   Birmingham City ordered to pay Southend £130,000 for poaching manager Barry Fry.

18   Don Howe, Dave Sexton and Bryan Robson join Venables' new England set-up.

19   Ireland defeat England 13-12 and Wales enjoy a 24-15 victory over France in the Five Nations Championship.

20   Norwegian speed-skater Johan Olav Koss becomes the most successful competitor at the Winter Games with 10,000m gold, having already won the 1500m and 5000m.

21   The Olympic ambition of Torvill and Dean falls short as they finish with a bronze medal in the Ice Dance competition.

22   Short track speed-skater Nicky Gooch is disqualified from the silver medal position in the Olympic 1000m event.

24   British Horseracing Board cancel all-weather hurdle races after the death of War Beat at Lingfield Park. It is the 13th death of a horse on a synthetic track in two months.
     West Indies win the 1st Test against England at Kingston, Jamaica by eight wickets.

25   Nancy Kerrigan takes silver in the Olympic Figure Skating behind Ukrainian Oksana Baiul. Harding finishes 8th.

26   Nicky Gooch wins a bronze in the Olympic 500m short track event.
     West Indies win the 2nd one-day match against England by 3 wickets.
     Nigel Benn beats Henry Wharton to retain his WBC super-middleweight title, whilst the WBA champion, Michael Nunn, surprisingly succumbs to Steve Little.

28   Geoff Cooke, who steered the England rugby union team to two grand slams, a World Cup final and 33 wins from 47 matches announces his retirement.

MARCH

1 National Hunt champion jockey, Richard Dunwoody, is banned for 14 days, ruling him out of the Cheltenham festival.
   Linford Christie breaks the European 60m indoor record when he clocks 6.48s.

2 England lose the third one-day international against the West Indies, at St Vincent, by 165 runs, leaving the West Indies 2-1 up.

5 Chelsea complete the double over Manchester United, inflicting the first defeat on the League leaders since they beat them 35 games and six months earlier.
   England defeat France 18-14 in Paris to set up a Five Nations Championship decider with Wales at Twickenham, while Scotland and Ireland draw 6-6 at Murrayfield.
   West Indies win the third one-day international to go 3-1 up in the five-match series.

6 Colin Jackson, at Sindelfingen, runs 7.30s to break the world 60m hurdles record
   England win the final one-day international against the West Indies.
   United Arab Emirates win the ICC cricket trophy for non-Test playing countries.

7 David Platt named as England captain against Denmark at Wembley, Venables' first match as coach.

9 Ray Illingworth becomes the chairman of selectors, to succeed Ted Dexter, after winning against M J K Smith, in a ballot of TCCB members.
   Platt scores to give England a 1-0 win against Denmark and 71,970 fans turn out.

13 Colin Jackson takes the European indoor title at 60m hurdles to add to the 60m flat crown the Welshman won a day earlier.

15 Flakey Dove wins the Champion Hurdle for Tom Price's modest Leominster stable.

16 John Toshack resigns as manager of Wales, just 34 days after accepting the job.
   Frank Bruno stops American Jesse Ferguson in 2min 22secs of his comeback fight.

17 Tonya Harding is given three years probation, fined $100,000 and ordered to perform 500 hours community service after admitting the charge of hindering the investigation into the assault on Nancy Kerrigan.
   French trained The Fellow wins the Cheltenham Gold Cup at the fourth attempt.

18 Jack Rowell is confirmed as the new manager of the England rugby union team.

19 Brian Lara scores 167 in the 2nd Test, a taste of things to come.
   England beat Wales 15-8, but Wales still take the Championship.
   Herbie Hide is a surprise winner of the WBO heavyweight title. His opponent, Michael Bentt, collapses in his dressing room and is rushed to hospital.

22 England lose by an innings in the 2nd Test against the West Indies.
   Mark Foster breaks the World 50m butterfly record at Sheffield's Speedo World Cup.

24 Frank Dick resigns as British Athletics director of coaching following cut-backs.

26 Cambridge cruise to a six and a half length victory in the 140th Boat Race.

27 Aston Villa win the Coca Cola Cup 3-1, so ending Manchester United's Treble hopes.

28 Graham Taylor, former England manager, takes over the reins at Wolves.

30 England score 46 in their 2nd innings, the 14th lowest Test score in history and the second lowest for England, and lose the third Test.
   Rugby union signs a £27m three-year deal with the BBC for coverage of the sport.

APRIL

1   Wendy Toms is to be the first female official in the Football League's history. The League announces Toms will be a lines(wo)man in the forthcoming season.
ENZA, a 92-foot catamaran, completes the fastest circumnavigation of the world under sail, 74 days, to win the Jules Verne Trophy.

2   Blackburn beat Manchester United 2-0 and reawaken their title hopes.

6   The England versus Germany international, having moved from Hamburg to Berlin, is called off for the second time because of fears of extremist violence.

7   Paul Gascoigne's career is threatened when he suffers a double fracture of his right leg when playing in a five-a-side training game for his club Lazio.

8   Following a British Athletics' inquiry, promotions officer Andy Norman is sacked.
Chinese athletes withdraw from NutraSweet London Marathon.

9   Miinnehoma, owned by comedian Freddie Starr, wins the Grand National. The race starts without incident.
Chelsea beat Luton 2-0 to reach the FA Cup final for the first time in 24 years.

10   José Maria Olazábal wins the US Masters, the sixth European golfer in seven years to don the Green Jacket.

11   Wade Dooley, England's most capped lock forward with 55 internationals, retires.

13   England enjoy a 208-run victory over the West Indies in the 4th Test. Alec Stewart becomes only the eighth Englishman to score a century in both innings of a Test.
Manchester United beat Oldham 4-1 in a replay and ensure their 12th FA Cup Final.

15   John Curry, the 1976 Olympic Figure Skating champion, dies aged 44.

17   Germany's Katrin Dörre wins her third successive London Marathon. Dionisio Ceron from Mexico, wins the men's race.
AC Milan take their third straight Serie A title when drawing 2-2 with Udinese.

18   Brian Lara breaks the world record for a Test innings when he scores 375 in the first innings of the 5th Test against England at St John's, Antigua. Sir Gary Sobers, whose 1958 record of 365 he breaks, is one of the first on the pitch to congratulate him.

19   Scott Gibbs, the British Lion and Welsh centre, joins St Helens rugby league club.

22   Michael Moorer beats Evander Holyfield in Las Vegas to win the WBA & IBF titles.

24   England's women lift the Rugby World Cup in Scotland, beating the US in the final.

24   Jeremy Bates becomes the first British male in 17 years to win an ATP tournament when he wins the Korean Open.

27   Wimbledon announce a 12.5% increase in prize money taking the total on offer for the 1994 Championships to £5,682,000.
Graeme Obree regains the world one hour record from rival Chris Boardman. Obree achieves 52.270km on the Bordeaux track.

28   Boxer Bradley Stone dies, two days after Richie Wenton knocks him out in a fight

29   Eleven days after his Test record, Lara scores 147 on his debut for Warwickshire.
Rubens Barrichello survives a 160mph crash during qualifying for the San Marino Grand Prix.

30   Austrian Roland Ratzenberger is killed in a crash during qualifying at San Marino.

MAY

1   Ayrton Senna becomes the second grand prix driver to die in successive days when the three-time world champion crashes into a concrete barrier during lap seven of the San Marino race at Imola

Wigan make it five successive League and Cup doubles when they defeat Leeds by 26-16 in the Challenge Cup at Wembley.

2   Manchester United retain the League title after nearest challengers Blackburn lose 2-1 at Coventry

Stephen Hendry wins his third successive world snooker title at the Crucible in Sheffield. Jimmy White is runner-up for the fifth time in a row.

Jump jockey Declan Murphy is seriously injured following a fall at Haydock Park, but comes off the danger list after four days in hospital.

3   Arsenal defeat Parma 1-0 in Copenhagen to land the European Cup Winners' Cup.

6   Forty years after Roger Bannister broke the four-minute mile, the worlds greatest milers, from Sydney Wooderson to Noureddine Morceli congregate in London.

Flat race jockey Steve Wood dies after a fall at Lingfield Park.

7   Lennox Lewis retains his WBC world title when the referee stops his fight against Phil Jackson in round eight to prevent the challenger taking further punishment.

Bath claim the Pilkington Cup, the club's 13th rugby union trophy in ten years.

8   Imran Khan's admission that he "occasionally scratched" the ball reopens the ball-tampering arguments. .

10   MPs vote to allow betting on Sundays.

11   Allan Border, the highest run-getter in Test history, retires. The Australian captain left the stage after 156 Tests and 11,174 runs at an average of 50.56.

12   Terry Venables' company Edennote is wound up in the High Court.

Racing driver Karl Wendlinger is injured after crashing during practice at Monaco.

14   Manchester United become only the fourth club this century to complete the League and FA Cup double this century when they beat Chelsea 4-0 at Wembley.

Barcelona clinch their fourth consecutive league title when their nearest challengers Deportivo La Coruña miss an 89th minute penalty in their game against Valencia.

15   As a tribute to Ayrton Senna, the front row of the grid at the Monaco Grand Prix is left empty. The race that Senna won six times is won by Michael Schumacher.

Imran Khan resigns from the cricket committee of the International Cricket Council.

16   Jennifer Capriati is arrested in Florida after drugs are found in her hotel room.

17   England, a team that didn't qualify for the World Cup, comprehensively outplay Greece, a team that did, 5-0 at Wembley.

18   In the first match of the South African tour and Jack Rowell's first as manager, England are unexpectedly beaten by Orange Free State 22-11.

David Broome retires after 35 years as an international show jumper.

AC Milan trounce Barcelona 4-0 in the European Cup final at Athens.

A section of the Millwall crowd invades the pitch at the New Den during the First Division play-off semi-final against Derby.

19   Monica Seles threatens to sue the German Tennis Federation £6.8m for losses
     incurred by the stabbing at Hamburg a year ago.
21   Chris Eubank narrowly defeats Ulsterman Ray Close for his 14th successful defence
     of his WBO super-middleweight world title.
22   England draw 0-0 with Norway at Wembley.
23   Chris Eubank signs up with Sky Television for an eight-fights-in-12-months deal
     which is said to guarantee the boxer over £10m. Promoter Barry Hearn pledges there
     will be no "patsies".
25   Valderrama is named as the host course for the 1997 Ryder Cup. Valderrama
     succeeds despite allegations from Seve Ballesteros of "bribery".
29   Nigel Mansell crashes in the Indianapolis 500 but escapes unhurt.
     Ireland beat Germany 2-0 in Hannover in a World Cup warm-up match.
30   Leicester City, after near misses in the past two seasons, finally earn a place in the
     Premier League when they defeat Derby 2-1 in the play-off final at Wembley.
     Ruud Gullit walks out on the Dutch World Cup squad.

JUNE

1   Willie Carson secures his fourth Derby success as Erhaab defeats the largest field, 25,
    for 16 years. Outsider Foyer falls and jocky Willie Ryan breaks three ribs.
2   Steffi Graf is overwhelmed by Mary Pierce in the semi-final of the French Open. It is
    the first time in her last 20 tournaments that Graf has failed to reach a final.
3   Brian Lara, having failed to equal the world record for six straight first-class
    centuries, nevertheless creates a new landmark with seven out of his last eight when
    he reaches 101 not out against Durham. His overnight score stands at 111 not out.
4   Graham Gooch scores 216 as England pile up the runs in the first Test against New
    Zealand at Trent Bridge.
    England's rugby union team come good at last on their South African tour, winning
    the first Test 32-15.
    Balachine, trained in Dubai, wins the Epsom Oaks.
5   Sergei Bruguera and Arantxa Sanchez-Vicario complete a Spanish double at the
    French Open.
    Haile Gebresilasie, an Ethiopian policeman, breaks Said Aouita's world 5000m
    record in Hengelo, Holland. Gebresilasie clocks 12:56.96.
6   England win the first Test against New Zealand by an innings and 90 runs.
    More than 7000 fans turn up at Dublin Airport to wave off the Irish World Cup team.
    Brian Lara scores 501 runs for Warwickshire against Durham, breaking Hanif
    Mohammed's record 499 for the highest first-class innings. Lara hit his runs off 427
    balls in 474 minutes. It takes Lara's county average to 235.20.
7   Tim Rodber becomes only the second Englishman to be dismissed while playing for
    his country when he is sent off against Eastern Province.
8   Bobby Charlton is knighted in the Queen's Birthday Honours list.

JUNE (CONTINUED)

8 Paul Elliott, the former Chelsea footballer, loses his High Court case against Dean Saunders. According to Mr Justice Drake, Elliott failed to prove that the Welshman was guilty of dangerous or reckless play.

11 South African balance the rugby union Test series 1-1, with a 27-9 win over England.

12 Eugeni Berzin is a surprise winner of the Giro d'Italia, temporarily breaking the stranglehold over the sport of the Spaniard Miguel Induráin, who finishes third.

14 Tottenham Hotspur are fined £600,000, banned from the FA Cup for a year and to have 12 points deducted from their next Premiership campaign, after being found guilty by the Football Association of making irregular payments to players.

16 James Florey, a 21-year-old student from Bracknell runs onto the course and into the path of the filly Papago in the Ribblesdale Stakes at Ascot. Remarkably, neither Papago nor Florey are seriously hurt.
Celtic FC sack Lou Macari after eight months as the club's manager.

17 World Cup, USA94, begins.

18 Ireland, in their opening game of USA94, defeat Italy 1-0, Ray Houghton the scorer.
Mary Pierce pulls out of Wimbledon, citing "reasons beyond my control".

19 Ernie Els, of South Africa, takes the US Open golf title after a play-off.

20 England draw the second Test against NZ. Dion Nash takes 11 wickets in the match.

21 Steffi Graf loses in the first round at Wimbledon.

23 Brian Lara continues his run rout scoring 197 in the Britannic Assurance championship game against Northants.

24 Mexico upset Ireland, winning 2-1 in Orlando. It leaves the Irish team needing a win against Norway to be sure of qualifying for the knock-out stage of the tournament.

25 Jack Charlton is banned from the touchline for Ireland's match against Norway because of "abuse of officials" during the first two Ireland games.
Jeremy Bates wins through to the last 16 at Wimbledon for the second time in his career. It is the fifth time in eight years he has been the best Briton at Wimbledon.

26 The filly Balanchine adds the Irish Derby to her Oaks triumph.

27 Germany win both the men's and women's European Cup athletic competitions, but second places from both the British teams at Birmingham ensure a double presence in the World Cup at Crystal Palace in September.
Western Samoa stifle the Welsh rugby union revival when they win 34-9.
For the second time in three years, Guy Forget ends the dream of Jeremy Bates of a quarter-final place at Wimbledon. The Frenchman wins 2-6, 6-1, 6-3, 6-1

28 After weeks of rumours, Williams Renault announce that Nigel Mansell will be joining the line-up for the French Grand Prix at Magny Cours on July 4th.

29 The Republic of Ireland squeeze through to the next stage of the World Cup by drawing 0-0 with Norway.

30 Diego Maradona, who was banned for 15 months in 1991 for cocaine use, tests positive for the drug Ephedrine in a random drugs test at the World Cup and is withdrawn from the competition

JULY

2   Martina Navratilova is denied a tenth singles Wimbledon title at her last time of asking. The 37-year-old is beaten 6-4, 3-6, 6-3 by the Spaniard Conchita Martínez.
Andrés Escobar, the Columbian defender whose own-goal cost his team a place in the next round of the World Cup, is gunned down in a car park in Medellín.
Chris Boardman convincingly wins the opening Prologue of the Tour de France in Lille and becomes the first Briton in 32 years to wear the Maillot Jaune of race leader.
Richard Johnson, Middlesex fast-medium bowler takes 10-45 against Derbyshire, the first bowler in the championship to take ten wickets in an innings since 1964.

3   Pete Sampras, hitting his first serve at an average 116mph, wins the Wimbledon title for the second succesive year. Sampras beats Goran Ivanisevic 7-6, 7-6, 6-0.
Michael Schumacher wins his sixth grand prix of the season, at Magny Cours, while Nigel Mansell is forced to retire.
Steve Redgrave and Mathew Pinsent win the Silver Goblets at Henley. It is the 13th Henley title for triple Olympic champion Redgrave.
Lew Hoad, Wimbledon singles champion in 1956 and 1957, dies in Spain aged 59.

4   Ireland's hopes disappear as they lose 2-0 to Holland in the World Cup. Holland's second goal slips through the fingers of goalkeeper Packie Bonner.

5   Chris Boardman loses the overall lead, just two days before the Tour reaches Britain.
The third Test against New Zealand ends in a draw, but England take the series 1-0.

6   The Tour de France arrives in Britain for two days. Tens of thousands turn out to watch the Dover-Brighton stage in which Boardman finishes fourth.
Leroy Burrell breaks the world 100m record of his Santa Monica clubmate Carl Lewis at the Lausanne GP, clocking 9.85 seconds.

8   Sean Yates becomes the second Englishman in a week to wear the Yellow Jersey of overall leader in the Tour de France.

9   Warwickshire win their first trophy of the summer when they defeat Worcester by 6 wickets in the Benson & Hedges Cup. There is plenty more to come.

10 Damon Hill wins the British Grand Prix at Silverstone, the one major trophy that eluded his father, Graham.
Germany, the defending champions, are knocked out of the World Cup by Bulgaria.

11 Miguel Induráin moves into the overall lead of the Tour de France and is never again headed in the race.

13 Italy win 2-1 against Bulgaria and Brazil beat Sweden 1-0 to qualify for the World Cup final.
Chris Boardman retires from the Tour de France on the 11th stage.
Michael Schumacher is summoned before the FIA over incidents at the British GP.

17 Brazil defeat Italy 3-2 on penalties after a disappointing World Cup final ends in a full time score of 0-0.
Nick Price takes his second major when he wins the Open Championship at Turnberry. Price, who won the USA PGA title two years ago, finishes one shot clear of Sweden's Jesper Parnevik.

17 Mark Petchey loses the fifth rubber and the British tennis team are defeated by Romania, 3-2. The defeat relegates Britain to Group Two of the Euro African zone, the lowest status they have known in the 94-year history of the Davis Cup.

21 South Africa's cricketers return to Lords for a Test match for the first time in 21 years. Captain Kepler Wessels rises to the occasion with a century.

22 William Sigei breaks the world 10,000m record at Oslo. Sigei clocks a time of 26:52.23 to become the third Kenyan in 13 months to break the 10,000m record.

23 Mike Atherton is captured on television apparently applying dirt to the ball during the first Test. Atherton is fined £2,000 by chairman of selectors Ray Illingworth; £1000 for lying to the match referee, Peter Burge, the second £1000 for having dirt in his pocket.

24 Miguel Induráin takes his fourth successive Tour de France title.
    England lose the Test against South Africa by 356 runs. In the second innings they score just 99 runs.
    Kevin Schwantz wins the British Motor Cycle Grand Prix at Donington Park.

26 Michael Schumacher is banned for two races and docked six points for failing to observe a 'black flag' penalty at the British Grand Prix.

28 Lester Piggott, in his 59th year, suffers head injuries following a fall at Goodwood.

29 Tottenham Hotspur sign Jürgen Klinsmann from Monaco for £2m.

31 Benetton driver Jos Verstappen survives a pit lane inferno during the Hockenheim Grand Prix. The team subsequently admit removing a refuelling valve.
    USA beat Australia 21-7 in the men's Lacrosse World Cup final.
    Great Britain's all-women team claim victory in the World Games Three-Day Event Championship at The Hague.

AUGUST

1 England's rugby union coach Dick Best is sacked. New manager Jack Rowell is to take overall responsibility for the coaching of the national side.
   Britain and Ireland draw with the USA 9-9 in golf's Curtis Cup at Tennessee. The women's team retain the amateur trophy that they won two years ago at Hoylake.

7 Solomon Wariso tests positive for the drug ephedrine and is sent home from the European Athletic Championships.

8 Linford Christie and Steve Backley, in the 100m and javelin respectively, retain their European titles in the Helsinki Championships.
   England draw the 2nd Test against South Africa at Headingley. Graeme Hick confirms his return to form with a 2nd innings 110.

9 Warwickshire beat Kent and Worcestershire beat Surrey in the NatWest Trophy semi-finals to set up a repeat of the Benson & Hedges final.

11 Du'aine Ladejo wins the European 400m title, relegating the two-time winner Roger Black to second place.
    Although almost 40% of American major league baseball players earn more than $1m a season, they decide to go on strike.

AUGUST (CONTINUED)

11	Erhaab, the Hamdan Al Maktoum owned, John Dunlop trained winner of the Epsom Derby, is retired after damaging a suspensory ligament. Baseball players in the US go on strike.
12	The Football League season starts. The Premiership gets under way a week later. Sally Gunnell and Colin Jackson win golds at the European Athletics Champs.
13	Brian Lara comes back to earth as, playing in a championships match against Notts he is dismissed twice in one day (the second time for a duck) and his season's average drops below 100 for the first time.
14	Mike Gatting is recalled to the England squad for the third Test against South Africa. Manchester United beat Blackburn 2-0 to win the Charity Shield. Nick Price, the Zimbabwe golfer, adds the US PGA title to his Open golf crown.
15	Graeme Obree is disqualified at the World Cycling Championships in Sicily and prevented from defending his 4000m pursuit title when the organisers introduce a last-minute ruling on riding positions. Tony Jacklin takes his first senior golf event when he wins the American Seniors Classic at Grand Rapids, Michigan just five weeks after his 50th birthday.
16	The TCCB land the largest deal in cricket's history, signing a TV contract with the BBC and BSkyB worth £60m over four years. British Athletics completes its deal with ITV for £3m over two years, plus an option for two more years. Chris Boardman captures the world 4000m pursuit title in Sicily.
17	Linford Christie confirms his status as the world's number one sprinter by winning the 100m at the Zürich Grand Prix meeting.
18	The Commonwealth Games begin in Victoria, Canada.
19	Mike Atherton is fined £1,250 for dissent in the Third Test. Peter Burge, the match referee, imposes the fine after Atherton reacts to being given out lbw. The England captain holds up his bat and points to it to indicate that he had touched the ball.
20	Devon Malcolm takes 9-57 at The Oval, the finest bowling return for England since Jim Laker's 19-wicket match haul in 1956.
21	England win the last Test to level the series against South Africa 1-1. Michael Doohan takes the world 500cc crown after victory at the Czech GP at Brno.
23	British officials at the Commonwealth Games admit that an English athlete has tested positive for drugs. Shot-putter Paul Edwards is presumed to be the offender.
24	Diego Maradona receives a 15-month ban for failing a World Cup drugs test.
25	British Athletics officials announce five drug positives. They are Diane Modahl, the 800m runner, Paul Edwards, and three unnamed athletes from the British League.
27	Martyn Moxon scores 274* against Worcester, a post-war record for Yorkshire.
28	Schumacher is stripped of Belgian GP victory after the Benetton car is found to infringe the technical regulations.
29	Ellery Hanley is appointed coach of the Great Britain rugby league team.
30	Nigel Mansell confirms that he will return to F1 for the last three races of the season
31	Liverpool pay £3.75m, a club record, for Coventry defender Phil Babb.

SEPTEMBER

1   The FA Cup is sponsored for the first time in its history. Pools company Littlewoods pay £20m over four years for the privilege.

2   Warwickshire beat Hampshire by an innings and 95 runs to claim their fourth county championship and the first since 1972.
    The England touring party to Australia is named. It is: Atherton, Stewart, Hick, Thorpe, Gooch, Crawley, Gatting, Rhodes, DeFreitas, Benjamin, Malcolm, Udal, McCague, Tufnell, Gough and White.

3   Billy Wright, of Wolves and England, dies. Wright, who played at centre-half, won 105 caps, captaining his country on 90 occasions.
    Noureddine Morceli and Jackie Joyner-Kersee win the overall Grand Prix athletics titles in Paris.

4   Worcestershire thwart Warwickshire's bid for the grand slam of cricket titles when they defeat the county champions in the NatWest final by 8 wickets.

6   The French Cycling Federation decide not to punish Miguel Induráin for taking the banned Salbutamol. Induráin had taken the drug for his asthma.

7   In European Championship qualifiers, Scotland beat Finland 2-0, Wales beat Albania 2-0, Ireland beat Latvia 3-0 and Northern Ireland lose 2-1 to Portugal.
    England beat the USA 2-0, in a friendly at Wembley.

8   After 42 years, the Epsom Derby is switched back to a Saturday for 1995.
    John Carr hits 261 not out for Middlesex and moves ahead of Lara in the averages.

10 Arantxa Sanchez-Vicario upsets favourite Steffi Graf to take the US Open title.
    Outsider Moonax wins the St Leger, the last classic of the season, at 40-1.

11 In the athletics World Cup at Crystal Palace, Europe win the women's competition, Africa the men's. The British men and women finish 2nd and 5th respectively.
    Andre Agassi, starting the competition unseeded, triumphs in the US Open
    Violence erupts at Birmingham's NEC as supporters of boxers Robert McCracken and Steve Foster clash.

13 Blackburn Rovers are embarrassed on their first ever excursion into European football, beaten at home 1-0 by Swedish club Trelleborgs in the UEFA Cup.

14 Manchester United enjoy a European Cup 4-2 victory over Gothenburg.
    Baseball's World Series is cancelled after 34 days of the players' strike.

18 Steven Redgrave and Matthew Pinsent retain their coxless pairs title at the World Championships in Indianapolis
    Warwickshire win the AXA Equity & Law League to complete a treble of titles.

19 Damon Hill's place in the Williams Renault team for the 1995 season is confirmed.

20 Will Carling is reappointed captain of England for the forthcomoing season.

21 Gary Lineker announces his retirement.

23 Scott Quinell signs for Wigan rugby league team at a fee purported to be £500,000.

25 Lennox Lewis loses his world heavyweight title as the referee stops the fight against Oliver McCall after 31 seconds of the second round.

28 Manchester United draw 0-0 at Galatasaray and qualify for the Champions League.

Lara's Theme

The statistics of a remarkable year

Brian Lara experienced a golden 50 days this summer. Not since the Bradman era have the record books been so comprehensively rewritten. The left-handed Trinidadian also provided the catalyst for Warwickshire's unique domestic treble, enriching the county scene with his sumptuous timing. Whilst his effort in the field (or lack of it) attracted criticism, it merely served to remind us that he wasn't quite perfect. Not quite.

WORLD TEST RECORD

B C Lara 375 West Indies v England Apr 16-18 Antigua

How he scored his runs

	1s	2s	3s	4s	Total
Fraser	18	7	1	11	79
Caddick	19	5	6	9	83
Tufnell	29	6	1	6	68
Lewis	21	9	2	15	105
Hick	12	6	0	4	40
Total	**99**	**33**	**10**	**45**	**375**

Progress

50:	154 mins	121 balls	7 fours
100:	232 mins	180 balls	16 fours
150:	327 mins	240 balls	22 fours
200:	440 mins	311 balls	27 fours
250:	515 mins	377 balls	32 fours
300:	610 mins	432 balls	38 fours
350:	721 mins	511 balls	42 fours
369:	748 mins	530 balls	44 fours *(record broken)*
375:	766 mins	538 balls	45 fours

HIGHEST TEST SCORES

375	12h 46m	B C Lara (24 yrs)	WI v Eng	1993-94
365*	10h 14m	G S Sobers (21)	WI v Pak	1957-58
364	13h 17m	L Hutton (22)	Eng v Aus	1938
337	16h 10m	Hanif Mo'med (23)	Pak v WI	1957-58
336*	5h 18m	W R Hammond (29)	Eng v NZ	1932-33
334	6h 23m	D G Bradman (21)	Aus v Eng	1930
333	10h 27m	G A Gooch (37)	Eng v Ind	1990
325	10h 0m	A Sandham (39)	Eng v WI	1929-30
311	12h 42m	R B Simpson (28)	Aus v Eng	1964
310*	8h 52m	J H Edrich (28)	Eng v NZ	1965
307	12h 7m	R M Cowper (25)	Aus v Eng	1965-66
304	7h 10m	D G Bradman (25)	Aus v Eng	1934
302	10h 12m	L G Rowe (25)	WI v Eng	1973-74

Other holders of the World Test Record

165	Charles Bannerman	Aus v Eng	1877
211	Billy Murdoch	Eng v Aus	1884
287	Reginald Foster	Eng v Aus	1903

Lara was involved in 3 century stands - 179 with J C Adams, 183 with K L T Arthurton and 219 with S Chanderpaul. Only Hanif Mohammed has bettered this, during his innings of 337 - 152 with Imtiaz Ahmed, 112 with Alimuddin, 154 with Saeed Ahmed and 121 with Wazir Mohammed.

FIRST CLASS RECORD

B C Lara 501 Warwicks v Durham June 3-6 Edgbaston

Lara's Milestones

111	Resumes at Friday's total of 210-2. Seventh hundred in eight innings.
148	Highest of his six championship centuries.
248	Highest score against Durham beating C C Lewis' 247 for Notts last year.
278	Highest score by a Warwickshire batsman beating Roger Twose's 277* v Glamorgan this season.
285	His 174 in a season beats Reg Santell's county best of 173 before lunch v Northants 1933.
300	First player to score triple century at Edgbaston.
306	Beats Frank Foster's Warwickshire record of 305* v Worcestershire at Dudley, 1911.
323	Highest score by a West Indian in England beating Viv Richard's 322 for Somerset v Warwicks in 1985.
325	Equals Don Bradman's feat of 1,000 runs in 7 innings in 1938
376	Highest score by a West Indies batsman beating his own 375 v England in April.
406	Beats Graeme Hick's 405* for Worcs v Somerset in 1988 - the highest in England this century.
425	Passes Archie McLaren's English record of 424 for Lancs v Somerset 1895.
453	Becomes second highest scorer in history surpassing Don Bradman's 452 for New South Wales v Queensland in 1930.
457	Fall of Charlie McCartney's 1921 world record of 345 in a day (Australia v Notts).
494	Surpasses the world record of 68 boundaries in an innings by Percy Perrin for Essex v Derbyshire at Chelmsford in 1904.
501*	Sets world record for the highest individual first class score beating Hanif Mohammed's 499 for Karachi v Bahawalpur in 1958-59.

Progress

			4s	6s
100:	144 mins	138 balls	14	0
150:	201 mins	193 balls	22	0
200:	224 mins	220 balls	30	2
250:	246 mins	245 balls	37	5
300:	280 mins	278 balls	44	7
350:	319 mins	311 balls	49	8
400:	367 mins	350 balls	53	8
450:	430 mins	398 balls	55	9
501:	474 mins	427 balls	62	10

Cup of Plenty

Jimmy Armfield reflects on USA '94, a competition to savour

I have to admit that I boarded the trans-Atlantic flight from Manchester in June as a sceptic. However, five weeks later I returned home fully convinced that the World Cup and indeed football itself was back on course. USA '94 was a total success. Despite the heat, the new directives to referees, the distances between venues and the absence of British teams, the tournament was a total contrast to Italia '90. Though four years ago, Bobby Robson's England did us proud, I left with an empty feeling, particularly after the dreadful final provided by Germany and Argentina. Not so this time, the organising committee in the States and the game's governing body, FIFA, did their homework and living up to the spectacle USA '94 provided will be something of a problem for France, the 1998 hosts.

FIFA's insistence that yellow and red cards should be used to cut out dissent, tackling from behind and time-wasting worked wonders. There was hardly a nasty moment in the entire tournament. Two uses of the elbow, ironically by players from the finalists Brazil and Italy, got just desserts. FIFA was not going to stand for any cynicism. The tough guys of the previous finals gave way to the technically better prepared and, despite the heat, every team looked remarkably fit. With no prima donnas on the pitch, dissent at a minimum and the arrival of the Africans onto the world stage, the crowds poured into the stadia.

It was a soccer carnival, though the games were never publicised in the manner that the American sports pages would for their own football, baseball or basketball. Even for the opening ceremony, with President Clinton present, the World Cup did not grab the headlines. There was more interest in the O J Simpson case and Houston's first success in the National Basketball League. Nevertheless, soccer did make its presence felt, especially when TEAM USA were playing.

The American team did its nation proud, winning through to the second stage from a difficult group that included Switzerland, Romania and Columbia, one of the pre-tournament favourites. The defeat of the Columbians by the USA resulted in the early exit of the South Americans, which later cost the life of defender Andrés Escobar, who was murdered when he returned home. Diego Maradona was withdrawn from the tournament when he tested positive for drugs, but the two incidents, one tragic the other merely sad, could not halt the freewheeling success of the tournament.

From start to finish, the interest did not wane. We expected the respective communities to get behind the likes of Mexico, Italy and Ireland. We knew, too, that Brazil would have a following, it always does in World Cup football. But it was the 60,000 plus gates that watched Morocco and Saudi Arabia in New York, Spain and South Korea in Dallas, that left us wondering if any other country could have matched the interest shown. I doubt it. The attendance figures were staggering. Maybe the Americans will yet learn that soccer, played in the right spirit, can be as exciting as any of their major sports. Make no mistake, though, the USA isn't ready yet for any takeover, although we constantly reminded them that soccer is the only real WORLD game.

Yet, whatever the sport, the Americans have a stadium to cater for it. Take Dallas; the World Cup games there were played in the Cotton Bowl, a 70,000 seater usually used for American football. Yet, also in the city are three other stadia. One plays host to the Dallas Cowboys, the Super Bowl champions, another the city's ice-hockey team, while the Texas Rangers baseball team plays at the third. Apparently, all three venues are more modern and better equipped than the Cotton Bowl. Even great stadia, however, don't guarantee good football. That is still in the hands, or the feet, of the players and the coaches. And this time they didn't let us down. Despite soaring temperatures and a schedule that meant they often had to travel through time zones for successive matches, they still provided more skill and excitement than we ought to expect with so much at stake.

I will never forget the magnificent games between Argentina and Romania, Holland and Brazil. Five goals in each, no boring defensive ploys, and the fans riveted. Even this ex-pro who has played in two World Cups and watched three others live, was left feeling that the game's future was in safe hands. Admittedly, the final was a bit of a let-down, but that was, in part, due to a comparison with what had gone before. Also, the Italians were handed the short straw.

Following a semi-final victory in Los Angeles, the Brazilians had only to travel an hour to the team hotel to await the final in the same Rose Bowl stadium three days later. The Italians, on the other hand, had to up sticks in New York, fly six hours to California, passing through two time zones. After a long arduous tournament, this was unfair, the organiser's one mistake. Surely, the final should have been played in one of the central zone venues; Chicago, Detroit or even Dallas.

I know the effect of air travel. I had 12 internal flights chasing the games and will never forget the weekend of July 9th and 10th. At the time, I was based in Los Angeles, but had to fly to Dallas - a 3 hours 40 minutes flight - for the quarter final between Brazil and Holland. When the game ended there was a dash to the airport for a 5pm flight to San Francisco. We arrived in time to find a delay for bad weather.

Eventually, we left Dallas at 11pm and reached Oakland at 3.30 in the morning. We hired a taxi - with a driver who had obviously taken driving lessons from Fred Flintstone - and reached our hotel across the bay at 4.15am, got into bed, and were awoken at 7.30am for the next day's game at Stanford stadium. When that game ended, Alan Green somehow got us to San Francisco airport (Damon Hill wouldn't have made it) and we boarded the 5pm shuttle with five minutes to spare, even though it took all three of us to carry Ron Jones' luggage. I slept well that night when we finally arrived back in our hotel in Santa Monica, even though the old adrenalin was still running.

Looking back now, I still recall it as a wonderful adventure. It was tiring, but I somehow never felt tired, the football saw to that. We did get in the odd trip and I vividly recall going to the Kennedy Museum in Dallas, Universal Studios and Disneyland in Los Angeles, and a return to Fifth Avenue and Central Park in New York. But the everlasting memory will be of the games.

I brought home two T-shirts and splashed across the front was a message clearly written by the soccer lovers within the States.

It says: "Soccer is life........the rest is just details" That sums it up.

Martina Moves On

Christine Janes pays tribute to a rare champion

Martina Navratilova was 16 years old when I lost to her on Court One in the first round of her first Wimbledon in 1973. It was toward the end of my playing career and my last Wimbledon and I always remember discussing the draw prior to the championships. It was at Queens Club with Virginia Wade among others and I was told about my opponent, a very promising Czech girl with an unpronounceable name. I was about to find out just how promising that Czech girl would be.

I was soundly beaten by her. The young prodigy had a powerful attacking game and I felt as though I was being swamped by her superior speed and ability. It seemed there was no weakness to exploit, especially on Wimbledon's fast grass. In fact, she did not win Wimbledon that year, but it was obvious even then that the world lay at her feet.

Her world turned out to be not quite so straightforward. At 18, Martina decided her only real chance of success was to defect from Czechoslovakia, then firmly under communist rule. She chose to move to the USA, where she would be free to compete and play tennis when and where she wanted. To leave her family behind at 18 must have been a daunting experience. Something that most 18 year olds would never have to contemplate; for tennis or otherwise. I have always admired her for that, for coping and succeeding during what must have been such a tough time. Fortune favours the brave, though, and Martina was justly rewarded by becoming the world's number one and the richest woman in professional sport.

Yet the natural talent that she had in abundance was, on its own, not enough. Before success came, Martina had to work hard on her fitness. She spent hours in the gym; she changed her diet to help keep her weight in check; and subdued a temperament which could be erratic, and threatened to mar her game. Martina left no stone unturned. She was totally dedicated and her reward was to become the best in the world - and the best female player that most of us have seen. During her peak, she was almost too good for the rest of the field. Only Chris Evert Lloyd was a match and between them was a fierce, but friendly, rivalry which set the standard for the women's game to follow.

This year, Martina announced her retirement at the age of 37. She wanted to have one last Wimbledon. Already the holder of nine Wimbledon singles titles, she very nearly made the ending a fairytale one. The crowds followed her progress to the final with overwhelming enthusiasm. In that emotionally charged atmosphere, it was all credit to Conchita Martínez, who produced her best form in her first Wimbledon final to win the title. No-one who saw the match will forget the occasion. Martina must have struggled with her emotions that day, we all did. Afterwards, perhaps still smiling slightly ruefully, she bent down and pulled out a few blades of grass from the Centre Court - a keepsake for one of Wimbledon's finest champions.

In 21 years, the little girl with the unpronounceable name had come a long way.

Le Tour En Angleterre

Simon Brotherton on two days when England embraced the Tour

Le Tour en Angleterre didn't start well for me. I awoke at the hotel in a panic thinking there were only five minutes to get ready for the early morning taxi to the start. It was only as I stood alone on the deserted street outside that I realised the trusty travel clock was still showing French time. It was a quarter to six in the morning and not quarter to seven and I sheepishly returned to the hotel. Thankfully, the day got better.

The response to the Tour in England was remarkable. We drove along the route half an hour ahead of the riders and the atmosphere was of an extended village fete, with bunting, banners and flags strewn across the verges and hedgerows. Everybody had brought out the picnics; smiling facesas they raised the second (or more) glass of the day. Kids loved it. Whether it was because it got them out of school (most likely) or they were the new generation of cycling devotees (less likely), their enthusiasm knew no bounds.

The Tour itself takes only a few seconds to pass, but the whole entourage of 1500 vehicles means the event is with you for over an hour. It helps to get people in the mood. Quite what a van with giant dancing vehicles has to do with the world's biggest cycling race is another matter. Still, it was popular as, I suspect, was the lorry promoting safe sex, from which free condoms were dispensed. The lorry hired by the chocolate company was a less successful enterprise. It ran into early trouble as the weather (very French for the day) was hot enough to melt all their products.

As the peloton drew near to Brighton, we travelled on roads where I had trained as a fourteen-year-old; where I was Sean Kelly or Stephen Roche on the twisting clumb of Ditchling. The reality now intruded on the old dream, but it was not the Kelly or Roche of my imagination, but the real Boardman and Yates we were trailing.

Boardman rose to the occasion. As the peloton swung into Elm Grove to climb Racehill for the first time, the Wirral rider was working his way towards the front. On the second circuit, to the delight of a crowd jostling for space on the hill, a crowd that had travelled from all over England for England's first glimpse of the Tour for over 20 years, Boardman forced himself out of the pack and into a clear fourth place. The timing was perfect, the Gan rider cheered up the hill to the echo. He could improve no further, though, and the stage went to the Spaniard, Francisco Cabello. A day later, Boardman suffered a reaction from his efforts and had an unhappy ride on the Portsmouth stage won with a spectacular sprint by Nicola Minali.

Yeet it was not Boardman's efforts, nor Canbello's lone victory, nor Minali's stunning sprint that was the highlight of the Tour en Angleterre. It was the sight of Sean Yates, soon himself to wear the Maillott Jaune for a day, as he approached his home village of Forest Row on the Dover-Brighton stage. There, prearranged with the other riders in the peloton, he stopped to greet his family, waiting in a lay-by, halfway up the hill into Ashdown Forest. The Tour may be a largely commercial exercise, but at moments like these, we can believe a little bit of romance still lingers.

Ten Years After

Eleanor Oldroyd catches up with Torvill and Dean

When I was told I was to be BBC Radio's Torvill and Dean correspondent at the Winter Olympics, my reaction was scornful. "Ice Dancing? It's a girly sport! You only want me to do it because I'm a girly! Anyway, it's not a sport at all, is it?" But my road to Lillehammer was to be a road to Damascus.

It all started over a cold weekend in Sheffield. I'd gone to watch Torvill and Dean begin their comeback on the ground floor; the British Ice Dance Championships. The couple who'd achieved perfection in Sarajevo ten years previously now had to go through the mill of qualifying against the best of the rest of British ice dancers. Of course, there was no competition. As Simon Barnes of *The Times* wrote, it was like watching a bunch of schoolkids who'd turned up for the French essay writing contest only to discover that Marcel Proust had also entered.

With a few exceptions, most of my fellow journalists were, like me, total novices when it came to covering ice dancing. Most of those who'd done it before hadn't done it since 1984. But we all knew as soon as they took to the ice, that Torvill and Dean were a different class. Maybe we didn't go quite as wild about 'Let's Face The Music And Dance' as we did about their sizzling rumba routine, but the judges had no doubt - straight sixes all the way. It was all so easy. Yet it was all going to become so complicated.

Off we trooped to Copenhagen for the European Championships. Slush surrounded the Brondby Hallen and the competition began to hot up. Enter Oksana Gritschuk, Yevgeny Platov, Maia Usova and Alexandr Zhulin. We learnt that Usova was married to Zhulin, but Zhulin had recently had an affair with Gritschuk (or was it Platov?). Jayne and Chris, despite a marriage apiece and an impending second in Chris' case, were still being asked the inevitable questions about their personal relationship. The slush was creeping inside the Bronby Hallen; but in truth,as you watched them melting the ice in the rumba, it was hard to believe that this amazing chemistry was produced by a purely professional relationship.

Competition began and we sat through interminable versions of the paso doble and the blues, the prescribed compulsory dances. Here came the first indication that not everybody was swept away by the euphoria for the Great Comeback. The Swiss judge gave them a 5.2 for the paso doble. The British media contingent were appalled. Jayne just shrugged and said they'd skated as well as they could.

So they were second after the Compulsories. Again came the rumba. Again it was electrifying and doubts were dispelled. It was all down to the free dance. Slight changes had been made since Sheffield. It still looked immensely slick and technically brilliant, but it still didn't quite bring the crowd to its feet. Gritschuk and Platov, skating last, did. By then, though, all seemed lost. Usova and Zhulin were already ahead of Torvill and Dean and the 5.9s and 6.0s of Gritschuk and Platov meant they had won the free dance. But it didn't mean they'd won the gold. In that instant a bunch of rookie ice dancing reporters had to become instant statistical geniuses.

Torvill and Dean were champions, but how? John Hennessy of *The Times* and Sandra Stevenson of *The Daily Telegraph* knew, so we all flocked round them. Eventually we had it clear in our minds: well, clearish. It was down to the order the judges placed each pair. Before G & P skated, U & Z placed first because more judges placed them first than T & D. But after G & P skated, the majority of judges had placed G & P first in the free dance. The gold medal then depended on which of T & D or U & Z came second in the section. To work that out, you had to count up the number of second places or better. T & D had six of those, U & Z had five - and that was enough to give T & D the title.

By the time I'd explained it on air to five local radio stations before eight the following morning, I thought I just about understood it. We hoped things wouldn't be so close in Lillehammer. As it happened, they weren't. But there were plenty of other controversies.

The narrow margin of victory in Copenhagen convinced Jayne and Chris that wholesale changes needed to be made to the free dance. The frustrating thing was that up until then they had strictly followed the directives of the International Skating Union. The ISU had indicated that they wanted to bring ice dance away from gimmickry and "back to the ballroom". Jayne and Chris had given them just that, but maybe the judges hadn't been listening. After all, they had gone wild for the showbizzy Gritschuk and Platov. Fine, said Chris, they want gimmicks, we can do gimmicks.

They had less than a month to reshape their Olympic challenge. When we watched the first practice at the Hamar rink, a frisson of uncertainty swept through the media corps. We'd got used to Torvill and Dean being perfect, here the edges were frayed. New jumps and lifts looked raw and the rhythm stuttered. Had they tried to change too much, too late?

On the night, as 23 million BBC viewers would testify, they looked as slick as ever. But it wasn't good enough for the judges. They marked them below Gritschuk and Platov and below Usova and Zhulin as well this time. An illegal lift at the end of the routine had cost them marks, the ISU explained. Ten years after the perfection of Bolero, Torvill and Dean had to make do with Olympic bronze. Back home, the papers were appalled: "GOLD ROBBERY!" screamed the headlines.

For many of us who had folowed them around, though, it wasn't much of a surprise. When I spoke to Chris and Jayne afterwards, they didn't seem totally surprised either. There was also a sense of relief in the camp. It had been an adventure, but they were glad it was all over. The audience had been their judges, they said, and as far as the audience was concerned they had won gold.

A few days later, Torvill and Dean skated in the exhibition; the chance for all of the medal winners to perform their party pieces. What else could they do but 'Bolero'? A group of Swedes in the crowd held up nine cards with '6.0' written on them. They were perfect still in the eyes of the fans. So should they have come back? Well, no doubt they added a few extra ticket sales to their 'Face The Music' tour, which followed immediately afterwards. More to the point, they gave an awful lot of entertainment to an awful lot of people, including me. I'm still not convinced about ice dancing's claims to be sport; it depends to much on the subjective views of nine people. But I thoroughly enjoyed my two months as BBC Radio Sport's showbiz and soap opera correspondent.

Lists

NEW YEAR HONOURS
United Kingdom recipients only listed

DBE: Gladys Marea Hartman, athletics
CBE: Lt Col John Robin Stephenson, cricket; Ernest William Swanton, cricket writer;
OBE: Andrew Gavin Hastings, rugby union; Nathaniel Lofthouse, football; Dr Robert James Price, disabled sport; Karen Smithies, cricket
MBE: Derek Atkins, tennis; Harry Henry Thomas Brind, cricket; Kenny Colaine, disabled sport; Richard Dillingham, community sport; Graham Reginald Garner, disabled sport; Gary Vincent Mabbutt, football; Peter James Winterbottom, rugby union

QUEEN'S BIRTHDAY HONOURS

Knights Bachelor: Robert Charlton, football; Timothy Miles Bindon Rice, music and sport
CBE: Trevor Edward Bailey, cricket
OBE: Ian Robert Emmerson, cycling; Richard Gwynne Robinson, CCPR; Garry Edward Schofield, rugby league; Susan Slocombe, hockey
MBE: Nicola Kim Fairbrother, judo; Gerald Anthony William Hicks, community sport; Thomas Alfred Benjamin Mahoney, rugby union; Alistair McCoist, football; Barry (Finbar Patrick) McGuigan, boxing; Karen Denis Pickering, swimming; William Prosser, rugby union; Albert Leslie Quick, swimming; John Regis, athletics; Jack Sokell, cricket; John Ronald Thomas, bowls; Adrian Stewart Tulloch, youth football; Francis Michael Turner, cricket

WILLIAM HILL'S TOP 10 EVENTS FOR BETTING TURNOVER
Excludes horse racing - as a comparison the Grand National turnover was £14m

1	Football World Cup	£17.0m
2	FA Cup	£10.0m
3	British Open golf	£1.5m
4	Wimbledon tennis	£1.25m
5	Five Nations rugby	£1.0m
6	World Snooker Champ'ship	£1.0m
7	Ryder Cup golf	£900,000
8	England v South Africa - cricket series	£800,000
9	US Masters golf	£750,000
10	US Open golf	£600,000

BBC SPORTS PERSONALITY OF THE YEAR AWARDS 1993

Winner: **Linford Christie**
International Award: **Greg Norman**
Team Award: **England rugby union team**

TELEVISION SPORTS RATINGS
From Oct 1 1993-Oct 1 1994

1 **Winter Olympics** *Feb 21* BBC1 23.95m*
Torvill & Dean
2 **Big Fight Live** *Oct 9* ITV 16.35m
Nigel Benn v Chris Eubank
3 **World Cup Football** *Oct 13* ITV 14.07m
Holland v England
4 **World Cup Grandstand** *July 17* BBC1 13.40m
Brazil v Italy (WC Final)
5 **Big Fight Live** *Feb 5* ITV 12.34m
Chris Eubank v Graciano Rocchigiani
6 **Eubank/Benn/Enemies** *Oct 9* ITV 11.79m
Big Fight Preview
7 **FA Cup Final** *May 14* BBC1 11.76m
Chelsea v Manchester United
8 **Big Fight Live** *May 21* ITV 11.55m
Chris Eubank v Ray Close
9 **World Cup '94** *June 18* ITV 11.23m
Ireland v Italy
10 **World Cup Grandstand** *July 4* BBC1 11.01m
Ireland v Holland
11 **Sportsnight Special** *Nov 17* BBC1 10.72m
England v San Marino/Wales v Romania
12 **European Match** *May 4* ITV 10.70m
Arsenal v Palma (Euro Cup Winners Final)
13 **World Cup Grandstand** *July 13* BBC1 10.66m
Italy v Bulgaria (Semi-final)
14 **World Cup Grandstand** *June 28* BBC1 10.54m
Ireland v Norway
15 **The Match** *Mar 2* ITV 10.31m
Man Utd v Sheff Wed (Coca Cola Cup S/F)
16 **The Match** *Mar 27* ITV 10.13m
Aston Villa v Man United (Coca Cola Cup Final)
17 **World Cup '94** *July 4* ITV 10.10m
Ireland v Holland
18 **Winter Olympics** *Feb 25* BBC2 10.02m**
Women's Free Skating (Kerrigan & Harding)

*The highest ever viewing figure for a single-channel showing of a sports programme.
*** The audience for the Harding & Kerrigan skate-off in the highest rating for **any** BBC2 programme .*

THE LONG AND THE SHORT OF BRITISH SPORT
The following is for top-level performers only

Tallest Men: Alan Bannister (basketball) 7ft 5in (2.26m)
Richard Metcalfe (rugby u) 7ft 3in (2.21m)
Smallest Man: Gary Bardwell (jockey) 4ft 6in (1.37m)
Heaviest Men: Paul Edwards* (athletics) 293lbs (133kg)
Elvis Gordon (judo) 291lbs (132kg)
Amarjit Singh (wrestling) 286lbs (130kg)
Tallest Woman: Chris Castle (basketball) 6ft 2in (1.88m)
Shortest Woman: Annika Reeder (gym) 4ft 4.5in (1.33m)
At just 63lbs (28.6kg), Reeder is surely the lightest as well
Heaviest Woman: Myrtle Augee (Athl) 211lbs (96kg)
*Tested positive for drugs and could be banned

BRITAIN'S TOP EARNING SPORTSMEN IN 1994

1 (2) **Nigel Mansell**   Motor Racing   £9.0m
A very profitable year for Mansell, who collected £5m for a year with Newman-Haas and in the region of £2m for his F1 outings

2 (1) **Lennox Lewis**   Boxing   £5.2m
Although Lewis lost his title, he did his bank balance no harm. Around £3m from the Oliver McCall fight and more than £1.5m from Jackson

3 (9) **Chris Eubank**   Boxing   £3.4m
Decent earners from fights against Amaral and Rocchigiani; around £2.1m already in from the Sky deal. No endorsements

4 (3) **Nick Faldo**   Golf   £2.4m
With endorsement contracts tied to success in the game, Faldo's earnings have fallen somewhat this year. Pringle of Scotland lead the endorsements

5 (4) **David Platt**   Football   £2.2m
No transfer for Platt means a drop. But add to a salary of not much less than a million, bonuses for winning the Italian cup & deals with Mizuno and Serraro you get a decent living

6 (5) **Paul Gascoigne**   Football   £1.5m
Gascoigne's broken leg has hit the pocket hard

6 (9) **Gary Lineker**   Football   £1.5m
One of only three British footballers to top the £1m, Lineker's contract with Grampus, which makes up the bulk of his income, finishs in November 1994

8 (11)**Stephen Hendry**   Snooker   £1.4m
Hendry has pocketed over £400,000 on table earnings and has a very healthy sponsorship deal with Sweater Shop (when he retained the world title they presented him with a vintage Bentley)

8 (-) **Colin Montgomerie** Golf   £1.4m
Almost a million in on-course earnings over the period, plus Pringle of Scotland and others

10 (8) **Nigel Benn**   Boxing   £1.2m
Just two fights, Wharton and Gimenez

10 (12)**Ian Woosnam**   Golf   £1.2m
A revival in Woosnam's fortunes with a Tour victory and a new Hippo clothing deal

11 (7) **Linford Christie**   Athletics   £1.1m
Over £400,000 from racing and deals with Lucozade, Puma, High & Mighty, Toyota and the Banana Group

12 (17)**Pat Eddery**   Horse Racing   £1.0m
Eddery's contract with Khaled Abdulluh is worth around two-thirds of a million, but ends this year. With retainers now out of fashion Eddery looks likely to slip off the list next year

Note: Because of our deadlines, these figures are estimated for a year that runs November - November

BEST-SELLING SPORTS BOOKS
Oct 1, 1993 to Oct 1, 1994
All editions are paperback, except where stated

1 **Fever Pitch**   £4.99
by Nick Hornby (Gollancz)

2 **My Favourite Year - A Collection of New Football Writing**   £9.99
Edited by Nick Hornby (Witherby)

3 **Rothmans Football Yearbook 1994-95** £16.99
Edited by Jack Rollin (Headline)

4 **A Game of Two Halves**   £6.99
Edited by Stephen Kelly (Mandarin)

5 **Botham - My Autobiography**   £15.99
(Collins Willow, hardback)

6 **Playfair Cricket Annual 1994**   £3.99
Edited by Bill Frindall (Headline)

7 **Just Champion**   £10.99
Alex Ferguson (Man United FC)

8 **We all Follow the Palace**   £9.95
Edited by Tony Matthews (Eagle Eye)

9 **All Played Out - Italia '90**   £5.99
Peter Davies (Mandarin)

10 **Physical Education and the Study of Sport**   £16.95
Davis, Bull, Roscoe & Roscoe (Mosby)

11 **When Push Comes to Shove - Rugby League, the People's Game**   £9.95
Clayton & Steele (Yorkshire Arts Circus)

12 **Cantona - My Story**   £15.99
Eric Cantona (Headline, hardback)

13 **Wisden Cricketers Almanack 1994***   £20.00
Edited by Matthew Engel (Wisden)

14 **The Kop - The End of an Era**   £5.99
Stephen Kelly (Mandarin)

15 **Rare Air - Michael on Michael**   £12.99
Michael Jordan (HarperCollins)

16 **Shot - A Photographic Record of Football in the Seventies**   £12.99
Compiled by Cheeseman, Alway & Lyons
(Witherby in assoc. with When Saturday Comes)

17 **Endless Winter - The Inside Story of the Rugby Revolution****   £14.99
Stephen Jones (Mainstream, hardback)

18 **Harvey Penick's Little Red Golf Book** £9.99
Penick with Shrake (HarperCollins, hardback)

19 **Visions of Sport - A Celebration of the Work of Allsport Photographic**   £14.95
Edited by Bob Martin (Kennedy West, hardback)

20 **Steve Waugh's Ashes Diary**   £16.50
Steve Waugh (Ironbark)

* Also sold in hardback at £22.50
** Winner of the William Hill Sports Book of the Year Award, 1993.

List Provided by Sportspages Bookshops
94-96 Charing Cross Road, London, 0171-240-9604
& St Ann's Square, Manchester, 0161 832 8530

Aerial Sports

Paragliding

European Championship

Preddvor, Slovenia   June 24-July 10
Open

1 Jimmy Pacher	ITA	6490
2 Hans Bollinger	SUI	6338
3 Richard Gallon	FRA	6215
11 John Silvester	GBR	5961
18 Jocky Sanderson	GBR	5585
20 John Pendry	GBR	5509

Women

1 Claire Bernier	FRA	5273
2 Nanou Berger	FRA	5178
3 Sarah Fenwick	GBR	4453

Team

1 France	19,141
2 Switzerland	18,730
3 Austria	17,936
6 Great Britain	17,282

PWC World Cup

Rounds in Brazil, Japan, Austria, Switzerland, Spain and France (2)
Overall Ranking

1 Jimmy Pacher	ITA
2 Hans Bollinger	SUI
3 Harry Buntz	Germany
12 John Silvester	GBR

Woman

1 Nanou Berger	FRA
2 Claire Bernier	FRA
3 Camilla Perner	AUT

Team

1 France
2 Switzerland
3 Austria
4 Great Britain

British National Accuracy Championships

Cerney, nr Cirencester   Aug 27-29
Overall

1 Mike Busby	18cm
2 Andy Webster	19cm
3 Mick Woodcock	24cm

Women

1 Fiona Macaskill	1.12m
2 Carol Quayle	4.05m
3 Sue Henry	5.96m

Team

1 Greed Dragons C	4.86m
2 Green Dragons A	5.1m
3 Bollington A	

British Nationals Championships

Championships held at three venues: Crickhowell, SE Wales (May 6-9); Hawes, Yorkshire Dales; Piedrahita, Spain (July 17-23). Competition at Hawes was cancelled due to inclement weather, or lots of wind and rain.
Overall

	Manufacturer/Glider	Pts
1 Patrick Holmes	Edel Rainbow	6151
2 Richard Carter	UP Kendo	5782
3 John Silvester	Edel Rainbow	5741
4 Steve Ham	Airwave Rave	5430
5 Sarah Fenwick	Nova Sphinx	5304
6 Rob Whittal	Edel Rainbow	5254
7 Rob Cruickshank	Apco Supra	4896
8 Jocky Sanderson	Nova Sphinx	4891
9 Judy Leden	Edel Rainbow	4677
10 Bruce Goldsmith	Airwave Rave	4494

British Open

(incorporating third day of Nationals)
Piedrahíta, Spain   July 17-23

1 Judy Leden	Edel Rainbow	3982
2 John Silvester	Edel Rainbow	3934
3 Rob Whittal	Edel Rainbow	3850

Hot Air Ballooning

World Champs

Châteaux d'Oex   Feb 2-6

1 V Dupuis	FRA	10310
2 J Petersen	GER	9965
3 O Lindstrom	SWE	8145
4 T Sage	GBR	8130
5 I Ashpole	GBR	7910
6 C Besnard	SUI	7530
7 N Charbonnier	ITA	7220
8 G Moyano	LUX	6845
9 F Taucher	GER	6545
10 F Buhlman	SUI	6340

American Football

It might be stretching fact to say that no other team in any sport has lost four championship finals in succession., but it's true enough to say that it requires a particular skill, even art, to achieve it. Buffalo Bills, unquestionably, have the Art. In 1993, they scored first and got trounced by the Cowboys. In 1994, the Bills actually led after the second quarter 13-6 and Destiny, for one brief moment, seemed thwarted. But, no. Help came in the form of running back Thurman Thomas, who should have been the Bills most potent attacking force. Thomas' second fumble of the game led to an equalising touchdown by Cowboy's James Washington and that was that. Dallas, with a club valued at $300m (Jones bought it for $65 in 1990), walked off with their second successive title and joined San Francisco and Pittsburg as the only teams on four Super Bowl victories. They also lost their first two games of the season (while Emmitt Smith was out of the team renegotiating his contract) and no other team has won the Super Bowl from that position before. Bill's record? Well, Denver once lost *two* Super Bowls in a row.

It was the year that saw the end of 38 years of CBS broadcasting the sport in America; an instituion dying, rather like the BBC losing Wimbledon. Rupert Murdoch's company Fox paid around £1 billion for future rights and, in a small change spin-off, have combined with the NFL to revive the World League in Europe, that died in 1992. In this incarnation, there will be no American clubs (seven from north America competed in 1991 and 1992), just the following six European team: Scottish Claymores (playing at Murrayfield, Edinburgh), London Monarchs (playing at Spurs), Amsterdam Admirals, Barcelona Dragons, Frankfurt Galaxy and Rhein Fire. The season kicks off in April with the provisional date for the World Bowl in mid-June.

QUOTES

"Let's make it five in '95" - **Buffalo Bills' player, following his team's fourth consecutive Super Bowl defeat.**

"I don't like the way they talk. They try to test your manhood, you shouldn't have to ridicule players" - **John Davis, Buffalo Bills player, on the sledging tactics of the Dallas Cowboys.**

"Come back next year Buffalo. It's easy pickings when you're around" - **Cowboys fans.**

"There are 500 coaches who could win the Super Bowl with our team" - **Jerry Jones, Cowboys owner, to coach Jimmy Johnson. Johnson resigned.**

"Every one of them was like a greased pig" - **Irv Eatman, of the Los Angeles Rams, who figured that the Houston Oilers were living up to their name by greasing their pants.**

"The idea that we were going to die overshadowed any point he was trying to make" - **Mike Duffy, senior lineman for Libertyville high school team. The coach, Dale Christensen staged a mock fight, in which he was apparently killed, in order to motivate his players. It didn't work. They lost. Christensen resigned.**

Super Bowl XXVIII

Dallas Cowboys		**30**
Buffalo Bills		**13**

Georgia Dome, Atlanta   *Jan 30*
Attendance 72,817

TEAMS

Dallas	Offense	Buffalo
Alvin Harper	WR	Don Beebe
Mark Tulnel	LT	John Fina
Nate Newton	LG	Glenn Parker
John Gesek	C	Kent Hull
Kevin Gogan	RG	John Davis
Erik Williams	RT	Howard Ballard
Jay Novacek	TE	Pete Metzelaars
Michael Irvin	WR	Bill Brooks
Troy Aikman	QB	Jim Kelly
Emmitt Smith	RB	Thurman Thomas
Daryl Johnston	RB-WR	Andre Read
	Defense	
Tony Tolbert	LE	Phil Hansen
Tony Casillas	LT-NT	Jeff Wright
Leon Lett	RT-RE	Bruce Smith
Charles Haley	RE-RILB	Cornelius Bennett
Darrin Smith	LLB-RILB	Mark Maddox
Darren Woodson	DB-LOLB	Marvcus Patton
Ken Norton	RLB-LOLB	Darryl Talley
Kevin Smith	LCB	Mickey Washington
Larry Brown	RCB	Nate Odomes
Thomas Everett	SB	Henry Jones
James Washington	FS	Mark Kelso

SUBSTITUTIONS

Dallas: K-Eddie Murray, P-John Jett, QB-Bernie Kosar, RB-Lincoln Coleman, Derrick Gainer, WR-Kevin Williams, GC-Frank Cornish, Dale Hellestrae, E-Jim Jeffcoat, T-Chad Hennings, Russell Maryland, DL-Jimmie Jones, DB-Bill Bates, Joe Fishback, Elvis Patlerson, LB-Dixon Edwards, Robert Jones, Godfrey Myles, Matt Vanderbeak, CB-Dave Thomas, S-Kenneth Gant, DNP RB-Derrick Lassic
Buffalo: K-Steve Christie, P-Chris Mohr, QB-Frank Reich, RB-Kenneth Davis, Carwell Gardner, WR-Russell Copeland, Steve Tasker, TE-Keith McKeller, T-Jerry Crafts, G-Jim Ritcher, C-Mike Devlin, Adam Lingner, E-Oliver Barnett, Mark Pike, NT-Mike Lodish, LB-Monty Brown, Keith Goganious, Richard Harvey, CB-Jerome Henderson, Thomas Smith, S-Matt Darby, Kurt Schulz, DNP RB-Nate Turner

SCORING

Dallas (NFC)	6	0	14	10		30
Buffalo (AFC)	3	10	0	0		13

Dallas	FG Murray 41
Buffalo	FG Christie 54
Dallas	FG Murray 24
Buffalo	Thomas 4 run (Christie kick)
Buffalo	FG Christie 28
Dallas	Washington 46 fumble return (Murray kick)
Dallas	E Smith 15 run (Murray kick)
Dallas	E Smith 1 run (Murray kick)
Dallas	FG Murray 20

TEAM STATISTICS

	Dallas	Buffalo
Total First Downs	20	22
Total Net Yardage	341	314
Rushing Yards	137	87
Passing Yards (Net)	204	227
Total Return Yardage	89	190
Punts/Average	4/43.8	5/37.6
Third Downs	5/13	5/17
Fourth Downs	1/1	2/3
Time of Possession	34:29	25:31

INDIVIDUAL STATISTICS

RUSHING

Dallas	No	Yds	LG	TD
Emmitt Smith	30	132	15t	2
Kevin Williams	1	6	6	0
Troy Aikman	1	3	3	0
Buffalo				
Thurman Thomas	16	37	6	1
Kenneth Davis	9	38	11	0
Jim Kelly	2	12	8	0

PASSING

Dallas	Att	Comp	Yds	TD	Int
Troy Aikman	27	19	207	0	1
Buffalo					
Jim Kelly	50	31	260	0	1

RECEIVING

Dallas	No	Yds	LG	TD
Michael Irvin	5	66	20	0
Jay Novacek	5	26	9	0
Emmitt Smith	4	28	10	0
Buffalo				
Bill Brooks	7	63	15	0
Thurman Thomas	7	52	24	0
Andre Reed	6	75	22	0

NFL Play-off Games

NATIONAL FOOTBALL CONFERENCE
Wild Card Play-off Games
Green Bay 28	Detroit 24
N Y Giants 17	Minnesota 10

Divisional Play-off Games
San Francisco 44	N Y Giants 3
Dallas 27	Green Bay 17

NFC Championship Game
Dallas 38	San Francisco 21

AMERICAN FOOTBALL CONFERENCE
Wild Card Play-off Games
Kansas City 27	Pittsburgh 24 (OT)
L A Raiders 42	Denver 24

Divisional Play-off Games
Buffalo 29	L A Raiders 23
Kansas City 28	Houston 20

AFC Championship Game
Buffalo 30	Kansas City 13

NFL Final League Standings - 1993

NATIONAL FOOTBALL CONFERENCE

Eastern Division

	W	L	T	Pct	PF	PA
Dallas	12	4	0	.750	376	229
N Y Giants*	11	5	0	.688	288	205
Philadelphia	8	8	0	.500	293	315
Phoenix	7	9	0	.438	326	269
Washington	4	12	0	.250	230	345

Central Division

	W	L	T	Pct	PF	PA
Detroit	10	6	0	.625	298	292
Minnesota*	9	7	0	.563	277	290
Green Bay*	9	7	0	.563	340	282
Chicago	7	9	0	.438	234	230
Tampa Bay	5	11	0	.313	237	376

Western Division

	W	L	T	Pct	PF	PA
San Francisco	10	6	0	.625	473	295
New Orleans	8	8	0	.500	317	343
Atlanta	6	10	0	.375	316	385
L A Rams	5	11	0	.313	221	367

*Wild cards

AMERICAN FOOTBALL CONFERENCE

Eastern Division

	W	L	T	Pct	PF	PA
Buffalo	12	4	0	.750	329	242
Miami	9	7	0	.563	349	351
N Y Jets	8	8	0	.500	270	247
New England	5	11	0	.313	238	286
Indianapolis	4	12	0	.250	189	378

Central Division

	W	L	T	Pct	PF	PA
Houston	12	4	0	.750	368	238
Pittsburgh*	9	7	0	.563	308	281
Cleveland	7	9	0	.438	304	307
Cincinnati	3	13	0	.188	187	319

Western Division

	W	L	T	Pct	PF	PA
Kansas City	11	5	0	.688	328	291
L A Raiders	10	6	0	.625	306	326
Denver	9	7	0	.563	373	284
San Diego	8	8	0	.500	322	290
Seattle	6	10	0	.375	280	314

SUPER BOWL HISTORY

Season		Winner	Loser	Score	Venue	Attendance	MVP	Team-Pos
I	15.1.67	Green Bay	Kansas City	35-10	Los Angeles	61,946	Bart Starr (GB-QB)	
II	14.1.68	Green Bay	Oakland	33-14	Miami	75,546	Bart Starr (GB-QB)	
III	12.1.69	New York Jets	Baltimore	16-7	Miami	75,389	Joe Namath (NY-QB)	
IV	11.1.70	Kansas City	Minnesota	23-7	New Orleans	80,582	Len Dawson (KC-QB)	
V	17.1.71	Baltimore	Dallas	16-13	Miami	79,204	Chuck Howley (D-LB)	
VI	16.1.72	Dallas	Miami	24-3	New Orleans	81,023	Roger Staubach (D-QB)	
VII	14.1.73	Miami	Washington	14-7	Los Angeles	90,182	Jake Scott (M-S)	
VIII	31.1.74	Miami	Minnesota	24-7	Houston	71,882	Larry Csonka (M-RB)	
IX	12.1.75	Pittsburgh	Minnesota	16-6	New Orleans	80,997	Franco Harris (P-RB)	
X	18.1.76	Pittsburgh	Dallas	21-7	Miami	80,187	Lynn Swann (P-WR)	
XI	9.1.77	Oakland	Minnesota	32-14	Pasadena	103,438	Fred Biletnikoff (O-WR)	
XII	15.1.78	Dallas	Denver	27-10	New Orleans	75,583	White & Martin (D-DT/DE)	
XIII	21.1.79	Pittsburgh	Dallas	35-31	Miami	79,484	Terry Bradshaw (P-QB)	
XIV	20.1.80	Pittsburgh	Los Angeles	31-19	Pasadena	103,985	Terry Bradshaw (P-QB)	
XV	25.1.81	Oakland	Philadelphia	27-10	New Orleans	76,135	Jim Plunkett (O-QB)	
XVI	24.1.82	San Francisco	Cincinnati	26-21	Pontiac	81,270	Joe Montana (SF-QB)	
XVII	30.1.83	Washington	Miami	27-17	Pasadena	103,667	John Riggins (W-RB)	
XVIII	22.1.84	LA Raiders	Washington	38-9	Tampa	72,920	Marcus Allen (LA-RB)	
XIX	20.1.85	San Francisco	Miami	38-16	Stanford	84,059	Joe Montana (SF-QB)	
XX	26.1.86	Chicago	New England	46-10	New Orleans	73,818	Richard Dent (CH-DE)	
XXI	25.1.87	New York Gts	Denver	39-20	Pasadena	101,063	Phil Simms (NY-QB)	
XXII	13.1.88	Washington	Denver	42-10	San Diego	73,302	Doug Williams (W-QB)	
XXIII	22.1.89	San Francisco	Cincinnati	20-16	Miami	75,129	Jerry Rice (SF-WR)	
XXIV	28.1.90	San Francisco	Denver	55-10	New Orleans	72,919	Joe Montana (SF-QB)	
XXV	27.1.91	New York Gts	Buffalo	20-19	Tampa	73,813	Ottis Anderson (NY-RB)	
XXVI	26.1.92	Washington	Buffalo	37-24	Minneapolis	63,130	Mark Rypien (W-QB)	
XXVII	31.1.93	Dallas	Buffalo	52-17	Pasadena	98,374	Troy Aikman (D-QB)	
XXVIII	30.1.94	Dallas	Buffalo	30-13	Atlanta	72,817	Emmitt Smith (D-RB)	

NFC Statistics

SCORING

	Td	Tdr	Tdp	Tdm	Xp	Fg	Saf	Pts
San Francisco	61	26	29	6	59	16	0	473
Dallas	41	20	18	3	40	30	0	376
Green Bay	35	14	19	2	35	31	1	340
Phoenix	37	12	21	4	37	21	2	326
New Orleans	33	10	18	5	33	28	1	317
Atlanta	34	4	28	2	34	26	0	316
Detroit	28	9	15	4	28	34	0	298
Philadelphia	35	7	23	5	31	16	2	293
N Y Giants	30	11	17	2	28	26	1	288
Minnesota	28	8	18	2	27	26	2	277
Tampa Bay	27	6	19	2	27	16	0	237
Chicago	22	10	7	5	21	27	0	234
Washington	26	11	11	4	24	16	1	230
L A Rams	25	8	16	1	23	16	0	221

SCORERS

Records: Points 176-Paul Hornung, Green Bay 1960
Touchdowns 24-John Riggins, Washington 1983
Field Goals 35-Ali Haji-Sheikh, New York 1983
Extra points 62-Mark Moseley, Washington 1983

Kickers

	Xp	Xpa	Fg	Fga	Pts
Jason Hanson (Detroit)	28	28	34	43	130
Chris Jacke (Green Bay)	35	35	31	37	128
Eddie Murray (Dallas)	38	38	28	33	122
Morten Andersen (New Orleans)	33	33	28	35	117
Norm Johnson (Atlanta)	34	34	26	27	112

Non-kickers

	Td	Tdr	Tdp	Tdm	Pts
Jerry Rice (San Francisco)	16	1	15	0	96
Andre Rison (Atlanta)	15	0	15	0	90
Sterling Sharpe (Green Bay)	11	0	11	0	66
Ricky Watters (San Francisco)	11	10	1	0	66
Edgar Bennett (Green Bay)	10	9	1	0	60
Emmitt Smith (Dallas)	10	9	1	0	60
Calvin Williams (Philadelphia)	10	0	10	0	60

PASSING

Records Completions: 353-Don Majkowski, GB 1989
Touchdowns: 36-Y A Tittle, NY 1963
Yards: 4,614-Neil Lomax, St L 1984
Longest for Td: 99yds-Frank Filchock, Was 1939;
George Izo, Was 1963; Karl Sweetan, Det 1966;
Sonny Jurgensen, Was 1968; Ron Jaworski, Phi 1985

	Att	Com	Pct	Yds	Ave	Td	Rating
Steve Young (SF)	462	314	68.0	4023	8.71	29	101.5
Troy Aikman (Dal)	392	271	69.1	3100	7.91	15	99.0
Phil Simms (NY-G)	400	247	61.8	3038	7.60	15	88.3
Bubby Brister (Phi)	309	181	58.6	1905	6.17	14	84.9
Bobby Hebert (Atl)	430	263	61.2	2978	6.93	24	84.0

PUNTING

Records Number: 114-Bob Parsons, Chicago 1981
Average: 51.4yds-Sammy Baugh, Washington 1940
Longest: 94yds-Joe Lintzenich, Chicago 1931

	No	Yds	Lg	Ave	Ret yds	Net ave
Jim Arnold (Det)	72	3207	68	44.5	377	36.8
Reggie Roby (Was)	78	3447	60	44.2	343	37.2
Rich Camarillo (Pho)	73	3189	61	43.7	267	37.8
Tom Barnhardt (NO)	77	3356	58	43.6	348	37.5
Harold Alexander (Atl)	72	3114	75	43.3	350	37.6

RUSHING

Records Carries: 407-James Wilder, Tampa Bay 1984
Yards: 2,105-Eric Dickerson, Los Angeles 1984
TDs: 24-John Riggins, Washington 1983

	Att	Yds	Avg	Long	TD
Emmitt Smith (Dal)	283	1486	5.3	62t	9
Jerome Bettis (Rams)	294	1429	4.9	71t	7
Erric Pegram (Atl)	292	1185	4.1	29	3
Barry Sanders (Det)	243	1115	4.6	42	3
Rodney Hampton(NYG)	292	1077	3.7	20	5

PASS RECEIVING

Records Receptions 108-Sterling Sharpe, Green Bay 1992
Yards 1570-Jerry Rice, San Francisco 1986
TDs 22-Jerry Rice, San Francisco 1987

	No	Yds	Avg	Long	TD
Sterling Sharpe (GB)	112	1274	11.4	54	11
Jerry Rice (SF)	98	1503	15.3	80t	15
Michael Irvin (Dal)	88	1330	15.1	61t	7
Andre Rison (Atl)	86	1242	14.4	53t	15
Cris Carter (Min)	86	1071	12.5	58	9

INTERCEPTIONS

Records Number: 14-Dick Lane, LA 1952
Yards: 301-Don Droll, Det 1949
Longest Return: 102yds - Bob Smith, Detroit 1949
Erich Barnes, NY 1961
TDs: 3-Dick Lynch, NY 1963; Herb Adderley, GB
1965; Monte Jackson, LA 1976; Rod Perry, LA 1976;
Ronnie Lott, SF 1981; Wayne Haddix, TB,1990;
Robert Massey, Pho 1992

	No	Yds	Avg	Long	TD
Deion Sanders (Atl)	7	91	13.0	41	0
Eric Allen (Phi)	6	201	33.5	94t	4
LeRoy Butler (GB)	6	131	21.8	39	0
Kevin Smith (Dal)	6	56	9.3	32t	1
Tom Carter (Was)	6	54	9.0	29	0

PUNT RETURNS

Records Number: 70-Danny Reece, Tampa Bay 1979
Yards: 646-Eddie Brown, Washington 1976
Longest for TD: 98yds-Gill Lefebvre, Cin 1933;
Charlie West, Min 1968; Dennis Morgan, Dal 1974

	No	FC	Yds	Avg	Long	TD
Tyrone Hughes (NO)	37	21	503	13.6	83t	2
Dexter Carter (SF)	34	20	411	12.1	72t	1
Kevin Williams (Dal)	36	14	381	10.6	64t	2
David Meggett (NY-G)	32	20	331	10.3	75t	1
Mel Gray (Det)	23	14	197	8.6	35	0

KICKOFF RETURNS

Records Number: 60-Drew Hill, Los Angeles 1981
Yards: 1,345-Buster Rhymes, Minnesota 1985
Longest: 106yds-Al Carmichael, GB 1956;Roy
Green, St L 1979
TDs: 4-Travis Williams, GB 1967; Cecil Turner, Chi
1970

	No	Yds	Avg	Long	TD
Robert Brooks (GB)	23	611	26.6	95t	1
Tyrone Hughes (NO)	30	753	25.1	99t	1
Tony Smith (Atl)	38	948	24.9	97t	1
Mel Gray (Det)	28	688	24.6	95t	1
Johnny Bailey (Pho)	31	699	22.5	48	0

AFC Statistics

SCORING

	Td	Tdr	Tdp	Tdm	Xp	Fg	Saf	Pts
Denver	42	13	27	2	41	26	1	373
Houston	40	11	23	6	39	29	1	368
Miami	40	10	27	3	37	24	0	349
Buffalo	37	12	20	5	36	23	1	329
Kansas City	37	14	20	3	37	23	0	328
San Diego	33	14	18	1	31	31	0	322
Pittsburgh	32	13	16	3	32	28	0	308
LA Raiders	29	10	17	2	27	35	0	306
Cleveland	36	8	23	5	36	16	2	304
Seattle	29	13	13	3	29	23	4	280
New York Jets	31	14	16	1	31	17	1	270
New England	26	9	17	0	25	19	0	238
Indianapolis	16	4	10	2	15	26	0	189
Cincinnati	16	3	11	2	13	24	3	187

SCORERS

Records: Points 155-Gino Cappelleti, Bos 1964
Touchdowns 23-O J Simpson, Buf 1975
Field Goals 34-Jim Turner, New York 1968
34-Nick Lowery, Kansas City 1990
Extra points 66-Uwe von Schamann, Mia, 1984

Kickers

	Xp	Xpa	Fg	Fga	Pts
Jeff Jaeger (LA Raiders)	27	29	35	44	132
Al Del Greco (Houston)	39	40	29	34	126
John Carney (San Diego)	31	33	31	40	124
Jason Elam (Denver)	41	42	26	35	119
Gary Anderson (Pittsburgh)	32	32	28	30	116

Non-kickers

	Td	Tdr	Tdp	Tdm	Pts
Marcus Allen (Kansas City)	15	12	3	0	90
Barry Foster (Pittsburgh)	9	8	1	0	54
Shannon Sharpe (Denver)	9	0	9	0	54
Gary Brown (Houston)	8	6	2	0	48
Tim Brown (LA Raiders)	8	0	7	1	48
Ben Coates (New England)	8	0	8	0	48
Robert Delpino (Denver)	8	8	0	0	48
Michael Jackson (Cleveland)	8	0	8	0	48
Natrone Means (San Diego)	8	8	0	0	48

PASSING

Records Completions: 404-Warren Moon, Houston 1991
Touchdowns: 48-Dan Marino, Miami 1984
Yards: 5,084-Dan Marino, Miami 1984
Longest for Td: 99yds-Jim Plunkett, Los Angeles '83

	Att	Com	Pct	Yds	Ave	Td	Rating
John Elway (Den)	551	348	63.2	4030	7.31	25	92.8
Joe Montana (KC)	298	181	60.7	2144	7.19	13	87.4
Vinny Testaverde (Cl)	230	130	56.5	1797	7.81	14	85.7
Boomer Esiason (NY)	473	288	60.9	3421	7.23	16	84.5
Scott Mitchell (Mia)	233	133	57.1	1773	7.61	12	84.2

PUNTING

Records Number: 105-Bob Scarpitto, Denver 1967
Average: 46.9-Greg Montgomery, Houston 1992
Longest: 98yds-Steve O'Neal, New York 1969

	No	Yds	Lg	Ave	Ret yds	Net ave
Greg Montgomery (Ho)	54	2462	77	45.6	249	39.1
Tom Rouen (Den)	67	3017	62	45.0	337	37.1
Rick Tuten (Sea)	90	4007	64	44.5	475	37.3
Brian Hansen (Cle)	82	3632	72	44.3	438	35.6
Lee Johnson (Cin)	90	3954	60	43.9	416	36.6

RUSHING

Records Carries: 390-Barry Foster, Pit,1992
Yards: 2,003-O J Simpson, Buf 1973
TDs: 19-Earl Campbell, Hou 1979
Chuck Muncie, SD 1981

	Att	Yds	Avg	Long	TD
Thurman Thomas (Buf)	355	1315	3.7	27	6
Leonard Russell (NE)	300	1088	3.6	21	7
Chris Warren (Sea)	273	1072	3.9	45t	7
Gary Brown (Hou)	195	1002	5.1	26	6
Johnny Johnson (NYJ)	198	821	4.1	57t	3
Rod Bernstine (Den)	223	816	3.7	24	4
Marcus Allen (KC)	206	764	3.7	39	12

PASS RECEIVING

Records Receptions 101-Charlie Hennigan, Houston 1964
Yards 1,746-Charlie Hennigan, Houston 1961
TDs 18-Mark Clayton, Miami 1984

	No	Yds	Avg	Long	TD
Reggie Langhorne (Ind)	85	1038	12.2	72t	3
Anthony Miller (SD)	84	1162	13.8	66t	7
Shannon Sharpe (Den)	81	995	12.3	63	9
Tim Brown (LA)	80	1180	14.8	71t	7
Brian Blades (Sea)	80	945	11.8	41	3
Webster Slaughter (Hou)	77	904	11.7	41	5
Terry Kirby (Mia)	75	874	11.7	47	3

INTERCEPTIONS

Records Number: 13-Lester Hayes, Oak 1980
Yards: 349-Charlie McNeil, SD 1961
Longest Return: 103yds-Venice Glenn, SD 1987
Louis Oliver, Mia 1992
TDs: 4-Ken Houston, Hou 1971; JimKearney,KC 1972

	No	Yds	Avg	Long	TD
Eugene Robinson (Sea)	9	80	8.9	28	0
Nate Odomes (Buf)	9	65	7.2	25	0
Rod Woodson (Pit)	8	138	17.3	63t	1
Marcus Robertson (Hou)	7	137	19.6	69	0
Darren Carrington (SD)	7	104	14.9	28	0
Brian Washington (NYJ)	6	128	21.3	62t	1

PUNT RETURNS

Records Number: 62-Fulton Walker, Los Angeles 1985
Yards: 692-Fulton Walker, Los Angeles 1985
Longest for TD: 98yds-Terance Mathis, NY 1990

	No	FC	Yds	Avg	Long	TD
Eric Metcalf (Cle)	36	11	464	12.9	91t	2
Darrien Gordon (SD)	31	15	395	12.7	54	0
Tim Brown (LA)	40	20	465	11.6	74t	1
OJ McDuffie (Mia)	28	22	317	11.3	72t	2
Glyn Milburn (Den)	40	11	425	10.6	54	0

KICKOFF RETURNS

Records Number: 55-Bruce Harper, NY 1978-9
David Turner, Cin 1979
Yards: 1,317-Bobby Jancik, Hou 1963
Longest: 106yds-Nolan Smith, KC 1967
TDs: 3-Ray Clayborn, NE 1977

	No	Yds	Avg	Long	TD
Raghib Ismail (LA)	25	605	24.2	66	0
OJ McDuffie (Mia)	32	755	23.6	48	0
Eric Ball (Cin)	23	501	21.8	45	0
Clarence Verdin (Ind)	50	1050	21.0	38	0
Ray Crittenden (NE)	23	478	20.8	44	0

Eurobowl VIII

Qualification Round 1
Luxembourg Mar 27
Copenhagen Towers (DEN) 28
Luxembourg Red Lions (LUX) 16
Feldkirch Apr 4
Oscar Dinos (AUT) 27
Basilisk Mean Machine
Qualification Play-off
Copenhagen Apr 4
Copenhagen Towers 38
Oscar Dinos 6

Quarter-finals
Malmo Apr 30
Limhamn Griffins (SWE) 6
East City Giants (FIN) 31
Den Haag May 1
Hague Raiders (HOL) 6
London Olympians 52
Bergamo Apr 23
Paris Castor/Sphinx (FRA) 20
Bergamo Lions (ITA) 23
Munich May 1
Munich Cowboys (GER) 35
Copenhagen Towers 16

Semi-finals
Helsinki May 22
East City Giants 20
London Olympians 22
Munich May 15
Bergamo Lions 25
Munich Cowboys 18

Final
Stuttgart June 4
London Olympians 26
Bergamo Lions 23

Angling

Fly Fishing

World Championships
Lillehammer, Norway   *Aug 13-14*
Team
1	Czech Republic	285 pts
2	Italy	286
3	England	290
4	Scotland	292
7	Wales	325
13	Ireland	366

Individual
1	P Coquard	FRA	13
2	H Morgan	WAL	30
3	P Cochito	ITA	32

European Championships
After two rounds at Dreux and Draycote, the leading team is England and the overall individual leader is Paul Canning (Eng). The final round is in Wales in October.

River Home International
St Boswells (River Tweed)   *July 1*
Team
1	England	51 placings
2	Scotland	52
3	Ireland	62
4	Wales	63

Individual
1	Jeremy Lucas	ENG
2	Jim Fairgreave	SCO*
3	Franz Grimley	WAL
4	Vince Gwillym	WAL
5	Ian Greenwood	ENG
6	Baz Reece	ENG

*Fairgreave caught the largest fish, a grayling of 56cms.

Boat Home International
Lough Conn   *May 21*
Team
1	Ireland	21 fish/28.25lbs
2	England	16/18.24lbs
3	Scotland	15/17.01lbs
4	Wales	12/11.15lbs

Individual
1 Pat Carson IRL 4/6.7lbs

English National River Championship
Dartmoor (East & West Dart)   *June 20*
1	Brian Easterbrook	West Country
2	Stuart Crofts	Yorkshire
3	Dennis Buck	North West
4	Jeremy Herrman	North West
5	IOliver Edwards	Yorkshire
6	Vic Knight	Severn-Trent

Coarse Angling

World Championships
Holme Pierrepont   *Sep 3-4*
Individual
1	R Nudd	ENG
2	R Stronck	LUX
3	J J Chaumet	FRA
4	M Barros	POR
5	D White	ENG
6	G Barbetta	ITA
7	D Guessard	FRA
8	C Branson	WAL
9	C Esteves	POR
10	K Bukrak	POL

Team
1	England (Nudd, Scotthorne, Gardener, White, Milsom)
2	France
3	Italy
4	Portugal
13	Wales
15	Ireland
21	Scotland

Jeanette Ford, a 39 year old travel agent from Felton, became the first woman ever to qualify for the England fly-fishing team when she competed in the home international at Loch Conn, in County Mayo. Ford chased her goal for 15 years and to say she is enthusiastic is, well, let her tell you......"I enjoy it. I like the company. I like the sport. If you see a fish rise it is the most exciting thing to me. You hook it in and you are obviously doing something right. It's all you think about......your knees are knocking. It's orgasmic, I suppose."

Archery

Euronations Cup
Lilleshall   *June 28*
1 England	7,322 pts
2 Scotland	7,130 pts
3 Republic of Ireland	7,082 pts

UK Masters Tournament
Lilleshall   *June 11-12*
Men's Individual (Olympic)
3rd/4th Place
R Broughton bt R Hallworth 107-101
Final
R Crich bt D Hughes 103-101

Men's Individual (Compound)
3rd/4th Place
L Macpherson bt K Phelps 109-100
Final
B Dicks bt A Yardy 110-109

The Petty Trophy
1 Mr S Hallard	1289
2 Mr S Terry	1256
3 Mr R Priestman	1234

Women's Individual (Olympic)
3rd/4th Place
Y Murton bt P Strettle 100-91
Final
L Milne bt A Williamson 104-103

Women's Individual (Compound)
3rd/4th Place
K Bent bt D Cannon 107-102
Final
N Simpson bt W Lesinski 106-104

The Ogden Trophy
1 Miss L Jones	1222
2 Mrs J Eley	1193
3 Miss Williamson	1191

All British & Open Field Archery Championships
Finsthwaite, Cumbria   *May 28-29*
Home International Competition
1 England	2330
2 Northern Ireland	1884
3 Wales	1803

Men's Freestyle
1 J Shales	"V" Archery	639
2 G Kinghorn	Worthing	627
3 A Scovell	Sellafield	619

Men's Compound Unlimited
1 D Jones	GNAS	653
2 S Tarplee	Eversham	638
3 B Jones	Merlin	628

Men's Traditional
1 R Hardy	BCA	464
2 M Berriman	Raven	451
3 J Geldard	Pendle	256

Men's Traditional Longbow
1 J Cope	Halesowen	400
2 A Newcombe	Kenwith	295
3 M Hughes	Pentref	271

Men's Compound Limited
1 J McCrea	Dundonald	486
2 M Watson	Foxhill	405
3 G Houghton	Foxhill	352

Men's Compound Bowhunter
1 D Danks	Halesowen	549
2 A Dennis	Exmouth	510
3 R Tucker	Pentref	414

Men's Barebow
1 G Edwards	Halesowen	586
2 P Mulligan	Scarva Road	582
3 R Mundon	Oaklands	579

Ladies Freestyle
1 L Oliver	Chantry	559
2 J Hartfield	Crawley	558
3 J Wilkinson	Maryport	542

Ladies' Barebow
1 P Lovell	Woodstock	589
2 C Farr	Pentref	455
3 M Norris	Halesowen	368

Ladies' Traditional
1 B Berriman	Raven	384
2 M Taylor	Capricorn	309
3 M Hughes	Pentref	271

Ladies' Traditional Longbow
1 R Moore	Lough Cuan	191
2 A Shooter	St Ives	92

Ladies' Compound Unlimited
1 A Shephard	New Century	606
2 B James	Meriden	582
3 C Jones	GNAS	572

Ladies' Compound Bowhunter
1 H Watson	Foxhill	404
2 K Edwards	Halesowen	376

Grand National Archery Meeting
Lilleshall   *June 29-July 1*
Double York Round
1 G Hardinges	2214
2 P Frost	2143
3 M Holden	2129

Challenge Cup (Men)
1 Hampshire	7203
2 Middlesex	7050

Compound Bows (Men)
1 P van Buren	2243

Double Hereford Round (Women)
1 A Williamson	2364
2 P Edwards	2350
3 B Thomas	2167

Walrond Cup (Women)
1 Berkshire	6347
2 Worcestershire	5910

Compound Bows
1 M Cooper	2236

National Indoor Target Championships
National Indoor Arena   *Mar 20*
Home International (Easton Cup)
1 England	2175
2 Wales	2130
3 Scotland	2110
4 N. Ireland	2053

Men's Recurve
1 P Frost	LAOFAC
2 R Crich	Rolls Royce
3 D Hughes	Dunlop

Men's Compound
1 S Tarplee	Evesham
2 R Howells	Margam
3 J Lesinski	Clophill

Women's Recurve
1 B Bird	Eccles
2 J Chandler	FOBB
3 J Collins	Buckland

Ladies' Compound
1 R Evans	GNAS
2 N Simpson	Oxford
3 W Lesinski	Clophill

Team Trophy
1 Bingham	217

Association Football

Few tournaments have been greeted with more early cynicism; the allocation of the World Cup to the USA was, as everyone knew, nothing more than a ploy to win over the planet's richest nation to the joys of soccer. João Havelange, the 79-year-old FIFA president, and a man not averse to a bit of richness in his sport, then barred Pele from the World Cup draw in Los Angeles. It was like throwing the Pope out of the Vatican. Had the old man gone mad? The element of farce continued at the opening ceremony in Chicago's Soldier Field. One minute, there was John Secada singing away to over a billion people worldwide, then there was no John Secada. He'd fallen through a hole in the stage.

Unable to extricate himself, the admirable Secada continued singing with only his head showing before security men eventually dragged him out and to hospital with a dislocated shoulder. It was possibly the first use of the electric cart in the tournament. The football followed a day later and things improved. Except for a decent final, USA 94 had everything (*see Front of Book*). Hagi burned brightly, Baggio flickered into occasional life and Maradona was banned. The new diktat to referees to stamp out foul play worked so well that Cantona was arrested and he wasn't even playing. For once, creative play was rewarded. It remains to be seen whether the referees, having tamed the wild tackles, will now be instructed to put a curb on the wild hairstyles. Valderrama's eccentricity we were prepared for; Mihaylov's transplant and Townsend's Harpic look, were unexpected additions.

The unsung stars of USA 94, though, were those who came to mow. The grounds were so sweetly manicured with circles and squares and chevrons that you fully expected them to mow in the half-time scores at the intervals. In short, USA 94 was a huge success and may even represent a sea-change in modern football. The rebirth of the imagination - or is that taking it a bit too far ?

England, Scotland, Wales and Northern Ireland all sat the competition out - for the first time since entry to the competition in 1950. In terms of managers, it was a costly experience. If Wales, with a team that fared passably well in the qualifying rounds, should lose a manager, then it is little wonder that Scotland

FIFA RANKINGS
As at July 1994
Figures in brackets show placings as at Dec 31, 1993

1 (3)	Brazil	65.21
2 (2)	Italy	62.89
3 (9)	Sweden	61.28
4 (1)	Germany	61.14
5 (7)	Holland	60.97
6 (5)	Spain	59.74
7 (13)	Romania	58.20
8 (4)	Norway	57.52
9 (8)	Argentina	57.46
10 (18)	Nigeria	56.28
11 (12)	Switzerland	55.80
12 (6)	Denmark	54.88
13 (10)	Republic of Ireland	53.68
14 (31)	Bulgaria	53.40
15 (16)	Mexico	53.10
16 (15)	France	52.82
17 (21)	Colombia	52.72
18 (11)	England	52.15
19 (14)	Russia	52.02
20 (25)	Belgium	50.17
21 (27)	Zambia	48.28
22 (22)	USA	47.68
23 (17)	Uruguay	47.23
24 (33)	Côte d'Ivoire	45.23
25 (20)	Portugal	44.73
26 (26)	Egypt	44.65
27 (23)	Cameroon	44.02
28 (37)	Ghana	43.32
29 (38)	Saudi Arabia	42.93
30 (30)	Morocco	42.71
33 (24)	Scotland	40.18
35 (29)	Wales	38.77
39 (39)	Northern Ireland	36.78

and England lost managers with alacrity. Roxburgh had already moved on long before the qualifying had finished, but Taylor's head rolled as the curtain came down. Taylor won less than 50% of his matches as England manager with 18 wins from 38 games. It can be said that Bobby Robson (47 from 95) fared little better, but Taylor just lost more of the important ones. As lowly as the results were, Taylor must have found the vitriol hard to take. If it's any solace, he can rest assured that as we speak idle tabloid pens are reconstructing Venables as a vegetable. Which particular variety will have to wait until the 1996 European Championship in England. Venables also has an Achilles heel, financial affairs of a mazy complexity. The media have already set about unravelling them. If it doesn't sound too cynical (and it probably does); as long as Venables is winning any potential financial scandals will have less appeal to the press.

Venables has started his term well - wins against Denmark, Greece and the USA, plus a draw with Norway - but the leeway he gains on not having to qualify for the European Champs is more than compensated by the expectation that will be heaped upon him as the tournament approaches. Doubtless there will be a few people to remind him (if he ever forgets) that England won the last big one held in England.

Yorath's departure from the Wales incumbency and Toshack's one match spell as manager showed just what a pig ear's you can make of hiring and firing. Northern Ireland did little better, causing something of a ruckus when Jimmy Nicholl didn't get the job and Bryan Hamilton did. Hamilton got off to the perfect start in March when his team beat Romania 2-0. Now, if we take a form line from that..........

A MANAGER'S LAMENT

"Do I not like that" - **Graham Taylor.**

"F****** Paul! F****** hit the space in there! Go Les! Hit Les, hit Les over the f****** top. F****** hell!" - **Taylor, as heard on Channel 4. There were 38 F-words on the Taylor documentary, which averages out at exactly one f*** or f****** for every game he was manager.**

"We are sorry if we disappointed some of our viewers, but 70 minutes into the England game it was clear that the miracle was not going to happen" - **BBC TV spokesperson justifying switching from the England v San Marino game to Wales v Romania.**

I would say 'Just make sure you don't lose, pal'. It's as simple as that. You've got to win. - **Taylor's advice to Venables.**

"I get letters from Princess Di thanking me for taking her out of the headlines" - **Taylor.**

"You've got to be joking. Even the Pope would have second thoughts about taking the job" - **Roy Hodgson, the manager of Switzerland, who didn't apply for the England job.**

"He did a magnificent job at Aston Villa and not a bad job for England - except for a few important games" - **Keith Pearson, the Wolves secretary, on Taylor's credentials.**

If crowds start chanting 'turnip, turnip, give us a wave' then you give them a wave" - **Taylor, on his new job at Wolves.**

Manchester United had almost run away with the League by Christmas. Fortunately, a few stumbles in the run-in gave added interest to the competition. Blackburn flattered, then deceived and the title was United's, with the highest number of points, 92, since the League turned to three points a game in the 1981-2 season. As Liverpool have won the title six times since then, it says much for the quality of Ferguson's current squad. The Cup provided stern competition in the semi-final and final. Joe Royle's Oldham had a fleeting brush with glory; it was only a last-minute equaliser that denied them their first appearance in an FA Cup final. In the replay Oldham were overrun and three weeks later, after a draw with Norwich, were relegated. United, having scored four in the second match against Oldham scored another four in the final. Quite how Chelsea, having looked the better side for half a game, managed to lose by such a convincing score remains a mystery. United, though, had their double; the sixth team in history following Preston North End in 1888-9, Aston Villa - 1896-7, Spurs - 1960-1, Arsenal - 1970-1, and Liverpool - 1985-6. Nor were they a million miles away from a treble, losing out to Aston Villa in the Coca Cola Cup final.

United had set a standard of attacking football which has to be admired. On the debit side, Alex Ferguson has also set a standard for spending money which others have quickly followed. In the last 12 months, Blackburn have spent over £10m, Tottenham and Newcastle £7.5m or so - and that's just for three players each. Chris Sutton cost a whacking £5m and even Norwich supporters don't know why.

By comparison, Arsenal have been almost parsimonious spending a mere £1.75m to lure Stefan Schwarz to Highbury. Maybe they don't feel there's a need for change, George Graham now having won six trophies in his time at Highbury. The victory against Parma in the Cup Winners' Cup Final the latest. The Italians had won the trophy in 1993 and expected to retain it. Arsenal, being Arsenal denied them in the way they know best. Alan Smith set it up with a stunning volley in the 20th minute and thereafter Parma were just squeezed out of the game. The final score was 1-0. It was the sixth time in their nine European games last year that the opposition hadn't scored.

THE MULTI-MILLION POUND MEN
Tranfers at over £2m from Oct 1 to Sep 30

£5,000,000			
Chris Sutton	Norwich	Blackburn	*Jul*
£3,600,000			
Phil Babb	Coventry	Liverpool	*Sep*
£3,000,000			
Daniel Amokachi	FC Bruges	Everton	*Aug*
John Scales	Wimbledon	Liverpool	*Sep*
£2,900,000			
Gheorghe Popescu	Eindhoven	Tottenham	*Sep*
£2,800,000			
Carlton Palmer	Sheff Weds	Leeds	*Jul*
£2,700,000			
Darren Peacock	QPR	Newcastle	*Mar*
David Batty	Leeds	Blackburn	*Oct*
£2,650,000			
Philippe Albert	Anderlecht	Newcastle	*Aug*
£2,600,000			
Ilie Dumitrescu	Steau Buch't	Tottenham	*Jul*
£2,500,000			
Bryan Roy	Foggia	Notts Forest	*Aug*
£2,400,000			
Tim Flowers	Southmptn	Blackburn	*Nov*
£2,300,000			
Paul Furlong	Watford	Chelsea	*May*
£2,250,000			
Ruel Fox	Norwich	Newcastle	*Feb*
£2,200,000			
Vinny Samways	Tottenham	Everton	*Aug*
£2,000,000			
Jürgen Klinsmann	Monaco	Tottenham	*Jul*
David Rocastle*	Leeds	Man City	*Dec*
David White*	Man City	Leeds	*Dec*

*Exchange valued at £2m

Arsenal's reticence to spend money certainly had nothing to do with the financial standing of the club, which announced a £4m profit in August from a turnover of £21.5m. If you wonder why the clubs change their strip every week, look no further than Arsenal's balance sheet. The club sold 220,000 strips in the two months from June to August, which means that around one person in every 250 in Britain owns an Arsenal strip, which is an alarming thought. Manchester United, one of only three clubs quoted on the Stock Exchange, enjoyed a similar profit (£4m) and their market value rose 7.5% when they won the double. Blackburn, on the other hand, lost over £6m in the financial year 1992-3, but that doesn't matter much as they've got a £10.25m loan from Jack Walker (*Sunday Times* estimate of wealth: £70m). Tottenham, also quoted on the Stock Exchange (the other club is Millwall), appear to have their benefactor in place now that Alan Sugar (*Sunday Times* EOW: £157m) has committed his funds so wholeheartedly to Spurs renaissance. After the purchase of Klinsmann and Dumitrescu, the price of Spurs shares rose to over 120p, easily the highest point of a year that saw them fall to 75p when the FA enquiry was in full flow.

Lest we forget, this was the year that Spurs lost 12 points,reduced to six, for improper payments to players. Quite how many club chairman were shifting uneasily in their seats when they heard, we can only guess. Millwall were fined £100,000 for the fights at the New Den (why change the habits of a lifetime, did you say?) and Everton £75,000 for poaching Mike Walker from Norwich. The story goes that they are currently offering Norwich more if they'll take him back again.

If Walker went willingly, most managers didn't - and so many went that we haven't even space to list them. Ian Branfoot deserves special mention. The Southampton manager received the dreaded director's message of support from the newly-appointed Lawrie McMenemy, then barely saw out a fortnight.

It was the year when Paul Elliott failed to persuade a court that Dean Saunders had meant to cripple him and the year that John Hill tragically died, watching the sport he loved. Hill was hit by a distress rocket at the Wales v Romania game.

It was the year football said goodbye to Sir Matt Busby, Sir Billy Wright and Danny Blanchflower, whose impeccable contributions to the sport will long outlast them.

Finally, it was Jack Charlton's year. The Irish made him a freeman of the city of Dublin before he even went to America and Guinness reported sales increases, in Britain, of 500% during Irish World Cup matches. Cheers.

WORLD CUP SCORERS

6 goals

Oleg Salenko	RUS	1p v Swe, 5(1p) v Cam
Hristo Stoichkov	BUL	2p v Gre, 1 v Arg, 1 v Mex, 1 v Ger, 1p v Ita

5 goals

Roberto Baggio	ITA	2 (1p) v Ngr, 1 v Esp, 2 v Bul
Jürgen Klinsmann	GER	1 v Bol, 1 v Esp, 2 v Kor, 1 v Bel
Romario	BRA	1 v Rus, 1 v Cam, 1 v Hol 2 v Swe (1 in each match)
Kennet Andersson	SWE	1 v Bra (group match) 2 v Sau, 1 v Rom, 1 v Bul

4 goals

Gabriel Batistuta	ARG	3 (1p) v Gre, 1p v Rom
Martin Dahlin	SWE	1 v Cam, 2 v Rus, 1 v Sau
Florian Raducioiu	ROM	2 v Col, 2 v Swe

3 goals

Bebeto	BRA	1 v Cam, 1 v USA, 1 v Hol
Denis Bergkamp	HOL	1 v Mar, 1 v Irl, 1 v Bra
Thomas Brolin	SWE	1p v Rus, 1 v Rom, 1 v Bul
Caminero	ESP	2 v Bol, 1 v Ita
Gheorghe Hagi	ROM	1 v Col, 1 v Sui, 1 v Arg

CAUTIONS
227 yellow cards   **15 red cards**

ATTENDANCES
3,567,415 at an average of 68,604 per game, easily the highest in World Cup history.
Highest game: 94,194 Brazil v Italy at LA
Lowest game: 44,132 Nigeria v Bulgaria at Dallas

QUOTES

"If I'm in Ireland, I'll buy a few of the Irish papers. I do a column for one of them, but I can't remember its name" - **Jack Charlton**

"There's me sitting in the directors' box. Do you expect me to have a geezer who's spent 25 percent of his book slagging me off, who's suing the arse off me and I've got to invite him in, shake his hand and smile?" - **Alan Sugar, on why Tel isn't welcome at Tottenham.**

"It doesn't bother me that we're not well liked. It's part of our history" - **George Graham, pretending he doesn't care.**

"If Ronnie Koeman hits a long ball, it's a great ball, but if an Englishman hits a long ball, it's a long ball" - **Graham again.**

He doesn't know a goal-line from a clothes-line" - **Barry Fry, discussing the merits of Birmingham City's owner, David Sullivan.**

If you continually play Russian roulette, eventually you're going to get the bullet" - **Dave Bassett, manager of Sheffield United, relegated after years on the edge.**

"At the moment, we couldn't hit a cow's arse with a banjo" - **Bassett again on the form of his Sheffield team.**

"That's the story of my managerial life. Buy in Woolworths, sell in Harrods" - **Joe Kinnear, manager of Wimbledon.**

"In many ways he's a nice guy. He has a very strong wife. It might have been better if I'd have made her manager" - **Ken Bates reflecting on the merits of former Chelsea manager John Hollins.**

"Fatboy waffles on about Bognor" - **Dummy headline that should have been taken out of the Sports Mail in Portsmouth before publication, but wasn't.**

"George would make a good manager - if he turned up for games" - **Pat Jennings on Best's interest in becoming the next Northern Ireland manager.**

"His knee played up in the supermarket. He's not used to pushing the trolley" - **Mick McGiven, Ipswich manager about his striker Ian Marshall's latest injury.**

"He nearly went to Middlesborough, but I told him that Newcastle was nearer London. Luckily footballers believe things like that" - **Kevin Keegan, on how he persuaded Robert Lee to sign.**

"We use a lot of first names..." - **Ken Patel, talking about a five-a-side tournament in Leicester where all 240 players were called Patel.**

"Football has lost the greatest ambassador it has ever known. No matter what era he had been manager, he would have been the greatest" - **Denis Law, on Sir Matt Busby.**

"He was my captain and always will be" - **Billy Bingham, paying tribute to Danny Blanchflower.**

World Cup Qualifying Rounds

Europe

GROUP 1 - Final Table

		P	W	D	L	GF	GA	Pts
1	Italy	10	7	2	1	22	7	16
2	Switzerland	10	6	3	1	23	6	15
3	Portugal	10	6	2	2	18	5	14
4	Scotland	10	4	3	3	14	13	11
5	Malta	10	1	1	8	3	23	3
6	Estonia	10	0	1	9	1	27	1

Italy and Switzerland qualified

Rome Oct 13, 1993 (61,178)
Italy (2) 3   **Scotland (1) 1**
Donadoni 3   *Gallacher 16*
Casiraghi 16, Eranio 81
One of the better qualifying performances from the Scots who could have made even more of a fight of it had Bryan Gunn not carelessly allowed Donadoni's shot to roll inside the post after only three minutes. Kevin Gallacher scored just seconds after Casiraghi had made it 2-0, but all the optimism of caretaker manager Craig Brown was not enough.
Italy: Pagliuca, Mussi (Lanna), Baresi, Costacurta, Benarrivo, Eranio, D Baggio, Donadoni, R Baggio, Stroppa (Zola), Casiraghi
Scotland: Gunn, McKimmie, McLaren, Irvine, Boyd, Bowman (McStay), Jess (Durrant), McAllister, Gallacher, Durie, McCall

Oporto Oct 13 (48,000)
Portugal (1) 1   **Switzerland (0) 0**
Joao Pinto II 9

Lisbon Nov 10 (100,000)
Portugal (2) 3   **Estonia (0) 0**
Futre 4, Oceano 40 (pen)
Rui Aguas 85

Milan Nov 17 (71,531)
Italy (0) 1   **Portugal (0) 0**
D Baggio 83

Ta Quali Nov 17 (8,000)
Malta (0) 0   **Scotland (1) 2**
                            McKinlay 16, Hendry 73
This was the first official outing for Craig Brown as the new manager of Scotland, and the Maltese minnows rarely threatened to spoil his big day. McAllister was outstanding in midfield and prised open the opposition defence with a pass for debutant Billy McKinlay to lift his shot over the keeper from 25 yards for the initial score. The Scottish captain was again the provider for Colin Hendry to seal the tie with a powerful header.
Malta: Cluett, Brincat, Galea, Buttigieg, Buhagiar (Saliba), S Vella, Busuttil, Spiteri, Laferla, Gregory, Suda (Scerri)
Scotland: Leighton, McLaren, Hendry, McKinnon, Irvine, Durrant (Boyd), McAllister, McKinlay (Booth), Nevin, Ferguson, Gallacher

Zurich Nov 17 (20,000)
Switzerland (3) 4   **Estonia (0) 0**
Knup 31, Herr 34
Ohrel 45, Chapuisat 61

GROUP 2 - Final Table

		P	W	D	L	GF	GA	Pts
1	Norway	10	7	2	1	25	5	16
2	Holland	10	6	3	1	29	9	15
3	England	10	5	3	2	26	9	13
4	Poland	10	3	2	5	10	15	8
5	Turkey	10	3	1	6	11	19	7
6	San Marino	10	0	1	9	2	46	1

Norway and Holland qualified

Rotterdam Oct 13, 1993 (48,000)
Holland (0) 2   **England (0) 0**
R Koeman 62, Bergkamp 68
England's World Cup aspirations were effectively ended by Ronald Koeman and German referee Kurt Assenacher. Assenacher refused to send off the Barcelona-based defender following a professional foul on Platt, and then allowed the Dutchman two attempts at a free kick, the second of which eluded Seaman to open the scoring. The referee's performance prompted one British tabloid to print his home phone number. Graham Taylor was fortunate enough to go ex-directory.
Holland: De Goey, De Wolf, R Koeman, F De Boer, Rijkaard, Wouters, Bergkamp, E Koeman, Overmars (Winter), R De Boer (Van Gobbel), Roy
England: Seaman, Parker, Dorigo, Palmer (Sinton), Adams, Pallister, Platt, Ince, Shearer, Merson (I Wright), Sharpe

Poznan Oct 13 (50,000)
Poland (0) 0   **Norway (0) 3**
                            Flo 68, Fjortoft 70
                            Johnsen 89

Istanbul Oct 27 (15,000)
Turkey (0) 2   **Poland (1) 1**
Hakan 53, K Bulent 67   *Kowalczyk 18*

Istanbul Nov 10 (10,500)
Turkey (2) 2   **Norway (0) 1**
Ertugrul 5,26   *Bohinen 47*

Bologna Nov 17 (2,378)
San Marino (1) 1   **England (3) 7**
Gualtieri 1   *Ince 21,73 Wright 32,46,78,88*
                            Ferdinand 37
At least the anaesthetic was quick; nine seconds (or less) into the match and England had succumbed to the fastest ever international goal. It disabused the most devoted English fan, there was no escape now. Wright went on to score four goals against a side that would struggle in the Pontin's League and England duly won their 400th international victory. All this in front of just 2,378 fans, the smallest ever to watch a full England team.
San Marino: Benedettini, Valentini (Gobby), Zanotti, Canti, Gennari, Guerra, Manzaroli, Della Valle, Bacciocchi (P Mazza), Bonini, Gualtieri
England: Seaman, Dixon, Pearce, Ince, Walker, Pallister, Ripley, I Wright, Ferdinand, Platt, Sinton

Poznan Nov 17 (20,000)
Poland (1) 1   **Holland (1) 3**
Lesniak 13   *Bergkamp 10, 56*
                            R De Boer 88

GROUP 3 - Final Table

	P	W	D	L	GF	GA	Pts
1 Spain	12	8	3	1	27	4	19
2 Republic of Ireland	12	7	4	1	19	6	18
3 Denmark	12	7	4	1	15	2	18
4 Northern Ireland	12	5	3	4	14	13	13
5 Lithuania	12	2	3	7	8	21	7
6 Latvia	12	0	5	7	4	21	5
7 Albania	12	1	2	9	6	26	4

Spain and Republic of Ireland qualified

Copenhagen   Oct 13, 1993   (40,200)
Denmark (0) 1   N Ireland (0) 0
B Laudrup 81
The European champions had to work hard to break down a spirited display from the Ulstermen and keep their World Cup hopes alive. Jimmy Quinn was unlucky to have a 70th minute header disallowed for a foul on Vilfort. Laudrup, who had earlier struck an upright, was set up for the winner by Arsenal's John Jensen, who fed the striker for a shot from the edge of the box.
Denmark: Schmeichel, Reiper, Olsen, Kjeldberg, Vilfort, Jensen, Nielsen, M Laudrup, B Laudrup, Povlsen, Pingel (H Larsen)
N Ireland: Wright, Fleming, Worthington, Taggart, McDonald, Donaghy, Magilton, Wilson (Black), Dowie (Quinn), Gray, Hughes

Dublin   Oct 13   (33,000)
Rep of Ireland (0) 1   Spain (3) 3
Sheridan 74   Caminero 12, Salinas 15,26
The party was ready to happen at Lansdowne Road, but Javier Clemente's team had no intention of joining in. "We've had a bad day" said Big Jack after watching three early goals throw open the race for qualification. The luck of the Irish was not in evidence as Irwin was denied by the crossbar and McGrath by the legs of Zubizaretta.
Rep of Ireland: Bonner, Irwin, Phelan, Moran (Sheridan), Kernaghan, Keane, McGrath, Houghton, Quinn, Whelan, Staunton (Cascarino)
Spain: Zubizaretta, Ferrer, Voro, Nadal, Giner, Hierro, Goicoechea, Camarasa, Luis Enrique, Salinas (Guardiola), Caminero (Bakero)

Windsor Park   Nov 17   (10,500)
N Ireland (0) 1   R of Ireland (0) 1
Quinn 73   McLoughlin 76
The Republic of Ireland secured World Cup qualification by the skin of their teeth in an emotionally charged Windsor Park. Jimmy Quinn sent the capacity crowd into raptures with his eighth goal in 37 internationals, which brought Billy Bingham to his feet in his 117th and final match in charge. Bingham, who had earlier clashed with Charlton over his description of the Republic's players as "mercenaries", was silenced three minutes later by an Alan McLoughlin equaliser. The Portsmouth midfielder who had previously played only walk-on roles in the Republic's performances, entered Irish folklore with an opportunist strike to seal the plane tickets to the USA.
N Ireland: Wright, Fleming, Worthington, Taggart, McDonald, Donaghy, Magilton, Wilson (Black), Quinn, Gray (Dowie), Hughes
R of Ireland: Bonner, Irwin, Phelan, Kernaghan, McGrath, Keane, Houghton (McLoughlin), Townsend, Quinn, Aldridge (Cascarino), McGoldrick

Seville   Nov 17   (50,000)
Spain (0) 1   Denmark (0) 0
Hierro 62

GROUP 4 - Final Table

	P	W	D	L	GF	GA	Pts
1 Romania	10	7	1	2	29	12	15
2 Belgium	10	7	1	2	16	5	15
3 RCS	10	4	5	1	21	9	13
4 Wales	10	5	2	3	19	12	12
5 Cyprus	10	2	1	7	8	18	5
6 Faeroes	10	0	0	10	1	38	0

Romania and Belgium qualified

Bucharest   Oct 13, 1993   (25,000)
Romania (0) 2   Belgium (0) 1
Raducioiu 67 (pen)   Scifo 87 (pen)
Dumitrescu 84

Cardiff   Oct 13   (10,000)
Wales (0) 2   Cyprus (0) 0
Saunders 70, Rush 82
Wales showed plenty of patience in breaking down a packed Cypriot defence which revelled in the physical side of the game to the extent that they ended the game with 9 men. Aizlewood and Hughes both picked up bookings which ruled them out of the Romania match.
Wales: Southall, Phillips, Horne, Aizlewood, Young, Symons (Goss), Giggs, Rush, Saunders, Hughes, Speed
Cyprus: Petridis, G Constantinou, Pittas, D Ioannou (Panayi), Evagoras, Yargoudakis (Xiuruppas), Charalambous, Kosta, Sotiriou, Larku, Papavasiliou

Kosice   Oct 27   (15,600)
RCS (2) 3   Cyprus (0) 0
Dubovsky 12, Hapal 23
Skuhravy 77

Brussels   Nov 17   (30,000)
Belgium (0) 0   RCS (0) 0

Cardiff   Nov 17   (40,000)
Wales (0) 1   Romania (1) 2
Saunders 60   Hagi 33, Raducioiu 83
Wales had failed to qualify for the last 8 finals, and this result made it 9. Romania, who had trounced Wales 5-1 17 months earlier, were pushed to the limit in front of a fervent crowd. A blunder by Southall and a penalty attempt by Bodin that would have graced a 5 Nations rugby match conspired to leave the Welshmen agonisingly short. In the stands, a tragic incident left Wales' fan John Hill dead, after a distress rocket was fired into the crowd.
Wales: Southall, Phillips, Melville, Bodin (Allen), Young, Symons (Goss), Giggs, Rush, Saunders, Horne, Speed
Romania: Prunea, Belodedici, Petrescu, Prodan, Selymes (Munteanu), Sabau, Popescu, Lupescu, Hagi, Raducioiu, Dumitrescu (Mihali)

GROUP 5 - Final Table

	P	W	D	L	GF	GA	Pts
1 Greece	8	6	2	0	10	2	14
2 Russia	8	5	2	1	15	4	12
3 Iceland	8	3	2	3	7	6	8
4 Hungary	8	2	1	5	6	11	5
5 Luxembourg	8	0	1	7	2	17	1

Russia and Greece qualified

Luxembourg Oct 12, 1993 (2,558)
Luxembourg (0) 1   **Greece (1) 3**
Fanelli 83   *Machlas 31, Apostolakis 65*
                       Saravakos 73

Budapest Oct 27 (1,500)
Hungary (1) 1   **Luxembourg (0) 0**
Detari 20

Athens Nov 17 (60,000)
Greece (0) 1   **Russia (0) 0**
Machlas 68

GROUP 6 - Final Table

		P	W	D	L	GF	GA	Pts
1	Sweden	10	6	3	1	19	8	15
2	Bulgaria	10	6	2	2	19	10	14
3	France	10	6	1	3	17	10	13
4	Austria	10	3	2	5	15	16	8
5	Finland	10	2	1	7	9	18	5
6	Israel	10	1	3	6	10	27	5

Sweden and Bulgaria qualified

Sofia Oct 13, 1993 (25,000)
Bulgaria (2) 4   **Austria (0) 1**
Penev 6, 76   *Herzog 51*
Stoichkov 33 (pen)
Lechkov 87

Paris Oct 13 (32,741)
France (2) 2   **Israel (1) 3**
Sauzee 30, Ginola 40 *R Harazi 21, Berkovich 85*
                       Atar 89

Stockholm Oct 13 (30,177)
Sweden (3) 3   **Finland (1) 2**
Dahlin 27,45   *Suominen 15*
H Larsson 40   *Litmanen 60*

Tel Aviv Oct 27 (27,000)
Israel (1) 1   **Austria (1) 1**
Rosenthal 3   *Reinmayr 15*

Vienna Nov 10 (25,000)
Austria (0) 1   **Sweden (0) 1**
Herzog 70   *Mild 67*

Tel Aviv Nov 10 (10,000)
Israel (0) 1   **Finland (0) 3**
R Harazi 90   *Hyrylainen 53, Paavola 72*
                       Hjelm 84

Paris Nov 17 (48,402)
France (1) 1   **Bulgaria (1) 2**
Cantona 33   *Kostadinov 36,90*

Africa
2ND ROUND
GROUP A - Final Table

		P	W	D	L	GF	GA	Pts
1	Nigeria	4	2	1	1	10	5	5
2	Côte d'Ivoire	4	2	1	1	5	6	5
3	Algeria	4	0	2	2	3	7	2

Nigeria qualified

Oct 8, 1993
Algeria (0) 1   **Nigeria (1) 1**

GROUP B - Final Table

		P	W	D	L	GF	GA	Pts
1	Morocco	4	3	0	1	6	3	6
2	Zambia	4	2	1	1	6	2	5
3	Senegal	4	0	1	3	1	8	1

Morocco qualified

Oct 10, 1993
Morocco (0) 1   **Zambia (0) 0**

GROUP C - Final Table

		P	W	D	L	GF	GA	Pts
1	Cameroon	4	3	0	1	7	3	6
2	Zimbabwe	4	0	2	2	3	6	4
3	Guinea	4	1	0	3	4	5	2

Cameroon qualified

Oct 10, 1993
Cameroon (3) 3   **Zimbabwe (1) 1**

Asia
Tournament in Qatar Oct 15-28
2ND ROUND - Final Table

		P	W	D	L	GF	GA	Pts
1	Saudi Arabia	5	2	3	0	8	6	7
2	South Korea	5	2	2	1	9	4	6
3	Japan	5	2	2	1	7	4	6
4	Iraq	5	1	3	1	9	9	5
5	Iran	5	2	0	3	8	11	4
6	North Korea	5	1	0	4	5	12	2

Saudi Arabia and South Korea qualified

North Korea (0) 3   **Iraq (1) 2**
Saudi Arabia (0) 0   Japan (0) 0
Iran (0) 0   **South Korea (1) 3**
North Korea (0) 1   Saudi Arabia (0) 2
Japan (0) 1   **Iran (1) 2**
Iraq (1) 2   South Korea (1) 2
North Korea (0) 0   **Japan (1) 3**
Iran (1) 1   Iraq (2) 2
South Korea (1) 1   **Saudi Arabia (1) 1**
Iraq (1) 1   Saudi Arabia (1) 1
Japan (0) 1   **South Korea (0) 0**
Iran (0) 2   North Korea (1) 1
South Korea (0) 3   **North Korea (0) 0**
Saudi Arabia (2) 4   Iran (1) 3
Iraq (0) 2   **Japan (1) 2**

Oceania/Concaf v 4th S America
Sydney Oct 31 (43,967)
Australia (1) 1   **Argentina (1) 1**
Aurelio Vidmar 42   *Balbo 37*

Buenos Aires Nov 17 (60,000)
Argentina (0) 1   **Australia (0) 0**
Batistuta 60

Argentina qualified

World Cup Finals

First Round

GROUP A

Detroit June 18 (77,557)
USA (1) 1   **Switzerland (1) 1**
Wynalda 45   *Bregy 40*
The first World Cup game to be played indoors had the highest attendance for a USA game to date. The two goals were both impressively executed free kicks.

Los Angeles June 18 (91,856)
Colombia (1) 1   **Romania (2) 3**
Valencia 42   *Raducioiu 15,87, Hagi 33*
Gheorghe Hagi engineered two goals and scored another with an outrageous 35-yard floater into the top corner.

Detroit June 22 (61,428)
Romania (1) 1   **Switzerland 4**
Hagi 36   *Sutter 16, Chapuisat 53*
     Knup 66,73
The previously impressive Romanians were swept aside by Roy Hodgson's lightweight team in the sauna-like atmosphere of the Silverdome.

Los Angeles June 23 (93,194)
USA (1) 2   **Colombia (0) 1**
Escobar (og) 35   *Valencia 90*
Stewart 53
This win consigned pre-tournament favourites Colombia to a early return whilst sparking huge celebrations amongst the home followers who were now assured of following their team through to the knock-out stage.

Los Angeles June 26 (93,869)
USA (0) 0   **Romania (1) 1**
     Petrescu 17
Romania showed another side of their game, playing disciplined defensive football. John Harkes was booked and thereby ruled out of the United States' next game.

San Francisco June 26 (83,769)
Switzerland (0) 0   **Colombia (1) 2**
     Gaviria 44, Lozano 90

Final Table

	P	W	D	L	GF	GA	Pts
1 Romania	3	2	0	1	5	5	6
2 Switzerland	3	1	1	1	5	4	4
3 USA	3	1	1	1	3	3	4
4 Colombia	3	1	0	2	4	5	3

Romania, Switzerland and USA qualified for Second Round

GROUP B

Los Angeles June 20 (83,959)
Cameroon (1) 2   **Sweden (1) 2**
Embe 32, Omam-Biyik 47   *Ljung 8, Dahlin 75*

San Francisco June 20 (81,061)
Brazil (1) 2   **Russia (0) 0**
Romario 26, Rai (pen) 53
Romario, described by his manager as a "gift from God", enlightened proceedings at Stanford Stadium with a display that showed that Brazilian football had recovered from its wilderness years.

San Francisco June 24 (83,410)
Brazil (1) 3   **Cameroon (0) 0**
Romario 39
Marcio Santos 65
Bebeto 73

Detroit June 25 (71,528)
Sweden (1) 3   **Russia (1) 1**
Brolin (pen) 39   *Salenko (pen) 4*
Dahlin 60,82

Detroit June 28 (77,217)
Brazil (0) 1   **Sweden (1) 1**
Romario 47   *K Andersson 24*

San Francisco June 28 (74,914)
Russia (3) 6   **Cameroon (0) 1**
Salenko 16, 41, 44 (pen)   *Milla*
72, 75, Radchenko 82
Oleg Salenko was unable to get a work permit to play for Tottenham as, according to the D of E, two caps for Ukraine was no guarantee of quality. Five goals in the World Cup was a little too late for Spurs (Salenko had long gone to Spain), but it was a new World Cup record.

Final Table

	P	W	D	L	GF	GA	Pts
1 Brazil	3	2	1	0	6	1	7
2 Sweden	3	1	2	0	6	4	5
3 Russia	3	1	0	2	7	6	3
4 Cameroon	3	0	1	2	3	11	1

Brazil and Sweden qualified for Second Round

GROUP C

Chicago June 17 (63,117)
Germany (0) 1   **Bolivia (0) 0**
Klinsmann 61
Not since England won their first match in 1970 have the holders won their opening game. Etcheverry, known as 'El Diablo', was the first red card culprit, talking an early bath only 5 minutes after coming on as substitute.

Dallas June 18 (56,247)
Spain (0) 2   **South Korea (0) 2**
Salinas 50   *Hong Myung-Bo 84*
Goicoechea 55   *Seo Jung-Won 90*
Spain looked to be cruising through to a victory when they were stunned by breakaway goals from the Koreans.

Chicago June 21 (63,113)
Germany (0) 1   **Spain (1) 1**
Klinsmann 48   *Goicoechea 14*
It became difficult to believe that Germany would retain their title after an unimaginative performance against Spain. The Spanish side, without their suspended sweeper Miguel Nadal, managed to hold on after Klinsmann's equalizer.

Boston June 24 (53,000)
South Korea (0) 0   **Bolivia (0) 0**
Not the most exciting game of the tournament, but the longest. Scottish referee Leslie Mottram did not blow for time until 103 minutes and 40 seconds had been played, making it probably the longest game in a World Cup.

Chicago   June 27   (63,089)
Bolivia (0) 1   **Spain (1) 3**
Erwin Sanchez 67   *Guardiola (pen) 20*
                             Caminero 66,71

Dallas   June 27   (63,998)
Germany (3) 3   **South Korea (0) 2**
Klinsmann 12,37   *Hwang Sun-Hong 52*
Riedle 20   *Hong Myung-Bo 63*
German coach Berti Vogts described the victory as
"lucky" and only some inspired goalkeeping from Illgner
kept the Koreans at bay. Two second-half strikes exposed
the Germany's frailty in defence. Post-match the German
midfielder Stefan Effenberg was told he would no longer
play for his country after 'showing his middle finger' to
German fans.
Final Table

	P	W	D	L	GF	GA	Pts
1 Germany	3	2	1	0	5	3	7
2 Spain	3	1	2	0	6	4	5
3 South Korea	3	0	2	1	4	5	2
4 Bolivia	3	0	1	2	1	4	1

Germany and Spain qualified for Second Round

GROUP D
Boston   June 21   (53,644)
Argentina (2) 4   **Greece (0) 0**
Batistuta 2,45,90 (pen)
Maradona 60
Greece were swept aside by a team inspired by the
presence of troubled star Maradona. Batistuta scored the
fastest goal of the tournament so far, and went on to
complete the Finals' first hat-trick.

Dallas   June 22   (44,932)
Bulgaria (0) 0   **Nigeria (2) 3**
                            Yekini 21, Amokachi 43
                            Amunike 54
The Super Eagles overpowered their East European
opponents mixing surging froward runs and intricate
tactical ploys. Coach Westerhof stated "we are afraid of
nobody. We have showed we can play football".

Boston   June 25   (54,453)
Argentina (2) 2   **Nigeria (1) 1**
Caniggia 22,29   *Siasia 9*
Nigeria dazzled with a brilliant early goal, but gradually
the Argentinians subdued the rampant Africans and the
second half was surprisingly one-sided. The half-time
foul-score was 24 by Nigeria, one by Argentina.

Chicago   June 26   (63,160)
Bulgaria (1) 4   **Greece (0) 0**
Stoichkov (pens) 5,56
Lechkov 66
Borimirov 90
Bulgaria won their first match in a World Cup finals with
a comfortable defeat of Greece. They had previously
played 17 games in six World Cups before the
breakthrough.

Boston   July 1   (53,001)
Greece (0) 0   **Nigeria (1) 2**
                            Finidi 45, Amokachi 90
Greece ended the Finals with the worst record of any
team playing, being the only team in the competition to
fail to score a point. No wonder England beat them 5-0.

Dallas   July 1   (63,998)
Argentina (0) 0   **Bulgaria (0) 2**
                            Stoichkov 61, Sirakov 90
In a match overshadowed by the ban on Maradona for
use of a outlawed stimulant, Bulgaria capitalised on a
dispirited opposition.
Final Table

	P	W	D	L	GF	GA	Pts
1 Nigeria	3	2	0	1	6	2	6
2 Bulgaria	3	2	0	1	6	3	6
3 Argentina	3	2	0	1	6	3	6
4 Greece	3	0	0	3	0	10	0

Nigeria, Bulgaria and Argentina qualified for the next round

GROUP E
New York   June 18   (73,511)
Italy (0) 0   **Rep. of Ireland (1) 1**
                            Houghton 12
Ray Houghton's left footed drive over Pagliuca proved
the decisive moment in this long awaited clash in the
debilitating heat of the Giants Stadium. It was the first
win over Italy that Ireland had recorded in the last eight
attempts. The Italians wilted with Baggio anonymous
and their much vaunted strike force rendered impotent
by the nous of McGrath and Babb.
Italy: Pagliuca, Tassotti, Baresi, Costacurta, Maldini,
Donadoni, D Baggio, Albertini, Evani (Massaro), R
Baggio, Signori (Berti)
Rep. of Ireland: Bonner, Irwin, McGrath, Babb, Phelan,
Houghton (McAteer), Keane, Sheridan, Townsend,
Staunton, Coyne (Aldridge)

Washington   June 19   (52,359)
Norway (0) 1   **Mexico (0) 0**
Rekdal 85
Verdens Gang, the Norwegian newspaper, backed their
country to become finalists at 12-1 against, but this was
the only time it looked even remotely possible.

New York   June 23   (74,624)
Italy (0) 1   **Norway (0) 0**
D Baggio 68
It took a spirited 10 man defence to keep Italy's hopes
alive following the dismissal of 'keeper Pagliuca and the
substitution of Roberto Baggio 22 minutes into the game.

Florida   June 24   (61,219)
Mexico (1) 2   **Rep. of Ireland (0) 1**
Luis Garcia 44,66   *Aldridge 84*
The game was played in a temperature of 103 degrees
and Ireland's game was riddled with errors. Tommy
Coyne was inches away and Townsend was denied by
the eccentric Campos whose luminous outfit was
probably responsible for distracting the midfielder. It
was left for Luis Garcia to prey upon defensive mistakes.
John Aldridge came off the bench to reduce the deficit.
Mexico: Campos, Del Olmo, Suarez, Juan de Dios,
Ramirez, Rodriguez (Salvador), Bernal, Ambriz, Luis
Garcia, Garcia Aspe, Hermosillo (Guiterrez), Zague
Rep. of Ireland: Bonner, Irwin, McGrath, Babb, Phelan,
Houghton, Keane, Sheridan, Townsend, Staunton
(Aldridge), Coyne (McAteer)

New York   June 28   (76,332)
Rep. of Ireland (0) 0   **Norway (0) 0**
Ireland eked out the draw that saw them through and
also saw the demise of an uninspiring Norwegian team.

Norway had to attack to progress in the competition, but you would never have believed it. They managed no shots at goal in the first half, preferring to hit long balls at 6' 5" Flo, known as The Lighthouse and about as mobile.
Rep. of Ireland: Bonner, G Kelly, McGrath, Babb, Staunton, Keane, McAteer, Sheridan, Townsend (Whelan), Houghton, Aldridge (D Kelly)
Norway: Thorstvedt, Berg, Bratseth, Johnsen, Halle (Jakobsen), Flo, Mykland, Leonhardsen (Bohinen), Rekdal, Bjornebye, Sorloth

Washington   June 28   (53,186)
Italy (0) 1   **Mexico (0) 1**
Massaro 48   *Bernal 58*
Daniele Massaro came on at the interval for Casiraghi and within three minutes had put Italy into the lead. Mexico's equaliser ensured them of top placing in Group E by virtue of the numbers of goals scored.
Final Table

	P	W	D	L	GF	GA	Pts
1 Mexico	3	1	1	1	3	3	4
2 Rep. Of Ireland	3	1	1	1	2	2	4
3 Italy	3	1	1	1	2	2	4
4 Norway	3	1	1	1	1	1	4

Mexico, Rep. of Ireland and Italy qualified for Second Round

GROUP F
Florida   June 19   (60,790)
Belgium (1) 1   **Morocco (0) 0**
Degryse 11
Belgium, seeded sixth in the competition, were lucky to hold off a Moroccan side which twice hit the woodwork.

Washington   June 21   (52,535)
Holland (0) 2   **Saudi Arabia (1) 1**
Jonk 50, Taument 87   *Amin 19*

Florida   June 25   (61,219)
Belgium (1) 1   **Holland (0) 0**
Albert 66
With the temperature again over 100" C in the Citrus Bowl, Belgium secured a much vaunted victory over Holland largely through their keeper Preud'homme.

New York   June 25   (72,404)
Saudi Arabia (1) 2   **Morocco (1) 1**
Al Jaber (pen) 8, Amin 46   Chaouch 28
The greatest result in Saudi Arabia's history. Both Saudi goals were against the run of play and they survived intense pressure in the second half.

Orlando   June 29   (60,578)
Morocco (0) 1   **Holland (1) 2**
Nader 47   *Bergkamp 43, Roy 78*

Washington   June 29   (52,959)
Belgium (0) 0   **Saudi Arabia (1) 1**
                              Owairan 5
Belgium appeared shocked when Saeed Owairan began a mazy dribble from 10 yards inside his own half and finished with a net-billowing shot inside the far post.
Final Table

	P	W	D	L	GF	GA	Pts
1 Holland	3	2	0	1	4	3	6
2 Saudi Arabia	3	2	0	1	4	3	6
3 Belgium	3	2	0	1	2	1	6
4 Morocco	3	0	0	3	2	5	0

Holland, Saudi Arabia and Belgium qualify for the next round

Second Round
Chicago   July 2   (60,246)
Germany (3) 3   **Belgium (1) 2**
Völler 6,39 Klinsmann 11 Grun 8 Albert 90
Belgium protested vigorously over a turned down penalty appeal when Helmer looked to have brought down Weber. However it was a rejuvenated Rudi Völler who smoothed Germany's passage to the next round.

Washington   July 2   (53,141)
Spain (1) 3   **Switzerland (0) 0**
Hierro 15
Luis Enrique 74
Beguiristain (pen) 86

Dallas   July 3   (60,277)
Saudi Arabia (0) 1   **Sweden (1) 3**
Al Ghesheyan 85   Dahlin 6, K Andersson 51,88

Los Angeles   July 3   (90,469)
Romania (2) 3   **Argentina (1) 2**
Dumitrescu 11,18   Batistuta (pen) 16
Hagi 58   Balbo 75
Argentina have appeared in the final of the last two World Cups, but with Maradona a sad spectator they succumbed to the irresistible skill of Hagi and Dumitrescu, the first 15 minutes of the game providing the finest football of the competition, Hagi executing a couple of exquisite passes for Dumitrescu's strikes.

Orlando   July 4   (61,355)
Holland (2) 2   **Rep. of Ireland (0) 0**
Bergkamp 12, Jonk 41
When Packie Bonner let Wim Jonk's shot slip between his hands for Holland's second, the fate of the Irish was effectively sealed. Bonner, a hero in Italia '90, was not alone in looking for holes to crawl into. Terry Phelan's flank was constantly pillaged by Overmars whose early cross set up a comfortable tap-in for Bergkamp. Whilst Houghton went close and McGrath's last minute effort was ruled out, the Dutch were worthy winners .
Holland: De Goey, Koeman, Valckx, De Boer, Rijkaard, Winter, Jonk, Witschge (Numan), Overmars, Bergkamp, van Vossen (Roy)
Rep. of Ireland: Bonner, Kelly, McGrath, Babb, Phelan, Houghton, Keane, Sheridan, Townsend, Staunton (McAteer), Coyne (Cascarino)

San Francisco   July 4   (84,147)
Brazil (0) 1   **USA (0) 0**
Bebeto 74
Brazil played the second half without Leonardo, dismissed for an elbow into Ramos' face. The Brazilians had most of the clever touches, but failed to score until Bebeto capitalised on some elusive running by Romario.

Boston   July 5   (54,367)
Nigeria (1) 1   **Italy (0) 2**
Amunike 26   R Baggio 87,(pen) 103 aet
Roberto Baggio finally lived up to his billing as the world's best player with a thrilling rescue act.
New York   July 5   (71,030)
Mexico (1) 1   **Bulgaria (1) 1**
Garcia Aspe (pen) 18   Stoichkov 7 aet
Bulgaria won 3-1 on penalties

Quarter Finals

Boston   July 9   (53,644)
Italy (1) 2   **Spain (0) 1**
D Baggio 26   *Caminero 59*
R Baggio 88

A Baggio double bill was sufficient to squeeze the Italians through yet another round. The Spaniard Caminero gained the dubious distinction of becoming the 200th player in the championships to be cautioned, for a foul on Conte. But luck stayed with Baggio who skipped round Zubizaretta to slot home the winner.

Dallas   July 9   (63,998)
Holland (0) 2   **Brazil (0) 3**
Bergkamp 63, Winter 76   *Romario 52, Bebeto 61*
                                  Branco 81

With Jan Wouters returning to the Dutch defence, the Brazilians found themselves cramped for room. However they upped a gear in the 2nd half and tore the Dutch apart at will to lead 2-0. The 2nd goal so enraged Holland, who believed that Romario was in an offside position, that they promptly equalised. Yet the South Americans clinched the tie with a rasping 30 yard free kick that skidded in off the far post.

New York   July 10   (72,416)
Bulgaria (0) 2   **Germany (0) 1**
Stoichkov 75   *Matthäus (pen) 48*
Lechkov 79

Giants Stadium witnessed one of the biggest upsets as the holders were sent crashing out. Talking later about his free kick equaliser, Stoichkov said "I thought about my little daughter and all my great years at Barcelona. That made me concentrate."

San Francisco   July 10   (81,715)
Sweden (0) 2   **Romania (0) 2**
Brolin 79   *Raducioiu 89,101*
K Andersson 115   *aet*
Sweden won 5-4 on penalties

Sweden's veteran 'keeper Thomas Ravelli thwarted both Belodedici and Petrescu to secure a victory on penalties.

English referee Philip Don had his work cut out to control some exuberant tackling, and the game seemed Sweden's until Raducioiu offered a glimmer of hope with a last minute leveller.

Semi Finals

New York   July 13   (77,094)
Italy (2) 2   **Bulgaria (1) 1**
R Baggio 21,26   *Stoichkov (pen) 44*

Baggio may not enjoy grinding out results, but big match player he is. His two strikes elevated an Italian performance that was by far their most impressive of the Finals. Mussi and Berti exploited the wide open spaces on Bulgaria's left flank, carving out openings for Casiraghi and Albertini. Stoichkov swept in a spot kick after Sirakov had been felled by Pagliuca, but it was not enough.

Los Angeles   July 13   (84,569)
Brazil (0) 1   **Sweden (0) 0**
Romario 80

A match that failed to live up to expectation, largely due to the cautious nature of the Swedes whose packed defence survived until Romario's late header won the game. Brazil only managed this paltry return from 29 shots, which was partly down to Ravelli's performance in his 116th international. It was ironic that Sweden's big central defence was eventually breached by the header from a man who stands at only 5' 6".

Third/Fourth Play Off

Los Angeles   July 16   (83,716)
Sweden (4) 4   **Bulgaria (0) 0**
Brolin 8, Mild 30
Larsson 37, K Andersson 39

Thomas Brolin orchestrated the rout of Bulgaria that led to Sweden's highest placing since they were second in 1958. With four goals in the first forty minutes, it was hardly surprising that the second half was something of an anti-climax. Especially for Stoichkov, who needed only one goal to become the competition's top scorer.

World Cup Final

Los Angeles   July 17   (94,194)
Brazil (0) 0   Italy (0) 0
aet
Brazil won 3-2 on penalties

Penalty Sequence: Baresi (shot over), Marcio Santos (saved), Albertini (scored), Romario (scored off upright), Evani (scored), Branco (scored), Massaro (saved), Dunga (scored), R Baggio (shot over)

Brazil's win in the Rose Bowl now means that they have won the Cup on a record four occasions, to the three of Germany and Italy. A dour game in which both teams successfully negated the attacking flair of the opposition, alway seemed likely to go the distance. The veteran Baresi was a surprise inclusion coming so soon after the Milan defender had undergone keyhole surgery on a knee problem. Massaro forced Taffarel into a save, but Pagliuca was the more troubled keeper, almost 'doing a Bonner' when a soft shot escaped his grasp and spun towards the goal. To his relief the ball cannoned into the post and popped back into his arms. Pagliuca however was required to make a superb save from a 53rd minute Bebeto header, but both sides missed gilt-edged opportunities to seal victory in extra time. The penalty lottery was lost as both Baresi and Baggio blasted high into cheering crowds of Brazilians. The Brazilians had exorcised the ghost of 1970, which had preyed upon successive teams and managers. It was therefore ironic to note that Brazil are the first Cup winners since Pele and Co. to go undefeated through the tournament.

Brazil: Taffarel, Jorginho (Cafu), Marcio Santos, Aldair, Branco, Mazinho, Mauro Silva, Dunga, Zinho (Viola), Bebeto, Romario **Italy:** Pagliuca, Mussi (Apolloni), Maldini, Baresi, Benarrivo, Donadoni, Albertini, D Baggio (Evani), Berti, R Baggio, Massaro

WORLD CUP QUOTES

"Me, they killed me, I'm completely dead....They cut my legs away from me....I think they've now cut my entire body away....I don't know where I stand.....I can't find myself" - **Diego Maradona.**

"I am upset at FIFA's stupidity. I consider ephedrine a medicine and I take it every day to be at my best for my public" - **Luciano Pavarotti, leaping to Maradona's defence.**

"He's been through drugs, he's been through drink and women and he's still there" - **John Fashanu appreciating Maradona - before the positive drug test.**

"I suppose I'll only know how they feel when I return on Thursday and if I have to pay for my own Guinness" - **Jack Charlton wondering what his post World Cup welcome would be in Ireland.**

"At least after the scan it proves to everyone that I do have a brain" - **Charlton again, following a health check-up.**

"He's a perfectionist. If he was married to Demi Moore, he'd expect her to be a good cook" - **Rick Davis, former New York Cosmos captain on the US manager, Boro Milutinovic.**

"Our coach speaks Spanish. He speaks six languages, unfortunately English isn't one of them" - **Roy Wegerle, on Milutinovic.**

"Soccer will never take over from baseball. Baseball's the only chance we blacks get to wave a bat at the white man without starting a riot" - **Eddie Murphy.**

"The boys called me Valderrama, but after the game I felt more like Val Doonican" - **Andy Townsend, who dyed his hair blond for a bet.**

"Germany weeps, the rest of the world laughs" - **Headline in *Blick*, the Swiss newspaper, after Germany lost to Bulgaria.**

"I've been looking for new kitchen curtains for a long time" - **Erik Thorstvedt, who swapped his jersey with the technicolour outfit of Mexican keeper, Jorge Campos.**

"A film called Passport to Terror will follow this game and I think the referee will be in it" - **Des Lynam, on referee Jamal Al-Sharif, who controlled the Mexico-Bulgaria game.**

"He tries that shot all the time in training. That's the first time I've seen it go in" - **Jack Charlton, on Ray Houghton's goal against Italy.**

"I'm over here, dad" - **Irish supporters to Eamonn Casey, the former Bishop of Galway, spotted at the game against Mexico.**

"The crazy thing about all these yellow cards given out is that this has been one of the cleanest World Cups in years" - **TV Commentator John Helm**

"There are 11 men sitting on yellow cards and that is a very uncomfortable position to be in' - **John Motson.**

British and Irish non-championship Matches

Wembley   Mar 9   (71,970)
England (1) 1   **Denmark (0) 0**
Platt
England: Seaman, Parker, Adams, Pallister, Le Saux, Anderton, Platt, Ince (Batty), Gascoigne (Le Tissier), Beardsley, Shearer
Denmark: Schmeichel, Kjeldberg, Olsen, Rieper, Vilfort (Hoegh), B Laudrup, M Laudrup, Larsen, Jensen, Dethlefsen, Christensen (Fredrikson)

Cardiff   Mar 9   (10,000)
Wales (0) 1   **Norway (1) 3**
Coleman   *Flo, Mykland, Jakobsen*
Wales: Southall, Melville, Young, Coleman, Perry, Horne, Phillips, Blake (Pembridge), Rush, Speed (Saunders), M Hughes (C Hughes)
Norway: Grodas, Loken, Berg, Pedersen, Bjornebye, Flo, Mykland, Rekdal (Solbakken), Bohinen, Jakobsen, Fjortoft (Frigaard)

Windsor Park   Mar 23   (5,500)
N Ireland (1) 2   **Romania (0) 0**
Morrow, Gray
N Ireland: Wright, Fleming, Donaghy, Taggart, Morrow, Wilson, Lomas, Magilton, Hughes (Black), Gray, Quinn (Dowie)
Romania: Prunea (Stelea), Petrescu, Lupescu (Mihali), Belodedici, Prodan, Munteanu, Sabau, Popescu (Gilca), Hagi, Dumitrescu, Raducioiu (Panduru)

Dublin   Mar 23   (34,000)
Rep. of Ireland (0) 0   Russia (0) 0
Rep. of Ireland: Bonner (A Kelly), G Kelly, Carey, Babb, McGoldrick, McAteer, O'Brien, Whelan, McLoughlin, D Kelly (Coyne), Cascarino
Russia: Kharine, Rakhimov, Gorlukovich, Kovtoun, Tetradze, Popov, Komeev (Tchertshev), Radchenko (Kossolapov), Borodyuk, Kuznetsov, Salenko

Hampden Park   Mar 23   (36,809)
Scotland (0) 0   **Holland (0) 1**
                                   Roy
Scotland: Goram, McKimmie, McLaren, Hendry, Levein (Boyd), Robertson (Collins), McCall, McStay (McKinlay), McAllister, Durie, Nevin (Jess)
Holland: De Goey, Van Gobbel, Blind, F De Boer, Witschge, Jonk, Rijkaard, Bosman (Winter), Taument (Overmars), Bergkamp (Gillhaus), Roy

Vienna   Apr 20   (35,000)
Austria (1) 1   **Scotland (1) 2**
Hutter   *McGinlay, McKinlay*
Austria: Wohlfahrt, Prosenik (Kuhbauer), Kogler, Schottel, Hochmaier, Hutter, Stoger, Herzog, Baur, Polster (Weissenberger), Cerny
Scotland: Leighton, McKimmie, McLaren, Hendry, Irvine, Boyd (I Ferguson), McKinlay, McAllister, Collins (McCall), McGinlay (Shearer), Jess (Nevin)

Tilburg   Apr 20   (30,000)
Holland (0) 0   **Rep. of Ireland (0) 1**
                                   Coyne
Holland: De Goey, Valckx, Koeman (De Wolf), F De Boer, Rijkaard, Jonk (Winter), Overmars, Bergkamp (Taument), Roy, R De Boer
Rep. of Ireland: Bonner, G Kelly, Moran, Babb, Phelan (McLoughlin), Whelan, McGoldrick (McAteer), Sheridan, Townsend, Staunton, Coyne (O'Coyle)

Wrexham   Apr 20   (4,694)
Wales (0) 0   **Sweden (0) 2**
                                   Larsson, Brolin
Wales: Southall, Horne, Melville, Neilson, Bodin, Bowen (Blackmore), Goss (Blake), Phillips, Speed, Roberts (C Hughes), Rush
Sweden: Ravelli, R Nilsson (M Nilsson), P Andersson, Bjorklund, Ljung, Larsson, Ingesson (Rehn), Schwarz, Limpar (Blomqvist), K Andersson, Brolin

Wembley   May 17   (23,659)
England (3) 5   **Greece (0) 0**
Anderton, Beardsley
Platt 2 (1 pen), Shearer
England: Flowers, Jones (Pearce), Adams, Bould, Le Saux, Anderton (Le Tissier), Richardson, Merson, Beardsley (Wright), Platt, Shearer
Greece: Karkamanis, Apostolakis, Kalitzakis, Kolitsidakis (Karataidis), Karagiannis, Tsalouchidis, Nioplias, Hantzidis (Saravakos), Kofidis (Kostis), Tsiantakis, Machlas (Mitropoulos)

Wembley   May 22   (64,327)
England (0) 0   **Norway (0) 0**
England: Seaman, Jones, Adams, Bould, Le Saux, Anderton (Le Tissier), Ince (Wright), Wise, Beardsley, Platt, Shearer
Norway: Thorstvedt (By Rise), H Berg, Johnsen, Bratseth, Nilsen (Haaland), Flo, O Berg (Ingebritsen), Rekdal, Bohinen, Jakobsen, Fjortoft (Sorloth)

Tallinn   May 23   (3,500)
Estonia (0) 1   **Wales (0) 2**
Reim (pen)   *Rush, Phillips*
Estonia: Poom, Kallaste, Lemsalu, Prins, Kaljend, Koauan, Olumets (Pari), Linnumae, Kristal, Reim, Lindmaa
Wales: Southall, Williams, Melville (Bodin), Neilson, Coleman, Phillips, Horne, R Jones, Hughes, Rush, J Bowen

Dublin   May 24   (32,500)
Rep. of Ireland (0) 1   Bolivia (0) 0
Sheridan
Rep. of Ireland: Bonner, Irwin (G Kelly), Moran (Kernaghan), Babb, Phelan, Houghton (McAteer), Keane, Townsend, Sheridan, Staunton, Coyne (Cascarino)
Bolivia: Trucco, Rimba, Quinteros, Sandy, Sporuco (J Pena), Baldivieso, Melgar, Cristaldo, Pinedo (Borja), A Pena (Castillo), Ramos (Moreno)

Utrecht   May 27   (17,500)
Holland (1) 3   **Scotland (0) 1**
Roy, Van Vossen   *Shearer*
Irvine (og)
Holland: De Goey, Valckx, Jonk, F De Boer, Winter, Wouters, Witschge, R De Boer (Numan), Overmars, Gullit (Van Vossen), Roy (Taument)

Scotland: Leighton (Gunn), Clarke, Hendry, Irvine, McKimmie, McCall, McKinlay (Nevin), McAllister, Collins (I Ferguson), McGinlay (Shearer), Durie (Jess)

Hannover May 29   (50,000)
Germany (0) 0   Rep. of Ireland (1) 2
                          Cascarino, G Kelly
Germany: Illgner, Kohler (Effenberg), Buchwald (Berthold), Strunz, Basler, Sammer, Wagner, Möller (Hässler), Klinsmann, Riedle (Völler)
Rep. of Ireland: A Kelly, Irwin (G Kelly), McGrath, Babb, Phelan, Keane, McAteer (Houghton), Sheridan (Whelan), Townsend, Staunton, Cascarino (Coyne)

Boston   June 4   (21,153)
Colombia (2) 2   N Ireland (0) 0
Perez, Valencia
Colombia: Cordoba, Escobar, Herrera, Gomez, Valderrama, Valencia (De Avila), Alvarez, Perea, Asprilla (Aristizabal), Perez, Rincon
N Ireland: Wright, Fleming, Worthington, Taggart, Donaghy, Magilton (Dennison), Wilson (Lomas), Morrow, Quinn (O'Boyle), Dowie (Patterson), Hughes

Dublin   June 5   (43,465)
Rep. of Ireland (1) 1   Czech Republic (1) 3
Townsend   Kuka 2 (1 pen), Suchoparek
Rep. of Ireland: Bonner, G Kelly, McGrath (Babb), Kernaghan, Phelan, McGoldrick (McAteer), Sheridan, Townsend, Staunton, Aldridge (Keane), Cascarino (Coyne)
Czech Republic: Kouba, Kubik, Kotulek, Repka, Suchoparek, Nemec, Novotny, Oborsky, Smejkal (Nedved), Frydek (Samec), Kuka

Miami   June 11   (8,418)
Mexico (2) 3   N Ireland (0) 0
Garcia 2 (1 pen)
Hermosillo
Mexico: Campos, Gutierrez, Perales, Suarez, Ambriz, Ramirez, Valdes, Del Olmo, Sanchez (Hermosillo), Garcia (Galindo) (Espinoza), Zague
N Ireland: Fettis (Wright), Fleming (Morrow), Donaghy, Taggart, Worthington, Wilson (Lennon), Lomas. Magilton (Patterson), Hughes, O'Boyle, Quinn (Dowie)

Wembley   Sep 7   (38,629)
England (2) 2   USA (0) 0
Shearer 33, 40
England: Seaman, Jones, Adams, Pallister, Le Saux, Venison, Anderton, Platt, Barnes, Shearer (Wright), Sheringham (Ferdinand
USA: Friedel (Sommer), Caligiuri, Lalas, Balboa, Agoos (Lapper), Perez (Wynalda), Dooley, Reyna (Moore), Sorber, Jones, Stewart (Klopas)

European Championships
Qualifying Matches

All games played on Sep 7 unless stated
GROUP 1
Romania (1) 3   Azerbaijan (0) 0
Belodedici 42
Petrescu 57
Raducioiu 87
Slovakia (0) 0   · France (0) 0

GROUP 2
Belgium (1) 2   Armenia (0) 0
Oliveira 3 Degryse 73
Cyprus (1) 1   Spain (2) 2
Sotiriou 36   Higuera 18, Evagoras (og) 26
Macedonia (1) 1   Denmark (0) 1
Boskoski 4   Povisen 87

GROUP 3
Hungary (2) 2   Turkey (0) 2
Kiprich 4 Halmai 45   Sukur 67 Bulent 71

GROUP 4
Sept 4
Estonia 0   Croatia 2
Slovenia (1) 1   Italy (1) 1
Udovic 14   Costacurta 16
Ukraine (0) 0   Lithuania (0) 2
                          Ianauskas 53
                          Fkarbelius 61

GROUP 5
Luxembourg (0) 0   Holland (1) 4
                          Roy 22, De Boer 62, 64 Jonk 90
Norway (0) 1   Belarus (0) 0
Frigaard 88
Czech Republic 6   Malta 1

GROUP 6
Apr 20
N Ireland (3) 4   Liechtenstein (0) 1
Quinn 2, Lomas, Dowie   Hasler
Latvia (0) 0   Republic of Ireland (2) 3
                          Aldridge 16, 75(pen) Sheridan 29
Liechtenstein (0) 0   Austria (3) 4
                          Polster 18, 44, 85 Aigner 23
Northern Ireland (0) 1   Portugal (1) 2
Quinn 58 (pen)   Costa 8, Oliveira 81

GROUP 7
Georgia (0) 0   Moldova (1) 1
                          Opriju 40
Wales (1) 2   Albania (0) 0
Coleman 9, Giggs 67

GROUP 8
Faroe Islands (0) 1   Greece (2) 5
Muller 89   Saraakos 12 Tshalouchidis 18, 85
                          Alexandris 55, 61
Finland (0) 0   Scotland (1) 2
                          Shearer 29 Collins 66

ENGLISH FOOTBALL

FA Carling Premiership 1993-94

		P	W	D	L	GF	GA	W	D	L	GF	GA	GD	Pts
1	Manchester United	42	14	6	1	39	13	13	5	3	41	25	+42	92
2	Blackburn Rovers	42	14	5	2	31	11	11	4	6	32	25	+27	84
3	Newcastle United	42	14	4	3	51	14	9	4	8	31	27	+41	77
4	Arsenal	42	10	8	3	25	15	8	9	4	28	13	+25	71
5	Leeds United	42	13	6	2	37	18	5	10	6	28	21	+26	70
6	Wimbledon	42	12	5	4	35	21	6	6	9	21	32	+3	65
7	Sheffield Wednesday	42	10	7	4	48	24	6	9	6	28	30	+22	64
8	Liverpool	42	12	4	5	33	23	5	5	11	26	32	+4	60
9	Queens Park Rangers	42	8	7	6	32	29	8	5	8	30	32	+1	60
10	Aston Villa	42	8	5	8	23	18	7	7	7	23	32	-4	57
11	Coventry City	42	9	7	5	23	17	5	7	9	20	28	-2	56
12	Norwich City	42	4	9	8	26	29	8	8	8	39	32	+4	53
13	West Ham United	42	6	7	8	26	31	7	6	8	21	27	-11	52
14	Chelsea	42	11	5	5	31	20	2	7	12	18	33	-4	51
15	Tottenham Hotspur	42	4	8	9	29	33	7	4	10	25	26	-5	45
16	Manchester City	42	6	10	5	24	22	3	8	10	14	27	-11	45
17	Everton	42	8	4	9	26	30	4	4	13	16	33	-21	44
18	Southampton	42	9	2	10	30	31	3	5	13	19	35	-17	43
19	Ipswich Town	42	5	8	8	21	32	4	8	9	14	26	-23	43
20	Sheffield United	42	6	10	5	24	23	2	8	11	18	37	-18	42
21	Oldham Athletic	42	5	8	8	24	33	4	5	12	18	35	-26	40
22	Swindon Town	42	4	7	10	25	45	1	8	12	22	55	-53	30

Quotes

"Glenn Hoddle is like Mozart among the hard rock men" - **Eric Cantona, after losing to Chelsea in the League.**

"That first night was the greatest. We were in the front row of the Kemlyn stand. The whole time my eyes were fixed on The Kop. I couldn't believe it. I was mesmerised. The steam was rising and the noise was incredible" - **Phil Thompson remembering his first visit to Anfield as an 11 year old and his first sight of The Kop, now gone.**

"The opposing fans even sing 'boring, boring, Arsenal' when we go out for our pre-match kick around" - **Ian Wright, who should be used to it by now.**

"I'm here to help Ian. I'm here to add my experience. There has not been a fooball director on the board since Ted Bates retired and they need someone here who has been through the mill" - **Lawrie McMenemy, shoring up Ian Branfoot's position as Southampton manager. Branfoot was sacked less than three weeks later.**

"I heard a crunch and saw the head fall out of the banking. It was ghastly" - **Worker at Ewood Park, where development work uncovered a body, interred for 15 years.**

"BOOZY SOCCER STAR'S CREAM CAKE TACKLE IN WINE BAR" - *Daily Star* headline to a story that Jason Dozzell had "pushed a pavlova" into a customer's face. **Desperate stuff.**

I scored against the blue team on Tuesday and eat two Weetabix every morning. Please tell me what time to turn up for training" - **Ben Glithero in a letter to Alex Ferguson. Ben is five.**

"It's a good job I don't play for Manchester United or one of those clubs that's won a lot or I'd look like I've got chicken pox" - **Vinnie Jones on his habit of tattooing himself after famous victories.**

"I wouldn't only not sign him, I wouldn't let him in the ground" - **Tommy Docherty's assessment of Vinnie Jones.**

"If there's a prat about in the world, he's the prat" - **Alex Ferguson, on Jimmy Hill.**

Goalscorers

	Lg	Cp	CC	Other	Total
Andy Cole (Newcastle)	34	1	6	0	41
Alan Shearer (Blackburn)	31	2	1	0	34
Chris Sutton (Norwich)	25	2	1	0	28
Matt Le Tissier (Southmptn)	25	0	0	0	25
Ian Wright (Arsenal)	23	1	6	3	33
Peter Beardsley (Newcastle)	21	2	1	0	24
Mark Bright (Sheff Weds)	19	2	2	0	23
Eric Cantona (Man United)	18	4	1	2	25
Dean Holdsworth (Wimb)	17	3	4	0	24
Rodney Wallace (Leeds)	17	0	0	0	17
Tony Cottee (Everton)	16	0	3	0	19
Les Ferdinand (QPR)	16	0	2	0	18
Ian Rush (Liverpool)	14	1	4	0	19
Kevin Campbell (Arsenal)	14	0	1	4	19

	Arsenal	Aston Villa	Blackburn	Chelsea	Coventry	Everton	Ipswich	Leeds	Liverpool	Man City	Man Utd	Newcastle	Norwich C	Oldham A	QPR	Sheff Utd	Sheff Weds	Southampton	Swindon	Tottenham	West Ham	Wimbledon
Arsenal	****	1-2	1-0	1-0	0-3	2-0	4-0	2-1	0-0	0-0	1-0	2-1	0-0	1-1	0-0	3-0	1-0	1-0	1-1	0-1	0-2	1-1
Aston Villa	1-2	****	0-1	0-0	0-0	0-1	0-1	1-2	2-1	3-0	0-2	0-2	2-3	0-1	4-1	1-0	2-2	0-2	5-0	1-0	3-1	0-1
Blackburn	1-1	1-0	****	0-0	0-1	0-3	0-2	1-0	3-3	0-2	3-1	1-1	1-1	2-1	1-3	2-1	2-2	2-0	3-1	0-2	0-1	3-0
Chelsea	0-2	1-2	2-0	****	2-0	1-1	0-0	2-1	0-1	2-2	0-1	0-0	1-5	1-0	0-1	0-0	1-1	2-0	2-0	4-3	1-0	1-1
Coventry	1-0	3-0	2-1	2-1	****	0-2	1-0	2-1	0-2	2-1	1-1	2-3	1-0	0-0	0-3	3-2	1-3	2-0	3-0	1-0	0-2	2-0
Everton	1-0	2-1	2-0	4-2	1-2	****	0-2	1-0	1-0	1-0	1-0	0-2	1-2	2-1	1-1	4-0	1-1	3-1	1-2	0-1	1-2	2-0
Ipswich	1-5	1-2	1-0	1-0	2-1	2-1	****	1-2	0-2	4-0	0-0	0-2	2-3	1-1	0-1	3-2	1-1	2-0	3-1	2-1	1-1	3-0
Leeds	2-1	2-0	3-3	4-1	1-0	4-2	0-0	****	0-4	0-0	1-0	1-0	2-1	1-0	0-1	1-1	1-1	3-1	4-0	0-2	1-0	4-0
Liverpool	0-0	2-1	2-1	2-1	1-0	0-1	2-0	2-0	****	2-1	2-0	0-2	0-1	2-1	3-2	0-1	4-2	0-0	2-0	1-1	2-0	1-1
Man City	0-0	3-0	0-2	2-2	0-2	1-0	4-0	2-1	2-1	****	2-3	4-1	0-4	1-0	3-0	2-1	1-3	1-0	4-2	2-1	0-0	0-1
Man Utd	1-0	0-2	3-1	0-1	1-1	1-0	0-0	1-1	3-2	2-3	****	1-1	2-2	3-2	2-1	0-0	5-0	2-0	7-1	0-1	0-0	0-1
Newcastle	2-0	3-1	1-1	0-0	4-0	2-0	2-0	1-0	2-2	3-3	1-1	****	1-2	3-2	1-2	4-0	0-0	0-1	1-2	0-1	2-0	4-0
Norwich C	1-1	1-2	2-2	1-1	1-0	0-1	1-5	2-0	1-0	0-2	2-3	1-2	****	1-1	0-4	3-0	1-3	4-5	0-0	1-2	0-1	3-1
Oldham A	0-0	1-1	2-1	2-1	3-0	1-0	0-3	1-1	0-3	1-1	3-3	1-3	3-0	****	1-0	0-0	1-3	1-1	7-1	0-2	0-1	0-0
QPR	1-1	2-2	1-0	3-3	0-0	2-1	2-1	1-0	1-3	0-0	2-3	1-2	2-2	1-1	****	2-1	0-4	0-2	1-0	1-2	2-0	1-1
Sheff Utd	1-1	1-1	1-2	3-1	0-0	5-1	5-0	0-1	3-1	1-1	0-3	2-0	1-1	2-1	4-1	****	1-1	2-1	0-0	2-2	3-2	2-0
Sheff Weds	0-1	1-2	1-2	3-1	1-0	0-0	1-1	3-3	4-2	0-1	2-3	0-1	0-1	1-1	3-4	2-1	****	1-0	3-3	0-2	0-2	0-1
Southampton	0-4	4-1	3-1	3-1	3-1	0-2	2-2	0-5	0-5	1-3	1-3	2-1	3-3	2-1	1-2	1-1	1-1	****	5-1	1-0	5-0	1-0
Swindon	0-4	1-2	1-3	1-3	1-0	1-1	0-1	1-0	1-2	0-1	2-2	2-2	3-3	0-1	1-0	0-1	1-3	2-1	****	1-0	0-0	2-1
Tottenham	0-1	1-1	0-2	1-1	1-2	3-2	3-2	0-1	2-0	1-1	0-1	1-2	1-3	1-3	0-1	3-3	1-0	1-0	1-1	****	1-3	2-4
West Ham	0-0	0-0	1-2	1-0	3-2	0-1	1-1	1-1	2-0	4-1	1-0	2-4	3-3	2-0	1-1	3-1	5-0	0-2	0-0	1-3	****	1-1
Wimbledon	0-3	2-2	4-1	1-1	1-1	1-1	0-2	2-1	1-1	1-0	1-0	1-0	3-1	3-0	1-1	2-0	2-1	1-0	3-0	0-0	1-2	****

Endsleigh Insurance League 1993-94
Division One

		P	W	D	L	GF	GA	W	D	L	GF	GA	PTS	GS
1	Crystal Palace	46	16	4	3	39	18	11	5	7	34	28	90	73
2	Nottingham Forest	46	12	9	2	38	22	11	5	7	36	27	83	74
3	Millwall	46	14	8	1	36	17	5	9	9	22	32	74	58
4	Leicester City	46	11	9	3	45	30	8	7	8	27	29	73	72
5	Tranmere	46	15	3	5	48	23	6	6	11	21	30	72	69
6	Derby County	46	15	3	5	44	25	5	8	10	29	43	71	73
7	Notts County	46	16	3	4	43	26	4	5	14	22	43	68	65
8	Wolverhampton Wandrs	46	10	10	3	34	19	7	7	9	26	28	68	60
9	Middlesbrough	46	12	6	5	40	19	6	7	10	26	35	67	66
10	Stoke City	46	14	4	5	35	19	4	9	10	22	40	67	57
11	Charlton Athletic	46	14	3	6	39	22	5	5	13	22	36	65	61
12	Sunderland	46	14	2	7	35	22	5	6	12	19	35	65	54
13	Bristol City	46	11	7	5	27	18	5	9	9	20	32	64	47
14	Bolton Wanderers	46	10	8	5	40	31	5	6	12	23	33	59	63
15	Southend United	46	10	5	8	34	28	7	3	13	29	39	59	63
16	Grimsby Town	46	7	14	2	26	16	6	6	11	26	31	59	52
17	Portsmouth	46	10	6	7	29	22	5	7	11	23	36	58	52
18	Barnsley	46	9	3	11	25	26	7	4	12	30	41	55	55
19	Watford	46	10	5	8	39	35	5	4	14	27	45	54	66
20	Luton Town	46	12	4	7	38	25	2	7	14	18	35	53	56
21	West Bromwich Albion	46	9	7	7	38	31	4	5	14	22	38	51	60
22	Birmingham City	46	9	7	7	28	29	4	5	14	24	40	51	52
23	Oxford United	46	10	5	8	33	33	3	5	15	21	42	49	54
24	Peterborough United	46	6	9	8	31	30	2	4	17	17	46	37	48

Quotes

"When I saw him, the world just stopped for me. I swore I'd never date a footballer. Now I'm in love with one of my own players" - **Karren Brady, Birmingham's managing director on Paul Peschisolido, club's leading goal-scorer**

"That's football. That's how it works" - **Karren Brady on the possibility that her club could sell Peschisolido.**

"From the Stadium of Light to the edge of darkness in three weeks" - **Birmingham City fan after Benfica winger Jose Domingues arrived for a 21 day trial.**

"The players have enough problems, without carrying such big numbers around" - **Barry Fry, Birmingham manager, explaining why the club was changing their squad-numbering system.**

"Do I not like Albion" - **A turnip's speech bubble on a T-shirt at Wolves.**

"It's got to be the safest job around because I can't get the sack" - **Chris Turner, chief executive of Peterborough United, who appointed himself manager of his club.**

"It was all down to a wonderful team talk by me at half-time. To be honest, what I said was just the usual cobblers. Sometimes it works, sometimes it doesn't" - **Mick McCarthy, Millwall's manager, cutting through the crap.**

"The Chinese say its the Year of the Dog. It isn't, it's the year of the underdog" - **David Pleat, after Luton knocked out Newcastle in the FA Cup.**

"In all fairness, the referee had a complete cerebral failure" - **Oldham winger Rick Holden, following the defeat of his side at Southend.**

"I think our fans know how to behave. I don't believe there will be any problems. Those days are behind us now" - **Reg Burr, Millwall chairman before the play-off game with Derby.**

Goalscorers

	Lg	Cp	CC	Other	Total
John McGinley (Bolton)	25	3	1	4	33
Chris Armstrong (Crystal P)	22	0	1	1	24
John Aldridge (Tranmere)	21	0	7	0	28
Stan Collymore (Notts F)	19	0	5	1	25
Bob Taylor (WBA)	18	0	1	2	21
Paul Furlong (Watford)	18	0	1	0	19
Wayne Allison (Bristol City)	15	4	0	1	20
Paul Wilkinson (Middles)	15	1	1	2	19
Gary McSwegan (Notts C)	15	0	1	1	17
Phil Gray (Sunderland)	14	0	3	0	17
Clive Mendonca (Grimsby)	14	0	2	1	17
Steve Bull (Wolves)	14	0	0	1	15
John Hendrie (Middles)	13	0	3	3	19
Tommy Johnson (Derby)	13	1	1	1	16
Paul Kitson (Derby)	13	1	0	1	15
Marco Gabbiadini (Derby)	13	0	2	0	15

(home \ away)	Barnsley	Birmingham	Bolton	Bristol City	Charlton	Crystal Pal	Derby Cty	Grimsby	Leicester	Luton Town	Middlesbro	Millwall	Notts Forest	Notts County	Oxford	Peterborough	Portsmouth	Southend	Stoke City	Sunderland	Tranmere	Watford	West Brom	Wolves
Barnsley	****	2-3	1-1	1-1	1-1	1-2	0-1	1-2	0-1	1-4	0-1	0-1	1-0	0-3	1-1	1-0	2-0	1-3	4-0	1-0	0-3	1-0	0-1	2-0
Birmingham	0-2	****	2-2	2-2	1-0	2-4	3-0	1-0	0-3	3-0	1-0	2-1	2-0	0-3	2-1	2-1	1-0	2-5	4-1	4-0	3-3	1-0	0-1	2-2
Bolton W	2-3	1-1	****	2-2	3-2	1-0	0-2	1-1	1-2	0-2	1-0	3-2	0-1	2-1	1-2	2-1	0-2	2-1	0-1	0-0	1-0	2-2	2-4	1-0
Bristol City	0-2	2-2	2-0	****	2-0	1-0	1-0	0-0	1-1	3-0	1-0	0-1	4-0	1-0	2-2	2-0	3-2	0-1	0-0	3-0	2-2	0-1	2-2	3-1
Charlton A	2-1	1-0	3-0	3-1	****	0-0	2-0	1-0	2-1	2-1	1-3	1-2	2-1	1-4	4-3	2-1	3-1	2-1	0-0	3-1	2-0	2-0	0-0	1-1
Crystal Palace	1-0	2-1	2-0	4-1	0-0	****	1-1	1-0	3-2	1-2	2-5	0-1	3-3	1-0	1-2	3-2	5-1	4-3	0-1	2-0	5-0	1-2	0-2	1-1
Derby County	2-0	1-1	1-0	1-0	2-0	3-1	****	2-1	1-0	2-1	0-1	2-0	0-1	1-2	2-1	2-0	4-1	1-0	1-3	4-2	4-0	1-2	5-3	0-4
Grimsby Town	2-0	1-0	1-0	0-0	1-0	1-1	1-1	****	2-1	1-0	0-1	2-1	2-0	1-1	2-1	1-1	1-1	2-1	0-1	4-2	4-0	2-2	2-2	2-0
Leicester	0-1	1-1	1-0	0-0	2-1	0-1	3-3	1-1	****	0-0	2-0	4-0	0-1	3-2	3-0	2-1	0-3	3-0	4-0	2-1	2-1	4-4	4-2	2-2
Luton Town	0-1	1-1	0-2	0-2	1-0	1-1	1-1	2-1	0-2	****	1-1	1-1	2-0	1-0	1-1	1-1	0-1	1-1	0-2	2-1	0-3	2-1	3-0	1-0
Middlesbrough	5-0	2-2	0-1	0-1	2-1	1-1	2-3	2-1	0-0	2-0	****	4-2	2-2	3-0	2-0	2-0	0-2	3-1	6-2	4-1	3-1	4-1	0-0	0-2
Millwall	2-0	2-1	1-0	0-1	3-0	3-0	1-0	1-0	0-0	2-1	1-1	****	2-3	3-0	1-0	1-0	0-0	1-0	1-0	4-1	3-1	2-1	3-2	1-0
Notts Forest	2-1	1-0	2-1	0-0	1-1	3-2	1-1	5-3	4-0	2-0	2-2	1-1	****	2-0	0-0	1-0	1-1	2-0	2-3	0-0	2-1	1-0	2-1	0-0
Notts County	3-1	2-1	2-0	2-0	3-3	4-1	1-2	2-1	1-2	2-3	1-3	2-1	2-2	****	2-1	1-2	3-2	1-1	1-0	0-3	0-0	2-1	1-0	0-2
Oxford Utd	1-1	2-0	0-2	4-2	2-2	1-3	0-1	2-2	2-2	2-2	1-2	0-2	1-0	2-1	****	1-2	3-2	2-1	1-0	0-3	0-0	2-3	1-1	4-0
Peterborough	4-1	1-0	2-3	0-2	0-1	1-1	2-2	1-2	1-1	3-1	1-0	0-0	2-3	2-1	0-2	****	2-2	3-1	2-2	1-3	0-0	2-1	3-0	0-1
Portsmouth	2-1	0-2	0-2	0-0	1-2	1-1	0-1	1-1	0-1	1-0	1-0	2-2	2-1	2-1	2-1	1-2	****	2-1	3-3	0-1	2-0	2-0	0-1	3-0
Southend	0-3	3-1	0-1	0-1	0-1	1-2	0-2	1-0	0-0	2-0	2-0	1-1	2-1	0-0	2-1	3-0	2-1	****	0-0	1-3	2-0	2-0	0-3	0-1
Stoke City	5-4	2-1	3-0	4-2	4-2	1-2	1-0	4-3	1-0	1-0	1-0	0-0	1-0	1-0	6-1	3-0	2-1	0-1	****	0-0	1-2	0-1	0-0	1-1
Sunderland	1-0	1-0	1-0	0-0	4-0	1-0	0-2	2-2	2-3	2-1	2-1	1-2	0-1	0-	2-3	2-0	1-2	0-1	0-1	****	3-2	2-0	1-0	0-2
Tranmere	0-3	1-2	2-1	3-1	1-0	2-3	1-1	1-0	2-3	3-1	3-1	1-2	1-1	3-1	1-1	2-1	1-3	1-1	3-3	1-0	****	1-2	2-0	1-1
Watford	0-2	5-2	4-3	1-1	2-0	4-4	1-1	1-0	1-2	2-2	2-0	2-0	0-2	3-1	2-3	2-1	4-1	2-2	0-1	0-1	2-1	****	0-1	3-2
West Brom	1-1	2-4	2-2	3-0	2-0	1-4	3-0	1-2	1-2	2-3	1-1	3-2	1-0	1-0	2-1	3-0	2-0	0-1	2-0	1-0	1-3	2-0	****	1-0
Wolves	1-1	3-0	1-0	3-1	1-1	1-1	2-2	2-2	2-0	1-0	1-0	2-0	1-1	3-0	2-1	0-1	1-1	3-0	0-1	1-1	1-1	1-1	1-2	***

Endsleigh Insurance League 1993-94
Division Two

		P	W	D	L	GF	GA	W	D	L	GF	GA	PTS	GS
1	Reading	46	15	6	2	40	16	11	5	7	41	28	89	81
2	Port Vale	46	16	6	1	46	18	10	4	9	33	28	88	79
3	Plymouth Argyle	46	16	4	3	48	26	9	6	8	42	30	85	88
4	Stockport County	46	15	3	5	50	22	9	10	4	24	22	85	74
5	York City	46	12	7	4	33	13	9	5	9	31	27	75	64
6	Burnley	46	17	4	2	55	18	4	6	13	24	40	73	79
7	Bradford City	46	13	5	5	34	20	6	8	9	27	33	70	61
8	Bristol Rovers	46	10	8	5	33	26	10	2	11	27	33	70	60
9	Hull City	46	9	9	5	33	20	9	5	9	29	34	68	62
10	Cambridge United	46	11	5	7	38	29	8	4	11	41	44	66	79
11	Huddersfield Town	46	9	8	6	27	26	8	6	9	31	35	65	58
12	Wrexham	46	13	4	6	45	33	4	7	12	21	44	62	66
13	Swansea City	46	12	7	4	37	20	4	5	14	19	38	60	56
14	Brighton & Hove Albion	46	10	7	6	38	29	5	7	11	22	38	59	60
15	Rotherham United	46	11	4	8	42	30	4	9	10	21	30	58	63
16	Brentford	46	7	10	6	30	28	6	9	8	27	27	58	57
17	AFC Bournemouth	46	8	7	8	26	27	6	8	9	25	32	57	51
18	Leyton Orient	46	11	9	3	38	26	3	5	15	19	45	56	57
19	Cardiff City	46	10	7	6	39	33	3	8	12	27	46	54	66
20	Blackpool	46	12	2	9	41	37	4	3	16	22	38	53	63
21	Fulham	46	7	6	10	20	23	7	4	12	30	40	52	50
22	Exeter City	46	8	7	8	38	37	3	5	15	14	46	45	52
23	Hartlepool United	46	8	3	12	28	40	1	6	16	13	47	36	41
24	Barnet	46	4	6	13	22	32	1	7	15	19	54	28	41

Quotes

"Even in the face of adversity we can laugh" - **Steve Birley, the commercial director of Exeter City who recycled the club's 'I'm following Exeter into the Third Division' stickers. Only in 1990, it meant they were being** *promoted*.

"Come on Fulham, you're 2-0 up, but you can still get a draw out of this....." - **Overheard at the Fulham - Hartlepool match.**

"If I want any guttering done, I'll give him a call" - **Ray Wilkins, QPR captain on Stockport's 6' 7" striker Kevin Francis, who scored one of the goals that knocked QPR out of the Cup.**

"We were both in love with Billy Rodaway, an attractive strapping lad who played for Burnley" - **Holly Johnson, former Frankie Goes to Hollywood singer, in his autobiography.**

"I considered myself a good bowler, but I was never able to get him out. I once tempted him to an outside edge, but that was all" - **Shaka Hislop, the Reading goalkeeper, on his days playing cricket against Brian Lara.**

"I'm prepared to buy players, but not ones who are useless and overpriced" - **Owen Oyston, Blackpool's owner, who could only just afford to be choosy.**

'Name the worst match of the season' - **The Orienteer, Leyton Orient's fanzine asked. They received 25 different answers.**

"Striker? He's a defender" - **Brentford manager Dave Webb's response to an enquiry after his player Denny Mundee. Webb, having learnt Mundee's true position, switched him into the attack and the player responded with 11 goals in 12 games.**

Goalscorers

	Lg	Cp	CC	Other	Total
Jimmy Quinn (Reading)	35	2	0	3	40
Gary Bennett (Wrexham)	32	3	0	1	36
Kevin Francis (Stockport)	28	3	1	2	34
Paul Barnes (York)	24	0	0	1	25
Dean Windass (Hull)	23	1	0	0	24
John Taylor (Bristol R)	23	0	0	0	23
Kurt Nogan (Brighton)	22	0	2	2	26
Andy Preece (Stockport)	21	2	0	5	28
Steve Castle (Plymouth)	21	0	0	1	22
Steve Butler (Cambridge)	21	0	0	0	21
Stuart Lovell (Reading)	20	0	0	1	21
David Eyres (Burnley)	19	4	3	1	27
Imre Varadi (Rotherham)	19	1	0	1	21
Martin Foyle (Port Vale)	18	0	1	2	21

	Bournemouth	Barnet	Blackpool	Bradford C	Brentford	Brighton	Bristol Rovers	Burnley	Cambridge	Cardiff City	Exeter City	Fulham	Hartlepool	Huddersfield	Hull City	Leyton Orient	Plymouth	Port Vale	Reading	Rotherham	Stockport	Swansea City	Wrexham	York City
Bournemouth	****	1-1	1-0	1-1	1-0	3-0	1-0	3-2	1-2	3-2	2-1	0-0	1-1	0-0	0-2	1-1	0-1	0-1	2-1	2-1	2-1	0-0	1-2	3-1
Barnet	1-2	****	3-1	1-2	1-1	2-1	0-2	3-1	2-3	0-0	1-1	2-1	0-1	2-1	0-1	1-2	1-1	0-1	2-3	1-1	2-1	1-2	4-1	1-3
Blackpool	2-1	3-1	****	0-0	2-3	2-0	1-0	0-1	2-3	0-1	3-1	2-3	6-2	3-0	1-2	0-2	2-1	2-3	0-4	1-2	2-1	2-0	0-1	0-5
Bradford City	0-0	2-1	1-3	****	1-0	1-1	1-2	1-1	0-0	1-0	2-1	1-0	4-1	2-1	1-3	2-1	1-5	1-1	2-4	1-3	2-0	1-2	4-1	0-0
Brentford	1-1	1-0	2-1	1-3	****	1-0	0-1	2-0	2-3	2-1	6-0	2-0	1-2	3-0	0-0	2-1	0-0	2-4	0-4	0-2	1-2	1-1	1-0	0-0
Brighton & HA	3-3	1-0	3-0	2-0	3-0	****	1-1	0-0	3-3	1-0	6-0	3-3	2-0	2-2	0-3	2-3	3-1	2-1	2-0	2-2	2-2	1-2	0-0	2-1
Bristol Rovers	0-1	5-2	1-0	4-3	1-4	1-0	****	3-1	2-1	2-1	1-0	4-1	3-0	0-1	2-1	2-1	1-1	1-4	2-0	2-1	1-1	1-1	2-1	0-1
Burnley	4-0	5-0	3-1	0-1	4-1	1-4	3-1	****	3-0	2-0	3-2	3-1	2-0	1-0	4-5	3-1	4-2	2-3	4-1	0-0	1-1	4-0	1-0	0-2
Cambridge Utd	3-2	3-1	3-2	2-1	0-1	1-0	3-1	0-1	****	1-1	3-0	3-2	1-0	4-5	3-4	2-0	4-2	2-3	3-1	0-1	0-0	1-1	3-1	0-2
Cardiff City	2-1	0-0	0-0	1-1	2-1	1-2	0-1	2-1	2-7	1-1	2-1	3-1	1-1	2-2	3-4	2-0	2-3	1-3	1-0	1-2	3-1	1-0	2-1	0-0
Exeter City	0-2	0-0	0-2	1-1	2-2	4-1	1-0	0-5	2-2	2-2	****	4-1	2-1	2-3	1-0	1-0	2-3	1-0	4-6	2-1	1-2	5-0	5-0	1-2
Fulham	0-2	3-0	1-0	1-1	0-1	3-2	1-0	3-2	2-1	1-3	1-0	****	0-1	2-2	0-1	2-3	1-1	0-0	1-0	1-0	1-2	1-0	0-0	0-1
Hartlepool	1-1	2-1	1-0	1-2	0-1	2-1	0-2	2-1	4-1	0-2	0-1	0-1	****	2-0	0-1	1-8	1-1	1-4	1-4	2-1	1-0	0-1	1-2	0-2
Huddersfield	1-1	1-2	2-1	1-1	1-3	2-2	4-1	3-2	0-2	3-0	1-2	4-1	2-0	****	1-4	1-1	0-2	1-8	1-1	2-3	2-1	1-0	3-0	3-2
Hull City	1-1	4-4	0-0	3-1	1-0	0-0	3-0	2-0	1-0	5-2	2-0	1-0	3-0	2-0	****	0-2	2-2	1-1	0-3	2-1	0-1	4-0	3-1	3-2
Leyton O	0-0	4-2	4-4	2-0	1-3	3-0	3-1	1-2	4-2	1-1	2-1	2-2	1-2	2-1	3-1	****	0-1	2-1	2-3	1-1	0-1	4-0	0-1	2-0
Plymouth A	2-0	1-0	2-1	3-1	3-2	0-3	3-2	1-0	2-1	1-2	0-3	3-1	2-0	2-0	3-1	3-1	****	2-1	3-1	4-2	0-3	3-1	3-0	2-0
Port Vale	2-1	6-0	2-0	0-0	1-1	4-0	0-0	1-1	2-2	2-2	4-0	2-0	3-0	2-1	2-1	2-1	2-1	****	2-0	0-4	2-1	3-0	3-0	2-1
Reading	3-0	4-1	1-1	0-0	2-1	2-0	2-0	3-2	2-1	1-1	2-0	2-4	1-0	1-0	1-1	1-0	3-2	1-2	****	0-0	2-0	1-0	3-0	2-1
Rotherham	1-2	1-1	0-2	2-1	2-0	0-1	3-2	2-1	2-0	5-2	3-0	2-4	7-0	5-0	2-3	3-0	0-3	1-2	2-2	****	0-0	1-2	1-1	2-1
Stockport C	0-2	2-1	1-0	4-1	3-1	0-2	2-1	2-1	3-1	1-1	0-2	3-1	2-1	0-2	3-1	3-0	0-3	0-2	0-4	0-0	****	1-2	4-0	2-1
Swansea City	1-1	2-0	2-3	2-0	1-1	1-3	2-0	4-0	1-1	1-1	3-1	1-0	1-0	3-1	3-0	4-2	3-1	2-3	0-1	2-0	1-2	****	1-0	1-2
Wrexham	2-1	4-0	4-4	0-3	1-2	1-3	0-1	1-0	0-0	1-0	1-1	2-1	3-1	1-0	3-0	1-1	1-1	0-0	2-1	0-3	0-1	3-2	****	1-1
York City	2-0	1-1	2-1	1-1	0-2	3-1	0-1	0-0	3-1	3-1	3-0	2-0	3-0	3-2	0-1	3-0	2-0	2-1	1-0	2-1	1-2	2-1	1-1	****

Endsleigh Insurance League 1993-94
Division Three

		P	W	D	L	GF	GA	W	D	L	GF	GA	PTS	GS
1	Shrewsbury Town	42	10	8	3	28	17	12	5	4	35	22	79	63
2	Chester City	42	13	5	3	35	18	8	6	7	34	28	74	69
3	Crewe Alexandra	42	12	4	5	45	30	9	6	6	35	31	73	80
4	Wycombe Wanderers	42	11	6	4	34	21	8	7	6	33	32	70	67
5	Preston North End	42	13	5	3	46	23	5	8	8	33	37	67	79
6	Torquay United	42	8	10	3	30	24	9	6	6	34	32	67	64
7	Carlisle United	42	10	4	7	35	23	8	6	7	22	19	64	57
8	Chesterfield	42	8	8	5	32	22	8	6	7	23	26	62	55
9	Rochdale	42	10	5	6	38	22	6	7	8	25	29	60	63
10	Walsall	42	7	5	9	28	26	10	4	7	20	27	60	48
11	Scunthorpe United	42	9	7	5	40	26	6	7	8	24	30	59	64
12	Mansfield Town	42	9	3	9	28	30	6	7	8	25	32	55	53
13	Bury	42	9	6	6	33	22	5	5	11	22	34	53	55
14	Scarborough	42	8	4	9	29	28	7	4	10	26	33	53	55
15	Doncaster Rovers	42	8	6	7	24	26	6	4	11	20	31	52	44
16	Gillingham	42	8	8	5	27	23	4	7	10	17	28	51	44
17	Colchester United	42	8	4	9	31	33	5	6	10	25	38	49	56
18	Lincoln City	42	7	4	10	26	29	5	7	9	26	34	47	52
19	Wigan Athletic	42	6	7	8	33	33	5	5	11	18	37	45	51
20	Hereford United	42	6	4	11	34	33	6	2	13	26	46	42	60
21	Darlington	42	7	5	9	24	28	3	6	12	18	36	41	42
22	Northampton Town	42	6	7	8	25	23	3	4	14	19	43	38	44

Quotes

"I predict that within ten years we will be among the ten wealthiest clubs in the country" - **Michael Knighton, chairman of Carlisle United.**

"She gave one tight off-side decision our way, which won the fans over" - **Mike Bateson, giving the Torquay fans verdict on lineswoman Wendy Toms first League outing.**

"When I went to tell the players this morning, they were in tears" - **Steve Wicks, on the day he was sacked from the Scarborough manager's job.**

"It's the fashion. As soon as they are shown not to be so good, the buyers will come back saying, 'Please Dario, can we have one of yours' " - **Dario Gradi, manager of Crewe, on the fashion for foreign players.**

"You could write the retained list on a postage stamp" - **Alan Murray, manager of Darlington.**

"I needed a midfield motivator and there he was sitting across the breakfast table from me" - **Keith Peacock, who signed his son Gavin from QPR, when he was Gillingham's manager.**

"We are a trend-setting club and we like blowing our own trumpet" - **Mike Bateson again. For once, Torquay almost had something to blow their trumpets about.**

Goalscorers

	Lg	Cp	CC	Other	Total
Tony Ellis (Preston NE)	26	2	1	1	30
Mark Carter (Bury)	20	0	0	0	20
Steve Norris (Chesterfield)	19	2	0	1	22
Matt Carmichael (Scunthorpe)	18	1	0	5	24
Dean Spink (Shrewsbury)	18	1	0	1	20
Chris Pike (Hereford)	18	1	0	0	19
Nick Forster (Gillingham)	18	0	0	0	18
Darren Rowbotham (Crewe)	15	1	1	0	17
Adrian Foster (Torquay)	15	0	1	0	16
Steve Whitehall (Rochdale)	14	1	0	0	15
Tony Naylor (Crewe)	13	1	0	2	16
David Reeves (Carlisle)	11	1	0	3	15

	Bury	Carlisle Utd	Chester City	Chesterfield	Colchester Utd	Crewe Alex	Darlington	Doncaster Rov	Gillingham	Hereford Utd	Lincoln City	Mansfield Town	Northampton T	Preston NE	Rochdale	Scarborough	Scunthorpe Utd	Shrewsbury	Torquay Utd	Walsall	Wigan Athletic	Wycombe W
Bury	****	2-1	1-1	2-1	0-1	1-0	5-1	4-0	0-0	5-3	1-0	2-2	0-0	1-1	5-1	0-1	2-0	2-3	1-1	1-2	3-0	1-2
Carlisle Utd	1-2	****	1-0	3-0	2-0	1-2	1-3	0-0	2-0	0-0	0-0	0-1	1-1	0-3	0-1	0-3	2-1	1-1	1-0	0-1	3-0	2-2
Chester City	3-0	1-0	****	1-2	2-0	2-1	1-2	3-4	1-2	0-0	0-5	0-3	1-0	1-0	2-0	0-1	1-1	3-0	1-3	1-1	2-1	3-1
Chesterfield	1-1	3-0	3-0	****	3-1	1-2	1-0	0-0	0-0	0-3	1-2	1-1	2-2	4-1	5-1	0-1	2-2	0-0	1-0	0-1	3-0	1-0
Colchester	4-1	2-1	2-0	3-1	****	0-0	0-0	2-1	1-1	5-0	3-0	1-1	1-1	1-0	0-2	1-1	1-2	2-1	1-1	1-2	2-3	3-1
Crewe Alex	2-4	2-3	2-1	2-1	2-1	****	2-1	3-1	2-1	1-0	1-2	1-2	1-2	0-2	2-2	1-0	1-2	2-2	2-2	2-2	4-1	2-1
Darlington	1-0	1-3	1-2	1-0	0-0	2-1	****	2-0	1-0	3-0	1-1	0-3	1-0	3-2	1-0	1-1	3-0	1-1	2-0	2-0	3-1	3-4
Doncaster R	1-3	0-0	3-4	0-0	2-1	3-1	2-0	****	1-3	0-1	1-3	0-1	0-0	1-0	2-1	1-3	3-0	3-0	0-1	0-2	4-0	0-3
Gillingham	1-0	2-0	1-2	0-0	1-1	2-1	1-0	1-3	****	1-0	1-0	3-0	0-1	0-2	1-0	0-1	2-2	1-1	0-1	2-2	0-0	0-1
Hereford Utd	3-0	0-0	0-0	0-3	5-0	1-0	3-0	2-1	2-0	****	2-0	2-3	1-1	2-3	3-1	5-1	1-2	1-0	2-2	1-1	3-1	3-4
Lincoln City	2-2	0-0	0-5	1-2	3-0	1-2	1-1	2-1	1-0	1-2	****	1-0	4-3	0-2	0-1	1-2	2-0	0-2	1-0	1-2	2-3	1-3
Mansfield	2-2	0-1	0-3	1-1	1-1	1-2	0-3	2-1	3-0	2-3	1-2	****	1-2	2-2	2-1	0-1	2-2	3-1	0-1	2-1	0-0	0-0
Northampton	0-1	1-1	1-0	2-2	1-1	1-2	1-0	0-0	0-1	1-1	4-3	1-2	****	1-0	4-3	0-1	3-2	2-1	1-3	1-0	2-3	1-0
Preston NE	3-1	0-3	1-0	4-1	1-0	0-2	3-2	1-0	0-2	2-3	0-2	2-2	1-0	****	2-0	0-1	2-2	6-1	3-1	2-0	3-0	1-0
Rochdale	2-1	0-1	2-0	5-1	0-2	2-2	1-0	2-1	1-0	3-1	0-1	2-1	4-3	2-0	****	2-1	2-1	2-1	1-3	1-1	2-2	1-1
Scarborough	1-0	0-3	0-1	0-1	1-1	1-0	1-1	1-3	0-1	5-1	1-2	0-1	0-1	0-1	2-1	****	2-0	2-0	2-0	0-1	4-1	1-1
Scunthorpe	1-1	2-1	1-1	2-2	1-2	1-2	3-0	3-0	2-2	1-2	2-0	2-2	3-2	2-2	1-2	2-2	****	0-0	1-1	0-2	3-1	0-0
Shrewsbury	1-0	1-1	3-0	0-0	2-1	2-2	1-1	3-0	1-1	1-0	0-2	3-1	2-1	6-1	1-3	1-3	1-4	****	1-3	2-5	0-1	1-0
Torquay Utd	0-0	1-0	1-3	1-0	1-1	2-2	2-0	0-1	0-1	2-2	1-0	0-1	1-3	3-1	1-2	1-3	1-2	3-2	****	1-2	1-2	3-1
Walsall	0-1	0-1	1-1	0-1	1-2	3-1	2-0	1-2	2-2	1-1	1-2	4-1	1-0	2-0	4-1	5-0	1-2	5-0	1-2	****	0-1	1-1
Wigan Ath	3-1	0-2	6-3	1-0	0-1	2-2	3-0	3-1	2-0	3-0	0-1	3-1	1-3	3-0	3-0	1-0	1-2	4-1	1-3	2-2	****	1-1
Wycombe W	2-1	2-0	1-0	1-0	2-5	3-1	2-0	3-1	1-1	3-2	2-3	1-0	1-0	1-0	1-1	1-1	1-1	1-0	1-1	4-2	0-1	****

English Non-League Football 1993-94

GM Vauxhall Conference

	P	W	D	L	GF	GA	PTS
Kidderminster Harriers	42	22	9	11	63	35	75
Kettering Town	42	19	15	8	46	24	72
Woking	42	18	13	11	58	58	67
Southport	42	18	12	12	57	51	66
Runcorn	42	14	19	9	63	57	61
Dagenham & Redbridge	42	15	14	13	62	54	59
Macclesfield Town	42	16	11	15	48	49	59
Dover Athletic	42	17	7	18	48	49	58
Stafford Rangers	42	14	15	13	56	52	57
Altrincham	42	16	9	17	41	42	57
Gateshead	42	15	12	15	45	53	57
Bath City	42	13	17	12	47	38	56
Halifax Town	42	13	16	13	55	49	55
Stalybridge Celtic	42	14	12	16	54	55	54
Northwich Victoria	42	11	19	12	44	45	52
Welling Utd	42	13	12	17	47	49	51
Telford Utd	42	13	12	17	41	49	51
Bromsgrove Rovers	42	12	15	15	54	66	51
Yeovil Town	42	14	9	19	49	62	51
Merthyr Tydfil	42	12	15	15	60	61	*49
Slough Town	42	11	14	17	54	58	47
Witton Albion	42	7	13	22	37	63	34

* 2 points deducted

Leading Scorers	League	Other
Paul Dobson (Gateshead)	25	9
Karl Thomas (Runcorn)	23	7
Paul Adcock (Bath City)	17	5
Terry Robbins (Welling Utd)	17	4
Mickey Spencer (Yeovil Town)	16	2
Clive Walker (Woking)	16	3

Northern Premier League

PREMIER DIVISION

	P	W	D	L	GF	GA	PTS
Marine	42	27	9	6	106	62	90
Leek Town	42	27	8	7	79	50	89
Boston Utd	42	23	9	10	90	43	78
Bishop Auckland	42	23	9	10	73	58	78
Frickley Athletic	42	21	12	9	90	51	75
Colwyn Bay	42	18	14	10	74	51	68
Morecambe	42	20	7	15	90	56	67
Barrow	42	18	10	14	59	51	64
Hyde Utd	42	17	10	15	80	71	61
Chorley	42	17	10	15	70	67	61
Whitley Bay	42	17	9	16	61	72	60
Gainsborough Trinity	42	15	11	16	64	66	56
Emley	42	12	16	14	63	71	52
Matlock Town	42	13	12	17	71	76	51
Buxton	42	13	10	19	67	73	49
Accrington Stanley	42	14	7	21	63	85	49
Droylsden	42	11	14	17	57	82	47
Knowsley Utd	42	11	11	20	52	66	44
Winsford Utd	42	9	11	22	50	74	38
Horwich RMI	42	8	12	22	50	74	*35
Bridlington Town	42	7	10	25	41	91	**28
Fleetwood Town	42	7	7	28	55	114	28

* 1 point deducted
** 3 points deducted

Leading scorers	League	Other
Tony McDonald (Chorley)	31	2
Andy Hayward (Frickley Ath.)	26	8
Chris Camden (Marine)	26	6
Brian Ross (Marine)	26	3
Neil Grayson (Boston Utd)	25	4

FIRST DIVISION

	P	W	D	L	GF	GA	PTS
Guiseley	40	29	6	5	87	37	93
Spennymoor Utd	40	25	6	9	95	50	81
Ashton Utd	40	24	7	9	85	41	79
Lancaster City	40	20	10	10	74	46	70
Netherfield	40	20	6	14	68	60	66
Alfreton Town	40	18	10	12	83	70	64
Warrington	40	17	11	12	52	48	62
Goole Town	40	16	11	13	72	58	59
Great Harwood Town	40	15	14	11	56	60	59
Gretna	40	16	7	17	64	65	55
Workington	40	14	10	16	70	74	52
Worksop Town	40	14	9	17	79	87	51
Bamber Bridge	40	13	11	16	62	59	50
Curzon Ashton	40	13	8	19	62	71	47
Congleton Town	40	12	9	19	53	68	45
Radcliffe Borough	40	10	14	16	43	59	44
Mossley	40	10	12	18	44	68	*39
Caernarfon Town	40	9	11	20	54	88	38
Farsley Celtic	40	6	16	18	42	77	34
Harrogate Town	40	8	9	23	40	86	33
Eastwood Town	40	7	11	22	47	63	32

* 3 points deducted

Leading scorers	League	Other
Kenny Clark (Worksop Town)	32	11
Andy Whittaker (Ashton/N'field)	29	9
Phil Stafford (Alfreton Town)	22	8
Mark Dobie (Gretna)	21	16
Mark Edwards (Ashton Utd)	19	16

Beazer Homes League

PREMIER DIVISION

	P	W	D	L	GF	GA	PTS
Farnborough Town	42	25	7	10	74	44	82
Cheltenham Town	42	21	12	9	67	38	75
Halesowen Town	42	21	11	10	69	46	74
Atherstone Utd	42	22	7	13	57	43	73
Crawley Town	42	21	10	11	56	42	73
Chelmsford City	42	21	7	14	74	59	70
Trowbridge Town	42	16	17	9	52	41	65
Sittingbourne	42	17	13	12	65	48	64
Corby Town	42	17	8	17	52	56	59
Gloucester City	42	17	6	19	55	60	57
Burton Albion	42	15	11	16	57	49	56
Hastings Town	42	16	7	19	51	60	55
Hednesford Town	42	15	9	18	67	66	54
Gresley Rovers	42	14	11	17	61	72	53
Worcester City	42	14	9	19	61	70	51
Solihull Borough	42	13	11	18	52	57	50
Cambridge City	42	13	11	18	50	60	50
Dorchester Town	42	12	11	19	38	51	47

Moor Green	42	11	10	21	49	66	43
Waterlooville	42	11	10	21	47	69	43
Bashley	42	11	10	21	47	80	43
Nuneaton Borough	42	11	8	23	42	66	41

Leading Scorers *(League and Cup)*
L Ryan (Cambridge) 28, T Senior (Farnborough) 26, C Boothe (Farnborough) 24, P Joinson (Halesowen) 22, L McRobert (Sittingbourne) 21, S Restarick (Chelms) 21

MIDLAND DIVISION

	P	W	D	L	GF	GA	PTS
Rushden & Diamonds	42	29	11	2	109	37	98
VS Rugby	42	28	8	6	98	41	92
Weston Super Mare	42	27	10	5	94	39	91
Newport AFC	42	26	9	7	84	37	87
Clevedon Town	42	24	10	8	75	46	82
Redditch Utd	42	19	11	12	79	62	68
Tamworth	42	19	7	16	82	68	64
Bilston Town	42	16	10	16	65	73	58
Stourbridge	42	17	6	19	71	75	57
Evesham Utd	42	16	8	18	50	60	56
Grantham Town	42	16	6	20	77	73	54
Bridgnorth Town	42	15	6	21	56	68	51
Racing Club Warwick	42	13	12	17	53	66	51
Dudley Town	42	13	10	19	64	61	49
Forest Green Rovers	42	12	12	18	61	84	48
Sutton Coldfield Town	42	12	8	22	53	75	44
Bedworth Utd	42	12	7	23	62	81	43
Hinckley Town	42	11	10	21	44	71	43
Leicester Utd	42	11	9	22	34	73	42
King's Lynn	42	9	11	22	47	72	38
Yate Town	42	10	6	26	48	86	36
Armitage	42	8	11	23	45	103	35

Leading Scorers
A Warner (VS Rugby) 33, M Nuttell (Rushden & D) 32, D Watkins (Rushden & D) 26, P McBean (Tamworth) 24, C Moss (Redditch) 23

SOUTHERN DIVISION

	P	W	D	L	GF	GA	PTS
Gravesend & Northfleet	42	27	11	4	87	24	92
Sudbury Town	42	27	8	7	98	47	89
Witney Town	42	27	8	7	69	36	89
Salisbury City	42	26	10	6	90	39	88
Havant Town	42	27	4	11	101	41	85
Ashford Town	42	24	13	5	93	46	85
Baldock Town	42	26	7	9	76	40	85
Newport IOW	42	22	8	12	74	51	74
Margate	42	20	8	14	76	58	68
Weymouth	42	18	9	15	71	65	63
Tonbridge	42	19	5	18	59	62	62
Buckingham Town	42	14	14	14	43	42	56
Braintree Town	42	16	7	19	72	84	55
Fareham Town	42	12	12	18	54	75	48
Poole Town	42	13	6	23	54	86	45
Burnham	42	10	9	23	53	92	39
Fisher 93	42	9	10	23	52	81	37
Dunstable	42	9	7	26	50	91	34
Erith & Belvedere	42	9	5	28	40	72	32
Canterbury City	42	8	7	27	35	80	31
Wealdstone	42	6	7	29	45	95	25
Bury Town	42	3	5	34	36	121	14

Leading Scorer
S Portway (Gravesend & N) 41, P Odey (Salisbury) 34, A Jones (Havant) 31, K Phillips (Baldock) 29, D Fosbury (Havant) 25

Diadora League

PREMIER DIVISION

	P	W	D	L	GF	GA	PTS
Stevenage Borough	42	31	4	7	88	39	97
Enfield	42	28	8	6	80	28	92
Marlow	42	25	7	10	90	67	82
Chesham Utd	42	24	8	10	73	45	80
Sutton Utd	42	23	10	9	77	31	79
Carshalton Athletic	42	22	7	13	81	53	73
St. Albans City	42	21	10	11	81	54	73
Hitchin Town	42	21	7	14	81	56	70
Harrow Borough	42	18	11	13	54	56	65
Kingstonian	42	18	9	15	101	64	63
Hendon	42	18	9	15	61	51	63
Aylesbury Utd	42	17	7	18	64	67	58
Hayes	42	15	8	19	63	72	53
Grays Athletic	42	15	5	22	56	69	50
Bromley	42	14	7	21	56	69	49
Dulwich Hamlet	42	13	8	21	52	74	47
Yeading	42	11	13	18	58	66	46
Molesey	42	11	11	20	44	62	44
Wokingham Town	42	11	6	25	38	67	39
Dorking	42	9	4	29	58	104	31
Basingstoke Town	42	5	12	25	38	86	27
Wivenhoe Town	42	5	3	34	38	152	18

Leading Scorers
Jimmy Bolton (Carshalton) 35, Martin Gittings (Stevenage) 27, David Lay (Marlow) 27

DIVISION 1

	P	W	D	L	GF	GA	PTS
Bishop's Stortford	42	24	13	5	83	31	85
Purfleet	42	22	12	8	70	44	78
Walton & Hersham	42	22	11	9	81	53	77
Tooting & Mitcham	42	21	12	9	66	37	75
Heybridge Swifts	42	20	11	11	72	45	71
Billericay Town	42	20	11	11	70	51	71
Abingdon Town	42	20	10	12	61	50	70
Worthing	42	19	11	12	79	46	68
Leyton	42	20	8	14	88	66	68
Boreham Wood	42	17	15	10	69	50	66
Staines Town	42	18	9	15	85	56	63
Bognor Regis Town	42	15	14	13	57	48	59
Wembley	42	16	10	16	66	52	58
Barking	42	15	11	16	63	69	56
Uxbridge	42	15	8	19	57	58	53
Whyteleafe	42	15	6	21	71	90	51
Maidenhead Utd	42	12	13	17	52	48	49
Berkhamsted Town	42	12	9	21	65	77	45
Ruislip Manor	42	10	8	24	42	79	38
Chalfont St. Peter	42	7	10	25	40	79	31
Windsor & Eton	42	8	7	27	47	94	31
Croydon	42	3	3	36	37	198	12

Leading Scorers
Leo Fortune-West (B Stortford) 28, Justin Mitchell (Walton & H) 27, Barry Popplewell (Leyton) 24

Association Football

Division 2

	P	W	D	L	GF	GA	PTS
Newbury Town	42	32	7	3	115	36	103
Chertsey Town	42	33	3	6	121	48	102
Aldershot Town	42	30	7	5	78	27	97
Barton Rovers	42	25	8	9	68	37	83
Witham Town	42	21	10	11	68	51	73
Malden Vale	42	20	10	12	70	49	70
Thame Utd	42	19	12	11	87	51	69
Metropolitan Police	42	20	9	13	75	54	69
Banstead Athletic	42	19	9	14	56	53	66
Aveley	42	19	5	18	60	66	62
Edgware Town	42	16	10	16	88	76	58
Saffron Walden Town	42	17	7	18	61	62	58
Hemel Hempstead	42	14	11	17	47	43	53
Egham Town	42	14	8	20	48	65	50
Ware	42	14	7	21	48	76	49
Hungerford Town	42	13	7	22	56	66	46
Tilbury	42	13	3	26	59	81	42
Hampton	42	12	5	25	42	70	41
Leatherhead	42	10	6	26	46	92	36
Lewes	42	8	10	24	38	85	34
Collier Row	42	7	8	27	37	88	29
Rainham Town	42	4	2	36	24	116	14

Leading Scorers
Matthew McDonald (Newbury) 42, Mario Russo (Metro. Police) 32, Scott McGleish (Edgware) 28, Mark Butler (Aldershot) 28, Lee Charles (Chertsey/Yeading) 28

Division 3

	P	W	D	L	GF	GA	PTS
Bracknell Town	40	25	8	7	78	29	83
Cheshunt	40	23	12	5	62	34	81
Oxford City	40	24	6	10	94	55	78
Harlow Town	40	22	11	7	61	36	77
Southall	40	17	12	11	66	53	63
Camberley Town	40	18	7	15	56	50	61
Hertford Town	40	18	6	16	67	65	60
Royston Town	40	15	11	14	44	41	56
Northwood	40	15	11	14	78	77	56
Epsom & Ewell	40	15	9	16	63	62	54
Harefield Utd	40	12	15	13	45	55	51
Cove	40	15	6	19	59	74	51
Kingsbury Town	40	12	14	14	57	54	50
Feltham & Hounslow	40	14	7	19	60	63	49
Leighton Town	40	12	11	17	51	64	47
East Thurrock Utd	40	10	15	15	65	64	45
Clapton	40	12	9	19	51	65	45
Hornchurch	40	12	8	20	42	60	44
Tring Town	40	10	11	19	48	64	41
Flackwell Heath	40	9	11	20	44	83	38
Horsham	40	6	8	26	43	86	26

Leading Scorers
Tony Wood (Bracknell/Flackwell) 33, Mark Randall (Northwood) 24, David Whitehead (Hertford) 23

Neville Ovenden Combination
Division 1

	P	W	D	L	GF	GA	PTS
Chelsea	38	24	8	6	79	41	80
Ipswich Town	38	19	8	11	71	52	65
Tottenham Hotspur	38	19	6	13	69	47	63
Crystal Palace	38	17	11	10	63	40	62
Norwich City	38	18	7	13	68	54	61
Wimbledon	38	16	13	9	53	48	61
Queen's Park Rangers	38	17	8	13	58	49	59
West Ham Utd	38	16	10	12	59	45	58
Swindon Town	38	18	4	16	54	53	58
Bristol Rovers	38	15	12	11	50	52	57
Southampton	38	15	10	13	62	66	55
Millwall	38	12	11	15	57	67	47
Charlton Athletic	38	13	7	18	61	62	46
Luton Town	38	12	9	17	64	70	45
Arsenal	38	13	6	19	67	76	45
Oxford Utd	38	11	10	17	53	66	43
Portsmouth	38	10	11	17	43	60	41
Brighton & Hove Albion	38	9	10	19	38	58	37
Watford	38	9	8	21	49	75	35
Bristol City	38	8	9	21	47	84	33

The Pontin's League
Division 1

	P	W	D	L	GF	GA	PTS
Manchester Utd	34	22	7	5	77	38	73
Aston Villa	34	18	9	7	61	29	63
Bolton Wanderers	34	15	10	9	88	65	55
Wolverhampton Wdrs	34	15	9	10	45	38	54
Derby County	34	14	8	12	55	51	50
Nottingham Forest	34	14	8	12	55	51	50
Sunderland	34	12	13	9	47	53	49
Blackburn Rovers	34	14	7	13	40	47	49
Leeds Utd	34	13	8	13	42	48	47
Coventry City	34	13	7	14	42	41	46
Sheffield Utd	34	12	9	13	57	60	45
Notts County	34	12	8	14	43	50	44
Everton	34	12	7	15	54	50	43
Liverpool	34	10	11	13	42	51	41
Newcastle Utd	34	10	8	16	46	53	38
Sheffield Wednesday	34	7	12	15	46	63	33
Leicester City	34	8	7	19	37	58	31
York City	34	6	10	18	36	67	28

It isn't just Pavarotti who still loves Maradona. Peter De Sisto, chairman of Petersfield Town, in the Jewson Wessex League, has written to Maradona's agent with an offer for him to play at the Hampshire club. "We are making every effort to get in touch with his agent," said De Sisto. "This is no joke.....we are prepared to put up an attractive financial offer."Maradona obviously doesn't know how pretty Petersfield is. He has yet to reply.....

English Cup Competitions
FA Challenge Cup

First Round

Crewe Alexandra 4 *(Edwards, Rowbotham, Gardiner, S Smith (pen))*
Darlington 2 *(Ellison, Painter)*

Leek Town 2 *(D Sutton 2)*
Wigan Athletic 2 *(Skipper, Morton)*

Wigan Athletic 3 *(McKearney (pen), Diskin (og), Duffy)*
Leek Town 0

Port Vale 2 *(Kerr, Foyle)*
Blackpool 0

Witton Albion 0
Lincoln City 2 *(West, Lormor)*

Runcorn 0
Hull City 2 *(Brown, Hargreaves)*

Halifax Town 2 *(Peake, Saunders)*
West Bromwich A 1 *(Hunt)*

Telford United 1 *(Bignot)*
Huddersfield Town 1 *(Rowe)*

Huddersfield Town 1 *(Jackson)*
Telford United 0

Wrexham 1 *(Watkin)*
Walsall 1 *(Lightbourne)*

Walsall 2 *(Lightbourne, McDonald)*
Wrexham 0

Rotherham United 1 *(Wilder (pen))*
Stockport County 2 *(Todd, Preece)*

Mansfield Town 1 *(Wilkinson)*
Preston North End 2 *(Ellis 2 (1 pen))*

Chesterfield 0
Rochdale 1 *(Stuart (pen))*

Scarborough 1 *(Young)*
Bury 0

Macclesfield Town 2 *(Sorvel, Macdonald)*
Hartlepool United 0

Bradford City 0
Chester City 0

Chester City 1 *(Lightfoot)*
Bradford City 0

Gretna 2 *(Townsley, Dobie)*
Bolton Wanderers 3 *(McGinlay (pen) Coyle 2)*

Accrington Stanley 2 *(Connor, Wood)*
Scunthorpe United 3 *(Toman, Goodacre 2)*

Shrewsbury Town 1 *(Gallen)*
Doncaster Rovers 1 *(Williamson)*

Doncaster Rovers 1 *(Williamson)*
Shrewsbury T 2 *(Spink, Walton) aet*

Knowsley United 1 *(Joyce (og))*
Carlisle United 4 *(Arnold 2, Davey, Reeves)*

Burnley 0
York City 0

York City 2 *(Canham, McCarthy)*
Burnley 3 *(Heath, Joyce, Eyres)*

Stalybridge Celtic 1 *(Aspinall)*
Marine 1 *(Rowlands)*

Marine 4 *(Camden 2, Murray, Doherty (pen))*
Stalybridge Celtic 4 *(Hill, Shaughnessy, Aspinall, Kirkham) aet*
Stalybridge won 4 2 on penalties

Colchester United 3 *(McGavin, S Brown, English)*
Sutton United 4 *(Quail, Smart, Newman, Morah)*

Enfield 0
Cardiff City 0

Cardiff City 1 *(Blake)*
Enfield 0

Slough Town 1 *(Scott)*
Torquay United 2 *(Sale, Moore)*

Yeading 0
Gillingham 0

Gillingham 3 *(Smith, Micklewhite, Baker)*
Yeading 1 *(James)*

Northampton Town 1 *(Aldridge)*
Bromsgrove Rovers 2 *(Shilvock, Carter)*

VS Rugby 0
Brentford 3 *(Allon 2 (1 pen), Gayle)*

Marlow 0
Plymouth Argyle 2 *(Dalton 2)*

Metropolitan Police 0
Crawley Town 2 *(Whitington, Van Sittart)*

Bristol Rovers 1 *(Archer)*
Wycombe Wanders 2 *(Langford, Carroll)*

Yeovil Town 1 *(Wallace)*
Fulham 0

Molesey 0
Bath City 4 *(Mings, Boyle, Adcock 2)*

Swansea City 1 *(Torpey)*
Nuneaton Borough 1 *(Shearer)*

Nuneaton Borough 2 *(Simpson 2)*
Swansea City 1 *(Torpey) aet*

Cambridge United 0
Reading 0

Reading 1 *(Gooding)*
Cambridge U 2 *(Nyamah, Heathcote)*

Kidderminster H 3 *(Brindley, Forsyth (pen), Davies)*
Kettering Town 0

Woking 2 *(S Wye, Dennis)*
Weston S Mare 2 *(Elson, Bowering)*

Weston Super Mare 0
Woking 1 *(Clement)*

Cambridge City 0
Hereford United 1 *(Pike)*

Barnet 2 *(Haag, Close)*
Carshalton Athletic 1 *(Annon)*

AFC Bournemouth 4 *(McGorry, Pennock, Masters, Wood)*
Brighton & Hove A 2 *(Kennedy 2)*

Farnborough Town 1 *(Jones)*
Exeter City 3 *(Worthington, Jepson, Ross)*

Leyton Orient 2 *(Lakin, Hackett)*
Gravesend & Northfleet 1 *(Portway)*

Association Football

Second Round

Lincoln City 1 *(D Johnson)*
Bolton Wanderers 3 *(Thompson, Brown, Coyle)*

Wigan Athletic 1 *(Gavin)*
Scarborough 0

Shrewsbury Town 0
Preston North End 1 *(Raynor)*

Burnley 4 *(Ryan (og), Eyres 3)*
Rochdale 1 *(Whitehall (pen))*

Chester City 2 *(Preece, Leonard)*
Hull City 0

Stockport County 5 *(Frain, Francis 2, Beaumont, Wallace)*
Halifax Town 1 *(Barr (pen))*

Port Vale 1 *(Tankard)*
Huddersfield Town 0

Carlisle United 3 *(Edmondson, Gallimore, Arnold)*
Stalybridge Celtic 1 *(Kirkham)*

Walsall 1 *(Wright)*
Scunthorpe United 1 *(Carmichael)*

Scunthorpe United 0
Walsall 0 *aet*
Scunthorpe win 7-6 on penalties

Crewe Alexandra 2 *(Lennon, Whalley)*
Macclesfield Town 1 *(Askey)*

Brentford 1 *(Gayle)*
Cardiff City 3 *(Westley (og), Stant, Bird)*

Torquay United 0
Sutton United 1 *(Jones)*

Kidderminster H 1 *(Forsyth (pen))*
Woking 0

Leyton Orient 1 *(Cooper)*
Exeter City 1 *(Bailey)*

Exeter City 2 *(Storer, Harris)*
Leyton Orient 2 *(Carter, Hackett) aet*
Exeter win 5-4 on penalties

Plymouth Argyle 2 *(Nugent 2)*
Gillingham 0

Crawley Town 1 *(Ford)*
Barnet 2 *(Rowe, Hoddle)*

Bath City 2 *(Brooks, Batty)*
Hereford United 1 *(Hall)*

Yeovil Town 0
Bromsgrove Rovers 2 *(Webb, Radburn)*

AFC Bournemouth 1 *(Watson)*
Nuneaton Borough 1 *(Green)*

Nuneaton Borough 0
AFC Bournemouth 1 *(Cotterill)*

Wycombe W 1 *(Hemmings)*
Cambridge United 0

Third Round

Swindon Town 1 *(Mutch)*
Ipswich Town 1 *(Marshall)*

Ipswich Town 2 *(Stockwell, Marshall)*
Swindon Town 1 *(Fjortoft) aet*

Oxford United 2 *(Elliott, Byrne)*
Tranmere Rovers 0

Preston NE 2 *(Moyes, Conroy)*
AFC Bournemouth 1 *(Aspinall (pen))*

Luton Town 1 *(Telfer)*
Southend United 0

Stockport County 2 *(Francis, Preece)*
Queens Pk Rangers 1 *(Barker)*

West Ham United 2 *(M Allen, Marsh)*
Watford 1 *(Porter (pen))*

Cardiff City 2 *(Stant, Thompson)*
Middlesbrough 2 *(Wilkinson, Moore)*

Middlesbrough 1 *(Kavanagh)*
Cardiff City 2 *(Stant, Blake) aet*

Wycombe W 0
Norwich City 2 *(Sutton 2)*

Bromsgrove Rovers 1 *(Crisp)*
Barnsley 2 *(Rammell, Archdeacon)*

Wolverhampton W 1 *(D Kelly)*
Crystal Palace 0

Sheffield Wednesday 1 *(Bright)*
Nottingham Forest 1 *(Cooper)*

Nottingham Forest 0
Sheffield Wednesday 2 *(Pearce, Bart-Williams)*

Millwall 0
Arsenal 1 *(Adams)*

Newcastle United 2 *(Cole, Beardsley)*
Coventry City 0

Charlton Athletic 3 *(Pardew, Leaburn, Grant)*
Burnley 0

Stoke City 0
Bath City 0

Bath City 1 *(Chenoweth)*
Stoke City 4 *(Regis 2, Cranson, Orlygsson)*

Bolton Wanderers 1 *(Patterson)*
Everton 1 *(Rideout)*

Everton 2 *(Barlow 2)*
Bolton Wanderers 3 *(McGinlay, Stubbs, Coyle) aet*

Plymouth Argyle 1 *(Nugent)*
Chester City 0

Wimbledon 3 *(Holdsworth 3)*
Scunthorpe United 0

Grimsby Town 1 *(Croft)*
Wigan Athletic 0

Barnet 0
Chelsea 0 *played at Stamford Bridge*

Chelsea 4 *(Burley, Peacock, Stein, Shipperley)*
Barnet 0

Bristol City 1 *(Allison)*
Liverpool 1 *(Rush)*

Liverpool 0
Bristol City 1 *(Tinnion)*

Birmingham City 1 *(Harding)*
Kidderminster H 2 *(Cartwright, Purdie)*

Exeter City 0
Aston Villa 1 *(Saunders (pen))*

Manchester City 4 *(Ingrebritsen 3, Kernaghan)*
Leicester City 1 *(Oldfield)*

Sheffield United 0
Manchester United 1 *(Hughes)*

Southampton 1 *(Dowie)*
Port Vale 1 *(Porter)*

Port Vale 1 *(Slaven)*
Southampton 0

Leeds United 3 *(Deane, Forrester 2)*
Crewe Alexandra 1 *(Naylor)*

Notts County 3 *(Draper, Agana, Devlin)*
Sutton United 2 *(Barrowcliffe, Smart)*

Oldham Athletic 2 *(Beckford, Holden)*
Derby County 1 *(Johnson)*

Blackburn Rovers 3 *(Shearer, Gallacher, Sherwood)*
Portsmouth 3 *(McLoughlin 3)*

Portsmouth 1 *(McLoughlin)*
Blackburn Rovers 3 *(Shearer, May, Wilcox)*

Sunderland 1 *(Ferguson)*
Carlisle United 1 *(Edmondson)*

Carlisle United 0
Sunderland 1 *(Howey) aet*

Peterborough United 1 *(Brissett)*
Tottenham Hotspur 1 *(Dozzell)*

Tottenham Hotspur 1 *(Barmby)*
Peterborough United 1 *(Charlery)*
aet Tottenham won 5-4 on penalties

Fourth Round
Port Vale 0
Wolverhampton W 2 *(Blades, Keen)*

Grimsby Town 1 *(Groves)*
Aston Villa 2 *(Houghton, Yorke)*

Newcastle United 1 *(Beardsley (pen))*
Luton Town 1 *(Thorpe)*

Luton Town 2 *(Hartson, Oakes)*
Newcastle United 0

Wimbledon 2 *(Scales, Fashanu)*
Sunderland 1 *(Smith)*

Stockport County 0
Bristol City 4 *(Shail, Allison 3)*

Norwich City 0
Manchester United 2 *(Keane, Cantona)*

Plymouth Argyle 2 *(Marshall, Dalton)*
Barnsley 2 *(Payton, Taggart)*

Barnsley 1 *(O'Connell)*
Plymouth Argyle 0

Ipswich Town 3 *(Marshall, Johnson, Thompson)*
Tottenham Hotspur 0

Oldham Athletic 0
Stoke City 0

Stoke City 0
Oldham Athletic 1 *(Beckford)*

Chelsea 1 *(Peacock)*
Sheffield Wednesday 1 *(Hyde)*

Sheffield Wednesday 1 *(Bright)*
Chelsea 3 *(Spencer, Peacock, Burley) aet*

Kidderminster H 1 *(Humphreys)*
Preston North End 0

Notts County 1 *(Lund)*
West Ham United 1 *(Jones)*

West Ham United 1 *(Chapman)*
Notts County 0 *aet*

Cardiff City 1 *(Blake)*
Manchester City 0

Charlton Athletic 0
Blackburn 0

Blackburn 0
Charlton Athletic 1 *(Pitcher)*

Oxford United 2 *(Dyer, Elliott)*
Leeds United 2 *(Speed, Wetherall)*

Leeds United 2 *(Strachan, White)*
Oxford United 3 *(Byrne, Allen, Magilton) aet*

Bolton Wanderers 2 *(McAteer, Coyle)*
Arsenal 2 *(Wright, Adams)*

Arsenal 1 *(Smith)*
Bolton Wanderers 3 *(McGinlay, McAteer, Walker) aet*

Fifth Round
Cardiff City 1 *(Stant)*
Luton Town 2 *(Oakes, Preece)*

Oldham Athletic 1 *(Ritchie)*
Barnsley 0

Kidderminster H 0
West Ham United 1 *(Chapman)*

Wolverhampton W 1 *(Kelly)*
Ipswich Town 1 *(Wark)*

Ipswich Town 1 *(Palmer)*
Wolverhampton W 2 *(Mills, Thompson)*

Bolton Wanderers 1 *(Stubbs)*
Aston Villa 0

Oxford United 1 *(Beauchamp)*
Chelsea 2 *(Spencer, Burley)*

Wimbledon 0
Manchester United 3 *(Cantona, Ince, Irwin)*

Bristol City 1 *(Tinnion)*
Charlton Athletic 1 *(Robson)*

Charlton Athletic 2 *(Pitcher (pen), Grant)*
Bristol City 0

Sixth Round
West Ham United 0
Luton Town 0

Luton Town 3 *(Oakes 3)*
West Ham United 2 *(M Allen, Bishop)*

Manchester United 3 *(Hughes, Kanchelskis 2)*
Charlton Athletic 1 *(Leaburn)*

Chelsea 1 *(Peacock)*
Wolverhampton Wanderers 0

Bolton Wanderers 0
Oldham Athletic 1 *(Beckford)*

Semi Finals
Chelsea 2 *(Peacock 2)*
Luton Town 0

Oldham Athletic 1 *(Pointon)*
Manchester United 1 *(Hughes) aet*

Manchester United 4 *(Irwin, Kanchelskis, Robson, Giggs)*
Oldham 1 *(Pointon)*

FA CUP FINAL
Wembley   May 14
Chelsea 0
Manchester United 4
(Cantona 2 pens), Hughes, McClair)
Chelsea: Kharine, Clarke, Sinclair, Kjeldberg, Johnsen, Burley (Hoddle), Spencer, Newton, Stein (Cascarino), Peacock, Wise
Manchester Utd: Schmeichel, Parker, Irwin (Sharpe), Bruce, Kanchelskis (McClair), Pallister, Cantona, Ince, Keane, Hughes, Giggs

Coca Cola Cup

First Round *(over 2 legs)*
Doncaster Rvrs 0
Blackpool 1 *(Watson)*

Blackpool 3 *(Watson, Quinn, Bamber)*
Doncaster Rvrs 3 *(Hulme, Harper, Wilcox)*
Blackpool won 4-3 on aggregate

Birmingham C 3 *(Parris, Frain, Peschisolido)*
Plymouth Arg 0

Plymouth Arg 2 *(Barlow, Marshall)*
Birmingham C 0
Birmingham won 3-2 on aggregate

Bolton Wdrs 0
Bury 2 *(Powell, Blissett)*

Bury 0
Bolton 2 *(Coyle, McGinlay)   aet*
2-2 on agg, Bolton won 3-0 on penalties

Bournemouth 3 *(Fletcher, Masters, Beardsmore)*
Cardiff C 1 *(Bird)*

Cardiff C 1 *(Morris (og))*
Bournemouth 1 *(Parkinson)*
Bournemouth won 4-2 on aggregate

Brentford 2 *(Peters, Westley)*
Watford 2 *(Furlong, Dyer)*

Watford 3 *(Holdsworth, Solomon, Dyer)*
Brentford 1 *(Westley)*
Watford won 5-3 on aggregate

Cambridge U 1 *(Claridge)*
Luton T 0

Luton T 0
Cambridge U 1 *(Claridge)*
Cambridge U won 2-0 on aggregate

Chesterfield 3 *(Turnbull (pen), Norris, Morris)*
Carlisle U 1 *(Davey)*

Carlisle U 1 *(Thomas)*
Chesterfield 1 *(Jules)*
Chesterfield won 4-2 on aggregate

Crewe Alex 0
Wrexham 1 *(Paskin)*

Wrexham 3 *(Connolly, Bennett (pen), Wilson (og))*
Crewe Alex 3 *(Lyons, Rowbotham, Ward)*
Wrexham won 4-3 on aggregate

Darlington T 1 *(Juryeff)*
Bradford C 5 *(McCarthy 3, Reid, Jewell)*

Bradford C 6 *(Jewell 2, McCarthy 2, Steele, Showler)*
Darlington T 0
Bradford won 11-1 on aggregate

Fulham 2 *(Betts (og), Farrell)*
Colchester U 1 *(Kinsella)*

Colchester U 1 *(McDonough)*
Fulham 2 *(Brazil, Farrell)*
Fulham won 4-2 on aggregate

Gillingham 1 *(Reinelt)*
Brighton & HA 0

Brighton & HA 2 *(Kennedy, Nogan)*
Gillingham 0
Brighton won 2-1 on aggregate

Hereford U 0
Torquay U 2 *(Trollope, Foster)*

Torquay U 0
Hereford U 2 *(May, Hall (pen))*
2-2 agg, Hereford won 4-3 on penalties

Huddersfield T 0
Scarborough 0

Scarborough 0
Huddersfield T 3 *(Dunn 2, Roberts)*
Huddersfield won 3-0 on aggregate

Leyton Orient 0
Wycombe W 2 *(Thompson, Langford)*

Wycombe W 1 *(Scott)*
Leyton Orient 0
Wycombe won 3-0 on aggregate

Notts Co 2 *(Lund, Cox)*
Hull C 0

Hull C 3 *(Abbott, Atkinson, Windass)*
Notts Co 1 *(Draper)*
aet; Notts Co won on away goals

Port Vale 2 *(Taylor, Slaven)*
Lincoln C 2 *(Lormor 2)*

Lincoln C 0
Port Vale 0
aet; Lincoln C won on away goals

Preston NE 1 *(Ellis)*
Burnley 2 *(Eyres (pen), Davis)*

Burnley 4 *(Russell, Eyres, Francis, Deary)*
Preston NE 1 *(Cartwright)*
Burnley won 6-2 on aggregate

Rochdale 2 *(Stuart, Flounders (pen))*
York C 0

York C 0
Rochdale 0
Rochdale won 2-0 on aggregate

Shrewsbury T 1 *(Evans)*
Scunthorpe U 0

Scunthorpe U 1 *(Martin)*
Shrewsbury T 1 *(Griffiths)*
Shrewsbury won 2-1 on aggregate

Stockport Co 1 *(Ryan)*
Hartepool U 1 *(West)*

Hartlepool U 2 *(Tait, Honour)*
Stockport Co 1 *(Francis)*
Hartlepool won 3-2 on aggregate

Sunderland 3 *(Goodman 2, Power)*
Chester C 1 *(Rimmer)*

Chester C 0
Sunderland 0
Sunderland won 3-1 on aggregate

Swansea 0
Bristol C 1 *(Robinson)*

Bristol C 0
Swansea 2 *(Bowen 2)*
Swansea won 2-1 on aggregate

Walsall 0
Exeter C 0

Exeter C 2 *(Jepson 2 (1 pen))*
Walsall 1 *(McDonald)*
Exeter won 2-1 on aggregate

Wigan Ath 0
Rotherham 1 *(Hazel)*

Rotherham 4 *(Banks, Gavin (og), Varadi, Law)*
Wigan Ath 2 *(Gavin, Morton)*
Rotherham won 5-2 on aggregate

Bristol R 1 *(Sterling)*
West Bromwich A 4 *(Burgess, Hunt, Donovan 2)*

West Bromwich A 0
Bristol R 0
West Bromwich won 4-1 on aggregate

Reading 3 *(Quinn, Lovell, Parkinson)*
Northampton T 0

Northampton T 0
Reading 2 *(Gray, Dillon)*
Reading won 5-0 on aggregate

Southend U 0
Barnet 2 *(Lynch, Walker)*

Barnet 1 *(Haag)*
Southend 1 *(Angell)*
Barnet won 3-1 on aggregate

Stoke C 2 *(Gleghorn, Carruthers)*
Mansfield T 2 *(Noteman,
    McLoughlin)*

Mansfield T 1 *(Stant)*
Stoke C 3 *(Stein 2, Regis)*
aet; Stoke won 5-3 on aggregate

Second Round *(over two legs)*
Barnet 1 *(Lynch)*
QPR 2 *(Ferdinand, Barker)*

QPR 4 *(Allen 3, Impey)*
Barnet 0
QPR won 6-1 on aggregate

Barnsley 1 *(Archdeacon (pen))*
Peterborough 1 *(Brissett)*

Peterborough 3 *(Philliskirk,
    McGlashan, Oliver)*
Barnsley 1 *(Bryson)*
aet; Peterborough won 4-2 on aggregate

Birmingham C 0
Aston Villa 1 *(Richardson)*

Aston Villa 1 *(Saunders)*
Birmingham C 0
Aston Villa won 2-0 on aggregate

Blackburn R 1 *(Shearer)*
Bournemouth 0

Bournemouth 0
Blackburn R 0
Blackburn won 1-0 on aggregate

Blackpool 3 *(Bamber 2, Watson)*
Sheffield U 0

Sheffield U 2 *(Davison, Ward)*
Blackpool 0
Blackpool won 3-2 on aggregate

Bolton W 1 *(Kelly (pen))*
Sheffield W 1 *(Bart-Williams)*

Sheffield W 1 *(Bright)*
Bolton W 0
Sheffield W won 2-1 on aggregate

Crystal Palace 3 *(Gordon, Southgate,
    Whyte)*
Charlton Ath 1 *(Leaburn)*

Charlton Ath 0
Crystal Palace 1 *(Armstrong)*
Crystal Palace won 4-1 on aggregate

Grimsby T 3 *(Dobbin, Mendonca 2)*
Hartlepool 0

Hartlepool 0
Grimsby T 2 *(Groves, Dobbin)*
Grimsby won 5-0 on aggregate

Huddersfield T 0
Arsenal 5 *(Wright 3, Campbell,
    Merson)*

Arsenal 1 *(Smith)*
Huddersfield T *(Dunn)*
Arsenal won 6-1 on aggregate

Ipswich T 2 *(Milton, Whitton)*
Cambridge U 1 *(Claridge (pen))*

Cambridge U 0
Ipswich T 2 *(Marshall, Kiwomya)*
Ipswich won 4-1 on aggregate

Lincoln C 3 *(D Johnson, Matthews
    Brown)*
Everton 4 *(Rideout 3, Cottee)*

Everton 4 *(Rideout, Snodin, Cottee 2)*
Lincoln 2 *(D Johnson, Baraclough
    (pen))*
Everton won 8-5 on aggregate

Middlesbro' 5 *(Hignett 4, Hendrie)*
Brighton & Hove A 0

Brighton & Hove A 1 *(Nogan)*
Middlesbrough 3 *(Wilkinson,
    Hignett, Hendrie)*
Middlesbrough won 8-1 on aggregate

Rochdale 1 *(Carey (og))*
Leicester C 6 *(Whitlow, Walsh,
    Thompson, Oldfield, Speedie,
    Ormondroyd)*

Leicester C 2 *(Ormondroyd, Joachim)*
Rochdale 1 *(Lancaster)*
Leicester C won 8-2 on aggregate

Rotherham U 0
Portsmouth 0

Portsmouth 5 *(Stimson, McLoughlin,
    Durnin, Walsh, Burns)*
Rotherham U 0
Portsmouth won 5-0 on aggregate

Sunderland 2 *(Goodman, P Gray)*
Leeds U 1 *(Speed)*

Leeds U 1 *(Whelan)*
Sunderland 2 *(Goodman, P Gray)*
Sunderland won 4-2 on aggregate

Swansea C 2 *(Torpey, Pascoe)*
Oldham Ath 1 *(Sharp)*

Oldham Ath 2 *(Halle, Bernard)*
Swansea C 0
Oldham won 3-2 on aggregate

Tranmere R 5 *(Aldridge 2, Nevin 3)*
Oxford U 1 *(Beauchamp)*

Oxford U 1 *(Wanless)*
Tranmere R 1 *(Irons)*
Tranmere won 6-2 on aggregate

Watford 0
Millwall 0

Millwall 4 *(Huxford, Murray,
    Moralee, Verveer)*
Watford 3 *(Porter, Nogan,
    Hessenthaler)*
aet; Millwall won 4-3 on aggregate

Wrexham 3 *(Bennett 2 (1 pen),Paskin)*
Nottingham F 3 *(Collymore 3)*

Nottingham F 3 *(Black, Crosby,
    Collymore)*
Wrexham 1 *(Pejic)*
Nottingham F won 6-4 on aggregate

Bradford C 2 *(McCarthy 2)*
Norwich C 1 *(Fox)*

Norwich C 3 *(Ekoku, Fox, Sutton)*
Bradford C 0
Norwich won 4-2 on aggregate

Burnley 0
Tottenham H 0

Tottenham H 3 *(Sheringham 2,
    Howells)*
Burnley 1 *(Eyres)*
Tottenham won 3-1 on aggregate

Coventry C 3 *(Morgan 2, Quinn)*
Wycombe W 0

Wycombe W 4 *(Ryan, Scott, Evans
    Cousins)*
Coventry C 2 *(Morgan, Babb)*
aet; Coventry won 5-4 on aggregate

Exeter C 1 *(Storer)*
Derby Co 3 *(Kitson, Simpson,
    Gabbiadini)*

Derby Co 2 *(Gabbiadini, Johnson)*
Exeter C 0
Derby won 5-1 on aggregate

Fulham 1 *(Farrell)*
Liverpool 3 *(Rush, Clough, Fowler)*

Liverpool 5 *(Fowler 5)*
Fulham 0
Liverpool won 8-1 on aggregate

Hereford 0
Wimbledon 1 *(Clarke)*

Wimbledon 4 *(Ardley, Jones,
    Holdsworth, Earle)*
Hereford 1 *(Hall)*
Wimbledon won 5-1 on aggregate

Manchester C 1 *(White)*
Reading 1 *(Lovell)*

Reading 1 *(Quinn)*
Manchester C 2 *(Lomas, Quinn)*
Manchester C won 3-2 on aggregate

Newcastle U 4 *(Cole 3, Bracewell)*
Notts Co 1 *(Srnicek (og))*

Notts Co 1 *(McSwegan)*
Newcastle U 7 *(Allen 2 (1 pen),*
Beardsley, Cole 3, Lee)
Newcastle won 11-2 on aggregate

Southampton 1 *(Moore)*
Shrewsbury T 0

Shrewsbury T 2 *(Summerfield,*
Brown)
Southampton 0
Shrewsbury won 2-1 on aggregate

Stoke C 2 *(Stein 2)*
Manchester U 1 *(Dublin)*

Manchester U 2 *(Sharpe, McClair)*
Stoke C 0
Manchester U won 3-2 on aggregate

Swindon T 2 *(Summerbee, Mutch)*
Wolverhampton W 0

Wolverhampton W 2 *(Mountfield,*
Burke)
Swindon T 1 *(Summerbee)*
Swindon won 3-2 on aggregate

West Bromwich A 1 *(Donovan)*
Chelsea 1 *(Shipperley)*

Chelsea 2 *(Wise 2)*
West Bromwich A 1 *(Taylor)*
Chelsea won 3-2 on aggregate

West Ham U 5 *(Morley 2 (1 pen),*
Chapman 2, Burrows)
Chesterfield 1 *(Norris)*

Chesterfield 0
West Ham U 2 *(M Allen, Boere)*
West Ham won 7-1 on aggregate

Third Round
Arsenal 1 *(Wright)*
Norwich C 1 *(Crook)*

Norwich 0
Arsenal 3 *(Wright 2, Merson)*

Blackburn R 0
Shrewsbury T 0

Shrewsbury T 3 *(Summerfield 2,*
MacKenzie (pen))
Blackburn R 4 *(Newell 2 (1 pen), May,*
Pearce) aet

Blackpool 2 *(Watson 2)*
Peterborough U 2 *(Hackett, Adcock)*

Peterborough U 2 *(Rush, Bradshaw)*
Blackpool 1 *(Howarth (og))*

Everton 2 *(Beagrie, Watson)*
Crystal Palace 2 *(Thorn, Southgate)*

Crystal Palace 1 *(Southgate)*
Everton 4 *(Watson 2, Ward (pen),*
Young (og))

Manchester C 1 *(White)*
Chelsea 0

Oldham Ath 2 *(Beckford, Sharp)*
Coventry C 0

Portsmouth 2 *(Durnin, Walsh)*
Swindon T 0

Sunderland 1 *(P Gray)*
Aston Villa 4 *(Atkinson 2, Richardson,*
Houghton)

Tranmere R 4 *(Aldridge 2, Vickers,*
Irons (pen))
Grimsby T 1 *(Okorie)*

Derby Co 0
Tottenham H 1 *(Barmby)*

Liverpool 3 *(Rush 3)*
Ipswich T 2 *(Marshall, Mason (pen))*

Manchester U 5 *(Bruce 2, McClair,*
Sharpe, Hughes)
Leicester C 1 *(Hill)*

Middlesbrough 1 *(Hendrie)*
Sheffield W 1 *(Palmer)*

Sheffield W 2 *(Watson, Palmer)*
Middlesbrough 1 *(Mustoe)*

Nottingham F 2 *(Black, Collymore)*
West Ham U 1 *(Morley)*

QPR 3 *(Sinclair, Barker, Ferdinand)*
Millwall 0

Wimbledon 2 *(Barton, Holdsworth)*
Newcastle U 1 *(Sellars)*

Fourth Round
Arsenal 0
Aston Villa 1 *(Atkinson)*

Everton 0
Manchester U 2 *(Hughes, Giggs)*

Peterborough U 0
Portsmouth 0

Portsmouth 1 *(Kristensen)*
Peterborough 0

Tranmere R 3 *(Brannan 2, Aldridge)*
Oldham Ath 0

Liverpool 1 *(Molby (pen))*
Wimbledon 1 *(Earle)*

Wimbledon 2 *(Holdsworth, Earle)*
Liverpool 2 *(Ruddock, Segers (og))*
aet Wimbledon won 4-3 on penalties

Nottingham F 0
Manchester C 0

Manchester C 1 *(Vonk)*
Nottingham F 2 *(Webb, Cooper)*

QPR 1 *(Meaker)*
Sheffield W 2 *(Jemson, Jones)*

Tottenham H 1 *(Campbell)*
Blackburn R 0

Fifth Round
Wimbledon 1 *(Holdsworth)*
Sheffield W 2 *(Watson, Bright)*

Manchester U 2 *(Giggs, Cantona)*
Portsmouth 2 *(Walsh 2)*

Portsmouth 0
Manchester U 1 *(McClair)*

Tottenham 1 *(Caskey)*
Aston Villa 2 *(Houghton, Barrett)*

Nottingham F 1 *(Gemmill)*
Tranmere R 1 *(Malkin)*

Tranmere R 2 *(Nevin, Thomas)*
Nottingham F 0

Semi Finals *(over 2 legs)*
Manchester U 1 *(Giggs)*
Sheffield W 0

Sheffield W 1 *(Hirst)*
Manchester U 4 *(McClair,*
Kanchelskis, Hughes 2)
Manchester U won 5-1 on aggregate

Tranmere R 3 *(Nolan, Hughes,*
Aldridge)
Aston Villa 1 *(Atkinson)*

Aston Villa 3 *(Saunders, Teale,*
Atkinson)
Tranmere R 1 *(Aldridge (pen))*
4-4 on aggregate, aet Aston Villa won
5-4 on penalties

COCA COLA CUP FINAL
Wembley   Mar 27
Aston Villa 3 *(Atkinson, Saunders 2,*
(1 pen))
Manchester Utd 1 *(Hughes)*
Aston Villa: Bosnich, Barrett,
Staunton (Cox), Teale, McGrath,
Richardson, Daley, Townsend,
Saunders, Atkinson, Fenton
Manchester Utd: Sealey, Parker,
Irwin, Bruce (McClair), Kanchelskis,
Pallister, Cantona, Ince, Keane,
Hughes, Giggs (Sharpe)

Autoglass Trophy

For clubs from Divisions 2 and 3

North Area Quarter Finals
Carlisle U 2 *(Reeves, Thomas)*
Mansfield T 1 *(Gray) aet*

Huddersfield T 3 *(Starbuck 2, Booth)*
Crewe Alex 2 *(Murphy, Naylor) aet*

Lincoln C 1 *(Brown)*
Chester C 0

Stockport Co 2 *(Preece, Francis)*
Scunthorpe U 0

South Area Quarter Finals
Colchester U 0
Wycombe W 1 *(Guppy)*

Fulham 1 *(Baah)*
Reading 0

Leyton Orient 1 *(Ludden)*
Brentford 0

Swansea C 1 *(Burns)*
Port Vale 0

Norh Area Semi Final
Carlisle U 2 *(Walling, Robinson)*
Lincoln C 1 *(D Johnson) aet*

Stockport Co 0
Huddersfield T 1 *(Dunn)*

South Area Semi Final
Fulham 2 *(Brazil 2)*
Wycombe W 2 *(Langford 2)*
aet; Wycombe won 4-2 on penalties

Leyton Orient 0
Swansea C 2 *(Chapple, Torpey)*

Northern Final *(over 2 legs)*
Huddersfield T 4 *(Jackson, Bullock,*
        Starbuck, Dunn)
Carlisle U 1 *(Davey (pen))*

Carlisle U 2 *(Mitchell (og), Joyce)*
Huddersfield T 0
Huddersfield won 4-3 on aggregate

Southern Final *(over 2 legs)*
Swansea C 3 *(Pascoe 2, Bowen)*
Wycombe W 1 *(Garner)*

Wycombe W 1 *(Hemmings)*
Swansea C 0
Swansea won 3-2 on aggegate

AUTOGLASS TROPHY FINAL
Wembley   Apr 24
Huddersfield T 1 *(Logan)*
Swansea C 1 *(McFarlane)*
aet Swansea won 3-1 on penalties
Huddersfield: Francis, Billy, Cowan,
Starbuck, Scully, Mitchell, Logan, P
Robinson, Booth, Bullock (Dunn),
Baldry
Swansea: Freestone, Jenkins, Clode
(Torpey), Basham, Harris, Pascoe,
Bowen, Ampadu, McFarlane,
Cornforth, Hodge (Ford)

Anglo-Italian Cup

For Division 1 clubs in England and Serie B clubs in Italy

INTERNATIONAL STAGE
Group A
Bolton W 5 *(McGinlay 2, McAteer,*
        Thompson, Phillips)
Ancona 0

Brescia 2 *(Chapple (og), Ambrosetti)*
Charlton Ath 0

Notts Co 4 *(Legg, Lund 2, Draper)*
Ascoli 2 *(Spinelli, D'Ainzara)*

Pisa 3 *(Lorenzini, Rovaris, Polidori)*
Middlesbrough 1 *(Hendrie)*

Ancona 1 *(Carruezzo)*
Charlton Ath 1 *(Bailey)*

Bolton W 3 *(Coyle, McGinlay, Green)*
Brescia 3 *(Ambrosetti 2, Hagi)*

Notts Co 3 *(Agana, Devlin, Lund)*
Pisa 2 *(Lorenzini 2)*

Brescia 3 *(Schenardi, Neri 2)*
Notts Co 1 *(Draper)*

Charlton Ath 0
Ascoli 3 *(Men'scina, Bierhoff, Troglio)*

Middlesbrough 0
Ancona 0

Pisa 1 *(Mattei)*
Bolton W 1 *(Phillips)*

Ascoli 3 *(Bierhoff, Menolascina,Maini)*
Middlesbrough 0

Ancona 0
Notts Co 1 *(McSwegan)*

Ascoli 1 *(Troglio)*
Bolton W 1 *(Seagraves)*

Charlton Ath 0
Pisa 3 *(Muzzi 3)*

Middlesbrough 0
Brescia 1 *(Ambrosetti)*

Group B
Fiorentina 3 *(Batistuta 2, Orlando)*
Southend U 0

Padova 0
Portsmouth 0

Stoke C 2 *(Carruthers, Orlygsson)*
Cosenza 1 *(Fabris)*

WBA 1 *(Taylor)*
Pescara 2 *(Borgonovo, Nobile)*

Cosenza 1 *(Fabris)*
Southend U 2 *(Angell 2)*

Pescara 2 *(Bivi, Compagno)*
Portsmouth 1 *(Doling)*

WBA 3 *(Hamilton,Ottoni (og),Garner)*
Padova 4 *(Montrone, Giordano,*
        Maniero, Ottoni)

Stoke C 0
Fiorentina 0

Fiorentina 2 *(Banchelli, Antonaccio)*
WBA 0

Padova 3 *(Maniero 2, Giordano)*
Stoke C 0

Portsmouth 3 *(Kristensen, Walsh 2)*
Cosenza 0

Southend 1 *(Lee)*
Pescara 3 *(Compagno,Sivebaek,Nobile)*

Cosenza 2 *(Fabris, Florio)*
WBA 1 *(Taylor)*

Pescara 2 *(Palladini, Mendy)*
Stoke C 1 *(Regis)*

Portsmouth 2 *(Hall, Dobson)*
Fiorentina 3 *(Banc'lli, Flachi, Malusci)*

Southend U 5 *(Lee, Edwards, G Jones*
        2, Otto)
Padova 2 *(Giordano, Cuicchi)*

Semi Finals *(over 2 legs)*
Brescia 1 *(Sabau)*
Pescara 0

Pescara 3 *(Sivebaek, Neri, Massara)*
Brescia 2 *(Hagi, Compagno)*
3-3 on agg.; Brescia won on away goals

Southend U 1 *(Gridelet)*
Notts Co 0

Notts Co 1 *(Devlin)*
Southend U 0
aet; Notts Co won 4-3 on penalties

ANGLO-ITALIAN CUP FINAL
Wembley   Mar 20
Notts Co 0
Brescia 1 *(Ambrosetti)*
Notts Co: Cherry, Wilson, Dijkstra, P
Turner, Johnson, Palmer, Devlin,
Draper, Lund, McSwegan (Agana),
Legg
Brescia: Landucci, Marangon,
Giunta, Domini, Baronchelli,
Bonometti, Schenardi, Sabau,
Ambrosetti (Piovanelli), Hagi, Gallo

SCOTTISH FOOTBALL 1993-4

PREMIER DIVISION

		P	W	D	L	GF	GA	W	D	L	GF	GA	GD	PTS
1	Glasgow Rangers	44	12	6	4	43	22	10	8	4	31	19	+33	58
2	Aberdeen	44	11	9	2	33	12	6	12	4	25	24	+22	55
3	Motherwell	44	11	7	4	31	20	9	7	6	27	23	+15	54
4	Glasgow Celtic	44	8	11	3	25	17	7	9	6	26	21	+13	50
5	Hibernian	44	11	7	4	29	15	5	8	9	24	33	+5	47
6	Dundee Utd.	44	5	11	6	26	25	6	9	7	21	23	-1	42
7	Heart of Midlothian	44	6	9	7	22	24	5	11	6	15	19	-6	42
8	Kilmarnock	44	6	10	6	18	19	6	6	10	18	26	-9	40
9	Partick Thistle	44	9	8	5	23	17	3	8	11	23	40	-11	40
10	St Johnstone	44	7	7	8	24	26	3	13	6	11	21	-12	40
11	Raith Rovers	44	3	12	7	25	35	3	7	12	21	45	-34	31
12	Dundee	44	6	7	9	26	26	2	6	14	16	31	-15	29

Goalscorers

	Lg	Cp	LCp	Total		Lg	Cp	LCp	Total
Mark Hateley (Rangers)	22	4	2	28	Roddy Grant (Partick)	13	0	2	15
Duncan Shearer (Aberdeen)	17	4	4	25	Gordon Durie (Rangers)	12	1	0	13
Craig Brewster (Dundee Utd)	16	4	0	20	John Robertson (Hearts)	10	1	2	13
Keith Wright (Hibernian)	16	1	2	19	Pat McGinlay (Celtic)	10	0	2	12
Albert Craig (Partick)	14	0	4	18	Billy McKinlay (Dundee Utd)	9	2	1	12
Tommy Coyne (Motherwell)	12	1	0	13	John Collins (Celtic)	8	0	0	8

	Aberdeen	Celtic	Dundee	Dundee Utd	Hearts	Hibernian	Kilmarnock	Motherwell	Partick T	Raith	Rangers	St Johnstone
Aberdeen		1-1	1-0	2-0	0-0	4-0	1-0	1-1	2-1	4-1	2-0	0-0
		1-1	1-1	1-0	0-1	2-2	3-1	0-0	2-0	4-0	0-0	1-1
Celtic	0-1		2-1	1-1	0-0	1-1	0-0	2-0	3-0	2-0	0-0	1-0
	2-2		1-1	0-0	2-2	1-0	1-0	0-1	1-1	2-1	2-4	1-1
Dundee	1-1	1-1		1-2	2-0	3-2	1-0	1-2	2-2	0-1	1-1	0-1
	0-1	0-2		1-1	0-2	4-0	3-0	1-3	1-0	2-2	1-1	0-1
Dundee Utd	1-1	1-0	1-0		0-0	2-2	0-0	0-0	2-2	2-2	1-3	2-0
	0-1	1-3	1-1		3-0	3-0	1-3	1-2	2-2	2-3	0-0	0-0
Hearts	1-1	1-0	1-2	1-1		1-0	0-1	2-3	2-1	1-0	2-2	1-1
	1-1	0-2	0-2	2-0		1-1	1-1	0-0	1-0	0-1	1-2	2-2
Hibernian	2-1	1-1	2-0	2-0	0-2		2-1	3-2	0-0	3-2	0-1	0-0
	3-1	0-0	2-0	0-1	0-0		0-0	0-2	5-1	3-0	1-0	0-0
Kilmarnock	1-1	2-2	1-0	1-1	0-0	1-1		0-1	3-1	1-0	0-2	0-0
	2-3	2-0	1-0	1-1	0-1	0-3		0-0	1-2	0-0	1-0	0-0
Motherwell	0-0	2-2	1-0	2-0	2-0	0-2	2-2		1-0	4-1	0-2	1-0
	1-1	2-1	3-1	1-2	1-1	0-0	1-0		2-2	3-1	2-1	0-1
Partick T	3-2	0-1	3-2	1-2	0-0	0-0	0-1	1-0		1-1	1-1	4-1
	1-1	1-0	1-0	1-0	0-1	1-0	1-0	0-0		2-2	1-2	0-0
Raith	1-1	1-4	2-1	1-1	1-0	1-2	2-2	0-3	2-2		1-1	1-1
	0-2	0-0	1-1	0-2	2-2	1-1	3-2	3-3	0-1		1-2	1-1
Rangers	2-0	1-2	3-1	0-3	2-1	2-1	1-2	1-2	1-1	2-2		2-0
	1-1	1-1	0-0	2-1	2-2	2-0	3-0	2-1	5-1	4-0		4-0
St Johnstone	1-1	2-1	2-1	1-1	2-0	1-3	0-1	3-0	1-3	1-1	1-2	
	0-1	0-1	1-1	1-1	0-0	2-2	0-1	2-1	1-0	2-0	0-4	

FIRST DIVISION

		P	W	D	L	GF	GA	W	D	L	GF	GA	GD	PTS
1	Falkirk	44	16	4	2	47	16	10	10	2	34	16	+49	66
2	Dunfermline Athletic	44	18	2	2	61	18	11	5	6	32	17	+58	65
3	Airdrieonians	44	9	9	4	28	18	11	5	6	30	20	+20	54
4	Hamilton Academicals	44	13	5	4	43	20	6	7	9	23	34	+12	50
5	Clydebank	44	11	5	6	30	28	7	9	6	26	20	+8	50
6	St Mirren	44	10	3	9	30	25	11	5	6	31	30	+6	50
7	Ayr Utd.	44	6	8	8	20	28	8	6	8	22	24	-10	42
8	Dumbarton	44	5	8	9	25	29	6	6	10	23	30	-11	36
9	Stirling Albion	44	7	6	9	23	30	6	3	13	18	38	-27	35
10	Clyde	44	6	7	9	18	20	4	5	13	17	38	-23	32
11	Morton	44	3	11	8	22	29	3	6	13	22	46	-31	29
12	Brechin City	44	4	3	15	13	34	2	4	16	17	47	-51	19

Goalscorers

	Lg	Cp	LCp	B&Q	Total		Lg	Cp	LCp	B&Q	Total
G Duffield (Hamilton)	19	0	0	0	19	A Tod (Dunfermline)	11	2	0	0	13
R Cadette (Falkirk)	18	0	4	6	28	R Alexander (Morton)	11	0	0	1	12
G O'Boyle (Dunfermline)	17	0	0	2	19	K Eadie (Clydebank)	11	0	0	0	11
H French (Dunfermline)	15	0	1	0	16	D Kirkwood (Airdrie)	10	4	1	0	15
C Gibson (Dumbarton)	13	0	0	0	13	B Laverty (St Mirren)	10	1	0	2	13
W Watters (Stirling Albion)	13	0	0	0	13	G Shaw (Falkirk)	10	0	0	0	10
S McGiven (Ayr Utd)	12	0	0	3	15	M Miller (Brechin)	10	0	0	2	12
C Flannigan (Clydebank)	11	0	0	2	13						

SECOND DIVISION

		P	W	D	L	GF	GA	W	D	L	GF	GA	GD	PTS
1	Stranraer	39	15	2	3	38	18	8	8	3	25	17	+28	56
2	Berwick Rangers	39	9	7	4	40	23	9	5	5	35	23	+29	48
3	Stenhousemuir	39	10	6	3	35	15	9	3	8	27	29	+18	47
4	Meadowbank Thistle	39	9	8	2	36	24	8	5	7	26	24	+14	47
5	Queen of the South	39	9	3	7	36	20	8	6	6	33	28	+21	43
6	East Fife	39	9	5	5	33	23	6	6	8	25	29	+6	41
7	Alloa	39	6	8	6	16	17	6	9	4	25	22	12	41
8	Forfar Athletic	39	6	6	8	27	32	8	5	6	31	26	0	39
9	East Stirling	39	7	3	9	29	31	6	8	6	25	26	-3	37
10	Montrose	39	6	5	8	24	25	8	3	9	32	36	-5	36
11	Queen's Park	39	10	4	6	34	32	2	6	11	18	44	-24	34
12	Arbroath	39	6	8	5	24	28	6	1	13	18	39	-25	33
13	Albion Rovers	39	3	5	12	18	33	4	5	10	19	33	-29	24
14	Cowdenbeath	39	1	4	15	19	39	5	4	10	21	33	-32	20

Goalscorers

	Lg	Cp	LCp	B&Q	Total		Lg	Cp	LCp	B&Q	Total
A Thompson (Queen of S)	29	2	0	1	32	D Grant (Montrose)	12	0	0	0	12
J O'Neill (Queen's Park)	18	0	0	0	18	W Hawke (Berwick)	12	0	0	0	12
M Scott (Albion)	17	1	1	1	20	M McCallum (East Stirling)	12	0	0	0	12
T Sloan (Stranraer)	16	8	0	0	24	W Callaghan (Cowdenbeath)	11	3	0	1	15
W Irvine (Berwick)	15	0	0	0	15	A Kennedy (Montrose)	11	1	0	2	14
M Mathieson (Stenhousemr)	14	0	1	0	15	L Bailey (Meadowbank)	11	0	0	1	12
D Bingham (Forfar)	13	3	0	1	17	S Mallan (Queen of S)	11	0	0	0	11
J Sludden (Stenhousemuir)	13	0	0	0	13	R Scott (East Fife)	10	3	1	0	14
I Little (Meadowbank)	12	0	1	2	15	D Diver (Arbroath)	10	0	0	1	11

Scottish Cup Competitions

SCOTTISH CUP
First Round
Albion Rovers 0
Huntly 0

Cowdenbeath 1 (Callaghan)
Queen's Park 1 (O'Neill)

East Fife 5 (Scott 3, Hope, Hildersley)
Rothes 0

Forfar Ath. 8 (Downie 2, Heddle 2,
    Bingham 3 (1 pen), Kopel)
Queen of Sth 3 (Mills, Thomson 2)

Ross Co. 11 (Grant 5 (1 pen),
    Williamson, Duff 3, Ferries 2)
St Cuthbert Wdrs 0

Stranraer 3 (Sloan 2, Henderson)
Whitehill Welfare 3 (Thorburn 2
    (2 pens), Sneddon)

First Round Replays
Queen's Park 2 (McPhee, Rodden)
Cowdenbeath 3 (Reilly, Henderson,
    Callaghan)

Whitehill Welfare 0
Stranraer 4 (Sloan 4)

Huntly 5 (De Barros, Stewart, Lennox,
    Murphy, Thomson (pen))
Albion R. 3 (Fraser, Scott (pen),
    McCaffrey)

Second Round
Berwick Rgrs 1 (Kane)
East Fife 0

East Stirling 4 (McAulay, Geraghty 2,
    Robertson)
Cove R 1 (Whyte)

Forfar Ath. 0
Ross Co. 4 (Grant 3, Wilson)

Meadowbank T. 1 (Rutherford)
Montrose 2 (Kennedy, Bailey (og))

Alloa 4 (McCulloch, Wilson (og),
    McCormick, Lamont)
Gala Fairydean 0

Cowdenbeath 1 (Hunter)
Stenhousemuir 0

Selkirk 0
Arbroath 3 (McKinnon, Adam,
    Buckley)

Huntly 1 (De Barros)
Stranraer 2 (Duncan (pen), Sloan)

Third Round
Aidrieonians 1 (Kirkwood (pen))
Dunfermline Ath. 1 (Tod)

Arbroath 2 (Sorbie, McKinnon)
Dundee Utd 3 (Crabbe, Brewster,
    McKinlay (pen))

Clydebank 1 (Henry)
Dundee 1 (Tosh)

Hibernian 2 (O'Neill, McAllister)
Clyde 1 (McCheyne)

Kilmarnock 2 (McSkimming,
    Black(pen))
Ayr Utd 1 (Bryce)

Morton 2 (McEwan, Lilley)
Cowdenbeath 2 (Henderson 2)

Motherwell 1 (Coyne)
Celtic 0

Partick Th. 0
Hearts 1 (M Johnston)

Raith Rvrs 2 (Dair, McStay)
Brechin City 0

Rangers 4 (Durie, Hateley (pen),
    Steven, Robertson)
Dumbarton 1 (Mooney (pen))

St Johnstone 2 (Dodds, McMartin)
Hamilton Acds. 0

St Mirren 2 (Elliot, Bone)
Montrose 0

Stirling Alb. 1 (Pew)
Berwick Rgrs 0

Stranraer 2 (Sloan, Ferguson)
Falkirk 1 (Hughes)

Alloa 2 (McAnenay, McAvoy)
Ross Co. 0

East Stirling 1 (Geraghty)
Aberdeen 3 (Craig (og), Shearer 2)

Third Round Replays
Cowenbeath 1 (Callaghan)
Morton 2 (Anderson, McEwan)

Dunfermline Ath. 1 (Tod)
Airdrieonians 3 (Kirkwood 2 (2 pens),
    Ferguson)

Dundee 2 (Britton, Shaw)
Clydebank 1 (Sweeney)

Fourth Round
Aberdeen 1 (Miller)
Raith Rvrs 0

Aidrieonians 1 (Kirkwood (pen))
Stranraer 0

Dundee Utd 2 (Brewster 2)
Motherwell 2 (Kirk, Philliben)

Morton 0
Kilmarnock 1 (Williamson)

Rangers 6 (I Ferguson, McPherson,
    McCoist 3 (1 pen), Newbigging (og))
Alloa 0

Dundee 3 (Britton 2 (1 pen), Shaw)
St Mirren 1 (Lavety)

Hibernian 1 (Wright)
Hearts 2 (Robertson, Foster)

St Johnstone 3 (Dodds 2, Ferguson)
Stirling Alb. 3 (Roberts 2, Armstrong)

Fourth Round Replays
Motherwell 0
Dundee Utd 1 (Welsh)

Stirling Alb. 0
St Johnstone 2 (Scott, Ferguson)

Quarter Finals
Aidrieonians 0
Dundee Utd 0

Kilmarnock 1 (Brown)
Dundee 0

Rangers 2 (Brown, Hateley)
Hearts 0

St Johnstone 1 (Dodds)
Aberdeen 1 (Booth)

Quarter Final Replays
Aberdeen 2 (Shearer, Richardson)
St Johnstone 0

Dundee Utd 2 (McLaren, McKinlay)
Aidrieonians 0

Semi Finals
Dundee Utd 1 (Welsh)
Aberdeen 1 (Shearer)

Kilmarnock 0
Rangers 0

Semi Final Replays
Dundee Utd 1 (McInally)
Aberdeen 0

Kilmarnock 1 (Black)
Rangers 2 (Hateley 2)

SCOTTISH CUP FINAL
Hampden Park   May 21
Dundee Utd 1 (Brewster)
Rangers 0
Dundee Utd: Van de Kamp, Cleland,
Malpas, McInally, Petric, Welsh,
Bowman, Hannah, McLaren
(Nixon), Brewster, Dailly
Rangers: Maxwell, G Stevens
(Mikhailichenko), D Robertson,
Gough, McPherson, McCall,
Murray, I Ferguson, McCoist (D
Ferguson), Hateley, Durie

SCOTTISH LEAGUE CUP

First Round

Alloa 1 *(Hendry)*
Berwick Rgrs 0

East Fife 1 *(Scott)*
Albion Rvrs 2 *(Fraser, Kerrigan)*

Queen's Park 0
Arbroath 1 *(Strachan)*

Stenhousemuir 3 *(Clouston, Irvine, Mathieson)*
Forfar Ath. 1 *(Hamill)*

Montrose 0
East Stirling 1 *(Conroy)*

Queen of the Sth 1 *(Shanks)*
Stranraer 2 *(Henderson 2)*

Second Round

Aberdeen 5 *(Shearer 3 (1 pen), McLeish, Richardson)*
Clydebank 0

Aidrieonians 2 *(Davenport, Kirkwood)*
Cowenbeath 1 *(Henderson)*

Ayr Utd 0
Motherwell 6 *(McGrillen 2, Arnott 2, Graham, Ferguson)*

Brechin City 0
St Mirren 1 *(Dick)*

Hamilton Acds. 0
Dundee Utd. 1 *(Connolly) aet*

Hibernian 2 *(Wright, Donald)*
Alloa 0

Kilmarnock 1 *(Mitchell)*

Morton 2 *(Tolmie, Lilley)*
Meadowbank Th. 1 *(Little)*
Dundee 1 *(Davidson (og)) aet Dundee won 3-1 on penalties*

Stenhousemuir 1 *(Fisher)*
Falkirk 2 *(Cadette, Duffy) aet*

Stirling Alb. 0
Celtic 2 *(McGinlay, McAvennie)*

Albion Rvrs 1 *(Scott)*
Partick Th. 11 *(Craig 2, Britton, English, Jamieson, Law, Cameron 4, Grant)*

Clyde 1 *(McAulay)*
St Johnstone 2 *(Wright (pen), Moore)*

Dunfermline 2 *(Robertson,French)*
East Stirling 0 *aet*

Hearts 2 *(Robertson 2)*
Stranraer 0

Raith Rvrs 1 *(Cameron)*
Arbroath 2 *(Elliot, Martin)*

Rangers 1 *(I Ferguson)*
Dumbarton 0

Third Round

Aberdeen 5 *(Shearer, Miller, Booth 2, Jess)*
Motherwell 2 *(Arnott, Shannon) aet*

Dunfermline Ath. 0
Rangers 2 *(T Steven, I Ferguson)*

Hibernian 2 *(Hunter, Wright)*
Dundee 1 *(Nielsen)*

Morton 0
Partick Th. 1 *(Craig)*

St Mirren 0
Dundee Utd 1 *(McKinlay)*

Arbroath 1 *(Tindal)*
Celtic 9 *(Nicholas, McGinlay, McAvennie 3, Payton 3, McNally)*

Hearts 0
Falkirk 1 *(May)*

St Johnstone 0
Aidrieonians 2 *(Lawrence, Balfour)*

Quarter Finals

Celtic 1 *(McAvennie)*
Aidrieonians 0

Dundee Utd 3 *(Clark 2, McLaren)*
Falkirk 3 *(Cadette 3) aet*
(Dundee Utd won 4-2 on penalties)

Partick Th. 2 *(Grant, Craig)*
Hibernian 2 *(McAllister 2) aet*
Hibernian won 3-2 on penalties

Rangers 2 *(Hateley (pen), I Ferguson)*
Aberdeen 1 *(Miller) aet*

Semi Finals

Dundee Utd 0
Hibernian 1 *(D Jackson)*

Celtic 0
Rangers 1 *(Hateley)*

SCOTTISH LEAGUE CUP FINAL
Celtic Park   Oct 24, 1993
Rangers 2 *(Durrant, McCoist)*
Hibernian 1 *(McPherson (og))*
Rangers: Maxwell, G Stevens, D Robertson, Gough, McPherson, McCall, T Steven, I Ferguson, Durrant, Hateley, Huistra (McCoist)
Hibernian: Leighton, Miller, Mitchell, Farrell, Tweed, Hunter, McAllister, Hamilton, Wright, D Jackson (Evans), O'Neill

B & Q Cup

Second Round

Airdrieonians 3 *(Abercromby, McIntyre, Black)*
Hamilton Acds. 1 *(Baptie)*

Ayr Utd 2 *(McGivern 2)*
Brechin City 1 *(Miller) aet*

Falkirk 3 *(Sloan, McDonald 2)*
Cowdenbeath 0

Morton 2 *(Alexander, Tolmie)*
St Mirren 4 *(Gallagher 2, Lavety, Harvie)*

Queen's Park 0
Clydebank 1 *(Lansdowne)*

Meadowbank Th. 2 *(Rutherford, Little)*
Stirling Alb. 0

Montrose 0

Stranraer 0 *aet*
Montrose won 6-5 on penalties

Queen of the Sth 0
Dunfermline Ath. 6 *(Den Bieman, O'Boyle 2, Laing 2, Smith)*

Quarter Finals

Aidrieonians 0
St Mirren 2 *(Gallagher 2)*

Ayr Utd 2 *(Murdoch (og), Burns (pen))*
Clydebank 0

Falkirk 4 *(Cadette 3, Drinkell)*
Dunfermline Ath. 1 *(Sharp)*

Meadowbank Th. 1 *(Rutherford)*
Montrose 1 *(Yeats) aet*
Meadowbank won 3-1 on penalties

Semi Finals

Ayr Utd 1 *(McGivern)*
St Mirren 2 *(Gallagher 2)*

Falkirk 3 *(Cadette 2, May)*
Meadowbank Th. 2 *(Little, G McLeod (pen))*

B & Q CUP FINAL
Fir Park, Motherwell   Dec 12
Falkirk 3 *(Duffy, Cadette, Hughes)*
St Mirren 0
Falkirk: Parks, Duffy, McQueen, Weir, McLaughlin, Hughes, May, Drinkell (Shaw), Cadette, McCall (Oliver), Rice
St Mirren: Money, Dawson, Baker, McWhirter, McLaughlin, Orr, Bone (R Gillies), Dick, Lavety, Hewitt (McIntyre), Elliot

Scottish Football

To absolutely nobody's surprise, Rangers added a 44th League title to the trophy cupboard, even though they dallied somewhat at the start of the season. For the second year in succession, though, the club failed badly to capitalise on that success and tumbled out of the European Cup - beaten by AEK Athens - almost before the new season had started. The signing of Basile Boli from Marseille was a adventurous move, but there may be clouds on the horizon. Boli's three-year deal will not have come cheaply, with £2.7m going to the beleaguered French team and a living wage or two to the French international. David Murray has pumped a small fortune into Rangers, but for the last three years his company Murray International has been trading at a loss. A businessman will always look for a return on his money; and the only return from Rangers comes with an extended run in Europe.

Celtic would have been grateful for such small mercies; six League titles in succession, four League Cups and two Scottish Cups is Rangers' recent record. Throughout that time, Celtic have not even finished as runners-up in the League and have not won anything at all since the 1989 Scottish Cup. Hope has sprung, though, in the buy-out of the club by Fergus McCann and the £21m refinancing in April. Before McCann's take-over in March, the Bank of Scotland was about to call in £10m of debt.

In July, Tommy Burns arrived as manager to add weight to the revival, but much to the annoyance of Kilmarnock. The club immediately reported Celtic to the League for poaching and they were duly fined £100,000. Kilmarnock meanwhile perceived that Burns was still technically employed by them, so proceded to pay him each month, then fine him the amount of his wages. Daft really, because presumably they would still have to pay his tax.

Dundee United beat Rangers in the Cup, but the biggest losers of the year were Elgin City, Gretna and Gala Fairydean who failed to win enough votes to join the new enlarged League. Gala, from the Borders, deserved better.

QUOTES

"If we don't make it, I'll go bunjee jumping without the rope" - **Matt Hall, the Gala Fairydean chairman on his plans if the club's League application failed. It did.**

"As far as Gala are concerned, we sometimes have to be a little selfish and the fact that we have a good-size supporters' club in the town may come into the equation - **Les Porteous, Hearts chairman, going some way to explain why Gala didn't get elected.**

"Apparently the only time he's been to Ibrox was for a Rod Stewart concert. If he gives a performance like Rod does on stage, I'll be happy" - **Billy Lamont, Alloa manager, on keeper Jim Butters before the 4th round Scottish Cup tie against Rangers. Alloa lost 6-0.**

"I had no language problem, I'd grown up with the music of The Kinks, Stones, Who, Troggs and Small Faces...." - **Ivan Golac, manager of Dundee United, recollecting his early days at Southampton. Golac came to Britain from Yugoslavia in 1982.**

Welsh Football
Konica League of Wales

FINAL TABLE

	P	W	D	L	GF	GA	Pts
Bangor City	38	26	5	7	82	26	83
Inter Cardiff	38	26	3	9	97	44	81
Ton Pentre	38	21	8	9	62	37	71
Flint Town United	38	20	6	12	70	47	66
Holywell Town	38	18	10	10	74	57	64
Newtown	38	18	9	11	52	48	63
Connah's Quay Nom.	38	16	11	11	59	47	59
Cwmbran Town	38	16	9	13	51	46	57
Ebbw Vale	38	16	9	13	68	66	57
Aberystwyth Town	38	15	10	13	57	56	55
Porthmadog	38	14	7	17	90	71	49
Llanelli	38	14	4	20	76	100	46
Conwy United	38	13	6	19	55	70	45
Mold Alexandra	38	12	7	19	59	75	43
Haverfordwest Coun.	38	10	10	18	40	81	40
Afan Lido	38	8	15	15	52	66	39
Caersws	38	9	12	17	39	56	39
Llansantffraid	38	9	7	22	46	77	34
Maesteg Park Athletic	38	8	9	21	43	71	33
Briton Ferry Athletic	38	8	9	21	53	84	33

Northern Irish Football
Smirnoff Irish League
FINAL TABLE

	P	W	D	L	GF	GA	Pts
Linfield	30	21	7	2	63	22	70
Portadown	30	20	8	2	76	21	68
Glenavon	30	21	5	4	69	29	68
Crusaders	30	17	7	6	53	30	58
Bangor	30	14	3	13	45	49	45
Ards	30	13	2	15	59	55	41
Distillery	30	11	8	11	41	40	41
Cliftonville	30	11	10	9	40	32	40*
Glentoran	30	10	7	13	46	43	37
Coleraine	30	10	7	13	41	50	37
Ballymena United	30	9	6	15	38	56	33
Ballyclare Comrades	30	9	6	15	36	58	33
Carrick Rangers	30	6	7	17	42	59	25
Newry Town	30	5	9	16	26	52	24
Omagh Town	30	6	5	19	32	58	23
Larne	30	5	7	18	30	62	22

* Cliftonville - 3 pts forefeited under Reg.31

Ulster Cup
Quarter Finals
Portadown 3 Glentoran 0
Crusaders 3 Larne 0
Linfield 1 Ballymena Utd 0
Bangor 2 Ballyclare Com. 0
Semi Finals
Crusaders 1 Portadown 0
Linfield 1 Bangor 2
FINAL
Windsor Park   *Oct 19*
Crusaders 1 Bangor 0

T.N.T. Gold Cup
Quarter Finals
Cliftonville 1 Distillery 1
Distillery won 3-1 on penalties
Crusaders 2 Linfield 5
Glenavon 3 Glentoran 3
Glentoran won 8-7 on penalties
Portadown 0 Bangor 4
Semi Finals
Distillery 2 Glentoran 1   *aet*
Linfield 0 Bangor 2
FINAL
Windsor Park   *Nov 2*
Distillery 3 Bangor 2 *aet*

Budweiser Cup
Semi Finals
Distillery 1 Linfield 3   *aet*
Cliftonville 2 Ards 3
FINAL
The Oval   *Dec 21*
Linfield 3 Ards 0

Wilkinson Sword League Cup
Semi Finals
Crusader 0 Linfield 1
Ards 1 Coleraine 2
FINAL
The Oval   *Apr 26*
Linfield 2 Coleraine 0

Nursing Times, whose reporters chronicle such things, noted that during the celebrations in Dublin that followed Ireland's 1-0 victory over Italy, four fans arrived at accident and emergency at St James' Hospital with bits of their ears missing. What sort of bet was that then?

Favourite World Cup headline (for the broadsheet reader)
'Jack back and will do it again'
The Guardian, courtesy of Steely Dan

Football pools, lotteries, spot the ball competitions; they're all a matter of skill as every winner will tell you. Jason Perritt doesn't pull that one. The 24 year old bank worker from Newbury won £500 quid on a Littlewoods spot-the-ball coupon and didn't try and kid anyone. "It's pot luck," he said. "It makes me laugh to think how people spend hours working out where to put their crosses." Jason just sat down with his mother, who helped him fill out the coupon. Jason is totally blind.

EUROPEAN LEAGUES 1993-4

Final League Tables, the teams below the line are those relegated

BELGIUM

	P	W	D	L	GF	GA	PTS
Anderlecht	34	24	7	3	79	31	55
FC Brugge	34	20	13	1	54	19	53
Seraing	34	15	13	6	50	27	43
Charleroi	34	18	5	11	61	49	41
Antwerp	34	14	13	7	44	38	41
Standard Liege	34	13	12	9	43	22	38
Ostend	34	10	16	8	45	41	36
Mechelen	34	11	11	12	42	40	33
Beveren	34	11	10	13	49	47	32
Ekeren	34	11	10	13	49	47	32
Lommel	34	10	10	14	41	50	30
CS Brugge	34	9	11	14	52	63	29
Liege	34	9	11	14	40	59	29
Lierse	34	7	14	13	30	42	28
Gent	34	7	13	14	43	57	27
RWD Molenbeek	34	7	11	16	32	49	25
Waregem	34	6	7	21	32	62	19
Genk	34	4	10	20	38	79	18

Anderlecht completed the double, beating FC Brugge 2-0 in the Cup final. Top scorer: Weber (CS Brugge) 31

DENMARK

	P	W	D	L	GF	GA	PTS
Silkeborg	14	8	2	4	23	15	31
FC Copenhagen	14	8	2	4	37	19	29
Odense	14	5	5	4	17	16	27
Brondby	14	6	5	3	21	14	27
Aalborg	14	4	6	4	18	19	23
Lyngby	14	5	1	8	17	21	21
Ikast	14	3	5	6	16	23	20
Aarhus	14	3	2	9	11	23	16

After drawing 0-0 with Naestved, Brondby won the cup final 3-1 on penalties. Teams play in an 18 match qualifying League. The top eight play off for the title; each team starts with half of their points from the qualifying table.

FRANCE

	P	W	D	L	GF	GA	PTS
Paris St Germain	38	24	11	3	54	22	59
Marseille	38	19	13	6	56	33	51
Auxerre	38	18	10	10	54	29	46
Bordeaux	38	19	8	11	54	37	46
Nantes	38	17	11	10	48	35	45
Cannes	38	16	12	10	50	43	44
Montpelier	38	15	13	10	41	37	43
Lyon	38	17	8	13	38	40	42
Monaco	38	14	13	11	55	37	41
Lens	38	13	13	12	49	40	39
St Etienne	38	12	13	13	38	36	37
Metz	38	12	13	13	36	35	37
Strasbourg	38	10	14	14	43	47	34
Sochaux	38	10	13	15	39	48	33
Lille	38	8	16	14	41	52	32
Caen	38	12	7	19	29	54	31
Le Havre	38	7	15	16	29	48	29
Martigues	38	5	17	16	37	58	27
Toulouse	38	4	15	19	26	60	23
Angers	38	4	13	21	37	63	21

Auxerre beat Montpelier 3-0 in the Cup and Marseille was relegated following the match-rigging revelations of 1993 Top scorers: Boli (Lens), Djorkaeff (M'co), Ouedec (Nantes) 20

GERMANY

	P	W	D	L	GF	GA	PTS
Bayern Munich	34	17	10	7	68	37	44
Kaiserslautern	34	18	7	9	64	36	43
Leverkusen	34	14	11	9	60	47	39
Borussia Dortmund	34	15	9	10	48	45	39
Eintracht Frankfurt	34	15	8	11	57	41	38
Karlsruhe	34	14	10	10	46	43	38
Stuttgart	34	13	11	10	51	43	37
Werder Bremen	34	13	10	11	51	44	36
Duisburg	34	14	8	12	41	52	36
Mönchengladbach	34	14	7	13	65	59	35
Cologne	34	14	6	14	49	51	34
Hamburg	34	13	8	13	48	52	34
Dynamo Dresden	34	10	14	10	33	44	34
Schalke	34	10	9	15	38	50	29
Freiburg	34	10	8	16	54	57	28
Nuremberg	34	10	8	16	41	55	28
Wattenscheid	34	6	11	17	48	70	23
Leipzig	34	3	11	20	32	69	17

Werder Bremen beat Rot-Weiss Essen 3-1 in the Cup final Top scorer: Kuntz (Kaiserslautern) 18

GREECE

	P	W	D	L	GF	GA	PTS
AEK Athens	34	25	4	5	63	28	79
Panathinaikos	34	22	6	6	82	32	72
Olympiakos	34	18	14	2	63	27	68
Aris Salonika	34	18	9	7	55	34	63
PAOK Salonika	34	14	9	11	45	38	51
Iraklis	34	13	10	11	59	45	49
Ofi Crete	34	13	8	13	55	42	47
Xanthi	34	12	9	13	62	63	45
Panionios	34	12	7	15	49	58	43
Levakiakos	34	11	9	14	38	45	42
Larissa	34	11	9	14	45	53	42
Athinaikos	34	11	7	16	34	50	40
Apollon	34	9	13	12	30	41	40
Edessaikos	34	11	6	17	41	56	39
Doxa Drama	34	11	5	18	37	64	38
Panachaiki	34	9	10	15	36	56	37
Kalamaria	34	8	8	18	42	66	32
Naussa	34	5	3	26	28	76	18

Panathinaikos beat AEK Athens 4-2 on penalties in the Cup final following a 3-3 draw.

HOLLAND

	P	W	D	L	GF	GA	PTS
Ajax	34	26	2	6	86	26	54
Feyenoord	34	19	13	2	61	27	51
PSV Eindhoven	34	17	10	7	60	36	44
Vitesse	34	17	6	11	63	37	40
Twente	34	15	9	10	57	43	39
Roda	34	15	8	11	55	40	38
NAC Breda	34	14	10	10	61	52	38
Willem II	34	15	7	12	48	42	37
Sparta	34	12	8	14	58	57	32
Maastricht	34	11	10	13	49	58	32
Volendam	34	13	4	17	46	55	30
Go Ahead	34	10	8	16	44	57	28
Heerenveen	34	9	10	15	35	61	28
Groningen	34	9	8	17	42	65	26
Utrecht	34	9	8	17	40	63	26
RKC Waalwijk	34	8	9	17	38	56	25
VVV Venlo	34	7	11	16	30	62	25
Cambuur	34	6	7	21	28	64	19

Feyenoord beat NEC Nijmegen 2-1 in the Cup final
Top scorer: Litmanen (Ajax) 26

IRELAND
Qualifying Table

	P	W	D	L	GF	GA	PTS
Shamrock Rovers	22	15	3	4	43	16	48
Cork City	22	12	5	5	43	24	41
Shelbourne	22	10	6	6	33	27	36
Galway United	22	9	7	6	30	26	34
Bohemians	22	8	7	7	23	17	31
Derry City	22	8	7	7	21	21	31
Monaghan United	22	9	3	10	27	27	30
Dundalk	22	7	8	7	25	20	29
St Patrick's Athletic	22	6	9	7	24	24	27
Cobh Ramblers	22	5	4	13	20	34	19
Limerick City	22	3	8	11	15	40	17
Drogheda United	22	4	5	13	16	44	17

Final Round

	P	W	D	L	GF	GA	PTS
Shamrock Rovers	32	21	3	8	62	30	66
Cork City	32	17	8	7	60	36	59
Galway United	32	14	8	10	47	42	50
Derry City	32	12	10	10	37	35	46
Shelbourne	32	11	10	11	42	42	43
Bohemians	32	11	8	13	34	35	41

Top six teams play each other twice

Promotion/Relegation

	P	W	D	L	GF	GA	PTS
Monaghan United	32	13	8	11	41	38	47
Dundalk	32	10	13	9	37	27	43
St Patrick's Athletic	32	9	12	11	32	38	39
Cobh Ramblers	32	8	8	16	31	41	32
Limerick City	32	6	11	15	23	50	29
Drogheda United	32	7	7	18	26	58	28

Sligo Rovers beat Derry City 1-0 in the Cup final.
Top scorer: Geoghean (Shamrock Rovers) 23

ITALY

	P	W	D	L	GF	GA	PTS
AC Milan	34	19	12	3	36	15	50
Juventus	34	17	13	4	58	25	47
Sampdoria	34	18	8	8	64	39	44
Lazio	34	17	10	7	55	40	44
Parma	34	17	7	10	59	35	41
Napoli	34	12	12	10	41	35	36
AS Roma	34	10	15	9	35	30	35
Torino	34	11	12	11	39	37	34
Foggia	34	10	13	11	46	46	33
Cremonese	34	9	14	11	41	41	32
Genoa	34	8	16	10	32	40	32
Cagliari	34	10	12	12	39	48	32
Internazionale	34	11	9	14	46	45	31
Reggiana	34	10	11	13	29	37	31
Piacenza	34	8	14	12	32	43	30
Udinese	34	7	14	13	35	48	28
Atalanta	34	5	11	18	35	65	21
Lecce	34	3	5	26	28	72	11

Sampdoria defeated Ancona 6-1 after a two leg Cup final.
Top scorer: Signori (Lazio) 23

POLAND

	P	W	D	L	GF	GA	PTS
Legia*	34	19	13	2	72	24	48
Katowice	34	18	12	4	52	28	48
Gornik Zabrze	34	17	12	5	56	32	46
LKS Lodz*	34	17	11	6	49	24	42
Pogon	34	11	19	4	39	24	41
Hutnik	34	12	15	7	34	28	39
Widzew	34	11	15	8	43	34	37
Ruch	34	13	10	11	48	41	36
Lech	34	12	11	11	39	32	35
Milliader	34	11	11	12	41	40	33
Stal	34	11	10	13	32	45	32
Wola	34	8	15	11	25	37	31
Zaglebie Lubin	34	9	12	13	40	47	30
Warta	34	11	8	15	32	45	30
Wisla*	34	6	13	15	30	46	22
Polonia	34	4	11	19	28	61	19
Siarka	34	4	10	20	25	57	18
Bydgoszcz	34	3	10	21	30	70	16

deducted 3 points
Legia completed the double by beating LKS Lodz 2-0 in the Cup final.
Top scorer: Burzawa (Milliader) 21

PORTUGAL

	P	W	D	L	GF	GA	PTS
Benfica	34	23	8	3	73	25	54
Porto	34	21	10	3	56	15	52
Sporting Lisbon	34	23	5	6	71	29	51
Boavista	34	16	6	12	46	31	38
Maritimo	34	13	12	9	45	40	38
Setubal	34	14	6	14	56	42	34
Farense	34	13	7	14	44	46	33
Estrela	34	9	15	10	39	36	33
Guimaraes	34	11	11	12	30	31	33
Uniao	34	11	9	14	36	42	31
Gil Vicente	34	10	11	13	27	47	31
Salgueiros	34	14	3	17	48	56	31
Belenenses	34	12	6	16	39	51	30
Beira Mar	34	9	11	14	28	38	29
Braga	34	9	10	15	33	43	28
Pacos	34	7	12	15	31	49	26
Famalicao	34	7	8	19	26	72	22
Estoril	34	5	8	21	22	57	18

Porto beat Sporting Lisbon 2-1 after a two-leg Cup final.
Top scorer: Yekini (Setubal) 21

ROMANIA

	P	W	D	L	GF	GA	PTS
Steaua	34	22	9	3	63	19	53
Uni Craiova	34	16	8	10	64	46	40
Dinamo	34	16	7	11	65	40	39
Rapid Bucharest	34	16	6	12	43	32	38
Petrolul	34	14	10	10	34	30	38
Farul	34	15	7	12	42	38	37
Gloria	34	16	3	15	47	43	35
Inter Sibiu	34	13	8	13	40	41	34
Piatra	34	11	10	13	27	40	32
UT Arad	34	12	8	14	35	49	32
Progresul Bucharest	34	14	4	16	44	42	32
Cluj	34	11	9	14	39	42	31
Brasov	34	13	5	16	38	52	31
Elect. Craiova	34	10	10	14	25	34	30
Otelul	34	12	5	17	38	47	29
Sportul	34	11	7	16	30	45	29
Timisoara	34	11	6	17	39	53	28
Brailia	34	9	6	19	33	53	24

Bistrita beat Uni Craiova 1-0 in the Cup final.
Top scorer: Gh. Craioveanu (Uni Craiova) 21

RUSSIA

	P	W	D	L	GF	GA	PTS
Spartak Moscow	34	21	11	2	81	18	53
Volgograd	34	17	8	9	56	35	42
Dynamo Moscow	34	16	10	8	65	38	42
Lokomotiv Moscow	34	14	11	9	45	29	39
Tekstilchik	34	14	11	9	45	34	39
Vladikavkaz	34	16	6	12	49	45	38
Torpedo Moscow	34	15	8	11	35	40	38
Ouralmach	34	16	4	14	51	52	36
CSKA Moscow	34	12	6	16	43	45	30
Kamaz	34	12	6	16	45	53	30
Novgorod	34	12	6	16	34	49	30
Stavropol	34	11	8	16	39	49	30
Zhemchonzhina	34	10	10	14	52	62	30
Sovekov	34	9	12	13	37	47	30
Vladivostok	34	11	7	16	29	56	29
Nakhodka	34	10	8	16	28	40	28
Rostselmach	34	8	12	14	35	52	28
Asmaral Moscow	34	7	6	21	28	53	20

Spartak Moscow completed the double, beating CSKA Moscow 4-2 on penalties following a 2-2 draw in the Cup final.
Top scorer: Poutchenko (Kamaz) 21

SPAIN

	P	W	D	L	GF	GA	PTS
Barcelona	38	25	6	7	91	42	56
La Coruña	38	22	12	4	54	18	56
Zaragoza	38	19	8	11	71	47	46
Real Madrid	38	19	7	12	61	50	45
Athletic Bilbao	38	16	11	11	61	47	43
Sevilla	38	15	12	11	56	42	42
Valencia	38	14	12	12	55	50	40
Santander	38	15	8	15	44	42	38
Oviedo	38	12	13	13	43	49	37
Tenerife	38	15	6	17	50	57	36
Real Sociedad	38	12	12	14	39	47	36
Atletico Madrid	38	13	9	16	54	54	35
Albacete	38	10	15	13	49	58	35
Sporting Gijon	38	15	5	18	42	57	35
Celta	38	11	11	16	41	51	33
Logrones	38	9	15	14	47	58	33
Rayo Vallecano	38	9	13	16	40	58	31
Valladolid	38	8	14	16	28	51	30
Lerida	38	7	13	18	29	48	27
Osasuna	38	8	10	20	34	63	26

Zaragoza beat Celta 5-4 on penalties after a scoreless Cup final.
Top scorer: Romario (Barcelona) 30

SWEDEN

	P	W	D	L	GF	GA	PTS
IFK Gothenburg	26	18	5	3	48	17	59
Norrkoping	26	17	3	6	56	23	54
AIK	26	14	4	8	49	43	46
Trelleborg	26	12	6	8	46	39	42
Halmstad	26	11	5	10	50	41	38
Hacken	26	11	4	11	44	49	37
Frolunda	26	11	4	11	38	45	37
Osters	26	10	6	10	43	34	36
Helsingborg	26	10	6	10	43	46	36
Malmo	26	10	5	11	43	38	35
Orebro	26	10	3	13	35	38	33
Degefors	26	6	5	15	32	54	23
Orgryte	26	5	6	15	26	44	21
Brage	26	4	4	18	26	68	16

Norrkoping beat Helsingborg 4-3 in extra time in the Cup final
Top scorer: Bertilsson (Halmstad) 18

It wasn't just the World Cup, where penalty misses broke hearts. In the final game of the Spanish season, Deportivo La Coruña had to beat Valencia to win the title. In the 88th minute, with the score 0-0, they were awarded a penalty. Miroslav Djukic stepped up and - missed. The title went instead to Barcelona, for the fourth year in a row.

Juventus, owned by Fiat, produced one of the great telephone number debts when they announced in March that the company losses amounted to 44 **billion** lire. Okay, it's not as bad as it sounds. 44 billion lire only translates to around 20 million pounds. Huh!

Italy didn't have a great run-up to the World Cup: in February they lost to France, in March to Germany, and in April to Pontedera. Yes, Pontedera, who play in the *Serie C2 B* (which is about GM Conference level). Pontedera scored in the 19th and 22nd minutes and 50 or so Pontedera fans at the practice game started chanting "We are not giving you any of our players" or the Italian equivalent, which I understand scans better.

Werder Bremen had an auspicious year, they won the German Cup and their manager announced that he had worked as a double agent in the seventies. "It was the Cold War, it was exciting" said Lemke, who claims to have fed dubious information to the KGB under instructions from the West German government. Okay, so who was Graham Taylor really working for?

European Cup Competitions

EUROPEAN CUP

Preliminary Round (*over 2 legs*)
Helsinki JK 1 *(Heinola)*
Norma Tallinn 1 *(Borisov)*

Norma Tallinn 0
Helsinki JK 1 *(Belokhovostov)*
Helsinki won 2-1 on aggregate
- - - - - - - - - - - - - - - - - - -
Ekranas 0
Floriana FC 1 *(Buttigieg)*

Floriana FC 1 *(Buttigieg)*
Ekranas 0
Floriana won 2-0 on aggregate
- - - - - - - - - - - - - - - - - - -
B68 Toftir 0
Croatia Zagreb 5 *(Cvitanovic, Leshak,
Vlaovic, Turkovic, Adzic)*

Croatia Zagreb 6 *(Zivkovic, Vlaovic 4
Hailovic)*
B68 Toftir 0
Zagreb won 11-0 on aggregate
- - - - - - - - - - - - - - - - - - -
Skonto Riga 0
Ol. Ljubljana 1 *(Milinovic)*

Ol. Ljubljana 0
Skonto Riga 1 *(Proitski)*
Riga won 12-10 on penalties
- - - - - - - - - - - - - - - - - - -
Cwmbran T 3 *(King (pen), Ford 2)*
Cork City 2 *(Caulfield, Buckley)*

Cork City 2 *(Morley, Glynn)*
Cwmbran 1 *(McNeil)*
4-4 on agg, Cork won on away goals
- - - - - - - - - - - - - - - - - - -
Tbilisi Dinamo 2 *(Arveladze,
Inalishvili)*
Linfield FC 1 *(Johnston)*

Linfield FC 1 *(Haylock)*
Tbilisi Dinamo 1 *(Arveladze)*
Tblisi won 3-2 on aggregate
- - - - - - - - - - - - - - - - - - -
Avenir Beggen 0
Rosenborg 2 *(Bragstad, Loken)*

Rosenborg 1 *(Skammelsrud)*
Avenir Beggen 0
Rosenborg won 3-0 on aggregate
- - - - - - - - - - - - - - - - - - -
Partizani Tirana 0
IA Akranes 0

IA Akranes 3 *(Hognasson,
Gudjohnsson 2)*
Partizani Tirana 0
Akranes won 3-0 on aggregate
- - - - - - - - - - - - - - - - - - -
Omonia FC 2 *(Shilikashvili 2)*
Aarau FC 1 *(Ratinho)*

Aarau FC 2 *(Stiel, Heldmann)*
Omonia FC 0
Aarau won 3-2 on aggregate
- - - - - - - - - - - - - - - - - - -
Zimbrul 1 *(Revda)*
Beitar Jerusalem 1 *(Harazi)*

Beitar Jerusalem 2 *(Harazi,
Greshnayev (pen))*
Zimbrul 0
Jerusalem won 3-1 on aggregate

First Round (*over 2 legs*)
Lech Poznan 3 *(Moskai, Podbrozny
(pen), Trzeciak)*
Beitar Jerusalem 0

Beitar Jerusalem 2 *(Ohana, Schwartz)*
Lech Poznan 4 *(Wilkashik, Scheczik
Brojana, Tapinski)*
Poznan won 7-2 on aggregate
- - - - - - - - - - - - - - - - - - -
Galatasaray 2 *(Turkyilmaz, Arif)*
Cork City 1 *(Barry)*

Cork City 0
Galatasaray 1 *(Turkyilmaz)*
Galatasaray won 3-1 on aggregate
- - - - - - - - - - - - - - - - - - -
Werder Bremen 5 *(Hobsch 3, Rufer 2)*
Dinamo Minsk 2 *(Gerassimez,
Velichko)*

Dinamo Minsk 1 *(Byelkevich)*
Werder Bremen 1 *(Rufer (pen))*
Werder won 6-3 on aggregate
- - - - - - - - - - - - - - - - - - -
Dinamo Kiev 3 *(Shkapenko, Leonerko
2 (1 pen))*
Barcelona 1 *(Koeman (pen))*

Barcelona 4 *(Laudrup, Bakero 2,
Koeman)*
Dinamo Kiev 1 *(Rebrov)*
Barcelona won 5-4 on aggregate
- - - - - - - - - - - - - - - - - - -
Monaco AS 1 *(Vlahos (og))*
AEK Athens 0

AEK Athens 1 *(Siskovic)*
Monaco AS 1 *(Djorkaeff)*
Monaco won 2-1 on aggregate
- - - - - - - - - - - - - - - - - - -
Kispest Honved 2 *(Szabados,
Stefanov)*
Manchester Utd 3 *(Keane 2, Cantona)*

Manchester Utd 2 *(Bruce 2)*
Kispest Honved 1 *(Salloi)*
Manchester Utd won 5-3 on aggregate
- - - - - - - - - - - - - - - - - - -
Glasgow Rangers 3 *(McPherson,
Hateley 2)*
Levski Sofia 2 *(Borimirov,Todorov)*

Levski Sofia 2 *(Sirakov, Todorov)*
Glasgow Rangers 1 *(Durrant)*
4-4 on agg, Sofia won on away goals
- - - - - - - - - - - - - - - - - - -
AIK Stockholm 1 *(Lidman)*
Sparta Prague 0

Sparta Prague 2 *(Siegl 2)*
AIK Stockholm 0
Prague win 2-1 on aggregate
- - - - - - - - - - - - - - - - - - -
Linfield FC 3 *(Haylock,
McConnell, Johnston)*
FC Copenhagen 0

FC Copenhagen 4 *(Moller, Johansen,
Hojer, Mikkelsen)*
Linfield FC 0
Copenhagen won 4-3 on aggregate
- - - - - - - - - - - - - - - - - - -
Helsinki JK 0
Anderl't 3 *(Bosman, Versavel,Boffin)*

Anderlecht 3 *(Nilis 3)*
Helsinki JK 0
Anderlecht won 6-0 on aggregate
- - - - - - - - - - - - - - - - - - -
IA Akranes 1 *(Thordarson)*
Feyenoord 0

Feyenoord 3 *(Refos, Obiku, Blinker)*
IA Akranes 0
Feyenoord won 3-1 on aggregate
- - - - - - - - - - - - - - - - - - -
Steaua Bucharest 1 *(Panduru)*
Croatia Zagreb 2 *(Cvitanovic, Jelicic)*

Croatia Zagreb 2 *(Vlaovic, Adziz)*
Steaua Buch 3 *(Panduru, Vladoiu 2)*
4-4 on agg.; Steaua won on away goals
- - - - - - - - - - - - - - - - - - -
Rosenborg 3 *(Tangen (pen),
Leonhardsen, Loeken)*
FK Austria 1 *(Zsak (pen))*

FK Austria 4 *(Nabekovas, Schmid,
Zsak, Kogler)*
Rosenborg 1 *(Dahlum)*
FK Austria won 5-4 on aggregate
- - - - - - - - - - - - - - - - - - -
Porto 2 *(Kostadinov, Semedo)*
Floriana FC 0

Floriana FC 0
Porto 0
Porto won 2-0 on aggregate
- - - - - - - - - - - - - - - - - - -
Skonto Riga 0
Spartak Moscow 5 *(Pogodin 2,
Rodionov 2, Bestchastnykh)*

Spartak Moscow 4 *(Tsymbalar 2,
Pisarev, Onopko)*
Skonto Riga 0
Spartak Moscow won 9-0 on aggregate
- - - - - - - - - - - - - - - - - - -

Aarau FC 0
AC Milan 1 *(Papin)*

AC Milan 0
Aarau FC 0
AC Milan won 1-0 on aggregate

Second Round *(over 2 legs)*
Barcelona 3 *(Koeman 2 (1 pen),*
  Quique)
FK Austria 0

FK Austria 1 *(Ogris)*
Barcelona 2 *(Stoichkov 2)*
Barcelona won 5-1 on aggregate
- - - - - - - - - - - - - - - - - - -
FC Copenhagen 0
AC Milan 6 *(Papin 2, Simone 2,*
  Laudrup, Orlando)

AC Milan 1 *(Papin)*
FC Copenhagen 0
AC Milan won 7-0 on aggregate
- - - - - - - - - - - - - - - - - - -
Lech Poznan 1 *(Podbrozny)*
Spartak Moscow 5 *(Pisarev 2, Karpin,*
  Onopko 2)

Spartak Moscow 2 *(Karpin, Khlestov)*
Lech Poznan 1 *(Dembilski)*
Spartak Moscow won 7-2 on aggregate
- - - - - - - - - - - - - - - - - - -
Levski Sofia 2 *(Yankov, Ginchev)*
Werder Bremen 2 *(Bode, Rufer)*

Werder Bremen 1 *(Basler)*
Levski Sofia 0
Werder Bremen won 3-2 on aggregate
- - - - - - - - - - - - - - - - - - -
Manchester Utd 3 *(Robson, Hakan*
  (og), Cantona)
Galatasaray 3 *(Arif, Turkyilmaz 2)*

Galatasaray 0
Manchester Utd 0
3-3 on agg; Galatasaray on away goals
- - - - - - - - - - - - - - - - - - -
Monaco 4 *(Ikpeba 2, Klinsmann 2)*
Steaua Bucharest 1 *(Dumitrescu*
  (pen))

Steaua Bucharest 1 *(Dumitrescu)*
Monaco 0
Monaco won 4-2 on aggregate
- - - - - - - - - - - - - - - - - - -
Porto 1 *(Domingos Oliveira)*
Feyenoord 0

Feyenoord 0
Porto 0
Porto won 1-0 on aggregate
- - - - - - - - - - - - - - - - - - -
Sparta Prague 0
Anderlecht 1 *(Nilis)*

Anderlecht 4 *(Bosman , Nilis 2,*
  Versavel)
Sparta Prague 2 *(Dvirnik, Vonasek)*
Anderlecht won 5-2 on aggregate

CHAMPIONS LEAGUE
Group A
Monaco 4 *(Klinsmann, Ikpeba,*
  Djorkaeff (pen), Thuram)
Spartak Moscow 1 *(Pisarev)*

Galatasaray 0
Barcelona 0

Spartak Moscow 0
Galatasaray 0

Barcelona 2 *(Beguiristain 2)*
Monaco 0

Monaco 3 *(Scifo, Djorkaeff,*
  Klinsmann)
Galatasaray 0

Spartak Moscow 2 *(Rodionov,Karpin)*
Barcelona 2 *(Stoichkov, Romario)*

Galatasaray 0
Monaco 2 *(Scifo, Gnako)*

Barcelona 5 *(Stoichkov, Amor,*
  Koeman 2, Romario)
Spartak Moscow 1 *(Karpin)*

Spartak Moscow 0
Monaco 0

Barcelona 3 *(Amor, Koeman (pen),*
  Eusebio)
Galatasaray 0

Monaco 0
Barcelona 1 *(Stoichkov)*

Galatasaray 1 *(Cihat)*
Spartak Moscow 2 *(Onopko, Karpin)*

Final Table
	P	W	D	L	F	A	Pt
Barcelona	6	4	2	0	13	3	10
Monaco	6	3	1	2	9	4	7
Spartak Moscow	6	1	3	2	6	12	5
Galatasaray	6	0	2	4	1	10	2
- - - - - - - - - - - - - - - - - - -
Group B
Porto 3 *(Domingos, Rui Jorge, Jose*
  Carlos)
Werder Bremen 2 *(Hobsch, Rufer)*

Anderlecht 0
AC Milan 0

AC Milan 3 *(Raducioiu, Panucci,*
  Massaro)
Porto 0

Werder Bremen 5 *(Rufer 2, Bratseth,*
  Hobsch, Bode)
Anderlecht 3 *(Albert, Boffin 2)*

AC Milan 2 *(Maldini, Savicevic)*
Werder Bremen 1 *(Basler)*

Anderlecht 1 *(Nilis)*
Porto 0
- - - - - - - - - - - - - - - - - - -
Werder Bremen 1 *(Rufer (pen))*
AC Milan 1 *(Savicevic)*

Porto 2 *(Drulovic, Secretario)*
Anderlecht 0

Werder Bremen 0
Porto 5 *(Rui Filipe, Kostadinov,*
  Secretario, Domingos, Timofte)

AC Milan 0
Anderlecht 0

Porto 0
AC Milan 0

Anderlecht 1 *(Bosman)*
Werder Bremen 2 *(Bode 2)*

Final Table
	P	W	D	L	F	A	Pt
AC Milan	6	2	4	0	6	2	8
Porto	6	3	1	2	10	6	7
Werder Bremen	6	2	1	3	11	15	5
Anderlecht	6	1	2	3	5	9	4

Semi Finals
Barcelona 3 *(Stoichkov 2, Koeman)*
Porto 0

AC Milan 3 *(Desailly, Albertini,*
  Massaro)
Monaco 0

EUROPEAN CUP FINAL
Athens   May 18
AC Milan   4 *(Massaro 2, Savicevic,*
  Desailly)
Barcelona   0
AC Milan: Rossi, Tassotti, Galli,
Maldini (Nava), Panucci, Boban,
Albertini, Desailly, Donadoni,
Savicevic, Massaro
Barcelona: Zubizaretta, Ferrer,
Koeman, Nadal, Beguiristain
(Eusebio), Bakero, Guardiola, Amor,
Sergi (Quique), Stoichkov, Romario

EUROPEAN CUP WINNERS CUP

Preliminary Round *(over 2 legs)*
British and Irish clubs only
Bangor 1 *(McAvoy)*
Apoel 1 *(Sotirou)*

Apoel 2 *(Milhaijovic, Pounas)*
Bangor 1 *(Glendinning)*
Apoel won 3-2 on aggregate

Karpaty Lvov 1 *(Yevtushok)*
Shelbourne 0

Shelbourne 3 *(Costello, Mooney,Lizzi)*
Karpaty Lvov 1 *(Masur)*
Shelbourne won 3-2 on aggregate

First Round *(over 2 legs)*
Apoel 0
Paris SG 1 *(Sassus)*

Paris SG 2 *(Le Guen, Gravelaine)*
Apoel 0
Paris SG won 3-0 on aggregate

Bayer Leverkusen 2 *(Hapal, Thom)*
Boby Brno 0

Boby Brno 0
Bayer Leverkusen 3 *(Kirsten, Fischer, Worns)*
Leverkusen won 5-0 on aggregate

Degerfors 1 *(Berger)*
Parma 2 *(Asprilla 2)*

Parma 2 *(Balleri, Brolin)*
Degerfors 0
Parma won 4-1 on aggregate

Valur 0
Aberdeen 3 *(Shearer, Jess 2)*

Aberdeen 4 *(Miller, Jess 2, Irvine)*
Valur 0
Aberdeen won 7-0 on aggregate

Benfica 1 *(Rui Agas)*
Katowice 0

Katowice 1 *(Kucz)*
Benfica 1 *(Vitor Paneira)*
Benfica won 2-1 on aggregate

CSKA Sofia 8 *(Shishkov 4, Andenov 2, Nankov 2 (1 pen))*
Balzers 0

Balzers 1 *(Kusters)*
CSKA Sofia 3 *(Andenov, Tanev, Ciric)*
CSKA Sofia won 11-1 on aggregate

Hajduk Split 1 *(Mornar)*
Ajax 0

Ajax 6 *(R de Boer, Davids 2, Litmanen F de Boer, Pettersson)*

Hajduk Split 0
Ajax won 6-1 on aggregate

Innsbruck 3 *(Danek, Westerthaler, Carracedo)*
Ferencvaros 0

Ferencvaros 1 *(Detari)*
Innsbruck 2 *(Westerhaler)*
Innsbruck won 5-1 on aggregate

Kosice 2 *(Danko 2 (1 pen))*
Besiktas 1 *(Sergen)*

Besiktas 2 *(Metin 2)*
Kosice 0
Besiktas won 3-2 on aggregate

Lillestrom 0
Torino 2 *(Silenzi, Jarni)*

Torino 1 *(Silenzi)*
Lillestrom 2 *(Sinigaglia (og), Mjielde)*
Torino won 3-2 on aggregate

Moscow Torpedo 1 *(Borisov)*
Maccabi Haifa 0

Maccabi Haifa 3 *(Mizrahi, Petz, Holzman)*
Moscow Torpedo 1 *(Kalaychev)*
Maccabi Haifa won 3-2 on aggregate

Odense 1 *(Keown (og))*
Arsenal 2 *(Wright, Merson)*

Arsenal 1 *(Campbell)*
Odense 1 *(Nielsen)*
Arsenal won 3-2 on aggregate

Panathinaikos 3 *(Donis, Saravakos, Warzycha)*
Shelbourne 0

Shelbourne 1 *(Mooney)*
Panathinaikos 2 *(Georgiadis, Saravakos)*
Panathinaikos won 5-1 on aggregate

Real Madrid 3 *(Djubovsky, Michel (pen), Fernandez (og))*
Lugano 0

Lugano 1 *(Subiat)*
Real Madrid 3 *(Hierro, Zamorano 2)*
Real Madrid won 6-1 on aggregate

Standard Liege 5 *(Bisconti, Wilmots 2 Cruz (pen), Asselman)*
Cardiff City 2 *(Bird)*

Cardiff City 1 *(James)*
Standard Liege 3 *(Wilmots, Lashaf, Bisconti)*
Liege won 8-3 on aggregate

Uni Craiova 4 *(Craioveanu, Gane 2, Calin)*
Havnar Boltfelag 0

Havnar Boltfelag 0
Uni Craiova 3 *(Gane 2, Vase)*
Uni Craiova won 7-0 on aggregate

Second Round *(over 2 legs)*
Ajax 2 *(Rijkaard, R de Boer)*
Besiktas 1 *(Mehmet)*

Besiktas 0
Ajax 4 *(Litmanen 3, Pettersson)*
Ajax won 6-1 on aggregate

Arsenal 3 *(Wright 2, Merson)*
Standard Liege 0

Standard Liege 0
Arsenal 7 *(Smith, Selley, Adams, Campbell 2, Merson, McGoldrick)*
Arsenal won 10-0 on aggregate

Benfica 3 *(Babunski (og), Rui Costa, Schwarz)*
CSKA Sofia 1 *(Andenov)*

CSKA Sofia 1 *(Andenov)*
Benfica 3 *(Rui Costa, Joao Pinto, Yuran)*
Benfica won 6-2 on aggregate

Innsbruck 1 *(Streiter)*
Real Madrid 1 *(Alfonso)*

Real Madrid 3 *(Michel, Butragueno, Alfonso)*
Innsbruck 0
Real Madrid won 4-1 on aggregate

Maccabi Haifa 0
Parma 1 *(Brolin)*

Parma 0
Maccabi Haifa 1 *(Mizrahi)*
1-1 on agg.; Parma won 3-1 on penalties

Panathinaikos 1 *(Warzycha)*
Bayer Leverkusen 4 *(P Sergio, Thom, Kirsten, Hapal)*

Bayer Leverkusen 1 *(Kirsten)*
Panathinaikos 2 *(Saravakos (pen), Georgiadis)*
Leverkusen won 5-3 on aggregate

Paris SG 4 *(Guerin, Ginola (pen), Bita (og), Valdo)*
Uni Craiova 0

Uni Craiova 0
Paris SG 2 *(Guerin 2)*
Paris SG won 6-0 on aggregate

Torino 3 *(Sergio, Fortunato, Aguilera)*
Aberdeen 2 *(Paatelainen, Jess)*

Aberdeen 1 *(Richardson)*
Torino 2 *(Carbone, Silenzi)*
Torino won 5-3 on aggregate

Quarter Finals (*over 2 legs*)
Benfica 1 (*Isaias*)
Bayer Leverkusen 1 (*Happe*)

Bayer Leverkusen 4 (*Kirsten 2,
    Schuster, Hapal*)
Benfica 4 (*Xavier, Joao Pinto, Kulkov*)
5-5 on agg.; Benfica won on away goals

Torino 0
Arsenal 0

Arsenal 1 (*Adams*)
Torino 0
Arsenal won 1-0 on aggregate

Ajax 0
Parma 0

Parma 2 (*Minotti, Brolin*)
Ajax 0
Parma won 2-0 on aggregate

Real Madrid 0
Paris SG 1 (*Weah*)

Paris SG 1 (*Ricardo*)
Real Madrid 1 (*Butragueno*)
Paris SG won 2-1 on aggregate

Semi Finals (*over 2 legs*)
Paris SG 1 (*Ginola*)
Arsenal 1 (*Wright*)

Arsenal 1 (*Campbell*)
Paris SG 0
Arsenal won 2-1 on aggregate

Benfica 2 (*Isaias, Rui Costa*)
Parma 1 (*Zola*)

Parma 1 (*Sensini*)
Benfica 0
2-2 on agg.; Parma won on away goals

CUP WINNERS CUP FINAL
Copenhagen May 4
Arsenal 1 (*Smith*)
Parma 0
Arsenal: Seaman, Dixon,
Winterburn, Davis, Bould, Adams,
Campbell, Morrow, Smith, Merson
(McGoldrick), Selley
Parma: Bucci, Benarrivo, Di Chiara,
Minotti, Apolloni, Sensini, Brolin,
Pin (Melli), Crippa, Zola, Asprilla

UEFA CUP

First Round (*over 2 legs*)
British and Irish results only
Bohemians 0
Bordeaux 1 (*Dugarry*)

Bordeaux 5 (*Zidane, Vercruysse 2,
    Paille, Fofana*)
Bohemians 0
Bordeaux won 6-0 on aggregate

Crusaders 0
Servette 0

Servette 4 (*Anderson, Sinval 2,
    Giallanza*)
Crusaders 0
Servette won 4-0 on aggregate

Hearts 2 (*Robertson, Colquhoun*)
Atletico Madrid 1 (*Kosecki*)

Atletico Madrid 3 (*Gonzalez, Manolo,
    Garcia*)
Hearts 0
Atletico Madrid won 4-2 on aggregate

Young Boys 0
Celtic 0

Celtic 1 (*Baumann (og)*)
Young Boys 0
aet Celtic won 1-0 on aggregate

Brondby 2 (*Vilfort, Kristensen*)
Dundee Utd 0

Dundee Utd 3 (*McKinlay, Crabbe,
    Clark*)
Brondby 1 (*Kristensen*)
aet Brondby won on away goals

Norwich C 3 (*Ekoku, Goss, Polston*)
Vitesse 0

Vitesse 0
Norwich C 0
Norwich won 3-0 on aggregate

Slovan Bratislava 0
Aston Villa 0

Aston Villa 2 (*Atkinson, Townsend*)
Slovan Bratislava 1 (*Tittel*)
Aston Villa won 2-1 on aggregate

Second Round (*over 2 legs*)
British and Irish results only
Bayern Munich 1 (*Nerlinger*)
Norwich C 2 (*Goss, Bowen*)

Norwich C 1 (*Goss*)
Bayern Munich 1 (*Valencia*)
Norwich won 3-2 on aggregate

La Coruna 1 (*Riesco*)
Aston Villa 1 (*Saunders*)

Aston Villa 0
La Coruna 1 (*Manjarin*)
La Coruna won 2-1 on aggregate

Celtic 1 (*Creaney*)
Sporting Lisbon 0

Sporting Lisbon 2 (*Cadete 2*)
Celtic 0
Lisbon won 2-1 on aggregate

Third Round

Bordeaux 1 (*Zidane*)
Karlsruhe 0

Karlsruhe 3 (*Schmitt 2, Kiriakov*)
Bordeaux 0
Karlsruhe won 3-1 on aggregate

Eint. Frankfurt 1 (*Dickhaut*)
La Coruna 0

La Coruna 0
Eint. Frankfurt 1 (*Gaudino*)
Frankfurt won 2-0 on aggregate

Ofi Crete 1 (*Velic*)
Boavista 4 (*A Oliveira 3, Owubokiri*)

Boavista 2 (*Nelson, Noguiera*)
Ofi Crete 0
Boavista won 6-1 on aggregate

Brondby 1 (*Kristensen*)
Boruss. Dortmund 1 (*Chapuisat*)

Boruss. Dortmund 1 (*Zorc*)
Brondby 0
Dortmund won 2-1 on aggregate

Juventus 3 (*Möller, R Baggio (pen),
    Ravanelli*)
Tenerife 0

Tenerife 2 (*Aguilera, Del Solar*)
Juventus 1 (*Möller*)
Juventus won 4-2 on aggregate

Norwich C 0
Internazionale 1 (*Bergkamp (pen)*)

Internazionale 1 (*Bergkamp*)
Norwich C 0
Internazionale won 2-0 on aggregate

Sporting Lisbon 2 (*Cherbakov,
    Cadete*)
Salzburg 0

Salzburg 3 (*Lainer, Hütter,
    Amerhauser*)
Sporting Lisbon 0
Salzburg won 3-2 on aggregate

Mechelen 1 (*Czerniatynski*)
Cagliari 3 (*Matteoli, Oliviera,
    Pusceddu*)

Cagliari 2 (*Firicano, Allegri*)
Mechelen 0
Cagliari won 5-1 on aggregate

Quarter Finals (*over 2 legs*)
Boavista 1 (*Owubokiri*)
Karlsruhe 1 (*Wittwer*)

Karlsruhe 1 (*Santos (og)*)
Boavista 0
Karlsruhe won 2-1 on aggregate

Boruss. Dortmund 1 *(Schulz)*
Internazionale 3 *(Jonk 2, Shalimov)*

Internazionale 1 *(Manicone)*
Boruss. Dortmund 2 *(Zorc, Zelic)*
Inter won 4-3 on aggregate

Cagliari 1 *(Dely Valdes)*
Juventus 0

Juventus 1 *(D Baggio)*
Cagliari 2 *(Firicano, Oliveira)*
Cagliari won 3-1 on aggregate

Salzburg 1 *(Hütter)*
Eint. Frankfurt 0

Eint. Frankfurt 1 *(Gaudino)*
Salzburg 0
1-1 on agg, Salzburg won on penalties

Semi Finals *(over 2 legs)*
Salzburg 0
Karlsruhe 0

Karlsruhe 1 *(Krieg)*
Salzburg 1 *(Stadler)*
1-1 on agg, Salzburg won on away goals

Cagliari 3 *(Oliveira, Criniti, Pancaro)*
Internazionale 2 *(Fontalan, Sosa)*

Internazionale 3 *(Bergkump (pen),*
Berti, Jonk)
Cagliari 0
Internazionale won 5-3 on aggregate

UEFA CUP FINAL
FIRST LEG
Vienna   Apr 26
Salzburg 0
Internazionale 1 *(Berti)*
Salzburg: Konrad, Lainer,
Winklhofer (Steiner), Furstaller,
Aigner, Amerhauser (Muzek),
Artner, Marquinho, Pfeifenberger,
Stadler

Internazionale: Zenga, Paganin,
Orlando, Jonk, Bergomi, Battistini,
Bianchi, Manicone, Berti, Bergkamp
(Dell'Anno), Sosa (Ferri)

SECOND LEG
Milan May 11
Internazionale 1 *(Jonk)*
Salzburg 0
Internazionale: Zenga, A Paganin,
Fontolan (Ferri), Jonk, Bergomi,
Battistini, Orlando, Manicone, Berti,
Bergkamp (M Paganin), Sosa
Salzburg: Konrad, Lainer, Weber,
Winklhofer (Amerhauser),
Furstaller, Aiguer, Jurcevic, Artner
(Steiner), Marquinho, Feiersinger,
Hütter
Internazionale won 2-0 on aggregate

Other Competitions

World Club Championship

Played annually between the winners of the European Cup and the winners of the South American Champions Cup (Copa Libertadores). AC Milan replaced Marseille who were stripped of their European Cup title in 1993.

Tokyo   Dec 12   (80,000)
AC Milan (0) 2   Sao Paulo (1) 3
Massaro 48   Palinha 19
Papin 81   Cerezo 60, Muller 87
AC Milan: Rossi, Panucci, Maldini,
Albertini (Orlando), Costacurta,
Baresi, Donadoni, Desailly, Papin,
Massaro, Raducioiu (Tassotti)
Sao Paulo: Zetti, Cafu, Valber,
Ronaldo, Doriva, Andre, Muller,
Dinho, Palinha (Juninho), Leonardo,
Cerezo

European Super Cup

Played annually between the winners of the Champions Cup and the Cup-Winners' Cup. AC Milan replaced Marseille in 1993-4

First Leg
Parma   Jan 12   (8,083)
Parma (0) 0   AC Milan (1) 1
                    Papin 43

Second Leg
Milan   Feb 2   (24,074)
AC Milan (0) 0   Parma (1) 2
                  Sensini 23
                  Crippa 95 aet

Copa Libertadores (South American Cup)

FINAL - FIRST LEG
Buenos Aires   Aug 24
Velez Sarsfield 1   Sao Paulo 0
Asad
Velez Sarsfield: Chilavert,
Sotomayor, Trotta, Cardozo,
Zandona, Gomez, Basualdo,
Bassedas, Pompei, Asad (Husain),
Flores (Fernandez)
Sao Paulo: Zetti, Vitor, Junior
Bahiano, Gilmar, Andre, Valber,
Axel, Cafu, Pahlinha (Juninho),
Euller, Muller

FINAL - SECOND LEG
Sao Paulo   Sep 1
Sao Paulo 1   Velez Sarsfield 0
Muller
Sao Paulo: Zetti, Vitor (Juninho),
Junior Bahiano, Gilmar, Andre,
Valber, Axel, Cafu, Pahlinha, Euller,
Muller
Velez Sarsfield: Chilavert,

Almandoz, Trotta, Pellegrino,
Cardozo, Zandona, Gomez,
Basualdo, Bassedas (Pompei), Asad,
Flores (Husain)
1-1 on agg.; Velez won 5-3 on penalties

South American Super Cup

Final *(over 2 legs)*
Flamengo 2   Sao Paulo 2
Sao Paulo 2   Flamengo 2
4-4 on agg, Sao Paulo won 5-3 on pens

South American Champions 1993-94

Argentina: **Velez Sarsfield**
Bolivia: **The Strongest**
Brazil: **Palmeiras**
Chile: **Colo Colo**
Colombia: **Junior**
Ecuador: **Emelec**
Paraguay: **Olimpia**
Peru: **Universitario**
Uruguay: **Penarol**
Venezuela: **Sport Maritimo**

In August, Kalman Meszoly was appointed Hungarian national coach for the third time. Meszoly's career also includes a conviction for match-rigging in 1989. It makes sense really. Hungary have had a dreadful time of it lately.

In the same month, April, that an amendment was added to the not-so-popular Criminal Justice and Public Order Bill to outlaw ticket touting, George Michael bid £50,000 in a charity auction for two World Cup final tickets. Expect a rush on gavels from former ticket touts.

Women's Football
NATIONAL LEAGUE
Premier Division

	P	W	D	L	GF	GA	Pts
Doncaster Belles	18	16	1	1	110	16	49
Arsenal	18	14	3	1	85	15	45
Knowsley United	18	13	2	3	63	30	41
Wembley	18	9	2	7	35	34	29
Millwall L	18	9	1	8	42	46	28
Leasowe Pacific	18	7	2	9	42	48	23
Stanton Rangers	18	6	5	7	32	38	23
Red Star Southampton	18	2	3	13	25	70	6
Ipswich Town	18	1	3	14	14	86	6
Wimbledon	18	2	0	16	16	81	3

Division One North

	P	W	D	L	GF	GA	Pts
Wolverhampton W	18	12	4	2	61	28	40
Sheffield Wednesday	18	13	1	4	46	20	40
Abbeydale	18	9	2	7	38	31	29
Bronte	18	8	4	6	46	26	28
Cowgate Kestrels	18	9	1	8	38	41	28
Villa Aztecs	18	8	3	7	37	34	27
St Helens	18	7	1	10	36	57	22
Langford	18	5	2	11	25	41	17
Nottingham Argyle	18	5	1	12	25	49	16
Kidderminster Harriers	18	3	3	12	24	49	12

Division One South

	P	W	D	L	GF	GA	Pts
Bromley Borough	18	14	3	1	68	16	45
Town & County	18	11	2	5	51	29	35
Bristol	18	11	1	6	50	34	34
Epsom & Ewell	18	10	2	6	37	26	32
Brighton & Hove Albion	18	9	4	5	36	23	31
Maidstone Town	18	8	5	5	37	28	29
Hemel Hempstead	18	4	6	8	33	44	18
Horsham	18	4	4	10	24	33	16
Oxford United	18	3	4	11	17	37	13
Hassocks	18	0	1	17	7	90	1

WFA LEAGUE CUP
First Round
Horsham 0 Arsenal 6
Nottingham A 1 Red Star 7
Leasowe 2 Cowgate 1
Langford 3 Hemel Hempstead 5
Villa 0 Wolves 5
Epsom & Ewell 1 Bromley Borough 2
Ipswich 1 Knowsley 4
Wembley 5 Hassocks 0
Millwall 4 Oxford 0
Doncaster 10 Maidstone 0
Bronte 0 Sheffield Weds 4
Kidderminster Town, Brighton, Wimbledon and Stanton received first round byes

Second Round
Kidderminster 0 Arsenal 6
Town & Country 1 Red Star 3
Brighton 2 Leasowe 6
Hemel Hempstead 3 Wimbledon 4
Wolves 1 Bromley 3
Knowsley 3 Wembley 1

Millwall 6 Stanton 5
Doncaster 9 Sheffield Weds 0
Third Round
Arsenal 9 Red Star 1
Leasowe 2 Wimbledon 2
Leasowe won on penalties
Bromley 1 Knowsley 5
Millwall 1 Doncaster 6

Semi-finals
Arsenal 4 Leasowe 1
Knowsley 0 Doncaster 4

Final
To be played

FA WOMEN'S CHALLENGE CUP
Fifth Round
Leasowe 9 Town & County 0
Epsom & Ewell 7 Inter-Cardiff 0
Brighton & Hove 1 Truro City 0
Doncaster 10 Bromley Borough 1
Wembley 2 Arsenal 4
Wakefield 1 Stanton Rangers 3
Knowsley 5 Huddersfield Town 2
Kidderminster 0 Preston Rangers 6

Sixth Round
Preston Rangers 2 Stanton Rangers 3
Arsenal 0 Knowsley 1
Doncaster 5 Brighton & Hove 1
Epsom & Ewell 2 Leasowe 3

Semi-finals
Stanton Rangers 0 Knowsley 1
Leasowe 0 Doncaster 6

Final
Doncaster 1 Knowsley 0

Athletics

Athletics had its fallow year in 1994. It had a European championships, a World Cup and a European Cup, a Commonwealth Games, 16 Grand Prix outdoor meetings, nine meetings designated Grands Prix II, a host of other international meetings and a full domestic programme. And that was just from June to September. If crops were rotated like athletics meetings, the soil would never recover.

The current policy of every governing body appears to be that there is no such thing as too much of a good thing. We might have expected that an overburdened sport would fray at the edges. Yet the story that did turn British Athletics upside down had little to do with a crowded calendar. Though it did have a lot to do with unfettered power. It broke with tragic force and it shook the roots of British Athletics with such ferocity, that the sport in Britain has yet to come to terms with it.

Sunday Times athletics writer Cliff Temple committed suicide in January. In April, an inquest attributed two contributory factors; the break-up of Temple's marriage and allegations issued against him by a BAF official, promotions officer Andy Norman. Six months before his death, Temple had written an article for his newspaper on the Chafford Hundred club, run by Norman's fiancée Fatima Whitbread. Prior to publication, Norman had called Temple and suggested he would reveal details of sexual impropriety between Temple and an athlete the journalist coached if Temple continued with the criticism.

Norman was eventually dismissed two weeks before the inquest reported its findings, but the state of the promotions officer's mind was best expressed by his own press release in which he denied ever making threats to Temple. As something approaching 10 million people had already heard the tape of the phone call on national television, it was difficult to understand why Norman was making such a facile statement. That the allegations were unfounded went without saying. Norman had simply reached that stage where his authority had been unchallenged for so long, that he thought he was above authority.

The crisis should have been dealt with expeditiously, but the affair dragged out over a period when the sport was without a chief executive. Those directors who could have excercised their influence constructively used it instead to prop up Norman's ailing arguments. When Peter Radford became executive chairman on February 1st, everybody at least knew where the buck stopped.

Radford's baptism has been a fearful one. He was pitched into a sea of troubles, with the Norman affair, Frank Dick's resignation and an apparent epidemic of drug-taking. Radford, though, knew the Norman storm was bubbling when he accepted the job - indeed as honorary chairman he had been party to the first decision to merely reprimand Norman over the Temple threats, then issue Norman another contract. When national coach Dick resigned over finances, in March, Radford made no attempt at reconciliation, at a time when having an old head in the Federation might have made sense. And the timing of the drug stories hardly left the Federation and its new executive with the whiff of roses clinging.

Radford's old allies went too. When the professor of sports science was made honorary chairman in March 1993, he was one of a four-hander whose election ticket was that they would bring the sport back to the clubs. The clubs were not convinced: in March Dave

Bedford and Bob Greenoak, two members of that quartet were voted out from their posts of secretary and vice-chairman. The clouds did at least break in mid-July when BAF announced a new two-year £3m deal with ITV for athletics coverage and as the contract has an option for a further two years, the sport boldly announced a £6m deal. The issues off the track diverted attention from the performances. Athletes complained; but the issues at stake were more important than a couple of results - even if they were good ones.

In a year without world or Olympic demands, the British performances did not rise to the magical level of 1993, though Colin Jackson came close. Unbeaten, almost untouched by the competition, Jackson is now riding on the plain of authority that Renaldo Nehemiah occupied in 1981. The American foresook hurdling for a career in American football. Jackson, who added the world indoor hurdles record to his CV last winter, is still only 27, doesn't play American football and could be around for a good while yet.

Linford Christie could claim no such invulnerability. He may look as if he changes in a telephone booth, but he was still beaten five times in a crowded summer. Christie has timing, though. Four losses in 1993, were scattered around that world crown in Stuttgart. Five defeats in 1994 were sprinkled around a European title (his third 100m title and only Valery Borzov can match that), a Commonwealth title (his second) and a victory at the one-day Olympics in Zürich. It was only a shame that, having decided to run in the Commonwealth Games, the man who is normally the British team captain scurried off so hastily before the relays, in order to get back on the money trail.

Sally Gunnell managed to earn a few bob *and* stay the full term in Victoria, anchoring the England 4 x 400m team to victory. Gunnell completed her season with just one loss over 400m hurdles, to American Kim Batten in Nice, retained her European and Commonwealth titles and, like Jackson, is sure to threaten her own world record in the 1995 season.

Kelly Holmes and Du'aine Ladejo translated promise into titles; Holmes with a Commonwealth gold, Ladejo with indoor and outdoor European 400m titles. Roger Black and Steve Backley returned after injury and illness had affected performances, Backley with particular gusto, reclaiming the brace of titles that he won in 1990.

WORLD OUTDOOR RECORDS 1994

MEN

100m	9.85 (+1.2)	Leroy Burrell	USA	Lausanne	Jul 6
3000m	7:25.11	Noureddine Morceli	ALG	Monte Carlo	Aug 2
2 Miles	8:09.01	Moses Kiptanui	KEN	Hechtel, Belgium	Jul 31
5000m	12:56.96	Haile Gebresilasie	ETH	Hengelo, Holland	Jun 4
10,000m	26:52.23	William Sigei	KEN	Oslo	Jul 22
20kmw (track)	1:17:25.5	Bernardo Segura	MEX	Fana, Norway	May 7
Pole Vault	6.14m	Sergey Bubka	UKR	Sestriere, Italy	Jul 31

WOMEN

2000m	5:25.36	Sonia O'Sullivan	IRL	Edinburgh	Jul 8
Hammer*	66.84m	Olga Kuzenkova	RUS	Adler, Russia	Feb 18

* *relatively new event recognised only as a world best, not yet as a world record.*

Team performances were impressive in the European Cup, when both the men's and women's teams placed second, and more than adequate in the European Championships (though not quite meeting the daunting standard of Split in 1990). However, the World Cup could hardly be taken at face value. When the USA do not even field a 4 x 400m men's team, it would be plain silly to read too much into Britain's second in the men's competition.

The World Cup is an unusual competition in that nations compete against continents. As the Americans clearly didn't fancy it and the Germans couldn't persuade two of their strongest athletes - Dieter Baumann and Heike Drechsler - to compete for nothing, it left only Britain, among the nations, taking it seriously. The continental teams generally find it hard to be cohesive units, but Africa is an exception. It was that team which gave the men's competition its credibility; Tanui, Morceli, Skah, and Kiptanui would enhance any event.

Noureddine Morceli must be the male athlete of the summer. The Algerian did fearful damage to Kiptanui's world 3000m record, reducing it by almost four seconds. Suddenly we are talking about two sub four-minute miles back to back. He talks a good record too, as did Saïd Aouita. But they have both been prodigious record breakers as well, and if it pleased a few that Morceli (after laying future claim to every world record from 800m to 10,000m) got his come-uppance over 800m, there are not many who would back against him cracking the rest of the set.

Moses Kiptanui took back a record when he broke Khalid Skah's two mile record in Belgium. His time, though, pales into insignificance when put alongside Morceli's metric equivalent. Haile Gebresilasie and William Sigei assaulted a couple of decent distance marks and Sergey Bubka eased the pole vault bar up another notch. We all know why Bubka only does it a centimetre at a time (more world record bonuses), but it doesn't stop it becoming a bit of a yawn. If he really can jump 6.20m, I wish he'd get on with it.

Leroy Burrell had a completely inauspicious season, except that in his first race in Europe he broke the world 100m record. The 100m has superseded the mile as the blue riband event, yet Burrell's record seemed strangely inglorious. It could be that this was because we all expected Christie would do it, but it may be too late for that now.

Sonia O'Sullivan was the female athlete of the year, though she often appeared to use racing as training. The two Grand Prix titles (and $130,000 each) went to Noureddine Morceli and Jackie Joyner-Kersee, but they were upstaged by Colin Jackson and Mike Powell who shared 20kg of gold (worth $280,000) after winning their events at each of the Golden Four meetings - Oslo, Zurich, Brussels and Berlin. It was the year that Liz McColgan got paid **not** to run the NutraSweet London Marathon and when the Chinese didn't run anywhere. It was also the year that Butch Reynolds lost his $27m award when the US Court of Appeal overturned the original Ohio Court judgment; when Steve Ovett got knocked off his bike and threatened the car driver with a more modest $100,000 claim.

It was the 40th anniversary of the four-minute mile and cause for the great names of miling to congregate in London for an extraordinary celebration. Eamonn Coghlan was present; in February, with a timely record, he became the first 40 year old in history to break the four minute barrier.

And it was the year the sport said goodbye to Dame Marea Hartman, who could tough out anything, except sadly, cancer.

European Championships

Helsinki   Aug 7-14

Men

100m	1	Linford Christie	GBR	10.14
(-0.5)	2	Geir Moen	NOR	10.20
	3	Aleksandr Parkhomovsky	RUS	10.31
	8	Jason John	GBR	10.46
		dnq Toby Box GBR, 10.45 for 6th in sf		
200m	1	Geir Moen	NOR	20.30
(-0.1)	2	Vladislav Dologodin	UKR	20.47
	3	Patrick Stevens	BEL	20.68
		dnq Philip Goedluck GBR, 21.11 for 7th in sf		
400m	1	Du'aine Ladejo	GBR	45.09
	2	Roger Black	GBR	45.20
	3	Matthias Rusterholtz	SUI	45.96
		dnq David McKenzie GBR 46.65 for 7th in sf		
800m	1	Andrea Benvenuti	ITA	1:46.12
	2	Vebjørn Rodal	NOR	1:46.53
	3	Tomás de Teresa	ESP	1:46.57
	6	Craig Winrow	GBR	1:47.09
		dnq Tom McKean GBR, 1:49.41 for 6th in heat		
1500m	1	Fermin Cacho	ESP	3:35.27
	2	Isaac Viciosa	ESP	3:36.01
	3	Branko Zorko	CRO	3:36.88
	11	Gary Lough	GBR	3:43.09
	12	David Strang	GBR	3:50.27
		dnq Kevin McKay GBR, 3:40.19 for 5th in heat		
5000m	1	Dieter Baumann	GER	13:36.93
	2	Rob Denmark	GBR	13:37.50
	3	Abel Antón	ESP	13:38.04
	5	John Nuttall	GBR	13:38.65
10,000m	1	Abel Antón	ESP	28:06.03
	2	Vincent Rousseau	BEL	28:06.63
	3	Stephane Franke	GER	28:07.95
	15	Gary Staines	GBR	28:25.60
	22	Justin Hobbs	GBR	29:28.08
Marathn	1	Martin Fiz	ESP	2:10:31
	2	Diego Garcia	ESP	2:10:46
	3	Alberto Juzdado	ESP	2:11:18
	4	Richard Nerurkar	GBR	2:11:56
	27	Peter Whitehead	GBR	2:16:40
	31	Bill Foster	GBR	2:17:12
	52	Steve Brace	GBR	2:24:21
		dnf Andy Green & Mark Flint GBR		

European Cup Team Result (aggregate of 4 runners)
  1 Spain 8:49:54, 2 Portugal 8:54:59
  3 France 8:47:56, 6 Great Britain 9:10:09

3000msc	1	Alessandro Lambruschini	ITA	8:22.40
	2	Angelo Carosi	ITA	8:23.53
	3	William van Dijck	BEL	8:24.86
	4	Mark Rowland	GBR	8:26.00
	10	Tom Hanlon	GBR	8:36.06
	11	Justin Chaston	GBR	8:36.83
110mh	1	Colin Jackson	GBR	13.08
(+1.1)	2	Florian Schwarthoff	GER	13.16
	3	Tony Jarrett	GBR	13.23
		dnq Andy Tulloch GBR, 13.62 for 5th in sf		
400mh	1	Oleg Tverdokhleb	UKR	48.06
	2	Sven Nylander	SWE	48.22
	3	Stéphane Diagana	FRA	48.23
	6	Peter Crampton	GBR	49.45
	8	Gary Cadogan	GBR	49.53
		dnq Lawrence Lynch GBR, 50.24 for 5th in heat		

HJ	1	Steinar Hoen	NOR	2.35m
	=2	Artur Partyka	POL	2.33m
	=2	Steve Smith	GBR	2.33m
	=9	Dalton Grant	GBR	2.25m
		dnq Brendan Reilly GBR, 2.20m for =16th		
PV	1	Rodion Gataullin	RUS	6.00m
	2	Igor Trandenkov	RUS	5.90m
	3	Jean Galfione	FRA	5.85m
		dnq Mike Edwards GBR, 5.20m for =24th		
LJ	1	Ivailo Mladenov	BUL	8.09m
	2	Milan Gombala	TCH	8.04m
	3	Konstandinos Koukodimos	GRE	8.01m
		dnq Barrington Williams GBR, 7.69m for 19th		
TJ	1	Denis Kapustin	RUS	17.62m
	2	Serge Hélan	FRA	17.55m
	3	Maris Bruzhiks	LAT	17.20m
	6	Jonathan Edwards	GBR	16.85m
	9	Julian Golley	GBR	16.35m
		dnq Frances Agyepong GBR, no jump		
Shot	1	Aleksandr Klimenko	UKR	20.78m
	2	Aleksandr Bagach	UKR	20.34m
	3	Roman Virastyuk	UKR	19.59m
		dnq Paul Edwards GBR, 18.54m for 13th		
Discus	1	Vladimir Dubrovchik	BLS	64.78m
	2	Dmitri Shevchenko	RUS	64.56m
	3	Jürgen Schult	GER	64.18m
		dnq Robert Weir GBR, 57.18m for 13th		
HT	1	Vasily Sidorenko	RUS	81.10m
	2	Igor Astapkovich	BLS	80.40m
	3	Heinz Weis	GER	78.48m
JT	1	Steve Backley	GBR	85.20m
	2	Seppo Räty	FIN	82.90m
	3	Jan Zelezny	TCH	82.58m
	6	Mick Hill	GBR	80.66m
		dnq Colin MacKenzie GBR, 74.00m for 22nd		
Decthln	1	Alain Blondel	FRA	8453pts
		(11.12/7.50m/13.78/1.99m/48.91/14.18/		
		45.08/5.40m/60.64m/4:20.48)		
	2	Henrik Dagård	SWE	8362pts
	3	Lev Lobodin	UKR	8201pts
20kmw	1	Mikhail Schennikov	RUS	1:18:45
	2	Yevgeny Misyuyla	BLS	1:19:22
	3	Valentin Massana	ESP	1:20:33
50kmw	1	Valery Spitsyn	RUS	3:41:07
	2	Thierry Toutain	FRA	3:43:52
	3	Giovanni Perricelli	ITA	3:43:55
4x100m	1	France		38.57
		(Lomba, Sangouma, Trouabal, Perrot)		
	2	Ukraine		38.98
	3	Italy		38.99
		dnq GBR, dropped baton in heat 1		
		Jarrett (2) to Braithwaite (3)		
4x400m	1	Great Britain		2:59.13
		(McKenzie 45.7, Whittle 45.3, Black 43.9,		
		Ladejo 44.2)		
	2	France		3:01.11
	3	Russia		3:03.10

Women

100m	1	Irina Privalova	RUS	11.02
(+0.6)	2	Zhanna Tarnopolskaya	UKR	11.10
	3	Melanie Paschke	GER	11.28

dnq, all GBR, Paula Thomas, 11.58 for 5th in sf
Stephanie Douglas 11.60 for 7th in sf
Marcia Richardson 11.71 for 7th in 2nd rd

200m	1	Irina Privalova	RUS	22.32
(+2.9)	2	Zhanna Tarnopolskaya	UKR	22.77
	3	Galina Malchugina	RUS	22.90

dnq, all GBR, Paula Thomas, 23.41 for 6th in sf
Katharine Merry, 23.55 for 8th in sf
Simmone Jacobs, 23.75 for 6th in heat

400m	1	Marie-José Pérec	FRA	50.33
	2	Svetlana Goncharenko	RUS	51.24
	3	Phylis Smith	GBR	51.30
	6	Melanie Neef	GBR	52.10

dnq Linda Keough GBR, 53.63 for 6th in sf

800m	1	Lyubov Gurina	RUS	1:58.55
	2	Natalya Dukhnova	BLS	1:58.55
	3	Lyudmila Rogachova	RUS	1:58.69
	5	Ann Griffiths	GBR	1:59.81

dnq Diane Modahl GBR, 2:02.18 for 6th in sf

1500m	1	Lyudmila Rogachova	RUS	4:18.93
	2	Kelly Holmes	GBR	4:19.30
	3	Yekaterina Podkopayeva	RUS	4:19.37

dnq A Davies GBR, 4:12.09 for 6th in heat
L ynn Gibson GBR, 4:13.89 for 10th in heat

3000m	1	Sonia O'Sullivan	IRL	8:31.84
	2	Yvonne Murray	GBR	8:36.48
	3	Gabriela Szabo	ROM	8:40.08
	6	Alison Wyeth	GBR	8:45.76
	11	Sonia McGeorge	GBR	8:51.55
10,000m	1	Fernanda Ribeiro	POR	31:08.75
	2	Conceição Ferreira	POR	31:32.82
	3	Daria Nauer	SUI	31:35.96
Marathn	1	Manuela Machado	POR	2:29:54
	2	Maria Curatolo	ITA	2:30:33
	3	Adriana Barbu	ROM	2:30.55
	11	Danielle Sanderson	GBR	2:36.29
	22	Marian Sutton	GBR	2:40:34
	30	Lesley Turner	GBR	2:45:16
	32	Linda Rushmere	GBR	2:45:24
	35	Teresa Dyer	GBR	2:50:23

100mh	1	Svetla Dimitrova	BUL	12.72
(w-1.7)	2	Yulia Graudyn	RUS	12.93
	3	Yordanka Donkova	BUL	12.93
	7	Jacqui Agyepong	GBR	13.17

dnq Clova Court GBR, 13.04 for 5th in sf
Sam Farquharson GBR, 13.33 in heat

400mh	1	Sally Gunnell	GBR	53.33
	2	Silvia Rieger	GER	54.68
	3	Anna Knoroz	RUS	54.68
	8	Gowry Retchakan	GBR	56.05
HJ	1	Britta Bilac	SLO	2.00m
	2	Yelena Gulyayeva	RUS	1.96m
	3	Nele Zilinskiene	LIT	1.93m

dnq Jill Bennett GBR, 1.85m for =19th
Debbie Marti GBR, 1.85m for 29th
Lea Haggett GBR, 1.75m for 34th

LJ	1	Heike Drechsler	GER	7.14m
	2	Inessa Kravets	UKR	6.99m
	3	Fiona May	ITA	6.90m
	9	Yinka Idowu	GBR	6.46m

dnq Denise Lewis GBR, 6.20m for 19th

TJ	1	Anna Biryukova	RUS	14.89m
	2	Inna Lasovskaya	RUS	14.85m
	3	Inessa Kravets	UKR	14.67m
	10	Michelle Griffiths	GBR	13.60m
	11	Rachel Kirby	GBR	13.45m

dnq Ashia Hansen GBR, 13,45m for 15th

SP	1	Viktoria Pavlysh	UKR	19.61m
	2	Astrid Kumbernuss	GER	19.49m
	3	Svetla Mitkova	BUL	19.49m

dnq Myrtle Augee GBR, 16.77m for 14th
Maggie Lynes GBR, 16.16m for 17th

DT	1	Ilke Wyludda	GER	68.72m
	2	Ellina Zveryova	BLS	64.46m
	3	Mette Bergmann	NOR	64.34m

dnq Jackie McKernan GBR, 57.56m for 13th

JT	1	Trine Hattestad	NOR	68.00m
	2	Karen Forkel	GER	66.10m
	3	Felicia Tilea	ROM	64.34m

dnq Sharon Gibson GBR, 53.82 for 17th
Sharon Holroyd GBR, 51.26 for 21st

Heptath	1	Sabine Braun	GER	6419pts

(13.33/1.84m/14.02/24.60/6.32m/48.54m/2:20.66)

	2	Rita Ináncsi	HUN	6404pts
	3	Urszula Wlodarczyk	POL	6322pts
10kmw	1	Sari Essayah	FIN	42:37
	2	Anna-Rita Sidoti	ITA	42:43
	3	Yelena Nikolayeva	RUS	42:43
	20	Vicky Lupton	GBR	46:30
	23	Verity Snook	GBR	47:23

disq Lisa Langford GBR

4x100m	1	Germany	42.90

(Paschke, Zipp, Knoll, Lichtenhagen)

	2	Russia	42.96
	3	Bulgaria	43.00
	5	Great Britain	43.63

(Douglas, Merry, Jacobs, Thomas)

4x400m	1	France (Landre, Dorsile, Elien, Pérec)	3:22.34
	2	Russia	3:24.06
	3	Germany	3:24.10
	4	Great Britain	3:24.14

(Neef, Keough, Smith, Gunnell)

Final Medal Table

	G	S	B
Russia	10	8	7
Great Britain	6	5	2
Germany	5	4	5
France	4	3	2
Ukraine	3	6	3
Spain	3	2	4
Norway	3	2	1
Italy	2	3	3
Portugal	2	1	0
Bulgaria	2	0	3
Belarus	1	4	0
Finland	1	1	0
Sweden	0	2	0
Belgium	0	1	2
Czech Republic	0	1	1
Poland	0	1	1
Hungary	0	1	0
Romania	0	0	3
Switzerland	0	0	2
Greece	0	0	1

World Cup
Crystal Palace   *Sep 8-10*

Men

100m	1	Linford Christie	GBR	10.21
(-0.3)	2	Olapade Adeniken	AFR	10.25
	3	Talal Mansour	ASI	10.31
200m	1	John Regis	GBR	20.45
(-1.4)	2	Frankie Fredericks	AFR	20.55
	3	Geir Moen	EUR	20.72
400m	1	Antonio Pettigrew	USA	45.26
	2	Du'aine Ladejo	GBR	45.44
	3	Inaldo de Sena	AME	45.67
800m	1	Mark Everett	USA	1:46.02
	2	William Tanui	AFR	1:46.84
	3	Craig Winrow	GBR	1:47.16
1500m	1	Noureddine Morceli	AFR	3:34.70
	2	Rudiger Stenzel	GER	3:40.04
	3	Mohamed Suleiman	ASI	3:40.52
5000m	1	Brahim Lahlafi	AFR	13:27.96
	2	John Nuttall	GBR	13:32.47
	3	Martin Bremer	GER	13:33.57
10,000m	1	Khalid Skah	AFR	27:38.74
	2	Antonio Silio	AME	28:16.54
	3	Rob Denmark	GBR	28:20.65
3000msc	1	Moses Kiptanui	AFR	8:28.28
	2	Sa'ed Shaddad Al-Asmari	ASI	8:35.74
	3	Alessandro Lambruschini	EUR	8:40.34
110mh	1	Tony Jarrett	GBR	13.23
(-1.6)	2	Allen Johnson	USA	13.29
	3	Emilio Valle	AME	13.45
400mh	1	Samuel Matete	ZAM	48.77
	2	Oleg Tverdokhleb	EUR	49.26
	3	Eronildo Nuñes de Araujo	AME	49.62
HJ	1	Javier Sotomayor	AME	2.40m
	2	Tim Forsyth	OCE	2.28m
	3	Steve Smith	GBR	2.28m
PV	1	Okkert Brits	AFR	5.90m *
	2	Jean Galfione	FRA	5.75m
	=3	Alberto Manzano	AME	5.40m
	=3	Andrey Tiwontschik	GER	5.40m
LJ	1	Fred Salle	GBR	8.10m
	2	Douglas de Souza	AME	7.96m
	3	Dion Bentley	USA	7.93m
TJ	1	Yoelvis Quesada	AME	17.61m
	2	Julian Golley	GBR	17.06m
	3	Oleg Sakirkin	ASI	16.81m
Shot	1	C J Hunter	USA	19.92m
	2	Aleksandr Klimenko	EUR	19.16m
	3	Courtney Ireland	OCE	18.93m
Discus	1	Vladimir Dubrovschcik	EUR	64.54m
	2	Alexis Elizalde	AME	61.50m
	3	Adewale Olukoju	AFR	60.22m
HT	1	Andrey Abduvaliyev	ASI	81.72m
	2	Lance Deal	USA	81.14m
	3	Heinz Weis	GER	80.32m
JT	1	Steve Backley	GBR	85.02m
	2	Raymond Hecht	GER	84.36m
	3	Gavin Lovegrove	OCE	82.28m
4x100m	1	Great Britain		38.46
		(Braithwaite, Jarrett, Regis, Christie)		
	2	Africa		38.97
	3	USA		39.33
4x400m	1	Great Britain		3:01.34
		(Whittle , Patrick, Black, Du'aine Ladejo)		
	2	Africa		3:02.66
	3	Europe		3:03.26

MEN'S FINAL TABLE: 1 Africa 116; 2 Great Britain 111; 3 Americas 95; 4 Europe 91; 5 Germany 85.5; 6 USA 78; 7 Asia 75; 8 Oceania 62.5

Women

100m	1	Irina Privalova	EUR	11.32
(-1.7)	2	Liliana Allen	AME	11.50
	3	Mary Onyali	AFR	11.52
200m	1	Merlene Ottey	AME	22.23
(-1.7)	2	Irina Privalova	EUR	22.51
	3	Cathy Freeman	OCE	22.72
400m	1	Irina Privalova	EUR	50.62
	2	Fatima Yusuf	AFR	50.80
	3	Jearl Miles	USA	51.24
800m	1	Maria Mutola	AFR	1:58.27
	2	Luciana Mendes	AME	2:00.13
	3	Natalya Dukhnova	EUR	2:02.81
1500m	1	Hassiba Boulmerka	AFR	4:01.05
	2	Angela Chalmers	AME	4:01.73
	3	Kelly Holmes	GBR	4:10.81
3000m	1	Yvonne Murray	GBR	8:56.81
	2	Robyn Meagher	AME	9:05.81
	3	Gabriela Szabo	EUR	9:15.16
10,000m	1	Elana Meyer	AFR	30:52.51
	2	Fernando Ribeiro	EUR	31:04.25
	3	Wei Li	ASI	32:37.94
100mh	1	Aliuska Lopez	AME	12.91
(-0.9))	2	Svetla Dimitrova	EUR	12.95
	3	Jacqui Agyepong	GBR	13.02
400mh	1	Sally Gunnell	GBR	54.80
	2	Silvia Rieger	GER	56.14
	3	Anna Knoroz	RUS	56.63
HJ	1	Britta Bilac	EUR	1.91m
	2	Charmaine Weavers	AFR	1.91m
	3	Silvia Costa	AME	1.91m
LJ	1	Inessa Kravets	EUR	7.00m
	2	Niurka Montalvo	AME	6.70m
	3	Christy Opara-Thompson	AFR	6.66m
TJ	1	Anna Biryukova	EUR	14.46m
	2	Sheila Hudson-Strudwick	USA	14.00m
	3	Ren Ruiping	ASI	13.84m
Shot	1	Huang Zhihong	ASI	19.45m
	2	Belsy Laza	AME	19.07m
	3	Astrid Kumbernuss	GER	18.89m
Discus	1	Ilke Wyludda	GER	65.30m
	2	Ellina Zvereva	EUR	63.86m
	3	Daniela Costian	OCE	63.38m
Javelin	1	Trine Hattestad	EUR	66.48m
	2	Isel Lopez	AME	61.40m
	3	Karen Forkel	GER	61.26m
4x100m	1	Africa		42.92
		(Idehen, Tombiri, Opara-Thompson, Onyali)		
	2	Germany		43.22
	3	Oceania		43.36
4x400m	1	Great Britain		3:27.36
		(Smith, Keough, Neef, Gunnell))		
	2	Germany		3:27.59
	3	Americas		3:27.91

WOMEN'S FINAL TABLE: 1 Europe 111; 2 Americas 98; 3 Germany 79; 4 Africa 78; 5 Great Britain 73; 6 Asia 67; 7 Oceania 57; 8 USA 48

European Cup Super League

Birmingham   *June 25-26*

Men

100m	1	Linford Christie	GBR	10.21
(+0.9)	2	Marc Blume	GER	10.37
	3	Pavel Galkin	RUS	10.42
200m	1	Linford Christie	GBR	20.67
(-0.1)	2	Sergey Osovitch	UKR	20.70
	3	Daniel Sangouma	FRA	21.04
400m	1	Roger Black	GBR	45.08
	2	Jean-Louis Rapnouil	FRA	46.43
	3	Dmitry Golovastov	RUS	46.58
800m	1	Nico Motchebon	GER	1:48.10
	2	Davide Cadoni	ITA	1:48.42
	3	Craig Winrow	GBR	1:48.76
1500m	1	Andrey Bulkovsky	UKR	3:49.33
	2	Rüdiger Stenzel	GER	3:49.38
	3	Gary Lough	GBR	3:49.57
5000m	1	Dieter Baumann	GER	13:48.95
	2	Abdelah Behar	FRA	13:49.12
	3	Ovidiu Olteanu	ROM	13:49.43
10,000m	1	Francesco Panetta	ITA	28:38.45
	2	Stephane Franke	GER	28:38.99
	3	Oleg Strizhakov	RUS	29:03.55
3000msc	1	Alessandro Lambruschini	ITA	8:24.98
	2	Steffen Brand	GER	8:27.83
	3	Justin Chaston	GBR	8:29.99
110mh	1	Florian Schwarthoff	GER	13.35
(+1.9)	2	Vladimir Belokon	UKR	13.62
	3	Andrew Tulloch	GBR	13.65
400mh	1	Sven Nylander	SWE	49.36
	2	Oleg Tverdokhleb	UKR	49.37
	3	Stephane Diagana	FRA	49.47
PV	1	Jean Galfione	FRA	5.70m
	2	Patrik Stenlund	SWE	5.60m
	3	Tim Lobinger	GER	5.60m
HJ	1	Hendryk Beyer	GER	2.25m
	2	Patrick Thavelin	SWE	2.20m
	3	Dalton Grant	GBR	2.20m
LJ	1	Stanislav Tarasenko	RUS	8.02m
	2	Dietmar Haaf	GER	7.84m
	3	Bogdan Tudor	ROM	7.78m
TJ	1	Denis Kapustin	RUS	17.30m
	2	Tord Henriksson	SWE	16.99m
	3	Serge Helan	FRA	16.92m
Shot	1	Paolo Dal Soglio	ITA	19.69m
	2	Roman Virastyuk	UKR	19.40m
	3	Gheorghe Guset	ROM	19.23m
Discus	1	Dmitri Shevchenko	RUS	64.74m
	2	Jürgen Schult	GER	64.42m
	3	Vladimir Zinchenko	UKR	62.80m
HT	1	Vasily Sidorenko	RUS	78.76m
	2	Andrey Skvaryuk	UKR	78.20m
	3	Christophe Epalle	FRA	78.16m
JT	1	Andrey Moruyev	RUS	87.34m
	2	Raymond Hecht	GER	85.40m
	3	Mike Hill	GBR	85.28m
4 x 100m	1	Great Britain		38.72
		(John, Wariso, Regis, Christie)		
	2	Ukraine		38.79
	3	Germany		38.81
4 x 400m	1	Great Britain		3:02.50
		(Whittle , Patrick, Black, Ladejo)		
	2	Russia		3:03.57
	3	France		3:03.74

Men's Final Table 1. Germany 121, 2. Great Britain 106.5, 3. Russia 101, 4. Ukraine 87, 5. Italy 84, 6. Sweden 81.5, 7. France 80, 8. Romania 56 *France and Romania relegated*

Women

100m	1	Zhanna Tarnopolskaya	UKR	11.26
(+0.8)	2	Katharine Merry	GBR	11.34
	3	Melanie Paschke	GER	11.37
200m	1	Silke Knoll	GER	23.04
(+2.9)	2	Katharine Merry	GBR	23.38
	3	Oksana Dyachenko	RUS	23.65
400m	1	Svetlana Goncharenko	RUS	52.08
	2	Melanie Neef	GBR	52.43
	3	Francine Landre	FRA	52.86
800m	1	Diane Modahl	GBR	2:02.81
	2	Patricia Djate	FRA	2:02.95
	3	Elena Zavadskaya	UKR	2:04.43
1500m	1	Liubov Kremlyova	RUS	4:05.97
	2	Kelly Holmes	GBR	4:06.48
	3	Violeta Beclea	ROM	4:09.26
3000m	1	Ludmilla Borisova	RUS	8:52.21
	2	Farida Fates	FRA	8:53.40
	3	Sonia McGeorge	GBR	8:55.47
10,000m	1	Kathrin Wessel	GER	32:26.85
	2	Rosario Murcia	FRA	32:59.80
	3	Rocio Rios	ESP	33:22.18
100mh	1	Jacqui Agyepong	GBR	13.00
(-1.4)	2	Yulia Graudyn	RUS	13.07
	3	Anne Piquereau	FRA	13.21
400mh	1	Sally Gunnell	GBR	54.62
	2	Tatyana Terechouk	UKR	55.04
	3	Tatyana Kurochkina	BLS	56.02
HJ	1	Tatyana Shevchik	BLS	1.94m
	2	Monica Iager	ROM	1.91m
	3	Elena Gulyayeva	RUS	1.88m
LJ	1	Heike Drechsler	GER	6.99m
	2	Olga Rublyova	RUS	6.65m
	3	Larisa Kuchinskaya	BLS	6.54m
TJ	1	Helga Radtke	GER	13.90m
	2	Redica Petrescu	ROM	13.83m
	3	Concepcion Paredes	ESP	13.81m
Shot	1	Astrid Kumbernuss	GER	19.63m
	2	Valentina Fedyushina	UKR	19.30m
	3	Larisa Peleshenko	RUS	18.86m
Discus	1	Ilke Wyludda	GER	68.36m
	2	Olga Nikishina	UKR	63.48m
	3	Ellina Zvereva	BLS	62.92m
Javelin	1	Natalia Shikolenko	BLS	69.00m
	2	Karen Forkel	GER	65.58m
	3	Felicia Tilea	ROM	63.88m
4 x 100m	1	Ukraine		43.38
	2	Great Britain		43.46
		(Douglas, Merry, Jacobs,Thomas)		
	3	Germany		44.24
4 x 400m	1	Great Britain		3:27.33
		(Goddard, Smith, Gunnell, Neef)		
	2	Germany		3:27.78
	3	Russia		3:28.85

Women's Final Table 1. Germany 98, 2. Great Britain 97, 3. Russia 95, 4. Ukraine 86, 5. Belarus 64, 6. France 60, 7. Romania 60, 8. Spain 50 *Romania and Spain are relegated*

European Cup - 1st League

Valencia   *June 11-12*

Men 100m: Alexandros Terzian GRE 10.25 (+1.8), 200m: Alexandros Terzian GRE 21.02 (+1.1), 400m: Papado'los GRE 47.00, 800m: Luis Gonzalez ESP 1:50.77, 1500m: Fermin Cacho ESP 3:40.82, 5000m: Antonio Serrano ESP 13:45.88, 10,000m: Juan Torres ESP 28:28.45, 3000msc: Antonio Peula ESP 8:40.09, 110mh: Csillag HUN 13.85 (-1.6), 400mh: Piotr Kotlarski POL 50.36, HJ: Jaroslaw Kotewicz POL 2.24m, PV: Gennady Sidorov BLS 5.65m, LJ: Konstandimos Koukodimos GRE 8.40 (+3.4), TJ: Milan Mikulás TCH 16.66m (+3.1), SP: Mañuel Martinez ESP 20.09m, DT: Atilla Horváth HUN 62.50m, HT: Vitaly Alisevich BLS 77.58m, JT: Costas Gatsioudis GRE 82.02m, 4 x 100m: Spain 39.91, 4 x 400m: Poland 3:06.52 **Men's Final Table** 1. Spain 113, 2. Poland 112.5, 3. Belarus 102, 4. Greece 95.5, 5. Hungary 89, 6. Czech Republic 83, 7. Bulgaria 71, 8. Denmark 52 *Spain and Poland promoted* **Women** 100m: Lucrécia Jardim POR 11.36 (+3.5), 200m: Erika Suchovska TCH 23.14 (+4.7), 400m: Elsbieta Killinska POL 52.98, 800m: Malgorzata Rydz POL 2:00.40, 1500m: Carla Sacramento POR 4:16.29, 3000m: Anna Brzezinska POL 8:57.50, 10,000m: Conceiçao Ferreira POR 31:54.65, 100mh: Carla Tuzzi ITA 12.97 (+1.1), 400h: Sylwia Pachut POL 57.45, HJ: Zuzana Kovacikova TCH 1.94m, LJ: Agata Karczmarek POL 6.89m (+1.4), TJ: Sarka Kasparkova TCH 14.19 (+3.0), SP: Danguolé Urbikiené LIT 18.68m, DT: Vladimira Malatova TCH 62.76m, JT: Genowefa Patla POL 61.60m, 4 x 100m: Italy 44.42, 4 x 400m: Czech Republic 3:30.17
Women's Final Table 1. Poland 105, 2. Italy 93, 3. Czech Republic 88, 4. Portugal 80, 5. Finland 71, 6. Switzerland 67, 7. Lithuania 63, 8. Austria 42 *Poland and Italy promoted*

European Cup - 2nd League

GROUP ONE
Dublin   *June 11-12*
Men's Final Table 1. Belgium 102, 2. Holland 97, 3. Portugal 95, 4. Ireland 90, 5.Lithuania 77, 6. Iceland 63, 7. Small Nations 35 **Women's Final Table** 1. Holland 99, 2. Belgium 88, 3. Greece 76, 4. Denmark 74, 5. Ireland 62, 6. Iceland 55, 7. Small Nations 22

GROUP TWO
Istanbul   *June 11-12*
Men's Final Table 1. Norway 107, 2. Switzerland 100, 3. Slovakia, 4. Cyprus 72, 5. Israel, 6. Croatia 68, 7. Turkey 54 **Women's Final Table** 1. Bulgaria 106, 2. Norway 97, 3. Turkey 74, 4. Slovakia 65, Croatia 49, 6. Cyprus 48, 7. Israel 36

GROUP THREE
Ljubljana   *June 11-12*
Men's Final Table 1. Finland 127, 2 Latvia 96, 3. Slovenia 90.5, 4. Austria 89.5, 5. Estonia 67, 6. Moldova 56, 7. Albania 30 **Women's Final Table** 1. Sweden 96, 2. Hungary 94, 3. Slovenia 86, 4. Latvia 61, 5. Estonia 58, 6. Moldova 52, 7. Albania 27

European Cup (Combined Events)

SUPER LEAGUE
Lyon   *Jul 2-3*
Men 1. Christian Plaziat FRA 8505 pts (10.94/7.88m/14.88m/2.10m/48.34/14.20/44.54m/5.10m

/57.32m/4:39.32), 2. Henrik Dagård SWE 8347, 3. Tomás Dvorak TCH 8313 **Men's Team** 1. France 24,864, 2. Czech Republic 23,836, 3. Spain 23, 723
Women 1. Svetlana Moskalets RUS 6507 (13.26/1.87m/13.20/23.75/6.70m/40.10m/2:16.84) 2. Nathalie Teppe FRA 6396, 3. Peggy Beer GER 6362, 12. Denise Lewis GBR 6069, 19. Kelly GBR 5826, 24. Schofield GBR 5671, 26. Johnson GBR 5486
Women's Team 1. Russia 18,876, 2. Ukraine 18,487, 3. France 18,474, 6. Great Britain 17,566

1ST LEAGUE
Bressanone, Italy   *Jul 2-3*
Men 1. Vitaly Kolpakov UKR 8257, 2. Lobodin UKR 8176, 3. Alex Kruger GBR 7963, 4. Simon Shirley GBR 7938, 11. Joseph GBR 7563, 16. Thomas GBR 7350 **Men's Team** 1. Ukraine 24,204, 2. Great Britain 23,464, 3. Russia 23,136
Women 1. Anzhela Atroshchenko BLS 6119, 2. Sharon Jaklofsky HOL 6068, 3. Tatyana Alisevich BLS 5995 **Women's Team** 1. Belarus 17,884, 2. Holland 17,537, 3. Italy 17,397

European Clubs Cups

Men   *Malaga, Spain* *May 28-29*
1. Larios Madrid ESP 129pts, 2. Fiamme Azzure Padova ITA 116, 3. Racing Club FRA 97.5, 4. Ujpesti Toma Egylet HUN 90.5, 5. Dukla Praha TCH 90, 6. Haringey GBR 86, 7. CSKA Sofia BUL 66, 8. Fenerbahce SK TUR 63.
Women   *Schwechat, Austria* *May 29*
1. Levski Sofia BUL 232, 2. Snam Gas Metano ITA,225.5, 3. LUCH Moskva RUS 222, 4. IBL Olimpija Ljubljana SLO 217.5, 5. Stade Français FRA 207, 6. Budapesti Honved SC HUN 207, 11. Essex Ladies GBR 174.5

World Junior Championships

Lisbon   *Jul 20-24*
Men 100m: Deji Aliu NGR 10.21 (+1.2), 200m: Tony Wheeler USA 20.62 (+1.7), 400m: Michael McDonald JAM 45.83, 800m: Paul Byrne AUS 1:47.42, 1500m: Julius Achon UGA 3:39.78, 5000m: Daniel Komen KEN 13:45.37, 10,000m: Komen KEN 28:29.74, 20k Road: Ciodoaldo Silva BRA 63:21, 3000msc: Paul Chemase KEN 8:31.51, 110mh: Frank Busemann GER 13.47 (+2.1), 400mh: Gennady Gorbenko UKR 50.56, HJ: Jagan Hames AUS 2.23m, PV: Viktor Chistyakov RUS 5.60m, LJ: Grega Cankar SLO 8.04m, TJ: Onochie (Larry) Achike GBR 16.67m, SP: Adam Nelson USA 18.34m, DT: Frants Kruger RSA 58.22m, HT: Vladislav Piskunov UKR 71.66m, JT: Marius Corbett RSA 77.98m, Dec: Benjamin Jensen NOR 7676, 10,000m walk: Jorge Segura MEX 40:26.93, 4x100m: GBR 39.60, 4x400m: USA 3:03.32
Women 100m: Sabrina Kelly USA 11.36 (+2.0), 200m: Heide Seyerling RSA 22.80 (+2.2), 400m: Olabisi Afolabi NGR 51.97, 800m: Miaoara Cosulianu ROM 2:04.95, 1500m: Anita Weyermann SUI 4:13.97, 3000m: Gabriela Szabo ROM 8:47.40, 10,000m: Yoko Yamazaki JPN 32:34.11, 100mh: Kirsten Bolm GER 13.26 (+0.5), 400mh: Ionela Tirlea ROM 56.25, HJ: Olga Kaliturina RUS 1.88m, LJ: Yelena Lysak RUS 6.72m, TJ: Yelena Lysak RUS 14.43m, SP: Chen Xiaoyan CHN 18.76m, DT: Corrie de Bruin HOL 55.18m, JT: Taina Uppa FIN 59.02m, Hept: Kathleen Gutjahr GER 5918, 5000mW: Irina Stankina RUS 21:05.41, 4x100m: JAM 44.01, 4x400m: USA 3:32.08

QUOTES

"If she was as much over the limit as the test supposes, she would be a big girl, with a deep voice and a beard. We'd all be calling her Barry White" - **World Cup winning hurdler Tony Jarrett on Diane Modahl.**

"No, I'm not an astro-turf. I wouldn't grass" - **Linford Christie, when asked if he would shop a fellow athlete that he suspected of taking drugs.**

"My view is that there are no more skeletons in the cupboard....." - **Peter Radford, executive chairman of the British Athletics Federation, after Solomon Wariso was withdrawn from the European Championship team.**

"Carl's a nut" - **Christie on Lewis.**

"I was hurting really badly, but I just left it in the hands of the Lord. If he could suffer that much on the cross for us then I could take it for a few more hours out there" - **Alberto Salazar, after his winning comeback, at 35, in the Comrades Marathon.**

"Darren's hand was wavering a bit, but I thought he had it" - **Tony Jarrett explaining how he and Darren Braithwaite had managed to mislay the baton during the heats of the European 4 x 100m relay for which Britain were the favourites.**

"The good thing about Australia is that there are no Americans there" - **Christie, on the advantages of training in Australia.**

"When I was at school I was nicknamed Grasshopper because I had a short body, long skinny legs and knobbly knees" - **Sally Gunnell reminiscing.**

"Eamonn called himself the fattest old git in the 1993 race. Now he can call himself the richest fat old git in the 1994 event" - **Mel Batty, coach and manager to 1993 London winner Martin, after they had negotiated a new six-figure deal in February for the 1994 and 1995 London Marathons.**

"You can't endorse a product without trying it first" - **Eamonn Martin, who is sponsored by Jiffy condoms.**

"There isn't a national federation in the world which comes close to promoting the events we do and every one of them envies us having Andy Norman" - **John Lister, BAF honorary treasurer, offering verbal support to Andy Norman after the first inquiry into his conduct.**

"There was no campaign of any kind by me against Mr Temple.....Cliff was a long-standing friend whom I held in the highest regard" - **Andy Norman, former British Athletics promotions officer.**

"YOU DICK HEADS" - *SUN* **headline the day after Frank Dick resigned.**

IAAF/Mobil Grand Prix I

SAO PAULO INTERNATIONAL
Sao Paulo, Brazil   May 21
Men
100m	1	Dennis Mitchell	USA	10.07
200m	1	Michael Johnson	USA	20.18
400m	1	Darnell Hall	USA	45.65
800m	1	William Tanui	KEN	1:46.38
1500m	1	Vénuste Niyongabo	BUR	3:35.18
3000m	1	Fita Bayesa	ETH	7:49.29
400mh	1	Samuel Matete	ZAM	48.41
HJ	1	Javier Sotomayor	CUB	2.36m
	-	Dalton Grant	GBR	no ht
PV	1	Dean Starkey	USA	5.92m
TJ	1	Mike Conley	USA	17.38m
Women
100m	1	Gwen Torrence	USA	11.07
200m	1	Dannette Young	USA	22.65
400m	1	Sandie Richards	JAM	51.25
3000m	1	Carmen De Oliveira	BRA	9:13.79
400mh	1	Kim Batten	USA	54.83
TJ	1	Inna Lasovskaya	RUS	14.63m
Discus	1	Barbara Echevarria	CUB	65.62m
Javelin	1	Natalya Shikolenko	BLS	67.10m

REEBOK GAMES
New York   May 22
Men
100m	1	Leroy Burrell	USA	10.27
200m	1	Kevin Braunskill	USA	20.73
	2	John Regis	GBR	20.76
400m	1	Antonio Pettigrew	USA	45.07
800m	1	Wilson Kipketer	KEN	1:45.06
400mh	1	Torrance Zellner	USA	49.65
HJ	1	Steinar Hoen	NOR	2.31m
LJ	1	Carl Lewis	USA	8.45m
TJ	1	Brian Wellman	BER	16.71m
	6	Tosi Fasinro	GBR	16.17m
Shot	1	Jim Doehring	USA	21.09m
Women
100m	1	Carlette Guidry	USA	11.31
400m	1	Marie-José Pérec	FRA	50.59
800m	1	Maria Mutola	MOZ	1:59.74
100mh	1	Michelle Freeman	JAM	13.09
LJ	1	Jackie Joyner-Kersee	USA	7.49m

BRUCE JENNER CLASSIC
San Jose City College Stadium   May 28
Men
100m	1	Andre Cason	USA	10.01
200m	1	Daniel Effiong	NGR	20.10
400m	1	Jason Rouser	USA	45.24
1500m	1	Simon Doyle	AUS	3:39.14
110mh	1	Mark Crear	USA	13.44
400mh	1	Derrick Adkins	USA	48.95
HJ	1	Hollis Conway	USA	2.30m
PV	1	Doug Fraley	USA	5.63m
TJ	1	Mike Conley	USA	17.54m
Shot	1	Kevin Toth	USA	21.07m
	9	Paul Edwards	GBR	18.53m
Hammer	1	Lance Deal	USA	75.98m
Discus	1	Nick Sweeney	IRL	61.96m

Women
100m	1	Gail Devers	USA	10.77
400m	1	Marie-José Pérec	FRA	50.65
1500m	1	Gina Procaccio	USA	4:08.77
3000m	1	Annette Peters	USA	8:58.3
100mh	1	Michelle Freeman	JAM	12.74
LJ	1	Jackie Joyner-Kersee	USA	7.30m
Discus	1	Daniela Costian	AUS	63.78m

GOLDEN GALA
Rome   June 8
Men
100m	1	Leroy Burrell	USA	10.06
400m	1	Samson Kitur	KEN	44.32
800m	1	Johnny Gray	USA	1:43.73
	6	Martin Steele	GBR	1:47.09
1500m	1	Vénuste Niyongabo	BUR	3:35.10
5000m	1	Mohamed Issangar	MAR	13:12.13
3000msc	1	Eliud Barngetuny	KEN	8:17.06
400mh	1	Samuel Matete	ZAM	48.11
HJ	1	Javier Sotomayor	CUB	2.37m
PV	1	Piotr Bochkaryov	RUS	5.70m
Shot	1	Kevin Toth	USA	21.01m
Hammer	1	Igor Astapkovich	BLS	83.14m
Women
100m	1	Juliet Cuthbert	JAM	11.22
400m	1	Pauline Davis	BAH	50.59
3000m	1	Roberta Brunet	ITA	8:42.97

3000m times are suspect, could be 6.6 seconds fast

100mh	1	Svetla Dimitrova	BUL	12.64
LJ	1	Heike Drechsler	GER	7.01m
Discus	1	Manuela Tirneci	ROM	64.04m

ATHLETISSIMA, 94
Lausanne, Switzerland   July 6
Men
100m	1	Leroy Burrell	USA	9.85 WR

(wind +1.2, reaction time of 0.140)

200m	1	Frankie Fredericks	NAM	20.10
	2	John Regis	GBR	20.17
800m	1	Wilson Kipketer	KEN	1:44.88
	11	Tom McKean	GBR	1:49.77
3000m	1	Alois Nizigama	BUR	7:40.73
	2	Rob Denmark	GBR	7:42.62
10000m	1	Haile Gebresilasie	ETH	27:15.00
110mh	1	Mark McKoy	AUT	13.19

McKoy's 1st international comp. as an Austrian

400mh	1	Derrick Adkins	USA	47.94
HJ	1	Javier Sotomayor	USA	2.37m
PV	1	Dean Starkey	USA	5.90m
LJ (+1.8)	1	Kareem Streete-Thompson	USA	8.51m
HT	1	Igor Astapkovich	BLS	79.92m
Women
100m(+.9)	1	Irina Privalova	RUS	10.77
200m	1	Irina Privalova	RUS	21.82
400m	1	Maicel Malone	USA	50.05
	7	Phylis Smith	GBR	51.53
1500m	1	Yekaterina Podkopayeva	RUS	4:06.13
	7	Alison Wyeth	GBR	4:08.37
100mh	1	Yordanka Donkova	BUL	12.64
	9	Jackie Agyepong	GBR	12.93
400mh	1	Sally Gunnell	GBR	54.06
JT	1	Natalya Shikolenko	BLS	69.58m

BNP D'ATHLETISME
Lille   *July 8*

Men

100m	1	Leroy Burrell	USA	10.12
200m	1	Oumar Loum	SEN	20.60
400m	1	Antonio Pettigrew	USA	45.29
1500m	1	Noureddine Morceli	ALG	3:30.61
	12	Matthew Yates	GBR	3:39.12
5000m	1	Khalid Skah	MAR	13:00.54
3000msc	1	Richard Kosgei	KEN	8:13.77
400mh	1	Derrick Adkins	USA	47.97
HJ	1	Troy Kemp	BAH	2.28m
PV	1	Okkert Brits	RSA	5.85m
TJ	1	Brian Wellman	BER	17.36m
JT	1	Jan Zelezny	TCH	91.28m

Women

100m	1	Irina Privalova	RUS	11.00
400m	1	Gwen Torrence	USA	50.20
800m	1	Natalya Dukhnova	BLS	2:00.41
	3	Diane Modahl	GBR	2:00.84
1500m	1	Yekaterina Podkopayeva	RUS	4:05.95
100mh	1	Yulia Graudyn	RUS	12.75
LJ (+1.3)	1	Heike Drechsler	GER	7.12m
JT	1	Natalya Shikolenko	BLS	66.98m

DN GALAN
Stockholm   *July 12*

Men

100m	1	Dennis Mitchell	USA	9.97
200m	1	Jeff Williams	USA	20.19
800m	1	Sammy Langat	KEN	1:44.78
1500m	1	Noureddine Morceli	ALG	3:34.09
Vets Mile	1	Dick Quax	NZL	4:39.81
5000m	1	Ismael Kirui	KEN	13:14.46
3000msc	1	Moses Kiptanui	KEN	8:09.16
	9	Tommy Hanlon	GBR	8:27.74
400mh	1	Derrick Adkins	USA	48.83
PV	1	Sergey Bubka	UKR	5.90m
TJ	1	Mike Conley	USA	17.46m
	6	Jonathan Edwards	GBR	16.73m
	9	Tosi Fasinro	GBR	16.35m
JT	1	Jan Zelezny	TCH	83.10m
	5	Mick Hill	GBR	81.26m
4x100m	1	International Team		39.12m

Women

100m	1	Irina Privalova	RUS	10.90
200m	1	Irina Privalova	RUS	22.02
1500m	1	Sonia O'Sullivan	IRL	4:00.46
	4	Kelly Holmes	GBR	4:02.52
5000m	1	Yelena Romanova	RUS	15:05.94
400mh	1	Kim Batten	USA	54.78
LJ	1	Heike Drechsler	GER	7.04m
TJ	1	Inessa Kravets	UKR	14.85m
	7	Michelle Griffith	GBR	13.04m
JT	1	Trine Hattestad	NOR	67.88m

TSB MEETING
London   *July 15*

Men

100m	1	John Drummond	USA	10.03
	2	Linford Christie	GBR	10.07
200m	1	John Regis	GBR	20.42
400m	1	Derek Mills	USA	44.68
	2	Du'aine Ladejo	GBR	45.00
	3	Roger Black	GBR	45.10

800m	1	Vebjørn Rodahl	NOR	1:45.10	
	5	Tom McKean	GBR	1:46.28	
1500m	1	Noureddine Morceli	ALG	3:30.72	
	6	David Strang	GBR	3:36.53	
5000m	1	William Sigei	KEN	13:06.72	
3000msc	1	Tom Buckner	GBR	8:36.77	
110mh	1	Tony Jarrett	GBR	13.32	
400mh	1	Samuel Matete	ZAM	48.22	
	4	Peter Crampton	GBR	49.78	
HJ	1	Javier Sotomayor	CUB	2.41m	
	3	Brendan Reilly	GBR	2.25m	
	4	Dalton Grant	GBR	2.25m	
PV	1	Maksim Tarasov	RUS	5.80m	
TJ	1	Mike Conley	USA	17.32m	
	3	Jonathan Edwards	GBR	16.71m	
JT	1	Mick Hill	GBR	84.22m	
	3	Steve Backley	GBR	79.64m	
4x100m	1	GBR		38.64	

Women

400m	1	Cathy Freeman	AUS	50.77	
800m	1	Kelly Holmes	GBR	1:59.43	
	3	Diane Modahl	GBR	2:00.50	
1500m	1	Lyn Robinson	GBR	4:12.05	
3000m	1	Sonia O'Sullivan	IRL	8:21.64	*ER*
	2	Yvonne Murray	GBR	8:29.60	
100mh	1	Michelle Freeman	JAM	13.03	
400mh	1	Sally Gunnell	GBR	54.04	
TJ (+1.3)	1	Ashia Hansen	GBR	14.04m	
JT	1	Natalya Shikolenko	BLS	71.40m	

NIKAIA-MOBIL MEETING
Nice   *July 18*

Men

100m	1	Dennis Mitchell	USA	10.19
800m	1	Wilson Kipketer	KEN	1:45.52
1500m	1	Vénuste Niyongabo	BUR	3:30.95
	7	Matthew Yates	GBR	3:36.47
3000m	1	Paul Bitok	KEN	7:34.36
3000msc	1	Richard Kosgei	KEN	8:11.83
	9	Justin Chaston	GBR	8:23.90
100mh	1	Mark McKoy	AUT	13.28
400mh	1	Derrick Adkins	USA	47.84
HJ	1	Javier Sotomayor	CUB	2.40m
	6	Dalton Grant	GBR	2.28m
PV	1	Sergey Bubka	UKR	5.90m
HT	1	Andrey Abduvaliyev	TJK	80.26m

Women

100m	1	Carlette Guidry	USA	11.17	
400m	1	Natasha Kaiser-Brown	USA	50.92	
1500m	1	Sonia O'Sullivan	IRL	3:59.10	
	5	Alison Wyeth	GBR	4:04.19	
3000m	1	Yelena Romanova	RUS	8:43.70	
100mh	1	Yordanka Donkova	BUL	12.70	
400mh	1	Kim Batten	USA	53.72	
	2	Sally Gunnell	GBR	53.91	
TJ	1	Innesa Kravets	UKR	14.58m	
DT	1	Ilke Wyludda	GER	65.28m	

MOBIL BISLETT GAMES
Oslo   *July 22*

Men

100m(+1.9)	1	Dennis Mitchell	USA	9.94
200m	1	Geir Moen	NOR	20.40
800m	1	Wilson Kipketer	KEN	1:43.29
	9	Tom McKean	GBR	1:46.20

Event	Pos	Name	Nat	Mark
Mile	1	Vénuste Niyongabo	BUR	3:48.94
	7	Kevin McKay	GBR	3:53.64
5000m	1	Khalid Skah	MAR	13:01.89
	11	Rob Denmark	GBR	13:32.60
10000m	1	William Sigei	KEN	26:52.23 WR
100mh	1	Colin Jackson	GBR	13.22
	2	Tony Jarrett	GBR	13.35
400mh	1	Derrick Adkins	USA	47.93
	3	Gary Cadogan	GBR	49.07
HJ	1	Steinar Hoen	NOR	2.35m
	=5	Brendan Reilly	GBR	2.20m
	10	Steve Smith	GBR	2.20m
JT	1	Patrik Bodén	SWE	83.38m
	4	Mick Hill	GBR	81.50m
	7	Steve Backley	GBR	80.98m
Women				
200m	1	Gwen Torrence	USA	21.94
1 Mile	1	Sonia O'Sullivan	IRL	4:17.25
	2	Yvonne Murray	GBR	4:22.64
100mh	1	Yordanka Donkova	BUL	12.76
	5	Jackie Agyepong	GBR	13.12
HJ	1	Hanne Haugland	NOR	1.97m
	8	Debbie Marti	GBR	1.80m
LJ	1	Jackie Joyner-Kersee	USA	7.33m
JT	1	Trine Hattestad	NOR	71.32m

GATORADE HERCULIS
Monte Carlo   Aug 2

Men

Event	Pos	Name	Nat	Mark
100m	1	Jon Drummond	USA	10.13
200m	1	Michael Johnson	USA	19.94
	2	John Regis	GBR	20.01
400m	1	Derek Mills	USA	44.73
	3	Du'aine Ladejo	GBR	44.94
	4	Roger Black	GBR	45.08
800m	1	Wilson Kipketer	KEN	1:43.68
1500m	1	Vénuste Niyongabo	BUR	3:32.25
3000m	1	Noureddine Morceli	ALG	7:25.11 WR
5000m	1	Simon Chemwoiyo	KEN	13:07.57
110mh	1	Colin Jackson	GBR	13.26
	3	Tony Jarrett	GBR	13.33
400mh	1	Samuel Matete	ZAM	47.90
3000msc	1	Eliud Barngetuny	KEN	8:10.84
TJ	1	Brian Wellman	BER	17.24m
	3	Jonathan Edwards	GBR	17.06m
JT	1	Dag Wennlund	SWE	84.36m
PV	1	Kory Tarpenning	USA	5.80m

Women

Event	Pos	Name	Nat	Mark
100m	1	Gwen Torrence	USA	10.87
400m	1	Marie-José Pérec	FRA	49.95
1500m	1	Yekaterina Podkopayeva	RUS	4:00.89
	8	Alison Wyeth	GBR	4:05.65
100mh	1	Svetla Dimitrova	BUL	12.53
400mh	1	Anna Knoroz	RUS	54.75
HJ	1	Britta Bilac	SLO	1.97m
LJ	1	Heike Drechsler	GER	7.15m
DT	1	Ilke Wyludda	GER	66.12m

WELTKLASSE
Zurich   Aug 17

Men

Event	Pos	Name	Nat	Mark
100m(-1.4)	1	Linford Christie	GBR	10.05
200m(-1.9)	1	Michael Johnson	USA	20.33
400m	1	Derek Mills	USA	44.93
	4	Roger Black	GBR	45.17
800m	1	Wilson Kipketer	KEN	1:46.12

Event	Pos	Name	Nat	Mark
1500m	1	Vénuste Niyongabo	BUR	3:36.15
	5	Matthew Yates	GBR	3:39.60
Mile	1	Andrey Bulkovsky	UKR	3:55.28
5000m	1	Noureddine Morceli	ALG	13:03.85
3000msc	1	Moses Kiptanui	KEN	8:08.80
110mh(-0.7)	1	Colin Jackson	GBR	13.19
400mh	1	Derrick Adkins	USA	47.90
HJ	1	Steve Smith	GBR	2.28m
	=5	Dalton Grant	GBR	2.20m
PV	=1	Sergey Bubka	UKR	5.70m
	=1	Rodion Gataullin	RUS	5.70m
	=1	Maksim Tarasov	RUS	5.70m
HT	1	Andrey Abduvaliev	TJK	83.24m
Women				
200m(-1.0)	1	Irina Privalova	RUS	22.15
800m	1	Maria Mutola	MOZ	1:55.19
Mile	1	Hassiba Boulmerka	ALG	4:22.09
100mh(-1.5)	1	Svetla Dimitrova	BUL	12.61
LJ(-0.8)	1	Inessa Kravets	UKR	7.09m
DT	1	Ellina Zveryova	BLS	66.58m

MEMORIAL IVO VAN DAMME
Brussels   Aug 19

Event	Pos	Name	Nat	Mark
100m(-0.1)	1	Linford Christie	GBR	10.03
200m(+0.6)	1	Michael Johnson	USA	20.02
800m	1	Patrick Konchellah	KEN	1:44.70
1500m	1	Vénuste Niyongabo	BUR	3:34.35
	7	Matthew Yates	GBR	3:37.82
5000m	1	James Kariuki	KEN	13:25.20
10,000m	1	Haile Gebresilasie	ETH	27:20.39
3000msc	1	Eliud Barngetuny	KEN	8:17.03
110mh(0.0)	1	Colin Jackson	GBR	13.22
		Tony Jarrett GBR disq - 2 false starts		
400mh	1	Samuel Matete	ZAM	48.15
HJ	1	Troy Kemp	BAH	2:31m
	2	Steve Smith	GBR	2.31m
PV	1	Sergey Bubka	UKR	5.95m
LJ(+0.2)	1	Mike Powell	USA	8.58m
JT	1	Jan Zelezny	TCH	88.34m
	3	Mick Hill	GBR	83.16m
Women				
100m(0.0)	1	Gwen Torrence	USA	10.83
200m(0.0)	1	Irina Privalova	RUS	22.22
1500m	1	Yvonne Graham	JAM	4:04.35
100mh(0.0)	1	Svetla Dimitrova	BUL	12.76
LJ	1	Jackie Joyner-Kersee	USA	7.11m
DT	1	Ellina Zveryova	BLS	67.44m

WELTKLASSE
Cologne   Aug 21

Men

Event	Pos	Name	Nat	Mark
100m(-0.3)	1	Dennis Mitchell	USA	10.13
800m	1	Mark Everett	USA	1:44.36
	3	Noureddine Morceli	ALG	1:44.89
		Morceli's 1st loss at any distance for almost 2 yrs		
1500m	1	Vénuste Niyongabo	BUR	3:31.98
3000m	1	Dieter Baumann	GER	7:34.69
110mh(+0.4)	1	Mark Crear	USA	13.13
400mh	1	Samuel Matete	ZAM	48.20
HJ	1	Javier Sotomayor	CUB	2.34m
PV	1	Rodion Gataullin	RUS	5.88m
TJ(-0.2)	1	Mike Conley	USA	17.20m
DT	1	Dmitry Shevchenko	RUS	64.24m

Women

100m(-0.1)	1	Gwen Torrence	USA	10.95
800m	1	Maria Mutola	MOZ	1:57.58
1500m	1	Yekaterina Podkopayeva	RUS	4:01.58
5000m	1	Sonia O'Sullivan	IRL	15:06.18
100mh(+0.9)	1	Svetla Dimitrova	BUL	12.67
400mh	1	Kim Batten	USA	54.47
LJ(-0.1)	1	Jackie Joyner-Kersee	USA	7.10m
JT	1	Trine Hattestad	NOR	70.44m

ISTAF '94

Berlin *Aug 30*

Men

100m(+1.0)	1	Dennis Mitchell	USA	10.00
	3	Linford Christie	GBR	10.02
400m	1	Michael Johnson	USA	44.04
	3	Roger Black	GBR	45.09
800m	1	Wilson Kipketer	KEN	1:43.95
1500m	1	Vénuste Niyongabo	BUR	3:31.16
	2	Matthew Yates	GBR	3:35.32
5000m	1	Dieter Baumann	GER	13:12.47
3000msc	1	Moses Kiptanui	KEN	8:09.16
	8	Mark Rowland	GBR	8:22.20
110mh(+0.9)	1	Colin Jackson	GBR	13.02
400mh	1	Samuel Matete	ZAM	48.22
HJ	=1	Troy Kemp	BAH	2.30m
	=1	Javier Sotomayor	CUB	2.30m
PV	1	Sergey Bubka	UKR	6.05m
LJ	1	Mike Powell	USA	8.20m
JT	1	Andrey Moruyev	RUS	85.18m
	5	Steve Backley	GBR	82.28m
	8	Mick Hill	GBR	77.18m

Women

200m(+0.4)	1	Merlene Ottey	JAM	22.07
1500m	1	Angela Chalmers	CAN	4:04.39
5000m	1	Alison Wyeth	GBR	15:10.38
100mh(+1.1)	1	Yulia Graudyn	RUS	12.62
LJ(-0.1)	1	Heike Drechsler	GER	6.91m
DT	1	Daniela Costian	AUS	66.06m

IAAF/MOBIL GRAND PRIX FINAL

Paris *Sep 3*

Men

100m(-0.6)	1	Dennis Mitchell	USA	10.12
	2	Linford Christie	GBR	10.13
		Christie's fifth defeat of the summer		
400m	1	Derek Mills	USA	45.22
	4	Roger Black	GBR	45.39
	7	Du'aine Ladejo	GBR	45.80
1500m	1	Noureddine Morceli	ALG	3:40.89
	4	Matthew Yates	GBR	3:42.79
5000m	1	Khalid Skah	MAR	13:14.63
110mh	1	Colin Jackson	GBR	13.08
(-0.8)		*Jackson's 33rd consecutive victory*		
400mh	1	Samuel Matete	ZAM	48.02
HJ	1	Javier Sotomayor	CUB	2.33m
PV	1	Sergey Bubka	UKR	5.90m
TJ	1	Mike Conley	USA	17.68m
SP	1	Randy Barnes	USA	20.60m
HT	1	Andrey Abduvaliyev	TJK	81.46m

Men's final Grand Prix standings
1. Noureddine Morceli 78pts ($100,000); 2. Samuel Matete ZAM 72 ($50,000); 3. Mike Conley USA 72 ($30,000); 4. Dennis Mitchell USA 72 ($20,000); 5. Javier Sotomayor 72 ($15,000); 6. Andrey Abduvaliyev TJK 68 ($13,000); 13. Linford Christie GBR 57.

Women

100m(+0.4)	1	Merlene Ottey	JAM	10.78
		Equals Ottey's best - only 3 women, Ashford		
		Privalova and Griffith-Joyner have run faster		
400m	1	Marie-José Pérec	FRA	49.77
1500m	1	Angela Chalmers	CAN	4:01.61
5000m	1	Sonia O'Sullivan	IRL	15:12.94
	3	Alison Wyeth	GBR	15:15.45
100mh	1	Svetla Dimitrova	BUL	12.66
(-0.5)				
LJ	1	Jackie Joyner-Kersee	USA	7.21m
DT	1	Ilka Wyludda	GER	65.84m
JT	1	Natalya Shikolenko	BLS	68.26m

Women's final Grand Prix standings
1. Jackie Joyner-Kersee USA 72 ($100,000); 2. Svetla Dimitrova BUL 72 ($50,000); 3. Sonia O'Sullivan IRL 72 ($30,000); 4. Natalya Shikolenko BLS 70 ($20,000); 5. Gwen Torrence USA 66 ($15,000); 6. Ilka Wyludda GER 66 ($13,000); 7. Heike Drechsler GER 63 ($12,000)

Grand Prix Prize Money
Morceli and Joyner-Kersee collect $100,000 as the overall GP winners, but they each also won another $30,000 as individual champions in the 1500m and Long Jump respectively.

IAAF/Mobil Grand Prix II

BRATISLAVA *June 1*
Men 100m: Daniel Effiong NGR 10.80 (+1.4), 6th Darren Braithwaite GBR 20.26; 200m: Daniel Effiong NGR 20.21 (+1.3), 3rd John Regis GBR 20.51; 1500m: Vénuste Niyongabo BUR 3:35.61; 3000m: Johnstone Kipkoech KEN 7:48.26; 110mh: Tony Jarrett GBR 13.40 (+0.7); 400mh: Samuel Matete ZAM 48.24, 5th Peter Crampton GBR 50.27; PV: Sergey Bubka UKR 5.85m; TJ: Vasily Sokov RUS 17.43 (+1.4), 4th Jonathan Edwards GBR 17.02 (+3.9); 5000mw: Sergey Korepanov KZK 19:21.51
Women 100m: Gwen Torrence USA 11.12 (+1.1); 200m: Dannette Young USA 22.49 (+1.3); 800m: Lyubov Kremlyova RUS 2:00.34; 5000m: Viktoria Nenasheva RUS 15:39.79; 400m: Sally Gunnell GBR 54.74; HJ: Yelena Gulyayeva RUS 1.95m; TJ: Inna Lasovskaya RUS 14.94m (+0.2); JT: Yekaterina Ivakina RUS 64.04m

HENGELO *June 4*
Men 100m: Leroy Burrell USA 10.08 (+0.9); 400m: Neil de Silva TRI 46.23; 800m: Vebjørn Rodal NOR 1:45.29; 1500m: Kevin McKay GBR 3:38.08; 5000m: Haile Gebresilasie 12:56.96 WR *(Kilometre splits 2:36.6/2:37.1/2:37.2/2:37.4/2:28.7)*; 110mh: Allen Johnson USA 13.50 (+1.2); PV: 1= Yevgeny Krasnov ISR & Scott Huffman USA 5.31m; LJ: Mike Powell USA 7.90m (-1.4); SP: Jim Doehring USA 20.19m; DT: Attila Horváth HUN 60.76m
Women 100m: Juliet Cuthbert JAM 11.24 (+0.9); 800m: Ellen van Langen HOL 2:00.38; 3000m: Lyudmila Borisova RUS 8:55.53; LJ: Mirela Dulgheru ROM 6.47m; SP: Astrid Kumbernuss GER 19.56m; DT: Daniela Costian AUS 62.32m

SEVILLE *June 5*
Men 100m: Linford Christie 10.31 (-2.0); 400m: Kennedy Ochieng KEN 45.20; 1500m: Rachid El Basir MAR 3:36.36; 5000m: Brahim Jabbour MAR 13:29.50; 10,000m: Paulo Guerra POR 28:25.62; 110mh: Emilio Valle CUB 13.81; 400mh: Oleg Tverdokhleb UKR 49.23; HJ: Javier Sotomayor CUB 2.42m; TJ: Denis Kapustin RUS 17.86 (+5.7); HT: Igor Astapkovich BLS 83.00m; 4 x 100m: Cuba 39.63
Women 200m: Dannette Young USA 22.65 (-1.9); 800m: Meredith Rainey USA 2:01.98; 1500m: Carla Sacramento POR 4:07.65; 5000m: Derartu Tulu ETH 15:40.29; 100mh: Svetla Dimitrova BUL 12.65; LJ: Ludmila Ninova AUT 7.09 (+1.6); JT: Natalya Shikolenko BLS 71.40m; 4 x 100m: Cuba 45.48

ST DENIS *June 10*
Men 200m: Frankie Fredericks NAM 20.45; 400m: Samson Kitur KEN 45.65; 1500m: Vénuste Niyongabo BUR 3:37.54; 5000m: Khalid Skah MAR 13:10.51; 300msc: Matthew Birir KEN 8:21.33; 110mh: Mark McKoy CAN 13.41; 400mh: Samuel Matete ZAM 48.82; PV: Sergey Bubka UKR 5.89m. LJ: Mike Powell 8.38m (+1.4); JT: Raymond Hecht GER 89.08m
Women Zhanna Tarnapolskaya UKR 11.12 (+1.1); 200m: Marie-José Pérec FRA 22.61; 800m: Ellen van Langen HOL 2:00.49; 10,000m: Derartu Tulu ETH 31:48.93; 100mh: Svetla Dimitrova BUL 12.50 (+2.7); 400mh: Deon Hemmings JAM 55.24; HJ: Inga Babakova UKR 1.95m; DT: Ellina Zveryova BLS 64.86m

HELSINKI *June 29*
Men 100m: Slip Watkins USA 10.30 (+0.6); 200m: Frankie Fredericks NAM 20.30 (+0.2); 400m: Antonio Pettigrew USA 45.10; 800m: Vebjørn Rodal NOR 1:44.30; 10,000m: Antonio Serrano ESP 27:56.99; 110mh: Eugene Swift USA 13.40 (+0.2); 400mh: Giorgio Frinoli ITA 49.47; PV: Scott Huffman USA 5.80m; LJ: Kareem Streete-Thompson USA 8.02 (+1.0); SP: C. J. Hunter USA 20.20m; JT: Jan Zelezny TCH 88.04m
Women 100m: Merlene Ottey JAM 11.02 (-0.1); 800m: Natalya Dukhnova BLS 1:58.29, 2nd Kelly Holmes GBR 2:00.48; 3000m: Kathy Franey USA 8:46.04; LJ: Nicole Boegman AUS 6.65m (+0.8); JT: Trine Hattestad NOR 69.96m; 4 x 100m: Great Britain 44.12

GATESHEAD *Jul 1*
Men. 100m: Linford Christie 10.46 (-2.0); 200m: Frankie Fredericks 20.75 (-1.0); 400m: Antonio Pettigrew USA 45.19; 800m: Mark Everett USA 1:47.16; Mile: Kevin McKay 3: 58.72; 110mh: Colin Jackson 13.51 (-2.8); 400mh: Torrance Zellner USA 49.95; HJ: Tim Forsyth AUS 2.28m; PV: Rodion Gataullin RUS 5.80m; TJ: Edrick Floreal CAN 17.13m; JT: Jan Zelezny TCH 91.68m.
Women. 400m: Jearl Miles USA 51.57; 800m: Ellen van Langen HOL 2:00.54; Mile: Sonia O'Sullivan IRL 4:25.77; 100mh: LaVonna Martin-Floreal USA 13.27(-4.7); 400mh: Sally Gunnell 54.69; TJ: Inna Lasovskaya RUS 14.40m; SP: Larisa Peleshenko RUS 18.98m; JT: Yekaterina Ivakina RUS 61.66m.

LINZ *Jul 4*
Men 100m: Davidson Ezinwa NGR 9.94 (+0.2) 3rd Linford Christie GBR 10.03; 200m: Daniel Effiong NGR 20.30 (+0.2); 800m: Wilson Kipketer KEN 1:45.35; 1500m: Branko Zorko CRO 3:40.07; 3000msc: Richard Kosgei

KEN 8:25.13; 110mh: Mark McKoy AUT 13.15 (-0.1); 400mh: Derrick Adkins USA 47.70; LJ: Kareem Streete-Thompson USA 8.63m (+0.5); SP: C. J. Hunter USA 20.31m; HT: Igor Astapkovich BLS 80.72m
Women 100m: Gwen Torrence USA 10.89 (+0.4); 400m: Natasha Kaiser-Brown USA 50.89; 1500m: Lyudmila Rogachova RUS 4:12.40; 3000m: Yvonne Graham JAM 8:56.15; 100mh: Tatyana Reshetnikova RUS 12.53 (+0.2); HJ: Britta Bilac SLO 1.94m; TJ: Inna Lasovskaya RUS 14.81m (+0.4); DT: Ilka Wyludda GER 65.52m

OTHER MEETINGS

GÖTZIS MULTI-EVENTS *May 28-29*
Decathlon 1. Eduard Hämäläinen BLS 8735 (10.50/7.26m/16.05m/2.11m/47.63/13.82/49.70/4.90m/ 60.32m/4:35.09), 2. Henrik Dagård SWE 8359 *NR*, 3. Stefan Schmid GER 8201, 7. Alex Kruger GBR 8078
Heptathlon 1. Sabine Braun 6665 (13.39/1.87m/14.57m/24.31/6.63m/49.68m/2:18.39), 2. Turchinskaya RUS 6596, 3. Rita Ináncsi HUN 6573 *NR*

CHINESE CHAMPIONSHIPS *Beijing, June 1-5*
100m: Chen Wenzhong 10.46; 200m: Chen Wenzhong 21.16; 400m: Lei Quan 46.66; 800m: Min Weiguo 1:47.14 *NR*; 1500m: Sun Mingyou 3:45.12; 5000m: Sun Reping 14:04.63; 3000msc: Gao Shuhai 8:31.56; 110mh: Zhen Yanhao 13.71; 400mh: Yang Xianjun 50.94; HJ: Tao Xu 2.28m; LJ: Huang Geng 8.15m; TJ: Zhou Sixin 16.47m; SP: Lin Hao 19.14m; DT: Ma Wei 58.98m; HT: Bi Zhong 72.46m; JT: Zhang Lianbiao 80.08m
Women 100m: Wang Xiaoyan 11.42; 200m: Chen Zhaojing 22.97; 400m: Ma Yuqin 50.45; 800m: Qu Yunxia 1:59.37; 1500m: Qu Yunxia 4:00.34, 3rd Wang Junxia 4:11.20; 3000m: Wang Xiaoxia 8:49.92, 5th Wang Junxia 8:50.79; 10,000m: Wang Junxia 31:38.17; 100mh: Zhang Yu 12.87; 400mh: Long Xueyan 56.28; PV: Cai Weiyan 3.85m; HJ: Lui Bo 1.85m; LJ: Li Jing 6.88m; TJ: Ren Ruiping 14.36m *WJR*; SP: Zhang Liuhong 20.54m; DT: Qiu Qiaoping 65.66m; JT: Zhang Li 61.34m; Hept: Zhang Xiaohui 6200 pts

MOSCOW *June 5*
Men 200m: Daniel Effiong NGR 20.76 (-1.1); 400m: Butch Reynolds USA 45.90; 800m: Charlez Nkazamyampi BUR 1:48.57; 1500m: Vyacheslav Shabunin RUS 3:40.57; 5000m: Ismael Kirui KEN 13:41.90; 110mh: Vladimir Belokon UKR 13.58 (-0.5); PV: Rodion Gataullin 5.85m; TJ: Oleg Sakirkin KZK 17.35m (+0.9); HT: Andrey Abduvaliyev TJK 81.20m.
Women 100m: Zhanna Tarnapolskaya UKR 11.16 (-0.8); 400m: Svetlana Goncharenko RUS 51.18; 800m: Yelena Storchevaya UKR 2:01.25; 1500m: Lyubov Kremlyova RUS 4:10.41; 100mh: Natalya Yudakova RUS 13.17; 400mh: Vera Ordina RUS 54.95; HJ: Yelena Gulyayeva RUS 1.98m;
TJ: Inna Lasovskaya RUS 14.48m; Shot: Larisa Peleshenko RUS 19.81m; Discus: Ilke Wyludda GER 65.12m.

US CHAMPIONSHIPS *Knoxville, June 14-18*
USA unless stated **Men** 100m: Dennis Mitchell 10.13 (-1.6); 200m: Ron Clark 20.77; 400m: Antonio Pettigrew 44.43; 800m: Mark Everett 1:46.08; 1500m: Terrance Herrington 3:37.77; 5000m: Matt Giusto 14:04.30; 10,000m: L Ansbury 29:01.84; 3000msc: Marc Croghan 8:23.47; 110mh: Mark Crear 13.36 (-0.8); 400mh: Derrick

Adkins 48.41; PV: Scott Huffman 5.97m *NR*; HJ: Hollis Conway 2.28m; LJ: Mike Powell 8.68m (+4.1); TJ: Mike Conley 17.51m (-0.8); SP:C.J.Hunter 20.82m; DT: Mike Gravelle 61.38m; HT: Lance Deal 82.50 *NR*; JT: Riech 77.86m; Dec: Dan O'Brien 8707 (10.31w/7.81m/15.87m/2.17m/48.19/13.98/ 46.34m/5.15m/62.28m/5:16.42)
Women 100m: Gail Devers 11.12 (-0.9); 200m: Carlette Guidry 22.71; 400m: Natasha Kaiser-Brown 50.73; 800m: Joetta Clark 2:00.41; 1500m: Regina Jacobs 4:07.71; 3000m: Annette Peters 9:01.69; 5000m: Ceci St Geme 15:57.71; 10,000m: Olga Appell MEX 32:23.76; 100mh: Jackie Joyner-Kersee 12.88; 400mh: Kim Batten 54.51; PV: Price 3.25m; HJ: Angie Bradburn 1.92m; LJ: Jackie Joyner-Kersee 7.14 (+2.3); TJ: Sheila Hudson-Strudwick 14.23 (+1.0) *NR*; SP: Connie Price-Smith 19.60m; DT Connie Price-Smith 59.46m; HT: Fitts 58.06; JT: Donna Mayhew 58.94m; Hept: Kym Carter 6371 (13.55/1.87m./16.07m/ 24.16/6.10m/32.88m/2:10.85)

HECHTEL, BELGIUM *July 30*
Men 100m: Mark Witherspoon 10.36 (0.0); 200m: Mark Witherspoon USA 20.66; 400m: Ogola UGA 46.38; 800m: Nixon Kiprotich KEN 1:44.48; 1500m: Benson Koech KEN 3:36.05; 2 Miles: Moses Kiptanui KEN 8:09.01 *WR*; 5000m: Ismael Kirui KEN 13:23.04; 3000msc: Barmasai KEN 8:20.96; 110mh: Courtney Hawkins USA 13.42 (+0.6); PV: Denis Petuschinsky RUS 5.70m
Women 100m: Jacqueline Poelman HOL 11.27; 400m: Solvi NOR 53.13; 800m:Lyubov Gurina RUS 1:56.53; 1500: Yekaterina Podkopayeva RUS 4:06.90; 5000m: Slegers 15:39.98; 100mh: Lynda Tolbert USA 13.80 (+0.7); SP: Huang Zhihong CHN 20.00m; DT: Mette Bergman NOR 66.26m

SESTRIERE, ITALY *July 31*
Men 100m: Leroy Burrell USA 10.00 (+3.5), 4th John Regis GBR 10.10; 200m: John Regis GBR 19.87 (+1.8) *ER*; 400m: Derek Mills USA 44.59; 800m: Patrick Konchellah KEN 1:46.73; 110mh: Colin Jackson GBR 12.94 (+2.8); 400m: Derrick Adkins USA 48.20, 3rd Gary Cadogan GBR 49.48; PV: Sergey Bubka UKR 6.14m *WR*; LJ: Mike Powell USA 8.95m (+3.9); SP: Kevin Toth USA 20.40m
Women 100m: Melinda Gainsford AUS 11.12 (+1.9); 100mh: Yulia Graudyn RUS 12.51 (+3.3); 400mH: Olga Nazarova RUS 55.41; LJ: Jackie Joyner-Kersee USA 7.49m (+1.7), 2nd Heike Drechsler 7.39 (+3.3)

USA v AFRICA *Durham, North Carolina, Aug 12-13*
Men 100m: Dennis Mitchell USA 9.94 (+0.5); 200m: Frankie Fredericks AFR 20.23 (+1.2); 400m: Michael Johnson USA 44.32; 800m: Mark Everett USA 1:44.86; 1500m: Seddiki AFR 3:40.48; 3000m: Paul Bitok AFR 7:44.41; 3000msc: William Mutwol AFR 8:35.05 *Matthew Birir finished first in 8:33.78 but ran as a guest*; 110mh: (+1.5) Mark Crear USA 13.20; 400mh: Samuel Matete AFR 47.90; HJ: Hollis Conway USA 2.23m; LJ: Mike Powell USA 8.02m; TJ: Kenny Harrison USA 17.38w; SP: Randy Barnes USA 20.75m; 4 x 100m: Africa 38.72; 4 x 400m: USA 3:01.70 **Match result** USA 147 Africa 115
Women 100m: Gwen Torrence USA 10.78 (0.0); 200m: Gwen Torrence USA 21.85 (-0.8); 400m: Maicel Malone USA 50.71; 800m: Maria Mutola AFR 1:58.15; 1500m: Regina Jacobs USA 4:10.24; 3000m: Annette Peters USA 9:14.87; 100mh: Jackie Joyner-Kersee USA 13.12 (+0.3);

400mh: Kim Batten USA 55.05; LJ: Christy Opara-Thompson 6.65w; 4 x 100m: USA 42.45; 4 x 400m: USA 3:26.63 **Match result** USA 68 Africa 46

GOTHENBURG *Aug 24*
Men 100m: Jon Drummond USA 10.21 (-0.1); 200m: Geir Moen NOR 20.54 (+0.5); 800m: Wilson Kipketer KEN 1:43.64; 1500m: Steve Holman USA 3:37.62; 2 miles: Marc Davis USA 8:12.74; 110mh: Mark Crear USA 13.30 (+0.2); 400mh: Oleg Tverdokhleb UKR 49.16; PV: Sergey Bubka UKR 5.80m; LJ: Stanislav Tarasenko RUS 8.28 (+2.9); JT: Jan Zelezny TCH 89.92m
Women 100m: Gwen Torrence USA 11.09 (-2.7); 200m: Merlene Ottey JAM 22.51 (-0.6); 1000m: Maria Mutola MOZ 2:33.02; 400mh: Anna Knoroz RUS 54.78; HJ: Yelena Topchina RUS 1.87m

COPENHAGEN *Aug 28*
Men 100m: Sam Jefferson 10.30 (-0.6); 200m: Michael Johnson USA 20.21 (+0.6); 800m: Wilson Kipketer KEN 1:44.51; 1500m: Andersen DEN 3:39.71; 5000m: William Sigei KEN 13:25.42; HJ: Steinar Hoen NOR 2.25m; PV: Igor Potapovich RUS 5.60m; JT: Patrik Boden SWE 81.98m
Women 100m: Merlene Ottey JAM 10.97 (+2.2); 200m: Danette Young USA 23.03; 800m: Regina Jacobs USA 2:01.89; 5000m: Hilde Stavik NOR 15:23.38; HJ: Britta Bilac SLO 1.91m; LJ: Renata Nielsen DEN 6.87m; JT: Jette Jeppesen DEN 60.24m

McDONALD'S GAMES
Sheffield *Sept 4*
Men 150: Linford Christie GBR 14.97 (+0.9) *NR*, 200 Frankie Fredericks NAM 20.35 (+0.9), 300m: Roger Black GBR 32.45, 800m: Patrick Konchellah KEN 1:46.31, 1m: John Mayock GBR 3:58.34, 110m: Colin Jackson 13.03 (+1.3), 400mh: Oleg Tverdokhleb UKR 49.29, HJ: Steve Smith GBR 2.24m, PV: Pat Manson USA 5.80m, TJ: Julian Golley GBR 16.75 (+2.1), JT: Jan Zelezny TCH 91.82m
Women 200m: Zhanna Tarnopolskaya UKR 22.86, 400m: Maicel Malone USA 50.77, 800m: Kelly Holmes GBR 2:01.56, 2000m: Angela Chalmers CAN 5:34.49 *NR*, 100mh: Svetla Dimitrova BUL 12.85 (+1.8), 400mh: Sally Gunnell GBR 55.24, TJ: Anna Biryukova RUS 14.70, SP: Hunag Zhihong CHN 19.54

MADRID *Sept 6*
Men 100m: Dennis Mitchell USA 10.12 (0.0), 200m: Frankie Fredericks NAM 20.26 (-0.1), 400m: Michael Johnson USA 43.90, 1000m: Vénuste Niyongabo BUR 2:15.91, 3000m: Aloÿs Nizigama BUR 7:47.49, 110m: Colin Jackson GBR 12.99 (-0.3), 400mh: Samuel Matete ZAM 48.03, HJ: Javier Sotomayor CUB 2.37m, LJ: Mike Powell USA 8.22m, JT: Juha Laukkanen FIN 83.50m
Women 100m: Irina Privalova RUS 11.02 (0.0), 400m: Sandra Myers ESP 50.33, 800m: Natalya Dukhnova BLS 1:58.88, HJ: Britta Bilac SLO 1.94m

TALENCE MULTI-EVENTS *France Sept 10-11*
Decathlon: 1. Dan O'Brien USA 8710 (10.43/7.75m/15.81m/2.06m/48.06/13.91/48.88m/5.20m /59.56m/4:56.58), 2. Eduard Hämäläinen BLS 8459, 3. Alain Blondel FRA 8439
Heptathlon: 1. Heike Drechsler GER 6741 (13.34/1.84m/13.58m/22.84/6.95m/40.64/2:11.53), 2. Nathalie Teppe FRA 6361, 3. Turchinskaya RUS 6294

Domestic Events

AAA CHAMPIONSHIPS

Sheffield　　　*June 11-12*

Men

100m	1	Linford Christie	TVH	9.91
(+3.7)	2	Toby Box	W & B	10.07
	3	Mike Rosswess	Birchfield	10.07
200m	1	Solomon Wariso	Haringey	20.67
(+3.2)	2.	Philip Goedluck	Belgrave	20.83
	3	Douglas Walker	GEC	20.85
400m	1	Roger Black	Team Solent	44.94
	2	Du'aine Ladejo	Belgrave	45.36
	3	Brian Whittle	Haringey	45.46
800m	1	Craig Winrow	Wigan	1:48.45
	2	V Malakwen	KEN	1:48.65
	3	Martin Steele	Longwood	1:48.68
1500m	1	Kevin McKay	Sale	3:40.59
	2	David Strang	Haringey	3:40.85
	3	Gary Lough	Annadale	3:41.71
5000m	1	Dermot Donnelly	Annadale	13:52.63
	2	Darren Mead	Belgrave	13:54.08
	3	Richard Findlow	Bradford	13:55.75
10,000m	1	Rob Denmark	Basildon	28:03.34
	2	Martin Jones	Horsham	28:33.18
	3	J Hobbs	Cardiff	28:45.86
3000msc	1	Justin Chaston	Belgrave	8:28.28
	2	Spencer Duval	Cannock	8:28.33
	3	Colin Walker	Gateshead	8:29.65
110mh	1	Andy Tulloch	W & B	13.70
(+0.8)	2	Paul Gray	Cardiff	13.76
	3	Lloyd Cowan	Haringey	14.09
400mh	1	Peter Crampton	Spenborough	49.82
	2	Steven Coupland	Sheffield	50.19
	3	Noel Levy	Blackheath	50.89
PV	1	Andy Ashurst	Sale	5.30m
	2	Kevin Hughes	Haringey	5.20m
	3	Mike Edwards	Belgrave	5.20m
HJ	1	Brendan Reilly	Loughborough	2.24m
	2	Geoff Parsons	Blue Circle	2.20m
	3	A Burke	IRL	2.15m
LJ	1	Barrington Williams	Cannock	7.77m
(+0.9)	2	Fred Salle	Belgrave	7.60m
	3	M Morgan	Belgrave	7.59m
TJ	1	Jonathan Edwards	Gateshead	17.39m
	2	Julian Golley	TVH	16.98m
	3	Francis Agyepong	Shaftesbury	16.95m
SP	1	Paul Edwards	Belgrave	18.32m
	2	J McNamara	AUS	17.16m
	3	Lee Newman	Blackheath	17.02m
DT	1	Kevin Brown	Birchfield	58.60m
	2	Robert Weir	Birchfield	57.94m
	3	Glen Smith	Solihull	56.22m
HT	1	Peter Vivian	TVH	70.80m
	2	Paul Head	Newham	69.08m
	3	Mike Jones	Shaftesbury	67.42m
JT	1	Mick Hill	Leeds	84.60m
	2	Steve Backley	Cambridge H	84.24m
	3	Colin McKenzie	N & EB	79.16m

Women

100m	1	Katharine Merry	Birchfield	11.27
(+2.9)	2	Stephanie Douglas	Sale	11.37
	3	Simmone Jacobs	Shaftesbury	11.39
200m	1	Katharine Merry	Birchfield	22.85
(+0.6)	2	Stephanie Douglas	Sale	23.17
	3	Paula Thomas	Trafford	23.33
400m	1	Melanie Neef	Glasgow	52.56
	2	Tracy Goddard	Basingstoke	53.59
	3	Sandra Douglas	Trafford	53.78
800m	1	Diane Modahl	Sale	2:01.35
	2	Dawn Gandy	Hounslow	2:03.75
	3	Sonya Bowyer	Sale	2:03.79
1500m	1	Kelly Holmes	Ealing	4:01.41
	2	Yvonne Murray	Motherwell	4:01.44
	3	Ann Griffiths	Sale	4:08.71
3000m	1	Sonia McGeorge	Brighton	9:03.80
	2	Laura Adam	Parkside	9:12.16
	3	Wendy Ore	Cardiff	9:14.72
10,000m	1	Zahara Hyde	Woking	33:23.25
	2	Carole Greenwood	Bingley	33:34.96
	3	Suzanne Rigg	Warrington	33:42.80
100mh	1	Clova Court	Birchfield	13.06
	2	Sally Gunnell	Essex Ladies	13.09
	3	Lesley-Anne Skeete	Trafford	13.43
400mh	1	Gowry Retchakan	Thurrock	57.08
	2	Jacqui Parker	Essex Ladies	57.31
	3	S McCann	Lisburn	58.09
PV	1	Katy Staples	Essex Ladies	3.65m
	2	P Wilson	Cannock	3.40m
	3	L Stanton	Rotherham	3.30m
HJ	1	Julia Bennett	Epsom	1.89m
	2	Debbie Marti	Bromley	1.86m
	3	Julie Major	Basildon	1.83m
LJ	1	Yinka Idowu	Essex	6.58m
	2	Denise Lewis	Birchfield	6.56m
	3	Ann Brooks	Hull	6.10m
TJ	1	Michelle Griffith	Windsor	14.08m
	2	Ashia Hansen	Essex Ladies	13.79m
	3	Rachel Kirby	Hounslow	13.29m
SP	1	Judy Oakes	Croydon	18.38m
	2	Myrtle Augee	Bromley	17.37m
	3	Maggie Lynes	Croydon	16.53m
DT	1	Jackie McKernan	Lisburn	56.94m
	2	Sharon Andrews	Essex Ladies	56.24m
	3	Debbie Callaway	Aldershot	54.94m
HT	1	L Shaw	Gloucester	59.58m
	2	D Holden	Hounslow	49.12m
	3	S Moore	Bristol	48.46m
Javelin	1	Shelley Holroyd	Sale	57.08m
	2	Sharon Gibson	Notts	56.90m
	3	K Costello	Derby	54.50m

TSB CHALLENGE　*Edinburgh　Jul 8*

Men. 100yds: Linford Christie 9.30 (+1.6), 200m: J Williams USA 20.41, 400m: Du'aine Ladejo 45.16, 800m: Atle Douglas NOR 1:44.71, 1500m: Steve Holman USA 3:38.30, 3000msc: Colin Walker 8:29.33, 100mh: Colin Jackson 13.05 (+2.5), 400mh: Gary Cadogan 49.21, HJ: Geoff Parsons 2.25m, PV: Pat Manson USA 5.80m, TJ: Jonathan Edwards 16.88m, JT: Mick Hill 83.40m
Women. 200m: Holli Hyche USA 22.86 (+2.3), 300m: Kim Graham USA 36.85, 2000m: Sonia O'Sullivan IRL 5:25.36 (WR), 100mh: Dawn Bowles USA 12.92 (+1.3), HJ: Alison Inverarity AUS 1.97m, LJ: Nicole Boegman AUS 6.53m.

GREAT BRITAIN v USA MATCH

Gateshead　　July 20

Men 100m: Kevin Braunskill USA 10.43 (-1.0), 200m: John Regis 20.44 (+1.5), 400m: Calvin Davis USA 45.34, 800m:

Craig Winrow 1:47.17, 1500m: Kevin McKay 3:45.70, 5000m: Harris USA 14:02.18, 3000msc: Mark Rowland 8:41.45, 110mh: Robert Reading USA 13.36 (+0.8), 400mh: Glenn Terry USA 49.73, HJ: Tony Barton USA 2.28m, PV: Kory Tarpenning USA 5.80m, LJ: Reggie Jones USA 8.15m, TJ: Jonathan Edwards 16.80m, SP: Greg Tafralis USA 20.89m, DT: Mike Gravelle USA 63.68m, HT: Lance Deal USA 78.28m, JT: Steve Backley 84.68, 4x100m: GBR 38.91, 4x400m: USA 3:01.38 **USA 206 GBR 180** **Women.** 100m: Cheryl Taplin USA 11.66 (-2.0), 200m: Flirtisha Harris USA 23.44(-1.2), 400m: Sally Gunnell 51.04, 800m: Beasley USA 2:02.80, 1500m: Yvonne Murray 4:04.19, 3000m: Sonia McGeorge 9:02.97, 100mh: Jacqui

Agyepong 13.34 (-2.6), 400mh: Tonja Buford USA 56.01, HJ: Debbi Marti 1.88m, LJ: Cynthea Rhodes USA 6.68m, TJ: Ashia Hansen 14.00m, SP: Judy Oakes 18.63m, DT: Lacy Barnes USA 56.94m, JT: Donna Mayhew USA 61.50m, 4x100m: USA 43.35, 4x400m: USA 3:26.99 **USA 168 GBR 152**

BRITISH LEAGUE
Men's Division One : Thames Valley Harriers
Women's Division One: Sale Harriers

GUARDIAN CUP **Winners:** Thames Valley Harriers

JUBILEE CUP **Winners:** Essex Ladies

WORLD BESTS 1994 & WORLD RECORDS

MEN
100m: 9.85 (+1.2) Leroy Burrell USA Lausanne, July 6
WR: As above
200m: 19.87A (+1.6) John Regis GBR Sestriere, July 31
WR: 19.72A Pietro Meannea ITA 1972
400m: 43.90 Michael Johnson USA Madrid, Sep 6
WR: 43.29 Butch Reynolds USA 1988
800m: 1:43.17 Benson Koech KEN Rieti, Aug 28
WR: 1:41.73 Sebastian Coe GBR 1981
1500m: 3:30.61 N Morceli ALG V. D'Ascq, Jul 8
WR: 3:28.86 Noureddine Morceli ALG 1992
One Mile: 3:48.67 N Morceli ALG St Peterb'g, Jul 26
WR: 3:44.39 Noureddine Morceli ALG 1993
3000m: 7:25.11 N Morceli ALG Monaco, Aug 2
WR: As above
5000m: 12:56.96 H Gebresilasie ETH Hengelo, June 4
WR: As above
10,000m: 26:52.23 William Sigei KEN Oslo, July 22
WR: As above
Marathon: 2:07:15 Cosmas Ndeti KEN Boston, Apr 18
WR: 2:06:50 Belayneh Dinsamo ETH 1988
3000msc: 8:08.80 Moses Kiptanui KEN Zurich, Aug 17
WR: 8:02.08 Moses Kiptanui KEN 1992
110mh: 12.98 (+0.2) Colin Jackson GBR Tokyo, Sept 15
WR: 12.91 (+0.5) Colin Jackson GBR 1993
400mh: 47.70 Derrick Adkins USA Linz, July 4
WR: 46.78 Kevin Young USA
PV: 6.14m Sergey Bubka UKR Sestriere, July 31
WR: As above
HJ: 2.42m Javier Sotomayor CUB Seville, June 5
WR: 2.45m Javier Sotomayor CUB 1993
LJ: 8.74mA Erich Walder USA El Paso, Apr 2
WR: 8.95m Mike Powell USA 1991
TJ: 17.68m Mike Conley USA Paris, Sep 3
WR: 17.97m Willie Banks USA 1985
SP: 21.09m Jim Doehring USA New York, May 22
WR: 23.12m Randy Barnes USA 1990
DT: 68.58m Attila Horváth HUN Budapest, June 24
WR: 74.08m Jürgen Schult GER 1986
HT: 83.36 Andrey Abduvaliyev TJK Budapest, June 3
WR: 86.74m Yuriy Sedykh URS 1986
JT: 91.82m Jan Zelezny TCH Sheffield, Sep 4
WR: 96.66m Jan Zelezny TCH 1993
Dec: 8735 Eduard Hämäläinen BLS Götzis, May 29
WR: 8891 Dan O'Brien USA 1992
4 x 100m: 37.79 Santa Monica TC USA Walnut, Apr 17
WR: 37.40 USA 1992 & 1993
4 x 400m: 2:59.13 Great Britain Helsinki, Aug 14
WR: 2:54.29 USA 1993

WOMEN
100m: 10.77 Irina Privalova RUS Lausanne, July 6
WR: 10.48 Florence Griffith-Joyner USA 1988
200m : 21.85 Gwen Torrence USA Durham, July 12
WR: 21.34 Florence G-Joyner USA 1988
400m : 49.77 Marie-José Pérec FRA Paris, Sep 3
WR: 47.60 Marita Koch GDR 1985
800m: 1:55.19 Maria Mutola MOZ Zürich, Aug 17
WR:1:53.28 Jarmila Kratochvilova TCH 1983
1500m: 3:59.10 Sonia O'Sullivan IRL Nice, July 18
WR: 3:50.46 Qu Yunxia CHN 1993
One Mile: 4:17.25 Sonia O'Sullivan IRL Oslo, July 22
WR: 4:15.61 Paula Ivan ROM 1989
3000m: 8:21.64 Sonia O'Sullivan IRL London, July 15
WR: 8:06.11 Wang Junxia CHN 1993
5000m: 15:05.94 Yelena Romanova RUS St'holm, July 12
WR: Ingrid Kristiansen NOR 1986
10,000m : 30:52.51 Elana Meyer RSA London, Sep 10
WR: 29:31.78 Wang Junxia CHN 1993
Marathon: 2:21:45 Uta Pippig GER Boston, Apr 18
WR: 2:21:06 Ingrid Kristiansen NOR 1985
100mh: 12.53 (+0.2) T Reshetnikova RUS Linz, July 4
& (-0.3) Svetla Dimitrova BUL Stara Zagora, July 16
WR: 12.21 Yrodanka Donkova BUL 1988
400mh: 53.33 Sally Gunnell GBR Helsinki, July 12
WR: 52.74 Sally Gunnell GBR 1993
PV: 4.01m Marina Andreyeva RUS Voronazh, June 18
WB: 4.11m Sun Caiyun CHN 1993
HJ: 2.00m Silvia Costa CUB Havana, June 26
WR: Stefka Kostadinova BUL 2.09m 1987
LJ: 7.49m Jackie Joyner-Kersee USA New York, May 22
WR: 7.52m Galina Chistyakova URS 1988
TJ: 14.98m Sofia Bozhanova BUL Stara Zagora, July 16
WR: 15.09m Anna Biryukova RUS 1993
SP: 20.56m Valentina Fedyushina UKR Kiev, May 27
WR: 22.63m Natalya Lisovskaya URS 1987
DT: 68.72m Daniela Costian AUS Auckland, Jan 22
WR: 76.80m Gabriele Reinsch GER 1988
HT: 66.84m Olga Kuzenkova RUS Adler, Feb 18
WB: As above
JT: 71.40m Natalya Shikolenko RUS Seville, June 5
WR: 80.00m Petra Felke GDR 1988
Hept: 6741 Heike Drechsler GER Talence Sep 10-11
WR: 7291 Jackie Joyner-Kersee USA 1988
4 x 100m: 42.45 USA Durham, Aug 12
WR: 41.37 GDR 1985
4 x 400m: 3:22.27 USA St Petersburg, July 29
WR: 3:15.17 URS 1988

Indoor Athletics
European Indoor Championships

Paris   Mar 11-13

Men

60m	1	Colin Jackson	GBR	6.49 CR
	2	Alexandros Terzian	GRE	6.51
	3	Michael Rosswess	GBR	6.54
200m	1	Daniel Sangouma	FRA	20.68
	2	Vladislav Dologodin	UKR	20.76
	3	George Panagiotopoulos	GRE	20.99
	5	Darren Braithwaite	GBR	21.30
400m	1	Du'aine Ladejo	GBR	46.53
	2	Mikhail Vdovin	RUS	46.56
	3	Rico Lieder	GER	46.82
	dnf	James Baulch (fell)	GBR	
800m	1	Andrey Loginov	RUS	1:46.38
	2	Luis Javier Gonzalez	ESP	1:46.69
	3	Ousmane Diarra	FRA	1:47.18
1500m	1	David Strang	GBR	3:44.57
	2	Branko Zorko	CRO	3:44.64
	3	Kader Chekhemani	FRA	3:44.65
3000m	1	Kim Bauermeister	GER	7:52.34
	2	Ovidiu Olteanu	ROM	7:52.37
	3	Rod Finch	GBR	7:53.99
60mh	1	Colin Jackson	GBR	7.41 CR
	2	Georg Boroi	ROM	7.57
	3	Mike Fenner	GER	7.58
HJ	1	Dalton Grant	GBR	2.37m
	2	Jean-Charles Gicquel	FRA	2.35m
	3	Hendrik Beyer	GER	2.33m
	7	Brendan Reilly	GBR	2.26m
PV	1	Pyotr Bochkaryov	RUS	5.90m CR
	2	Jean Galfione	FRA	5.80m
	3	Igor Trandenkov	RUS	5.75m
LJ	1	Dietmar Haaf	GER	8.15m
	2	Konstant' Koukodimos	GRE	8.09m
	3	Bogdan Tudor	ROM	8.07m
TJ	1	Leonid Voloshin	RUS	17.44m
	2	Denis Kapustin	RUS	17.35m
	3	Vasily Sokov	RUS	17.31m
	13	Francis Agyepong	GBR	16.27m
	14	Julian Golley	GBR	16.17m
SP	1	Aleksandr Bagach	UKR	20.66m
	2	Dragan Peric	IP	20.55m
	3	Petur Gudmundsson	ISL	20.04m
Hept	1	Christian Plaziat	FRA	6268pts
	2	Henrik Dagård	SWE	6119pts
	3	Alain Blondel	FRA	6084pts
	dnf	Alex Kruger	GBR	
5000mw	1	Mikhail Shchennikov	RUS	18:34.32
	2	Ronald Weigel	GER	18:40.32
	3	Denis Langlois	FRA	18:43.20

Women

60m	1	Nelli Cooman	HOL	7.17
	2	Melanie Paschke	GER	7.19
	3	Patricia Girard	FRA	7.19
200m	1	Galina Malchugina	RUS	22.41
	2	Silke Knoll	GER	22.96
	3	Jacqueline Poelman	HOL	23.43
400m	1	Svetlana Goncharenko	RUS	51.62
	2	Tatyana Alekseyeva	RUS	51.77
	3	Viviane Dorsile	FRA	51.92
800m	1	Natalya Dukhnova	BLS	2:00.42
	2	Ella Kovacs	ROM	2:00.49
	3	Carla Sacramento	POR	2:01.12
1500m	1	Yekaterina Podkopayeva	RUS	4:06.46
	2	Lyudmila Rogachova	RUS	4:06.60
	3	Malgorzata Rydz	POL	4:06.98
3000m	1	Fernanda Ribeiro	POR	8:50.47
	2	Margareta Keszeg	ROM	8:55.61
	3	Anna Brzezinska	POL	8:56.90
	6	Alison Wyeth	GBR	9:04.35
	8	Sonia McGeorge	GBR	9:14.04
60mh	1	Yordanka Donkova	BUL	7.85
	2	Eva Sokolova	RUS	7.89
	3	Anne Piquereau	FRA	7.91
HJ	1	Stefka Kostadinova	BUL	1.98m
	2	Desislava Alexandrova	BUL	1.96m
	3	Sigrid Kirchmann	AUT	1.96m
LJ	1	Heike Drechsler	GER	7.06m
	2	Lyudmila Ninova	AUT	6.78m
	3	Inessa Kravets	UKR	6.72m
TJ	1	Inna Lasovskaya	RUS	14.88m CR
	2	Ana Biryukova	RUS	14.72m
	3	Sofia Bozhanova	BUL	14.52m
	10	Michelle Griffiths	GBR	13.55m
SP	1	Astrid Kumbernuss	GER	19.44m
	2	Larissa Peleshenko	RUS	19.16m
	3	Svetla Mitkova	BUL	19.09m
Pent	1	Larissa Turchinskaya	RUS	4801pts
	2	Rita Ináncsi	HUN	4775pts
	3	Urszula Wlodarczyk	POL	4668pts
3000mw	1	Annarita Sidoti	ITA	11:54.32
	2	Beate Gummelt	GER	11:56.01
	3	Yelena Arshintseva	RUS	11:57.48

Medal Table

	G	S	B	Total
Russia	9	7	3	19
Great Britain	5	0	2	7
Germany	4	4	3	11
France	2	2	7	11
Bulgaria	2	1	2	5
Ukraine	1	1	1	3
Holland	1	0	1	2
Portugal	1	0	1	2
Belarus	1	0	0	1
Italy	1	0	0	1
Romania	0	4	1	5
Greece	0	2	1	3
Austria	0	1	1	2
Croatia	0	1	0	1
Hungary	0	1	0	1
Individual	0	1	0	1
Spain	0	1	0	1
Sweden	0	1	0	1
Poland	0	0	3	3
Iceland	0	0	1	1

IAAF Indoor

HAMILTON, ONTARIO
Jan 14

Men

50m	Henry Neal	USA	5.69
1000m	George Kersh	USA	2:24.12
Mile	Marcus O'Sullivan	IRL	4:02.40
3000m	Reuben Reina	USA	7:41.04

The competitors ran 1 lap (146M) short.

HJ	Steinar Hoen	NOR	2.24m
PV	Bill Payne	USA	5.50m
LJ	Obinna Eregbu	NGR	7.83m

Women

50m	Juliet Cuthbert	JAM	6.30
500m	Jearl Miles	USA	1:11.06
800m	Shola Lynch	USA	2:10.42
1500m	Paula Schnurr	CAN	4:11.80
HJ	Yolanda Henry	USA	1.85m

MONTREAL GRAND PRIX
Jan16

Men

60m	Bruny Burin	CAN	6.54
200m	Chris Robinson	CAN	22.16
400m	Ian Morris	TRI	47.16
800m	Davide Cadoni	ITA	1:52.75
1000m	Sean Kaley	CAN	2:31.83
Mile	Marcus O'Sullivan	IRL	3:59.72
60mh	Michel Brodeur	CAN	8.12
HJ	Steinar Hoen	NOR	2.27m
PV	Gerald Baudouin	FRA	5.65m
LJ	Tony Walton	CAN	7.92m

Women

60m	Michelle Freeman	JAM	7.22
200m	France Gareau	CAN	25.08
400m	Juliet Campbell	JAM	54.00
800m	Sarah Howell	CAN	2:05.48
1000m	Kristan Marvin	CAN	2:58.13
60mh	Michelle Freeman	JAM	8.00
HJ	Yolanda Henry	USA	1.86m
LJ	Christy Opara	NGR	6.37m

MILLROSE GAMES
New York   Feb 4

Men

60m	Henry Neal	USA	6.55
400m	Antonio McKay	USA	48.04
500m	Mark Everett	USA	1:01.19
800m	George Kersh	USA	1:49.71
Vets Mile	Eamonn Coghlan	IRE	4:04.55
Mile	Niall Bruton	USA	3:58.71
3000m	Reuben Reina	USA	7:50.16
60mh	Greg Foster	USA	7.61
HJ	Tony Barton	USA	2.23m
PV	Brent Burns	USA	5.70m
SP	C J Hunter	USA	20.52m
Weight	Lance Deal	USA	23.48m

Women

60m	Gail Devers	USA	7.00
400m	Maicel Malone	USA	53.89
800m	Maria Mutola	MOZ	2:00.23
Mile	Hassiba Boulmerka	ALG	4:30.01
60mh	Michelle Freeman	JAM	7.90
HJ	Tisha Waller	USA	1.92m
SP	Connie Price-Smith	USA	17.21m

SAMSUNG CUP
Budapest   Feb 5

Men

200m	Vladislav Dologodin	UKR	20.89
400m	Kostas Kenderis	GRE	47.45
800m	Anatolij Makarevic	BLS	1:47.24
60mh	Georg Boroi	ROM	7.51
PV	Zoltan Farkas	HUN	5.40m

Women

1500m	Tudorita Chidu	ROM	4:07.85
60mh	Eva Sokolova	RUS	8.01
HJ	Zuzanna Kovacikova	TCH	1.92m
TJ	Ludmila Dubkova	RUS	13.87m

MOBIL INTERNATIONAL
Fairfax, USA   Feb 6

Men

60m	Michael Green	JAM	6.59
400m	Michael Johnson	USA	45.81
800m	David Kiptoo	KEN	1:48.43
Vets Mile	Eamonn Coghlan	IRE	4:03.28
Mile	David Strang	GBR	3:57.38
3000m	Roy Keith	USA	7:49.83
60mh	Allen Johnson	USA	7.64
HJ	Randy Jenkins	USA	2.25m
PV	Denis Petushinsky	RUS	5.70m

Women

60m	Juliet Cuthbert	JAM	7.14
200m	Carlette Guidry	USA	23.55
400m	Maicel Malone	USA	52.56
800m	Maria Mutola	MOZ	2:00.14
Mile	Hassiba Boulmerka	ALG	4:28.64
HJ	Tisha Waller	USA	1.96m

YOMIURI CHITOSE INTERNATIONAL
Osaka, Japan   11 Feb

Men

60m	Michael Green	JAM	6.53
800m	Tomonari Ono	JAP	1:55.00
60mh	Jack Pierce	USA	7.62
HJ	Takahiro Kimino	JPN	2.20m
LJ	Obinna Eregbu	NGR	7.94m
TJ	Shigehisa Matsumoto	JPN	16.45m
PV	Sergey Bubka	UKR	5.85m

Women

60m	Gail Devers	USA	7.04
1500m	Yoshiko Ichikawa	JPN	4:25.18
60mh	Michelle Freeman	JAM	7.98
HJ	Stefka Kostadinova	BUL	1.95m

TROPHÉE PAS DE CALAIS
Lievin, France   Feb 13

Men

60m	Bruny Surin	CAN	6.52
200m	Frank Fredericks	NAM	20.71
3000m	Moses Kiptanui	KEN	7:40.94
60mh	Georg Boroi	ROM	7.50
TJ	Leonid Voloshin	RUS	17.21m
PV	Rodion Gataullin	RUS	5.90m

Women

60m	Irina Privalova	RUS	6.93	
1000m	Natalya Dukhnova	BLS	2:36.84	
60mh	Yordanka Donkova	BUL	7.83	
HJ	Tatyana Shevchik	BLS	1.94m	
TJ	Inna Lasovskaya	RUS	14.90	WR
3000mw	Beate Anders	GER	12:06.24	

IAAF INTERNATIONAL
Genoa, Italy   16 Feb
Men

60m	Yoel Isasi	CUB	6.69
200m	Giorgio Marras	ITA	21.15
400m	Andrea Nuti	ITA	46.96
800m	Vénuste Niyongabo	BUR	1:49.27
60mh	Li Tong	CHN	7.71
LJ	Giovanni Evangelisti	ITA	7.87m
HJ	Federico Rodeghiero	ITA	2.20m
PV	Danny Krasnov	ISR	5.50m
Shot	Marco Dodoni	ITA	18.69m

Women

60m	Sonia Vigati	ITA	7.35
200m	Giada Gallina	ITA	23.98
400m	Pauline Davis	USA	54.73
800m	Nicoletta Tozzi	ITA	2:06.33
60mh	Carla Tuzzi	ITA	8.12

SUNKIST INTERNATIONAL
Los Angeles   Feb 19
Men

500yds	Antonio McKay	USA	58.7
880yds	David Kiptoo	KEN	1:51.25
Mile	Marcus O'Sullivan	IRE	4:00.31
3000m	Reuben Reina	USA	7:58.00
50mh	Li Tong	CHN	6.50
PV	Brent Burns	USA	5.70m
Shot	Randy Barnes	USA	20.20m

Women

50m	Irina Privalova	RUS	6.08
440yds	Donalda Duprey	CAN	55.91
880yds	Maria Mutola	MOZ	2:00.21
Mile	Suzy Hamilton	USA	4:36.43
50mh	Jackie Joyner-Kersee	USA	6.87

TSB INTERNATIONAL
Birmingham   Feb 26
Men

60m	Linford Christie	GBR	6.58
200m	Frank Fredericks	NAM	20.62
400m	Michael Johnson	USA	45.17
800m	Martin Steele	GBR	1:47.78
1000m	Benson Koech	KEN	2:20.22
1500m	Matthew Hibberd	GBR	3:43.23
60mh	Colin Jackson	GBR	7.38
TJ	Vladimir Melikhov	RUS	16.87m
HJ	Javier Sotomayor	CUB	2.40m
PV	Istvan Bagyula	HUN	5.60m

Women

200m	Dannette Young	USA	23.13
400m	Sally Gunnell	GBR	52.84
60mh	Aliuska Lopez	CUB	8.10
TJ	Michelle Griffith	GBR	13.74m

HALLENLEICHTATHLETIK
Karlsruhe   Mar 1
Men

60m	Linford Christie	GBR	6.48
200m	Patrik Stevens	BEL	20.99
400m	Rico Lieder	GER	46.68
800m	Paul Ereng	KEN	1:46.19
Mile	Jens-Peter Herold	GER	3:53.74
60mh	Mark McKoy	CAN	7.52
HJ	Troy Kemp	BAH	2.31m

Women

60m	Merlene Ottey	JAM	7.11	
800m	Ella Kovacs	ROM	1:59.66	
LJ	Heike Drechsler	GER	7.06m	
PV	Nichole Rieger	GER	4.08m	WB

SAN SEBASTIAN
Mar 13
Men

60m	Linford Christie	GBR	6.52
200m	A Porkhomovsky	RUS	20.88
400m	Wesley Russell	USA	46.81
800m	Robert Kibet	KEN	1:46.90
1500m	Vénuste Niyongabo	BUR	3:40.32
3000m	Mohamed Choumassi	MAR	7:52.67
60mh	Colin Jackson	GBR	7.46
SP	Manuel Martinez	ESP	19.90m
PV	Javier Garcia Chico	ESP	5.50m

Women

60m	Liliana Allen	CUB	7.21
200m	Galina Malchugina	RUS	22.70
800m	Patricia Djate	FRA	2:02.78
60mh	Aliuska Lopez	CUB	8.20
TJ	Inna Lasovskaya	RUS	14.31m

DN GAMES
Stockholm   Mar 8
Men

60m	Dennis Mitchell	USA	6.61
200m	Joakim Öhman	SWE	21.58
400m	Troy Douglas	BER	47.15
800m	Benson Koech	KEN	1:47.65
5000m	Mohamed Issangar	MAR	13:26.84
60mh	Colin Jackson	GBR	7.42
PV	Jani Lehtonen	FIN	5.83m
LJ	Ivailo Mladenov	BUL	8.09m
Shot	Petur Gudmundsson	ISL	20.07m

Women

60m	Merlene Ottey	JAM	7.09
800m	Olga Kuznyetsova	RUS	2:02.39
1500m	Mitica Constantin	ROM	4:16.74
60mh	Brigita Bukovec	SLO	8.04
HJ	Stefka Kostadinova	BUL	2.00m
LJ	Ana Biryukova	RUS	6.69m

IAAF WORLD CROSS-COUNTRY CHAMPIONSHIPS

Budapest   Mar 26

Senior Men		(12,060m)
1	William Sigei KEN	34.29
2	Simon Chemoiywa KEN	34.30
3	Haile Gebresilasie ETH	34.32
4	Paul Tergat KEN	34.36
5	Khalid Skah MAR	34.56
6	James Songok KEN	35.02
7	Addis Abebe ETH	35.11
8	Ayele Mezgebu ETH	35.14
9	Shem Kororia KEN	35.15
10	Mat. Ntawulikura RWA	35.19
11	Salah Hissou MAR	35.23
12	Dominic Kirui KEN	35.26
13	Paulo Guerra POR	35.27
14	Larbi Khattabi MAR	35.34
15	Khalid Boulami MAR	35.39
16	Mohamed Issangar MAR	35.40
17	Wilson Omwoyo KEN	35.41
18	Mustapha Essaid FRA	35.41
19	Pedro Arco ESP	35.42
20	Vincenzo Modica ITA	35.42

Others include

32	John Nuttal GBR	36.00
54	David Clarke GBR	36.24
63	Martin Jones GBR	36.33
71	Dominic Bannister GBR	36.44
95	Eamonn Martin GBR	36.56
124	Barry Royden GBR	37.16
132	Darren Mead GBR	37.24
146	Steve Tunstall GBR	37.33
-	Andy Bristow GBR	DNF

Teams
1.Kenya 34 pts; 2. Morocco 83; 3. Ethiopia 133; 4. Spain 174; 5. Portugal 210; 6. Italy 312; 7. France 319; 8. Great Britain 439; 28 Teams finished.

Junior Men		(8,140m)
1	Philip Mosima KEN	24.15
2	Daniel Komen KEN	24.17
3	Abreharn Tsige ETH	24.46
4	Philip Kemei KEN	24.49
5	Lemma Alemayehu ETH	25.00
6	Pablo Olmedo MEX	25.04
7	Tibebu Reta ETH	25.04
8	Reyes Estevez ESP	25.11
9	Melk Mothuli RSA	25.13
10	Salah Ghazi MAR	25.15

Other include:

27	Darrius Burrows GBR	25.53
49	Ben Noad GBR	26.15
93	Neil Caddy GBR	26.50
118	Scott West GBR	27.12
129	Matthew O'Dowd GBR	27.19
135	Kevin Holland GBR	27.31

Teams 1.Kenya 18 pts.; 2.Ethiopia 27; 3.Morocco 78; 4.South Africa 96; 5.Japan 118; 16. Great Britain 287. 31 Teams finished.

Senior Women		(6,220m)
1	Helen Chepngeno KEN	20.45
2	Cath McKiernan IRL	20.52
3	Concei. Ferreira POR	20.52
4	Merima Denboba ETH	20.57
5	Albertina Dias POR	20.59
6	Elana Meyer RSA	21.00
7	Zola Pieterse RSA	21.01
8	Farida Fates FRA	21.01
9	Olga Churbanova RUS	21.05
10	Fernanda Ribeiro POR	21.05
11	Margareta Keszeg ROM	21.06
12	Daria Nauer SUI	21.10
13	Silvia Sommaggio ITA	21.12
14	Getenesh Urge ETH	21.13
15	Claudia Stalder SUI	21.17
16	Julia Vaquero ESP	21.18
17	Sumie Yamaguchi JPN	21.20
18	Joyce Koech KEN	21.22
19	Gegi Asha ETH	21.24
20	Estela Estevez ESP	21.26

Others include:

45	Laura Adam GBR	21.44
77	Tanya Blake GBR	22.06
78	Wendy Ore GBR	22.07
80	Vicky McPherson GBR	22.11
119	Carol Greenwood GBR	22.49
121	Jane Spark GBR	22.53

Teams 1.Portugal 55 pts.; 2.Ethiopia 65; 3.Kenya 75; 4.Russia 84; 5.Spain 111; 6.South Africa 124; 14.Great Britain 280. 25 Teams finished.

Junior Women		(4,330m)
1	Sally Barsosio KEN	14.04
2	Rose Cheruiyot KEN	14.05
3	Elizabeth Yeptanui KEN	14.15
4	Gabriela Szabo ROM	14.25
5	Ruth Biwott KEN	14.27
6	Naomi Mugo KEN	14:29
7	Pam Chepchumba KEN	14.36
8	Azumi Miyazaki JPN	14.37
9	Shori Hotesa ETH	14.46
10	Berhane Dagne ETH	14.48

Others include:

11	Nicola Slater GBR	14.49
26	Heidi Moulder GBR	15.24
40	Cathryn Berry GBR	15.41
42	Clare O'Connor GBR	15.42
50	Sarah Simmons GBR	15.47
78	Michelle Matthews GBR	16.05

Teams
1.Kenya 11 pts.; 2.Ethiopia 46; 3.Japan 60; 4.Romania 83; 5.Great Britain 119 23 teams finished.

Taking all four races into account (and the union of the domestic nations in 1988), the 1994 World Cross-country Championships represented Britain's worst ever showing with only one athlete, Nicola Slater, finishing in the top 20. Since the Championships became an official world title, in 1973, only two British athletes have taken a senior title. Zola Budd, whose connection with Britain was convenient, to say the least, and Ian Stewart. The senior winners since 1973 are:

	Men	Women		Men	Women
1973	Pekka Paivarinto (FIN)	Paolo Cacchi (ITA)	1984	Carlos Lopes (POR)	Maricica Puica (ROM)
1974	Eric de Beck (BEL)	Paolo Cacchi (ITA)	1985	Carlos Lopes (POR)	Zola Budd (ENG)
1975	Ian Stewart (SCO)	Julie Brown (USA)	1986	John Ngugi (KEN)	Zola Budd (ENG)
1976	Carlos Lopes (POR)	Carmen Valero (ESP)	1987	John Ngugi (KEN)	Annette Sergent (FRA)
1977	Leon Schots (BEL)	Carmen Valero (ESP)	1988	John Ngugi (KEN)	Ingrid Kristiansen (NOR)
1978	John Treacy (IRL)	Grete Waitz (NOR)	1989	John Ngugi (KEN)	Annette Sergent (FRA)
1979	John Treacy (IRL)	Grete Waitz (NOR)	1990	Khalid Skah (MAR)	Lynn Jennings (USA)
1980	Craig Virgin (USA)	Grete Waitz (NOR)	1991	Khalid Skah (MAR)	Lynn Jennings (USA)
1981	Craig Virgin (USA)	Grete Waitz (NOR)	1992	John Ngugi (KEN)	Lynn Jennings (USA)
1982	Mohamed Kedir (ETH)	Maricica Puica (ROM)	1993	William Sigei (KEN)	Albertina Dias (POR)
1983	Bekele Debele (ETH)	Grete Waitz (NOR)	1994	William Sigei (KEN)	Helen Chepngeno (KEN)

IAAF World Cross Challenge

Date	Venue	Men's Winner		Women's Winner	
Nov 28	Bolbec, France	Khalid Boulami	MAR	Catherina McKiernan	IRL
Dec 19	Brussels, Belgium	Ismael Kirui	KEN	Albertina Dias	POR
Jan 1	Durham, England	Haile Gebresilasie	ETH	Paula Radcliffe	GBR
Jan 8	Belfast, N.Ireland	Ismael Kirui	KEN	Paula Radcliffe	GBR
Jan 23	Seville, Spain	William Sigei	KEN	Yelena Romanova	RUS
Jan 30	San Sebastián, Spain	Haile Gebresilasie	ETH	Yelena Romanova	RUS
Feb 6	Tourcoing, France	Ezequiel Bitok	KEN	Zola Pieterse	RSA
Feb 13	Açoteias, Portugal	Ondoro Osoro	KEN	Catherina McKiernan	IRL
Feb 20	Diekirch, Luxemburg	Tendai Chimusasi	ZIM	Catherina McKiernan	IRL
Feb 20	Chiba, Japan	Gert Thys	RSA	Galianova Nadezhda	RUS
Mar 5	San Vittore, Italy	Albertina Dias	POR	Fita Bayessa	ETH

Final Standings - Men

1	Haile Gebresilasie	ETH	107 pts
2	William Sigei	KEN	97
3	Ismael Kirui	KEN	91
4	Paulo Guerra	POR	85
5	Ezequiel Bitok	KEN	77
6	Jonah Kiprono	KEN	68
7	Steve Tunstall	GBR	67
8	Rudi Walem	BEL	65
9	Charles Omwoyo	KEN	62
10	Robert Stefko	SVK	61

Final Standings - Women

1	Catherina McKiernan	IRE	141
2	Albertina Dias	POR	123
3	Margareta Keszeg	ROM	97
4	Farida Fates	FRA	86
=5	Olga Bondarenko	RUS	74
=5	Iulia Negura	ROM	74
7	Tecla Lorupe	KEN	72
8	Daria Nauer	SUI	62
9	Vicki McPherson	GBR	54
=10	Conceição Ferreira	POR	53
=10	Zola Pieterse	RSA	53

UK World Cross-country Trials

Alnwick   Feb 19

Senior Men (12km)

1	Steve Tunstall	Preston	36:37
2	Andy Bristow	Brighton	36:48
3	Richard Nerurkar	Bingley	36:50
4	Dominic Bannister	Shaftesbury	37:02
5	Martin Jones	Horwich	37:04
6	Eamonn Martin	Basildon	37:08
7	Dave Clarke	Hercules	37:13
8	Barry Royden	Medway	37:23
9	Darren Mead	Norfolk O	37:26

Junior Men (6km)

1	Darrius Burrows	Birchfield	23:21
2	Neil Caddy	Newquay	23:35
3	Scott West	Birchfield	23:51
4	Ben Noad	Bristol	24:05
5	Kevin Holland	Crawley	24:05
6	Matthew O'Dowd	Swindon	24:06

Senior Women (6km)

1	Paula Radcliffe	Bedford	19:27
2	Laura Adam	Parkside	19:55
3	Bev Hartigan	Tipton	19:57
4	Tanya Blake	Blackheath	19:59
5	Vikki McPherson	Glasgow	20:00
6	Wendy Ore	Cardiff	20:01

Junior Women (4km)

1	Nicola Slater	Radley	14:43
2	Heidi Moulder	Westbury	14:47
3	Cathryn Berry	Kingston	14:58
4	Sarah Simmons	Medway	14:58
5	Michelle Matthews	Bedford	14:59
6	Clare O'Connor	Oldham	15:03

BAF Inter-county Championships

Stopsley Common, Luton   Jan 15

Men

1	Andrew Pearson	Yorks	36:48
2	Spencer Duval	Staffs	37:10
3	Craig Mochrie	Leics	37:18

Men's Team

1	Yorkshire	95 pts
2	Leicester	230
3	North East	264

Women

1	Sonia McGeorge	Sussex	20:35
2	Anthea Duke	N/E	20:36
3	Jane Spark	G Man	20:39

Women's Teams

1	Sussex	206
2	Hants	238
3	Gtr Manchester	290

European Men's Clubs Championship

Amorebieta, Spain   Feb 6

1	Dionisio Castro	POR	31:20
2	Million	FRA	31:29
3	Jean-Pierre Lautredoux	FRA	31:34
4	Pinilla	ESP	31:39
5	Ezequiel Canario	POR	31:51
6	Carlos Monteiro	ESP	31:53

Teams

1	Sporting Lisboa	POR	22 pts
2	Reebok Racing Club	ESP	28
3	Jogging Marignanals	FRA	49
4	Swansea	WAL	108
5	Bingley	ENG	110

ROAD RUNNING

IAAF Events

IAAF World Half Marathon Championships
Brussels   Oct 3

Men	1	Vincent Rousseau	BEL	61:06
	2	Steve Moneghetti	AUS	61:10
	3	Carl Thackery	GBR	61:13
Teams		1. Kenya 3:05:40, 2. Australia 3:05:43, 3. Great Britain 3:06:10		
Women	1	Conceição Ferreira	POR	70:07
	2	Mari Tanigawa	JPN	70:09
	3	Tecla Lorupe	KEN	70:12
Teams		1. Romania 3:32:18, 2. Japan 3:32:22, 3. Portugal 3:34:12, 4. Great Britain 3:38:54		

IAAF World Marathon Cup
San Sebastian   Oct 31

Men	1	Richard Nerurkar	GBR	2:10:03
	2	Severino Bernardini	ITA	2:10:12
	3	Kebede Gemechu	ETH	2:10:16
Teams		1. Ethiopia 6:31:17, 2. Italy 6:32:41, 3. Great Britain 6:34:06		
Women	1	Wang Junxia	CHN	2:28:16
	2	Zhang Linli	CHN	2:29:42
	3	Zhang Lirong	CHN	2:29:45
Team		1. China 7:27:43, 2. Spain 7:33:55, 3. Russia 7:44:07, 8. Great Britain 7:56:15		

IAAF World Road Relay Championship
Litochoro, Greece   Apr 17

Men	1	Morocco		1:57:56
		(Jabbour 13:35, Khattabi 28:44, El Guerrouj 13:43, Hissou 27:57, B Boutayeb 13:53, Skah 20:04)		
	2	Ethiopia		1:58:51
	3	Kenya		2:00:51
	5	Great Britain		2:02:12
		(Cullen 14:01, Clarke 29:41, Taylor 14:07 M Jones 28:58, Moore 14:21, Royden 21:04)		
Women	1	Russia		2:17:19
		(Pentukova 16:12, Galyamova 32:59, Kopytova 15:45, Solominskaya 33:21, Romanova 15:48, Churbanova 23:14)		
	2	Ethiopia		2:19:09
	3	Romania		2:19:18
	8	Great Britain		2:21:52
		(Sutton 16:42, McPherson 33:42, Blake 16:41, Thompson 34:43, McGeorge 15:50, Adam 24:14)		

UK Events

Morpeth to Newcastle (14.1m)
Jan 1

Men	1	Colin Walker	GBR	69.50
Women	1	Lyn Harding	GBR	80:00

Nutra Sweet London Marathon
Apr 17

Men	1	Dionicio Ceron	MEX	2:08:53
	2	Abebe Mekkonen	ETH	2:09:17
	3	German Silva	MEX	2:09:18
	4	Salvatore Bettiol	ITA	2:09:40
	5	Grzegorz Gadjus	POL	2:09:49
	6	Martin Pitayo	MEX	2:10:58

Women	1	Katrin Dörre	GER	2:32:34
	2	Lisa Ondieki	AUS	2:33:17
	3	Janet Mayal	BRA	2:34:21
	4	Sally Ellis	GBR	2:37:06
	5	Sally Eastall	GBR	2:37:08

St Neots Half Marathon
May 29

Men	1	Muwinda	KEN	63:01
Women	1	Danielle Sanderson	GBR	73:11

BAF 10km Championships
Stoke   Aug 7

Men	1	Julius Koech	KEN	29:09
	2	Martin McLoughlin	GBR	29:21
		McLoughlin becomes national champion		
Women	1	Wendy Ore	GBR	33:41

BUPA GREAT RUN SERIES

BUPA Great Caledonian Run (10km)
Edinburgh   Oct 3, 1993

Men	1	Gary Staines	GBR	28:37
	2	J Kibor	KEN	28:43
	3	John Treacy	IRL	29:04
Women	1	Lyubov Borisova	RUS	33:37
	2	A Wright	GBR	35:12
	3	S Ridley	GBR	35:52

BUPA Great South Run (10 miles)
Portsmouth   Oct 10, 1993

Men	1	Gary Staines	GBR	46:11
	2	John Treacy	IRL	46:25
	3	Paul Davies-Hale	GBR	47:00
Women	1	Iulia Negura	ROM	53:01
	2	Suzanne Rigg	GBR	53:42
	3	Marion Sutton	GBR	54:17

BUPA Aberdeen Road Races
May 22
5km

Men	1	Ismael Kirui	KEN	13:37
Women	1	Sonia O'Sullivan	IRL	15·18

1 Mile

Men	1	Kevin McKay	GBR	4:06

BUPA Great London Run (Women - 10km)
Hyde Park   July 10

	1	Yelena Vyasova	RUS	33:55
	2	Suzanne Rigg	GBR	34:02
	3	A Wright	GBR	34:11

BUPA Great Welsh Run (10km)
Cardiff   July 31

Men	1	Paul Evans	GBR	28:23
	2	Richard Nerurkar	GBR	28:25
	3	Jonah Koech	KEN	28:35
Women	1	Marion Sutton	GBR	32:55
	2	Wendy Ore	GBR	33:15
	3	S Jepkorir	KEN	33:21

BUPA Great North Run (Half-marathon)
Tyneside   Sep 18

Men	1	Benson Masya	KEN	1:00:02
	2	Moses Tanui	KEN	1:00:03
	3	Paul Tergat	KEN	1:00:42
Women	1	Rosanna Munerotto	ITA	1:11:29
	2	Andrea Wallace	GBR	1:11:34
	3	Mañuela Machado	POR	1:11:48

INTERNATIONAL EVENTS

Kosice Peace Marathon
Oct 3

Men	1	Wieslaw Palczynski	POL	2:14:11
Women	1	Elena Platinina	UKR	2:42:11

Marathon Adidas de la Republica Argentina
Oct 10

Men	1	Toribio Gutierrez	ARG	2:19:55
Women	1	Adao Arlete	BRA	2:44:37

Venice Marathon for UNICEF
Oct 10

Men	1	Arthur Castro	BRA	2:10:06
	2	Salvatore Bettiol	ITA	2:11:44
Women	1	Helena Javornik	SLO	2:37:27

Beijing International Marathon
Oct 17

Men	1	Hu Gangjun	CHN	2:10:57
	2	Tokunga Daisuke	JPN	2:11:09
	3	Belayneh Densimo	ETH	2:12:11
Women	1	Li Yemei	CHN	2:30:36
	2	Wang Xiuting	CHN	2:32:03
	3	Yvonne Danson	GBR	2:32:42

DB-Marathon Frankfurt
Oct 17

Men	1	Stephan Freigang	GER	2:11:53
	2	Karol Dolega	POL	2:12:59
	3	Terje Naess	NOR	2:13:11
Women	1	Sissel Grottenberg	NOR	2:36:50

Maratona D'Italia
Carpi   *Oct 24*

Men	1	Graziano Calvaresi	ITA	2:11:49
	2	Luigi De Lello	ITA	2:12:07
	3	Diamantoni Dos Santos	BRA	2:12:22
Women	1	Marian Freriks	HOL	2:39:53

Reims Marathon
Oct 17

Men	1	Vincent Rousseau	BEL	2:09:13
	2	Leszek Beblo	POL	2:10:24
	3	Slawomir Gurny	POL	2:10:31
Women	1	Judit Nagy	HUN	2:32:07
	2	Linda Milo	BEL	2:34:12
	3	Farkas	HUN	2:35:19

Citibank Auckland International Marathon
Oct 24

Men	1	Kerry Rodger	NZL	2:19:58
Women	1	Raewyn Rodger	NZL	2:46:17

Chicago Marathon
Oct 24

Men	1	Luis Dos Santos	BRA	2:13:14
	2	Eddy Hellebuyck	BEL	2:14:39
	3	Antoni Niemczak	POL	2:15:06
Women	1	Ritva Lemettinen	FIN	2:33:18
	2	Linda Somers	USA	2:34:25
	3	Silvana Peirera	BRA	2:37:57

Golden Pages Dublin Marathon
Oct 26

Men	1	John Treacy	IRL	2:14:40
Women	1	Cathy Shum	IRL	2:38:14

New York City Marathon
Nov 14

Men	1	Andres Espinosa	MEX	2:10:04
	2	Bob Kempainen	USA	2:11:03
	3	Arturo Barrios	MEX	2:12:21
	4	Joachim Pinheiro	POR	2:12:40
	5	Kevin Brantly	USA	2:12:49
	6	Innocencio Miranda	MEX	2:12:52
Women	1	Uta Pippig	GER	2:26:24
	2	Olga Appell	MEX	2:28:56
	3	Nadia Prasad	FRA	2:30:16
	4	Marcia Narloch	BRA	2:32:23
	5	Alena Peterkova	TCH	2:33:43
	6	Emma Scaunich	ITA	2:35:02

Tokyo International Women's Marathon
Nov 21

Women	1	Valentina Egorova	RUS	2:26:40
	2	Mari Tanigawa	JPN	2:28:22
	3	Katrin Dörre	GER	2:28:52

Ekiden Relay
Chiba, Japan Nov 23

Men	1	Morocco	2:01:13
	2	Ethiopia	2:01:33
	3	Great Britain	2:02:19
Women	1	Japan	2:17:57
	2	Russia	2:19:52
	3	Australia	2:21:56
	5	Great Britain	2:24:06

Discoveries Marathon Lisbon
Nov 28

Men	1	Saïd Ermili	MAR	2:12:28
Women	1	Manuela Machado	POR	2:31:31

Fukuoka International Men's Marathon
Dec 5

Men	1	Dionisio Ceron	MEX	2:08:51
	2	Gert Thys	RSA	2:09:31
	3	Valdenor Dos Santos	BRA	2:10:21

Macao International Marathon
Dec 5

Men	1	Hu Gangjun	CHN	2:19:11
Women	1	Li Yemei	CHN	2:39:19

Palermo Marathon
Dec 8

Men	1	Boay Akonay	TAN	2:13:52

Costa De Calvia International Marathon
Dec 12

Men	1	Ian Bloomfield	GBR	2:17:44
Women	1	Elena Sipatova	RUS	2:42:09

Honolulu Marathon
Dec 12

Men	1	Bong Ju Lee	KOR	2:13:16
	2	Cosmas Ndeti	KEN	2:13:40
Women	1	Carla Beurskens	HOL	2:32:20

Tiberias Marathon
Jan 12

Men	1	Ahmed Hussein	ETH	2:14:52

Kathmandu International Marathon
Jan 16

Men	1	Purna Akshya	NEP	2:27:50
Women	1	Susan Bitzer	GER	3:06:50

Vietnam Marathon - Ho Chi Minh City
Jan 16

Men	1	Doug Kurtis	USA	2:26:19
Women	1	Lucy Christina Ramwell	GBR	2:56:15

Osaka Ladies International Marathon
Jan 30

Women	1	Tomoe Abe	JPN	2:26:09
	2	Nobuko Fujimura	JPN	2:26:09
	3	Junko Asari	JPN	2:26:10

Las Vegas International Marathon
Feb 5

Men	1	Michael Dudley	USA	2:16:54
Women	1	Roxi Erickson	USA	2:40:14

Marathon Popular de Valencia
Feb 6

Men	1	Eugeni Zaratovski	RUS	2:16:20
Women	1	Zinaida Semenova	RUS	2:34:08

Beppu-Oita Mainichi Marathon
Feb 6

Men	1	Hajime Nakatomi	JPN	2:11:28
	2	Kenichiro Takeuchi	JPN	2:11:39
	3	Uirga Girma	ETH	2:11:41

Tokyo International Men's Marathon
Feb 13

Men	1	Steve Moneghetti	AUS	2:08:55
	2	Vincent Rousseau	BEL	2:09:08
	3	Toshiyuki Hayata	JPN	2:10:19

Women's Ekiden Relay
Beijing   Feb 20

	1	China	2:16:03

Ohme Hochi Road Race 30Km
Feb 20

Men	1	Yasuyuki Watanabe	JPN	1:31:22
Women	1	Eriko Asai	JPN	1:44:52

Maraton Ciudad de Sevilla
Feb 27

Men	1	Jose Apalanza	ESP	2:16:09
Women	1	Ana Isabel Alonso	ESP	2:33:18

Hiroshima Marathon
Mar 6

Men	1	Kenichi Suzuki	JPN	2:11:05

Nagoya International Women's Marathon
Mar 6

Women	1	Eriko Asai	JPN	2:30:30
	2	Ramilia Burangulova	RUS	2:31:12
	3	Anna Rybicka	POL	2:31:43

City of Los Angeles Marathon
Mar 6

Men	1	Paul Pilkington	USA	2:12:13
	2	Luca Barzaghi	ITA	2:12:52
	3	Andrzej Krystin	POL	2:13:21
Women	1	Olga Appell	USA	2:28:12

Lisbon Half Marathon
Mar 13

Men	1	Andres Espinoza	MEX	61:34
	2	Antonio Pinto	POR	61:55
	3	Andrew Masai	KEN	61:56
Women	1	Tecla Lorupe	KEN	69:27
	2	Carmen de Oliveira	BRA	69:31

Maraton Catalunya Barcelona
Mar 13

Men	1	Benito Ojeda	ESP	2:15:14
Women	1	Marina Ivanova	RUS	2:40:30

Kyoto Half Marathon
Mar 20

Men	1	Valdenor dos Santos	BRA	61:53
	2	Moses Tanui	KEN	61:57
	3	Stephan Freigang	GER	62:00
Women	1	Uta Pippig	GER	67:59

Vigaranomaratona
Mar 20

Men	1	Marco Di Lieto	ITA	2:19:41
Women	1	Dana Hajna	CZE	2:48:57

Dong-A International Marathon
Gyeongju, South Korea   Mar 20

Men	1	Manuel Matias	POR	2:08:33
	2	Wan-Ki Kim	KOR	2:08:34
	3	Isidro Rico	MEX	2:09:14
Women	1	Mi-Kyung Lee	KOR	2:35:44

Ohlsson's Two Oceans Marathon 56Km
Apr 2

Men	1	Phineas Mokaba	RSA	3:15:06
Women	1	Carolyn Hunter-Rowe	GBR	3:51:36

Splendid International Half-Marathon
Italy   Apr 4

Men	1	John Kiprono	KEN	1:01:26
Women	1	Maria Venturelli	ITA	1:20:54

Berlin Half-Marathon
Apr 10

Men	1	Tendai Chimusasa	ZIM	1:01:45
	2	Venderlei Lima	BRA	1:02:01
	3	Julius Ondieki	KEN	1:02:20
Women	1	Kathrin Wessel	GER	1:10:47

Vienna City Marathon
Apr 10

Men	1	Joaquim Silva	POR	2:10:42
	2	Davide Milesi	ITA	2:12:44
Women	1	Sissel Grottenberg	NOR	2:36:17

Women's Ekiden Relay
Seoul   Apr 10

	1	Russia	2:17:16
	9	Great Britain	2:24:01

Nike Rotterdam Marathon
Apr 17

Men	1	Vincent Rousseau	BEL	2:07:51
	2	Willie Motolo	RSA	2:10:17
	3	Hu Gangjun	CHN	2:10:26
Women	1	Miyoko Asahina	JPN	2:25:52
	2	Ritva Lemettinen	FIN	2:29:16
	3	Carla Beurskens	HOL	2:29:43
	6	Mañuela Machado	POR	2:34:15

BAA Boston Marathon
Apr 18

Men	1	Cosmas Ndeti	KEN	2:07:15
	2	Andres Espinosa	MEX	2:07:19
	3	Jackson Kipngok	KEN	2:08:08
	4	Hwang Young-Cho	KOR	2:08:09
	5	Arturo Barrios	MEX	2:08:28
	6	Boay Akonay	TAN	2:08:35

Women	1	Uta Pippig	GER	2:21:45
	2	Valentina Yegorova	RUS	2:23:33
	3	Elena Meyer	RSA	2:25:15
	4	Alena Peterková	TCH	2:25:19
	5	Carmen de Oliveira	BRA	2:27:41
	6	Monica Pont	ESP	2:29:36

Belgrade Marathon
Apr 23   **Belgrade course may be short*
Men	1	Vladimir Bukhanov	UKR	2:12:25
Women	1	Cristina Pomacu	ROM	2:33:06

Shell Hanse-Marathon Hamburg
Apr 24
Men	1	Eduard Tuhbatulin	RUS	2:12:58
	2	Barnabas Qamunga	TAN	2:13:02
	3	Carsten Eich	GER	2:13:35
Women	1	Angeline Kanana	KEN	2:29:59

Maraton Popular de Madrid
Apr 24
Men	1	Abdelkader El Mouaziz	MAR	2:17:39
Women	1	Marina Ivanova	RUS	2:43:48

Paris Marathon
Apr 24
Men	1	Said Ermili	MAR	2:10:57
	2	Antonio Pinto	POR	2:10:58
	3	Andrew Masai	KEN	2:11:01
Women	1	Mari Tanigawa	JPN	2:27:55

Turin Marathon
Apr 24
Men	1	Michael Kapkiai	KEN	2:10:08
	2	Turbo Tummo	ETH	2:10:24
Women	1	Laura Fogli	ITA	2:31:45

San Francisco Bay to Breakers, 12km
May
Men	1	Ismael Kirui	KEN	34:03
Women	1	Tecla Lorupe	KEN	39:10

Pittsburgh Marathon
May 1
Men	1	Abel Gisemba	KEN	2:13:51
Women	1	Slusser	USA	2:37:14

Torun Marathon
Torun, Poland   May 8
Men	1	T Wojcik	POL	2:13:55
Women	1	Nikiel	POL	2:37:07

Gothenburg Half Marathon
May 7
Men	1	Onesmo Ludago	TAN	1:03:08
Women	1	Ritva Lemettinen	FIN	1:13:04

25Km von Berlin
May 8
Men	1	Tendai Chimusasa	ZIM	1:14:45
Women	1	Alena Peterkova	CZE	1:25:46

Diadora Marathon Munich
May 15
Men	1	Gidamis Shahanga	TAN	2:17:27
Women	1	Svetlana Kasatkina	RUS	2:53:45

Fabricolor Marathon Pardubice
May 15
Men	1	Juma Mnyampanda	TAN	2:17:32
Women	1	Alena Peterkova	CZE	2:31:47

Toronto Marathon
May 15
Men	1	Peter Maher	CAN	2:16:07
Women	1	Carole Rouillard	CAN	2:32:49

Conseil General International 15Km Road Race
May 29
Men	1	Paul Tergat	KEN	WB	42:12
	2	Andrew Masai	KEN		42:33
	3	Antonio Pinto	POR		43:35
Women	1	Fernanda Ribeiro	POR		48:45
	2	Iulia Negura	ROM		49:32
	3	Olga Bondarenko	RUS		49:39

Maratona de Porto Alegre
May 29
Men	1	Luis Carlos Da Silva	BRA	2:12:59
Women	1	Cleusa Maria Irineu	BRA	2:43:31

Comrades Marathon
Durban to Pietermaritzburg (86.7km)   May 31
Men	1	Alberto Salazar	USA	5:38:39
Women	1	Lyakhova	RUS	6:42:18

Stockholm Marathon
Jun 4
Men	1	Tesfaye Bekele	ETH	2:14:16
Women	1	Irina Sklarenko	RUS	2:40:34

St Petersburg Half Marathon
June 12
Men	1	Simon Robert Naali	TAN	62:28
Women	1	Olga Bondarenko	RUS	70:37

IAU 100km World Challenge
Hokkaido, Japan   June 26
Men	1	Alexey Volgin	RUS	6:22:43
	2	Jarostaw Janicki	POL	6:23:33
	3	Kazimiertz Bak	GER	6:24:29
Women	1	Valentin Shatyaeva	RUS	7:34:58
	2	Trudy Thompson	GBR	7:42:17
	3	Irina Petrova	RUS	7:46:35

Peachtree 10km
Atlanta   July 4
Men	1	Benson Masya	KEN	28:01
Women	1	Anne Marie Letko	USA	31:57

San Francisco Marathon
July 31
Men	1	Muturi	KEN	2:17:34
Women	1	Karolina Szabó	HUN	2:44:34

Helsinki Marathon
Aug 6
Men	1	Zerihun Gizaw	ETH	2:20:02
Women	1	Renz	GER	2:41:35

Badminton

Doubles remains the strong suit of English Badminton, with Commonwealth titles for Wright and Muggeridge in the women's doubles, Clark and Hunt in the mixed. Clark, would have enjoyed her Victoria success, having missed out in the European mixed event earlier in the year when the selectors determined that her fitness wasn't good enough. "I have not only been the most consistent player in England, I have possibly been the most consistent in the world," said an irate Clark. England also won the team title establishing a monopoly of some note; since the team title was introduced to the Games in 1974, no other team has won it. *For results, see Commonwealth section.*

It is only in the mixed doubles, that any British players have climbed into the top ten of the IBF rankings. Ponting and Wright made it up the IBF ladder to third, while Gillian Gowers and Denmark's Michael Sogaardclimbed as high as second. In January, a new ranking system comes out. Suffice to say it won't worry Steve Butler. The 30-year-old retired in March to take up a coaching post in Germany. He left on a high note; his IBF ranking of 20 was the highest he had ever placed. Darren Hall was one rank higher, but it wasn't the happiest of years. Hampered by a back injury, Hall missed both the English Open and the Commonwealth Games. The good news is that he has returned to full fitness for the forthcoming season.

That season will include a five-event Grand Slam circuit, supported by Friends Provident and designed to create a stronger domestic game. From last season's seven-match circuit, the current national rankings have been drawn up. The men's singles reads: 1. Darren Hall; 2. Peter Bush; 3. Anthony Bush. Women: 1. Sue Louis Lane; 2. Fiona Smith; 3. Alison Humby.

IBF WORLD RANKINGS

As at April 20, 1994 - this is the final ranking under the old points system, a new system comes into operation on Jan 1,1995

Men

1	Joko Suprianto	INA
2	Ardy B Wiranata	INA
3	Heryanto Arbi	INA
4	Harmawen Susanto	INA
5	Poul-Erik Hoyer-Larsen	DEN
6	Allan Budi Kusuma	INA
7	Thomas Stuer-Lauridson	DEN
8	Jens Olsson	SWE
19	Darren Hall	ENG
20	Stephen Butler	ENG
46	Anders Nielson	ENG

Men's Pairs

1	Gunawan/Suprianto	INA
2	Holst-Christensen/Lund	DEN
3	Subagya/Mainaky	INA
4	Axelsson/Jonsson	SWE
5	Chen Kang/Chen Hongyang	CHN
9	Hunt/Archer	ENG

Women

1	Susi Susanti	INA
2	Ye Zhaoying	CHN
3	Soo Hyun Bang	KOR
4	Camilla Martin	DEN
5	Han Jingna	CHN
6	Kim Ji Hyun	KOR
7	Liu Yuhang	CHN
8	Lim Xiaoqing	SWE
29	Joanne Muggeridge	ENG
41	Alison Humby	ENG
46	Sarah Hore	ENG

Women's Pairs

1	Chung/Gil	KOR
2	Finarsih/Tampi	INA
3	Ge Fei/Gu Jun	CHN
4	Shim Eun Jung/Jang 'lye Ock	KOR
5	Chen Ying/Wu Yuhong	CHN
12	Clark/Bradbury	ENG
16	Clark/Wright	ENG

Mixed Pairs

1	Bengtsson/Lund	SWE/DEN
2	Gowers/Sogaard	ENG/DEN
3	Ponting/Wright	ENG
4	Antonsson/Crabo	SWE
5	Holst-Christ/Nedergaard	DEN
11	Clark/Ponting	ENG

European Championships

Den Bosch, Holland   Apr 10-17

Anders Nielsen (ENG)
Tomasz Mendreck (CZE)
Jeroen van Dijk (HOL)
Rickard Magnusson (SWE)
Alexandr Tsigankov (UKR)
Michael Sogaard (DEN)
Tomas Johansson (SWE)
Hans Sperre (NOR)
Pedro Vanneste (BEL)
Jyri Aalto (FIN)
Colin Houghton (ENG)
Jens Olsson (SWE)
Oliver Pongratz (GER)
Pontus Jäntii (FIN)
Stephen Butler (ENG)
Poul-Erik Hoyer Larsen (DEN)

Men's Singles
from 3rd round

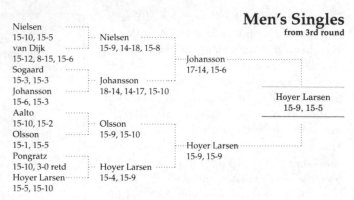

British players' results
1st Round:
Anders Nielsen (ENG) bt Alexj Siderov (RUS) 15-7, 15-2
Jeroen van Dijk (HOL) bt David Gilmour (SCO) 15-4, 15-7
Luigi Dalli-Cardillo (BEL) bt Peter Knowles (ENG) w/o
Alexandr Tsigankov (UKR) bt John Leung (WAL) 11-15,
15-8, 15-8
Hannes Fuchs (AUT) bt Bruce Topping (IRL) 15-7, 15-4
Mikhail Korshuk (BLS) bt Bruce Flockhart (SCO) 18-13,
15-11

Peter Espersen (DEN) bt Geraint Lewis (WAL) 15-2, 15-4
Colin Houghton (ENG) bt Chris Rees (WAL) 18-13, 15-4
Oliver Pongratz (GER) bt Graham Henderson (IRE) 15-0,
15-1
Stephen Butler (ENG) bt Henrik Bengtsson (SWE) 13-18,
15-5, 15-10
2nd Round:
Anders Nielsen bt Sören Nielsen (DEN) 15-10, 15-4
Colin Houghton bt Etienne Thobois (FRA) 15-2, 15-3
Stephen Butler bt Erik Lia (NOR) 15-5, 15-6

Camilla Martin (DEN)
Kelly Morgan (WAL)
Catrine Bengtsson (SWE)
Julia Mann (ENG)
Christine Magnusson (SWE)
Irina Yakusheva (RUS)
Anne Sondergaard (DEN)
Astrid van der Knaap (HOL)
Anne Gibson (SCO)
Jo Muggeridge (ENG)
Silvia Albrecht (SUI)
Pernille Nedergaard (DEN)
Sandra Dimbour (FRA)
Marina Andrievskaya (RUS)
Monique Hoogland (HOL)
Lim Xiaoqing (SWE)

Women's Singles
from 3rd round

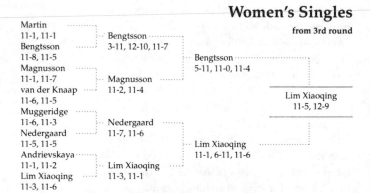

British players' results.
1st Round:
Sonya McGinn (IRE) bt Mateja Slatnar (SLO) 11-2, 11-0
Kelly Morgan (WAL) bt Heidi Vrancken (BEL) 11-2, 11-0
Julia Mann (ENG) bt Eva Lacinová (CZE) 11-2, 11-3
Christine Magnusson (SWE) bt Gail Davies (WAL) 11-0,
11-1
Sue Louis Lane (ENG) bt Diana Koleva (BUL) 11-6, 11-0
Jennifer Allen (SCO) bt Gudrun Juliusdottir (ISL) 11-2,11-0
Anne Gibson (SCO) bt Nicole Baldewein (GER) 12-9, 11-7
Jo Muggeridge (ENG) bt Rachel Phipps (WAL) 11-1, 11-4
Stephanie Müller (GER) bt Aileen Travers (SCO) 11-7, 11-8

Alison Humby (ENG) bt Birna Peterson (ISL) 11-1, 11-3
Elena Nozdran (UKR) bt Emma Duggan (IRE) 11-2, 11-0
2nd Round:
Camilla Martin (DEN) bt Sonya McGinn 11-3, 11-2
Kelly Morgan bt Vigdis Asgeirsdottir (ISL) 11-1, 11-1
Julia Mann bt Irina Koloskova (UKR) 5-11, 11-0, 11-4
Anne Sondergaard bt Sue Louis Lane(DEN) 11-6, 11-4
Astrid van der Knapp (HOL) bt Jennifer Allen 11-8, 11-3
Anne Gibson bt Victoria Hristova (BUL) 11-7, 11-1
Jo Muggeridge bt Georgy Trouerbach (HOL) 11-6, 11-2
Monique Hoogland (HOL) bt Alison Humby 11-4, 10-12,
11-7

Men's Doubles

Second Round *(British results only)*
Rickard Magnusson/Pär-Gunnar Jönsson (SWE) bt
Geraint Lewis/John Leung (WAL) 15-2, 15-4
Chris Hunt/Simon Archer (ENG) bt
Richard Hozbik/Tomasz Mendrek (CZE) 15-4, 15-6
David Gilmour/Gordon Haldane (SCO) bt
Lasso Lindelöf/Mikael Segercrantz (FIN) 15-4, ret.
Kenny Middlemiss/Russell Hogg (SCO) bt
Chris Rees/David Tonks (WAL) 15-13, 15-2
Julian Robertson/Nick Ponting (ENG) bt
Mihail Popov/Svetoslav Stoyanov (RUS) 15-6, 15-6

Third Round *(British results only)*
Hunt/Archer bt
Gilmour/Haldane w/o
Andrej Antropov/Nicolaj Zuev (RUS) bt
Middlemiss/Hogg 15-6, 15-1
Robertson/Ponting bt
Pierre Pelupessy/Ruud Kuitjen (HOL) 15-5, 15-12

Quarter-finals
Christian Jakobsen/Jens Eriksen (DEN) bt
Magnusson/Jonsson 15-7, 12-15, 18-16
Hunt/Archer bt
Quinten van Dalm/Ron Michels (HOL) 15-2, 15-7
Antropov/Zuev bt
Jan-Erik Antonsson/Mikael Rosén (SWE) 15-11, 15-7
Henrik Svarrer/Jim Laugesen (DEN) bt
Robertson/Ponting 15-8, 15-8

Semi-finals
Hunt/Archer bt
Jakobsen/Eriksen 15-12, 7-15, 15-12
Antropov/Zuev bt
Svarrer/Laugesen 15-11, 6-15, 15-7

Final
Hunt/Archer bt
Antropov/Zuev 18-16, 15-4

Women's Doubles

Third Round *(British results only)*
Lisbet Stuer-Lauridsen/Lotte Olsen (DEN) bt
Jayne Plunkett/Malin Virta (IRE) 15-2, 15-4
Georgy Trouerbach/Nicole van Hooren (HOL) bt
Aileen Travers/Jillian Haldane (SCO) 15-8, 15-13
Gillian Gowers/Joanne Wright (ENG) bt
Camilla Silwer/Tove Hol (NOR) 15-0, 15-4
Gillian Clark/Julie Bradbury (ENG) bt
Irina Yakusheva/Nadezhda Chervjakova (RUS) 15-4,15-8
Christine Magnusson/Lim Xiao Qing (SWE) bt
Elinor Allen/Jennifer Allen (SCO) w/o

Quarter-finals
Stuer-Lauridsen/Olsen bt
Trouerbach/van Hooren 15-0, 15-10
Erica van den Heuvel/Maria Bengtsson (HOL/SWE) bt
Gowers/Wright 8-15, 15-3, 15-4
Clark/Bradbury bt
Anne-Mette Bille/Marlene Thomsen (DEN) 11-15, 15-11,
15-5
Magusson/Lim Xiao Qing bt
Katrin Schmit/Kerstin Ubben (GER) 15-10, 15-10

SEMI FINALS
Stuer-Lauridsen/Olsen bt

van den Heuvel/Bengtsson 15-2, 15-8
Magnusson/Lim Xiao Qing bt
Clark/Bradbury 15-11, 12-15, 18-14

Final
Magnusson/Lim Xiao Qing bt
Stuer-Lauridsen/Olsen 17-14, 15-12

Mixed Doubles

Second Round *(British results only)*
Russell Hogg/Aileen Travers (SCO) bt
Peter Axelsson/Marlene Thomsen (DEN) w/o
Quinten van Dalm/Nicole van Hooren (HOL) bt
Bruce Topping/Sonya McGinn (IRE) 15-3, 15-11
Michael Sogaard/Catrine Bengtsson (DEN/SWE) bt
Gordon Haldane/Jillian Haldane (SCO) 15-3, 10-15, 15-11
Chris Hunt/Gillian Gowers (ENG) bt
Alexej Siderov/Irina Yakusheva (RUS) 15-3, 15-3
Jens Eriksen/Anne-Mette Bille (DEN) bt
Chris Rees/Rachel Phipps (WAL) 15-1, 15-2
Mikael Segercrantz/Nina Sarnesto (FIN) bt
David Tonks/Kelly Morgan (WAL) 15-4, 15-12
Jürgen Koch/Irina Serova (AUT) bt
Nick Ponting/Joanne Wright (ENG) 15-11, 15-6
Simon Archer/Joanne Davies (ENG) bt
Nicolaj Zuev/Marina Andievskaya (RUS) 13-15, 15-6,
15-11

Third Round *(British results only)*
van Dalm/van Hooren bt Hogg/Travers 15-10, 15-4
Eriksen/Bille bt
Hunt/Gowers 15-7, 15-3
Jan-Erik Antonsson/Astrid Crabo (SWE) bt
Archer/Davies 15-12, 15-10

Quarter-finals
Pår-Gunnar Jönsson/Maria Bengtsson (SWE) bt van
Dalm/van Hooren 15-6, 15-6
Sogaard/Bengtsson bt
Eriksen/Bille 15-8, 18-16
Ron Michels/Erica van den Heuvel (HOL) bt
Kock/Serova 18-15, 5-15, 17-16
Christian Jakobsen/Lotte Olsen (SWE) bt
Antonsson/Crabo 15-6, 11-15, 15-9

Semi-finals
Sogaard/Bengtsson bt Jönsson/Bengtsson 15-6, 15-6
Jakobsen/Olsen bt
Michels/van den Heuvel 15-5, 15-2

Final
Sogaard/Bengtsson bt
Jakobsen/Olsen 15-6, 15-9

Thomas Cup
Glasgow   *July 11*
QUALIFYING - FIRST STAGE
Group A
Belarus bt Ireland 4-1; bt Slovenia 5-0; bt Wales 3-2
Wales bt Ireland 3-2; bt Slovenia 5-0
Ireland bt Slovenia 5-0
Group B
Norway bt Israel 5-0; bt South Africa 5-0; bt USA 3-2
USA bt Israel 5-0; bt South Africa 4-1
South Africa bt Israel 5-0
Group C
Iceland bt Spain 5-0; bt Bulgaria 5-0; bt Barbados 5-0
Bulgaria bt Spain 4-1; bt Barbados 5-0
Spain bt Barbados 5-0
Group D
Austria bt Cyprus 5-0; bt France 5-0 bt Belgium 4-0
France bt Cyprus 5-0; bt Belgium 4-1
Belgium bt Cyprus 5-0
Group E
Poland bt Slovakia 5-0; bt Portugal 4-1; bt Guatemala 5-0
Portugal bt Slovakia 4-1; bt Guatemala 5-0
Guatemala bt Slovakia 3-2
Group F
Switzerland bt Czech 4-1; bt Peru 4-1; bt Italy 5-0
Peru bt Czech 3-2; bt Italy 5-0
Czech bt Italy 5-0

SEMI-FINAL STAGE
Group W
Denmark bt Russia 5-0; bt Austria 5-0; bt Belarus 5-0
Russia bt Austria 4-1; bt Belarus 5-0
Group X
Finland bt Netherlands 3-2; bt Canada 3-2; bt Switzerland 5-0;
Netherlands bt Canada 5-0; bt Switzerland 4-1
Group Y
England bt Scotland 5-0; bt Iceland 5-0; bt Poland 5-0
Scotland bt Iceland 5-0; beat Poland 4-1
Poland bt Iceland 3-2

SEMI-FINALS
Denmark bt Finland 4-1
Sweden bt England 3-2

3RD/4TH PLAY-OFF
Finland bt England 3-2

FINAL
Denmark bt Sweden
Denmark, Sweden and Finland qualified for the finals

QUALIFYING - FIRST STAGE
Singapore   *July 11-13*
Group A
Singapore bt Iran 5-0; bt Sri Lanka 3-2
Sri Lanka bt Iran 5-0
Group B
India bt Mexico 5-0; bt Pakistan 5-0
Pakistan bt Mexico 5-0
Group C
Australia bt Macau 5-0; bt Napal 5-0; bt Mauritius 5-0
Mauritius bt Macau 4-1; bt Nepal 4-1
Macau bt Napal 3-2

SEMI-FINAL STAGE
Group X
Korea bt Chinese-Taipei 4-1; bt India 4-1; bt Singapore 5-0
Chinese-Taipei bt India 4-1; bt Singapore 5-0; India bt Singapore 4-1
Group Y
China bt Thailand 5-0; bt Japan 4-1; bt Australia 5-0
Thailand bt Japan 5-0; bt Australia 5-0
Japan bt Australia 5-0

SEMI-FINALS
Korea bt Thailand 5-0
China bt Chinese-Taipei 5-0

3RD/4TH PLAY-OFF
Thailand bt Chinese-Taipai 4-1

FINAL
China bt Korea 3-2
China, Korea & Thailand qualified for the finals

THOMAS CUP - FINAL ROUNDS
Jakarta
Group A
Indonesia bt Finland 5-0; bt China 5-0; bt Sweden 5-0
China bt Finland 5-0; bt Sweden 4-1
Sweden bt Finland 5-0
Group B
Malaysia bt Denmark 4-1; bt Thailand 5-0; bt Korea 3-2
Korea bt Denmark 3-2; bt Thailand 4-1
Denmark bt Thailand 5-0

SEMI-FINALS
Indonesia bt Korea 4-1
Malaysia bt China 4-1

FINAL
Indonesia bt Malaysia 3-0

Uber Cup
Glasgow
Group A
Iceland bt Israel 4-1; bt Spain 4-1; bt Belgium 3-2
Spain bt Israel 3-2; bt Belgium 3-2
Belgium bt Israel 3-2
Group B
Switzerland bt Peru 5-0; bt Cyprus 5-0; bt Slovenia 5-0; bt Portugal 5-0
Slovenia bt Peru 3-2; bt Cyprus 5-0; bt Portugal 5-0
Peru bt Cyprus 5-0
Portugal bt Cyprus 3-2
Group C
France bt Belarus 3-2; bt Wales 4-1; bt South Africa 4-1
Wales bt Belarus 5-0; bt South Africa 4-0
Belarus bt South Africa 4-1
Group D
Norway bt Finland 3-2; bt USA 5-0; bt Italy 5-0
Finland bt Hungary 3-2; bt USA 3-2; bt Italy 5-0
Hungary bt Norway 3-2; bt USA 3-2; bt Italy 5-0
USA bt Italy 5-0

SEMI-FINAL STAGE
Group W
Denmark bt Germany 5-0; bt Poland 5-0; bt Norway 5-0
Germany bt Poland 4-1; bt Norway 5-0
Poland bt Norway 4-1
Group X
England bt Netherlands 4-1; bt New Zealand 4-1; bt
Iceland 5-0
Netherlands bt New Zealand 3-2; bt Iceland 5-0
New Zealand bt Iceland 5-0
Group Y
Russia bt Canada 5-0; bt Czech Rep 5-0;
bt Switzerland 5-0
Canada bt Czech Rep 5-0; bt Switzerland 5-0
Switzerland bt Czech Rep 3-2
Group Z
Sweden bt Scotland 4-1; bt Bulgaria 5-0; bt France 5-0
Scotland bt Bulgaria 5-0; bt France 5-0; France bt Bulgaria
4-1
SEMI-FINALS
Denmark bt England 3-2
Russia bt Sweden 3-2

3RD/4TH PLACE PLAY-OFF
Sweden bt England 4-1

FINAL
Denmark bt Russia 4-1
Denmark, Russia and Sweden qualified for the finals

QUALIFYING - FIRST STAGE
Singapore
Group A
Singapore bt Sri Lanka 4-1; bt Kazakhstan 3-2
Sri Lanka bt Kazakhstan 3-2
Group B
India bt Nepal 5-0; bt Mexico 5-0
Mexico bt Nepal 3-2

SEMI-FINAL STAGE
Group X
Korea beat Australia 5-0; bt Hong Kong 5-0
bt Singapore 5-0
Australia bt Hong Kong 3-2; bt Singapore 4-1
Group Y
Japan bt Thailand 4-1; bt Malaysia 5-0; bt India 5-0
Thailand bt Malaysia 4-1; bt India 5-0
Malaysia bt India 3-2

SEMI-FINALS
Korea bt Thailand 5-0
Japan bt Australia 4-1

3RD/4TH PLACE PLAY-OFF
Thailand bt Australia 5-0
FINAL
Korea bt Japan 4-1
Korea, Japan and Thailand qualified for the finals

FINAL ROUNDS
Group A
China bt Korea 3-2; bt Japan 4-1; bt Russia 5-0
Korea bt Japan 5-0; bt Russia 5-0
Japan bt Russia 5-0

Group B
Indonesia bt Thailand 5-0; bt Denmark 3-2; bt Sweden 5-0
Sweden bt Thailand 3-2; bt Denmark 3-2
Denmark bt Thailand 5-0

SEMI-FINALS
China bt Sweden 3-2
Indonesia bt Korea 4-1

FINAL
Indonesia bt China 3-2

World Cup
Ho Chi Minh City, Vietnam
MEN'S SINGLES
Semi-finals
T Stuer-Lauridsen DEN bt J Suprianto INA 9-15, 15-12,
15-6
H Arbi INA bt A Wiranata INA 15-10, 15-11
FINAL
H Arbi bt T Stuer-Lauridsen 9-7, retired

WOMEN'S SINGLES
Semi-finals
S Susanti INA bt C Martin DEN 12-10, 11-1
Bang Soo-Hyun KOR bt Ye Zhaoying CHN 11-2, 11-4
Final
S Susanti bt Bang Soo-Hyun 12-9, 11-6

MEN'S DOUBLES
Semi-finals
B Suprianto & R Gunawan INA bt T Lund & M Sogaard
DEN 15-2, 15-10
Cheah Soon Kit & Soo Beng Kiang MAL bt Yap Kim
Hock & Tan Kim Her MAL 6-15, 15-11, 15-8
Final
Cheah Soon Kit & Soo Beng Kiang bt B Suprianto & R
Gunawan 18-13, 13-18, 18-16

WOMEN'S DOUBLES
Semi-finals
Chung Soo-Young & Gil Young-Ah KOR bt Wu Yuhong
& Chen Ying CHN 15-10, 15-7
Lili Tampi & Finarsih INA bt L Stuer-Lauridsen & L
Olsen DEN 15-3, 15-5
Final
Lili Tampi & Finarsih bt Chung Soo-Young & Gil Young-
Ah 15-11, 15-12

MIXED DOUBLES
Semi-finals
T Lund DEN & C Bengtsson SWE bt J-E Antonsson & A
Crabo SWE 18-16, 15-12
Cheng Xingdong & Gu Jun CHN bt A Miranat & P Riseu
INA 15-10, 15-6
Final
T Lund & C Bengtsson bt Cheng Xingdong & Gu Jun 10-
15, 15-10, 15-2

European Team Championships
Den Bosch, Holland   Apr 10-12
Group A
Sweden bt Scotland 5-0
Russia bt Scotland 4-1
Sweden bt Russia 5-0

Group B
Denmark bt Germany 5-0
England bt Germany 3-2
Denmark bt England 4-1
Group C
Netherlands bt Wales 5-0
Wales bt Norway 3-2
Netherlands bt Norway 5-0
Group D
Poland bt Iceland 4-1
Finland bt Iceland 3-2
Poland bt Finland 3-2
Group E
Belgium bt Ireland 3-2
Austria bt Czech Republic 4-1
Czech Republic bt Belgium 4-1
Austria bt Ireland 4-1
Austria bt Belgium 4-1
Ireland bt Czech Republic 3-2
Group F
Ukraine bt Bulgaria 4-1
Switzerland bt France 4-1
Ukraine bt France 5-0
Bulgaria bt Switzerland 3-2
Bulgaria bt France 3-2
Ukraine bt Switzerland 3-2

PLAY-OFFS
19/20th place
Belgium bt France 3-2
17/18th place
Switzerland bt Ireland 4-1
15/16th place
Czech Republic bt Bulgaria 4-1
13/14th place
Austria bt Ukraine 4-1
11/12th place
Norway bt Iceland 3-2
9/10th place
Wales bt Finland 3-2
7/8th place
Netherlands bt Poland 5-0
5/6th place
Germany bt Scotland 3-2
3/4th place
England bt Russia 4-1
Men's Singles: Anders Nielsen bt Andrey Antropov 8-15 15-5 15-8
Ladies' Singles: Sue Louis Lane lost to Marina Andrievskaya 8-11 11-1 12-10
Men's Doubles: Simon Archer & Chris Hunt bt Nicolai Zuev & Sergej Meinikov 51-8 15-2
Ladies' Doubles: Julie Bradbury & Gillian Clark bt Irina Yakusheva & Nadezhda Chervjakova 15-8 15-11
Mixed Doubles: Nick Ponting & Joanne Wright bt Nicolai Zuev & Marina Andrievskaya 17-14, 15-8
FINAL
Sweden bt Denmark 3-2

Open Events

GERMAN OPEN
Leverkusen   *Sep 29-Oct 3*
(Finals Only)
Men's Singles
Thomas Stuer-Lauridsen (DEN) bt Allan Budi Kusuma (INA) 15-5 15-2
Women's Singles
Susi Susanti (INA) bt Ye Zhaoying (CHN) 11-6 11-8
Men's Doubles
Lund/Holst-Chr (DEN) bt Mainaky/Subagja (INA) 17-14 15-12
Women's Doubles
Tampi/Finarsih (INA) bt Chen Ying/Wu Yuhong (CHN) 15-3 15-10
Mixed Doubles
Lund/Heuvel (DEN/HOL) bt Sogaard/Gowers (DEN/ENG) 15-4 15-12

DUTCH OPEN
's-Hertogenbosch   *Oct 6-10*
Men's Singles
Poul-Erik Hoyer Larsen (DEN) bt Allan Budi Kusuma (INA) 11-15 15-5 15-11
Men's Doubles
Cheah Soon Kit/Soo Beng Kiang (CHN) bt Xion/Qui (CHN) 15-4 17-14
Mixed Doubles
Antonsson/Crabo(SWE) bt Jonsson/Bengtsson (SWE) 18-13 9-15 15-9

SLOVENIAN OPEN
Slovenia Ljubljana   *Oct 22-24*
Men's Singles
P Espersen (DEN) bt Peter Rasmussen (DEN) 15-4 15-5
Women's Singles
Camilla Martin (DEN) bt Pernille Nedergaard (DEN) 11-12 12-11 11-7
Men's Doubles
Jakobsen/Svarrer (DEN) bt Antonsson/Rosen (SWE) 15-7 17-15
Women's Doubles
Thomsen/Martin (DEN) bt Yakusheva/Andrievskaya (RUS) 15-1 15-3
Mixed Doubles
Antonsson/Crabo (SWE) bt Jakobsen/Thomsen (DEN) 15-10 15-11

DANISH OPEN
Aarhus   *Oct 13-17*
Men's Singles
Poul-Erik Hoyer Larsen (DEN) bt Jens Olsson (SWE) 15-11 15-2
Women's Singles
Ye Zhaoying (CHN) bt Liu Yuhang (CHN) 11-8 11-1
Men's Doubles
Holst-Chr/Lund (DEN) bt Svarrer/Laugesen (DEN) 15-5 15-5
Women's Doubles
Stuer-Lauridsen/Olsen (DEN) bt Koike/Hirota (JPN) 15-4 15-2
Mixed Doubles
Lund/Bengtsson (DEN/SWE) bt Antonsson/Crabo (SWE) 15-4 15-4

RUSSIAN OPEN
Moscow *Oct 28-31*
Men's Singles
H Fuchs (AUT) bt V Tikhomirov (RUS) 15-6 15-3
Women's Singles
M Andrievskaya (RUS) bt I Yakusheva (RUS) 11-1 11-4
Men's Doubles
Korshuk/Shmakov (RUS) bt Cotterill/Quinn (ENG) 15-10 15-12
Women's Doubles
Andrievskaya/Yakusheva (RUS) bt Cha Yoon Sook/Yoo Eun Young (KOR) 13-15 15-13 15-1
Mixed Doubles
Zuev/Andrievskaya (RUS) bt Melnikov/Yakusheva (RUS) 17-14, 15-7

THAI OPEN
Bangkok *Nov 2-7*
Men's Singles
Joko Suprianto (INA) bt Hermawan Susanto (INA) 15-11, 15-3
Women's Singles
Susi Susanti (INA) bt Somharuethai Jaroensiri (THA) 12-10 11-2
Men's Doubles
Gunawan/Bambang (INA) bt Imay/Dicky(INA)15-5 15-7
Women's Doubles
Gu Fei/Gu Jun (CHN) bt Li Oi/Han Jingna (CHN) 15-5 15-10
Mixed Doubles
Liu Jianjun/Wang Xiaoyuan (CHN) bt Chen Xingdon/Sun Man (CHN) 15-5 15-11

CHINESE OPEN
Hangzhou-Zhejiang *Nov 9-14*
Men's Singles
Joko Suprianto (INA) bt Ardy B Wiranta (INA) 15-8 5-15 15-7
Women's Singles
Han Jingna (CHN) bt Ye Zhaoying (CHN) 12-10 11-1
Men's Doubles
Gunawan/Bambang Suprianto (INA) bt Chen Kang/Chen Hongyong (CHN) 15-12 15-12
Women's Doubles
Wu Yuhang/Chen Ying (CHN) bt Lin Yanfen/Pan Li (CHN) 4-15 15-12 15-4
Mixed Doubles
Chen Xingdong/Sun Man (CHN) bt Yoo Yangaung/Jang Kycock (KOR) 12-15 15-9 15-8

SCOTTISH OPEN
Glasgow *Nov 25-28*
Men's Singles
Steven Butler (ENG) bt Thomas Stuer-Lauridsen (DEN) 15-12 15-10
Women's Singles
Camilla Martin (DEN) bt Denyse Julien (CAN) 11-6 11-8
Men's Doubles
Holst-Christensen/Lund (DEN) bt Melnikov/Zuev (RUS) 15-4 15-7
Women's Doubles
Olsen/Stuer-Lauridsen (DEN) bt Bille/Thomsen (DEN) 11-15 15-10 15-7
Mixed Doubles
Lund/Bengtsson (SWE) bt Holst-Christensen/Nedergaard (DEN) 15-2 15-11

TAIWAN OPEN
Taipei *Jan 11-16*
Men's Singles
Heryanto Arbi (IND) bt Thomas Stuer-Lauridsen (DEN) 15-3 15-2
Women's Singles
Susi Susanti (INA) bt Kim Ji Hyun (KOR) 11-2 11-5
Men's Doubles
Gunawan/Suprianto (INA) bt Jacobsen/Eriksen (DEN) 15-1 15-8
Women's Doubles
Finarsih/Tampi (INA) bt Olsen/Stuer-Lauridsen (DEN) 15-9 15-4
Mixed Doubles
Sagaard/Gowers (DEN/ENG) bt Axelsson/Thomsen (SWE/DEN) 18-14 15-10

JAPANESE OPEN
Tokyo *Jan 18-23*
Men's Singles
Ardy Wiranata (INA) bt Heryanto Arbi (INA) 12-15 15-6 15-3
Women's Singles
Susi Susanti (INA) bt Ye Zhaoying (CHN) 11-6 10-12 11-8
Men's Doubles
Subagdja/Kantono (INA) bt Thongsari/Teerawiwatana (THA) 15-11 12-15 18-16
Women's Doubles
Gil Young Ah/Chung Soo Young (KOR) bt Finarsih/Tampi (INA) 15-11 15-11
Mixed Doubles
Holst-Christensen/Bengtsson (DEN/SWE) bt Sogaard/Gowers (DEN/ENG) 15-7 15-9

SWISS OPEN
Basle *Mar 2-6*
Men's Singles
Thomas Stuer-Lauridsen (DEN) bt Paul-Erik Hoyer-Larsen (DEN) 17-18 17-16 15-3
Women's Singles
Camilla Martin (DEN) bt Henny Ika (INA) 11-5 11-1
Men's Doubles
Jonsson/Axelsson (SWE) bt Yap Kim Hock/Tan Kim Her (MAL) 15-7 15-8
Women's Doubles
Olsen/Stuer-Lauridsen (DEN) bt Bille/Thomsen (DEN) 15-6 3-15 15-4
Mixed Doubles
Axelsson/Thomsen (SWE/DEN) bt Holst-Christensen/Bengtsson (DEN/SWE) 18-13, 15-9

SWEDISH OPEN
Lund *Mar 10-13*
Men's Singles
Jens Olsson (SWE) bt Lioe Tiong Ping (INA) 15-10 15-2
Women's Singles
Bang Soo Hyun (KOR) bt Kim Ji Hyun (KOR) 6-11 11-5 11-3
Men's Doubles
Mainaky/Subagdja (INA) bt Jonsson/Axelsson (SWE) 15-11 15-12
Women's Doubles
Chung Soo Yong/Gil Young Ah(KOR) bt Shim Eun Jung/Jang Hye Ock (KOR) 15-9 15-11
Mixed Doubles
Yoo Young Sun/Jang Hye Ock (KOR) bt Michaels/van den Heuvel (HOL) 15-9 10-15 18-17

ENGLISH OPEN
Birmingham   *Mar 15-16*
(Finals Only)
Men's Singles
Heryanto Arbi (INA) bt Ardy Wiranata (INA) 15-12 17-14
Women's Singles
Susi Susanti (INA) bt Ye Zhaoying (CHN) 11-5 11-9
Men's Doubles
Gunawan/Suprianto (INA) bt Mainaky/Subagya (INA)
15-12 15-12
Women's Doubles
Chung Soo Young/Gil Young Ah (KOR) bt Jang Hye
Ock/Shim Eun Jung (KOR) 7-15 15-8 15-4
Mixed Doubles
Ponting/Wright (ENG) bt Hunt/Clark (ENG) 15-10 15-11

FRENCH OPEN
Paris   *Mar 23-27*
(Finals Only)
Men's Singles
Sun Jung (CHN) bt Robert Libequist (FIN) 15-1 16-17 15-2
Women's Singles
Ning Zhang (CHN) bt Lin Yuhang (CHN) 7-11 11-7 11-7
Men's Doubles
Santosa/Razak (INA) bt Jakobsen/Svarrer (DEN) 16-18
17-16 15-12
Women's Doubles
Olsen/Kirkegaard (DEN) bt Oktaviani/Zanati (INA) 15-1
15-7
Mixed Doubles
Liang/Peng (CHN) bt Mitteldorf/Schmidt (GER) 15-13
15-2

INDONESIAN OPEN
Jakarta   *Aug 10-14*
(Finals Only)
Men's Singles
Ardi Wiranata (INA) bt Joko Suprianto (INA) 15-9, 15-8
Women's Singles
Susi Susanti (INA) bt Bang Soo Hyun (KOR) 2-11, 11-0,
11-?
Men's Doubles
Subagdja/Mainaky (INA) bt B Suprinato/Gunawan
(INA) 10-15, 15-4, 18-20
Women's Doubles
Finarsih/Lili Tampi (INA) bt Chung Soo Young/Gil
Young Ah (KOR) 10-15, 15-9, 15-?*
Mixed Doubles
Jiang Xin/Zhang Jin (CHN) bt Flandi Limpile/Dede
Hasanah (INA) 15-3, 15-11
* *Incomplete results supplied*

English National Championships
Norwich Sport Village   *Feb 11-13*
MEN'S SINGLES
Semi-Finals
Darren Hall(Essex) bt Peter Bush (Wilts) w/o
Peter Knowles (Kent) bt Anders Nielsen (Surrey) 15-12
15-8
Final
Darren Hall bt Peter Knowles 15-3 15-13

WOMEN'S SINGLES
Semi-Finals
Sue Louis-Lane (Devon) btAlison Humby (Hants) 6-11
11-6 11-2
Fiona Smith (Surrey) bt Sarah Hore (Hants) 11-3 12-10
Final
Sue Louis-Lane bt Fiona Smith 11-4 11-1

MEN'S DOUBLES
Semi-Finals
Simon Archer (Worcs)/Chris Hunt (Lancs) bt Mike
Adams/Dave Wright (Yorks) 15-4 15-3
Nick Ponting (Herts)/Julian Robertson (Northants) bt
Neil Cottrill/John Quinn (Middx) 15-9 12-15 15-5
Final
Archer/Hunt bt Ponting/Robertson 15-8 18-17

WOMEN'S DOUBLES
Semi-Finals
Gillian Gowers (Herts)/Joanne Wright (Sussex) bt Tracey
Dineen (Essex)/Alison Humby (Hants) 15-6 15-9
Julie Bradbury (Oxon)/Gillian Clark (Surrey) bt Nichola
Beck (Bucks)/Emma Chaffin (Surrey) 15-5 15-0
Final
Gowers/Wright bt Bradbury/Clark 15-7 ret'd

MIXED DOUBLES
Semi-Finals
Nick Ponting (Herts)/Joanne Wright (Sussex) bt Dave
Wright (Yorks)/Gillian Gowers (Herts) 15-3 15-9
Chris Hunt (Lancs)/Gillian Clark (Surrey) bt Julian
Robertson (Northants)/Julie Bradbury (Oxon) 15-9 18-15
Final
Ponting/Wright bt Hunt/Clark 15-9 15-9

Baseball

Whenever sport gets too serious, you can always rely on the element of farce to intrude. Last year, the Grand National didn't start, this year the World Series is cancelled; one by accident, one by design, but both risible in their way. Ken Evans, the recall man who took much of the National flak, might not relish the comparison. While he pocketed £28 a day (around $45) for his part in last year's pantomime, the average Major League player earns over £2,000 a day, or not a penny less than £750,000 a year. Some, like San Francisco's Barry Bonds, can watch their bank account grow to the annual tune of $7.1m, while Bobby Bonilla, of the New York Mets, who earns $6.3m, doesn't have to walk past the smoked salmon counter at Sainsburys. You get the picture, these sportsmen are seriously rich.

To labour the point, if it hasn't been already, the lowest salary - that which a rookie earns - is still $109,000 a year. Given those figures, it hardly comes as a surprise that the salary bills of the major clubs are huge; New York Yankees adds up to almost $45m a year, while at the other end of the scale even the relatively poor San Diego Padres must shell out almost $15m. The estimate from the owners is that 58% of revenue goes back in salaries.

So it was, that when the labour deal expired at the beginning of the season, that the owners resolved to introduce a salary cap, asserting that the smallers clubs would go under if they didn't. Yet the owners couldn't really rush out the accountants to support their claims. The figures on the other side of the ledger don't make such bad reading.

In the 1993 season, baseball revenues reached almost $1.8 billion and the total attendance was a record 71 million. The franchises for Miami and Denver went for $100m and Eli Jacobs sold the Baltimore Orioles for $173m; he had paid just $70m when he bought the club four years earlier. There are claims that 19 of the 28 clubs will lose money this year, but the value of the clubs has stayed high (Steinbrenner's Yankees are allegedly worth $250m) and there is no rush to sell.

So, stalemate, and the brightest season for years is snuffed out just when it is all about to happen. Ken Griffey, of Seattle Mariners, and Matt Williams, of the Giants, were both chasing the single season record of 61 home runs, held by Roger Maris, of the Yankees. At the All-Star break, each had 33 which gave them two more than Maris had at the same point. Frank Thomas, of Chicago White Sox, also had 32 home runs under his belt at that stage, but Thomas was chasing three of the immortal Babe Ruth's records; the number of walks, total bases and runs.

On the evening of August 12th, the strike began; the eighth in the last 22 years. However, the previous seven had been resolved before the main event was threatened. This time, after 34 days, what two world wars and the Great Depression couldn't stop, was halted by the intransigence of the players and owners. For the first time in baseball history, a history that goes back to four years after the civil war, there was no World Series.

QUOTES

"It"ll be a long one. We"re going to lose the World Series this year. The players are hard as nails. The owners are pretty tough too....You mark my words, if a strike occurs.......Clinton will have to step in and there will have to be government arbitration. Why not do it now if you're going to do it then?" - **Ted Turner, media man and owner of Atlanta Braves, as the crisis approached at the end of July.**

"We'll play for free" - **Houston Astro fans poster.**

"Let baseball know you are tired of being kicked around, like the kids in a messy divorce" - **Wallace Matthews, columnist in the *New York Post*, inciting the fans to boycott before the players did.**

"...the last few meetings haven't been very pretty. To answer the question today, I think it could get ugly and it could be for a while" - **Al Martin, Pittsburgh outfielder and the Pirates' player representative.**

"As far as I knew, they had vanished into the Black Hole of Calcutta" - **Donald Fehr, Players Association executive director, on the players' proposals and where the owners had put them.**

"We have reached the point where it is no longer practical to complete the remainder of the season or to preserve the integrity of post-season play" - **Bud Selig, on September 14th, when the acting commissioner for the sport cancelled the World Series.**

"In Memoriam" - **New York Times front page headline.**

Have you ever wondered why there's all that ball tampering in cricket, but nobody ever tampers with a bat. They do in baseball. America's equivalent to cricket closed its bat-tampering case in July when Albert Belle, of the Cleveland Indians, dropped his appeal after his suspension was reduced from ten games to seven. Belle's bat had a forbidden cork centre, making the bat lighter. Belle didn't have the greatest disciplinary record before that, having twice charged pitchers and once hit a heckler in the crowd with a baseball. On this occasion, though, his suspension didn't much matter; ten days later they were all on strike anyway.

Michael Jordan, not so long ago the greatest sports star in the whole wide world, is performing on a smaller stage these days. Jordan hit the first home run of his professional baseball career in July, when he helped Birmingham Barons to a 6-1 win over the Carolina Mudcats in a minor league game.

If you can't go to the game, go to the cinema. An estimated 10 million more cinema tickets were sold in the first eight months of 1994 than the previous year. It wasn't all down to the strike, which was only on for two weeks of the period in question, but it will be interesting to see the September and October figures.

The wife of Detroit Tigers Cecil Fielder was a put-up to win the Mrs Michigan title; at least that's what four of the other contestants are claiming. They have filed a lawsuit stating that the pageant organisers helped her lose weight and cancelled the swimsuit competition to improve Mrs Fielder's chances. They also allege the promoters arranged for Fielder to obtain breast implants and that they rigged the scores. Well, if that lot's true, they weren't taking any chances, were they?

Would you believe it? The highest paid sports star in Japan is none other than a baseball player. Hiromiysu Ochiai, of the Yomiuri Giants, was paid 360 million yen (around £2.5m) for his last year's work.

AMERICAN LEAGUE
CHAMPIONSHIP SERIES

CHICAGO WHITE SOX v TORONTO BLUE JAYS
Game 1
Chicago   Oct 5, 1993

Toronto	0	0	0	2	3	0	2	0	0	**7**	**17**	**1**
Chicago	0	0	0	3	0	0	0	0	0	**3**	**6**	**1**

GUZMAN, Cox(7) and Ward (9)
MCDOWELL, Deleon (7), Radinsky (8), McCaskill (9)
HR: Toronto (1) Molitor
Time: 3:38
Att: 46,246

Game 2
Chicago   Oct 6, 1993

Toronto	1	0	0	2	0	0	0	0	0	**3**	**8**	**0**
Chicago	1	0	0	0	0	0	0	0	0	**1**	**7**	**2**

STEWART, Leiter(7) and Ward(S)(9)
A FERNANDEZ and Hernandez(9)
Time: 3:00
Att: 46,101

Game 3
Toronto   Oct 8, 1993

Chicago	0	0	5	1	0	0	0	0	0	**6**	**12**	**0**
Toronto	0	0	1	0	0	0	0	0	0	**1**	**7**	**1**

ALVAREZ
HENTGEN, Cox(4), Eichhorn(7) and Castillo(9)
Time: 2:56
Att: 51,783

Game 4
Toronto   Oct 9, 1993

Chicago	0	2	0	0	0	3	1	0	1	**7**	**11**	**0**
Toronto	0	0	3	0	0	1	0	0	0	**4**	**9**	**0**

Bere, BELCHER(3), McCaskill(7), Radinsky(8) and
Hernandez(S)(9)
STOTTLEMYRE, Leiter(7) and Timlin(7)
HR: Chicago(2)-Johnson, Thomas
Time: 3:30
Att: 51,889

Game 5
Toronto   Oct 10, 1993

Chicago	0	0	0	0	1	0	0	0	2	**3**	**5**	**1**
Toronto	1	1	1	1	0	0	1	0	x	**4**	**9**	**0**

McDOWELL, DeLeon(3),Radinsky(7),Hernandez(7)
GUZMAN,Castillo(8) and Ward(9)
HR: Chicago(2)-Ventura,Burks
Time: 3:09
Att: 51,375

Game 6
Chicago   Oct 12, 1993

Toronto	0	2	0	1	0	0	0	0	3	**6**	**10**	**0**
Chicago	0	0	2	0	0	0	0	0	1	**3**	**5**	**3**

STEWART and Ward(S)(8)
A FERNANDEZ,McCaskill(8),Radinsky(9) and
Hernandez(9)
HR: Toronto(1)-White: Chicago(1)-Newson
Time: 3:31
Att: 45,527

Score by Innings

Toronto	2	3	5	6	3	1	3	0	3	**26**	**65**	**2**
Chicago	1	2	7	4	1	3	1	0	4	**23**	**46**	**7**

NATIONAL LEAGUE
CHAMPIONSHIP SERIES

ATLANTA BRAVES v PHILADELPHIA PHILLIES
Game 1
Philadelphia   Oct 6, 1993

Atlanta	0	0	1	1	0	0	0	0	1	0	**3**	**9**	**0**
Philadelphia	1	0	0	1	0	1	0	0	0	1	**4**	**9**	**1**

Avery, Mercker(7) and McMICHAEL(9)
Schilling and WILLIAMS(9)
HR: Philadelphia(1)-Incaviglia
Time: 3:33
Att: 62,012

Game 2
Philadelphia   Oct 7, 1993

Atlanta	2	0	6	0	1	0	0	4	1	**14**	**16**	**0**
Philadelphia	0	0	0	2	0	0	0	0	1	**3**	**7**	**2**

MADDUX, Stanton(8) and Wohlers(9)
GREENE, Thigpen(3), Rivera(4), Mason(6), West(8) and
Andersen(9)
HR: Atlanta(4)-McGriff,Blauser,Berryhill,Pendleton:
Philadelphia(2)-Hollins,Dykstra
Time: 3:14
Att: 62,436

Game 3
Atlanta   Oct 9, 1993

Philadelphia	0	0	0	1	0	1	0	1	1	**4**	**10**	**1**
Atlanta	0	0	0	0	0	5	4	0	x	**9**	**12**	**0**

MULHOLLAND, Mason(6), Andersen(7), West(7) and
Thigpen(8)
GLAVINE,Mercker(8) and McMichael(9)
HR: Philadelphia(1)-Kruk
Time: 2:44
Att: 52,032

Game 4
Atlanta   Oct 10, 1993

Philadelphia	0	0	0	2	0	0	0	0	0	**2**	**8**	**1**
Atlanta	0	1	0	0	0	0	0	0	0	**1**	**10**	**1**

JACKSON and Williams(S)(8)
SMOLTZ, Mercker(7) and Wohlers(8)
Time: 3:33
Att: 52,032

Game 5
Atlanta   Oct 11, 1993

Philadelphia	1	0	0	1	0	0	0	0	1	1	**4**	**6**	**1**
Atlanta	0	0	0	0	0	0	3	0	0	0	**3**	**7**	**1**

Schilling, WILLIAMS(9) and Andersen(S)(10)
Avery, Mercker(8), McMichael(9) and Wohlers(10)
HR: Philadelphia(2)-Daulton, Dykstra
Time: 3:21
Att: 52,032

Game 6
Philadelphia   Oct 13, 1993

Atlanta	0	0	0	0	1	0	2	0	0	**3**	**5**	**3**
Philadelphia	0	0	2	0	2	2	0	0	x	**6**	**7**	**1**

MADDUX, Mercker(6), McMichael(7), Whohlers(7)
GREENE, West(8) and Williams(S)(9)
HR: Atlanta(1)-Blauser: Philadelphia(1)-Hollins
Time: 304
Att: 62,502

Score by Innings

Philadelphia	2 0 2	7 2 4	0 1 3	2	**23**	**47**	**7**
Atlanta	2 1 7	1 2 5	6 4 5	0	**33**	**59**	**5**

World Series
PHILADELPHIA PHILLIES V TORONTO BLUE JAYS
Game 1
Toronto Oct 16, 1993

Philadelphia	2 0 1	0 1 0	0 0 1	**5**	**11**	**1**
Toronto	0 2 1	0 1 1	3 0 x	**8**	**10**	**3**

SCHILLING,West(7),Andersen(7) and Mason(8)
Guzman,LEITER(6)and Ward(S)(8)
HR: Toronto(2)-White,Olerud
Time: 3:27
Att: 52,011

Game 2
Toronto Oct 17, 1993

Philadelphia	0 0 5	0 0 0	1 0 0	**6**	**12**	**0**
Toronto	0 0 0	2 0 1	0 1 0	**4**	**8**	**0**

MULHOLLAND, Mason(6) and Willimas(S)(8)
STEWART, Castillo(7), Eichorn(8) and Timlin(8)
HR: Philadelphia(2)-Dykstra, Eisenreich; Toronto(1)-Carter
Time: 3:35
Att: 52,062

Game 3
Philadelphia Oct 19, 1993

Toronto	3 0 1	0 0 1	3 0 2	**10**	**13**	**1**
Philadelphia	0 0 0	0 0 1	1 0 1	**3**	**9**	**0**

HENTGEN,Cox(7) and Ward(9)
JACKSON, Rivera(6),Thigpen(7) and Andersen(9)
HR: Toronto(1)-Molitor; Philadelphia(1)-Thompson
Time: 3:16
Att: 62,688

Game 4
Philadelphia Oct 20, 1993

Toronto	3 0 4	0 0 2	0 6 0	**15**	**18**	**0**
Philadelphia	4 2 0	1 5 1	1 0 0	**14**	**14**	**0**

Stottlemyre, Leiter(3), CASTILLO(5), Timlin(8), Ward (5)
Greene, Mason (3), West (6), Anderson (7), Williams (8) and Thigpen(9)
HR: Philadelphia(3)-Dykstra2, Daulton
Time: 4:14
Att: 62,731

Game 5
Philadelphia Oct 21, 1993

Toronto	0 0 0	0 0 0	0 0 0	**0**	**5**	**1**
Philadelphia	1 1 0	0 0 0	0 0 x	**2**	**5**	**1**

GUZMAN and Cox(8)
SCHILLING
Time:2:53
Att: 62,706

Game 6
Toronto Oct 23, 1993

Philadephia	0 0 0	1 0 0	5 0 0	**6**	**7**	**0**
Toronto	3 0 0	1 1 0	0 0 3	**8**	**10**	**2**

Mulholland,Mason(6),West(8),Andersen(8) and WILLIAMS(9)
Stewart, Cox(7), Leiter(7) and WARD(9)
HR: Philadelphia(1)-Dykstra; Toronto(2)-Molitor, Carter
Time: 3:27   Att: 52,195

Score by Innings

Toronto	7 3 6	2 6 2	8 0 2	**36**	**58**	**2**
Philadelphia	9 2 6	3 2 5	6 7 5	**45**	**64**	**7**

Final League Standings 1993

AMERICAN LEAGUE

East Division	W	L	Pct	GB
1 Toronto	95	67	.586	-
2 New York	88	74	.543	7
3 Baltimore	85	77	.525	10
4 Detroit	85	77	.525	10
5 Boston	80	82	.494	15
6 Cleveland	76	86	.469	19
7 Milwaukee	69	93	.426	26

West Division				
1 Chicago	94	68	.580	-
2 Texas	86	76	.531	8
3 Kansas City	84	78	.519	10
4 Seattle	82	80	.506	12
5 California	71	91	.438	23
6 Minnesota	71	91	.438	23
7 Oakland	68	94	.420	26

NATIONAL LEAGUE

East Division				
1 Philadelphia	97	65	.599	-
2 Montreal	94	68	.580	3
3 St Louis	87	75	.537	10
4 Chicago	84	78	.519	13
5 Pittsburgh	75	87	.463	22
6 Florida	64	98	.395	33
7 New York	59	103	.364	38

West Division				
1 Atlanta	104	58	.642	-
2 San Francisco	103	59	.636	1
3 Houston	85	77	.525	19
4 Los Angeles	81	81	.500	23
5 Cincinatti	73	89	.451	31
6 Colorado	67	95	.414	37
7 San Diego	61	101	.377	43

Basketball

World Championships

Hamilton & Toronto, Canada   Aug 4-14

Preliminary Round

Group A
China 97 (38)   Brazil 93 (30)*
United States 115 (59)   Spain 100 (51)
Brazil 67 (36)   Spain 73 (30)
United States 132 (71)   China 77 (38)
Spain 76 (46)   China 78 (31)
United States 105 (48)   Brazil 82 (36)
* *Score at the end of normal time 77-77*

Group B
Croatia 85 (45)   Cuba 65 (27)
Australia 87 (59)   Korea 85 (44)
Croatia 104 (52)   Korea 53 (30)
Cuba 87 (42)   Australia 93 (42)
Cuba 92 (46)   Korea 79 (44)
Croatia 83 (43)   Australia 69 (39)

Group C
Canada 83 (39)   Angola 52 (30)
Russia 84 (48)   Argentina 64 (31)
Canada 91 (30)   Argentina 73 (30)
Russia 94 (46)   Angola 57 (34)
Argentina 67 (36)   Angola 59 (34)
Russia 73 (36)   Canada 66 (41)

Group D
Puerto Rico 102 (48)   Egypt 74 (35)
Greece 68 (31)   Germany 58 (35)
Greece 69 (37)   Egypt 53 (28)
Puerto Rico 74 (41)   Germany 81 (42)
Puerto Rico 72 (35)   Greece 64 (39)
Germany 78 (39)   Egypt 56 (28)

Quarter-finals

Group A
Russia 101 (51)   Puerto Rico 85 (47)
United States 130 (62)   Australia 74 (48)
Canada 61 (30)   Croatia 92 (45)
Puerto Rico 83 (25)   United States 134 (62
Australia 94 (51)   Puerto Rico 81 (41)
Croatia 81   Greece 55

Group B
Croatia 105 (61)   China 73 (41)
Greece 74 (40)   Canada 71 (34)
Australia 76 (30)   Russia 103 (55)
China 61 (30)   Greece 77 (35)
China 58 (37)   Canada 90 (43)
United States 111   Russia 94

Group C
Spain 98 (53)   Korea 57 (39)
Argentina 91 (52)   Egypt 66 (30)
Egypt 52 (18)   Spain 94 (40)
Korea 83 (45)   Argentina 105 (50)
Spain 72 (37)   Argentina 70 (34)
Korea 89 (49)   Egypt 81 (34)

Group D
Cuba 76 (39)   Brazil 82 (35)
Germany 86 (32)   Angola 76 (45)
Angola 71 (39)   Cuba 75 (38)

Brazil 76 (49)   Germany 96 (48)
Cuba 74 (34)   Germany 86 (39)
Brazil 78 (44)   Angola 79 (52)

Semi-finals
Korea 75 (47)   Angola 71 (46)
Egypt 69 (34)   Cuba 54 (28)
Spain 90 (43)   Brazil 85 (34)
Argentina 85 (44)   Germany 71 (41)
Australia 95 (44)   China 57 (27)
Puerto Rico 85 (48)   Canada 82 (47)
Greece 58 (30)   United States 97 (40)
Russia 66 (31)   Croatia 64 (22)

FINALS

15th/16th place
Angola 67 (38)   Cuba 75 (40)
13th/14 place
Korea 76 (41)   Egypt 69 (35)
11th/12th place
Brazil 93 (48)   Germany 71 (42)
9th/10th place
Spain 65 (25)   Argentina 74 (39)
7th/8th place
China 76 (41)   Canada 104 (51)
5th/6th place
Australia 96 (57)   Puerto Rico 83 (47)
3rd/4th place
Croatia 78 (36)   Greece 60 (32)
1st/2nd
United States 137 (73)   Russia 91 (40)

FINAL PLACINGS
 1 United States
 2 Russian
 3 Croatia
 4 Greece
 5 Australia
 6 Puerto Rico
 7 China
 8 Canada
 9 Argentina
10 Spain
11 Brazil
12 Germany
13 Korea
14 Egypt
15 Cuba
16 Angola

European Championship for Men's Clubs

Preliminary Rounds
IPS-Budivelnik UKR 58 Guildford Kings GBR 84
Guildford Kings 85 IPS-Budivelnik 85

Guildford Kings 86 Hapoel Galil Elyon 78
Hapoel Galil Elyon 71 Guildford Kings 65

Competition Proper
Guildford results only
Guildford Kings 71 Maes Pils BEL 97
Olympiakos GRE 96 Guildford Kings 51
Guildford Kings 73 Limoges FRA 80
Leverkusen GER 105 Guildford Kings 57
Guildford Kings 64 FC Barcelona ESP 109
Guldford Kings 72 Real Madrid ESP 81
Trévise ITA 93 Guildford Kings 71
Maes Pils 91 Guildford Kings 65
Guildford Kings 51 Olympiakos 71
Limoges 72 Guildford Kings 55
Guildford Kings 54 Leverkusen 72
FC Barcelona 94 Guildford Kings 55
Real Madrid 104 Guildford Kings 75
Guildford Kings 75 Trévise 76
Semi-final
Tel Aviv
Olympiakos 77 Panathinaikos GRE 72
7UP-Joventut, Badalona ESP 79 FC Barcelona 65
3rd/4th place
Panathinaikos 100 FC Barcelona 83
Final
7UP-Joventut, Badalona 59 Olympiakos 57

European Cup for Men's Clubs
Lausanne   Mar 15
Final
Smelt Olimpia, SLO 91 Taugres ESP 81

European Radivoj Korac Cup
Final - *over two legs*
Salonique   Mar 9
PAOK-Bravo GRE 75 Pall Trieste ITA 66
Trieste   Mar 16
Pall, Trieste 91 PAOK-Bravo 100

European Cup for Women's Clubs
Poznan, Poland   Mar 31
Final
SFT Como 79 Godella-Valencia 68

European Liliana Ronchetti Cup
Final - *over two legs*
Cesena, Italy   Mar 9
Ahena ITA 78 Parma Primizie 65
Parma, Italy   Mar 16
Parma Primizie 68 Ahena 66

6th McDonald's Open
Munich   Oct 21-23, 1993
Semi-finals
Phoenix Suns USA 145 Real Madrid ESP 115
CSP Limoges FRA 85 Buckler Bologna ITA 101
3rd/4th place
Real Madrid 123 CSP Limoges 119
Final
Phoenix Suns 112 Buckler Bologna 90

Commonwealth Championships
Malaysia   July
Full Results
Canada 107 Singapore 42
England 59 Nigeria 49
Hong Kong 72 Malaysia 88
England 95 Hong Kong 51
Malaysia 108 Singapore 63
Canada 59 Nigeria 64
England 81 Malaysia 49
Canada 110 Hong Kong 68
Singapore 42 Nigeria 107
Malaysia 43 Canada 97
Nigeria 85 Hong Kong 49
England 70 Singapore 40
Singapore 69 Hong Kong 81
Nigeria 105 Malaysia 74
England 50 Canada 64

Final Table	P	W	L	Pts
1 Canada	5	4	1	8
2 England	5	4	1	8
3 Nigeria	5	4	1	8
4 Malaysia	5	2	3	4
5 Hong Kong	5	1	4	2
6 Singapore	5	0	5	0

Budweiser League
MEN
Premier Division

1 Thames Valley Tigers	36	31	5	3356	2777	62
2 Worthing Bears	36	30	6	3342	3031	60
3 Manchester Giants	36	29	7	3516	2903	58
4 Guildford Kings	36	24	12	3100	2845	48
5 London Towers	36	21	15	3093	3124	42
6 Birmingham Bullets	36	21	15	3044	2914	42
7 Leicester Riders	36	20	16	2974	2917	40
8 Derby Bucks	36	17	19	3139	3132	34
9 Doncaster Panthers	36	13	23	2917	3105	26
10 Sunderland Scorpions	36	13	23	3190	3394	26
11 Chester Jets	36	11	25	2927	3073	22
12 H Hempstead Royals	36	3	33	2998	3552	6
13 Oldham Celtics	36	1	35	2729	3558	2

Division One

1 Coventry Crusaders	18	16	2	1498	1338	32
2 Crystal P Mavericks	18	12	6	1483	1333	24
3 Cardiff Heat	18	11	7	1533	1426	22
4 Sheffield Forgers	18	10	8	1489	1434	20
5 Brixton Topcats	18	10	8	1512	1413	20
6 Stockton Mohawks	18	9	9	1558	1607	18
7 Ware Rebels	18	8	10	1455	1568	16
8 Solent Stars	18	7	11	1390	1448	14
9 Bury Lobos	18	4	14	1552	1699	8
10 Plymouth Raiders	18	3	15	1451	1655	6

Division Two

1	Nottingham Cobras	20	18	2	1696	1200	36
2	Chiltern Fastbreak	20	15	5	1470	1368	30
3	Swindon Sonics	20	13	7	1530	1452	26
4	Guildford Storm	20	13	7	1717	1510	26
5	Liverpool Atac	20	12	8	1550	1528	24
6	Stevenage Phoenix	20	12	8	1765	1684	24
7	Mid Sussex Magic	20	11	9	1751	1673	22
8	Northampton 89'ers	20	8	12	1457	1522	16
9	London Elephants	20	4	16	1441	1848	7
10	Leicester Falcons	20	3	17	1353	1629	6
11	Lewisham Lightning	20	1	19	1472	1788	2

PREMIER DIVISION
Play-off Semi-finals
Manchester 72 Guildford 82
Worthing 77 Derby 75
Play-off Final
Guildford 65 Worthing 71

DIVISION ONE
Play-off Final
Cardiff 69 Coventry 65

DIVISION TWO
Play-off Final
Guildford 69 Swindon 54

CHRYSALIS MEN'S CUP
Final
Thames Valley 83 Worthing 92

BASKETBALL LEAGUE TROPHY
Final
Manchester 73 Thames Valley 79

CHRYSALIS MEN'S NATIONAL TROPHY
Final
Plymouth 60 Sheffield 62

NBL Women's League

Division One

1	Sheffield Hatters	22	21	1	1610	1128	42
2	Northampton 76ers	22	20	2	1709	1195	40
3	Thames Valley Ladies	22	14	8	1492	1204	28
4	Barking & D Bobcats	22	14	8	1477	1402	28
5	Ipswich	22	12	10	1270	1332	24
6	Birmingham Quality	22	11	11	1254	1231	22
7	Nottingham Wildcats	22	11	11	1081	1206	22
8	Chester Cats	22	8	14	1203	1407	16
9	London Jets	22	8	14	1280	1384	16
10	Rhondda	22	6	16	1149	1451	12
11	Brixton Lady Top Cats	22	5	17	1098	1327	10
12	South Tyneside	22	2	20	1226	1582	4

Division Two

1	London Heat	18	17	1	1237	774	34
2	Cardiff Flyers	18	15	3	1093	943	30
3	Leicester Ladies	18	13	5	1085	929	26
4	Spelthorne Acers	18	10	8	1041	993	20
5	Doncaster Free Press	18	9	9	931	937	18
6	Luton Accs Raiders	18	8	10	947	1109	16
7	Sunderland Ladies	18	7	11	883	877	14
8	Manchester Flames	18	6	12	910	1027	12
9	Harlesden Amazons	18	4	14	855	1000	8
10	Plymouth Racers	18	1	17	819	1212	2

DIVISION ONE
Play-off Final
Sheffield 56 Thames Valley 60

DIVISION TWO
Play-off Final
London Heat 83 Leicester 59

WOMEN'S NATIONAL TROPHY
Final
London Heat 54 Cardiff 59

NBA
(Final Standings 1993-4)

ATLANTIC DIVISION

	W	L	%	GB
New York	57	25	.695	-
Orlando	50	32	.610	7
New Jersey	45	37	.549	12
Miami	42	40	.512	15
Boston	32	50	.390	25
Philadelphia	25	57	.305	32
Washington	24	58	.293	33

CENTRAL DIVISION

Atlanta	57	25	.695	-
Chicago	55	27	.671	2
Cleveland	47	35	.573	10
Indiana	47	35	.573	10
Charlotte	41	41	.500	16
Detroit	20	52	.244	37
Milwaukee	20	62	.244	37

MIDWEST DIVISION

Houston	58	24	.707	-
San Antonio	55	27	.671	3
Utah	53	29	.646	5
Denver	42	40	.512	16
Minnesota	20	62	.244	38
Dallas	13	69	.159	45

PACIFIC DIVISION

Seattle	63	19	.768	-
Phoenix	56	26	.683	7
Golden State	50	32	.610	13
Portland	47	35	.573	16
LA Lakers	33	49	.402	30
Sacramento	28	54	.341	35
LA Clippers	27	55	.329	36

NBA PLAY-OFFS
FIRST ROUND
EASTERN CONFERENCE
Atlanta Hawks v Miami Heat
Atlanta 88 Miami 93
Atlanta 104 Miami 86
Miami 90 Atlanta 86
Miami 89 Atlanta 103
Atlanta 102 Miami 91
Atlanta win series 3-2

New York Knicks v New Jersey Nets
New York 91 New Jersey 80
New York 90 New Jersey 81
New Jersey 93 New York 92
New Jersey 92 New York 102
New York win series 3-1
Chicago Bulls v Cleveland Cavaliers
Chicago 104 Cleveland 96
Chicago 105 Cleveland 96
Cleveland 92 Chicago 95
Chicago win series 3-0
Orlando Magic v Indiana Pacers
Orlando 88 Indiana 89
Orlando 101 Indiana 103
Indiana 99 Orlando 86
*Indiana win series 3-0***WESTERN CONFERENCE**
Seattle Supersonics v Denver Nuggets
Seattle 106 Denver 82
Seattle 97 Denver 87
Denver 110 Seattle 93
Denver 94 Seattle 85
Seattle 94 Denver 98
Denver win series 3-2
Houston Rockets v Portland Trail Blazers
Houston 114 Portland 104
Houston 115 Portland 104
Portland 118 Houston 115
Portland 89 Houston 92
Houston win series 3-1
Phoenix Suns v Golden State Warriors
Phoenix 111 Golden State 104
Phoenix 117 Golden State 111
Golden State 133 Phoenix 140
Phoenix win series 3-0
San Antonio Spurs v Utah Jazz
San Antonio 106 Utah 89
San Antonio 84 Utah 96
Utah 105 San Antonio 72
Utah 95 San Antonio 90
Utah win series 3-1

EASTERN CONFERENCE SEMI-FINAL
Chicago Bulls v New York Nicks
New York 90 Chicago 86
New York 96 Chicago 91
Chicago 104 New York 102
Chicago 95 New York 83
New York 87 Chicago 86
New York 87 Chicago 77
New York win series 4-3
Atlanta Hawks v Indiana Pacers
Atlanta 85 Indiana 96
Atlanta 92 Indiana 69
Indiana 101 Atlanta 81
Indiana 102 Atlanta 86
Atlanta 88 Indiana 76
Indiana 98 Atlanta 79
Indiana win series 4-2

WESTERN CONFERENCE SEMI-FINAL
Phoenix Suns v Houston Rockets
Houston 87 Phoenix 91
Houston 117 Phoenix 124
Phoenix 102 Houston 118

Phoenix 96 Houston 107
Houston 107 Phoenix 96
Phoenix 103 Houston 86
Houston 104 Phoenix 94
Houston win series 4-3
Denver Nuggets v Utah Jazz
Utah 100 Denver 91
Utah 104 Denver 94
Denver 109 Utah 111
Denver 83 Utah 82
Utah 101 Denver 109
Denver 94 Utah 91
Utah 91 Denver 81
Utah win series 4-3

EASTERN CONFERENCE FINAL
New York Knicks v Indiana Pacers
New York 100 Indiana 89
New York 89 Indiana 78
Indiana 88 New York 68
Indiana 83 New York 77
New York 86 Indiana 93
Indiana 91 New York 98
New York 94 Indiana 90
New York win series 4-3

WESTERN CONFERENCE FINAL
Houston Rockets v Utah Jazz
Houston 100 Utah 88
Houston 104 Utah 99
Utah 95 Houston 86
Utah 78 Houston 80
Houston 94 Utah 83
Houston win Series 4-1

NBA FINALS
Houston Rockets v New York Knicks
Houston 85 New York 78
Houston 83 New York 91
New York 89 Houston 93
New York 91 Houston 82
New York 91 Houston 84
Houston 86 New York 84
Houston 90 New York 84
Houston win series 4-3

The Commonwealth Championship in Malaysia didn't get off to the best of starts. New Zealand and Australia declined to attend, Northern Ireland and Scotland withdrew at the last minute, and Tanzania, Western Samoa and Swaziland all failed to show. Basketball has never been part of the Games proper. Now we know why.

"I have three versions. The million dollar smile, the two million dollar smile, and the three million dollar smile" - **Shaquille O'Neal, who has a $42m-seven-year contract with Orlando Magic, taking the mick out of himself. Nah, second thoughts, he's serious.**

Billiards

World Championships

Bombay, India   *Oct 1-5, 1993*

ROUND 1	ROUND 2	QUARTER-FINAL	SEMI-FINAL	FINAL
Clive Everton ENG 963 / John Caven SCO 480	Geet Sethi IND 1685 / Clive Everton 563	Geet Sethi 2038	Geet Sethi 1598	Geet Sethi 2139
David Edwards WAL 989 / Nalin Patel IND 1021	Michael Ferreira IND 1122 / Nalin Patel 912	Michael Ferreira 606		
David Barton ENG 576 / Roxton Chapman ENG 1171	Ian Williamson ENG 596 / Roxton Chapman 603	Roxton Chapman 1120	Roxton Chapman 1024	
Subhash Agarwal IND 1718 / Des Heald ENG 800	Peter Gilchrist ENG 1420 / Subhash Agarwal 864	Peter Gilchrist 1007		**Geet Sethi**
John Murphy ENG 1116 / David Rees ENG 676	Robbie Foldvari AUS 1356 / John Murphy 526	Robbie Foldvari 794	Norman Dagley 1237	
Mark Wildman ENG 947 / Howard Griffiths WAL 826	Norman Dagley ENG 1306 / Mark Wildman 615	Norman Dagley 1118		Mike Russell 1140
Derendra Joshi IND 1236 / Manoj Kothari IND 1127	Bob Close ENG 1438 / Derendra Joshi 562	Bob Close 997	Mike Russell 1317	
Hugh Nimmo SCO 976 / David Sneddon SCO 1034	Mike Russell ENG w/o	Mike Russell 1367		

Strachan UK Pro Championships

Qualifying-Aldershot   Apr 3-5   *Final-Plymouth Pavilions   Apr 7*

First Round
Derendra Joshi 799 bt
Howard Griffiths 408

John Murphy 503 bt
David Sneddon

Hugh Nimmo 553 bt
John Caven 358

S Hardcastle 640 bt
Mark Wildman 265

Michael Ferreira 1015 bt
David Rees 271

Clive Everton 468 bt
Des Heald 235

Roxton Chapman 593 bt
Nalin Patel 463

Eddie Charlton 571 bt
A Kumar 442

Second Round
Robbie Foldvari 546 bt
Derendra Joshi 256

Bob Close 492 bt
John Murphy 433

Ian Williamson 716 bt
Hugh Nimmo 202

Peter Gilchrist 617 bt

S Hardcastle 530

Mike Russell 946 bt
Subhash Agarwal 459

Michael Ferreira 544 bt
Clive Everton 323

Norman Dagley 366
Roxton Chapman 365

Geet Sethi 735
Eddie Charlton 380

Quarter-finals
Bob Close 601 bt
Robbie Foldvari 449

Peter Gilchrist 648 bt
Ian Williamson 390

Mike Russell 1291 bt
Michael Ferreira 223

Geet Sethi 1100 bt
Norman Dagley 393
Semi-finals
Peter Gilchrist 699 bt
Bob Close 418

Mike Russell 787 bt
Geet Sethi 653
FINAL
**Mike Russell 1072 bt
Peter Gilchrist 330**

Third Radiant Grand Slam

Qualifying-Sheffield   Feb 2-3
Final-Hyderabad, India   Feb 5 7

Semi-final
Geet Sethi 5
Norman Dagley 2

Mike Russell 5
Subhash Agarwal 0

FINAL
**Geet Sethi bt
Mike Russell**

First Goldflake Grand Slam

Qualifying-Sheffield   July
Final-Madras, India   July 28-31

Semi-final
Mike Russell 5
Roxton Chapman 2

Robbie Foldvari 5
Geet Sethi 3

FINAL
**Mike Russell 6
Robbie Foldvari 3**

Bobsleigh/Luge

BOBSLEIGH WORLD CUP
Kunsteisbahn am Königssee, Germany   Nov 4-6
Two Man (Round 1)

1	Gustav Weder/Donat Acklin	SUI I	1:38.04
2	Sepp Dostthaler/Mike Sehr	GER III	1:38.61
3	Christoph Langen/Günther Eger	GER I	1:38.73
9	Mark Tout/Jason Wing	GBR II	1:39.26
23	Sean Olsson/George Farrell	GBR I	1:40.63
31	Peter Gunn/Alvin Walker	GBR III	1:42.54

Winterberg, Germany   Nov 11-17
Two Man (Round 2)

1	Gustav Weder/Donat Acklin	SUI I	1:51.81
2	Pierre Lueders/David MacEachern	CAN I	1:52.28
3	Christoph Langen/Günther Eger	GER I	1:52.44
9	Mark Tout/Jason Wing	GBR I	1:53.02
22	Sean Olsson/Lenny Paul	GBR II	1:53.87
35	Peter Gunn/Vernon Bramble	GBR III	1:55.60

Four Man (Round 1)

1	Hubert Schösser	AUT I	1:49.43
2	Dirk Wiese	GER III	1:49.47
3	Gustav Weder	SUI I	1:49.54
13	Mark Tout	GBR I	1:50.28
15	Sean Olsson	GBR II	1:50.55
29	Peter Gunn	GBR III	1:52.16

Altenberg, Germany   Nov 21-28
Two Man (Round 3)

1	Christoph Langen/Peer Jöchel	GER I	1:53.08
2	Günther Huber/Stefano Ticci	ITA I	1:53.29
3	Zintis Ekmanis/Aldis Intlers	LAT I	1:53.38
5	Mark Tout/Eric Sekwalor	GBR I	1:53.66
16	Sean Olsson/Lenny Paul	GBR II	1:54.71
34	Peter Gunn/Vernon Bramble	GBR III	1:57.50

Four Man (Round 2)

1	Dirk Wiese	GER II	1:51.29
2	Hubert Schösser	AUT I	1:51.35
3	Mark Tout	GBR I	1:51.58
6	Sean Olsson	GBR II	1:51.83

Four Man (Round 3)

1	Dirk Wiese	GER II	1:51.86
2	Mark Tout	GBR I	1:51.88
3	Hubert Schösser	AUT I	1:51.96
14	Sean Olsson	GBR II	1:52.77

Calgary, Canada   Dec 19-22
Two Man (Round 4)

1	Pierre Lueders/David MacEachern	CAN I	1:52.13
2	Gunther Huber/Stefano Ticci	ITA I	1:52.23
3	Sean Olsson/Lenny Paul	GBR II	1:52.25
11	Mark Tout/Eric Sekwalor	GBR I	1:53.08
21	Peter Gunn/John Herbert	GBR III	1:55.70

Four Man (Round 4)

1	Pierre Lueders	CAN I	1:52.22
2	Chris Lori	CAN II	1:52.38
3	Pasquale Gesuito	ITA I	1:52.65
4	Mark Tout	GBR I	1:52.69
7	Sean Olsson	GBR II	1:53.02
18	Peter Gunn	GBR III	1:54.76

St Moritz, Switzerland   Jan 27-30
Two Man (Round 5)

1	Pierre Lueders/David MacEachern	CAN I	2:08.45
2	Reto Götchi/Guido Acklin	SUI I	2:08.82
3	Jiri Dzmura/Pavel Polovsky	CZE I	2:09.34
5	Mark Tout/Lenny Paul	GBR I	2:09.47
10	Sean Olsson/Paul Field	GBR II	2:10.13

Four Man (Round 5)

1	Gustav Weder	SUI I	2:05.58
2	Hubert Schösser	AUT I	2:05.75
3	Mark Tout	GBR I	2:05.90
10	Sean Olsson	GBR II	2:06.89

WORLD CUP FINAL STANDINGS

1	Pierre Lueders/David MacEachern	CAN	136
2	Christoph Langen/Günther Eger	GER	124
3	Günther Huber/Stefano Ticci	ITA	122
6	Mark Tout/Lenny Paul	GBR	100

EUROPEAN CHAMPIONSHIPS
La Plagne, France   Jan 19
Two Man

1	Christoph Langen/Peer Jöchel	GER I	2:00.45
2	Günther Huber/Stefano Ticci	ITA I	2:00.51
3	Gustav Weder/Donat Acklin	SUI II	2:00.69
8	Sean Olsson/Paul Field	GBR II	2:01.36
9	Mark Tout/Paul Lenny	GBR I	2:01.45

Four Man

1	Günther Huber	ITA I	1:57.92
2	Mark Tout	GBR I	1:58.11
3	Dirk Wiese	GER I	1:58.19
9	Sean Olsson	GBR II	1:58.78

LUGE

WORLD CUP   Final Standings
Men

1	Markus Prock	AUT	160
2	Duncan Kennedy	USA	148
3	Georg Hackl	GER	140

Women

1	Gabi Kohlisch	GER	83
2	Jana Bode	GER	82
3	Susi Erdmann	GER	60
	Andrea Tagwerker	AUT	60

Doubles

1	Krause/Behrendt	GER	95
2	Schiegl/Schiegl	AUT	71
3	Skel/Wöller	GER	65

EUROPEAN CHAMPIONSHIPS
Kunsteisbahn-am-Königssee   Jan 18-23
Men

1	Markus Prock	AUT	1:35.907
20	Paul Hix	GBR	1:40.014
28	Keith Yandell	GBR	1:42.160
29	Ian Whitehead	GBR	1:42.298

Women

1	Gerda Wiessensteiner	ITA	1:30.185

Men's Doubles

1	Joerg Raffl/Norbert Huber	ITA	1:30.137

Bowls

INDOOR - MEN
World Championship

Preston   Feb 27-Mar 5
SINGLES
Quarter Finals
A Thomson (ENG) bt W Wood (SCO) 7-0, 7-3, 5-7, 6-7, 7-4
M McMahon (HKG) bt G Robertson (SCO) 7-5, 7-4, 7-3
S Rees (WAL) bt W Richards (ENG) 7-2, 7-5, 7-6
R Corsie (SCO) bt I Taylor (AUS) 7-6, 5-7, 3-7, 7-4, 7-4
Semi Finals
R Corsie bt M McMahon 7-3, 7-1, 2-7, 7-4
A Thomson bt S Rees 1-7, 1-7, 7-4, 7-4, 7-1
Final
A Thomson bt R Corsie 7-2, 7-0, 6-7, 7-6
PAIRS
Final
C Curtis/I Schuback (AUS) bt G Smith/A Thomson ENG
7-1, 7-6, 5-7, 7-0

English Championships

Melton Mowbray   Apr 10-17
Singles
M King (Pinewood Park) bt P Bennett (Bodmin) 21-12
Pairs
G Smith/R Vickers (Cyphers) bt M Newman/R Newman
(Whiteknights) 23-22
Triples
Lockhart/Holt/Burrows (Blackpool Boro') bt Bull/
Sekjer/Smith (Cyphers) 27-4
Fours
Booth/Heppell/Sekjer/Smith (Cyphers) bt Harman/
Lines/Smyth/Halmai (Paddington) 19-16

Inter-County
Somerset CIBA bt Kent CIBA

Under 25s Double Rink
Cumbria IBC bt City of Ely IBC

EIBA Champion of Champions Singles

Nottingham   Feb 4-5
Senior
M King (Pinewood Pk) bt R Hitchens (Huddersfield) 21-4
Under 25s
K Cousins (Five Rivers) bt K Mills (Brit. Cellophane) 21-6

EIBA Club Championship

Lawton Park   Feb 18-19
Semi Finals
Stanley IBC bt Teignbridge IBC 85-61
City of Ely IBC bt Cambridge Park IBC 72-70
Final
City of Ely bt Stanley 80-79

EIBA Mixed Fours
Church Gresley   Mar 26-27
Semi Finals
Sunderland bt Teignbridge 19-7
Cambridge Park bt Isis 14-12
Final
Sunderland bt Cambridge park 18-14

Welsh Team Championship
Ogwr   Mar 19
Porthkerry bt Oxwich 82-64

INDOOR - WOMEN
World Championship

Cumbernauld   Apr 23
Semi Finals
M Price (ENG) bt J Conlan (SCO) 7-3, 0-7, 7-2
J Woodley (SCO) bt A Simon (GUE) 7-3, 7-6, 7-5
Final
Woodley bt Price 5-7, 7-1, 7-5, 5-7, 7-5

English Championships

Darlington   Mar 5-12
Singles
M Price (Desborough) bt D Hunt (Swinton) 21-18
Doubles
J Hills/J Tester (Dartford Stone Lodge) bt J Beardsley/
J Baker (South Forest) 18-17
Triples
Barwell *(V Thompson/P Sutton/J Meakin)* bt Taunton 21-14
Fours
Swinton *(J Cropper/B Barker/I Howlett/D Hunt)* bt Crystal
Palace 21-20

Champion of Champions
S Rickman (King George Field) bt S Curtis (Eccles) 21-2
Under 31 Singles (winner)
J Thomas (Nottingham)
Unbadged Pairs
M Coles/B Tricker (Ipswich) bt D Burton/C Templeton
(Croydon) 26-13

Inter-Clubs Championships

Darlington   Mar 12-13
Semi Finals
Boston bt Stevenage 101-58
Rugby Thornfield bt Banister Park 83-62
Final
Boston bt Rugby Thornfield 93-87

OUTDOOR - MEN

Mazda International Jack High Tournament

Tweed Heads, Gold Coast, Australia   Apr 17
Semi Finals
A Thomson (ENG) bt R Corsie (SCO) 9-4, 9-7
D Stockham (AUS) bt R Parrella (AUS) 9-6, 9-5
Final
Thomson bt Stockham 9-4, 9-5

Toshiba International Singles

Tiverton   Sept 9-11
Semi Finals
D Drew (Stenalees) bt D Bryant (England) 21-20
W Richards (England) bt J Evans (England) 21-10
Final
Richards bt Drew 21-8

British Championships

Ayr   July 5-12
Singles
C Best (IRE) bt G Whitelaw (SCO) 21-20
Triples
Ireland *(Moffet/Henry/McClure)* bt Wales 16-15
Fours
Scotland *(Wells/Wilson/Lyall/Amos)* bt England 23-21

English Championships

Worthing   Aug 29-Sept 9
Singles
Nottinghamshire B *(P Wilkinson)* bt Derbyshire B *(K Morley)* 21-14
Pairs
Northumberland B *(Wood/Bennett)* bt Durham B *(Theobald/Webb)* 26-6
Triples
Devon A *(Colling/Evans/Denison)* bt Berkshire A *(Waldron/R Newman/M Newman)* 15-12
Fours
Gloucestershire A *(Wills/Gillett/Jones/Alcock)* bt Hampshire A *(Manderson/Archibald/Line/Standley)* 21-13

English Players' Association Championship

Wellingborough   Apr 23-24
Semi Finals
M Biggs (Thamesdown) bt B Bass (Cambridge Park, Twickenham) 7-4, 1-7, 7-2
R Morgan (E Dorset) bt R Vinter (Boston) 2-7, 7-2, 7-1
Final
Morgan bt Biggs 1-7, 7-1, 7-0

Champion of Champions

Worthing   Aug 28
Singles
Michael Arnold (Kent) bt Mark Christmas (Essex) 21-18

Middleton (County) Cup

Worthing   Sept 10
Cumbria bt Middlesex 102-98

National Club Two Fours

Worthing   Sept 11
Bath bt Bolton 51-26

National Under 25s Championship

Daventry   Aug 21
Stephen Mead (Beds) bt David Baxter (Cumbria) 21-16

Scottish Championships

Singles
Colin Peacock (Marchmount) bt James McGuire (Lochgelly) 21-14
Pairs
Maybole bt Prestonpans-Castlepark 16-11
Triples
Houldsworth bt Hawick 16-10
Fours
Drongan bt Spittal 19-14

Welsh Championships

Singles
Alan McCarley (Brynhyfryd) bt Roger Davies (St Gabriels) 21-19
Pairs
R Thomas/R Kent (Sketty) bt J Forey/M Bishop (Brynhyfryd) 21-11
Triples
Cardiff *(Dickens/Blake/Watson)* bt Prestelgne *(Phillips/B Weale/R Weale)* 22-6
Fours
Cardigan *(Culley/Thomas/Goodman/Bowen)* bt Penhill *(Edwards/Bullock/Letman/Rowlands)* 24-16
Mixed Pairs
Betty Morgan/Robert Weale (Llandrindod Wells) bt Lisa Oliver/Jonathan Forey (Strady) 23-15

Welsh County Championship

South Glamorgan bt Carmarthenshire

Irish Championships

Singles
G McCloy (Portrush) bt S Braniff (Musgrave) 21-12
Pairs
Henry/Moffett (Portrush) bt Saunders/Montgomery (NICS) 23-14
Triples
Lisnagarvey *(Aicken/McCloughlin/Graham)* bt Cookstown 21-14
Fours
Cliftonville *(Smith/Gray/Patterson/Johnson)* bt Brooke Park 27-7

WOMEN - OUTDOOR
English Championships
Royal Leamington Spa   July 28-Aug 7
Singles
I Betke (Thaxsted) bt P Kirk (Wealdstone) 21-12
2 Wood Singles
B Whitehead (Norfolk BC) bt G Fitzgerald (Kettering
Lodge) 16-9
Pairs
Carpenter/Darling (Milton Park) bt Hodge/Stern
(Northolt) 18-15
Triples
Egham *(Winter/Garden/Hankin)* bt Penryn 17-8
Fours
Peterborough & Dist. *(S & V Newson/Brundle/Anton)* bt
Carlton Conway 25-8
Champion of Champions
J Baker (Derbys) bt P Garden (Surrey) 21-10
Under 25s Singles
L Whitehead (Norfolk) bt K Hindley (Wilts) 21-13

Home Internationals
Llandrindod Wells   June 24-26
England bt Ireland 131-84
Scotland bt Wales 147-110
England bt Wales 125-119
Scotland bt Ireland 143-94
England bt Scotland 110-107
Wales bt Ireland 130-114
Final Standings: 1. England 6pts, 2. Scotland 4, 3. Wales
2, 4. Irealnd 0

British Isles Championships
Llandrindod Wells   June 24-26
Singles
D Prior (Hewell) bt M Rosser (Skewen) 25-9
Pairs
J Davies/B Morgan (Llandrindod Wells) bt I Minnis/F
Elliott (Knock) 30-19
Triples
Gt Baddow *(Buckingham/Haste/Polley)* bt Sophia Gardens
16-13
Fours
Wingrave *(Killen/McGarrity/Hand/Martin)* bt Kirn &
Hunter's Quay 23-17

Boxing

It was when Lennox Lewis won the WBC title by beating Tony Tucker in Las Vegas that the French sports paper, *L'Équipe*, described the winner as "sans panache". Less than 18 months later, Lewis was still sans panache and also sans title and, in terms of his future in the ring, quite possibly sans everything. It was such a silly way to go. Call it pride, call it hubris, call it just plain stupidity. There is no business that takes you from King to Clown so quickly and Lewis forgot that. The world champion's camp did everything wrong; from the moment of Pepe Correa's buffoonery with a suspender belt at the first press conference, McCall was given reasons to be angry. His anger exploded in the fight and Lewis, fighting so lazily it looked like he felt he couldn't lose, was caught within thirty seconds of the second round and was sans mentis, you could say.

It was a shock, but the heavyweight division has been one long shock of late. Don King, McCall's promoter, would have done well to get his £250,000 bet on his boxer, who was quoted at around 4-1 against winning. Yet just think what kind of accumulator he could have laid with Holyfield, Moorer, Bentt and Hyde in the past year. All won unexpectedly and only Lewis, albeit with unimpressive performances against Bruno and Jackson, had been a winning favourite in the division. Whither goest Lewis now? People may avoid him. He is not easy to beat, but not popular enough to make it a large payday to compensate.

Hyde's title victory, before a sparse crowd at Millwall's new stadium, served to remind us not how brilliant the Norwich heavyweight is, but what a fine line boxers tread. Bentt was rushed to hospital with concussion and advised never to box again. Holyfield had already received the same medical advice for a heart condition, following his defeat by Michael Moorer. Two withdrawals that have changed the heavyweight scene and just to complete the shuffling of the pack, Mike Tyson could return to the ring in the spring.

The deal of the year was made by Chris Eubank with BSkyB television. It was presented as a £10m-8 fight-12 month package. The numbers almost certainly don't add up to that, but they could fall the right side of £5m. Whatever, it may well be a reflection on what Sky thought about the deal that the architect, Kelvin McKenzie, has moved on. Eubank's performances won't have caused a rush for satellite dishes.

Nigel Benn had successful defences - his fifth and sixth for the WBC title - against Wharton and Gimenez, but can feel justly aggrieved that it was the fight that went on outside the ring that cornered the publicity on the Gimenez bill. For those of a statistical bent (and what are you doing reading this book if you're not?) Julio César Chavez lost to Frankie Randall after 91 victories and James Miller became the first parachutist to land in a world title fight ring when he interrupted the Bowe-Holyfield fight. Finally, the full list of British boxers who fought for world titles in the past year is:

Heavyweight Lennox Lewis (won 2, lost 1), Hyde (W1), Bruno (L1) **Light-heavyweight** Nicky Piper (L1) **Super-middleweight** Benn (W2, D1), Eubank (W3, D1) **Middleweight** Chris Pyatt (W1, L1) **Light-welterweight** Andy Holligan (L1) **Super-featherweight** Lloyd Havard (L1) **Featherweight** Robinson (W3), Colin McMillan (L1), Paul Hodkinson (L1) **Flyweight** Francis Ampofo (L1) **Light-flyweight** Paul Weir (L1)

PROFESSIONAL BOXING
World Title Fights

HEAVYWEIGHT
WBA/IBF
Las Vegas   Nov 6, 1993
Evander Holyfield (USA) bt
Riddick Bowe (USA)
Points

Las Vegas   Apr 22
Michael Moorer (USA) bt
Evander Holyfield
Points

WBC
Cardiff   Oct 1, 1993
Lennox Lewis (ENG) bt
Frank Bruno (ENG)
Referee stopped fight, round 7

Atlantic City   May 6
Lennox Lewis bt
Phil Jackson (USA)
Rsf, round 8

Wembley   Sep 25
Oliver McCall (USA) bt
Lennox Lewis
Rsf, round 2

WBO
Tulsa   Oct 29, 1993
Michael Bentt (USA) bt
Tommy Morrison (USA)
Kst, round 1

London   Mar 19
Herbie Hyde (ENG) bt
Michael Bentt
Ko, round 7

CRUISERWEIGHT
WBA
Paris   Nov 6, 1993
Orlin Norris (USA) bt
Marcelo Figueroa (ARG)
Ko, round 6, Norris won vacant title

Las Vegas   Mar 4
Orlin Norris bt
Arthur Williams (USA)
Points

Las Vegas   July 2
Orlin Norris bt
Arthur Williams
Ko, round 3

IBF
Atlantic City   Nov 17, 1993
Alfred Cole (USA) bt
Vincent Boulware (USA)
Rsf, round 5

Bismarck, N Dakota   July 23
Alfred Cole bt
Nate Miller (USA)
Points

WBC
Levallois Perret, Paris   Oct 16, 1993
Anaclet Wamba (FRA) bt
Akim Tafer (FRA)
Retired, round 8

Monte Carlo   July 14
Anaclet Wamba drew with
Adolpho Washington (USA)
12 rounds, Wamba retained title

WBO
Hamburg   Nov 20, 1993
Nestor Giovanni (ARG) bt
Markus Bott (GER)
Points

LIGHT-HEAVYWEIGHT
WBA
Fargo, N Dakota   Nov 16, 1993
Virgil Hill (USA) bt
Saul Montana (MEX)
Rsf, round 10

Dec 17, 1993 Minot, N Dakota
Virgil Hill bt
Guy Waters (AUS)
Points

Bismarck, N Dakota   July 23
Virgil Hill bt
Frank Tate (USA)
Points

IBF
Dusseldorf   Dec 11, 1993
Henry Maske (GER) bt
David Vedder (USA)
Points

Dortmund   Mar 26
Henry Maske bt
Ernie Magdelano (USA)
Rsf, round 9

Dortmund   June 4
Henry Maske bt
Andrea Magi (ITA)
Points

WBC
Bismarck, N Dakota   July 23
Mike McCallum (JAM) bt
Jeff Harding (AUS)
Points

WBO
Cardiff   Jan 29
Leeonzer Barber (USA) bt
Nicky Piper (WAL)
Rsf, round 9

SUPER-MIDDLEWEIGHT
WBA
Puebla, Mexico   Dec 18, 1993
Michael Nunn (USA) bt
Merqui Sosa (DOM)
Points

London   Feb 26
Steve Little (USA) bt
Michael Nunn
Points

Tucumán, Argentina   Aug 12
Frank Liles (USA) bt
Steve Little
Points

IBF
Tulsa, Oklahoma   Oct 29, 1993
James Toney (USA) bt
Tony Thornton (USA)
Points

Los Angeles   Mar 5
James Toney bt
Tim Littles (USA)
Rsf, round 4

Las Vegas   July 29
James Toney bt
Prince Charles Williams (USA)
Ko, round 12

WBC/WBO
Manchester   Oct 9, 1993
Nigel Benn (ENG) drew with
Chris Eubank (ENG)
12 rounds, Benn retained the WBC
title, Eubank the WBO title

WBC
London   Feb 26
Nigel Benn bt
Henry Wharton (ENG)
Points

Birmingham   Sep 10
Nigel Benn bt
Juan Carlos Gimenez (PAR)
Points

WBO
Berlin   Feb 5
Chris Eubank bt
Graciano Rocchigiani (GER)
Points

Belfast   *May 21*
Chris Eubank bt
Ray Close (IRL)
Points

London   *July 9*
Chris Eubank bt
Mauricio Amaral (BRA)
Points

Cardiff   *Aug 27*
Chris Eubank bt
Sam Storey (IRL)
Rsf, round 7

MIDDLEWEIGHT
WBA
Buenos Aires   Oct 2, 1993
John David Jackson (USA) bt
Reggie Johnson (USA)
Points . In May, Jackson was
stripped of his WBA title

Tucumán, Argentina   Aug 12
Jorge Castro (ARG) bt
Reggie Johnson
Points-Castro took the vacant title

IBF
Las Vegas   May 27
Roy Jones (USA) bt
Thomas Tate (USA)
Rsf, round 2

WBC
Las Vegas   Mar 4
Gerald McClellan (USA) bt
Gilbert Baptist (USA)
Rsf, round 1

Las Vegas   May 7
Gerald McClellan bt
Julian Jackson (VIR)
Ko, round 1

WBO
Brentwood   Feb 9
Chris Pyatt (ENG) bt
Mark Cameron (RSA)
Ko, round 1

Sheffield   May 11
Steve Collins (IRL) bt
Chris Pyatt
Rsf, round 5

LIGHT-MIDDLEWEIGHT
WBA
Alma Ata, Kazakhstan   Jan 22
Julio Cesar Vasquez (ARG) bt
Juan Medina Padilla (ESP)
Points

Las Vegas   Mar 4
Julio Cesar Vasquez bt
Armand Picar (PHI)
Rsf, round 2

Tucumán, Argentina   Apr 8
Julio Cesar Vasquez bt
Ricardo Nuñez (ARG)
Points

Belfast   May 21
Julio Cesar Vasquez bt
Ahmet Dottuev (RUS)
Rsf, round 10

St Jean de Luz, France   Aug 21
Julio Cesar Vasquez bt
Ronald Wright (USA)
Points

IBF
Las Vegas   Mar 4
Gianfranco Rosi (ITA) drew with
Vincent Pettway (USA)
Technical draw, Rosi retained title

WBC
Puebla, Mexico   Dec 18, 1993
Simon Brown (JAM) bt
Terry Norris (USA)
Ko, round 4

Las Vegas   Jan 29
Simon Brown bt
Troy Waters (AUS)
Points

Las Vegas   May 7
Terry Norris bt
Simon Brown
Points

WBO
Phoenix, Arizona   Oct 30, 1993
Verno Phillips (USA) bt
Lupe Aquino (MEX)
Rsf, rd 7, Phillips took vacant title

Inglewood   July 25
Verno Phillips bt
Jaime Llanes (MEX)
Rsf, round 7

WELTERWEIGHT
WBA
Manchester   Oct 9, 1993
Crisanto España (VEN) bt
Donovan Boucher (CAN)
Rsf, round 10

Levallois Perret, Paris   June 4
Ike Quartey (GHA) bt
Crisanto España
Rsf, round 11

IBF
Fort Lauderdale, Florida   Oct 23, 1993
Felix Trinidad (PUR) bt
Anthony Stephens (USA)
Rsf, round 10

Las Vegas   Jan 29
Felix Trinidad bt
Hector Camacho (PUR)
Points

Las Vegas   Sep17
Felix Trinidad bt
Luis Ramon Campas (MEX)
Rsf, round 4

WBC
Norfolk, Virginia   Apr 9
Pernell Whitaker (USA) bt
Santos Cardona (PUR)
Points

WBO
Oct 12, 1993
Gert Bo Jacobsen (DEN) vacated
title

Belfast   Oct 16, 1993
Eamonn Loughran (IRL) bt
Lorenzo Smith (USA)
Points, Loughran took vacant title

Las Vegas   Jan 22
Eamonn Loughran bt
Alessandro Duran (ITA)
Points

LIGHT-WELTERWEIGHT
WBA
Tucumán, Argentina   Dec 17, 1993
Juan Martin Coggi (ARG) bt
Eder Gonzalez (COL)
Rsf, round 7

Las Vegas   Mar 18
Juan Martin Coggi bt
Eder Gonzalez
Rsf, round 3

Las Vegas   Sep 17
Frankie Randall (USA) bt
Juan Martin Coggi
Points

WBO
Atlantic City Nov 19, 1993
Charles Murray (USA) bt
Courtney Hooper (USA)
Retired, round 6

Atlantic City Feb 13
Jake Rodriguez (USA) bt
Charles Murray
Points

Ledyard   Apr 21
Jake Rodriguez bt
Ray Oliveira (USA)
Points

Bushkill, Pennsylvania   Aug 27
Jake Rodriguez bt
George Scott (SWE)
Rsf, round 9

WBC
Puebla, Mexico   Dec 18, 1993
Julio Cesar Chavez (MEX) bt
Andy Holligan (ENG)
Retired, round 5

QUOTES

"'Hurtful' was how he described our opening offer. If raised a few wry smiles on our side of the table. There was, after all,more than just a couple of million on offer" - **Vic Wakeling, head of Sky Sport, on negotiations with Chris Eubank.**

"If anyone says this schedule is insane, I've never really said I'm sane" - **Chris Eubank, after signing the Sky deal.**

"Before conception, I had wanted a girl. It's uncanny how I always get what I want." - **Chris Eubank, after the birth of his first child.**

"What else am I going to be? A nuclear scientist?" - **Mike Tyson, on his decision to resume boxing when he leaves prison.**

"I can argue with a doctor. I can argue with an expert. But I can't argue with Allah. I will not fight again" - **Michael Bentt, on his decision not to fight again following the Hyde fight.**

"No, Daddy, please don't do it. You're too old" - **Blaine McGuigan, ten year old son of the former world featherweight champion, when his father started talking of a comeback.**

"I only hope that Frank Warren is right when he say there will be no problem with security at the forthcoming contest between Robert McCraken and Steve Foster....I have had the misfortune to be at events where both men have fought.....on both occasion their supporters have behaved disgracefully" - **Mr Roper, in a letter to Boxing News on September 2nd, eight days before the fight.**

"This is the worst I have seen at any contest. These were just low-life scum who have nothing to do with boxing" - **Frank Warren, who promoted the fight bill at the NEC Birmingham at which supporters of Robert McCraken and Steve Foster fought.**

"Just exuberance" - **Conservative party chairman Jeremy Hanley, putting a slightly different complexion on the events at the NEC.**

"It's definite that I will be a world champion. I will be a world champion at three different weights. I'm planning to be a millionaire at the age of 25" - **Naseem Hamed, the very confident European bantamweight champion.**

"It seems a lot to pay, but Rocky was a great fighter and I'm proud to own them" - **Robert Hillman, who bought a pair of Rocky Marciano's gloves for £1,400 at a Bonham's auction in August. Muhammed Ali's gloves made £1,200, Henry Cooper's £320 and Frank Bruno's just £250. Make of that what you will.**

"I realised how big he was when I stepped on his feet" - **Phil Jackson, stopped in eight rounds by Lewis.**

"When I do my homework in Hackney and punch the bag in Casey's gym, I keep thinking of all those guys who hope my performance will be a parody of a male contest" - **Anna Limos, a heavyweight boxer (11st 12lb) who topped the bill on the first all-women's billing at the York Hall in February.**

Las Vegas   *Jan 29*
Frankie Randall (USA) bt
Julio Cesar Chavez
Points

Las Vegas   *May 7*
Julio Cesar Chavez bt
Frankie Randall
Technical decision, round 8

Las Vegas   *Sep 17*
Julio Cesar Chavez bt
Meldrick Taylor (USA)
Rsf, round 8

WBO
Arezzo, Italy   Nov 19, 1993
Zack Padilla (USA) bt
Efrem Calamati (ITA)
Retired, round 8

Ledyard   *Dec 16, 1993*
Zack Padilla bt
Ray Oliveira
Points
Rotterdam   *Apr 18*
Zack Padilla bt
Harold Miller (USA)
Retired, round 6

Los Angeles   July 24
Zack Padilla bt
Juan Laporte (PUR)
Retired, round 11

LIGHTWEIGHT
WBA
Johannesburg Oct 30, 1993
Olzubek Nazarov (RUS) bt
Dingaan Thobela (RSA)
Points

Hammanskraal, South Africa   Mar 19
Olzubek Nazarov bt
Dingaan Thobela
Points

IBF
Las Vegas   *May 27*
Rafael Ruelas (USA) bt
Mike Evgen (USA)
Rsf, round 3

WBC
Mexico City   Nov 27, 1993
Miguel Angel Gonzalez (MEX) bt
Wilfrido Rocha (COL)
Rsf, round 10

Paris   *Mar 29*
Miguel Angel Gonzalez bt
Jean Baptiste Mendy (FRA)
Rsf, round 5

Ciudad Juárez, Mexico   Aug 6
Miguel Angel Gonzalez bt
Leavander Johnson (USA)
Rsf, round 8

WBO
Las Vegas   *July 29*
Oscar De La Hoya (USA) bt
Jorge Paez (MEX)
Ko, round 2, De La Hoya took the
vacant title

SUPER-FEATHERWEIGHT
WBA
Inglewood   *Oct 11, 1993*
Genaro Hernandez (USA) bt
Harold Warren (USA)
Points

Inglewood   *Mar 19*
Genaro Hernandez bt
Jorge Ramirez (MEX)
Rsf, round 8

IBF
San Juan, Puerto Rico   *Oct 9, 1993*
John John Molina (PUR) bt
Bernard Taylor (USA)
Ko, round 8

Cardiff   *Jan 22*
John John Molina bt
Floyd Havard (WAL)
Retired, round 6

Las Vegas   *Apr 22*
John John Molina bt
Gregorio Vargas (MEX)
Points

WBC
Las Vegas   *May 7*
Jesse James Leija (MEX) bt
Azumah Nelson (GHA)
Points

WBO
Los Angeles   *Mar 5*
Oscar De La Hoya bt
Jimmi Bredahl (DEN)
Retired, round 10

Las Vegas   *May 27*
Oscar De La Hoya bt
Giorgio Campanella (ITA)
Rsf, rd 3. De La Hoya vacated title

FEATHERWEIGHT
WBA
Kwangmyong, S Korea   Dec 4, 1993
Eloy Rojas (VEN) bt
Yung-Kyun Park (KOR)
Points

Kobe, Japan   *Mar 19*
Eloy Rojas bt
Seiji Asakawa (JPN)
Ko, round 5

IBF
Marseille   *Nov 30, 1993*
Tom Johnson (USA) bt
Stéphane Haccoun (FRA)
Rsf, round 9

St Louis   *Feb 12*
Tom Johnson bt
Orlando Soto (PAN)
Points

Atlantic City June 11
Tom Johnson bt
Benny Amparo (DOM)
Rsf, round 12

WBC
Reno, Nevada Dec 4, 1993
Kevin Kelley (USA) bt
Gregorio Vargas (MEX)
Points

Atlantic City May 6
Kevin Kelley bt
Jesse Benavides (USA)
Points

WBO
Cardiff   *Oct 23, 1993*
Steve Robinson (WAL) bt
Colin McMillan (ENG)
Points

Cardiff   *Mar 12*
Steve Robinson bt
Paul Hodkinson (ENG)
Ko, round 12

Cardiff   *June 4*
Steve Robinson bt
Freddy Cruz (DOM)
Points

SUPER-BANTAMWEIGHT
WBA
Tokyo   *Nov 18, 1993*
Wilfredo Vasquez (PUR) bt
Horoaki Yokota (JPN)
Points

Tokyo   *Mar 2*
Wilfredo Vasquez bt
Yuichi Kasai (JPN)
Rsf, round 1

Las Vegas   *July 2*
Wilfredo Vasquez bt
Jae-Won Choi (KOR)
Rsf, round 2

IBF
Lake Tahoe, California   Oct 17, 1993
Kennedy McKinney (USA) bt
Jesus Salud (USA)
Points

South Padre Island, S Africa   Apr 16
Kennedy McKinney bt
Welcome Neita (RSA)
Points

Hammanskraal, S Africa   Aug 20
Vuyani Bungu (RSA) bt
Kennedy McKinney
Points

WBC
Reno, Nevada Apr 9
Tracy Harris Patterson (USA)
Richard Duran (USA)
Points

Atlantic City Aug 26
Hector Acero Sanchez (DOM) bt
Tracy Harris Patterson
Points

WBO
Zaragoza, Spain   Oct 29, 1993
Daniel Jimenez (PUR) bt
Felix Garcia Losada (ESP)
Rsf, round 5

Palma, Majorca   Jan 7
Daniel Jimenez bt
Felix Garcia Losada
Points

Seville, Spain June 25
Daniel Jimenez bt
Cristobal Pascual (ESP)
Points

Wiener Neustadt   Sep 4
Daniel Jimenez bt
Harry Geier (AUT)
Ko, round 1

BANTAMWEIGHT
WBA
Atlantic City Oct 23, 1993
Junior Jones (USA) bt
Jorge Julio (COL)
Points

New York   Jan 8
Junior Jones bt
Elvis Alvarez (COL)
Points

Las Vegas   Apr 22
John Michael Johnson (USA) bt
Junior Jones
Rsf, round 11

Bangkok   July 16
Daorung MP Petroleum (THA) bt
John Michael Johnson
Rsf, round 1

IBF
Hammanskraal, S Africa Nov 20, 1993
Orlando Canizales (USA) bt
Juvenal Berrio (COL)
Points

San Jose, California   Feb 26
Orlando Canizales bt
Gerardo Martinez (USA)
Rsf, round 4

South Padre Island, S Africa   June 7
Orlando Canizales bt
Rolando Bohol (PHI)
Ko, round 5

WBC
Nagoya, Japan Dec 23, 1993
Yasuei Yakushiji (JPN) bt
Jung-Il Byun (KOR)
Points

Nagoya   Apr 16
Yasuei Yakushiji bt
Josefino Suarez (MEX)
Ko, round 10

Nagoya   Aug 1
Yasuei Yakushiji bt
Jung-Il Byun
Rsf, round 11

WBO
London   July 30
Alfred Kotey (GHA) bt
Rafael Del Valle (PUR)
Points

SUPER-FLYWEIGHT
WBA
Tokyo   Nov 15, 1993
Katsuya Onizuka (JPN) bt
Thanomsak Sithbaobay (THA)
Points

Tokyo   Apr 3
Katsuya Onizuka bt
Seungkoo Lee (KOR)
Points

IBF
Hermosillo, Mexico   Nov 26, 1993
Julio Cesar Borboa (MEX) bt
Rolando Pascua (PHI)
Rsf, round 4

Inglewood   Apr 25
Julio Cesar Borboa bt
Jorge Luis Roman (MEX)
Rsf, round 4

Hammanskraal, S Africa   May 21
Julio Cesar Borboa bt
Jaji Sibali (RSA)
Rsf, round 9

Inglewood   Aug 29
Harold Grey (USA) bt
Julio Cesar Borboa
Points

WBC
Seoul, S Korea   Nov 13, 1993
Jose Luis Bueno (MEX) bt
Sung-Kil Moon (KOR)
Points

Yokohama, Japan   May 4
Hiroshi Kawashima (JPN) bt
Jose Luis Bueno
Points

Tokyo   Aug 7
Hiroshi Kawashima bt
Carlos Salazar (ARG)
Points

WBO
Korsør, Denmark   Oct 29, 1993
Johnny Bredahl (DEN) bt
Eduardo Nazario (PUR)
Nazario disqualified round 4

Barnholme, Denmark   Mar 25
Johnny Bredahl bt
Eduardo Nazario
Points . Bredahl relinq title in Aug

FLYWEIGHT
WBA
Puerto La Cruz, Venezuela Oct 4, 1993
David Griman (VEN) bt
Alvaro Mercado (COL)
Points

Bangkok   Feb 13
Saensor Ploenchit (THA) bt
David Griman
Points

Bangkok   Apr 10
Saensor Ploenchit bt
Jesus Rojas (VEN)
Points

Bangkok   June 12
Saensor Ploenchit bt
Aquiles Guzman (VEN)
Points

IBF
Chaiyaphum, Thailand   Oct 3, 1993
Pichit Sithbangprachan (THA) bt
Miguel Martinez (MEX)
Rsf, round 9

Surat Thani, Thailand   Jan 23
Pichit Sithbangprachan bt
Arthur Johnson (USA)
Points

Rajaburi, Thailand   May 8
Pichit Sithbangprachan bt
José Luis Zepeda (MEX)
Points

WBC
Kyoto, Japan   Dec 13, 1993
Yuri Arbachakov (RUS) bt
Nam-Hook Cha (KOR)
Points

Tokyo   Aug 1
Yuri Arbachakov bt
Hugo Rafael Soto (ARG)
Ko, round 8

WBO
Sun City, S Africa   Dec 4, 1993
Jake Matlala (RSA) bt
Luigi Camputaro (ITA)
Retired, round 8

London   June 11
Jake Matlala bt
Francis Ampofo (ENG)
Retired, round 9

LIGHT-FLYWEIGHT
WBA
Tokyo   Oct 21, 1993
Leo Gamez (VEN) bt
Shiro Yahiro (JPN)
Rsf, round 9

Panama City   Feb 6
Leo Gamez bt
Juan Torres (PAN)
Rsf, round 7

Bangkok   June 27
Leo Gamez drew with
Kaj Ratchabandit (THA)
Gamez retained the title

IBF & WBC
Phoenix   Oct 30, 1993
Michael Carbajal (USA) bt
Domingo Sosa (DOM)
Rsf, round 5

Inglewood   Feb 19
Humberto Gonzalez (MEX) bt
Michael Carbajal
Points

WBO
Glasgow   Feb 2
Josue Camacho (PUR) bt
Paul Weir (SCO)
Points

Phoenix   July 15
Michael Carbajal bt
Josue Camacho
Points

STRAWWEIGHT
WBA
Pichit, Thailand   Nov 28, 1993
Chana Porpaoin (THA) bt
Rafael Torres (DOM)
Ko, round 4

Chonburi, Thailand   Mar 27
Chana Porpaoin bt
Carlos Murillo (PAN)
Points

Petchaboon, Thailand   Aug 27
Chana Porpaoin bt
Keunyoung Kang (KOR)
Points

Patthalung, Thailand   Sep 3
Chana Porpaoin bt
Keunyoung Kang
Points

IBF
Suphanburi, Thailand   Dec 10, 1993
Ratanapol Sorvorapin (THA) bt
Felix Naranjo (COL)
Rsf, round 2

Bangkok   Feb 27
Ratanapol Sorvorapin (THA) bt
Ronnie Magrama (PHI)
Points

Bangkok   May 14
Ratanapol Sorvorapin bt
Roger Espanola (PHI)
Rsf, round 6

Thailand   Aug 13
Ratanapol Sorvorapin bt
Marcelino Bolivar (VEN)
Rsf, round 4

WBC
Lake Tahoe, California   Dec 18, 1993
Ricardo Lopez (MEX) bt
Manny Melchor (PHI)
Ko, round 11

Las Vegas   May 7
Ricardo Lopez bt
Kermin Guardia (COL)
Points

Las Vegas   Sep 17
Ricardo Lopez bt
Yodsing Au Saengmorokot (THA)
Ko round 1

WBO
Dec 1993
Paul Weir (SCO) vacated the title

San Juan, Puerto Rico   Dec 22, 1993
Alex Sanchez (PUR) bt
Orlando Malone (USA)
Rsf, round 1

Palma, Majorca   Jan 7
Alex Sanchez bt
Arturo Garcia Mayen (USA)
Rsf, round 1

Bayamon, Puerto Rico   Aug 13
Alex Sanchez bt
Carlos Juan Rodriguez (DOM)
Ko, round 1

European Title Fights

HEAVYWEIGHT
London   Dec 1, 1993
Henry Akinwande (ENG) bt
Biagio Chianese (ITA)
Rsf, round 4

Berlin   July 23
Henry Akinwande bt
Mario Shiesser (GER)
Ko, round 7

CRUISERWEIGHT
Ferrara, Italy   Feb 2
Carl Thompson (ENG) bt
Massimiliano Duran (ITA)
Ko, round 8

Epernay, France   June 14
Carl Thompson bt
Akim Tafer (FRA)
Ko, round 6

LIGHT-HEAVYWEIGHT
Castelnau-le-Nez,France   Nov 13, 1993
Eddy Smulders (HOL) bt
Eric Nicoletta (FRA)
Points

Lyon, France   Mar 5
Fabrice Tiozzo (FRA) bt
Eddy Smulders
Rsf, round 7

SUPER-MIDDLEWEIGHT
Marino, Italy   Nov 26, 1993
Vincenzo Nardiello (ITA) bt
Mauro Galvano (ITA)
Points, Nardiello took vacant title

Toulon, France   June 11
Frederic Seillier (FRA) bt
Vincenzo Nardiello
Retired, round 5

MIDDLEWEIGHT
Dec 11, 1993   Berck-Sur-Mer, France
Agostino Cardamone (ITA) bt
Frederic Seillier
Points

Vitoria, Spain   Apr 14
Agostino Cardomone bt
Gino Lelong (FRA)
Points

Solofra, Italy   July 20
Agostino Cardamone bt
Neville Brown (ENG)
Rsf, round 7

LIGHT-MIDDLEWEIGHT
Dijon, France   Oct 5, 1993
Bernard Razzano (FRA) bt
Laurent Boudouani (FRA)
Retired, round 9

Dijon   Jan 11
Javier Castillejo (ESP) bt
Bernard Razzano
Retired, round 6

Madrid   Feb 19
Javier Castillejo bt
Santa Colombo (ITA)
Rsf, round 3

Cordoba, Spain   Mar 25
Javier Castillejo bt
Valentino Mance (ITA)
Retired, round 3

Las Palmas, Canary Isles   May 20
Javier Castillejo bt
Patrick Vungbo (BEL)
Points

Boiro   Jul 23
Javier Castillejo bt
Ludovic Proto
Retired, round 8

WELTERWEIGHT
Paris   Feb 1
Gary Jacobs (SCO) bt
Tek N'Kalankete (FRA)
Points

Glasgow   Apr 13
Gary Jacobs bt
Alessandro Duran (ITA)
Ko, round 8

LIGHT-WELTERWEIGHT
Levallois Perret, Paris   Dec 4, 1993
Christian Merle (FRA) bt
Valery Kayumba (FRA)
Rsf, round 2

Clermont-Ferrand, France   Apr 17
Valery Kayumba bt
Christian Merle
Rsf, round 3

Levallois Perret, Paris   June 4
Khalid Rahilou (FRA) bt
Valery Kayumba
Points

LIGHTWEIGHT
Dijon   Oct 5, 1993
Jean Baptiste Mendy (FRA) bt
Angel Mona (FRA)
Retired, round 9

Aalborg, Denmark   Apr 22
Racheed Lawal (DEN) bt
Paul Burke (ENG)
Ko, round 4, Lawal took vacant title

SUPER-FEATHERWEIGHT
Cayenne, France   Oct 2, 1993
Jacobin Yoma (FRA) bt
Areski Bakir (FRA)
Rsf, round 8

Cayenne   Jan 28
Jacobin Yoma bt
Rimvidas Bilius (LIT)
Rsf, round 8

Cayenne   May 14
Jacobin Yoma bt
Neil Haddock (WAL)
Retired, round 6

FEATHERWEIGHT
Charleroi, France   Mar 22
Stefano Zoff (ITA) bt
Stéphane Haccoun (FRA)
Retired, round 9

BANTAMWEIGHT
Glasgow   Feb 2
Vicenzo Belcastro (ITA) bt
Drew Docherty (SCO)
Points

Sheffield   May 11
Naseem Hamed (ENG) bt
Vincenzo Belcastro
Points

Sheffield   Aug 17
Naseem Hamed bt
Antonio Picardi (ITA)
Rsf, round 3

FLYWEIGHT
London   Apr 27.
Luigi Camputaro (ITA) bt
Mickey Cantwell (ENG)
Points

Whitchurch   Aug 3
Luigi Camputaro bt
Darren Fifield (ENG)
Points

Commonwealth Title Fights

CRUISERWEIGHT
Waregem, Belgium   Jan 28
Franco Wanyama (UGA) bt
Tony Booth (ENG)
Rsf, round 2, Wanyama took vacant title

MIDDLEWEIGHT
West Bromwich   Oct 27, 1993
Richie Woodhall (ENG) bt
Gerry Meekison (CAN)
Points

LIGHT-MIDDLEWEIGHT
London   Feb 26
Lloyd Honeghan (ENG) bt
Kevin Adamson (ENG)
Rsf, round 6

WELTERWEIGHT
London   Oct 5, 1993
Andrew Murray (GUY) bt
Tony Swift (ENG)
Rsf, rd 6, Murray took vacant title

LIGHT-WELTERWEIGHT
Bristol   May 25
Ross Hale (ENG) bt
Andy Holligan (ENG)
Rsf, round 3

LIGHTWEIGHT
Watford   Nov 10, 1993
Billy Schwer (ENG) bt
Paul Burke (ENG)
Points

Stevenage   May 11
Billy Schwer bt
Howard Grant (CAN)
Rsf, round 9

SUPER-FEATHERWEIGHT
London   July 30
Tony Pep (CAN) bt
J T Williams (WAL)
Rsf, round 1

FEATHERWEIGHT
Sunderland   May 24
Billy Hardy (ENG) bt
Alan McKay (ENG)
Rsf, round 8

BANTAMWEIGHT
London   Jan 14
Johnny Armour (ENG) bt
Rufus Adebayo (NGR)
Rsf, round 7

FLYWEIGHT
London   Oct 13, 1993
Daren Fifield (ENG) bt
Danny Porter (ENG)
Rsf, round 9, Fifield took vacant title

London   Feb 9
Daren Fifield bt
Danny Porter
Rsf, round 6

British Titles

LIGHT-HEAVYWEIGHT
Bethnal Green Dec 1, 1993
Maurice Gore bt
Simon Harris
Rsf, round 11

SUPER-MIDDLEWEIGHT
Bethnal Green Mar 11
Cornelius Carr bt
James Cook
Points

MIDDLEWEIGHT
Bethnal Green Nov 10, 1993
Neville Brown bt
Frank Grant
Rsf, round 7

Birmingham   Jan 26
Neville Brown bt
Andy Flute
Retired, round 7

LIGHT-MIDDLEWEIGHT
Watford   Feb 23
Robert McCraken bt
Andy Till
Points

Birmingham   Sep 10
Robert McCraken bt
Steve Foster
Points

WELTERWEIGHT
Dagenham   Feb 17
Del Bryan bt
Derek Grainger
Ko, round 7

Birmingham   Sep 10
Del Bryan bt
Lindon Scarlett
Points

LIGHT-WELTERWEIGHT
Bristol   May 25
Ross Hale bt
Andy Holligan
Rsf, round 3

Whitchurch   Aug 3
Ross Hale bt
Hugh Forde
Rsf, round 7

LIGHTWEIGHT
Watford   Nov 10, 1993
Billy Schwer bt
Paul Burke
Points

Stevenage   Feb 16
Billy Schwer bt
Sean Murphy
Rsf, round 3

SUPER-FEATHERWEIGHT
Cardiff   Mar 23
Floyd Havard bt
Neil Haddock
Rsf, round 10

FEATHERWEIGHT
Manchester   Dec 18, 1993
Duke McKenzie bt
John Davidson
Rsf, rd 4, McKenzie took vacant title

Sunderland   May 24
Billy Hardy bt
Alan McKay
Rsf, rd 8, Hardy took vacant title

SUPER-BANTAMWEIGHT
Bethnal Green Apr 26
Richie Wenton bt
Bradley Stone
Rsf, round 10, Wenton took
inaugural title.
Stone later died in hospital

FLYWEIGHT
Edinburgh   Sep 21
Francis Ampofo bt
James Drummond
Rsf, round 3

AMATEUR BOXING

ABA Championships
Birmingham Arena   May 4
LIGHT-FLYWEIGHT (48KG)
Gary Jones (Sefton) bt
Darren Fox (RAF)

FLYWEIGHT (51KG)
Danny Costello (Hollington) bt
Owen Spensley (RAF)

BANTAMWEIGHT (54KG)
Spencer Oliver (Finchley) bt
John McLean (Basingstoke)

FEATHERWEIGHT (57KG)
Dean Pithie (Willenhall) bt
Stephen Smith (Repton)

LIGHTWEIGHT (60KG)
Andrew Green (Phil Thomas) bt
Ian Smith (St Pancras)

**LIGHT-WELTERWEIGHT
(63.5KG)**
Alan Temple (Hartlepool) bt
Richie Edwards (St Patricks)

WELTERWEIGHT (67KG)
Kevin Short (Army) bt
Mark Santine (Birmingham)

LIGHT-MIDDLEWEIGHT (71KG)
Wayne Alexander (Lynn) bt
Steve Bendall (Triumph)

MIDDLEWEIGHT (75KG)
David Starie (Hurstleigh) bt
Eddie Stuart (Leonis)

LIGHT-HEAVYWEIGHT (81KG)
Kelly Oliver (Bracebridge) bt
Paul Rogers (Penhill)

HEAVYWEIGHT (91KG)
Steve Burford (Army) bt
Israel Ajose (All Stars)

SUPER-HEAVYWEIGHT (91KG+)
Danny Watts (Army) bt
Mohammed Khamkhoer (Fitzroy)

AIBA World Rankings
As at June 30

LIGHT-FLYWEIGHT (48KG)

1 Petrov	BUL	263
2 Munchian	ARM	180
3 Lozano	ESP	140

FLYWEIGHT (51KG)

1 Font	CUB	280
2 Khadpo	THA	170
3 Sunee	MRI	150

BANTAMWEIGHT (54KG)

1 Christov	BUL	300
2 Casamayor	CUB	150
3 Kovacs	HUN	145

FEATHERWEIGHT (57KG)

1 Huste	GER	193
2 Todorov	BUL	185
3 Casamayor	CUB	120

LIGHTWEIGHT (60KG)

1 Rudolph	GER	240
2 Soltani	ALG	205
3 Gonzalez	CUB	176

**LIGHT-WELTERWEIGHT
(63.5KG)**

1 Vinent	CUB	300
2 Urkel	GER	282
3 Oaida	ROM	129

WELTERWEIGHT (67KG)

1 Hernandez J	CUB	210
2 Otto	GER	205
3 Buonanno	ITA	185

LIGHT-MIDDLEWEIGHT (71KG)

1 Vastag	ROM	364
2 Duvergel	CUB	260
3 Veit	GER	110

MIDDLEWEIGHT (75KG)

1 Hernandez A	CUB	315
2 Schenk	GER	181
3 Eigenbrodt	GER	135

LIGHT-HEAVYWEIGHT (81KG)

1 Gerbey	CUB	272
2 Ottke	GER	150
3 Benguisma	ALG	135

HEAVYWEIGHT (91KG)

1 Savon	CUB	360
2 Kandelaki	GEO	190
3 Monse	GER	155

SUPER-HEAVYWEIGHT (91KG+)

1 Balado	CUB	390
2 Rusinov	BUL	145
3 Beloussov	RUS	110

Canoeing

Slalom Racing

World Cup

1ST SERIES
Nottingham   *June 25-26*

K1 - Men
1	Ian Raspin	GBR
2	Shaun Pearce	GBR
3	Oliver Fix	GER

C1 - Men
1	Danko Herceg	CRO
2	Gareth Marriott	GBR
3	Patrice Estanguet	FRA

C2 - Men
1	Adisson/Forgues	FRA
2	Berro/Trummer	GER
3	Kolomanski/Staniszewski	POL

K1 - Women
1	Rachel Crosbee	GBR
2	Stepanka Hilgertova	TCH
3	Lynn Simpson	GBR

2ND SERIES
Augsburg, Germany   *July 2-3*

K1 - Men
1	Jochen Lettmann	GER
2	Shaun Pearce	GBR
3	Vincent Fondeviole	FRA

C1 - Men
1	Sören Kaufmann	GER
2	Gareth Marriott	GBR
3	Emmanuel Brugvin	FRA

C2 - Men
1	Saidi/Delrey	FRA
2	Simek/Rohan	TCH
3	Ehrenberg/Senft	GER

K1 - Women
1	Lynn Simpson	GBR
2	Angela Radermacher	GER
3	Kordula Striepecke	GER

3RD SERIES
Bourg-St-Maurice, France   *July 9-10*

K1 - Men
1	Scott Shipley	USA
2	Pierpaolo Ferrazzi	ITA
3	Oliver Fix	GER

C1 - Men
1	Gareth Marriott	GBR
2	Danko Herceg	CRO
3	David Hearn	USA

C2 - Men
1	Simek/Rohan	TCH
2	Briau/Daille	FRA
3	Saidi/Delrey	FRA

K1 - Women
1	Anouk Loubie	FRA
2	Rachel Crosbee	GBR
3	Stepanka Hilgertova	TCH

4TH SERIES
Seu d'Urgell, Spain   *July 16-17*

K1 - Men
1	Oliver Fix	GER
2	Albin Cizman	SLO
3	Ian Willey	IRL

C1 - Men
1	Lukas Pollert	TCH
2	Patrice Estanguet	FRA
3	Danko Herceg	CRO

C2 - Men
1	Saidi/Delrey	FRA
2	Simek/Rohan	TCH
3	Berro/Trummer	GER

K1 - Women
1	Danielle Woodward	AUS
2	Marcela Sadilova	TCH
3	Isabelle Despres	FRA

FINAL SERIES
Yahagi, Japan   *Sept 17-18*

K1 - Men
1	Shaun Pearce	GBR
2	Ian Raspin	GBR
3	Scott Shipley	USA

C1 - Men
1	Gareth Marriott	GBR
2	Lukas Pollert	TCH
3	Herve Delamarre	FRA

C2 - Men
1	Haller/Haller	USA
2	Adisson/Forgues	FRA
3	Simek/Rohan	TCH

K1 - Women
1	Lynn Simpson	GBR
2	Kordula Striepecke	GER
3	Marcela Sadilova	TCH

OVERALL PLACINGS
K1 - Men
1	Shaun Pearce	GBR
2	Ian Raspin	GBR
3	Scott Shipley	USA

C1 - Men
1	Gareth Marriott	GBR
2	Lukas Pollert	CZE
3	Danko Herceg	CRO

C2 - Men
1	Simek/Rohan	CZE
2	Saidi/Delrey	FRA
3	Haller/Haller	USA

K1 - Women
1	Lynn Simpson	GBR
2	Rachel Crosbee	GBR
3	Kordula Striepecke	GER

British Championships
Llangollen   *Oct 23-24, 1993*

K1 - Men
1	Andrew Raspin	161.22
2	Shaun Pearce	161.47
3	Rob Wright	163.62

C1 - Men
1	Richard Dumoney	179.22
2	Mark Delaney	179.49
3	Bill Horsman	181.71

C2 - Men
1	Green/Green	184.44
2	Millar/Pitt	187.97
3	Walling/Walling	204.56

K1 - Women
1	Lynn Simpson	179.59
2	Maria Lunc	185.43
3	Penny Briscoe	185.62

Scottish International
River Tay, Grandtully

K1 - Men
1	Shaun Pearce ENG	121.39
2	Ian Wilkie IRE	125.80
3	M Jones ENG	125.86

C1 - Men
1	Gareth Marriott ENG	139.93
2	Mark Delaney SCO	142.90
3	Nick Smith ENG	147.12

C2 - Men
1	Millar/Pitt SCO	165.62
2	Walling/Walling ENG	166.76
3	Reardon/Roden ENG	169.43

K1 - Women
1	Heather Corrie ENG	146.26
2	Rachel Crosbee ENG	149.50
3	Lynn Simpson ENG	150.45

Sprint Racing

World Championships
Xochimilco, Mexico   Sep 21-25

MEN'S 200M

K1
1 Sergey Kalesnik   BLS
2 Vince Fehervari   HUN
3 Miguel Garcia   ESP

K2
1 Freimut/Wysocki   POL
2 Serban/Stoian   ROM
3 Bluhm/Gutsche   GER

K4
1 Russia
2 Romania
3 Ukraine

C1
1 Nikolai Buchalov   BUL
2 Ervin Hoffman   HUN
3 Michail Slivinsky   UKR

C2
1 Masojkov/Dovgalionok   BLS
2 Kolonics/Horvath   HUN
3 Boivin/Hoyer   FRA

C4
1 Russia
2 Hungary
3 France

MEN'S 500M

K1
1 Zsombor Borhi   HUN
2 Daniel Collins   AUS
3 Knut Holmann   NOR

K2
1 Bluhm/Gutsche   GER
2 Androvicz/Rajna   HUN
3 Hunter/Robinson   AUS

K4
1 Russia
2 Romania
3 Hungary

C1
1 Nikolai Buchalov   BUL
2 Imre Pulai   HUN
3 Michail Slivinsky   UKR

C2
1 Andriev/Obreja   ROM
2 Kolonics/Horvath   HUN
3 Stoyanov/Marinov   BUL

C$
1 Hungary
2 Romania
3 Slovakia

MEN'S 1000M

K1
1 Clint Robinson   AUS
2 Zsombor Borhi   HUN
3 Knut Holmann   NOR

K2
1 Staal/Nielsen   DEN
2 Rossi/Scarpa   ITA
3 Bee/Szijjarto   HUN

K4
1 Russia
2 Poland
3 Germany

C1
1 Ivan Klementiyev   POL
2 Nikolai Buchalov
3 Victor Partnoi

C2
1 Dittmer/Kirchbach
2 Novak/Boldiszar   HUN
3 Koszykowski/Goliasz   POL

C4
1 Hungary
2 Romania
3 Mexico

WOMEN'S 200M

K1
1 Rita Koban   HUN
2 Anna Olsson   SWE
3 Caroline Brunet   CAN

K2
1 Koban/Laky   HUN
2 Schmidt/Gleue   GER
3 Hajcel/Urbanczyk   POL

K4
1 Hungary
2 Germany
3 Canada

K1
1 Birgit Schmidt   GER
2 Rita Koban   HUN
3 Josefa Idem   ITA

K2
1 Urbanczyk/Hajcel   POL
2 Czigany/Mednyanszky   HUN
3 Schmidt/Gleue   GER

K4
1 Germany
2 Hungary
3 Sweden

British Championships
Holme Pierrepont   July 2-3

MEN'S 200M

K1
1 G Bourne (Elmbridge)
36.08
2 S Tingay (Leighton Buzzard)
37.33
3 D Battershell (Weybridge)
37.74

K2
1 Lawler/Bourne
(Elmbridge)   33.21
2 Battershell/Easterling
(Weybridge)   34.85
3 Parsons/Bland
(Fladbury)   34.94

K4
1 Masters/Turrell/ Bland/
Parsons   32.03
2 West/Morgan/Tingay/Elliott
32.28
3 Battershell/Easterling/

Oliver/Roesseur   32.51

C1
1 E Jamieson (Weybridge)
44.60
2 A Crowther (Fladbury)
45.60
3 J Love (Leamington Spa)
46.74

C2
1 Train/Train (Fladbury)
40.08
2 Crowther/Crowther (Fladbury)
40.66
3 Martin/Driscoll (Fladbury)
43.08

MEN'S 1000M

K1
1 G Bourne (Elmbridge)
3:37.46
2 I Lawler (Elmbridge)
3:39.06
3 G Mawer (Richmond)
3:41.77

C1
1 S Train (Fladbury)
4:05.01
2 A Train (Fladbury)
4:05.24
3 E Jamieson (Weybridge)
4:18.04

WOMEN'S 200M

K1
1 H Dresser (Richmond)
43.68
2 A Thorogood (Newham)
44.53
3 B Train (Fladbury)
45.16

K2
1 Dresser/Ormerod (Richmond)
42.60
2 Train/Train (Fladbury)
42.89
3 Bennett/Campbell (Fladbury)
43.71

K4
1 Thorogood/Bennett/Kilby/
Green
2 Dresser/Keane/Selwood/
Dawes
3 Train/Cheyne/Hardy/
Ormerod

Nottingham Regatta
Holme Pierrepont   June 3-5

MEN'S 200m

K1 G Bourne GBR   40.99
K2 Heinz/Lopez MEX   38.40
K4 Mexico   34.79
C1 T Love GBR   48.38
C2 Martinez/Ferrer MEX   43.28
C4 Mexico   39.21

MEN'S 500m

K1 G Bourne GBR   1:51.35
K2 Block/Burgess GBR   1:49.87

K4	Ireland	1:40.82
C1	S Train GBR	2:11.69
C2	Martinez/Ferrer MEX	2:00.54
C4	Mexico	1:55.75

MEN'S 1000m

K1	G Bourne GBR	4:00.01
K2	Mawer/Maloney IRE	3:35.44
K4	Great Britain	3:21.57
C1	S Train GBR	4:33.68
C2	Train/Train GBR	3:49.75
C4	Mexico	3:44.13

MEN'S 10,000m

K1	J Block GBR	44:24.01
C1	S Train GBR	46.14.00

WOMEN'S 200m

K1	R Hernandez MEX	49.70
K2	Hernandez/Rosas MEX	42.92

WOMEN'S 500m

K1	A Thorogood GBR	2:16.50
K2	Hernandez/Rosas MEX	2:03.39

WOMEN'S 6000m

K1	A Thorogood GBR	28:58.00

Duisburg Regatta
Duisburg, Germany   June 24-26
MEN
K2

1	Kalesnik/Plitkin BLS	34.53
5	Lawler/Bourne GBR	36.20

C2

1	Boldiszar/Novak HUN	3:47.71
2	Train/Train GBR	3:47.86

WOMEN'S 200M
K1

1	R Koban HUN	42.79
9	H Dresser GBR	45.54

Milan Regatta
Milan   Aug 6-7
MEN
K1 - 1000m

1	K Holman NOR	3:31.46
2	M Kolelimaimen FIN	3:33.70
3	D Hofmann GER	3:34.18
7	I Lawler GBR	3:39.20

K2- 200m

1	Lawler/Bourne GBR	34.72
2	Lioult/Obertin FRA	34.75
3	Dresossi/Bonomi ITA	34.91

Marathon Racing

World Championships
Amsterdam   Sept 3-4   (over 42.7km)
K1 - MEN

1	L Loch DEN	2:59.46
2	T Kranz SWE	2:59.50
3	R Herreveld RSA	2:59.59
8	G Slater GBR	3:03.53
9	S Dark GBR	3:13.07

C1 - MEN

1	A Neilsson DEN	3:20.38
2	G Kolozsvari HUN	3:28.41

3	K Scales DEN	3:28.56
14	J Lee GBR	3:42.13
19	M Marshall GBR	3:50.49

K2 - MEN

1	Lawler/Harris GBR	2:46.50
2	Laszlo/Toth HUN	2:46.51
3	Christiansen/Slogard DEN	2:46.52

C2 - MEN

1	Bohacs/Gyulia HUN	3:06.31
2	Train/Train GBR	3:06.33
3	Pedro/Bienvenido ESP	3:14.58

K1 - WOMEN

1	S Gunnersen SWE
2	D Cooper AUS
3	A Pitz HUN
7	A Hemmings GBR

K2- WOMEN

1	Cooper/Jesney AUS	3:00.57
2	Selmer/Lassen DEN	3:10.37
3	Biro/Erdodi HUN	3:11.47
5	Thorogood/Gilby GBR	3:13.40

British Champions'ps
River Severn, Worcester   Aug 27-28
K1 - MEN *(15km)*

1	G Mawer (Richmond)	1:39.42
2	G Slater (Lichfield)	1:39.45
3	S Dark (Stratford-on-A)	1:39.49

K2 - MEN

1	Lawler/Harris (Elmbridge)	1:33.32
2	Dark/Gibbons (Strat./Reading)	1:34.27
3	Kirk/Clark (Royal)	1:34.28

K1 - WOMEN *(10km)*

1	A Hemmings (Elmb'dge)	1:39.00
2	S Bennett (Fladbury)	1:41.35
3	L Dawe (Exeter)	1:42.29

K2 - WOMEN

1	Dallaway/Gilby (Elmbridge)	1:32.14
2	Dresser/Keane (Richmond)	1:32.20
3	Chapman/Brough (Reading)	1:32.54

Devizes-Westminster

1	Phillips/Lewis (RNKC/B on A)	15h 43m
2	Belcher/Cornish (AUS/RSA)	15:51
3	Greenham/Wallis (Wok'ham)	16:30

Wild Water Racing

British Championships
Series Final
River Usk, Crickhowell   Dec 4
MEN

K1	I Tordoff (Chester)	22.46
C1	R Pumphrey (Shadwell)	27.22.7

C2	Warne/Anderson (Chelmsford)	28.11.5

WOMEN

K1	L Rae (Loughboro)	26.34.3

British Open
Tryweryn, Bala   May 15
K1 - MEN

1	I Tordoff (Chester)	22:01.15
2	A Tordoff (Chester)	22:08.63
3	M Swallow (Chester)	23:00.68

C1 - MEN

1	R Pumphrey (S'dwell)	26:04.05
2	J Willacy (RAFC)	26:35.72
3	R Pearton (Herts)	27:49.45

C2 - MEN

1	Belbin/Caunt (NKC)	25:37.62
2	Clough/Clough (Tees)	26:09.21
3	Blackman/Blackman (RAFCA)	26:13.04

K1 - WOMEN

1	A Tordoff (Chester)	24:47.58
2	T Parsons (NKC)	25:19.78
3	C Berry (Forth)	25:27.81

Canoe Polo

World Championships
Pond's Forge, Sheffield   July 8-10
MEN
Semi Finals
Australia 5 Holland 1
Germany 2 Great Britain 1
3rd/4th Play Off
Holland 1 Great Britain 2
Final
Australia 6 Germany 1

WOMEN
Semi Finals
Great Britain 2 France 1
Australia 6 Germany 4
3rd/4th Play Off
France 5 Germany 3
Final
Great Britain 0 Australia 2

Canoe Sailing

European Championships
Carnac, France   July 18-22

1	Robin Wood (GBR)	12.75
2	Jens Osterlund (SWE)	21.75
3	Mark Goodchild (GBR)	24.00

British Championships
Rock SC, Cornwall   May 29-June 3

1	Lee Noble in 'Stingray' (Ullswater)	6.75
2	Lester Noble in 'Sundance' (Ullswater)	9.50
3	Robin Wood in 'Splinter' (British Steel)	9.7

Cricket

Cricket 'anoraks' have had a field day this year. Wisdens and Playfairs have been thumbed to extinction following the records that have been destroyed - not to mention the *Rules of Cricket* section, poured over with relish. The authors of those cricketing volumes primarily have messrs Lara, Malcolm, Atherton and the Warwickshire side to thank for increased sales - with a little assistance from England in Trinidad. At St Johns, Lara surpassed Garfield Sobers' Test record then overtook Hanif Mohammed's 499 first class score (although the Pakistani player was run out believing he had passed 500) against Durham at Edgbaston. Malcolm had his radar working when battering the South Africans into submission at The Oval with 9-57. Warwickshire took an unprecedented three titles and came within a whisper of a fourth. And Mike Atherton...well there was a story.

The clean-cut Lancashire captain ended up out-of-pocket for substances that appeared in it. *The Sun* offered readers the opportunity to dry their hands on packets of "Mike's Super Soil", whilst every old buffer with a stripey tie was wheeled in front of the cameras to call for the cat-o'-nine-tails and the return of the saintly Gatting. It might well have been the memories of Gatting's dignified era - remember those chats with the umpire, that night at the hotel - that helped to keep Atherton his job.

Ball tampering had raised its head periodically allowing newspaper artists and scientists to fill up sections usefully entitled "How to swing a cricket ball". First Pakistan paceman Sarfraz took his old mate Allan Lamb to court on libel charges, then Imran, the doyen of swing bowlers, admitted to being a dab hand with a bottle top and all hell was let loose. Not to be outdone, Derek Pringle admitted interference with the ball during his Essex days, though the idea of Pringle and reverse swing is a bit suspect. About as likely as a Devon Malcom century before lunch or Allan Border walking.

Botham had a quiet time in his first year of retirement. He replaced David Mellor as the anchor of Radio 5 Live's 'Six-O-Six' phone in and brought out his much awaited biography, imaginatively titled "Botham: my autobiography" which is a touch tautological, but that hasn't stopped it rocketing into the best seller lists. His old mate, Border, also decided it was time to hang up his bat. His Test career spanned 156 Tests comprising a record 11,174 runs at an average of 50.56. Border's decision was not entirely without controversy as he accused Board officials of forcing him from his post to be replaced by a man who has been known to

KAPIL DEV'S WICKETS									LEADING TEST WICKET TAKERS					
As at Feb , 1994									*As at Feb, 1994*					
Opposition	*Mts*	*Rns*	*Wkts*	*Ave*	*BB*	*5w*	*10w*			*Ctry*	*Tests*	*Wkts*	*5w*	*10w*	*BB*
Australia	20	2003	79	25.35	8-106	7	-		Kapil Dev	India	130	432	23	2	9-83
England	27	3174	85	37.34	6-91	4	-		R J Hadlee	NZ	86	431	36	9	9-52
New Zealand	9	792	23	34.43	4-34	-	-		I T Botham	England	102	383	27	4	8-34
Pakistan	29	2982	99	30.12	8-85	7	1		M D Marshall	W Indies	81	376	22	4	7-22
South Africa	4	299	8	37.38	3-43	-	-		Imran Khan	Pakistan	88	362	23	6	8-58
Sri Lanka	14	1173	45	26.06	5-110	1	-		D K Lillee	Australia	70	355	23	7	7-81
West Indies	25	2216	89	24.90	9-83	4	1		R G D Willis	England	90	325	16	0	8-43
Total	**130**	**12773**	**432**	**29.56**	**9-83**	**23**	**2**		L R Gibbs	W Indies	79	309	18	2	8-38

smile at least once in his career, Mark Taylor. The problems down under pale into insignificance when compared to the latest round of Sri Lankan intrigue following the introduction of a fitness test criterion into the selection process. At first the level was fixed at 75% fitness but this was lowered to 55% after none of the team qualified for selection. Even with the lowered rate of fitness, 12 of the 26 squad members were ruled unfit, including captain Arjuna Ranatunga. Lalitha Ratnayake, the doctor conducting the tests, then had to drop the level to 50% so that the Sri Lankans could raise a squad to take to the Australasia Cup in Sharjah. He cited bad eating habits, lack of exercise and an over-indulgence in sex as the reasons behind the recent poor performances and complained that "Ranatunga's pot belly had raised his centre of gravity, causing problems of balance." Mike Gatting beware.

Still in the subcontinent, India's premier all-rounder of the past decade, Kapil Dev, surpassed Sir Richard Hadlee's Test tally of 431 with the dismissal of (the very fit) Hashan Tillekeratne. Kapil was obviously taking life easier than the dashing Kiwi needing 44 more Tests to get one more Test wicket. Kapil has also scored over 5,000 runs in a Test career stretching back to 1978. Curtly Ambrose passed his particular milestones in Georgetown when he splayed Mike Atherton's stumps in the 2nd Test to register his 200th Test victim. He became only the 8th West Indian to achieve that feat, with the list headed by former Hampshire strike bowler, Malcolm Marshall, with 376.

LOWEST TEST INNINGS

26	New Zealand v England (Auckland)	1954-55
30	South Africa v England (Port Elizabeth)	1895-96
30	South Africa v England (Edgbaston)	1924
35	South Africa v England (Cape Town)	1898-99
36	Australia v England (Edgbaston)	1902
36	South Africa v Australia (Melbourne)	1931-32
42	Australia v England (Sydney)	1887-88
42	New Zealand v Australia (Wellington)	1945-46
42	India v England (Lord's)	1974
43	South Africa v England (Cape Town)	1889-90
44	Australia v England (The Oval)	1896
45	England v Australia (Melbourne)	1886-87
45	South Africa v Australia (Melbourne)	1931-32
46	**England v West Indies (Port of Spain)**	**1994**

Another Malcolm, but this time of the Devon variety, has had an undulating season. Forced to return from the West Indies to have a knee operation after the 1st Test defeat he returned only to be a spectator as England won and drew in the last two Tests. After a modest start to the summer, he returned to the wilds of Derbyshire following his exclusion from the Test squads and settled down to the more sedate life of county cricket. With The Oval wicket being the cricketing equivalent of a bouncy castle, Dev was recalled for one last bash at the tourists. Obviously the 6' 2" speedster fancied a winter break down under as he peppered the bewildered Boks and in doing so recorded the 6th best Test figures in history.

To take nine wickets in an innings is impressive, to get 10 is about as impressive as you can get, particularly when they are all bowled. Alex Kelly, a 17 year old who plays for Bishop Auckland, did just this during a match in the Millburngate Durham County Junior League. Kelly entered the fray with opponents Newton Aycliffe at a healthy 36-0 chasing a total of 130. Twenty-seven balls later and without conceding a run, Kelly had clean bowled all ten Newton Aycliffe batsmen. Mr Harry Smurthwaite, the Bishop Auckland secretary, left the reporters in no doubt as to the worth of the schoolboy record holder "You can forget greats like Lillee, Trueman and Holding - this is the lad to watch". Keep that passport handy, Alex.

One thing that bowlers will be relishing is the change from one bouncer an over to two decided on by the International Cricket Council. The ICC have also changed rules applying to qualification periods and turned down a proposal to increase the minimum overs bowled from 90 to 96. Though only two bouncers an over will be permitted it is now legitimate to propel them both at the same batsman. Pretty radical meeting. Referees were also encouraged to mete out stiffer penalties after one fine handed out to Merv Hughes led one Australian observer to brand the whole system as a joke. "Big Merv spends more on a round of drinks," he said.

On the domestic front Raymond Illingworth became the new chairman of selectors. He roundly criticised a number of the players in the West Indies, fined his captain £1000 for having dirt in his pocket (though he wasn't doing anything illegal with it?) and then dropped his highest rated bowler, Fraser, for the tour of Australia. But yes, they did win two Tests as well. Notwithstanding this crushing success, Illy determined to make further radical changes and banned God from the changing room. Perhaps God wanted to

TOP TEST WICKET HAULS

10-53	**J C Laker** Eng v Australia (Manchester)	1956
9-28	**G A Lohmann** Eng v S Africa (Jo'burg)	1896
9-37	**J C Laker** Eng v Australia (Manchester)	1956
9-52	**R J Hadlee** NZ v Australia (Brisbane)	1986
9-56	**Abdul Qadir** Pak v England (Lahore)	1988
9-57	**D E Malcolm** Eng v S Africa (The Oval)	1994
9-69	**J M Patel** Ind v Australia (Kanpur)	1960
9-83	**Kapil Dev** Ind v W Indies (Ahmedabad)	1984
9-86	**Sarfraz Nawaz** Pak v Australia (Melb'ne)	1979
9-95	**J M Noriega** WI v India (Port of Spain)	1971

play four seamers and not have a left hander in the top six. Perhaps God really wanted Alec Stewart to remain as wicketkeeper and have Alan Igglesden take the new ball. Illingworth wasn't saying. The chairman simply grasped the nettle and rid the squad of the divisive interference from team chaplain The Rev. Andrew Wingfield-Digby. Digby had been present for 11 defeats in 15 Tests before the Illingworth dynasty stepped in, not a great record for the Great Selector in the sky. As old toughie Illingworth put it, "I don't want players who need shoulders to cry on".

There wasn't a dry eye in the house at Lord's, however, when South Africa came out to bat after 29 years in the wilderness. The wonderful spirit of togetherness didn't last too long as Atherton nicked a handful of top-soil and England collapsed for a dismal 99 (God works in mysterious ways). South African coach Mike Proctor had his wrist slapped for parading the new national flag (though it miraculously later appeared in his hand at the moment of Wessels' century) and that well known trouble-maker, Archbishop Desmond Tutu fell foul of the Lord's stewards. The country's leading Anglican cleric popped into the South African dressing room at tea on the first day, only to be stopped by the stewards (generously known in the game as the "gauleiters") as he was dressed in mufti and therefore not wearing a jacket. As Peter Deeley observed "Archbishop Tutu might well have observed that it is easier for a camel to pass through the eye of a needle than for a jacketless

TOP ONE-DAY INTERNATIONAL BOWLERS

	Wkts	S/Rate
Wasim Akram (Pakistan)	254	28.43
Kapil Dev (India)	251	22.65
Imran Khan (Pakistan)	182	24.40
Craig McDermott (Australia)	170	26.99
Richard Hadlee (New Zealand)	158	25.56
Malcolm Marshall (W Indies)	157	21.88
Curtly Ambrose (W Indies)	151	27.07
Steve Waugh (Australia)	151	22.24
Waqar Younis (Pakistan)	149	34.43
Joel Garner (W Indies)	146	27.39

man to enter the Lord's pavilion."

There have been a few interesting reasons for cricketing absenteeism this year. Phil Tufnell was too busy locking up his former girlfriend in a cupboard and attending court proceedings over an alleged assault charge to concentrate too much on regaining his Test place. During one Middlesex second team match Tufnell apparently became so disinterested in proceedings that when wandering back to fine-leg he didn't stop at the boundary rope and continued into his car and disappeared. 'The Cat', so called for his habit of cat-napping, turned up safe and well in time for an appearance in the 2nd Test against the South Africans. Other interesting sick-notes came from one Lulma Masikazana who should have been keeping wicket for Eastern Province in their match against England A on the tour of South Africa. Unfortunately Masikazana could not take the field as he was too busy being circumcised, a tribal rite of passage in the region. This allowed a debut to Grant Morgan, who didn't have any such worries, and notched up an unbeaten 60.

Looking ahead to next season Worcestershire begin their defence of the NatWest Trophy at home to Cumberland, whilst Warwickshire face a tough trip to Taunton to face Somerset. Holland's debut in the competition is at Northampton for whom Curtly Ambrose will be missing due to Test commitments.

INTERNATIONAL RATINGS
As at September 1

Test Matches		One Day	
West Indies	68	Pakistan	67
Pakistan	66	Australia	59
Australia	65	England	56
India	56	West Indies	56
South Africa	49	India	55
England	40	South Africa	45
New Zealand	32	New Zealand	43
Sri Lanka	21	Sri Lanka	36
Zimbabwe	20	UAE	14
		Zimbabwe	12

NATWEST TROPHY DRAW 1995

First Round *(to be played on June 27)*
Cambridgeshire v Derbyshire.....Cheshire v Essex.....Cornwall v Middlesex.....Durham v Herefordshire.....Glamorgan v Dorset.....Gloucestershire v Suffolk.....Lancashire v Norfolk Leicestershire v Hampshire.....Northamptonshire v Holland......Nottinghamshire v Scotland Staffordshire v Kent.....Surrey v Berkshire.....Sussex v Devon.....Warwickshire v Somerset Worcestershire v Cumberland.....Yorkshire v Ireland

BENSON & HEDGES CUP GROUP DRAW 1995
(competition begins Sunday April 23)

Group A	Group B	Group C	Group D
Minor Counties	Scotland	Combined Univs.	Ireland
Durham	Derbyshire	Essex	Kent
Lancashire	Northamptonshire	Glamorgan	Somerset
Leicestershire	Worcestershire	Gloucestershire	Surrey
Nottinghamshire	Yorkshire	Hampshire	Sussex
Warwickshire		Middlesex	

QUOTES

"You guys are history. You are going to pay for it" - **Fast bowler Devon Malcolm after being hit on the head by a bouncer from Fanie de Villiers. The England bowler went on to get 9-57.**

"It's no secret that I prefer the quicker bowlers...I just hope they don't shake a coconut tree and a black Shane Warne pops out" - **England batsman Robin Smith before the tour of the West Indies .**

"About two grand a game" - **Graham Thorpe, revealing the difference between Test and county cricket.**

"The only England captain to have led a team who scored fewer than 46 runs in a Test match was Arthur Shrewsbury...and he shot himself" - **Journalist Ian Wooldridge offering sound advice after the debacle in Trinidad.**

"Chris Lewis: the enigma with no variation" - **Former Test spinner Vic Marks on the Notts and England all-rounder.**

"I still don't think I am batting as well as I can" - **Brian Lara after setting a Test record 375, then hitting 501 against Durham.**

"I'm struggling to see the funny side, but I suppose in time it will be good to know I was part of history" - **Durham wicketkeeper Chris Scott after dropping Lara on 18.**

"It would have been better if he'd got one run more or one run less" - **Spokesman for Lara's sponsor, Joe Bloggs' Jeans, after his Levi equalling 501.**

"When you support Birmingham City, you have to look for a hero from somewhere else" - **Warwickshire supporter at the B & H semi-final v Surrey.**

"I couldn't understand why there was such a fuss, but when I saw the pictures I realised it had looked suspicious." - **England captain Mike Atherton after being 'caught' on TV applying dirt to the ball in the First Test v South Africa at Lord's.**

"I don't think you continue seeing someone just because you can get a holiday in the West Indies" - **Susie Carman, the ex-girlfriend of Mike Atherton, after their split-up.**

"It looks like something out of a puzzle book and you can only work it out by a process of elimination" - **Autograph collector trying to work out Athertons's signature.**

"We came to play cricket but lost at skittles" - **Kent's Alan Igglesden after losing a controversial 'bowl out' to Warwickshire.**

England v South Africa

1ST TEST
Lord's   July 21-24

SOUTH AFRICA - First Innings

			Min	Bls	
A C Hudson	c Gooch	b Gough	6	41	32
G Kirsten	c DeFreitas	b Hick	72	204	145
W J Cronje	c Crawley	b Fraser	7	27	18
K C Wessels*	c Rhodes	b Gough	105	298	217
P N Kirsten	c Rhodes	b Gough	8	38	37
J N Rhodes		b White	32	107	78
B M McMillan	c Rhodes	b Fraser	29	131	76
D J Richardson†	lbw	b Gough	26	37	35
C R Matthews		b White	41	54	36
P S de Villiers	c Rhodes	b Fraser	8	41	31
A A Donald	not out		5	18	14
Extras (LB9, NB9)			18		
Total (118.5 overs)			357		

Fall of wickets: 18 (Hudson), 35 (Cronje), 141 (G Kirsten), 164 (P Kirsten), 239 (Rhodes), 241 (Wessels), 281 (Richardson), 334 (Matthews), 348 (McMillan), 357 (DeVilliers)
Bowling: DeFreitas 18-5-67-0, Gough 28-6-76-4, Salisbury 25-2-68-0, Fraser 24.5-7-72-3, Hick 10-5-22-1, White 13-2-43-2

ENGLAND - First Innings

			Min	Bls	
M A Atherton*	c Wessels	b Donald	20	90	64
A J Stewart		b Donald	12	14	11
J P Crawley	c Hudson	b de Villiers	9	29	16
G A Hick	c Richardson	b de Villiers	38	135	88
G A Gooch	lbw	b de Villiers	20	45	39
C White	c Richardson	b Donald	10	101	63
J Rhodes†		b McMillan	15	33	27
I D K Salisbury	not out		6	60	38
P A J DeFreitas	c Wessels	b Donald	20	9	10
D Gough		c&b Donald	12	18	15
A R C Fraser	run out (G Kirsten)		3	8	7
Extras (B2, LB5, NB8)			15		
Total (61.3 overs)			180		

Fall of wickets: 19(Stewart), 41(Crawley), 68(Atherton), 107(Gooch), 119(Hick), 136(Rhodes), 141(White), 161(DeFreitas), 176(Gough), 180(Fraser)
Bowling: Donald 19.3-5-74-5, de Villiers 16-5-28-3, Matthews 16-6-46-0, McMillan 10-1-25-1

SOUTH AFRICA - Second Innings

			Min	Bls	
G Kirsten	st Rodes	b Hick	44	171	126
A C Hudson	lbw	b Fraser	3	12	4
W J Cronje	c Fraser	b Gough	32	98	67
K C Wessels*	c Crawley	b Salisbury	28	115	108
P N Kirsten		b Gough	42	163	129
J N Rhodes		b Gough	32	102	68
B M McMillan	not out		39	99	65
D J Richardson†	c Rhodes	b Fraser	3	31	24
C R Matthews		b Gough	25	63	38
P S deVilliers					
A A Donald					
Extras (B8, LB10, NB12)			30		
Total (8 wkts dec, 102.3 overs)			278		

Fall of wickets: 14 (Hudson), 73 (Cronje), 101 (G Kirsten), 141 (Wessels), 208 (Rhodes), 209 (P Kirsten), 220 (Richardson), 278 (Matthews)
Bowling: Fraser 23-5-62-2, Gough 19.3-5-46-4, DeFreitas 14-3-43-0, Hick 24-14-38-1, Salisbury 19-4-53-1, White 3-0-18-0

ENGLAND - Second Innings

			Min	Bls	
M A Atherton*	c McMillan	b de Villiers	8	50	37
A J Stewart	c Richardson	b Matthews	27	142	82
J P Crawley	c Hudson	b McMillan	7	39	24
G A Hick	lbw	b McMillan	11	9	7
G A Gooch	lbw	b Donald	28	66	51
C White	c Wessels	b Matthews	0	1	1
S J Rhodes†	not out		14	73	43
P A J DeFreitas	c G Kirsten	b Matthews	1	6	6
I D K Salisbury		b Donald	0	7	5
D Gough	retired hurt		0	11	6
A R C Fraser	lbw	b McMillan	1	23	14
Extras (B1, LB1)			2		
Total (45.5 overs)			99		

Fall of wickets: 16(Atherton), 29(Crawley), 45 (Hick), 74(Stewart), 74(White), 82(Gooch), 85(DeFreitas), 88(Salisbury), 99(Fraser)
Bowling: Donald 12-5-29-2, de Villiers 12-4-26-1, Matthews 14-6-25-3, McMillan 6.5-2-16-3, Cronje 1-0-1-0

Toss: South Africa   **Man of the Match:** K C Wessels
Umpires: H D Bird & S G Randell   (TV) M J Kitchen

SOUTH AFRICA WON BY 356 runs

It was 29 years since South Africa had last trod upon the hallowed turf at Lord's which has in recent years proved a graveyard for the home side and a source of inspiration to visiting nations. Following their 356 run capitulation the burial party were rubbing their hands in anticipation. Atherton was first to the gallows following TV pictures of him applying dirt to the ball and then failing to give a full explanation to Australian referee Peter Burge. In the end the gallows remained unused as Illingworth jumped in with a £2000 fine to usurp any more dramatic action being taken. Whilst pocketing dirt was common practice in effecting 'Wooden Horse' escapes in World war II, even Atherton's delve into the grey area of cricketing law could not extricate his side from the watchful eye of captain Wessels. His dogged century, brought up with two 4s off White, set up the platform for the visiting seamers to skittle out a lacklustre England. The declaration left England five sessions to make 456. In the end only two were needed as McMillan and Matthews ripped the heart out of the top order and paid back Gough with a number of short deliveries, one of which caught him on the forearm causing the 23 year old Barnsley paceman to leave the field in distress. Even though Gooch took his Test aggregate past Viv Richards' 8540 total, Wessels revelled in "the most satisfying" of Test wins since their return.

2ND TEST
Headingley   Aug 4-8
ENGLAND- First Innings

			Min	Bls	
G A Gooch	c McMillan	b de Villiers	23	45	40
M A Atherton*		c & b McMillan	99	320	224
G A Hick	c McMillan	b de Villiers	25	87	61
G P Thorpe	c Rhodes	b McMillan	72	156	112
A J Stewart		b McMillan	89	225	171
J P Crawley	lbw	b Matthews	38	157	113
S J Rhodes†	not out		65	202	144
P A J DeFreitas		b Donald	15	49	34
D Gough	run out		27	74	60
A R C Fraser	c Cronje	b de Villiers	6	34	18
P C R Tufnell					
Extras (B1, LB5, NB12)			18		
Total (9 wkts dec, 160.3 overs, 682 mins)			477		

Fall of wickets: 34 (Gooch), 84 (Hick), 228 (Thorpe), 235 (Atherton), 350 (Crawley), 367 (Stewart), 394 (DeFreitas), 447 (Gough), 477 (Fraser).
Bowling: Donald 29-2-135-1, de Villiers 39.3-12-108-3, Matthews 39-7-97-1, McMillan 37-12-93-3, Cronje 16-3-38-0

ENGLAND - Second Innings

			Min	Bls	
G A Gooch	c Richardson	b Matthews	27	100	77
M A Atherton*	c sub(Cullinan)	b McMillan	17	65	42
G A Hick	lbw	b McMillan	110	272	192
G P Thorpe	run out		73	173	125
A J Stewart	not out		36	65	37
J P Crawley	c Cronje	b McMillan	0	1	2
S J Rhodes†					
P A J DeFreitas					
D Gough					
A R C Fraser					
P C R Tufnell					
Extras (LB1, NB3)			4		
Total (5 wkts dec, 78.3 overs, 468 mins)			267		

Fall of wickets: 39 (Atherton), 57 (Gooch), 190 (Thorpe), 267 (Hick), 267 (Crawley)
Bowling: de Villiers 25-3-98-1, McMillan 15.3-0-66-2, Matthews 24-8-53-1, G Kirsten 2-1-10-0, Cronje 12-3-39-0

SOUTH AFRICA- First Innings

			Min	Bls	
A C Hudson	c Atherton	b Gough	19	18	19
G Kirsten	c Rhodes	b DeFreitas	7	37	21
D J Richardson†		b Fraser	48	99	73
W J Cronje		b DeFreitas	0	1	1
K C Wessels*	c Crawley	b Fraser	25	56	102
P N Kirsten	c Stewart	b DeFreitas	104	295	226
J N Rhodes	c Rhodes	b Gough	46	131	97
B M McMillan		b Tuffnel	78	204	140
C R Matthews	not out		62	147	100
P S de Villiers	st Rhodes	b Tuffnel	13	21	23
A A Donald	c Crawley	b DeFreitas	27	50	47
Extras (B8, LB7, NB13)			28		
Total (133.1 overs, 555 mins)			447		

Fall of wickets: 13 (Hudson), 31 (G Kirsten), 31 (Cronje), 91 (Richardson), 105 (Wessels), 199 (Rhodes), 314 (P Kirsten), 391 (McMillan), 410 (de Villiers), 447 (Donald)
Bowling: Gough 37-3-153-2, DeFreitas 29.1-6-89-4, Fraser 31-5-92-2, Tufnell 32-13-81-2, Gooch 3-0-9-0, Hick 1-0-8-0

SOUTH AFRICA - Second Innings

			Min	Bls	
G Kirsten	c Rhodes	b DeFreitas	65	153	128
A C Hudson		c & b Tufnell	12	79	66
W J Cronje	not out		13	133	124
K C Wessels*		b Tufnell	7	20	29
P N Kirsten	not out		8	28	31
J N Rhodes					
B M McMillan					
D J Richardson†					
C R Matthews					
P S de Villiers					
A A Donald					
Extras (B2, LB2, NB7)			11		
Total (3 wkts, 60 overs, 214 mins)			116		

Fall of wickets: 43 (Hudson), 93 (G Kirsten), 104 (Wessels)
Bowling: DeFreitas 14-3-41-1, Gough 10-5-15-0, Tufnell 23-8-31-2, Fraser 7-2-19-0, Hick 6-3-6-0

Toss: **England**   Man of the Match: **P N Kirsten**
Umpires: **D R Shepherd & R S Dunne**
(TV) **J C Balderstone**

MATCH DRAWN

It was an improvement. England showed resilience, but after Gary Kirsten steadied the South African ship the match petered out into only the 5th draw in 20 years at Headingley. England's innings was enlightened by a flurry of strokes from the recalled Thorpe, who whirled to his half century in only 60 balls. Captain Atherton had decided that the middle was the only sanctuary from the tabloids and ground out 99 before McMillan held onto a straight drive. 'Big Mac', looking as if he'd stepped straight off a Viking longship, had a hand in the first five wickets to fall before he set about pillaging the English bowling with a bucolic array of blows. Peter Kirsten was felled by Gough only to recover to register his century in the 3rd last over of the day before top edging to short third man. England's problems were compounded by their inability to remove Matthews and the injured Donald, who frustrated the crowd until the 2nd over after lunch. To have any chance of victory England needed quick runs, so it was curious to see the caution with which Gooch and Atherton approached the task. A hamstrung Gooch continued his miserable run of form playing down the wrong line to Matthews, before the livewire Thorpe injected fresh impetus into proceedings with another fiery cameo. The effect this had on Hick was to transform the leaden-footed wooden No. 3 into the free scoring genius of Worcester legend. Unleashed from his mental shackles, Hick's 2nd Test century set up a South African target of 298 in a possible 70 overs. But with the younger Kirsten impregnable, South Africa ensured at least a share of the spoils in the series.

3RD TEST
The Oval   Aug 18-21
SOUTH AFRICA- First Innings

			Min	Bls	
G Kirsten	c Rhodes	b DeFreitas	2	13	12
P N Kirsten		b Malcolm	16	57	30
W J Cronje	lbw	b Benjamin	38	93	65
K C Wessels*	lbw	b Benjamin	45	115	84
D J Cullinan	c Rhodes	b DeFreitas	7	11	11
J N Rhodes	retired hurt		8	20	14
B M McMillan	c Hick	b DeFreitas	93	269	193
D J Richardson†	c Rhodes	b Benjamin	58	125	89
C R Matthews	c Hick	b Benjamin	0	8	4
P S de Villiers	c Stewart	b DeFreitas	14	61	50
A A Donald	not out		14	34	21
Extras (B8, LB10, W1, NB18)			37		
Total (9 wkts, 92.2 overs, 410 mins)			332		

Fall of wickets: 2 (G Kirsten), 43 (P Kirsten), 73 (Cronje), 85 (Cullinan), 136 (Wessels), 260 (Richardson), 266 (Matthews), 301 (de Villiers), 332 (McMillan)
Bowling: DeFreitas 26.2-5-93-4, Malcolm 25-5-81-1, Gough 19-1-85-0, Benjamin 17-2-42-4, Hick 5-1-13-0

SOUTH AFRICA - Second Innings

			Min	Bls	
P N Kirsten	c DeFreitas	b Malcolm	1	16	13
G Kirsten		c & b Malcolm	0	6	3
W J Cronje		b Malcolm	0	11	7
K C Wessels*	c Rhodes	b Malcolm	28	91	61
D J Cullinan	c Thorpe	b Gough	94	217	134
B M McMillan	c Thorpe	b Malcolm	25	81	63
D J Richardson†	lbw	b Malcolm	3	7	7
C R Matthews	c Rhodes	b Malcolm	0	3	2
J N Rhodes	c Rhodes	b Malcolm	10	36	20
P S de Villiers	not out		0	5	2
A A Donald		b Malcolm	0	1	2
Extras (LB5, NB9)			14		
Total (50.3 overs, 244 mins)			175		

Fall of wickets: 0 (G Kirsten), 1 (P Kirsten), 1 (Cronje), 73 (Wessels), 137 (McMillan), 143 (Richardson), 143 (Matthews), 175 (Cullinan), 175 (Rhodes), 175 (Donald)
Bowling: DeFreitas 12-3-25-0, Malcolm 16.3-2-57-9, Gough 9-1-39-1, Benjamin 11-1-38-0, Hick 2-0-11-0

ENGLAND- First Innings

			Min	Bls	
G A Gooch	c Richardson	b Donald	8	61	43
M A Atherton*	lbw	b de Villiers	0	5	1
G A Hick		b Donald	39	137	85
G P Thorpe		b Matthews	79	157	115
A J Stewart		b de Villiers	62	153	106
J P Crawley	c Richardson	b Donald	5	26	12
S J Rhodes†	lbw	b de Villiers	11	53	33
P A J DeFreitas	run out (Cullinan)		37	52	31
D Gough	not out		42	66	42
J E Benjamin	lbw	b de Villiers	0	7	7
D E Malcolm	c sub (Shaw)	b Matthews	4	7	4
Extras (B1, W1, NB15)			17		
Total 76.5 overs, 371 mins)			304		

Fall of wickets: 1 (Atherton), 33 (Gooch), 93 (Hick), 145 (Thorpe), 165 (Crawley), 219 (Rhodes), 222 (Crawley), 292 (DeFreitas), 293 (Benjamin), 204 (Malcolm)
Bowling: Donald 17-2-76-3, de Villiers 19-3-62-4, Matthews 20.5-4-82-2, McMillan 12-1-67-0, Cronje 8-3-16-0

ENGLAND - Second Innings

			Min	Bls	
G A Gooch		b Matthews	33	27	20
M A Atherton*	c Richardson	b Donald	63	161	113
G A Hick	not out		81	151	81
G P Thorpe	not out		15	18	14
A J Stewart					
J P Crawley					
S J Rhodes†					
P A J DeFreitas					
D Gough					
A R C Fraser					
D E Malcolm					
Extras (LB6, NB7)			13		
Total (2 wkts, 35.3 overs, 180 mins)			205		

Fall of wickets: 56 (Gooch), 180 (Atherton)
Bowling: Donald 12-1-96-1, de Villiers 12-0-66-0, Matthews 11.3-4-37-1

Toss: England   Man of the Match: **D E Malcolm**
Umpires: **K E Palmer & R S Dunne**
(TV) **A G T Whitehead**

ENGLAND WON BY 8 WICKETS

It was not a happy match for Fanie de Villers. Having been fined £550 for the team's over rate, he had a further financial penalty imposed at the hands of international despot, Peter Burge, allegedly for 'dissent'. Burge had previously warmed up with £1,250 imposition on the beleaguered Atherton for 'shaking his head'. However, it was de Villiers who made the worst mistake of the game when he planted a bouncer straight between the eyes of Devon Malcolm. The Derbyshire tail-ender, squared up his 6' 2" frame and growled "You guys are history". And history it became as Malcolm ripped out the South African top 3 for 1 run. With the Oval pitch playing like a trampoline the procession of departing batsmen grew longer as the Jamaican-born strike bowler recorded the 6th best Test figures of all time with a shattering third spell of 5.3-1-17-5. The catalyst for this display occurred on Friday night when Gough and DeFreitas brought England back into the game with a Bothamesque disregard of the bowling. Alan Donald, so feared by the top order, disappeared to various parts of South London as the pair played with a flourish that would make even John Daly blanch. South Africa, who had palpably over-relied on the moutainous McMillan all summer, all but came apart at the seams. Whilst Malcolm took his Test haul to 98 wickets, debutant Joey Benjamin made an impressive opening to his account bagging 4 wickets on his home pitch. With memories of Trinidad still fresh, the batsmen tucked into a dispirited Donald who began to resemble a 'buffet' bowler offering up a staple diet of help-yourself deliveries. At long last England has something to crow about.

BATTING AVERAGES

England	M	In	NO	Rns	HS	Avge	100s	50s
G P Thorpe	2	4	1	239	79	79.66	-	3
G A Hick	3	6	1	304	110	60.80	1	1
A J Stewart	3	5	1	226	89	56.50	-	2
S J Rhodes	3	4	2	105	65*	52.50	-	1
D Gough	3	4	2	81	42*	40.50	-	-
M A Atherton	3	6	0	207	99	34.50	-	2
G A Gooch	3	6	0	139	33	23.16	-	-
P A J DeFreitas	3	4	0	73	37	18.25	-	-
J P Crawley	3	5	0	59	38	11.80	-	-
I D K Salisbury	1	2	1	6	6*	6.00	-	-
C White	1	2	0	10	10	5.00	-	-
D E Malcolm	1	1	0	4	4	4.00	-	-
A R C Fraser	2	3	0	10	6	3.33	-	-
J E Benjamin	1	1	0	0	0	0.00	-	-
P C R Tufnell	1	0	-	-	-	-	-	-

South Africa	M	In	NO	Rns	HS	Avge	100s	50s
B M McMillan	3	5	1	264	93	66.00	-	2
D J Cullinan	1	2	0	101	94	50.50	-	1
K C Wessels	3	6	0	238	105	39.66	1	-
P N Kirsten	3	6	1	179	104	35.80	1	-
J N Rhodes	3	5	1	128	46	32.00	-	-
C R Matthews	3	5	1	128	62*	32.00	-	1
G Kirsten	3	6	0	190	72	31.66	-	2
D J Richardson	3	5	0	138	58	27.60	-	1
A A Donald	3	4	2	46	27	23.00	-	-
W J Cronje	3	6	1	90	38	18.00	-	-
P S de Villiers	3	4	1	35	14	11.66	-	-
A C Hudson	2	4	0	30	12	7.50	-	-

BOWLING

England	O	M	R	W	Avge	Best	S/Rate
D E Malcolm	41.3	7	138	10	13.80	9-57	24.90
J E Benjamin	28	3	80	4	20.00	4-42	42.00
P C R Tufnell	55	21	112	4	28.00	2-31	82.50
C White	16	2	61	2	30.50	2-43	48.00
A R C Fraser	85.5	19	245	7	35.00	3-72	73.57
D Gough	122.3	21	414	11	37.63	4-46	66.82
P A DeFreitas	113.3	25	358	9	39.77	4-89	75.67
G A Hick	48	23	98	2	49.00	1-22	144.00
I D K Salisbury	44	6	121	1	121.00	1-53	264.00
G A Gooch	3	0	9	0	-	-	-

South Africa	O	M	R	W	Avge	Best	S/Rate
B M McMillan	81.2	16	267	9	29.66	3-16	54.22
P S de Villiers	123.3	27	388	12	32.33	4-62	61.75
A A Donald	89.3	15	410	12	34.16	5-74	44.75
C R Matthews	125.3	35	340	8	42.50	3-25	94.16
G Kirsten	2	1	10	0	-	-	-
W J Cronje	37	9	94	0	-	-	-

Tetley Bitter Tour Matches

SA V KENT

Canterbury   June 25-27

Kent	292 (G R Cowdrey 114, S A Marsh 57, W J Cronje 4-47)
	2nd innings forfeited
S Africa	0-0 dec
	258 (D J Richardson 88, T G Shaw 66, D W Headley 5-60)

Kent won by 34 runs

SA V SUSSEX

Hove   June 29-July 1

Sussex	358-7 dec (N J Lenham 76, P W Jarvis 70*)
	91-6 (P L Symcox 5-29)
S Africa	613-8 dec (B M McMillan 132, P N Kirsten 130 W J Cronje 94, K C Wessels 77, G F J Liebenberg 64*)

Match Drawn

SA V HAMPSHIRE

Southampton   July 2-4

Hampshire	300-8 dec (V P Terry 75, A A Donald 5-58)
	198-5 (R S M Morris 101*)
S Africa	264-9 dec (J N Rhodes 77, G Kirsten 50, S D Udal 5-63)

Match Drawn

SA V GLOUCESTERSHIRE

Bristol   July 6-8

Gloucs	278-9 dec (M W Alleyne 75, R I Dawson 71, P S de Villiers 5-118)
	201-7 (M W Alleyne 86)
S Africa	129-6 dec (K C Wessels 52)

Match Drawn

SA V DURHAM

Chester-le-Street   July 12-14

Durham	228 (G Fowler 68, C W Scott 53, B M McMillan 4-47, P S de Villiers 4-80)
	301-7 dec (G Fowler 61, P Bainbridge 50)
S Africa	428-4 dec (G Kirsten 201*, A C Hudson 64, K C Wessels 53)

Match Drawn

SA V NORTHAMPTONSHIRE

Northampton   July 16-18

S Africa	296-7 dec (K C Wessels 70, J N Rhodes 59, B M McMillan 50)
	216-3 dec (G Kirsten 102)
Northants	250-5 dec (K M Curran 81, M B Loye 50)
	131-4

Match Drawn

SA V NOTTINGHAMSHIRE

Trent Bridge   July 27-29

S Africa	327-6 dec (W J Cronje 108, J N Rhodes 71*, P N Kirsten 57)
	164-3 dec (D J Cullinan 61*)
Notts	218 (R T Robinson 82)
	139 (P L Symcox 5-44, T G Shaw 4-29)

South Africa won by 134 runs

SA V LEICESTERSHIRE

Leicester   July 30-Aug 1

S Africa	270-8 dec (D J Cullinan 66, G F Liebenberg 59)
	163-5 dec (G Kirsten 62, W J Cronje 54)
Leics	167 (P S de Villiers 6-67)
	216-7 (J J Whitaker 59)

Match Drawn

SA V GLAMORGAN

Pontypridd   Aug 13-15

Glamorgan	337-5 dec (D L Hemp 126, P A Cottey 84, A J Dalton 51*)
	222-9 dec (M P Maynard 101)
S Africa	288-6 dec (R P Snell 94, W J Cronje 78)
	140-3 (G Kirsten 76*)

Match Drawn

1st One Day International

Edgbaston   Aug 25

SOUTH AFRICA

			Min	Bls	
K C Wessels*		b DeFreitas	4	7	8
G Kirsten	c DeFreitas	b Lewis	30	62	48
P N Kirtsen	c Rhodes	b DeFreitas	8	30	27
J N Rhodes	c Thorpe	b Cork	35	61	52
D J Cullinan		b DeFreitas	45	105	87
W J Cronje		b Lewis	36	61	66
D J Richardson†	not out		20	33	18
R P Snell	c Gough	b Lewis	2	4	4
T G Shaw	not out		17	22	22
C R Matthews					
P S deVilliers					
Extras(LB6, W10, NB2)			18		
Total (55 overs) (7 wkts)			215		

Fall of wickets: 5 (Wessels), 30 (P Kirsten), 58 (G Kirsten), 103 (Rhodes), 174 (Cronje), 176 (Cullinan), 182 (Snell)

Bowling: DeFreitas 9-1-38-3, **Gough** 11-2-40-0, **Lewis** 8-0-32-3, **Udal** 11-0-34-0, **Cork** 11-0-46-1, **Hick** 5-1-19-0

Umpires: **J C Balderstone & H D Bird**
TV Umpire: **P Willey**
Man of the Match: **G A Hick**   Toss: **South Africa**

ENGLAND

			Min	Bls	
M A Atherton*	run out		49	121	80
A J Stewart	c de Villiers	b Shaw	32	65	70
G A Hick	c Shaw	b Snell	81	136	116
G P Thorpe	run out		26	51	41
N H Fairbrother	not out		19	29	19
S J Rhodes†	not out		0	1	0
C C Lewis					
D G Cork					
P A J DeFreitas					
D Gough					
S Udal					
Extras (B9, W2, NB1)			12		
Total (54 overs) (4 wkts)			219		

Fall of wickets: 57 (Stewart), 126 (Atherton), 181 (Thorpe), 215 (Hick)

Bowling: de Villiers 11-2-27-0, **Matthews** 11-1-42-0, **Shaw** 11-0-34-1, **Cronje** 9-0-50-0, **Snell** 11-0-49-1, G Kirsten 1-0-8-0,

ENGLAND WON BY 6 WICKETS

Atherton had the pleasure of accepting a cheque for £6000 rather than writing one following a controlled team performance in Birmingham. Udal and DeFreitas never allowed the South African batting to settle and were aided by some quicksilver fielding. Hick, relishing his new-found freedom, continued the onslaught after Stewart and Atherton had created the base for the middle order. Only de Villiers found any rhythm in an attack that began to look jaded and one-paced in the face of enterprising batting.

2nd One Day International

Old Trafford   Aug 27

SOUTH AFRICA

G Kirsten	c Lewis	b Cork	30
K C Wessels*	lbw	b DeFreitas	21
W J Cronje	run out		0
J N Rhodes	lbw	b Cork	0
D J Cullinan	run out		54
B M McMillan	st Rhodes	b Udal	0
D J Richardson†	c Lewis	b Gough	14
T G Shaw		b Gough	6
C R Matthews		b Cork	26
P S de Villiers	not out		14
A A Donald	not out		2
Extras (LB6, W4, NB4)			14
Total (55 overs) (9 wkts)			181

Fall of wickets: 1-43, 2-47, 3-47, 4-64, 5-68, 6-113, 7-121, 8-163, 9-163

Bowling: DeFreitas 11-4-12-1, Gough 10-1-39-2, Lewis 9-0-44-0, **Udal** 11-2-17-1, **Cork** 11-1-49-3, **Hick** 3-0-14-0

Umpires: **M J Kitchen & K E Palmer**
Man of the Match: **S J Rhodes**   Toss: **England**

ENGLAND

M A Atherton*	c Wessels	b Matthews	19
A J Stewart	c Cullinan	b Donald	11
G A Hick	lbw	b Donald	0
G P Thorpe	c Cullinan	b Shaw	55
N H Fairbrother	run out		3
S J Rhodes†	run out		56
C C Lewis	not out		17
P A J DeFreitas	not out		7
D G Cork			
D Gough			
S Udal			
Extras (W4, NB10)			14
Total (48.2 overs) (6 wkts)			182

Fall of wickets: 1-27, 2-28, 3-42, 4-60, 5-130, 6-171

Bowling: Donald 10.2-1-47-2, de Villiers 8-1-29-0, McMillan 10 1 53 0, **Matthews** 9-2-20-1, **Shaw** 11-0-33-1

ENGLAND WON BY 4 WICKETS

England took the series with a gritty performance on the second day of a rain affected match. The sparse crowds watched Rhodes and Thorpe - named as Atherton's players of the summer - steer England to a deserved triumph. Both recorded their first 50s in one-day internationals. Earlier Cork had staked a claim for the winter with a useful bowling display, and Gough had rediscovered the fire and pace that have made him a regular this summer. Only Cullinan mastered the conditions for the visitors, although the penurious Udal exerted a control that only DeFreitas bettered with figures of 1-12 from 11 overs. This was not matched by Donald who, in the space of a month, seems to have lost the mystique which previously shrouded the man deemed 'fastest white man on earth'. As Jim Morrison can testify, speed is not everything.

England v New Zealand

1st TEST

Trent Bridge   June 2-6

NEW ZEALAND - First Innings

			Min	Bls	
B A Young	c Hick	b DeFreitas	15	83	57
B R Hartland	c Hick	b DeFreitas	6	37	32
K Rutherford*	lbw	b DeFreitas	25	99	71
M D Crowe	c Rhodes	b White	16	31	29
S P Fleming	c White	b DeFreitas	54	111	102
S A Thomson	c Hick	b Fraser	14	44	36
A C Parore†	c Rhodes	b Malcolm	38	110	83
G R Larsen	c Fraser	b Such	8	50	30
M N Hart	c Hick	b Fraser	36	97	78
D J Nash	c Rhodes	b Malcolm	19	94	60
H T Davis	not out		0	6	5
Extras (LB 6, NB 14)			20		
Total (93.4 overs)			251		

Fall of wickets: 13(Hartland), 37(Young), 66(Crowe), 78(Rutherford), 108(Thomson), 169(Fleming), 188(Parore), 194(Larsen), 249(Hart), 251(Nash)
Bowling: Malcolm 17.4-5-45-2, Fraser 21-10-40-2, DeFreitas 23-4-94-4, Such 19-7-28-1, White 13-3-38-1

ENGLAND - First Innings

			Min	Bls	
M A Atherton*	c Parore	b Larsen	101	325	264
A J Stewart	c Larsen	b Davis	8	22	14
G A Gooch	c Crowe	b Thomson	210	417	317
G A Hick		b Nash	18	51	43
R A Smith	run out (Larsen)		78	218	168
C White	c Larsen	b Hart	19	53	47
S J Rhodes†	c Thomson	b Nash	49	170	140
P A J DeFreitas	not out		51	88	59
A R C Fraser	c Fleming	b Larsen	8	21	13
P M Such					
D E Malcolm					
Extras (LB9, W6, NB10)			25		
Total (174.4 overs) (8 wkts dec)			567		

Fall of wickets: 16 (Stewart), 279 (Atherton), 314 (Hick), 375 (Gooch), 414 (White), 482 (Smith), 528 (Rhodes), 567 (Fraser)
Bowling: Davis 21-0-93-1, Nash 36-5-153-2, Larsen 44.4-11-116-2, Hart 35-7-123-1, Thomson 38-6-73-1

NEW ZEALAND - Second Innings

			Min	Bls	
B R Hartland	lbw	b DeFreitas	22	46	31
B A Young	c Rhodes	b Fraser	53	114	87
K Rutherford*	c Atherton	b Such	14	63	57
M D Crowe	lbw	b DeFreitas	28	98	73
S P Fleming	c White	b Hick	11	58	54
S A Thomson	c White	b Such	6	42	37
A C Parore†	c Rhodes	b DeFreitas	42	216	159
G R Larsen	c Stewart	b DeFreitas	2	18	14
M N Hart	lbw	b Fraser	22	127	109
D J Nash	c Rhodes	b DeFreitas	5	50	33
H T Davis	not out		0	7	5
Extras (LB 1, NB 20)			21		
Total (106.3 overs)			226		

Fall of wickets: 59(Hartland), 95(Rutherford), 95(Young), 122(Fleming), 141(Crowe), 141(Thomson), 147(Larsen), 201(Hart), 224(Nash), 226(Parore)
Bowling: Malcolm 10-2-39-0, Fraser 23.8-6-53-2, DeFreitas 22.3-4-71-5, Such 34-12-50-2, White 3-3-0-0, Hick 14-6-12-1

Umpires: H D Bird (ENG) & S J Bucknor (WI)
(TV) M J Kitchen

Man of the Match: G A Gooch   Toss: New Zealand

ENGLAND WON BY AN INNINGS & 90 RUNS

New Zealand were doomed to lose after making poor use of a flat track, from which only Philip DeFreitas got any real assistance. It was ironic for the much travelled seamer that it was only the injuries to Gough and Caddick that ensured his selection, and he celebrated by hitting his first Test 50 in his 34th Test. The game was effectively lost for the Kiwis as Atherton and Gooch flayed the lightweight attack for a 2nd-wicket partnership of 263. Gooch was particularly savage on anything short and reached three figures off 170 balls, whilst Atherton was relatively sedate bringing up his landmark off 243 balls. Gooch always looked a contender for a double century and duly obliged before edging to slip. A cumbersome heave by Fraser brought the innings to a close 45 minutes into the fourth day, leaving the way clear for DeFreitas to emphasise his rejuvenation by collecting his 100th Test wicket at the expense of Hartland. Malcolm was subjected to a vicious early onslaught from Young, but when he tickled one to Rhodes, who marked his debut with six dismissals, the resistance had all but crumbled. With Crowe and Rutherford failing to show a lead the young New Zealand side were left rudderless and succumbed to a revitalised English side much in need of success.

2ND TEST
Lord's　　　*June 16-20*

NEW ZEALAND - First Innings

B A Young	lbw	b Fraser	0
B A Pocock	c Smith	b Such	10
K Rutherford*	c Stewart	b DeFreitas	37
M D Crowe	c Smith	b DeFreitas	142
S P Fleming	lbw	b Fraser	41
S A Thomson	run out (Taylor)		69
A C Parore†	c Rhodes	b Taylor	40
M N Hart		b Such	25
D J Nash		b White	56
C Pringle	c Hick	b DeFreitas	14
M B Owens	not out		2
Extras: (B 3, LB 15, W 1, NB 21)			40
Total			476

Fall of wickets: 0(Young), 39(Pocock), 67(Rutherford), 140(Fleming), 318(Thomson), 350(Crowe), 391(Parore), 397(Hart), 434(Pringle), 476(Nash)

Bowling: Fraser 36-9-102-2, DeFreitas 35-8-102-3, **Taylor** 20-4-64-1, **Such** 30-8-84-2, **White** 21.1-5-84-1, **Gooch** 5-1-13-0, **Hick** 2-0-9-0

NEW ZEALAND - Second Innings

B A Pocock	lbw	b DeFreitas	2
B A Young	c Hick	b Such	94
K Rutherford*	lbw	b DeFreitas	0
M D Crowe		b DeFreitas	9
S P Fleming	lbw	b Taylor	39
S A Thomson	not out		38
A C Parore†	not out		15
M N Hart			
D J Nash			
C Pringle			
M B Owens			
Extras: (LB 4, NB 10)			14
Total: (5 wkts dec)			211

Fall of wickets: 9(Pocock), 9(Rutherford), 29(Crowe), 144(Fleming), 170(Young)

Bowling: Fraser 15-0-50-0, DeFreitas 16-0-63-3, Such 25-5-55-1, **White** 4-1-21-0, **Hick** 2-2-0-0, **Taylor** 6-2-18-1

ENGLAND - First Innings

				Min	Bls
M A Atherton*	lbw	b Hart	28		
A J Stewart	c Parore	b Nash	45		
G A Gooch	lbw	b Nash	13		
R A Smith		c & b Nash	6		
G A Hick	c Young	b Pringle	58		
C White	run out (Nash/Parore)		51		
S J Rhodes†	not out		32		
P A J DeFreitas	c Parore	b Thomson	11		
A R C Fraser		c & b Nash	10		
J P Taylor	c Parore	b Nash	0		
P M Such	c Parore	b Nash	4		
Extras: (B4, LB12, NB7)			23		
Total			281		

Fall of wickets: 65(Stewart), 95(Gooch), 95(Atherton), 101(Smith), 193 (White), 225(Hick), 241(DeFreitas), 265(Fraser), 271(Taylor), 281(Such)

Bowling: Owen 7-0-34-0, Nash 25-6-76-6, Pringle 23-5-65-1, **Hart** 44-21-50-1, **Thomson** 22-8-40-1

ENGLAND - Second Innings

				Min	Bls
M A Atherton*	c Young	b Nash	33		
A J Stewart	c Crowe	b Nash	119		
G A Gooch	lbw	b Nash	0		
R A Smith	c Parore	b Nash	23		
G A Hick	lbw	b Pringle	37		
C White	c Thomson	b Nash	9		
S J Rhodes†	not out		24		
P A J DeFreitas	lbw	b Owens	3		
A R C Fraser	lbw	b Hart	2		
J P Taylor	not out		0		
P M Such					
Extras: (B2, LB1, NB1)			4		
Total (8 wkts)			254		

Fall of wickets: 60(Atherton), 60(Gooch), 136(Smith), 210(Hick), 217(Stewart), 240(White), 244(DeFreitas), 250(Fraser)

Bowling: Nash 29-8-93-5, **Owens** 10-3-35-1, **Hart** 41-23-55-1, **Pringle** 16-5-41-1, **Thomson** 12-4-27-0

Umpires: **N T Plews (ENG), S A Bucknor(WI)**
Man of the Match: **D J Nash**　Toss: New Zealand

(TV) R Palmer
MATCH DRAWN

Just when English followers start to believe that the corner has been turned, England try to conjure defeat against an ordinary New Zealand side. Fortunately for them the Nos. 7 and 10 managed to negotiate the last 23 minutes in an enveloping gloom. Taking first use of a benign pitch, New Zealand made England work spearheaded by their only world class batsman, Martin Crowe. The ex-Somerset bat, took a liking for the tavern boundary, planting three different bowlers over the perimeter to bring up his 16th Test hundred and take his run tally over the 5000 mark. England's response was a throwback to the anaemia of past performances as the cameos came and went. Indeed it was only Rutherford's inexplicable caution in delaying the declaration that prevented more acute embarrassment. With Nash a revelation it took a bold innings from Stewart to hold up one end as wickets tumbled to the 22-year-old in only his 5th Test. Stewart fed off Rutherford's misconception that the Surrey captain is susceptible to the short-pitched delivery as he reached his 7th Test century with 17 fours in the 64th over of the innings. With the obdurate Rhodes digging in, to be joined by a bemused Taylor England saw themselves to a scratchy draw. Nash's match figures of 11-169 were the first 10-wicket haul by any Kiwi bowler at Lord's and only the 7th time by an overseas bowler at that venue since the War.

3RD TEST
Old Trafford   June 30-July 5
ENGLAND - First Innings

			Min	Bls
M A Atherton*	lbw	b Nash	111	408	307
A J Stewart	c Pringle	b Nash	24	45	31
G A Gooch	c Young	b Nash	0	1	1
R A Smith		b Owens	13	61	40
G A Hick	c Nash	b Owens	20	95	67
C White	c Hart	b Owens	42	169	129
S J Rhodes†	c Parore	b Nash	12	40	26
P A J DeFreitas		b Owens	69	150	107
D Gough	c sub(Davis)	b Pringle	65	157	126
A R C Fraser	c Thomson	b Hart	10	41	30
P M Such	not out		5	16	17
Extras: (LB8, W1,NB2)			11		
Total			382		

Fall of wickets: 37 (Stewart), 37 (Gooch), 68 (Smith), 104 (Hick), 203 (White), 224 (Rhodes), 235 (Atherton), 365 (DeFreitas), 372 (Fraser), 382 (Gough)
Bowling: Nash 39-9-107-4, **Owens** 34-121-99-4, **Pringle** 39-12-95-1, **Hart** 27.3-9-50-1, **Thomson** 7-1-23-0

NEW ZEALAND - First Innings

			Min	Bls
B A Young	c Rhodes	b DeFreitas	25	132	84
MJ Greatbatch	c Hick	b Gough	0	7	5
K Rutherford*	c Gooch	b DeFreitas	7	23	18
S P Fleming	c Rhodes	b Gough	14	65	55
M D Crowe	c Gooch	b White	70	146	91
M N Hart	c Atherton	b Gough	0	14	9
S A Thomson	c Rhodes	b DeFreitas	9	32	28
A C Parore†	c Rhodes	b White	7	32	26
D J Nash	not out		8	42	29
C Pringle		b White	0	1	2
M B Owens	c Stewart	b Gough	4	8	7
Extras: (NB 7)			7		
Total (57.3 overs, 260 mins)			151		

Fall of wickets: 2 (Greatbatch), 12 (Rutherford), 47 (Fleming), 82 (Young), 93 (Hart), 113 (Thomson), 125 (Parore), 140 (Crowe), 140 (Pringle), 151 (Owens)

Bowling: Fraser 12-3-17-0, **Gough** 14-1-47-4, **DeFreitas** 17-2-61-3, **Such** 5-2-8-0, **White** 7-1-18-3

Umpires: **D R Shepherd (ENG), S B Lambson (ZIM)**
        (TV) **A G T Whitehead**
Man of the Match: **P A J DeFreitas** Toss: **England**
Men of the Series: **D J Nash & P A J DeFreitas**

NEW ZEALAND - Second Innings

			Min	Bls
B A Young		b DeFreitas	8	7	13
M J Greatbatch	c DeFreitas	b White	21	116	58
K Rutherford*	c Rhodes	b Gough	13	43	31
S P Fleming	c Hich	b Fraser	11	27	23
M D Crowe	c Hick	b DeFreitas	115	333	237
S A Thomson	c Smith	b Gough	21	64	38
A C Parore†	c Gooch	b DeFreitas	71	213	158
M N Hart	not out		16	63	56
D J Nash	not out		6	44	30
C Pringle					
M B Owens					
Extras: (B8, LB 13, NB 5)			26		
Total: (7 wkts, 106.2 overs, 462 mins)			308		

Fall of wickets: 8 (Young), 34 (Rutherford), 48 (Fleming), 73 (Greatbatch), 132 (Thomson), 273 (Parore), 287 (Crowe)

Bowling: DeFreitas 30-6-60-3, **Gough** 31.2-5-105-2, **Fraser** 19-7-34-1, **White** 14-3-36-1, **Such** 10-2-39-0, **Gooch** 2-0-13-0

MATCH DRAWN
ENGLAND WIN SERIES 1-0

It never rains in Manchester...it just pours. And so it was that the final match of the series departed to a watery grave at 3.30pm on the final day. Atherton, on his home pitch, notched up another hundred with exemplary patience, whilst Gough and DeFreitas carved and heaved their way to an 8th wicket partnership of 130 in 207 balls. Their bravado lifted England from an umpromising 235-7 to an altogether more respectable total. Gough was fired up and soon removed the miserable Greatbatch 5th ball, fending off a riser to 2nd slip. DeFreitas and White entered into the spirit of the occasion before Crowe emerged to thwart the onslaught. Crowe, who was suffering from an illness, blazed his 50 from 51 balls before hooking the feisty White straight down the throat of the man on the backward square-leg boundary. With the follow-on enforced, New Zealand again showed alarming top order frailty before Crowe showed his supreme mastery of the conditions and the bowlers. He found an admirable partner in the diminutive form of Adam Parore whose half century only took 15 overs to complete. With only 18 overs possible on the fourth day it only remained for the pairing to see off the second new ball, which was not best used by an increasingly frustrated seam attack. When Crowe eventually departed flashing an expansive drive to 2nd slip, the match was already beyond England's grasp.

BATTING AVERAGES

England	M	In	NO	Rns	HS	Avge	100s	50s
M A Atherton	3	4	0	273	111	68.25	2	-
D Gough	1	1	0	65	65	65.00	-	1
S J Rhodes	3	4	2	117	49	58.50	-	-
G A Gooch	3	4	0	223	210	55.75	1	-
A J Stewart	3	4	0	196	119	49.00	1	0
P A J DeFreitas	3	4	1	134	69	44.66	-	2
G A Hick	3	4	0	133	58	33.25	-	1
C White	3	4	0	121	51	30.25	-	1
R A Smith	3	4	0	120	78	30.00	-	1
P M Such	3	2	1	9	5*	9.00	-	-
A R C Fraser	3	4	0	30	10	7.50	-	-
J P Taylor	1	2	1	0	0*	0.00	-	-
D E Malcolm	1	0	0	0	0		-	-

New Zealand	M	In	NO	Rns	HS	Avge	100s	50s
M D Crowe	3	6	0	380	142	63.33	2	1
A C Parore	3	6	1	213	71	42.60	-	1
B A Young	3	6	0	195	94	32.50	-	2
S A Thomson	3	6	1	157	69	31.40	-	1
D J Nash	3	5	2	94	56	31.33	-	1
S P Fleming	3	6	0	170	54	28.33	-	1
M N Hart	3	5	1	99	36	24.75	-	-
K R Rutherford	3	6	0	96	37	16.00	-	-
B R Hartland	1	2	0	28	22	14.00	-	-
M J Greatbatch	1	2	0	21	21	10.50	-	-
C Pringle	2	2	0	14	14	7.00	-	-
B A Pocock	1	2	0	12	10	6.00	-	-
M B Owens	2	2	1	6	4	6.00	-	-
G R Larsen	1	2	0	10	8	5.00	-	-
H T Davis	1	2	2	0	0*		-	-

BOWLING

England	O	M	R	W	Avge	Best	S/Rate
G A Hick	18	8	21	1	21.00	1-12	108.00
P A DeFreitas	151.3	24	451	21	21.47	5-71	43.29
D Gough	47.5	7	152	6	25.33	4-47	47.83
C White	62.1	15	197	6	32.83	3-18	62.17
J P Taylor	26	6	82	2	41.00	1-18	78.00
D E Malcolm	27.4	7	84	2	42.00	2-45	83.00
A R C Fraser	126	37	296	7	42.28	2-40	108.00
P M Such	123	36	264	6	44.00	2-50	123.00
G A Gooch	7	1	26	0	-	-	-

New Zealand	O	M	R	W	Avge	Best	S/Rate
D J Nash	129	28	429	17	25.23	6-76	45.53
M B Owens	51	15	168	5	33.60	4-99	61.20
G R Larsen	44.4	11	116	2	58.00	2-116	134.00
C Pringle	78	22	201	3	67.00	1-41	156.00
M N Hart	147.3	60	278	4	69.50	1-50	221.25
S A Thomson	79	19	163	2	81.50	1-40	237.00
H T Davis	21	0	93	1	93.00	1-93	126.0

Tetley Bitter Tour Matches

NZ V WORCESTERSHIRE
Worcester   May 4-6
Worcs   343-7 dec (S J Rhodes 100*, G R Haynes 82,
           G A Hick 67)
           103-6 dec (G R Larsen 4-13)
N Zealand 194-7 dec (K R Rutherford 84)
           153-4 (K R Rutherford)
Match Drawn

NZ V SOMERSET
Taunton   May 7-9
Somerset   364-8 dec (R J Turner 104*, A N Hayhurst 84,
           I Fletcher 51)
N Zealand 182 (B A Pocock 61, M D Crowe 56, Mushtaq
           Ahmed 5-57)
           247-2 (M D Crowe 102*, B A Pocock 51*)
Match Drawn

NZ V MIDDLESEX
Lord's   May 12-14
N Zealand 249-6 (S P Fleming 118*)
           101-9
Middlesex 156-4 (J D Carr 57*)
Match Drawn

NZ V YORKSHIRE
Headingley   May 24-26
Yorkshire 408-5 dec (R J Blakey 84*, D Byas 68, R B
           Richardson 63, C White 59, M B Owens 4-89)
N Zealand 173 (C White 5-42)
           202
Yorkshire won by an innings and 33 runs

NZ V ESSEX
Chelmsford   May 28-30
N Zealand 428-5 dec (K R Rutherford 129, B A Young
           122, S A Thomson 52*)
           108-3
Essex   334 (R C Irani 83, N Hussain 71, M N Hart
           4-106)
Match Drawn

NZ V GLAMORGAN
Swansea   June 8-10
Glamorgan 361 (O D Gibson 85, H Morris 84, C Pringle
           5-58)
           226-6 dec (P A Cottey 90*)
N Zealand 282-5 dec (S P Fleming 151)
           306-2 (K R Rutherford 115*, B A Young 95,
           S A Thomson 50*)
New Zealand win by 8 wickets

NZ V GLOUCESTERSHIRE
Bristol   June 11-13
Gloucs   286-9 dec (M W Alleyne 70, D J Nash 4-59)
           368-7 dec (M G N Windows 106, R I Dawson
           87)
N Zealand 295-5 dec (B A Pocock 103*, B A Young 87,
           222-9 (M J Greatbatch 53, A M Smith 4-59)
Match Drawn

NZ V DERBYSHIRE
Derby   June 25-27
Derbyshire 424-9 dec (T J G O'Gorman 143, M E Cassar
           66)
N Zealand 210 (M J Greatbatch 84, A C Parore 50, S J
           Base 4-58)
           196 (B R Hartland 65)
Derbyshire won by an innings and 18 runs

England v New Zealand (Texaco Trophy)

1st One Day International
Edgbaston   May 19

ENGLAND

			Min	Bls
M A Atherton*	run out		81	158 137
A J Stewart	c Nash	b Pringle	24	38 30
R A Smith	c Parore	b Thomson	15	51 38
G A Gooch		b Thomson	23	45 40
G A Hick		b Pringle	18	40 32
D A Reeve	c Fleming	b Pringle	16	32 26
S J Rhodes†	c Thomson	b Pringle	12	16 13
C C Lewis		b Pringle	19	12 10
S D Udal	not out		3	9 4
D Gough				
A R C Fraser				
Extras(B1, LB5, W7)			13	
Total (55 overs) (8 wkts)			**224**	

Fall of wickets: 33 (Stewart), 84 (Smith), 140 (Gooch), 161 (Atherton), 180 (Hick), 199 (Reeve), 199 (Rhodes), 224 (Lewis)

Bowling: Morrison 6-0-31-0, **Pringle** 11-1-45-5, **Nash** 6-1-20-0, **Larsen** 10-1-43-0, **Hart** 11-0-45-0, **Thomson** 11-0-34-2

NEW ZEALAND

			Min	Bls
B A Young		b Gough	65	149 114
M D Crowe	c Stewart	b Gough	0	8 3
A C Parore†		b Udal	42	72 65
K Rutherford*	lbw	b Udal	0	7 5
S P Fleming		c & b Hick	17	31 28
S A Thomson	c Lewis	b Hick	7	23 25
G R Larsen		c & b Lewis	13	20 25
D J Nash		b Lewis	0	1 2
M N Hart	c Stewart	b Lewis	13	48 28
C Pringle	c Hick	b Fraser	3	3 3
D K Morrison	not out		17	
Extras (LB4, W1)			5	
Total (52.5 overs)			**182**	

Fall of wickets: 2 (Crowe), 78 (Parore), 81 (Rutherford), 110 (Fleming), 134 (Young), 136 (Thomson), 136 (Nash), 149 (Larsen), 152 (Pringle), 182 (Hart)

Bowling: Fraser 10-0-37-1, **Gough** 11-1-36-2, **Udal** 11-0-39-2, **Reeve** 4-0-15-0, **Lewis** 9.5-2-20-3, **Hick** 7-0-31-2

Umpires: R Palmer & N T Plews
Man of the Match: **M A Atherton** Toss: **New Zealand**

ENGLAND WON BY 42 RUNS

This was Raymond Illingworth's first game at the helm of English cricket, and a home one-day game against weak opposition offered little insight into the true worth of the new regime. Whilst the victory was comfortable, the new chairman rewarded his team with a 7 out of 10 although there were a few blips, "We set high standards and I am not too happy about the dropped catches". The major plus was the pace and control of Yorkshire's Darren Gough whose 'Waqaresque' inswinging Yorker proved the downfall of Bryan Young. It was Young and Parore who kept New Zealand in the chase with a 76-run 2nd wicket stand before the Kiwi 'keeper was deceived by England's other debutant Shaun Udal. Yet the total always looked beyond the visitors after Atherton had anchored the innings before falling to a direct throw from Crowe at backward point. The only plus for New Zealand was Chris Pringle's analysis of 5-45 which was the best Texaco Trophy figures in the 36th of these games covering the last 11 seasons.

2nd One Day International
Lord's   May 21
Match abandoned due to torrential rain. England won the series 1-0

England v West Indies

1ST TEST

Sabina Park, Kingston, Jamaica   *Feb 19-24*

ENGLAND - First Innings

			Min	Bls
M A Atherton*	c Murray	b K Benjamin	55	227 189
A J Stewart	c Murray	b K Benjamin	70	192 118
G P Thorpe		b K Benjamin	16	125 69
R A Smith		b Walsh	0	5 6
G A Hick		b Adams	23	79 65
M P Maynard	lbw	b K Benjamin	35	99 68
R C Russell†	lbw	b K Benjamin	0	3 4
C C Lewis	c Adams	b Ambrose	8	35 27
A R Caddick	c Adams	b K Benjamin	3	29 27
A P Igglesden	not out		3	29 16
D E Malcolm	run out (Arthurton/Murray)		6	4 5
Extras (B2, LB5, W4, NB4)			**15**	
Total (98.1 overs)			**234**	

Fall of wickets: 121(Stewart), 133(Atherton), 134(Smith), 172(Hick), 172(Thorpe), 172(Russell), 194(Lewis), 209(Caddick), 227(Maynard), 234 (Malcolm)
Bowling: Ambrose 22-8-46-1, Walsh 23-6-41-1, K.C.G. Benjamin 24-7-66-6, W.K.M. Benjamin 19.1-7-43-0, Adams 10-1-31-1

ENGLAND - Second Innings

			Min	Bls
M A Atherton*	c Adams	b Walsh	28	113 78
A J Stewart	run out (K Benjamin)		19	43 27
R A Smith	c. Adams	b Walsh	2	18 12
G A Hick	c. sub*	b K Benjamin	96	310 187
M P Maynard	c. Murray	b W Benjamin	0	4 3
R C Russell†	c. Adams	b W Benjamin	32	76 55
G P Thorpe		b W Benjamin	14	51 41
C C Lewis	lbw	b Ambrose	21	94 69
A R Caddick	not out		29	84 50
A P Igglesden	c Adams	b K Benjamin	0	11 10
D E Malcolm		b Walsh	18	44 22
Extras (B1, LB3, W2, NB2)			**8**	
Total (91.5 overs)			**267**	

Fall of wickets: 34(Stewart), 39(Thorpe), 58(Atherton), 63(Hick), 126(Maynard), 155(Russell), 213(Lewis), 226(Smith), 228(Igglesden), 267(Malcolm)
Bowling: Ambrose 24-6-67-1, Walsh 24.5-6-67-3, W.K.M. Benjamin 20-3-56-3, K.C.G. Benjamin 18-2-60-2, Adams 2-0-9-0, Simmons 3-1-4-0
*sub R A Harper

WEST INDIES - First Innings

			Min	Bls
D L Haynes	c Thorpe	b Malcolm	4	14 13
P V Simmons	c Russell	b Caddick	8	18 10
R Richardson*	c Maynard	b Malcolm	5	29 13
B C Lara		b Hick	83	186 131
K L Arthurton	c Lewis	b Malcolm	126	323 232
J C Adams	not out		95	342 226
J R Murray†	lbw	b Igglesden	34	73 47
W K Benjamin		b Caddick	38	71 58
C E L Ambrose		b Caddick	0	4 4
K C Benjamin		b Lewis	0	2 1
C A Walsh	lbw	b Lewis	0	23 8
Extras (LB10, W1, NB3)			**14**	
Total (123 overs)			**407**	

Fall of wickets: 12(Haynes), 12(Simmons), 23(Richardson), 167(Lara), 256(Arthurton), 319(Murray), 389(W Benjamin), 389(Ambrose) 390(K Benjamin) 407(Walsh)
Bowling: Malcolm 23-3-113-3, Caddick 29-5-94-3(nb4), Lewis 26-4-82-2 (w1,nb1), Igglesden 24-5-53-1, Hick 21-4-55-1

WEST INDIES - Second Innings

			Min	Bls
D L Haynes	not out		43	110 77
P V Simmons	lbw	b Igglesden	12	55 27
B C Lara		b Caddick	28	44 35
R Richardson*	not out		4	10 20
K L Arthurton				
J C Adams				
J R Murray†				
W K Benjamin				
C E L Ambrose				
K C Benjamin				
C A Walsh				
Extras (B5, LB3)			**8**	
Total (2 wkts, 26.2 overs)			**95**	

Fall of wickets: 38(Simmons),87(Richardson)
Bowling: Malcolm 5-1-19-0, Caddick 6-1-19-1, Lewis 3-0-6-0, Igglesden 7-0-36-1, Hick 3-1-2-0, Stewart 2.2-0-5-0

Umpires: SA Bucknor (WI) & ID Robinson (Zim)
Man of the Match: **JC Adams**   Toss: **England**

WEST INDIES WON BY 8 WICKETS

2ND TEST

Bourda, Georgetown, Guyana March 17-22

ENGLAND - First Innings

			Min	Bls	
M A Atherton*	c Murray	b Ambrose	144	412	296
A J Stewart		b Walsh	0	5	4
M Ramprakash	lbw	b Walsh	2	6	6
R A Smith	c Lara	b K Benjamin	84	217	160
G A Hick	c Richardson	b Ambrose	33	96	77
G P Thorpe		b Ambrose	0	18	13
I D K Salisbury	lbw	b W Benjamin	8	86	60
R C Russell†	c Richardson	b Ambrose	13	116	72
C C Lewis	c Richardson	b K Benjamin	17	98	63
A R C Fraser	not out		0	9	4
A P Igglesden		b K Benjamin	0	1	2
Extras (LB14, NB7)			21		
Total			322		

Fall of wickets: 0(Stewart),2(Ramprakash),173(Smith), 245(Hick), 253(Thorpe) 276(Atherton), 281(Salisbury) 322(Russell), 322(Lewis), 322 (Igglesden)
Bowling: Ambrose 30-8-58-4, **Walsh** 26-7-69-2, **K.C.G. Benjamin** 23.5-5-60-3, **W.K.M. Benjamin** 26-9-62-1, **Adams** 3-1-10-0, **Chanderpaul** 16-2-49-0

WEST INDIES - First Innings

			Min	Bls	
D L Haynes	c Russell	b Salisbury	63	212	135
R Richardson*	c Lewis	b Fraser	35	100	86
B C Lara	c Atherton	b Lewis	167	256	210
K L Arthurton	c Thorpe	b Salisbury	5	29	16
J C Adams	lbw	b Igglesden	137	414	262
S Chanderpaul		b Salisbury	62	163	135
J R Murray†	lbw	b Salisbury	0	1	1
W K Benjamin		b Fraser	44	59	53
C E L Ambrose	c Russell	b Lewis	10	21	14
K C Benjamin	c Russell	b Lewis	1	17	15
C A Walsh	not out		10	28	10
Extras (B2, LB6, W1,NB13)			22		
Total			556		

Fall of wickets:
63(Richardson),177(Haynes),203(Arthurton), 315 (Lara), 441(Chanderpaul), 441(Murray), 505(W Benjamin), 520(Ambrose), 532(K Benjamin), 556(Adams)
Bowling: Lewis 28-1-110-3, **Igglesden** 24.3-3-94-1, **Fraser** 29-5-85-2, **Salisbury** 37-4-163-4, **Hick** 20-1-61-0, **Ramprakash** 15-1-35-0
Umpires: **S Venkataraghavan (Ind) & C Duncan (WI)**
Man of the match: **BC Lara** Toss: **West Indies**

ENGLAND - Second Innings

			Min	Bls	
M A Atherton*		b Ambrose	0	4	4
A J Stewart		b K Benjamin	79	218	137
M Ramprakash		b Ambrose	5	43	27
R A Smith	c Richardson	b Ambrose	24	83	52
G A Hick		b K Benjamin	5	8	5
G P Thorpe		b Walsh	20	96	61
R C Russell†	c Murray	b Ambrose	6	56	38
C C Lewis	c Adams	b K Benjamin	24	143	102
I D K Salisbury		b Walsh	19	120	82
A R C Fraser		b K Benjamin	0	1	1
A P Igglesden	not out		1	7	3
Extras (B2, LB2, W1, NB2)			7		
Total			190		

Fall of wickets: 0(Atherton), 30(Ramprakash), 91(Smith), 96(Hick), 129(Stewart), 140(Thorpe), 150(Russell), 185(Lewis), 186(Fraser), 190(Salisbury)
Bowling: Ambrose 23-5-37-4, **Walsh** 25-4-71-2, **K C G Benjamin** 19-6-34-4, **WKM Benjamin** 16-4-44-0, **Adams** 2-2-0-0

WEST INDIES WON BY AN INNINGS & 44 RUNS

3RD TEST
Queens Park Oval, Port of Spain, Trinidad   Mar 25-30

WEST INDIES - First Innings

			Min	Bls
D L Haynes		b Salisbury	38	127	98
R Richardson*	lbw	b Salisbury	63	267	172
B C Lara		b Lewis	43	141	104
K L Arthurton	lbw	b Lewis	1	21	17
J C Adams	c Smith	b Lewis	2	10	10
S Chanderpaul		b Fraser	19	65	52
J R Murray†	not out		27	131	77
W K Benjamin		b Fraser	10	17	15
C E L Ambrose	c Thorpe	b Fraser	13	39	31
K C Benjamin		b Fraser	9	10	9
C A Walsh	lbw	b Lewis	0	1	1
Extras (B1, LB13, W1, NB12)			27		
Total			252		

Fall of wickets: 66(Haynes), 158(Richardson), 158(Lara), 163(Adams), 164(Arthurton,)201(Chanderpaul), 212(W Benjamin), 241(Ambrose), 251(K Benjamin), 252(Walsh)
Bowling: Fraser 24-9-49-4, **Caddick** 19-5-43-0, **Lewis** 25.2-3-61-4, **Salisbury** 22-4-72-2, **Ramprakash** 2-1-8-0, **Hick** 3-1-5-0

WEST INDIES - Second Innings

			Min	Bls
D L Haynes		b Lewis	19	105	68
R Richardson*		c & b Caddick	3	34	28
B C Lara	c Salisbury	b Caddick	12	35	18
K L Arthurton	c Stewart	b Caddick	42	144	88
J C Adams	c Russell	b Salisbury	43	137	97
S Chanderpaul	c Fraser	b Caddick	50	197	124
J R Murray†	c Russell	b Caddick	14	52	37
W K Benjamin	c Fraser	b Lewis	35	70	51
C E L Ambrose		b Caddick	12	21	13
K C Benjamin	not out		5	28	19
C A Walsh	lbw	b Lewis	1	6	4
Extras (B8, LB13, NB12)			33		
Total			269		

Fall of wickets 15(Richardson), 37(Lara), 51(Haynes), 131(Arthurton), 143(Adams), 167(Murray), 227(W Benjamin) 247(Ambrose), 267(Chanderpaul), 269(Walsh)
Bowling: Fraser 25-6-71-0, **Caddick** 26-5-65-6, **Lewis** 27.5-6-71-3, **Salisbury** 9-1-41-1

ENGLAND - First Innings

			Min	Bls
M A Atherton*	c Murray	b W Benjamin	48	137	103
A J Stewart		b Ambrose	6	28	13
M Ramprakash	c &	b W Benjamin	23	85	55
R A Smith	lbw	b Ambrose	12	59	29
G A Hick	lbw	b Walsh	40	106	70
G P Thorpe	c Lara	b Ambrose	86	244	167
R C Russell†		b Ambrose	23	133	108
C C Lewis		b Ambrose	9	28	21
I D Salisbury	c Lara	b Walsh	36	92	65
A R Caddick	c Lara	b W Benjamin	6	28	24
A R C Fraser	not out		8	49	32
Extras (B10, LB9, W1, NB11)			31		
Total			328		

Fall of wickets: 16(Stewart), 82(Ramprakash), 87(Atherton), 115(Smith) 167,(Hick), 249(Russell), 273(Lewis), 281(Thorpe), 294(Caddick), 328(Salisbury)
Bowling: Ambrose 29-6-60-5, **Walsh** 27.2-3-77-2, **K Benjamin** 20-5-70-0, **W Benjamin** 24-3-66-3, **Adams** 4-0-18-0, **Chanderpaul** 5-0-13-0, **Arthurton** 3-0-5-0

Umpires: **S Bucknor (WI) & S Venkataraghavan (Ind)**
Man of the Match: **C E L Ambrose**Toss: **West Indies**

ENGLAND - Second Innings

			Min	Bls
M A Atherton*	lbw	b Ambrose	0	1	1
A J Stewart		b Ambrose	18	45	23
M Ramprakash	run out (Walsh/Murray)		1	3	4
R A Smith		b Ambrose	0	6	2
G A Hick	c Murray	b Ambrose	6	17	14
G P Thorpe		b Ambrose	3	45	28
I D Salisbury	c Lara	b Walsh	0	6	3
R C Russell†	c sub*	b Ambrose	4	15	12
C C Lewis	c W B'min	b Walsh	6	29	17
A R Caddick	c Lara	b Walsh	1	13	12
A R C Fraser	not out		0	5	0
Extras (LB6, NB1)			7		
Total			46		

Fall of wickets: 0(Atherton), 1(Ramprakash), 5(Smith),21(Hick), 26(Stewart), 27(Salisbury), 37(Russell), 40(Thorpe), 45(Caddick), 46(Lewis)
Bowling: Ambrose 10-1-24-6, **Walsh** 9.1-1-16-3, *Sub:Phil Simmons

WEST INDIES WON BY 147 RUNS

4TH TEST

Kensington Oval, Bridgetown, Barbados   April 8-13

ENGLAND - First Innings

M A Atherton*	c Lara	b K Benjamin	85
A J Stewart		b W Benjamin	118
M Ramprakash	c Murray	b W Benjamin	20
R A Smith	c Murray	b W Benjamin	10
G A Hick	c Murray	b Ambrose	34
G P Thorpe	c sub*	b K Benjamin	7
R C Russell†	c Chander'l	b Ambrose	38
C C Lewis	c Murray	b Ambrose	0
A R Caddick		b Ambrose	8
A R C Fraser	c Chander'l	b Walsh	3
P C R Tufnell	not out		0
Extras (LB8, NB24)			32
Total			355

Fall of wickets: 171-223-242-265-290-307-307-327-351-355
Bowling: Ambrose 24.2-5-86-4, Walsh 24-3-88-1, W Benjamin 22-4-76-3, K Benjamin 20-5-74-2, Chanderpaul 10-4-23-0.
*Sub:Phil Simmons

ENGLAND - Second Innings

M A Atherton*	c Lara	b Walsh	15
A J Stewart		b Walsh	143
M Ramprakash	c Chander'l	b Walsh	3
R A Smith	lbw	b K Benjamin	13
G A Hick	c Lara	b Walsh	59
G P Thorpe	c Arthurton	b Walsh	84
R C Russell†	not out		17
C C Lewis	c Walsh	b Adams	10
A R Caddick			
A R C Fraser			
P C R Tufnell			
Extras (B8, LB6, NB36)			50
Total (7 wkts dec)			394

Fall of wickets: 33-43-79-194-344-382-394
Bowling: Ambrose 22-4-75-0, Walsh 28-5-94-5, W Benjamin 22-3-58-0, K Benjamin 20-1-92-1, Chanderpaul 10-3-30-0, Adams 6.5-0-31-1

WEST INDIES - First Innings

				Min	Bls
D L Haynes	c Atherton	b Fraser	35		
R B Richardson*	c Atherton	b Fraser	20		
B C Lara	c sub*	b Lewis	26		
K L T Athurton	c Russell	b Fraser	0		
J C Adams	c Thorpe	b Fraser	26		
S Chanderpaul	c Ramp'kash	b Tufnell	77		
J R Murray†	c Thorpe	b Fraser	0		
W K Benjamin	c Hick	b Fraser	8		
C E L Ambrose	c Hick	b Fraser	44		
K C Benjamin	not out		43		
C A Walsh	c Tufnell	b Fraser	13		
Extras (LB1, NB11)			12		
Total			304		

Fall of wickets: 55-55-95-126-126-126-134-205-263-304
Bowling: Fraser 28.5-7-75-8, Caddick 24-2-92-0, Tufnell 32-12-76-1, Lewis 17-2-60-1

Umpires: **L H Barker (WI) & D B Hair (Aus)**
Man of the Match: **A J Stewart** Toss:**West Indies**

WEST INDIES - Second Innings

				Min	Bls
R B Richardson*	c Ramp'sh	b Caddick	33		
J C Adams	c Russell	b Caddick	12		
B C Lara	c Tufnell	b Caddick	64		
K C Benjamin	c Hick	b Caddick	0		
K L T Athurton		b Tufnell	52		
S Chanderpaul	c sub*	b. Hick	5		
J R Murray†	c Thorpe	b Caddick	5		
D L Haynes	c Thorpe	b Tufnell	15		
W K Benjamin	c Stewart	b Tufnell	3		
C E L Ambrose		b Lewis	12		
C A Walsh	not out		18		
Extras (B1, LB7 NB 10)			18		
Total			237		

Fall of wickets 43-43-128-150-164-179-195-199-216-237
Bowling: Fraser 17-7-40-0, Caddick 17-3-63-5, Tufnell 36-12-100-3, Lewis 8.2-1-23-1, Hick 4-2-3-1
*Sub:Nasser Hussain

ENGLAND WON BY 208 RUNS

5TH TEST

Antigua Recreation, St John's, Antigua   *April 16-21*

WEST INDIES - First Innings

P V Simmons	lbw	b Caddick	8
S C Williams	c Caddick	b Fraser	3
B C Lara	c Russell	b Caddick	375
J C Adams	c sub*	b Fraser	59
K L Arthurton	c Russell	b Caddick	47
S Chanderpaul	not out		75
J R Murray†			
W K Benjamin			
C E L Ambrose			
K C Benjamin			
C A Walsh*			
Extras (LB3, NB23)			26
Total (5 wkts dec)			593

Fall of wickets: 11-12-191-374-593
Bowling: Fraser 43-4-121-2, Caddick 47.2-8-158-3,
Tufnell 39-8-110-0, Lewis 33-1-140-0, Hick 18-3-61-0
*Sub:Nasser Hussain

WEST INDIES - Second Innings

P V Simmons	not out	22
S C Williams	not out	21
B C Lara		
J C Adams		
K L Arthurton		
S Chanderpaul		
J R Murray†		
W K Benjamin		
C E L Ambrose		
K C Benjamin		
C A Walsh		
Extras		
Total (0 wkts)		43

Bowling: Fraser 2-1-2-0, Caddick 2-1-11-0, Tufnell
6-4-5-0, Smith 8-2-11-0, Ramprakash 3-1-5-0
Thorpe 2-1-1-0, Stewart 1-0-8-0

ENGLAND - First Innings

M A Atherton*	c Murray	b Ambrose	135
A J Stewart	c Ambrose	b K Benjamin	24
M Ramprakash	lbw	b K Benjamin	19
R A Smith	lbw	b K Benjamin	175
G A Hick		b K Benjamin	20
G P Thorpe	c Adams	b Chanderpaul	9
R C Russell†	c Murray	b W Benjamin	62
C C Lewis	not out		75
A R Caddick	c W B'min	b Adams	22
A R C Fraser		b Adams	0
P C R Tufnell	lbw	b W Benjamin	0
Extras (B9, LB20, NB23)			52
Total			593

Fall of wickets: 40-70-373-393-401-417-535-585-589-593
Bowling: Ambrose 40-18-66-1 Walsh 40-9-123-0,
W Benjamin 41.1-15-93-2, K Benjamin 37-7-110-4,
Chanderpaul 24-1-94-1, Adams 22-4-74-2,
Arthurton 2-1-4-0

Umpires: **D Hair (Aus) & S Bucknor (WI)**
Man of the Match: **B C Lara**   Toss **West Indies**

MATCH DRAWN
WEST INDIES WIN SERIES 3-1

BATTING AVERAGES

West Indies	M	In	NO	Rns	HS	Avge	100s	50s
B C Lara	5	8	0	798	375	99.75	2	2
J C Adams	5	7	1	374	137	62.33	1	2
S Chanderpaul	4	6	1	288	77	57.60	-	4
K L T Arthurton	5	7	0	273	126	39.00	1	1
D L Haynes	4	7	1	217	63	36.16	-	1
R B Richardson	4	7	1	163	63	27.16	-	1
S C Williams	1	2	1	24	21*	24.00	-	-
W K M Benjamin	5	6	0	138	44	23.00	-	-
P V Simmons	2	4	1	50	22*	16.66	-	-
J R Murray	5	6	1	80	34	16.00	-	-
C E L Ambrose	5	6	0	91	44	15.16	-	-
K C G Benjamin	5	6	2	58	43*	14.50	-	-
C A Walsh	5	6	2	42	18*	10.50	-	-

England	M	In	NO	Rns	HS	Avge	100s	50s
M A Atherton	5	9	0	510	144	46.66	2	2
A J Stewart	5	9	0	477	143	53.00	2	2
R A Smith	5	9	0	320	175	35.55	1	1
G A Hick	5	9	0	316	96	35.11	-	2
G P Thorpe	5	9	0	239	86	26.55	-	2
R C Russell	5	9	1	195	62	24.37	-	1
C C Lewis	5	9	1	170	75*	21.25	-	1
M P Maynard	1	2	0	35	35	17.50	-	-
I D K Salisbury	2	4	0	63	36	15.75	-	-
A R Caddick	4	6	1	69	29*	13.80	-	-
D E Malcolm	1	2	0	24	18	12.00	-	-
M R Ramprakash	4	7	0	73	23	10.42	-	-
A R C Fraser	4	6	3	11	8*	3.66	-	-
A P Igglesden	2	4	2	4	3*	2.00	-	-
P C R Tufnell	2	2	1	0	0*	0.00	-	-

BOWLING

West Indies	O	M	R	W	Avge	Best	S/Rate
C E L Ambrose	224.2	59	519	26	19.96	6-24	51.77
K C Benjamin	181.5	38	566	22	25.72	6-66	49.59
C A Walsh	227.2	44	646	19	34.00	5-94	71.79
W K Benjamin	190.2	48	498	12	41.50	3-56	95.17
J C Adams	49.5	8	173	4	43.25	2-74	74.75
S Chanderpaul	65	10	209	1	209.00	1-94	390.00
P V Simmons	3	1	4	0	-	-	-
K L T Arthurton	5	1	9	0	-	-	-

England	O	M	R	W	Avge	Best	S/Rate
A R C Fraser	168.5	39	443	16	27.68	8-75	63.31
A R Caddick	170.2	30	545	18	30.27	6-65	56.78
I D Salisbury	68	9	276	7	39.42	4-163	58.29
C C Lewis	168.3	18	553	14	39.50	4-61	72.21
D E Malcolm	28	4	132	3	44.00	3-113	56.00
A P Igglesden	55.3	8	183	3	61.00	1-36	111.00
P C Tufnell	113	36	291	4	72.75	3-100	169.50
G A Hick	77	14	198	2	99.00	1-3	231.00
G P Thorpe	2	1	1	0	-	-	-
A J Stewart	3.2	0	13	0	-	-	-
M Ramprakash	20	3	48	0	-	-	-

Cricket

1st One Day International

Kensington Oval, Bridgetown, Barbados   Feb 16

ENGLAND

			Min	Bls
M A Atherton*	c Richardson	b Cummins	86	147
A J Stewart†	c Lara	b Benjamin	11	34
G P Thorpe	c Adams	b Benjamin	4	14
R A Smith		c& b Harper	12	23
G A Hick	c Simmons	b Cummins	47	63
M P Maynard	not out		22	16
C C Lewis	not out		6	7
S L Watkin				
A P Igglesden				
P C R Tufnell				
D E Malcolm				
Extras(B4, LB7, NB3)			14	
Total (50 overs) (5wkts)			202	

Fall of wickets: 35(Stewart), 45(Thorpe), 73(Smith), 166(Atherton), 176(Hick)
Bowling: Ambrose 10-2-35-0, **Walsh** 10-0-42-0, **Benjamin** 10-2-38-2, **Cummings** 10-1-28-2, **Harper** 10-0-48-1

Umpires: **L. H Barker (WI) & C R Duncan (WI)**
Man of the Match: **MA Atherton** Toss: England

WEST INDIES

			Min	Bls
D L Haynes	c Malcolm	b Igglesden	17	38
B C Lara	c Igglesden	b Malcolm	9	16
R Richardson*	c Maynard	b Lewis	12	28
K L T Athurton		b Lewis	6	23
P V Simmons		b Lewis	0	1
J C Adams†	c Thorpe	b Igglesden	29	55
R A Harper	lbw	b Watkin	11	22
A C Cummins	c Thorpe	b Malcolm	24	38
W K Benjamin	c Thorpe	b Tufnell	0	5
C E L Ambrose	c Smith	b Malcolm	10	18
C A Walsh	not out		1	1
Extras (B1, LB10, W11)			22	
Total (40.4 overs)			141	

Fall of wickets: 17(Lara), 43(Haynes), 48(Richardson), 48(Simmons), 55(Arthurton), 82(Harper), 121(Adams), 122(W Benjamin), 136(Cummins), 141 (Ambrose)
Bowling: Malcolm 8.4-1-41-3, **Watkin** 8-1-27-1, **Lewis** 8-2-18-3, **Igglesden** 8-2-12-2, **Tufnell** 8-0-32-1

ENGLAND WON BY 61 RUNS

2nd One Day International

Sabina Park, Kingston, Jamaica   Feb 26

ENGLAND

			Min	Bls
M A Atherton*	c Athurton	b Harper	46	147
A J Stewart†	run out (Lara/Harper)		66	88
R A Smith	c Harper	b K Benjamin	56	64
G A Hick	c Cummins	b Arthurton	31	36
M P Maynard		b Cummins	22	19
N Hussain	c Richardson	b Cummins	10	14
C C Lewis		b K Benjamin	0	3
S L Watkin		b K Benjamin	0	1
A P Igglesden	not out		2	3
P C R Tufnell	not out		2	2
A R C Fraser				
Extras (LB9, W7, NB2)			18	
Total (50 overs) (8wkts)			253	

Fall of wickets: 112(Stewart), 128(Atherton), 209(Hick), 214(Smith), 247(Hussain), 248(Lewis), 248(Watkin), 249(Maynard)
Bowling: Walsh 5-1-26-0, **K C G Benjamin** 10-1-44-3, **Cummins** 8-1-42-2, **W K M Benjamin** 8-0-33-0, **Harper** 8-0-45-1, **Simmons** 7-0-32-0, **Arthurton** 4-0-22-1

Umpires: **L H Barker (WI) & S A Bucknor (WI)**
Man of the Match: **J C Adams** Toss: West Indies

WEST INDIES

			Min	Bls
D L Haynes		c & b Hick	53	83
B C Lara	lbw	b Watkin	8	21
P V Simmons		b Fraser	39	65
K L Arthurton	st Stewart	b Hick	12	9
R B Richardson*	c Fraser	b Watkin	32	39
J C Adams†	not out		52	46
R A Harper	lbw	b Watkin	0	2
A C Cummins	c Smith	b Watkin	16	10
W K Benjamin	not out		9	5
K C Benjamin				
C A Walsh				
Extras (B3,L7,W6,NB3)			19	
Total (45.5 overs) (7wkts)			240	

Fall of wickets: 13(Lara), 111(Haynes,) 128(Simmons), 130(Arthurton), 186(Richardson) ,186(Harper), 223(Cummins)
Bowling: Igglesden 7-1-29-0, **Watkin** 9.5-1-49-4, **Fraser** 9-0-50-1, **Lewis** 9-0-48-0, **Tufnell** 4-0-22-0, **Hick** 7-0-32-2

WEST INDIES WON ON FASTER SCORING RATE

3rd One Day International

Arnos Vale, St. Vincent   March 2

WEST INDIES

				Bls
D L Haynes	c Lewis	b Tufnell	83	95
P V Simmons	c Hussain	b Tufnell	63	99
B C Lara	c Stewart	b Fraser	60	41
K L Arthurton	c Smith	b Watkin	28	25
R Richardson*	not out		52	26
J C Adams†	c Smith	b Watkin	6	4
R A Harper	run out (Lewis)		15	12
A C Cummins	not out		0	0
W K M Benjamin				
C E L Ambrose				
K C Benjamin				
Extras (LB4,W2)			6	
Total (50 overs) (6 wkts)			313	

Fall of wickets: 145(Simmons), 156(Haynes), 230(Lara), 242(Arthurton), 256(Adams), 300(Harper)
Bowling: Igglesden 10-1-65-0, **Watkin** 9-0-61-2, **Lewis** 9-0-67-0, **Fraser** 10-1-46-1, **Hick** 3-0-18-0, **Tufnell** 9-0-52-2

Umpires: **L H Barker (WI)** & **G T Johnson (WI)**
Man of the Match: **D L Haynes**   Toss: **England**

ENGLAND

				Bls
C C Lewis	lbw	b Cummins	2	10
A J Stewart†	c Adams	b K Benjamin	13	20
R A Smith		b Ambrose	18	35
G A Hick	c Cummins	b Harper	32	85
M P Maynard	c Simmons	b Cummins	6	19
N Hussain		c & b Harper	16	28
M A Atherton*	not out		19	41
S L Watkin	c Lara	b Arthurton	4	22
A P Igglesden	c Ambrose	b Lara	18	28
A R C Fraser	st Adams	b Lara	1	8
P C R Tufnell	not out		0	4
Extras (B1, LB12,W6)			19	
Total (50 overs) (9wkts)			148	

Fall of wickets: 7(Lewis), 24(Stewart), 41(Smith), 64(Maynard), 98(Hussain), 105(Hick), 119(Watkin), 144(Igglesden), 148(Fraser)
Bowling: K C G Benjamin 6-0-21-1, **Cummins** 8-1-22-2, **W K M Benjamin** 5-1-15-0, **Ambrose** 6-2-13-1, **Simmons** 7-1-18-0, **Harper** 10-0-29-2, **Arthurton** 6-1-12-1, **Lara** 2-0-5-2

WEST INDIES WON BY 165 RUNS

4th One Day International

Queen's Park Oval, Port of Spain, Trinidad   March 5

WEST INDIES

				Bls
D L Haynes		b Lewis	115	112
P V Simmons	c Hick	b Lewis	16	19
B C Lara	lbw	b Fraser	19	25
K L Arthurton	c Stewart	b Fraser	0	2
R Richardson*	c Ramp'kash	b Caddick	13	34
J C Adams†	c Caddick	b Fraser	40	68
R A Harper		b Lewis	23	12
A C Cummins	not out		13	7
W K Benjamin	not out		0	0
C E L Ambrose				
K C Benjamin				
Extras (B4,LB4,W13, NB5)			26	
Total (45.4 overs) (7wkts)			265	

Fall of wickets: 45(Simmons), 75(Lara), 75(Arthurton), 98(Richardson), 222(Adams), 238(Haynes), 265(Harper)
Bowling: Igglesden 3-0-16-0, **Caddick** 10-0-60-1, **Fraser** 10-0-31-3, **Lewis** 9.4-1-59-3, **Hick** 4-0-33-0, **Salisbury** 9-0-58-0

Umpires: **S A Bucknor (WI)** & **C E Cumberbatch (WI)**
Man of the Match: **D L Haynes**   Toss: **England**

ENGLAND

				Bls
M A Atherton*		b K Benjamin	41	56
A J Stewart†		b K Benjamin	2	15
R A Smith		b Harper	45	59
G A Hick		c & b Harper	10	21
M P Maynard		b Harper	8	9
M Ramprakash		b Ambrose	31	25
C C Lewis	c Lara	b Harper	4	8
A R Caddick	not out		20	17
I D K Salisbury		b Cummins	5	6
A P Igglesden	run out (Arthurton/Adams)		0	0
A R C Fraser	not out		4	3
Extras (B1,LB9,W11,NB2)			23	
Total (36 overs) (9wkts)			193	

Fall of wickets: 23(Stewart), 86(Atherton), 110(Smith), 121(Hick), 130(Maynard), 145(Lewis), 177(Ramprakash), 184(Salisbury), 184(Igglesden)
Bowling: K C G Benjamin 8-0-37-2, **Cummins** 6-0-34-1, **Ambrose** 8-0-34-1, **W K M Benjamin** 7-0-38-0, **Harper** 7-0-40-4

WEST INDIES WON ON FASTER SCORING RATE

5th One Day International
Queen's Park Oval, Port of Spain, Trinidad   March 6

WEST INDIES

		Min	Bls
P V Simmons	b Salisbury	84	104
J C Adams†	c Atherton b Salisbury	23	61
B C Lara	c Stewart b Caddick	16	29
K L Arthurton	c Ramp'ash b Lewis	17	19
R Richardson*	c Stewart b Salisbury	15	23
R I C Holder	run out (Lewis)	26	16
R A Harper	c&b Lewis	37	33
A C Cummins	c Smith b Lewis	11	10
W K Benjamin	c Ramp'ash b Lewis	8	6
K C Benjamin	not out	0	0
C A Walsh			
Extras: (B1, LB10,W1,NB1)		13	
Total: (50 overs) (9 wkts)		250	

Fall of wickets: 89(Adams), 126(Simmons), 135(Lara), 164(Richardson), 164(Arthurton), 230(Harper), 232(Holder), 248(Cummins), 250(W Benjamin)
Bowling: Fraser 10-2-41-0, **Watkin** 10-0-56-0, **Lewis** 10-0-35-4, **Caddick** 10-0-66-1, **Salisbury** 10-0-41-3

Umpires: **S A Bucknor (WI) & C E Cumberbatch (WI)**
Man of the Match: **A J Stewart** Toss: **West Indies**

ENGLAND

			Min	Bls
M A Atherton*		b K Benjamin	51	79
A J Stewart†		b Cummins	53	38
R A Smith	lbw	b Cummins	4	16
G A Hick	not out		47	60
M P Maynard	c Adams	b K Benjamin	1	6
M Ramprakash	c Adams	b Walsh	10	11
C C Lewis	not out		16	19
A R Caddick				
I D K Salisbury				
S L Watkin				
A R C Fraser				
Extras: (B2, LB9, W4, NB4)			19	
Total (36.4 overs) (5wkts)			201	

Fall of wickets: 62(Stewart), 83(Smith), 151(Atherton), 156(Maynard), 174(Ramprakash)
Bowling: W K M Benjamin 8-1-33-0, **Walsh** 10-0-58-1, **Cummins** 7.4-0-36-2 **K C G Benjamin** 9-0-55-2 **Harper** 2-0-8-0

ENGLAND WON ON FASTER SCORING RATE

Other Matches

ENGLAND XI v LEEWARD ISLANDS
St Johns, Antigua   Feb 3-6
Leeward Is	181 (C W Walwyn 65, C C Lewis 3-21)
	173 (I D K Salisbury 4-59)
England XI	312 (M A Atherton 77, R C Russell 56 H A G Anthony 3-51)
	44-3

England won by 7 wickets

ENGLAND XI v BARBADOS
Bridgetown   Feb 10-13
Barbados	348 (R I C Holder 85, S L Campbell 83 P A Wallace 57, D E Malcolm 7-134)
	192 - 5 dec. (S L Campbell 54)
England XI	302 (M A Atherton 108, R A Smith 59, O D Gibson 5-87)
	48-0

Match Drawn

ENGLAND XI v PRESIDENT'S XI
Georgetown, Guyana   Mar 10-13
England XI	308-2 dec (M R Ramprakash 154*, G P Thorpe 84)
	170-1 dec (N Hussain 103*)
President's XI	181-7 dec (K F Semple 76, Salisbury 3-52)
	170-3 (R G Samuels 56)

Match Drawn

ENGLAND XI v BOARD XI
St George's, Grenada   Apr 2-5
England XI	319 (M R Ramprakash 91, A J Stewart 65, G A Hick 59, R N Lewis 5-95)
Board XI	313 (R I C Holder 116, D E Malcolm 4-81 P C Tufnell 4-87)
	172-2 (S C Williams 102*)

Board XI won by 8 wickets

FIRST CLASS AVERAGES 1993-1994

England	M	In	NO	Rns	HS	Avge	100s	50s
M A Atherton	7	12	0	704	144	58.66	3	3
A J Stewart	7	12	0	590	143	49.16	2	3
N Hussain	3	5	2	144	103*	48.00	1	-
M R Ramprakash	8	14	2	457	154*	38.08	1	2
G A Hick	8	14	1	480	96	36.92	-	4
R A Smith	8	15	1	491	175	35.07	1	2
R C Russell	8	12	2	268	62	26.80	-	2
G P Thorpe	9	14	0	370	86	26.42	-	3
M P Maynard	4	6	1	103	40*	20.60	-	-
C C Lewis	7	10	1	176	75*	19.55	-	1
A R Caddick	6	7	1	105	36	17.50	-	-
I D K Salisbury	4	5	0	66	36	13.20	-	-
S L Watkin	3	3	1	24	19	12.00	-	-
A R C Fraser	6	7	3	20	9	5.00	-	-
D E Malcolm	3	5	0	24	18	4.80	-	-
P C R Tufnell	4	5	3	6	5*	3.00	-	-
A P Igglesden	4	7	3	8	3*	2.00	-	-

England	O	M	R	W	Avge	Best	R/over
A R C Fraser	205.5	51	539	20	26.95	8-75	2.62
I D Salisbury	145	29	462	17	27.17	4-59	3.19
A R Caddick	231.2	43	746	25	29.84	6-65	3.23
D E Malcolm	91	8	444	14	31.71	7-134	4.88
C C Lewis	190	22	614	19	32.31	4-61	3.23
S L Watkin	69	13	235	5	47.00	2-43	3.41
M Ramprakash	21.2	3	50	1	50.00	1-2	2.33
A P Igglesden	113.3	16	403	8	50.37	2-13	3.55
P C R Tufnell	212.3	61	554	10	55.40	4-87	2.61
G A Hick	116	20	310	4	77.50	1-3	2.67
G P Thorpe	4	1	6	0	-	-	1.50
A J Stewart	3.2	0	13	0	-	-	3.94

CHAMPIONS TROPHY

Sharjah, UAE   *Oct-Nov 1993*

FIRST MATCH
Sri Lanka   172 (48.5 overs)
               (A Ranatunga 83*, A C Cummins 3-32
               K C G Benjamin 3-34)
West Indies 173-2 (46 overs)
               (P V Simmons 92, R B Richardson 69*)
West Indies won by 8 wickets
Match Award: P V Simmons

SECOND MATCH
West Indies 267-7 (50 overs)
               (K L T Arthurton 84, J C Adams 81*,
               Wasim Akram 3-36)
Pakistan   228-9 (50 overs)
               (Asif Mujtaba 60*, Hooper 3-33)
West Indies won by 39 runs
Match Award: J C Adams

THIRD MATCH
Pakistan   313-3 (50 overs)
               (Asif Mujtaba 113*, Saeed Anwar 107)
Sri Lanka   199-7 (50 overs)
               (S T Jayasuriya 58)
Pakistan won by 114 runs
Match Award: Asif Mujtaba

FOURTH MATCH
West Indies 260-9 (50 overs)
               (P V Simmons 81, K L T Arthurton 63,
               Wasim Akram 4-40, Mushtaq Ahmed 3-46)
Pakistan   261-5 (49 overs)
               (Saeed Anwar 131)
Pakistan won by 5 wickets
Match Award: Saeed Anwar

FIFTH MATCH
Sri Lanka   270-6 (50 overs)
               (S T Jayasuriya 65, P A de Silva 62)
Pakistan   271-8 (49.4 overs)
               (Saed Anwar 111, Inzamam-ul-Haq 53,
               D K Liyanage 3-49)
Pakistan won by 2 wickets
Match Award: Saeed Anwar

SIXTH MATCH
Sri Lanka   182-9 (50 overs)
West Indies 183-2 (38.4 overs)
               (P V Simmons 90*)
West Indies won by 8 wickets
Match Award: P V Simmons

FINAL
Pakistan   284-4 (50 overs)
               (Basit Ali 127*, Salim Malik 84)
West Indies 285-4 (45.3 overs)
               (B C Lara 153)
West Indies won by 6 wickets
Match Award: B C Lara

Australia v New Zealand

1ST TEST
W A C A Ground, Perth   *Nov 12-16*
Australia   398 (I A Healy 113*, M A Taylor 64,
               C L Cairns 4-113)
               323-1 dec (M A Taylor 142*, M J Slater 99)
N Zealand   419-9 dec (A H Jones 143, C L Cairns 78, C J
               McDermott 3-127)
               166-4
Match Drawn

2ND TEST
Bellerive Oval, Hobart   *Nov 26-29*
Australia   544-6 dec (M J Slater 168, M E Waugh 111,
               D C Boon 106)
N Zealand   161 (T B A May 5-65, S K Warne 3-36)
               161 (K R Rutherford 55, S K Warne 6-31)
Australia won by an innings and 222 runs

3RD TEST
Woolloongabba, Brisbane   *Dec 3-7*
N Zealand   233 (A H Jones 56, C J McDermott 4-39, S K
               Warne 4-66)
               278 (K R Rutherford 86, B A Young 53, S K
               Warne 4-59, G D McGrath 3-66)
Australia   607-6 dec (S R Waugh 147*, A R Border 105,
               D C Boon 89, S K Warne 74*)
Australia won by an innings and 96 runs

TEST AVERAGES
BATTING

Australia	M	In	NO	Rns	HS	Avge	100s	50s
S R Waugh	3	3	2	216	147*	216.00	1	-
M A Taylor	3	4	1	286	142*	95.33	1	2
D C Boon	3	4	1	262	106	87.33	1	2
S K Warne	3	2	1	85	74*	85.00	-	1
M J Slater	3	4	0	305	168	76.25	1	1

New Zealand	M	In	NO	Rns	HS	Avge	100s	50s
M D Crowe	1	2	1	73	42	73.00	-	-
A H Jones	3	6	0	324	143	54.00	1	1
B A Young	1	2	0	91	53	45.50	-	1
K R Rutherford	3	6	0	250	86	41.66	-	2
T E Blain	3	5	1	165	42*	41.25	-	-

BOWLING

Australia	O	M	R	W	Avge	Best	R/over
S K Warne	151.3	49	305	18	16.94	6-31	2.01
M E Waugh	48	18	94	5	18.80	1-7	1.96
T B A May	93.3	33	202	9	22.44	5-65	2.16

New Zealand	O	M	R	W	Avge	Best	R/over
C L Cairns	65	11	253	5	50.60	4-113	3.89
W Watson	24	11	52	1	52.00	1-52	2.16
S B Doull	54	5	204	3	68.00	2-105	3.77

Hero Cup

IST MATCH
Kanpur   *Nov 7*
Sri Lanka   203 (49.4 overs)
             (R S Mahanama 73, J Srinath 5-24)
India   205-3 (44.4 overs)
             (V G Kambli 78, M Azharuddin 75*)
India won by 7 wickets

2ND MATCH
Wankhede Stadium, Bombay   Nov 9
West Indies 268-8 (50 overs)
             (B C Lara 67, J C Adams 55, R Kalpage 3-64)
Sri Lanka   222-8 (50 overs)
             (H P Tillekeratne 104, Benjamin 5-22)
West Indies won by 46 runs

3RD MATCH
Bangalore   *Nov 10*
S Africa   22-1 (9 overs)
No result

4TH MATCH
Brabourne Stadium, Bombay   Nov 14
S Africa   180-5 (40 overs)
             (D J Cullinan 70*)
West Indies 139 (37 overs)
             (P L Symcox 3-20)
South Africa won by 41 runs

5TH MATCH
Patna   *Nov 15*
Sri Lanka   263-6 (50 overs)
             (P A de Silva 68, A Ranatunga 59)
Zimbabwe   208 (49 overs)
             (A C Waller 55, S T Jayasuriya 4-19)
Sri Lanka won by 55 runs

6TH MATCH
Ahmedabad   *Nov 16*
West Indies 202-7 (50 overs)
             (A R Kumble 3-24)
India   100 (28.3 overs)
             (Hooper 3-9, Benjamin 3-27)
West Indies won on faster scoring rate

7TH MATCH
Indore   *Nov 18*
India   248-5 (50 overs)
             (M Prabhakar 91, V G Kambli 55,
             M Azharuddin 54*, S G Peall 3-54)
Zimbabwe   248 (50 overs)
             (A Flower 56, J Srinath 3-44)
Match tied

8TH MATCH
Gauhati   *Nov 19*
S Africa   214-7 (50 overs)
             (K C Wessels 53, S T Jayasuriya 3-31)
Sri Lanka   136 (40.1 overs)
             (R P Snell 4-12)
South Africa won by 78 runs

9TH MATCH
Hyderabad   *Nov 21*
West Indies 233-9 (50 overs)
             (D L Haynes 75, R I C Holder 50)
Zimbabwe   99 (36.3 overs)
             (P V Simmons 3-23)
West Indies won by 134 runs

10TH MATCH
Mohali   *Nov 22*
India   221 (49.2 overs)
             (V G Kambli 86, W J Cronje 3-29)
S Africa   178-9 (50 overs)
             (J N Rhodes 56, S A Ankola 3-33)
India won by 43 runs

1ST SEMI-FINAL
Calcutta   *Nov 24*
India   195 (50 overs)
             (M Azharuddin 90, P S de Villiers 3-19,
             R P Snell 3-33)
S Africa   193-9 (50 overs)
             (A C Hudson 62)
India won by 2 runs

2ND SEMI-FINAL
Calcutta   *Nov 25*
Sri Lanka   188-6 (50 overs)
             (P A de Silva 68)
West Indies 190-3 (41.5 overs)
             (B C Lara 82, K L T Arthurton 72*)
West Indies won by 7 wickets

FINAL
Calcutta   *Nov 27*
India   225-7 (50 overs)
             (V G Kambli 68, A C Cummins 3-38)
West Indies 123 (40.1 overs)
             (A R Kumble 6-12)
India won by 102 runs

Australia v South Africa

IST TEST
Melbourne Cricket Ground   Dec 26-30
Australia   342-7 dec (M A Taylor 170, M E Waugh 84,
             C R Matthews 3-68)
S Africa   258-3 (W J Cronie 71, A C Hudson 64*)
Match Drawn

2ND TEST
Sydney Cricket Ground   Jan 2-6
S Africa   169 (G Kirsten 67, S K Warne 7-56)
             239 (J N Rhodes 76*C J McDermott 4-62,
             S K Warne 5-72)
Australia   292 (M J Slater 92, D R Martyn 59, A A
             Donald 4-83, P S de Villiers 4-80)
             111 (P S de Villiers 6-43, A A Donald 3-34)
South Africa won by 5 runs

3RD TEST
Adelaide Oval Jan 28-Feb 1
Australia   469-7 dec (S R Waugh 164, A R Border 84,
A A Donald 3-122, B M McMillan 3-89)
124-6 dec
S Africa   273 (A C Hudson 90, P N Kirsten 79, C J
McDermott 3-49, S R Waugh 4-26)
129 (C J McDermott 4-33, S K Warne 4-31)
Australia won by 191 runs

TEST AVERAGES
BATTING

Australia	M	In	NO	Rns	HS	Avge	100s	50s
S R Waugh	1	2	0	165	164	82.50	1	-
M A Taylor	3	5	0	304	170	60.80	1	1
M J Slater	3	5	0	185	92	37.00	-	2
C J McDermott	3	2	1	35	29*	35.00	-	-
D C Boon	3	5	0	156	50	31.20	-	1

South Africa	M	In	NO	Rns	HS	Avge	100s	50s
P N Kirsten	1	2	0	121	79	60.50	-	1
K C Wessels	2	3	1	84	63*	42.00	-	1
J N Rhodes	3	5	2	124	76*	41.33	-	1
A C Hudson	3	5	1	157	90	39.25	-	2
G Kirsten	3	5	0	174	67	34.80	-	1

BOWLING

Australia	O	M	R	W	Avge	Best	R/over
S R Waugh	24	10	30	4	7.50	4-26	1.25
S K Warne	175.1	63	307	18	17.05	7-56	1.75
C J McDermott	115.1	33	246	14	17.57	4-33	2.14

South Africa	O	M	R	W	Avge	Best	R/over
P S de Villiers	132.3	37	311	11	28.27	6-43	2.35
A A Donald	127.2	26	373	13	28.69	4-83	2.93
B M McMillan	41	3	122	4	30.50	3-89	2.97

World Series Cup

1ST MATCH
Melbourne Cricket Ground Dec 9
Australia   189 (45.5 overs)
(M J Slater 73, P S de Villiers 3-30)
S Africa   190-3 (48.4 overs)
(W J Cronje 91*, K C Wessels 70)
South Africa won by 7 wickets

2ND MATCH
Adelaide Dec 11
New Zealand v South Africa
Match abandoned without a ball bowled

3RD MATCH
Adelaide Dec 12
N Zealand   135 (48.2 overs)
(S K Warne 4-25, G D McGrath 4-32)
Australia   136-2 (38.5 overs)
(D C Boon 51*, M L Hayden 50*)
Australia won by 8 wickets

4TH MATCH
Sydney Dec 14
Australia   172-9 (50 overs)
(C R Matthews 3-23, P S de Villiers 3-37)
S Africa   69 (28 overs)
(P R Reiffel 4-13)
Australia won by 103 runs

5TH MATCH
Melbourne Dec 16
Australia   202-5 (50 overs)
(M A Taylor 81)
N Zealand   199-9 (50 overs)
(S K Warne 4-19)
Australia won by 3 runs

6TH MATCH
Hobart Dec 18
S Africa   147-7 (50 overs)
(C Pringle 3-28)
N Zealand   148-6 (44.1 overs)
(B A Young 74, C R Matthews 4-38)
New Zealand won by 4 wickets

7TH MATCH
Brisbane Jan 8
N Zealand   256-7 (50 overs)
(C L Cairns 70, S A Thomson 68)
S Africa   219-8 (39 overs)
(P N Kirsten 97, C Pringle 3-38)
New Zealand won on faster scoring rate

8TH MATCH
Brisbane Jan 9
Australia   230-9 (50 overs)
(D M Jones 98, D B Rundle 4-42)
S Africa   182 (46.5 overes)
(G Kirsten 51, G D McGrath 4-24)
Australia won by 48 runs

9TH MATCH
Sydney Jan 11
N Zealand   198-9 (50 overs)
(K R Rutherford 65, M J Greatbatch 50,
G D McGrath 3-29)
Australia   185 (48.3 overs)
(D C Boon 67, C Pringle 4-40)
New Zealand won by 13 runs

10TH MATCH
Perth Jan 14
N Zealand   150 (44.2 overs)
(A A Donald 3-15, B M McMillan 3-39)
S Africa   151-5 (30.3 overs)
(P N Kirsten 50, C Pringle 3-24)
South Africa won by 5 wickets

11TH MATCH
Perth Jan 16
S Africa   208-7 (50 overs)
(G Kirsten 55)
Australia   126 (41 overs)
(R P Snell 3-26)
South Africa won by 82 runs

12TH MATCH
Melbourne Jan 19
Australia   217-3 (50 overs)
(D M Jones 82, D C Boon 65)
N Zealand   166 (47.5 overs)
(S K Warne 3-28, P R Reiffel 3-35)
Australia won by 51 runs

1ST FINAL

Melbourne   *Jan 21*

S Africa   230-5 (50 overs)
              (G Kirsten 112*)

Australia   202 (48.5 overs)
              (R P Snell 5-40)

South Africa won by 28 runs

2ND FINAL

Sydney   *Jan 23*

Australia   247-6 (50 overs)
              (M E Waugh 107, A A Donald 4-40)

S Africa   178 (45.5 overs)
              (J N Rhodes 52, C J McDermott 3-39, S K
              Warne 3-42)

Australia won by 69 runs

3RD FINAL

Sydney   *Jan 25*

Australia   223-8 (50 overs)
              (D C Boon 64, M E Waugh 60)

S Africa   188-9 (50 overs)

Australia won by 35 runs

Pakistan v Zimbabwe

1ST TEST

Defence Stadium, Karachi   *Dec 1-6*

Pakistan   423-8 dec (Shoaib Mohammad 81,
              Javed Miandad 70, Rashid Latif 68*, E A
              Brandes 3-106)
              131-3 dec
              (Inzamam-ul-Haq 57*)

Zimbabwe   289 (A Flower 63, Waqar Younis 7-91)
              134 (Waqar Younis 6-44)

Pakistan won by 131 runs

2ND TEST

Rawalpindi Stadium   *Dec 9-14*

Pakistan   245 (Asif Mujtaba 54*, D H Brain 4-41, H H
              Streak 3-58, E A Brandes 3-82)
              248 (Rashid Latif 61, Asif Mujtaba 51, H H
              Streak 5-56, E A Brandes 3-71)

Zimbabwe   254 (M H Dekker 68, A D R Campbell 63,
              Waqar Younis 5-88)
              187 (A D R Campbell 75, M H Dekker 68*
              Wasim Akram 5-65, Waqar Younis 4-50)

Pakistan won by 52 runs

3RD TEST

Gaddafi Stadium, Lahore   *Dec 16-21*

Pakistan   147 (D H Brain 5-42, E A Brandes 3-45)
              174-1 (Asif Mujtaba 65*, Shoaib Mohammad
              53*)

Zimbabwe   230 (A Flower 62*, D L Houghton 50, Waqar
              Younis 5-100, Wasim Akram 4-70)

Match drawn

TEST AVERAGES
BATTING

Pakistan	M	In	NO	Rns	HS	Avge	100s	50s
Asif Mujtaba	3	6	3	184	65*	61.33	-	3
Rashid Latif	3	4	1	169	68*	56.33	-	2
Shoaib Moh'ad	3	5	1	179	81	44.75	-	2
Inzamam-ul-Haq	3	5	1	163	57*	40.75	-	1
Javed Miandad	3	5	0	143	70	28.60	-	1

Zimbabwe	M	In	NO	Rns	HS	Avge	100s	50s
A D R Campbell	3	5	0	205	75	41.00	-	3
A Flower	3	5	1	158	63	39.50	-	2
M H Dekker	3	5	1	143	68*	35.75	-	2
D L Houghton	3	5	1	123	50	24.60	-	1
G W Flower	3	5	0	79	30	15.80	-	-

COOPERS & LYBRAND RATINGS
As at September 1st - brackets is previous position

Test Batsmen

1	(7)	Brian Lara (West Indies)	871
2	(6)	Sachin Tendulkar (India)	762
3	(4)	David Boon (Australia)	749
4	(1)	Desmond Haynes (W Indies)	734
5	(34)	Inzamam-ul-Haq (Pakistan)	718
6	(19)	Steve Waugh (Australia)	717
7	(18)	Alec Stewart (England)	709
8	(3)	Richie Richardson (W Indies)	698
9	(13)	Vinod Kambli (India)	689
10	(2)	Graham Gooch (England)	682
11	(8)	Martin Crowe (N Zealand)	681
12	(16)	Michael Atherton (England)	668
13	(26)	Moham. Azharuddin (India)	666
14	(30)	Navjot Sidhu (India)	654
15	(33)	Michael Slater (Australia)	651
16	(5)	Salim Malik (Pakistan)	644
17	(26)	Graham Thorpe (England)	643
18	(26)	Graeme Hick (England)	639
19	(16)	Hashan Tillekeratne (S Lanka)	618
20	(22)	Mark Taylor (Australia)	612

Test Bowlers

1	(1)	Waqar Younis (Pakistan)	904
2	(2)	Curtly Ambrose (W Indies)	903
3	(5)	Shane Warne (Australia)	876
4	(3)	Anil Kumble (India)	861
5	(9)	Wasim Akram (Pakistan)	791
6	(6)	Allan Donald (South Africa)	713
7	(15)	Craig McDermott (Australia)	634
8	(7)	Merv Hughes (Australia)	631
9	(8)	Angus Fraser (England)	611
10	(21)	Philip DeFreitas (England)	602
11	(14)	Kapil Dev (India)	595
12	(17)	Winston Benjamin (W Indies)	592
13	(31)	Venkat. Raju (India)	581
14	(13)	Courtney Walsh (W Indies)	571
15	(18)	Manoj Prabhakar (India)	553
16	(20)	Mutt. Muralitharan (S Lanka)	551
17	(47)	Kenny Benjamin (W Indies)	522
18	(11)	Tim May (Australia)	520
19	(24)	Devon Malcolm (England)	519
20	(16)	Danny Morrison (N Zealand)	506

BOWLING

Pakistan	O	M	R	W	Avge	Best	R/over
Waqar Younis	130.4	31	373	27	13.81	7-91	2.85
Wasim Akram	76.2	14	203	11	18.45	5-65	2.66
Ata-ur-Rehman	66	22	134	6	22.33	2-20	2.03

Zimbabwe	O	M	R	W	Avge	Best	R/over
D H Brain	95	24	184	12	15.33	5-42	1.94
E A Brandes	141	26	394	13	30.30	3-45	2.79
H H Streak	110.5	22	284	8	35.50	5-56	2.56

1ST ONE DAY INTERNATIONAL
Karachi　　　　　　　*Dec 24*
Zimbabwe 143 (38 overs)
　　(D L Houghton 52, Wasim Akram 5-15)
Pakistan 147-3 (33.5 overs)
　　(Saeed Anwar 68)
Pakistan won by 7 wickets

2ND ONE DAY INTERNATIONAL
Rawalpindi　　　　　　*Dec 25*
Zimbabwe 195-5 (40 overs)
　　(A D R Campbell 74, D L Houghton 57)
Pakistan 196-4 (39.4 overs)
　　(Asif Mujtaba 61)
Pakistan won by 6 wickets

3RD ONE DAY INTERNATIONAL
Lahore　　　　　　　*Dec 27*
Pakistan 216-4 (40 overs)
　　(Inzamam-ul-Haq 80*, Javed Miandad 55)
Zimbabwe 141-9 (40 overs)
　　(Mustaq Ahmed 3-19, Salim Malik 3-22)
Pakistan won by 75 runs

Sri Lanka v West Indies
ONLY TEST
Moratuwa　　　　　　*Dec 8-13*
Sri Lanka 190 (P A de Silva 53, W K M Benjamin 4-46
　　C E L Ambrose 3-14)
　　43-2
West Indies 204 (C L Hooper 62, R B Richardson 51,
　　M Muralitharan 4-47, S D Anurasiri 3-77)
Match drawn

1ST ONE DAY INTERNATIONAL
Colombo　　　　　　*Dec 1*
West Indies 197-3 (39 overs)
　　(B C Lara 89)
Sri Lanka 35-1 (12.1 overs)
No result

2ND ONE DAY INTERNATIONAL
Colombo　　　　　　*Dec 16*
West Indies 229-8 (49 overs)
　　(B C Lara 65, D L Haynes 51, K L T
　　Arthurton 50* R S Kalpage 4-45)
Sri Lanka 230-7 (48.1 overs)
　　(A Ranatunga 66*, P A deSilva 51
　　A C Cummins 4-33
Sri Lanka won by 3 wickets

3RD ONE DAY INTERNATIONAL
Colombo　　　　　　*Dec 18*
Sri Lanka 103-5 (23 overs)
　　(C A Walsh 3-24)
West Indies 107-4 (22.1 overs)
West Indies won by 6 wickets

India v Sri Lanka
1ST TEST
Babu Stadium, Lucknow　　*Jan 18-22*
India 511 (S R Tendulkar 142, N S Sidhu 124, S V
　　Manjrekar 61, M Muralitharan 5-162)
Sri Lanka 218 (R S Mahanama 73, A R Kumble 4-69)
　　174 (A R Kumble 7-59)
India won by an innings & 119 runs

2ND TEST
Bangalore　　　　　*Jan 26-30*
India 541-6 dec (M Azharuddin 108, N S Sidhu 99,
　　S R Tendulkar 96, M Muralitharan 4-179)
Sri Lanka 231 (R S Kalpage 63, M Prabhakar 4-82, A R
　　Kumble 3-50, Kapil Dev 3-73)
　　215 (H E Tillekeratne 80, A R Kumble 3-64)
India won by an innings & 95 runs

3RD TEST
Gujarat Stadium, Ahmedabad　*Feb 8-12*
Sri Lanka 119 (Venkatapathy Raju 5-38, R K Chauhan
　　3-8)
　　222 (R S Mahanama 63, Venkatapathy Raju
　　6-87, R K Chauhan 3-45)
India 358 (M Azharuddin 152, V G Kambli 57,
　　P A de Silva 3-50, M Muralitharan 3-79)
India won by an innings & 17 runs

TEST AVERAGES
BATTING

India	M	In	NO	Rns	HS	Avge	100s	50s
M Azharuddin	3	3	0	307	152	102.33	2	-
N S Sidhu	3	3	0	266	124	88.66	1	1
S R Tendulkar	3	3	0	244	142	81.33	1	1
Kapil Dev	3	3	1	99	53*	49.50	-	1
V G Kambli	3	3	0	144	82	48.00	-	2

Sri Lanka	M	In	NO	Rns	HS	Avge	100s	50s
R S Mahanama	3	6	0	282	73	47.00	-	2
H P Tillekeratne	3	6	0	179	80	29.83	-	1
M Muralitharan	3	6	4	46	20*	23.00	-	-
P B Dassanayake	3	6	1	98	36	19.60	-	-
A Ranatunga	3	6	0	107	29	17.83	-	-

BOWLING

India	O	M	R	W	Avge	Best	R/over
Venkatapathy R	106.2	16	228	16	14.25	6-87	2.14
A R Kumble	136.3	36	317	18	17.61	7-59	2.32
R K Chauhan	92	34	181	10	18.10	3-8	1.97

Sri Lanka	O	M	R	W	Avge	Best	R/over
P A de Silva	23	5	50	3	16.66	3-50	2.17
M Muralitharan	143	21	420	12	35.00	5-162	2.94
D K Liyanage	17	6	55	1	55.00	1-55	3.24

1ST ONE DAY INTERNATIONAL
Rajkot   *Feb 15*
India   246-5 (50 overs)
    (N S Sidhu 108, M Prabhakar 67)
Sri Lanka   238-8 (50 overs)
    (P A de Silva 69, A R Kumble 3-41, S R
    Tendulkar 3-43)
India won by 8 runs

2ND ONE DAY INTERNATIONAL
Hyderabad   *Feb 18*
Sri Lanka   226-7 (50 overs)
    (A Ranatunga 98, R S Kalpage 51, M
    Prabhakar 5-35)
India   227-3 (48.2 overs)
    (N S Sidhu 79, V G Kambli 56*)
India won by 7 wickets

3RD ONE DAY INTERNATIONAL
Jalhandar   *Feb 20*
India   213-9 (50 overs)
    (S R Tendulkar 52)
Sri Lanka   141-6 (32.5 overs)
    (Venkatapathy Raju 3-19)
Sri Lanka won on faster scoring rate

New Zealand v Pakistan
1ST TEST
Eden Park Auckland   *Feb 10-12*
N Zealand   242 (A H Jones 66, Waqar Younis 4-46)
    110 (Wasim Akram 6-43)
Pakistan   215 (S B Doull 5-66)
    141-5 (Aamir Sohail 78)
Pakistan won by 5 wickets

2ND TEST
Basin Reserve, Wellington   *Feb 17-20*
N Zealand   175 (Wasim Akram 4-60)
    361 (T E Blain 78,A H Jones 76, K R
    Rutherford 63, Wasim Akram 7-119)
Pakistan   548-5 dec (Saeed Anwar 169, Salim Malik 140
    Inzamam-ul-Haq 135*, Basit Ali 85)
Pakistan won by an innings and 12 runs

3RD TEST
Lancaster Park, Christchurch   *Feb 24-28*
Pakistan   344 (Basit Ali 103, Saeed Anwar 69, Aamir
    Sohail 60, D K Morrison 4-105)
    179 (Basit Ali 67, D K Morrison 4-66)
N Zealand   200 (A H Jones 81, Waqar Younis 6-78)
    324-5 (S A Thomson 120*, B A Young 120)

TEST AVERAGES
BATTING

New Zealand	M	In	NO	Rns	HS	Avge	100s	50s
A H Jones	3	6	0	298	81	49.66	0	3
S A Thomson	3	6	1	206	120*	41.20	1	0
B A Young	3	6	0	191	120	31.83	1	0
D K Morrison	2	3	1	53	42	26.50	0	0
T E Blain	3	6	1	127	78	25.40	0	1
Pakistan	**M**	**In**	**NO**	**Rns**	**HS**	**Avge**	**100s**	**50s**
Inzamam-ul-Haq	3	5	2	223	135*	74.33	1	0
Basit Ali	3	5	0	287	103	57.40	1	2
Saeed Anwar	3	5	0	261	169	52.20	1	1
Salim Malik	3	5	0	210	140	42.00	1	0
Aamir Sohail	3	5	0	159	78	31.80	0	2

BOWLING

New Zealand	O	M	R	W	Avge	Best
S B Doull	88	11	332	12	27.66	5-66
D K Morrison	76.3	12	310	10	31.00	4-66
M N Hart	58.2	16	186	5	37.20	3-47
Pakistan	**O**	**M**	**R**	**W**	**Avge**	**Best**
Wasim Akram	159.4	41	431	25	17.24	7-119
Waqar Younis	118.2	21	405	18	22.50	6-78
Mushtaq Ahmed	17	1	79	3	26.33	3-79

FIRST ONE DAY INTERNATIONAL
Dunedin   *Mar 3*
N Zealand   122-9 (30 overs)
    (Akram Raza 3-18)
Pakistan   123-5 (26.1 overs)
    (Saeed Anwar 60*)
Pakistan won by 5 wickets

SECOND ONE DAY INTERNATIONAL
Auckland   *Mar 6*
Pakistan   146 (43.3 overs)
    (Aamir Sohail 48, S A Thomson 3-14)
N Zealand   110 (44.3 overs)
    (Wasim Akram 4-23)
Pakistan won by 36 runs

THIRD ONE DAY INTERNATIONAL
Wellington   *Mar 9*
Pakistan   213-6 (48 overs)
    (Inzamam 88, Aamir Sohail 78, D K Morrison
    3-32)
N Zealand   202-8 (48 overs)
    (K R Rutherford 46)
Pakistan won by 11 runs

FOURTH ONE DAY INTERNATIONAL
Auckland   *Mar 13*
Pakistan   161-9 (50 overs)
    (G R Larsen 4-24)
N Zealand   161 (49.4 overs)
    (K R Rutherford 47, Waqar Younis 6-30)
Match tied

FIFTH ONE DAY INTERNATIONAL
Christchurch   *Mar 16*
Pakistan   145-9 (50 overs)
    (Basit Ali 57, D K Morrison 3-20, C Pringle
    3-21)
N Zealand   146-3 (34.3 overs)
    (B R Hartland 68*, S A Thomson 48*)
New Zealand won by 7 wickets

New Zealand v India
ONLY TEST
Hamilton   *Mar 19-23*
N Zealand   187 (K R Rutherford 63, J Srinath 4-60)
    368-7 dec (S P Fleming 92, B A Young 85, K R
    Rutherford 59)
India   246 (M Azharuddin 63, D K Morrison 4-52)
    177-3 (N S Sidhu 98)
Match drawn

FIRST ONE DAY INTERNATIONAL
Napier   Mar 25
N Zealand   240-5 (50 overs)
(S P Fleming 90, S A Thomson 83)
India   212 (50 overs)
(A D Jadeja 55, D K Morrison 3-35)
New Zealand won by 28 runs

SECOND ONE DAY INTERNATIONAL
Auckland   Mar 27
N Zealand   142 (49.4 overs)
(C Z Harris 50*, R K Chauhan 3-43)
India   143-3 (23.3 overs)
(S R Tendulkar 82*)
India won by 7 wickets

THIRD ONE DAY INTERNATIONAL
Wellington   Mar 30
India   255-5 (50 overs)
(N S Sidhu 71*, S R Tendulkar 63, A D Jadeja 56)
N Zealand   243-9 (50 overs)
(S A Thomson 60, A C Parore 47, C Z Harris 44, A R Kumble 5-33, J Srinath 3-31)
India won by 12 runs

FOURTH ONE DAY INTERNATIONAL
Christchurch   Apr 2
India   222-6 (50 overs)
(A D Jadeja 68, S R Tendulkar 40, N R Mongia 40*)
N Zealand   223-4 (49.4 overs)
(K R Rutherford 61, A C Parore 47*, B A Young 43, S A Thomson 40*)
New Zealand won by 6 wickets

South Africa v Australia
1ST TEST
Wanderers, Johannesburg   Mar 4-8
S Africa   251 (J N Rhodes 69)
450 (W J Cronje 122, A C Hudson 60, P N Kirsten 53, K C Wessels 50, S K Warne 4-86)
Australia   248
256 (D C Boon 83)
South Africa won by 197 runs

2ND TEST
Newlands, Cape Town   Mar 17-21
S Africa   361 (A C Hudson 102, B M McMillan 74, P N Kirsten 70)
164 (S R Waugh 5-28)
Australia   435 (D C Boon 96, S R Waugh 86, M A Taylor 70, I A Healy 61, C R Matthews 5-80, P S de Villiers 4-117)
92-1
Australia won by 9 wickets

3RD TEST
Kingsmead, Durban   Mar 25-29
Australia   269 (S R Waugh 64, I A Healy 55, C R Matthews 4-65)
297-4 (M E Waugh 113*, M J Slater 95)
S Africa   422 (B M McMillan 84, J N Rhodes 78, A C Hudson 65, D J Richardson 59, S K Warne 4-92)

TEST AVERAGES
BATTING

South Africa	M	In	NO	Rns	HS	Avge	100s	50s
A C Hudson	3	5	0	293	102	58.60	1	2
J N Rhodes	3	5	0	193	78	38.60	0	2
W J Cronje	3	5	0	190	122	38.00	1	0
P N Kirsten	3	5	0	187	70	37.40	0	2
B M McMillan	3	5	0	185	84	37.00	0	2
Australia	**M**	**In**	**NO**	**Rns**	**HS**	**Avge**	**100s**	**50s**
S R Waugh	3	4	1	297	13	22.84	0	2
M E Waugh	3	5	1	233	113*	58.25	1	0
D C Boon	3	6	1	277	96	55.40	0	2
M J Slater	3	6	1	251	95	50.20	0	1
I A Healy	3	4	0	157	61	39.25	0	2

BOWLING

South Africa	O	M	R	W	Avge	Best
C R Matthews	134	44	297	13	22.84	5-80
A A Donald	128	21	425	12	35.41	3-66
P S de Villiers	148.3	33	405	11	36.81	4-117
Australia	**O**	**M**	**R**	**W**	**Avge**	**Best**
S R Waugh	77.5	29	130	10	13.00	5-28
S K Warne	190.5	69	336	15	22.40	4-86
P R Reiffel	30	7	77	2	38.50	2-77

FIRST ONE DAY INTERNATIONAL
Johannesburg   Feb 19
S Africa   232-3 (50 overs)
(W J Cronje 112, J N Rhodes 47*, P N Kirsten 47)
Australia   227-5 (50 overs)
(D C Boon 58, S R Waugh 46*, D M Jones 42)
South Africa won by 5 runs

SECOND ONE DAY INTERNATIONAL
Verwoerdburg   Feb 20
S Africa   265-5 (50 overs)
(W J Cronje 97, A Kuiper 47*, J N Rhodes 44)
Australia   209 (42.4 overs)
(S R Waugh 86, A R Border 41, C R Matthews 3-26)
South Africa won by 56 runs

THIRD ONE DAY INTERNATIONAL
Port Elizabeth   Feb 22
Australia   281-6 (50 overs)
(D C Boon 76, D M Jones 67, M E Waugh 60)
S Africa   193 (43 overs)
(W J Cronje 45, S K Warne 4-36)
Australia won by 88 runs

FOURTH ONE DAY INTERNATIONAL
Durban   Feb24
Australia   154 (43.2 overs)
(A R Border 69*, C R Matthews 4-10)
S Africa   157-3 (45 overs)
(W J Cronje 50*, K C Wessels 40*)
South Africa won by 7 wickets

FIFTH ONE DAY INTERNATIONAL
East London   Apr 2
S Africa   158 (49.5 overs)
(P N Kirsten 53, A R Border 3-27)
Australia   159-3 (40 overs)
(S R Waugh 67*)
Australia won by 7 wickets

SIXTH ONE DAY INTERNATIONAL
Port Elizabeth   Apr 4
S Africa   227-6 (50 overs)
                (J N Rhodes 66, A C Hudson 63)
Australia   201 (49.1 overs)
                (P R Reiffel 58, S K Warne 55)
South Africa won by 26 runs

SEVENTH ONE DAY INTERNATIONAL
Cape Town   Apr 6
Australia   242-6 (50 overs)
                (M E Waugh 71, M A Taylor 63, A R Border
                40*, C R Matthews 4-47)
S Africa   206-5 (50 overs)
                (A C Hudson 62, S K Warne 3-31)
Australia won by 36 runs

EIGHTH ONE DAY INTERNATIONAL
Bloemfontein   Apr 8
Australia   203-6 (50 overs)
                (D C Boon 45, S R Waugh 41, I A Healy 41*,
                C R Matthews 3-40)
S Africa   202-8 (50 overs)
                (A C Hudson 84)
Australia won by 1 run

Australasia Cup
UNITED ARAB EMIRATES (UAE) V INDIA
Sharjah   Apr 13
India   273-5 (50 overs)
                (V G Kambli 82*, M Azharuddin 81, S R
                Tendulkar 63)
UAE   202-9 (50 overs)
                (M Hussain 70, V Mehra 43, Bhupinder
                Singh 3-34, Srinath 3-49)
India won by 71 runs
Match Award: V G Kambli

AUSTRALIA V SRI LANKA
Sharjah   Apr 14
Sri Lanka   154 (49.3 overs)
                (H P Tillekeratne 64, S K Warne 3-29)
Australia   158-1 (36.5 overs)
                (M A Taylor 68*, M E Waugh 64*)
Australia won by 9 wickets
Match Award: M E Waugh

INDIA V PAKISTAN
Sharjah   Apr 15
India   219 (46.3 overs)
                (S R Tendulkar 73, N S Sidhu 47)
Pakistan   223-4 (44.3 overs)
                (Basit Ali 75*, Saeed Anwar 71)
Pakistan won by 6 wickets
Match Award: Saeed Anwar

AUSTRALIA V NEW ZEALAND
Sharjah   Apr 16
N Zealand   207-9 (50 overs)
                (B A Young 63, S K Warne 4-34, D W
                Fleming 4-39)
Australia   208-3 (47.5 overs)
                (D C Boon 68, M L Hayden 67)
Australia won by 7 wickets
Match Award: S K Warne

UAE V PAKISTAN
Sharjah   Apr 17
UAE   145 (49.5 overs)
                (Waim Akram 3-19, Ata-ur-Rehmann 3-32,
                Salim Malik 3-42)
Pakistan   146-1 (23.1 overs)
                (Aamir Sohail 51*, Inzamam-ul-Haq 50*)
Pakistan won by 9 wickets
Match Award: Ata-ur-Rehmann

NEW ZEALAND V SRI LANKA
Sharjah   Apr 18
N Zealand   217-8 (50 overs)
                (S A Thomson 50)
Sri Lanka   215-9 (50 overs)
                (A P Gurusinha 117*, D J Nash 3-43, C
                Pringle 3-46)
New Zealand won by 2 runs
Match Award: A P Gurusinha

Semi-Finals
AUSTRALIA V INDIA
Sharjah   Apr 19
Australia   244-9 (50 overs)
                (S R Waugh 53, M L Hayden 48, J Srinath 3-
                32, A R Kumble 3-50)
India   245-3 (45.4 overs)
                (A Jadeja 87, N S Sidhu 80)
India won by 7 wickets
Match Award: Inzamam-ul-Haq

NEW ZEALAND V PAKISTAN
Sharjah   Apr 20
Pakistan   328-2 (50 overs)
                (Inzamam-ul-Haq 137*, Aamir Sohail 134)
N Zealand   266-7 (50 overs)
                (A C Paroro 82, S A Thomson 62)
Pakistan won by 62 runs
Match Award: Inzamam-ul-Haq

Australasia Cup Final
INDIA V PAKISTAN
Sharjah   Apr 22
Pakistan   250-6 (50 overs)
                (Aamir Sohail 69, Basit Ali 57, R K
                Chauhan, J Srinath 3-56)
India   211 (47.4 overs)
                (V G Kambli 56, A C Bedade 44)
Pakistan won by 39 runs

England 'A' in South Africa
TRANSVAAL V ENGLAND A
Johannesburg   Dec 10-12
Transvaal   161 (M D Haysman 52, A Dale 3-34)
                200 (M W Rushmere 64*, M D Haysman 52,
                M C Ilott 6-61)
England A   293 (M N Lathwell 83, M R Hobson 4-76,
                S D Jack 3-76)
                69-1
England A won by 9 wickets

EASTERN PROVINCE V ENGLAND A
Port Elizabeth   *Dec 17-20*
England A 566-5 dec (J P Crawley 286, A P Wells 126)
E Province 192 (G Morgan 60*, R D B Croft 5-41,
            D G Cork 3-47)
            304 (A Botha 74, E A E Baptiste 58)
England A won by an innings and 70 runs

WESTERN PROVINCE V ENGLAND A
Cape Town   *Dec 26-28*
W Province 177 (D Jordaan 65, M C Ilott 3-42, D Gough
            3-47, D G Cork 3-52)
            178 (D Gough 4-57, M C Ilott 3-26)
England A   321 (M B Loye 68, A Dale 64, A C Dawson
            5-42)
            35-0
England A won by 10 wickets

NATAL V ENGLAND A
Durban   *Jan 1-4*
Natal   458 (C R B Armstrong 97, D J Watson 87,
            A Dale 3-95, P M Such 3-130)
England A   116 (D N Crookes 4-35, S M Pollock 3-33, L
            Klusener 3-37)
            285 (J P Crawley 81, M B Loye 68, L Klusener
            4-61, D N Crookes 4-103)
Natal won by an innings and 57 runs

NORTHERN TRANSVAAL V ENGLAND A
Verwoerdburg   *Jan 7-9*
N Transvaal 138 (B J Sommerville 60, M C Ilott 4-32, M J
            M McCague 3-34)
            162 (D G Cork 4-50, MC Ilott 3-64)
England A   205 (H Morris 57, S Elworthy 4-55, T Bosch
            3-31)
            96-2
England A won by 8 wickets

ORANGE FREE STATE V ENGLAND A
Bloemfontein   *Jan 14-17*
O F S   370 (G F J Liebenberg 82, P J R Steyn 80,
            M J McCague 4-84, D Gough 3-77)
            262-9 dec (J M Arthur 106 P M Such 3-88)
England   180 (A P Wells 53, F D Stephenson 3-48)
            321-5 (J P Crawley 128, H Morris 64, N Boje
            3-89)
Match Drawn

BORDER V ENGLAND A
East London   *Jan 21-24*
England A   320 (S J Rhodes 108, M B Loye 71, I L Howell
            3-49)
            175-5 dec (H Morris 55, B C Fourie 3-59)
Border   200 (B M Osbourne 50, M C Ilott 3-30)
            189-9 (P M Such 4-51)
Match Drawn

SOUTH AFRICA A V ENGLAND A
Port Elizabeth   *Jan 27-31*
S Africa A 357 (E O Simons 88, G F J Liebenberg 79,
            M C Ilott 4-71)
            221 (P J R Steyn 69, M C Ilott 5-43, D Gough
            5-81)
England A   329 (A P Wells 130, M B Loye 51)
            126-4 (A Martyn 3-23)
Match Drawn

FIRST-CLASS AVERAGES
BATTING

England	M	In	NO	Rns	HS	Avge	100s	50s
J P Crawley	8	13	1	779	286	64.91	2	2
A P Wells	8	14	3	593	130	53.90	2	1
S J Rhodes	8	11	4	293	108	41.85	1	-
M B Loye	8	12	1	439	71	39.90	-	4
H Morris	8	14	1	402	79	30.92	-	4
M P Bicknell	1	2	1	27	22	27.00	-	-
R D B Croft	5	4	1	69	32*	23.00	-	-
A Dale	7	11	2	196	64	21.77	-	1
D Gough	5	6	2	75	24	18.75	-	-
M N Lathwell	7	13	1	215	83	17.91	-	1
D G Cork	4	3	0	32	16	10.66	-	-
M C Ilott	6	5	1	40	18*	10.00	-	-
P M Such	6	6	2	25	12*	6.25	-	-
M J McCague	5	5	0	31	14	6.20	-	-
J P Taylor	2	3	0	12	11	4.00	-	-

BOWLING

England	O	M	R	W	Avge	Best	R/over
M C Ilott	229.1	60	525	37	14.18	6-61	2.29
D G Cork	129.1	34	333	17	19.58	4-50	2.57
D Gough	192.1	34	589	23	25.60	5-81	3.06
R D B Croft	177	52	397	14	28.35	5-41	2.24
M J McCague	150	32	434	15	28.93	4-84	2.89
A Dale	120	24	333	11	30.27	3-34	2.78
P M Such	272.3	76	623	19	32.78	4-51	2.29
J P Taylor	62	8	205	5	41.00	2-65	3.31
M P Bicknell	4	2	4	0	-	-	-

Britannic Assurance County Championship

FINAL TABLE

Last year's position in brackets

		P	W	L	D	Bt	Bl	Pts
1	Warwickshire (16)	17	11	1	5	41	55	272
2	Leicestershire (9)	17	8	7	2	42	60	230
3	Nottinghamshire (7)	17	8	5	4	39	51	218
4	Middlesex (1)	17	7	3	7	43	57	212
5	Northants (4)	17	8	4	5	28	53	209
6	Essex (11)	17	7	5	5	32	63	207
7	Surrey (6)	17	7	7	3	32	57	201
8	Sussex (10)	17	7	5	5	28	60	200
9	Kent (8)	17	6	7	4	44	58	198
10	Lancashire (13)	17	8	6	3	32	59	194 *
11	Somerset (5)	17	7	7	3	32	47	191
12	Gloucestershire (17)	17	5	8	4	28	56	172**
13	Hampshire (13)	17	4	7	6	32	55	159**
14	Yorkshire (12)	17	4	6	7	38	57	159
15	Worcestershire (2)	17	4	6	7	42	52	158
16	Durham (18)	17	4	10	3	32	57	153
17	Derbyshire (15)	17	4	9	4	25	54	143
18	Glamorgan (3)	17	2	8	7	29	50	111

* Lancs deducted 25pts for unsuitable pitch
** Gloucs & Hants include 8pts for level scores in drawn games

SEASON'S STATISTICS
Top Individual Scores

501	B C Lara (Warwicks v Durham)
294	D M Ward (Surrey v Derbyshire)
281*	J P Crawley (Lancashire v Somerset)
277*	R G Twose (Warwicks v Glamorgan)
274*	M D Moxon (Yorkshire v Worcs)
261*	J D Carr (Middlesex v Gloucs)
261	P V Simmons (Leics v Northants)
250	J P Crawley (Lancashire v Notts)

Leading Run Scorers

2066	B C Lara (Warwicks)
1747	G A Gooch (Essex)

First to 1000 Runs
B C Lara (Warwicks), June 6

First (and only) to 2000 Runs
B C Lara (Warwicks), Sept 1

Highest Partnership
322* Lara/Piper (5th) Warwicks v Durham

Leading Wicket Takers

90	M M Patel (Kent)
89	C A Walsh (Gloucestershire)

Best Bowling (Match)
15-147 M J McCague (Kent v Derbyshire)

Best Bowling (Innings)
10-45 R L Johnson (Middlesex v Derbyshire)

Highest Team Score
810-4d Warwicks v Durham

Lowest Team Score

73	Oxford Univ. v Durham
73	Worcs v Yorkshire
73	Derbyshire v Yorkshire

Leading Catcher
34 N Hussain (Essex)

Leading Wicketkeeper
74 S A Marsh (Kent) (69ct, 5st)

Edgbaston is not usually the place for county triumphs. It is a concrete bowl with little of the rustic charm that is often associated with the much maligned county championship. But this year the ranks of season ticket holders has swelled and the entertainment has been truly first class. The arrival of Brian Lara proved the catalyst to many of the perennial journeymen on the Warwickshire staff to raise their first championship since 1972. Whilst Lara cracked his 501 (much to the annoyance of his jean sponsor Joe Bloggs), Dermot Reeve was moulding an impressive outfit around his effervescent talents. Tim Munton with 81 wickets was the backbone of the bowling, churning out almost 700 overs, whilst the New Zealand bound Twose and the portly Moles both completed double centuries. There will also be a few happy bank managers in the Birmingham area, as the county's dressing room kitty has swollen to £132,600, half of which seems to have gone to Moet & Chandon.

Elsewhere, last years champions Middlesex could only reflect on a couple of individual triumphs notably John Carr's effort to pip Lara at the top of the averages. Carr, who averaged 90.7, is not a household name, and it may be true to say that the selectors are not acquainted with the blond haired right hander either. If Carr is not well known then Richard Johnson is positively anonymous. The Middlesex seamer first came into the news when he prevented Lara from making his 6th successive first-class hundred and then went up to Derby and captured all 10 2nd innings wickets. His figures of 10-45 also proved the most economical championship figures since Hedley Verity's 10-10 for Yorkshire in 1932.

The Pakistan trio of Wasim, Waqar and Mushtaq also disappeared from the county scene for Test duty, whilst Richie Richardson realised that he really can't play on English wickets and went home, prompting calls for restrictions on overseas players (again). More permanent absentees are to be Durham's David Graveney and Kent's purveyor of booming outswingers, Richard Ellison, who have unscrewed their spikes for the last time.

Finally it was an ominous sign that Walsh and Ambrose bagged 166 wickets between them at a combined average of 15.95 - what odds on another blackwash?

1994 Final Averages - All First-Class Matches

BATTING
Qualification: 6 Innings

	M	In	NO	Rns	HS	Avge	100s	50s
J D Carr (M)	20	27	10	1542	261*	90.70	6	7
B C Lara (Wk)	15	25	2	2066	501*	89.82	9	3
M W Gatting (M)	19	27	3	1671	225	69.62	6	6
G A Gooch (E)	17	29	2	1747	236	64.70	6	5
C C Lewis (Nt)	12	19	4	881	220*	58.73	2	5
B McMillan (SA)	9	11	3	467	132	58.37	1	3
M D Moxon (Y)	17	30	4	1458	274*	56.07	4	6
S J Rhodes (Wc)	18	27	11	896	100*	56.00	1	5
G A Hick (Wc)	17	29	1	1538	215	54.92	5	5
C L Hooper (K)	16	29	0	1579	183	54.44	5	7
R G Twose (Wk)	18	31	5	1411	277*	54.26	3	6
G P Thorpe (Sy)	16	25	4	1136	190	54.09	2	7
M Ramp'kash (M)	18	26	2	1271	135	52.95	4	6
A N Hayhurst (So)	18	30	6	1250	121	52.08	2	10
D J Bicknell (Sy)	18	30	4	1354	235*	52.07	3	7
C J Hollins (OU)	8	10	2	415	131	51.87	1	2
P A Cottey (Gm)	19	33	6	1393	191	51.59	3	6
A J Moles (Wk)	11	20	3	863	203*	50.76	1	5
J P Crawley (La)	20	34	3	1570	281*	50.64	3	6
N Fairbrother (La)	12	22	2	1002	204	50.10	4	1
P N Kirsten (SA)	10	16	5	549	130	49.90	2	1
R S M Morris (Ha)	9	17	3	686	174	49.00	2	3
K M Curran (Nr)	15	25	5	973	114	48.65	1	8
M Trescothick (So)	11	20	1	924	121	48.63	2	8
A D Brown (Sy)	17	24	2	1049	172	47.68	2	6
N V Knight (Ex)	12	21	1	944	157	47.20	4	3
G Kirsten (SA)	11	19	3	751	201*	46.93	2	5
A J Stewart (Sy)	16	23	3	936	142	46.80	3	4
M D Crowe (NZ)	9	16	2	654	142	46.71	3	3
N J Speak (La)	19	34	6	1304	143	46.57	3	7
T M Moody (Wc)	18	28	3	1160	159	46.40	3	6
R J Bailey (Nr)	20	36	9	1236	94*	45.77	-	11
M C Nicholas (Ha)	19	32	6	1182	145	45.46	3	5
D Leatherdale (Wc)	17	25	3	987	139	44.86	2	3
M Azharuddin (De)	9	17	1	712	205	44.50	2	1
A Fordham (Nr)	11	20	1	844	158	44.42	3	4
D M Ward (Sy)	16	22	1	921	294*	43.85	1	5
N R Taylor (Kt)	16	27	3	1049	139	43.70	3	4
J E R Gallian (La)	12	20	0	874	171	43.70	2	5
P E Robinson (Le)	5	7	0	305	86	43.57	-	3
R A Smith (Ha)	17	29	0	1263	162	43.55	5	4
R J Bailey (Nr)	18	33	5	1214	129*	43.35	3	7
P Johnson (Nt)	17	29	2	1170	132	43.33	4	5
A J Lamb (Nr)	15	22	1	908	131	43.23	2	5
D P Ostler (Wk)	18	29	2	1161	186	43.00	2	6
R I Dawson (Gc)	16	30	4	1112	127*	42.76	1	7
T R Ward (Kt)	19	33	1	1368	125	42.75	3	10
D L Hemp (Gm)	21	38	4	1452	136	42.70	4	8
R T Robinson (Nt)	19	31	1	1276	182	42.53	2	10
K C Wessels (SA)	12	18	2	679	105	42.43	1	4
J E Morris (Du)	20	35	1	1433	204	42.14	4	6
R C Irani (Ex)	18	29	6	965	119	41.95	2	8
R J Harden (So)	18	31	5	1061	131*	40.80	2	7
W Larkins (Du)	16	27	3	976	158*	40.66	1	6
K R Brown (Mx)	20	25	9	639	102*	39.93	1	1
M B Loye (Nr)	15	26	3	914	132	39.73	3	5
M N Lathwell (So)	18	32	1	1230	206	39.67	2	9
M A Lynch (Sy)	4	7	1	238	60	39.66	-	1
S P Fleming (NZ)	9	16	1	591	151	39.40	2	1

BOWLING
Qulaification: 10 wickets

	O	M	R	W	Avge	Best
K J Barnett (De)	54.2	5	173	13	13.30	5-31
C E L Ambrose (Nr)	540	159	1113	77	14.45	7-44
C A Walsh (Gc)	506.1	119	1535	89	17.24	7-42
M J McCague (Kt)	341.1	67	1084	57	19.01	9-86
I D Austin (La)	251.5	72	662	33	20.06	5-23
F D Stephenson (Sx)	480.5	108	1345	67	20.07	6-50
J E Benjamin (Sy)	591.2	130	1658	80	20.72	6-27
T A Munton (Wk)	699.4	181	1748	81	21.58	7-52
M M Patel (Kt)	811.2	202	2058	90	22.86	8-96
C White (Yk)	235.2	53	761	33	23.06	5-40
S R Lampitt (Wc)	512.4	127	1484	64	23.18	5-33
A R Caddick (So)	373.1	73	1186	51	23.25	6-51
C C Lewis (Nt)	345.2	69	1082	46	23.52	5-55
G R Larsen (NZ)	226.4	73	494	21	23.52	5-24
M C Ilott (Ex)	497.5	115	1391	59	23.57	6-24
Wasim Akram (La)	213.2	44	646	27	23.92	8-30
P S de Villiers (SA)	277.3	59	922	38	24.26	6-67
W K M Benjamin (Ha)	281	97	585	24	24.37	6-46
E S H Giddins (Sx)	450.4	89	1463	60	24.38	5-38
C A Connor (Ha)	574.4	131	1764	72	24.50	7-47
D Gough (Yk)	479.2	100	1526	62	24.61	6-66
P A J DeFreitas (De)	530	108	1621	65	24.93	6-39
M B Owens (NZ)	127	31	424	17	24.94	5-74
D J Millns (Le)	532	99	1901	76	25.01	6-44
V J Wells (Le)	301.5	78	1053	42	25.07	5-50
A C S Pigott (Sy)	268.3	73	737	29	25.41	6-46
P V Simmons (Le)	300.5	81	769	30	25.63	4-68
J E Emburey (Mx)	674	204	1514	59	25.66	6-89
G D Rose (So)	344.1	70	1136	44	25.81	4-40
D M Cousins (Ex)	112	21	337	13	25.92	6-35
R A Pick (Nt)	507.2	122	1413	54	26.16	6-62
G C Small (Wk)	339	79	946	36	26.27	5-46
R L Johnson (Mx)	350.4	85	1059	40	26.47	10-45
Mushtaq Ahmed (So)	404	114	1196	45	26.57	7-94
G Chapple (La)	458.4	110	1474	55	26.80	6-48
A R C Fraser (Mx)	532.5	142	1343	50	26.86	3-16
M W Alleyne (Gc)	351.3	68	1103	41	26.90	5-78
R S Yeabsley (OU)	174.4	27	567	21	27.00	6-54
S D Udal (Ha)	678	174	1872	69	27.13	6-79
P L Symcox (SA)	280.5	86	761	28	27.17	5-29
G Yates (La)	320.5	70	1013	37	27.37	5-34
G J Parsons (Le)	462.2	131	1208	44	27.45	5-34
D W Headley (Kt)	295.3	48	989	36	27.47	5-60
P W Trimby (OU)	243.3	48	718	26	27.61	5-84
I D K Salisbury (Sx)	474	143	1336	48	27.83	6-55
P J Hartley (Yk)	562.1	116	1701	61	27.88	5-89
S J E Brown (Du)	578.5	88	2108	75	28.10	6-68
M A Ealham (Kt)	265.4	62	762	27	28.22	7-53
P C R Tufnell (Mx)	463.5	128	1107	39	28.38	6-35
K E Cooper (Gc)	418.2	99	1095	38	28.81	4-38
V Pike (Gc)	199	51	578	20	28.90	6-41
M Watkinson (La)	631.1	173	1823	63	28.93	8-30
E E Hemmings (Sx)	422	140	959	33	29.06	7-66
D E Malcolm (De)	551.3	97	2015	69	29.20	9-57
P J Martin (La)	614.4	177	1580	54	29.25	5-61
R C Irani (Ex)	249.4	42	834	28	29.78	4-27
K P Evans (Nt)	411.5	105	1141	38	30.02	4-46
D G Cork (De)	329.1	55	1112	37	30.05	6-29
C E Cuffy (Sy)	389.3	107	1082	36	30.05	4-70

Benson and Hedges Cup

(All Matches over 55 overs)

FIRST ROUND   *all April 26*

SCOTLAND V SUSSEX   *Hove*
Scotland   157-7 (55 overs)
            (J D Love 53, F D Stephenson 2-24)
Sussex   161-2 (40.4 overs)
            (D M Smith 65*, A P Wells 51*)
Sussex won by 8 wickets
Gold Award: D M Smith

IRELAND V LEICESTERSHIRE   *Leicester*
Ireland   160-9 (55 overs)
            (S J S Warke 53, A D Mullally 2-30)
Leics   164-1 (50.1 overs)
            (N E Briers 70*, P V Simmons 64)
Leicestershire won by 9 wickets
Gold Award: P V Simmons

MIDDLESEX V NORTHANTS   *Lord's*
Northants   232-7 (55 overs)
            (M B Loye 71*, P C R Tufnell 3-32, J E
            Emburey 3-37)
Middlesex   236-4 (53.5 overs)
            (M R Ramprakash 119*)
Middlesex won by 6 wickets
Gold Award: M R Ramprakash

COMBINED UNIS V LANCS   *The Parks*
Comb. Us.   191-3 (55 overs)
            (R R Montgomerie 52, G Steer 43)
Lancs   193-3 (51.3 overs)
            (J P Crawley 73, N H Fairbrother 41*, J Bovill
            2-21)
Lancs won by 7 wickets
Gold Award: J P Crawley

NOTTS V MINOR COUNTIES   *Trent Bridge*
Minor Cs.   191-4 (55 overs)
            (I Cockbain 54*, S D Myles 43, G W Mike 2-
            35)
Notts   195-7 (53.5 overs)
            (C C Lewis 48*, J C Adams 40, D R Thomas
            3-36, A Smith 3-40)
Notts won by 3 wickets
Gold Award: I Cockbain

SURREY V SOMERSET   *Oval*
Surrey   288-3 (55 overs)
            (A J Stewart 167*, D M Ward 50)
Somerset   253 (53.2 overs)
            (M N Lathwell 120, M P Bicknell 4-49, M A
            Butcher 3-37)
Surrey won by 35 runs
Gold Award: A J Stewart

SECOND ROUND   *all May 10*

KENT V GLOUCESTERSHIRE   *Canterbury*
Gloucs   189-9 (55 overs)
            (A J Wright 55, A P Igglesden 3-26)
Kent   193-6 (54 overs)
            (M R Benson 47)
Kent won by 4 wickets
Gold Award: M V Fleming

ESSEX V LEICESTERSHIRE   *Chelmsford*
Leics   241-9 (55 overs)
            (P V Simmons 57, J J Whitaker 53, M C Ilott
            3-28)
Essex   246-2 (51.5 overs)
            (G A Gooch 130*, N Hussain 59)
Essex won by 8 wickets
Gold Award: G A Gooch

DERBYSHIRE V LANCASHIRE   *Derby*
Lancs   280-5 (55 overs)
            (M A Atherton 100, J P Crawley 73)
Derbys   282-6 (54.5 overs)
            (A S Rollins 70, D G Cork 63*)
Derbyshire won by 4 wickets
Gold Award: D G Cork

MIDDLESEX V WARWICKSHIRE   *Lord's*
Middlesex   150 (54.3 overs)
            (M R Ramprakash 42, T A Munton 3-27, N M
            K Smith 3-29)
Warwicks   151-7 (53.2 overs)
            (P N Weekes 3-32)
Warwickshire won by 3 wickets
Gold Award: T A Munton

SURREY V GLAMORGAN   *Oval*
Glamorgan   236-6 (55 overs)
            (H Morris 55, P A Cottey 43, J E Benjamin 3-
            52)
Surrey   240-7 (54.4 overs)
            (D J Bicknell 90, G P Thorpe 51)
Surrey won by 3 wickets
Gold Award: D J Bicknell

HAMPSHIRE V YORKSHIRE   *Southampton*
Yorkshire   178-6 (55 overs)
            (M D Moxon 40, R J Blakey 40)
Hampshire   182-2 (51 overs)
            (T C Middleton 63*, R A Smith 58)
Hampshire won by 8 wickets
Gold Award: T C Middleton

DURHAM V WORCESTERSHIRE   *Stockton*
Durham   190-8 (55 overs)
            (P J Newport 2-14, R K Illingworth, 3-51)
Worcs   191-2 (45.4 overs)
            (G A Hick 104*, T M Moody 65*)
Worcs won by 8 wickets
Gold Award: P J Newport

NOTTS V SUSSEX   *Trent Bridge*
Sussex   239-9 (55 overs)
            (A P Wells 51, N J Lenham 44, M A Crawley
            4-43, J A Afford 3-34)
Notts   241-3 (49.2 overs)
            (R T Robinson 91*, J C Adams 86, P W Jarvis
            34-2)
Notts won by 7 wickets
Gold Award: R T Robinson

Cricket

QUARTER FINALS May 2425

DERBYSHIRE V WORCS *Derby*

Derbys   98 (44 overs)
          (S R Lampitt 6-26, T M Moody 3-14)
Worcs   100-1 (18.2 overs)
          (G A Hick 40*)
Worcs won by 9 wickets
Gold Award: S R Lampitt

HAMPSHIRE V ESSEX *Southampton*

Essex   124-3 (19 overs)
          (J P Stephenson 47)
Hampshire 127-1 (17.2 overs)
          (R A Smith 73*, M C J Nicholas 46*)
Match reduced by rain to 19 overs per side.
Hampshire won by 9 wickets
Gold Award: R A Smith

NOTTINGHAMSHIRE V SURREY *Trent Bridge*

Notts   275-8 (55 overs)
          (P R Pollard 104, A J Hollioake 3-48)
Surrey   278-4 (51.4 overs)
          (D J Bicknell 109, D M Ward 73)
Surrey won by 6 wickets
Gold Award: D M Ward

WARWICKSHIRE V KENT *Edgbaston*
No play was possible on either of the allocated days.
Warwicks went through after winning 5-4 in a bowl out.

SEMI-FINALS *June 7/8*

SURREY V WARWICKSHIRE *Oval*

Surrey   267-7 (55 overs)
          (G P Thorpe 87, D M Ward 61, D A Reeve 3-48, N M K Smith 3-54)
Warwicks 270-6 (54.1 overs)
          (B C Lara 70, D A Reeve 46*, A C S Pigott 3-43)
Warwicks won by 4 wickets
Gold Award: D A Reeve

WORCS V HAMPSHIRE *Worcester*

Hampshire 244-6 (55 overs)
          (R A Smith 108)
Worcs   245-7 (52.4 overs)
          (G R Haynes 65, T M Moody 56, N G Cowans 4-36)
Worcs won by 3 wickets
Gold Award: G R Haynes

THE FINAL
WARWICKSHIRE v WORCESTERSHIRE
Lord's July 9

WORCESTERSHIRE

T S Curtis*	c Piper	b Small	13
A C H Seymour		b Munton	3
G A Hick	lbw	b P Smith	27
T M Moody	run out		47
G R Haynes	c Piper	b N Smith	22
D Leatherdale	c Ostler	b P Smith	4
S J Rhodes†	lbw	b Twose	0
S R Lampitt	c Penney	b P Smith	1
R Illingworth	lbw	b Reeve	18
N V Radford	not out		23
P J Newport	not out		1
Extras (LB2, W5, NB4)			11
Total (9 wickets, 55 overs)			170

Fall of wickets: 1-10, 2-28, 3-55, 4-100, 5-124, 6-124, 7-125, 8-126, 9-168
Bowling: **Small** 11-4-26-1, **Munton** 11-3-29-1, **P Smith** 11-1-34-3, **Reeve** 9-1-38-1, **N Smith** 5-0-16-1, **Twose** 8-1-25-1

WARWICKSHIRE

D P Ostler	run out		55
R G Twose	run out		37
B C Lara	c Hick	b Newport	8
P A Smith	not out		42
Asif Din	c Rhodes	b Moody	15
D A Reeve*	not out		9
Extras (LB1, W5)			6
Total (4 wickets, 44.2 overs)			172

Did not bat: T L Penney, K J Pipert, N M K Smith, G C Small, T A Munton
Fall of wickets:1-91, 2-98, 3-103, 4-147
Bowling: **Moody** 11-2-31-1, **Newport** 8-0-29-1, **Lampitt** 9.2-1-38-0, **Illingworth** 6-0-22-0, **Radford** 8-0-39-0, **Hick** 2-0-12-0

Toss: Warwickshire
Umpires: H D Bird & K E Palmer
Third Umpire: B Leadbetter   *Gold Award:* P A Smith

As has often proved the case in recent years, the toss was the most important part of the mornings proceedings. Tim Curtis called wrong and from then on it was always going to be a struggle for the Worcestershire batting. A crowd close on 29,000 watched as they crawled their way to 50 off 22 overs, as even Graeme Hick struggled to find the emptier reaches of the ground. His 27 took 80 balls before Paul Smith nipped one back to trap him LBW and leave Worcester in dire straits at 55-3. Worcester's other big gun Moody hit but two of his team's meagre total of 10 fours before departing for 47. Warwickshire's tempestuous seamer Smith, all permed hair and flapping shirt-tails, provided the aggressive intent that rewarded him with figures of 3-34 in his 11-over spell. The target never really looked in doubt as Ostler and Twose played with panache to record an opening stand of 91 from 24 overs. The massed crowd was awaiting the entrance of the latest wonder-boy, Brian Lara who emerged after tea following Haynes' run-out of Twose. Yet with the stage set and the audience on the edge of their seats, their was a palpable sense of deflation as the Trinidadian chipped Newport into the bucket-like hands of Hick at midwicket. It was left to Smith to tuck in his shirt and stride to the crease to dispel any negative thoughts that may have begun to surface. His unbeaten 42 along with his spell of bowling was enough to earn him the accolade of Man-of-the-Match.

176

NatWest Trophy

(All matches played over 60 overs)

FIRST ROUND *(June 21-22)*

BERKSHIRE V KENT   *Finchampstead*
Kent   384-6 (60 overs)
             (C L Hooper 136*, T R Ward 120, P J Oxley 5-87)
Berkshire   241-5 (60overs)
             (J R Wood 88, D A Shaw 57)
Kent won by 143 runs
Match Award: C L Hooper (136, 10-0-20-0)*
Kent recorded their highest NWT score, whilst Hooper's 136* was his highest score in limited overs cricket for Kent

CAMBRIDGESHIRE V HAMPSHIRE   *March*
Cambs   107 (57.1 overs)
             (C A Connor 4-11)
Hampshire   110-1 (31.1 overs)
             (R A Smith 59*)
Hampshire won by 9 wickets
Match Award: C A Connor (11.1-5-11-4)

CHESHIRE V DURHAM   *Bowden*
Cheshire   107-9 (47 overs)
             (J D Gray 51*, S J E Brown 5-22)
Durham   108-5 (33.1 overs)
Durham won by 5 wickets
Match Award: S J E Brown (10-2-22-5)

CUMBERLAND V LEICESTERSHIRE   *Netherfield*
Cumberl'd   188-7 (60 overs)
Leics   192-3 (50.2 overs)
             (J J Whitaker 73*, B F Smith 63*)
Leicestershire won by 7 wickets
Match Award: B F Smith (63)*

DEVON V YORKSHIRE   *Exmouth*
Devon   242-5 (60 overs)
             (P M Roebuck 83)
Yorkshire   246-6 (59.2 overs)
             (C White 65*)
Yorkshire won by 4 wickets
Match Award: P M Roebuck (83, 12-1-39-1 and captain)

GLAMORGAN V LINCOLNSHIRE   *Swansea*
Glamorgan   344-5 (60 overs)
             (S P James 123, A Dale 110, M P Maynard 75)
Lincs   184-9 (60 overs)
Glamorgan won by 160 runs
Match Award: S P James 123

GLOUCESTERSHIRE V DERBYSHIRE   *Bristol*
Gloucs   228-8 (60 overs)
             (R I Dawson 60)
Derbys   229-7 (59.2 overs)
             (K J Barnett 113*, C J Adams 52)
Derbyshire won by 3 wickets
Match Award: K J Barnett (113, 1 ct and captain)*

LANCASHIRE V SCOTLAND   *Old Trafford*
Scotland   178-9 (60 overs)
             (G N Reifer 72)
Lancs   179-5 (53.3 overs)
             (M A Atherton 50)
Lancashire won by 5 wickets
Match Award: G N Reifer (72, 6.3-3-14-0)

MINOR COUNTIES WALES V MIDDLESEX   *Mold*
Wales   104 (53.3 overs)
             (J E Emburey 2-5)
Middlesex   108-1 (16.2 overs)
             (D L Haynes 64*)
Middlesex won by 9 wickets
Match Award: K R Brown (5 ct, 1 st - equalling NWT record)

NORFOLK V WORCESTERSHIRE   *Lakenham*
Worcs   309-8 (60 overs)
             (G R Haynes 98, T S Curtis 78)
Norfolk   172 (56.4 overs)
             (S G Plumb 57)
Worcestershire won by 137 runs
Match Award: G R Haynes (98, 7-1-9-1)

NORTHAMPTONSHIRE V IRELAND   *Northampton*
Ireland   182-6 (60 overs)
             (S G Smyth 61)
Northants   183-3 (55.1 overs)
             (R J Warren 100*)
Northamptonshire won by 7 wickets
Match Award: R J Warren (100 - on NWT debut)*

NORTHUMBERLAND V NOTTS   *Jesmond*
Notts   344-6 (60 overs)
             (P Johnson 146, C C Lewis 89, R T Robinson 62)
North'd   116 (39 overs)
             (K P Evans 6-10)
Nottinghamshire won by 228 runs
Match Award: P Johnson (146, 1 ct)
Notts recorded their highest NWT score, and Kevin Evans set the best Notts bowling analysis with 7-3-10-6

OXFORDSHIRE V SOMERSET   *Aston Rowant*
Somerset   349-4 (60 overs)
             (M E Trecothick 116, R J Harden 105*, M N Lathwell 64)
Oxon   130 (43 overs)
             (A P van Troost 5-22)
Somerset won by 219 runs
Match Award: M E Trescothick (116, 1 ct - on NWT debut)

SURREY V STAFFORDSHIRE   *Oval*
Staffs   165-8 (60 overs)
             (S D Myles 71)
Surrey   166-1 (38.4 overs)
             (G P Thorpe 84*, D J Bicknell 56*)
Surrey won by 9 wickets
Match Award: J E Benjamin (12-2-26-3)

SUSSEX V ESSEX   *Hove*
Essex   272-5 (60 overs)
             (G A Gooch 86, J P Stephenson 55)
Sussex   256 (59.2 overs)
             (N J Lenham 82*, D M Smith 64, R C Irani 4-59)
Essex won by 16 runs
Match Award: R C Irani (11, 12-2-59-4)

WARWICKS V BEDFORDSHIRE   *Edgbaston*
Warwicks   361-8 (60 overs)
             (R G Twose 110, D P Ostler 81)
Bedford   164 (56.3 overs)
             (J D Robinson 67)
Warwickshire won by 197 runs
Match Award: R G Twose (110, 11-1-30-2)

SECOND ROUND   *July 6-7*

DURHAM V DERBYSHIRE   *Darlington*
Durham   278 (60 overs)
          (P Bainbridge 85, J E Morris 67, D G Cork 5-43)
Derbys   280-6 (58.1 overs)
          (T J G O'Gorman 89, M Azharuddin 74*,
          A C Cummins 4-48)
Derbyshire won by 4 wickets
Match Award: T J G O'Gorman (86)

GLAMORGAN V ESSEX   *Cardiff*
Glamorgan 316-8 (60 overs)
          (M P Maynard 78, P A Cottey 57, R D B Croft
          50, M S Kasprowicz 5-60)
Essex   240-9 (60 overs)
          (N Shaid 85*)
Glamorgan won by 76 runs
Match Award: O D Gibson (44, 9-1-34-3)

HAMPSHIRE V KENT   *Southampton*
Hampshire 187 (59.1 overs)
          (M C J Nicholas 62)
Kent   188-6 (46.5 overs)
Kent won by 4 wickets
Match Award: M C J Nicholas (62 and captain)

LEICESTERSHIRE V WARWICKSHIRE   *Leicester*
Warwicks 296-6 (60 overs)
          (T L Penney 65*, P A Smith 50)
Leicester 168 (47.3 overs)
          (T J Boon 55)
Warwickshire won by 128 runs
Match Award: T L Penney (65, 1 ct)*
Dermot Reeve (34) and T L Penney shared a record NWT sixth wicket partnership of 123

MIDDLESEX V NORTHAMPTONSHIRE   *Uxbridge*
Middlesex 259-6 (60 overs)
          (M A Roseberry 67)
Northants 262-3 (54 overs)
          (A J Lamb 129*, R J Bailey 52)
Northants won by 7 wickets
Match Award: A J Lamb (129, 1 ct and captain)*
Lamb's 129 was the highest of his 4 hundreds in the NWT*

SURREY V LANCASHIRE   *Oval*
Surrey   343-6 (60 overs)
          (G P Thorpe 145*, D M Ward 87)
Lancs   218 (49.3 overs)
          (I D Austin 57, Wasim Akram 50, C E Cuffy
          4-43)
Surrey won by 125 runs
Match Award: G P Thorpe (145, 2 ct)*
Surrey recorded their highest total in limited overs cricket and the fourth highest against a 1st class county in NWT. Thorpe made his highest score in limited overs matches and his first century in NWT.

WORCESTERSHIRE V NOTTS   *Worcester*
Worcs   263-6 (60 overs)
          (G A Hick 97)
Notts   174 (52.4 overs)
Worcestershire won by 89 runs
Match Award: G A Hick 97

YORKSHIRE V SOMERSET   *Headingley*
Yorkshire 215 (59.5 overs)
          (D Byas 71, A N Hayhurst 4-29)
Somerset 216-7 (59.5 overs)
          (R J Harden 64)
Somerset won by 3 wickets
Match Award: A N Hayhurst (24, 6.5-0-29-4, 1 ct and capt.)

QUARTER FINALS   *July 26-27*

DERBYSHIRE V KENT   *Derby*
Derbys   128 (43.5 overs)
          (D G Cork 62, M A Ealham 4-10, A P
          Igglesden 3-37)
Kent   129-5 (47.3 overs)
Kent won by 5 wickets
Match Award: M A Ealham (26, 8.5-2-10-4)*

GLAMORGAN V SURREY   *Swansea*
Glamorgan 161 (55.4 overs)
          (A J Murphy 6-26, C E Cuffy 2-9, A J Stewart
          7 ct)
Surrey   165-5 (48.4 overs)
          (G P Thorpe 56)
Surrey won by 5 wickets
Match Award: A J Murphy (12-3-26-6)

SOMERSET V WARWICKSHIRE   *Taunton*
Somerset 124 (50.2 overs)
          (N M K Smith 4-26)
Warwicks 125-2 (24.1 overs)
          (D P Ostler 47, A J Moles 41*)
Warwickshire won by 8 wickets
Match Award: N M K Smith (8.2-1-26-4)

WORCESTERSHIRE V NORTHANTS   *Worcester*
Northants 128 (46.1 overs)
          (P J Newport 4-30, S J Rhodes 4 ct, 1 st)
Worcs   129-8 (45.1 overs)
          (T M Moody 40, C E L Ambrose 3-16)
Worcestershire won by 2 wickets
Match Award: S J Rhodes (24, 4 ct, 1 st)*

SEMI FINALS   *Aug 9*

WARWICKSHIRE V KENT   *Edgbaston*
Warwicks 265-8 (60 overs)
          (A J Moles 105*, R G Twose 49, M V Fleming
          3-28)
Kent   257 (59.5 overs)
          (T R Ward 80, N R Taylor 64, C L Hooper 44,
          D A Reeve 3-44)
Warwickshire won by 8 runs
Match Award: A J Moles (105)*

SURREY V WORCESTERSHIRE   *Oval*
Worcs   357-2 (60 overs)
          (T M Moody 180*, T S Curtis 136*)
Surrey   350 (59.5 overs)
          (D J Bicknell 89, A J Hollioake 60, A D Brown
          52, G P Thorpe 49, G A Hick 4-54)
Worcestershire won by 7 runs
Match Award: T M Moody (180, 8-0-43-2, 1 ct)*
Tom Moody registered the second highest score in NWT, as well as being the highest innings for Worcester in limited overs matches. He faced 160 balls hitting 3 sixes and 25 fours. His unbroken 3rd wicket partnership of 309 with Tim Curtis (136 off 180 balls) set a world record for all limited over matches. It*

surpassed the previous best of 303 by Alan Barrow (202*) and Henry Fotheringham (128*) for Natal's third wicket against an African XI at Durban in October 1975. Surrey's total of 350 was their highest in limited over matches and established a

world record for the highest second innings total in limited over cricket. The match aggregate of 707 beat the previous highest of 697 by Eastern Province and Western Province in 1969-70.

THE FINAL
WARWICKSHIRE V WORCESTERSHIRE
Lord's   Sept 3-4

WARWICKSHIRE

A J Moles	c Rhodes	b Newport	8
D P Ostler	c Lampitt	b Newport	4
B C Lara	c Hick	b Haynes	81
P A Smith	c Haynes	b Moody	13
R G Twose	c L'dale	b Newport	22
T L Penney	lbw	b Radford	18
D A Reeve*	c Rhodes	b Newport	13
N M K Smith	c Ill'worth	b Lampitt	20
K J Pipert	not out		16
G C Small	run out		5
T M Munton	not out		0
Extras (B1, LB8, W10, NB4)			23
Total (9 wickets, 60 overs)			223

Fall of wickets:1-8(Ostler), 2-17(Moles), 3-50(P Smith), 4-90(Twose), 5-150(Penney), 6-171(Lara), 7-188(Reeve), 8-215(N Smith), 9-222(Small)

Bowling: **Moody** 12-4-17-1, **Newport** 12-2-38-4, **Radford** 12-1-45-1, **Lampitt** 11-1-45-1, **Illingworth** 6-0-35-0, **Haynes** 7-0-34-1

WORCESTERSHIRE

T S Curtis*		b Reeve	11
D B D'Oliveira	c Lara	b Munton	12
G A Hick	not out		93
T M Moody	not out		88
Extras (LB6, W11, NB6)			23
Total (2 wickets, 49.1 overs)			223

Did not bat: G R Haynes, D A Leatherdale, S J Rhodest, S R Lampitt, P J Newport, R K Illingworth, N V Radford
Fall of wickets: 1-29(D'Oliveira), 2-29(Curtis)
Bowling: **Small** 12-0-40-0, **Munton** 12-3-23-1, **Reeve** 6-1-30-1, **P Smith** 7-1-54-0, **Twose** 5-0-36-0, **N Smith** 7-0-34-0, **Penney** 0.1-0-4-0

Toss: Worcestershire
Umpires: D R Shepherd & N T Plews
Match Award: T M Moody

Worcestershire turned the tables on their traditional rivals and cruised to victory on the second day of a rain affected final. The Warwickshire dream of a grand slam probably faltered on the loss of the toss and on the the ability of Worcester's middle order to dominate one of the best seam attacks in the country. With both Hick and Moody in full flow the target of 223 always looked a modest one, as it proved when Warwickshire were overhauled with 10 overs and five balls to spare. Hick hit 12 fours and a six, whilst Moody clubbed 10 fours and two sixes in an unbeaten 198-run partnership which is the second highest stand in a NatWest final. The ending was played out in front of only 10,000 due to the interference of rain which halted Warwickshire at 88-3 on Saturday afternoon. Newport and Moody used the conditions to maximum effect before the entrance of the feted Brian Lara. He quickly showed his gift of timing, pulling and square driving with effortless ease. Richard Illingworth was singled out for particular attention, but as Lara flowed past his 50 Gavin Haynes was brought in as a makeshift sixth bowler. Having hit seven fours and a six, Lara clipped Haynes sweetly off his legs only to see Hick emerge from the shadow of the grandstand to claim the vital catch. Flu victim Reeve and Neil Smith could not find the necessary acceleration and Warwickshire finished their stint a good 30 runs short. However, with Hick and Moody on song any total was going to be within range.

NATWEST RECORDS
Batting

206	A I Kallicharran	Warwicks v Oxfordshire	Birmingham	1984
180 *	T M Moody	Worcestershire v Surrey	The Oval	1994
177	C G Greenidge	Hampshire v Glamorgan	Southampton	1975
172 *	G A Hick	Worcestershire v Devon	Worcester	1987
165 *	V P Terry	Hampshire v Berkshire	Southampton	1985

Partnerships

1st	248	D M Smith/C W J Athey	Sussex v Hampshire	Hove	1993
2nd	286	I S Anderson/A Hill	Derbyshire v Cornwall	Derby	1986
3rd	309 *	T S Curtis/T M Moody	Worcester v Surrey	The Oval	1994
4th	234 *	D Lloyd/C H Lloyd	Lancs v Glamorgan	Manchester	1978
5th	166	M A Lynch/G J R Roope	Surrey v Durham	The Oval	1982

Bowling

8-21	M A Holding	Derbyshire v Sussex	Hove	1988
8-31	D L Underwood	Keny v Scotland	Edinburgh	1987
7-15	A L Dixon	Kent v Surrey	The Oval	1967
7-15	R P Lefebvre	Somerset v Devon	Torquay	1990
7-19	N V Radford	Worcester v Bedfordshire	Bedford	1991

AXA Equity & Law League
Played on Sundays over 40 overs

FINAL TABLE
Last year's position in brackets

		P	W	L	T	NR	Pts
1	Warwickshire (10)	17	13	3	5	1	54
2	Worcestershire (16)	17	12	4	0	1	50
3	Kent (2)	17	12	5	0	0	48
4	Lancashire (6)	17	11	5	0	1	46
5	Yorkshire (9)	17	10	6	0	1	42
6	Surrey (3)	17	9	5	0	3	42
7	Glamorgan (1)	17	9	6	1	1	40
8	Derbyshire (11)	17	8	7	0	2	36
9	Durham (7)	17	6	7	1	3	32
10	Leicestershire (14)	17	7	9	0	1	30
11	Nottinghamshire (17)	17	6	8	0	3	30
12	Hampshire (15)	17	7	10	0	0	28
13	Northants (5)	17	6	9	1	1	28
14	Middlesex (8)	17	6	10	0	1	26
15	Sussex (4)	17	5	11	0	1	22
16	Somerset (18)	17	5	12	0	0	20
17	Essex (12)	17	4	11	1	1	20
18	Gloucestershire (13)	17	4	12	0	1	18

SEASON'S STATISTICS

Top Batsmen

1	C L Hooper (Kent)	773 runs	£3,000
2	D Byas (Yorkshire)	702	£1,500
3	A D Brown (Surrey)	688	
4	R A Smith (Hants)	676	
5	J C Adams (Notts)	674	
6	P V Simmons (Leics)	660	
7	A P Wells (Sussex)	618	
8	M W Alleyne (Gloucs)	588	
9	D M Ward (Surrey)	578	
10	M R Ramprakash (Mx)	561	

Top Bowlers

1	C A Connor (Hants)	26 wkts	£2,250
2	N M K Smith (Warks)	26	£2,250
3	P J Martin (Lancs)	25	
3	P J Newport (Worcs)	25	
3	A Walker (Durham)	25	
3	V J Wells (Leics)	25	
7	R P Lefebvre (Glam)	24	
7	N V Radford (Worcs)	24	
9	S R Lampitt (Worcs)	23	
10	S R Barwick (Glam)	21	
10	R D B Croft (Glam)	21	
10	M V Fleming (Kent)	21	
10	K D James (Hants)	21	

Top Wicketkeepers

1	A N Aymes (Hants)	26 dis.	£1,500
2	C P Metson (Glam)	24	
3	K M Krikken (Derbys)	22	
4	S J Rhodes (Worcs)	21	
5	C W Scott (Durham)	20	
6	S A Marsh (Kent)	19	
7	R J Blakey (Yorks)	17	
7	P A Nixon (Leics)	17	

There are 16 counties that will not want to look back on 1994 with any sense of fondness. But the traditional rivals from the West Midlands will be rubbing their hands with glee at all the lovely bonus money flowing into their coffers. Warwickshire usurped their Worcester neighbours in the one-day competitions, leaving Bob Woolmer to reflect (with the help of Meatloaf) "two out of three ain't bad". With the championship already in the bag, the 'Bears' had to win their last AXA match at Bristol to lift an historic treble. With Lara arriving in his black BMW for his final appearance the scene was set for for the final champagne spray of a magical season. However their were a few red faces around as the Warwickshire boys lost three wickets without a run on the board. Lara swished to 38 and Reeve swept to 50 to give some respectability.

Needing 184 to win, you should never underestimate the ability of Gloucestershire to conjure up appalling displays just when the eyes of the country are upon them. Only three players reached double figures (young lads who obviously don't know better) before collapsing in a disorganised mess 46 runs short. Looking like a seventies dance troupe in their gaudy polyester yellow suits, Dermot Reeve's men duly received their cheque for £31,000 and partied their way into the record books.

Whilst the Warwickshire committee were celebrating their £230,000 'Yankee' (controversially limited to £100,000 by their bookmakers), Worcestershire duly jumped ahead of Kent in the battle for second place with their victory over Durham. For most of the season they have ridden in the wake of the Brummie showboat, although it was the emphatic NatWest victory that prevented the grand slam (and the ruination of a bookmaker or two).

Next season sees the reintroduction of zonal games into the Benson and Hedges competition, whilst the NatWest competition will see Holland compete in place of one of the minor counties. On the 50th anniversary of Arnhem, the TCCB's Tim Lamb described the move as "part of a deliberate policy to build a bridgehead into Europe". With Holland beating representative XI's from England, and more recently, South Africa, let's hope that it is not a bridge too far for county cricket.

Australia 1993-94
Sheffield Shield

QUEENSLAND V SOUTH AUSTRALIA
Brisbane   *Oct 21-24*
S Australia 522 (D S Webber 176, D S Lehmann 128,
             P W Jackson 4-90, C J McDermott 4-111)
Queensland 352 (M L Hayden 125, T B A May 4-112, B N
             Wigney 3-95)
             416-4 (A R Border 125*, T J Barsby 116, S G
             Law 100)
Match Drawn
Points: Q'd 0, SA 2

SOUTH AUSTRALIA V VICTORIA
Adelaide   *Oct 27-30*
Victoria   357-9 dec (W N Phillips 60, D J Ramshaw 58,
            P E McIntyre 4-101, S P George 3-73)
            198 (M T G Elliott 99, P E McIntyre 5-61, T B
            A May 5-80)
S Australia 430 (P C Nobes 141, J A Brayshaw 134,
            S H Cook 5-114, S K Warne 4-119)
            127 (P C Nobes 63*, J A Brayshaw54*)
South Australia won by 9 wickets
Points: SA 6 Vic 0

WESTERN AUSTRALIA V QUEENSLAND
Perth   *Oct 29-Nov 1*
W Australia 211 (J L Langer 65, D R Martyn 59,
            C J McDermott 5-62, C G Rackemann 3-57)
            373 (J L Langer 96, D R Martyn 56,
            C G Rackemann 6-93)
Queensland 430 (T J Barsby 82, I A Healy 79)
            158-1 (M L Hayden 96*)
Queensland won by 9 wickets
Points: WA0 Q'd 6

QUEENSLAND V NEW SOUTH WALES
Brisbane   *Nov 4-7*
Queensland 257 (A R Border 85, P J S Alley 4-45)
           281 (M L Hayden 173*)
NSW   382 (G R Robertson 85, M E Waugh 61, P W
           Jackson 4-86)
           157-2 (M E Waugh 85)
New South Wales won by 8 wickets
Points Q'd 0, NSW 6

VICTORIA V WESTERN AUSTRALIA
Melbourne   *Nov 4-7*
W Australia 322 (J L Langer 144, A I C Dodemaide 5-85)
            185 (D R Martyn 89*, S K Warne 6-42,
            S H Cook 3-38)
Victoria   230 (B J Hodge 95, J Angel 3-38, D J Spencer
            3-66)
            278-4 (M T G Elliott 175*)
Victoria won by 6 wickets
Points: WA 2 Vic 6

TASMANIA V WESTERN AUSTRALIA
Hobart   *Nov 11-14*
W Australia 473-5 dec (J L Langer 135, D R Martyn 100,
            T M Moody 65, M R J Veletta 65*)
Tasmania   514 (M J DiVenuto 125, R T Ponting 105,
            S Young 63, J Angel 3-188)
Match Drawn
Points: Tas 2, WA0

VICTORIA V NEW SOUTH WALES
Melbourne   *Nov 19-22*
NSW   227 (M J Slater 77, M E Waugh 58,
            S K Warne 4-72)
            268-7 dec (S R Waugh 122, M A Taylor 50, P
R   Reiffel 5-73)
Victoria   233 (D J Ramshaw 85, B J Hodge 54, B E
            McNamara 6-43)
            263-9 (B J Hodge 92, D M Jones 72)
Victoria won by 1 wicket
Points: Vic 6, NSW 0

NEW SOUTH WALES V TASMANIA
Sydney   *Nov 25-28*
NSW   353-5 dec (M G Bevan 141, R Chee Quee 69,
            G R J Matthews 55*)
            274-9 dec (R Chee Quee 133*, S Herzberg
            4-82, S Young 3-68)
Tasmania   343 (D F Hills 88, N C P Courtney 55,
            M J Di Venuto 53, C D Matthews 7-99)
            215 (R J Tucker 4-64, C D Matthews 4-82)
NSW won by 69 runs
Points: NSW 6, Tas 0

SOUTH AUSTRALIA V QUEENSLAND
Adelaide   *Nov 25-28*
Queensland 330 (M L Hayden 165, D A Reeves 3-52,
           B N Wigney 3-78)
           351-4 dec (T J Barsby 129, M L Hayden 116)
S Australia 420 (P C Nobes 140, D S Webber 100)
           262-5 (P C Nobes 106, D S Lehmann 50, S G
           Law 3-42)
South Australia won by 5 wickets
Points: SA 6, Q'd 0

TASMANIA V VICTORIA
Hobart   *Dec 10-13*
Tasmania   328 (R J Tucker 107, D F Hills 71, S H Cook
            4-84, D W Fleming 3-77)
            308-6 dec (R T Ponting 66, D F Hills 59,
            C Howard 5-112)
Victoria   329-3 dec (D M Jones 158, B J Hodge 106)
            267-8 (D M Jones 60, D J Ramshaw 53)
Match Drawn
Points: Tas 0 Vic 2

WESTERN AUSTRALIA V NEW SOUTH WALES
Perth   *Dec 10-11*
W Australia 503-8 dec (D R Martyn 197, G R Marsh 128,
            T M Moody 68, P J S Alley 5-101)
NSW   73 (B P Julian 5-34, J Angel 3-25)
            177 (M G Bevan 50, J Angel 5-57, B P
Julian 3-45)
Western Australia won by an innings and 253 runs
Points: WA 6, NSW 0

NEW SOUTH WALES V VICTORIA
Sydney   *Dec 18-21*
Victoria   264 (W N Phillips 57, B J Hodge 57,
    G D McGrath 4-60,W J Holdsworth 3-73)
    324-6 dec (D M Jones 155, D J Ramshaw 80)
NSW   283 (M E Waugh 119, S K Warne 5-77,
    D W Fleming 3-63)
    275-9 (M G Bevan 81, R Chee Quee 76P R R
    Reiffel 4-68, S K Warne 3-90)
Match Drawn
Points: NSW 2, Vic 0

WESTERN AUSTRALIA V SOUTH AUSTRALIA
Perth   *Dec 18-20*
S Australia   179 (D S Webber 58, T M Moody 4-43,
    J Angel 3-30)
    283 (J D Siddons 129, J Angel 5-59,
    D R Martyn 3-29)
W Australia 304 (T M Moody 65, S P George 3-54, T B A
    May 3-96)
    160-1 (J L Langer 90*, M R J Veletta 62*)
Western Australia won by 9 wickets
Points: WA 6, SA 0

QUEENSLAND V TASMANIA
Brisbane   *Dec 31-Jan 3*
Queensland 245 (S Young 3-38, C R Miller 3-41)
    339-6 dec (M L Love 138, M L Hayden 121)
Tasmania   190 (S Young 55, M S Kasprowicz 4-56)
    329-7 (D J Buckingham 77, R T Ponting 64)
Match Drawn
Points: Q'd 2, Tas 0

SOUTH AUSTRALIA V NEW SOUTH WALES
Adelaide   *Dec 31-Jan 3*
NSW   395-9 dec (M G Bevan 103, S R Waugh 73,
    N D Maxwell 61, S P George 5-102)
    337 (M G Bevan 89, S P Goerge 3-31,
    P E McIntyre 3-128)
S Australia 465-8 dec (G S Blewett 93, D S Lehmann 85,
    P C Nobes 78, G R Robertson 3-83)
    158 (G R Robertson 5-43, N D Maxwell 3-27)
New South Wales won by 109 runs
Points: SA 2, NSW 6

SOUTH AUSTRALIA V WESTERN AUSTRALIA
Adelaide   *Jan 7-10*
W Australia 446-7 dec (G R Marsh 98, J L Langer 96,
    D J Marsh 3-65, S P George 3-120)
    174-3 (J L Langer 56*)
S Australia   437 (D S Lehmann 200, J A Brayshaw 146
    D J Spencer 4-85, B P Julian 4-108)
Match Drawn
Points: SA 0, WA 1.8

TASMANIA V NEW SOUTH WALES
Hobart   *Jan 7-10*
NSW   398 (S R Waugh 190*, M G Bevan 71,
    C R Miller 7-83)
    296-4 dec (M G Bevan 117*, M J Slater
    107)
Tasmania   401-6 dec (D F Hills 158*, D J Buckingham
    52, P J S Alley 3-84)
    294-6 (D J Buckingham 88*, D F Hills 68)
Tasmania won by 4 wickets
Points: Tas 6, NSW 0

QUEENSLAND V VICTORIA
Brisbane   *Jan 13-16*
Queensland 247 (M L Hayden 126, J P Maher 70,
    M G Hughes 5-70, A I C Dodemaine 3-74)
    331-6 dec (M L Hayden 155, S G Law 76)
Victoria   272 (G J Allardice 86, A J Bichel 4-69, M S
    Kasprowicz 4-76)
    212 (B J Hodge 64, C G Rackemann 5-32)
Queensland won by 194 runs
Points: Q'd 6, Vic 0

QUEENSLAND V WESTERN AUSTRALIA
Brisbane   *Jan 19-22*
Queensland 244 (S G Law 118, J Angel 4-64)
    375-8 (J P Maher 122, M L Love 119)
W Australia 413 (J L Langer 89, M J R Veletta 80*, T J
    Zoehrer 69)
Match Drawn
Points: Q'd 0, WA 2

TASMANIA V SOUTH AUSTRALIA
Hobart   *Jan 18-21*
S Australia 519 (J D Siddons 161, D S Lehmann 137, G S
    Blewett 51, C R Miller 4-108)
    209-3 dec (J D Siddons 89*)
Tasmania   401-8 dec (S Young 124*, D F Hills 63, D J
    Buckingham 57)
    329-6 (M J Di Venuto 112)
Tasmania won by 4 wickets
Points: Tas 6, SA 2

VICTORIA V SOUTH AUSTRALIA
Melbourne   *Jan 28-31*
Victoria   377-9 dec (D M Jones 145, M T G Elliott 72)
    337-1 dec (W N Phillips 156*, D M Jones
    152*)
S Australia 499 (G S Blewett 268, D S Lehmann 86,
    D W Fleming 4-130, C Howard 4-144)
    177-8 (D S Lehmann 67, D W Fleming 4-65)
Match Drawn
Points: Vic 0, SA 2

NEW SOUTH WALES V WESTERN AUSTRALIA
Sydney   *Feb 2-5*
W Australia 379 (T M Moody 115, J Angel 84*, M J R
    Veletta 71)
    135 (G R Robertson 5-71)
NSW   409 (M G Bevan 203*, R J Davison 56, P A
    Emery 50, W K Wishart 4-90)
    106-1 (R Chee Quee 50)
NSW won by 9 wickets
Points: NSW 6, WA 0

TASMANIA V QUEENSLAND
Hobart   *Feb 10-13*
Queensland 339 (A J Bichel 61*, G I Foley 52)
    208-9 dec (J P Maher 89, C R Miller 4-56)
Tasmania   248 (S Young 68, D Tazelaar 5-49)
    293-6 (D F Hills 91, J Cox 81, C G Rackemann
    4-72)
Match Drawn
Points: Tas 0, Q'd 2

NEW SOUTH WALES V SOUTH AUSTRALIA
Sydney *Feb 16-18*
NSW 391 (N D Maxwell 75, M G Bevan 67, B E
McNamara 59, R Chee Quee 58)
S Australia 123 (N D Maxwell 4-31)
198 (G S Blewett 90, G R Robertson 6-54)
NSW won by an innings and 70 runs
Points: NSW 6, SA 0

VICTORIA V TASMANIA
Melbourne *Feb 17-20*
Tasmania 444-9 dec (M J Di Venuto 89, C D
Matthews 75,
D J Buckingham 71, S H Cook 4-114)
213-2 dec (J Cox 103*, D F Hills 52)
Victoria 331 (W N Phillips 130, B J Hodge 62, R J
Tucker 4-56, S Young 4-85)
236-9 (B J Hodge 72, G J Allardice 65, S
Herzberg 4-66)
Match drawn
Points: Vic 0, Tas 2

WESTERN AUSTRALIA V TASMANIA
Perth *Feb 24-27*
W Australia 454 (J L Langer 233, M R J Veletta 66, M
W Ridgway 4-127)
286-6 dec (G R Marsh 81, D R Martyn 58)
Tasmania 487-4 dec (J Cox 129, R T Ponting 101, D
J Buckingham 100*)
53-1
Match drawn
Points: WA 0, Tas 2

VICTORIA V QUEENSLAND
Melbourne *Feb 24-27*
Victoria 242 (I A Wrigglesworth 58)
250 (M T G Elliott 113, C G Rackemann
4-38)
Queensland 275 (W A Seccombe 95, G I Foley 89, D
W Fleming 5-61)
214 (J P Maher 90, S G Law 58, S M
McCooke 6-35)
Victoria won by 3 runs
Points: Vic 5.6, Q'd 2

NEW SOUTH WALES V QUEENSLAND
Sydney *Mar 17-20*
NSW 412-6 dec (S Lee 104*, R J Davison 81)
207-4 dec (M G Bevan 69*)
Queensland 200 (M D Maxwell 4-45)
368 (S G Law 108, G I Foley 68)
New South Wales won by 51 runs
Points: NSW 6, Q'd 0

SOUTH AUSTRALIA V TASMANIA
Adelaide *Mar 17-20*
S Australia 489 (G S Blewett 214, D S Lehmann 157,
C R Miller 5-82)
246-6 dec (G S Blewett 80, M P Faull 66)
Tasmania 370-5 dec (D F Hills 114, J Cox 98, R T
Ponting 84*)
366-6 (R T Ponting 161, D F Hills 126, P
E McIntyre 4-97)
Tasmania won by 4 wickets
Points: SA 2, Tas 6

WESTERN AUSTRALIA V VICTORIA
Perth *Mar 17-19*
Victoria 118
155 (G J Allardice 53, B A Reid 5-34)
W Australia 112 (D W Fleming 5-34, S H Cook 4-41)
162-7 (S H Cook 4-43)
Western Australia won by 3 wickets
Points: WA 6, Vic 1.4

SHEFFIELD SHIELD - FINAL TABLE

	P	W	D	L	Pts
1 New South Wales	10	6	1	3	38
2 Tasmania	10	3	6	1	24
3 Western Australia	10	3	4	3	23.8
4 South Australia	10	2	3	5	22
5 Victoria	10	3	4	3	21
6 Queensland	10	2	4	4	20

SHEFFIELD SHIELD FINAL
NEW SOUTH WALES V TASMANIA
Sydney *Mar 25-29*
Tasmania 255 (S Young 62, B E McNamara 4-24)
126 (P J S Alley 5-24, N D Maxwell 4-50)
NSW 442 (B E McNamara 128, M G Bevan 113,
M T Haywood 73)
New South Wales won by an innings and 61 runs

AUSTRALIAN FIRST CLASS AVERAGES 1993-4
Batting *(Excluding visiting players)*

	M	In	NO	Rns	HS	Ave
M L Hayden (Q'd)	6	12	3	1136	173*	126.22
S R Waugh (NSW/A)	9	15	4	976	190*	88.72
M G Bevan (NSW)	12	22	5	1312	203*	77.17
D M Jones (Vic)	7	14	2	918	158*	76.50
J L Langer (WA)	11	19	2	1198	233	70.47

Bowling *(Excluding visiting players)*

	O	M	Rns	W	Ave	Best
S K Warne (Vic/A)	574.2	176	1255	63	19.92	7-56
B E McNamara (NSW)	165.3	57	363	18	20.16	6-43
S M McCooke (Vic)	88.4	25	223	11	20.27	6-35
N D Maxwell (NSW)	221.2	52	641	31	20.67	4-31
G R Matthews (NSW)	160.2	40	412	19	21.68	7-99

Minimum 10 wickets to qualify

New Zealand 1993-94
Shell Trophy

CENTRAL DISTRICTS V WELLINGTON
Wanganui   Dec 11-14
C Districts 308 (S W J Wilson 105, C D Ingham 72, H T
             Davis 4-61)
             186 (R G Twose 81, M C Goodson 6-48)
Wellington   506-4 dec (M H Austen 202, R T Hart 120, M
             W Douglas 95)
Wellington won by an innings and 12 runs

CANTERBURY V AUCKLAND
Rangiora   Dec 11-13
Canterbury   128 (C M Brown 6-50, J T C Vaughan 4-27)
             146 (S P Fleming 57, C M Brown 4-40)
Auckland   121 (C W Flanaghan 6-30)
             105 (C W Flanaghan 5-37)
Canterbury won by 48 runs

OTAGO V NORTHERN DISTRICTS
Hamilton   Dec 11-13
N Districts 82 (D J Nash 5-18)
             254 (G E Bradburn 61, A J Gale 5-72)
Otago   233 (J M Allan 56)
             104-3 (R A Lawson 54*)
Otago won by 7 wickets

CENTRAL DISTRICTS V OTAGO
Dunedin   Dec 16-19
C Districts 95-1 dec
             116-3 dec (C D Ingham 54)
Otago   First innings forfeited
             182-7 (P W Dobbs 82, D J Nash 51)
Match drawn

AUCKLAND V NORTHERN DISTRICTS
Auckland   Dec 16-19
Auckland   291 (A C Parore 87*, A T Reinholds 71, J T C
             Vaughan 69)
             215-9 dec (J T C Vaughan 79*,M N Hart 5-66)
N Districts 221 (G P Burnett 71)
             244 (B G Cooper 87, M D Bailey 57, S W
             Brown 5-56)
Auckland won by 41 runs

WELLINGTON V CANTERBURY
Wellington Dec 16-19
Wellington   287 (E B McSweeney 111, D S McHardy 60)
             281-7 (E B McSweeney 99, M W Douglas 57,
             C W Flanaghan 4-50)
Canterbury   257 (B R Hartland 65, L G Howell 60, J D
             Wells 6-59)
Match drawn

NORTHERN DISTRICTS V CANTERBURY
Hamilton   Jan 18-21
Canterbury   407 (S P Fleming 105, D J Murray 95, L K
             Germon 89, M J Stephens 5-101)
N Districts 138 (M W Priest 4-32)
             254 (G E Bradburn 63, M W Priest 4-54)
Canterbury won by an innings and 15 runs

CENTRAL DISTRICTS V AUCKLAND
Palmerston North   Jan 18-21
C Districts 449 (R G Twose 99, R K Brown 90, M E L
             Lane 84, C D Ingham 73)
             33-0
Auckland   151
             330 (J I Pamment 98, D N Patel 59, S W Duff
             4-111)
Central Districts won by 10 wickets

WELLINGTON V OTAGO
Wellington Jan 18-21
Wellington   330 (M H Austen 89, L J Doull 79, R P Wixon
             5-95)
             165 (E J Marshall 5-95)
Otago   272 (L C Breen 73, M C Goodson 4-65)
             124 (M C Goodson 5-40)
Wellington won by 99 runs

NORTHERN DISTRICTS V CENTRAL DISTRICTS
Nelson   Feb 3-6
C Districts 272 (G P McRae 62, S W Duff 59, J B M
             Furlong 51*, R P de Groen 5-89)
             247-6 dec (T E Blain 50)
N Districts 217 (M D Bailey 84, M E Parlane 75)
             300-9 (M E Parlane 89, G E Bradburn 73*,
             K A Wealleans 51, D J Hartshorn 4-124)
Match drawn

AUCKLAND V WELLINGTON
Auckland   Feb 3-5
Wellington   116 (M L Su'a 6-56)
             152 (M H Austen 58, D N Patel 6-43)
Auckland   266 (G R Jonas 4-85)
             3-0
Auckland won by 10 wickets

OTAGO V CANTERBURY
Rangiora   Feb 3-5
Otago   179 (P W Dobbs 63, G R Baker 53)
             145 (M W Priest 6-72)
Canterbury   303 (D J Boyle 117, N J Astle 69, A J Gale
             6-75)
             22-1
Canterbury won by 9 wickets

CANTERBURY V CENTRAL DISTRICTS
Christchurch   Feb 10-13
Canterbury   341 (M W Priest 73*, D J Murray 70)
             400-4 (C Z Harris 140*, D J Murray 85, B R
             Hartland 55, N J Astle 52*)
C Districts 261 (S J Roberts 5-70)
Match drawn

OTAGO V AUCKLAND
Dunedin   Feb 10-13
Auckland   141 (J W Wilson 4-29)
             269 (A C Parore 133, A T Reinholds 61, R P
             Wixon 5-83)
Otago   163 (C Pringle 7-63)
             173 (C Pringle 7-56)
Auckland won by 74 runs

NORTHERN DISTRICTS V WELLINGTON
Hamilton   Feb 10-13
Wellington 218 (M W Douglas 66, R L Hayes 4-41)
            255 (M W Douglas 106)

N Districts 312 (G P Burnett 131, H T Davis 4-95)
             164-4
Wellington won by 6 wickets

SEMI FINALS
CANTERBURY V CENTRAL DISTRICTS
Christchurch   Feb 17-20
C Districts 195 (S W Duff 85)
             241 (R G Twose 70, M W Priest 4-76)
Canterbury 559 (L K Germon 114, G R Stead 113*, M W
            Priest 102, C Z Harris 70, W Wisneski 5-115)
Canterbury won by an innings and 123 runs

AUCKLAND V WELLINGTON
Auckland   Feb 17-20
Auckland   170 (A T Reinholds 52, H T Davis 4-48, G R
            Jonas 4-48)
            322-4 dec (A C Parore 84, D N Patel 84)
Wellington 108 (M L Su'a 5-44, W Watson 4-30)
Match Drawn

Shell Trophy Final
Rangiora   Feb 25-28
Auckland   179
            204 (A C Parore 91, M F Sharpe 4-59)
Canterbury 94 (W Watson 4-31)
            290-7 (D J Boyle 92*, M W Priest 88)
Canterbury won by 3 wickets

NEW ZEALAND FIRST CLASS AVERAGES 1993-4
Batting

	M	In	NO	Rns	HS	Ave
C Z Harris (Cant)	4	6	1	301	140*	60.20
R G Twose (C Dist)	6	9	2	395	99	56.42
M W Priest (Cant)	5	6	1	279	102	55.80
M H Austen (Well)	6	10	0	484	202	48.40
G E Bradburn (N Dist)	6	11	3	362	73*	45.25

Bowling

	O	M	Rns	W	Ave	Best
J T C Vaughan (Auck)	68.2	26	117	10	11.70	4-27
C W Flanaghan (Cant)	162.3	63	335	23	14.56	6-30
M F Sharpe (Cant)	122	31	299	19	15.73	4-59
M W Priest (Cant)	261.2	102	458	28	16.35	6-72
C M Brown (Auck)	145.1	51	330	20	16.50	6-50

India 1993-94 Duleep Trophy
WEST ZONE V SOUTH ZONE
Municipal Corporation Stadium, Rajkot   Oct 10-13, 1993
West Zone 551-8 dec (V G Kambli 151, S V Manjrekar
           144, R J Shastri 77, K S More 58)
South Zone 289 (A Viadya 55, A Kuruvilla 4-85)
           207 (R J Shastri 5-55)
West Zone won by an innings and 86 runs
Points: WZ 6, SZ 0

NORTH ZONE V CENTRAL ZONE
Motibaug Palace Grounds, Baroda   Oct 10-13
Cent. Zone 250 (P K Amre 71, A R Kapoor 4-60)
            361 (P K Amre 114*, A R Khurasiya 103,
            Yusuf Ali Khan 62, Maninder Singh 4-70)
North Zone 708 (A D Jadeja 264, Ajay Sharma 151, A R
            Kapoor 103*, R K Chauhan 5-195)
North Zone won by an innings and 97 runs
Points: CZ 0, NZ 6

SOUTH ZONE V EAST ZONE
Municipal Corporation Ground, Rajkot   Oct 19-22
East Zone 206 (C S Pandit 67, S C Ganguly 51, J Srinath
           4-41)
           80 (A R Kumble 3-7)
South Zone 333 (Robin Singh 109, V B Chandrasekhar 67,
           J Srinath 55, U Chatterjee 4-57)
South Zone won by an innings and 47 runs
Points: EZ 0, SZ 6

NORTH ZONE V WEST ZONE
Motibaug Palace Grounds, Baroda   Oct 19-22
West Zone 187 (S V Manjrekar 63, S S Bhave 55)
           169 (S V Jedhe 51)
North Zone 403 (Ajay Sharma 110, Bhupinder Sni 50)
North Zone won by an innings and 47 runs
Points: WZ 0, NZ 6

SOUTH ZONE V NORTH ZONE
Sarder Patel Stadium, Bulsar   Oct 28-30
North Zone 170 (V Prasad 7-38)
           99 (Subramaniam 5-14, Robin Singh 4-30)
South Zone 200 (S Sharath 61, Robin Singh 60, Obaid
           Kamal 4-25)
           73-3
South Zone won by 7 wickets
Points: NZ 0, SZ 6

EAST ZONE V CENTRAL ZONE
Wankhede Stadium, Bombay   Oct 28-31
East Zone 462 (C S Pandit 125, S J Kalyani 114, S T
           Banerjee 81, S Saba Karim 60, N D Hirwani
           4-133)
Cent. Zone 197 (P K Dwvedi 50, P S Vaidya 4-41)
           242 (G K Pandey 106*, U Chatterjee 4-80)
East Zone won by an innings and 23 runs
Points: EZ 6, CZ 0

WEST ZONE V EAST ZONE
Lalbhai Contractor Stadium, Vesu, Surat   Nov 6-8
West Zone 235 (S V Manjrekar 113)
           103 (Banerjee 6-48)
East Zone 439 (S Saba Karim 79, L S Rajput 73, Iqbal
           Siddiqui 4-97)
East Zone won by an innings and 101 runs
points: WZ 0, EZ 6

CENTRAL ZONE V SOUTH ZONE
Poona Club Ground, Pune   Nov 6-10

Cent. Zone 252 (M S Mudgal 65, G K Pandey 64, Robin
                Singh 4-50)
            387 (Rizwan Shamshad 141, P V Gandhe 80,
                M Venkataramana 4-77)
South Zone 200 (D Vasu 77, N D Hirwani 4-72)
            154 (N D Hirwani 5-48)

Central Zone won by 285 runs
Points: CZ 6, SZ 0

WEST ZONE V CENTRAL ZONE
Wankhede Stadium, Bombay   Nov 15-19

West Zone   407 (R J Shastri 87, N R Mongia 81, T B
                Arothe 63)
            328-6 dec (R J Shastri 126, S V Manjrekar 116,
                N D Hirwani 4-109)
Cent. Zone 424 (Rizwan Shamshad 133, G K Pandey 104)
            232 (G K Pandey 72, Iqbal Siddiqui 5-55)

West Zone won by 79 runs
Points: WZ 6, CZ 2

NORTH ZONE V EAST ZONE
Poona Club Ground, Pune   Nov 15-19

North Zone 415 (Rajesh Puri 151, Bhupinder Snr 73)
            274-8 dec (Bantoo Singh 63, A D Jadeja 62)
East Zone   329 (S Saba Karim 78, L S Rajput 64, C S
                Pandit 60)
            208-6 (Chetan Sharma 60, S Saba Karim 52*,
                A D Jadeja 4-99)

Match drawn
Points: NZ 2, EZ 2

Final Table	NZ	WZ	EZ	SZ	CZ	Pts
1 North Zone	--	6	2	0	6	14
2 West Zone	0	--	0	6	6	12
3 East Zone	0	6	--	0	6	12
4 South Zone	6	0	6	--	6	12
5 Central Zone	0	2	0	6	--	8

INDIAN AVERAGES
(Qualification 600 runs, includes Ranji, Duleep Trophies and International matches)

Batting	M	In	NO	Rns	HS	Avge
S S Sugwekar	5	8	2	728	225	121.33
M Azharuddin	8	9	1	677	155	84.62
Rizwan Shamshad	8	12	1	867	169	78.81
M V Sridhar	7	11	1	757	366	75.70
S V Manjrekar	12	18	3	1100	156	73.33
Vikram Rathore	11	19	2	1047	250	61.58
A C Bedade	7	11	0	657	159	59.72
R J Shastri	12	18	1	963	151	56.64
J Arun Lal	8	14	1	729	177	56.07
R S Dravid	13	20	4	846	151*	52.87

Bowling	O	M	Rns	W	Ave	Best
K N A Padmanabhan	258.4	80	511	33	15.48	8-57
S L Venkata Raju	335.5	109	678	42	16.14	6-87
Utpal Chatterjee	362	111	811	49	16.55	7-71
Pradeep Jain	328.4	99	814	46	17.69	8-67
Bharati Vij	279.1	63	786	44	17.86	7-58
B K Venkat Prasad	411.2	124	930	50	18.60	7-37
Chetan Sharma	344.5	62	1059	54	19.61	6-30
M Venkataramana	245.2	67	594	30	19.80	5-29
Bhupinder Singh Snr	431.4	127	1068	53	20.15	7-46
P S Vaidya	372.1	77	1081	53	20.39	5-68

South Africa 1993-94
Castle Cup

Final Table	P	W	D	L	Pts
Orange Free State	7	4	3	0	24
Western Province	7	3	2	2	20
Transvaal	7	2	4	1	16
Eastern Province	7	1	5	1	16
Border	7	2	3	2	14
Natal	7	1	4	2	12
Boland	7	1	3	3	10
Northern Transvaal	7	1	2	4	8

Benson & Hedges Series

Final Table	P	W	L	NR	Pts
Natal	8	7	1	0	28
Orange Free State	8	6	1	1	26
Western Province	8	5	2	1	22
Border	8	5	2	1	22
Eastern Province	8	4	4	0	16
Northern Transvaal	8	3	5	0	12
Transvaal	8	2	5	1	10
Impalas	8	1	7	0	4
Boland	8	1	7	0	4

B & H NIGHT SERIES FINAL
Kingsmead, Durban   Mar 11

Natal   103 (36.2 overs)
                (B T Player 5-27, A A Donald 4-21)
Orange F S 108-3 (28.1 overs)
                (J F Venter 37*)

Orange Free State won by 7 wickets
Match Award: B T Player

FIRST CLASS AVERAGES
(Excluding overseas players, qualification 300 runs, 20 wkts)

Batting	M	In	NO	Rns	HS	Avge
D J Cullinan (Tvl)	4	6	2	459	337*	114.75
D J Callaghan (EP)	4	6	2	400	113	100.00
C J van Heerden (OFS)	6	8	3	364	126*	72.80
W J Cronje (OFS)	7	13	0	870	251	66.92
T N Lazard (Bol)	9	16	3	853	307*	65.61
P N Kirsten (Bdr)	9	14	0	872	271	62.28
S J Cook (Tvl)	8	14	2	745	136	62.08
M D Marshall (Ntl)	8	11	4	420	120*	60.00

Bowling	O	M	Rns	W	Ave	Best
M J Vandrou (Tvl)	217.1	67	476	26	18.30	5-42
L Klusener (Ntl)	201.4	37	567	27	21.00	4-38
M W Pringle (WP)	258.4	68	607	28	21.67	4-43
C R Matthews (WP)	214.3	64	456	21	21.71	5-80
A G Elgar (Bol)	195.1	73	475	21	22.61	4-83
M Erasmus (Bol)	240.1	63	554	24	23.08	5-54
A Bodenhorst (Bdr)	233	46	650	27	24.07	5-52
E A E Baptiste (EP)	316.3	106	629	25	25.16	5-41

West Indies 1993-94
Red Stripe Cup

Final Table	P	W	D	L	Pts
Leeward Islands	5	3	1	1	61
Trinidad & Tobago	5	3	1	1	56
Guyana	5	1	3	1	41
Jamaica	5	1	2	2	28
Barbados	5	0	5	0	24
Windward Islands	5	0	2	3	8

Top Century Makers

206	B C Lara (T&T) v Barbados	Port-of-Spain
180	B C Lara v Jamaica	Port-of-Spain
169	B C Lara v Guyana	Pointe-a-Pierre
160	N O Perry (Jam) v Windwards	Kingston
157	S C Williams (Lee) v Barbados	Bridgetown
151	R B Richardson (Lee) v Jamaica	Kingston
142	K F Semple (Guy) v Jamaica	Kingston
141	S L Campbell (Bar) v Leewards	Bridgetown

Best Bowling

8-51	R Dhanraj (T&T) v Barbados	Port-of-Spain
6-81	C E Cuffy (Win) v Jamaica	Kingston
6-82	R C Haynes (Jam) v T&T	Port-of-Spain
6-109	C A Walsh (Jam) v Barbados	Bridgetown
5-19	K C Benjamin (Lee) v T&T	Montserrat
5-27	B S Browne (Guy) v T&T	Pointe-a-Pierre
5-38	R A Harper (Guy) v Leewards	Georgetown
5-48	D Ramnarine (T&T) v Jamaica	Port-of-Spain

Bowling	O	M	Rns	W	Ave	Best
G J Whittal (Mata)	135	33	323	16	20.18	6-34
D Matambanadzo (U24)	92.5	15	286	13	22.00	3-43
M P Jarvis (Mash)	357.3	119	753	33	22.81	6-74
E Matambanadzo (U24)	78	17	241	10	24.10	3-20
J A Rennie (Mata)	222.5	54	651	23	28.30	6-34
H J Hira (U24)	121.1	36	322	11	29.27	3-43
S G Peall (Mash)	165	36	453	14	32.35	4-39
G J Crocker (Dist)	127.2	33	337	10	33.70	6-84

Zimbabwe 1993-94 Lonrho
Logan Cup

Final Table	P	W	L	wf	lf	Bt	Bl	Pts
Mashonaland U24	3	1	0	1	1	12	29	56
Matabeleland	3	1	0	1	1	12	22.5	49.5
Mash'land C Districts	3	0	1	1	1	15	20	40
Mashonaland	3	0	1	1	1	10	22.5	37.5

wf: won on first innings, lf: lost on first innings, Bt: batting bonus points, Bl: bowling bonus points

Lonrho Logan Cup Final

Harare Sports Club   Mar 18-20

Mashonaland U24	286 (G J Rennie 76)
	245 (S V Carlisle 54, G J Whittal 6-34)
Matabeleland	140 (W R James 52*, D D Stannard 4-23)

Mashonaland Under 24 won by virtue of their 1st innings lead

FIRST CLASS AVERAGES
(Qualification 200 runs, 10 wkts)

Batting	M	In	NO	Rns	HS	Avge
W R James (Mata)	6	10	1	620	215	68.88
A Flower (Mash)	5	8	1	392	113	56.00
G W Flower (U24)	6	12	1	534	96	48.54
G K B-Jackson (Dist)	6	12	1	496	130	45.09
S V Carlisle (U24)	6	11	1	385	111*	38.50
I P Butchart (Zim XI)	4	7	1	209	60*	34.83
A C Waller (Dist)	3	6	0	206	62	34.33
G A Paterson (Dist)	5	8	0	250	73	31.25

Curling

World Championships
Oberstdorf   *Apr 9-17*
MEN
Semi Finals
Canada bt Germany 6-5
Sweden bt Switzerland 6-4
Final
Canada (Folk/Ryan/Gretzinger/Richard) bt
Sweden (Nassen/Loof/Ljungberg/Satter) 3-2
Game Scores (in final)

Toss	1	2	3	4	5	6	7	8	9	10	Total
Sweden	0	0	1	0	0	0	0	0	1	0	2
Canada	1	0	0	0	0	1	0	0	1	0	3

Final Standings

		Wins	Losses	Toss won
1	Canada	10	1	4
2	Sweden	7	2	6
3	Switzerland	8	2	6
3	Germany	6	5	6
5	USA	5	5	6
6	Norway	4	5	5
7	Holland	3	6	5
7	Denmark	3	6	3
7	Scotland	3	6	4
10	Australia	1	8	5

WOMEN
Semi Finals
Canada bt Germany 10-6
Scotland bt Sweden 10-6
Final
Canada (Peterson/Betker/McCusker/Gudereit) bt
Scotland (Cannon/Milne C/Milne M/Watt) 5-3
Game Scores (in final)

Toss	1	2	3	4	5	6	7	8	9	10	Total
Scotland	0	0	1	0	1	0	0	0	1	X	3
Canada	1	0	0	1	0	0	2	1	0	X	5

Final Standings

		Wins	Losses	Toss won
1	Canada	10	1	10
2	Scotland	7	4	5
3	Sweden	6	4	3
3	Germany	6	5	6
5	Norway	5	5	2
6	Switzerland	4	5	2
6	Finland	4	5	5
6	USA	4	5	5
9	Denmark	2	7	3
10	Japan	1	8	7

Bell's Scottish Championships
Summit Centre, Glasgow   *Feb 23-27*
MEN'S TEAM
Livingstone (Hamilton/Kelly/Moran/Barr) bt
Stranraer (Wilson/Wilson/Wilson/Torrance)

Royal Bank of Scotland Scottish Ladies Championships
Summit Centre, Glasgow   *Feb 17-20*
WOMEN'S TEAM
Stranraer (Cannon/Milne/Milne/Watt) bt
Greenacres (Martin/MacMillan/Bayne/Weir) 7-4

Scottish Seniors Championship
Livingstone   *Mar 11-13*
MEN'S TEAM
Lockerbie (Porteous/Thomson/Halliday/Parker) bt
Aberdeen (Shand/McKinnon/Davidson/Cumming)
WOMEN'S TEAM
Hamilton (Smith/Allan/Dykes/Forrest) bt
Inverness (Fraser/Macleod/MacPherson/Barrie)

English Championships
Pitlochry, Scotland   *Feb*
MEN
Final Positions
1 Alistair Burns, 2 Jim Brown, 3 Eric Laidler, 3 Martyn
Deakin, 5 Richard Lumsden, 5 John Brown

WOMEN
Final Positions
1 Joan Reed, 2 Joan Ross, 3 Janice Manson, 4 Alison
Arthur, 5 Caroline Cumming

Cycling

To the real world, it's known as Banco Español de Credito; to those who follow the fortunes of Miguel Induráin, it's better known as Banesto, the team that pays in excess of £2m a year for the services of the best road racer since Bernard Hinault. It was not the best start to the year when Banesto had to be refinanced to the tune of £3.2 **billion.** Did it worry Induráin? Apparently not, for the Spaniard won his fourth successive Tour with rather more ease than the three that preceded it. Tony Rominger, who strolled away with the Vuelta, was the most obvious threat. Yet his stomach (literally, not metaphorically) was not up to the task. Above Lourdes, on the hill of Hautacam, Induráin claimed the race. When the peloton reached Cahors, a day later, Induráin's lead, of 7:56, was the largest at that point of the Tour since Luis Ocaña in 1973. Ocaña, who had breached the dominance of Eddy Merckx, died a month before this year's Tour began.

Where do you place Induráin in the pantheon now? He sits only fifth in the number of Grands Tours won, but no rider since its inception in 1903 has won five Tour de France in a row. The Spaniard now equals Merckx and Anquetil with four straight successes. Does he go straight to the top if he wins next year? Already Induráin's dominance is being felt. This year's finishers (just over 61% of those that began the race) did not include **one** previous winner of the event.

Boardman at least nurtured our hopes. The Wirral rider became the first Briton since Tommy Simpson to wear the Yellow Jersey - and for three whole days too. *(See Front of Book)*

Thanks largely to Boardman (and a bit to Sean Yates too) the Tour en Angleterre was a spectacular success. The idea that more than three million turned out was stretching the imagination, but it was a good few hundred thousand and the crowds were filled with enthusiasm. It just needs to come back a bit sooner next time.

Boardman could have wrapped up his summer there and then, but he drew breath and proceeded to knock off two world titles in Sicily. The first Briton ever to come away with a brace of titles. Poor Obree, in contrast, had a disaster. A last minute rule that rendered his riding position unacceptable, eliminated him from the pursuit and in the time trial he flagged behind Boardman. Even the hour record, that he retook in April, became Induráin's in September. Obree needed a silver lining and a two year contract with Le Groupement, signed in September, could be it.

HISTORY'S PELOTON

EDDY MERCKX
11 Grands Tours
Tour de France: 1969, 1970, 1971, 1972, 1974
Giro d'Italia: 1968, 1970, 1972, 1973, 1974
Vuelta a España: 1973

BERNARD HINAULT
10 Grands Tours
Tour de France: 1978, 1979, 1981, 1982, 1985
Giro d'Italia: 1980, 1982, 1985
Vuelta a España: 1978, 1983

JACQUES ANQUETIL
8 Grands Tours
Tour de France: 1957, 1961, 1962, 1963, 1964
Giro d'Italia: 1960, 1964
Vuelta a España: 1963

FAUSTO COPPI
7 Grands Tours
Tour de France: 1949, 1952
Giro d'Italia: 1940, 1947, 1949, 1952, 1953

MIGUEL INDURÁIN
6 Grands Tours
Tour de France: 1991, 1992, 1993, 1994
Giro d'Italia: 1992, 1993

World Track Championships

Palermo, Sicily   Aug 15-22

MEN

Kilometre

1 Florian Rousseau   FRA   1:03.163
2 Hartwell   USA   1:03.795
3 Shane Kelly   AUS   1:03.846

4000m Pursuit

Semi-finals
Francis Moreau FRA 4:32.267 bt
Fulst GER 4:33.073

Chris Boardman GBR 4:27.742 bt
Jens Lehmann GER 4:30.004
Final
Chris Boardman 4:27.742 bt
Francis Moreau 4:39.301

Sprint

Semi-finals
Darryn Hill AUS bt Jens Fieldler GER 2-1
10.965, 11.173, 11.006
Martin Nothstein USA bt Michael Hübner GER 2-1
11.117, 10.931, 11.092
3rd/4th place
Michael Hübner bt Jens Fiedler 2-0
11.432, 11.096
Final
Martin Nothstein bt Darryn Hill 2-0
11.173, 11.006

4000m Team Pursuit

Semi-finals
Germany 4:17.136 bt France 4:19.434
USA 4:18.390 bt Australia 4:18.417
Final
Germany (Nach, Fulst, Hondo, Lehmann) 4:15.668 bt
USA (Aitkin, McGee, O'Grady, O'Shannessey) 4:17.372

Points race

1 Bruno Risi   SUI   35 pts
2 Jan-Bo Petersen   DEN   18
3 Franz Stocher   AUT   14

Tandem

Semi-finals
Raasch/Glucklich GER bt Drcmanek/Hargas TCH 2-0
11.217, 10.387
Colas/Magné FRA bt Chiappa/Paris ITA 2-0
10.551, 10.990
Final
Colas/Magné bt Chiappa/Paris 2-0
10.576, 10.903

Motor-paced

Final Placings
1 Carsten Podlesch   GER   85 pts
2 Roland Konigshofer   AUT   57
3 Allessandro Tresin   ITA   42

Keirin

1 Bruno Risi   SUI   35 pts
2 Jan-Bo Peterseon   DEN   18
3 Franz Stocher   AUT   14

WOMEN

3000m Pursuit

Semi-finals
Svetlana Samohvalova RUS 3:50.026 bt
Eickoff USA 3:52.531

Marion Clignet FRA 3:46.686 bt
Belluti ITA 3:54.107
Final
Marion Clignet FRA 3:43.399 bt
Svetlana Samohvalova RUS 3:50.898

Sprint

Semi-finals
Félicia Ballanger FRA bt Grishina RUS 2-1
12.354, 12.241, 12.781
Enioukhina RUS bt Tyler AUS 2-0
12.391, 12.420
3rd/4th place
Grishina bt Tyler
12.499, 12.275
Final
Enioukhina bt Félicia Ballanger 2-1
12.176, 12.177, 11.593

Points Race

1 Ingrid Haringa   HOL   24 pts
2 Svetl. Samohvalova   RUS   18
3 Gorojanskaya   BLS   16

Medal Table			
	G	S	B
France	3	2	0
Germany	2	2	2
United States	2	2	1
Russia	1	2	1
Great Britain	1	0	0
Holland	1	0	0
Switzerland	1	0	0
Australia	0	1	2
Austria	0	1	1
Denmark	0	1	0
Italy	0	0	3
Belarus	0	0	1

World Road Race Championships

Sicily Aug 22-28

MEN

Professional Road Race (251.8km)
1	Luc Leblanc	FRA	6:33:54
2	Claudio Chiapucci	ITA	at 9
3	Richard Virenque	FRA	ST

Time Trial (42km)
1	Chris Boardman	GBR	49:34.5
2	Andrea Chiurato	ITA	50:22.8
3	Jan Ullrich	GER	51:25.3
30	Graeme Obree	GBR	54:54.5

100km time trial
1	Italy	1hr 57m
2	France	at 2:48
3	Germany	3:01

Amateur Road Race (185.2km)
1	Alex Pedersen	DEN	4:24:38
2	Milan Dvorscik	SLO	ST
3	Christophe Mengin	FRA	ST

WOMEN

Road Race (86.4km)
1	Monica Valvik	NOR	2:08:03
2	Patsy Maegerman	BEL	ST
3	Jeanne Golay	USA	ST

Time Trial (30km)
1	Karen Kurreck	USA	38:22.8
2	Anne Samplonius	CAN	39:00.7
3	Jeannie Longo-Ciprelli	FRA	39:44.1

50km Team Race
1	Russia	1:44:55
	(Sokolova, Ilaliaseva, Boubnenkova, Pohlanova)	
2	Lithuania	at 44
3	United States	58

The Hours of Induráin and Obree
	Obree (27 Apr)	Indurain (Sep 3)
5km	5:38.99	5:43.947
10km	11:18.13	11:20.097
15km	16:57.04	16:58.938
20km	22:39.03	22:38.510
25km	28:21.95	28:18.363
30km	34:04.34	33:58.341
35km	39:46.94	39:33.489
40km	45:30.76	45:13.850
45km	51:14.03	50:55.942
50km	56:54.51	56:34.263
Total	**52.713km**	**53.040km**

National Track Championships

Leicester   Jul 23-31

MEN

4000m Pursuit
Final
Graeme Obree (Maxim) 4:34.656 bt
Bryan Steel (Team Haverhill) 4:43.823

4000m Team Pursuit
Final
North Wirral Velo 4:24.38 bt
Team Haverhill 4:25.97

1000m Sprint
Final
S Brydon (Edinburgh) bt
G Hibbert (Clayton) 2-0

Kilometre Time Trial
1	Robert Hayles	Haverhill	1:7.829
2	G Sword	N Wirrall	1:8.728
3	R Prince	St Raphael	1:9.356

40km
1	Simon Lillistone	N Wirral	50 pts
2	Tony Doyle	Creatabolin	28
3	A Stirrat	Edinburgh	20

Tandem Sprint
final
Boyd/Hibbert (Clayton) bt
Rowe (Leo)/Phillips (Stoke) 2-0

Omnium
1	A Wallis	Olympia	12 pts
2	G Coltman	Raleigh	17
3	R Butler	G Butler	20

Keirin
1	P McHugh	PCA
2	P Jacques	Manchester
3	M Libbrizzi	Edinburgh

WOMEN

Points Race (25km)
1	Sally Hodge	VC Ajax	53 pts
2	Sally Dawes	Team Raleigh	38
3	Maria Lawrence	Rockingham	13

3000m Pursuit
Final
Yvonne McGregor (Swaledale) 3:56.340 bt
Maxine Johnson (Oundle) 3:57.364

1000m Sprint
Final
Wendy Everson (RAF) bt
Sally Boyden (Swaledale) 2-0

Kilometre Time Trial
1	Maxine Johnson	Oundle	1:17.137
2	R Jones	Abergavenny	1:18.789
3	Sally Dawes	Raleigh	1:18.813

Tour de France

July 2-24

Date	Stage	Route (distance)	Winner(Team)		Race Leader
Jul 2	Prologue	Lille (7.2km)*	**Chris Boardman (GAN)**	GBR	Boardman
Jul 3	1	Euralille - Armentières (234km)	**Djamo. Abduzhaparov (Polti)**	UZB	Boardman
Jul 4	2	Roubaix - Boulogne-sur-Mer (203.5km)	**Jean-Paul van Poppel (Festina)**	HOL	Boardman
Jul 5	3	Calais - Eurotunnel (66.5km)**	**GB-MG**		Museeuw
Jul 6	4	Dover - Brighton (204km)	**Francisco Cabello (Kelme)**	ESP	Vanzella
Jul 7	5	Portsmouth - Portsmouth (187km)	**Nicola Minali (Gewiss)**	ITA	Vanzella
Jul 8	6	Cherbourg - Rennes (270.5km)	**Gianluca Bortolami (M-Clas)**	ITA	Yates
Jul 9	7	Renne - Futuroscope (259.5km)	**Jan Svorada (Lampre)**	SLO	Museeuw
Jul 10	8	Poitiers - Trésillac (218.5km)	**Bo Hamburger (TVM)**	DEN	Museeuw
Jul 11	9	Périgueux - Bergerac (64km)***	**Miguel Induráin (Banesto)**	ESP	Induráin
Jul 12	10	Bergerac - Cahors (160.5km)	**Jacky Durand (Castorama)**	FRA	Induráin
Jul 13	11	Cahors - Lourdes Hautacam (170.5km)	**Luc Leblanc (Festina)**	FRA	Induráin
Jul 15	12	Lourdes - Luz Ardiden (204.5km)	**Richard Virenque (Festina)**	FRA	Induráin
Jul 16	13	Bagnères de Bigorre - Albi (223km)	**Bjarne Riis (Gewiss)**	DEN	Induráin
Jul 17	14	Castres - Montpellier (202km)	**Rolf Sorensen (GB-MG)**	DEN	Induráin
Jul 18	15	Montpellier - Carpentras (231km)	**Eros Poli (Mercatone)**	ITA	Induráin
Jul 19	16	Valréas - L'Alpe d'Huez (224.5km)	**Roberto Conti (Lampre)**	ITA	Induráin
Jul 20	17	Bourg d'Oisans - Val Thorens (147km)	**Nelson Rodriguez (ZG-Mobili)**	COL	Induráin
Jul 21	18	Moûtiers - Cluses (170.5km)	**Piotr Ugroumov (Gewiss)**	LAT	Induráin
Jul 22	19	Cluses - Avoriaz (45km)****	**Piotr Ugroumov (Gewiss)**	LAT	Induráin
Jul 23	20	Morzine - Lac St Point (208km)	**Djamo. Abduzhaparov (Polti)**	UZB	Induráin
Jul 24	21	Euro Disney - Paris (188km)	**Eddy Seigneur (GAN)**	FRA	Induráin

* Individual Time Trial ** Team Time Trial *** Individual Time Trial **** Mountain Indiv. Time Trial

FINAL CLASSIFICATION

	Rider	Team/Country	Time		Rider	Team/Country	Time
1	**Miguel Induráin**	**Banesto/ESP**	103:38:38	23	Frederico Munoz	Kelme/COL	48:33
2	Piotr Ugroumov	Gewiss/LAT	at 5:39	24	Jim Van De Laer	Lotto/BEL	48:35
3	Marco Pantani	Carrera/ITA	7:19	25	Bruno Cenghialta	Gewiss/ITA	51:30
4	Luc Leblanc	Festina/FRA	10:03	26	Charly Mottet	Novemail/FRA	51:44
5	Richard Virenque	Festina/FRA	10:10	27	Beat Zberg	Carrera/SUI	57:06
6	Roberto Conti	Lampre/ITA	12:19	28	Gerd Audehm	Telecom/GER	57:44
7	Alberto Elli	GB-MG/ITA	20:17	29	Erik Breukink	ONCE/HOL	59:55
8	Alex Zülle	ONCE/SUI	20:35	30	Abraham Olana	Mapei-Clas/ESP	1:01:29
9	Udo Bolts	Telekom/GER	25:19	71	Sean Yates	Motorola/GBR	2:04:45
10	Vladimir Poulnikov	Carrera/UKR	25:28				
11	Pascal Lino	Festina/FRA	26:01	**Points (Green Jersey)**			
12	Fernando Escartin	Mapei-Clas/ESP	30:38	1	Djamo Abduzhaparov	Polti/UZB	322
13	Gianluca Bortolami	Mapei-Clas/ITA	32:35	2	Silvie Martinello	Mercatone/ITA	273
14	Bjarne Riis	Gewiss/DEN	33:32	3	Jan Svorada	Lampre/TCH	230
15	Oscar Pellicioli	Polti/ITA	34:55	**King of the Mountains (Polka-dot Jersey)**			
16	Nelson Rodriguez	ZG-Mobil/COL	35:18	1	Richard Virenque	Festina/FRA	392
17	Jean-François Bernard	Banesto/FRA	36:44	2	Marco Pantani	Carrera/ITA	243
18	Hernan Buenahora	Kelme/COL	38:00	3	Piotr Ugrumov	Gewiss/LIT	219
19	Rolf Sorenson	GB-MG/DEN	42:39	**Teams**			
20	Bo Hamburger	TVM/DEN	44:07	1	Festina-Andorra		311:28:53
21	Thomas Davy	Castorama/FRA	46:41		(Leblanc, Bagot, Hervé, Hodge, Lino, Torres, Van		
22	Eric Caritoux	Chazal/FRA	47:19		Poppel, Vermote, Virenque)		
				2	Gewiss-Ballan 312:11:50, 3 Mapei-Clas		312:13:31

Vuelta a España
(Tour of Spain)
Apr 25-May 15
STAGE WINNERS
1 Valladolid time trial 9km
  Tony Rominger (Mapei-Clas) SUI   10:35
2 Valladolid-Salamanca 178.4km
  Laurent Jalabert (ONCE)   FRA   4:34:53
3 Salamanca-Caceres 239.3km
  Laurent Jalabert (ONCE)   FRA   5:53:27
4 Almendralejo-Cordoba 235.6km
  Endrio Leone ((Jolly)   ITA   6:36:33
5 Cordoba-Granada 167km
  Laurent Jalabert (ONCE)   FRA   4:24:10
6 Granda-Sierra Nevada 150km
  Tony Rominger (Mapei-Clas) SUI   4:18:09
7 Baza-Alicante 250km
  Simone Biacsi (Mercatone)   ITA   6:08:03
8 Benidorm-Benidorm time trial 39.5km
  Tony Rominger (Mapei-Clas) SUI   48:44
9 Benidorm-Valencia 166km
  Jean-Paul Van Poppel (Festina) HOL   3:55:09
10 Igualada-Andorra 205km
  Angel-Yesid Camargo (Kelme)COL   5:18:59
11 Andorra-Cerler 195km
  Tony Rominger (Mapei-Clas) SUI   5:42:50
12 Benasque-Zaragoza 226.7km
  Laurent Jalabert (ONCE)   FRA   5:44:39
13 Zaragoza-Pamplona 200km
  Laurent Jalabert (ONCE)   FRA   5:24:29
14 Pamplona-Alto Cruz de la Demanda 174km
  Tony Rominger (Mapei-Clas) SUI   4:23:42
15 Santo Domingo de la C-Santander 220km
  Alessio Di Basco (Amore e Vita) ITA   5:44:29
16 Oviedo-Lagos de Covadonga 147kn
  Laurent Jalabert (ONCE)   FRA   3:42:20
17 Cangas de Onis-Alto del Naranco 150km
  Bart Voskamp (TVM)   HOL   3:52:02
18 Avila-Avila 189km
  Guiseppe Calcaterre (Amore) ITA   5:12:53
19 Avila-Segovia 171km
  Marino Alonso (Banesto)   ESP   4:21:04
20 Segovia-Destilerias DYC 52km
  Tony Rominger (Mapei-Clas) SUI   1:08:59
21 Destilerias DYC-Madrid 170km
  Laurent Jalabert (ONCE)   FRA   4:26:55

FINAL CLASSIFICATION
1 **Tony Rominger** (Mapei-Clas) SUI   92:07:48
2 Mikel Zarrabeitia (Banesto)   ESP   at 7:28
3 Pedro Delgado (Banesto)   ESP   9:27
4 Alex Zülle (ONCE)   SUI   10:54
5 Oliver Rinçon (ONCE)   COL   13:09
6 Luc Leblanc (Festina)   FRA   15:27
7 Vicente Aparicio (Banesto)   ESP   15:48
8 L Perez (Castellblanch)   ESP   16:46
9 Fernando Escartin (Mapei-Clas) ESP   16:54
10 Angel Camargo (Kelme)   COL   20:35
King of the Mountains
1 Luc Leblanc (Festina)   FRA   158
2 Michele Copolillo (Navigare)   ITA   148
3 Tony Rominger (Mapei-Clas) SUI   136
Points
1 Laurent Jalabert (ONCE)   FRA   243

Giro D'Italia (Tour of Italy)
Bologna-Milan   May 22-June 12
STAGE WINNERS
1 /1 Bologna-Bologna 86km
  Endrio Leoni (Jolly)   ITA   2:00:01
1 /2 Bologna time trial 7km
  Armand De Las Cuevas (Cast) FRA   7:52
2 Bologna-Osimo 232km
  Moreno Argentin (Gewiss)   ITA   6:13:31
3 Osimo-Loreto Aprutino 185km
  Gianni Bugno (Polti)   ITA   4:25:20
4 Montesilvano-Campitello 204km
  Evgeni Berzin (Gewiss-Ballan) RUS   5:33:37
5 Campobasso-Melfi 158km
  Endrio Leone (Jolly)   ITA   3:41:39
6 Potenza-Caserta 215km
  Marco Saligari (GB-MG)   ITA   5:39:38
7 Fiuggi-Fiuggi 119km
  Laudelino Cubino (Kelme)   ESP   2:56:12
8 Grosseto-Follonica time trial 44km
  Evgeni Berzin (Gewiss-Ballan) RUS   50:46
9 Castiglione Della Pescaia-Pontedera 153km
  Jan Svorada (Lampre)   SLO   3:25:07
10 Marostica-Marostica 115km
  Djamo Abduzhaparov (Polti) UZB   2:33:07
11 Marostica-Bibione 165km
  Jan Svorada (Lampre)   SLO   4:08:05
12 Bibione-Kranj 204km
  Andrea Ferrigato (ZG Mobili) ITA   4:47:04
13 Kranj-Lienz 204km
  Michele Bartoli (Mercatone)   ITA   5:56:49
14 Lienz-Merano 235km
  Marco Pantani (Carrera)   ITA   7:43:04
15 Merano-Aprica 195km
  Marco Pantani (Carrera)   ITA   6:55:58
16 Sondrio-Stradella 220km
  Max Sciandri (GB-MG)   ITA   6:24:36
17 Santa Maria la Versa-Lavagna 200km
  Jan Svorada (Lampre)   SLO   5:26:04
18 Chiavari-Passo del Boco time trial 35km
  Evgeni Berzin (Gewiss-Ballan) RUS   59:52
19 Lavagna-Bra 212km
  Massimo Ghirotto (ZG Mobili)ITA   5:26:50
20 Cuneo-Les Deuz Alpes 201km
  Vladimir Poulnikov (Carrera) UKR   6:28:50
21 Les Deux Alpes-Sestriere 121km
  Pascal Richard (GB-MG)   SUI   3:30:53
22 Turin-Milan 198km
  Stefano Zanini (Navigare)   ITA   4:54:38

FINAL CLASSIFICATION
1 **Evgeni Berzin** (Gewiss-Ballan) RUS 100:41:21
2 Marco Pantani (Carrera)   ITA   at 2:51
3 Miguel Induráin (Banesto)   ESP   3:23
4 Pavel Tonkov (Lampre)   RUS   11:16
5 Claudio Chiappucci (Carrera) ITA   11:58
6 J Rodriguez (Mapei-Clas)   ESP   13:17
7 Massimo Podenzana (Navigare) ITA   14:35
8 Gianni Bugno (Polti)   ITA   15:26
9 Armand de las Cuevas (Cast) FRA   15:35
10 Andy Hampsten (Motorola)   USA   17:21
95 Brian Smith   GBR   3:22:35
King of the Mountains: Pascal Richard
Points: Evgeni Berzin

QUOTES

"It's like being a big fish in a little pond, then going out to sea" - **Chris Boardman, on the transition from Olympic cyclist to professional.**

"Incroyable! Ce n'est pas l'Alpe d'Huez, c'est la côte de Ditchling Beacon" - **French TV presenter overwhelmed by the numbers that had turned out to watch the Tour in Sussex.**

"It's unbelievable. Everyone knew that he was in with a shout, but I never dreamed that he would demolish the guys like that. It must be the biggest margin ever in the prologue" - **Sean Yates, on the exploits of Boardman at Lille.**

"It's like being a cross between a decathlete, a racehorse and a chess player" - **Boardman, on what it takes.**

"A clairvoyant called mystic Meg told her that I was going to have a good month" - **Boardman, recallling what his wife told him before the Tour.**

"How's my form? My three-year-old son is going better than me" - **Johan Museeuw, at the Tour de Med.**

"I had five punctures and three crashes. If I had had only four punctures, I would have won" - **Franco Ballerini, after the Paris-Roubaix.**

"Yes, but I sold them a long time ago" - **Induráin, when asked if he had any Banesto shares.**

I read that I am certain to ride the Vuelta in 1995. Well - it's the first I heard of it" - **Miguel Induráin, who was reportedly offered £2.5m to ride the Vuelta in 1995. Maybe he hadn't heard the price?**

"Induráin can beat me any day he likes up to the day before the Tour. After that the Tour will be mine" - **Tony Rominger, touted as this year's threat to Induráin in the Tour.**

"Making a thick muscled sprinter climb a 2000 metre mountain is like asking Linford Christie to run a marathon" - **Sean Yates, on the demands of the Tour.**

"It shouldn't be banned" - **Miguel Induráin's verdict, in April, on the Obree bike.**

"It was so vague: nobody could give me any figures or designs and they were jabbering away in Italian. I didn't know what they wanted so I thought stuff it, I'm just going to do my usual ride" - **Graeme Obree, after his disqualification in Sicily.**

"I would not administer drugs. However, I would understand a rider who told me he had used them. The basic thing in cycling is to win. They are professionals and if an anti-doping control doesn't detect a substance, it's the fault of the system, not of the rider or the doctor" - **Doctor Michele Ferrari, who advises a number of cyclists including Tony Rominger and Armand de las Cuevas.**

World Cup Series

Milan-San Remo (294km)
Mar 19
1 Giorgio Furlan (Gewiss-Ballan) ITA 7:05:37
2 Mario Cipollini (Mercatone) ITA at 20
3 Adriano Baffi (Mercatone) ITA St

Tour of Flanders (268km)
Apr 3
1 Gianni Bugno (Polti) ITA 6:45:20
2 Johan Museeuw (GB-MG) BEL St
3 Andrei Tchmil (Lotto) RUS St

Paris-Roubaix (270km)
Apr 10
1 Andrei Tchmil (Lotto) RUS 7:28:02
2 Fabio Baldato (GB-MG) ITA at 1:13
3 Franco Ballerini (Mapei-Clas) ITA St

Liège-Bastogne-Liège (268km)
Apr 17
1 Evgeni Berzin (Gewiss-Ballan) RUS 7:16:30
2 Lance Armstrong (Motorola) USA at 1:37
3 Giorgio Furlan (Gewiss) ITA St

Amstel Gold (250km)
Apr 23
1 John Museeuw (GB-MG) BEL 6:42:34
2 Bruno Cenghialta (Gewiss) ITA St
3 Marco Saligari (GB-MG) ITA at 7

San Sebastian Classic (238km)
Aug 6
1 Armand de las Cuevas (Cast) FRA 5:24:37
2 Lance Armstrong (Motorola) USA at 1:56
3 Stefano Della Santa (Mapei) ITA 1:57

Leeds International Classic (231km)
Aug 14
1 Gianluca Bortalami (Mapei) ITA 6:03:29
2 Viatcheslav Ekimov (WordP) RUS St
3 Bo Hamburger (TVM) DEN at 11

Zurich Classic (243.6km)
Aug 21
1 Gianluca Bortalami (Mapei) ITA 6:14:11
2 Johan Museeuw (GB-MG) BEL St
3 Maurizio Fondriest (Lampre) ITA St

WORLD CUP POINTS (*two events remaining*)
1 Johan Museeuw (GB-MG) BEL 125 pts
2 Gianluca Bortalami (Lampre) ITA 116
3 Andrei Tchmil (Lotto) RUS 115
4 Giorgio Furlan (Gewiss) ITA 87

1993 World Cup

Paris-Tours (251km)
Oct 3, 1993
1 John Museeuw (GB-MG) BEL 6:34:50
2 Maurizio Fondriest (Lampre) ITA St
3 Alexandre Gontchenkov (Lam) UKR at 5

Tour of Lombardy (242km)
Oct 10, 1993
1 Pascal Richard (Ariostea) SUI 6:04:38
2 Giorgio Furlan (Ariostea) ITA St
3 Maximilian Sciandri (Mot) ITA at 7

Grand Prix des Nations (62.5km)
Oct 17, 1993
1 Armand de las Cuevas (Cast) FRA 1:20:54
2 Stephen Hodge (ONCE) AUS at 1:02
3 Eddy Seigneur (Gan) FRA 1:27
4 Chris Boardman (Gan) GBR 2:39
15 Graeme Obree (Bic) GBR 5:59

World Cup 1993 - Final Classification
1 Maurizio Fondriest (Lampre) ITA 287 pts
2 Johan Museeuw (GB-MG) BEL 172
3 Maximilian Sciandri (Mot) ITA 114
24 Sean Yates (Motorola) GBR 12

Milk Race
Aug 8-12
STAGE WINNERS
1 Glasgow 128.8 miles
  Maurizio Fondriest (Lampre) ITA 5:20:29
2 Carlisle-Blackpool 113 miles
  Viebren Weenstra (Collstrop) HOL 5:15:46
3 Bolton 7.8 miles time trial
  Maurizio Fondriest (Lampre) ITA 14:58.86
4 Chester-Leicester 120.2 miles
  Olaf Ludwig (Telekom) GER 4:40:32
5 Nottingham-Manchester 92.4 miles
  Jan Svorada (ONCE) TCH 3:51:19

FINAL CLASSIFICATION
1 Maurizio Fondriest (Lampre) ITA 20:54:53
2 Viatcheslav Ekimov (WordP) RUS at 21
3 Olaf Ludwig (Telekom) GER 27
4 Jan Svorada (Lampre) TCH 46
5 Rolf Aldag (Telekom) GER 53
6 Sean Yates (Motorola) GBR 55
Points: Olaf Ludwig 47 pts
King of the Mountains: S Sunderland (TVM) AUS 68 pts
Sprints: Ben Luckwell (FS Maestro) GBR 24 pts

Other Events

Dauphiné Libéré (Evian-Chambéry)
May 30-June 6

Prologue(6.7km)	Chris Boardman (Gan)	GBR	8:50
Stage 1(224km)	Marcel Wust (Nov)	GER	5:54:47
S 2(208km)	E Magnien (Cast)	FRA	5:30:36
S 3(38.2kmTT)	Chris Boardman (Gan)	GBR	47:27
S 4(196.5km)	E Magnien (Cast)	FRA	5:08:27
S 5(173.5km)	Pascal Hervé (Festina)	FRA	5:29:19
S 6(203.5km)	Ronan Pensec (NOv)	FRA	5:33:25
S 7(157km)	Chris Boardman (Gan)	GBR	3:44:03

Final Overall: 1. Laurent Dufaux (ONCE) SUI 32:21:53
   Also 20. Chris Boardman (Gan) GBR at 13:25

USPRO championship (156m)
Philadelphia   June 5
1 Sean Yates GBR 6:04:25
2 B Boscardin USA at 56
3 B Walton USA St

CYCLO-CROSS

World Championships

Koksijde, Belgium   Jan 29-30
15 Miles

1	P Herijgers	BEL	1:00:38
2	R Groenendaal	HOL	1:00:44
3	E Verveccken	BEL	1:01:15
33	R Hammond	GBR	1:05:54
36	C Young	GBR	1:06:16
37	P Stevenson	GBR	1:06:42

National Championships

Southampton   Jan 9
Men

1	Roger Hammond	VC Bad	1:11:43
2	Nick Craig	Diamond Back	at 14
3	Steve Douce	BCCA Pro	52

Women

1	Caroline Alexander	Louis Garneau	44:59
2	Sally Hibberd	BCCA Prio	at 3:31
3	Isla Rowntree	Black Country	4:05

Junior Men

1	Brian Curtis	Festival RC	41:35

Veterans

1	Les Lloyd	Didcot Phnx	1:00:13

Juvenile

1	James Allaway	Fat Tracks	25:03

National Trophy Series

ROUND 1
Stockport   Oct 17, 1993

1	Steve Douce	BCCA Pro
2	Roger Hammond	VC Bad
3	Peter Stevenson	Middridge

ROUND 2
Wolverhampton   Nov 14, 1993

1	Roger Hammond	VC Bad
2	Peter Stevenson	Middridge
3	Steve Douce	BCCA Pro

ROUND 3
Leicester   Dec 5, 1993

1	Roger Hammond	VC Bad
2	Barrie Clarke	Team Raleigh
3	Richard Thackray	Braford Olympic

ROUND 4
Northallerton   Jan 22-23

1	R Poelvoorde	BEL	1:01:07
2	S Douce	BCCA	1:03:11
3	P Stevenson	GBR	1:03:36

OVERALL

1	Steve Douce	BCCA Pro
2	Roger Hammond	VC Bad
3	Peter Stevenson	Middridge

BCCA International

Birmingham   Oct 31
Men

1	Dariuz Gil	POL	1:02:18
2	Roger Hammond	GBR	at 1
3	Steve Douce	BCCA Pro	2

MOUNTAIN BIKING

World Championships

Vail, Colorado   Sep 18
Men's Cross-country 29 miles

1	H Djernis	DEN	2:33:57
2	D Tinker Juarez	USA	at 37
3	B Brentjens	HOL	3:34

Women's Cross-country 22.34 miles

1	A Sydor	CAN	2:12:07
2	S DeMattei	USA	at 3:19
3	S Ballantyne	USA	3:45

CYCLING WEEKLY — More News Faster

Darts

Embassy World Championship

Lakeside CC, Frimley Green   Jan 1-8
Second Round
Kevin Kenny ENG bt Nick Gedney ENG	3-2
Bobby George ENG bt Martin Phillips WAL	3-1
Martin Adams ENG bt Bob Taylor SCO	3-1
Magnus Caris SWE bt Leo Laurens BEL	3-0
John Part CAN bt Paul Lim USA	3-0
Steve McCollum ENG bt Colin Monk ENG	3-1
Troels Rusel DEN bt Ian Sarfas ENG	3-1
Ronnie Sharp SCO bt Roland Scholten(3) HOL	3-1

Quarter-finals
Bobby George bt Kevin Kenny	4-2
Magnus Caris bt Martin Adams	4-2
John Part bt Steve McCollum	4-0
Ronnie Sharp bt Troels Rusel	4-1

Semi-finals
Bobby George bt Magnus Caris	5-4
John Part bt Ronnie Sharp	5-1

FINAL
John Part bt Bobby George	6-0

Skol World Championship

Purfleet   Dec 30-Jan 2
Quarter-finals
Peter Evison (Hayes) bt Rod Harrington (Chelms.)	4-1
Phil Taylor (Stoke) bt Bob Anderson (Swindon)	4-2
S Brown (USA) bt Alan Warriner (Lancaster)	4-3
Dennis Priestley (Mexboro') bt T Kirby (IRE)	4-2

Semi-finals
Dennis Priestley bt Peter Evison	5-3
Phil Taylor bt S Brown	5-0

3rd/4th Play-off
S Brown bt Peter Evison	5-1

FINAL
Dennis Priestley bt Phil Taylor	6-1

Proton Cars World Matchplay

Blackpool   Aug 4-7
Quarter-finals
D Priestley (ENG) bt J Harvey (SCO)	11-4
R Harrington (ENG) bt J Watkins (USA)	11-7
L Butler (USA) bt J Wilson (SCO)	11-4
S Burgess (ENG) bt B Anderson (ENG)	11-8

Semi-finals
D Priestley bt R Harrington	11-4
L Butler bt S Burgess	11-7

3rd/4th Play-off
R Harrington bt S Burgess	11-9

FINAL
L Butler bt D Priestley	16-12

Winmau World Masters

Park Inn Hotel, London   Dec 3-4, 1993
Semi-finals
Steve Beaton (ENG) bt Ian Carpenter (ENG)	3-1
Leslie Wallace (SCO) bt Paul Williams (ENG)	3-2

FINAL
Steve Beaton bt Leslie Wallace	3-1

British Matchplay Championship
Great Yarmouth, Norfolk   Oct 10, 1993
Steve Beaton (Wilts) bt Ronnie Baxter (Lancs)   5-2

Embassy Gold Cup
Men's Singles: Shayne Burgess (Kent)
Women's Singles: Jayne Stubbs (Cheshire)
Men's Pairs: Ronnie Sharp & Alan Brown (Ayrshire)
Women's Pairs: Tammy Montgomery & Val Windle (Yorkshire)

British Open 1993
Men: Martin Adams (ENG) bt Stefan Nagy (SWE) 2-0
Women: Sandra Greatbatch (ENG) bt Sue Talbot (ENG) 3-0

Women's World Championships
Park Inn Hotel, London   Dec 3-4
Mandy Solomons (ENG) bt Kathy Maloney (USA) 3-1

British Championships
Men			Women	
1	England	4pts	Wales	3 pts
2	Wales	2	Scotland	2
3	Scotland	0	England	1

Mediterranean Open
Men's Singles: Paul Williams
Men's Pairs: Clive Pearce & Carl Williams
Women's Singles: Maggie Sutton
Women's Pairs: Lisa & Trina Shergold

Inter-County Championships
Men (Premier)		(Scotland)	
1 Yorkshire	65	Fife	63
2 Glamorgan	62	Ayrshire	62
3 London	60	Lothian	55
Women (Premier)		**(Scotland)**	
1 London	40	Grampian	33
2 Cambridgeshire	34	Lothian	28
3 Yorkshire	32	Fife	27

Equestrianism

Equestrianism is one of only two Olympic sports where women compete equally with men (shooting is the other) and after Britain's performance in the World Three-Day Eventing Championship at The Hague, you could argue that it's the men that are competing unequally. The four women riders - Karen Dixon, Mary Thompson, Charlotte Bathe and Kristina Gifford - that made up the three-day team led the competition from the first day, the dressage, extended it in the cross-country discipline and, despite a predictable wobble at the treble by King William, won with a couple of fences in hand.

A clear round by King William would have brought Thompson the individual title as well, but Dixon's bronze with Thompson a place behind was the eventual reward. New Zealand's Vaughn Jefferies recovered some ground for the male sex by winning the individual title and it was some compensation for the double Olympic champion Mark Todd, his compatriot who tumbled out in the cross-country. The course for the cross-country had come in for some early criticism as it was considered not a stern enough test. Yet, in the end it took its toll, notably on America's Bruce Davidson, who with Pirate Lion looked sure to be in contention until he took an early bath at the second water. His demise assured the British team of a clear lead going into the jumping.

The horses also suffered because of the heat; a problem which was highlighted earlier in the year when a warning report from the Animal Health Trust at Newmarket, suggested that the conditions at Atlanta could threaten the well-being of the horses. In August, the Trust, partly funded by the International Equestrian Federation and Volvo, sent a group of horses to Atlanta for a three-day event at Bouckaert Farm, approximately 70 miles north of the Olympic site. The results of tests taken during that competition could determine whether the three-day event remains on the 1996 Olympic programme.

British interests will be hoping the horses, having had time to acclimatise will bear up well. In the world championships we have won the team title four times in the eight championships that have been held since its inception in 1970. We have also supplied three individual winners and, just to emphasise the point, Karen Dixon currently tops the FEI world rankings.

George Bowman, a 59 year old carpet dealer from Cumbria, earned Britain's highest individual honour at the World Games when he took the silver in the carriage driving championship. Driving with three Cumberland Cobs and a last minute substitute Lippizaner, Bowman came within an whisker of his lifetime's ambition, finishing just 3.3 points behind Germany's Michael Freund. Britain's show jumpers, though, had a disaster at The Hague, placing sixth in the team competition and never in the hunt for individual honours. Michael Whitaker could afford a rueful smile, however. He has won Grands Prix in Ascona, Calgary and Dublin in the second half of the year and the sport has never been richer as a quick reference to our owners' list shows. For example, when Jos Landsink dominated the Volvo World Cup final at 's-Hertogenbosch he picked up a cheque for £86,000. Don't tear the golf club or the tennis racket from your kids' hands just yet, but if they ask you to go pony trekking, go buy the helmet.

World Equestrian Games
The Hague, Holland   July 27-Aug 7

SHOW JUMPING
Team Championship
1 Germany   16.88
   (Sloothaak/von Ronne/Hafemeister/Beerbaum)
2 France   31.63
   (Bost/Rozier/Navet/Robert)
3 Switzerland   45.69
   (Fuchs/Lauber/Fuchs/McNaught-Mandli)
6 Great Britain   63.66
   (Skelton/Whitaker/Brown/Whitaker)

Individual Championship
After 3 competitions
1	Franke Sloothaak	GER	6.67
	on San Patrignano Weihaiwej		
2	Ludger Beerbaum	GER	9.05
	on Almox Ratina Z		
3	Michel Robert	FRA	11.78
	on Miss San Patrignano		

Final Exchange of Horses
1	Franke Sloothaak	GER	0 faults
2	Michel Robert	FRA	0.5
3	Soren von Ronne	GER	4
	on Taggi		
4	Ludger Beerbaum	GER	12

DRESSAGE
Team Championship
1 Germany   5269
   (Uphoff-Becker/Balkenhol/Werth/Rehbein)
2 Holland   5196
   (Bontje/Rothenberger/van Grunsven)
3 United States   4787
   (Raine/Dover/Rockwell/Lavell)
7 Great Britain   4577
   (Bredin/Fry/Faurie/Eilberg)

Grand Prix
1	Anky van Grunsven (Olympic Bonfire)	HOL	1819
2	Isabell Werth (Gigolo FRH)	GER	1810
3	Nicole Uphoff-Becker (Rembrandt B)	GER	1742
10	Emile Faurie (Virtu)	GBR	1635
27	Jane Bredin (Cupido)	GBR	1534
54	Laura Fry (Quarrman II)	GBR	1409
57	Ferdi Eilberg (Arun Tor)	GBR	1350

Grand Prix Special
1	Isabell Werth (Gigolo FRH)	GER	1605
2	Nicole Uphoff-Becker (Rembrandt B)	GER	1592
3	Sven Rothenberger (Dondolo)	HOL	1495
4	Emile Faurie (Virtu)	GBR	1469

Freestyle To Music
1	Anky van Grunsven (Olympic Bonfire)	HOL	83.08
2	Klaus Balkenhol (Goldstern)	GER	82.40
3	Karin Rehbein (Donerhall)	GER	77.07
11	Jane Bredin (Cupido)	GBR	67.72

THREE-DAY EVENTING
Team Championship
1 Great Britain   198.80
   (Dixon/Thomson/Bathe/Gifford)
2 France   213.20
   (Bigot/Teulere/Duroy)
3 Germany *(Overesch/Mysegaes/Ehrenbrink)*
   279.60

Individual Championship
1	Vaughan Jefferis (Bounce)	NZL	55.60
2	Dorothy Trapp (Holokai)	USA	56.80
3	Karen Dixon (Get Smart)	GBR	60.80
4	Mary Thomson (King William)	GBR	64.80
12	Charlotte Bathe (Cool Customer)	GBR	73.20
17	Kristina Gifford (General Jock)	GBR	81.80
22	Helen Bell (Troubleshooter)	GBR	93.40

DRIVING
Team Championship
1 Germany *(Sandmann/Freund/Hammann)*
   256.6
2 Belgium *(Brasseur/van Dijck/Standaert)*
   271.4
3 Holland *(Aarts/Chardon/de Ruyter)*
   283.4
5 Great Britain *(Bowman/Holder)*
   315.4

Horses Four-in-Hand
1	Michael Freund	GER	122.5
2	George Bowman	GBR	125.8
3	Ijsbrand Chardon	HOL	127.6
21	Alwyn Holder	GBR	189.6
26	Richard Margrave	GBR	207.2
40	Karen Bassett	GBR	411.9

ENDURANCE
Team Championship
1 France *(Fleury/Jollivet/David/Atger)*
   1915.85
2 Spain *(Vila/Cobos/Albarran/Amain)*
   2119.71
3 Austria *(Forrester/de Jong/Timms/Wade)*
   2126.02
11 Great Britain *(Smedley/Helme/Wiggans/Brown)*

Individual
1	Valerie Kanavy (Pieraz)	USA	601.93
2	Dennis Pesce (Melfenik)	FRA	607.85
3	Stephane Fleury (Roc'H)	FRA	626.58
9	Jill Thomas (Egypt. Khalifa)	GBR	675.30
33	Gill Smedley (Charlie)	GBR	769.58
34	Donna Helme (Bobby)	GBR	769.58

VAULTING
Team Competition
1	Switzerland (Casanova V CH)	8.434
2	Germany (Rodeo)	8.285
3	Sweden (Picasso)	7.687
13	Great Britain (Verona)	6.168

Individual (Men)
1	Thomas Fiskbaek (Hamlet)	DEN	9.391
2	Christoph Lensing (Aladin)	GER	9.332
3	Thomas Föcking (Aladin)	GER	9.252
29	Merlyn Forrer (Negus)	GBR	6.517
31	Ronan Brown (Gusta)	GBR	6.248

Individual (Women)
1	Tanja Benedetto (Zarewitsch)	GER	9.344
2	Kerith Lemon (Maxwell 8)	USA	9.086
3	Mieke Lorentz (Falun)	GER	9.078
41	Louise Townsend (Gusta)	GBR	5.778

Show Jumping

Volvo World Cup (1993-94)

WESTERN EUROPEAN LEAGUE
Final Standings *(after 14 competitions)*

1	Jos Lansink	HOL	127 pts
2	Franke Sloothaak	GER	99
3	Michael Whitaker	GBR	92
4	John Whitaker	GBR	69
5	Hugo Simon	AUT	63
6	Lesley McNaught-M	SUI	53

NORTH AMERICAN LEAGUE
Final Standings *(after 8 competitions)*

1	Hap Hansen	USA	74 pts
2	Sarah Baldwin-Cline	USA	63
3	Michael Endicott	USA	58

PACIFIC LEAGUE
Final Standings *(after 16 competitions)*

1	John Fahey	AUS	126 pts
2	Alison Rowland	AUS	118
3	Sharon Scott	AUS	107

NEW ZEALAND SUB-LEAGUE
Final Standings *(after 7 competitions)*

1	Maurice Beatson	NZL	60 pts
2	Harvey Wilson	NZL	56
3	Leanne Chambers	NZL	55

MEXICAN SUB-LEAGUE
Final Standings *(after 6 competitions)*

1	Jaime Guerra	MEX	47 pts
2	C Lorenza O'Farril	MEX	45
3	Fernandos Senderos	MEX	44

VOLVO WORLD CUP FINAL
's-Hertogenbosch, Holland   Apr 13-17

1	Jos Lansink (Bollvorm's Libero H)	HOL	0 pens
2	Franke Sloothaak (San P. Weihaiwej)	GER	9.5
3	Michael Whitaker (Ev. Midnight M.)	GBR	14
4	Hugo Simon (Apricot D)	AUT	14.25
5	Dirk Hafemeister (P S Priamos)	GER	16
6	Jenny Zoer (Desteny AZ)	HOL	18
7	Roelof Bril (Bollvorm's Let's Go)	HOL	19
	Beat Grandjean (Sir Archy)	SUI	19
9	Nick Skelton (Ev. Limited Edition)	GBR	20.5
10	Mark Leone (Crown Royal Artos Z)	USA	21.5

GRAND SLAM FINAL STANDINGS
After 4 events (Berlin, London, Brussels, Paris)

1	Franke Sloothaak	GER	99 pts
2	Ludger Beerbaum	GER	94
3	Hugo Simon	AUT	83
4	Dirk Hafemeister	GER	75
5	Michael Whitaker	GBR	68

Volvo World Cup (1994-95)

CENTRAL EUROPEAN LEAGUE
Round 1 *Iwno, Poland   May 14*

1	Zbigniew Koscienski (Bosman)	POL	20 pts

Round 2 *Vilnius, Lithuania   May 29*

1	Tonu Rahn (Omer)	EST	20 pts

Round 3 *Warsaw, Poland   June 5*

1	Ante Simlesa (Sandro Song)	CRO	20 pts

Round 4 *Piatra Neamt, Romania   June 19*

1	Victor Poganovski (Bahus)	UKR	17 pts

Round 5 *Bojourishte, Bulgaria   June 26*

1	Radu Ilioi (Naum)	ROM	20 pts

Round 6 *Hortobagy, Hungary   July 3*

1	Zbigniew Koscienski (Bosman)	POL	20 pts

Round 7 *Tallinn, Estonia   July 17*

1	Pille Elson (Baltija)	EST	9 pts
	Urmas Tomps (Haiko)	EST	9
	Rein Pill (Pretoria)	EST	9
	Konstantin Prohorov (Divident)	EST	9

Round 8 & Round 9 - Cancelled

Round 10 *Bratislava, Slovakia   Aug 14*

1	Istvan Bogar (Meran)	HUN	20 pts

SOUTH AMERICAN LEAGUE
Round 1 *Buenos Aires, Argentina   May 1*

1	Ricardo Dircie (Apolo)	ARG	20 pts

Round 2 *Montevideo, Uruguay   May 8*

1	Jorge Johannpeter (Lendel Joter)	BRA	11 pts

CANADIAN LEAGUE
Round 1 *Calgary, Canada   June 4*

1	Beth Underhill (Monopoly)	CAN	20 pts

Round 2 *Bromont, Canada   June 26*

1	Mario Deslauriers (Alemao)	CAN	15 pts

Nations Cup (1993)
Final Standings *(over 24 events, Apr 27-Nov 20)*

1	Germany	36.00
2	Switzerland	31.50
3	Holland	29.50
4	Great Britain	28.00
5	France	27.50
6	United States	23.00

TOP 10 OWNERS
Aug 1, 1993-July 31, 1994

1	M Whitaker	£194,586
2	C Whitaker	£177,058
3	J Haller	£173,398
4	Everest	£120,138
5	S Welch	£113,788
6	Lady P Harris	£83,196
7	Gascoines C S	£54,012
8	K H Fisher	£52,644
9	Senator International	£48,740
10	Countess of Inchcape	£46,348

Nations Cup (1994)

Rome, Italy   *Apr 23-27*
1 Switzerland 12 pens*(McNaught-Mändli/Fuchs/Lauber/
                              Fuchs)*
2 Germany 12 *(Gravemeier/Weinberg/Becker/Sloothaak)*
Switzerland won jump off
3 Great Britain 16 *(Skelton/Popely/Clarke/M Whitaker)*

Kiskunhalas, Hungary   *Apr 28-May 1*
1 Switzerland 0 pens *(Buholzer/Fah/Brandlin/Friedlf)*
2 Austria 8 *(Domaingo/Frischeis/Fischer/Boor)*
3 Hungary 8.25 *(Varro/Rezga/Hevesy/Bogar)*
4 Great Britain 9.50 *(Goodwin/Priest/Bevan/Barton)*

Lucerne, Switzerland   *May 12-15*
1 Sweden 8.75 pens *(Eriksson/Zetterman/Lanner/Gretzer)*
2 Holland 12 *(Tops/Zoer/Harmsen/Lansink)*
3 Great Britain *(Skelton/Popely/Clarke/M Whitaker)*

Hickstead, England   *May 19-22*
1 Italy 36 pens *(Bologni/Bartalucci/Sozzi/Arioldi)*
2 Great Britain 36.25 *(Skelton/Whitaker/Bowen/Whitaker)*
3 Ireland 40 *(Charles/Mullins/Chesney/Ledingham)*

Barcelona, Spain   *June 2-5*
1 Italy 8.50 pens *(Smith/Baroni/Govoni/Dominici)*
2 Great Britain 12 *(Billington/Goosen/Edgar/Skelton)*
2 France 12 *(Rozier/Robert/Godignon/Ledermann)*

Aachen, Germany   *June 14-19*
1 Great Britain 8 pens *(Whitaker/Brown/Popely/Whitaker)*
2 Ireland 8 *(Charles/Ledingham/Chesney/Macken)*
3 Germany 12 *(Beerbaum/Beerbaum/Gravemeier/
                    Sloothaak)*

Falsterbo, Sweden   *July 7-10*
1 Germany 12 pens *(Nagel/Scheppers/Bökman/Becker)*
2 Sweden 16 *(Eriksson/Zetterman/Schultz/Gretzer)*
3 Switzerland 24 *(Friedli/Fäh/Fuchs/Mändli)*

Geesteren-Twente, Holland   *July 7-10*
1 Germany 12.25 pens *(von Ronne/Schneider/
                              Hafemeister/Sloothaak)*
2 Holland 21 *(Romp/Zoer/Schans/Lansink)*
3 Switzerland 24.25 *(Fuchs/Grandjean/Lauber/Mändli)*

La Baule, France   *July 14-17*
1 Ireland 12 pens *(Charles/Ledingham/Chesney/Macken)*
2 Switzerland 16 *(Estermann/Oberson/Fuchs/Melliger)*
3 Brazil 16.25 *(Pessoa/Diniz/Johanpeter/Pessoa)*

Luxembourg   *July 15-17*
1 Germany 4 pens*(Beerbaum/von Ronne/Hafemeister/ S
                        Sloothaak)*
2 Holland 4 *(Raymakers/Vleuten/Hendrix/Lansink)*
Germany won after jump off
3 Switzerland 16 *(Fuchs/Buholzer/Lauber/Fuchs)*

San Remo, Italy   *July 1-3*
1 France 24 pens *(Kolnik/Labeyrie/Chartier/Grangier)*
2 Italy 35.50 *(di Stefano/Pecora/Rolli/Enrico)*
3 Portugal 65 *(da Costa/Guimaraes/Pinheiro/Oliveira)*

Dublin, Italy   *Aug 9-13*
1 Great Britain 0 pens *(Skelton/Whitaker/Bradley/
                              Whitaker)*
2 Germany 4 *(Gundel/Schepers/Hetzel/Becker)*
2 France 4 *(Nicolas/de Balanda/Bonneau/Bourdv)*
2 Switzerland 4 *(M Fuchs/Sprunger/Oberson/Buholzer)*

Calgary, Canada   *Sept 7-11*
1 USA 25 pens *(Kursinski/McMullen/Grubb/Lenehan)*
2 Canada 29.50 *(Lamaze/Henselwood/Millar/Underhill)*
3 Ireland 31.75 *(Charles/Mullins/Ledingham/Macken)*

Presidents Cup (1993)

Final Standings *(over 29 events, Apr 24-Nov 29)*
1 Germany   36.00
2 Switzerland   36.00
3 France   35.50
4 Great Britain   31.00
5 Holland   30.00
6 United States   23.00

TOP 30 HORSES
August 1, 1993-July 31, 1994

1	Everest Dollar Girl	£173,398
2	Everest Mon Santa	£119,836
3	Everest Midnight Madness	£83,196
4	Everest Grannusch	£79,733
5	Everest Two Step	£74,750
6	Everest Limited Edition	£73,694
7	Everest Gammon	£72,853
8	Everest My Mesieur	£52,210
9	Everest Winstar	£40,967
10	Everest Showtime	£37,232
11	Senator Lannegan	£32,946
12	Bowriver Queen	£31,280
13	Everest Elton	£29,969
14	Bluebird	£28,412
15	Comex	£27,701
16	Everest Major Wager	£22,167
17	Benjumin II	£19,969
18	Endeavour	£19,477
19	Everest Flarepath	£19,030
20	Rhapsody	£17,296
21	Tees Hanauer	£17,228
22	Bond Gringo	£16,701
23	Alfredo	£16,588
24	Suntory	£15,898
25	Everest Sure Thing	£15,511
26	Wessex Zakatak	£15,475
27	Everest Milton	£15,342
28	It's The Business	£14,960
29	Everest Roddy's Revenge	£13,487
30	Everest Costa Classics	£12,633

Grands Prix

Rome, Italy   *Apr 23-27*

1	Arnaldo Bologni (May Day)	ITA	34.91
2	Hervé Godignon (Twist du Valon)	FRA	36.11
3	Otto Becker (Herrmann's Ascalon)	GER	36.32

Kiskunhalas, Hungary   *Apr 28-May 1*

1	Urs Fäh (Jeremia)	SUI	40.13
2	Thomas Buholzer (Wapiti)	SUI	41.67
3	Paul Bevan (Belotti)	GBR	4 flts

Hickstead, England   *May 19-22*

1	Gerry Mullins (Pallas Green)	IRL	56.68
2	Michael Whitaker (Ev. Midnight M.)	GBR	4 flts
3	Roger-Yves Bost (President Papillon)	FRA	4 flts

Aachen, Germany   *June 14-19*

1	Rodrigo Pessoa (L P Special Envoy)	BRA	47.96
2	Thomas Fuchs (Major AC Folien)	SUI	48.88
3	Nelson Pessoa (L P Chouman)	BRA	48.89

Barcelona, Spain   *June 2-5*

1	Markus Fuchs (Interpane Blue Point)	SUI	35.16
2	Michel Robert (Miss San Patrignano)	FRA	37.26
3	Rodrigo Pessoa (L P Tom Boy)	BRA	4 flts

Falsterbo, Sweden   *July 7-10*

1	Emile Hendrix (Anadolu Bikker)	HOL	43.54
2	Eric van der Vleuten (O V's El Band)	HOL	44.07
3	Royne Zetterman (Irco Mena)	SWE	44.09

Geesteren-Twente, Holland   *July 7-10*

1	Franke Sloothaak (S P Joli Coeur)	GER	39.92
2	Markus Fuchs (Interpane Goldlights)	SUI	42.12
3	Jaime Guerra (Renata La Silla)	MEX	44.33

La Baule, France   *July 14-17*

1	Alexandra Ledermann (Rochet M)	FRA	89.12
2	Eric Navet (Waiti Quito de Baussy)	FRA	91.63
3	Rodrigo Pessoa (L P Special Envoy)	BRA	4 flts

Luxembourg   *July 15-17*

1	Franke Sloothaak (S P Weihaiwej)	GER	31.19
2	Nick Skelton (Everset Dollar Girl)	GBR	31.22
3	Ludger Beerbaum (Almox Ratina Z)	GER	31.35

Dublin, Ireland   *Aug 9-13*

1	John Whitaker (Everset Grannusch)	GBR	37.46
2	Debbie Dolan (Quantum Leap)	USA	38.96
3	Peter Charles (La-Ina)	IRL	39.35

Calgary, Canada   *Sept 7-11*

1	John Whitaker (Everset Grannusch)	GBR	55.80
2	Thomas Fuchs (Major AC Folien)	SUI	56.94
3	Eric Navet (Waiti Quito de Baussy)	FRA	4 flts

Horse of the Year Show

Wembley Arena   *Oct 5-10, 1993*

British Championship (Women)

1	Alison Bradley (Endeavour)	29.98	£2,000
2	Marie Edgar (Everest Winstar)	30.92	£1,400
3	Julia Cleeland (Finance)	32.40	£900

Toggi Grand Prix

1	John Whitaker (Everset Grannusch)	33.89	£6,000
2	Warren Clarke (Benjumin II)	34.76	£4,500
3	Nick Skelton (Everset Dollar Girl)	4 flts	£3,000

The Olympia International

The Grand Hall, Olympia   *Dec 17-20*

P & O Grand Prix

1	Peter Charles (Impulse)	IRL	28.20	£9,000
2	Ludger Beerbaum (Al. Ratina Z)	GER	28.38	£7,000
3	Peter Eriksson (Robin Z)	SWE	29.16	£4,700

Volvo World Cup Preliminary Round

1	Michael Whitaker (Ev. Two Step)	GBR	37.70	£9,000
2	Dirk Hafemeister (PS Priamos)	GER	38.31	£5,500
3	Geoff Billington (Rhapsody)	GBR	41.36	£3,500

Royal International Horse Show

Hickstead   *July 7-10*

King George V Gold Cup

1	M Whitaker (Ev. Midnight M.)	GBR	41.66	£7,500
2	N Skelton (Ev. Limited Edition)	GBR	42.15	£4,000
3	D Bowen (Ben Hur)	GBR	46.70	£3,500

Queen Elizabeth II Cup

1	D Lampard (Abbervail Dream)	GBR	63.36	£2,000
2	M Edgar (Everest Winstar)	GBR	4 flts	£1,000
3	L Edgar (Everest Premier)	GBR	4 flts	£800

July Stakes

1	J Whitaker (Ev. Roddy's Rev.)	GBR	41.90	£1,000
2	R Runge (Goliath)	GER	43.40	£600
3	J Kraus (Pikora)	GER	Elim	£400

Kraus eliminated in jump-off

Redland Roof Tiles Stakes

1	G Luckett (Everest Vantage)	GBR	39.93	£1,000
2	E J Brown (Bond Diamond)	GBR	43.91	£600
3	D Cojuanco (Chouman)	PHI	44.12	£400

BSJA TOP RIDERS

Jan 1-July 31

(1993 positions in brackets)

1	(2)	M Whitaker	3,773.10
2	(1)	J Whitaker	2,053.80
3	(3)	N Skelton	1,700.30
4	(4)	M Edgar	1,369.22
5	(6)	G Billington	885.84
6	(15)	J Fisher	782.44
7	(5)	R Smith	731.78
8	(22)	W Funnell	671.24
9	(36)	G Glazzard	662.64
10	(10)	M Lucas	531.74
11	(38)	J Renwick	516.42
12	(43)	A Bradley	516.22
13	(20)	T Stockdale	432.30
14	(24)	W Clarke	404.24
15	(104)	R Hoekstra	398.50
16	(34)	K Brown	393.52
17	(30)	M Lanni	389.52
18	(47)	G Goodwin	384.60
19	(18)	J Popely	378.44
20	(7)	P Murphy	375.78

Speed Classic

1	G Luckett (Everest Fire One)	GBR 79.10	£1,000
2	J Whitaker (Ev. Roddy's Rev.)	GBR 81.82	£600
3	J Renwick (Clover)	GBR 86.92	£400

Sussex Stakes

1	M Lucas (Senator Lannegan)	GBR 44.71	£1,000
2	M Edgar (Everest Winstar)	GBR 45.01	£600
3	R Smith (Silver Dust)	GBR 48.23	£400

Dressage

Volvo World Cup Final

Göteborg, Sweden   Apr 3-4

Grand Prix

1	Monica Theodorescu (Ganimedes T.)	GER	1684
2	Nicole Uphoff-Becker (H's G Gilbert)	GER	1645
3	Kyra Kyrklund (Edimburg)	FIN	1596

Grand Prix Freestyle

1	Monica Theodorescu (Ganimedes T.)	GER	77.30
2	Klaus Balkenhol (Goldstern 078)	GER	75.89
3	Nicole Uphoff-Becker (H's G Gilbert)	GER	75.26

Final Results

1	Monica Theodorescu (Ganimedes T.)	GER	100 pts
2	Nicole Uphoff-Becker (H's G Gilbert)	GER	92
3	Kyra Kyrklund (Edimburg)	FIN	87

Official International Events

AACHEN, GERMANY   *June 14-19*

Team Event

1	Germany	5251
	(Werth/Theodorescu/Balkenhol/Uphoff-Becker)	
2	Holland	4855
	(van Grunsven/Rothenberger/Strijk/Bartels)	
3	Sweden	4622
	(Hakanson/Solmell/Johansson/Brink)	

Grand Prix

1	Isabell Werth (Gigolo FRH)	GER	1779
2	Monica Theodorescu (Grunox Tec.)	GER	1778
3	Klaus Balkenhol (Goldstern)	GER	1694

Grand Prix Special

1	Isabell Werth (Gigolo FRH)	GER	1602
2	Monica Theodorescu (Grunox Tec.)	GER	1573
3	Nicole Uphoff-Becker (Rembrandt B.)	GER	1520

Grand Prix Freestyle

1	Anky van Grunsven (Olym. Cocktail)	HOL	80.31
2	Klaus Balkenhol (Goldstern)	GER	77.64
3	Karin Rehbein (Donnerhall)	GER	76.26

ARNHEM, HOLLAND   *June 23-25*

Team Event

1	Holland *(van Grunsven/Bontje/Rothenberger/Bartels)* 4980	
2	Germany *(Klimke/Kemmer/Werth)* 4781	
3	USA *(McPhail/Raine/Lavell/Rockwell)* 4658	

Grand Prix

1	Anky van Grunsven (Olym. Cocktail)	HOL	1730
2	Ellen Bontje (Heuriger)	HOL	1658
3	Robert Dover (Devereaux)	USA	1643

Grand Prix Special

1	Ellen Bontje (Heuriger)	HOL	1483
2	Robert Dover (Devereaux)	USA	1431
3	Michael Klimke (Chan)	GER	1424

Grand Prix Freestyle

1	Heike Kemmer (Borsalino)	GER	72.03
2	Carole Lavell (Gifted)	USA	72.03
3	Sven Rothenberger (Bo)	HOL	71.82

Three Day Eventing

Badminton, England

May 5-8

1	Mark Todd (Horton Point)	NZL	41.40
2	Blyth Tait (Delta III)	NZL	53.80
3	Vaughn Jefferies (Bounce)	NZL	57.00
4	Bruce Davidson (Eagle Lion)	USA	57.00
5	Mark Todd (Just an Ace)	NZL	62.20
6	Karen Dixon (Get Smart)	GBR	63.40
7	Kristina Gifford (General Jock)	GBR	68.65
8	Mandy Stibbe (King's Jester)	HOL	69.15
9	Helen Bell (Troubleshooter)	GBR	73.10
10	Felicity Cribb (Carmody St.)	AUS	73.20

AVARE, BRAZIL   *Nov 12-14*

1	Almir Lustosa Vieira (Black Jack)	BRA	140.8
2	Serguei Fofanoff (Fri Ribe Off)	BRA	154.4
3	José Ortelli (Como Vos)	ARG	161.0

PUKEKOHE, NEW ZEALAND   *Dec 2-5*

1	Jo Wilson (Stylish Diplomat)	NZL	55.60
2	Joe Meyer (Alleutian)	NZL	62.20
3	Neil Sharpe (Winter Oak)	NZL	68.75

LOCHINVAR, AUSTRALIA   *Mar 24-27*

1	Kylie Gallagher (Sunbird)	AUS	264.20

SAMUR, FRANCE   *Apr 21-24*

1	Jean Teulere (Rodosto)	FRA	49.20
2	Robert Lemieux (Kayem)	CAN	61.00
3	David O'Connor (On a Mission)	USA	63.20

LEXINGTON, USA   *Apr 28-May 1*

1	Julie Gomena (Treaty)	USA	51.20
2	Bruce Davidson (Regnt Lion)	USA	58.35
3	Kelli McM. Temple (King's Revenge)	USA	59.75

CHECKMATE, CANADA   *May 13-15*

1	Phyllis Dawson (Half Magic)	USA	80.35
2	Jill Walton (Patrona)	USA	85.55
3	Mike Huber (Hoopde)	USA	99.20

PUNCHESTOWN, IRELAND   *May 20-23*

1	Karen Dixon (Too Smart)	GBR	56.40
2	Clayton Fredericks (Bundaberg)	AUS	59.80
3	Susan Shortt (Park Hall)	IRL	63.60

LUHMUHLEN, GERMANY   *May 26-29*

1	Pila Pantsu (Cyna)	FIN	53.40
2	Marina Loheit (Jelly Lorum)	GER	57.00
3	Ingrid Klimke (Grand Prix)	GER	59.00

TAUPO, NEW ZEALAND   *May 19-22*

1	Trudy Boyce (Van Gogh)	NZL	64.80
2	Bryce Newman (Darby)	NZL	69.25
3	Sally Clark (Squirrel Hill)	NZL	69.40

COMPIEGNE, FRANCE *May 25-29*

1	Marie-Christine Duroy (U P B Ferry)	FRA	60.40
2	Michel Bouquet (Un d'Escla)	FRA	66.65
3	Kristina Gifford (Midnight Blue II)	GBR	67.00

Duroy also won the Continental Cup Final (Europe)

BRAMHAM, ENGLAND *June 9-12*

1	Blyth Tait (Aspyring)	NZL	50.00
2	Ian Stark (Kilcoran)	GBR	52.00
3	Andrew Nicholson (Walk on Cloud)	NZL	56.60

GAWLER, AUSTRALIA *Aug 11-13*

1	John Bird (Corporal Clyde)	AUS	69.40
2	Samantha Seaton (Past Time)	AUS	83.80
3	Brian Schrapel (Boongarry)	AUS	91.45

Sonja Johnson on Floating Dollar (93.85) won the Continental Cup Final (AUS/NZ)

BURGHLEY, ENGLAND *Sept 2-4*

1	William Fox-Pitt (Chaka)	GBR	49.80
2	Mary Thomson (King Kong)	GBR	51.40
3	Karen Dixon (Too Smart)	GBR	52.40
4	Mary Thomson (Star Appeal)	GBR	54.40
5	Karen O'Connor (Pr'ce Panache)	USA	58.80

BLENHEIM, ENGLAND *Sept 16-18*

1	Nina Melkonian (West Star)	GER	52.60
2	Terry Boon (Vital Decision)	GBR	54.10
3	Stefano Brecciaroli (Pinezzo)	ITA	58.40
4	Franck Bourny (Royal Reseda)	FRA	59.20
5	Nick Campbell (Nietzsche)	GBR	64.20

FEI WORLD RANKINGS
As at Sept 25

| 1 | Karen Dixon | GBR | 322 |

6th Badminton, 1st Punchestown, 8th Bramham, 3rd WEG, 3rd Burghley

| 2 | Andrew Nicholson | NZL | 315 |

6th Punchestown, 4th Compiegne, 3rd Bramham, 7th Burghley, 1st & 5th Achselschwang

| 3 | Mark Todd | NZL | 278 |

6th Samur, 1st & 5th Badminton, 10th Chantilly, 2nd & 7th Falsterbo

| 4 | Mary Thomson | GBR | 269 |

11th Badminton, 4th WEG, 2nd & 4th Burghley

| 5 | Blyth Tait | NZL | 229 |

2nd Badminton, 1st Bramham, 1st Chantilly, 4th Blenheim

| 6 | Bruce Davidson | USA | 228 |

2nd & 7th Lexington, 4th Badminton, 1st Blenheim

| 7 | Matt Ryan | AUS | 174 |

12th Badminton, 5th Compiegne, 11th Bramham, 6th Burghley

| 8 | Vaughn Jefferies | NZL | 173 |

3rd Badminton, 1st WEG

| 9 | Kristina Gifford | GBR | 172 |

7th Badminton, 3rd Compiegne, 7th Bramham, 17th WEG

| 10 | Ian Stark | GBR | 172 |

8th Punchestown, 2nd Bramham, 3rd Blair Castle, 11th Burghley

Driving

Pairs Driving World Championships
Gladstone, USA   Oct 6-10

Team

1	Austria (Moser/Pointl/Wolfmayr)
2	Germany
3	Poland

Individual

1	Georg Moser	AUT
2	Vilmos Lazer	HUN
3	Horst Schepper	GER

AACHEN, GERMANY *June 14-19*
Nations Cup

1	Germany 234 (Freund/Hammann/Sandmann)
2	Belgium 254 (Standaert/van Dijk/Brasseur)
3	Sweden 261 (Eriksson/Gustafsson/Pahlsson)

Horses Four-in-Hand

1	Michael Freund	GER	111.8
2	Jan-Erik Pahlson	SWE	120.0
3	Felix Brasseur	BEL	120.8

Fencing

World Championships

Athens   July 3-8

Men's Foil

1	Rolando Tuckers	CUB
2	Alessandro Puccini	ITA
3	Thorsten Weidner	GER
3	Oscar Garcia	CUB

Women's Foil

1	Reka Szabo-Lazar	ROM
2	Valentina Vezzali	ITA
3	Francesca Bortalozzi	ITA
3	Laurence Modaine	FRA

Men's Epee

1	Pavel Kolobkov	RUS
2	Olivier Jacquet	SUI
3	Jean-MarieHenry	FRA
3	Arndt Schmitt	GER

Women's Epee

1	Laura Chiesa	ITA
2	Katja Nass	GER
3	Minna Lehtola-Kaaritianen	FIN
3	Corinna Panzeri	ITA

Men's Sabre

1	Felix Becker	GER
2	Stanislaw Pozdniakov	RUS
2	Bence Szabo	HUN

World Junior Championships

Mexico   Mar 31-Apr 2

Men's Foil

1	Matteo Zennaro	ITA
2	Tomer Or	ISR
3	Piotr Blaszczak	POL
3	Laurenzo Taddei	ITA

Women's Foil

1	Valentina Vezzali	ITA
2	Aida Mohamed	HON
3	Monique De Bruin	USA
3	Anna Rybicka	POL

Men's Epee

1	Gabor Boxzko	HON
2	Andrey Maly	UKR
3	Evgeny Fedossyev	RUS
3	Dirk Kunzelmann	GER

Women's Epee

1	Shaogi Yang	CHI
2	Imke Duplitzer	GER
3	Simona Iluti	ROM
3	Isabella Tarchini	SUI

Men's Sabre

1	Sergey Charikov	RUS
2	Domonkos Ferjancsik	HUN
3	Hervé Charron	FRA
3	Alexei Ermolaev	RUS

British Senior Championship

London   May 12

Men's Foil

1	Laurent Harper	Boston
2	Mark Heath	Salle Paul
3	Khaled Beydoun	Sussex H.
3	Tony Bartlett	Salle Paul

Women's Foil

1	Fiona McIntosh	Salle Paul
2	L Strachan	Salle Paul
3	Sarah Kellett	Boston
3	Sarah Mawby	Salle Paul

Men's Epee

1	John Llewellyn	Reading
2	Steven Paul	Poly
3	John Chalmers	Bristol
3	Tony Perity	Salle B.

Women's Epee

1	Carol Greenway	
2	Sheila Pearce	Watford
3	Karen Young	MPAGB
3	Helen Nicholas	MPAGB

Men's Sabre

1	Nick Fletcher	Salle Froh
2	James Williams	Salle Froh
3	Richard Cohen	Salle Froh
3	Ian Williams	H'smith

Women's Sabre

1	Sue Benny	
2	Lyn Bournemitza	

Challenge Martini

London   Mar 5

Men's Epee

1	Marius Strzalka	GER
2	Olivier Jaquet	SUI
3	Stefano Pantano	ITA
3	Kaido Kaabermai	EST
64	George Liston	GBR

Ipswich Cup

Ipswich   Apr 23-24

Women's Epee

1	Gyongyi Szalay	HUN
2	Katja Nass	GER
3	Hedwig Funkenhauser	GER
3	Isabelle Pentucci	SUI
15	Carol Greenway	GBR

Eden Cup

London   Nov 20,1993

Men's Foil

1	Lorenzo Taddei	ITA
2	Sven Hein	GER
3	Alessandro Cominotti	ITA
3	Thomas Engel	GER
20	Paul Walsh	GBR

Corble Cup

Hendon   May 7

Men's Sabre

1	Kirk Zavieh	GBR
2	Ian Williams	GBR
3	Gary Fletcher	GBR
3	Peter Ujvario	AUS

Commonwealth Championships

Whistler, Canada   June 20-24

Men's Foil

1	T Wong	HKG
2	D Waller	CAN
3	P Walsh	ENG
3	D McKenzie	SCO

Women's Foil

1	M-F Hervieu	CAN
2	S Mawby	ENG
3	S Wetterberg	CAN
3	L Harris	ENG

Men's Sabre

1	L Nowosielski	CAN
2	P Hoenigmann	SCO
3	N Fletcher	ENG
3	J Tanner	ENG

Men's Epee

1	L Shong	CAN
2	S Austin	WAL
3	S Weymouth	AUS
3	S Aspinall	ENG

Women's Epee

1	C Read	ENG
2	K-I Ro	HKG
3	H Landymore	CAN
3	C Greenway	ENG

Men's Foil Team
1.Canada 2.England 3.Hong Kong
Women's Foil Team
1.England 2.Scotland 3.Canada
Sabre Team
1.Scotland 2.Wales 3.Canada
Epee Team: Men
1.Canada 2.England 3.Australia
Epee Team: Women
1.England 2.Canada 3.Hong Kong
Overall Placing
1.Canada 2.England 3.Scotland

Richard Cohen finished third in the men's sabre at the national championships. It wasn't for the first time. Cohen, a 47-year-old editor, has placed in every national championships since 1969, the year The Beatles made Get Back. That long ago.

Golf

It was, unquestionably, Nick Price's year. In 1993, he won money - around $2.79m of it. In 1994, he won fame. It was evident the way he wrapped his arms round the Open trophy that fame was something he appreciated. He held the silver as you might hold a child. Two months later, he'd done it again, cuddling another cup as he took the US PGA title. Price is already a distance clear in the money winning stakes and another Sun City satchel could even see him exceed last year's amount. Yes, a good year Nick. Now back to Zimbabwe for a sport of fishing; return renewed and refreshed for the Masters and, if you can keep the roll going, the first man since Ben Hogan in 1953 to win three majors in a row.

Olazábal's victory at Augusta was blessed relief for a man who had played prince for rather too long; in his stead Ernie Els assumed the princedom. Though his victory in the US Open suggested that Els may already have his eyes on Price's lately established kingdom. Between them, Els, Price and Olazábal achieved something that no-one else has. They combined to prevent an American winning any one of the Majors. Since the inception of the Masters in 1934, one tournament at least (and very often all four) has been claimed by an American golfer. This year it has been two African golfers (another first) and if you want the statistics to back that argument up, the Sony Rankings at the end of September show four African golfers in the top 16; the same number as American golfers. Okay, the logic falls down if you count up the total number of golfers from the USA in the top 30 - over half at 16. Yet, there still isn't one American golfer in the top five. Make of that what you will.

Els won his Major in a furnace. It was hot enough at Oakmont for Montgomerie's caddie to need treatment. Montgomerie himself toiled heroically without help, though he did go a bit redder than usual. Notwithstanding a miserable play-off that he never got to grips with, it was still the performance of the year by a British male golfer. Montgomerie also returned from an average performance in the US PGA to win two European Tour events back-to-back which doesn't happen too often.

Tony Jacklin, who you may remember was the last British golfer to win the US Open, took another American Tour victory this year - 24 years later. Jacklin resigned from the Ryder Cup committee last December, presumably to work on his game approaching his fiftieth birthday and a place on the Senior Tour. It did not look such a great idea when he played the British Senior event - his first serious event since the birthday party - and was disqualified. Jacklin hit a ball in the bunker which bounced back and hit him in the chest. As Jacklin didn't know the penalty, he filled in the wrong score on his card and was disqualified. After thirty years, you might reckon he ought to know these things (like how much you lose when a ball bounces off your chest) but it happened at the thirteenth, so maybe he really was unlucky.

Anyway, to keep it short, five weeks later Jacklin wins the First of America Classic tournament and pockets a first prize of $97,000. It could be the start of something big for Jacklin. As you can see from our money earners lists, the Senior Tour in America is extremely serious business. In 1993, Dave Stockton and Bob Charles earned more money on the US Senior Tour than Colin Montgomerie (who led the field) on the European Tour.

Anders Forsbrand can probably lay claim to the worst professional round of the year. While the older members of the Senior Tour might chase the illusory target of trying to play their age, Forsbrand achieved the not inconsiderable one of playing three times his. At the French Open, on the National course at Paris, the 33-year-old Forsbrand had reached 93 strokes for 17 holes before he ran out of balls on the 18th. By that stage, the Swede had lost five balls in water and two more in waist-high rough. As he would have been playing his sixth shot on the 18th and faced a 115-yard pitch over water to reach the green, it is fair to estimate that he would have scored over 100. That would make him the first man on the Tour to achieve that since Mark James played one-handed in Sardinia in 1978. As Forsbrand could not return a score, he did not - according to officials - keep his card. However, we have managed to reconstruct the round and the details are as follows. Forsbrand , who probably wouldn't want to be reminded of it, should take some consolation that for many of us, breaking 100 (or even 110) is a significant leap forwards.

It wasn't a completely terrible year for Forsbrand who upheld a place in the top twenty

Forsbrand's Bad Day at the Office

Hole	1	2	3	4	5	6	7	8	9	out	10	11	12	13	14	15	16	17	18	in
Yardage	380	185	485	400	370	345	405	190	515	3275	345	175	400	375	505	385	160	430	470	3245 6520
Par	4	3	5	4	4	4	4	3	5	36	4	3	4	4	5	4	3	4	5	36 72
Forsbrand	4	5	5	5	4	4	8	4	4	43	4	3	9	10	6	8	3	7	8*	58 101
Over Par	-	+2	+2	+3	+3	+3	+7	+8	+7		+7	+7	+7	+12	+18	+19	+23	+23	+26	

* Estimated score

money winners for most of the season and must have been cheered by the selection of Valderrama as the 1997 venue for the Ryder Cup. Forsbrand is attached to the club. Seve Ballesteros was less enamoured of the decision. The Spaniard suggested, alleged and claimed that he had been offered an inducement of almost $1m to support the Valderrama bid and then implied, insinuated and inferred that the Ryder Cup committee members might also have been subject to similar inducements. Well, it was enough to rouse David Huish, a member of the Ryder Cup committee. "If Seve said that to my face, I'd punch him on the nose," he said. We have no reports that Ballesteros did say it to his face, but the Spaniard was on dodgy ground all round on this one. His support was for the rival bid of Novo Sancti Petri, but it was hardly an impartial advocacy. Ballesteros designed the course. Needless to say, after Ballesteros' attack the committee voted for Valderrama - which is not to say that they wouldn't have done anyway.

Ballesteros was on more solid ground with his complaint against original exclusion from the World Matchplay at Wentworth (he was later enlisted). No player has won the event more than Ballesteros (he shares the record of five wins with Gary Player) and he remains a potent attraction for spectators. That rejection of Ballesteros' highlights the ambiguity that arises when the promoter, players' agent, commentator, etc are all the same person. Mark McCormack is not a world- class golfer, which is fortunate, otherwise he would be ringing himself to negotiate with himself on behalf of himself to participate in an event that he himself was promoting. He could then appear on television and tell us how good the event was, how well he had put the field together, how marvellous it was dealing with a respectable agent like himself, how well he was playing and, of course, what a good commentator he is.

McCormack realised many rounds ago that there was money in golf, but even he might have been surprised by the value of a common-or-garden old golf ball. Actually, it wasn't so common or garden, it was feather-filled in Musselburgh in 1840 and still in mint condition. At auction, in July, it raised £12,075. Bobby Locke's ball when he won the Open at Troon, by comparison, made just £1,400.

It was the year in which one report talked of the growing number of anti-golf societies that are springing up, which seems a particularly futile exercise, and it was the year that a Nottinghamshire golfer, John Buckingham, spent something in the region of quarter of a million pounds to prove that he hadn't cheated and that Graham Rusk and Reginald Dove were lying. The jury dismissed the libel, thereby illustrating that the whole exercise was utterly futile and that the anti-golf societies might be right after all.

Paul Azinger put such trivia in perspective. The 1993 US PGA winner had the best season of his career last year, but in December a biopsy revealed the beginning of lymphoma cancer. Azinger underwent chemotherapy and for six months golf, in his words, "was pretty insignificant". He returned to the Tour in August, after completing just three rounds of golf, to an emotional response. At the Buick Open he shot a first round 76 and was cheered from the first tee to the last green. "Now I know what it feels like to be John Daly," said Azinger.

Britain and Ireland's women had the strongest nerves of the summer, holding on to the Curtis Cup that they won in Hoylake two years ago by the very narrowest of margins. It went, as they say, to the wire. Janice Moodie was the last of Britain's golfers of step out for the Sunday singles. She faced American Carol Semple Thompson in a match that was destined to decide the competition. Moodie, who is studying at San José State University, held her nerve in a match that went to the eighteenth. The final score at Chattanooga was nine all, enough to bring back the Cup. Moodie, who has won five college tournaments in the US, could probably make a reasonable living in the professional ranks now, but by her own admission is having too good a time at college to worry about that yet.

When she does, it will be some time before she can attack the record of Laura Davies who celebrated her 30th victory on the Tour when she won the Irish Holidays Open. Davies has won at least one tournament a year for the past ten years. She immediately followed the Irish Open victory with a success in the Scottish Open at Dalmahoy and her career earnings on the European Tour are now approaching £450,000. Liselotte Neumann hit the seasonal jackpot when she triumphed in the Weetabix British Open. The $52,500 prize money for the event makes it the richest competition on the European Tour by £18,000. In 1994, the Women's European Tour enjoyed £1,800,000 in prize money. It hasn't quite climbed back to the heady boom days of 1990, when it reached £1.9m, but the women's game, in both the professional and amateur ranks, is doing quite nicely, thank you.

David Johnson is a 49-year-old policemen who plays off six. Joe Jackson is a 47-year-old publican who plays off 15. Together they were playing the 140 yard 10th at Ravensworth Golf Club, Tyne and Wear. Johnson teed off first and the ball went straight into the hole. Jackson followed and his ball took the same path. "When we discovered the two balls in the hole, we went straight to the 19th to celebrate," said Johnson.

Odds against it happening: in the region of 1,845,000,000 -1. Bet they can't do it again.

The 123rd Open Championship

Turnberry Hotel, Scotland   *July 14-17*

268	**Nick Price (ZIM)**	**69 66 67 66**
	(£110,000)	
269	Jesper Parnevik (SWE)	68 66 68 67
	(£88,000)	
271	Fuzzy Zoeller (USA)	71 66 64 70
	(£74,000)	
273	Anders Forsbrand (SWE)	72 71 66 64
	Mark James (ENG)	72 67 66 68
	David Feherty (NIR)	68 69 66 70
	(£50,666 each)	
274	Brad Faxon (USA)	69 65 67 73
	(£36,000)	
275	Colin Montgomerie (SCO)	72 69 65 69
	Tom Kite (USA)	71 69 66 69
	Nick Faldo (ENG)	75 66 70 64
	(£30,000 each)	
276	Tom Watson (USA)	68 65 69 74
	Frank Nobilo (NZL)	69 67 72 68
	Ronan Rafferty (NIR)	71 66 65 74
	Jonathan Lomas (ENG)	66 70 72 68
	Russell Claydon (ENG)	72 71 68 65
	Larry Mize (USA)	73 69 64 70
	Greg Norman (AUS)	71 67 69 69
	Mark Calcavecchia (USA)	71 70 67 68
	Mark McNulty (ZIM)	71 70 68 67
	(£19,333.33 each)	
277	Peter Senior (AUS)	68 71 67 71
	Mark Brooks (USA)	74 64 71 68
	Vijay Singh (FIJ)	70 68 69 70
	Greg Turner (NZL)	65 71 70 71
	(£12,500 each)	
278	Loren Roberts (USA)	68 69 69 72
	Tom Lehman (USA)	70 69 70 69
	Peter Jacobsen (USA)	69 70 67 72
	Andrew Coltart (SCO)	71 69 66 72
	Paul Lawrie (SCO)	71 69 70 68
	Bob Estes (USA)	72 68 72 66
	Mike Springer (USA)	72 67 68 71
	Craig Stadler (USA)	71 69 66 72
	Ernie Els (RSA)	69 69 69 71
	Jeff Maggert (USA)	69 74 67 68
	Terry Price (AUS)	74 65 71 68
	(£7972.73 each)	
279	Lee Janzen (USA)	74 69 69 67
	Gary Evans (ENG)	69 69 73 68
	Mark Davis (ENG)	75 68 69 67
	(£6,700 each)	
280	Jose Maria Olazábal (ESP)	72 71 69 68
	Jean Van de Velde (FRA)	68 70 71 71
	Darren Clarke (NIR)	73 68 69 70
	Masashi Ozaki (JPN)	69 71 66 74
	David Gilford (ENG)	72 68 72 68

	Davis Love III (USA)	71 67 68 74
	Seve Ballesteros (ESP)	70 70 71 69
	Domingo Hospital (ESP)	72 69 71 68
	Brian Marchbank (SCO)	71 70 70 69
	(£6,100 each)	
281	Howard Twitty (USA)	71 72 66 72
	David Edwards (USA)	68 68 73 72
	Jim Gallagher Jr (USA)	73 68 69 71
	Greg Kraft (USA)	69 74 66 72
	(£5,450 each)	
282	David Frost (RSA)	70 71 71 70
	Tsukasa Watanabe (JPN)	72 71 68 71
	Mats Lanner (SWE)	69 74 69 70
	Katsuyoshi Tomori (JPN)	69 69 73 71
	(£4,925 each)	
283	Tommy Nakajima (JPN)	73 68 69 73
	John Cook (USA)	73 67 70 73
	Peter Baker (ENG)	71 72 70 70
	Brian Watts (USA)	68 70 71 74
	Ross McFarlane (ENG)	68 74 67 74
	(£4,700 each)	
284	Robert Allenby (AUS)	72 69 68 75
	Gordon Brand Jr (SCO)	72 71 73 68
	Bernhard Langer (GER)	72 70 70 72
	Per-Ulrik Johansson (SWE)	73 69 69 73
	Hajim Meshiai (JPN)	72 71 71 70
	Wayne Grady (AUS)	68 74 67 75
	Christy O'Connor Jr (IRE)	71 69 71 73
	(£4,350 each)	
285	Lennie Clements (USA)	72 71 72 70
	Carl Mason (ENG)	69 71 73 72
	Steve Elkington (AUS)	71 72 73 69
	Mark Roe (ENG)	74 68 73 70
	Ruben Alvarez (ARG)	70 72 71 72
	(£4,050 each)	
286	Wayne Riley (AUS)	77 66 70 73
	Warren Bennett (ENG)*	72 67 74 73
	(£3,900 each)	
287	Sandy Lyle (SCO)	71 72 72 72
	(£3,850)	
288	Colin Gillies (ENG)	71 70 72 75
	Craig Ronald (ENG)	71 72 72 73
	(£3,775 each)	
289	Joakim Haeggman (SWE)	71 72 69 77
	Ben Crenshaw (USA)	70 73 73 73
	Craig Parry (AUS)	72 68 73 76
	(£3,650 each)	
291	Nic Henning (RSA)	70 73 70 78
	(£3,550)	
292	John Daly (USA)	68 72 72 80
	(£3,500)	

* *Denotes Amateur*

Price and Parnevik - final round

Hole	1	2	3	4	5	6	7	8	9	out	10	11	12	13	14	15	16	17	18	in
Yardage	350	428	462	167	441	222	528	430	452	3480	452	177	448	411	440	209	410	498	432	3477
Par	4	4	4	3	4	3	5	4	4	35	4	3	4	4	4	3	4	5	4	35
Price	4	5	4	2	5	3	4	4	4	35	4	3	3	4	4	3	3	3	4	31	66
Parnevik	4	4	4	3	4	3	5	4	4	35	4	2	3	3	4	4	4	3	5	32	67

Final Scores (cont.)

The following did not make the cut:

144
Mikael Krantz (SWE)	70 74
Costantino Rocca (ITA)	73 71
D A Weibring (USA)	72 72
José Rivero (ESP)	72 72
Kevin Stables (SCO)	74 70
Howard Clark (ENG)	71 73
John Huston (USA)	71 73
Paul McGinley (IRE)	71 73
Christopher D Gray (AUS)	69 75
Miguel Angel Martin (ESP)	69 75

145
Eduardo Romero (ARG)	73 72
Miguel A Jiménez (ESP)	71 74
Gary Player (RSA)	72 73
Stephen Robertson (ENG)	75 70
Barry Lane (ENG)	73 72
Jack Nicklaus (USA)	72 73
Tony Johnstone (ZIM)	75 70
Michael Campbell (NZL)	72 73
Lee James (ENG)*	75 70

146
Mike Clayton (AUS)	71 75
Steven Richardson (ENG)	69 77
Peter Mitchell (ENG)	74 72
Fulton Allem (RSA)	73 73
Mike Harwood (AUS)	77 69
Andre Bossert (SUI)	74 72
Bradley Hughes (AUS)	72 74
Scott Simpson (USA)	73 73

147+
Bruce Vaughan (USA)	69 78
Paul Curry (ENG)	73 74
Andrew Magee (USA)	67 80
Lee Trevino (USA)	75 72
Sam Torrance (SCO)	74 73
Kirk Triplett (USA)	71 76
Hiroshi Goda (JAP)	71 76
Wayne Westner (RSA)	73 74
Gabriel Hjertstedt (SWE)	71 76
Craig Jones (AUS)	71 76
Gary Emerson (ENG)	75 73
Payne Stewart (USA)	74 74
Kenny Walker (SCO)	72 76
James Wright (ENG)	71 77
Steen Tinning (DEN)	75 73
Carlos D Franco (PAR)	72 76
Andrew Oldcorn (ENG)	77 71
Paul Broadhurst (ENG)	73 75
Jim McGovern (USA)	78 70
Gary Orr (SCO)	76 72
Francis Quinn (USA)	77 71
Gill Morgan (USA)	73 76
Des Smyth (IRE)	80 69
José Maria Cañizares (ESP)	80 69
Peter Smith (SCO)	73 76
John Harris* (USA)	73 76
Craig Evans* (ZIM)	74 75
Ian Baker-Finch (AUS)	73 77
Fredrik Lindgren (SWE)	78 72
Keith Walters (ENG)	75 75
Chip Beck (USA)	76 75
Cory Pavin (USA)	75 76
Carl Green (ENG)	75 76
Pierre Fulke (SWE)	77 74
Mark Mouland (WAL)	76 76
Ian Woosnam (WAL)	79 73
Phil Mickelson (USA)	78 74
Craig Cassells (ENG)	77 75
Bob Charles (NZ)	74 79
Rodger Davis (AUS)	77 76
Anders Gillner (SWE)	74 79
Paul Eales (ENG)	76 78
Joe Higgins (ENG)	78 76
Stephen Pullan* (ENG)	81 74
Eduardo Herrera (COL)	77 79
Andrew George (ENG)	74 83
Lee Fickling (ENG)	80 80

How fortunes vary. On day one, Jonathan Lomas, who had only qualified for the European Tour on his fourth attempt last year, took a mere 66 to be one off the leader (Greg Turner) after the first day. Nick Faldo, three-time winner of the championship and the golfer who has stayed longest at the top of the Sony Rankings, hit a despairing 75, which included a penalty for playing the wrong ball at the 17th. "This was not the cleverest thing that I've done," admitted Faldo, who had assumed his partner Jim McGovern had outdriven him (as he had all day) and did not identify his ball before striking it. Even at this stage, Faldo's misery was as nothing to Woosnam who hit a 79. Tom Watson took all the plaudits on the second day, taking a 65 on a Turnberry course that held fond memories. It was here in 1977 that Watson shook off the attentions of Nicklaus to record the second of his five British Open victories. However, already the bookmakers had earmarked the man they considered most likely; Nick Price. The Zimbabwean struck a 66 to move into fourth place. Norman and Els stayed in contention, while Faldo enjoyed a face-saving 66. No cut for Faldo. No trophy either. As the field concertinaed on day three, it was apparent that the serious business was all left to the final day. Watson, Brad Faxon and Ronan Rafferty all fell away from challenging positions. Fuzzy Zoeller and David Feherty sustained the pace, but couldn't quite match the play of Parnevik and Price. It looked to be the Swede's championship as he birdied at the 11th, 12th and 13th. The 16th and 17th, when Price struck a birdie followed by a giant putt for an eagle, tilted the balance. Price's score of 268 equalled the Turnberry Open record set by Watson - when he beat Price. The British born Zimbabwean hugged the trophy like he couldn't believe it. It was, after all, only his second major championship in almost twenty years on the circuit and he could hardly then have known how close the next was. He dedicated it to his mum in Norfolk which is some compensation for the fact that a Briton didn't win. Mark James and Feherty, who spent most of the summer on the US PGA Tour, came closest in shared fourth. Faldo and Montgomerie shared a respectable eighth place.

US Masters

Augusta National Course, Augusta, Georgia   *Apr 7-10*

279	**José Maria Olazábal (ESP)** ($306,000)	**74 67 69 69**
281	Tom Lehman (USA) ($216,000)	70 70 69 72
282	Larry Mize (USA) ($136,000)	68 71 72 71
283	Tom Kite (USA) ($96,000)	69 72 71 71
285	Jay Haas (USA)	72 72 72 69
	Loren Roberts (USA)	75 68 72 70
	Jim McGovern (USA) ($73,000 each)	72 70 71 72
286	Corey Pavin (USA)	71 72 73 70
	Ernie Els (RSA) ($60,000 each)	74 67 74 71
287	John Huston (USA)	72 72 74 69
	Ray Floyd (USA)	70 74 71 72
	Ian Baker-Finch (AUS) ($50,000 each)	71 71 71 74
288	Tom Watson (USA) ($42,000)	70 71 73 74
289	Can Forsman (USA) ($38,000)	74 66 76 73
291	Mark O'Meara (USA)	75 70 76 70
	Brad Faxon (USA)	71 73 73 74
	Chip Beck (USA) ($34,000 each)	71 71 75 74
292	Seve Ballesteros (ESP)	70 76 75 71
	Hale Irwin (USA)	73 68 79 72
	Bill Glasson (USA)	72 73 75 72
	Ben Crenshaw (USA)	74 73 73 72
	Lanny Wadkins (USA)	73 74 73 72
	David Edwards (USA)	72 73 73 74
	Greg Norman (AUS) ($24,343 each)	70 70 75 77
293	Bernhard Langer (GER)	74 74 72 73
	Jeff Sluman (USA) ($16,800 each)	74 75 71 73
294	Scott Simpson (USA)	74 74 73 73
	Curtis Strange (USA)	74 70 75 75
	Vijay Singh (FIJ) ($14,800 each)	70 75 74 75
295	Lee Janzen (USA)	75 71 76 73
	Craig Parry (AUS) ($13,300 each)	75 74 73 73

296	Nick Faldo (ENG) ($12,400)	76 73 73 74
297	Sam Torrance (SCO)	76 73 74 74
	Russ Cochrane (USA) ($11,550 each)	71 74 74 78
298	Nick Price (ZIM)	74 73 74 77
	David Frost (RSA)	74 71 75 78
	Fuzzy Zoeller (USA) ($10,300 each)	74 72 74 78
299	Sandy Lyle (SCO)	75 73 78 73
	Fred Funk (USA)	79 70 75 75
	Fulton Allem (RSA) ($9,000 each)	69 77 76 77
300	Costantino Rocca (ITA)	79 70 78 73
	Mike Standly (USA)	77 69 79 75
	Andrew McGee (USA)	74 74 76 76
	Hajim Meshiai (JPN)	71 71 80 78
	Wayne Grady (AUS) ($7,400 each)	74 73 73 80

301 Ian Woosnam (WAL)76 73 77 75, John Cook (USA) 77 72 77 75 ($6,000 each)
304 John Daly (USA) 76 73 77 78, Howard Twitty (USA) 73 76 74 81($5,250 each)
305 Jeff Maggert (USA) 75 73 82 75 ($5,000)J Harris* 72 76 80 77

The following did not make the cut: 150
Mark Calcavecchia (USA) 75 75; Rick Fehr (USA) 77 73; Nolan Hencke (USA) 77 73; Johnny Miller (USA) 77 73; Colin Montgomerie (SCO) 77 73; Jumbo Ozaki (JPN) 76 74; Gil Morgan (USA) 74 76;Gary Player (RSA) 71 79; Craig Stadler (USA) 76 74; Jim Gallagher Jr 74 77; Dudley Hart (USA) 76 75; Billy Mayfair (USA) 74 77; Brett Ogle (USA) 74 77; Danny Ellis (USA) 78 74; John Inman (USA) 76 76; Jack Nicklaus (USA) 78 74; Grant Waite (USA) 74 78; Peter Baker (ENG) 78 75; Bob Estes (USA) 77 76; John Adams (USA) 76 78; Billy Casper (USA) 77 77; Charles Coody (USA) 80 74; Anders Forsbrand (SWE) 80 74; Scott Hoch (USA) 75 79; Davis Love III 76 78; Steve Elkington (AUS) 81 74; Arnold Palmer (USA) 78 77; Tommy Aaron (USA) 76 80; Payne Stewart (USA) 78 78; Jeffrey Thomas* (USA) 78 78; Blaine McCallister (USA) 79 78; Barry Lane (ENG) 76 82; Iain Pyman* (ENG) 82 79; Gay Brewer (USA) 84 79; Doug Ford (USA) 85 withdrew

"I had struggled for too long," said Olazábal, whose form in 1993 had dragged him down to 18th on the European Tour money list. The attentions of John Jacobs (hired by the Spanish Golf Federation) to his wayward swing was enough to put him back on the road to good times. It was 1991 when Olazábal was last in sight of the Masters title, finishing runner-up that year to Woosnam. Since then, no green jacket, but rather the promise of the world's best young golfer has hung uncomfortably around his shoulders. The Spaniard came into the tournament in good form, having set his season off on the right course with a March win in the Turespaña Open. However, a first round 74 was hardly a blasting opener. It was on the second day, playing alongside Fuzzy Zoeller, that Olazábal found his feet. In a capricious wind, the Spaniard scored five birdies in a round of 67 to move into the slipstream of Larry Mize and Tom Lehman. With Olazábal and Lehman holding up on the third day with 69s and Mize slipping away, the field entered the final day in crocodile formation. In the final round, it took Olazábal eight holes to catch Lehman, another four to move ahead. Even then it was far from over. The Spaniard's teetered on the edge of the water at the 15th, Lehman contributed his share by missing a birdie putt at the 16th and Olazábal three-putted at the 17th. When he struck a four at the final hole, you could probably hear the sighs from back in Fuenterrabia. Olazábal, although only 28, at last had won a Major title. It was fitting that the second European home was Ballesteros, so inspirational in the development of Olazábal.

US Open

Oakmont Country Club, Pennsylvania   June 16-19

279	Ernie Els (RSA)	66 71 69 73
	Els won after a play-off. See below	
	($320,000)	
	Colin Montgomerie (SCO)	71 65 73 70
	Loren Roberts (USA)	76 69 64 70
	($141,827 each)	
280	Curtis Strange (USA)	70 70 70 70
	($75,728)	
282	John Cook (USA)	73 65 73 71
	($61,318)	
283	Clark Dennis (USA)	71 71 70 71
	Greg Norman (AUS)	71 71 69 72
	Tom Watson (USA)	68 73 68 74
	($49,485 each)	
284	Duffy Waldorf (USA)	74 68 73 69
	Jeff Maggert (USA)	71 68 75 70
	Jeff Sluman (USA)	72 69 72 71
	Frank Nobilo (NZL)	69 71 68 76
	($37,179 each)	
285	Jim McGovern (USA)	73 69 74 69
	Scott Hoch (USA)	72 72 70 71
	David Edwards (USA)	73 65 75 72
	($29,767 each)	
286	Fred Couples (USA)	72 71 69 74
	Steve Lowery (USA)	71 71 68 76
	($25,899 each)	
287	Scott Verplank (USA)	70 72 75 70
	Seve Ballesteros (ESP)	72 72 70 73
	Hale Irwin (USA)	69 69 71 78
	$22,477 each)	
288	Sam Torrance (SCO)	72 71 76 69
	Steve Pate (USA)	74 66 71 77
	$19,464 each)	

289 Bernhard Langer (GER) 72 72 73 72, Kirk Triplett (USA) 70 71 71 77 ($17,223 each); 290 Mike Springer (USA) 74 72 73 71, Craig Parry (AUS) 78 68 71 73, Chip Beck (USA) 73 73 70 74 ($14,705 each); 292 Davis Love III (USA)74 72 74 72, Jim Furyk (USA) 74 69 74 75, Lennie Clements (USA) 73 71 73 75, Jack Nicklaus (USA) 69 70 77 76, Masashi Ozaki (JPN) 70 73 69 80 ($11,514 each); 293 Mark Carnevale (USA) 75 72 76 70, Tom Lehman (USA) 77 68 74 76, Fulton Allem (RSA) 73 70 74 76, Tom Kite (USA) 73 71 72 77, Ben Crenshaw (USA) 71 74 70 78, Brad Faxon (USA) 73 69 71 80 ($9,578 each), 294 Bradley Hughes (AUS) 71 72 77 74, Peter Baker (ENG) 73 73 73 75, Gordon Brand Jr (SCO)73 71 73 77, Brandt Jobe (USA) 72 74 68 80 ($8,005 each); Francis Quinn (USA)75 72 73 75 ($7,222); 296 Paul Goydos (USA) 74 72 79 71, Fred Funk (USA) 74 71 74 77, Don Walsworth (USA) 71 75 73 77 ($6,585 each); 297 Tim Dunlavey (USA) 76 70 78 73, Olin Browne (USA) 74 73 77 73, Barry Lane (ENG) 77 70 76 74, Mike Emery Jr (USA) 74 73 75 75, David Berganio Jr (USA) 73 72 76 76, Jim Gallagher (USA) 74 68 77 78, Wayne Levi (USA) 76 70 73 78, Phil Mickelson (USA)75 70 73 79 ($5,105 each); 298 Tommy Armour III (USA) 73 73 79 73, Hugh Royer (USA) 72 71 77 78, Scott Simpson (USA) 73 74 73 78 ($4,324 each);299 Steven Richardson (ENG) 74 73 76, Fuzzy Zoeller (USA) 76 70 76 77 ($4,105 each); 301 Dave Rummells (USA) 71 74 82 74, Doug Martin (USA) 76 70 74 81 ($3,967 each); 302 Ed Humenik (USA) 74 72 81 75, Emlyn Aubrey (USA) 72 69 81 80, Mike Smith (USA 74 73 78 77 ($3,800 each).

*Those who missed cut include:*Nick Faldo (ENG)73 75, Nick Price (ZIM) 76 72, Ian Woosnam (WAL) 77 75

The Play-off

Hole	1	2	3	4	5	6	7	8	9	out	10	11	12	13	14	15	16	17	18	in
Yardage	463	342	421	560	378	195	431	249	474	3513	458	378	598	181	356	467	228	315	452	3433
Par	*4*	*4*	*4*	*5*	*4*	*3*	*4*	*3*	*5*	*36*	*4*	*4*	*5*	*3*	*4*	*4*	*3*	*4*	*4*	*35*	*71*
Els	5	7	3	5	4	3	3	4	4	38	5	4	6	3	4	4	3	3	4	36	74
Roberts	4	5	4	5	·6	2	4	4	4	38	5	4	5	3	4	4	4	3	4	36	74
Montgomerie	4	6	6	5	4	4	4	4	5	42	4	6	5	2	4	4	3	4	4	36	78

Els beat Robert on the second extra hole.

Tom Watson had forecast scores closer to the nineties that the sixties in his criticisms of the course. Watson, whose only victory in the Open was at Pebble Beach in 1982, defied his own predictions by leading the field through the first day with a 68. On his heels was Nicklaus, a four-time Open winner, who gets nearer playing his age as each year progresses. At 54, he hit a 69. Okay, there's way to go, but it was still impressive. Nicklaus, though, lacks the stamina to stay in contention, especially in conditions like Oakmont, where the sun was almost cripplingly hot. Montgomerie suffered, but still came his closest yet to winning a Major. Montgomerie, on a course that rewards the straight hitter, set up his chances with a sparkling second round 65. The Scot faltered slightly on the third day as the impressive Els took just 30 shots to the turn. It was Loren Roberts, though, who posted the lowest score of the tournament with a 64 the same day. On day four, Montgomerie and Roberts were steady; Els less so. At the end of the day, the three could not be divided and set up the first three-way play-off in the US Open since 1963. Day five began badly for both Montgomerie and Els, as they took a six and seven respectively at the par four second. Els recovered to take a three at the third, the Scot never did recover. At the turn, Els and Roberts were four shots clear as Montgomerie played some of his worst golf of the year. "I never got to grips with my game," he admitted. At the end of 18 holes, Els and Roberts were still inseparable and it took two more holes (sudden death this time) before Els could claim his first Major title.

QUOTES

"Go there. Be patient. You know what you have got to do. You're the best in the world" - **Seve Ballesteros' message, pinned to Olazábal's locker at Augusta.**

"I felt like I was staring at a grey prison wall. Now I'm on the other side and it's all green with trees and lakes and flowers" - **José Marie Olazábal, after having won the Masters.**

"Bunkers are not meant to be places of pleasure. They are supposed to be for repentance" - **Michael Bonallack, secretary of the R & A, at the Open.**

"Every time I made a birdie, I heard yet another roar from behind me. I thought, 'Shoot' someone must be playing unbelievably back there" - **Jesper Parnevik, feeling the breath of Nick Price on the final round of the Open.**

"In 1982, I had my left hand on it. In 1988, I had my right hand on it. And now I've got both hands on it and doesn't it feel good" - **Nick Price, on winning the Open after twice being runner-up.**

"I've got to believe now that I'm actually quite good at this game" - **Colin Montgomerie, having deposed Nick Faldo as Europe's number one.**

"The cheques are so small these days, I can't afford to eat much" - **Seve Ballesteros, on how he's slimmed down.**

"At one point I got into so much rough that I found a sabre-toothed tiger and a woolly mammoth" - **Mark Roe, on a bad day at the Turespaña Open.**

"I wouldn't be surprised if he came on holiday with us" - **Glendryth Woosnam, wife of Ian, on John Daly, who has regularly ended up playing with her husband in tournaments.**

"It's the longest relationship I've ever had" - **John Daly, on Ian Woosnam.**

"It's been so bad people think I must have been having too many beers" - **Ian Woosnam, on his lack of form.**

"This is the first time I've won when sober" - **Daly again, after winning the Bell South Classic in May.**

"When I turn professional I want to make a lot of money, I don't want to be making up the numbers" - **Janice Moodie, Curtis Cup player, on why she isn't turning professional just yet.**

"There'll only be three players in the field. They'll play one hole a day for three days and the winner is the guy who can remember his score" - **Lee Trevino, on his plan for a Super Super Super Super Super Seniors' Tour, for players aged 95 and over.**

"I know that people are going to look at me differently because I've had cancer, are going to admire me maybe more than I deserve. I'm no hero" - **Paul Azinger, after returning to golf following chemotherapy for cancer.**

US PGA

Southern Hills GC, Tulsa   *Aug 11-14*

269	**Nick Price (ZIM)**	67 65 70 67
	($310,000)	
275	Corey Pavin (USA)	70 67 69 69
	($160,000)	
276	Phil Mickelson (USA)	68 71 67 70
	($110,000)	
277	Nick Faldo (ENG)	73 67 71 66
	Greg Norman (AUS)	71 69 67 70
	John Cook (USA)	71 67 69 70
	($76,666 each)	
278	Steve Elkington (AUS)	73 70 66 69
	José Maria Olazábal (ESP)	72 66 70 70
	($57,500 each)	
279	Ian Woosnam (WAL)	68 72 73 66
	Tom Kite (USA)	72 68 69 70
	Loren Roberts (USA)	69 72 67 71
	Tom Watson (USA)	69 72 67 71
	Ben Crenshaw (USA)	70 67 70 72
	($41,000 each)	
280	Jay Haas (USA)	70 67 68 75
	($32,000)	
281	Larry Mize (USA)	72 72 67 70
	Kevin Triplett (USA)	71 69 71 70
	Mark McNulty (ZIM)	72 68 70 71
	Glen Day (USA)	70 69 70 72
	($27,000 each)	
282	Mark McCumber (USA)	73 70 71 68
	Craig Stadler (USA)	70 70 74 68
	Fuzzy Zoeller (USA)	69 71 72 70
	Bill Glasson (USA)	71 73 68 70
	Craig Parry (AUS)	70 69 70 73
	($18,666 each)	
283	Bernhard Langer (GER)	73 71 67 72
	Barry Lane (ENG)	70 73 68 72
	David Frost (RSA)	70 71 69 73
	Jeff Sluman (USA)	70 72 66 75
	Ernie Els (RSA)	68 71 69 75
	($13,000 each)	
284	Brad Faxon (USA)	72 73 73 66
	Wayne Grady (AUS)	75 68 71 70
	Lennie Clements (USA)	74 70 69 71
	Sam Torrance (SCO)	69 75 69 71
	Bob Boyd (USA)	72 71 70 71
	Richard Zokol (CAN)	77 67 67 73
	($8,458 each)	
285	Chip Beck (USA)	72 70 72 71
	Colin Montgomerie (SCO)	67 76 70 72
	Blaine McCallister (USA)	74 64 75 72
	($7,000 each)	
286	Fred Couples (USA)	68 74 75 69
	Billy Mayfair (USA)	73 72 71 70
	Hale Irwin (USA)	75 69 68 74
	Tom Lehman (USA)	73 71 68 74
	Gil Morgan (USA)	71 68 73 74
	($6,030 each)	
287	Neal Lancaster (USA)	73 72 72 70
	David Edwards (USA)	72 70 74 71
	David Gilford (ENG)	69 73 73 72
	($5,200 each)	
288	Billy Andrade (USA)	71 71 78 68
	Andrew McGee (USA)	70 74 71 73
	Bob Estes (USA)	72 71 72 73
	Fulton Allem (RSA)	74 67 74 73
	Greg Kraft (USA)	74 69 70 75
	Frank Nobilo (NZL)	72 67 74 75
	Masashi Ozaki (JPN)	71 69 72 76
	DA Weibring (USA)	69 73 70 76
	($4,112 each)	

289 Dudley Hart (USA) 72 71 75 71, Fred Funk
(USA) 76 69 72 72, Hal Sutton (USA) 76 69 72 72,
Tom Dolby (USA) 73 68 75 73, Kenny Perry (USA)
78 67 70 74, Mike Springer (USA) 77 66 69 77
($3,158 each); 290 Raymond Floyd (USA) 69 76 73
72, Tommy Nakajima (JPN) 73 71 74 72, Ron
McDougal (USA) 76 69 72 73, Lanny Wadkins (USA)
69 73 73 75, Bruce Fleisher (USA) 75 68 72 75 ($2,800
each); 291 Payne Stewart (USA) 72 73 72 74, Lee
Janzen (USA) 73 71 73 74, Jay Don Blake (USA) 72
71 74 74, John Inman (USA) 70 72 72 76, Todd Smith
(USA) 74 69 71 77 ($2,600 each); 292 Donnie
Hammond (USA) 74 69 76 73, Peter Senior (AUS) 74
71 70 77 ($2,512 each); 297 Sandy Lyle (SCO) 75 70
76 76, Dicky Pride (USA) 75 69 73 80 ($2,462); 298
Brian Henninger (USA) 77 65 78 78, Hajim Meshiai
(JPN) 74 71 74 79 ($2,412 each)
Those who missed the cut include: John Daly (USA) 73
73, Peter Baker (ENG) 76 71, Joakim Haegmann
(SWE) 72 75, Costantino Rocca (ITA) 73 77, Jesper
Parnevik (SWE) 79 73, Seve Ballesteros 78 76

Nick Price won his second Major of the season in a canter. The Florida-based Zimbabwean had said, a couple of days before the tournament, that every championship winner has : "One very good round, two good rounds and one no-so-good round". It defined his performance perfectly. A good round on the first day was good enough for a share of the lead, a brilliant second round (a 65 that only McCallister could better over the four days) took him clear. The dodgy round came on day three, when a five-stroke lead was reduced to two. Eleven straight pars were followed by a bogey on the twelfth and though Price recovered to finish the day on level par, it kept the championship open on the final day. Price had feared Norman, five shots off the lead as they entered the final round. In the end, he only had to fear himself. Only a self-inflicted wound could have deprived him of the title. Price became the first man since Walter Hagan to take the Open/PGA double and the first since Tom Watson, in 1982, to take successive Majors. No British golfer has ever won the PGA Championship so it has to be considered a good day when two Britons place in the top ten. Faldo finished top European after his final round of 66, but suffered on the greens earlier in the week. Woosnam's star is flickering again, if not yet burning brightly, and the Welshman started and finished the tournament well enough to suggest that he may yet add to the single Major he has so far collected. For Torrance, Gilford and Montgomerie in particular (the Scot shared the first-round lead), their first day was their best. For Montgomerie, at least, his performance shook him up. He returned to the European Tour and procceded to take the next two tournaments.

Sony Rankings

As at September 25th, 1994

	Player	Ctry	Pts/Evts	Average		Player	Ctry	Pts/Evts	Average
1	Nick Price	ZIM	1743/80	21.79	51	Gordon Brand Jr	SCO	402/85	4.65
2	Greg Norman	AUS	1458/70	20.83	52	Payne Stewart	USA	391/84	4.65
3	Nick Faldo	ENG	1207/73	16.53	53	Tony Johnstone	ZIM	428/92	4.63
4	Bernhard Langer	GER	1232/76	16.21	54	Mark James	ENG	315/68	4.60
5	José Maria Olazábal	ESP	1131/78	14.50	55	Mark Calcavecchia	USA	446/97	4.60
6	Fred Couples	USA	1027/74	13.88	56	Darren Clarke	ENG	377/82	4.59
7	Colin Montgomerie	SCO	1186/95	12.48	57	Robert Allenby	AUS	399/87	4.57
8	Ernie Els	RSA	1098/88	12.48	58	Chip Beck	USA	407/89	4.57
9	Corey Pavin	USA	914/85	10.75	59	Bill Glasson	USA	286/64	4.47
10	David Frost	RSA	1029/98	10.50	60	Rodger Davis	AUS	374/84	4.45
11	Masashia Ozaki	JPN	678/70	9.69	61	Craig Stadler	USA	362/83	4.36
12	Tom Kite	USA	719/75	9.59	62	Joakim Haeggman	SWE	322/74	4.35
13	Ian Woosnam	WAL	689/76	9.07	63	Constantino Rocca	ITA	375/87	4.31
14	Tom Lehman	USA	743/86	8.64	64	Bob Estes	USA	359/85	4.22
15	Vijay Singh	FIJ	869/105	8.28	65	Wayne Westner	RSA	340/85	4.00
16	Mark McNulty	ZIM	570/69	8.26	66	Naomichi Ozaki	JPN	391/99	3.95
17	Davis Love III	USA	684/88	7.77	67	Raymond Floyd	USA	234/60	3.90
18	Paul Azinger	USA	574/74	7.76	68	Steve Lowery	USA	307/79	3.89
19	Fuzzy Zoeller	USA	461/60	7.68	69	Anders Forsbrand	SWE	360/93	3.87
20	Loren Roberts	USA	602/79	7.62	70	Rick Fehr	USA	291/76	3.83
21	Seve Ballesteros	ESP	535/73	7.33	71	Brett Ogle	AUS	292/77	3.79
22	John Cook	USA	549/76	7.22	72	Sandy Lyle	SCO	316/85	3.72
23	Phil Mickelson	USA	480/69	6.96	73	Andrew McGee	USA	337/93	3.62
24	Larry Mize	USA	526/79	6.66	74	Mark O'Meara	USA	312/87	3.59
25	Brad Faxon	USA	571/87	6.56	75	Nolan Henke	USA	311/87	3.57
26	Tom Watson	USA	386/60	6.43	76	John Daly	USA	303/85	3.56
27	Jeff Maggert	USA	578/90	6.42	77	David Feherty	NIR	303/86	3.52
28	Hale Irwin	USA	398/67	5.94	78	Mike Springer	USA	304/87	3.49
29	Lee Janzen	USA	568/96	5.92	79	Todd Hamilton	USA	302/87	3.47
30	Barry Lane	ENG	592/103	5.75	80	Gil Morgan	USA	235/69	3.41
31	John Huston	USA	508/90	5.64	81	Duffy Waldorf	USA	292/86	3.40
32	Frank Nobilo	NZL	470/84	5.60	82	Tsukasa Watanabe	JPN	356/106	3.36
33	David Gilford	ENG	463/83	5.58	83	Bruce Lietzke	USA	204/61	3.34
34	Jesper Parnevik	SWE	404/73	5.53	84	Howard Clark	ENG	224/67	3.34
35	Tsun'ki Nakajimn	JPN	477/87	5.48	85	Jeff Sluman	USA	326/99	3.29
36	David Edwards	USA	422/77	5.48	86	Fulton Allem	RSA	299/92	3.25
37	Scott Hoch	USA	404/77	5.46	87	Ronan Rafferty	IRL	301/93	3.24
38	Steve Elkington	AUS	428/80	5.35	88	Dan Forsman	USA	264/82	3.22
39	Jay Haas	USA	465/87	5.34	89	Billy Andrade	USA	290/92	3.15
40	Sam Torrance	SCO	448/85	5.27	90	Carl Mason	ENG	262/84	3.12
41	Peter Senior	AUS	482/93	5.18	91	Peter Baker	ENG	269/87	3.09
42	Ben Crenshaw	USA	400/78	5.13	92	Retief Goosen	RSA	253/84	3.01
43	Craig Parry	AUS	474/93	5.10	93	Greg Turner	AUS	234/78	3.00
44	Curtis Strange	USA	376/74	5.08	94	Roger Mackay	AUS	206/69	2.99
45	Miguel A Jiménez	ESP	456/90	5.07	95	Masahito Kuramoto	JPN	256/86	2.98
46	Mark McCumber	USA	335/67	5.00	96	Lennie Clements	USA	200/69	2.90
47	Mark Roe	ENG	410/85	4.82	97	Steven Richardson	ENG	321/111	2.89
48	Eduardo Romero	ARG	372/78	4.77	98	Robert Karlsson	SWE	210/73	2.88
49	Scott Simpson	USA	367/77	4.77	99	Brian Watts	USA	186/65	2.86
50	Jim Gallagher jnr	USA	407/86	4.73	100	Rocco Mediate	USA	204/73	2.79

VOLVO EUROPEAN TOUR

Date	Tournament	Venue	Winner	Score	1st Prize	Runner(s)-up	Margin
Sep 30 Oct 3	Mercedes German Masters	Mönsheim Stuttgart	**Steven Richardson** (ENG)	271 (-7)	£100,000	Karlsson	2
Oct 7 -10	Alfred Dunhill Open	Royal Zoute Knokke-le-Zoute	**Darren Clarke** (NIR)	270 (-14)	£100,000	Nick Faldo Vijay Singh	2
Oct 14 -17	Alfred Dunhill Cup	Old Course St Andrews	**United States**	2-1	£300,000 (team)	England	
Oct 21 -24	Toyota Match Play Championship	Wentworth	**Corey Pavin** (USA)	1 hole	£160,000	Nick Faldo	
Oct 28 -31	Madrid Open	Puerto de Hierro Madrid	**Des Smyth** (IRL)	272 (-16)	£66,660	Westner, Rivero Hospital, Roe	3
Nov 4 -7	Volvo Masters	Valderrama	**Colin Montgomerie** (SCO)	274 (-10)	£125,000	Darren Clarke	1
Nov 11 -14	World Cup Golf by Heineken	Lake Nona Florida	**USA**	556	$130,000 (each)	Zimbabwe	5
Jan 13 -16	Madeira Island Open	Campo de Golfe da Madeira	**Mats Lanner** (SWE)	206 (-10)	£41,660	Mathias Grönberg Hedblom, Clark	2
Jan 20 -23	Moroccan Open	Golf Royal de Agadir	**Anders Forsbrand** (SWE)	276 (-12)	£58,330	Howard Clarke	4
Feb 3 -6	Johnnie Walker Classic	Blue Canyon C.C. Phuket, Thailand	**Greg Norman** (AUS)	277 (-11)	£100,000	Fred Couples	1
Feb 10 -13	Turespaña Open de Tenerife	Golf del Sur	**David Gilford** (ENG)	278 (-10)	£41,660	Wayne Riley Andrew Murray	2
Feb 17 -20	Open de Extremadura	Golf del Guadiana Badajoz	**Paul Eales** (ENG)	281 (-7)	£41,600	Peter Hedblom	1
Feb 24 -27	Turespaña Masters Open de Andalucia	Montecastillo Golf Resort, Jerez	**Carl Mason** (ENG)	278 (-10)	£50,535	José Maria Olazábal	2
Mar 3 -6	Turespaña Open Mediterrania	Villa Martin, Torrevieja	**José Maria Olazábal** (ESP)	276 (-12)	£50,000	Paul McGinley	-
Mar 10 -13	Turespaña Iberia Open de Baleares	Son Vida Majorca	**Barry Lane** (ENG)	269 (-19)	£41,616	Jim Payne	2
Mar 17 -20	Portuguese Open	Penha Longa GC Lisbon	**Phillip Price** (WAL)	278 (-6)	£50,000	David Gilford Eales, Goosen	4
Apr 1 -4	Open V33	Lyon GC Villette d'Anthon	**Stephen Ames** (TRI)	282 (-6)	£37,500	Pedro Linhart Gabriel Hjertstedt	2
Apr 14 -17	Tournoi Perrier de Paris	Golf de Saint-Cloud Paris	**David J Russell** (ENG)	260 (-20)	£70,000	Mark Mouland Spence, Baker	1
Apr 21 -24	Heineken Open Catalonia	Pais, Girona	**José Coceres** (ARG)	275 (-13)	£50,000	Jean Louis Guepy	3
Apr 28 May 1	Air France Cannes Open	Cannes Mougins	**Ian Woosnam** (WAL)	271 (-17)	£50,000	Colin Montgomerie	5
May 5 -8	Benson & Hedges International Open	St Melion Plymouth	**Seve Ballesteros** (ESP)	281 (-17	£108,330	Nick Faldo	3
May 12 -15	Peugeot Open de España	Club de Campo Madrid	**Colin Montgomerie** (SCO)	277 (-11)	£83,330	Mark Roe Richard Boxall Mark McNulty	1
May 19 -22	Tisettanta Italian Open	Marco Simone GC Rome	**Eduardo Romero** (ARG)	272 (-16)	£75,000	Greg Turner	1

Date	Tournament	Venue	Winner	Score	Prize	Runner-up	
May 27 -30	Volvo PGA Championship	Wentworth	**José Maria Olazábal** (ESP)	271 (-17)	£133,330	Ernie Els	1
June 2 -5	Alfred Dunhill Open	Royal Zoute GC Belgium	**Nick Faldo** (ENG)	279 (-5)	£100,000	Joakim Haeggman	-
June 9 -12	Honda Open	Gut Kaden Hamburg	**Robert Allenby** (AUS)	276 (-12)	£83,330	Miguel A. Jiménez	-
June 16 -19	Jersey European Airways Open	La Moye GC St Brelade	**Paul Curry** (ENG)	266 (-22)	£58,330	Mark James	3
June 23 -26	Peugeot Open de France	National GC Paris	**Mark Roe** (ENG)	274 (-14)	£91,660	Gabriel Hjertstedt	1
June 30 -July 3	Murphy's Irish Open	Mount Juliet GC Co Kilkenny	**Bernhard Langer** (GER)	275 (-13)	£98,765	Robert Allenby John Daly	1
July 6 -9	Bell's Scottish Open	Gleneagles Perthshire	**Carl Mason** (ENG)	265 (-15)	£100,000	Peter Mitchell	1
July 21 -24	Heineken Dutch Open	Hilversum GC Utrecht	**Miguel A Jiménez** (Spain)	270 (-18)	£108,330	Howard Clark	2
July 28 --31	Scandinavian Open	Drottningholm GC Stockholm	**Vijay Singh** (FIJ)	268 (-20)	£108,330	Mark McNulty	3
Aug 4 -7	BMW International Open	St Eurach GC Munich	**Mark McNulty** (ZIM)	274 (-14)	£87,500	Seve Ballesteros	1
Aug 11 -14	Hohe Brücke Open	GC Waldviertel Litschau, Austria	**Mark Davis** (ENG)	270 (-18)	£41,660	Philip Walton	2
Aug 18 -21	Murphy's English Open	Forest of Arden Warwickshire	**Colin Montgomerie** (SCO)	274 (-14)	£100,000	Barry Lane	1
Aug 25 -28	Volvo German Open	Hubbelrath Dusseldorf	**Colin Montgomerie** (SCO)	269 (-19)	£108,330	Bernhard Langer	1
Sep 1 -4	Canon European Masters	Crans-sur-Sierre Switzerland	**Eduardo Romero** (ARG)	266 (-22)	£111,290	Pierre Fulke	1
Sep 8 -11	European Open Championship	East Sussex National, Uckfield	**David Gilford** (ENG)	275 (-13)	£100,000	Costantino Rocca	5
Sep 15 -18	Dunhill British Masters	Woburn G & GC Bucks	**Ian Woosnam** (WAL)	271 (-17)	£108,330	Seve Ballesteros	4
Sep 22 -25	Trophé Lancôme	St Nom la Bretèche Paris	**Vijay Singh** (FIJ)	263 (17)	£100,000	Miguel A Jiménez	1

EUROPEAN MONEY LIST 1993
As at Dec 31, 1993

1	Colin Montgomerie	SCO	613,682.70
2	Nick Faldo	ENG	558,738.33
3	Ian Woosnam	WAL	501,353.41
4	Bernhard Langer	GER	469,569.64
5	Sam Torrance	SCO	421,328.19
6	Costantino Rocca	ITA	403,866.48
7	Peter Baker	ENG	387,988.84
8	Darren Clarke	NIR	369,675.08
9	Gordon Brand Jr	SCO	367,589.10
10	Barry Lane	ENG	339,218.47
11	Mark James	ENG	335,589.34
12	Ronan Rafferty	NIR	311,125.03
13	Steven Richardson	ENG	304,015.12
14	Frank Nobilo	NZL	294,598.76
15	Joakim Haegmann	SWE	287,370.84
16	David Gilford	ENG	273,301.31
17	Jesper Parnevik	SWE	272,511.73
18	José Maria Olazábal	ESP	249,493.14
19	Paul Broadhurst	ENG	243,588.17
20	Wayne Westner	RSA	226,297.89

EUROPEAN MONEY LIST 1994
As at September 30

1	Colin Montgomerie	SCO	602,919.58
2	Bernhard Langer	GER	418,945.85
3	José Maria Olazábal	ESP	399,607.57
4	Miguel Angel Jiménez	ESP	368,353.22
5	Seve Ballesteros	ESP	350,723.78
6	David Gilford	ENG	294,779.45
7	Mark Roe	ENG	289,139.66
8	Nick Faldo	ENG	269,142.64
9	Ernie Els	RSA	257,599.66
10	Eduardo Romero	ARG	253,197.04
11	Barry Lane	ENG	250,534.50
12	Vijay Singh	FIJ	248,545.00
13	Ian Woosnam	WAL	238,327.14
14	Howard Clark	ENG	236,345.60
15	Mark McNulty	ZIM	232,049.66
16	Robert Allenby	AUS	222,322.01
17	Peter Mitchell	ENG	208,869.73
18	Carl Mason	ENG	191,349.31
19	Anders Forsbrand	SWE	177,181.17
20	Jesper Parnevik	SWE	161,983.33

PGA EUROPEAN SENIORS TOUR

Date	Tournament	Venue	Winner	Score	Prize Money	1st Prize
May 13 -15	St Pierre Seniors Classic	St Pierre GC Chepstow	**Tommy Horton** (ENG)	212 (-1)	£50,000	£8,330
May 20 -22	La Manga Spanish Open	La Manga GC Cartagena	**Brian Huggett** (WAL)	215 (-1)	£100,000	£16,660
June 8 -10	D-Day Seniors Open	Omaha Beach GC Bayeux	**Brian Waites** (ENG)	206 (-10)	£50,000	£8,330
June 24 -26	Northern Electric Seniors	Slaley Hall Northumberland	**John Morgan** (ENG)	219 (+3)	£50,000	£8,330
June 30 July 2	The Tandem Open	Stockley Pk GC Heathrow	**Malcolm Gregson** (ENG)	205 (-11)	£52,000	£8,330
July 20 -23	Senior British Open	Royal Lytham &St Annes	**Tom Wargo** (USA)	280 (-8)	£220,000	£36,650
July 27 -29	Lawrence Batley Seniors	Woodsome Hall Huddersfield	**John Morgan** (ENG)	202 (-8)	£65,000	£10,170
Aug 5 -7	Forte PGA Seniors	Sunningdale GC Berks	**John Morgan** (ENG)	203 (-7)	£75,000	£12,500
Aug 12 -14	Belfast Telegraph Irish Masters	Malone GC Belfast	**Tommy Horton** (ENG)	208 (-5)	£60,000	£9,665
Aug 23 -25	Joe Powell Memorial Classic	Collingtree GC Northampton	**Liam Higgins** (IRL)	210 (-6)	£52,000	£8,330
Sep 2 -4	Shell Scottish Open	Royal Aberdeen	**Antonio Garrido** (ESP)	201 (-9)	£100,000	£16,660
Sep 22 -24	Zurich Pro-am Lexus Trophy	Breitenloo GC Zurich	**Liam Higgins** (IRL)	200 (-16)	£47,000	£7,850

The Amateur Championship

Nairn Golf Club   May 30-June 4
Fifth Round
Allan Turnbull (Peebles) bt
Martin Erlandsson (Sweden) 19th
Lee James (Broadstone) bt
Craig Watson (East Renfrewshire) 5&4
Gordon Sherry (Limarnock-Barassie)
bt Robert Shiels (Moray) 2&1
Kalle Brink (Sweden) bt Carl Duke (Porters Park) 19th
Semi-finals
Lee James bt Allan Turnbull 2&1
Gordon Sherry bt Kalle Brink 4&3
Final
Lee James bt Gordon Sherry 2&1

Seniors Amateur Championship

Formby & Southport/Ainsdale Aug 3-5
1	C W Green	Dumbarton	223 (72, 77, 74)
2	Curtis Wagner	USA	227 (78, 77, 72)
3	Idwal Fisher	West Bowling	227 (76, 77, 74)

Boys Amateur Championship

LIttle Aston GC Aug 8-12
Final
Christopher Smith (Scarborough) bt
Chris Rogers (Royal Mid-Surrey) 2&1

Youths Amateur Championship

Royal St Davids   Aug 11-13
1	F Jacobson	SWE	277 (66, 67, 71, 73)
2	S Hurd	Horsforth	279 (69, 68, 68, 74)
3	R Tate	Meon Valley	280 (71, 70, 67, 72)
3	S Davis	Kedleston Park	280 (68, 67, 73, 72)

English Amateur Championship

Moortown, Leeds   July 25-30
Final
M Foster (Worksop) bt A Johnson (Wyke Green) 8&7

Scottish Amateur Championship

Renfrew   July 25-30
Final
H McKibbin (Troon Welbeck) bt
A Reid (Barassie) at 39th

Welsh Amateur Championship

Royal Porthcawl   July 25-30
Final
C Evans (West Monmouth) bt
M Smith (Ross-on-Wye) 5&4

US PGA MONEY LIST 1993
As at Dec 31, 1993

	Player	Ctry	Evnts	Money $
1	Nick Price	ZIM	18	1,478,557
2	Paul Azinger	USA	24	1,458,456
3	Greg Norman	AUS	15	1,359,653
4	Jim Gallagher Jr	USA	27	1,078,870
5	David Frost	RSA	22	1,030,717
6	Payne Stewart	USA	26	982,875
7	Lee Janzen	USA	26	932,335
8	Tom Kite	USA	20	887,811
9	Fulton Allem	RSA	28	851,345
10	Fred Couples	USA	19	796,579
11	Jeff Maggert	USA	28	793,023
12	Davis Love III	USA	26	777,059
13	Larry Mize	USA	22	724,660
14	Scott Simpson	USA	22	707,166
15	John Huston	USA	30	681,441
16	Rocco Mediate	USA	24	680,623
17	Steve Elkington	AUS	23	675,383
18	Corey Pavin	USA	24	675,087
19	Vijay Singh	FIJ	14	657,831
20	David Edwards	USA	21	653,086
Also				
91	Nick Faldo	ENG	6	188,886

US PGA MONEY LIST 1994
As at Sep 25

	Player	Ctry	Evnts	Money $
1	Nick Price	ZIM	16	1,442,927
2	Greg Norman	AUS	14	1,255,164
3	Tom Lehman	USA	20	978,689
4	José Maria Olazábal	ESP	8	969,900
5	Loren Roberts	USA	19	920,570
6	Corey Pavin	USA	18	825,305
7	Hale Irwin	USA	20	759,836
8	Jeff Maggert	USA	21	712,475
9	Mike Springer	USA	21	710,717
10	Scott Hoch	USA	23	705,559
11	Steve Lowery	USA	27	701,048
12	Mark McCumber	USA	18	644,009
13	John Huston	USA	21	626,299
14	Ernie Els	RSA	10	624,440
15	Tom Kite	USA	21	604,089
16	Phil Mickelson	USA	15	601,316
17	Fuzzy Zoeller	USA	16	587,883
18	Ben Crenshaw	USA	22	562,852
19	Fred Couples	USA	12	561,854
20	Brad Faxon	USA	23	560,305
Also				
74	Nick Faldo	ENG	9	221,146
76	Colin Montgomerie	SCO	5	213,828

PGA SENIORS MONEY LIST 1993
As at Dec 31, 1993

	Player	Ctry	Evnts	Money $
1	Dave Stockton	USA	34	1,175,944
2	Bob Charles	NZL	29	1,046,823
3	George Archer	USA	32	963,124
4	Lee Trevino	USA	25	956,591
5	Chi Chi Rodriguez	USA	32	798,857
Also				
26	Gary Player	RSA	22	360,272
42	Jack Nicklaus	USA	6	206,028
64	Arnold Palmer	USA	18	106,232

PGA SENIORS MONEY LIST 1994
As at Oct 2

	Player	Ctry	Evnts	Money $
1	Dave Stockton	USA	27	1,268,885
2	Lee Trevino	USA	22	1,200,569
3	Ray Floyd	USA	17	1,121,074
4	Jim Albus	USA	30	1,032,533
5	Jim Colbert	USA	28	923,795
Also				
41	Tony Jacklin	ENG	11	185,222
99	Tommy Horton	ENG	5	14,894

PGA/NIKE TOUR MONEY LIST 1993
As at Dec 31, 1993

	Player	Ctry	Evnts	Money $
1	Sean Murphy	USA	26	166,293
2	Doug Martin	USA	20	147,003
3	Stan Utley	USA	22	144,127

PGA TOUR ALL-TIME MONEY
As at Oct 2

	Player	Ctry	Money $
1	Tom Kite	USA	9,104,818
2	Greg Norman	AUS	7,862,727
3	Fred Couples	USA	6,825,349

Nike Tour

Utah Classic	Sean Murphy	204	$27,000	Gtr Greenville	Scott Gump	272	$31,500
Boise Open	Tommy Moore	199	$36,000	Miami Valley	Tommy Armour	266	$36,000
Sonoma Cty	Sean Murphy	274	$27,000	Cleveland Open	Tommy Armour	275	$36,000
Bakersfield Open	Clark Dennis	202	$27,000	Dominion Open	Sonny Skinner	271	$36,000
Tour Champ'shp	David Duval	277	$36,000	Carolina Classic	Skip Kendall	276	$36,000
Inland Empire	Skip Kendall	197	$36,000	Gateway Classic	Brad Fabel	279	$36,000
Monterrey Open	Scott Gump	269	$36,000	Wichita Open	Den Postlewait	271	$31,500
Louisiana Open	Bill Porter	276	$31,500	Dakota Dunes	Pat Bates	276	$36,000
Pensacola Clssc	Bruce Vaughan	271	$36,000	Ozarks Open	Jerry Haas	272	$36,000
Mississippi	John Elliott	276	$31,500	Texarkana Open	Mike Brisky	266	$36,000
Panama City	Keith Fergus	202	$31,500	Permian Open	Bruce Vaughan	269	$31,500
Shreveport Open	Omar Uresti	270	$31,500	New Mexico	Jim Carter	272	$31,500
Alabama Classic	Tommy Tolles	274	$36,000	Utah Classic	Chris Perry	205	$31,500
Carolina Classic	Charlie Rymer	274	$31,500	Boise Open	Keith Fergus	198	$36,000
Georgia Open	Rick Pearson	273	$31,500	Tri-Cities Open	Jerry Haas	203	£31,500
Knoxville Open	Vic Wilk	275	$36,000				

US PGA TOUR

Date	Tournament	Venue	Winner	Score	1st Prize	Runner(s)-up	Margin
Sep 30 Oct 3	Buick Southern Open	Calloway Gardens Pine Mountain, GA	**John Inman** (USA)	278 (-10)	$126,000	Estes, Brooks Bryant, Andrade	Play-off
Oct 6 -9	Walt Disney World Oldsmobile Classic	Walt Disney Resort L. Buena Vista, FL	**Jeff Maggert** (USA)	265 (-23)	$180,000	Greg Kraft	3
Oct 13 -16	H-E-B Texas Open	Oak Hills GC San Antonio, TX	**Jay Haas** (USA)	263 (-21)	$180,000	Bob Lohr	Play-off
Oct 20 -23	Las Vegas Invitational	TPC at Summerlin Desert Inn, LV	**Davis Love III** (USA)	331 (-29)	$234,000	Craig Stadler	8
Oct 27 -30	THE TOUR Championship	The Olympic Club San Francisco	**Jim Gallagher Jr** (USA)	277 (-7)	$340,000	Simpson, Norman Frost, Huston	1
Nov 3 -6	Lincoln Mercury Kapalua Interntl	Kapalua Resort Maui, HI	**Fred Couples** (USA)	274 (-16)	$180,000	Blaine McCallister	
Nov 10 -13	World Cup of Golf	Lake Nona Resort Orlando, FL	**United States**	555 (-20)	$130,000 each	Zimbabwe	5
Nov 17 -20	Franklin Funds Shark Shootout	Sherwood CC Thousand Oaks, CA	**Steve Elkington & Raymond Floyd**	188 (-28)	$150,000 each	four teams	1
Nov 26 -27	The Skins Game	Bighorn GC Palm Desert, CA	**Payne Stewart** (USA)		$280,000	Fred Couples	
Dec 1 -4	JCPenney Classic	Innisbrook Resort Tarpon Springs, FL	**Mike Springer & Melissa McNamara**	265 (-19)	$120,000 each	five teams	
Jan 6 -9	Mercedes Championship	La Costa Carlsbad, CA	**Phil Mickelson** (USA)	276 (-12)	$180,000	Fred Couples	Play-off
Jan 13 -16	United Airlines Hawaiian Open	Waialae CC Honolulu, HI	**Brett Ogle** (AUS)	269 (-19)	$216,000	Davis Love III	1
Jan 20 -23	Northern Telecom Open	Tucson National Starr Pass, AZ	**Andrew McGee** (USA)	270 (-18)	$198,000	Roberts, Singh Blake, Stricker	2
Jan 27 -30	Phoenix Open	TPC of Scottsdale Scottsdale, AZ	**Bill Glasson** (USA)	268 (-16)	$216,000	Bob Estes	3
Feb 3 -6	AT & T Pebble Beach Pro-Am	Pebble Beach, CA	**Johnny Miller** (USA)	281 (-7)	$225,000	Maggert, Triplett Pavin, Watson	
Feb 10 -13	Nissan Los Angeles Open	Riviera CC Pacific Palisds, CA	**Corey Pavin** (USA)	271 (-13)	$180,000	Fred Couples	2
Feb 16 -20	Bob Hope Chrysler Classic	Indian Wells, CA	**Scott Hoch** (USA)	334 (-26)	$198,000	Fuzzy Zoeller Gallagher, Clements	1
Feb 24 -27	Buick Invitational	Torrey Pines GC La Jolla, CA	**Craig Stadler** (USA)	268 (-20)	$198,000	Steve Lowery	1
Mar 3 -6	Doral-Ryder Open	Doral Resort & CC Miami, FL	**John Huston** (USA)	274 (-14)	$252,000	Billy Andrade Brad Bryant	3
Mar 10 -13	Honda Classic	Weston Hills CC Ft Lauderdale, FL	**Nick Price** (ZIM)	277 (-8)	$198,000	Craig Parry	1
Mar 17 -20	Nestlé Invitational	Bay Hill Club Orlando, FL	**Loren Roberts** (USA)	275 (-13)	$216,000	Vijay Singh, Nick Price, Fuzzy Zoeller	1
Mar 24 -27	THE PLAYERS Championship	TPC at Sawgrass Ponte Vedre, FL	**Greg Norman** (AUS)	264 (-24)	$450,000	Fuzzy Zoeller	4
Mar 31 Apr 3	Freeport-McMoRan Classic	English Turn G&CC New Orleans, LA	**Ben Crenshaw** (USA)	273 (-15)	$216,000	José Maria Olazábal	3
Apr 7 -10	The Masters	Augusta national Augusta, GA	**José Maria Olazábal** (ESP)	279 (-9)	$360,000	Tom Lehman	2

Date	Tournament	Venue	Winner	Score	1st Prize	Runner(s)-up	Margin
Apr 14 -17	MCI Heritage Classic	Harbour Town GL Hilton Head, SC	Hale Irwin (USA)	266 (-18)	$225,000	Greg Norman	2
Apr 21 -24	Kmart Greater Greensboro Open	Forest Oaks CC Greensboro, NC	Mike Springer (USA)	275 (-13)	$270,000	Hale Irwin, Brad Bryant, Ed Humenik	3
Apr 28 May 1	Shell Houston Open	TPC at Woodlands The Woodlands, TX	Mike Heinen (USA)	272 (-16)	$234,000	Hal Sutton, Jeff Maggert, Tom Kite	3
May 5 -8	BellsSouth Classic	Atlanta CC Marietta, GA	John Daly (USA)	274 (-14)	$216,000	Nolan Henke Brian Henninger	1
May 12 -15	GTE Byron Nelson Classic	TPC at Las Colinas Irving, TX	Neal Lancaster (USA)	132 (-9)	$216,000	Yoshi Mizumake, Play-off Ogrin, Byrum	
May 19 -22	Memorial Tournament	Muirfield Village Dublin, OH	Tom Lehman (USA)	268 (-20)	$270,000	Greg Norman	1
May 26 -29	Southwestern Bell Colonial	Colonial CC Fort Worth, TX	Nick Price (ZIM)	266 (-14)	$252,000	Scott Simpson	Play-off
June 2 -5	Kemper Open	TPC at Avenel Potomac, MD	Mark Brooks (USA)	271 (-13)	$234,000	D.A. Weibring Bobby Wadkins	3
June 9 -12	Buick Classic	Westchester CC Harrison, NY	Lee Janzen (USA)	268 (-16)	$216,000	Ernie Els	3
June 16 -19	US Open	Oakmont CC Oakmont, PA	Ernie Els (RSA)	279 (-5)	$320,000	Loren Roberts Play-off Colin Montgomerie	
June 23 -26	Canon Greater Hartford Open	TPC at R. Highlands Cromwell, CT	David Frost (RSA)	268 (-12)	$216,000	Greg Norman	1
June 30 July 3	Motorola Western Open	Cog Hill G & CC Lemont, IL	Nick Price (RSA)	277 (-11)	$216,000	Greg Kraft	1
July 7 -10	Anheuser Busch Golf Classic	Kinsmill GC Williamsburg, VA	Mark McCumber (USA)	267 (-17)	$198,000	Glen Day	3
July 14 -17	Deposit Guaranty	Annandale GC Madison, MS	Brian Henninger (USA)	135 (-9)	$126,000	Mike Sullivan	
July 21 -28	New England Classic	Pleasant Valley CC Sutton, MA	Kenny Perry (USA)	268 (-16)	$180,000	David Feherty	1
July 28 -31	Federal Express St Jude Classic	TPC at Southwind Memphis, TN	Dicky Pride (USA)	267 (-17)	$225,000	Hal Sutton Play-off Gene Sauers	
Aug 4 -7	Buick Open	Warwick Hills CC Grand Blanc, MI	Fred Couples (USA)	270 (-18)	£198,000	Corey Pavin	2
Aug 11 -14	PGA Championship	Southern Hills CC Tulsa, OK	Nick Price (ZIM)	269 (-11)	$310,000	Corey Pavin	6
Aug 18 -21	The Sprint International	Castle Pines GC Castle Rock, CO	Steve Lowery (USA)	35 pts	$252,000	Rick Fehr	Play-off
Aug 25 -28	NEC World Series of Golf	Firestone CC Akron, OH	José Maria Olazábal (ESP)	269 (-11)	$360,000	Scott Hoch	1
Sep 1 -4	Greater Milwaukee Open	Brown Deer Pk GC Milwaukee, WI	Mike Springer (USA)	268 (-16)	$180,000	Loren Roberts	
Sep 8 -11	Bell Canadian	Glen Abbey GC Oakville, Ontario	Nick Price (ZIM)	275 (-13)	$234,000	Mark Calcavecchia	1
Sep 15 -18	BC Open	En-Joie GC Endicott, NY	Mike Sullivan (USA)	266 (-18)	$162,000	Jeff Sluman	4
Sep 22 -25	Hardee's Golf Classic	Oakwood CC Coal Valley, IL	Mark McCumber (USA)	265 (-15)	$180,000	Kenny Penny	1

Golf

SENIOR PGA TOUR

Date	Tournament	Venue	Winner	Score	1st Prize	Runner(s)-up	Margin
Sep 27 Oct 3	Vantage Championship	Tanglewood GC Clemmons, NC	Lee Trevino	198 (-18)	$90,000	D Weaver	5
Oct 4 -10	The Transamerica	Silverado CC Napa, CA	Dave Stockton	203 (-13)	$90,000	Lee Trevino Simon Hobday	1
Oct 11 -17	Raley's Senior Gold Rush	Rancho Muriela GC CA	George Archer	202 (-14)	$90,000	Bob Charles Chi Chi Rodriguez	1
Oct 18 -24	Ralphs Senior Classic	Rancho Park GC Los Angeles	Dale Douglass	196 (-17)	$97,000	Jim Dent	Play-off
Oct 25 -31	PING Kaanapali Classic	Kaanapali Resort Kaanapali, HI	George Archer	199 (-14)	$82,500	Lee Trevino Dave Stockton	Play-off
Dec 6 -12	Hyatt Senior TOUR Championship	Hyatt Dorado Puerto Rico	Simon Hobday	199 (-17)	$150,000	Ray Floyd L Gilbert	2
Jan 3 -9	Mercedes Championships	La Costa CC Carlsbad, CA	Jack Nicklaus	279 (-9)	$100,000	Bob Murphy	1
Jan 24 -30	Senior Skins Game	Mauni Lani Kohala Coast, HI	Raymond Floyd		$240,000	Arnold Palmer	
Jan 31 Feb 6	Royal Caribbean Classic	The Links Key Biscayne	Lee Trevino	205 (-8)	$120,000	Kermit Zarley	Play-off
Feb 7 -13	GTE Suncoast Classic	TPC of Tampa Bay Lutz, FL	Rocky Thompson	201 (-12)	£105,000	Raymond Floyd	1
Feb 14 -20	IntelliNet Challenge	The Vineyards Naples, FL	Mike Hill	201 (-15)	$75,000	Tom Wargo	3
Feb 21 -27	Chrysler Cup	TPC at Prestancia Sarasota, FL	George Archer	203 (-13)	$55,000	Simon Hobday	Play-off
Feb 28 Mar 6	GTE West Classic	Ojai Valley Inn Ojai, CA	Jay Sigel	198 (-12)	$82,500	Jim Colbert	Play-off
Mar 7 -13	Vantage at The Dominion	Dominion CC San Antonio TX	Jim Albus	208 (-8)	$97,500	Lee Trevino G Marsh, G Archer	1
Mar 21 -27	Doug Sanders Celebrity Classic	Deeerwood Club Kingwood, TX	Tom Wargo	209 (-7)	$75,000	Bob Murphy	1
Mar 21 -27	American Express Grandslam	Oak Hills CC Chiba-Ken, Japan	Lee Trevino	207 (-9)	$86,000	Gary Player	7
Apr 11 -17	PGA Seniors' Championship	PGA National GC Palm Beach Gdns, FL	Lee Trevino	279 (-9)	$115,000	Jim Colbert	1
Apr 18 -24	Dallas Reunion Pro-Am	Oak Cliff Dallas, TX	Larry Gilbert	202 (-8)	$75,000	George Archer Rocky Thompson	1
Apr 25 May 1	Las Vegas Senior Classic	TPC at Summerlin Las Vegas, NV	Raymond Floyd	203 (-13)	$135,000	Tom Wargo	
May 2 -8	Liberty Mutual Legends fo Golf	Barton Creek CC Auston, TX	Douglass/Coody	188 (-28)	$200,000	Rodriguez/Dent Murphy/Colbert	1
May 9 -15	PaineWebber Invitational	TPC at Piper Glen Charlotte, NC	Lee Trevino	206 (-13)	$112,500	Jim Colbert Jimmy Powell	1
May 16 -22	Cadillac NFL Golf Classic	Upper Montclair CC Clifton, NJ	Raymond Floyd	206 (-10)	$135,000	Bob Murphy Gary Player	
May 23 -29	Bell Atlantic Classic	Chester Valley GC Malvern, PA	Lee Trevino	206 (-4)	$105,000	Mike Hill	2
May 30 june 5	Bruno's Memorial Classic	Greystone GC Birmingham, AL	Jim Dent	201 (-15)	$150,000	Kermit Zarley B Charles & L Gilbert	2

Date	Tournament	Venue	Winner	Score	1st Prize	Runner(s)-up	Margin
June 6 -12	Nationwide Championship	CC of the South Alpharetta, GA	Dave Stockton	198 (-18)	$172,500	Bob Murphy	1
June 13 -19	Bell South Senior Classic at Opryland	Springhouse GC Nashville, TN	Lee Trevino	199 (-17)	$157,500	Dave Stockton Jim Albus	1
June 20 -26	Ford Senior Players Championship	TPC of Michigan Dearborn, MI	Dave Stockton	271 (-17)	$210,000	Jim Albus	6
June 27 July 3	US Senior Open	Pinehurst CC Pinehurst, NC	Simon Hobday	274 (-10)	$145,000	Jim Albus Graham Marsh	1
July 4 -10	Kroger Senior Classic	GC at Kings Island Mason, OH	Jim Colbert	199 (-14)	$127,500	Raymond Floyd	2
July 11 -17	Ameritech Senior Open	Stonebridge CC Aurora, IL	John Paul Cain	202 (-14)	$112,500	Jim Colbert Simon Hobday	1
July 18 -24	Southwestern Bell Classic	Loch Lloyd CC Belton, MO	Jim Colbert	196 (-14)	$105,000	Larry Gilbert Isao Aoki	2
July 25 -31	Northville Long Island Classic	Meadow Brook Jericho, NY	Lee Trevino	200 (-16)	$97,500	Jim Colbert	7
Aug 1 -7	Bank of Boston Senior Golf Classic	Nashawtue CC Concord, MA	Jim Albus	203 (-13)	$112,500	Raymond Floyd Bob Brue	2
Aug 8 -14	First of America Classic	Egypt Valley GC Ada, MI	Tony Jacklin	136 (-8)	$97,500	Dave Stockton	1
Aug 15 21	Burnet Senior Classic	Bunker Hills GC Coon Rapids, MN	Dave Stockton	203 (-13)	$157,500	Jim Albus	1
Aug 22 -28	Franklin Quest Championship	Park Meadows GC Park City, UT	Tom Weiskopf	204 (-12)	$75,000	Dave Stockton	Play-off
Aug 29 Sep 4	GTE Northwest Classic	Inglewood CC Kenmore, WA	Simon Hobday	209 (-7)	$82,500	Jim Albus	Play-off
Sep 5 -11	Quicksilver Classic	Quicksilver GC Midway, PA	Dave Eichelberger	209 (-7)	$157,500	Homero Blancas Raymond Floyd	2
Sep 12 -18	Bank One Classic	Kearney Hill Links Lexington, KY	Isao Aoki	202 (-14)	$87,500	Chi Chi Rodriguez	3
Sep 19 -25	Brickyard Crossing Championship	Brickyard Crossing Speedway, IN	Isao Aoki	133 (-11)	$105,000	Tom Wargo Jimmy Powell	

FNB TOUR (PGA OF SOUTH AFRICA)

Date	Tournament	Venue	Winner	Score	1st Prize	Runner(s)-up	Margin
Nov 1 -4	FNB Players Championship	Royal Johannesburg GC	**Mark McNulty** (ZIM)	273 (-15)	R90,850	Roger Wessels	5
Nov 25 -28	Zimbabwe Open	Chapman GC	**Tony Johnstone** (ZIM)	273 (-15)	R47,400	Nic Henning	8
Dec 9 -12	Philips South African Open	Durban Country Club	**Tony Johnstone** (ZIM)	267 (-21)	R90,850	Ernie Els	7
Jan 6 -9	Bells Cup	Fancourt Country Club	**Tony Johnstone** (ZIM)	271 (-17)	R82,950	Ernie Els	3
Jan 13 -16	Lexington PGA	Wanderers GC	**David Frost** (RSA)	259 (-21)	R90,850	Nick Price	7
Jan 20 -23	ICL International	Zwartkop Country Club	**Nick Price** (ZIM)	267 (-21)	R79,000	David Frost	9
Jan 27 -30	Telkom SA Masters	Lost City Country Club	**Chris Davidson** (RSA)	281 (-7)	R79,000	Bruce Vaughan	2
Feb 3 -6	Holland Insurance RS Sun Classic	Royal Swazi Sun GC	**Omar Uresti** (USA)	274 (-14)	R79,000	Andrew Pitts	2
Feb 10 -13	Autopage Mount Edgecombe Trophy	Mount Edgecombe Country Club	**Bruce Vaughan** (USA)	275 (-13)	R79,000	Tony Johnstone	P/off

PGA TOUR OF AUSTRALASIA

Date	Tournament	Venue	Winner	Score	1st Prize	Runner(s)-up	Margin
Oct 20 -24	Meru Valley GC Malaysia	Meru Valley Perak Masters	**Anthony Painter** (AUS)	275 (-13)	$36,000	John Senden	1
Nov 4 -7	Woodlands GC	Victoria Open	**Lucas Parsons** (AUS)	276 (-12)	$200,000	Bradley Hughes	3
Nov 11 -14	Royal Adelaide GC	Eagle Blue Open	**Wayne Smith** (AUS)	210 (-9)	$36,000	Jim Kennedy Kevin Miskimins	Play-off
Nov 18 -21	Concord GC Sydney	Ford Australian PGA Championship	**Ian Baker-Finch** (AUS)	275 (-9)	$63,000	Grant Waite Peter Fowler	Play-off
Nov 25 -28	Metropolitan GC	Heineken Australian Open	**Brad Faxon** (USA)	275 (-13)	$153,000	Michael Clayton Jeff Woodland	2
Dec 2 -5	The Lakes	Greg Norman's Holden Classic	**Curtis Strange** (USA)	274 (-18)	$126,000	John Wade	2
Dec 9 -12	The Grange GC Auckland	Air New Zealand Shell Open	**Terry Price** (AUS)	277 (-3)	$44,280	Michael Campbell B Faxon W Riley	1
Dec 16 -19	Hyatt Regency Coolum	Coolum Classic	**David Diaz** (AUS)	275 (-13)	$36,000	David Ecob Jeff Wagner	4
Jan 6 -9	Remuera Auckland	AMP New Zealand Open	**Craig Jones**	277 (-7)	$43,740	Frank Nobilo	1
Jan 20 -23	Kingston Heath Victoria	Optus Players Championship	**Patrick Burke**	280 (-8)	$54,000	Bradley Hughes	1
Jan 27 -30	The Vines Resort WA	Heineken Classic	**Michael Clayton** (AUS)	279 (-9)	$63,000	Wayne Smith	3
Feb 17 -20	Huntingdon Victoria	Microsoft Australian Masters	**Craig Parry** (AUS)	282 (-10)	$135,000	Ernie Els	3
Feb 24 -27	Castle Hill NSW	Canon Challenge	**Peter Senior** (AUS)	276 (-12)	$54,000	Chris Gray	Play-off

Women's Golf

Weetabix British Open

Woburn G & CC, Beds   *Aug 11-14*
Yardage: 6258   *Par: 73*

280	**Liselotte Neuman (SWE)**	**71 67 70 72**
	(£52,500)	
283	Dottie Mochrie (USA)	73 66 74 70
	Annika Soremstam (SWE)	69 75 69 70
	(£27,250 each)	
284	Laura Davies (ENG)	74 66 73 71
	Corinne Dibnah (AUS)	75 70 67 72
	(£14,625 each)	
285	Cindy Figg-Currier (USA)	69 74 68 74
	(£10,750)	
286	Helen Alfredsson (SWE)	71 76 71 68
	(£9,250)	
287	Tracy Hanson (USA)	74 73 66 74
	(£8,000)	
288	Suzanne Strudwick (ENG)	71 71 71 75
	Val Skinner	77 71 66 74
	Caroline Pierce	70 75 71 72
	(£6,250 each)	
289	Hiromi Kobayashi (JPN)	73 73 69 74
	(£5,100)	
290	Sarah Gautrey (AUS)	69 74 72 75
	(£4,800)	
291	Tania Abitbol (ESP)	76 68 75 72
	Penny Grice-Whittaker (ENG)	77 72 72 70
	Marnie McGuire (NZL)	71 73 78 69
	(£4,526 each)	
292	S Gronberg Whitmore (SWE)	71 69 74 78
	Li Wen-Lin (TAI)	73 70 73 76
	Jane Geddes (USA)	74 72 72 74

	Estefania Knuth (ESP)	78 69 72 73
	(£4,100 each)	
293	Pamela Wright (SCO)	68 75 78 72
	Karen Pearce (AUS)	70 74 75 74
	Kris Tschetter (USA)	68 76 75 74
	(£3,740 each)	
294	Kay Cockerill (USA)	71 77 73 73
	Amy Alcott (USA)	74 74 75 71
	Betsy King (USA)	73 74 69 78
	Alice Ritzman (USA)	69 76 75 74
	(£3,425 each)	

295 Susan Moon (ENG), Alison Nicholas (ENG), Dale Reid (SCO), Mardi Lunn (AUS), Kathryn Marshall (SCO), Lora Fairclough (ENG), Susan Redman (USA); 296 Trish Johnson (ENG), Evelyn Orley (SUI), Kristi Albers; 297 Leigh Ann Mills (USA) , Heidi Person (USA), Caroline Hall (ENG), Laura Navarro (ESP), Lori West (USA); 298 Tina Barrett; 299 Marta Figueras-Dotti (ESP), Karina Orun (DEN), Weny Doolan (AUS), Tina Fischer (GER)*, Julie Forbes (SCO); 300 Marie Laure De Lorenzi (FRA), Carin Hjalmarsson (SWE), Isabella Maconi (ITA); 301 Xonia Wunsch-Ruiz (ESP), Laree Sugg (USA), Karen Noble (USA); 302 Federico Dassu (ITA), Marjan De Boer (HOL), Gillian Stewart (SCO), Florence Descampe (BEL), Catrin Nilsmark (SWE), Sally Prosser (ENG), Muffin Spencer-Devlin (USA), Shani Waugh (AUS), Helen Wadsworth (WAL), Sandrine Mendiburu (FRA), Sara Robinson (ENG); 303 Nancy Scranton ; 304 Diane Barnard (ENG), Lisa Hackney (ENG), Elaine Crosby; 306 Mette Hageman (HOL); 307 Beverley New (ENG), Malin Burstrom (SWE), Nicola Moult (ENG), Mary Lawrence Wengler (USA); 309 Jennifer Lawrence (ENG), Sophie Gustafson (SWE) * *denotes amateur*

SPALDING
ORDER OF MERIT 1993

	Player	Ctry	Evnts	Money £
1	Karen Lunn	AUS	5	81,266
2	Laura Davies	ANG	9	64,938
3	Annika Sorenstam	SWE	9	55,927
4	Marie Laure de Lorenzi	FRA	10	46,479
5	Liselotte Neumann	SWE	4	39,530
6	Helen Dobson	ENG	6	38,179
7	Corinne Dibnah	AUS	10	34,429
8	Lora Fairclough	ENG	10	28,625
9	Frederica Dassu	ITA	10	27,707
10	Dale Reid	SCO	10	25,553
11	Mardi Lunn	AUS	8	23,495
12	Laurette Maritz-Atkins	RSA	10	23,145
13	Alison Nicholas	ENG	8	22,772
14	Catrin Nilsmark	SWE	10	21,052
15	Carin Hjalmarsson	SWE	10	19,309
16	Amaia Arruti	ESP	6	18,579
17	Trish Johnson	ENG	7	17,452
18	Janet Soulsby	ENG	10	16,393
19	Karina Orum	DEN	10	15,841
20	Mette Hageman	HOL	9	15,664

FORD
ORDER OF MERIT 1994
As at Sep 25

	Player	Ctry	Evnts	Money $
1	Lisselotte Neuman	SWE	4	102,750
2	Helen Alfredsson	SWE	5	63,315
3	Laura Davies	ENG	7	59,384
4	Annika Sorenstam	SWE	5	58,360
5	Corinne Dibnah	AUS	13	55,956
6	Tracy Hanson	USA	5	44,205
7	Lora Fairclough	ENG	12	43,369
8	Helen Wadsworth	WAL	11	41,979
9	Alison Nicholas	ENG	9	36,954
10	Sarah Gautrey	AUS	11	34,379
11	Florence Descampe	BEL	6	31,862
12	Karina Orum	DEN	13	29,610
13	Catrin Nilsmark	SWE	11	29,284
14	Trish Johnson	ENG	8	28,069
15	Joanna Morley	ENG	13	25,632
16	Dale Reid	SCO	12	25,427
17	Kristal Parker	USA	9	23,637
18	Susan Moon	USA	12	21,684
19	Laura Navarro	ESP	12	21,254
20	Sofia Gronberg Whitmore	SWE	9	20,453

Date	Tournament	Venue	Winner	Score	1st Prize	Runner(s)-up	Margin
Apr 21 -24	Ford Golf Classic	Woburn, Beds	**Catrin Nilsmark** (SWE)	284 (-12)	$15,000	Trish Johnson Joanne Morley	4
May 19 -22	Costa Azul Open	Montado & Aroeira Lisbon	**Sandrine Mendiburu** (FRA)	140 (-4)	£7,500	Lora Fairclough	1
Jun 9 -12	Evian Masters	Royal GC Evian	**Helen Alfredsson** (SWE)	287 (-1)	$34,875	Sarah Gautrey Lora Fairclough	3
Jun 16 -19	OVB Open	Kaprun GC nr Salzburg	**Florence Descampe** (BEL)	277 (-15)	$15,000	Tracy Hanson	Play-off
Jun 23 -26	BMW European Masters	Golf de Bercuit nr Brussels	**Helen Wadsworth** (WAL)	278 (-14)	$24,000	Tracy Hanson	3
Jun 30 -Jul 3	Hennessy Cup	Cologne GC Germany	**Lisselotte Neumann** (SWE)	277 (-11)	$33,000	Alison Nicholas	1
Jul 28 -31	Irish Holidays Open	St Margaret's CC Dublin	**Laura Davies** (ENG)	282 (-6)	£11,500	Carin Hjalmarsson Helen Wadsworth	8
Aug 4 -7	The New Skoda Scottish Open	Dalmahoy G & CC Kirknewton	**Laura Davies** (ENG)	278 (-10)	£11,250	Karina Orum	1
Aug 18 -21	Trygg Hansa Open	Haninge GC nr Stockholm	**Liselotte Neuman** (SWE)	274 (-18	$15,000	Corinne Dibnah	4
Sep 1 -4	Waterford Dairies English Open	The Tytherington Macclesfield	**Patricia Meunier** (FRA)	288 (-)	$9,000	M L de Lorenzi Corinne Dibnah	2
Sep 9 -11	Sens Dutch Open	Het Rijk Van Nijmegen	**Liz Weima** (HOL)	214 (-2)	$8,250	Sofia G Whitmore	2
Sep 22 -25	BMW Italian Open	Lignano GC nr Venice	**Corinne Dibnah** (AUS)	277 (-11)	$10,500	Dale Reid	Play-off

The Curtis Cup

Chattanooga, Tennessee   *July 30-31*

Singles - British/Irish names first

Saturday

J Hall halved with J McGill
J Moodie lost to E Klein 3&2
L Walton beat W Ward 1 hole
M McKinley lost to C Semple Thompson 2&1
M McKay lost to E Port 2&1
C Matthew beat S Sparks 1 hole

Foursomes

Saturday

Speak/McKay lost to Semple Thompson/Klein
Hall/Walton beat Kaupp/Part 6&5
Matthews/Moodie halved with McGill/Ingram

Foursomes

Sunday

Hall/Walton beat McGill/Ingram 2&1
McKinley/Rose Power lost to Sem Thompson/Klein 4&2
Matthews/Moodie beat Ward/Sparks

Singles

Sunday

J Hall lost to J McGill 4&3
M McKay lost to E Port 7&5
C Matthew beat E Klein 2&1
M McKinley beat W Kaupp 3&2
L Walton lost to W Ward 4&3
J Moodie beat C Semple Thompson 2 holes

Match Result

Great Britain & Ireland 9   United States 9
Great Britain & Ireland retain trophy

British Amateur Championship

Newport, Gwent   *June 7-11*

Third Round

J Hall (Felixstowe) bt M McKay (Turnberry) 5&4
C Matthew (N Berwick) bt K McKenna (Tynem'th) 8&7
C M D'Algue (FRA) bt A Rose (Stirling) 4&3
K Egford (Crane Valley) bt M Sutton (Blackheath) 2&1
A Adamson (RSA) bt K Speak (Clitheroe) 2&1
E Duggleby (Malton) bt C Grady (Bawburgh) 3&1
M Alsguren (FRA) bt S Lambert (Coombe H) 2&1
K Stupples (Cinque P) bt M McKenna (Donabate) 5&4

Quarter-finals

C Matthew bt J Hall 2&1
C M D'Algue bt K Egford 2&1
A Adamson bt M Alsguren 2 holes
E Duggleby bt K Stupples 19th

Semi-finals

C M D'Algue bt C Matthew 20th
E Duggleby bt A Adamson 2&1

Final

E Duggleby bt C M D'Algue 3&1

Gymnastics

Artistic Gymnastics
Individual
World Championships

Brisbane   *April 20-24*

MEN
ALL ROUND

1	Ivan Ivankov	BLR	57.012

(Floor: 9.450, P Horse: 9.562, Rings: 9.525, Vault: 9.500, P Bars: 9.375, H Bar: 9.450)

2	Alexel Voropaev	RUS	56.924
3	Vitaly Scherbo	BLR	56.350
16	Neil Thomas	GBR	55.200

(9.375, 9.125, 9.100, 9.425, 9.075, 9.100)

36	Paul Bowler	GBR	53.325

(8.625, 9.000, 8.475, 9.425, 8.775, 9.025)

40	Marvin Campbell	GBR	53.275

(8.675, 8.900, 8.825, 9.200, 9.025, 8.650)

APPARATUS

Floor

1	Vitaly Scherbo	BLR	9.725
2	Ioannis Melissandis	GRE	9.687
2	Neil Thomas	GBR	9.687

Pommel Horse

1	Marius Urzica	ROM	9.712
2	Eric Poujade	FRA	9.700
3	Li Donghua	SUI	9.662

Rings

1	Yuri Chechi	ITA	9.787
2	Paul O'Neill	USA	9.725
3	Dan Burinca	ROM	9.700

Vault

1	Vitaly Scherbo	BLS	9.674
2	Xiaoshuang Li	CHN	9.618
3	Hong-Chul Yeo	KOR	9.600

Parallel Bars

1	Liping Huang	CHN	9.775
2	Rustam Charipov	UKR	9.612
3	Alexei Nemov	RUS	9.575

High Bars

1	Vitaly Scherbo	BLR	9.687
2	Zoltan Supola	HUN	9.537
3	Ivan Ivankov	BLR	9500

WOMEN
All round

1	Shannon Miller	USA	39.274

(Vault: 9.812, Asym.bars: 9.850, Beam: 9.862, Floor: 9.750)

2	Lavinia Milosovici	ROM	39.236
3	Dina Kochetkova	RUS	39.125
38	Karin Szymko	GBR	36.142

(9.268, 9.300, 8.912, 8.662)

44	Annika Reeder	GBR	35.806

(8.881, 8.500, 8.925, 9.500)

47	Zita Lusack	GBR	35.518

(9.056, 9.175, 8.050, 9.237)

APPARATUS

Vault

1	Gina Gogean	ROM	9.812
2	Svetlana Chorkina	RUS	9.800
3	Lavinia Milosovici	ROM	9.787

Asymmetric Bars

1	Li Luo	CHN	9.912
2	Svetlana Chorkina	RUS	9.875
3	Dina Kochetkova	RUS	9.850

Beam

1	Shannon Miller	USA	9.875
2	Lilia Podkopayeva	UKR	9.737
3	Oxana Fabrichnova	RUS	9.712

Floor

1	Dina Kochetkova	RUS	9.850
2	Lavinia Milosovici	ROM	9.837
3	Gina Gogean	ROM	9.762

European Championships -Men

Prague   *June 2-5*

TEAM

1	Belarus	170.286

(Floor: 28.262, P Horse: 28.675, Rings: 28.250, Vault: 28.225, P Bars: 28.699, H Bar: 28.175)

2	Russia	169.848
3	Germany	168.911
12	Great Britain	159.725

(25.100, 26.350, 26.900, 27.125, 26.925, 27.275)

ALL ROUND

1	Ivan Ivankov	BLR	57.549

(Floor: 9.625, P Horse: 9.525, Rings: 9.612, Vault: 9.550, P Bars: 9.637, H Bar: 9.600)

2	Igor Korobchinski	UKR	56.799
3	Evgeni Chabaev	RUS	56.749

APPARATUS

Floor

1	Ivan Ivanov	BUL	9.687

Pommel Horse

1	Marius Urzica	ROM	9.787

Rings

1	Yuri Chechi	ITA	9.787

Vault

1	Vitaly Scherbo	BLS	9.662

Parallel Bars

=1	Alexey Nemov	RUS	9.725
=1	Rustam Charipov	UKR	9.725

High Bars

1	Aljaz Pegan	SLO	9.762

European Championships - Women

Stockholm   May 12-15
TEAM
1 Romania   117.785
   (*Vault: 29.549, Asym.bars: 29.325, Beam: 29.537,*
   Floor: 29.374)
2 Russia   115.422
3 Ukraine   115.221
11 Great Britain   108.884
   (*27.349, 26.987, 26.262, 28.286*)
ALL ROUND
1 Gina Gogean   ROM   39.411
   (*9.837, 9.825, 9.912, 9.837*)
2 Svetlana Chorkina RUS   39.224
2 Dina Kochetkova   RUS   39.224
14 Karin Szymko   GBR   37.305
   (*9.481, 9.312, 9.250, 9.262*)
APPARATUS
Vault
1 Lavinia Milosovici ROM   9.800
Asymmetric Bars
1 Svetlana Chorkina RUS   9.887
Beam
1 Gina Gogean   ROM   9.900
Floor
1 Lilia Podkopayeva UKR   9.937
7 Annika Reeder   GBR   9.675

Birmingham Classic

Birmingham Indoor Arena   Sep 30
Men
1 Ivan Ivankov   BUL   57.250
7 Lee McDermott   GBR   54.175
Women
1 Lavinia Milosovici ROM   38.913
1 Zita Lusack   GBR   37.650

Birmingham Classic - 1993

Birmingham Indoor Arena   Oct 8, 1993
Men
1 Sergey Kharkov   RUS   56.000
7 Paul Bowler   GBR   53.750
Women
1 Lavinia Milosovici ROM   38.300
7 Jackie Brady   GBR   37.325

Women's Internationals

Great Britain v Israel v Greece
Glasgow   Mar 6
1. Great Britain 185.10, 2. Israel 182.925,
3. Greece 181.85

Great Britain v Romania
Liverpool   Mar 26-27
1 Romania   194.675
   (*Milosovici 39.375, Hatagan 38.925, Amonar 38.800,*
   Gogean 38.625, Cacovean 38.475, Fuchs 37.625)
2 Great Britain   189.675
   (*Lusack 38.425, Brady 37.950, Szymko 37.300*
   Reeder 37.275, Leman 37.225, Acklam 36.800)

British Individual Championships - Men

Birmingham   Sep 23-25
OVERALL
1 Lee McDermott   Sutton   98.50
APPARATUS
Floor
1 Craig Heap   Lilleshall   9.25
Pommel Horse
1 Lee McDermott   Sutton   9.15
Rings
1 Lee McDermott   Sutton   9.60
Vault
1 A Minshall   Liverpool   8.925
Parallel Bars
=1 Lee McDermott   Sutton   9.2
=1 Craig Heap   Lilleshall   9.2
High Bars
1 Lee McDermott   Sutton   9.3

British Individual Championships 1993 - Men

Liverpool   Oct 1-3
OVERALL
1 Marvin Campbell   Manchester   104.10
APPARATUS
Floor
1 Paul Bowler   Manchester   8.90
Pommel Horse
=1 Marvin Campbell   Manchester   8.85
=1 Lee Rickets   N Staffs   8.85
=1 Robert Barber   N Staffs   8.85
Rings
1 Paul Bowler   Manchester   9.20
Vault
1 Paul Bowler   Manchester   9.00
Parallel Bars
1 Paul Bowler   Manchester   9.00
High Bars
1 Craig Heap   Manchester   9.20
1 Paul Bowler   Manchester   9.20

British Team Championships -Men

Liverpool   Feb 19-20
Adams Shiel: City of Liverpool GC 209.50
Williams Trophy: Central Manchester 'A' 202.90
Continental Cup: Central Manchester 205.45

British Individual Championships - Women

Guildford   Sep 24-25
ALL ROUND
1 Zita Lusack   Heathrow   73.637
APPARATUS
Vault
=1 Sonia Lawrence   Spelthorne   9.343
=1 Anna-Liese Acklam Camberley   9.343

Asymmetric Bars

| 1 Zita Lusack | Heathrow | 9.312 |

Beam

| 1 Anna-Liese Acklam | Camberley | 9.150 |

Floor

| 1 Annika Reeder | Loughton | 9.612 |

British Individual Championships - Women

Crawley   Oct 2, 1993

ALL ROUND

| 1 Jackie Brady | Alderwood | 36.5625 |

(9.5375, 9.050, 9.700, 9.275)

APPARATUS

Vault

| 1 Jackie Brady | Alderwood | 9.399 |

Asymmetric Bars

| 1 Jackie Brady | Alderwood | 9.187 |

Beam

| 1 Jackie Brady | Alderwood | 8.800 |

Floor

| 1 Jackie Brady | Alderwood | 9.537 |

Rhythmic Gymnastics

World Championships

Alicante   Nov 4-7

TEAM

| 1 Bulgaria | 94.750 |

(Rope: 18.700, Hoop: 19.050, Ball: 19,200, Clubs: 19.050, Ribbon: 18.750)

2 Ukraine	94.400
3 Russia	94.200
21 Great Britain	84.950

(18.650, 16.850, 17.300, 16.800, 17.150)

ALL ROUND

| 1 Maria Petrova | BUL | 38.975 |

(Hoop: 9.775, Ball: 9.675, Clubs: 9.700, Ribbons: 9.825)

| 2 Ekaterina Serebrianskaya | UKR | 38.775 |
| 3 Amina Zaripova | RUS | 39.025 |

Debbie Southwick GBR finished 27th

EXERCISES

Rope

| 1 Ekaterina Serebrianskaya | UKR | 9.775 |

Hoop

| 1 Maria Petrova | BUL | 9.825 |

Ball

| 1 Maria Petrova | BUL | 9.800 |

Clubs

| 1 Carmon Acedo | ESP | 9.775 |

Ribbon

| 1 Maria Petrova | BUL | 9.775 |

European Championships

Thessaloniki   May 26-29

TEAM

| 1 Ukraine | 95.700 |

(Rope: 19.150, Hoop: 19.450, Ball: 19,350, Clubs: 18.850, Ribbon: 18.900)

| 18 Great Britain | 85.600 |

(16.600, 17.500, 17.550, 16.750, 17.200)

ALL ROUND

| 1 Maria Petrova | BUL | 39.075 |

(9.750, 9.750, 9.800, 9.775))

APPARATUS

Rope

| 1 Elena Vitrichenko | UKR | 9.725 |

Ring

| 1 Elena Vitrichenko | UKR | 9.750 |

Ball

| 1 Amina Zaripova | RUS | 9.850 |

Clubs

| 1 Amina Zaripova | RUS | 9.825 |

Ribbon

| 1 Elena Vitrichenko | UKR | 9.775 |

ALL ROUND GROUP EXERCISES

| 1 Greece | 38.675 |

Rhythmic British Championships

Bletchley   Mar 26

ALL ROUND

| 1 Debbie Southwick | Mersey | 36.00 |

(9.250, 9.250, 9.225, 8.70)

Sports Acrobatics

European Championships

Antwerp   Nov 22-28, 1993

OVERALL RESULTS

Women's Tumbling

| 1 Svetlana Ivanova | UKR | 29.46 |
| 10 Minn Brodie | GBR | 27.56 |

Men's Tumbling

1 Pascal Eouzan	FRA	29.07
1 Sergei Bondarchuk	UKR	29.07
8 Craig Lowther	GBR	28.16
9 Craig Smith	GBR	27.95

Men's Pairs

| 1 Latchkov/Vladev | BUL | 29.32 |

Mixed Pairs

| 1 Perelygina/Perelygin | RUS | 29.58 |
| 6 Barton/Wilcox | GBR | 28.88 |

Women's Pairs

| 1 Redkovolosova/Antipova | | UKR | 29.60 |

Women's Groups

| 1 Petrova/Pankova/Ivanova | | BUL | 29.60 |
| 8 Harris/Thorne/Young | | GBR | 27.56 |

Men's Groups

| 1 Pas/Szczygiel/Gutszmit/Kozlowski | POL | 29.22 |
| 4 Bowes/Heslop/Smith/Burlison | GBR | 28.40 |

British Championships

OVERALL RESULTS

Women's Tumbling

| 1 Minn Brodie | Spelthorne | 27.12 |

Men's Tumbling

| 1 Craig Lowther | Wakefield | 29.06 |

Mixed Pairs

| 1 Griffith/Crocker | Spelthorne | 29.25 |

Women's Pairs

| 1 Boultwood/Robinson | Spelthorne | 29.09 |

Women's Groups

| 1 Gooding/Rogers/Hardy | King Edmund | 28.22 |

Men's Groups

| 1 Heslop/Bowes/Thompson/Burlison | DV | 27.52 |

Handball

Women's World Championship

Norway   *Nov 24-Dec 5*
Group 1*
Norway 21 Korea 18
Hungary 24 Russia 24
Poland 25 Denmark 30
Russia 19 Norway 14
Korea 37 Poland 29
Denmark 37 Hungary 23
Norway 28 Denmark 23
Poland 22 Russia 21
Hungary 33 Korea 31

Final Standings

		P	W	D	L	PF	PA	Pts
1	Denmark	5	4	0	1	143	122	8
2	Norway	5	4	0	1	104	91	8
3	Russia	5	2	1	2	113	109	5
4	Hungary	5	1	2	2	120	135	4
5	Poland	5	1	1	3	117	136	3
6	Korea	5	1	0	4	136	140	2

Group 2*
Romania 15 Austria 16
Sweden 30 USA 11
Germany 22 UCS 21
USA 12 Germany 24
UCS 21 Romania 25
Austria 17 Sweden 11
Germany 25 Austria 10
Romania 30 USA 15
Sweden 19 UCS 18

Final Standings

		P	W	D	L	PF	PA	Pts
1	Germany	5	4	0	1	109	82	8
2	Romania	5	3	0	2	111	93	6
3	Sweden	5	3	0	2	95	80	6
4	Austria	5	3	0	2	83	78	6
5	UCS**	5	2	0	3	99	99	4
6	USA	5	0	0	5	69	134	0

* *Incomplete match details*
***United team of Czech and Slovak Republics*
Play Off Round
11th/12th
USA 21 Korea 29
9th/10th
Poland 17 UCS 22
7th/8th
Austria 9 Hungary 16
5th/6th
Russia 25 sweden 19
3rd/4th
Romania 19 Norway 20
Final
Denmark 21 Germany 22 (aet)

European Cup 1993-94
Men

Group A	P	W	D	L	PF	PA	Pts
ABC Braga (POR)	6	3	2	1	139	135	8
USAM Nimes (FRA)	6	2	3	1	142	135	7
Sandefjord HK (NOR)	6	3	1	2	146	142	7
Badel 1862 Zagreb (CRO)	6	0	2	4	135	147	2
Group B							
TEKA Santander (ESP)	6	4	0	2	136	136	8
SG Wallau-M'heim(GER)	6	3	0	3	128	127	6
UHK West Wien	6	3	0	3	116	121	6
Celje 'Pivov. Lasko'(SLO)	6	2	0	4	120	116	4

Final *(2 legs: Apr 23 & 30)*
TEKA Santander 45 ABC Braga 43

Women

Group A	P	W	D	L	PF	PA	Pts
Hypo N'österreich(AUT)	6	6	0	0	141	110	12
CB Mar Valencia (ESP)	6	2	0	4	126	133	4
Chimistul Vilcea (ROM)	6	2	0	4	138	147	4
Podravka Koprivnica (CRO)	6	2	0	4	123	138	4
Group A							
Vasas Budapest (HUN)	6	4	1	1	137	103	9
TV Giessen-Lützell'n (GER)	6	4	1	1	153	123	9
Gjerpen IF Skien (NOR)	6	2	0	4	140	157	4
WAT Fünfhaus (AUT)	6	1	0	5	128	175	2

Final *(2 legs: May 7 & 14)*
Hypo Niederösterreich 45 Vasas Budapest 39

Cup Winners Cup
Men's Final *(2 legs: Apr 24 & 30)*
FC Barcelona (ESP) 46 OM Vitrolles (FRA) 37
Women's Final *(2 legs: May 8 & 15)*
Walle Bremen (GER) 45 Spectrum Budapest (HUN) 44

EHF Cup
Men's Final *(2 legs: Apr 23 & 30)*
CBM Alzira Avidesa (ESP) 44 Linde Linz (AUT) 41
Women's Final *(2 legs: May 8 & 14)*
Viborg HK (DEN) 44 DVSC Debrecen (HUN) 44
(Viborg win on away goals)

City Cup
Men's Final *(2 legs: Apr 24 & May 1)*
TUSEM Essen (GER) 58 Drott Halmstad (SWE) 43
Women's Final *(2 legs: May 7 & 15)*
Buxtehuder SV (GER) 45 Baekkelagets Oslo (NOR) 43

British Cup
Eccles Sports Centre   *June 11*
Men's Final
Ruislip 22 MVS 16
Women's Final
Ruislip 16 Halewood Town 11

Hockey

England's women plummeted out of the World Cup in Dublin after exhibiting a Rolf Harris-like ability to do nothing but draw. Sue Slocombe's team set off with a semi final place a realistic goal, only to come unstuck against the unfancied Americans. Even the livewire Jane Sixsmith could not influence England's dismal performance in front of goal, as they managed only 5 goals in 7 games. The European Champions were left to hack about in the lower reaches to secure an Olympic qualifying spot by finishing 9th.

The re-structured women's National League saw Leicester clinch their first title, whilst the men's equivalent was won for the third time by Havant. The mandarins in the Hockey Association also decided to throw out a proposal for a premier league which England coach David Whitaker saw as central to improving the chances of the national side. This was no surprise as at the time the administration of the sport was preoccupied with designing a national stadium in the hockey hot-bed of Milton Keynes. The stadium was due to play host to the prestigious Champions Trophy tournament in 1995. It was a marvellous idea, brilliantly conceived, a Tour de Force. Only one thing was missing. Money. Silly thing to forget, eh?

So, the HA has been forced to make a late withdrawal. There will be no tournament in Milton Keynes because there isn't a stadium to hold it in and the HA will have to go back to the drawing board - but not to design another stadium, please.

OLYMPIC GAMES WINNERS
Men

1908	England	1964	India
1920	England	1968	Pakistan
1928	India	1972	West Germany
1932	India	1976	New Zealand
1936	India	1980	India
1948	India	1984	Pakistan
1952	India	1988	Great Britain
1956	India	1992	Germany
1960	Pakistan		

Women

1980	Zimbabwe	1988	Australia
1984	Holland	1992	Spain

WORLD CUP WINNERS

Men		Women	
1971	Pakistan	1974	Holland
1973	Holland	1976	West Germany
1975	India	1978	Holland
1978	Pakistan	1981	West Germany
1982	Pakistan	1983	Holland
1986	Australia	1986	Holland
1990	Holland	1990	Holland

NATIONAL CUP CHAMPIONS

Men		Women	
1972-3	Hounslow	1979	Chelmsford
1974-5	Southgate	1980	Norton
1976	Nottingham	1981	Sutton Coldfield
1977	Slough	1982-3	Slough

1978	Guildford	1984	Sheffield
1979-81	Slough	1985	Ipswich
1982	Southgate	1986	Slough
1983	Neston	1987-9	Ealing
1984	East Grinstead	1990-1	Sutton Coldfield
1985-8	Southgate	1992	Hightown
1989	Hounslow	1993	Leicester
1990	Havant		
1991-3	Hounslow		

EUROPEAN CHAMPIONS CUP
Men

1969-70	Club Egara de Terrasa (ESP)
1971-5	Frankfurt 1880 (FRG)
1976-8	Southgate (ENG)
1979	Klein Zwitserland (HOL)
1980	Slough (ENG)
1981	Klein Zwitserland (HOL)
1982-3	Dynamo Alma-Ata (URS)
1984	TG 1846 Frankental (FRG)
1985	Atletico Terrasa (ESP)
1986	Kampong, Utrecht (HOL)
1987	Bloemendaal (HOL)
1988-93	Uhlenhorst Mülheim (FRG/GER)

Women

1974	Harvestehuder, Hamburg (FRG)
1976-82	Amsterdam (HOL)
1983-7	HGC Wassenaar (HOL)
1988-90	Amsterdam (HOL)
1991	HGC Wassenaar (HOL)
1992	Amsterdam (HOL)

Men's Hockey

Champions Trophy

Lahore, Pakistan   *Mar 17-25*
Pool Matches
Mar 17
Great Britain 1 Pakistan 4
Germany 2 Australia 1
Spain 4 Holland 4

Mar 18
Australia 3 Holland 2
Pakistan 3 Spain 1

Mar 19
Great Britain 0 Germany 1

Mar 20
Pakistan 2 Holland 1
Germany 3 Spain 2
Australia 5 Great Britain 4

Mar 21
Pakistan 2 Australia 0

Mar 22
Great Britain 1 Spain 1
Germany 1 Holland 1

Mar 23
Great Britain 2 Holland 5
Pakistan 1 Germany 1
Spain 0 Australia 2

League Standings

		P	W	D	L	GF	GA	Pts
1	Pakistan	5	4	1	0	12	4	9
2	Germany	5	3	2	0	8	5	8
3	Australia	5	3	0	2	11	10	6
4	Holland	5	1	2	2	13	12	4
5	Spain	5	0	2	3	8	13	2
6	Great Britain	5	0	1	4	8	16	1

5th/6th Place Play-off
Great Britain 2 Spain 4
3rd/4th Place Play-off
Holland 2 Australia 2
Holland won 8-7 on penalty strokes
FINAL
Pakistan 2 Germany 2
Pakistan won 7-6 on penalty strokes

NCM Trophy

Amstelveen, Holland   *June 25-July 3*

25 June
Holland 2 Germany 2
Malaysia 0 Argentina 3

26 June
Pakistan 6 Malaysia 2
Holland 6 South Afria 1
Germany 2 Australia 3

June 27
Argentina 0 Pakistan 1
South Africa 2 Australia 5

June 28
Argentina 1 Germany 1
Holland 7 Malaysia 0
June 29
South Africa 1 Pakistan 6
Australia 6 Malaysia 0

June 30
Germany 5 South Africa 1
Australia 4 Argentina 0
Holland 6 Pakistan 2

July 1
Germany 5 Malaysia 1
Holland 3 Argentina 1

July 2
Malaysia 0 South Africa 3
Australia 2 Pakistan 7

July 3
South Africa 2 Argentina 3
Pakistan 1 Germany 2
Holland 2 Australia 2

Final Standings

		P	W	D	L	GF	GA	Pts
1	Holland	6	4	2	0	26	8	10
2	Australia	6	4	1	1	22	13	9
3	Pakistan	6	4	0	2	22	13	8
4	Germany	6	3	2	1	16	9	8
5	Argentina	6	2	1	3	8	11	5
6	South Africa	6	1	0	5	9	24	2
7	Malaysia	6	0	0	6	3	30	0

EUROPEAN INDOOR NATIONS CHAMPIONSHIPS
Bonn   *Jan 30*
Final
Germany 9 England 2

EUROPEAN CLUB CHAMPIONSHIP
Bloemedaal, Holland   *May 20-23*
3rd/4th Place Play-off
Durkheim (GER) 2 Hounslow (GBR) 1
Final
Uhlenhorst (GER) 2 Bloemendaal (HOL) 1

EUROPEAN CLUB CUP WINNERS CUP A DIVISION
Terrassa, Spain   *April 1-4*
3rd/4th Place Play-off
Teddington (GBR) 5 Harvestehuder (GER) 3
Final
HGC (HOL) 3 Atletico Terrassa (ESP) 3
(HGC won 5-4 on penalty strokes)

Pizza Express National Hockey League

Division 1

		P	W	D	L	GF	GA	Pts
1	Havant	17	14	2	1	39	13	44
2	Hounslow	17	12	3	2	48	14	39
3	Old Loughtonians	17	10	6	1	48	19	36
4	Southgate	17	10	4	3	45	15	34
5	Teddington	17	10	3	4	36	23	33
6	Cannock	17	7	7	3	31	21	28
7	Stourport	17	8	4	5	26	16	28
8	East Grinstead	17	8	4	5	32	23	28
9	Reading	17	8	2	7	30	27	26
10	Trojans	17	6	2	9	25	32	20
11	Indian Gymkhana	17	4	6	7	18	29	18
12	Welton	17	5	2	10	18	35	17
13	Bournville	17	5	1	11	23	34	16
14	Firebrands	17	3	7	7	15	30	16
15	Canterbury	17	3	5	9	20	39	14
16	Slough	17	4	2	11	17	37	14
17	St Albans	17	4	1	12	15	42	13
18	Bromley	17	1	1	15	8	45	4

Division 2

		P	W	D	L	GF	GA	Pts
1	Guildford	17	14	2	1	58	25	44
2	Surbiton	17	13	4	0	53	18	43
3	Barford Tigers	17	9	5	3	39	23	32
4	Oxford University	17	9	3	5	40	24	30
5	Brooklands	17	8	5	4	35	24	29
6	Richmond	17	8	4	5	25	23	28
7	Edgbaston	17	8	2	7	33	36	26
8	Harleston Magpies	17	6	5	6	29	33	23
9	Gloucester City	17	6	3	8	27	25	21
10	Sheffield	17	5	6	6	28	30	21
11	Isca	17	6	2	9	29	36	20
12	Beeston	17	4	6	7	28	37	18
13	Cambridge City	17	4	5	8	23	35	17
14	Neston	17	4	4	9	19	29	16
15	Harborne	17	4	4	9	22	38	16
16	Doncaster	17	3	4	10	21	37	13
17	Cheltenham	17	3	4	10	15	31	13
18	Warrington	17	3	4	10	19	39	13

Harborne were relegated following play-offs. Crostyx, Whitchurch and Hampstead & Westminster are promoted.

Player of the Season: Ian Jennings (Guildford)
Top Goal Scorer: Ian Jennings 34 goals

Scottish National League

Division 1

		P	W	D	L	GF	GA	Pts
1	McMahon Kelburne	18	15	1	2	50	13	46
2	Grange	18	14	2	2	51	15	44
3	Torbrex Wanderers	18	9	4	5	40	27	31
4	Menzieshill	18	9	2	7	28	28	29
5	T R Gordonians	18	7	4	7	27	32	25
6	Edinburgh MIM	18	5	7	6	18	20	22
7	Western	18	4	6	8	21	34	18
8	Insights Inverlieth	18	5	3	10	19	35	18
9	D W Clydesdale	18	3	5	10	21	35	14
10	Hazelhead	18	1	2	15	12	48	5

HA Cup

5th Round
Beeston 2 Warrington 1
Bournville 1 Old Loughtonians 5
Bromley 1 Havant 2
East Grinstead 1 Hounslow 3
Harrogate 2 Trojans 1
Reading 2 Cannock 1
Southgate 2 St Albans 1
Teddington 2 Surbiton 1
6th Round
Harrogate 0 Reading 7
Old Loughtonians 3 Havant 0
Southgate 1 Hounslow 1
(Hounslow won 6-5 on penalty strokes)
Teddington 2 Beeston 1

Semi-finals
Mar 13
Teddington 2 Hounslow 2
(Teddington won 4-2 on penalty strokes)
Old Loughtonians 3 Reading 2

Final
University of Birmingham   May 15
Teddington 1 Old Loughtonians 0

NORWICH UNION COUNTY CHAMPIONSHIP
Final
Abbeydale, Sheffield   May 8
Staffordshire 3 Surrey 1

HA INDOOR CLUB CHAMPIONSHIP
Final
Crystal Palace NSC   Jan 21
St Albans 2 East Grinstead 2
(St Albans win 6-5 on penalty strokes)

HA TROPHY
Final
University of Birmingham   May 15
Ashford (Middx) 3 Bowdon 2

HA YOUTH CUP
U16 Final
Cannock Hockey Club   May 2
Homerton House 2 St George's College, Weybridge 1
U18 Final
Cannock Hockey Club   May 2
Kingston Gram Sch 3 Bedford Sch 1

COMMERCIAL UNION UAU CHAMPIONSHIPS
Cannock Hockey Club   Mar 16
Final
Bristol 2 Exeter 2 *(title shared)*

Women's Hockey
World Cup
Dublin, Ireland July 13-24
Pool Results
July 13
Russia 2 Australia 1
Ireland 0 Argentina 3
Spain 3 Korea 3
Canada 0 Germany 2

July 14
Netherlands 1 China 0
England 0 USA 1
Russia 0 Korea 4
Argentina 1 Australia 3

July 15
Spain 1 Ireland 1
China 0 England 0
USA 1 Germany 1
Canada 0 Netherlands 3

July 16
Argentina 1 Russia 0
Korea 2 Ireland 0
Australia 1 Spain 1

July 17
Germany 3 England 0
China 2 Canada 0
Netherlands 1 USA 2

July 18
Korea 0 Argentina 1
Spain 3 Russia 1
Australia 4 Ireland 0
Canada 1 USA 0

July 19
Germany 1 China 2
Netherlands 1 England 0
Ireland 0 Russia 0
Argentina 1 Spain 0

July 20
Australia 4 Korea 1
England 3 Canada 0
China 0 USA 1
Netherlands 1 Germany 2

Pool rankings
Pool A

		P	W	D	L	GF	GA	Pts
1	Germany	5	3	1	1	9	4	7
2	USA	5	3	1	1	5	3	7
3	Netherlands	5	3	0	2	7	4	6
4	China	5	2	1	2	4	3	5
5	England	5	1	1	3	3	5	3
6	Canada	5	1	0	4	1	10	2

Pool B

		P	W	D	L	GF	GA	Pts
1	Argentina	5	4	0	1	7	3	8
2	Australia	5	3	1	1	13	5	7
3	Korea	5	2	1	2	10	8	5
4	Spain	5	1	3	1	8	7	5
5	Russia	5	1	1	3	3	9	3
6	Ireland	5	0	2	3	1	10	3

Play-offs
July 22-23
Korea 4 China 1
Spain 0 Netherlands 2
Russia 1 Canada 1 *(Canada won 4-2 on penalty strokes)*
Ireland 1 England 1 *(England won 2-0 on penalty strokes)*

Semi-finals
Argentina 2 USA 0
Australia 2 Germany 0

July 23-24
11th/12th places
Russia 2 Ireland 3
9th/10th places
Canada 0 England 1
7th/8th places
China 2 Spain 1
5th/6th places
Korea 2 Netherlands 0
3rd/4th places
USA 2 Germany 1

Final
July 24
Argentina 0 Australia 2

Australia have qualified for 1996 Olympic Games
Australia/Argentina/Germany/Korea/Netherlands/USA have
qualified from 9th World Cup

INTERNATIONALS
Basingstoke   *Mar 12-13*
England 1 India 1
England 1 India 1
India won series 4-3 on penalty strokes

Lilleshall   *May 31-June 1*
England 1 Australia 2
England 0 Australia 3

Madrid, Spain   *June 10-12*
Spain 1 England 3
Spain 0 England 2

Dublin, Ireland   *June 25-26*
Ireland 0 England 0
Ireland 0 England 1

Bisham Abbey   *July 6-7*
England 2 South Africa 2
England 1 South Africa 0

ARGENTINIAN TOURNAMENT
Buenos Aires, Argentina   Mar 9-17
England 1 Argentina 3
England 2 South Africa 1
England 0 Australia 2
England 2 USA 0
Final Placings: 1 Australia, 2 Argentina, 3 England, 4 USA, 5 South Africa

EUROPEAN U21 INDOOR CUP
Llodio, Bilbao, Spain   Jan 21-23
Final Placings: 1 Spain, 2 England, 3 Slovakia, 4 Belarus, 5 France, 6 Czech Republic, 7 Austria

EUROPEAN INDOOR CLUB CHAMPIONSHIPS
Russelsheim, Germany   Feb 18-20
A Division
Final Standings: 1 Russelsheim (GER), 2 Berliner (GER), 3 Edinburgh (SCO), 4 Hightown (ENG)

EUROPEAN CLUBS CUP WINNERS CUP
Cardiff, Wales   April 1-4
A Division
Final Standings: 1 Bayer Leverkusen (GER), 2 SKIF Moscow (RUS), 3 Balsam Leicester (ENG) 4, Stade Francais (FRA)

EUROPEAN CUP FOR CLUB CHAMPIONS
Bloemendaal, Netherlands   May 20-23
A Division
Final Standings: 1 HGC (HOL), 2 Russelsheim (GER), 3 Ipswich (ENG), 4 Glasgow (SCO)

National League
Premier League

		P	W	D	L	GF	GA	Pts
1	Balsam Leicester	14	9	3	2	23	11	30
2	Ipswich	14	8	4	2	24	8	28
3	F P Sutton Coldfield	14	8	3	3	19	14	27
4	Slough	14	7	4	3	19	8	25
5	Hightown	14	8	1	5	20	12	25
6	Clifton	14	2	3	9	10	24	9
7	Chelmsford	14	2	1	11	9	31	7
8	Ealing	14	1	3	10	10	26	4*

Ealing deducted 2 points and a goal for using an unregistered player

First Division

		P	W	D	L	GF	GA	Pts
1	Bracknell	14	8	3	3	17	9	27
2	Trojans	14	6	6	2	18	14	24
3	Wimbledon	14	6	5	3	19	14	23
4	Doncaster	14	4	7	3	18	13	19
5	Bradford S'bank	14	3	6	5	21	26	15
6	Exmouth	14	4	3	7	15	20	15
7	Blueharts	14	3	5	6	13	18	14
8	Pickwick	14	3	3	8	13	20	12

Second Division

		P	W	D	L	GF	GA	Pts
1	Canterbury	14	9	2	3	19	7	29
2	Sunderland Bedans	14	7	3	4	18	11	24
3	Olton	14	7	1	6	16	18	22
4	Sherwood	14	4	8	2	15	13	20
5	Great Harwood	14	5	5	4	14	13	20
6	Woking	14	5	3	6	16	19	14
7	Harleston Magpies	14	3	5	6	16	19	14
8	Colwall	14	1	3	19	5	31	6

Harleston Magpies relegated after play-offs. Loughborough Students and St Albans are promoted.

COMMERCIAL UNION UAU CHAMPIONSHIPS
Cannock Hockey Club   Mar 9
Final
Heriot Watt 4 Bristol 2

Scottish National League
First Division

		P	W	D	L	GF	GA	Pts
1	Glasgow West KP	16	15	1	0	89	1	46
2	Edinburgh Ladies	16	12	3	1	52	4	39
3	Grove	16	9	1	6	30	15	28
4	Hyndland	16	8	3	5	20	13	27
5	Royal High Gym'sts	16	5	6	5	21	22	21
6	Glasgow West KP II	16	5	5	6	19	26	20
7	Heriot Watt SCPE	16	3	4	9	15	38	13
8	Grange	16	0	4	12	3	55	4
9	Melrose	16	0	3	13	1	76	3

Horse Racing

The winds of recession have blown coldly through racing and at the end of the 1993 flat season, as many as ten group one races were seeking new sponsors. It was the news that the batteries were running out on the Ever Ready Derby, though, that was the gravest concern. The Derby has suffered grievously in recent times, falling away in popularity, its place as a protected species under threat. The betting turnover - a reasonable guide on such matters - showed the Derby, at around £30m, lagging behind the £75m Grand National by a distance.

It came then as something of a relief when Vodafone, with money to burn, decided to burn £3.5m of it on sponsoring the Derby - and the Epsom meeting - for the next three years. The key to winning Vodafone's heart was the change of days; the meeting will now be run on Friday to Sunday, with The Derby on Saturday. Vodafone's money should also enhance the quality of the undercard. When the Thursday programme starts with the Mrs Beeton Auction Stakes, a class E maiden worth £3,635 to the winner, it's difficult to believe you're at one of the world's great race meetings. With all that sorted, Epsom could be set fair: all they need now is a course that a few more horses can act on and we really could have the world's greatest race.

Erhaab acted on it all right. As he swept past the field in the final half furlong, the near-black colt looked like one for the history book. A month later the bubble burst at the Eclipse. 'Unable qckn' said The Form Book as the odds on favourite was defeated by Ezzoud and Bob's Return. A hamstring injury was the original diagnosis, but when he then finished seventh in the King George VI & Queen Elizabeth the stable was forced to look for other reasons. Stud beckoned (he was a Derby winner after all) and we were forced to look elsewhere for our horse of the year.

Kings Theatre gave us a hard ridden victory in that King George, but in truth there were no singing horses this year; no Nashwan or Nijinsky, although the aptly named Lochsong gave us a few verses. The Arc summed it up; five horses with little more than a length between them as they passed the line. In a year of accidents - over 58 logged by the end of August including Foyer in the Derby - the saddest by far was at Lingfield in May when Kalar fell in the 5 furlong Moorhen Handicap, a fall that cost Jockey Steve Wood his life. Declan Murphy's fall at Haydock in May put him on the critical list, but for a thankfully brief time. National Hunt jockeys know they take criminal risks with their well-being, flat race jockeys - the fall percentage has almost doubled on last season - may have to reassess the risks.

The Fellow takes first prize in the National Hunt year, having finally won a Cheltenham Gold Cup. Miinnehoma won the National, which started properly this year. Miinnehoma's owner is Freddie Starr who, according to the anecdote in Graham Sharpe's racing book *Racing Shorts*, bid for his horse at the Doncaster Sales by sticking his tongue out at the auctioneer. Well, he would, wouldn't he? There was a fleeting reprise of the 1993 National at Folkestone on February 9th when the starting tape failed to rise for the 4.10 race. The horses, obviously having watched the National farrago on television, knew exactly what to do. Instead of charging the tape, they tried to jump it.

QUOTES

"I think I'd rather retire and go there myself" - **Richard Price, trainer of Champion Hurdle winner Flakey Dove, on whether his horse should be retired to stud.**

"There can't be anyone left in County Carlow" - **Tom Foley, trainer of Cheltenham Festival winner Danoli, on the ecstatic reception to his horse's victory.**

"I can clearly remember what she looked like, but not her name. That's been the case with quite a few along the way" - **John... er what's-'is-name, you know the one with the curly hair who does the racing on television.**

"My jockey said that after the first fence he didn't find them difficult. He said that he was still going well when he fell" - **Francis Doumen, trainer of The Fellow, with the same old Aintree story.**

"They say there may be traffic problems with a big field, but that's rubbish" - **Willie Carson, before the Derby.**

"It was carnage out there. There were bad horses everywhere I went and I'm sure they were responsible for a lot of the better ones being beaten" - **Willie Carson, after the Derby, which he nevertheless won - on Erhaab.**

"It was ridiculous, the worst and roughest race I have ever ridden in" - **Michael Roberts, another jockey disenamoured of the 1994 Derby.**

"Look at it. Better than Ascot. That's for the elite. This is racing for the mob and they love it" - **Dave Pipe, bookmaker father of trainer Martin, enthusing over the new floodlit racing at Wolverhampton.**

"I've seen jockeys pick up the stick and bring it down without making contact with the horse. I find it quite hilarious. Anyone watching from a distance...can be fooled by it" - **Steve Smith-Eccles, on how jockeys pretended they were trying. Smith-Eccles catalogued a list of 'crimes' in race riding, but presumably the stewards would approve of the one above.**

"That's the way she is. You're throwing the reins at her and growling at her and you think she's going nowhere and all of a sudden she takes off" - **Sue Scargill, on the wayward ways of Lincoln winner, Our Rita.**

"You've got to think it was great entertainment for a quid" - **Ladbrokes spokesperson, after Jason Mosley's £1 win 11 horse accumulator, made in his local Ladbrokes, went down on the last horse. Mosley, who stood to win £43,000, might be inclined to use William Hill after a comment like that.**

"I couldn't even remember seeing a horse, let alone hitting one" - **James Florey, who ran into the path of the three year old Papago, during the Ribblesdale Stakes at Ascot. I suppose that's what they mean when they say blind-drunk.**

"She's pretty unbelievable. It will take some horse to match her" - **Dettori, on Balanchine. Though they changed the goalposts by including the all-weather wins, Dettori still had a "pretty unbelievable" season himself**

C=colt, f=filly, the weight carried is in brackets after the horse's name, the starting price follows the jockey's name, the prize money is after the trainer

THE CLASSICS

MADAGANS 1000 GUINEAS
Newmarket, Apr 28   3y f (1m)
LAS MENINAS (9-0)
John Reid   12/1
T Stack (Ireland)   £112,705

MADAGANS 2000 GUINEAS
Newmarket, Apr 30   3y c&f (1m)
MISTER BAILEYS (9-0)
Jason Weaver   16/1
M Johnston   £131,948

EVER READY DERBY
Epsom, June 1
3y c & f (1m 4f 10y)
ERHAAB (9-0)
Willie Carson   7/2F
J L Dunlop   £473,080

ENERGIZER OAKS
Epsom, June 4
3y f (1m 4f 10y)
BALANCHINE (9-0)
Frankie Dettori   6/1
H Ibrahim (Dubai)   £147,500

**TELECONNECTION
ST LEGER STAKES**
Doncaster, Sep 10
3y c & f   (1m 6f)
MOONAX (9-0)
Pat Eddery   40/1
B W Hills   £153,346

GROUP 1

**EVER READY
CORONATION CUP**
Epsom, June 3
3y+ (1m 4f10y)
APPLE TREE (9-0)
Thierry Jarnet   12/1
A Fabre (France)   £91,950

ST JAMES'S PALACE STAKES
Royal Ascot, June 14   3y c&f (1m)
GRAND LODGE (9-0)
Michael Kinane   6/1
W Jarvis   £130,329

CORONATION STAKES
Royal Ascot, June 15   3y f (1m)
KISSING COUSIN (9-0)
Michael Kinane   13/2
H R A Cecil   £128,583

GOLD CUP
Royal Ascot, June 16   3y+ (2m 4f)
ARCADIAN HEIGHTS (6-9-2)
Michael Hills   20/1
G Wragg   £111,843

CORAL-ECLIPSE STAKES
Sandown, July 2   3y+ (1m2f7y)
EZZOUD (5-9-7)
Walter Swinburn   5/1
M R Stoute   £177,504

JULY CUP
Newmarket, July 7   3y+ (6f)
OWINGTON (3-8-13)
Paul Eddery   3/1
G Wragg   £85,194

**KING GEORGE & QUEEN
ELIZABETH DIAMOND STAKES**
Ascot, July 23   3y+ (1m 4f)
KINGS'S THEATRE (3-8-9)
Michael Kinane   12/1
H R A Cecil   £265,808

SUSSEX STAKES
Goodwood, July 27   3y+ (1m)
DISTANT VIEW (8-13)
Pat Eddery   4/1
H R A Cecil   £97,960

**JUDDMONTE INTERNATIONAL
STAKES**
York, Aug 16   3+ (1m2f 85y)
EZZOUD (5-9-6)
Walter Swinburn   4/1
M R Stoute   £151,454

**ASTON UPTHORPE YORKSHIRE
OAKS**
York, Aug 17   3+ f & m
(1m3f195y)
ONLY ROYALE (5-9-7)
Frankie Dettori   15/2
L M Cumani   £79,424

**KEENELAND NUNTHORPE
STAKES**
York, Aug 18   3y+ (5f)
PICCOLO (3-9-3)
John Reid   14/1
M R Channon   £85,391

HAYDOCK PARK SPRINT CUP
Haydock, Sep 3   3+ (6f)
LAVINIA FONTANA (5-8-9)
Jason Weaver   11/2
J L Dunlop   £72,464

FILLIES' MILE
Ascot, Sep24   2y f (1m)
AQAARID (8-10)
Willie Carson   11/2
J L Dunlop   £94,635

QUEEN ELIZABETH STAKES
Ascot, Sep 24   3y+ (1m)
MAROOF (4-9-4)
Richard Hills   66/1
R W Armstrong   £190,005

....

1993 Races

DEWHURST STAKES
Newmarket, Oct 15, 1993   2y c & f (7f)
GRAND LODGE (9-0)
John Reid   9/4F
W Jarvis   £117,724

DUBAI CHAMPION STAKES
Newmarket, Oct 16, 1993   3y+ (1m 2f)
HATOOF (4-9-0)
Walter Swinburn   5/2F
Mrs C Head   £205,707

RACING POST TROPHY
Doncaster, Oct 23, 1993
2y c & f (6f)
KING'S THEATRE (9-0)
Willie Ryan   4/1
H R A Cecil   £86,779

GROUP 2

GARDNER MERCHANT MILE
Sandown, Apr 22   3y+ (1m 14y)
PENNY DROPS (5-8-11)
David Harrison   8/1
Lord Huntingdon   £35,406

**MADAGANS JOCKEY CLUB
STAKES**
Newmarket, Apr 29   3y+ (1m 4f)
SILVER WISP (5-8-9)
Michael Hills   20/1
D Nicholson   £33,285

**HOMEOWNERS DANTE
STAKES**
York, May 11   3y (1m 2f 85y)
ERHAAB (9-0)
Willie Carson   11/2
J L Dunlop   £73,884

YORKSHIRE CUP
York, May 12   3y+
(1m5f194y)
KEY TO MY HEART (8-9)
John Reid   16/1
D Moffatt   £54,628.84

**JUDDMONTE LOCKINGE
STAKES**
Newbury, May 13   3y+ (1m)
EMPEROR JONES (4-9-0)
Frankie Dettori   11/2
J H M Gosden   £44,280

TRIPLEPRINT TEMPLE STAKES
Sandown, May 30   *3y+ (5f 6y)*
LOCHSONG (6-9-7)
Frankie Dettori   **4/9F**
I A Balding   £35,325

QUEEN ANNE STAKES
Royal Ascot, June 14   *3y+ (1m)*
BARATHEA (9-8)
Michael Kinane   **3/1**
L M Cumani   £56,793

PRINCE OF WALES STAKES
Royal Ascot, June 14   *3y+ (1m 2f)*
MUHTARRAM (9-7)
Willie Carson   **6/4F**
J H M Gosden   £66,355

KING EDWARD VII STAKES
Royal Ascot, June 14
3y c & g (1m 4f)
FOYER (8-8)
Michael Kinane   **7/2**
M R Stoute   £69,033

RIBBLESDALE STAKES
Royal Ascot, June 16
3y f (1m 4f)
BOLAS (8-8)
Pat Eddery   **3/1F**
B W Hills   £62,697

HARDWICKE STAKES
Royal Ascot, June 17   *3y+ (1m 4f)*
BOBZAO (5-8-9)
John Reid   **11/1**
T G Mills   £63,630

KING'S STAND STAKES
Royal Ascot, June 17   *3y+ (5f)*
LOCHSONG (6-9-0)
Frankie Dettori   **3/10F**
I A Balding   £64,893

PRINCESS OF WALES'S STAKES
Newmarket, July 5   *3y+ (1m4f)*
WAGON MASTER (4-9-0)
Richard Hills   **7/1**
A C Stewart   £36,446

FALMOUTH STAKES
Newmarket, July 6   *3y (1m)*
LEMON SOUFFLE (8-6)
Lester Piggott   **6/5F**
R Hannon   £34,158

RICHMOND STAKES
Goodwood, July 28
2y c&g (6f)
SRI PEKAN (8-11)
Richard Quinn   **9/4**
P F I Cole   £27,145

VODAFONE NASSAU STAKES
Goodwood, July 30
3y f & m (1m2f)
HAWAJISS (8-6)
Walter Swinburn   **4/1F**
M R Stoute   £44,130

**TRIPLEPRINT GEOFFREY
FREER STAKES**
Newbury, Aug 13
3+ (1m 5f 61yf)
RED ROUTE (3-8-5)
Willie Ryan   **11/10**
H R A Cecil   £41,726

GREAT VOLTIGEUR STAKES
York, Aug 16
3y c&g (1m2f)
SACRAMENT (8-9)
Walter Swinburn   **6/1**
M R Stoute   £48,829

**SCOTTISH EQUITABLE
GIMCRACK STAKES**
York, Aug 17   *2y c&g (6f)*
CHILLY BILLY (9-0)
Kieran Fallon   **12/1**
Mrs J R Ramsden   £61,537

TALKLAND LOWTHER STAKES
York, Aug 18   *2y f (6f)*
HARAYIR (8-11)
Willie Carson   **2/1**
Major W R Hern   £43,477

**TRIPLEPRINT CELEBRATION
MILE**
Goodwood, Aug 27   *3y+ (1m)*
MEHTHAAF (3-8-11)
Willie Carson   **5/2**
J L Dunlop   £38,722

**LAURENT-PERRIER
CHAMPAGNE STAKES**
Doncaster, Sep 9   *2y c & g (7f)*
SRI PEKAN (9-0)
Michael Kinane   **100/30**
P F I Cole   £36,984

**TELEPRINT FLING CHILDERS
STAKES**
Doncaster, Sep 10   *2y (5f)*
RAAH ALGHARB (8-11)
Walter Swinburn   **7/1**
M R Stoute   £25,795

ROYAL LODGE STAKES
Ascot, Sep 24   *2y c & g (1m)*
ELTISH (8-10)
Pat Eddery   **7/4**
H R A Cecil   £66,177

SUN CHARIOT STAKES
Newmarket, Oct 1   *3+ f (1m 2f)*
LA CONFEDERATION (3-8-8)
Kevin Darley   **5/1**
D Loder   £33,662

....

1993 Races
CHALLENGE STAKES
Newmarket, Oct 14, 1993   *3+ (7f)*
CATRAIL (3-8-11)
Michael Roberts   **4/5F**
M R Stoute   £17,750

**VODAPHONE HORRIS HILL
STAKES**
Newbury, Oct 21, 1993
2y (7f 64y)
TATAMI (8-12)
Michael Roberts   **4/1**
L Cumani   £25,376

GROUP 3

**SHADWELL STUD NELL GWYN
STAKES**
Newmarket, Apr 12   *3y f (7f)*
MEHTHAAF (8-9)
Willie Carson   **100/30**
J L Dunlop   £20,580

EARL OF SEFTON STAKES
Newmarket, Apr 13   *3y+ (1m1f)*
DEL DEYA (4-8-7)
Frankie Dettori   **8/1**
J H M Gosden   £19,884

CRAVEN STAKES
Newmarket, Apr 14   *3y c&g (1m)*
KING'S THEATRE (9-0)
Michael Kinane   **5/1**
H R A Cecil   £19,884

**GAINSBOROUGH STUD FRED
DARLING STAKES**
Newbury, Apr 15   *3y f (7f64y)*
BULAXIE (9-0)
Willie Carson   **5/2**
J L Dunlop   £20,400

**LANES END JOHN PORTER
STAKES**
Newbury, Apr 16   *3y+ (1m 4f 5y)*
RIGHT WIN (4-9-3)
Pat Eddery   **15/2**
R Hannon   £20,400

**SINGER & FRIEDLANDER
GREENHAM STAKES**
Newbury, Apr 16   *3y +c &g (7f)*
TURTLE ISLAND (3-9-0)
John Reid   **2/1**
P W Chapple-Hyam   £20,220

THRESHER CLASSIC TRIAL
Sandown, Apr 23   3y (1m 2f 7y)
LINNEY HEAD (8-10)
Frankie Dettori   9/4
J H M Gosden   £42,980

T.G.I. FRIDAY'S GORDON RICHARD'S STAKES
Sandown, Apr 23   3y+ (1m 2f 7y)
SCRIBE (4-8-10)
Willie Carson   11/2
J L Dunlop   £20,400

INSULPAK SAGARO STAKES
Ascot, Apr 27   3y+ (2m 45y)
SAFETY IN NUMBERS (4-8-8)
Kevin Darley   7/2
Lady Herries   £24,716

PALACE HOUSE STAKES
Newmarket, Apr 30   3y+ (5f)
LOCHSONG (9-2)
Frankie Dettori   7/2
I A Balding   £20,406

DALHAM CHESTER VASE
Chester, May 3   3y (1m 4f 66y)
BROADWAY FLYER (8-10)
Michael Hills   4/5
J W Hills   £28,710

ORMONDE STAKES
Chester, May 5
3y+ (1m 5f 89y)
SHAMBO (9-2)
Michael Roberts   6/1
C E Brittain   £29,250

JARDINE INSURANCE BROKERS DERBY TRIAL STAKES
Lingfield, May 7   3y (1m3f106y)
HAWKER'S NEWS (8-7)
Walter Swinburn   5/1
M R Stoute   £31,400

TATTERSALLS MUSIDORA STAKES
York, May 10   3y f (1m2f85y)
HAWAJISS (8-10)
Walter Swinburn   7/1
M R Stoute   £22,589

DUKE OF YORK STAKES
York, May 12   3y+ (6f)
OWINGTON (3-8-9)
Michael Hills   4/1
G Wragg   £21,300

BONUSPRINT HENRY II STAKES
Sandown, May 30   3y+ (2m 78y)
MY PATRIARCH (4-8-10)
Pat Eddery   15/8F
J L Dunlop   £26,040

BRIGADIER GERARD STAKES
Sandown, May 31   3y+ (1m 2f 7y)
CHATOYANT (4-8-10)
Michael Kinane   7/1
J W Watts   £21,480

DIOMED STAKES
Epsom, June 1   3y+ (1m 114y)
BLUEGRASS PRINCE (3-8-6)
Brent Thomson   11/2
R Hannon   £23,000

COVENTRY STAKES
Royal Ascot, June 14   2y (6f)
SRI PEKAN (8-13)
Richard Quinn   6/1
P F I Cole   £26,270

JERSEY STAKES
Royal Ascot, June 15   3y (7f)
GNEISS (8-10)
Paul Eddery   10/1
Mrs J Cecil
RIVER DEEP (8-10)
Richard Quinn   20/1
P F I Cole   £26,962
Horses dead-heated

QUEEN MARY STAKES
Royal Ascot, June 15   2y f (5f)
GAY GALLANTA (8-8)
Walter Swinburn   16/1
M R Stoute   £26,714

QUEEN'S VASE
Royal Ascot, June 15   3y (2m 45y)
SILVER WEDGE (8-11)
Michael Hills   20/1
G Lewis   £33,908

CORK & ORRERY STAKES
Royal Ascot, June 16   3y+ (6f)
OWINGTON (3-8-10)
Michael Hills   4/1F
G Wragg   £36,848

NORFOLK STAKES
Royal Ascot, June 16   2y (5f)
MIND GAMES (8-13)
John Carroll   5/2
J Berry   £22,100

VAN GEEST CRITERION STAKES
Newmarket, June 25   3y+ (7f)
HILL HOPPER (3-8-4)
Philip Robinson   6/1
J H M Gosden   £20,232

LANCASHIRE OAKS
Haydock, July 2   3y+ f&m (1m3f200y)
STATE CRYSTAL (3-8-4)
Willie Ryan   5/2
H R A Cecil   £20,860

HILLSDOWN CHERRY HINTON STAKES
Newmarket, July 5   2y f (6f)
RED CARNIVAL (8-9)
Walter Swinburn   11/4
M R Stoute   £18,840

SBJ GROUP JULY STAKES
Newmarket, July 6   2y c&g (6f)
FALLOW (8-10)
Frankie Dettori   11/2
D R Loder   £18,666

TENNENTS SCOTTISH CLASSIC
Ayr, July 18   3y+ (1m2f)
BENEFICIAL (4-9-7)
Michael Hills   12/1
G Wragg   £22,494

PRINCESS MARGARET STAKES
Ascot, July 23   2y f (6f)
TAJANNUB (8-8)
Willie Carson   2/1F
R W Armstrong   £22,916

BEESWING STAKES
Newcastle, July 25   3y+ (7f)
GABR (4-9-0)
Richard Hills   4/1
R W Armstrong   £22,200

GORDON STAKES
Goodwood, July 26   3y (1m4f)
BROADWAY FLYER (8-13)
Michael Hills   11/2
J W Hills   £19,536

KING GEORGE STAKES
Goodwood, July 26   3y+ (5f)
LOCHSONG (6-9-7)
Frankie Dettori   10/11F
I A Balding   £28,400

LANSON CHAMPAGNE VINTAGE STAKES
Goodwood, July 27   2y (7f)
ELTISH (8-11)
Pat Eddery   8/11F
H R A Cecil   £23,380

TIFFANY GOODWOOD CUP
Goodwood, July 28   3y+ (2m)
TIOMAN ISLAND (9-5)
Richard Quinn   10/1
P F I Cole   £33,450

MOLECOMB STAKES
Goodwood, July 29   2y (5f)
HOH MAGIC (8-10)
Michael Hills   Evens F
M Bell   £20,400

TOPLIST HUNGERFORD STAKES
Newbury, Aug 12   *3+ (7f34y)*
YOUNG ERN **(4-9-3)**
Willie Ryan   **9/2**
S Dow   16,892

SUNSET BOULEVARD SOLARIO STAKES
Sandown, Aug 19   *2y (7f 16y)*
LOVELY MILLIE **(8-9)**
Frankie Dettori   **7/4F**
D R Loder   £20,760

PRESTIGE STAKES
Goodwood, Aug 26   *2y f (7f)*
PURE GRAIN **(8-9)**
John Reid   **2/1**
M R Stoute   £17,750

BONUSPRINT SEPTEMBER STAKES
Kempton, Sep 3   *3+ (1m 3f 30y)*
WAGON MASTER **(4-9-5)**
Willie Carson   **2/1F**
A C Stewart   £24,246

WORTHINGTON BEST BITTER PARK HILL STAKES
Doncaster, Sep 7 3+ f&m (1m 6f 132y)
COIGACH **(3-8-5)**
Willie Ryan   **13/2**
H R A Cecil   £21,308

ABU DHABI AIRPORT DUTY FREE MAY HILL STAKES
Doncaster, Sep 8   *2f (1m)*
MAMLAKAH **(8-8)**
Richard Hills   **7/1**
H Thompson Jones   £26,976

KIVETON PARK STAKES
Doncaster, Sep 8   *3+ (1m)*
SOVIET LINE **(4-9-0)**
Walter Swinburn   **4/1**
M R Stoute   £22,848

DONCASTER CUP
Doncaster, Sep 8   *3+ (2m 2f)*
ARCADIAN HEIGHTS **(6-9-7)**
Frankie Dettori   **7/2F**
G Wragg   £21,491

CUMBERLAND LODGE STAKES
Ascot, Sep 22   *3+ (1m 4f)*
WAGON MASTER **(4-9-5)**
Willie Carson   **11/8F**
A C Stewart   £26,720

DIADEM STAKES
Ascot, Sep 24   *3+ (6f)*
LAKE CONISTON **(3-8-11)**
Pat Eddery   **85/40F**
G Lewis   £41,160

JOCKEY CLUB CUP
Newmarket, Oct 1   *3+ (2m)*
FURTHER FLIGHT **(8-9-3)**
Michael Hills   **11/8F**
B W Hills   £18,621

CHARLTON HUNT SUPREME STAKES
Goodwood, Sep 30   *3+ (7f)*
SOVIET LINE **(4-9-2)**
Walter Swinburn   **2/1F**
M R Stoute   £20,580

....

1993 RACES
TATTERSALLS ROCKFEL STAKES
Newmarket, Oct 15, 1993
RELATIVELY SPECIAL **(8-8)**
Ray Cochrane   **11/8F**
Luca Cumani   £16,425

MAJOR HANDICAPS

WILLIAM HILL LINCOLN H'CAP
Doncaster, Mar 26   *3y+ (1m2f)*
OUR RITA **(5-8-5)**
Darryll Holland   **16/1**
J D Scargill   £47,340

LADBROKE CHESTER CUP
Chester, May 4
3+ (2m2f 147y)
DOYLE **(5-7-10)**
Gary Bardwell   **14/1**
R J R Williams   £29,162

WILLIAM HILL TROPHY
York, June 11   *3y (6f)*
ENCORE M'LADY **(...)**
N Carlisle   **20/1**
F H Lee   30,954

ROYAL HUNT CUP
Royal Ascot, June 15 *3y+ (1m)*
FACE NORTH **(8-3)**
Alan Munro   **25/1**
R Akehurst   £52,621

WOKINGHAM HANDICAP
Royal Ascot, June 17 *3y+ (6f)*
VENTURE CAPITALIST **(5-8-12)**
John Reid   **20/1**
R Hannon   £52,475

NEWCASTLE BROWN ALE NORTHUMBERLAND PLATE
Newcastle, June 25   *3+ (2m 19y)*
QUICK RANSOM **(6-8-8)**
Jason Weaver   **25/1**
M Johnston   £60,606

ROYAL HONG KONG JOCKEY CLUB TROPHY
Sandown, July 1   *3+ (1m2f7y)*
KNOWTH **(5-7-8)**
Jimmy Quinn   **13/2**
R Akehurst   £46,182

JOHN SMITH'S MAGNET CUP
York, July 9   *3y+ (1m2f85y)*
CEZANNE **(5-9-12)**
Gary Hind   **9/2**
H Ibrahim   £36,390

WEATHERBY'S SUPER SPRINT
Newbury, July 16   *2y (5f34y)*
BRIEF GLIMPSE
Michael Hills   **7/2**
Major D N Chappell   68,778

WILLIAM HILL CUP
Goodwood, July 26   *3y+ (1m2f)*
DESERT SHOT **(4-8-13)**
Jason Tate (3)   **12/1**
M R Stoute   £35,500

TOTE GOLD TROPHY
Goodwood, July 27   *3y+ (1m4f)*
MIDNIGHT LEGEND **(9-7)**
Jason Weaver   **9/2**
L M Cumani   £36,100

EUROLINK SPITFIRE
Goodwood, July 29   *3y (1m 2f)*
FRUSTRATION **(8-6)**
David Harrison   **5/1**
Lady Herries   £32,460

TOTE EBOR HANDICAP
York, Aug 17   *3+ (1m5f194y)*
HASTEN TO ADD **(4-9-3)**
George Duffield   **13/2F**
Sir M Prescott   £97,361

LADBROKE (AYR) GOLD CUP
Ayr, Sep 17   *3+ (6f)*
DARING DESTINY **(3-8-0)**
J Tate (3)   **18/1**
K R Burke   £51,760

TOTE FESTIVAL HANDICAP
Ascot, Sep 24   *3+ (7f)*
WIZARD KING **(3-8-7)**
George Duffield   **13/2F**
Sir Mark Prescott   £50,200

ASCOT HANDICAP
Ascot, Sep 24   *3+ (1m 4f)*
WHITECHAPEL **(6 8 5)**
Michael Hills   **6/1**
Lord Huntingdon   £48,298

WILLIAM HILL CAMBRIDGESHIRE
Newmarket, Oct 1   *3+ (1m 1f)*
HALLING **(3-8-8)**
Frankie Dettori   **8/1F**
J Gosden   £51,280

....

1993 Races

TOTE CESAREWITCH
Newmarket, Oct 16,1993
AAHSAYLAD (7-8-12)
John Williams 12/1
J White £50,915

WILLIAM HILL NOVEMBER HANDICAP
Doncaster, Nov 7, 1993
QUICK RANSOM
Jason Weaver 6-1F
M Johnston

FRANCE

PRIX GANAY
Longchamp, May 1   3y+ c & f
(1m2f110y)
MARILDO (7-9-2)
G Guignard 185/10f
France £57,208

DUBAI POULE D'ESSAI DES POULAINS
Longchamp, May 8   3y c (1m)
GREEN TUNE (9-2)
O Doleuze
France £114,416

DUBAI POULE D'ESSAI DES POULICHES
Longchamp, May 15   3y f (1m)
EAST OF THE MOON (9-2)
Cash Asmussen 17/10
France £114,416

PRIX LUPIN
Longchamp, May 15   3y c & f
(1m2f110y)
CELTIC ARMS (9-2)
Gerald Mosse 59/10
France £45,767

PRIX SAINT-ALARY
Longchamp, May 22   3y f (1m 2f)
MOONLIGHT DANCE (9-2)
Thierry Jarnet 7/10
France £56,476

PRIX D'ISPAHAN
Longchamp, May 29   3y+ c & f
(1m1f55y)
BIGSTONE (9-2)
Olivier Peslier 7/2F
France £57,208

PRIX JEAN PRAT
Longchamp, May 29
3y c & f (1m1f55y)
MILLKOM (9-2)
J R Dubosc 4/5F
France £45,767

PRIX DU JOCKEY-CLUB
Chantilly, June 5   3y c&f (1m4f)
CELTIC ARMS (9-2)
Gerald Mosse 53/10
France £286,041

PRIX DE DIANE HERMES
Chantilly, June 12   3y f (1m2f110y)
EAST OF THE MOON (9-2)
Cash Asmussen 4/5F
France £160,183

GRAND PRIX DE PARIS
Longchamp, June 26   3y c&f (1m2f)
MILLKOM (9-2)
J R Dubosc 34/10f
France £137,000

GRAND PRIX DE SAINT-CLOUD
Saint-Cloud, July 3   3y+ (1m 4f)
APPLE TREE (9-8)
Thierry Jarnet 13/10
France £137,300

PRIX EUGENE ADAM
Saint-Cloud, July 14   3y (1m 2f)
CARNEGIE (8-11)
Thierry Jarnet 16/10
A Fabre £34,325

PRIX ROBERT PAPIN
Maisons-L, July 17   2y c & f (5f 110y)
GENERAL MONASH (8-11)
Brent Thomson 87/10F
P W Chapple-Hyam £40,046

PRIX DU HARAS *Deauville, Aug 14*
3+ c & f (1m)
EAST OF THE MOON (3-8-8)
Cash Asmussen 9/10
France £114,416

PRIX MORNAY
Deauville, Aug 21   2y c & f (6f)
HOH MAGIC (8-10)
Michael Hills 24/10
M Bell £91,553

PRIX DU MOULIN DE LONGC'P
Longchamp, Sep 4   3+ c & f (1m)
SKI PARADISE (4-8-13)
Yutaka Take 92/10
France £102,975

PRIX DE LA SALAMANDRE
Longchamp, Sep 11   2y c & g (7f)
PENNEKAMP (8-11)
Thierry Jarnet 3/5F
France £45,767

PRIX VERMEILLE
Longchamp, Sep 11   3y f (1m 4f)
SIERRA MADRE (3-9-2)
Gerald Mosse 27/10
France £91,533

GRAND CRITERIUM
Longchamp, Oct 1   2y c & f (1m)
GOLDMARK (8-11)
S Guillot
A Fabre £114,416

PRIX DU CADRAN
Lonchamp, Oct 1   3+ (2m 4f)
MOLESNES (4-8-13)
Olivier Peslier
M Rolland £57,208

PRIX DE L'ABBAYE
Longchamp, Oct 2   2+ (5f)
LOCHSONG (6-9-0)
Frankie Dettori 17/10
I A Balding £57,208

FORTE PRIX DE L'ARC DE TRIOMPHE
Longchamp, Oct 2   3+ (1m 4f)
CARNEGIE (3-8-11)
Thierry Jarnet 19/10
A Fabre £456,666

GERMANY

ARAG PREIS
Dusseldorf, May 1   3y f (1m)
LIFE'S LUCK (8-11)
T Hellier
Germany £46,693

HOLSTEN TROPHY
Hamburg, July 2   3y+ (6f)
SHARP PROD (9-4)
Alan Munro
Lord Huntington £46,693

BMW DEUTSCHES DERBY
Hamburg, July 3
3y c & f (1m 4f)
LAROCHE (9-2)
S Eccles 181DM
Germany £116,732

BERLIN-BRANDENBURG-TROPHY-DER LANDESBANK
Hoppegarten, July 10   3y+ (1m)
ROYAL ABJAR (8-5)
Bruce Raymond 16DM
Germany £77,821

PREIS DER PRIVATBANKIERS
Dusseldorf, July 24   3y+ (1m4f)
STERNKONIG (9-7)
A Helfenbein
Germany £93,385

ARAL-POKAL
Gelsenkirchen, Aug 7   3+ (1m4f)
HEVER GOLF ROAS (3-8-8)
Jason Weaver 26DM
T J Naughton 81,712

IRELAND

FIRST NATIONAL BUILDING SOCIETY 2000 GUINEAS
Curragh, May 15   3y c&f (1m)
TURTLE ISLAND (9-0)
John Reid   **5/4F**
P W Chapple-Hyam   £109,381

AIRLIE/COOLMORE IRISH 1000 GUINEAS
Curragh, May 21   3y f (1m)
MEHTHAAF (9-0)
Willie Carson   **5/2**
J L Dunlop   £93,857

BUDWEISER IRISH DERBY
Curragh, June 26   3y c & f (1m4f)
BALANCHINE (8-11)
Frankie Dettori   **5/1**
H Ibrahim   £331,429

KILDANGAN IRISH OAKS
Curragh, July 9   3y f (1m4f)
BOLAS (9-0)
Pat Eddery   **5/2F**
B W Hills   £107,476

HEINZ 57 PHOENIX STAKES
Leopardstown, Aug 7   2y (6f)
EVA LUNA (8-11)
Kevin Manning   **6/1**
Ireland   £80,476

TATTERSALLS BREEDERS
Curragh, Aug 27   2y (6f)
LOVEYOUMILLIONS (8-10)
Jason Weaver   **3.70 Tote**
M Johnston   £70,000

GUINNESS CHAMPION STAKES
Leopardstown, Sep 10
3+ (1m 2f)
CEZANNE (5-9-4)
Michael Kinane   **7/2**
M R Stoute   £93,143

MOYGLARE STUD STAKES
Curragh, Sep 11   2y f (7f)
BELLE GENIUS (8-11)
Jason Weaver   **20/1**
P A Kelleway   £55,333

NATIONAL STAKES
Curragh, Sep 17   2y c & f (7f)
DEFINITE ARTICLE (9-0)
Michael Kinane   **4/1**
Ireland   £59,143

JEFFERSON SMURFIT MEMORIAL IRISH ST LEGER
Curragh, Sep 17   3+ (1m 6f)
VINTAGE CROP (7-9-8)
Michael Kinane   **7/4**
D Weld   £83,413

ITALY

PREMIO PAROLI
Capannelle, May 1   3y c&f (1m)
POLIUTO (9-2)
F Jovine
Italy   £64,781

PREMIO PRESIDENTE
Capannelle, May 14   3y+ c&f (1m 2f)
MUHTARRAM (5-9-2)
Willie Carson
J H M Gosden   £43,428

OAKS D'ITALIA
San Siro, May 22   3y f (1m4f)
SHAHMIAD (8-11)
F Jovine
Italy   £67,117

DERBY ITALIANO
Capannelle, May 29   3y c&f (1m4f)
TIME STAR (9-2)
Richard Quinn
P F I Cole   £157,922

GRAN PREMIO DI MILANO
San Siro, June 19   3y+ c&f
(1m4f)
PETIT LOUP (9-6)
Walter Swinburn
France   £98,701

JAPAN

YASUDA KINEN
Tokyo, May 15   3y+ (1m)
NORTH FLIGHT (8-9)
K Tsunoda
Japan   £565,407

UNITED STATES

SAN LUIS REY STAKES
Santa Anita, Mar 27   3y+ (1m4f)
BIEN BIEN (8-12)
Chris McCarron
(America)   £101,351

CAESARS INTERNATIONAL
Atlantic C, June 26   3y+ (1m1f110y)
LURE (8-11)
Mike Smith
America   £202,703

AMERICAN DERBY
Arlington Park, July 24   3y (1m1f110y)
OVERBURY & VAUDEVILLE
(3-8-3)   (3-8-2)
S Sellers   A Lopez
D R Loder   America
Horses dead-heated   £81,081 each

BEVERLY D STAKES
Arlington Park, Aug 27
3+ f & m (1m 1f 110y)
HATOOF (5-8-11)
Walter Swinburn   **7.20 Tote**
France   £202,703

ARLINGTON MILLION
Arlinton Park, Aug 27   3+ (1m 2f)
PARADISE CREEK (5-9-0)
Pat Day   **5.60 Tote**
America   £405,405
All races Santa Anita, Nov 6

BREEDERS' CUP SPRINT
3y+ (6f dirt)
CARDMANIA
Eddie Delahoussaye $12.60/$2
D Meredith in US

BDRS' CUP JUVENILE FILLIES
2y f (1m110y dirt)
PHONE CHATTER
L Pincay jnr   **$6.60/$2**
R Mandella in US

BREEDERS' CUP DISTAFF
3+f (1m1f dirt)
HOLLYWOOD WILDCAT
Eddie Delahoussaye $4.60/$2
N Drysdale in US

BREEDERS' CUP MILE
3y+ (1m dirt)
LURE
Mike Smith   **$4.60/$2**
C McGaughey in US

BREEDERS' CUP JUVENILE
2y c&f (1m110y dirt)
BROCCO
Gary Stevens   **$8.00/$2**
R Winick in US

BREEDERS' CUP TURF
Santa Anita, Nov 6   3y+ (1m4f turf)
KOTASHAAN
K Desormeaux   **$5.00/$2**
R Mandella in US

BREEDERS' CUP CLASSIC
Santa Anita, Nov 6   3y+ (1m2f dirt)
ARCANGUES
J Bailey   **$269.20/$2**
A Fabre in France

Final Figures for 1993

Top Trainers - by money

		Wins	£	%
1	H R A Cecil	94	1,248,318	23.0
2	R Hannon	182	1,228,146	15.0
3	M R Stoute	65	1,071,842	15.5
4	J Gosden	110	1,020,975	24.3
5	J L Dunlop	93	700,736	17.4
6	J Berry	133	555,410	16.3
7	G Wragg	35	428,417	17.3
8	C E Brittain	38	416,141	8.4
9	P Chapple-Hyan	52	407,059	21.8
10	I A Balding	50	383,636	14.6

Top Jockeys - by wins

		Wins	£	%
1	Pat Eddery	169	1,659,078	20.8
2	Frankie Dettori	149	1,048,678	16.5
3	Kevin Darley	143	554,458	17.2
4	Richard Quinn	123	652,513	13.9
5	Willie Carson	115	996,497	13.7
6	George Duffield	115	456,389	15.2
7	Michael Roberts	114	1,326,907	15.9
8	John Reid	108	793,012	14.1
9	Willie Ryan	96	663,027	14.5
10	John Carroll	94	416,908	14.7

1994 - As at Oct 4th

Top Trainers - by money

		Wins	£	%
1	M R Stoute	97	1,297,780	19.0
2	J L Dunlop	70	1,248,159	16.3
3	H R A Cecil	64	983,723	23.5
4	J H M Gosden	83	694,296	18.1
5	R Hannon	100	595,890	10.1
6	M Johnston	71	479,912	14.9
7	P F I Cole	61	451,827	12.2
8	G Wragg	28	415,118	17.8
9	L M Cumani	42	411,441	17.7
10	J Berry	98	401,078	13.7

Top Jockeys - by wins

		Wins	£	%
1	Pat Eddery	169	1,659,078	20.8
2	Frankie Dettori	149	1,048,678	16.5
3	Kevin Darley	143	554,458	17.2
4	Richard Quinn	123	652,513	13.9
5	Willie Carson	115	996,497	13.7
6	George Duffield	115	456,389	15.2
7	Michael Roberts	114	1,326,907	15.9
8	John Reid	108	793,012	14.1
9	Willie Ryan	96	663,027	14.5
10	John Carroll	94	416,908	14.7

Raceform Speed Figures As at Oct 1, 1994

Two Year Olds

5f-6f

1	Hoh Magic	74
2	Bruttina	68
3	Silca Blanca	67
4	Princely Hush	66
5	Istidaad	65
6	Options Open	65
7	Statom	65
8	Tereshkova	64
9	Gay Gallanta	63
10	Pentire	63

7f and upwards

1	Belle Genius	73
2	Eltish	72
3	Juyush	69
4	Stiletto Blade	69
5	Tereshkova	68
6	Eva Luna	66
7	Fahal	65
8	Aqaarid	61
9	Classic Cliche	61
10	Wijara	61

Three Year Olds and Upwards

5f-6f

1	Lochsong	97
2	Lake Coniston	94
3	First Trump	91
4	Tropical	88
5	College Chapel	87
6	Lavinia Fontana	87
7	Midhish	87
8	Margaret's Gift	86
9	Thousla Rock	85
10	Ridgewood Ben	80

7f-9f

1	Barathea	95
2	Lower Egypt	95
3	Bigstone	93
4	Muhtarram	92
5	Alflora	91
6	Sayyadati	91
7	Emperor Jones	90
8	Fraam	90
9	Soviet Line	90
10	Young Ern	90

10f-12f

1	Only Royale	97
2	Bob's Return	96
3	East of the Moon	93
4	Erhaab	93
5	Her Ladyship	92
6	Millkom	92
7	Urgent Request	92
8	Bobzao	91
9	George Augustus	91
10	Dancing Bloom	89
11	Mister Baileys	89
12	Wagon Master	89
13	Cezanne	88
14	Weigh Anchor	88
15	Agathe	87
16	Kings Theatre	87
17	Belle Argentine	87
18	Cheviot Amble	86
19	Darrery	86
20	Beauchamp Hero	85

National Hunt

All UK races valued at over £12,000 are listed

DESERT ORCHID SOUTH WESTERN CHASE
Wincanton, Oct 21   (2m 5f)
PANTO PRINCE (12-11-8)
Sean McNeill   5/1
C L Popham   £15,550

CHARLIE HALL CHASE
Wetherby, Oct 30   (3m 110y)
BARTON BANK (7-11-2)
Adrian Maguire   12/1
D Nicholson   £15,440

UNITED HOUSE CONSTRUCTION HANDICAP CHASE
Ascot, Oct 30   (2m)
STORM ALERT (7-11-1)
Sean McNeill   9/4
Andrew Turnell   £15,313

PLYMOUTH GIN HALDON GOLD CHALLENGE CUP
Exeter, Nov 2   (2m 2f)
TRAVADO (7-11-0)
Jamie Osborne   11/10
N J Henderson   £15,925

TOTE SILVER TROPHY
Chepstow, Nov 6   (2m 4f 110y)
TRIPLE WITCHING (7-10-10)
Adrian Maguire   17/2
D Nicholson   £16,633

STEEL PLATE & SECTIONS YOUNG CHASERS CHAMPIONSHIP FINAL
Cheltenham, Nov 12   (3m 1f)
LIGHT VENEER (8-10-5)
Mick Fitzgerald   10/1
Merrita Jones   £13,420

MURPHY'S HANDICAP HURDLE
Cheltenham, Nov 13   (2m 110y)
LEOTARD (6-12-0)
Jamie Osborne   3/1
O Sherwood   £13,550

MACKESON GOLD CUP
Cheltenham, Nov 13   (2m 4f 110y)
BRADBURY STAR (8-11-8)
Declan Murphy   13/2
J T Gifford   £32,143

COOPERS & LYBRAND ASCOT HURDLE
Ascot, Nov 19   (2m 4f)
KING CREDO (8-11-0)
Adrian Maguire   5/2
S Woodman   £13,329

CROWTHER HOMES BECHER HANDICAP CHASE
Aintree, Nov 20   (3m 3f 30y)
INDIAN TONIC (7-10-6)
Chris Maude   4/1
N A Twiston-Davies   £18,729

HENNESSY COGNAC GOLD CUP
Newbury, Nov 27   (3m 2f 110y)
COGENT (9-10-1)
D Fortt   10/1
Andrew Turnell   £35,152

WILLIAM HILL HANDICAP HURDLE
Sandown, Dec 4   (2m 110y)
LAND AFAR (6-11-2)
Warren Marston   13/2
J Webber   £20,750

MITSUBISHI SHOGUN TINGLE CREEK TROPHY
Sandown, Dec 4   (2m)
SYBLLIN (7-11-9)
Peter Niven   6/1
J G FitzGerald   £15,550

BULA HURDLE
Cheltenham, Dec 11   (2m 1f)
STAUNCH FRIEND (5-11-8)
Declan Murphy   6/1
M H Tompkins   £21,560

TRIPLEPRINT GOLD CUP
Cheltenham, Dec 11   (2m 5f)
FRAGRANT DAWN (9-10-2)
Declan Murphy   14/1
M C Pipe   £31,215

LONG WALK HURDLE
Ascot, Dec 18   (3m 1f 110y)
SWEET DUKE (6-11-7)
Carl Llewellyn   7/2
N A Twiston-Davies   £25,372

TRIPLEPRINT FELTHAM NOVICES' CHASE
Kempton, Dec 27   (3m)
SEE MORE INDIANS (6-11-7)
Graham Bradley   7/2
P F Nicholls   £19,140

KING GEORGE VI TRIPLEPRINT CHASE
Kempton, Dec 27   (3m)
BARTON BANK (7-11-10)
Adrian Maguire   9/2
D Nicholson   £51,780

BONUSPRINT CHRISTMAS HURDLE
Kempton, Dec 28   (2m)
MUSE (6-11-7)
Mark Richards   3/1
D R C Elsworth   £33,960

FINALE JUNIOR HURDLE
Chepstow, Dec 28   3y (2m 110y)
MYSILV (10-9)
Adrian Maguire   11/10F
D Nicholson   £16,153

VICTOR CHANDLER HANDICAP CHASE
Warwick, Jan 15   (2m)
VIKING FLAGSHIP (7-10-10)
Richard Dunwoody   3/1
D Nicholson   £19,328

BIC RAZOR LANZAROTE HANDICAP HURDLE
Kempton, Jan 22   (2m)
NIJMEGEN (6-10-6)
Jamie Osborne   5/1
J G FitzGerald   £16,995

PETER MARSH HANDICAP CHASE
Haydock, Jan 22   (3m)
ZETA'S LAD (11-10-10)
Robbie Supple   5/1
John R Upson   £15,475

GREAT YORKSHIRE HANDICAP CHASE
Doncaster, Jan 29   (3m)
CARBISDALE (8-11-4)
Peter Niven   13/2
Mrs M Reveley   £19,008

MASON ORGANISATION PATTERN NOVICES' CHASE
Ayr, Jan 29   (3m 1f)
KILLULA CHIEF (7-11-5)
Mark Dwyer   5/4F
J G M O'Shea   £12,024

SCILLY ISLES NOVICES' CHASE
Sandown, Feb 5   (2m 4f 110y)
BAYDON STAR (7-11-6)
Richard Dunwoody   6/4
D Nicholson   £19,991

SANDOWN H'CAP HURDLE
Sandown, Feb 5   (2m 6f)
DARK HONEY (9-9-11)
Tony Dicken   8/1
S Dow   £13,520

AGFA HANDICAP CHASE
Sandown, Feb 5 *(3m 110y)*
SECOND SCHEDUAL (9-10-7)
Richard Dunwoody **6/1**
D Nicholson £18,570

MARSTON MOOR HANDICAP CHASE
Wetherby, Feb 5 *(2m 4f 110y)*
BLAZING WALKER (10-11-10)
Chris Grant **14/1**
P Cheesbrough £15,996

COMET HANDICAP CHASE
Ascot, Feb 9 *(3m 110y)*
DUBACILLA (8-12-0)
Dean Gallagher **11/4**
J T Cole £13,745

REYNOLDSTOWN NOVICES' CHASE
Ascot, Feb 9 *(3m 110y)*
ONE MAN (6-11-5)
Neil Doughty **2/1**
G Richards £15,029

MITSUBISHI SHOGUN GAME SPIRIT CHASE
Newbury, Feb 12 *(2m 1f)*
VIKING FLAGSHIP (7-11-10)
Adrian Maguire **3/1**
D Nicholson £15,480

TOTE GOLD TROPHY
Newbury, Feb 12 *(2m 110y)*
LARGE ACTION (6-10-8)
Jamie Osbourne **9/2**
O Sherwood £33,305

KINGWELL HURDLE
Wincanton, Feb 24 *(2m)*
VALFINET (7-11-7)
Richard Dunwoody **4/7**
M C Pipe £12,320

PENDIL NOVICES' CHASE
Kempton, Feb 26 *(2m 4f 110y)*
MONSIEUR LE CURE (8-11-3)
Norman Williamson **9/4**
J A C Edwards £12,110.25

RACING POST HANDICAP CHASE
Kempton, Feb 26 *(3m)*
ANTONIN (6-10-4)
John Burke **7/1**
Mrs S A Bramall £29,700

GREENALLS GOLD CUP
Kempton, Feb 26 *(3m 4f 110y)*
MASTER OATS (8-10-2)
Norman Williamson **11/4**
K C Bailey £22,159

SUNDERLANDS IMPERIAL CUP
Sandown, Mar 12 *(2m 110y)*
PRECIOUS BOY (8-11-7)
Lorcan Wyer **33/1**
M G Meagher £19,365

CITRÖEN NOVICES' HURDLE
Cheltenham, Mar 15 *(2m 110y)*
ARCTIC KINSMAN (6-11-8)
Carl Llewellyn **50/1**
N A Twiston-Davies £35,908

GUINNESS ARKLE CHALLENGE TROPHY
Cheltenham, Mar 15 *(2m)*
NAKIR (6-11-8)
Jamie Osborne **9/1**
S Christian £43,290

SMURFIT CHAMPION HURDLE
Cheltenham, Mar 15 *(2m 110y)*
FLAKEY DOVE (8-11-9)
Mark Dwyer **9/1**
R J Price £99,933

RITZ CLUB N.H. H'CAP CHASE
Cheltenham, Mar 15 *(3m 1f)*
ANTONIN (6-11-5)
John Burke **4/1F**
Mrs S A Bramall £31,045

FULKE WALWYN KIM MUIR CHALLENGE CUP
Cheltenham, Mar 15 *(3m 1f)*
FIGHTING WORDS (8-10-0)
T McCarthy **9/2F**
J T Gifford £17,636

HAMLET CIGARS GOLD CARD HANDICAP HURDLE
Cheltenham, Mar 15 *(3m 2f)*
TINDARI (6-10-9)
P Williams **20/1**
J M Jefferson £23,052

SUN ALLIANCE HURDLE
Cheltenham, Mar 16 *(2m 5f)*
DANOLI (6-11-7)
Charlie Swan **7/4F**
Thomas Foley, Ire. £39,504

NATIONAL HUNT 1993-4

Top Trainers

		Wins	£	%
1	M C Pipe	127	570,281	22.2
2	D Nicholson	81	555,355	23.7
3	N A Twiston-Davies	72	407,444	16.1
4	K C Bailey	87	339,418	23.1
5	Mrs M Reveley	103	313,186	25.6
6	J T Gifford	51	241,357	15.6
7	P J Hobbs	64	203,426	20.9
8	N H Henderson	48	194,941	17.8
9	O Sherwood	41	174,490	19.6
10	G Richards	48	172,571	15.8
11	R J Price	9	158,836	15.3
12	J H Johnson	32	150,433	15.0
13	Mrs S Bramall	21	140,748	15.4
14	J A C Edwards	18	139,543	20.5
15	J White	53	131,671	19.0
16	J G Fitzgerald	23	127,878	12.1
17	P F Nicholls	29	126,966	17.7
18	F Doumen (France)	2	121,233	28.6
19	M D Hammond	44	121,172	13.7
20	Capt T A Forster	33	109,214	13.5

Top Jockeys

		1st	2nd	3rd	Total
1	R Dunwoody	198	145	117	891
2	A Maguire	194	175	112	915
3	J Osborne	105	75	54	497
4	N Williamson	104	103	65	582
5	P Niven	89	71	44	410
6	M Fitzgerald	68	53	73	556
7	G McCourt	65	58	50	397
8	D J Murphy	58	52	51	371
9	D Bridgwater	58	38	41	398
10	L Wyer	48	36	42	266
11	A Dobbin	45	48	32	348
12	M Dwyer	41	43	44	331
13	P Hobbs	39	42	27	237
14	C Llewellyn	39	42	40	312
15	G Bradley	37	24	26	211
16	T Reed	37	19	24	232
17	W Marston	34	32	20	322
18	B Storey	34	60	40	356
19	B Powell	34	55	52	446
20	M Richards	33	35	24	245

QUEEN MOTHER CHAMPION CHASE
Cheltenham, Mar 16   (2m)
VIKING FLAGSHIP (7-12-0)
Adrian Maguire   4/1
D Nicholson   £74,381

CORAL CUP
Cheltenham, Mar 16   (2m 5f)
TIME FOR A RUN (7-11-8)
Charlie Swan   11/1
E J O'Grady, Ire   £37,924

SUN ALLIANCE NOV CHASE
Cheltenham, Mar 16   (3m 1f)
MONSIEUR LE CURE (8-11-4)
Peter Niven   15/2
J A C Edwards   £49,017

NH CHALLENGE CUP
Cheltenham, Mar 16   (4m)
CHRISTMAS GORSE (8-12-4)
Mr M Armytage   14/1
N A Gaselee   £15,530

MILDMAY OF FLETE CHALLENGE CUP
Cheltenham, Mar 16   (2m 4f 110y)
ELFAST (11-11-4)
Graham McCourt   8/1
J Webber   £26,337

DAILY EXPRESS TRIUMPH HURDLE
Cheltenham, Mar 17   4y (2m 1f)
MYSILV (10-9)
Adrian Maguire   2/1F
D Nicholson   £36,372

BONUSPRINT STAYERS' HURDLE
Cheltenham, Mar 17   (3m 110y)
BALASANI (8-11-10)
Mark Perrett   9/2JF
M C Pipe   £46,625

TOTE CHELTENHAM GOLD CUP
Cheltenham, Mar 17   (3m 2f 110y)
THE FELLOW (9-12-0)
Adam Kondrat   7/1
F Doumen   £118,770

CHRISTIES FOXHUNTER CHASE
Cheltenham, Mar 17   (3m 2f 110y)
DOUBLE SILK (10-12-0)
Mr Ron Treloggen   2/5F
R C Wilkins   £13,580

GRAND NATIONAL ANNUAL CHALLENGE CUP
Cheltenham, Mar 17   (2m 110y)
SNITTON LANE (8-10-0)
David Bridgwater   33/1
W Clay   £24,309

CATHCART CHALLENGE CUP
Cheltenham, Mar 17   (2m 5f)
RAYMYLETTE (7-11-0)
Mick Fitzgerald   7/4
N J Henderson   £29,240

COUNTY HANDICAP HURDLE
Cheltenham, Mar 17   (2m 1f)
DIZZY (6-10-0)
Tony Dobbin   12/1
P Monteith   £22,250

MILDMAY OF FLETE CHALLENGE CUP
Cheltenham, Mar 16   (2m 4f 110y)
ELFAST (11-11-4)
Graham McCourt   8/1
J Webber   £26,337

BET WITH THE TOTE NOVICES HANDICAP CHASE
Uttoxeter, Mar 19   (3m 2f)
TARAMOSS (7-11-8)
Jamie Osborne   9/2F
J A C Edwards   £14,395

TETLEY MIDLANDS NATIONAL
Uttoxeter, Mar 19   (4m 2f)
GLENBROOK D'OR (10-10-0)
Brian Clifford   10/1
A J Wilson   £32,810

LETHEBY & CHRISTOPHER LONG DISTANCE HURDLE
Ascot, Mar 30   (3m)
SWEET GLOW (7-11-7)
Richard Dunwoody   9/2
M C Pipe   £13,100

DAILY TELEGRAPH NOVICES' HANDICAP CHASE
Ascot, Apr 6   (2m 3f 110y)
WELL BRIEFED (7-10-3)
Brendan Powell   4/1F
R H Buckler   £14,005

MARTELL CUP
Aintree, Apr 7   (3m 1f)
DOCKLANDS EXPRESS (12-11-5)
Richard Dunwoody   5/2
K C Baily   £28,820

SANDEMAN MAGHULL NOVICES' CHASE
Aintree, Apr 7   (2m)
NAKIR (6-11-10)
Jamie Osborne   6/5F
S Christian   £26,337

JOHN HUGHES MEMORIAL TROPHY
Aintree, Apr 7   (2m 6f)
INDIAN TONIC (8-10-4)
Chris Maude   5/1F
N A Twiston-Davies   £24,319

Chaseform Speed Figures 1993-94

Novice Hurdlers
1	Large Action	88
2	Arctic Kinsman	80
3	Morceli	71
4	Dreams End	70
5	Minella Lad	69
	Monalee River	69
7	Barna Boy	65
	Super Coin	65
9	Brief Gale	64
	Danoli	64
	Here He Comes	64

Senior Hurdlers
1	Oh So Risky	92
2	Flakey Dove	85
	Mole Board	85
4	Muse	80
5	Sweet Duke	79
6	Precious Boy	78
7	Granville Again	76
8	Absalom's Lady	75
9	Arabian Gold	72
	Avro Anson	72
	Her Honour	72
	Nahar	72
	Staunch Friend	72

Novice Chasers
1	Baydon Star	83
2	Monsieur Le Cure	81
3	Current Express	75
4	Lord Relic	74
	Crystal Spirit	74
	Martomick	74
7	Nakir	72
8	Belvederean	70
9	Big Beat	69
10	Easy Buck	67

Senior Chasers
1	Remittance Man	92
2	Viking Flagship	90
3	Deep Sensation	89
4	Space Fair	83
	Young Snugfit	83
6	Storm Alert	81
	Travado	81
	Uncle Ernie	81
9	Elfast	80
10	Sybillin	79

Juveniles
1	Winter Forest	68
2	Moorish	66
3	Pridwell	65
4	Mysilv	64

GLENLIVET HURDLE
Aintree, Apr 7   4y (2m 110y)
TROPICAL LAKE (10-9)
K F O'Brien   10/1
M Hourigan   £25,176

MILDMAY OF FLETE CHALLENGE CUP
Cheltenham, Mar 16   (2m 4f 110y)
ELFAST (11-11-4)
Graham McCourt   8/1
J Webber   £26,337

MUMM MELLING CHASE
Aintree, Apr 8   (3m 1f)
KATABATIC (11-11-10)
Sean McNeill   14/1
J T Gifford   £38,898

MUMM MILDMAY NOVICES' CHASE
Aintree, Apr 8   (3m 1f)
MONSIEUR LE CUE (8-11-9)
Peter Niven   7/4F
J A C Edwards   £20,652

ODDBINS HANDICAP HURDLE
Aintree, Apr 8   (2m 4f)
KADI (5-11-7)
Adrian Maguire   7/1
D Nicholson   £13,177

CORDON BLEU HANDICAP HURDLE
Aintree, Apr 9   (2m 110y)
FOR REG (5-10-1)
Adrian Maguire   4/1
P J Flynn   £18,342

MARTELL AINTREE HANDICAP CHASE
Aintree, Apr 8   (2m)
UNCLE ERNIE (9-10-8)
Mark Dwyer   3/1
J G Fitzgerald   £26,110

MARTELL AINTREE HURDLE
Aintree, Apr 8   (2m 4f)
DANOLI (6-11-7)
Charlie Swan   9/2
T Foley   £30,585

MARTELL GRAND NATIONAL
Aintree, Apr 8   (4m 4f)
MIINNEHOMA (11-10-8)
Richard Dunwoody   16/1
M C Pipe   £115,606

EDINBURGH MILL'S FUTURE CHAMPIONS NOVICE CHASE
Ayr, Apr 16   (2m 4f)
SEE MORE INDIANS
Richard Dunwoody   7/2
P F Nicholls   £19,560

STAKIS SCOTTISH GRAND NATIONAL
Ayr, Apr 16   (4m 1f)
EARTH SUMMIT (6-10-0)
David Bridgwater   16/1
N A Twiston-Davies   £29,700

EBF NOVICES' H'CAP HURDLE
Cheltenham, Apr 20   5,6 & 7y (2m 4f)
GOSPEL (5-11-3)
David Bridgwater   7/1
N A Twiston-Davies   £17,125

WHITBREAD GOLD CUP
Sandown, Apr 23   (3m 5f 110y)
USHERS ISLAND (8-10-0)
Charlie Swan   25/1
J H Johnson   £58,415

CHELTENHAM SILVER TROPHY
Cheltenham, Apr 27   (2m 5f)
GALE AGAIN (7-11-4)
Declan Murphy   6/4F
T Stack   £16,225

SWINTON HANDICAP
Haydock, May 2   (2m)
DREAMS END (6-11-4)
M Hourigan
P J Hobbs   £23,555

OVERSEAS

PRIX HEROS XII (CHASE)
Auteuil, Oct 16   (2m 6f)
UCELLO II (7-11-2)
C Aubert
France   £35,842

GRANDE COURSE DE HAIES DE CAGNES
Cagnes-Sur-Mer, Jan 13 (2m4f)
LE ROI THIBAULT (5-10-8)
J-L Y Beaurain
France   £22,883

HENNESSY COGNAC GOLD CUP
Leopardstown, Feb 13   (3m)
JODAMI (9-12-0)
Mark Dwyer   5/4
P Beaumont   £41,071

JAMESON IRISH GRAND NATIONAL
Fairyhouse, Apr 4   (3m 5f)
SON OF WAR (7-10-10)
F Woods   12/1
Ireland   £52,571

HEINEKEN GOLD CUP
Punchestown, Apr 27   (3m 1f)
MERRY GALE (6-12-0)
K O'Brien   5/2
Ireland   £31,143

PRIX AMADOU
Auteuil, Apr 30   4y (2m 6f)
TOPKAR (4-9-13)
C Gombeau
France   £40,046

Brian Lara's achievements this summer have led to a long list of those claiming to have bettered the great man. Josh Gifford must feature quite high on the list. In a benefit match at Hove in 1991, Gifford not only bowled Lara out, for the singularly unexceptional score of ten, but proceeded to score 11 runs himself before losing his wicket to - yes, Lara.

These pages were compiled with the invaluable assistance of Raceform, the Form Book

Ice Hockey

Britain's return to Pool A after a 32-year absence was to be a short-lived excursion ending with a 5-2 defeat by Norway in the relegation match. Britain were effectively outclassed and outplayed throughout a tournament boosted by players released from NHL teams at the end of the regular season. However, the British attitude seemed one of enjoying the occasion, especially as most of the team had only met on the outward plane journey. Rick Fera, Britain's man-of-the-match against the Russians, summed up the feeling: "None of us in our wildest dreams thought we'd ever pull on shirts in Pool A of the world championship against the Russians, and I would rather lose 12-3 in that than win a gold medal in Pool B." British coach Alex Dampier was similarly impressed with the workings of the 'Red Machine' "We're not used to so many players who can shoot so well" he lamented.

The view of Durham Wasps' coach, Paul Smith, was less starry-eyed when assessing Britain's chances prior to the tournament: "If Britain turn out to be the Eddie the Eagle of the world championships it would do untold harm to the domestic game".

The ongoing controversy over foreign players continued with statistics at the World Championships showing that, apart from the Canadians in their national side there were 50 others playing as dual nationals. Great Britain boasted 15, Italy 9 and even the USA managed to have one. It is not all one-way traffic though - Steve Thomas of the New York Islanders was the last name added to the Canadian squad...and he was born in Stockport.

World Championship

Pool A

Milan, Italy   Apr 25-May 8

Preliminary Round

GROUP A

				GROUP B			
Italy	1	Canada	4	Sweden	3	Norway	3
Austria	2	Germany	2	Finland	4	Czech R.	4
G Britain	3	Russia	12	France	1	USA	5
Canada	6	Austria	1	Czech R.	5	France	2
G Britain	4	Germany	0	USA	7	Norway	2
Russia	7	Italy	0	Sweden	3	Finland	5
Russia	1	Canada	3	Czech R.	3	USA	5
Italy	3	Austria	1	France	0	Sweden	6
Canada	3	Germany	2	Norway	1	Finland	5
Austria	1	Russia	4	France	1	Finland	8
Italy	10	G Britain	2	Czech R.	2	Norway	2
Germany	0	Russia	6	USA	2	Sweden	6
Canada	8	G Britain	2	Norway	1	France	4
G Britain	0	Austria	10	USA	2	Finland	7*
Italy	3	Germany	1	Sweden	4	Czech R.	1

* FResult amended after a doping positive USA 0 Finland 7.

Final Group Standings

GROUP A

	P	W	D	L	GF	GA	Pts
1 Canada	5	5	0	0	24	7	10
2 Russia	5	4	0	1	30	7	8
3 Italy	5	3	0	2	17	15	6
4 Austria	5	1	1	3	15	15	3
5 Germany	5	1	1	3	9	14	3
6 Great Britain	5	0	0	5	7	44	0

GROUP B	P	W	D	L	GF	GA	Pts
1 Finland	5	4	1	0	29	11	9
2 Sweden	5	3	1	1	22	11	7
3 USA	5	3	0	2	19	19	6
4 Czech Republic	5	1	2	2	15	17	4
5 France	5	1	0	4	8	25	2
6 Norway	5	0	2	3	9	21	2

Quarter Finals

Russia	1	USA	3
Sweden	7	Italy	2
Canada	3	Czech R.	2
Finland	10	Austria	0

Relegation Game

G Britain	2	Norway	5

Semi Finals

Finland	8	USA	0
Sweden	0	Canada	6

3rd/4th Play Off

Sweden	7	USA	2

FINAL

Finland   1   Canada   2

(after penalty shoot-out - 1-1 at full time)

Pool B

Copenhagen, Denmark   Apr 7-17

Final Standings

		P	W	D	L	GF	GA	Pts
1	Switzerland	7	6	1	0	52	9	13
2	Latvia	7	6	0	1	61	9	12
3	Poland	7	5	1	1	45	21	11
4	Japan	7	3	1	3	37	38	7
5	Denmark	7	3	0	4	31	27	6
6	Holland	7	2	1	4	23	33	5
7	Romania	7	1	0	6	18	43	2
8	China	7	0	0	7	11	98	0

Switzerland promoted to Pool A, China relegated to Pool C

Pool C (Group 1)

Spisska Nova Ves, Slovakia   Mar 18-27

Final Standings

		P	W	D	L	GF	GA	Pts
1	Slovakia	6	4	2	0	43	3	10
2	Belarus	6	5	0	1	35	11	10
3	Ukraine	6	3	2	1	49	7	8
4	Kazakhstan	6	3	2	1	52	12	8
5	Slovenia	6	2	0	4	26	27	4
6	Hungary	6	1	0	5	14	47	2
7	Bulgaria	6	0	0	6	3	115	0
8	DPR Korea	withdrew

Slovakia promoted to Pool B, Korea relegated

Pool C (Group 2)

Barcelona, Spain   Mar 13-19

Final Standings

TOP 4		P	W	D	L	GF	GA	Pts
1	Estonia	3	3	0	0	27	0	6
2	Spain	3	1	1	1	11	13	3
3	Korea	3	1	1	1	4	13	3
4	Croatia	3	0	0	3	3	19	0

BOTTOM 4		P	W	D	L	GF	GA	Pts
1	Belgium	3	3	0	0	23	6	6
2	Australia	3	2	0	1	17	11	4
3	Israel	3	1	0	2	13	12	2
4	South Africa	3	0	0	3	5	29	0

Estonia promoted to Pool C (Group 1)

Women's World Championship

Lake Placid, USA   Apr 11-17

Semi Finals

Canada 4 Finland 1   USA 14 China 3

3rd/4th Play Off

Finland 8 China 1

FINAL

Canada 6 USA 3

National League

PREMIER DIVISION

		P	W	D	L	GF	GA	Pts
1	Cardiff Devils	44	39	0	5	422	220	78
2	Fife Flyers	44	27	2	15	304	192	56
3	Sheffield Steelers*	44	28	4	12	313	198	55
4	Nottingham P'thers	44	26	4	12	288	224	54
5	Murrayfield Racers*	44	27	2	15	385	286	51
6	Durham Wasps	44	24	2	18	316	284	50
7	Whitley Warriors	44	23	4	17	282	298	50
8	Humberside Hawks	44	18	4	22	301	308	40
9	Basingstoke Beavers	44	11	6	27	255	344	28
10	Bracknell Bees	44	11	3	30	220	320	25
11	Peterborough Pirates	44	9	3	32	239	398	21
12	Teesside Bombers	44	5	0	39	238	491	10

* Five points deducted for breaking wage-capping regulations

Leading Scorers	P	Goals	Assists	Pts
Tony Hand (Mur)	44	72	150	222
Chris Palmer (Mur)	44	114	97	211
Rick Brebant (Car)	44	88	120	208
Hilton Ruggles (Car)	43	100	77	177
Richard Laplante (Mur)	42	69	90	159

Leading Netminders	P	Shots	GA	Ave.
John McCrone (Fif)	43	1249	171	4.18
Martin McKay (She)	39	1283	165	4.63
Jason Wood (Car)	43	1372	183	4.76

DIVISION ONE

North		P	W	D	L	GF	GA	Pts
1	Milton Keynes Kings	44	38	0	6	485	233	76
2	Telford Tigers	44	34	5	5	452	252	73
3	Blackburn Hawks	44	24	6	14	373	284	54
4	Trafford Metros	44	24	3	17	392	335	51
5	Paisley Pirates	44	20	3	21	412	368	43
6	Solihull Barons	44	13	4	27	313	369	30
7	Dumfries Vikings	44	11	5	28	336	444	27
8	Oxford City Stars	44	1	2	41	222	743	4

South		P	W	D	L	GF	GA	Pts
1	Slough Jets	44	35	3	6	433	231	73
2	Romford Raiders	44	27	5	12	328	235	59
3	Medway Bears	44	25	3	16	309	237	53
4	Swindon Wildcats	44	20	4	20	373	325	44
5	Guildford Flames	44	19	2	23	293	308	40
6	Lee Valley Lions	44	14	1	29	330	451	29
7	Streatham Redskins	44	11	2	31	222	344	24
8	Chelmsford Ch'tains	44	10	2	32	260	374	22

British Championship

Wembley   Apr 22-24

Semi Finals

Sheffield Steelers 8 Nottingham Panthers 0

Cardiff Devils 8 Fife Flyers 4

Final

Cardiff 12 Sheffield 1

Benson & Hedges Cup

Sheffield   Dec 6

Final   (5,865)

Cardiff Devils 2 *(Chinn, Brebant)*

Murrayfield Racers 6 *(T Hand 2, Palmer 2, Pentland, Lovell)*

B & H All-Star Challenge
Sheffield   Dec 6
North 11 *(Little 2, Morrison 2, Matulik, Robertson, Payne,*
*   Kaese, Longstaff, Norton, Odelein)*
South 11 *(Belanger 4, Whistle 3, Adey 2, Dickie, King)*
South won 3-2 after penalty shootout

European Cup
Riga, Latvia   Oct 8-10
Sokol Eskulap Kiev UKR bt Cardiff Devils GBR 9-1
Pardaugava Riga LAT bt Energ. Elek. Vilnius LTU 12-0
Sokol Eskulap Kiev bt Energ. Elek. Vilnius 11-1
Pardaugava Riga bt Cardiff Devils 11-4
Cardiff Devils bt Energ. Elek. Vilnius 10-3
Sokol Eskulap Kiev drew with Pardaugava Riga 2-2

Final Standings	P	W	D	L	GF	GA	Pts
1 Pardaugava Riga	3	2	1	0	25	6	5
2 Sokol Eskulap Kiev	3	2	1	0	22	4	5
3 Cardiff Devils	3	1	0	2	15	23	2
4 Energ. Vilnius	3	0	0	3	33	4	0

National Hockey League
Eastern Conference
NORTHEAST DIVISION
	P	W	L	T	GF	GA	Pts
Pittsburgh Penguins	84	44	27	13	299	285	101
Boston Bruins	84	42	29	13	289	252	97
Montreal Canadiens	84	41	29	14	283	248	96
Buffalo Sav.	84	43	32	9	282	218	95
Québec Nordiques	84	34	42	8	277	292	76
Hartford Whalers	84	27	48	9	227	288	63
Ottawa Senators	84	14	61	9	201	397	37

ATLANTIC DIVISION
	P	W	L	T	GF	GA	Pts
New York Rangers	84	52	24	8	299	231	112
New Jersey Devils	84	47	25	12	306	220	106
Washington Capitals	84	39	35	10	277	263	88
New York Islanders	84	36	36	12	282	264	84
Florida Panthers	84	33	34	17	233	233	83
Philadelphia Flyers	84	35	39	10	294	314	80
Tampa Bay Lightning	84	30	43	11	224	251	71

Western Conference
CENTRAL DIVISION
	P	W	L	T	GF	GA	Pts
Detroit Red Wings	84	46	30	8	356	275	100
Toronto Maple Leafs	84	43	29	12	280	243	98
Dallas Stars	84	42	29	13	286	265	97
St Louis Blues	84	40	33	11	270	283	91
Chicago Blackhawks	84	39	36	9	254	240	87
Winnipeg Jets	84	24	51	9	245	344	57

PACIFIC DIVISION
	P	W	L	T	GF	GA	Pts
Calgary Flames	84	42	29	13	302	256	97
Vancouver Canucks	84	41	40	3	279	276	85
San Jose Sharks	84	33	35	16	252	265	82
Anaheim Mighty Ducks	84	33	46	5	229	251	71
Los Angeles Kings	84	27	45	12	294	322	66
Edmonton Oilers	84	25	45	14	261	305	64

Conference Quarter Finals
EASTERN CONFERENCE *(Best of 7 series)*
New York Rangers bt New York Islanders 4-0
Washington Capitals bt Pittsburgh Penguins 4-2
New Jersey Devils bt Buffalo Sav. 4-3
Boston Bruins bt Montreal Canadiens 4-3

WESTERN CONFERENCE *(Best of 7 series)*
San Jose Sharks bt Detroit Red Wings 4-3
Vancouver Canucks bt Calgary Flames 4-3
Toronto Maple Leafs bt Chicago Blackhawks 4-2
Dallas Stars bt St Louis Blues 4-0

Conference Semi Finals
EASTERN CONFERENCE *(Best of 7 series)*
New York Rangers bt Washington Capitals 4-1
New Jersey Devils bt Boston Bruins 4-2
WESTERN CONFERENCE *(Best of 7 series)*
Toronto Maple Leafs bt San Jose Sharks 4-3
Vancouver Canucks bt Dallas Stars 4-1

Conference Finals
EASTERN DIVISION *(Best of 7 series)*
New York Rangers bt New Jersey Devils 4-3
WESTERN DIVISION *(Best of 7 series)*
Vancouver Canucks bt Toronto Maple Leafs 4-1

NHL Stanley Cup Championship
Best of 7 series   May 31-June 14
Game 1: New York Rangers 2 Vancouver Canucks 3 (OT)
Game 2: New York Rangers 3 Vancouver Canucks 1
Game 3: Vancouver Canucks 1 New York Rangers 5
Game 4: Vancouver Canucks 2 New York Rangers 4
Game 5: New York Rangers 3 Vancouver Canucks 6
Game 6: Vancouver Canucks 4 New York Rangers 1
Game 7: (Deciding Match)
Madison Square Garden   June 14 (18,000)
New York Rangers 3 Vancouver Canucks 2

NHL STANLEY CUP WINS
1928 onwards

1928	N Y Rangers	1954-5	Detroit Red Wings
1929	Boston Bruins	1956-1960	
1930-1	Montreal C'diens		Montreal C'diens
1932	Toronto Maple Ls	1961	Chicago Blackh'ks
1933	N Y Rangers	1962-4	Toronto Maple Ls
1934	Chicago Blackh'ks	1965-6	Montreal C'diens
1935	Montreal Maroons	1967	Toronto Maple Ls
1936-7	Detroit Red Wings	1968-9	Montreal C'diens
1938	Chicago Blackh'ks	1970	Boston Bruins
1939	Boston Bruins	1971	Montreal C'diens
1940	N Y Rangers	1972	Boston Bruins
1941	Boston Bruins	1973	Montreal C'diens
1942	Toronto Maple Ls	1974-5	Philadelphia Flyers
1943	Detroit RedWings	1976-9	Montreal C'diens
1944	Montreal C'diens	1980-3	N Y Islanders
1945	Toronto Maple Ls	1984-5	Edmonton Oilers
1946	Montreal C'diens	1986	Montreal C'diens
1947-9	Toronto Maple Ls	1987-8	Edmonton Oilers
1950	Detroit Red Wings	1989	Calgary Flames
1951	Toronto Maple Ls	1990	Edmonton Oil'
1952	Detroit Red Wings	1991-2	Pittsburgh P'guins
1953	Montreal C'diens	1993	Montreal C'diens

Ice Skating

World Championships

Chiba, Japan   Mar 22-27

PAIRS

Two elements: technical & free-skating.

			TP	FS	Ttl
1	Evgenia Shishkova Vadim Naumov	RUS	1	1	1.5
2	Isabelle Brasseur Lloyd Eisler	CAN	2	2	3.0
3	Marian Eltsova Andrey Bushkov	RUS	3	3	4.5
25	Dana Mednick Jason Briggs	GBR	25	-	

ICE DANCING

Four elements; 2 compulsory, original and free dances.

			D1	D2	OD	FD	Total
1	Oksana Gritschuk Evgeny Platov	RUS	1	1	1	1	2.0
2	Sophie Moniotte Pascal Lavanchy	FRA	2	2	2	2	4.0
3	Susanna Rahkamo Petri Kokko	FIN	3	3	3	3	6.0
16	Marika Humphreys Justin Lanning	GBR	16	16	16	16	32.0

FIGURE SKATING

Men

			TP	FS	Ttl
1	Elvis Stojko	CAN	1	1	1.5
2	Philippe Candeloro	FRA	2	2	3.0
3	Viacheslav Zagorodniuk	UKR	3	3	4.5
10	Steven Cousins	GBR	7	11	14.5

Women

			TP	FS	Ttl
1	Yuka Sato	JPN	1	1	1.5
2	Surja Bonaly	FRA	2	2	3.0
3	Tanja Szewczenko	GER	4	3	5.0
18	Charlene Von Saher	GBR	16	18	26.0

European Championships

Copenhagen, Denmark   Jan 18-23

PAIRS

			TP	FS	Ttl
1	Ekaterina Gordeeva Sergey Grinkov	RUS	1	1	1.5
2	Evgenia Shishkova Vadim Naumov	RUS	2	3	4.0
3	Natalia Mishkutenok Artur Dmitriev	RUS	5	2	4.5
17	Dana Mednick Jason Briggs	GBR	19	15	24.5

ICE DANCING

			D1	D2	OD	FD	Ttl
1	Jayne Torvill Christopher Dean	GBR	3	2	1	2	3.6
2	Oksana Gritschuk Evgeny Platov	RUS	2	3	3	1	3.8
3	Maya Usova Alexandr Zhulin	RUS	1	1	2	3	4.6

FIGURE SKATING

Men

			TP	FS	Ttl
1	Victor Petrenko	UKR	1	1	1.5
2	Viacheslav Zagorodniuk	UKR	3	2	3.5
3	Alexei Urmanov	RUS	6	3	6.0
11	Steven Cousins	GBR	13	10	16.5

Women

			TP	FS	Ttl
1	Surya Bonaly	FRA	1	1	1.5
2	Oksana Baiul	UKR	2	2	3.0
3	Olga Markova	RUS	3	3	4.5
23	Stephanie Main	GBR	18	24	33.5

World Junior Championships

Colorado, USA   Nov 28-Dec 4

PAIRS

			TP	FS	Ttl
1	Maria Petrova Anton Sikharulidze	RUS	1	1	1.5
2	Caroline Haddad Jean-Sebastien Fecteau	CAN	3	2	3.5
3	Galina Maniachenko Evgeny Gigursky	UKR	2	3	4.0

ICE DANCING

			D1	D2	OD	FD	Ttl
1	Sylwia Nowak Sebastian Kolasinski	POL	2	2	1	1	2.4
2	Ekaterina Svirina Sergey Sahnovskiy	RUS	1	1	2	2	3.6
3	Agnes Jacquemard Alexis Gayet	FRA	3	3	5	3	7.2
12	Julie Keeble Lasantha Salpadoru	GBR	13	12	11	12	23.6

FIGURE SKATING

Men

			TP	FS	Ttl
1	Michael Weiss	USA	1	1	1.5
2	Naoki Shigematsu	JPN	6	3	6.0
3	Jere Michael	USA	5	4	6.5
22	Stuart Bell	GBR	22	22	33.0

Women

			TP	FS	Ttl
1	Michelle Kwan	USA	1	1	1.5
2	Krisztine Czako	HUN	2	2	3.0
3	Irina Slutskaja	RUS	3	3	4.5
24	Stephanie Main	GBR	21	24	34.5

British Championships

Sheffield   Jan 7-8

ICE DANCING

			D1	D2	OD	FD	Ttl
1	Jayne Torvill Christopher Dean	NISA	1	1	1	1	2.0
2	Marika Humphreys Justin Lanning	Slough	2	2	2	2	4.0
3	Michelle Fitzgerald Vincent Kyle	Slough	3	3	3	4	7.0

Basingstoke   Dec 8-12

FIGURE SKATING

Men

			Tp	FS	Ttl
1	Steven Cousins	Deeside	.5	1.0	1.5
2	John Martin	Kyle	1.0	2.0	3.0
3	D Ings	Swindon	1.5	3.0	4.5

Women

1	Stephanie Main	Murrayfield	.5	1.0	1.5
2	N Gorbenko-Risk	Aly-Pally	1.0	2.0	3.0
3	Emma Warmington	Sun'land	2.0	3.0	5.

Judo

"You can't go in expecting to win," said Nicola Fairbrother, prior to the 1993 World Championships in Ontario last October. Fairbrother might have understated her own chances, but she was highly enough thought of to be the only British player tipped in the Japanese magazine *Kindai Judo*. The Japanese, yet to be as strong in the women's branch of the sport as they are in the men's, got it spot-on. Fairbrother took the world lightweight title against one of their own, Chiyori Tateno. Throwing the Japanese with a *sode-tsuri-komi-goshi* for a seven point *waza-ari*. It was a throw that Fairbrother had never before used in top level competition. "I had been practising with Tateno in a training camp....and I knew that if I went into ground work with her I was history. I had to throw her," acknowledged Fairbrother.

Her career has been a steady progression. She won silver at the European Junior Championships in 1986 and moved on to gold a year later. In 1990, Fairbrother won a senior European bronze, then took the title two years later. In that same year, 1992, she missed an Olympic gold by a narrow margin. The victory of the 24-year-old from Sandhurst means she becomes the seventh British women to hold a world title. With a silver from Kate Howey and two bronzes to add to the team total, Britain's women stood equal second to the Japanese in the women's medal table.

The predictability that took Fairbrother to the world title did not extend to the European Championships in May, but the British team was none the poorer for it. Fairbrother succumbed to Jessica Gal at Gdansk and Ray Stevens, who might have warily been circling the gold medal, also had to be satisfied with silver. It was left to the living and training partners Ryan Birch and Rowena Sweatman to pull off an exceptional double gold. Birch defeated an overconfident Johans Laats. The Belgian having beat him thrice before, it was fourth time lucky for Birch. While Sweatman, a 26-year-old engineering graduate from the same Pinewood club as Fairbrother, overcame Austria's Angleburger. With another silver coming from former champion Diane Bell and bronzes from Kate Howey and Debbie Allan, it was a thoroughly conspicuous championship. Given the ructions in the sport in 1993 - and not entirely absent this year with the suspension of national squad coach Mark Earle - the performances on the mat ensured that the sport has been getting the headlines that it prefers. That said, the coverage from Gdansk still suggests that the sport has a major problem in persuading the media to take it seriously at any level.

BRITISH WORLD CHAMPIONS

Men

- 78kg	Neil Adams	1981

Women

-61kg	Diane Bell	1986
	Diane Bell	1987
-56kg	Ann Hughes	1986
	Nicola Fairbrother	1993
-52kg	Loretta Doyle	1982
	Sharon Rendle	1987
	Sharon Rendle	1989
-48kg	Jane Bridge	1980
	Karen Briggs	1982
	Karen Briggs	1984
	Karen Briggs	1986
	Karen Briggs	1989

World Championships

Sept 30 - Oct 3   Hamilton, Canada

MEN

-60kg
1	Ryuki Sonoda	JPN
2	Nazim Gousseinov	AZE
3	Georgi Vazagachvili	GEO
3	Richard Trautmann	GER

-65kg
1	Yukimasa Nakamura	JPN
2	Eric Born	SUI
3	Uda Quellmalz	GER
3	Sergey Kosmynine	RUS

-71kg
1	Hoon Chung	KOR
2	Bertalan Hajtos	HUN
3	Rogerio Cardoso	BRZ
3	Daisuke Hideshima	JPN

-78kg
1	Ki-Young Chun	KOR
2	Hidehiko Yoshida	JPN
3	Darcel Yandzi	FRA
3	Jason Morris	USA

-86kg
1	Yoshio Nakamura	JPN
2	Nicolas Gill	CAN
3	Leon Villar	SPN
3	Adrian Croitoru	ROM

-95kg
1	Antal Kovacs	HUN
2	Aurelio Miguel	BRZ
3	Stephane Traineau	FRA
3	Marc Meiling	GER

+95kg
1	David Douillet	FRA
2	Dav Khakhaleichvili	GEO
3	Frank Moller	GER
3	Sergei Kossorotov	RUS

Open
1	Rafael Kubacki	POL
2	Henry Stohr	GER
3	Naoyo Ogawa	JPN
3	Dav Khakhaleichvili	GEO

WOMEN

-48kg
1	Ryoko Tamura	JPN
2	Aiyue Li	CHN
3	Giovanna Tortora	ITA
3	Joyce Heron	GBR

-52kg
1	Rodriguez Verdecia	CUB
2	Almudena Munoz	SPN
3	Wakaba Suzuki	JPN
3	Cecile Nowak	FRA
5	Sharon Rendle	GBR

-56kg
1	Nicola Fairbrother	GBR
2	Chiyori Tateno	JPN
3	Jessica Gal	HOL
3	Morales Gonzalez	CUB

-61kg
1	Caveye De Van	BEL
2	Yael Arad	ISR
3	Diane Bell	GBR
3	Zulueta Beltran	CUB

-66kg
1	Min-Sun Cho	KOR
2	Liiko Ogasawa	USA
3	Di Zhang	CHN
3	Odalys Reve Jimerez	CUB
7	Chloe Cowan	GBR

-72kg
1	Chunhui Leng	CHN
2	Kate Howey	GBR
3	Mi Jung Kim	KOR
3	Victoria Kazounina	RUS

+72kg
1	Johanna Hagn	GER
2	Noriko Anno	JPN
3	Monique Van Der Lee	HOL
3	Svetlana Goundarenko	RUS

Open
1	Beata Maksymow	POL
2	Angelique Seriese	HOL
3	Ying Zhang	CHN
3	Ji-Yoon Moon	KOR

Medal Table *(top ten only)*

	G	S	B
Japan	4	3	3
Korea	3	-	2
Poland	2	-	-
Germany	1	1	4
Great Britain	1	1	2
China	1	1	2
Hungary	1	1	-
Cuba	1	-	3
France	1	-	3
Belgium	1	-	-

European Championships

May 19-22   Gdansk, Poland

MEN

-60kg
1	Girola Giovinazzo	ITA
2	Nazim Gousseinov	AZE
3	Franck Chambily	FRA
3	Geor Revazichvili	GEO

-65kg
1	Vladimir Dratchko	RUS
2	Jaroslaw Lewak	POL
3	Salim Abanoz	TUR
3	Benoit Campargue	FRA

-71kg
1	Sergey Kosmynine	RUS
2	Patrick Rosso	FRA
3	Bertalan Hajtos	HUN
3	Rene Sporleder	GER

-78kg
1	Ryan Birch	GBR
2	Johans Laats	BEL
3	Mark Huizinga	HOL
3	Patrick Reiter	AUT

-86kg
1	Oleg Maltsev	RUS
2	Vincent Carabetta	FRA
3	Iverl Djikurauki	GEO
3	Adrian Croitoru	ROM

-95kg
1	Pawel Nastula	POL
2	Ray Stevens	GBR
3	Dmitri Serfueev	RUS
3	Mike Hax	GER

+95kg
1	David Douillet	FRA
2	Rafal Kubacki	POL
3	Igor Moller	GER
3	Selim Tataroglu	TUR

Open
1	Laurent Crost	FRA
2	Harry Van Berneveld	BEL
3	Evgeny Petchourov	RUS
3	Davidashvili	GEO

WOMEN

-48kg
1	Jolanda Soler	ESP
2	Sylvie Meloux	FRA
3	T Kouvchinova	RUS
3	Justina Pinheiro	POR

-52kg
1	Ewa Krause	POL
2	Alessandra Giungi	ITA
3	A Von Schichow	GER
3	Debbie Allan	GBR

-56kg
1	Jessica Gal	HOL
2	Nicola Fairbrother	GBR
3	Magalle Baton	FRA
3	Ursula Myren	SWE

-61kg
1	G Van De Cavaye	HUN
2	Diane Bell	GBR
3	Miriam Blasco	ESP
3	Mir Janosikova	SVK

-66kg
1	Rowena Sweatman	GBR
2	A Angleberger	AUT
3	Claudia Zwiers	HOL
3	Radke Stusakova	TCH

-72kg
1	Ulla Werbrouck	BEL
2	Estha Essombe	FRA
3	Kate Howey	GBR
3	Cristina Curto	ESP

+72kg
1	Angelique Seriese	HOL
2	Beata Maksymov	POL
3	Svetlana Gundarenko	RUS
3	Raquel Barrientos	ESP
5	Josie Horton	GBR

Open
1	Monique Van Der Lee	HOL
2	Christine Cicot	FRA
3	Irina Rodina	RUS
3	Beata Maksymov	POL

Medal Table *(top ten only)*

	G	S	B
Russia	3	-	5
Holland	3	-	2
France	2	5	3
Great Britain	2	3	2
Poland	2	3	1
Belgium	2	2	-
Italy	1	1	-
Spain	1	-	3
Austria	-	1	1
Azerbayan	-	1	-

British Open Championships

April 9, 1994   Birmingham

MEN

-60kg
1 Manuel Orgaz — ESP
2 Thierry Dibert — FRA
3 Ewan Berton — CAN
3 James Johnson — GBR

-65kg
1 Julian Davies — GBR
2 Tsuyoshi Uchida — JPN
3 Paul Leishman — GBR
3 Grasmuch Jurgen — GER

-71kg
1 E Zymna — GER
2 Billy Cusack — GBR
3 T Bucholz — GER
3 Patrick Loon — HOL

-78kg
1 Ryan Birch — GBR
2 Edelmar Zandl — BRA
3 Philip Waydelich — FRA
3 Kowak Knut — GER

-86kg
1 Tamaz Saakachvilei — FRA
2 Stephance Norris — FRA
3 Nicholas Gill — CAN
3 Alex Borderieux — FRA

-95kg
1 Ray Stevens — GBR
2 M Hax — GER
3 M Wirth — GER
3 D Knorret — GER

+95kg
1 Georges Mathonnet — FRA
2 Laurent Crost — FRA
3 Kasim Dahu — FRA
3 Rolf Koser — GER

WOMEN

-48kg
1 Ana Fernandez — ESP
2 Yuka Eto — JPN
3 Brite Siemens — GER
3 Yolanda Soler — ESP

-52kg
1 Fatira Merah — FRA
2 Lizzie Floodgate — GBR
3 A Takeda — JPN
3 Elise Summers — GBR

-56kg
1 Karina Nedellec — FRA
2 Narelle Hill — AUS
3 Barbara Dohmen — GER
3 Cheryl Peel — GBR

-61kg
1 Carol Kelly — GBR
2 Miriam Blasco — ESP
3 Kirsti Weir — GBR
3 Yuko Emoto — JPN

-66kg
1 Karen Roberts — GBR
2 Yoko Nakatachi — JPN
3 Sophie Roberge — CAN
3 Nicole Bruns — GER

-72kg
1 Kate Howey — GBR
2 Heli Syrja — FIN
3 Laurence Sionneau — FRA
3 Katarina Hakansen — SWE

+72kg
1 Monique Van der Lee — HOL
2 Claudia Weber — GER
3 Karin Kutz — GER
3 Heba Rashid — EGY

British Closed Championships

Crystal Palace   Dec 4, 1993

WOMEN

-48kg
1 Joyce Heron — SJF

-52kg
1 Debbie Allen — Sth

-56kg
1 Cheryl Peel — NHC

-61kg
1 Kirsti Weir — SJF

-66kg
1 Chloe Cowan — Nth

-72kg
1 Kate Howey — Sth

+72kg
1 Michelle Rogers — NW

MEN

-60kg
1 Jamie Johnson — Mids

-65kg
1 Simon Moss — Mids

-71kg
1 Danny Kingston — NHC

-78kg
1 William Cusack — SJF

-86kg
1 Fitzroy Davis — Mids

-95kg
1 Lloyd Alexander — Lon

+95kg
1 William Etherington — NW

British Ranking List

MEN

-60kg
1 John Newton — Y&H — 564
2 Jamie Johnson — Mid — 515
3 Junior Morrison — Lon — 407

-65kg
1 Simon Moss — Mid — 700
2 Jean Paul Bell — Mid — 641
3 David Somerville — SJF — 468

-71kg
1 Danny Kingston — Sth — 980
2 Ian Freeman — Sth — 940
3 Stephen Ravenscroft — NW — 564

-78kg
1 Ryan Birch — Y&H — 752
2 Martin McSorley — Mid — 610
3 Daniel Kissen — Y&H — 470

-86kg
1 Gary Edwards — SJF — 610
=2 David Southby — Sth — 560
=2 Keith Davies — Lon — 560

-95kg
=1 Danny Sargent — Sth — 470
=1 Dale Webb — Mid — 470
3 R Giles — Sth — 397

+95kg
1 Nick Kokotaylo — NW — 710
2 William Etherington — NW — 515
3 Dean Pitcher — NHC — 405

WOMEN

-48kg
1 Joyce Heron — SJF — 940
2 Philippa Gemmill — NHC — 704
3 Fiona Robertson — SJF — 424

-52kg
1 Elise Summers — NHC — 867
2 Sharon Rendle — Y&H — 610
3 Elizabeth Floodgate — Sth — 560

-56kg
1 Cheryl Peel — NHC — 700
2 Debbie Allen — Sth — 637
3 Ceri Richards — Mid — 620

-61kg
1 Diane Bell — Nth — 980
2 Kirsti Weir — SJF — 560
3 Rosie Felton — Mid — 530

-66kg
1 Chloe Cowan — Nth — 940
2 Rowena Sweatman — NW — 614
3 Eva Webster — West — 537

72kg
1 Kate Howey — Sth — 980
2 Josie Horton — Sth — 800
=3 Elaine Morgan — WJA — 420
=3 Stacey Smith — Lon — 420

+72kg
1 Michelle Rodgers — NW — 840
2 Lisa Maddaford — West — 520
3 Suzanne Simpkins — Mid — 447

Karate/Taekwondo

Karate World Championships

Johannesburg, South Africa   Nov

INDIVIDUAL KATA

Men		Women	
1 N Aramoto	JPN	L Hayashi	JPN
2 S Dorfman	RSA	L Greenspan	RSA
3 Y Yamaguchi	JPN	E Vanzyl	RSA

INDIVIDUAL KUMITE

Men		Women	
1 N Aramoto	JPN	S Inove	JPN
2 Y Yamaguchi	JPN	B Monareng	RSA
3 R Amos	GBR	K Marriott	AUS
3 F Hatanaka	JPN		

European Championships

Birmingham   May

MEN

Team Kumite	Team Kata
1 Italy	France
2 France	Italy
3 Switzerland	Spain
3 England	

Individual Kata	Open
1 M Milon FRA	C Della Rocca ITA
2 L Sanz ESP	E Idrizi CRO
3 P Acri ITA	J Stupka SVK
3	G Petermann AUT

-60kg	-65kg	-70kg
1 H Yagli TUR	M Braun FRA	R Anselmo FRA
2 D Luque ESP	T Stephens ENG	A Soykan TUR
3 P Eriksson SWE	D Simmi ITA	S Azadi GER
3 D Dovy FRA	S Cunn'ham SCO	M Oggianu ITA

-75kg	-80kg	+80kg
1 W Otto ENG	G Cherdieu FRA	O Olivares ESP
2 G Talarico ITA	D Benetello ITA	V Jokovic INP
3 A Varo FRA	C Meana ESP	J Roddie SCO
3 D Devigili AUT	G Berg SWE	L Salzillo ITA

WOMEN

Team Kumite	Team Kata
1 France	Spain
2 Sweden	France
3 Italy	Germany
3 Spain	

Individual Kata	Open
1 C Colajacomo ITA	C Hernandez ESP
2 N Dumont FRA	N Beniot FRA
3 S Mansouri GER	P Duggin ENG
3	S Laine FIN

-53kg	-60kg	+60kg
1 S Laine FIN	C Bux ITA	S Jean-Pierre FRA
2 M Mazurier FRA	T Petrovic INP	R Ortega ESP
3 J Toney ENG	C Garcia ESP	K Olsson SWE
3 E Tuccitto ITA	L Karat'nova RUS	K Coulter SCO

English Championships

Wembley   June

MEN

Team Kumite
1. FEKO, 2. HIGASHI, 3. SHUKOKAI
3. BRITISH SPORTS

-75kg	-78kg	+78kg
1 Tim Stephens	Wayne Otto	Ian Cole
2 Frank Lee	Gerard Burke	Milton Hector
3 Pat Wallace	Danny Arthur	Keith Morton
3 Steve Gull	Junior Campbell	Eddie Gillespie

WOMEN

Team Kumite
1. ISHINRYU (A), 2. ISHINRYU (B), 3. SKU, 3. SEKU

-53kg	-60kg	+60kg
1 Vikky Fisher	Molly Samuels	Janice Francis
2 Astra Annan	Juliet Toney	Dianne Reilly
3 Vicky Aldersley	Angela Webb	Helen Gibson
3 Marie Long	Sarah Knight	Brenda Hayden

Taekwondo World Cup

George Town, Cayman Islands   July 21-23

MEN

Fin	Fly	Bantam
1 TJ Seung KOR	SG Seo KOR	IG Kim KOR
2 G Salim DEN	TM Farahat EGY	R Zuniga MEX
3 M Tuncer TUR	J Argudo ESP	A Evcimen TUR
3 S Lopez USA	A Haider DEN	G Esparza ESP
Feather	**Light**	**Welter**
1 W Cordova MEX	SJ Park KOR	T-I Liu TPE
2 E Boyali TUR	A Acharki GER	E Ozkuru GER
3 F Zas ESP	O Sanchez ESP	T Mort'nsen DEN
3 T Doss'tos CAN	A Taraya PHI	S Goodwin CAN
Middle	**Heavy**	
1 V Estrada MEX	WK Allam EGY	
2 DW Lee KOR	P Gentil FRA	
3 M Nitschke GER	G Weissfich USA	
3 M-H Ho TPE	P-Y Wu TPE	

WOMEN

Fin	Fly	Bantam
1 C Falco ESP	S-H Chen TPE	H-W Tang TPE
2 L Aguirre MEX	EE Anis EGY	D Murray USA
3 KY Chaing USA	M Sprengel GER	A Yazici TUR
3 Y-Y Lo TPE	B Ortiz PUR	A Manar EGY
Feather	**Light**	**Welter**
1 C-C Liu TPE	J-A Nash GBR	E Benitez ESP
2 M Karpat'li GRE	E Evans USA	S Seidal GER
3 V Marquez MEX	Y-A Chen TPE	M De Real MEX
3 K Walker GBR	N Deliktas TUR	O Malpica VEN
Middle	**Heavy**	
1 A Salado ESP	H-Y Huang TPE	
2 CH Yang KOR	B Hipf GER	
3 G Anke GER	K Bassi GRE	
3 B Kunkle USA	A Widehov SWE	

Korfball

International Results

Havirov, Czech Republic	Oct 22

Czech Rep 7 Netherlands 9

Hajduszoboszlo, Hungary	Oct 23

Hungary 10 Belgium 13

Stiens, Netherlands	Oct 23

Netherlands 10 Great Britain 13

Dordrecht, Netherlands	Oct 24

Netherlands 11 Belgium 10

Lisbon, Portugal	Oct 30

Portugal 9 Netherlands 21

Olomouc, Czech Republic	Nov 6

Czech Republic 9 Germany 13

Bergisch Gladbach, Germany	Feb 26

Germany 8 Netherlands 8

Zwijdgrecht, Netherlands	Mar 3

Netherlands 20 France 6

Oude Pekela, Netherlands	Mar 26

Netherlands 16 Poland 10

World Championships for National Youth Teams

Taipei, Taiwan	Apr 4-7

First Rounds

Netherlands 29 Great Britain 4
Belgium 29 Chinese-Taipei 10
Hungary 5 Australia 18
South Africa 2 Chinese-Taipei 18
Great Britain 8 Hungary 10
Chinese-Taipei 15 Czech Republic 6
Australia 8 Netherlands 30
South Africa 1 Belgium 30
Hungary 6 Netherlands 38
Belgium 18 Czech Republic 9
Australia 12 Great Britain 5
South Africa 4 Chinese-Taipei 20

7th/8th Place
South Africa 6 Great Britain 14
5th/6th Place
Czech Republic 23 Hungary 8
3rd/4th Place
Australia 10 Chinese Taipei 18
Final
Netherlands 14 Belgium 5

European Champions Cup

QUALIFYING ROUND

Chateauroux, France	Oct 9-10

KC Godoolo (HUN) 8 Egara '85 (SPA) 12
AWF Warszawa (POL) 6 Sangalhos (POR) 10
Bourges (FRA) 14 KC Godoolo 5
Egara '85 14 AWF Warszawa 11
Sangalhos 18 Bourges 10
Godollo 15 AWF Warszawa 9
Egara '85 7 Sangalhos 18
AWF Warszawa 6 Bourges 10

FINALS

Olomouc, Czech Republic	Jan 8-9

Bourgerhout (BEL) 14 Sangalhos (POR) 8
Grun-Weiss '67 (GER) 14 KC Kolin (Czech Rep) 8
Vultrix (ENG) 14 Armsikopi (ARM) 13
Deetos (HOL) 27 Egara '85 (SPA) 13
Sangalhos 12 KC Kolin 15
Armiskopi 16 Egara 12
Borgerhout 22 Grun-Weiss '67 14
Vultrix 11 Deetos 30

Play-offs
7th/8th Place
Sangalhos 14 Egara '85 11
5th/6th Place
KC Kolin 18 Armsikopi 13
3rd/4th Place
Grun-Weiss '67 11 Vultrix 11-9
Final
Deetos 20 Borgerhout 7

National League 1992-3

Premier Division

	P	W	D	L	GF	GA	Pts
1 Mitcham	12	11	0	1	209	131	22
2 Vultrix 1	12	10	0	2	193	122	20
3 Nomads 1	12	8	1	3	207	135	17
4 Croydon	12	5	0	7	158	178	10
5 Bec	12	3	3	6	119	163	9
6 Vultrix II	12	2	2	8	129	180	6
7 Nomads II	12	0	0	12	100	196	0

Senior Division 1

	P	W	D	L	GF	GA	Pts
1 Kingfisher	12	10	0	2	163	104	20
2 Mitcham II	12	6	2	4	144	138	14
3 Bor. Green	12	6	1	5	132	133	13
4 Invicta	12	5	2	5	136	126	12
5 Croydon II	12	5	2	5	145	149	12
6 Trojans	12	4	2	6	131	149	10
7 Bec II	12	1	1	10	97	149	3

Senior Division 2

	P	W	D	L	GF	GA	Pts
1 North Downs	13	11	1	0	221	83	25
2 Nottingham	13	10	3	0	192	97	23
3 Sheffield	14	8	0	6	134	105	16
4 Invicta II	14	7	2	5	169	151	16
5 Woking	14	7	0	7	141	154	14
6 Kingfisher II	14	5	2	7	159	190	12
7 Egham	14	2	0	12	92	221	4
8 Norwich	14	0	0	14	97	204	0

North Downs v Nottingham final match declared void

Lacrosse

MEN

World Cup
Manchester, England   July 20-30

PREMIER DIVISION
Semi Finals
USA 25 *(Morrill 6, Cook 4, Dixon 3, B Miller 3, Tucker 2,*
Wade 2, M Miller, Lockwood, Sombrotto, Soudan,
Rastelli (og))
England 3 *(Moore 2, Lynch)*

Canada 17 *(T Marechek 6, P Gait 3, G Gait 2, Dean,*
Alexander, Tavares, B Marechek)
Australia 18 *(Brown 5, Gibson 3, Toomey 2, Warren,*
Buchanan, Brewer, Cornish, Purdie)
5th/6th Play Off
Iroquois Nationals 19 Japan 13
3rd/4th Play Off
England 10 *(McManus 3, Gosnay 2, Morley 2, Baythorpe,*
Moore, Gosnay)
Canada 25 *(Martin 5, B Marechek 3, T Marechek 3, Govett 3,*
Aird 3, Tavares 3, P Gait 2, Cordingley, Game,
Dean, Hamilton)

WORLD CUP FINAL
Bury Football Club   July 30
United States 21 *(Millon 4, Morrill 4, Dixon 4, Pietramala 2,*
Marino 2, Shek 2, Cook, Lockwood, Detommaso)
Australia 7 *(Purdie 2, Buchanan 2, Gibson, Brewer, Toomey)*

Division 1 Final (Centurion Trophy)
Scotland 12 Wales 7

Northern League

Division 1	P	W	D	L	GF	GA	Pts
1 Mellor	20	18	1	1	195	83	37
2 Timperley	20	16	1	3	222	119	33
3 Cheadle	20	16	0	4	224	134	32
4 Heaton Mersey	20	14	2	4	248	147	30
5 Stockport	20	11	1	8	187	155	23
6 Poynton	20	9	0	11	211	191	18
7 Old Waconians	20	8	1	11	170	230	17
8 Sheffield Steelers	20	5	1	14	137	157	11
9 Sale	20	5	1	14	140	234	11
10 Hulmeians	20	3	0	17	121	224	6
11 Rochdale	20	1	0	19	140	321	2

Southern League

Division 1	P	W	D	L	GF	GA	Pts
1 Hillcroft	16	15	0	1	168	66	30
2 Kenton	15	13	0	2	209	86	26
3 Purley	16	10	0	6	156	115	20
4 Bath	16	9	0	7	117	101	**16
5 Croydon	16	6	0	10	100	180	*11
6 Buckhurst Hill	16	5	0	11	108	152	*9
7 Hitchin	15	4	0	11	78	144	8
8 Beckenham	16	3	0	13	108	200	6
9 Hampstead	16	6	0	10	107	84	***5

* 1 point deducted, ** 2 points deducted, *** 7 points deducted

Flags Knockout Competitions

South Senior Final *(Apr 9)*
Purley 7 Kenton 18

South Intermediate Final *(Apr 9)*
Orpington 8 Oxford 11

North Senior Champions
Mellor

North Junior Champions
Boardman & Eccles

WOMEN

Home Internationals
Scotland 4 Wales 5 *(Penarth, Wales   Apr 9)*
England 6 Wales 6 *(Wycombe Abbey, Bucks   Apr 23)*
England 2 Scotland 5 *(Heriott Watt, Edinburgh Apr 16)*
Wales win the Home Nations title

England v Japan
1st Test *(Komazawa Stadium, Tokyo   June 12)*
Japan 1 England 22

2nd Test *(Kyoto   June 19)*
Japan 0 England 24

National Clubs and Colleges Final
Cobham, Surrey   Mar 26
Birmingham Univ. 5 Centaurs Club 4

National C & C Mixed Final
Cobham, Surrey   Mar 27
Hillcroft Rosemeadians 2 Beckenham Beetles 1 (aet)

Senior Territorial Tournament
Malvern Boys School, Worcs   Feb 12-13 & Feb 26-27
South 9 North 2

UAU Championship
Leicester University   Mar 9
Birmingham Univ. 9 Univ. of Brighton 4

National Schools Championship
Milton Keynes Sports Club   Mar 19
Berkhamstead Girl's School 1 Haberdasher's Aske's 1
Title shared between the two schools

Modern Pentathlon

If you could criticize Richard Phelps for anything, it's timing. The Gloucestershire scrap-dealer trots off to Darmstadt in 1993, wins the world title and nobody notices. This year, when the championship is on his native soil, he is out of contention before they even reach the pool and in truth, Phelps chance had all but disappeared after the first event, the shooting. Greg Whyte worked hard to compensate with fine shows in the fencing and shooting, but the effort told in the swimming, usually his strongest event. Thereafter, it was simply a matter of how high the team would place. A medal was almost assured following the qualifying competition. Only four nations had the required three competitors in the final. The French, with Ruer and Deleigne both placing in the top six, were always out of reach, but the British trio did more than enough to keep ahead of Belarus and Russia for the silver medal. None of Britain's women qualified for the final, with Kate Houston failing by just a single place to reach the top 32.

In anxiety over its Olympic status, the sport continued to juggle its component parts. The shooting was altered to a fixed target and the sequence for the world championships read: shooting, fencing, swimming, running and riding - although we have kept the traditional results sequence below. The changes have left some, like Phelps, unhappy. His argument is that the sport should have made one radical change, rather than chip away at the traditional format. Phelps likes the idea of a knock-out modern pentathlon competition. The Grail, to retain a place in the Olympics beyond Atlanta, has still not been realised although there was much talk that a decision would be made in Paris, at the International Olympic Committee meeting in September. Yet still the doubts linger.......

World Championships

Sheffield, England   Aug 11-16

MEN'S INDIVIDUAL		Fence	Swim	Shoot	Run	Ride	Total
1 Dmitriy Svatkovskii	RUS	910	1224	1012	1357	1040	5543
2 Christophe Ruer	FRA	820	1328	1012	1288	1070	5518
3 Janos Martinék	HUN	820	1228	1096	1261	1100	5505
4 Peter Steinmann	SUI	910	1272	952	1324	1010	5468
5 László Fábián	HUN	940	1248	1048	1192	1037	5465
6 Sebastien Deleigne	FRA	850	1236	1048	1291	1040	5465
7 Maciej Czyzowicz	POL	850	1284	1060	1246	992	5432
8 Vladan Jesensky	CZE	790	1212	1108	1198	1100	5408
9 A Zadnieprowskis	LTU	670	1308	1000	1324	1100	5402
10 Gintaras Staskevicius	LTU	790	1344	892	1285	1070	5381
12 Greg Whyte	GBR	880	1284	1036	1126	1040	5366
20 Graham Brookhouse	GBR	670	1272	1084	1222	989	5237
22 Richard Phelps	GBR	790	1304	964	1288	844	5109

WOMEN'S INDIVIDUAL		Fence	Swim	Shoot	Run	Ride	Total
1 Eva Fjellerup	DEN	1030	1232	1048	1210	1070	5590
2 Zhanna Shubionok	BLS	910	1180	952	1280	1070	5392
3 Emese Köblö	HUN	970	1276	904	1165	1040	5355
4 Eszter Hortobágyi	HUN	940	1220	1000	1245	904	5309
5 Margrit Toomann	EST	820	1244	1072	1125	1010	5271
6 Csilla Furi	HUN	700	1304	916	1255	1070	5245
7 Kerstin Danielsson	SWE	820	1236	1084	1100	987	5227
8 Diane Nash	AUS	880	1240	868	1255	983	5226
9 Vannessa Richey	USA	640	1332	940	1220	1055	5187
10 Barbara Boccolari	ITA	850	1208	1036	1080	995	5169

MEN'S TEAM

1 France	16,194
2 Great Britain	15,793
3 Belarus	15,396

MEN'S RELAY

1 Hungary	5,279
2 Poland	5,112
3 Russia	5,070

WOMEN'S TEAM

1 Italy	15,352
2 Poland	15,352
3 Hungary	14,683

WOMEN'S RELAY

1 Poland	5,114
2 Hungary	4,969
3 Denmark	4,949

British Open Championships

Stowe and Milton Keynes   July 16-17

MEN'S FINAL STANDINGS

1	Dominic Mahony	Army	5433
2	Richard Phelps	Spartan	5366
3	Shawn Morgan	Army	5217
4	James Greenwell	Individual	5166
5	Greg Whyte	Lygea	5112
6	Simeon Robbie	SEALions	5023
7	David Storer	Evesham	4996
8	Ed Egan	Oxford Univ	4862
9	Sean Kinsey	Spartan	4830
10	Alex Paddon	Army	4731

MEN'S TEAM

1	Army *(Mahony/Morgan/Paddon)*	15,381
2	Spartan *(Brookhouse/Phelps/Sweeting)*	13,538
3	SEALions *(Bancroft/Robbie/Smale)*	13,406

WOMEN'S FINAL STANDINGS

1	Rachel Wilmot	East Midlands	5487
2	Kate Houston	SEALions	5371
3	Julia Allen	Cambridge Univ.	5244
4	Kate Allenby	Individual	5161
5	Vicky Rowe	SEALions	5144
6	Michelle Kimberley	Evesham	5106
7	Nicki Andrews	SEALions	5074
8	Helen Griffiths	Wales & Borders	5050
9	Gwen Lewis	Dumfries Dolphins	5009
10	Lisa Willcocks	Oxford Univ.	4907

WOMEN'S TEAM

1	SEALions *(Andrews/Houston/Rowe)*	15,589
2	Oxford Univ. *(Carpenter/Hutton/Willcocks)*	12,999

National Tetrathlon Championships

Sheffield   Feb 19

Men			Women		
1	S Morgan (Army)	4,249	1	K Houston (Ind)	4,211
2	G Whyte (Ind)	4,131	2	H Griffiths (E.M)	4,181
3	J Greenwell (Ind)	4,075	3	V Rowe (Ind)	4,175

Biathlon World Cup Final

Canmore, Canada   Mar 15-20

MEN

Individual 20 km	PS	Run	Total
1 Hubert Leitgeb ITA	1 0 0 1	52.15	54.15
2 Vadim Sashurin BLS	0 0 1 0	53.17	54.17
3 Jon Age Tyldum NOR	0 1 0 0	53.19	54.19

Sprint 10 km	PS	Total
1 Sylfest Glimsdal NOR	0 0	26:22.2
2 Victor Maigurov BLS	0 0	26:26.5
3 Patrice Bailly-Salins FRA	0 2	27:03.6

Team 10 km	Total
1 Italy *(Carrara/Leitgeb/Zingerle/Pallhuber)*	26:26.5
2 Russia *(Dratchev/Kobelev/Kirienko/Tarasov)*	26:27.8
3 Germany *(Hoos/Morgenstern/Sendel/Steinigen)*	26:34.3

Relay 4x7.5 km	Total
1 Russia *(Kobelev/Dratchev/Tarasov/Tropnicov)*	1:16.06.6
2 Belarus *(Maigurov/Ryshenkov/Popov/Sash'n)*	1:16.52.0
3 Italy *(Favre/Pallhuber/Carrara/Zingerle)*	1:17.24.3

WOMEN

Individual 15 km	PS	Run	Total
1 Uschi Disl GER	0 1 0 0	46:30.5	47:30.5
2 Myriam Bedard CAN	2 0 0 1	45:50.3	48:50.3
3 Nathalie Santer ITA	1 1 1 1	45:01.5	49:01.5

Sprint 7.5 km	PS	Total
1 Nadegda Talanova RUS	0 0	21:31.1
2 Svetlana Paraygina BLS	1 0	21:33.7
3 Nathalie Santer ITA	0 1	21:42.4

Team 7.5 km	Total
1 Belarus *(Per'ova/Ry'kova/Kokouwa/Par'gina)*	23:37.1
2 Norway *(Skjelbreid/Idland/Sikveland/Fossen)*	23:47.6
3 France *(Claret/Beausire/Niogret/Claudel)*	23:57.6

Relay 4x7.5 km	Total
1 Germany *(Disl/Petter/Harvey/Schaaf)*	1:31.53.3
2 USA *(Coats/Smith/Tavares/Skinner)*	1:32.50.6
3 Norway *(Skjelbreid/Idland/Fossen/Sikveland)*	1:32.57.6

European Championships

Kontiolahti, Finland   Mar 17-20

MEN

Individual 20 km	PS	Run	Total
1 Tor E Kristiansen NOR	0 0 0 1	58:55.8	59:55.8
2 Bertrand M-Joly FRA	0 0 1 1	58:20.7	1:00:20.7
3 Ville Räikkönen FIN	1 1 1 0	57:21.5	1:00:21.5

Sprint 10 km	PS	Total
1 Holger Schönthier GER	0 1	29:20.6
2 Rene Cattarinussi ITA	0 0	29:25.6
3 Vesa Hietalahti	0 0	29:42.3

Relay 4x7.5 km	Total
1 Russia *(Muslimov/Vavilov/Klykov/Rajbov)*	1:28.26.5
2 Poland *(Ziemianin/Ziemianin/Sikora/Wojtas)*	1:28.52.8
3 Belarus *(Khokhr'ov/Krivel/Karpinkin/Redkin)*	1:28.59.8

WOMEN

Individual 15 km	PS	Run	Total
1 Halina Piton POL	0 0 1 0	51:36.7	52:36.7
2 Martina Jasikova SVK	0 0 1 2	50:34.2	53:34.2
3 Irina Mihelschina RUS	2 2 1 0	50:47.5	55:47.5

Sprint 7.5 km	PS	Total
1 Irina Mihelschina RUS	0 0	25:59.6
2 Jirina Pelcova CZE	0 1	26:55.6
3 Kathi Schwaab GER	0 1	26:58.2

Relay 4x7.5 km	Total
1 Russia *(Novoseljskaj/Dumnova/Mihelschina)*	1:20.06.4
2 Slovakia *(Jasicova/Murinova/Mihokova)*	1:20.36.5
3 Ukraine *(Tserbe/Petrova/Ogurtsova)*	1:20.38.4

Motor Cycling

It was all Mick Doohan's year. Six straight victories in a row from Jerez to Le Mans set up an unassailable lead for the Australian and he clinched the world title in Brno, with his seventh victory from eleven races. The Czech band played Waltzing Matilda, but Doohan, even with the adrenalin of victory flowing through his veins, was hardly in any shape to waltz. Two years ago, surgeons pieced together his leg following a crash in the Dutch Grand Prix and, like so many on the circuit, he wears the badge of a wild courage. The Honda rider still walks with a pronounced limp and looks more comfortable on the bike than off it.

Kevin Schwantz had his own knock-about year, with precious little going right. Having broken his wrist pre-season, the American broke it again in Holland and drove most of the races with his left wrist in a cast. Even when things went his way, as in the British Grand Prix, the defending champion still had the kind of crash, in qualifying, that most people don't walk away from. Schwantz stayed in the saddle, though never in the running, until the US Grand Prix at Laguna Seca in September, when another crash in practice (which dislocated his left hip and broke his other wrist) persuaded the Texan that maybe even Texans aren't *that* tough.

With Schwantz out, the opportunity arose for Britain's Sean Emmett to acquire a desperately sought-after factory ride. Emmett, who likes the idea of being Britain's next Barry Sheene, knows his only real chance of emulation comes with a contract from one of the factory teams. The 23-year-old had his chance for the Lucky Strike team at Barcelona, in the European Grand Prix, and it would be a fine thing to report that he took it with both hands. But he didn't. Emmett crashed the Suzuki and scored no points at all. Yet, he was in contention for seventh place when he bombed out. If that doesn't sound a world-beating perfomance, consider only that the 'Privateers' - those in the non-factory teams - seldom place that high, and it was certainly virgin track for Emmett.

Carl Fogarty, who spent most of the summer tussling with Scott Russell and Aaron Slight for the World Superbike title, had a fleeting glimpse of a factory ride in the British Grand Prix when the Cagiva team offered him a spare ride. Fogarty rides for Ducati in the Superbike series and both companies are owned by the Castiglione brothers, which is how it all came about. But Fogarty, unlike Emmett, didn't even get to the start line and the troupe of British fans, with 'Foggy' T-shirts to the fore, had to find other heroes.

Niall MacKenzie has never let them down. For an awful long time now, the 33-year-old Scot, has been the top ranking Briton on the grand prix circuit. For the eighth time in nine years, his consistency gave him the edge and he finished the season the leading British scorer ahead of John Reynolds and Jerry McWilliams. But neither McKenzie, nor Reynolds, nor even McWilliams, is the future hero.

Wayne Rainey returned to the circuit as manager of the Yamaha 250cc team. Yamaha had a dire season at 500cc, with Team Roberts having to wait till the US race before the Luca Cadalora earned them a victory. Roberts looks disenamoured of the sport and it's possible that Rainey may move up to take over the helm. Wheelchair or not, he remains the most charismatic man in the sport.

Australian GP

Eastern Creek   Mar 27

500CC (29 laps - 113.970km)

1	John Kocinski (Cagiva)	USA	44:37.026	25
2	Luca Cadalora (Yamaha)	ITA	+6.480	20
3	Michael Doohan (Honda)	AUS	+9.246	16
4	Kevin Schwantz (Suzuki)	USA	+26.654	13
5	Shininchi Itoh (Honda)	JPN	+30.829	11
6	Alex Criville (Honda)	SPA	+33.319	10
Also				
10	John Reynolds (Yamaha)	GBR	+1:22.062	6
14	Sean Emmett (Yamaha)	GBR	+1:33.338	2

250CC (28 laps - 110.040km)

1	Massimiliano Biaggi (Aprilia)	ITA	43:42.148	25
2	Doriano Romboni (Honda)	ITA	+0.668	20
3	Loris Capirossi (Honda)	ITA	+0.696	16
4	Jean Phillipe Ruggia (Aprillia)	FRA	+4.380	13
5	Tadayuki Okada (Honda)	JPN	+22.590	11
6	Takuma Aoki (Honda)	JPN	+22.636	10
Also				
24	Allan Patterson (Honda)	GBR	2 laps	

125CC (26 laps - 102.180km)

1	Kazuto Sakata (Aprilia)	JPN	43:05.474	25
2	Peter Oettl (Aprilia)	GER	+5.199	20
3	Garry McCoy (Aprilia)	AUS	+11.537	19
4	Fausto Gresini (Honda)	ITA	+15.540	13
5	Oliver Petrucciani (Aprilia)	SUI	+24.593	11
6	Akira Saito (Honda)	JPN	+27.472	10
Also				
34	Neil Hodgson (Honda)	GBR	DNF	

Malaysian GP

Shah Alam   April 10

500CC (33 laps - 115.665km)

1	Michael Doohan (Honda)	AUS	47:36.874	25
2	John Kocinski (Cagiva)	USA	+5.225	20
3	Shinichi Itoh (Honda)	JPN	+7.978	16
4	Luca Cadalora (Yamaha)	ITA	+8.915	13
5	Albert Puig (Honda)	SPA	+19.814	11
6	Kevin Schwantz (Suzuki)	USA	+23.345	10
Also				
11	Niall Mackenzie (Yamaha)	GBR	1:15.155	5
12	John Reynolds (Yamaha)	GBR	1:23.835	4
13	Sean Emmett (Yamaha)	GBR	1 lap	3
14	Jerry McWilliams (Yamaha)	GBR	1 lap	2
30	Kevin Mitchell (Yamaha)	GBR	DNF	

Points after 2 rounds: Kocinski 45, Doohan 41, Cadalora 33, Itoh 27, Schwantz 23, Puig 20 - GBR: Reynolds 10, Mackenzie 13, Emmett 14, McWilliams 17

250CC (31 laps - 108.655km)

1	Massimiliano Biaggi (Aprilia)	ITA	45:26.300	25
2	Tadayuki Okada (Honda)	JPN	+5.808	20
3	Loris Capirossi (Honda)	ITA	+9.177	16
4	Jean Phillipe Ruggia (Aprilia)	FRA	+13.972	13
5	Doriano Romboni (Honda)	ITA	+29.783	11
6	Ralf Waldmann (Honda)	GER	+31.037	10
Also				
22	Allan Patterson (Honda)	GBR	1 lap	

Points after 2 rounds: Biaggi 50, Capirossi 32, Romboni 31, Okada 31, Ruggia 26, Waldmann 19

125CC (29 laps - 101.645km)

1	Noboru Ueda (Honda)	JPN	45:09.031	25
2	Kazuto Sakata (Aprilia)	JPN	+1.357	20
3	Jorge Martinez (Yamaha)	SPA	+4.775	16
4	Dirk Raudies (Honda)	GER	+6.725	13
5	Takeshi Tsujimura (Honda)	JPN	+14.007	11
6	Fausto Gresini (Honda)	ITA	+24.225	10
Also				
17	Neil Hodgson (Honda)	GBR	+1:07.618	

Points after 2 rounds: Sakata 45, Ueda 34, Gresini 23, Oettl 20, McCoy 20, Petrucciani 20

Japanese GP

Suzuka   April 24

500CC (21 laps - 123.145km)

1	Kevin Schwantz (Suzuki)	USA	45:49.996	25
2	Michael Doohan (Honda)	AUS	+3.474	20
3	Shinichi Itoh (Honda)	JPN	+7.989	16
4	Luca Cadalora (Yamaha)	ITA	+1:08.016	13
5	Alexandre Barros (Suzuki)	BRA	+1:16.543	11
6	Toshihiko Honma (Yamaha)	JPN	+1:17.325	10
Also				
12	John Reynolds (Yamaha)	GBR	+2:55.410	4
13	Jeremy McWilliams (Yamaha)	GBR	+3:14.792	3

Points after 3 rounds: Doohan 61, Kocinski 52, Schwantz 48, Cadalora 46, Itoh 43, Puig 28, Barros 28

250CC (19 laps - 111.416km)

1	Tadayuki Okada (Honda)	JPN	42:28.242	25
2	Loris Capirossi (Honda)	ITA	+0.128	20
3	Tohru Ukawa (Honda)	JPN	+0.314	16
4	Massimiliano Biaggi (Aprilia)	ITA	+2.109	13
5	Nobuatsu Aoki (Honda)	JPN	+3.841	11
6	Doriano Romboni (Honda)	ITA	+10.296	10

Points after 3 rounds: Biaggi 63, Okada 56, Capirossi 52, Romboni 41, Ruggia 35, D'Antin 22

125CC (18 laps - 105.553km)

1	Takeshi Tsujimura (Honda)	JPN	42:13.168	25
2	Kazuto Sakata (Aprilia)	JPN	+0.670	20
3	Hideyuki Nakajo (Honda)	JPN	+13.352	16
4	Peter Oettl (Aprilia)	GER	+15.923	13
5	Akira Saitoh (Honda)	JPN	+18.234	11
6	Masaki Tokudome (Honda)	JPN	+18.316	10

Points after 3 rounds: Sakata 65, Tsujimura 36, Ueda 34, Oettl 33, Saito 29, McCoy 27

Spanish GP

Jerez   May 8

500CC (27 laps - 119.421km)

1	Michael Doohan (Honda)	AUS	47:31.082	25
2	Kevin Schwantz (Suzuki)	USA	+0.489	20
3	John Kocinski (Cagiva)	USA	+9.265	16
4	Alexandre Barros (Suzuki)	BRA	+13.258	13
5	Alex Criville (Honda)	SPA	+14.825	11
6	Albert Puig (Honda)	SPA	+21.122	9
Also				
30	Kevin Mitchell (Yamaha)	GBR	DNF	

Points after 4 rounds: Doohan 86, Kocinski 68, Schwantz 68, Cadalora 46, Itoh 43, Barros 41

250CC (26 laps - 114.998km)

1	Jean Philippe Ruggia (Aprilia)FRA		46:16.824	25
2	Doriano Romboni (Honda)	ITA	+0.645	20
3	Tadayuki Okada (Honda)	JPN	+0.856	10
4	Ralf Waldmann (Honda)	GER	+0.955	13
5	Takuma Aoki (Honda)	JPN	+8.466	11
6	Luis D'Antin (Honda)	SPA	+31.582	15

Also

22	John Robinson (Honda)	GBR	1 Lap	
32	Allan Patterson (Honda)	GBR	DNF	

Points after 4 rounds: Okada 69, Biaggi 63, Romboni 61, Ruggia 60, Capirossi 52, Waldmann 35

125CC (23 laps - 101.729km)

1	Kazuto Sakata (Aprilia)	JPN	43:05.188	25
2	Peter Oettl (Aprilia)	GER	+6.802	20
3	Herri Torrontegui (Aprilia)	SPA	+10.048	16
4	Noboru Ueda (Honda)	JPN	+11.650	13
5	Dirk Raudies (Honda)	JPN	+12.183	11
6	Takeshi Tsujimura (Honda)	JPN	+26.358	10

Also

28	Neil Hodgson (Honda)	GBR	DNF	

Points after 4 rounds: Sakata 90, Oettl 53, Ueda 47, Tsujimura 46, Torrontegui 39, Martinez 32

Austrian GP
Salzburgring   May 22

500CC (29 laps - 122.815km)

1	Michael Doohan (Honda)	AUS	37:54.120	25
2	Kevin Schwantz (Suzuki)	USA	+12.610	20
3	Alex Criville (Honda)	SPA	+15.432	16
4	Shinichi Itoh (Honda)	JPN	+21.230	13
5	John Kocinski (Cagiva)	USA	+24.306	11
6	Albert Puig (Honda)	SPA	+28.928	17

Also

9	Niall Mackenzie (Yamaha)	GBR	+1:10906	7
10	John Reynolds (Yamaha)	GBR	1 Lap	6
12	Sean Emmett (Yamaha)	GBR	1 Lap	4
16	Jeremy McWilliams (Yamaha)	GBR	1 Lap	

Points after 5 rounds: Doohan 111, Schwantz 88, Kocinski 79, Itoh 56, Criville 54, Barros 50

250CC (26 laps - 110.110km)

1	Loris Capirossi (Honda)	ITA	35:29.052	25
2	Massimiliano Biaggi (Aprilia)	ITA	+0.500	20
3	Doriano Romboni (Honda)	ITA	+19.434	16
4	Tadayuki Okada (Honda)	JPN	+19.604	13
5	Ralf Waldermann (Honda)	GER	+19.663	11
6	Jean Phillipe Ruggia (Aprilia)	FRA	+39.143	10

Also

20	Allan Patterson (Honda)	GBR	+ 1 lap	

Points after 5 rounds: Okada 85, Biaggi 83, Capirossi 77, Romboni 77, Ruggia 70, Waldmann 43

125CC (24 laps - 101.640km)

1	Dirk Raudies (Honda)	GER	35:55.23	25
2	Noboru Ueda (Honda)	JPN	+4.001	20
3	Garry McCoy (Aprilia)	AUS	+4.232	16
4	Peter Oettl (Aprilia)	GER	+16.007	13
5	Kazuto Sakata (Aprilia)	JPN	+16.047	11
6	Stefano Perugini (Aprilia)	ITA	+16.687	10

Also

27	Neil Hodgson (Honda)	GBR	+1:29.995	

Points after 5 rounds: Sakata 101, Ueda 67, Oettl 65, Raudies 55, Mc Coy 48, Tsujimura 46.

German GP
Hockenheim   June 12

500CC (18 laps - 122.256km)

1	Michael Doohan (Honda)	AUS	35:58.994	25
2	Kevin Schwantz (Suzuki)	USA	+13.982	20
3	Albert Puig (Honda)	SPA	+15.764	16
4	Alex Criville (Honda)	SPA	+19.536	13
5	Alexandre Barros (Suzuki)	BRA	+33.120	11
6	Shinichi Itoh (Honda)	JPN	+33.293	10

Also

10	John Reynolds (Yamaha)	GBR	+1:36.643	6
11	Sean Emmett (Yamaha)	GBR	+1:37.062	5
16	Kevin Mitchell (Yamaha)	GBR	+1 lap	

Points after 6 rounds: Doohan 136, Schwantz 108, Kocinski 79, Criville 67, Itoh 66, Puig 64

250CC (16 laps - 118.672km)

1	Loris Capirossi (Honda)	ITA	33:43.516	25
2	Massimiliano Biaggi (Aprilia)	ITA	+0.284	20
3	Doriano Romboni (Honda)	ITA	+0.425	16
4	Nobuatsu Aoki (Honda)	JPN	+1.292	13
5	Tadayuki Okada (Honda)	JPN	+1.625	11
6	Ralf Waldmann (Honda)	GER	+13.566	10

Points after 6 rounds: Biaggi 103, Caprirossi 102, Okada 96, Romboni 93, Ruggia 78, Waldmann 53

125CC (15 laps - 101.880km)

1	Dirk Raudies (Honda)	GER	34:44.974	25
2	Kazuto Sakata (Aprilia)	JPN	+ 17.025	20
3	Tomomi Manako (Honda)	JPN	+17.025	16
4	Peter Oettl (Aprilia)	GER	+17.345	13
5	Stefano Perugini (Aprilia)	ITA	+17.946	11
6	Noboru Ueda (Honda)	JPN	+30.406	10

Also

16	Neil Hodgson (Honda)	GBR	+1:06.782	

Points after 6 rounds: Sakata 121, Raudies 80, Oettl 79, Ueda 77, McCoy 48, Tsujimura 46

Dutch GP
Assen   June 25

500CC (20 laps - 120.980km)

1	Michael Doohan (Honda)	AUS	41:35.272	25
2	Alexandre Barros (Suzuki)	BRA	+1.90	20
3	Alex Criville (Honda)	ESP	+7.446	16
4	Alberto Puig (Honda)	ESP	+17.956	13
5	Kevin Schwantz (Suzuki)	USA	+23.859	11
6	Doug Chandler (Cagiva)	USA	+24.464	10

Also

17	Kevin Mitchell (Yamaha)	GBR	+ 1 lap	

Points after 7 rounds: Doohan 161, Schwantz 119, Kocinski 87, Criville 83, Barros 81, Puig 77

250CC (18 laps - 108.882km)

1	Massimiliano Biaggi (Aprilia)	ITA	38:19.086	25
2	Tadayuki Okada (Honda)	JPN	+28.702	20
3	Wilco Zeelenberg (Honda)	HOL	+28.966	16
4	Ralph Waldmann (Honda)	GER	+29.221	13
5	Nobuatsu Aoki (Honda)	JPN	+29.732	11
6	Jean-Michel Bayle (Aprilia)	FRA	+29.939	10

Points after 7 rounds: Biaggi 128, Okada 116, Capirossi 102, Romboni 93, Ruggia 78, Waldmann 66

125CC (17 laps - 102.833km)

1	Takeshi Tsujimura (Honda)	JPN	39:07.728	25
2	Jorge Martinez (Yamaha)	ESP	+0.230	20
3	Loek Bodelier (Honda)	HOL	+0.942	16
4	Kazuto Sakata (Aprilia)	JPN	+1.354	13
5	Masaki Tokudome (Honda)	JPN	+17.249	11
6	Herri Torrontegui (Aprilia)	JPN	+17.254	10

Points after 7 rounds: Sakata 134, Raudies 80, Oettl 79, Ueda 77, Tsujimura 71, Martinez 61

Italian GP
Mugello   July 3

500CC (23 laps - 120.635km)

1	Michael Doohan (Honda)	AUS	44:20.402	25
2	Luca Cadalora (Yamaha)	ITA	+5.784	20
3	Kevin Schwantz (Suzuki)	USA	+17.336	16
4	Alberto Puig (Honda)	ITA	+24.104	13
5	Schinichi Itoh (Honda)	JPN	+24.182	11
6	Darryl Beattie (Yamaha)	AUS	+28.736	10

Also

9	Niall Mackenzie (Yamaha)	GBR	+1:01.510	7
14	Sean Emmett (Yamaha)	GBR	+1:33.838	2
15	Jerry McWilliams (Yamaha)	GBR	+1:34.572	1
30	John Reynolds (Yamaha)	GBR	DNF	
31	Kevin Mitchell (Yamaha)	GBR	DNF	

Points after 8 rounds: Doohan 186, Schwantz 135, Barros 90, Puig 90, Kocinski 87, Criville 83

250CC (21 laps - 110.145km)

1	Ralph Waldmann (Honda)	GER	41:05.128	25
2	Tetsuya Harada (Yamaha)	JPN	+2.060	20
3	Loris Capirossi (Honda)	ITA	+5.204	16
4	Jean-Philippe Ruggia (Aprilia)	FRA	+8.457	13
5	Marcellino Lucchi (Aprilia)	ITA	+9.248	11
6	Luis D'Antin (Honda)	ESP	+41.106	10

Points after 8 rounds: Biaggi 128, Okada 125, Capirossi 118, Romboni 93, Ruggia 91, Waldmann 91

125CC (20 laps - 104.900km)

1	Noboru Ueda (Honda)	JPN	41:25.510	25
2	Kazuto Sakata (Aprilia)	JPN	+3.470	20
3	Takeshi Tsujimura (Honda)	JPN	+8.738	16
4	Peter Oettl (Aprilia)	GER	+8.800	13
5	Dirk Raudies (Honda)	GER	+17.833	11
6	Masaki Tokudome (Honda)	JPN	+25.432	10

Points after 8 rounds: Sakata 154, Ueda 102, Oettl 92, Raudies 91, Tsujimura 86, Martinez 70

French GP
Le Mans   July 17

500CC (27 laps - 119.610km)

1	Michael Doohan (Honda)	AUS	47:28.917	25
2	John Kockinski (Cagiva)	USA	+6.101	20
3	Alex Criville (Honda)	ESP	+11.313	16
4	Albert Puig (Honda)	ESP	+12.327	13
5	Shinichi Itoh (Honda)	JPN	+20.087	11
6	Alexandre Barros (Suzuki)	BRA	+26.069	10

Also

8	Jeremy McWilliams (Yamaha)	GBR	+1:12.759	8
16	Kevin Mitchell (Yamaha)	GBR	+1 lap	

Points after 9 rounds: Doohan 211, Schwantz 135, Kocinski 107, Puig 103, Barros 100, Criville 99

250CC (25 laps - 110.750km)

1	Loris Capirossi (Honda)	ITA	43:46.089	25
2	Doriano Romboni (Honda)	ITA	+0.689	20
3	Massimiliano Biaggi (Aprilia)	ITA	+1.181	16
4	Ralf Waldermann (Honda)	GBR	+5.123	13
5	Jean-Michel Bayle (Aprilia)	FRA	+5.528	11
6	Nobuatsu Aoki (Honda)	JPN	+5.528	10

Points after 9 rounds: Biaggi 144, Capirossi 143, Okada 132, Romboni 113, Walderman 104, Ruggia 100

125CC (23 laps - 101.890km)

1	Noboru Ueda (Honda)	JPN	42:59.000	25
2	Takeshi Tsujimura (Honda)	JPN	+0.112	20
3	Kazuto Sakata (Aprilia)	JPN	+3.118	16
4	Peter Oettl (Aprilia)	GER	+4.034	13
5	Dirk Raudies (Honda)	GER	+9.738	11
6	Jorge Martinez (Yamaha)	ESP	+9.830	10

Also

20	Neil Hodgson (Honda)	GBR	+1:12.794	

Points after 9 rounds: Sakata 170, Ueda 127, Tsujimura 107, Oettl 105, Raudies 102, Martininez 80

British GP
Donington Park   July 24

500CC (30 laps - 120.690km)

1	Kevin Schwantz (Suzuki)	USA	47:31.632	25
2	Mick Doohan (Honda)	AUS	+2.366	20
3	Luca Cadalora (Yamaha)	ITA	+5.810	16
4	John Kocinski (Cagiva)	USA	+12.260	13
5	Doug Chandler (Cagiva)	USA	+16.464	11
6	Alex Criville (Honda)	ESP	+19.774	10

Also

8	Niall McKenzie (Yamaha)	GBR	+60.783	8
10	Jeremy McWilliams (Yamaha)	GBR	+72.378	6
12	Sean Emmett (Yamaha)	GBR	+85.088	4
14	John Reynolds (Yamaha)	GBR	1 lap	2

Points after 10 rounds: Doohan 231, Schwantz 160, Kocinski 120, Puig 112, Criville 109, Barros 100

250CC (27 laps - 108.621km)

1	Loris Capirossi (Honda)	ITA	43:18.624	25
2	Tadayuki Okada (Honda)	JPN	+3.233	20
3	Doriano Romboni (Honda)	ITA	+3.356	16
4	Tetsuya Harada (Yamaha)	JPN	+3.876	13
5	Jean-Michel Bayle (Aprilia)	FRA	+5.516	11
6	Jean Philippe Ruggia (Aprilia)	FRA	+6.107	10

Also

20	Eugene McManus (Yamaha)	GBR	1 lap	

Points after 10 rounds: Capirossi 168, Okada 152, Biaggi 144, Romboni 129, Walderman 113, Ruggia 110

125CC (26 laps - 104.598km)

1	Takeshi Tsujimura (Honda)	JPN	44:22.659	25
2	Stefano Perugini (Aprilia)	ITA	+0.267	20
3	Peter Oettl (Aprilia)	GER	+1.459	16
4	Kazuto Sakata (Aprilia)	JPN	+1.631	13
5	Herri Torrontegui (Aprilia)	ESP	+1.853	11
6	Noboru Ueda (Honda)	JPN	+16.690	10

Also

21	Neil Hodgson (Honda)	GBR	+66.813	

Points after 10 rounds: Sakata 183, Ueda 137, Tsujimura 132, Oettl 121, Raudies 110, Martininez 86

Czech Republic GP

Brno   Aug 21

500CC (22 laps - 118.668km)

1	Mick Doohan (Honda)	AUS	45:39.974	25
2	Shinichi Itoh (Honda)	JPN	+3.322	20
3	Luca Cadalora (Yamaha)	ITA	+8.822	16
4	Alex Criville (Honda)	ESP	+24.136	13
5	Alberto Puig (Honda)	ESP	+30.504	11
6	Norifumi Abe (Yamaha)	JPN	+39.996	10

Also

9	Niall McKenzie (Yamaha)	GBR	+56.504	7
10	Jeremy McWilliams (Yamaha)	GBR	+1:08.220	6
12	John Reynolds (Yamaha)	GBR	+1:10.328	4
13	Sean Emmett (Yamaha)	GBR	+1:38.539	3

Points after 11 rounds: Doohan 256, Schwantz 169, Puig 123, Criville 122, Kocinski 120, Itoh 115

250CC (20 laps - 107.880km)

1	Massimiliano Biaggi (Aprilia)	ITA	42:09.445	25
2	Ralf Waldermann (Honda)	GER	+6.425	20
3	Jean Philippe Ruggia (Aprilia)	FRA	+9.583	16
4	Nobuatsu Aoki (Honda)	JPN	+32.565	13
5	Tadayuki Okada (Honda)	JPN	+37.479	11
6	Jean -Michel Bayle (Aprilia)	FRA	+37.523	10

Points after 11 rounds: Biaggi 169, Capirossi 168, Okada 163, Walderman 133, Romboni 129, Ruggia 126

125CC (19 laps - 102.486km)

1	Kazuto Sakata (Aprilia)	JPN	42:34.015	25
2	Noboru Ueda (Honda)	JPN	+2.639	20
3	Stefano Perugini (Aprilia)	ITA	+3.295	16
4	Jorge Martinez (Yamaha)	ESP	+3.397	13
5	Takeshi Tsujimura (Honda)	JPN	+14.431	11
6	Masaki Tokudome (Honda)	JPN	+14.569	10

Also

28	Neil Hodgson (Honda)	GBR	12 laps	

Points after 11 rounds: Sakata 208, Ueda 157, Tsujimura 143, Oettl 121, Raudies 119, Martinez 99

United States GP

Laguna Seca   Sep 11

500CC (33 laps - 116.622km)

1	Luca Cadalora (Yamaha)	ITA	48:00.370	25
2	John Kocinski (Cagiva)	USA	+7.896	20
3	Mick Doohan (Honda)	AUS	+24.876	16
4	Shinichi Itoh (Honda)	JPN	+36.125	13
5	Doug Chandler (Cagiva)	USA	+36.130	11
6	Norifumi Abe (Yamaha)	JPN	+44.454	10

Also

9	Jeremy McWilliams (Yamaha)	GBR	+1:15.888	7
10	Niall McKenzie (Yamaha)	GBR	+1:22.916	6
11	Sean Emmett (Yamaha)	GBR	+1:27.047	5

Points after 12 rounds: Doohan 272, Schwantz 169, Kocinski 140, Cadalora 139, Puig 132, Itoh 128, Criville 122

250CC (31 laps - 109.554km)

1	Doriano Romboni (Honda)	ITA	46:01.397	25
2	Massimiliano Biaggi (Aprilia)	ITA	+1.433	20
3	Tetsuya Harada (Yamaha)	JPN	+1.631	16
4	Tadayuki Okada (Honda)	JPN	+2.575	13
5	Nobuatsu Aoki (Honda)	JPN	+2.749	11
6	Luis D'Antin (Honda)	ESP	+24.541	10

Points after 12 rounds: Biaggi 189, Okada 176, Capirossi 168, Romboni 154, Walderman 139, Ruggia 126

125CC (29 laps - 102.486km)

1	Takeshi Tsujimura (Honda)	JPN	54:21.102	25
2	Stefano Perugini (Aprilia)	ITA	+0.974	20
3	Peter Oettl (Aprilia)	GER	+1.552	16
4	Haruchika Aoki (Honda)	JPN	+14.715	13
5	Jorge Martinez (Yamaha)	ESP	+17.852	11
6	Hideyuki Nakajo (Honda)	JPN	+18.070	10

Also

22	Neil Hodgson (Honda)	GBR	+1:29.492	

Points after 12 rounds: Sakata 208, Ueda 164, Tsujimura 168, Oettl 137, Raudies 127, Martinez 110

Argentinian GP

Buenos Aires   Sep 25

500CC (33 laps - 116.622km)

1	Mick Doohan (Honda)	AUS	48:12.812	25
2	Doug Chandler (Cagiva)	USA	+8.742	20
3	John Kocinski (Cagiva)	USA	+16.969	16
4	Shinichi Itoh (Honda)	JPN	+28.281	13
5	Alberto Puig (Honda)	ESP	+33.383	11
6	Luca Cadalora (Yamaha)	ITA	+40.069	10

Also

9	Jeremy McWilliams (Yamaha)	GBR	+56.749	7
10	Sean Emmett (Yamaha)	GBR	+58.171	6
11	Niall McKenzie (Yamaha)	GBR	+1:12.954	5

Points after 13 rounds: Doohan 297, Schwantz 169, Kocinski 156, Cadalora 149, Puig 143, Itoh 141

250CC (31 laps - 109.554km)

1	Tadayuki Okada (Honda)	JPN	45:09.167	25
2	Massimiliano Biaggi (Aprilia)	ITA	+5.283	20
3	Tetsuya Harada (Yamaha)	JPN	+5.603	16
4	Jean Phillipe Ruggia (Aprilia)	FRA	+6.513	13
5	Loris Capirossi (Honda)	ITA	+13.867	11
6	Kenny Robert Jr (Yamaha)	USA	+19.601	10

Points after 13 rounds: Biaggi 109, Okada 201, Capirossi 179, Romboni 154, Walderman 147, Ruggia 139

125CC (29 laps - 102.486km)

1	Jorge Martinez (Yamaha)	ESP	43:37.658	25
2	Noboru Ueda (Honda)	JPN	+0.376	20
3	Stefano Perugini (Aprilia)	ITA	+1.334	16
4	Gianluigi Scalvini ((Aprilia)	ITA	+3.114	13
4	Haruchika Aoki (Honda)	JPN	+3.643	11
6	Dirk Raudies (Honda)	GER	+14.007	10

Points after 13 rounds: Sakata 215, Ueda 184, Tsujimura 177, Oettl 140, Raudies 137, Martinez 125

European GP *(Brief results only)*

Barcelona   Oct 9

500CC: 1. Luca Cadalora 46:03.356, 2. Mick Doohan +3.488, 3. John Kocinski +6.536, 4. Alex Criville +7.486
250CC: 1. Massimiliano Biaggi 42:44.818, 2. Loris Capirossi +1.940, 3. Doriano Romboni +2.608
125CC: 1. Dirk Raudies 43:26.974, 2. Peter Oettl +2.137, 3. Haruchika Aoki +4.956

FINAL STANDINGS
500CC: 1. Mick Doohan 317pts, 2. Luca Cadalora 174, 3. John Kocinski 172, 10. Niall McKenzie 69, 12. Jeremy McWilliams 49, 14. John Reynolds 43, 15. Sean Emmitt 34
250CC: 1. Massim'o Biaggi 234, 2. Tadayuki Okada 214, 3. Loris Capirossi 199
125CC: 1. Kazuto Sakata 224, 2. Noboru Ueda 194, 3. Takeshi Tsujimura 190

SIDECAR WORLD CHAMPIONSHIP

British GP

Donington Park - 25 laps   May 2

1	**Derek Brindley (Honda)**	GBR	41:31.89	25
2	Marcus Bösiger (ADM)	SUI	+9.71	20
3	Steve Webster (Krauser)	GBR	22.04	16
4	Barry Brindley (Yamaha)	GBR	+22.75	13
5	Paul Guedel (ADM)	SUI	+25.38	11

German GP

Hockenheim - 13 laps (88.296km)   June 6

1	**Rolf Biland (Swiss Auto)**	SUI	28:35.190	25
2	Steve Webster (Krauser)	GBR	+5.426	20
3	Steve Abbott (Krauser)	GBR	+5.780	16
4	Klaus Klaffenbock (Bartol)	AUT	+5.978	13
5	Barry Brindley (Yamaha)	GBR	+6.437	11

Dutch GP

Assen - 17 laps (102.833km)   June 25

1	**Rolf Biland (Swiss Auto)**	SUI	37:44.428	25
2	Klaus Klaffenbock (Bartol)	AUT	+4.572	20
3	Derek Brindley (Yamaha)	GBR	+8.217	16
4	Ralph Bohnhorst (Steinh'sen)	GER	+10.811	13
5	Paul Guedel (ADM)	SUI	+13.700	11

Austrian GP

Zeltweg- 16 laps (66.98 miles)   July 17

1	**Darren Dixon (ADM)**	GBR	34:36.887	25
2	Marcus Bösiger (ADM)	SUI	+9.257	20
3	Rolf Biland (Swiss Auto)	SUI	+9.517	16
4	Paul Guedel (ADM)	SUI	+15.208	13
5	Steve Webster (Krauser)	GBR	+25.545	11

British GP2

Donington - 26 laps (104.598km)   July 24

1	**Rolf Biland (Swiss Auto)**	SUI	42:54.342	25
2	Derek Brindley (Honda)	GBR	+0.672	20
3	Steve Webster (Krauser)	GBR	+22.620	16
4	Klaus Klaffenboek (Bartol)	AUT	+29.497	13
5	Paul Guedel (ADM)	SUI	+29.806	11

Czech Republic GP

Brno - 19 laps (102.486km)   Aug 21

1	**Rolf Biland (Swiss Auto)**	SUI	40:52.767	25
2	Marcus Bösiger (ADM)	SUI	+4.113	20
3	Steve Webster (Krauser)	GBR	+4.798	16
4	Derek Brindley (Honda)	GBR	+6.285	13
5	Ralph Bohnhorst (Steinh'sen)	GER	+19.809	11

Dutch GP2

Assem - 17   Sep 10-11

1	**Rolf Biland (Swiss Auto)**	SUI	36:56.51	25
2	Darren Dixon (Yamaha)	GBR	+5.72	20
3	Steve Webster (Krauser)	GBR	+6.13	16
4	Klaus Klaffenbock (Bartol)	AUT	+6.65	13
5	Derek Brindley (Honda)	GBR	+7.00	11

European GP *(Brief results only)*

1. **Darren Dixon 50:02.148**, 2. Paul Guedel +9.969, 3. Steve Abbott +56.11

FINAL PLACINGS: 1. Rolf Biland/Kurt Waltisperg 141 pts, 2. Steve Webster/Adolf Hanni 104, 3. Derek Brindley/Paul Hutchinson 96, 4. Markus Bösiner/Jorg Egli 88, 5. Paul Guedel/Charly Guedel 86

SUPERBIKE WORLD CHAMPIONSHIP

British GP

Donington Park - 25 laps   May 2

RACE 1

1	**Carl Fogarty (Ducati)**	GBR	40:16.42	20
2	Aaron Slight (Honda)	NZL	+1.33	17
3	Fabrizio Pirovani (Ducati)	ITA	+2.01	15
8	Brian Morrison (Honda)	GBR	+43.68	9

RACE 2

1	**Scott Russell (Kawasaki)**	USA	40:05.37	20
2	Carl Fogarty (Ducati)	GBR	+9.40	17
3	Troy Corser (Ducati)	AUS	+14.99	15

German GP

Hockenheim - 14 laps   May 8

RACE 1

1	**Scott Russell (Kawasaki)**	USA	29:08.36	20
2	Aaron Slight (Honda)	NZL	+0.35	17
3	Terry Rymer (Kawasaki)	GBR	+8.47	15

RACE 2

1	**Scott Russell (Kawasaki)**	USA	29:07.49	20
2	Fabrizio Pirovano (Ducati)	ITA	+0.25	17
3	Doug Polen (Honda)	USA	+0.53	15

Italian GP

Santa Monica - 25 laps   May 29

RACE 1

1	**Scott Russell (Kawasaki)**	USA	40:44.221	20
2	Giancarlo Falappa (Ducati)	ITA	+14.503	17
3	Aaron Slight (Honda)	NZL	+55.823	15

RACE 2

1	**Biancarlo Falappa (Ducati)**	ITA	40:35.836	20
2	Scott Russell (Kawasaki)	USA	+0.168	17
3	Mauro Lucchiari (Bucati)	ITA	+1.924	15

Spanish GP

Albacete - 28 laps   June 19

RACE 1

1	**Carl Fogarty (Ducati)**	GBR	44:21.492	20
2	Aaron Slight (Honda)	NZL	+8.808	17
3	James Whitham (Ducati)	GBR	+15.425	15

RACE 2

1	**Carl Fogarty (Ducati)**	GBR	44:33,685	20
2	Aaron Slight (Honda)	NZL	+6.972	17
3	James Whitham (Ducati)	GBR	+17.796	15

Austrian GP

Österreichring - 18 laps   July 17

RACE 1

1	**Carl Fogarty (Ducati)**	GBR	33:32.0	20
2	Andreas Meklau (Ducati)	AUT	+0.7	17
3	Doug Polen (Honda)	USA	+0.9	15

RACE 2

1	**Carl Fogarty (Ducati)**	GBR	33:33.0	20
2	Andreas Meklau (Ducati)	AUT	+3.1	17
3	Doug Polen (Honda)	USA	+3.2	15

Indonesian GP
Sentul - 25 Aug 21
RACE 1

1 **James Whitham (Cinelli)**	GBR	37:13.265	20
2 Aaron Slight (Honda)	NZL	+0.330	17
3 Scott Russell (Kawasaki)	USA	+13.144	15

RACE 2

1 **Carl Fogarty (Ducati)**	GBR	31:01.075	20
2 Aaron Slight (Honda)	NZL	+2.801	17
3 Scott Russell (Kawasaki)	USA	+10.979	15

Japanese GP
Sportsland SUGO - 25 laps Aug 28
RACE 1

1 **Scott Russell (Kawasaki)**	USA	38:49.703	20
2 Fabrizio Pirovano (Ducati)	ITA	+3.425	17
3 Yasutomo Nagai (Yamaha)	JPN	+3.702	15

RACE 2

1 **Scott Russell (Kawasaki)**	USA	38:38.123	20
2 Carl Fogarty (Ducati)	GBR	+0.668	17
3 Keiichi Kitagawa (Kawasaki)	JPN	+1.258	15

Dutch GP
Circuit Van Drenthe - 16 Sep 10-11
RACE 1

1 **Carl Fogarty (Ducati)**	GBR	34:11.40	20
2 Paulo Casoli (Yamaha)	ITA	+3.81	17
3 Aaron Slight (Honda)	NZL	+5.15	15

RACE 2

1 **Carl Fogarty (Ducati)**	GBR	34:06.65	20
2 Aaron Slight (Honda)	NZL	+6.65	17
3 Mauro Lucchiari (Ducati)	ITA	+8.20	15

Italian GP2
Mugello Sep 25
RACE 1

1 **Scott Russell (Kawasaki)**	USA	39:07.53	20
2 Carl Fogarty (Ducati)	GBR	+3.58	17
3 Troy Corser (Ducati)	USA	+7.18	15

RACE 2

1 **Carl Fogarty (Ducati)**	GBR	39:12.62	20
2 Aaron Slight (Honda)	NZL	+6.12	17
3 Mauro Lucchiari (Ducati)	ITA	+11.29	15

Standings after 9 rounds (3 remaining): Fogarty 255, Slight 237, Russell 223, Polen 144, Whitham 126

SUPERSPORT EUROPEAN CHAMPIONSHIP

British GP
Donington Park - 25 laps May 2

1 **Yves Briguet (Honda)**	SUI	42:50.10	20
2 Mike Edwards (Yamaha)	GBR	+0.27	17
3 Ian Simpson (Yamaha)	GBR	+18.38	15

German GP
Hockenheim - 14 laps May 8

1 **Fred Bayens (Honda)**	AUS	31:38.02	20
2 Frank Heidger (Honda)	GER	+0.27	17
3 Rachel Nicotte (Honda)	FRA	+0.53	15

Italian GP
Santa Monica - 23 laps May 29

1 **Ives Briguet (Honda)**	SUI	39:26.283	20
2 Enrico Eugeni (Honda)	ITA	+8.368	17
3 Francesco Bastianini (Honda)	ITA	+10.974	15

Spanish GP
Albacete - 28 laps June 19

1 **Ives Briguet (Honda)**	SUI	47:00.393	20
2 Jose Sagardogui (Yamaha)	ESP	+0.208	17
3 Idalio Gavifa (Honda)	ESP	+10.75	15

Austrian GP
Österteichring - 16 laps July 17

1 **Christian Zwedorn (Honda)**	AUT	31:54.452	20
2 Gavira Eustaquie (Honda)	ESP	+0.006	17
3 Yves Briquet (Honda)	SUI	+0.046	15

Dutch GP
Assen - 16 laps Sep 8-9

1 **Ives Briguet (Honda)**	SUI	36:35.95	20
2 Christian Zwedorn (Honda)	AUT	+0.65	17
3 Eric Mahe (Honda)	FRA	+8.92	15

MOTOCROSS WORLD CHAMPIONSHIPS
FINAL STANDINGS
500CC: 1. Marcus Hansson (Honda) 328 points; 2. Jacky Martens (Husqvarna) 321; 3. Joel Smets (Vertemati) 299
250CC: 1. Greg Albertyn (Suzuki) RSA 403; 2. Stefan Everts (Kawasaki) BEL 392; 3. Yves Demaria (Honda) FRA 367
125CC: 1. Bob Moore (Yamaha) USA 364; 2. Alessio Chiodi (Honda) ITA 316; 3. Pedro Tragter (Suzuki) HOL 264
Sidecar: 1. Fuhrer/Kaiser (VMC) GER 232; 2. Fussenegger/Meusburger (EML) AUT 204; 3. Weinmann/Weinmann (EML) GER 199

BRITISH SUPERCUP
Final Standings
Supersport 600: 1. Ian Simpson 188; 2. Mike Edwards 173; 3. Iain Duffus 111
125CC: 1. Steve Patrickson 144; 2. Kevin Maudsley 134; 3. Robin Appleyard 133
Superbike: 1. Ian Simpson 319; 2. Jim Moodie 287; 3. Phil Borley 284
Single Cylinder: 1. David Rawlins 113; 2. Mike Edwards 109; 3. Steve Ruth 81
250CC: 1. Jason Vincent 165; 2. Eugene McManus 143; 3. Steve Sawford 121
Formula 2 Sidecars: 1. Boddice/Wells 67; 2. Bell/Roache 67; 3. Molyneux/Hill 66

Isle of Man TT
June 10
Senior TT

1 S Hislop (Honda)	1:53:53.8
2 P McCallen (Honda)	1:55:08.8
3 J Dunlop (Honda)	1:56:20.2

Motor Racing

It had been such a long time since a driver had died at a grand prix event - Ricardo Paletti at the Canadian Grad Prix in 1982 - that it was beginning to look as if the sport had somehow contained the risks. There were seven fatal crashes in the sixties, eight in the seventies, then none for twelve years. Yet when the reminder came, on the weekend of the Imola Grand Prix, it was the most brutal possible. On Friday, April 29, Rubens Barrichella crashed at Variente Bassa at 160mph, but walked away. If you could call back History, you would cancel the race there and then. On Saturday, Roland Ratzenberger crashed doing 195mph at Villeneuve, the corner named after the late Canadian driver, and died. The 31-year-old Austrian was in his first Formula One season.

On Saturday, seven lap into the race proper, Ayrton Senna failed to negotiate Tamburello corner and his Williams Renault flew across a narrow grass verge and into the concrete retaining wall. Senna was flown by helicopter to the Maggiore Hospital in Bologna, but the Brazilian had died instantly. To date, the causes of the crash have not been discovered, although a report in the French sports paper, *L'Equipe*, claimed that a broken steering column was to blame. The crashes came a fortnight before a new safety committee of the drivers was due to meet.

Formula One has known enough tragedies, but none comparable. Senna was the senior driver in the sport, the only former world champion racing still racing in F1. The most charismatic driver by a good dozen laps. It is a measure of the regard he was held in that in Brazil, three days of mourning were declared. His death will more than tarnish the sport, it could damage it irreparably.

Mansell is returning. To add lustre, or what? The 41-year-old has become more important to F1 since the death of Senna. The theory is that the drama of the Hill-Schumacher conflict will pale in comparison with the theatrics of the former champion. Mansell getting out of bed, as they say, would make more news. Well, not quite. In the midst of a year when success has looked just round the bend for Schumacher and Benetton, they have made their news not with the tales of glory, but by courting controversy.

Cakewalking the championship after six victories from seven races, Schumacher ignored a black flag at Silverstone and was banned for two races. Benetton were fined £330,000. At the German Grand Prix, Jos Verstappen, the second Benetton driver, is engulfed in flames in the pit lane. The suggestion was that a refuelling filter was removed, but Benetton were later cleared of that offence. At the Belgian Grand Prix, Schumacher wins, but the Benetton car is disqualified because the skid-block under the car is too thin.

If Schumacher and Benetton weren't happy, the bans at least kept the world championship title running till the last three grands prix. Damon Hill may or may not miss out, we go to press too early for that, but he does at least have a place in the Williams team for next year. With Mansell shouldering his way back for the final three races on the 1994 calendar, poor old David Coulthard probably won't.

QUOTES

"He should take a few boxing tips over the winter and if he's not had lessons in self-defence, he should take some" - **Nigel Mansell, offering advice to Damon Hill when he learnt that Senna was to be Hill's team-mate.**

"He used us and I hope we don't see him again. He must think there's a big sign in the pit lane saying 'public convenience'" - **Bernie Ecclestone, on the departing Alain Prost.**

"He comes up to you on the grid and shakes you by the hand which is very sporting and makes him seem like a normal person. But when he gets into the car and puts his helmet on he turns into some sort of demon" - **Damon Hill, on the errant Mika Hakkinen after the Finn had taken Hill out of the Pacific Grand Prix in April.**

"God has had his hand over F1 for a long time. This weekend, he took it away" - **Nikki Lauda, after San Marino.**

"It went on despite everything and death itself was made into a brutal spectacle - the spark of the sponsors prevailed over death...." - **Statement from The Vatican deploring the continuation of the Imola race.**

"....I was still certain he would win the title. I don't know why, but this was always what I had in my mind. He was always my target. It felt strange when he was gone" - **Michael Schumacher, on Senna.**

"He was the master of his craft. I was proud to race against him" - **Alain Prost, on Senna.**

"Schumacher, virtually pedalling his Benetton back with his fists" - **Murray Walker, but we know what he means....roughly.**

"The engine just died on me. A pity......I could already taste the champagne" - **David Coulthard, who ran out of petrol less than a mile from the finish of the Italian Grand Prix when in second place.**

"He just bulldozes everyone off the track and there's nothing you can do about it. The guy's got a serious problem" - **Paul Tracey on Michael Andretti, who returned to Indy Car because he was getting just that kind of flak in F1.**

"I'm too old, the physical part of my life is pretty much over" - **Paul Newman, 69, who is to give up racing because he keeps crashing.**

"Given the opportunity and motivation, I can win another world title without batting an eye. I can beat Schumacher. I can beat anyone. Believe me, when you have won a world championships and you have won all those races, you know how to get the job done" - **Nigel Mansell, doing his own publicity.**

"He has burnt his boats with every team he has been involved with. I don't even know if he is fit enough for F1's rigours. He has all the money he needs, beautiful homes, a boat and a jet. It is time for him to make way for the new generation" - **Jackie Stewart, giving a different slant on Mansell.**

Brazilian Grand Prix

Interlagos   March 27
Laps: 71 x 4.325km   Total distance: 307.075km

1 **Michael Schumacher GER (Benetton-F) 1:36:38.759**
                                                      (192.600 kmh)

2	Damon Hill GBR (Williams-Renault) at	1 lap
3	Jean Alesi FRA (Ferrari)	1 lap
4	Rubens Barrichello BRA (Jordan-Hart)	1 lap
5	Ukyo Katayama JPN (Tyrrell-Yamaha)	2 laps
6	Karl Wendlinger AUT (Seuber-Mercedes)	2 laps
7	Johnny Herbert GBR (Lotus-Mugen-Honda)	2 laps
8	Pierreluigi Martini ITA (Minardi-Ford)	2 laps
9	Erik Comas FRA (Larrousse-Ford)	3 laps
10	Pedro Lamy POR (Lotus-Mugen-Honda)	3 laps
11	Olivier Panis FRA (Ligier Renault)	3 laps
12	David Brabham AUS (Simtek-Ford)	4 laps

Pole position: Ayrton Senna
Fastest lap: Schumacher 1:18.455 (198.4 kmh)

Schumacher's third F1 victory was greeted by half empty stands as thousands poured from the circuit following Senna's spin on lap 55. While the home favourite failed, the young pretender drove flawlessly to finish well clear of Hill and Alesi. Martin Brundle, on his debut with McLaren, was the victim of a spectacular pile-up on the apex of the long Descida do Lago corner involving Eddie Irvine. The Northern Irishman was later suspended and fined $10,000 by the race stewards. Hill was relatively content with his second placing after two disappointing days during qualifying. "I gambled on one stop and it wasn't really the best way to go, but second place is a firm base on which to build a challenge for the world championship," he said.

World Championship Standings
Drivers: Schumacher 10, Hill 6, Alesi 4, Barrichello 3, Katayama 2, Wendlinger 1.
Constructors: Benetton-Ford 10, Williams-Renault 6, Ferrari 4, Jordan-Hart 3, Tyrrell-Yamaha 2, Sauber-Mercedes 1.

Pacific Grand Prix

Aida (Japan)   April 17
Laps: 83 x 3.703km   Total distance: 307.349km

1 **Michael Schumacher GER (Benetton-F) 1:46:01.693**
                                                      (173.9 kmh)

2	Gerhard Berger AUT (Ferraro) at	1:15.300
3	Rubens Barrichello BRA (Jordan-Hart)	1 lap
4	Christian Fittipaldi BRA (Footwork-Ford)	1 lap
5	Heinz-Harald Frentzen GER (Sauber-Mercedes)	1 lap
6	Erik Comas FRA (Larrousse-Ford)	3 laps
7	Johnny Herbert GBR (Lotus-Mugen-Honda)	3 laps
8	Pedro Lamy POR (Lotus-Mugen-Honda)	4 laps
9	Olivier Panis FRA (Ligier-Renault)	5 laps
10	Eric Bernard FRA (Ligier Renault)	5 laps
11	Roland Ratzenberger AUT (Simtak -Ford)	5 laps

Pole position: Ayrton Senna
Fastest lap: Schumacher 1:14.023 (180.0 kmh)

The newly constructed circuit in southern Japan witnessed a superb display of measured aggression from Schumacher, who took the lead at the first bend and was never headed. The first corner was not such a pleasant experience for Senna, who was starting from the 64th pole of his career. With wheelspin on the green light, Hakkinen's nudge was enough to send Senna shunting into Farrini and an angry retirement. Not content with one Williams' driver, the Finn went in search of a second.

It took him 49 laps to catch Hill, but catch him he did. "He's a bit of a wild boy," said Hill, in the understatement of the day.

World Championship standings
Drivers: Schumacher 20, Barrichello 7, Hill 6, Berger 6, Alesi 4, Fittipaldi 3, Katayama 2, Frentzen 2, Comas 1, Wendlinger 1.
Constructors: Benetton-Ford, Ferrari 10, Jordan-Hart 7, Williams-Renault 6, Sauber-Mercedes 3, Footwork-Ford 3, Tyrrell-Yamaha 2, Larrousse 1.

San Marino Grand Prix

Imola   May 1
Laps: 61 x 5.040km   Total distance: 307.440km

1 **Michael Schumacher GER (Benetton-F) 1:28:28.642**
                                                      (198.2 kmh)

2	Nicola Larini FRA (Ferrari) at	54.942
3	Mika Hakkinen FIN (McLaren-Peugeot)	1:10.679
4	Karl Wendlinger AUT (Sauber-Mercedes)	1:13.658
5	Ukyo Katayama JPN (Tyrrell-Yamaha)	1 lap
6	Damon Hill GBR (Williams-Renault)	1 lap
7	Heinz-Harold Frentzen GER (Sauber-Mercedes)	1 lap
8	Martin Brundle GBR (McLaren-Peugeot)	1 lap
9	Mark Blundell GBR (Tyrrell-Yamaha)	2 laps
10	Johnny Herbert GBR (Lotus-Mugen-Honda)	2 laps
11	Olivier Panis FRA (Ligier-Renault)	2 laps
12	Eric Bernard FRA (Ligier-Renault)	3 laps

Pole position: Ayrton Senna
Fastest lap: Schumacher 1:24.438 (214.8 kmh)

Imola was the scene of one of the most tragic weekends in F1 history with the deaths of Roland Ratzenburger and Ayrton Senna. Ratzenburger's Simtek ploughed into a concrete retaining wall at close to 200mph after 18 minutes of the final qualifying session. With teams still in shock, the following day saw Senna lead the field from pole position, oblivious of the start line fracas until he saw the safety car emerge a lap later. After the debris from Lehto and Lamy's cars was cleared from the circuit, Senna sped away from Schumacher. On the sixth lap and increasing his lead over the German, Senna entered the Tamburello curve only to fly across the grass verge and into a concrete barrier at 190mph. Senna died instantly of massive head injuries.

World Championship standings
Drivers: Schumacher 30, Hill 7, Barrichello 7, Berger 6, Larini 6, Alesi 4, Katayama 4, Wendlinger 4, Hakkinen 4, Fittipaldi 3, Frentzen 2, Comas 1
Constructors: Benetton-Ford 30, Ferrari 16, Jordan-Hart 7, Williams-Renault 7, Sauber-Mercedes 6, Tyrrell-Yamaha 4, McLaren-Peugeot 4, Footwork-Ford 3, Larrousse-Ford 1.

Monaco Grand Prix

Monte Carlo   May 15
Laps: 78 x 3.328km   Total distance: 259.584km

1 **Michael Schumacher GER (Benetton-F) 1:23:07.262**
                                                      (141.734 kmh)

2	Martin Brundle GBR (McLaren-Peugeot) at	35.716
3	Gerhard Berger AUT (Ferrari)	43.806
4	Andrea De Cesaris ITA (Jordan-Hart)	1 lap
5	Jean Alesi FRA (Ferrari)	1 lap
6	Michele Alboreto ITA (Minardi-Ford)	1 lap
7	J J Lehto FIN (Benetton-Ford)	1 lap
8	Johnny Herbert GBR (Lotus-Mugen-Honda)	2 laps
9	Olivia Beretta MON (Larrousse-Ford)	2 laps
10	Olivier Panis FRA (Ligier-Renault)	2 laps

11	Erik Comas FRA (Larrousse-Ford)	2 laps
12	Pedro Lamy POR (Lotus-Mugen-Honda)	3 laps
13	Paul Belmondo FRA (Pacific-Ilmor)	7 laps
14	Bertrand Gachot FRA (Pacific-Ilmor)	10 laps
15	Christian Fittipaldi BRA (Footwork-Ford)	12 laps
16	David Brabham AUS (Simtek-Ford)	14 laps
17	Mark Blundell GBR (Tyrrell-Yamaha)	19 laps
18	Ukyo Katayama JPN (Tyrrell Yamaha)	21 laps
19	Eric Bernard FRA (Ligier-Renault)	25 laps
20	Rubens Barrichello BRA (Jordan-Hart)	32 laps

Pole position: Michael Schumacher
Fastest lap: Schumacher 1:21.076 (147.772 kmh)

With the front row of the grid left vacant as a tribute to the two victims of Imola, the principality took on a subdued air. With the spectre of 6-time winner Senna hanging palpably over the race, the drivers had to contend with another hospitalisation as Karl Wendlinger's Sauber failed to negotiate the harbour-front chicane in practice. Again the race was dominated from the green light by Schumacher who had built up a four-second lead by the end of the first lap. As 2nd placed Brundle conceded: "Schuey's taking the mick, isn't he? He's completely on it: the car's together and so is he". Hakkinen and Hill continued their feud following their joint exit at the first corner, whilst Blundell's exploding engine proved the only nervous moment for the German leader:"It gave me a very big moment. I almost hit the barrier". Brundle's 2nd place added further weight to his demands to be installed for the season, though as Ron Dennis told him:"If you want to drive a McLaren, earn it".

World Championship Standings
Drivers: Schumacher 40, Berger 10, Hill 7, Barrichello 7, Larini 6, Alesi 6, Brundle 6, Hakkinen 4, Wendlinger 4, Katayama 4, Fittipaldi 3, De Cesaris 3, Frentzen 2, Comas 1, Alboreto 1.

Constructors: Benetton-Ford 40, Ferrari 22, Jordan-Hart 10, McLaren-Peugeot 10, Williams-Renault 7, Sauber-Mercedes 6, Tyrrell-Yamaha 4, Footwork-Ford 3, Minardi-Ford 1, Larrousse 1.

Spanish Grand Prix
Jarama   May 29
Laps: 65 x 4.747km   Total distance: 308.555km

1	**Damon Hill GBR (Williams-Renault)**	**1:36:14.374**
		(192.366 kmh)
2	Michael Schumacher GER (Benetton-F) at	24.166
3	Mark Blundell GBR (Tyrrell-Yamaha)	1:26.969
4	Jean Alesi FRA (Ferrari)	1 lap
5	Pierreluigi Martini ITA (Minardi-Ford)	1 lap
6	Eddie Irvine GBR (Jordan-Hart)	1 lap
7	Olivier Panis FRA (Ligier-Renault)	2 laps
8	Eric Bernard FRA (Ligier Renault)	3 laps
9	Alessandra Zanardi ITA (Lotus-Mugen Hond)	3 laps
10	David Brabham AUS (Simtak-Ford)	4 laps
11	Martin Brundle GBR (McLaren-Peugeot)	DNF

Pole position: Michael Schumacher
Fastest lap:Schumacher 1:25.155 (200.683 kmh)

May wasn't a merry month for the Williams team, but Damon Hill went some way to lift the gloom by triumphing in an incident free race at the Circuit de Catalunya. Schumacher was denied a fifth consecutive victory due to a faulty gearbox which left him to nurse his crippled Benetton home in second. This was Hill's first victory since Monza 1993 and he immediately dedicated it to the team and to Senna "I don't think I've

known such a difficult month or so before. To win was better than I expected to do". Schumacher was equally happy with his drive after becoming stuck in 5th gear: "I resorted to things I had learned from my Group C sportscar racing days and managed to find a new line. I never imagined I could finish second so it feels as good as a win to me".

World Championship Standings
Drivers: Schumacher 46, Hill 17, Berger 10, Alesi 9, Barrichello 7, Larini 6, Brundle 6, Blundell 4, Hakkinen 4, Wendlinger 4, Katayama 4, Fittipaldi 3, De Cesaris 3, Frentzen 2, Martini 2, Comas 1, Alboreto 1, Irvine 1.

Constructors: .Benetton-Ford 46, Ferrari 25, Williams-Renault 17, Jordan-Hart 11, McLaren-Peugeot 10

Canadian Grand Prix
Circiut Gilles Villeneuve, Montreal   June 12
Laps: 69 x 4.430km   Total distance: 305.670km

1	**Michael Schumacher GER (Benetton-F) 1:44:31.887**	
		(188.006 kmh)
2	Damon Hill GBR (Williams-Renault) at	39.660
3	Jean Alesi FRA (Ferrari)	1:13.368
4	Gerhard Berger AUT (Ferrari)	1:15.609
5	David Coulthard GBR (Williams-Renault)	1 lap
6	JJ Lehto FIN (Benetton-Ford)	1 lap
7	Rubens Barrichello BRA (Jordan-Hart)	1 lap
8	Johnny Herbert GBR (Lotus-Mugen-Honda)	1 lap
9	Piereluigi Martini ITA (Minardi-Ford)	1 lap
10	Mark Blundell GBR (Tyrrell Yamaha)	DNF
11	Michele Alboreto ITA (Minardi-Ford)	2 laps
12	Olivier Panis FRA (Ligier-Renault)	2 laps
13	Eric Bernard FRA (Ligier-Renault)	3 laps
14	David Brabham AUS (Simtek-Ford)	4 laps
15	Alessandra Zanardi ITA (Lotus-Mugen-Honda)	DNF

Pole position: Michael Schumacher
Fastest lap: Schumacher 1:28.927 (192.171 kmh)

This was the first race under the new ruling that ordinary fuel must be used instead of the high performance 'jungle juice' previously available. Perhaps they should also check what brand of orange juice Schumacher drinks for breakfast as once again he blasted away the opposition. Neither Hill nor Alesi could match the Benetton's performance, although Alesi had to constantly fight with a jumping gearbox. Hill had more man-made problems in the shape of new team-mate David Coulthard: "I got a bit cheesed off being behind Coulthard, because I was able to go quicker. I'll be having a word with him later". A brief sprinkling of rain threatened to enliven the procession. "Briefly it made one or two sections of the track tricky, but it didn't last long" said Schumacher.

World Championship Standings
Drivers: Schumacher 56, Hill 23, Berger 13, Alesi 13, Barrichello 7, Larini 6
Constructors: Benetton-Ford 57, Ferrari 32, Williams-Renault 25, Jordan-Hart 11, McLaren-Peugeot 10, Tyrrell-Yamaha 8

French Grand Prix
Magny Cours   July 3
Laps:72 x 4.250km   Total distance:306.000km

1	**Michael Schumacher GER (Benetton-F) 1:38:35.704**	
		(186.216 kmh)
2	Damon Hill GBR (Williams-Renault) at	12.642
3	Gerhard Berger AUT (Ferrari)	52.765
4	Heinz-Harold Frentzen GER (Sauber-Mercedes)	1 lap

5	Pierreluigi Martini ITA (Minardi-Ford)	2 laps
6	Andrea De Cesaris ITA (Sauber-Mercedes)	2 laps
7	Johnny Herbert GBR (Lotus-Mugen-Honda)	2 laps
8	Christian Fittipaldi BRA (Footwork-Ford)	2 laps
9	Maurizio Gounon FRA (Simtek-Ford)	4 laps
10	Mark Blundell GBR (Tyrrell-Yamaha)	DNF

Pole position: Damon Hill
Fastest lap: Hill 1:19.678 (192.022kmh)

All eyes were on the transatlantic star who had come to grace F1 with a guest appearance. IndyCar's Nigel Mansell did not disappoint in qualifying with a drive that landed him on the front row alongside team-mate Hill. The euphoria that existed within the Williams team was dissipated after 3 seconds of the race as Schumacher swept past the two Britons to begin a familiar sequence of events. Hill was bewildered: "I was pretty pleased with my start, but I was beaten to the first corner anyway". Whilst Schumacher put it down to good timing, later revelations about Benetton's 'launch control' developments cast suspicion about the legality of the start. Mansell experienced difficulty in keeping third place from Berger and eventually retired. The Austrian described his tactics: "I kept an eye on his pitboards and I could see them counting him down to come in again. So I think, OK, I push, make him use his tyres, maybe make him tired. Then something happened to him and he pulled off". Hill who briefly held the lead during a Schumacher pitstop, said of the German: "I don't know how we're going to do it, but we've got to stop this man".

World Championship Standings
Drivers: Schumacher 66, Hill 29, Berger 17, Alesi 13, Barrichello 7, Larini 6, Brundle 6, Frentzen 5
Constructors: Benetton-Ford 67, Ferrari 36, Williams-Renault 31, Jordan-Hart 11, McLaren-Peugeot 10, Sauber-Mercedes 10, Tyrrell-Yamaha 8

British Grand Prix

Silverstone   July 10
Laps: 60 x 4.430km   Total distance:191.66km

1	**Damon Hill GBR (Williams-Renault) 1:30:03.640**	
	(202.143 kmh)	
2	Michael Schumacher GER (Benetton-Ford) at	18.778
3	Jean Alesi FRA (Ferrari)	1:08.128
4	Mika Hakkinen FIN (McClaren-Peugeot)	1:40.659
5	Rubens Barrichello BRA (Jordan-Hart)	1:41.751
6	David Coulthard (GBR)	1 lap
7	Ukyo Katayama JPN (Tyrrell-Yamaha)	1 lap
8	Heinz-Harold Frentzen GER (Sauber-Mercedes)	1 lap
9	Jos Verstappen HOL (Footwork-Ford)	1 lap
10	Christian Fittipaldi BRA (Footwork-Ford)	2 laps
11	Pierreluigi Martini ITA (Minardi-Ford)	2 laps
12	Johnny Herbert GBR (Lotus-Mugen-Honda)	2 laps
13	Olivier Panis FRA (Ligier-Renault)	2 laps
14	Eric Bernard FRA (Ligier-Renault)	2 laps
15	Olivier Beretta MON (Larrousse-Ford)	2 laps
16	David Brabham AUS (Simtek Ford)	3 laps
17	Jean-Marc Gounon FRA (Simtek-Ford)	3 laps

Pole position: Damon Hill
Fastest lap: Hill 1:27.100 (209.014 kmh)

Before the race Hill was in a dark mood as he faced media criticism that he was not up to the job: "I've never heard such a lot of bollocks in all my life. I'm very, very pissed off". The mild mannered image was ditched as Hill took pole by 0.003 seconds from Schumacher, who

showed his displeasure by illegally overtaking the Williams on the warm-up lap. This resulted in the German being given a 5 second stop-go penalty which he refused to obey until the 27th lap. The FIA were not impressed and slapped a fine and a 2-race ban on the championship leader, though this could not take the gloss off a famous victory for Hill. Unsurprisingly Hill was overwhelmed "I had a lot of motivation to win, not least because my father never did. It's funny, but I almost feel it was my destiny to win this race. I feel everything in my life has come together to this point."

World Championship Standings
Drivers: Schumacher 72, Hill 39, Berger 17, Alesi 17, Barrichello 9, Hakkinen 7, Larini 6, Brundle 6, Frentzen 5
Constructors: Benetton-Ford 73, Williams-Renault 42, Ferrari 40, McLaren-Peugeot 13, Jordan-Hart 13, Sauber-Mercedes 10

German Grand Prix

Hockenheim   July 31
Laps: 45 x 6.815km   Total distance:306.675km

1	**Gerhard Berger AUT (Ferrari)**	**1:22:37.272**
		(222.976 kmh)
2	Olivier Panis FRA (Ligier-Renault) at	54.779
3	Eric Bernard FRA (Ligier-Renault)	1:05.042
4	Christian Fittipaldi BRA (Footwork-Ford)	1:21.609
5	Gianni Morbidelli ITA (Footwork-Ford)	1:30.540
6	Erik Comas FRA (Larousse-Ford)	1:45.445
7	Olivier Beretta MON (Larrousse-Ford)	1 lap
8	Damon Hill GBR (Williams-Renault)	1 lap

Pole position: Gerhard Berger
Fastest lap: Coulthard 1:46.211

Berger completed Ferrari's first victory since Alain Prost won the Spanish GP in 1990. With Schumacher cleared to race after his appeal, 150,000 flocked to the wooded circuit and saw half of the field wiped out on the first lap. 'Hit man' Hakkinen was again up to his old tricks on the first corner and landed a one-race ban for his part in the pile up. Hill retired soon after after clipping Katayama, only to rejoin 2 laps down on the rest of the field. The delight of the crowd was short-lived when the championship leader coasted out of the race with engine problems. Benetton's problems continued with a faulty fuel hose showering Jos Verstappen with gallons of fuel during a routine pit stop. The Dutchman was soon engulfed in flames as the mechanics scattered, though the fire was quickly doused. It was therefore ironic that Berger, who had himself been engulfed in flames 2 years ago, went on to complete only his first win since 1992.

World Championship Standings
Drivers: Schumacher 66, Hill 39, Berger 27, Alesi 19, Barrichello 10, Hakkinen 8, Larini 6, Brundle 6, Panis 6
Constructors: Benetton-Ford 67, Ferrari 52, Williams-Renault 43, Jordan-Hart 14, McLaren-Peugeot 14, Sauber-Mercedes 10, Ligier-Renault 10

Hungarian Grand Prix

Hungaroring   Aug 14
Laps: 77 x 3.968km   Total distance:305.536km

1	**Michael Schumacher GER (Benetton-F) 1:48:00.185**	
	(169.744 kmh)	
2	Damon Hill GBR (Williams-Renault) at	20.827
3	Jos Verstappen HOL (Benetton-Ford)	1:10.329
4	Martin Brundle GBR (McLaren-Peugeot)	1 lap

5	Mark Blundell GBR (Tyrrell-Yamaha)	1 lap
6	Olivier Panis FRA (Ligier-Renault)	1 lap
7	Michele Alboreto ITA (Minardi-Ford)	2 laps
8	Erik Comas FRA (Larrousse-Ford)	2 laps
9	Olivier Beretta MON (Larrousse-Ford)	2 laps
10	Eric Bernard FRA (Ligier-Renault)	2 laps
11	David Brabham AUS (Simtek-Ford)	3 laps
12	Gerhard Berger AUT (Ferrari)	5 laps
13	Alessandro Zanardi ITA (Lotus-Mug.-Honda)	5 laps
14	Christian Fittipaldi BRA (Footwork-Ford)	8 laps

Pole position: Michael Schumacher
Fastest lap: Schumacher 1:18.258

Benetton's response to their mounting troubles was to claim two podium finishes in a masterly tactical display with Hill sandwiched in between. Schumacher chose to make three stops in the 77-lap race compared to two by Hill and Williams. The lighter and better balanced Benetton led for all but nine of the laps prompting Schumacher to say afterwards: "I would not say this is the most satisfying victory of my career, but it's certainly the most important". Brundle's misery was complete; after running a strong second his Peugeot engine suffered electrical failure on the final lap to give Verstappen his first top 3 finish in his 6th grand prix race.

World Championship Standings
Drivers: Schumacher 76, Hill 45, Berger 27, Alesi 19, Barrichello 10, Brundle 9, Hakkinen 8, Panis 7
Constructors: Benetton-Ford 81, Ferrari 52, Williams-Renault 49, McLaren-Peugeot 17, Jordan-Hart 14, Tyrrell-Yamaha 11, Ligier-Renault 11

Italian Grand Prix

Monza — *Sept 11*
Laps: 53 x 5.800km — *Total distance:307.400*

1	**Damon Hill GBR (Williams-Renault)**	**1:18:02.754**
		(234.96 kmh)
2	Gerhard Berger AUT (Ferrari) at	4.930
3	Mika Hakkinen FIN (McLaren-Peugeot)	25.640
4	Rubens Barrichello BRA (Jordan-Hart)	50.634
5	Martin Brundle GBR (McLaren-Peugeot)	1:25.575
6	David Coulthard GBR (Williams-Renault)	1 lap
7	Eric Bernard FRA (Ligier-Renault)	1 lap
8	Erik Comas FRA (Larrousse-Ford)	1 lap
9	JJ Lehto FIN (Benetton-Ford)	1 lap
10	Olivier Panis FRA (Ligier-Renault)	2 laps

Pole position: Jean Alesi
Fastest lap: Hill 1:25.930

With the cheers of the *tifosi* roaring on the Ferrari of Berger, Damon Hill completed the victory that cut the championship lead to 11 points. With Schumacher sidelined for his misdemeanours at Silverstone, Hill and Coulthard took full advantage of the early retirement of pole man Jean Alesi. Coulthard evetually had to settle for 6th after running out of fuel when only metres from the finish whilst holding off Berger's challenge. Whilst 'Mad Mika' calmed down enough to claim third, his mantle was carried on by Eddie Irvine whose shunt on Johnny Herbert caused the race to be red-flagged and restarted. Herbert, who had made an impressive start was unimpressed: "He should be banned from Formula One - he is always driving like this and causing trouble".

World Championship Standings
Drivers: Schumacher 76, Hill 65, Berger 33, Alesi 19, Hakkinen 18, Barrichello 13, Brundle 11, Verstappen 8,

Blundell 8, Coulthard 8, Panis 7
Constructors: Benetton-Ford 85, Williams-Renault 73, Ferrari 58, McLaren-Peugeot 29, Jordan-Hart 17, Tyrrell-Yamaha 13, Ligier-Renault 11, Sauber-Mercedes 10

Portuguese Grand Prix

Estoril — *Sept 25*
Laps: 71 x 4.350km — *Total distance:308.850km*

1	**Damon Hill GBR (Williams-Renault)**	**1:41:10.165**
		(183.589)
2	David Coulthard GBR (Williams-Renault) at	0.603
3	Mika Hakkinen FIN (McLaren-Peugeot)	20.193
4	Rubens Barrichello BRA (Jordan-Hart)	28.003
5	Jos Verstappen HOL (Benetton-Ford)	29.385
6	Martin Brundle GBR (McLaren-Peugeot)	52.702
7	Eddie Irvine GBR (Jordan-Hart)	1 lap
8	Christian Fittipaldi BRA (Footwork-Ford)	1 lap
9	Gianni Morbidelli ITA (Footwork-Ford)	1 lap
10	Eric Bernard FRA (Ligier-Renault)	1 lap
11	Johnny Herbert GBR Lotus-Mugen-Honda)	1 lap
12	Pierluigi Martini ITA (Minardi-Ford)	2 laps
13	Michele Alboreto ITA (Minardi-Ford)	2 laps
14	Yannick Dalmas FRA (Larrousse-Ford)	2 laps
15	Jean-Marc Gounon FRA (Simtek-Ford)	4 laps
16	P Adams BEL (Lotus-Mugen-Honda)	4 laps

Pole position: Gerhard Berger
Fastest lap: Coulthard 1:22.466 (190.379 kmh)

With Schumacher watching the race on German TV, Williams completed their first one-two of the season, and in doing so reduced the championship lead to one point. Hill was happy to have made the most of Schumacher's absence: "I have maximised the opportunity and I couldn't have hoped for more" Coulthard was an impressive second in his final race before Mansell returned from across the pond. The young Scot pushed Hill hard and the frostiness between them afterwards suggested more than competitive friction.

World Championship Standings
Drivers: Schumacher 76, Hill 75, Berger 33, Hakkinen 22, Alesi 19, Barrichello 16, Coulthard 14, Brundle 12, Verstappen 10, Blundell 8
Constructors: Williams-Renault 89, Benetton-Ford 87, Ferrari 58, McLaren-Peugeot 34, Jordan-Hart 20, Tyrrell-Yamaha 13, Ligier-Renault 11, Sauber-Mercedes 10

1993 Season

Japanese Grand Prix

Suzuka — *Oct 24*
Laps:53 x 5.864km — *Total distance:310.792km*

1	**Ayrton Senna BRA (McLaren-Ford)**	**1:40:27.912**
		(185.512 kmh)
2	Alain Prost FRA (Williams-Renault)	11.435
3	Mika Hakkinen FIN (McLaren-Ford)	26.129
4	Damon Hill GBR (Williams-Renault)	1:23.538
5	Rubens Barrichello BRA (Jordan-Hart)	1:35.101
6	Eddie Irvine GBR (Jorda-Hart)	1:48.421
7	Mark Blundell GBR (Ligier-Renault)	1 lap
8	JJ Lehto GBR (Sauber)	1 lap
9	Martin Brundle GBR (Ligier-Renault)	2 laps
10	Pierreluigi Martini ITA (Minardi-Ford)	2 laps
11	Johnny Herbert GBR (Lotus-Ford)	2 laps

12	T Suzuki JPN (Larrousse-Lamborghini)	2 laps
13	Pedro Lamy POR (Lotus-Ford)	4 laps
14	Derek Warwick GBR (Footw.-Mugen-Honda)	5 laps

Fastest lap:Prost 1:41.176 (129.649 kmh)

Senna won the race comfortably enough in front of 162,000 spectators, although the race claimed 13 out of 24 starters. Senna will be more remembered though for the left hook that floored debutant Eddie Irvine, following the Ulsterman's first championship point. The Brazilian took exception to some robust driving which also left Derek Warwick fuming after being shunted from the track. Senna had become embroiled when looking to lap both Irvine and Hill who were wheel-to-wheel. After the fracas in the pit lane Irvine was less than complimentary about the former world champion: "I think the guy is a nutter. He is completely out of control".

World Championship Standings
Drivers: Prost 95, Hill 65, Senna 63, Schumacher 52, Patrese 20, Alesi 13, Brundle 12, Herbert 11, Blundell 10, Berger 10, Andretti 7, Wendlinger 7
Constructors: Williams-Renault 158, McLaren-Ford 74, Benetton-Ford 72, Ferrari 23, Ligier-Renault 22, Lotus-Ford 12, Sauber 12, Minardi-Ford 7, Footwork-Mugen-Honda 4

Australian Grand Prix

Adelaide *Nov 7*
Laps:79 x 3.780km *Total distance: 298.62km*

1	**Ayrton Senna BRA (McLaren Ford)**	**1:43:27.476**	
		(173.183 kmh)	
2	Alain Prost FRA (Williams-Renault)	9.259	
3	Damon Hill GBR (Williams-Renault)	33.902	
4	Jean Alesi FRA (Ferrari)	1 lap	
5	Gerhard Berger AUT (Ferrari)	1 lap	

6	Martin Brundle GBR (Ligie-Renault)	1 lap
7	Aguri Suzuki JPN (Footwork-Mugen-Honda)	1 lap
8	Ricardo Patrese ITA (Benetton-Ford)	2 laps
9	Mark Blundell GBR (Ligier-Renault)	2 laps
10	David Warwick GBR (Footw.-Mugen-Honda)	3 laps
11	Rubens Barrichello BRA (Jordan-Hart)	3 laps
12	Erik Comas FRA (Larrousse-Lamborghini)	3 laps
13	Andrea De Cesaris ITA (Tyrrell-Yamaha)	4 laps
14	T Suzuki JPN (Larrousse-Lamborghini)	5 laps
15	Karl Wendlinger AUT (Sauber)	6 laps

Fastest lap:Hill 1:15.381 (180.523 kmh)

The victory by Senna established the Woking based McLaren team as the most successful in F1 history with 104 wins. It was also the Brazilian's 41st triumph in 158 races. Prost, driving in his last grand prix, was never in the hunt and had to use all his wiles to fight off a spirited challenge from Hill who set a new circuit record of 1:15.381. The race itself belonged to Senna who led into the first corner and kept the lead throughout, save for a brief spell after an early pit stop. Prost was left to contemplate retirement: "I hope I don't get fat and lazy, that's for sure. I will feel a little bit more free and my life should be a little bit better."

WORLD CHAMPIONSHIP FINAL STANDINGS
Drivers: Prost 99, Senna 73, Hill 69, Schumacher 52, Patrese 20, Alesi 16, Brundle 13, Berger 12, Herbert 11, Blundell 10, Andretti 7, Wendlinger 7, Fittipaldi 5, Lehto 5, Hakkinen 4, Warwick 4, Alliot 2, Barrichello 2, Barbazza 2, Zanardi 1, Comas 1, Irvine 1
Constructors: Williams-Renault 168, McLaren-Ford 84, Benetton-Ford 72, Ferrari 28, Ligier-Renault 23, Lotus-Ford 12, Sauber-Mercedes 12, Minardi-Ford 7, Footwork-Mugen-Honda 4, Larrousse-Lamborghini 3, Jordan-Hart 3

Le Mans 24 Hours

Circuit de la Sarthe, Le Mans June 18-19
344 laps Distance: 2912 miles

1	**Le Mans Porche Team (Dauer-Porsche)**	**Yannick Dalmas/Hurley Haywood/Mauro Baldi**	**344 laps**
2	Toyota Team SARD (Toyota)	Eddie Irvine/Mauro Martini/Jeff Krosnoff	343
3	Le Mans Porche Team (Dauer-Porsche)	Hans Stuck/Danny Sullivan/Thierry Boutsen	343
4	Nisso Trust Racing Team (Toyota)	Steven Andskar/George Fouche/Bob Wollek	328
5	Nissan/Cunnigham Racing (Nissan)	Steve Millen/Johnny O'Connell/John Morton	317
6	Gulf Oil Racing (Kremer-Porsche)	Derek Bell/Robin Donovan/Jurgen Laessig	316
7	Courage Competition (Courage-Porsche)	Jean-Louis Ricci/Andy Evans/Phillipe Olczyk	310
8	Larbre Competition (Porsche Carrera)	Dominique Dupuy/Carlos Palau/Jesus Pareja	307
9	Ecurie Beinoise (Porsche Carrera)	Enzo Calderari/Lilian Bryner/Renato Mastropietro	299
10	Konrad Motorsport (Porsche Carrera)	Tomlje Matjaz/Patrick Huisman/Cor Euser	295
11	Repsol Ferrari Espana (Ferrari)	Alfonso Borbon/Tomas Saldana/Andreas Vilarino	276
12	Rent A Car Racing Team (Dodge Viper)	René Arnoux/Justin Bell/ Bertrand Balas	273
13	Legeay Sports (Alpine)	Luc Galmard/Jean-Claude Police/Benjamin Roy	272
14	Kremer Honda Racing (Honda)	Armin Hahne/Bertrand Gachot/Christophe Bouchut	257
15	Team Artnature (Mazda)	Yojiro Terada/Pierre de Thoisy/Franck Freon	250
16	Kremer Honda Racing (Honda)	Kazuo Shimizu/Phillipe Favre/Hideki Okada	240
17	Augusta Racing Team (Venturi)	Jean-Louis Sirera/Xavier Camp/Antonio Puig	225

Winner's Average Speed: 121.33 mph
Fastest Laps: Thierry Boutsen BEL 3:52.54 (130.81 mph)
              Eddie Irvine GBR 3:53.92 (130.06 mph)

Indy Car World Series (PPG)

The Indy Car Series comprises 16 races; 15 in north America and one in Australia(the first). In the race charts below, the drivers are given in finish positions, the numbers in brackets after the placings refer to the start grid position. The Laps column gives the position of the driver when the winner crossed the line - if the car withdrew, then it will show on which lap. If the driver was also in the final lap, the Status column shows an average speed figure. Otherwise, the Status column shows Running if the car was still racing (but not on the final lap) or the reason for withdrawal. The placings in brackets refer to the qualifying times

Australian FAI Grand Prix (Race 1)
Surfers' Paradise, Queensland   *Mar 20*

Driver	Ctry	Car	Laps	Status	Pts	Total
1 (2) Michael Andretti	USA	Target-Scotch R941 Ford-Cos XB	55	80.994	21	21
2 (3) Emerson Fittipaldi	BRA	Marlboro Penske 94 Ilmor V8	55	80.978	16	16
3 (19) Mario Andretti	USA	Kmart Caltex L94 Ford-Cos XB	55	80.900	14	14
4 (10) Jimmy Vasser	USA	Conseco-STP R941 Ford-Cos XB	55	80.501	12	12
5 (12) Stefan Johansson	SWE	Alumax Penske 93 Ilmor V8	55	80.190	10	10
6 (7) Mauricio Gugelmin	BRA	Hollywood Indy Car R941 Ford-Cos XB	55	79.946	8	8
7 (11) Teo Fabi	ITA	Pennzoil Special R941 Ilmor V8	54	96.925	6	6
8 (14) Mike Groff	USA	Motorola L94 Honda V8	54	97.633	5	5
9 (1) Nigel Mansell	GBR	Kmart Caltex L94 Ford-Cos XB	54	94.877	5	5
10 (17) Scott Goodyear	CAN	Budweiser King L94 Ford-Cos XB	53	97.835	3	3
11 (18) Scott Sharp	USA	PacWest Racing L94 Ford-Cos XB	53	97.940	2	2
12 (26) Dominic Dobson	USA	PacWest Racing L94 Ford-Cos XB	52	99.779	1	1
Also						
14 (5) Al Unser Jr.	USA	Marlboro Penske 94 Ilmor V8	51	96.394	0	0

Time of Race: 1:53:52.770 Margin of Victory: 1.326 secs. Lap Leaders: Michael Andretti 1-55.

An eventful start to the Indy Car season with storm weather forcing the race to start two hours late and finish 10 laps early in the dim glow of the Surfers' Paradise street lamps. With two restarts and cars spinning off at regular intervals, it was Michael Andretti, in his first race back in Indy Cars, who picked his way through the carnage. Andretti had a face-off with the reigning champion, Mansell, afer one of the restarts. "How many shunts did you have in F1, sonny?" Mansell was reported to have said. It was Mansell, though, who spun twice, leaving the door open for Andretti to outpace the evergreen Fittipaldi and go some way to exorcising that nightmare year in Formula 1.

Valvoline 200 (Race 2)
Phoenix, Arizona   *Apr 10*

Driver	Ctry	Car	Laps	Status	Pts	Total
1 (6) Emerson Fittipaldi	USA	Marlboro Penske 94 Ilmor V8	200	107.437	21	37
2 (9) Al Unser Jr.	USA	Marlboro Penske 94 Ilmor V8	200	107.221	16	16
3 (3) Nigel Mansell	GBR	Kmart Caltex L94 Ford-Cos XB	199	Running	14	19
4 (15) Stefan Johansson	SWE	Alumax Penske 93 Ilmor V8	197	Running	12	22
5 (11) Jimmy Vasser	USA	Conseco-STP R941 Ford-Cos XB	197	Running	10	22
6 (20) Mike Groff	USA	Motorola L94 Honda V8	196	Running	8	13
7 (7) Robby Gordon	USA	Valvoline-Cummins L94 Ford-Cos	195	Running	6	6
8 (5) Raul Boesel	BRA	Duracell Charger L94 Ford-Cos XB	195	Running	5	5
9 (13) Scott Sharp	USA	PacWest Racing L94 Ford-Cos XB	194	Running	4	6
10 (16) Adrian Fernandez	MEX	Tecate-Quaker State R941 Ilmor V8	194	Running	3	3
11 (10) Scott Goodyear	CAN	Budweiser King L94 Ford-Cos XB	192	Running	2	5
12 (17) Davy Jones	USA	Foyt-Copenhagen Racing L94 Ford-Cos	190	Running	1	1
Also						
21 (4) Mario Andretti	USA	Kmart Caltex L94 Ford-Cos	156	Contact	0	14
23 (1) Paul Tracy	CAN	Marlboro Penske 94 Ilmor V8	62	Contact	1	1

Time of Race: 1:51:41:615 Margin of Victory: 13.482 secs. Lap Leaders: Tracy 1-10, Mansell 11-29, Tracy 30-62, Gordon 63, Fittipaldi 64-141, Unser Jr. 142-146, Gordon 147-154, Fittipaldi 155-200.

Ovals can be tough on cars and drivers and Phoenix was just that with accidents accounting for no less than eight of the starters. On the front of the grid was the first all-Canadian line-up, but Villeneuve and Tracy gained no advantage from their grid positions, both being ruled out by crashes. The stock-cat mentality had Fittipaldi describing it as, "one of the most intense races I've ever participated in." However, it didn't prevent the 48 year old veteran from claiming his first victory of the season. Mansell, who was equally awed by the "scariest" of races, finished a lap adrift in third.

Toyota Grand Prix of Long Beach (Race 3)
Long Beach, California   *Apr 17*

Driver	Ctry	Car	Laps	Status	Pts	Total
1 (2) Al Unser Jr.	USA	Marlboro Penske 94 Ilmor V8	105	99.283	21	37
2 (4) Nigel Mansell	GBR	Kmart Texaco L94 Ford-Cos	105	98.646	16	35

3 (5)	Robby Gordon	USA	Valvoline-Cummins L94 Ford-Cos XB	105	98.530	14	20
4 (7)	Raul Boesel	BRA	Duracell Fuji Film L94 Ford-Cos XB	104	Running	12	17
5 (6)	Mario Andretti	USA	Kmart Texaco L94 Ford-Cos XB	104	Running	10	24
6 (9)	Michael Andretti	USA	Target-Scotch R941 Ford-Cos XB	104	Running	8	29
7 (8)	Mauricio Gugelmin	BRA	Hollywood R941 Ford-Cos XB	104	Running	6	14
8 (19)	Adrian Fernandez	MEX	Tecate-Quaker State R941 Ilmor V8	104	Running	5	8
9 (12)	Teo Fabi	ITA	Pennzoil Special R941 Ilmor V8	104	Running	4	10
10 (10)	Stefan Johansson	SWE	Alumax Penske 93 Ilmor V8	102	Fuel	3	25
11 (16)	Arie Luyendyk	HOL	Eurosport-Boost Mon L94 Ilmor V8	102	Running	2	2
12 (27)	Frank Freon	FRA	Marcelo Group L93 Ford-Cos XB	101	Running	1	1
Also							
20 (1)	Paul Tracy	CAN	Marlboro Penske 94 Ilmor V8	75	Gearbox	1	2
21 (3)	Emerson Fittipaldi	BRA	Marlboro Penske 94 Ilmor V8	66	Gearbox	0	37
24 (23)	Jimmy Vasser	USA	Conseco-STP R941 Ford-Cos XB	36	Suspension	0	22

Time of Race: 1:40:53:582 *Lap Leaders:* Tracy 1-20, Unser Jr. 21-39, Fittipaldi 40-41, Unser Jr. 42, Fittipaldi 43-62, Unser Jr. 63-80, Gordon 81-82, Unser Jr. 83-105.

Al Unser Jr is to Long Beach what British F1 drivers are to Silverstone. It's not quite more often than not, but five wins from 11 outings is not a bad track record. Unser, who had to nurse a suspect gearbox, finished comfortably ahead of Mansell, who admitted that he just couldn't catch the Penske car. Paul Tracy was again unfortunate, stalling his car after having made much of the early running. When the other front runners made their final pit stops for fuel and fresh tyres, Mansell pulled himself up to second place for his best finish of the season so far.

Indianapolis 500 (Race 4)

Speedway, Indianapolis *May 29*

	Driver	Ctry	Car	Laps	Status	Pts	Total
1 (1)	Al Unser Jr.	USA	Marlboro Penske 94 Mercedes	200	Running	21	58
2 (4)	Jacques Villeneuve	CAN	Player's Ltd. R941 Ford-Cos XB	200	Running	16	16
3 (28)	Bobby Rahal	USA	Miller Genuine Draft Penske 93 Ilmor	199	Running	14	14
4 (16)	Jimmy Vasser	USA	Conseco-STP R941 Ford-Cos XB	199	Running	12	34
5 (19)	Robby Gordon	USA	Valvoline-Cummins L94 Ford-Cos XB	199	Running	10	30
6 (5)	Michael Andretti	USA	Target-Scotch R941 Ford-Cos XB	198	Running	8	37
7 (24)	Teo Fabi	ITA	Pennzoil Special R941 Ilmor V8	198	Running	6	16
8 (11)	Eddie Cheever	USA	Quaker-State Special L94 Ford-Cos XB	197	Running	5	5
9 (22)	Bryan Herta	USA	Foyt-Copenhagen L94 Ford-Cos XB	197	Running	4	4
10 (10)	John Andretti	USA	Foyt-Jonathan Byrd's L94 Ford-Cos XB	196	Running	3	3
11 (30)	Mauricio Gugelmin	BRA	Hollywood Indy Car R941 Ford-Cos XB	196	Running	2	16
12 (21)	Brian Till	USA	The Mi-Jack Car L93 Ford-Cos XB	194	Running	1	1
Also							
15 (27)	Stefan Johansson	SWE	Alumax Penske 93 Ilmor V8	192	Running	0	25
17 (3)	Emerson Fittipaldi	BRA	Marlboro Penske 94 Mercedes	184	Contact	1	38
22 (7)	Nigel Mansell	GBR	Kmart/Texaco L94 Ford-Cos XB	92	Contact	0	35
32 (20)	Mario Andretti	USA	Kmart/Texaco L94 Ford-Cos XB	23	Fuel system	0	24

Time of Race: 3:06:29.006 *Lap Leaders:* Unser Jr. 1-23, Fittipaldi 24-61, Villeneuve 62-63, Fittipaldi 64-124, Villeneuve 125-129, Fittipaldi 130-133, Unser 134-138, Fittipaldi 139-164, Unser 165-168, Fittipaldi 169-184, Unser 185-200.

The Roger Penske domination of Indy Car continued when Unser romped home in the blue riband of the Indy Car season. Unser picked up a cheque for $700,000 for his victory, but the money looked to be going to Emerson Fittpaldi after the Brazilian led with just 16 laps remaining. On the next circuit, Fittipaldi ploughed into the concrete wall and the veteran was left to rue what might have been."The car was flying. It was my mistake," he admitted. other cars were flying, notably that of Dennis Vitolo, which landed on Mansell's car in the pit lane. Mansell, who had not even survivied half a race, was so incensed that he discharged himself from the medical centre before the doctor could complete his examination.

Miller Genuine Draft 200 (Race 5)

Milwaukee, Wisconsin *June 5*

	Driver	Ctry	Car	Laps	Status	Pts	Total
1 (11)	Al Unser Jr.	USA	Marlboro Penske 94 Ilmor V8	192	118.804	21	79
2 (8)	Emerson Fittipaldi	BRA	Marlboro Penske 94 Ilmor V8	192	118.774	16	54
3 (2)	Paul Tracy	CAN	Marlboro Penske 94 Ilmor V8	190	Running	14	16
4 (12)	Michael Andretti	USA	Target-Scotch R941 Ford-Cos XB	189	Running	12	49
5 (9)	Nigel Mansell	GBR	Kmart Texaco L94 Ford-Cos XB	189	Running	10	45
6 (3)	Robby Gordon	USA	Valvoline-Cummins L94 Ford-Cos XB	189	Running	8	38
7 (19)	Bobby Rahal	USA	Miller Genuine Draft L94 Honda V8	189	Running	6	20
8 (1)	Raul Boesel	BRA	Duracell Charger L94 Ford-Cos XB	188	Running	6	23
9 (4)	Jacques Villeneuve	CAN	Player's Ltd. R941 Ford-Cos XB	187	Running	4	20

10 (7)	Bryan Herta	USA	A.J.Foyt Copenhagen L94 Ford-Cos	187	Running	3	7
11 (16)	Jimmy Vasser	USA	Conseco-STP R941 Ford-Cos	187	Running	2	36
12 (15)	Scott Sharp	USA	PacWest Racing L94 Ford-Cos	186	Running	1	7
Also							
14 (13)	Mario Andretti	USA	Kmart Texaco L94 Ford-Cos XB	185	Running	0	24
26 (14)	Stefan Johansson	SWE	Alumax PC93 Ilmor V8	163	Engine	0	25

Time of Race: 1:36:57.964 sec. *Lap Leaders:* Tracy 1-22, Fittipaldi 23-30, Unser Jr. 31-68, Fittipaldi 69-71, Unser 72-128, Fittipaldi 129-132, Unser Jr. 133-192.

"This team is just awesome," said Unser, as the orange overalls of the Penske team took all three tiers of the podium for the first time since Michigan in 1980. Unser himself completed a hattrick of wins and even Michael Andretti concede that there were two races being run and that he was happy enough to finish fourth and win the second one. It was also a remarkable race in that only one car failed to finish, that of Swede Stefan Johansson, due to engine failure after 163 laps.

ITT Automotive Detroit Grand Prix (Race 6)
Detroit, Michigan.   *June 12*

	Driver	Ctry	Car	Laps	Status	Pts	Total
1 (3)	Paul Tracy	CAN	Marlboro Penske 94 Ilmor V8	77	86.245	20	36
2 (4)	Emerson Fittipaldi	BRA	Marlboro Penske 94 Ilmor V8	77	86.127	16	70
3 (10)	Robby Gordon	USA	Valvoline-Cum. L94 Ford-Cos XB	77	86.113	14	52
4 (8)	Teo Fabi	ITA	Pennzoil Special R941 Ilmor V8	77	85.932	12	28
5 (17)	Michael Andretti	USA	Target-Scotch R941 Ford-Cos XB	77	85.909	10	59
6 (6)	Bobby Rahal	USA	Miller Genuine Draft L94 Honda V8	77	85.899	8	28
7 (7)	Jacques Villeneuve	CAN	Player's Ltd. R941 Ford-Cos XB	77	85.764	6	26
8 (5)	Mauricio Gugelmin	BRA	Hollywood Indy Car R941 Ford-Cos XB	77	85.597	5	21
9 (18)	Bryan Herta	USA	Foyt-Copenhagen L94 Ford-Cos XB	77	85.584	4	11
10 (2)	Al Unser Jr.	USA	Marlboro Penske 94 Ilmor V8	77	85.579	4	83
11 (21)	Scott Goodyear	CAN	Budweiser King L94 Ford-Cos XB	76	Running	2	7
12 (16)	Christian Danner	GER	Marcelo Anvil-Lola L93 Ford-Cos XB	76	Running	1	1
Also							
18 (9)	Mario Andretti	USA	Kmart Texaco L94 Ford-Cos XB	75	Running	0	24
20 (19)	Jimmy Vasser	USA	Conseco-STP R941 Ford-Cos XB	74	Contact	0	36
21 (1)	Nigel Mansell	GBR	Kmart Texaco L94 Ford-Cos XB	65	Throttle M	1	46

Time of Race: 1:52:29.642 *Lap Leaders:* Mansell 1, Unser Jr.. 2-48, Tracy 49, Unser 50-54, Tracy 55-77.

It was something of a novelty to see Mansell and the Newman Haas Lola back on the front of the grid. The novelty didn't last long. Mansell rammed into the back of a braking Fittipaldi on lap 2 and had to limp back into the pits. Paul Tracy tried a similar maneouvre on his teammate, and race-leader Unser, but this time it was the car that was hit which said goodnight. Tracy might have worried what Penske would say, but he still went on to win the race. Just for a change, there was only two Penskes on the podium, while back in fourth place Italy's Teo Fabi had his best race of the year.

Budweiser/G I Joe's 200 (Race 7)
Portland, Oregon   *June 26*

	Driver	Ctry	Car	Laps	Status	Pts	Total
1 (1)	Al Unser Jr.	USA	Marlboro Penske 94 Ilmor V8	102	107.777	21	105
2 (3)	Emerson Fittipaldi	BRA	Marlboro Penske 94 Ilmor V8	102	107.748	16	86
3 (4)	Paul Tracy	CAN	Marlboro Penske 94 Ilmor V8	102	107.253	14	50
4 (7)	Robby Gordon	USA	Valvoline-Cummins L94 Ford-Cos XB	102	106.871	12	64
5 (2)	Nigel Mansell	GBR	Kmart Texaco L94 Ford-Cos XB	102	106.871	10	56
6 (5)	Jacques Villeneuve	CAN	Players Ltd R94 Ford-Cos XB	101	Running	8	34
7 (21)	Alessandro Zampedri	ITA	The Mi-Jack Car L93 Ford Cos XB	101	Running	6	6
8 (13)	Stefan Johansson	SWE	Alumax Penske 93 Ilmor V8	101	Running	5	30
9 (16)	Mario Andretti	USA	Kmart Texaco L94 Ford-Cos XB	100	Running	4	28
10 (14)	Adrian Fernandez	MEX	Tecate-Quaker State R941 Ilmor V8	100	Running	3	11
11 (20)	Mike Groff	USA	Motorola L94 Honda V8	99	Running	2	15
12 (17)	Bobby Rahal	USA	Miller Genuine Draft L94 Honda V8	99	Running	1	29
Also							
31 (9)	Michael Andretti	USA	Target-Scotch R941 Ford Cos XB	11	Contact	0	59

Time of Race: 1:50:43.706 *Margin of Victory:* 1.830 secs. *Lap Leaders:* Unser Jr. 1-32, Tracy 33-34, Unser Jr. 35-68, Fittipaldi 69-70, Tracy 71-72, Unser Jr. 73-102.

It took the Penske team 14 years to acheive that clean sweep in Milwaukee. Twenty-one days later, they repeated the feat in Portland. Unser, now daring to dream of a second Indy Car title, took his fourth race of the summer. Fittipaldi, 16 years his senior, was again the driver snapping at his heels. Mansell has something of a tussle with the third Penske driver, Paul Tracy, but having lost that battle was ultimately taken on the line by Robby Gordon. "I never drove so hard for a fifth place," said a dispirited Mansell.

Motor Racing

Budweiser Cleveland GP (Race 8)
Cleveland, Ohio — *July 10*

	Driver	Ctry	Car	Laps	Status	Pts	Total
1 (1)	Al Unser Jr.	USA	Marlboro Penske 94 Ilmor V8	85	138.026	22	127
2 (4)	Nigel Mansell	GBR	Kmart Texaco L94 Ford-Cos XB	85	137.426	16	72
3 (2)	Paul Tracy	CAN	Marlboro Penske 94 Ilmor V8	85	Running	14	64
4 (5)	Jacques Villeneuve	CAN	Players Ltd R94 Ford-Cos XB	85	Running	12	46
5 (8)	Stefan Johansson	SWE	Alumax Penske 93 Ilmor V8	84	Running	10	40
6 (19)	Raul Boesel	BRA	Duracell Charger L94 Ford-Cos XB	84	Running	8	31
7 (14)	Adrian Fernandez	MEX	Tecate-Quaker State R941 Ilmor V8	84	Running	6	17
8 (7)	Mauricio Gugelmin	BRA	Hollywood Indy Car R941 Ford-Cos XB	84	Running	5	26
9 (13)	Teo Fabi	ITA	Pennzoil Special R941 Ilmor V8	83	Running	4	32
10 (23)	Alessandro Zampedri	ITA	The Mi-Jack Car L93 Ford Cos XB	83	Running	3	9
11 (6)	Robby Gordon	USA	Valvoline-Cummins L94 Ford-Cos XB	82	Running	2	66
12 (27)	Willy T Ribbs	USA	Service Merchandise L94 Ford-Cos XB	82	Running	1	1
Also							
18 (17)	Michael Andretti	USA	Target-Scotch R941 Ford Cos XB	77	Engine	0	59
20 (3)	Emerson Fittipaldi	BRA	Marlboro Penske 94 Ilmor V8	65	Fire	0	86

Time of Race: 1:27:32.000 *Margin of Victory:* 0.60 secs *Lap Leaders:* Unser Jr. 1-28, Fittipaldi 29, Unser Jr. 30-57, Mansell 58, Fittipaldi 59, Unser Jr. 60-85.

It was 5 out of 6 for Unser Jnr on the bumpy Cleveland street circuit leaving Mansell 23 seconds behind in second place. Even with a 41-point lead over Fittipaldi, Unser Jnr was reserved about his chances of claiming the title: "In 1985 I had a 36-point lead and lost the championship to my dad (Al Snr) by one point". Mansell himself was modest about his drive "I drove my ass off" he droned, having earlier sent team-mate Mario Andretti spinning into retirement with damaged front suspension.

Molson Indy Toronto (Race 9)
Toronto, Canada — *July 17*

	Driver	Ctry	Car	Laps	Status	Pts	Total
1 (6)	Michael Andretti	USA	Target-Scotch R941 Ford Cos XB	98	96.673	21	80
2 (9)	Bobby Rahal	USA	Miller Genuine Draft L94 Honda V8	98	96.572	16	45
3 (4)	Emerson Fittipaldi	BRA	Marlboro Penske 94 Ilmor V8	98	96.561	14	100
4 (10)	Mario Andretti	USA	Kmart Texaco L94 Ford-Cos XB	98	95.753	12	40
5 (5)	Paul Tracy	CAN	Marlboro Penske 94 Ilmor V8	97	Running	10	74
6 (1)	Robby Gordon	USA	Valvoline-Cummins L94 Ford-Cos XB	97	Running	9	75
7 (13)	Andrea Montermini	ITA	Budweiser King L94 Ford-Cos XB	97	Running	6	6
8 (12)	Teo Fabi	ITA	Pennzoil Special R941 Ilmor V8	97	Running	5	37
9 (15)	Jacques Villeneuve	CAN	Players Ltd R94 Ford-Cos XB	97	Running	4	50
10 (18)	Scott Goodyear	CAN	Budweiser King L94 Ford-Cos XB	97	Running	3	10
11 (16)	Dominic Dobson	USA	PacWest Racing Gp. LT94 Ford-Cos	97	Running	2	3
12 (17)	Raul Boesel	BRA	Duracell Fuji Film L94 Ford-Cos XB	97	Running	1	32
Also							
23 (2)	Nigel Mansell	GBR	Kmart Texaco L94 Ford-Cos XB	66	Handling	0	72
25 (8)	Jimmy Vasser	USA	Conseco-STP R941 Ford-Cos XB	43	Off Course	0	36
29 (3)	Al Unser Jr.	USA	Marlboro Penske 94 Ilmor V8	2	Engine	0	127

Time of Race: 1:48:15.978 *Lap Leaders:* Gordon 1-12, Mansell 13-25, Michael Andretti 26-38, Rahal 39-40, Michael Andretti 41-98

Michael Andretti recorded his 2nd win of the year and the 29th of his career to tie him with Rick Mears for fifth on the all-time victory list. Andretti seems to have an affinity for the street circuit on which he has completed a record 4 victories. His father celebrated his 400th start in Indy Cars by finishing fourth, whilst Bobby Rahal's second was his best finish since Vancouver in 1993. With the race coinciding with the World Cup Final, and with thousands of Italian fans in attendance, the giant TV screens at the circuit remained in action into the evening for a post-race football party.

Marlboro 500 (Race 10)
Brooklyn, Michigan — *July 31*

	Driver	Ctry	Car	Laps	Status	Pts	Total
1 (12)	Scott Goodyear	CAN	Budweiser King L94 Ford-Cos XB	250	159.800	20	30
2 (26)	Arie Luyendyk	HOL	Eurosport-Boost Monaco LT94 Ilmor V8	249	Running	16	18
3 (9)	Dominic Dobson	USA	PacWest Racing L94 Ford-Cos XB	248	Running	14	17
4 (8)	Teo Fabi	ITA	Pennzoil Special R941 Ilmor V8	246	Running	12	49
5 (25)	Mark Smith	USA	Craftsman Tools L94 Ford-Cos XB	240	Running	10	10
6 (20)	Hiro Matsushita	JPN	Panasonic-Duskin L94 Ford-Cos XB	239	Running	8	8
7 (23)	Willy T Ribbs	USA	Service Merchandise L94 Ford-Cos XB	236	Running	6	7

8 (14) Al Unser Jr.	USA	Marlboro Penske 94 Ilmor V8	231	Engine	5	132
9 (2) Raul Boesel	BRA	Duracell Charger L94 Ford-Cos XB	225	Engine	5	37
10 (7) Emerson Fittipaldi	BRA	Marlboro Penske 94 Ilmor V8	209	Engine	3	103
11 (15) Marco Greco	BRA	INT Sports Ltd L94 Ford-Cos XB	195	Running	2	2
12 (18) Scott Sharp	USA	PacWest Racing L94 Ford-Cos	185	Drive Line	1	8
Also						
16 (11) Paul Tracy	CAN	Marlboro Penske 94 Ilmor V8	150	Fuel Pressure	0	74
22 (3) Michael Andretti	USA	Target-Scotch R94l Ford-Cos XB	66	Contact	0	80
26 (1) Nigel Mansell	GBR	Kmart Texaco L94 Ford-Cos XB	35	Throttle Link	1	73

Time of Race: 3:7:44.099 *Lap Leaders:* Mansell 0-26, Michael Andretti 27-67, Goodyear 68, Boesel 69-121, Unser Jr. 122-124, Boesel 125-158, Unser Jr. 159-164, Goodyear 165-169, Unser Jr. 170-191, Boesel 192-224, Unser Jr. 225-230, Goodyear 231-250

On the fastest race track in the world, Scott Goodyear claimed only his second IndyCar victory whilst giving team owner Kenny Bernstein his first in the sport. Mansell set the early pace and built up a comfortable cushion before a sticking throttle made the car uncontrollable on the unforgiving circuit: "I've had to change my pants three times. I just can't drive it if I can't stop" bemoaned the reigning champion. It was also significant for the fact that all three Penskes failed to finish for the first time this season, leaving only eight cars running at the conclusion of the race. Even the eventual winner, Goodyear, ran out of fuel at one point but was fortunate to be able to coast down the pit lane and refire his engine without squandering the lead.

Miller Genuine Draft 200 (Mid Ohio) (Race 11)
Lexington, Ohio　　　　　　　*Aug 14*

Driver	Ctry	Car	Laps	Status	Pts	Total
1 (1) Al Unser Jr.	USA	Marlboro Penske 94 Ilmor V8/D	83	110.387	21	153
2 (2) Paul Tracy	CAN	Marlboro Penske 94 Ilmor V8/D	83	110.357	17	91
3 (3) Emerson Fittipaldi	BRA	Marlboro Penske 94 Ilmor V8/D	83	110.731	14	117
4 (10) Robby Gordon	USA	Valvoline-Cummins L94 Ford-Cos XB	82	Running	12	87
5 (8) Michael Andretti	USA	Target-Scotch R94l Ford-Cos XB	82	Running	10	90
6 (14) Adrian Fernandez	MEX	Tecate-Quaker State R94l Ilmor V8	82	Running	8	25
7 (4) Nigel Mansell	GBR	Kmart Texaco L94 Ford-Cos XB	82	Running	6	79
8 (17) Raul Boesel	BRA	Duracell Charger L94 Ford-Cos XB	82	Running	5	42
9 (6) Jacques Villeneuve	CAN	Player's Ltd R94l Ford-Cos XB	82	Running	4	54
10 (15) Mario Andretti	USA	Kmart Texaco L94 Ford-Cos XB	82	Running	3	43
11 (18) Scott Sharp	USA	PacWest Racing L94 Ford-Cos XB	82	Running	2	10
12 (21) Stefan Johansson	SWE	Alumax Penske 93 Ilmor V8	81	Running	1	41

Time of Race: 1:40:59.436 *Lap Leaders:* Tracy 1-28, Fittipaldi 29, Tracy 30-57, Unser Jr. 58-83

Ohio saw a another all Penske podium as Al Unser Jr. drove himself into a 36 point lead. He was aided by a controversial stop-go penalty to team-mate Paul Tracy who was adjudged to have contravened a yellow flag when lapping the skidding car of Robby Gordon. Unser's win equalled his personal record of six wins in a season which he set in 1990. His appreciation of Penske was obvious: "They're going to have to take a crane or a big ball to get me out of this team".

Slick 50 200 (Race 12)
Loudon, New Hampshire　　　　　*Aug 21*

Driver	Ctry	Car	Laps	Status	Pts	Total
1 (10) Al Unser Jr.	USA	Marlboro Penske 94 Ilmor V8	200	122.635	20	173
2 (4) Paul Tracy	CAN	Marlboro Penske 94 Ilmor V8	200	122.618	16	107
3 (1) Emerson Fittipaldi	BRA	Marlboro Penske 94 Ilmor V8	200	122.601	16	133
4 (2) Raul Boesel	BRA	Duracell Charger L94 Ford-Cos XB	198	Running	12	54
5 (17) Michael Andretti	USA	Target-Scotch R94l Ford-Cos XB	198	Running	10	100
6 (6) Dominic Dobson	USA	PacWest Racing L94 Ford-Cos XB	197	Running	8	25
7 (12) Jimmy Vasser	USA	Coseco-STP R94l Ford-Cos XB	195	Running	6	42
8 (8) Adrian Fernandez	MEX	Tecate-Quaker State R94l Ilmor V8	195	Running	5	30
9 (19) Bobby Rahal	USA	Miller Genuine Draft L94 Honda V8	193	Running	4	49
10 (24) Willy T Ribbs	USA	Service Merchandise L94 Ford-Cos XB	192	Running	3	10
11 (23) Scott Goodyear	CAN	Budweiser King L94 Ford-Cos XB	192	Running	2	32
12 (15) Mark Smith	USA	Craftsman Tools L94 Ford-Cos XB	192	Running	1	11
Also						
18 (3) Nigel Mansell	GBR	Kmart Texaco L94 Ford-Cos XB	127	Handling	0	79

Time of Race: 1:43:31.594 *Lap Leaders:* Fittipaldi 1-46, Tracy 47-69, Unser Jr. 70-81, Mansell 82-85, Unser Jr. 86-151, Fittipaldi 152-195, Unser Jr. 196-200

Any mathematical chance of Mansell retaining his crown was lost as he clashed with Mario Andretti at half distance. Mansell had been running 'Little Al' Unser close when he cannoned his Newman-Haas team-mate into the wall on turn 1. Fittipaldi led both Unser and Tracy by almost a lap before a blistered front right tyre forced him into an unscheduled third pitstop. The three Penskes eventually crossed the finish less than 2 seconds apart, to complete another clean sweep

Molson Indy Vancouver (Race 13)

Vancouver, Canada   *Sept 4*

	Driver	Ctry	Car	Laps	Status	Pts	Total
1 (8)	Al Unser Jr.	USA	Marlboro Penske 94 Ilmor V8	102	89.166	20	193
2 (1)	Robby Gordon	USA	Valvoline-Cummins L94 Ford-Cos XB	102	89.136	17	104
3 (3)	Michael Andretti	USA	Target-Scotch R941 Ford-Cos XB	102	89.073	14	114
4 (4)	Scott Goodyear	CAN	Budweiser King L94 Ford-Cos XB	102	89.003	12	44
5 (13)	Mauricio Gugelmin	BRA	Hollywood Indy Car R941 Ford-Cos XB	102	88.998	10	36
6 (18)	Arie Luyendyk	HOL	Eurosport-Boost Monaco L94 Ilmor V8	102	88.972	8	26
7 (15)	Bobby Rahal	USA	Miller Genuine Draft L94 Honda V8	102	88.935	6	55
8 (16)	Mark Smith	USA	Craftsman Tools L94 Ford-Cos XB	102	88.744	5	16
9 (12)	Emerson Fittipaldi	BRA	Marlboro Penske 94 Ilmor V8	101	Contact	4	137
10 (2)	Nigel Mansell	GBR	Kmart Texaco L94 Ford-Cos XB	101	Contact	4	83
11 (10)	Mario Andretti	USA	Kmart Texaco L94 Ford-Cos XB	101	Running	2	45
12 (14)	Scott Sharp	USA	PacWest Racing L94 Ford-Cos XB	101	Running	1	11

Also

	Driver	Ctry	Car	Laps	Status	Pts	Total
20 (6)	Paul Tracy	CAN	Marlboro Penske 94 Ilmor V8	94	Suspension	0	107

Time of Race: 1:53:27.345 *Margin of Victory:* 2.239s. *Lap Leaders:* Gordon 1-36, Mansell 37-75, Fernandez 76, Unser Jr. 77-102. Unser must have sprayed more champagne than Olly Reed and collected more trophies than Buffalo Bill. The 32-year-old New Mexican shrugged off the effects of food poisoning and negotiated 7 yellow flags to record his 8th win of the season. Mansell tried to outbrake Fittipaldi in their battle for 4th spot, only for the two former World F1 champions to come into contact. Fittipaldi wasn't impressed: "He hit me like a torpedo. He said he was committed. I think he was committed to stopping his car with mine".

Texaco/Havoline 200 (Race 14)

Elkhart Lake, Wisconsin   *Sept 11*

	Driver	Ctry	Car	Laps	Status	Pts	Total
1 (2)	Jacques Villeneuve	CAN	Player's Ltd R941 Ford-Cos XB	50	116.922	20	74
2 (4)	Al Unser Jr.	USA	Marlboro Penske 94 Ilmor V8/D	50	116.911	16	209
3 (9)	Emerson Fittipaldi	BRA	Marlboro Penske 94 Ilmor V8/D	50	116.873	14	151
4 (15)	Teo Fabi	ITA	Pennzoil Special R941 Ilmor V8	50	116.471	12	61
5 (6)	Adrian Fernandez	MEX	Tecate-Quaker State R941 Ilmor V8	50	116.400	10	40
6 (10)	Raul Boesel	BRA	Duracell Charger 94 Ford-Cos XB	50	116.317	8	62
7 (14)	Scott Goodyear	CAN	Budweiser King L94 Ford-Cos XB	50	116.280	6	50
8 (19)	Stefan Johansson	SWE	Alumax Penske 93 Ilmor V8	50	116.239	5	46
9 (16)	Bobby Rahal	USA	Miller Genuine Draft L94 Hinda V8	50	116.224	4	59
10 (13)	Scott Sharp	USA	PacWest Racing 94 Ford-Cos XB	50	116.216	3	14
11 (12)	Dominic Dobson	USA	PacWest Racing 94 Ford-Cos XB	50	115.933	2	27
12 (21)	Christian Danner	GER	No Touch-Van Dyne 93 Ford-Cos XB	50	115.724	1	2

Also

	Driver	Ctry	Car	Laps	Status	Pts	Total
13 (3)	Nigel Mansell	GBR	Kmart Texaco L94 Ford-Cos XB	50	115.308	0	83
17 (20)	Michael Andretti	USA	Target-Scotch R941 Ford-Cos XB	46	Exhaust	0	114
18 (1)	Paul Tracy	CAN	Marlboro Penske 94 Ilmor V8	43	Engine	2	109
25 (5)	Robby Gordon	USA	Valvoline-Cummins 94 Ford-Cos XB	16	Transmission	0	104

Time of Race: 1:42:37.930 *Margin of victory:* 0.609 secs. *Lap Leaders:* Tracy 1-35, Villeneuve 36-50. Villeneuve may have fought hard to claim victory, but Unser's 2nd place was sufficient to clinch his second IndyCar World Cup crown, and the ninth title for Roger Penske. The race ended Fittipaldi's hopes of a late challenge and he paid tribute to the new champion: "He has done a great job for the team and I know he will be a great champion and ambassador for our sport." When Unser last won the title with Rick Galle's team in 1990 he was in hospital after crashing during the race at Nazareth. "This feels better," said Unser, "We were able to roll the car onto the trailer today".

Bosch Spark Plug GP (Race 15)

Nazareth, Pennsylvania   *Sept 18*

	Driver	Ctry	Car	Laps	Status	Pts	Total
1 (2)	Paul Tracy	CAN	Marlboro Penske 94 Ilmor V8	200	131.141	21	130
2 (18)	Al Unser Jr.	USA	Marlboro Penske 94 Ilmor V8	200	130.939	16	225
3 (1)	Emerson Fittipaldi	BRA	Marlboro Penske 94 Ilmor V8	200	130.803	15	166
4 (6)	Raul Boesel	BRA	Duracell Charger L94 Ford-Cos XB	196	Running	12	74
5 (10)	Stefan Johansson	SWE	Alumax Penske 93 Ilmor V8	195	Running	10	56
6 (15)	Teo Fabi	ITA	Pennzoil Special R941 Ilmor V8	194	Running	8	69
7 (7)	Jacques Villeneuve	CAN	Player's Ltd R941 Ford-Cos XB	193	Running	6	80
8 (21)	Scott Goodyear	CAN	Budweiser King L94 Ford-Cos XB	191	Running	5	55
9 (19)	Michael Andretti	USA	Target-Scotch R941 Ford-Cos XB	191	Running	4	118

10 (14)	Mauricio Gugelmin	BRA	Hollywood Indy Car R941 Ford-Cos XB	190	Running	3	39
11 (20)	Mike Groff	USA	Motorola L94 Honda V8	190	Running	2	17
12 (8)	Mark Smith	USA	Craftsman Tools L94 Ford-Cos XB	189	Running	1	17

Also

22 (3)	Nigel Mansell	GBR	Kmart Texaco L94 Ford-Cos XB	87	Handling	0	83
23 (4)	Robby Gordon	USA	Valvoline-Cummins L94 Ford-Cos XB	63	Wheel Bearing	0	104

Time of Race: 1:31:30.292 *Margin of victory:* 1.830 secs. *Lap Leaders:* Tracy 1-47, Unser Jr. 48-50, Tracy 51-124, Unser Jr. 125-126, Fittipaldi 127-129, Tracy 130-200 Tracy notched up his first oval victory of his IndyCar career as the white and orange colours of the Marlboro Penskes swept over the finish 4 laps ahead of the rest of the field. "Today our cars were head and feet above any other car out there" said new champion Unser. Mario Andretti had an unfortunate final return to his home track when he was involved in an accident with Eddie Cheever after the retiring Indy legend had suffered from dire handling. Unser needs just 10 points to beat Michael Andretti's modern record of 234 points in one season.

PPG Indycar Final Round (Race 16)
Laguna Seca, California   *Oct 10*

	Driver	Ctry	Car	Laps	Status	Pts	Total
1 (1)	Paul Tracy	CAN	Marlboro Penske 94 Ilmor V8/D	84		22	152
2 (8)	Raul Boesel	BRA	Duracell Charger L94 Ford-Cos XB	84		16	90
3 (2)	Jacques Villeneuve	CAN	Player's Ltd R941 Ford-Cos XB	84		14	94
4 (9)	Emerson Fittipaldi	BRA	Marlboro Penske 94 Ilmor V8/D	84		12	178
5 (7)	Teo Fabi	ITA	Pennzoil Special R941 Ilmor V8	84		10	79
6 (10)	Arie Luyendyk	HOL	Eurosport-Boost Monaco LT94 Ilmor V8	84		8	34
7 (25)	Adrian Fernandez	MEX	Tecate-Quaker State R941 Ilmor V8	84		6	36
8 (3)	Nigel Mansell	GBR	Kmart Texaco L94 Ford-Cos XB	83		5	88
9 (23)	Andrea Montermini	ITA	Budweiser King L94 Ford-Cos XB	83		4	10
10 (14)	Dominic Dobson	USA	PacWest Racing L94 Ford-Cos XB	83		3	30
11 (23)	Willy T Ribbs	USA	Service merchandise L94 Ford-Cos XB	83		2	12
12 (6)	Stefan Johansson	SWE	Alumax Penske 93 Ilmor V8	83		1	57

Time of Race: 2:00:00.763

Paul Tracy bowed out from the all-conquering Penske team with his third victory of the season. It left Penske with a 1-2-3 on the season's overall honours list. They will lose the Canadian for next season as Tracey moves on to occupy the berth at Newman-Haas that our Nigel filled so impressively last year, but a little less formidably this. Mansell, who ended the Indy season in eighth place overall, moves back to the Isle of Man and a place, presumably, in the Williams team. It was only the 31st Indy race in Mansell's brief transatlantic career, but it was number 407 for Mario Andretti, who once boasted a few F1 races himself. Andretti, in his final Indy race, didn't depart with a bang, but a smoke. Unfortunately the smoke was from his engine and it took him into the pits, four laps from home, for the final time.

Formula 3000 International Championship

ROUND 1
Silverstone, England   May 2 (over 38 laps)
1 **Franck Lagorce FRA (Reynard-Cos)**   **1:01:56.79**
                                                 (192.33 kmh)
2   David Coulthard GBR (Reynard-Cos) at   4.10
3   Gil De Ferran BRA (Reynard-Zytek-Judd)   7.52

ROUND 2
Pau, France   May 23 (over 71 laps)
1 **Gil De Ferran BRA (Reynard-Z-Judd)**   **1:25:39.269**
                                                 (137.267 kmh)
2   Vincenzo Sospiri ITA (Reynard-Cos) at   5.472
3   Didier Cottaz FRA (Reynard-Zytek-Judd)   11.848

ROUND 3
Barcelona, Spain   May 28 (over 41 laps)
1 **Massimilliano Papis ITA (Reynard-Judd) 1:05:41.393**
                                                 (177.768 kmh)
2   Fabrizio De Simone ITA (Reynard-Judd) at   23.432
3   Vincezo Sospiri ITA (Reynard-Cos)   23.909

ROUND 4
Enna Pergusa, Italy   July 17 (over 41 laps)
1 **Gil De Ferran BRA (Reynard-Z-Judd)**   **57:41.731**
                                                 205.908 kmh)
2   Franck Lagorce FRA (Reynard-Cos) at   10.626
3   Hideki Noda JPN (Reynard-Cos)   14.114

ROUND 5
Hockenheim, Germany   July 30 (over 29 laps)
1 **Franck Lagorce FRA (Reynard-Cos)**   **58:07.686**
                                                 (203.056 kmh)
2   Jules Boullion FRA (Reynard-Cos) at   7.798
3   Gil De Ferran BRA (Reynard-Cos)   20.403

ROUND 6
Spa-Francorchamps, Belgium   Aug 27 (over 27 laps)
1 **Jules Boullion FRA (Reynard-Cos)**   **1:11:34.525**
                                                 (157.536 kmh)
2   Didier Cottaz FRA (Reynard-Zytek-Judd) at   16.939
3   Kenny Brack SWE (Reynard-Zytek-Judd)   38.173

ROUND 7
Estoril, Portugal   Sept 24
1 **Jules Boullion FRA (Reynard-Cos)**   **1:08:32.879**
                                                 (167.826 kmh)
2   Vincenzo Sospiri ITA (Reynard-Cos) at   21.460
3   Guillaume Gomez FRA (Reynard-Cos)   23.635

ROUND 8
Magny-Cours, France   Oct 2 (over 48 laps)
1 **Jules Boullion FRA (Reynard-Cos)**   **1:10:41.298**
                                                 (172.16 kmh)
2   Franck Lagorce FRA (Reynard-Cos) at   4.363
3   Guillaume Gomez FRA (Reynard-Cos)   11.840
Final Championship Standings
*Boullion 36, Lagorce 34, De Ferran 28, Sospiri 24, Papis 13,
Cottaz 13, Gomez 12, De Simone 7*

Formula 3000 - 1993
Final Race

ROUND 9
Nogaro, France   Oct 10 (over 55 laps)
1 **Franck Lagorce FRA (Reynard-Cos)**   **1:14:44.597**
                                                 (160.533 kmh)
2   Jules Boullion FRA (Reynard-Cos) at   0.447
3   Emmanuel Collard FRA (Reynard-Cos)   1.108
Final Championship Standings
*Olivier Panis 32, Pedro Lamy 31, David Coulthard 25, Franck
Lagorce 21, Gil De Ferran 21, Olivier Beretta 20*

**The World's Most
Authoritative
Motorsport Magazine**

Netball

International Matches

ENGLAND V TRINIDAD & TOBAGO
1st Test
England 40   Trinidad & Tobago 35
2nd Test
England 40   Trinidad & Tobago 36
3rd Test
England 50   Trinidad & Tobago 37
4th Test
England 48   Trinidad & Tobago 36

HOME INTERNATIONALS
England 50   Scotland 21
England 60   N Ireland 34
England 78   Rep. of Ireland 22
England 48   Wales 34

Domestic Fixtures

NATIONAL CLUBS CUP
Round 3
Cliftonettes 56   Falcons 57
Chester 43   St Austell Brend 37
Kent County 54   Unit 7 49
Leeds Athletic 61   Pennine 25
All Stars 44   Alpha Services 11
Kelly 57   Fairlands 44
Moredon 432   Auto Electric 51
Astrosyn Arupian 32   Watford Premier 34
Dudley Leisure 54   Greatfield 48
Notts City 19   Bramhall 34
Wasps 33   The Downs 57
Hillcrest 57   Alpha 38
Oldham 28   Ipswich Ladies 48
Sheffield Open 10   GEC 91
Grasshoppers won   Tor conceded
Oakwood 46   Bristol United 19
Round 4
Falcons 44   Chester 46
Leeds Athletic 42   Kent County 33
All Stars 48   Kelly 53
Auto Electric 38   Watford Premier 42
Bramhall 30   Dudley Leisure 51
The Downs 65   Hillcrest 49
Ipswich 40   GEC 46
Oakwood 65   Grasshoppers 43
Quarter-finals
Leeds Athletic 38   Chester 27
Watford Premier 41   Kelly 36
The Downs 44   Dudley Leisure 38
GEC 49   Oakwood 51
Semi-finals
Oakwood 59   The Downs 48
Leeds Athletic 44   Watford Premier 33
Final
Oakwood 44   Leeds Athletic 37

National League
DIVISION 1

		P	W	D	L	GF	GA	Pts
1	New Cambell	7	6	1	0	348	274	33
2	Linden	7	5	1	1	355	322	29
3	Aquila	7	5	0	2	314	304	27
4	Harborne	7	3	1	4	345	350	21
5	Tongham	7	3	0	4	304	343	19
6	Hertford Hornets	7	2	1	4	302	330	17
7	Toucans	7	1	2	4	267	281	15
8	BICC	7	0	0	7	265	296	7

DIVISION 2

		P	W	D	L	GF	GA	Pts
1	Hirondelles	7	6	1	0	383	305	33
2	Vauxhall Golds	7	5	0	2	335	304	27
3	Crawley Sports	7	4	1	2	307	244	24
4	Academy	7	3	2	2	306	295	23
5	OPA	7	3	0	4	281	321	18
6	Henley	7	2	1	4	283	303	16
7	YWCA	7	1	0	6	333	349	11
8	Hornsey	7	1	1	5	311	418	11

SOMERSET PLATE COMPETITION
Semi-finals
Ipswich Ladies 8   Gauntlettes 4
Old Chelts 5   Grasshoppers 6
Final
Ipswich Ladies 10   Grasshoppers 1

ENGLISH COUNTIES LEAGUE WINNERS
Winner: Essex Metropolitan
INTER-COUNTY CHAMPIONSHIP
Winner: Essex Metropolitan
INTER-REGIONAL CHAMPIONSHIP
Winner: Eastern Region

Orienteering

World Championships

West Point, USA   Oct 10-14, 1993
MEN
SHORT RACE FINAL
Oct 10   Dist: 4.75km   Climb: 135m

1	Petter Thoreson	NOR	22.34
2	Timo Karppinen	FIN	23.00
3	Martin Johansson	SWE	23.26
=4	Steve Hale	GBR	23.27
=4	Jon Tvedt	NOR	23.27

WOMEN
SHORT RACE FINAL
Oct 10   Dist: 3.66km   Climb: 85

1	Anna Bogron	SWE	20.39
2	Marita Skogum	SWE	21.10
3	Eija Koskivaara	FIN	21.11
9	Yvette Hague	GBR	22.32

MEN
CLASSIC RACE
Oct 12   Dist: 13.475km   Climb: 690m

1	Allan Mogensen	DEN	87.36
2	Jorgen Martensson	SWE	88.07
3	Petter Thoresen	NOR	89.28
16	Steve Palmer	GBR	94.37

WOMEN
CLASSIC RACE
Oct 12   Dist:8.62   Climb: 410m

1	Marita Skogum	SWE	62.27
2	Annika Viilo	FIN	64.42
3	Yvette Hague	GBR	66.09

MEN
4 X 10 KM RELAY
Oct 13

1	Switzerland	217.16
2	Great Britain	217.31
3	Finland	218.20

WOMEN
4 X 6.8 KM RELAY
Oct 13

1	Sweden	168.48
2	Finland	176.59
3	Czech Republic	180.29
8	Great Britain	192.37

World Cup Series

WORLD CUP 1

New Zealand   3rd April 1994
MEN
CLASSIC INDIVIDUAL
Dist: 10.85 km   Climb: 570 m

1	Alistair Landels	NZL	60.44

WOMEN
CLASSIC INDIVIDUAL
Dist: 6.55 km   Climb: 370 m

1	Gunilla Svard	SWE	60.25

WORLD CUP 2

Australia   6th April 1994
MEN
SHORT DISTANCE INDIVIDUAL
Dist: 5 km   Climb 5%

1	Janne Salmi	FIN	27.44

WOMEN
SHORT DISTANCE INDIVIDUAL
Dist: 4 km   Climb: 4%

1	Hanne Staff	NOR	27.42

MEN'S RELAY
April 8th   Dist: 9 km   Climb: 4%

1	Norway

WOMEN'S RELAY
April 8th   Dist: 7.4 km   Climb: 4%

1	Czechoslovakia

British Championships

Mar 19-20
MEN'S INDIVIDUAL
16.19km   680m climb

1	Neil Conway	East Pennine	1:29:31
2	Jonathan Musgrave	MAROC	1:32:25
3	Robert Lee	Interpolers	1:33:28

WOMEN'S INDIVIDUAL
10.22km   430 climb

1	Yvette Hague	Warrior O	1:09:40
2	Heather Munro	Warrior O	1:11:12
3	Jenny James	South Yorks	1:14:05

MEN'S RELAY
3 x 7.8km

1	South Yorkshire	2:13:54

WOMEN'S RELAY
3 x 5.3km

1	South Yorkshire	1:53:23

Ski-Orienteering World Championships

Val di Non, Itlay   Jan 31-Feb 6
MEN'S LONG DISTANCE

1	Nicolo Corradino	ITA	1:45:58

WOMEN'S LONG DISTANCE

1	Pepa Miloucheva	BUL	1:17:30
42	Sally Sahni	GBR	2:02:19
50	Fiona Russell-Mills	GBR	2:58:36

MEN'S SHORT DISTANCE

=1	Nicolo Corradino	ITA	42:37
=1	Ivan Kouzmine	RUS	42:37

WOMEN'S SHORT DISTANCE

1	Virpi Juutilainen	FIN	27:40
34	Sally Sahni	GBR	38:16
49	Fiona Russell-Mills	GBR	46:44

MEN'S RELAY

1	Norway	2:37:27

WOMEN'S RELAY

1	Sweden	2:46:50

Polo

FIP European Championships
Beaufort   Sep 7-11th
Great Britain 11   Italy 2
Great Britain 14   Spain 3
Great Britain 9   France 4¹⁄₂
Italy 5   France 4¹⁄₂
Italy 7   Spain 4
France 8¹⁄₂ Spain 6
Great Britain qualify for the World Championship in St Moritz in July 1995

Cartier International Day (Coronation Cup)
Guards Polo Club   July 24
England 11   South Africa 1

Davidoff Gold Cup
Cowdray Park   June 25-July 17
Final
Ellerston Black 13   Pegasus 11

Queens Cup
Guards Polo Club   May 18-June 5
Semi-finals
Black Bears 10   Aspen Midhurst 6
Ellerston White 10   Maple Leafs 9
Final
Black Bears 12   Ellerston White 11

Alfred Dunhill Cup
Semi-finals
Les Lions 10   Pegasus 6
Royal Pahang 10   Labegorce 7
Final
Royal Pahang 9   Les Lions 7

Warwickshire Cup
Cirencester Park   June 7-26
League 1

	P	L	GF	GA	GD	Ranking
Ellerston White	3	0	34	27	+7	1
Bulldogs	2	1	30	26	+4	2
Palmera	1	2	25	27	-2	3
Fish Creek	0	3	22	31	-9	4

League 2

	P	L	GF	GA	GD	Ranking
Black Bears	3	0	32	26	+6	1
Ellerston Black	2	1	32	28	+4	2
Los Clocos	1	2	27	27	0	3
Labegorce	0	3	23	33	-10	4

Final
Black Bears 11   Ellerston White 10

Prince of Wales' Trophy
Royal Berkshire Polo Club   June 11
Final
Cowdray 10   Maple Leafs 9

Gerald Balding Cup
Cirencester Park   May 10-22
Final
Black Bears 6   Bulldogs 1

Dollar Cup
Cowdray Park   May 24-29
Final
Indio 8   Geebung 7¹⁄₂

Royal Windsor Cup
Guards Polo Club   May 31-June 19
Final
Ellerston White 9   Beaufort 8¹⁄₂

Archie David Cup
Guards Polo Club   June 12-18
Final
JHPA 8   Impala 6¹⁄₂

Eduardo Moore Tournament
Royal Berkshire Polo Club   June 20-July 10
Final
Ash Park 13   Azurra 3

Harrison Cup
Cowdray Park   July 30
Final
Azurra 6   Rio Pardo 5

Prince Philip Trophy
Guards Polo Club   July 31
Final
Ellerston Black 12   Palmera 8

Cowdray Park Challenge Cup
Cowdray Park   July 31
Final
Black Bears 11   C S Brooks 7

Kirtlington Summer Cup
Kirtlington   Aug 4-7
Final
Indio 4   Leopards 3¹⁄₂

Sylvester Stallone stunned (well, almost) the polo world when he announced that he would have to give up the sport. Stallone had been so keen on the game that he had polo fields built on his estates in Miami and California. The man who played Rocky and Rambo in eight films of unmitigated violence has had to retire because polo is too dangerous.

Rackets/Real Tennis

## Rackets	## Real Tennis

Rackets

Manchester Gold Racquet
Manchester   Oct 22-24
Singles
J Male bt S Shenkman 15-0, 15-4
Doubles
G Barker/S Shenkman bt J Male/C Worlidge 15-12, 15-10

World Doubles Challenge
New York (First Leg)   Nov 6
S Hazell/N Smith bt J Male/J Prenn   97-76
Queen's Club (Second Leg)   Nov 13
J Male/J Prenn bt S Hazell/N Smith   84-70
Aggregate score
Hazell/Smith bt Male/Prenn   166-160

Pro-Am Trophy
Queen's Club   Nov 6-7
Amateurs bt Profesionals   6-3

Amateur Championships
SINGLES
Queen's Club   Nov 23-Dec 5
Semi Finals
W Boone bt T Cockroft 15-13, 17-16, 15-7
J Prenn bt M Hue Williams 10-15, 15-8, 15-7, 15-18, 15-13
Final
Boone bt Prenn 18-13, 9-15, 15-2, 15-9
DOUBLES
Queen's Club   Mar 12-15
Final
W Boone/T Cockroft bt R Owen-Browne/J Prenn 7-15,
17-18, 15-8, 15-7, 15-7, 15-7

Professional Championships
Malvern   Jan 28-30
SINGLES
Semi Finals
P Brake bt R Wakely 7-15, 11-15, 15-3, 15-3, 15-1
N Cripps bt D Makey 15-5, 14-15, 15-12, 12-15, 15-8
Final
Brake bt Cripps 15-12, 15-6, 15-9
DOUBLES
Final
J Eaton/R Tolchard bt M/R Crosby 9-15, 15-4, 15-7

Open Championships
Queen's Club
SINGLES   Feb 2-13
Semi Finals
N Smith bt T Cockroft 17-18, 15-10, 15-8, 15-9, 15-12
R Owen-Browne bt W Boone 17-16, 15-10, 15-7, 15-3
Final
Smith bt Owen-Br. 15-7, 15-12, 15-9, 11-15, 6-15, 8-15, 15-6
DOUBLES   Apr 15-24
Final
W Boone/T Cockroft bt R Owen-Browne/J Prenn 18-13,
15-12, 15-7, 7-15, 15-4

Real Tennis

Manchester Gold Racquet
Manchester   Oct 22-24
Singles
J Snow bt J Male 10-2
Doubles
M McMurragh/J Snow bt J Male/N Pendrigh 8-7

Browning Cup (Pro Handicap)
The Oratory   Oct 7-10
Final
M Gooding bt T Heughan 6-5, 1-6, 6-3

Open Championships
Queen's Club   Nov 20-29
Singles Final
J Snow bt R Fahey 4-6, 2-1 (retired)
Doubles Final (1993)
C Bray/M Gooding bt J Snow/N Wood 6-3, 6-4, 6-2
Queen's Club   Apr 15-24
Doubles Final (1994)
W Boone/T Cockroft bt R Owen-Browne/J Prenn 18-13,
15-12, 15-7, 7-15, 15-4

Professional Championships
Singles Final
Holyport   May 2-8
L Deuchar bt M Devine 6-5, 6-3, 6-2
Doubles Final
Queen's Club   Jan 7-9
L Deuchar/R Fahey bt C Bray/M Gooding 5-6, 6-3, 6-0, 6-3

Amateur Championships
Singles Final
Queen's Club   Mar 12-20
Snow bt Pendrigh 6-3, 6-3, 6-3
Doubles Final
Hatfield   Apr 29-May 2
Acheson-Gray/Pendrigh bt McMurragh/Snow 1-6, 6-5,
5-6, 6-1, 6-3

European Open Doubles
Queen's Club   Mar 23-26
Final
W Davies/L Deuchar bt M Devine/K Sheldon 6-3, 6-5, 6-2

Amateur Singles Handicap
Leamington   Jan 29-30
Final
E Slater bt M Wolton 6-4

Ladies Open Championships
Singles Final
Seacourt   Apr 28-May 2
A Garside bt S Jones 6-3, 6-1
Doubles Final
Canford   Jan 14-16
F Deuchar/M Happell won by default

Rowing

It always feels good when the wind is in your sails and Matthew Pinsent and Steven Redgrave must have felt very good at the world championships in Indianapolis. The following wind gave them a timing, in the coxless pairs, that was a world championship record by three seconds. More importantly, nobody else in the race could match the power of the British pair and they pulled ahead of the German crew of Peter Höltzenbein and Thorsten Streppelhoff - more familiar in Britain as members of the victorious Cambridge Boat Race crew - to take a third successive title. We believe that makes the British rowers the only crew in world championships history to have achieved a hattrick of titles with the same oarsman.

In world championship terms, Peter Haining is a mere novice compared to Redgrave, having only the one notch on his oar, the lightweight sculling title he won in Roudnice last year. Throughout this summer, it looked likely that the title would be resolved between Haining and Niall O'Toole, the 1991 winner from Ireland. At Duisberg, O'Toole twice beat Haining; at Lucerne, Haining pulled one back. In Indianapolis, he won the one that mattered, catching the Irishman at the 1500m mark and drawing away to a two length win. Britain's third gold came in the lightweight eights, in which the GB crew just got the measure of the Danish eight. There was disappointment for the lightweight coxless four, which had destroyed the world record in Paris - they could only come eighth - but a tally of three golds, a silver and a bronze from Indianapiolis was a fair week's work

QUOTES

"Scotland - eat it!" - **Wade Hall-Craggs, as he crossed the finish line ahead of Peter Haining in the Thames World Sculling Challenge.**

"Cambridge could have done a 360 degree turn and looped the loop and they'd still have beaten us" - **Liz Chick, the Oxford cox, after her crew lost by 20 seconds in the Boat Race.**

"Everyone appeared to feel good by yesterday lunchtime with the possible exception of a marshal's launch which was sunk by a safety boat, presumably on a job creation scheme" - **Paul Weaver in the *Daily Telegraph* reporting on the Fours Head.**

"You don't look the type to row. Don't your tits get in the way" - **A cynic of women's rowing, to Oxford oarswoman Lucy Bannon.**

"We are intent on stopping pot-hunting" - **Mike Sweeney, chairman of the Henley stewards, on new measures designed to stop crews entering races below their standard of rowing.**

"Fred just turned up and said: 'Didn't you guys know?' Six months of our life has been vapourised. I've been coaching for 16 years and I coach on feeling good. I doubt I'll even watch the race on Saturday. My garden needs fixing" - **Tim Bramfitt, the Oxford assistant coach who, along with head coach Richard Tinkler, was replaced by Fred Smallbone the week before the Boat Race.**

World Championships

Indianapolis   Sep 11-18
The starred name (*) is the cox.

MEN

Single Sculls

1	Andre Willms	GER	6:46.33
2	Xeno Müller	SUI	6:48.10
3	Iztok Cop	SLO	6:49.33

Double Sculls

1	Thorsen/Bjoenness	NOR	6:08.33
2	Uhrig/Händle	GER	6:08.88
3	Lamarque/Barathay	FRA	6:10.03

Quads

1	Italy	5:37.68
2	Ukraine	5:39.11
3	Germany	5:39.71

Coxless Pairs

1	Redgrave/Pinsent	GBR	6:18.65
2	Höltzenbein/Strepplehoff	GER	6:19.75
3	Walker/Wearne	AUS	6:20.25

Coxed Pairs

1	Boraska/Frakovic/Razov*	CRO	6:42.16
2	Abbagnale C/Cascone/Cirillo*	ITA	6:42.98
3	Ungemach/Zeidler/Gross*	ROM	6:46.99
10	Cross/Redgrave/Bass*	GBR	6:55.84

Coxless Fours

1	Italy	5:48.44
2	France	5:49.82
3	Great Britain	5:50.37
	(Foster/Searle/Searle/Obholzer)	

Coxed Fours

1	Romania	6:06.69
2	USA	6:06.98
3	Holland	6:07.72
10	Great Britain	6:14.76
	(Gaylor/Morrison/Nolan/Smith/Tompsett*)	

Eights

1	USA	5:24.50
2	Holland	5:25.10
3	Romania	5:27.08
7	Great Britain	5:32.58
	(Bridge/Parish/Hamilton/Phelps/Manners/Hunt-Davis/Walker/Cracknell/Herbert*)	

MEN'S LIGHTWEIGHT

Single Sculls

1	Peter Haining	GBR	6:53.48
2	Niall O'Toole	IRL	6:56.33
3	Karsten Nielsen	DEN	6:56.99

Double Sculls

1	Esposito/Crispi	ITA	6:18.10
2	Hamill/Rodger	NZL	6:20.14
3	Geir/Geir	SUI	6:20.85
6	Whitelaw/Sinton	GBR	6:26.01

Quads

1	Austria	5:46.75
2	Italy	5:48.83
3	Portugal	5:49.64

Coxless Pairs

1	Pettinari/Gaddi	ITA	6:34.70
2	Mitiouchev/Tchdumatchenko	RUS	6:39.92
3	Maxwell/O'Connor	IRL	6:39.96
6	Everington/Partridge	GBR	6:46.26

Coxless Fours

1	Denmark	5:53.77
2	Austria	5:56.24
3	Germany	5:57.07
7	Great Britain	5:59.68
	(Butt/Watson/Strange/Helm)	

Eights

1	Great Britain	5:31.00
	(Bates/Cox/Lemon/Smith/Ellis/McNiven/Kay Hessian/Deakin*)	
2	Denmark	5:31.56
3	Italy	5:34.63

WOMEN

Single Sculls

1	Trine Hansen	DEN	7:23.98
2	Kathrin Boron	GER	7:24.90
3	Anne-Elise Bredael	BEL	7:25.56
8	Guin Batten	GBR	7:41.32

Double Sculls

1	Baker P/Lawson B	NZL	6:45.30
2	McBean/Heddle	CAN	6:46.17
3	Thieme/Schuster	GER	6:47.16

Quads

1	Germany	6:11.73
2	China	6:15.74
3	Ukraine	6:18.05

Coxless Pairs

1	Gosse/Cortin	FRA	7:01.77
2	Bobeica/Lipa	ROM	7:05.45
3	Ozollns/Klomp	AUS	7:07.60
5	Turvey/Batten	GBR	7:11.50

Coxless Fours

1	Holland	6:30.76
2	USA	6:31.92
3	Australia	6:32.85

Eights

1	Germany	6:07.42
2	USA	6:08.24
3	Romania	6:08.55

WOMEN'S LIGHTWEIGHT

Single Sculls

1	Constanta Pipota	Rom	7:34.17
2	Laurien Vermulst	HOL	7:35.81
3	Pia Vogel	SUI	7:38.63
11	Patricia Coreless	GBR	7:53.46

Double Sculls

1	Wiebe/Miller	CAN	6:54.85
2	Alfang Zhong/Shaoyan Ou	CHN	6:56.83
3	Burns/Zarzecny	USA	6:57.76
10	Mangan/White	GBR	7:09.79

Coxless Fours

1	USA	6:36.40
2	Great Britain	6:37.28
	(Brownless/Hall/Stapleton/Williams)	
3	USA	6:49.47

Henley Regatta

June 29-July 3
TEMPLE CHALLENGE CUP
Eights
Final
Imperial College London 'A' bt
Trinity College, Dublin

WYFOLD CHALLENGE CUP
Coxless Fours
Final
Nottinghamshire County bt
Lea Rowing Club

PRINCESS ELIZABETH CHALLENGE CUP
Eights
Final
St Paul's School, Concord, USA bt
Atlantic City High School, USA

STEWARDS' CHALLENGE CUP
Coxless Fours
Final
Boulogne and Lyon, France bt
London Rowing Club

DOUBLE SCULLS CHALLENGE CUP
Final
Mitring/Dani, Hungary bt
Uhrig/Handle, Germany

BRITANNIA CHALLENGE CUP
Coxed Fours
Final
Belfast Rowing Club bt
University of London 'A'

VISITORS' CHALLENGE CUP
Coxless Fours
Final
Imperial College, London bt
University of London

DIAMOND CHALLENGE SCULLS
Final
X Müller, Switzerland bt
M Hansen, Denmark

GRAND CHALLENGE CUP
Eights
Final
Charles River RA, San Diego, USA bt
Sport Nautique Compiégne, France

SILVER GOBLETS & NICKALLS CHALLENGE CUP
Coxless Pairs
Final
Redgrave/Pinsent, Leander bt
Van Driessche/Goiris, Vereniging, Belgium

LADIES' CHALLENGE PLATE
Eights
Final
College Boat Club, USA bt
London RC & Nottinghamshire County RA

WOMEN'S SINGLE SCULLS
Final
Marnie McBean, Canada bt
Kathrin Boron, Germany

FAWLEY CHALLENGE CUP
Coxless Fours
Final
Windsor RC & Maidenhead RC bt
Bedford School

PRINCE PHILIP CHALLENGE CUP
Coxed Fours
Final
Nottinghamshire County RA bt
Leander Club

THAMES CHALLENGE CUP
Eights
Final
Goldie Boat Club bt
Brown University, USA

QUEEN MOTHER CHALLENGE CUP
Coxless Fours
Final
Treviris & Böllberg, Germany bt
London Rowing Club 'A'

Duisberg Regatta

May 21-22

Saturday's Events

MEN
Coxless Pairs

1	Germany	6:24.42
4	Great Britain	6:30.49
	(Walker/Singfield)	

Coxed Fours

1	Romania	6:03.47
2	Univ of London	6:06.61

Eights

1	Germany	5:27.65
5	Oxford, Brookes Univ	5:49.92

MEN'S LIGHTWEIGHT
Single Sculls

1	Niall O'Toole	IRL	6:55.15
2	Peter Haining	GBR	6:59.45

Coxless Pairs

1	Ireland	6:31.95
5	Scottish Rowing	6:49.95

Fours

1	Denmark	5:52.47
2	London RC	5:54.09

WOMEN
Coxless Pairs

1	France	7:00.32
2	Great Britain	7:03.76
	(Turvey/Batten)	

WOMEN'S LIGHTWEIGHT
Single Sculls

1	Laurien Vermulst	HOL	7:35.18
2	Helen Mangan	GBR	7:42.46
5	Patricia Coreless	GBR	7:55.60

Sunday's Events

MEN

Coxed Fours

1 Nereus — HOL — 6:14.02
3 Univ of London — GBR — 6:20.11

Coxless Fours

1 France — 5:56.99
2 Molesey — 5:59.00

MEN'S LIGHTWEIGHT

Single Sculls

1 Niall O'Toole — IRL — 6:56.54
2 Peter Haining — GBR — 6:58.25

Coxless Pairs

1 Germany — 6:40
3 Scottish Rowing — 6:46
  (Harris/Gillespie)

Coxless Fours

1 Notts County — 5:59.75

WOMEN

Coxless Pairs

1 Britain — 7:15.88
  (Turvey/Batten)

Coxless Fours

1 Holland — 6:36.84
5 Great Britain — 6:49.39

WOMEN'S LIGHTWEIGHT

Single Sculls

1 Laurien Vermulst — HOL — 7:42.81
3 Helen Mangan — GBR — 7:53.91

Lucerne Regatta

July 15-17

MEN

Double Sculls

1 Thorsen/Bjonness — NOR — 6:13.14

Quad Sculls

1 Germany — 5:40.92

Coxless Pairs

1 Redgrave/Pinsent — GBR — 6:18.34 *WR*

Coxed Pairs

1 Frankovic/Boroska — CRO — 6:46.04
3 Cross/Singfield — GBR — 6:51.66

Coxless Fours

1 France — 5:54.58

Eights

1 Germany — 5:27.27
7 Great Britain — 5:40.27

LIGHTWEIGHT MEN

Single Sculls

1 Peter Haining — GBR — 6:57.41
2 Niall O'Toole — IRL — 6:57.60

Double Sculls

1 Esposito/Crispi — ITA — 6:23.51

Quad Sculls

1 Austria — 5:54.12

Coxless Pairs

1 O'Connor/Maxwell — IRL — 6:38.82

Coxless Fours

1 Denmark — 5:56.21
2 Great Britain — 5:57.50

Eight

1 Great Britain — 5:37.36

WOMEN

Double Sculls

1 Thieme/Schuster — GER — 6:51.05

Quad Sculls

1 Germany — 6:18.15

Coxless Pairs

1 Cortin/Grosse — FRA — 7:14.65
2 Turvey/Batten — GBR — 7:16.79

Coxless Fours

1 Holland — 6:40.47
5 Scottish ARA — 6:54.26

Eights

1 USA — 6:12.30

LIGHTWEIGHT WOMEN

Single Sculls

1 Constanta Pipota — ROM — 7:37.40

Double Sculls

1 Miller/Wiebe — CAN — 7:05:10
5 White/Mangan — GBR — 7:15.62

Coxless Fours

1 USA — 6:44.20
2 Great Britain — 6:49.72

French International Championships

Arne La Vallée, Paris   June 18-19

Saturday's Events

MEN

Coxless Fours

1 Van Driessche/Goiris — BEL — 6:24.79
7 Singfield/McLennan — GBR — 6:37.63

Coxed Pairs

1 Romania — 6:09.56

Coxless Fours

1 Poland — 5:51.05 *WR*
4 Moseley — 5:53.58

MEN LIGHTWEIGHT

Double Sculls

1 Schmolzer/Rantasa — AUT — 6:18.92
4 Sinton/Long — GBR — 6:23.20
6 Booth/Haining — GBR — 6:26.63

WOMEN

Coxless Pairs

1 Cortin/Gosse — FRA — 7:09.60
2 Turvey/Batten — GBR — 7:14.34

WOMEN LIGHTWEIGHT

Double Sculls

1 White/Mangan — GBR — 7:05.15

On the T-shirts of one of the more illustrious British crews at the World Championships in Indianapolis the slogan read:
'The Undesirables - too old, too fat, too slow'
The crew in question was Martin Cross, Steven Redgrave and cox Hayden Bass. We leave you to work out which adjective applies to which oarsman, but Martin Cross is 37 if that's a help.

Sunday's Events

MEN
Double Sculls
1 Galtarossa/Corona ITA   6:11.46
2 Nichol/Jahnich GBR   6:34.34
Coxless Pairs
1 Van Driessche/Goiris   BEL   6:24.83
5 Singfield/McLennan   GBR   6:36.27
Coxed Pairs
1 Abbagnale/Cascone   ITA   6:51.41
3 Stanhope/Cross   GBR   7:05.54
Coxless Fours
1 Italy   5:51.61
6 GBR (Moseley)   5:59.09
Coxed Fours
1 France   6:04.56
2 Univ of London   6:08.84
Eights
1 Romania   5:28.17
3 GBR (composite)   5:29.57
MEN LIGHTWEIGHT
Single Sculls
1 Niall O'Toole   IRL   6:51.67
2 Peter Haining   GBR   6:52.62
Double Sculls
1 Schmolzer/Rantasa AUS   6:24.38
Coxless Pairs
1 O'Connor/Maxwell IRL   6:26.61 *WR*
Coxless Fours
1 Great Britain   5:48.86 *WR*
Eights
1 GBR (composite)   5:35.85
WOMEN
Coxless Pairs
1 Cortin/Gosse   FRA   7:04.28
2 Turvey/Batten   GBR   7:11.98
Coxless Fours
1 Romania   6:37.62
2 Great Britain   6:41.33
WOMEN LIGHTWEIGHT
Single Sculls
1 Constanta Pipota   ROM   7:28.15
Double Sculls
1 White/Mangan   GBR   6:59.63

World Cup Singles Sculling

Duisberg   May 22
Men
1 Vaclav Chalupa   TCH   6:48.57
2 André Willms   GER   6:50.42
Women
1 Marnie McBean   CAN   7:24.73
2 Annelise Bredael   BEL   7:25.51
Arne La Vallé, Paris   June 19
Men
1 Xeno Müller   SUI   6:398.74
2 Horst Nussbaumer AUT
Women
1 Annelise Bredael   BEL   7:17.60
2 Trine Hansen   DEN   7:21.35

Henley   July 3
Men
1 Xeno Müller   SUI   6:35
2 Martin Halbo Hansen   DEN
Women
1 Marnie McBean   CAN   7:35
2 Kathrin Boron
Lucerne   July 17
Men
1 Xeno Müller   SUI   6:38.97 *WR*
2 Nicolae Taga   ROM   6:40.25
Women
1 Silken Laumann   CAN   7:17.09 *WR*
2 Marnie McBean   CAN   7:20.12

OVERALL WORLD CUP STANDINGS
Men: 1. Xeno Müller (SUI) 56 points; 2. Martin Halbo
Hansen (DEN) 36; 3. Vaclav Chalup (TCH) 29.
Women: 1. Marnie McBean (CAN) 51; 2. Trine Hansen
(DEN) 39; 3. Annelise Bredael (BEl) 36.

National Championships

Nottingham   July 16-17
MEN
Single Sculls
1 D W Nicoll   U Thames 7:12
Double Sculls
1 Moseley   6:29
Quad Sculls
1 Tideway Scullers   6:02
Coxless Pairs
1 Cambridge 99   6:52
Coxed Pairs
1 Thames Tradesmen   7:18
Coxless Fours
1 Thames   6:05
Coxed Fours
1 London RC   6:15
Eights
1 London RC   5:40
MEN LIGHTWEIGHT
Single Sculls
1 C Elmitt   Colet   7:09
Double Sculls
1 London RC   6:40
Quad Sculls
1 Tideway Scullers   6:09
Coxless Pairs
1 Marlow   7:04
Coxless Fours
1 London RC   6:05
Eights
1 London RC   5:43
WOMEN
Single Sculls
1 S Appelboom   Mortlake 7:45
Double Sculls
1 Tideway Scullers   7:13
Quad Sculls
1 Gros/Notts/Tideway/Chester   6:43
Coxless Pairs
1 Edinburgh Uni   7:35
Coxed Fours
1 Bedford   7:09

Coxless Fours
1 Thames T/London U 6:51
Eights
1 Cap/Marl/Thames T 6:23
WOMEN LIGHTWEIGHT
Single Sculls
1 S Appelboom   Mortlake 7:45
Coxless Pairs
1 Upper Thames   7:37
Coxless Fours
1 Thames Tradesmen 6:57

Thames World Sculling Challenge

Putney - Mortlake   Nov 13
1 Wade Hall-Craggs   Tideway Scullers
2 Peter Haining   Scottish Rowing
3 Steven Redgrave   Leander
Times; Hall-Craggs, Haining, Redgrave
Mile: 4:21, 4:27; 4:28
Hammersmith Bridge: 7:54, 7:54.5, 8:02
Chiswick Steps: 12:40, 12:41, 12:57
Barnes Bridge: 17:30, 17:31, Redgrave no time taken
Finish: 21:02, 21:08, Redgrave ntt

The 140th Boat Race
Putney to Mortlake   Mar 26
Senior Race
Cambridge beat Oxford bt 6½ lengths
Times (Cambridge first)
Mile: 3:58, 4:03
Hammersmith Bridge: 7:12, 7:20
Chiswick Steps: 11:12, 11:28
Barnes Bridge: 15:07, 15:23
Finish: 18:09, 18:29

Reserve Race
Goldie (Cambridge) beat Isis (Oxford) by 13 lengths
Times (Goldie first)
Mile: 4:10, 4:16
Chiswick Steps: 11:32, 11:53
Barnes Bridge: 15:23, 15:53
Finish: 18:27, 19:06

Lightweight Race
Henley   Mar 20
Oxford beat Cambridge by ¾ length
Time: 5 mins 45 secs

The Women's Boat Race
Henley   Mar 20
Senior Race
Cambridge beat Oxford by 1 length
Time: 6 mins 11 secs
Reserve Race
Cambridge beat Oxford by a canvas
Time: 6 mins 22 sec
Lightweight Race
Cambridge beat Oxford by 1 foot
Time: 6 mins 23 secs

Head of the River Race
Mortlake to Putney   Mar 26
1 Münster von 1882   GER   16:55.02
2 Leander   GBR   16:57.08
3 London   GBR   17:06.23
4 Molesey   GBR   17:09.93
5 University of London GBR 17:11.32
6 Notts County   GBR   17:11.82
7 Imperial College   GBR   17:14.62
8 Mulheim II   GER   17:21.25

Scullers Head
Tideway, 4.25 miles Apr 9
Single Sculls - Men
1 Peter Haining   Auriol   19:53.4 *(Record)*
Women
1 Ali Hall   Upper Thames 21:36.4

Indoor Rowing World Championships
Boston   Feb 20
Open Men
1 Matthias Siejkowski POL   7:23.1
2 Jean Rolland   FRA   7:29.6
3 Tom Bohrer   USA   7:32.6
Lightweight Men
1 Wolfgang Siegl   AUT   7:52.9
2 John Roberts   USA   7:53.1
3 Maichael Gier   SUI   7:53.8
Open Women
1 Maria Brandin   SWE   8:13.6 *WR*
2 Zhang Xiuyun   CHN   8:31.8
3 Betsy McCagg   USA   8:37.9
Lightweight Women
1 Annamarie Stapleton* GBR   8:54.6 *WR*
2 Benedicte Luzuy   FRA   9:01.3
3 Li Fei   CHN   9:05.6
   *née Dryden

British Championships
Bracknell   Nov 27, 1993
Open Men
1 Simon Gore   GBR   7:44.1
Masters I, Men
1 Andy Ripley   7:53.6
Lightweight Men
1 Pepyn Aardewijn   HOL   7:49.9
Open Women
1 Ali Hall   GBR   8:46.8
Lightweight Women
1 Annamarie Dryden GBR   9:01.5

Rugby League

In publicity terms, the League had had a bonanza year. Va'aiga Tuigamala, Scott Gibbs and, the most telling of them all, Scott Quinnell in September; all switched codes. New Zealand rugby will not founder in the absence of Tuigamala, though the distinctive Samoan was one of the best known faces of the game; Welsh rugby will survive the departure of Gibbs who had previously flirted with a league transfer; but the secession of Quinnell was a bitter blow. The 23-year-old's departure means nobody is sacrosant. The Welsh Rugby Union needs no reminding that 16 players have switched codes in the last eight years for around £2m.

Both Tuigamala and Quinnell moved to Central Park. So if anybody was looking for flaws in the Wigan diamond, look again. The Challenge Cup final performance should have persuaded any doubters. Offiah showed that he was as sparkling an athlete as ever with a wonderful 13th minute try that took him past Harmon, Innes, Cummins and Schofield. What makes it all the more exasperating is that the man doesn't even *look* as if he's travelling fast. As well as the League and Cup double (the fifth year in a row) and the Regal Trophy, Wigan also triumphed at Brisbane in the World Cup Challenge match against the Broncos.

Given that a substantial part of the England team is made up of players from Wigan, it was perhaps no surprise that Ellery Hanley became the new England manager, following the decision of Malcolm Reilly to end his seven year tenure and move to the Australian club Newcastle Knights. For Hanley, who had hardly spoken to any of the media for six years, the hardest part of the job maybe off the field, not on it.

QUOTES

"Complacency permeated the game. Many clubs were spending far beyond their means on players and lurching from crisis to crisis" - **Maurice Lindsay, chief executive of Rugby League on the state of the game when he took on the job two years ago.**

"It was very difficult. I think they must have had him under armed escort" - **Jack Robinson, chairman of Wigan, on his negotiations to sign All Black winger Va'aiga Tuigamala.**

"High, deliberate and disgusting" - **Andy Thompson's description of the tackle that broke his jaw in January. It was the second time in three months that Thompson broke it.**

"Scott Gibbs will never be welcome in our club again. He has abused the trust and efforts of a number of people. To me, he is not a rugby professional, but a rugby prostitute" - **Mike James, chairman of Swansea rugby union club.**

"And he's got the icepack on his groin there, so possibly not the old shoulder injury" - **Ray French, commentating on BBC**

"They must have provoked me because I don't normally waste good beer" - Mike McClennan, St Helen's manager, who admitted pouring beer over a fan.

"I should have left the bugger at Rosslyn Park" - **Doug Laughton, the Leeds coach, after Martin Offiah had scored a memorable try in the Challenge Cup final. It was Laughton who had introduced Offiah to rugby league**

British International Matches

Wembley   Oct 16
Great Britain 17   New Zealand 0
Tries: Robinson (2)
*   Devereux*
Goals: Davies (2)
DG: Davies
GB: Davies, Robinson, Newlove, Connolly, Devereux, Schofield (capt), Edwards, Harrison, Dermott, Fairbank, Betts, Joynt, Clarke
NZ: Edwards, Halligan, Iro, Watson, Hoppe, Mgamu, Freeman (capt), Lomax, Mann, Stuart, Kearney, Pongia, Nikau

Central Park, Wigan   Oct 30
Great Britain 29   New Zealand 12
Tries: Devereux (2)   Tries: Watson
*   Schofield   Ropati*
*   Offiah, Newlove   Goals: Botica (2)*
Goals: Davies (4)
DG: Schofield
GB: Davies, Offiah, Newlove, Connolly, Devereux, Schofield (capt), Edwards, Harrison, L Jackson, Fairbank, Nickle, Joynt, Clarke
NZ: Watson, Botica, Iro, Ropati, Hoppe, Kemp, Freeman (capt), Solomona, Mann, Stuart, Kearney, Pongia, Mackie

Leeds   Nov 6
Great Britain 29   New Zealand 10
Tries: Fairbank   Try: Williams
*   Clarke, Davies   Goals: Botica (3)*
*   Offiah, Farrell*
Goals: Davies (4)
DG: Davies
GB: Davies, Offiah, Newlove, Connolly, Devereux, Schofield (capt), Edwards, Skerrett, L Jackson, Fairbank, Farrell, Joynt, Clarke
NZ: Watson, Botica, Iro, Ropati, Williams, Kemp, Whittaker, Solomona, Johnston, Stuart, Kearney (capt), Pongia, Mackie

Carcassonne, France   Mar 20
France 4   Great Britain 12
Tries: Newlove,   Try: Martial
*   Edwards*

CHAMPIONSHIP WINNERS

	Division 1	Division 2
1979-80	Bradford N.	Featherstone Rovers
1980-81	Bradford N.	York
1981-82	Leigh	Oldham
1982-83	Hull	Fulham
1983-84	Hull Kingston R	Barrow
1984-85	Hull Kingston R	Swinton
1985-86	Halifax	Leigh
1986-87	Wigan	Hunslet
1987-88	Widnes	Oldham
1988-89	Widnes	Leigh
1989-90	Wigan	Hull Kingston Rovers
1990-91	Wigan	Salford
1991-92	Wigan	Sheffield Eagles
1992-93	Wigan	Featherstone Rovers
1993-94	**Wigan**	**Workington Town**

Goals: Crooks, Farrell
GB: Steadman, Bentley, Connolly, Newlove, Offiah, Schofield (capt), Edwards, Crooks, L Jackson, Molloy, Farrell, Fairbank, Joynt
France: Frison, Garcia, Martial, Fraise, Sirvent, Fages, Entat, Teixido, Torreilles, Llong, Divet, Cabestany, Grandjean

Swansea City FC   Oct 3
Wales 19   New Zealand 24
Tries: Cordle (2)   Tries: Hoppe, Mackie
Goals: Davies (5)   Ropati
DG: Griffiths   Goals: Halligan (6)
Wales: Ford, Cordle, Bateman, Devereux, Sullivan, J Davies (capt), Ellis, M Jones, Williams, Young, Marlow, Phillips, J Griffiths
NZ: Edwards, Halligan, Ropati, Taewa, Hoppe, Ngamu, Freeman (capt), Lomax, Mann, Stuart, Kearney, Pomgia, Mackie

Cardiff City FC   Mar 4
Wales 13   France 12
Try: Webster   Tries: Entat, Garcia
Goals: Davies (4)   Goals: Torreilles (2)
DG: Davies
Wales: Ford, Cordle, Bateman, J Davies, Sullivan, J Griffiths, Ellis, M Jones, Williams, Young, Moriaty, Phillips, Perrett

New Zealand 1993 Tour Results
Excluding Test results v Great Britain & Wales

Bradford   Oct 6 (5,015)
Bradford Northern 17 New Zealand 10

Wigan   Oct 10 (13,669)
Wigan 18 New Zealand 25

Castleford   Oct 12 (4,927)
Castleford 16 New Zealand 4

St Helens   Oct 20 (8,165)
St Helens 8 New Zealand 14

Leeds   Oct 24 (6,898)
Leeds 6 New Zealand 35

Workington   Oct 26 (3,099)
G Britain U21s 24 New Zealand 37

Widnes   Nov 2 (5,646)
Widnes 10 New Zealand 18

Perpignan, France   Nov 11 (5,000)
Roussillon Select 22 New Zealand 24

Carpentras, France   Nov 14 (2,000)
French Select 4 New Zealand 45

St Gaudens, France   Nov 17 (1,900)
Midi-Pyrenees Select 2 New Zealand 30

Carcassonne, France   Nov 21 (3,500)
France 11 New Zealand 36

Stones Bitter Championship
DIVISION 1

		P	W	D	L	PF	PA	Pts
1	Wigan	30	23	0	7	780	403	46
2	Bradford N	30	23	0	7	784	555	46
3	Warrington	30	23	0	7	628	430	46
4	Castleford	30	19	1	10	787	466	39
5	Halifax	30	17	2	11	682	581	36
6	Sheffield E	30	16	2	12	704	671	34
7	Leeds	30	15	2	13	673	680	32
8	St Helens	30	15	1	14	704	537	31
9	Hull	30	14	2	14	536	530	30
10	Widnes	30	14	0	16	523	642	28
11	Featherstone R	30	13	1	16	651	681	27
12	Salford	30	11	0	19	554	650	22
13	Oldham	30	10	1	19	552	651	21
14	Wakefield T	30	9	1	20	458	708	19
15	Hull K R	30	9	0	21	493	782	18
16	Leigh	30	2	1	27	370	912	5

DIVISION 2

		P	W	D	L	PF	PA	Pts
1	Workington T	30	22	2	6	760	331	46
2	Doncaster	30	22	1	7	729	486	45
3	London C	30	21	2	7	842	522	44
4	Batley	30	21	1	8	707	426	43
5	Huddersfield	30	20	0	10	661	518	40
6	Keighley C	30	19	1	10	856	472	39
7	Dewsbury	30	18	1	11	766	448	37
8	Rochdale H	30	18	0	12	704	532	36
9	Ryedale Y	30	17	1	12	662	516	35
10	Whitehaven	30	14	4	12	571	437	32
11	Barrow	30	13	1	16	581	743	27
12	Swinton	30	11	0	19	528	681	22
13	Carlisle	30	9	0	21	540	878	18
14	Hunslet	30	3	1	26	445	814	7
15	Bramley	30	3	0	27	376	957	6
16	Highfield	30	1	1	28	267	1234	3

Stones Bitter Premiership
First Round

Castleford 28	Halifax 23
Bradford N 42	Leeds 16
Warrington 16	Sheffield E 32
Wigan 34	St Helens 16

Semi Finals

Central Park, Wigan	*May 13*
Wigan 52	Sheffield E 18
Oddsall Stadium, Bradford	*May 15*
Bradford N 16	Castleford 24

Final

Old, Trafford, Manchester	*May 22*
Wigan 24	**Castleford 20**
Tries: Farrell, Panapa	*Tries: Sampsom, Sykes*
Botica, Betts	*Steadman*
Goals: Botica (4)	*Goals: Crooks (2), Steadman (2)*

Wigan: Atcheson, Robinson, Panapa, Connolly, Offiah, Botica, Edwards (capt), Skerrett, Hall, Cowie, Betts, Farrell, Clarke
Castleford: Ellis, Smith, Blackmore, Smith, Middleton, Steadman, Ford, Crooks (capt), Russell, Sampson, Ketteridge, Hay, Nikau

Stones Bitter Second Division Premiership
First Round

Batley 28	Huddersfield 17
Doncaster 48	Dewsbury 18
London C 66	Keighley C 12
Workington T 50	Rochdale H 6

Semi Finals

Tattersfield, Doncaster	*May 15*
Doncaster 6	London C 16
Derwent Park, Workington	*May 15*
Workington T 19	Batley 4

Final

Old, Trafford, Manchester	*May 22*
Workington T 30	**London C 22**
Tries: Cocker (2)	*Tries: Johnson (3)*
Byrne, Kay	*Campbell*
Drummond	*Goals: Gallagher (3)*
Mulligan	
Goals: Marwood (3)	

Workington: Mulligan, Drummond, Kay, Burns, Cocker, Kitchin, Marwood, Pickering, McKenzie, Armstrong (capt), Hepi, Oglanby, Byrne
London C: Stoop, Gallagher, Roskell, Campbell, Johnson, McIvor, Riley, Whiteley, Carter, Rotheram, Rosolen, Stewart (capt), Ramsey

Silk Cut Challenge Cup
First Round

Askam 36	Orchard Park 20
Barrow Island 26	Moorends 13
Beverley 84	Cambridge City Eagles 10
Blackpool Gladiators 10	Park Amateurs 28
Dewsbury Celtic 38	Fulham Travellers 15
Dudley Hill 8	Thatto Heath 22
East Leeds 25	Kells 12
Eastmoor 4	Irlam Hornets 12
Egremont 28	Ace 6
Gretland 0	Ellenborough 18
Hemel Hempstead 18	Hensingham 22
Heworth 24	Wigan St Judes 8
Leigh East 15	Farnworth 10
Leigh M W 34	Eureka 14
Lock Lane 13	Mysons 16
Mayfield 24	Hull Dockers 12
Milford 18	Cardiff Institute 8
Millom 18	Westgate Redoubt 10

1994 AWARDS

Man of Steel: Jonathan Davies (Warrington)

1st Division Player: Jonathan Davies (Warrington)

2nd Division Player: Martin Oglanby (Workington)

Young Player: Andrew Farrell (Wigan)

Coach: John Joyner (Castleford)

Referee: John Connolly (Wigan)

Moldgreen 23	Skirlaugh 5
Oldham St Annes 32	Bisons 8
Oulton 27	Queens 6
Redhill 16	Littleborough 12
Saddleworth 13	Seaton 2
Shaw Cross 12	Fryston 6
Walney Central 11	Simms Cross 0
West Hull 36	Ovenden 9
Wigan St Patricks 13	Wath Brow 6
Woolston Rovers 54	Upton & Frickley 12
York Acorn 32	Orrell St James 32
Chorley B 30	Elland 2
Nottingham C 8	Clayton 24
York Acorn 5	Orrell St James 24

Second Round

Askam 8	Chorley B 3
Blackbrook 8	Beverley 17
Clayton 6	Oulton 23
East Leeds 14	Egremont 10
Ellenborough 4	Woolston Rovers 9
Hensingham 40	Mysons 0
Leigh East 14	Millom 24
Leigh M W 13	Moldgreen 11
Mayfield 14	Wigan St Patricks 32
Milford 19	Irlam Hornets 20
Redhill 32	Orrell St James 18
Saddleworth 12	Oldham St Annes 4
Walney Central 4	Barrow Island 6
West Hull 47	Park Amateurs 14
Dewsbury Celtic 18	Heworth 10
Shaw Cross 11	Thatto Heath 4

Third Round

Batley 58	Dewsbury Celtic 2
Barrow 34	East Leeds 10
Bramley 46	Redhill 20
Carlisle 42	Askam 8
Dewsbury 64	Hensingham 6
Doncaster 36	Wigan St Patricks 4
Highfield 16	Saddleworth 13
Huddersfield 42	Woolston Rovers 6
Hunslet 58	Barrow Island 2
Keighley C 68	Oulton 0
London C 40	Shaw Cross 14
Rochdale H 32	Millom 0
Ryedale Y 52	Leigh MW 2
Swinton 30	Irlam Hornets 0
Whitehaven 44	West Hull 4
Workington T 24	Beverley 10

Fourth Round

Halifax 18	Warrington 22
Barrow 30	Bradford N 58
Batley 8	Keighley C 29
Bramley 11	Widnes 20
Carlisle 12	Workington T 13
Castleford 36	Salford 4
Doncaster 18	Dewsbury 6
Highfield 4	Whitehaven 15
Huddersfield 16	St Helens 23
Hull KR 16	Ryedale 6
Hunslet 20	Oldham 30
London C 14	Featherstone R 28
Rochdale H 18	Leeds 40

Sheffield E 42	Leigh 10
Swinton 12	Hull 18
Wigan 24	Wakefield T 16

Fifth Round

Leeds 38	Warrington 4
Doncaster 20	Oldham 0
Hull 21	Wigan 22
Hull KR 8	Featherstone R 30
Keighley C 14	Castleford 52
Whitehaven 4	St Helens 46
Widnes 22	Sheffield E 6
Workington T 0	Bradford N 32

Quarter Finals

Castleford 30	Widnes 6
Leeds 33	Bradford N 10
St Helens 40	Doncaster 9
Wigan 32	Featherstone R 14

Semi Finals

Knowsley Rd, St Helens	*Mar 26*
St Helens 8	Leeds 20
Wieldon Rd, Castleford	*Mar 12*
Castleford 6	Wigan 20

SILK CUT CHALLENGE CUP FINAL
Wembley   *Apr 30*

Leeds 16	**Wigan 26**
Tries: Offiah (2)	*Tries: Fallon, Schofield*
Farrell, Panapa	*Cummins*
Goals: Botica (5)	*Goals: Holroyd (2)*

Leeds: Tait, Fallon, Iro, Innes, Cummins, Holroyd, Schofield, Harmon, Lowes, Howard, Mercer, Eyres, Hanley (capt)

Wigan: Connolly, Tuigamala, Bell (capt), Mather, Offiah, Botica, Edwards, Skerett, Dermott, Platt, Betts, Farrell, Clarke

CHALLENGE CUP WINNERS
Since 1960

1960	Wakelfield T	1977	Leeds
1961	St Helens	1978	Leeds
1962	Wakefield T	1979	Widnes
1963	Wakefield T	1980	Hull Kingston R
1964	Widnes	1981	Widnes
1965	Wigan	1982	Hull
1966	St Helens	1983	Featherstone R
1967	Featherstone R	1984	Widnes
1968	Leeds	1985	Wigan
1969	Castleford	1986	Castleford
1970	Castleford	1987	Halifax
1971	Leigh	1988	Wigan
1972	St Helens	1989	Wigan
1973	Featherstone R	1990	Wigan
1974	Warrington	1991	Wigan
1975	Widnes	1992	Wigan
1976	St Helens	1993	Wigan
		1994	**Wigan**

Regal Trophy

Preliminary Round

Carlisle 28	Wakefield T 12
Halifax 19	Keighley C 10
Highfield 8	Oldham 26
Leigh 20	Huddersfield 12
London C 26	Featherstone R 12
Rochdale H 10	Bramley 11
Ryedale Y 12	Workington T 11
Swinton 14	Hull 36
Warrington 58	Hunslet 16
Whitehaven 8	Wigan 22
Widnes 24	Doncaster 4
Hull KR 12	Castleford 16

First Round

Dewsbury 56	West Bowling 10
Barrow 54	Leigh MW 12
Batley 64	Queens 1
Bramley 17	Woolston Rovers 8
Carlisle 36	Carcassonne 24
Doncaster 62	Mysons 4
Highfield 30	Ellenborough 22
Huddersfield 36	Irlam Hornets 8
Hunslet 30	Chorley B 19
Keighley C 72	Nottingham C 12
London C 48	St Esteve 16
Rochdale H 80	Blackpool Gladiators 10
Ryedale Y 66	Hemel Hempstead 14
Swinton 24	Saddleworth 13
Whitehaven 46	Egremont 0

Second Round

Dewsbury 6	St Helens 20
Salford 21	Leeds 12
Barrow 8	Bradford N 28
Batley 8	Sheffield E 6
Carlisle 28	Wakefield T 12
Halifax 19	Keighley C 10
Highfield 8	Oldham 26
Leigh 20	Huddersfield 12
London C 26	Featherstone R 12
Rochdale H 10	Bramley 11
Ryedale Y 12	Workington T 11
Swinton 14	Hull 36
Warrington 58	Hunslet 16
Whitehaven 8	Wigan 22
Widnes 24	Doncaster 4
Hull KR 12	Castleford 16

Third Round

St Helens 8	Warrington 16
Carlisle 34	Bramley 4
Hull 10	Widnes 6
Oldham 8	Wigan 16
Ryedale Y 10	London C 42
Castleford 54	Leigh 14
Batley 8	Salford 12
Bradford N 16	Halifax 8

Quarter Finals

Warrington 10	Wigan 27
Castleford 44	Carlisle 4
London C 10	Bradford N 22
Salford 26	Hull 6

Semi Finals

Oddsall, Bradford   *Jan 1*
Bradford N 10	Castleford 23

The Willows, Salford   *Jan 8*
Salford 12	Wigan 18

Final

Headingley   *Jan 22*

Castleford 33	**Wigan 2**
Tries: Ketteridge (2)	*Goal: Botica*
Nikau, Anderson	
Crooks	

Goals: Crooks (6)

DG: Kemp

Castleford: Steadman, Ellis, Blackmore, Anderson, Middleton, Kemp, Ford, Crooks (capt), Russell, Ketteridge, Morrison, Smales, Nikau

Wigan: Lydon, Robinson, Mather, Connolly, Offiah, Botica, Edwards, Skerrett, Dermott, Platt (capt), Cowie, Farrell, Clarke

---

KNOCKOUT TROPHY

First held in 1971-2, it was originally called the Player's No 6 Trophy, then the John Player Trophy, then the John Player Special Trophy until, in 1989, it was renamed the Regal Trophy

1972	Halifax	1983	Wigan
1973	Leeds	1984	Leeds
1974	Warrington	1985	Hull Kingston R
1975	Bradford N	1986	Wigan
1976	Widnes	1987	Wigan
1977	Castleford	1988	St Helens
1978	Warrington	1989	Wigan
1979	Widnes	1990	Wigan
1980	Bradford N	1991	Warrington
1981	Warrington	1992	Widnes
1982	Hull	1993	Wigan
		1994	**Wigan**

Rugby Union

It was a paradoxical year for rugby union. Wales won the Five Nations, but lost to England. England defeated New Zealand, but pressured their manager, Geoff Cooke, into resignation. New Zealand, unbelievably, lost three Tests in a row, but remain second favourites for the World Cup. The peaceful transition to democracy in South Africa ensured the World Cup would go ahead in that country, though everything else (the refereeing, the fighting, the administration) seemed to suggest it was not such a great idea. The BBC paid £27m for a three-year Five Nations deal - almost treble the amount they paid before - but the home unions still reject payments for players. Three major names secede to rugby league as union officials maintain rules that would be illegal if they were based on colour or sex.

One revolution, at least, is coming. In June, Labour MP Dave Hinchcliffe brought a bill before Parliament that would prevent discrimination of players who have appeared in a different sport. Lack of Parliamentary time meant the bill went no further, but Hinchcliffe promises it will reappear. At the heart of it all is the refusal of rugby union to pay its players; the arguments have never had such a hearing. Whether from former international prop, Stuart Evans, who threatened to take legal action to be reinstated or New Zealand officials wanting to pay openly, the controversy continued. Will Carling, who plays a bit of rugby, was generally reckoned to be earning six figures a year from his 'promotional' activities and was quoted as saying that: "There is no such thing as non-rugby related earnings as far as I am concerned. Every penny I earn is down to who I am and what I have achieved in the game. To suggest otherwise, or turn a blind eye, is sheer hypocrisy". The International Rugby Board set up a working party, to report back in March 1995. It will all change, sooner rather than later. Canute never saw a tide like it.

On the pitch, Carling's England had a year of peaks and troughs. Magnificent wins against New Zealand and South Africa - in the first Test - were counterbalanced by a Five Nations defeat at Twickenham by Ireland and the remainder of the South African tour, in which seven other matches elicited only two more victories, but injuries that were close to criminal. Earlier along the way, Cooke resigned (ousted in all but name) and Jack Rowell was appointed. Rowell proceeded to clear the decks all round; stepping down as coach for Bath, resigning from Golden Wonder, where he made the crisps crisper, and sacking Dick Best, who worked with Cooke in the England set-up.

Wales also had a funny old year. Losing to Western Samoa, at the Apia ground, was bad enough. Losing to Canada, in Cardiff, was downright humiliating. Yet, the team that had been written off before the season started, came away with the Five Nations championship title. They won't want to look at the videos of their game against France, though. As good as it was, it will simply remind them of how much they'll miss Scott Quinnell (*see Rugby League section*).

Of Scotland, we shall talk little. Without Iain McGeechan and without luck (Argentina even managed to have 16 players on the field when they defeated them) they achieved little. They can count themselves unfortunate to lose at Twickenham, but it was rubbing salt in to the wounds when Scottish Provident decided to sponsor the *England* team.

Five Nations Championship

Parc des Princes, Paris Jan 15
France 35   **Ireland 15**
Tries: Benetton   *PG: Elwood (5)*
    Lacroix
    Saint-André
    Merle
Conv: Lacroix (3)
PG: Lacroix (3)
France: Sadourny, Bernat-Salles, Sella, Lacroix, Saint-André, Penaud, Galthié, Armary, Gonzalès, Gallart, Merle, Roumat*, Benetton, Cécillon, Benazzi
Ireland: O'Shea, Wallace, Danaher, Cunningham, Geoghegan, Elwood, Bradley*, Popplewell, Kingston, Clohessy (Halpin), Johns, Francis, Galwey, Robinson, O'Connell

National Stadium, Cardiff Jan 15
Wales 29   **Scotland 6**
Tries: Rayer (2)   *PG: G Hastings (2)*
    I Evans
Conv: N Jenkins
PG: N Jenkins (4)
Wales: Clement, I Evans*, Hall, N Davies, Walker (Rayer), N Jenkins, R Moon, R Evans, G Jenkins, J Davies, P Davies, G Llewellyn, Lewis, Quinnell, Perego
Scotland: G Hastings*, Stanger, Townsend, Jardine, Logan, Chalmers (Wyllie), Nicol, Wright, K Milne, Burnell, Edwards, Munro, Turnbull, Wainwright, Morrison (Weir)

Murrayfield, Edinburgh Feb 5
Scotland 14   **England 15**
Try: Wainwright   *PG: Callard (5)*
PG: G Hastings (2)
DG: Townsend
Scotland: G Hastings*, Stanger, S Hastings (Jardine), Wyllie, Logan, Townsend, Armstrong, Sharp, K Milne, Burnell, Reed, Munro, Walton, Wainwright (Smith), Weir
England: Callard, T Underwood, Carling*, de Glanville, R Underwood, Andrew, Bracken, Leonard, Moore, Ubogu, Johnson, Bayfield, Hall, Back, Ojomoh

Lansdowne Rd., Dublin Feb 5
Ireland 15   **Wales 17**
PG: Elwood (5)   *Try: N Jenkins*
              PG: N Jenkins (4)
Ireland: O'Shea, Wallace, McCall, Danaher, Geoghegan, Elwood, Bradley*, Popplewell, Kingston, Clohessy, Galwey, Francis, Robinson, McBride, Johns
Wales: Clement, I Evans*, Hall, N Davies, Proctor, N Jenkins, R Moon, R Evans, G Jenkins, J Davies, P Davies, G Llewellyn, Lewis, Quinnell, Perego

Twickenham, London Feb 19
England 12   **Ireland 13**
PG: Callard (4)   *Try: Geoghegan Conv: Elwood*
              PG: Elwood (2)
England: Callard, T Underwood, Carling*, De Glanville, R Underwood, Andrew, Bracken, Leonard, Moore, Ubogu, Johnson, Bayfield, Rodber, Back, Ojomoh
Ireland: O'Shea, Wallace, Field, Danaher, Geoghegan, Elwood, Bradley*, Popplewell, Kingston, Clohessy, Galwey, Francis, Robinson, McBride, Johns

National Stadium, Cardiff Feb 19
Wales 24   **France 15**
Tries: Quinnell   *Tries: Roumat*
    Walker   *Sella*
Conv: N Jenkins   *Conv: Lacroix*
PG: N Jenkins (4)   *PG: Lacroix*
Wales: Rayer, Hill, Hall, Clement, Walker, N Jenkins, R Moon, R Evans, G Jenkins, J Davies, G Llewellyn*, Lewis, Quinnell, Perego
France: Sadourny, N'Tamack, Sella, Lacroix, Saint-André, Penaud, Galthié, Armary, Gonzalès, Gallart, Merle, Roumat*, Benetton, Benazzi, Cécillon

Parc des Princes, Paris Mar 5
France 14   **England 18**
Try: Benazzi   *PG: Andrew (5)*
PG: Lacroix (3)   *DG: Andrew*
France: Sadourny, Saint-André, Sella, Lacroix, Techoueyres, Penaud, Galthié, Benezech, Gonzalès, Gallart, Merle, Roumat*, Benetton, Cabannes, Benazzi
England: Pears, Hunter, Carling*, de Glanville, R Underwood, Andrew, Morris, Leonard, Moore, Ubogu, Johnson, Redman, Rodber, Clarke, Ojomoh

Lansdowne Rd., Dublin Mar 5
Ireland 6   **Scotland 6**
PG: Elwood (2)   *PG: G Hastings (2)*
Ireland: O'Shea, Wallace, Field, Danaher, Geoghegan, Elwood, Bradley*, Popplewell, Kingston, Clohessy, Galwey, Francis, Robinson, McBride, Johns
Scotland: G Hastings* (Dods), Stanger, S Hastings, Wyllie, Logan, Townsend, Armstrong, Sharp, K Milne, Burnell, Reed, Munro, Walton, Smith, Weir

Murrayfield, Edinburgh Mar 19
Scotland 12   **France 20**
PG: G Hastings (4)   *Tries: Sadourny*
              Saint-André
              Conv: Lacroix
              Montlaur
              PG: Lacroix (2)
Scotland: G Hastings*, Stanger, S Hastings, Wyllie, Logan, Townsend, Redpath, Sharp, K Milne, Burnell, Reed, Munro, Walton, Smith, Weir
France: Sadourny, Saint-André*, Sella, Delaigue, Techoueyres, Lacroix (Montlaur), Macabiau, Benezech, Gonzalès, Seigne, Merle, Brouzet, Benetton, Cabannes, Benazzi

Twickenham, London Mar 19
England 15   **Wales 8**
Tries: R Underwood   *Try: Walker*
    Rodber   *PG: N Jenkins*
Conv: Andrew
PG: Andrew
England: Hunter, T Underwood, Carling*, de Glanville, R Underwood, Andrew (Catt), Morris, Leonard, Moore, Ubogu, Johnson, Redman, Rodber, Clarke, Richards

Wales: Rayer, I Evans*, Hall, N Davies, Walker, N Jenkins, R Moon, R Evans, G Jenkins, J Davies, P Davies, G Llewellyn, Lewis (Copsey), Quinnell, Perego

FINAL 5 NATIONS TABLE

		P	W	D	L	PF	PA	Diff	Pts
1	Wales	4	3	0	1	78	51	+27	6
2	England	4	3	0	1	60	49	+11	6
3	France	4	2	0	2	84	69	+15	4
4	Ireland	4	1	1	2	49	70	-21	3
5	Scotland	4	0	1	3	38	70	-32	1

British International Matches
Excluding Five Nations Championship

England in South Africa
1st Test
Pretoria   June 4

South Africa 15	England 32
PG: Joubert (5)	Tries: Clarke
	Andrew
	Conv: Andrew (2)
	PG: Andrew (5)
	DG: Andrew

South Africa: Joubert, Small, Muller, Venter, Williams, H le Roux, Van der Westhuizen, A-H le Roux, Allan, Swart, Strydom, Atherton, Pienaar*, van Heerden, Strauss
England: Hull, T Underwood, Carling*, de Glanville, R Underwood, Andrew, Morris, Leonard, Moore, Ubogu, Bayfield, Redman, Rodber, Clarke, Richards (Ojomoh)

2nd Test
Cape Town   June 11

South Africa 27	England 9
Tries: H le Roux	PG: Andrew (3)
Joubert	
Conv: Joubert	
PG: H le Roux (3)	
Joubert (2)	

South Africa: Joubert, Small, Muller, Venter (Van Der Westhuizen), Williams, H le Roux, Roux, Swart, Allan, J le Roux, Andrews, Atherton, Pienaar*, MacDonald (Van Heerden), Richter
England: Hull, T Underwood, Carling*, de Glanville, R Underwood, Andrew, Morris, Leonard, Moore, Ubogu, Bayfield, Redman, Rodber, Ojomoh, Clarke,

TOUR MATCHES
Bloemfontein   May 18
Orange Free State 22 England 11

Durban   May 21
Natal 21 England 6

Potchefstroom   May 25
Western Transvaal 24 England 26

Johannesburg   May 28
Transvaal 24 England 21

Kimberley   May 31
South Africa A 19 England 16

Port Elizabeth   June 7
Eastern Province 13 England 31

Scotland in Argentina
1st Test
Buenos Aires   June 4

Argentina 16	Scotland 15
Try: Teran	PG: Dods (5)
Conv: Meson	
PG: Meson (3)	

Argentina: Meson, Teran, Cuesta-Silva, Loffreda*, Jorge, Del Castillo, Miranda, Corral, Angelillo, Noriego, Sporleder, Llanes, Viel, Camerlinckx, Temperley
Scotland: Dods, Joiner, Jardine, Shiel, Logan, Townsend, Redpath, Sharp, McKenzie, Burnell, Munro, Reed*, Walton, Hogg, Smith

2nd Test
Buenos Aires   June 11

Argentina 19	Scotland 17
Try: Martin	Try: Logan
Conv: Meson	PG: Shiel (2), Dods
PG: Meson (3)	DG: Townsend
DG: Del Castillo	

Argentina: Meson, Teran, Cuesta Silva, Loffreda*, Jorge, Del Castilla, Miranda, Mendez, Angelillo, Noriego, Sporleder, Llanes, Martin, Santamarina, Viel
Scotland: Dods, Joiner, Jardine, Shiel, Logan (Nichol), Townsend, Redpath, Sharp (Watt), McKenzie, Burnell, Munró, Reed*, Walton, Hogg, Smith

TOUR MATCHES
Buenos Aires   May 25
Buenos Aires 24 Scotland 24

Mendoza   May 28
Cuyo 25 Scotland 11

Cordoba   May 31
Cordoba 14 Scotland 40

Newell's Old Boys   June 7
Rosario 27 Scotland 16

Ireland in Australia
1st Test
Ballymore   June 4

Australia 33	Ireland 13
Tries: Tabua	Try: Johns
Lynagh	Conv: Elwood
Campese	PG: Elwood
Burke	O'Shea
Smith	
Conv: Lynagh	
PG: Lynagh (2)	

Australia: Pini, Campese, Burke, O'Connor, Smith, Lynagh*, Slattery, Daly, Kearns, McKenzie, Eales, Morgan, Tabua, Wilson, Gavin
Ireland: O'Shea (Field), Geoghegan, Bell, Danaher, Woods, Elwood, Bradley*, Fitzgerald, Wood, Clohessy, Galwey (McBride), Francis, Robinson, Corkery, Johns

2nd Test
Sydney   June 11

Australia 32	Ireland 18
Tries: Herbert	*Tries: Clohessy*
Wilson	*Francis*
Tabua	*Conv: O'Shea*
Conv: Lynagh	*PG: O'Shea*
PG: Lynagh (5)	*DG: O'Shea*

Australia: Burke, Campese, Tombs, Herbert, Smith (Constable), Lynagh*, Slattery, Daly, Kearns, McKenzie, Eales, Morgan, Tabua, Wilson, Gavin
Ireland: O'Shea, Geoghegan, Bell, Danaher, Woods, Elwood, Bradley*, Fitzgerald, Wood, Clohessy, Fulcher, Francis, Robinson, Corkery, Johns

TOUR MATCHES
Perth   May 18
Western Australia 8 Ireland 64

Sydney   May 21
New South Wales 55 Ireland 18

Canberra   May 25
ACT 22 Ireland 9

Brisbane   May 29
Queensland 29 Ireland 26

Mount Isa   June 1
Australia XV 57 Ireland 9

Lismore   June 8
NSW Country 18 Ireland 20

Wales in Canada and South Pacific
1st Test
Toronto   June 11

Canada 15	Wales 33
PG: Rees (5)	*Tries: Hall (2)*
	I Evans
	Conv: N Jenkins (3)
	PG: N Jenkins (4)

Canada: Stewart, Toews, Gray, Stuart*, Lougheed, Rees, Graf, Evans, Svoboda, Jackart, James, Charron, Grodon, MacKenzie (Ennis), MacKinnon
Wales: Rayer, I Evans* (Clement), Hall, N Davies, Proctor, N Jenkins, Moon, R Evans, G Jenkins, J Davies, P Davies, G Llewellyn, Taylor, Quinnell, Collins

2nd Test
Suva   June 18

Fiji 8	Wales 23
Try: Veitayaki	*Tries: Rayer*
PG: Bogisa	*Collins*
	Conv: A Davies (2)
	PG: A Davies (3)

Fiji: Bogisa, Vidiri, Toloi, Nauga, Tuidraki, Rayasi, McLennan, Williams, Batimala, Veitayaki, Tawake*, Savai, Matalulu, Campbell (Korovou), Mocelutu
Wales: Rayer, I Evans*, Boobyer, N Davies, Proctor, A Davies, Moon, R Evans, McBryde, Williams-Jones, Copsey, Arnold, Taylor, Collins, Lewis (P Davies)

3rd Test
Nukualofa   June 22

Tonga 9	Wales 18
PG: S Tu'ipulotu (3)	*PG: Jenkins (6)*

Tonga: S Tu'ipulotu, Va'enuku, Manukia, Latu, Taupeaafu, E Vunipola, M Vunipola, Lutua, F Vunipola, Fa, Mali, Taumoepeaw, Loto'ahea, Vikilani, K Tu'ipolotu
Wales: Clement, I Evans*, Hall (N Davies), Boobyer, Wilkins, N Jenkins, John, Buckett, G Jenkins, Williams-Jones, Copsey, G Llewellyn, Taylor, Collins, Williams

4th Test
Apia   June 25

Western Samoa 34	Wales 9
Tries: Lima (2)	*PG: N Jenkins (3)*
Lam	
Conv: Kellett (2)	
PG: Kellett (5)	

Western Samoa: Aiolupo, Lima, Vaega, Tuilagi, Samania, Kellett, Vitale, Fatialofa*, Leiasamaivao, Latu, Birtwhistle, Keenan (Kaleta), Vaifale, Iupeli, Lam (Mika)
Wales: Rayer, I Evans*, Clement, N Davies, Proctor, N Jenkins, Moon, R Evans (Williams-Jones), G Jenkins, J Davies, P Davies (Copsey), G Llewellyn, Lewis, Quinnell (Taylor), Collins

Other Match
Hamilton   June 8
Canada Select XV 19 Wales 28

New Zealand in Britain
1st Test
Murrayfield   Nov 20, 1993

Scotland 15	New Zealand 51
PG: G Hastings (4)	*Tries: Ellis (2)*
Chalmers	*Wilson (3)*
	Brooke
	Bunce
	Conv: Cooper (4)
	Wilson
	PG: Cooper (2)

Scotland: G Hastings*, Stanger, Jardine, Shiel, S Hastings, Chalmers (Wyllie), Nicol, Watt, K Milne, Burnell, Cronin (Hogg), Macdonald, McIvor, Wainwright, Weir
New Zealand: Timu, Wilson, Bunce, Cooper (Clarke), Tuigamala, Ellis, Forster, Dowd, Fitzpatrick*, Brown, Jones, Gordon, Joseph, Brooke, Pene

2nd Test
Twickenham   Nov 27, 1993

England 15	New Zealand 9
PG: Callard (4)	*PG: Wilson (3)*
DG: Andrew	

England: Callard, T Underwood, Carling*, de Glanville, R Underwood, Andrew, Bracken, Leonard, Moore, Ubogu, Johnson, Redman, Rodber, Clarke, Richards
New Zealand: Timu, Wilson, Bunce, Clarke, Tuigamala, Ellis, Forster, Dowd, Fitzpatrick*, Brown, Jones, Gordon, Joseph, Brooke, Pene

QUOTES

"I thought we could have made it a hundred. We lost concentration for a while" - **Zinzan Brooke, after the New Zealand tourists had beaten South of Scotland 84-5**

His initials are J C and he got fairly close to him today" - **Dick Best, England coach, on Jonathan Callard after the England full-back had scored all England's points against Scotland, including a last-minute penalty to win the game.**

"I wasn't satisfied with my overall game. Someone said it was a bit like J P R Williams in the second half. It was more like Kenneth Williams in the first" - **Jonathan Callard, on the same game.**

"Don't ask me about the level of emotion in the Welsh dressing-room. I'm someone who cries when he watches *Little House on the Prairie*" - **Robert Norster, Wales manager, after his team beat Five Nations favourites France.**

"If anybody had said in January that, in just two months, our Welsh captain would be receiving the Five nations Trophy from the Queen, they would have strapped him in a straight-jacket and thrown away the key" - **Nigel Walker, following the England which Wales lost. It did not prevent them from winning the championship, though.**

"We do appreciate a good fight up here" - **The Mayor of Kimberley, after the South Africa 'A' game against England.**

"Increasingly, penalties have become one of life's mysteries" - **Jack Rowell, England manager, on the controversial refereeing during the South African tour.**

"Together we are building a new nation. Now all that we have to do is build a new team" - **F W de Klerk, South African vic-president, after England defeated the Sprinboks in the first Test.**

"At the end of the day, it's only a game" - **Sean Fitzpatrick, New Zealand captain *before* he had a large chunk bitten out of his ear by South Africa's Johan Le Roux.**

"All this talk now is that forwards should not be fat and slow, but ball-handlers. That's rubbish. What they should be is man-handlers" - **Ray Prosser, former prop for Wales and the British Lions.**

"I think Brian's gnashers are the sort you get from a DIY shop and hammer in yourself. He's the only player we have who looks like a French forward" - **Paul Rendall on England hooker Brian Moore.**

"My image is shot to pieces. None of my oponents is going to be the least bit frightened of me now" - **Mickey Skinner, after admitting that he got down on one knee to propse to his girlfriend.**

"I love it when you tackle someone and you can hear their teeth rattle" - **Frances Gifford, 17-year-old women's rugby player.**

TOUR MATCHES
Twickenham Oct 23, 1993
London/SE 12 New Zealand 39

Leicester Oct 26
Midlands 6 New Zealand 12

Redruth Oct 30
South West 15 New Zealand 19

Manchester Nov 2
North 21 New Zealand 27

Gateshead Nov 7
England A 12 New Zealand 26

Galashiels Nov 10
South of Scotland 5 New Zealand 84

Glasgow Nov 13
Scotland A 9 New Zealand 20

Edinburgh Nov 16
Scotland Development XV 12 New Zealand 31

Gloucester Nov 23
Emerging England 19 New Zealand 30

Devonport Nov 30
Combined Services 3 New Zealand 13

Cardiff Dec 4
Barbarians 12 New Zealand 25

Other International Matches
National Stadium, Cardiff Oct 16

Wales 55	**Japan 5**
Tries: Evans (2), Gibbs (2)	*Try: Williams*
Jenkins, Moon, Lewis	
Rayer, Clement	
Conv: Jenkins (5)	

Parc des Princes, Paris Nov 6

France 3	**Australia 24**
PG: Lacroix	*Tries: Roebuck, Gavin*
	Conv: Roebuck
	PG: Roebuck (4)

National Stadium, Cardiff Nov 10
Wales 24   **Canada 26**

Lansdowne Rd, Dublin Nov 13
Ireland 25   **Romania 3**

Nepean June 4
Canada 18   **France 16**

Brisbane June 18

Australia 23	**Italy 20**
Tries: Herbert, Burke	*Try: Bonomi*
Conv: Lynagh, Wallace	*PG: Troiani (5)*
PG: Lynagh (2), Wallace	

Sydney June 25
Australia 20   **Italy 7**

Christchurch June 25

New Zealand 8	**France 22**
Try: Bunce	*Try: Benetton*
PG: Cooper	*Conv: Lacroix*
	PG: Lacroix (2)
	DG: Sadourny, Deylaud (2)

Auckland July 2
New Zealand 20   **France 23**

Dunedin July 9

New Zealand 22	**South Africa 14**
Try: Kirwan	*Try: Straeuli*
Conv: Howarth	*PG: Joubert (3)*
PG: Howarth (5)	

Auckland Aug 6

New Zealand 18	**South Africa 14**
PG: Howarth (6)	*Tries: Johnson, Venter*
	Conv: Johnson
	PG: Johnson (2)

Sydney Aug 6

Australia 73	**Western Samoa 3**
Tries: Little (2), Smith (2)	*PG: Kellett*
Ofahengaue, Howard,	
Campese, Gavin,	
Pini, Junee, Gregan	
Conv: Knox (6)	
PG: Knox (2)	

BLEDISLOE CUP
Played annually between Australia and New Zealand
Sydney Aug 17

Australia 20	**New Zealand 16**
Tries: Little, Kearns	*Howarth*
Conv: Knox (2)	*Howarth*
PG: Knox (2)	*Howarth (3)*

World Cup Qualifying Round
SOUTH AMERICAN GROUP
Ascuncion, Paraguay Oct 2
Paraguay 3 Uruguay 67

Montevideo, Uruguay Oct 9
Uruguay 14 Chile 6

Buenos Aires, Argentina Oct 11
Argentina 70 Chile 7

Buenos Aires, Argentina Oct 16
Argentina 51 Paraguay 3

Montevideo, Uruguay Oct 23
Uruguay 10 Argentina 19

Hamilton, Canada Mar 12
Bermuda 3 USA 60

AMERICAN PLAY OFF
Long Beach California, USA May 28
USA 22 Argentina 28

Buenos Aires, Argentina June 20
Argentina 16 USA 11

AFRICAN GROUP
Tunis, Tunisia   Oct 26
Tunisia 16 Ivory Coast 19
Tunisia 5 Morocco 6
Morocco 3 Ivory Coast 15

Casablanca, Morocco   June 14-18
Morocco 17 Ivory Coast 9
Namibia 25 Zimbabwe 20
Zimbabwe 21 Morocco 9
Ivory Coast 13 Namibia 12
Zimbabwe 10 Ivory Coast 17
Morocco 16 Namibia 16

EUROPE CENTRAL GROUP
Den Haag, Holland   Oct 31
Israel 10 Sweden 26
Czech Republic 6 Holland 42

Apeldoorn, Holland   Nov 3
Holland 56 Israel 0
Czech Republic 34 Sweden 7

Amsterdam, Holland   Nov 6
Holland 31 Sweden 6
Czech Republic 28 Israel 0

EUROPE EAST GROUP
Bucharest, Romania   May 2-7
Romania 60 Germany 6
Russia 67 Germany 5
Romania 30 Russia 0

Brescia, Italy   May 15-21
Holland 33 Czech Republic 9
Italy 104 Czech Republic 8 *(World record score)*
Italy 63 Holland 9

EUROPE WEST GROUP
Lisbon, Portugal   May 17
Portugal 11 Wales 102

Madrid, Spain   May 21
Spain 0 Wales 54

Madrid, Spain   May 28
Spain 35 Portugal 19

EUROPEAN GROUP CLASSIFICATION
Bucharest, Romania   Sept 17
Romania 9 Wales 16

HONG KONG SEVENS
Hong Kong   Mar 26-7
Quarter Finals
Western Samoa 21 President's VII 12
Argentina 0 Australia 43
New Zealand 21 France 12
South Africa 12 Fiji 14
Semi Finals
Western Samoa 17 Australia 20 (aet)
New Zealand 28 Fiji 14
FINAL
New Zealand 32 Australia 20

COURAGE CLUBS CHAMPIONSHIP

DIVISION 1

		P	W	D	L	PF	PA	Pts
1	Bath	18	17	0	1	431	181	34
2	Leicester	18	14	0	4	425	210	28
3	Wasps	18	10	1	7	362	340	21
4	Bristol	18	10	0	8	331	276	20
5	Northampton	18	9	0	9	331	276	18
6	Harlequins	18	8	0	10	333	287	16
7	Orrell	18	8	0	10	327	302	16
8	Gloucester	18	6	2	10	247	356	14
9	London Irish	18	4	0	14	217	391	8
10	Newcastle Gos.	18	2	1	15	190	483	5

DIVISION 2

		P	W	D	L	PF	PA	Pts
1	Sale	18	13	2	3	438	160	28
2	West Hartlepool	18	13	2	3	369	271	28
3	Saracens	18	11	1	6	299	238	23
4	Wakefield	18	8	3	7	347	240	19
5	Moseley	18	9	1	8	266	220	19
6	Nottingham	18	8	1	9	254	326	17
7	Waterloo	18	6	2	10	231	346	14
8	London Scottish	18	6	0	12	232	325	12
9	Rugby	18	5	1	12	186	302	11
10	Otley	18	4	1	13	235	449	9

DIVISION 3

		P	W	D	L	PF	PA	Pts
1	Coventry	18	14	0	4	406	259	28
2	Fylde	18	13	0	5	339	219	26
3	Bedford	18	12	0	6	332	219	24
4	Blackheath	18	11	0	7	305	222	22
5	Rosslyn Park	18	10	1	7	372	240	21
6	Exeter	18	9	1	8	308	271	19
7	Richmond	18	9	0	9	337	300	18
8	Morley	18	6	0	12	245	334	12
9	Havant	18	3	0	15	203	432	6
10	Redruth	18	2	0	16	178	488	4

DIVISION 4

		P	W	D	L	PF	PA	Pts
1	Clifton	18	16	2	0	477	205	34
2	Harrogate	18	14	2	2	479	219	30
3	Liverpool St H.	18	11	1	6	396	275	23
4	Plymouth Alb.	18	9	0	9	286	416	18
5	Aspatria	18	8	0	10	303	372	16
6	Leeds	18	7	0	11	243	318	14
7	Askeans	18	6	1	11	268	358	13
8	Broughton Park	18	6	0	12	243	356	12
9	Sheffield	18	5	1	12	287	310	11
10	Sudbury	18	4	1	13	240	393	9

CIS INSURANCE DIVISIONAL CHAMPIONSHIP
Newcastle Gosforth   Oct 16
Northern 21 London/SE 22

Bath   Oct 16
Southern 31 Midlands 3

Gloucester   Oct 23
South West 29 Northen 16

Leicester   Oct 30
Midlands 14 London/SE 23

Northampton   Nov 6
Midlands 9 Northern 31

Twickenham   Jan 3
London/SE 17 South West 25
South West Division are Divisional Champions

CIS INSURANCE COUNTY CHAMPIONSHIP

AREA NORTH
League 1

	P	W	D	L	PF	PA	Pts
1 Yorkshire	3	3	0	0	83	14	6
2 Durham	3	1	0	2	62	63	2
3 Lancashire	3	1	0	2	40	72	2
4 Northumberland	3	1	0	2	44	80	2

League 2

	P	W	D	L	PF	PA	Pts
1 Cheshire	3	3	0	0	65	47	6
2 Cumbria	3	2	0	1	57	46	4
3 Leicestershire	3	1	0	2	51	53	2
4 Warwickshire	3	0	0	3	51	78	0

League 3

	P	W	D	L	PF	PA	Pts
1 Staffordshire	3	3	0	0	84	59	6
2 North Midlands	3	2	0	1	73	41	4
3 Notts,Lincs,Derby	3	1	0	2	59	63	2
4 East Midlands	3	0	0	3	48	101	0

AREA SOUTH
League 1

	P	W	D	L	PF	PA	Pts
1 Cornwall	3	3	0	0	48	37	6
2 Gloucestershire	3	2	0	1	78	39	4
3 Hampshire	3	1	0	2	30	56	2
4 Middlesex	3	0	0	3	38	62	0

League 2

	P	W	D	L	PF	PA	Pts
1 Surrey	3	2	1	0	48	28	5
2 Devon	3	1	1	1	31	40	3
3 Kent	3	1	0	2	52	41	2
4 Dorset & Wilts	3	1	0	2	49	71	2

League 3

	P	W	D	L	PF	PA	Pts
1 Sussex	3	2	0	1	45	37	4
2 Bucks.	3	2	0	1	36	40	4
3 Hertfordshire	3	1	0	2	48	44	2
4 Somerset	3	1	0	2	37	45	2

League 4

	P	W	D	L	PF	PA	Pts
1 Oxfordshire	2	2	0	0	57	21	4
2 Berkshire	2	1	0	1	54	47	2
3 East. Counties	2	0	0	2	20	63	0

Semi Finals
Otley Jan15
Yorkshire 13 Gloucestershire 12

Redruth Feb 5
Cornwall 9 Durham 14

FINAL
Twickenham   Apr 16
Yorkshire 26 Durham 3

Middlesex Sevens
Twickenham   May 14
Quarter Finals
Rosslyn Park 21 Harlequins 10
Orrell 10 Fiji Spartans 7
Loughborough Univ. 0 Bath 24
London Irish 5 Saracens 26
Semi Finals
Rosslyn Park 7 Orrell 10
Bath 19 Saracens 0
Final
Bath 19 Orrell 12

THE PILKINGTON CUP
Fourth Round
Dec 18, 1993
Rosslyn Park 22 Coventry 15
Bristol 46 Henley 6
Bath 24 Wasps 11
Nottingham 9 Gloucester 29
Orrell 55 Stourbridge 3
Otley 20 Wharfedale 5
London Scottish 6 Fylde 8
Northampton 22 Waterloo 3
Newcastle Gosforth 53 Bridgwater & Albion 10
Harlequins 52 Basingstoke 3
Blackheath 10 Leicester 16
Wakefield 17 West Hartlepool 18
Rugby 13 Sale 17
Moseley 42 Winnington Park 6
Havant 13 London Irish 18
Saracens 26 Birmingham/Solihull 3

Fifth Round
Jan 22
Rosslyn Park 12 Saracens 29
Newcastle Gosforth 7 Orrell 12
Leicester 43 London Irish 10
Moseley 15 Fylde 6
Harlequins 23 West Hartlepool 15
Gloucester 11 Northampton 6
Bath 14 Bristol 9
Otley 7 Sale 58

Quarter Finals
Feb 26
Saracens 6 Bath 23
Gloucester 3 Orrell 10
Leicester 12 Moseley 6
Harlequins 26 Sale 13

Semi Finals
Apr 2
Harlequins 25 Bath 26
Orrell 18 Leicester 31

PILKINGTON CUP FINAL
Twickenham   May 7

Bath 21	**Leicester 9**
Tries: Swift, Call	*PG: Harris (3)*
Conv: Callard	
PG: Callard (3)	

Bath: Callard, Swift, de Glanville, Catt, Adebayo, Barnes, Hill, Hilton, Dawe, Ubogu, Redman, Reed, Robinson (Ojomoh), Hall (capt), Clarke
Leicester: Kilford, T Underwood, Potter, Boyle, R Underwood, Harris, Kardooni, Rowntree, Cockerill, Garforth, Johnson, Poole, Wells, Back, Richards (capt)
The attendance of 68,000 set a new record for a British club rugby match. Richard Hill, in his last game for Bath, became the first player to appear in eight cup winning final teams. The replacement of Andy Robinson by Steve Ojomoh 9 minutes into the second half brought to 14 the number of international players in Bath's winning team, equalling the cup record also set by Bath in 1987.

Pilkington Shield
Semi Finals
Apr 2
Malvern 8 Hucclecote Old Boys 6
Old Hamptonians 10 Kidderminster Carolians 6
Final
Twickenham   May 7
Malvern 8 Old Hamptonians 6

WORTHINGTON NATIONAL 10'S CHAMPIONSHIP
Final
Kingsholm, Gloucester
Gloucester 5 Bristol 26

COMMERCIAL UNION UAU FINAL
Twickenham   Mar 23
Univ. of Northumbria 13 West London Inst. 9

Heineken Welsh League
DIVISION 1

		P	W	D	L	PF	PA	Pts
1	Swansea	22	20	0	2	549	264	40
2	Neath	22	17	2	3	581	286	36
3	Pontypridd	22	17	1	4	571	299	35
4	Cardiff	22	15	2	5	668	240	32
5	Llanelli	22	13	1	8	461	366	27
6	Bridgend	22	10	1	11	466	434	21
7	Newport	22	8	2	12	362	472	18
8	Newbridge	22	7	1	14	367	440	15
9	Pontypool	22	7	0	15	312	626	14
10	Dunvant	22	6	1	15	288	464	13
11	Aberavon	22	6	1	15	242	464	13
12	Cross Keys	22	0	0	22	239	751	0

DIVISION 2

		P	W	D	L	PF	PA	Pts
1	Treorchy	22	20	1	1	425	200	41
2	Abertillery	22	15	1	6	473	242	31
3	Maesteg	22	13	1	8	376	259	27
4	S Wales Police	22	12	0	10	367	333	24
5	Tenby Utd	22	10	0	12	308	366	20
6	Llanharan	22	9	2	11	259	349	20
7	Narberth	22	10	0	12	273	294	20
8	Penarth	22	9	0	13	291	372	18
9	Ebbw Vale	22	8	2	12	279	321	18
10	Llandovery	22	8	1	13	269	370	17
11	Mountain Ash	22	8	0	14	275	333	16
12	Glamorgan W.	22	6	0	16	262	418	12

SWALEC CUP
Round 6
Cardiff 15 Bridgend 6
Dunvant 8 Newbridge 18
Llanelli 57 Llandovery 5
Maesteg 11 Bonymaen 9
Maesteg Celtic 14 South Wales Police 37
Pontypridd 13 Swansea 3
Tenby Utd 25 Narberth 14
Ystradgynlais 3 Neath 26

Quarter Finals
Maesteg 35 Tenby Utd 17
Neath 3 Llanelli 7
Pontypridd 32 Newbridge 10
Cardiff 20 South Wales Police 13

Semi Finals
Llanelli 23 Maesteg 7
Cardiff 8 Pontypridd 6

SWALEC CUP FINAL
National Stadium, Cardiff   May 7
Cardiff 15   **Llanelli 8**
Tries: Hall, Rayer   Evans
Conv: Davies   PG: Stephens
PG: Davies
Cardiff: Rayer, Ford, Hall (capt), Laity, Walker, Davies, Moore, Griffiths, Humphreys, Mustoe, Rees, Jones, Bennett, Budd, Williams
Llanelli: Boobyer, Evans, Davies (Jones), Davies, Proctor, Stephens, Moon, Evans, Lamerton, Williams-Jones, Davies (Jones), Copsey, Lewis, Perego, Quinnell

Scottish League
DIVISION 1

		P	W	D	L	PF	PA	Pts
1	Melrose	13	12	0	1	410	192	24
2	Gala	12	9	0	3	274	214	18
3	Edinburgh Acs.	13	8	1	4	265	183	17
4	Heriots F.P.	12	7	0	5	230	224	14
5	Watsonians	13	7	0	6	276	337	14
6	Stirling County	12	6	1	5	227	163	13
7	Hawick	12	6	1	5	218	178	13
8	Jed-Forest	13	6	0	7	231	199	12
9	Currie	12	6	0	6	230	285	12
10	Stewarts Mel.	13	5	1	7	157	190	11
11	Boroughmuir	12	5	0	7	214	228	10
12	West of Scotland	13	4	1	8	235	279	9
13	Kelso	13	4	0	9	175	296	8
14	Selkirk	13	0	1	12	138	312	1

Irish League
DIVISION 1

		P	W	D	L	PF	PA	Pts
1	Garryowen	10	8	0	2	172	108	16
2	Cork Const.	10	7	0	3	201	123	14
3	Blackrock Coll.	10	7	0	3	137	99	14
4	Dungannon	10	5	0	5	181	130	10
5	Lansdowne	10	5	0	5	162	167	10
6	St Mary's Coll.	10	5	0	5	157	163	10
7	Young Munster	10	5	0	5	102	149	10
8	Shannon	10	4	0	6	107	104	8
9	Old Wesley	10	4	0	6	114	138	8
10	Greystones	10	4	0	6	97	156	8
11	Wanderers	10	1	0	9	141	234	2

FRENCH CHAMPIONSHIP
Final
Parc des Princes
Toulouse 22 Montferrand 16

NEW ZEALAND CHAMPIONSHIP 1993
Final
Auckland 27 Otago 18

SUPER TEN CHAMPIONSHIPS
(Played by teams from Australia, New Zealand and S Africa)
Pool A
Queensland 44 Transvaal 19
Transvaal 35 Eastern Province 15
Eastern Province 10 Queensland 41
Transvaal 44 Otago 19
Otago 24 Queensland 18
Eastern Province 21 North Harbour 31
North Harbour 23 Otago 19
Otago 57 Eastern Province 24
North Harbour 19 Transvaal 6
Queensland 13 North Harbour 10

Pool B
Waikato 16 New South Wales 43
New South Wales 25 Western Samoa 23
Auckland 27 Waikato 10
Waikato 18 Western Samoa 32
Natal v New South Wales *(Walk over for Natal)*
Western Samoa 15 Auckland 13
Natal 30 Waikato 24
Natal 48 Western Samoa 26
New South Wales 22 Auckland 19
Natal 14 Auckland 12

Final
Durban, South Africa May 14
Natal 10 Queensland 21

Steve Spiller, a Welsh rugby fan, sold the slates off his roof to raise the money for a ticket to the England-Wales game at Twickenham. Spiller, who got £200 for the slates, covered his house in felt and set off for the game. "He was determined to go, so I have to forgive him," said his wife Debbie, who must get a diploma in martyrdom.
Or she was lying.

At Penryn, Cornwall in March, the Vyvyan family made history by supplying all the members of a seven-a-side team. Richard (33), Jonathan (31), Simon (29), Charles (28), Paul (24), James (21) and Hugh (18) were the brothers in question.

Women's World Championships
Scotland Apr 11-24
Pool A
USA 110 Sweden 0
Sweden 5 Japan 10
USA 121 Japan 0
Pool B
England 66 Russia 0
Scotland 51 Russia 0
Scotland 0 England 26
Pool C
France 77 Scottish Students 0
Scottish Students 5 Ireland 51
France 31 Ireland 0
Pool D
Canada 5 Wales 15
Wales 29 Kazakhstan 8
Canada 28 Kazakhstan 0

Quarter Finals
USA 76 Ireland 0
England 24 Canada 10
France 99 Japan 0
Wales 8 Scotland 0

Semi Finals
Gala Apr 20
USA 56 Wales 15
England 18 France 6

3rd/4th Play Off
Raeburn Place, Edinburgh Apr 24
France 27 Wales 0

FINAL
Raeburn Place, Edinburgh Apr 24
England 38 USA 23

Women's National League
DIVISION 1

	P	W	D	L	PF	PA	Pts
1 Saracens	11*	10	0	1	365	63	30
2 Richmond I	12	10	0	2	260	73	30
3 Wasps I	12	8	1	3	193	105	25
4 Clifton	11*	5	1	5	174	135	16
5 Blackheath	12	5	0	7	142	202	15
6 Cardiff	12	3	0	9	101	291	9 **
7 Eton Manor	12	0	0	12	35	401	0 ***

* Clifton v Saracens was not played: 0 pts each
** Cardiff defaulted v Clifton (3 pts)
*** Eton Manor defaulted v Wasps (3 pts) & Richmond (3 pts)
DIVISION 2

	P	W	D	L	PF	PA	Pts
1 Waterloo	12	11	0	1	333	66	33
2 Leeds	12	9	0	3	179	47	27
3 Richmond II	12	9	0	3	213	146	27
4 Wasps II	12	7	0	5	212	144	21
5 Northampton	12	3	1	8	52	216	10
6 Sale	12	2	0	10	90	263	6
7 Medway	12	0	1	11	43	240	1 *

* Medway defaulted v Leeds (3 pts)

COMMERCIAL UNION UAU WOMEN'S FINAL
Richmond Mar 9
Loughborough Univ. 32 Greenwich Univ. 5

Shooting

UIT World Championships

July 21-Aug 3

300m Rifle Events
Tolmezzo, Italy
FREE RIFLE 3 X 40M
Individual
1 Glenn Dubis   USA   1175
2 Norbert Sturny   SUI   1169
3 Eric Chollet Durnad SUI 1168
Team
1 Belarus   3480
2 Finland   3487
3 Czech Republic   3477
FREE RIFLE 60 SHOTS PRONE
Individual
1 Bernd Rücker   GER   600
2 Petr Kurka   TCH   599
3 Roger Chasset   FRA   597
Team
1 Finland   1787
2 Czech Republic   1785
3 Switzerland   1783
STANDARD RIFLE 3 X 20M
Individual
1 Jukka Salonen   FIN   584
2 Milan Bakes   TCH   582
3 Harri Marjala   FIN   580
Team
1 United States   1736
2 Finland   1728
3 Germany   1716

Rifle, Pistol & Running Target Men
Milan, Italy
50M FREE RIFLE 3 X 40M
Individual
1 Petr Kurka   TCH   1268.5
2 Tommy Tamas   USA   1266.3
3 Wolfram Wiabel   AUT   1265.1
Team
1 France   3479
2 Ukraine   3478
3 Czech Republic   3470
50M RIFLE 60 SHOTS PRONE
Individual
1 Li Wenjie   CHN   700.5
2 Stevan Pletikosic IOP   699.2
3 Christian Klees   GER   698.4
Team
1 Ukraine   1784
2 France   1784
3 Russia   1783

AIR RIFLE
Individual
1 Boris Polak   694.1
2 Anatoli Klimenko   691.8
3 Frank Dobler   GER   691.8
Team
1 Belarus   1766
2 Czech Republic   1764
3 Russia   1764
FREE PISTOL
Individual
1 Wang Yifu   CHN   663.5
2 Victor Makarov   UKR   659.7
3 Franck Dumoulin   FRA   657.7
Team
1 Ukraine   1675
2 Russia   1674
3 China   1673
RAPID FIRE PISTOL
Individual
1 Krzysztof Kucharczynk POL 691.4
2 Emil Milev   BUL   690.2
3 Ralf Schumann   GER   689.7
Team
1 Poland   1753
2 China   1749
3 Hungary   1747
CENTRE FIRE PISTOL
Individual
1 Paal Hembre   NOR   588
2 Christian Kezel   FRA   585
3 Oleg Tkatchev   UKR   585
Team
1 Russia   1741
2 Ukraine   1740
3 Korea   1739
STANDARD PISTOL 3 X 20M
Individual
1 Lee Sang Hak   KOR   575
2 Hansrudolf Schneider SUI 574
3 Seppo Makinen   FIN   574
Team
1 Finland   1706
2 China   1706
3 Switzerland   1701
AIR PISTOL
Individual
1 Franck Dumoulin   FRA   683.7
2 Igor Basinski   BLS   682.2
3 Roberto Di Donna   ITA   681.6
Team
1 China   1732
2 Italy   1731
3 Hungary   1731
50M RUNNING TARGET 30+30
Individual
1 Shu Qingquan   CHN   592
2 Lubos Racansky   THC   590
3 Gennadi Avramenko UKR   580

Team
1	China	**1759**	
2	Hungary	1759	
3	Germany	1758	

50M RUNNING TARGET MIXED
Individual
1	**Lubos Racansky**	**TCH**	**398**	
2	Gennadi Avramenko	UKR		395
3	Adam Aathoff	USA	394	

Team
1	**Czech Republic**	**1181**
2	Russia	1173
3	China	1166

10M RUNNING TARGET 30+30
Individual
1	**Manfred Kurzer**	**GER**	**676.3**
2	Krister Holmberg	FIN	676.0
3	Carlo Colombo	ITA	675.1

Team
1	**Czech Republic**	**1706**
2	United States	1697
3	Hungary	1690

10M RUNNING TARGET MIXED
Individual
1	**Roy Hill**	**USA**	**385**
2	Miroslav Janus	TCH	384
3	Krister Holmberg	FIN	381

Team
1	**Czech Republic**	**1139**
2	Russia	1138
3	United States	1131

Women

50M STANDARD RIFLE 3 X 20M
Individual
1	**Anna Malukhina**	**RUS**	**679.4**
2	Lessia Leskiv	UKR	676.0
3	Irina Gerasimeonok	RUS	673.9

Team
1	**Germany**	**1729**
2	Russia	1725
3	China	1720

50M STANDARD RIFLE 60 SHOTS PRONE
Individual
1	**Petra Horneber**	**GER**	**596**
2	Beth Herzman	USA	592
3	Nata Fernandez	ESP	592

Team
1	**Russia**	**1758**
2	Norway	1755
3	Ukraine	1754

10M AIR RIFLE
Individual
1	**Sonja Pfeilschifter**	**GER**	**496.9**
2	Christine Chuard	FRA	495.6
3	Renata Mauer	POL	495.5

Team
1	**Germany**	**1177**
2	Russia	1174
3	Korea	1174

25M SPORT PISTOL
Individual
1	**Boo Soon Hee**	**KOR**	**683.8**

2	Julita Macur	POL	679.5
3	Li Duihong	CHN	679.2

Team
1	**China**	**1734**
2	Korea	1732
3	Belarus	1723

10M AIR PISTOL
Individual
1	**Jasna Sekaric**	**IOP**	**484.6**
2	Margit Stein	GER	484.1
3	Galina Beliaeva	KZK	483.7

Team
1	**China**	**1144**
2	Bulgaria	1137
3	Germany	1135

10M RUNNING TARGET 20+20
Individual
1	**Kim Moon Sun**	**KOR**	**354**
2	Csilla Madari	HUN	352
3	Ann Sjokvist	FIN	347

Shotgun Events
Men

Fagnano, Italy
TRAP 125
Individual
1	**Dmitri Monakov**	**UKR**	**148,0**
2	Christopher Vicard	FRA	146,0
3	Lance Bade	USA	146,0

Team
1	**Italy**	**363**
2	Portugal	355
3	Germany	353

SKEET 125
Individual
1	**Bruno Rossetti**	**ITA**	**148,0**
2	Alexander Cherkasov	RUS	145,0
3	Ennio Falco	ITA	145,0

Team
1	**Italy**	**366**
2	Russia	354
3	Germany	353

DOUBLE TRAP 150
Individual
1	**Mark Russell**	**AUS**	**189,0**
2	Kevin Gill	GBR	189,0
3	Albano Pera	ITA	187,0

Team
1	**Great Britain**	**406**
2	Australia	406
3	Italy	406

Women
TRAP 125
Individual
1	**Paola Tattini**	**ITA**	**112**
2	Deena Julin	USA	112
3	Denise Morrison	USA	112

Team
1	**Italy**	**329**
2	United States	323
3	Germany	321

SKEET 125
Individual

1	Erdjanik Avetisian	ARM	116
2	Diana Igaly	HUN	113
3	Daniela Bolis	ITA	111

Team

1	Hungary	323
2	United States	321
3	italy	316

DOUBLE TRAP
Individual

1	Satu Pusila	FIN	140,0
2	Elena Shishirina	RUS	139,0
3	Svetlana Demina		139,0

Team

1	Russia	306
2	Finland	302
3	China	296

UIT World Cup
Ford Benning, Atlanta   Apr 20
Men's Air Rifle

1	V Becvar	TCH	697
5	N Wallace	GBR	692.8

Men's Air Pistol

1	B Kokorev	RUS	684.0
3	M Gault	GBR	680.4

Women's Air Rifle

1	G Beliaeva	KZK	486.8
26	C Page	GBR	371.0

NRA Imperial Meeting
Bisley   July 16-23
Queen's Prize

1	M Miller	Comber	291.34
2	J Jackman	O Johnians	291.29
3	A Ringer	Uppingham	289.35

Kolapore Cup

1	Great Britain	1,183.180
2	Canada	1,169.159
3	Jersey	1,153.131

Mackinnon Trophy

1	Scotland	1,146.115
2	England	1,140.114
3	Canada	1,127.101

Universities Long Range

1	Birmingham	382.38

Land Rover Discovery Challenge

1	R Vary	Camb Uni	73.7

St George's Challenge Vase

1	S Collings	Windsor	150.21

Prince of Wales' Prize

1	N Brasier	LMRA	25.5

European Women's Air Pistol Championships
Strasbourg   Mar 5

1	M Grozdeva	BUL	484.4
2	D Iorgeva	BUL	483.9
3	J Sekaric	IOP	482.6
8	C Page	GBR	477.5

Pistol 94
Bisley   May 26-30
MEN

Annual Challenge Trophy: C Valentine	142	
The Elite Trophy: A Hobdell		
The Dubai Cup: C Somers	175	
The Feinwerkbrau Trophy: A Lamont	568	
FIOCCHI Free Pistol Trophy: M Gault	570	
The McQueen Trophy: J H Rolfe	578	
The Hammerli Trophy: A Lamont	562	
The Buffalo Trophy: M Gault	587 *R*	
The Long John Cup: S Pengelly	581	
The D & P Guns Trophy: P Vanderhove	551	
The Burton Shield: M Gault 296		

WOMEN

The Hammerli Bell: T Roland	535
The Hapoel Trophy: T Roland	365

Clay Pigeon Shooting
WORLD CHAMPIONSHIPS
Montebello Club, nr Venice   June 16-19
Men: 1. Italy; 2. Italy; 3. Italy
Women: 1. Italy; 2. Great Britain (Dionne Rogers); 3. Italy
Team: 1. United States; 2. Italy; 3. France; 5. Great Britain

FITASC SPORTING EUROPEAN CHAMPIONSHIP
La Rabot, France   July 17
Men

1	George Digweed	185
2	Barry Simpson	184
3	Stuart Clarke	182

Women

1	Denise Eyre	GBR	163
2	V Girardet	FRA	153
3	C Van	USA	153

Team

1	France
2	Great Britain
3	Belgium

ROLEX BRITISH GRAND PRIX OLYMPIC TRAP
North Wales SS   Aug 11-13
Men

1	Giovanni Pellielo	ITA	218
2	Peter Boden	GBR	215+1*
3	Vittorio Tailoa	ITA	215+0*

Women

1	Anita North	GBR	125
2	Mary Rowley	GBR	120
3	Micky Evans	GBR	119

BRITISH OPEN SPORTING CHAMPIONSHIP
West Midlands   Aug 10-14
High Gun: George Digweed   97*
Runner-up: C Bloxham   97
* Shoot-off

BRITISH OPEN SKEET CHAMPIONSHIP
Lakenheath   Aug 4-7

1	A Coy	100/100*

ABT BRITISH OPEN CHAMPIONSHIP
Bywell SG   June 4-5

1	Ian Peel	220

Skiing

Ulrike Maier's death cast a long shadow over the season. The Austrian died when she crashed at Garmisch on January 29th, in a downhill race, an event she did not usually compete in. The 28-year-old mother was the first woman to be killed in a World Cup race. Her death advanced the case against the Olympic course at Kvitfjell, deemed by many to be too quick for women skiers. However, the Games went ahead without problems and though there were a high number of fallers in the women's downhill, there were no serious injuries.

Kjetil Andre Aamodt won the overall men's World Cup and was favoured for as many as four gold medals in Lillehammer *(for results, see Winter Olympic section)*, but the Norwegian skier had to make do with a couple of silvers and a bronze, and the unlikely skiing hero of the Games was Germany's Markus Wasmeier, who had never won a World Cup ski in his life, but took gold in the super-G and the giant slalom. In the women's events, Vreni Scheider bowed out with the overall World Cup title and an Olympic gold medal.

Graham Bell enjoyed the highest British placing at Kitzbuhel for many a year, when he placed 12th in the downhill, but there was little else to warm British hearts. Emma Carrick-Anderson, in whom much hope for the future resides, had a dreadful year failing to complete either the slalom or the giant slalom in both the Olympic Games and the World Junior Championships.

Men's Downhill

VAL GARDENA, ITALY
Dec 17   Dist 3446m/Drop 839m   Snow hard

1	Markus Foser	LIE	2:08.90
21	Martin Bell	GBR	2:10.40
35	Graham Bell	GBR	2:10.87

Dec 18

1	Patrick Ortlieb	AUT	2:04.14
38	Graham Bell	GBR	2:06.49
45	Martin Bell	GBR	2:06.83

BORMIO-VATELLINA, ITALY
Dec 29   Dist 3582m/Drop 1010m   Snow hard

1	Hennes Trinkl	AUT	1:55.76
26	Martin Bell	GBR	1:58.05
38	Graham Bell	GBR	1:59.09
dns	Roger Walker	GBR	

SAALBACH-HINTERGLEMM, AUSTRIA
Jan 6   Dist 1515m/Drop 485m   Snow hard

1	Ed Podivinsky	CAN	2:09.83
22	Martin Bell	GBR	2:11.28
dnq	Graham Bell	GBR	

KITZBUHEL, AUSTRIA
Jan 15   Dist 3351m/Drop 860m

1	Patrick Ortlieb	AUT	2:00.12
12	Graham Bell	GBR	2:01.79
51	Martin Bell	GBR	2:05.11

WENGEN, SWITZERLAND
Jan 22   Dist 4230m/Drop 1028m   Snow hard

1	William Besse	SUI	2:28.88
36	Graham Bell	GBR	2:32.01
54	Martin Bell	GBR	2:34.46

CHAMONIX, FRANCE
Jan 29   Dist 3343m/Drop 870m   Snow Hard

1	Kjetil Andre Aamodt	NOR	1:58.35
37	Martin Bell	GBR	2:01.39
53	Graham Bell	GBR	2:02.13

ASPEN, USA
Mar 4   Dist 3005m/Drop 792m   Snow hard

1	Hannes Trinkl	AUT	1:38.95
46	Graham Bell	GBR	1:41.16
48	Martin Bell	GBR	1:41.54
58	Roger Walker	GBR	1:43.67
60	Andrew Freshwater	GBR	1:44.71

Mar 5

1	Cary Mullen	CAN	1:38.21
39	Graham Bell	GBR	1:40.87
57	Martin Bell	GBR	1:41.97
61	Roger Walker	GBR	1:42.84
62	Andrew Freshwater	GBR	1:43.65

WHISTLER MOUNTAIN, CANADA
Mar 12   Dist 3807m/Drop 1000m   Snow spring

1	Atle Skaardal	NOR	2:11.30
50	Graham Bell	GBR	2:15.03
59	Martin Bell	GBR	2:15.64
68	Andrew Freshwater	GBR	2:18.43
69	Roger Walker	GBR	2:19.01

VAIL, USA
Mar 16   Dist 2692m/Drop 667m   Snow hard

1	William Besse	SUI	1:38.17

FINAL DOWNHILL STANDINGS

1	Marc Girardelli	LUX	556
2	Hannes Trinkl	AUT	536
3	Patrick Ortlieb	AUT	488
4	Cary Mullen	CAN	461

Men's Slalom

PARK CITY, USA
Nov 28   Drop 180m   Snow hard
1 **Thomas Stangassinger** AUT   **1:35.54**
STONEHAM, CANADA
Dec 5   Drop 220m   Snow wet
1 **Alberto Tomba**   ITA   **1:47.57**
SESTRIERE, ITALY
Dec 14   Drop 210m   Snow hard
1 Alberto Tomba   ITA   1:58.38
MADONNA DI CAMPIGLIO, ITALY
Dec 20   Drop 180m   Snow hard
1 **Jure Kosir**   SLO   **1:34.69**
dnf William Gaylord   GBR
KRANJSKA GORA, SLOVENIA
Jan 9   Drop 199m   Snow hard
1 **Finn Chr. Jagge**   NOR   **1:43.46**
KITZBÜHEL, AUSTRIA
Jan 16   Drop 180m   Snow hard
1 **Thomas Stangassinger** AUT   **1:37.85**
CHAMONIX, FRANCE
Jan 30   Drop 203m   Snow hard
1 **Alberto Tomba**   ITA   **2:01.37**
dns William Gaylord   GBR
dns Spencer Pession   GBR
GARMISCH, GERMANY
Feb 6   Drop 200m   Snow hard
1 **Alberto Tomba**   ITA   **1.32.47**
ASPEN, USA
Mar 6   Drop 336m   Snow hard
1 **Fredrik Nyberg**   SWE   **1.51.26**

FINAL SLALOM STANDINGS
1 **Alberto Tomba**   ITA   **540**
2 Thomas Stangassinger   AUT   452
3 Jure Kosir   SLO   421
4 Finn Chr. Jagge   NOR   389

Men's Giant Slalom

SÖLDEN, AUSTRIA
Oct 30   Drop 350m   Snow hard
1 **Franck Piccard**   FRA   **1:56.32**
PARK CITY, USA
Nov 27   Drop 366m   Snow hard
1 **Günther Mader**   AUT   **2:00.61**
VAL D'ISERE, FRANCE
Dec 13   Drop 420m   Snow hard
1 **Christian Mayer**   AUT   **2:29.96**
ALTA BADIA, ITALY
Dec 19   Drop 448m   Snow hard
1 **Steve Locher**   SUI   **2:37.54**
KRANJSKA GORA, SLOVENIA
Jan 8   Drop 394m   Snow hard
1 **Fredrik Nyberg**   SWE   **2:09.81**
HINTERSTODER, AUSTRIA
Jan 11   Drop 440m   Snow hard
1 **Kjetil Andre Aamodt** NOR   **2:49.63**
CRANS MONTANA, SWITZERLAND
Jan 18   Drop 390m   Snow hard
1 **Jan Einar Thorsen**   NOR   **2:32.83**
ASPEN, USA
Mar 6   Drop 336m   Snow hard
1 **Fredrik Nyberg**   SWE   **1:51.26**

VAIL, USA
Mar 19   Drop 375m   Snow hard
1 **Kjetil Andre Aamodt** NOR   **2:25.62**

FINAL GIANT SLALOM STANDINGS
1 **Christian Mayer**   AUT   **496**
2 Kjetil Andre Aamodt   NOR   494
3 Franck Piccard   FRA   414
4 Fredrik Nyberg   SWE   384

Men's Super G

VAL D'ISERE, FRANCE
Dec 12   Dist 2200m/Drop620m   Snow hard
1 **Günther Mader**   AUT   **1:28.25**
49 Martin Bell   GBR   1:30.41
59 Graham Bell   GBR   1:30.89
LECH, AUSTRIA
Dec 22   Dist 1700m/Drop 460m   Snow hard
1 **Hannes Trinkl**   AUT   **1:04.42**
WENGEN, SWITZERLAND
Jan 23   Dist 2880m/Drop 683m   Snow hard
1 **Marc Girardelli**   LUX   **1:41.30**
58 Martin Bell   GBR   1:45.93
59 Graham Bell   GBR   1:46.05
WHISTLER MOUNTAIN, CAN
Mar 13   Dist 2455m/Drop 662m   Snow Spring
1 **Tommy Moe**   USA   **1:31.22**
58 Martin Bell   GBR   1:35.44
64 Graham Bell   GBR   1:36.45
VAIL, USA,
Mar 17   Dist 1863m/Drop 478m Snow wet
1 **Jan Einar Thorsen**   NOR   **1:15.82**

FINAL SUPER G STANDINGS
1 **Jan Einar Thorsen**   NOR   **280**
2 Marc Girardelli   LUX   275
3 Tommy Moe   USA   242
4 Kjetil Andre Aamodt   NOR   202

Women's Downhill

TIGNES, FRANCE
Dec 4   Dist 1960m/Drop 575m   Snow hard
1 **Kate Pace**   CAN   **1:16.56**
ST. ANTON, AUSTRIA
Dec 18   Dist m/Drop 710m   Snow hard
1 **Anja Haas**   AUT   **2:19.25**
CORTINA, ITALY
Jan 14   Dist 2600m/Drop 710m   Snow hard
1 **Katja Seizinger**   GER   **1:25.72**
GARMISCH, GERMANY
Jan 29   Dist 2865m/Drop 800m   Snow hard
1 **Isolde Kostner**   ITA   **1:44.04**
SIERRA NEVADA, SPAIN
Feb 2   Dist 3532m/Drop 800m   Snow hard
1 **Hilary Lindh**   USA   **2:04.21**
WHISTLER MOUNTAIN, CANADA
Mar 6   Dist 2801m/Drop 762m   Snow hard
1 **Katya Seizinger**   GER   **1:50.96**
VAIL, USA
Mar 16   Dist 2726m/Drop 667m   Snow hard
1 **Katja Seizinger**   GER   **1:47.08**

FINAL DOWNHILL STANDINGS

1	Katja Seizinger	GER	482
2	Kate Pace	CAN	398
3	Melanie Suchet	FRA	258
4	Isolde Kostner	ITA	230

Women's Slalom

ST CATERINA, ITALY
Nov 28   Drop 160m   Snow hard
1 **Vreni Schneider** SUI 1:38.93
dnf Claire De Pourtales GBR
dnf E Carrick-Anderson GBR

VEYSONNAZ, SWITZERLAND
Dec 12   Drop 200m   Snow hard
1 **Pernilla Wiberg** SWE 1:26.16

ST ANTON, AUSTRIA
Dec 19   Drop 180m   Snow hard
1 **Vreni Schneider** SUI 1:47.84
dnf Claire De Pourtales GBR
dnf E Carrick-Anderson GBR

MORZINE, FRANCE
Jan 6   Drop 200m   Neige, Humide
1 **Pernilla Wiberg** SWE 1:49.39

ALTENMARKT, AUSTRIA
Jan 9   Drop 180m   Snow Hard
1 **Vreni Schneider** SUI 1:36.41
dnf E Carrick-Anderson GBR
   Clair De Pourtales disqualified

MARIBOR, SLOVENIA
Jan 22   Drop 191m   Snow Hard
1 **Urska Hrovat** SLO 1:55.19
dnf E Carrick-Anderson GBR
dnf Claire De Pourtales GBR

MARIBOR, SLOVENIA
Jan 23   Drop 191m   Snow Hard
1 **Vreni Schneider** SUI 1:47.94
dnf E Carrick-Anderson GBR
dnf Claire De Pourtales GBR

SIERRA NEVADA, SPAIN
Feb 5   Drop 200m   Snow Hard
1 **Vreni Schneider** SUI 1:41.30

MAMMOTH MOUNTAIN, USA
Mar 10   Drop 177m   Snow Hard
1 **Vreni Schneider** SUI 1:18.52

VAIL, USA
Mar 20   Drop 164m   Snow Wet
1 **Vreni Schneider** SUI 1:35.91

FINAL SLALOM STANDINGS

1	Vreni Schneider	SUI	860
2	Pernilla Wiberg	SWE	620
3	Urska Hrovat	SLO	386
4	Martina Ertl	GER	312

Women's Giant Slalom

SÖLDEN, AUSTRIA
Oct 31   Drop 350m   Snow hard
1 **Anita Wachter** AUT 2:14.57

ST CATERINA, ITALY
Nov 26   Drop 343m   Snow hard
1 **Anita Wachter** AUT 2:17.31

ST CATERINA, ITALY
Nov 27   Drop 343m   Snow hard
1 **Ulrike Maier** AUT 2:20.84

TIGNES, FRANCE
Dec 5   Drop 355m   Snow hard
1 **Deborah Compagnoni** ITA 2:15.43

VEYSONNAZ, SWITZERLAND
Dec 11   Drop 400m   Snow hard
1 **Deborah Compagnoni** ITA 2:29.86

MORZINE, FRANCE
Jan 5   Drop 360m   Snow wet
1 **Deborah Compagnoni** ITA 2:14.47

CORTINA, ITALY
Jan 16   Drop 400m   Snow hard
1 **Anita Wachter** AUT 2:38.80

MARIBOR, SLOVENIA
Jan 21   Drop 385m   Snow hard
1 **Ulrike Maier** AUT 2:28.83

VAIL, USA
Mar 19   Drop 341m   Snow hard
1 **Martina Ertl** GER 2:18.54

FINAL GIANT SLALOM STANDINGS

1	Anita Wachter	AUT	635
2	Vreni Schneider	SUI	516
3	Deborah Compagnoni	ITA	515
4	Ulrike Maier	AUT	432

Women's Super G

FLACHAU, AUSTRIA
Dec 22   Drop 480m/Distance 1513m   Snow hard
1 **Katja Koren** SLO 1:15.62

CORTINA, ITALY
Jan 15   Drop 518m/Distance 1725m   Snow hard
1 **Katja Seizinger** GER 1:11.96

CORTINA, ITALY
Jan 17   Drop 518m/Distance 1725m   Snow hard
1 **Alenka Dovzan** SLO 1:20.64
1 **Pernilla Wiberg** SWE 1:20.64

SIERRA NEVADA, SPAIN
Feb 6   Drop 600m/Distance 2320m   Snow hard
1 **Hilde Gerg** GER 1:47.80

MAMMOTH MOUNTAIN, USA
Mar 9   Drop 536m/Distance 2030m   Snow hard
1 **Katja Seizinger** GER 1:20.07

VAIL, USA
Mar 17   Drop 478m/Distance 1822m   Snow hard
1 **Diann Roffe** USA 1:24.93

FINAL SUPER `G' STANDINGS

1	Katja Seizinger	GER	416
2	Bibiana Perez	ITA	266
3	Hilde Gerg	GER	200
4	Alenka Dovzan	SLO	198

WORLD CUP OVERALL

Men

1	Kjetil Andre Aamodt	NOR	1392
2	Marc Girardelli	LUX	1007
3	Alberto Tomba	ITA	822
4	Günther Mader	AUT	820
5	Hannes Trinkl	AUT	701
6	Jan Einer Thorsen	NOR	657
7	Lasse Kjus	NOR	651
8	Tommy Moe	USA	650
9	Atle Skaardal	NOR	641
10	Cary Mullen	CAN	535

Women

1	Vreni Schneider	SUI	1656
2	Pernilla Wiberg	SWE	1343
3	Katja Seizinger	GER	1195
4	Anita Wachter	AUT	1057
5	Martina Ertl	GER	943
6	Deborah Compagnoni	ITA	841
7	Ulrike Maier	AUT	711
8	Bibiana Perez	ITA	667
9	Marianne Kjoerstad	NOR	570
10	Urska Hrovat	SLO	523

World Junior Championships

Lake Placid, USA   Mar 5-15

MEN

Downhill

1	Kevin Wert	CAN
20	David Cook	GBR

Super G

1	Benjamin Melquoin	FRA
50	Tim Fawke	GBR
dnf	David Cook	GBR

Giant Slalom

1	Stefan Stankalla	GER
33	Tim Fawke	GBR
dnf	David Cook	GBR

Slalom

1	Benjamin Covili	FRA
dnf	Tim Fawke	GBR

WOMEN

Giant Slalom

1	Melanie Turgeon	CAN
dnf	Emma C-Anderson	GBR
dnf	Shona Robertson	GBR

Slalom

1	Laurent Piquenout	FRA
dnf	Emma C-Anderson	GBR
dnf	Shona Robertson	GBR

British Ski Championships

Tignes, France   Jan 22-29

MEN

Slalom

1	Bill Gaylord	1:23.89
2	Alain Baxter	1:24.56
3	Sean Langmuir	1:25.65

Giant Slalom

1	Alain Baxter	1:55.14
2	Spenser Pession	1:55.25
3	Mark Reilly	1:59.68

Combined Championship (Fedden Cup)

1	Alain Baxter

WOMEN

Slalom

1	Emma C-Anderson	1:17.36
2	Kelly Morris	1:25.16
3	Anna Lees Jones	1:25.19

Giant Slalom

1	Lesley McKenna	2:01.37
2	Marjory Adam	2:01.50
3	Sophie Lockyer	2:02.11

Combined Championship (Lillywhite Gretton Trophy)

1	Kelly Morris

Freestyle World Cup

WOMEN

Ballet

1	Ellen Breen	USA	792
2	Oksana Kutschenko	RUS	764
3	Cathy Fechoz	FRA	764
12	Vicki Simpson	GBR	476

Mogul

1	Donna Weinbrecht	USA	800
2	Stine Lise Hattestad	NOR	756
3	Candice Gilg	FRA	704
36	Jilly Curry	GBR	68

Aerial

1	Lina Tcherjazova	UZB	792
2	Colette Brand	SUI	720
3	Nikki Stone	USA	688
20	Jilly Curry	GBR	324

Combined

1	Maja Schmid	SUI	684
2	Katherine Kubenk	CAN	680
3	Natalia Orekhova	RUS	672

OVERALL

1	Kristean Porter	USA	156.00
2	Natalia Orekhova	RUS	154.50
3	Katherina Kubenk	CAN	140.00
32	Vicki Simpson	GBR	59.50
41	Jilly Curry	GBR	49.00

MEN

Ballet

1	Fabrice Becker	FRA	788
2	Heini Baumgartner	SUI	768
3	Rune Kristiansen	NOR	760
30	Martin Fielden	GBR	92

Mogul

1	Edgar Grospiron	FRA	780
2	Sergei Shupletsov	RUS	748
3	Jean Luc Brassard	CAN	744
44	Hugh Hutchison	GBR	68

Aerial

1	Phillippe Laroche	CAN	744
2	Lloyd Langlois	CAN	680
3	Nicolas Fontaine	CAN	672

Combined

1	David Belhumeur	CAN	588
2	Sergei Shupletsov	RUS	580
3	Darcy Downs	CAN	568

OVERALL

1	Sergei Shupletsov	RUS	157.50
2	David Belhumeur	CAN	125.50
3	Trace Worthington	USA	116.00
47	Richard Cobbing	GBR	48.00

British Championships

MEN
Ballet

1 Mark Hussey	ENG	17.85

Moguls

1 Nathan Gardner	ENG	25.56

Aerials

1 Richard Cobbing	ENG	160.73

Combined

1 Robin Bell	SCO	27.13

WOMEN
Ballet

1 Vicki Simpson	ENG	21.00

Moguls

1 Kim Smith	ENG	17.49

Aerials

1 Kathryn Spellerberg	ENG	82.03

Combined

1 Gia Benson	ENG	30.0

World Cup Ski Jumping

PLANICA, SLOVAKIA
Dec 11

1	Epsen Bredesen	NOR	100
2	Takanobu Okabe	JPN	80
3	Andreas Goldberger	AUT	60

Dec 12

1	Jens Weissflog	GER	100
2	Andreas Goldberger	AUT	80
3	Espen Bredesen	NOR	60

PREDAZZO, ITALY
Dec 14

1	Jens Weissflog	GER	100
2	Espen Bredesen	NOR	80
3	Andreas Goldberger	AUT	60

COURCHEVEL, FRANCE
Dec 17

1	Andreas Goldberger	AUT	100
2	Jinya Nishikata	JPN	80
3	Jaroslav Sakala	CZE	60

ENGELBERG, SWITZERLAND
Dec 19

1	Janne Ahonen	FIN	100
2	Sylvain Freiholz	SUI	80
3	Bjoern Myrbakken	NOR	60

OBERSDORF, GERMANY
Dec 31

1	Jens Weissflog	GER	100
2	Espen Bredesen	NOR	80
3	Andreas Goldberger	AUT	60

GARMISCH-PARTENKIRCHEN, GERMANY
Jan 1

1	Espen Bredesen	NOR	100
2	Jens Weissflog	GER	80
3	Takanobu Okabe	JPN	60

INNSBRUCK, AUSTRIA
Jan 4

1	Andreas Goldberger	AUT	100
2	Jens Weissflog	GER	80
3	Noriaki Kasai	JPN	60

BISCHOFSHOFEN, AUSTRIA
Jan 6

1	Espen Bredesen	NOR	100
2	Noriaki Kasai	JPN	80
3	Jens Weissflog	GER	80

MURAU, AUSTRIA
Jan 8

1	Noriaki Kasai	JPN	100
2	Espen Bredesen	NOR	80
3	Dieter Thoma	GER	60

LIBEREC, CZECH REPUBLIC
Jan 15

1	Espen Bredesen	NOR	100
2	Jaroslav Sakala	CZE	80
3	Roberto Cecon	ITA	60

Jan 16

1	Jaroslav Sakala	CZE	100
2	Espen Bredesen	NOR	80
3	Lasse Ottesen	NOR	60

SAPPORO, JAPAN
Jan 22

1	Jens Weissflog	GER	100
2	Andreas Goldberger	AUT	80
3	Jiri Parma	CZE	60

Jan 23

1	Jens Weissflog	GER	100
2	Espen Bredesen	NOR	80
3	Jinya Nishikata	JPN	60

LAHTI, FINLAND
Mar 5

1	Jens Weissflog	GER	100
2	Christain Moser	AUT	80
3	Noriaki Kasai	JPN	60

ORNSKOLDSVIK, SWEDEN
Mar 9

1	Roberto Cecon	ITA	100
2	Kenji Suda	JPN	80
3	Jens Weissflog	GER	60

PLANICA, SLOVENIA
Mar 20

1	Jaroslav Sakala	CZE	100
2	Espen Bredesen	NOR	80
3	Roberto Cecon	ITA	60

THUNDER BAY, CANADA
Mar 26

1	Gard Siegmund	GER	100
2	Andreas Goldberger	AUT	80
3	Roberto Cecon	ITA	60

May 27

1	Jens Weissflog	GER	100
2	Takanobu Okabe	JPN	80
3	Espen Bredesen	NOR	60

FINAL STANDINGS

1	Espen Bredesen	NOR	1203
2	Jens Weissflog	GER	1110
3	Andreas Goldberger	AUT	927
4	Jaroslav Sakala	CZE	751
5	Roberto Cecon	ITA	710
6	Noriaki Kasai	JPN	562

Cross CountryWorld Cup

Santa Caterina, Italy   Dec 11-12
Men's 30km (Classic)
1 Vladimir Smirnov (KAZ)   1:22:50.9
Women's 5km (Classic)
1 Elena Vaelbe (RUS)   14:40.2
Women's Relay 4 x 5km (Classic)
1 Russia   1:00:21.2

Davos, Switzerland   Dec 18-19
Men's 15km (Free)
1 Bjorn Daehlie (NOR)   36:28.8
Men's Relay 4 x 10km (Free)
1 Norway   1:42:35.2
Women's 10km (Free)
1 Elena Vaelbe (RUS)   26:11.5

Toblach, Italy   Dec 21-22
Men's 10km (Classic)
1 Vladimir Smirnov (KZK)   24:02.8
Men's 15km (Pursuit)
1 Vladimir Smirnov (KZK)   59:04.9
Women's 15km (Classic)
1 Manuela Di Centa (ITA)   44:18.6
Women's Relay 4x5km (Classic)
1 Russia   49:49.0

Kavgolovo, Russia Jan 8-9
Men's 15km (Classic)
1 Vladimir Smirnov (KZK)   41:54.4
Women's 10km (Classic)
1 Lubov Egorova (RUS)   30:29.3

Holmenkollen, Norway Jan 15-16
Men's 15km (Free)
1 Vladimir Smirnov (KZK)   36:44.7
Men's Relay 4x10km (Free)
1 Finland   1:31:56.2
Women's 15km (Free)
1 Lubov Egorova (RUS)   41:16.2
Women's Relay 4x5km (Classic)
1 Russia   50:39.3

Lillehammer   Feb 13-27
X country events count towards World Cup standings.
Results in Winter Olympics Section

Lahti, Finland   Mar 4-6
Men's 15km (Free)
1 Vladimir Smirnov (KZK)   36:44.2
Men's Relay 4x10km (Classic)
1 Finland   1:47:15.7
Women's 30km (Free)
1 Manuela Di Centa (ITA)   1:22:50.6
Women's Relay 4x5km (Classic)
1 Norway   59:46.5

Falun, Sweden   Mar 12-13
Men's 30km (Classic)
1 Harri Kirvesniemi (FIN)   1:22:44.3
Men's Relay 4x10km (Free)
1 Norway   1:32:26.4
Women's 10km (Free)
1 Manuela Di Centa (ITA)   28:31.6
Women's Relay 4x5km (Classic)
1 Russia   49:25.0

Thunder Bay, Canada   Mar 19-20
Men's 50km (Free)
1 Alexj Prokurorov (RUS)   1:54:46.3
Men's Relay 4x10km (Free)
1 Norway   1:35:00.7
Women's 5km (Classic)
1 Larisa Lazhutina (RUS)   13:11.0
Women's 10km (Free)
1 Manuela Di Centa (ITA)   38:18.3

FINAL STANDINGS
Men (Individual)
1 Vladimir Smirnov (KZK)   830
2 Bjorn Daehlie (NOR)   680
Men (Team)
1 Norway   3451
23 Great Britain   26
Women (Individual)
1 Manuela Di Centa (ITA)   790
2 Lyubov Egorova (RUS)   740
Women's (Team)
1 Russia   4533
Combined Team
1 Norway   6025

British Nordic & Biathlon Championships

Les Saisies, France   Jan 19-27
MEN'S BIATHLON
20km Individual
1 Jason Sklenar   1:22:50
2 David Rodgers   1:23:56
3 Ceri Thomas   1:24:33
10km Sprint
1 Paul Ryan   30:43.00
2 Clive Brown   33:55.60
3 Ceri Thomas   33:58.90
MEN'S CROSS-COUNTRY
15km Classical
1 David Belam   29:19.2
2 Glen Scott   31:02.8
3 John Read   31:32.0
10km Free
1 David Belam   26:50.1
2 David Brown   29:04.2
3 Ed Nicoll   29:35.0
WOMEN'S BIATHLON
15km Individual
1 Julie Farmer   1:13:38
2 Tina Edwards   1:32:46
3 Nicky George   1:43:17
7.5km Sprint
1 Julie Farmer   31:37.0
2 Christina Sullivan   35:37.3
3 Nicky George   35:37.4
WOMEN'S CROSS-COUNTRY
15km Classical
1 Julie Farmer   39:30.5
2 Nicky George   42:05.8
3 Tina Edwards   42:13.2
10km Free
1 Julie Farmer   35:23.4
2 Tina Edwards   40:16.0
3 Nicky George   43:09.0

Snooker

'White signs one of the biggest contracts in snooker history', ran the story in September when Jimmy White agreed a new five year deal worth £2m to join Steve Davis and Ronnie O'Sullivan in the Barry Hearn stable. It will ensure that White is kept in the manner to which he has become accustomed and it makes the 120 hours community service (for drink-driving) a bit more bearable, but it won't guarantee him the one title that has eluded him almost willfully and eluded him again this year. White has made the final on six occasions, but has yet to claim the title, beaten by Steve Davis in 1984, John Parrott in 1991 and four times by Stephen Hendry - 1990, 1992, 1993 & 1994.

At least he can claim he is getting better. Last year against Hendry, he was trounced 18 frames to 5. This year it went to the wire; 18-17 and a missed black by White in that last frame that would have given him the title. Hendry, who had incurred a hairline fracture in his left elbow during the competition admitted that his legs went to jelly during the last frame. It wasn't quite Taylor against Davis in 1985, but it was superb snooker.

The extremes occurred on Sunday night as Hendry took six of the first seven frames which looked impressive until White took seven in a row. Overnight, White had inched a 9-7 lead. On the final day, it was nip and tuck all the way. At no point in the 19 frames that were played on Monday did either player assume control. Hendry was two frames ahead at 16-14, but White drew level at 16 frames each, winning the 32nd frame on the black. When Hendry then slipped a frame ahead, White made a 75 clearance to take the match to the 35th and last frame. The television audience grew as the match progressed and, while the average was not especially high, the viewing figure for the final frame was 13.4 million viewers, which compares favourably with the 18 million who watched Taylor beat Davis nine years ago.

While Hendry's victory reaffirmed him as the outstanding player of his generation, there is little doubt who leads the next generation. The world ranking for the end of the 1992-3 season had Ronnie O'Sullivan at 57th place. Still only 18, O'Sullivan won both the UK title and the British Open in the spring of 1994 and moved into ninth place on the world list. There were leaps and bounds too for Stephen Lee, who came from nowhere into 40th, and Dave Harrold who mover from 50th to 19th, but had the misfortune to draw Stephen Hendry in the World Championship quarter-final and was roundly trounced 13-2. Peter Ebdon is hardly a generation younger than Hendry - there's just two years between them - but it was Ebdon's turn to stake a claim. The Londoner won his first ranking tournament at Reading when he took the Skoda Grand prix title beating Ken Doherty in the final 9-5, but more significantly toppling Hendry along the way.

Off the table, Alan McManus parted company with his manager, Willie Thorne parted company with his money (or was that last year?) and Jimmy White admitted he was, "bang out of order" when he drove while drunk. But the quote of the year goes to *Today* astrologist Penny Thornton, on her friendship with Alex Higgins. "We are friends," acknowledged Thornton, "But it is a friendship born out of astrological interest". Well, as Higgins *climbed* the ranking list 13 places in 1994, it must be working.

Embassy World Championship

Crucible Theatre, Sheffield   *April 16 - May 2*

ROUND 9		ROUND 10		ROUND 11	Q/F	S/F

ROUND 9		ROUND 10		ROUND 11		Q/F		S/F	
Mark Bennett	7	Stephen Hendry	10						
Surinder Gill	10	Surinder Gill	1	Stephen Hendry	13				
				Dave Harold	2				
Alain Robidoux	8	David Roe	8			Stephen Hendry	13		
Dave Harold	10	Dave Harold	10			Nigel Bond	8		
Tony Drago	5	Nigel Bond	10						
Cliff Thorburn	10	Cliff Thorburn	9	Nigel Bond	13				
				Terry Griffiths	8				
Jason Ferguson	9	Terry Griffiths	10					Stephen Hendry	16
Mark Davis	10	Mark Davis	7					Steve Davis	9
Peter Ebdon	10	James Wattana	10						
Stefan Mazrocis	4	Peter Ebdon	6	James Wattana	13				
				Brian Morgan	9				
Dean Reynolds	8	Martin Clark	9			James Wattana	9		
Brian Morgan	10	Brian Morgan	10			Steve Davis	13		
Doug Mountjoy	9	Steve James	10						
Les Dodd	10	Les Dodd	9	Steve James	3				
				Steve Davis	13				
Dene O'Kane	10	Steve Davis	10						
Stephen Lee	6	Dene O'Kane	3						
Joe Swail	4	Jimmy White	10						
Billy Snaddon	10	Billy Snaddon	6	Jimmy White	13				
				Neal Foulds	10				
Joe Johnson	9	Neal Foulds	10			Jimmy White	13		
Anthony Davies	10	Anthony Davies	7			Ken Doherty	10		
Tony Knowles	9	Ken Doherty	10						
Alex Higgins	10	Alex Higgins	6	Ken Doherty	13				
				Alan McManus	11				
Mick Price	4	Alan McManus	10					Jimmy White	16
Fergal O'Brien	10	Fergal O'Brien	7					Darren Morgan	8
Mark Johnston-A	9	Willie Thorne	10						
Gary Ponting	10	Gary Ponting	2	Willie Thorne	12				
				Darren Morgan	13				
Gary Wilkinson	9	Darren Morgan	10			Darren Morgan	13		
Mark A King	10	Mark A King	5			John Parrott	11		
Tony Jones	8	Dennis Taylor	6						
Ronnie O'Sullivan	10	Ronnie O'Sullivan	10	Ronnie O'Sullivan	3				
				John Parrott	13				
Mike Hallett	5	John Parrott	10						
Drew Henry	10	Drew Henry	9						

Stephen Hendry 18
Jimmy White 17

Major Tournaments

Date	Tournament	Venue	Status	Final (winner bold)	S/Finalists	Prize Money
Sep 22 -26	Regal Masters	Motherwell	Invitation	**Ken Doherty** Alan McManus		£140,000
Oct 1 -8	Dubai Duty Free	Al Nasr Sports Hall	Ranking	**Stephen Hendry** Steve Davis	R O'Sullivan Alan McManus	£375,000
Oct 18 -31	New Skoda Grand Prix	The Hexagon Reading	Ranking	**Peter Ebdon** Ken Doherty	John Parrott Steve Davis	£224,000
Nov 12 -28	Royal Liver Ass. UK Championship	Guild Hall Preston	Ranking	**Ronnie O'Sullivan** Stephen Hendry	Darren Morgan John Parrott	£325,000
Dec 13 -19	Humo European Open	Sporthal Arena Antwerp	Ranking	**Stephen Hendry** Ronnie O'Sullivan	John Parrott Jimmy White	£150,000
Jan 3- Feb 5	Regal Welsh Open	Newport Centre	Ranking	**Steve Davis** Alan McManus	James Wattana Peter Ebdon	£150,000
Feb 6 -13	Benson & Hedges Masters	Wembley CC	Invitation	**Alan McManus** Stephen Hendry	Ken Doherty James Wattana	£415,000
Feb 13 -19	International Open	Bournemouth Intern Centre	Ranking	**John Parrott** James Wattana	Jimmy White Alan McManus	£150,000
Mar 4 -12	Kloster Thailand Open	Bangkok	Ranking	**James Wattana** Steve Davis	Jimmy White Alan McManus	£180,000
Mar 22 -27	Benson & Hedges Irish Masters	Goffs Co. Kildare	Invitation	**Steve Davis** Alan McManus	Jimmy White Fergal O'Brien	IR190,000
Mar 31 Apr 7	British Open	Pavilions Plymouth	Ranking	**Ronnie O'Sullivan** James Wattana	Stephen Hendry Steve Davis	£200,000
Apr 16 May 2	Embassy World Championship	Crucible Sheffield	Major Ranking	**Stephen Hendry** Jimmy White	Steve Davis Darren Morgan	£1,068,000
Until May 29	European League	Various	Invitation	**Stephen Hendry** won play off final John Parrott		

Money Winners
Top 40 1993-4

1	Stephen Hendry	£419,770		21	Fergal O'Brien	£29,763
2	Alan McManus	£276,571		22	Gary Wilkinson	£28,660
3	Steve Davis	£238,983		23	Tony Knowles	£28,025
4	Jimmy White	£200,057		24	Joe Swail	£27,000
5	Ronnie O'Sullivan	£179,500		25	Dene O'Kane	£24,725
6	James Wattana	£170,645		26	Anthony Hamilton	£24,049
7	Ken Doherty	£160,619		27	Mike Hallett	£23,170
8	John Parrott	£159,645		28	Brian Morgan	£23,950
9	Peter Ebdon	£118,849		29	Andy Hicks	£22,715
10	Darren Morgan	£105,525		30	Doug Mountjoy	£21,085
11	Nigel Bond	£83,990		31	Alain Robidoux	£19.815
12	Neal Foulds	£69,290		32	Drew Henry	£19,890
13	Willie Thorne	£64,589		33	Stephen Lee	£19,725
14	Terry Griffiths	£60,429		34	Dean Reynolds	£19,565
15	Steve James	£53,990		35	Mick Price	£19,305
16	Dennis Taylor	£48,720		36	Jason Ferguson	£19,135
17	Martin Clark	£44,605		37	Tony Jones	£18,975
18	David Roo	£40,175		38	Billy Snaddon	£18,185
19	Dave Harold	£35,572		39	Mark Bennett	£16,830
20	Tony Drago	£31,735		40	John Higgins	£16,685

World Ranking List 1994

1	(1)	Stephen Hendry	53300.00	55	(36)	Paul J Davies	16970.00
2	(4)	Steve Davis	52300.00	56	(40)	Jim Wych	16800.00
3	(5)	James Wattana	49000.00	57	(33)	Silvino Francisco	16560.00
4	(3)	Jimmy White	49000.00	58	(-)	Mark J Williams	16376.00
5	(2)	John Parrott	48300.00	59	(74)	Paul McPhillips	15935.00
6	(6)	Alan McManus	46750.00	60	(34)	Eddie Charlton	15890.00
7	(11)	Ken Doherty	42020.00	61	(38)	Peter Francisco	15650.00
8	(10)	Darren Morgan	41500.00	62	(56)	Steve Newbury	15280.00
9	(57)	Ronnie O'Sullivan	37620.00	63	(60)	Steve Murphy	15280.00
10	(21)	Peter Ebdon	35240.00	64	(90)	Anthony Davies	15230.00
11	(9)	Nigel Bond	34730.00	65	(91)	Mark C Davies	14860.00
12	(25)	Joe Swail	32680.00	66	(47)	Cliff Wilson	14790.00
13	(16)	David Roe	32580.00	67	(83)	Karl Broughton	14725.00
14	(8)	Terry Griffiths	31250.00	68	(-)	Stephen C O'Connor	14605.00
15	(7)	Willie Thorne	31250.00	69	(51)	Tony Meo	14490.00
16	(20)	Tony Drago	30250.00	70	(55)	Ian Graham	13220.00
17	(13)	Steve James	30200.00	71	(62)	Eugene Hughes	13080.00
18	(12)	Martin Clark	29560.00	72	(39)	Bob Chaperon	12600.00
19	(50)	Dave Harold	28920.00	73	(-)	Stefan Mazrocis	11995.00
20	(22)	Dene O'Kane	28820.00	74	(77)	Troy Shaw	11985.00
21	(23)	Tony Knowles	28090.00	75	(86)	Brian Rowswell	11915.00
22	(17)	Gary Wilkinson	27610.00	76	(-)	Jimmy Michie	11785.00
23	(19)	Mike Hallett	27300.00	77	(58)	Jack McLaughlin	11710.00
24	(15)	Dennis Taylor	26700.00	78	(-)	Karl Payne	11625.00
25	(14)	Neal Foulds	25620.00	79	(89)	Craig Edwards	11255.00
26	(30)	Doug Mountjoy	24560.00	80	(-)	Sean Lanigan	11210.00
27	(27)	Mick Price	24420.00	81	(87)	Joe Grech	11145.00
28	(32)	Jason Ferguson	24300.00	82	(-)	Mark Rowing	11100.00
29	(28)	Dean Reynolds	23750.00	83	(-)	Shokat Ali	10845.00
30	(37)	Brian Morgan	23720.00	84	(-)	Mark A Flowerdew	10785.00
31	(24)	Mark Bennett	23530.00	85	(-)	Steve Judd	10740.00
32	(18)	Alain Robidoux	23170.00	86	(98)	Chris Small	10615.00
33	(54)	Andy Hicks	22515.00	87	(78)	John Read	10560.00
34	(29)	Tony Jones	22510.00	88	(81)	Paul Tanner	10345.00
35	(49)	Anthony Hamilton	22230.00	89	(-)	Mark A King	10250.00
36	(59)	Billy Snaddon	21940.00	90	(75)	Nick Dyson	10180.00
37	(26)	Joe Johnson	20280.00	91	(-)	Terry M Murphy	10125.00
38	(53)	Nick Terry	20040.00	92	(-)	David McDonnell	9730.00
39	(64)	Drew Henry	19980.00	93	(-)	Jamie Woodman	9595.00
40	(-)	Stephen Lee	19530.00	94	(85)	Shaun Mellis	9455.00
41	(63)	Dave Finbow	19530.00	95	(-)	Andrew Cairns	9445.00
42	(100)	Fergal O'Brien	19115.00	96	(-)	Sean Storey	9370.00
43	(46)	Les Dodd	18820.00	97	(-)	Darren D Clarke	9255.00
44	(31)	Mark Johnston-Allen	18700.00	98	(68)	Brady Gollan	9225.00
45	(45)	Rod Lawler	18630.00	99	(-)	Dominic Dale	9086.00
46	(35)	Danny Fowler	18380.00	100	(-)	Darryn Walker	9075.00
47	(42)	Jason Prince	18190.00				
48	(61)	Alex Higgins	17820.00			Also	
49	(52)	Nigel Gilbert	17420.00	159	(72)	John Virgo	4925.00
50	(44)	Jonathan Birch	17320.00	192	(123)	Rex Williams	3825.00
51	(-)	John Higgins	17320.00	202	(234)	Allison Fisher	3365.00
52	(43)	Wayne Jones	17200.00	241	(134)	Ray Edmonds	2250.00
53	(48)	Tony Chappel	17150.00				
54	(41)	Cliff Thorburn	17000.00				

The 1994 rankings above apply throughout the 1994/5 season.

HIGHBALL WORLD CHAMPIONSHIP
New Delhi   May 19-21
Quarter-finals
Allison Fisher 5 Sarah Smith 0
Tessa Davidson 5 Kelly Fisher 4
Stacey Hillyard 5 Kim Shaw 0
Karen Corr 5 Sharon Dickson 3
Semi-finals
Allison Fisher 6 Tessa Davidson 3
Stacey Hillyard 6 Karen Corr 3
Final
Allison Fisher 7 Stacey Hillyard 3
HB: Stacey Hillyard 108

BERKSHIRE LADIES CLASSIC
Semi-finals
Allison Fisher 3 Ann-Marie Farren 0
Stacey Hillyard 3 Sharon Dickson 1
Final
Allison Fisher 3 Stacey Hillyard 1
Highest Break: Allison Fisher 106

REGAL MASTERS
Stirling   Nov 13-14
Semi-finals
Ann-Marie Farren 4 Karen Corr 1
Stacey Hillyard 4 Lynette Horsburgh 3
Final
Stacey Hillyard 4 Ann-Marie Ferran 3
HB: Stacey Hillyard 98

PONTINS BRITISH OPEN CHAMPIONSHIPS
Prestatyn   Dec 4-5
Semi-finals
Allison Fisher 3 Tessa Davidson 1
Karen Corr 3 Kim Shaw 1
Final
Allison Fisher 3 Karen Corr 1
HB: Ann-Marie Ferran 79

NATIONAL LADIES CHAMPIONSHIP
Tooting   Mar 6
Semi-finals
Allison Fisher 4 Ann-Marie Ferran 0
Karen Corr 4 Stacey Hillyard 2
Final
Karen Corr 4 Allison Fisher 0
HB: Allison Fisher 129

PONTINS UK CHAMPIONSHIPS
Lowestoft   Mar 19-20
Semi finals
Stacey Hillyard 4 Tessa Davidson 3
Kare Corr 4 Lynette Horsburgh 1
Final
Karen Corr 4 Stacey Hillyard 3
HB: Karen Corr 107

GREEN BAIZE CLASSIC
Cirencester   Apr 17
Semi-finals
Allison Fisher 3 Tessa Davidson 1
Karen Corr 3 Stacey Hillyard 1
Final
Allison Fisher 3 Karen Corr 2
HB: Tessa Davidson 77

PONTINS SPRING BOWL
Prestatyn   May 7-14
Semi-finals
Karen Corr 3 Kim Shaw 1
Lisa Quick 3 Allison Fisher 2
Final
Karen Corr 4 Lisa Quick 1
HB: Tessa Davidson 103

LLANELLI CLASSIC
June 27-28
Semi-finals
Stacey Hillyard 4 Tessa Davidson 0
Allison Fisher 4 Kelly Fisher 1
Final
Allison Fisher 4 STacey Hillyard 2
HB: Stacey Hillyard 98

WORLD RANKING LIST
As at end of 1993/94 season
Last seasons's ranking in brackets

1	(1) Allison Fisher	Hadlow	364
2	(2) Karen Corr	Bourne	361
3	(3) Stacey Hillyard	Christchurch	357
4	(4) Tessa Davidson	Bicester	275
5	(5) Ann-Marie Farren	Nottingham	233
6	(6) Kim Shaw	Wisbech	225
7	(7) Kelly Fisher	Wisbech	224
8	(9) Sarah Smith	Sheffield	206
9	(11) Lisa Quick	Weston S M	184
10	(8) Lynette Horsburgh	Blackpool	181
11	(10) Sharon Dickson	Newport	175
12	(7) Mandy Fisher	Wisbech	145
13	(14) Caroline Walch	Sunbury	131
14	(16) June Banks	Llanelli	129
15	(20) Helen Audus	Leeds	120
16	(12) Georgina Aplin	Royston	106
17	(-) Julie Kelly	Wexford	86
18	(18) Maria Tart	Hounslow	86
19	(22) Carla Jolly	Reading	83
20	(15) Julie Gillespie	Doune	81
21	(-) Emma Bonney	Portsmouth	78
22	(23) Teresa Carlisle	Mitcham	72
23	(-) Jenny Poulter	Maidstone	69
24	(21) Maureen Seto	Canada	64
25	(-) Helen Lazell	Southend	49

Speed Skating

Long Track

WORLD CHAMPIONSHIPS - MEN
Mar 12-13   Gothenburg, Sweden

500m

1	Ids Postma	HOL	**38.39**
2	Hiroyuki Noake	JPN	38.50
3	Naoki Kotake	JPN	38.90

1500m

1	Johann Olav Koss	NOR	1:59.68
2	Andrey Anufrienko	RUS	2:00.76
3	Hiroyuki Noake	JPN	2:00.95

5000m

1	Kjell Storelid	NOR	7:11.63
2	Johann Olav Koss	NOR	7:14.21
3	Jaromir Radke	POL	7:16.05

10,000m

1	Johann Olav Koss	NOR	14:49.58
2	Kjell Storelid	NOR	14:51.68
3	Ids Postma	HOL	14:54.93

Overall

1	Johann Olav Koss	NOR	**167.233**
2	Ids Postma	HOL	168.457
3	Rintje Ritsma	HOL	168.567

WORLD CHAMPIONSHIPS - WOMEN
Feb 5-6   Butte, Montana, USA

500m

1	Ulrike Adeberg	GER	**41.36**
2	Emese Hunyady	AUT	41.80
3	Emese Antal	AUT	41.84

1500m

1	Emese Hunyady	AUT	2:07.13
2	Mikaela Dascalu	ROM	2:07.22
3	Anni Friesinger	GER	2:07.93

3000m

1	Emese Hunyady	AUT	4:30.59
2	Ulrike Adeberg	GER	4:30.71
3	Mikaela Dascalu	ROM	4:32.41

5000m

1	Emese Hunyady	AUT	8:02.06
2	Anni Friesinger	GER	8:04.77
3	Ludmila Prokashev	KZK	8:04.97

Overall

1	Emese Hunyady	AUT	**177.480**
2	Ulrike Adeberg	GER	178.733
3	Mikaela Dascalu	ROM	178.859

WORLD CUP
MEN
500m: Dan Jansen USA 186
1000m: Dan Jansen USA 122
1500m: Falko Zandstra HOL 105
5000m: Johann Olav Koss NOR 135
WOMEN
500m: Bonnie Blair USA 172
1000m: Bonnie Blair USA 125
1500m: Emese Hunyady AUT 119
3000m: Gunda Niemann-Kleemann GER 150

Short Track

WORLD CHAMPIONSHIPS
Mar 31-2 Apr   Guildford, Great Britain
Only the 7 leading points scorers qualified for the 3000m event. The overall winner was determined by the points won in the four finals.
MEN

500m

			Time	Pts
1	Frederic Blackburn	CAN	44.07	5
2	Derrick Campbell	CAN	44.10	3
3	Ki-Hoon Kim	KOR	44.24	2

1000m

1	Marc Gagnon	CAN	1:33.08	5
2	Frederic Blackburn	CAN	1:33.08	3
3	Derrick Campbell	CAN	1:33.13	2

1500m

1	Ji-Hoon Chae	KOR	2:26.45	5
2	Marc Gagnon	CAN	2:27.15	3
3	Derrick Campbell	CAN	2:27.55	2
5	Nicky Gooch	GBR	2:31.60	

3000m

1	Orazio Fagone	ITA	5:55.36	5
2	Ji-Hoon Chae	KOR	5:55.58	3
3	Marc Gagnon	CAN	5:55.77	2

Overall
1. Marc Gagnon CAN 10 final points (37 in total);
2=. Frederic Blackburn CAN 9 (41); 2=. Ji-Hoon Chae
KOR 9 (34); 8. Nicky Gooch GBR 0 (22)

5000m Relay

1	Japan	7:20.11
2	Australia	7:22.57
3	Canada	7:31.06

WOMEN

500m

1	Marinella Canclini	ITA	47.09	5
2	Nathalie Lambert	CAN	47.43	3
3	Yang Yang	CHN	48.16	2

Debbie Palmer (GBR) was eliminated in heats

1000m

1	Nathalie Lambert	CAN	1:45.46	5
2	So-Hee Kim	KOR	1:45.54	3
3	Ryang-Hee Kim	KOR	1:45.56	2

Debbie Palmer (GBR) was eliminated in heats

1500m

1	So-Hee Kim	KOR	2:43.03	5
2	Nathalie Lambert	CAN	2:43.12	3
3	Ryang-Hee Kim	KOR	2:43.14	2

3000m

1	Nathalie Lambert	CAN	6:23.21	5
2	Ryang-Hee Kim	KOR	6:23.23	3
3	Yang Yang	CHN	6:24.46	2

Overall
1. Nathalie Lambert CAN 16 (54) pts; 2. So-Hee Kim
KOR 8 (43); 3. Ryang-Hee Kim KOR 7 (34); 25 Debbie
Palmer GBR (4)

3000m Relay

1	Canada	4:30.89
2	China	4:31.16
3	Korea	4:31.28

Speedway

World Final
Vojens, Denmark   Aug 20

Final

1	Tony Rickardsson	SWE	**12pts** *(after run off)*
2	Hans Nielsen	DEN	12 *(after run off)*
3	Craig Boyce	AUS	12 *(after run off)*
4	Greg Hancock	USA	11
5	Tommy Knudsen	DEN	10
6	Marvyn Cox	GER	9
7	Mark Loram	ENG	9
8	Henrik Gustafsson	SWE	9
9	Josh Larsen	USA	7
10	Jan Stæchmann	DEN	7
11	Chris Louis	ENG	6

World Championship

British Final
Coventry   May 1
1. Andy Smith 12, 2. Joe Screen 11, 3. Steve Schofield 11, 4. Gary Havelock 11

Commonwealth Final
Kings Lynn   May 22
1. Mark Loram 14, 2. Martin Dugard 13, 3. Joe Screen 12,

Overseas Final
Coventry   June 12
1. Sam Ermolenko 14, 2. Greg Hancock 12, 3. Craig Boyce 12

World Team Championship
Brokstedt, Germany   Sept 18

1	Sweden	23	(Rickardsson 12, Gustansson 11)
2	Poland	20	(T Gollob 16, J Gollob 4)
3	Denmark	17	(Knudsen 12, Nielsen 5)
4	Australia	17	(Boyce 9, Adams 8)
5	United States	16	(Ermolenko 12, Hancock 5)
6	England	16	(Loram 9, Louis 4, Havelock 3)

World Under 21 Championship
Elgane, Norway   Aug 14

1	Mikael Karlsson	SWE	**14pts** *(after run off)*
2	Rune Holta	NOR	14
3	Jason Crump	AUS	12

England v Sweden

First Test *Exeter   July 17*
England 70 Sweden 38

Second Test *Ipswich   July 21*
England 65 Sweden 43

Third Test *Oxford   July 22*
England 75 Sweden 32

1993 British League

Division 1	M	W	D	L	PF	PA	BP	Pts
Belle Vue	40	24	1	15	2287	2017	14	63
Wolverhampton	40	23	0	17	2284	2029	17	63
Eastbourne	40	23	1	16	2189	2087	14	61
Arena Essex	40	21	1	18	2203	2113	10	53
Coventry	40	18	3	19	2172	2142	13	52
Reading	40	20	1	19	2181	2129	10	51
Bradford	40	19	3	18	2109	2174	7	48
Ipswich	40	17	0	23	2081.5	2202.5	8	42
King's Lynn	40	15	4	21	2002.5	2215.2	6	40
Poole	40	17	0	23	2033	2281	6	40
Cradley Heath	40	16	0	24	2080	2232	5	37

Division 2	M	W	D	L	PF	PA	BP	Pts
Glasgow	40	27	1	12	2418	1900	19	74
Long Eaton	40	25	0	15	2302	1970	13	63
Peterborough	40	24	0	16	2260	2012	13	61
Swindon	40	23	1	16	2217.5	2088.5	13	60
Edinburgh	40	20	1	19	2272	2041	15	56
Newcastle	40	21	2	17	2138.5	2133.5	8	52
Middlesbrough	40	21	0	19	2125	2189	8	50
Rye House	40	20	0	20	2133	2177	9	49
Sheffield	40	15	0	25	1959	2320	5	35
Exeter	40	12	0	28	1881	2429	3	27
Oxford	40	9	1	30	1934	2378	4	23

Division 1 Riders Championship
Swindon   Oct 31
1. Per Jonsson 14, 2. Henrik Gustafsson, 3. Chris Louis 13, 4. Leigh Adams 11, 5. Hans Neilsen 10

British League Team Championship
Peterborough   Aug 7

Division 1 Final
1. Poole 28 *(Crump 9, Boyce 7, Rossiter 6, Schofield 6)*
2. Cradley Heath 20 *(Nashlin 8, Cross 7, Hamill 3, Hancock 2)*
3. Eastbourne 15 *(Norris 5, M Dugard 4, Barker 4, Andersson 2)*
4. Coventry 9 *(Jorgensen 6, Andersen 2, Olsen 1)*

Division 2 Final
1. Oxford 24 *(Goodwin 11, Poole 7, Karlsson 5, Grahame 1)*
2. Long Eaton 17 *(Dixon 7, Collins 5, Johnston 4, Hellsen 1)*
3. Peterborough 16 *(Tesar 7, Monaghan 4, Pedersen 3, Sullivan 1, Nicholls 1)*
4. Edinburgh 15 *(Lamb 5, McKinna 4, Andersen 3, Collins 3)*

Division 2 Pairs Championship
Arena Essex   May 28
1. Swindon *(Tony Olsson & Tony Langdon)*
2. Glasgow *(Nigel Crabtree & David Walsh)*
3. Peterborough *(Sam Tesar & Eric Monaghan)*
4. Edinburgh *(Les Collins & Vesa Yilnen)*

Speedway Star Knockout Cup Final
Glasgow 118 Swindon 98

Squash

Men's World Open Championship 1994

Barcelona *Sep 9-14*
First Round (selected)
Jansher Khan (PAK) bt Craig Rowland (AUS) 15-7, 15-6, 15-9
Philip Whitlock (GBR) bt Craig Wapnick 15-8, 15-12, 15-13
Chris Walker (GBR) bt Austin Adarraga 15-3, 15-7, 15-9
Zarak Jahan Khan (PAK) bt Michael Puertas (GBR) 15-9, 15-13, 15-4
Rodney Eyles (AUS) bt Stephen Meads (GBR) 15-11, 15-10, 6-15, 15-13
Simon Parke (GBR) bt Del Harris (GBR) 17-15, 15-10, 14-15, 15-13
Ross Norman (NZL) bt Paul Johnson (GBR) 15-12, 15-13*
Anthony Hill (AUS) bt Mark Cairns (GBR) 15-10, 15-9, 15-9
Jason Nicolle (GBR) bt Paul Gregory (GBR) 15-8, 6-15, 11-15, 15-12, 15-9
Rodney Martin (AUS) bt Mir Zaman Gul (PAK) 15-16, 15-12, 15-8*
Paul Steel (NZL) bt Tony Hands (GBR) 15-10, 15-9, 12-15, 15-12
Peter Marshall (GBR) bt Lucas Buit (HOL) 15-7, 15-4, 15-4
Sami Elopuro (FIN) bt Craig Van Der Wath (RSA) 15-7, 15-8, 15-9
Peter Nicol (GBR) bt Abdul Faheem Khan (HKG) 15-11, 16-6, 15-11
Daniel Meddings (GBR) bt Glen Wilson (NZL) 15-12, 15-7, 15-9
Brett Martin (AUS) bt Angus Kirkland 15-6, 17-16, 15-12
Second Round
Jansher Khan bt Philip Whitlock 15-9, 15-8, 15-8
Chris Walker bt Zarak Jahan Khan 15-10, 15-7, 10-15, 15-9
Rodney Eyles bt Simon Parke 15-12, 15-6, 15-10
Anthony Hill bt Ross Norman 15-9, 17-15, 15-9
Rodney Martin bt Jason Nicolle*
Peter Marshall bt Paul Steel 15-2, 15-8, 16-17, 15-8
Peter Nicol bt Sami Elopuro 15-8, 15-12, 15-6
Brett Martin bt Daniel Meddings 15-13, 15-8, 15-13
Quarter-finals
Jansher Khan bt Chris Walker 15-11, 15-6, 15-10
Rodney Eyles bt Anthony Hill 15-6, 15-10, 15-8
Peter Marshall bt Rodney Martin 15-7, 13-15, 15-5, 15-3
Peter Nicol bt Brett Martin 15-10, 15-11, 6-15, 15-10
Semi-finals
Jansher Khan bt Rodney Eyles 15-7, 15-12, 15-13
Peter Marshall bt Peter Nicol 15-7, 13-15, 15-5, 15-3
FINAL
Jansher Khan bt Peter Marshall 10-15, 15-11, 15-8, 15-4
* *Incomplete results supplied*

WORLD RANKINGS
Men
As at August 31

1	Jansher Khan	PAK	1159.028
2	Brett Martin	AUS	706.875
3	Peter Marshall	GBR	688.125
4	Rodney Eyles	AUS	628.125
5	Rodney Martin	AUS	455.781
6	Chris Walker	GBR	455.156
7	Peter Nicol	GBR	402.813
8	Ross Norman	NZL	290.938
9	Zarak Jahan Khan	PAK	272.568
10	Philip Whitlock	GBR	231.094
11	Tony Hands	GBR	226.563
12	Anthony Hill	AUS	217.150
13	Sami Elopuru	FIN	186.875
14	Jason Nicolle	GBR	185.469
15	Daniel Meddings	GBR	175.833
16	Paul Gregory	GBR	174.125
17	Mark Cairns	GBR	170.333
18	Simon Parke	GBR	164.063
19	Del Harris	GBR	158.825
20	Mark Carlyon	AUS	144.694
21	Stephen Meads	GBR	140.295
22	Paul Steel	NZL	136.531
23	Paul Johnson	GBR	133.906
24	Angus Kirkland	GBR	126.222
25	Julien Bonetat	FRA	125.361
26	Abdul Faheem Khan	HKG	124.066
27	Craig Van Der Wath	RSA	120.763
28	Hansi Wiens	GER	115.556
29	Mir Zaman Gul	PAK	108.938
30	Derek Ryan	IRL	107.600

Women

1	Michelle Martin	AUS	1666.15
2	Liz Irving	AUS	969.40
3	Suzanne Horner	GBR	804.00
4	Cassandra Jackman	GBR	748.59
5	Sarah Fitz-Gerald	AUS	608.50
6	Carol V Owens	AUS	541.73
7	Susan Wright	GBR	528.30
8	Fiona Geaves	GBR	454.00
9	Claire Nitch	RSA	377.30
10	Martine LeMoignan	GBR	352.30

Men's World Open Championship 1993

Karachi   Nov 18-23, 1993
First Round (selected)
Jansher Khan (PAK) bt Paul Gregory (GBR)
15-11, 15-7, 15-7
Peter Nicol (GBR) bt Hansi Weiss (GER)
15-8, 15-12, 15-12
Rodney Eyles (AUS) bt Jason Nicolle (GBR) 13-15, 15-11,
15-9, 15-4
Mir Zaman Gul (PAK) bt Simon Parke (GBR) 8-15, 17-15,
15-12, 15-12
Peter Marshall (GBR) bt Mark Cairns (GBR) 15-11, 11-15,
15-9, 15-8
Philip Whitlock (GBR) bt Stephens Meads (GBR)
15-3, 15-6, 15-3
Tony Hands (GBR) bt Anthony Hill (AUS) 13-15, 15-7, 15-
9, 15-3
Ross Norman (NZL) bt Del Harris (GBR) 15-9, 15-7,
10-15, 15-14
Daniel Meddings (GBR) bt Mark Mcleans (SCO) 15-5,
15-9, 15-7
Chris Walker (GBR) bt Mark Carlyon (AUS) 13-15, 15-7,
15-12, 15-5
Zarak J Khan (PAK) bt Adrian Davies (GBR) 13-15, 15-13,
12-15, 15-3, 15-14
Second Round
Jansher Khan bt Peter Nicol 15-4, 15-11, 15-5
Rodney Eyles bt Mir Zaman Gul 15-9, 10-15, 15-7, 15-4
Peter Marshall bt Philip Whitlock 15-13, 13-15, 15-8, 15-12
Tony Hands bt C Van Der Wath (RSA) 15-8, 15-17, 15-13,
15-13
Jahangir Khan bt Ross Norman 15-7, 15-12, 9-15, 15-12
Brett Martin (AUS) bt Daniel Meddings 15-12, 15-10,
15-11
Chris Walker bt Tristan Nancarrow (AUS) 15-13, 15-8,
15-6
Rodney Martin (AUS) bt Zarak J Khan 15-12, 15-8, 15-11
Quarter-finals
Jansher Khan bt Rodney Eyles 15-7, 15-7, 15-7
Peter Marshall bt Tony Hands 15-8, 15-12, 15-14
Jahangir Khan bt Brett Martin 17-16, 17-15, 15-11
Chris Walker bt Rodney Martin 13-15, 17-14, 15-10, 15-11
Semi-finals
Jansher Khan bt Peter Marshall 15-5, 15-6, 15-8
Jahangir Khan bt Chris Walker 15-7, 15-5, 9-15, 15-4
FINAL
Jansher Khan bt Jahangir Khan 14-15, 15-9, 15-5, 15-5

World Championship 1993
Seedings

1. **Jansher Kahn PAK**	5. **Rodney Eyles AUS**
2. **Rodney Martin AUS**	6. **Ross Norman NZL**
3. **Brett Martin AUS**	7. **Sami Elopuro FIN**
4. **Peter Marshall ENG**	8. **Chris Walker ENG**

Men's World Team Championships

Karachi   Nov 24-29, 1993
Final Placings
1. Australia; 2. Australia; 3. England; 4. Finland; 5. New
Zealand; 6. Egypt; 9. Scotland; 10, Ireland; 14. Wales.

European Team Championships

Zoetermeer, Holland   Apr 28-May 1
MEN
Semi-finals
Germany bt Scotland 2-2 (on games)
England bt France 4-0
Final
England bt Germany 4-0
England players first
Tony Hands bt Hansi Wiens 1-9, 9-3, 9-3, 9-1
Philip Whitlock bt Simon Frenz 2-9, 10-8, 9-3, 9-2
Jason Nicolle bt Oliver Rucks 9-4, 9-1, 6-9, 9-2
Stephen Meads bt Florian Possl 9-1, 9-1, 9-4
WOMEN
Semi-final
Germany bt Ireland 3-0
England bt Holland 3-0
Final
England bt Germany 3-0
Suzanne Horner bt Sabine Schone 9-1, 9-0, 9-6
Cassie Jackman bt Sabine Baum 9-2, 9-5, 9-3
Fiona Greaves bt Silke Bartel 9-3, 9-5, 9-0

World Junior Men's Championships

Christchurch, New Zealand   July 31-Aug 12
INDIVIDUAL
Semi-finals
Ahmed Barada (EGY) bt Thierry Lincou (FRA)
9-2, 9-0, 9-2
Omar El Borolossy (EGY) bt Iain Higgins (GBR)
9-7, 9-2, 9-5
Final
Ahmed Barada (EGY) bt Omar El Borolossy (EGY)
9-0, 7-9, 3-9, 9-3, 9-2
TEAM
Final Placings
1. Egypt; 2. England; 3. Finland; 16. Wales; 20. Scotland

European Junior Championships

Bolzano, Italy   Apr
BOYS
Final
T Lincou (FRA) bt O Kowalski (GER) 1-9, 10-8, 9-3, 9-3
GIRLS
Final
V Atkinsson (HOL) bt C Waddell (SCO) 9-7, 1-9, 9-7, 9-1
MIXED TEAMS
Final Placings: 1. England; 2. Germany; 3. Holland; 4.
Ireland; 5. Scotland; 14. Wales

Hi-Tec British Open
Early Rounds: Lambs   Apr 6-7
Final Rounds: Wembley CC   Apr 9-11
MEN
Quarter-finals
Jansher Kahn (PAK) bt Rodney Eyles (AUS) 9-2, 9-4, 9-5
Peter Marshall (GBR) bt Anthony Hill (AUS) 9-1, 9-1, 9-1
Chris Walker (GBR) bt Mark Cairns (GBR)
9-7, 4-9, 9-3, 9-2
Brett Martin (AUS) bt Zarak Khan (PAK) 9-3, 9-5, 9-0
Semi-finals
Jansher Khan bt Peter Marshall 9-2, 7-9, 9-4, 9-3
Brett Martin bt Chris Walker 9-7, 7-9, 9-7, 9-4
Final
Jansher Khan bt Brett Martin 9-1, 9-0, 9-10, 9-1
WOMEN
Quarter-finals
Michelle Martin (AUS) bt Martine Le Moignan (GBR) 9-2,
9-3, 9-2
Sarah Fitz-Gerald (AUS) bt Claire Nitch (RSA) 9-3, 3-9,
9-2, 10-8
Suzanne Horner (GBR) bt Fiona Geaves (GBR)
9-2, 9-2, 9-3
Liz Irving (AUS) bt Carol Owens (AUS) 9-4, 9-1, 8-10, 9-4
Semi-finals
Michelle Martin bt Sarah Fitz-Gerald 9-6, 9-6, 9-5
Liz Irving bt Suzanne Horner 7-9, 9-7, 9-2, 9-7
Final
Michelle Martin bt Liz Irving 9-6, 9-6, 9-5

Men's International Events

Qatar International
Doha Qatar   Nov 12-17
Final
Jansher Khan (PAK) bt Rodney Martin (AUS)
15-7, 15-8, 15-9

Leekes Classic
Cardiff   Feb 21-26
Final
Brett Martin (AUS) bt Peter Marshall (GBR)
12-15, 15-2, 15-5, 15-10

Andersen Portuguese Open
Lisbon   Mar 8-12
Final
Jansher Khan (PAK) bt Peter Marshall (GBR)
16-17, 15-12, 15-8, 15-7

Austrian Open
Linz   Mar 30-Apr 3
Final
Jansher Khan (PAK) bt Rodney Eyles (AUS)
15-11, 15-10, 15-14

USA Open
New York   Apr 16-21
Final
Rodney-Eyles (AUS) bt Brett Martin (AUS)
9-15, 15-12, 15-12, 17-14

Internationaux de France
Tours, France   May 16-22
Final
Jansher Khan (PAK) bt Peter Marshall (GBR)
15-12, 15-14, 15-13

Hong Kong Women's Open
Hong Kong   Aug 30-Sep 3
Final
Jansher Khan (PAK) bt Peter Nicol (GBR) 15-7, 15-10, 15-6

Women's International Events

Leekes Classic
Cardiff   Feb 21-26
Final
Liz Irving (AUS) bt Michelle Martin (AUS)
5-15, 17-15, 15-6, 15-12

JSM Supersquash
Tokyo   May 31-June 5
Final
Michelle Martin (AUS) bt Cassie Jackman (GBR)
9-3, 9-5, 9-5

Hong Kong Women's Open
Hong Kong   June 14-19
Final
Michelle Martin (AUS) bt Cassie Jackman (GBR)
9-6, 9-5, 7-9, 10-8

Domestic Events

SRA National Championships
Welwyn Garden City   Jan 13-18
MEN
Semi-finals
Peter Marshall (Leics) bt Tony Hands (Essex) 9-4, 9-2, 9-5
Peter Nicol (SCO) bt Jason Nicolle (Hants) 9-5, 10-9, 9-0
Final
Peter Marshall bt Peter Nicol 9-6, 9-7, 9-4
WOMEN
Semi-finals
Suzanne Horner (Yorks) bt Jane Martin (Northumbria)
9-6, 9-2, 9-6
Sue Wright (Kent) bt Lisa Opie (Notts) 9-6, 9-5, 8-10, 9-4
Final
Suzanne Horner bt Sue Wright 9-4, 9-1, 9-1

SRA National League - Men
PREMIER DIVISION

		MW	ML	GW	GL	Pts
1	Leekes Wizards	28	12	94	53	44
2	WF Village Manc'ster	24	16	82	64	38
3	Manchester Northern	21	19	82	72	37
4	Rackets	21	19	80	70	32
5	ICL-PMD Herts	15	25	57	86	21
6	Lingfield	11	29	50	100	16

Inter County Championships

Men: 1. Yorkshire; 2. Essex; 3. Lancashire; 4. Sussex
Women: 1. Essex; 2. Kent; 3. Yorkshire; 4. Bedfordshire

Swimming

Let's start with the good news. In men's swimming two performers were outstanding; Alexander Popov, who broke Matt Biondi's world record at Monte Carlo in June, and Kieren Perkins. In the Commonwealth Games, the Australian was under instructions from his coach, John Carew, *not* to attack the world 1500m record. "I knew I was going to get into trouble, but I saw all those Aussies clapping and waving," said the ingenuous Perkins and off he went for the record. Perkins lopped 1.82 seconds from his Barcelona swim and took the 800m on the way. They were his eighth and ninth world records. In Rome, at the World Championships, he added a tenth, breaking the 400m record as he took both 400m and 1500m titles. Sensational swimming, but nobody was calling him out for drug-taking.

In women's swimming throughout the year, but especially in Rome, there was some sensational swimming too, but everybody was making accusations. Karen Pickering, who won Britain's first ever women's world title when she won the 200m freestyle at the short-course championships in Palma, was mortified when her swim at Rome left her last in the final behind Jingyi Le. "I was really shocked that I swan like that and was joint last. I will have to watch it again, but I cannot believe the winner's time. That's a man's time. That is the sort of time that some men are doing at our national championships," said Pickering, joining the queue of swimmers protesting. If it's true, FINA (the International Swimming Federation) have only themselves to blame for lagging behind in random testing. If it's not, (or even if it is) it's a good job the Chinese don't know much about the laws of libel.

World Championships

Rome   Sep 1-11

50m Freestyle
1 Alexander Popov	RUS	22.17
2 Gary Hall	USA	22.44
3 Raimundas Majolis	LIT	22.52
6 Mark Foster	GBR	22.76

100m Freestyle
1 Alexander Popov	RUS	49.12
2 Gary Hall	USA	49.41
3 Gustavo Borges	BRA	49.52

200m Freestyle
1 Antti Kasvio	FIN	1:47.32
2 Anders Holmertz	SWE	1:48.24
3 Danyon Loader	NZL	1:48.49

400m Freestyle
1 Kieren Perkins	AUS	3:43.80	WR
2 Antti Kasvio	FIN	3:48.55	
3 Danyon Loader	NZL	3:48.62	

1500m Freestyle
1 Kieren Perkins	AUS	14:50.52
2 Daniel Kowalski	AUS	14:53.42
3 Steffen Zesner	GER	15:09.20
8 Graeme Smith	GBR	15:29.24

100m Backstroke
1 Martin Lopez Zubero	ESP	55.17
2 Jeff Rouse	USA	55.51
3 Tama Deutsch	HUN	55.69
8 Martin Harris	GBR	56.21

200m Backstroke
1 Vladimir Selkov	RUS	1:57.42
2 Martin Lopez Zubero	ESP	1:58.75
3 Royce Sharp	USA	1:58.86
6 Adam Ruckwood	GBR	2:00.15

100m Breaststroke
1 Norbert Rosza	HUN	1:01.24
2 Karoly Guttler	HUN	1:01.44
3 Frederic Deburghgraeve	BEL	1:01.79

200m Breaststroke
1 Norbert Rosza	HUN	2:12.81
2 Eric Wunderlich	USA	2:12.87
3 Karoly Guttler	HUN	2:14.12
4 Nick Gillingham	GBR	2:14.25

100m Butterfly
1 Rafal Szukala	POL	53.51
2 Lars Frolander	SWE	53.65
3 Denis Pankratov	RUS	53.68

200m Butterfly
1 Denis Pankratov	RUS	1:56.54
2 Danyon Loader	NZL	1:57.99
3 Chris-Carol Bremer	GER	1:58.11

200m Individual Medley
1 Jani Sievinen	FIN	1:58.16	WR
2 Greg Burgess	USA	2:00.86	
3 Attila Czene	HUN	2:01.84	

400m Individual Medley
1 Tom Dolan	USA	4:12.30	WR
2 Eric Sievinen	FIN	4:13.29	
3 Eric Namesik	USA	4:15.69	

4 x 100m Freestyle

1 United States	3:16.90	
2 Russia	3:18.12	
3 Brazil	3:19.35	

4 x 200m Freestyle

1 Sweden	7:17.74	
2 Russia	7:18.13	
3 Germany	7:19.10	

4 x 100m Medley

1 United States	3:37.74	
2 Russia	3:38.28	
3 Hungary	3:39.47	

1 Metre Platform

1 Evan Stewart	ZIM	382.14
2 Wei Lan	CHN	375.96
3 Brian Earley	USA	361.59

3 Metre Platform

1 Zhuocheng	CHN	655.44
2 Dmitri Sautin	RUS	646.59
3 Tianling Wang	CHN	638.22

10 Metre Platform

1 Dmitri Sautin	RUS	634.71
2 Shuwei Sun	CHN	630.03
3 Vladimir Timoshinin	RUS	607.32

WOMEN

50m Freestyle

1 Jingyi Le	CHN	24.51	WR
2 Natalie Mesheryakova	RUS	25.10	
3 Amy Van Dyken	USA	25.18	

100m Freestyle

1 Jingyi Le	CHN	54.01	WR
2 Lu Bin	CHN	54.15	
3 Franziska van Almsick	GER	54.77	
=7 Karen Pickering	GBR	55.79	

200m Freestyle

1 Franziska van Almsick	GER	1:56.78	WR
2 Lu Bin	CHN	1:56.89	
3 Claudia Poll	CRC	1:57.61	

400m Freestyle

1 Aihua Yang	CHN	4:09.64
2 Cristina Teuscher	USA	4:10.21
3 Claudia Poll	CRC	4:10.61

800m Freestyle

1 Janet Evans	USA	8:29.85
2 Hayley Lewis	AUS	8:29.94
3 Brooke Bennett	USA	8:31.30

100m Backstroke

1 Cihong He	CHN	1:00.57
2 Nina Zhivanevskaya	RUS	1:00.83
3 Babara Bedford	USA	1:01.32

Cihong WR in qualifying - 1:00.16

200m Backstroke

1 Cihong He	CHN	2:07.40
2 Krisztina Egerszegi	HUN	2:09.10
3 Lorenza Vigarani	ITA	2:10.92

100m Breaststroke

1 Samantha Riley	AUS	1:07.69	WR
2 Guohong Dai	CHN	1:09.26	
3 Yuan Yuan	CHN	1:10.19	

200m Breaststoke

1 Samantha Riley	AUS	2:26.87
2 Yuan Yuan	CHN	2:27.38
3 Brigitte Becue	BEL	2:28.85

100m Butterfly

1 Limin Liu	CHN	58.98
2 Yub Qu	CHN	59.69
3 Susan O'Neill	AUS	1:00.11

200m Butterfly

1 Limin Liu	CHN	2:07.25
2 Yun Qu	CHN	2:07.42
3 Susan O'Neill	AUS	2:09.54

200m Individual Medley

1 Lu Bin	CHN	2:12.34
2 Allison Wagner	USA	2:14.40
3 Elli Overton	AUS	2:15.26

400m Individual Medley

1 Guohong Dai	CHN	4:39.14
2 Allison Wagner	USA	4:39.98
3 Kristine Quence	USA	4:42.21

4 x 100m Freestyle Relay

1 China	3:37.91	WR
2 United States	3:42.94	
3 Germany	3:45.38	
5 Great Britain	3:45.52	

4 x 200m Freestyle Relay

1 China	7:57.98	
2 Germany	8:01.37	
3 United States	8:03.16	

4 x 100m Medley Relay

1 China	4:01.67	WR
2 United States	4:06.53	
3 Russia	4:06.70	

WOMEN'S DIVING

I Metre Springboard

1 Lixia Chen	CHN	279.30
2 Shuping Tan	CHN	276.00
3 Annie Pelletier	CAN	273.84

3 Metre Springboard

1 Shuping Tan	CHN	548.49
2 Vera Ilyina	RUS	498.60
3 Claudia Bockner	GER	480.15

10 Metre Platform

1 Mingxia Fu	CHN	434.04
2 Bin Chi	CHN	420.24
3 Maria José Alcala	MEX	396.48

SYNCHRONISED SWIMMING

Solo

1 Becky Dyroen Lance	USA	191.040
2 Fumiko Okuno	JPN	187.306
3 Lisa Alexander	CAN	186.826

Duet

1 Lancer/Sidduth	USA	187.009
2 Okuno/Tachibana	JPN	186.259
3 Alexander/Woodley	CAN	186.259
8 Vakil/Shacklock	GBR	177.674

Teams

1 United States	185.883
2 Canada	183.263
3 Japan	183.215

LONG DISTANCE SWIMMING

Men

1 Greg Streppel	CAN	5:35:26.56
2 David Bates	AUS	5:36:31.70
3 Alexei Akatlev	RUS	5:37:26.43

Women

1 Melissa Cunningham	AUS	5:48:25.04
2 Rita Kovacs	HUN	5:50:13.76
3 Shelley Taylor-Smith	AUS	5:53:12.82

World Short Course Swimming Championships

Palma, Majorca   Dec 2-5, 1993

MEN

50m Freestyle
1	Mark Foster	GBR	**21.84**
2	Bin Hu	CHN	21.93
3	Robert Abernethy	AUS	21.97

100m Freestyle
1	Fernan. de Queiroz	BRA	**48.38**
2	Gustavo Borges	BRA	48.42
3	Jon Olsen	USA	48.49

200m Freestyle
1	Antiti Kasvio	FIN	**1:45.21**
2	Trent Bray	NZL	1:45.53
2	Artur Wojdat	POL	1:45.53

400m Freestyle
1	Daniel Kowalski	AUS	**3:42.95**
2	Antiti Kasvio	FIN	3:42.98
3	Paul Palmer	GBR	3:45.07

1500m Freestyle
1	Daniel Kowalski	AUS	**14:42.04**	
2	Jorg Hoffmann	GER	14:53.09	
3	Piotr Albinski	POL	14:53.97	
4	Graeme Smith	GBR	14:54.45	BR

100m Backstroke
1	Tripp Schwenk	USA	**52.98**	
2	Martin Harris	GBR	53.93	BR
3	Rodolfo Falcon	CUB	54.00	

200m Backstroke
1	Tripp Schwenk	USA	**1:54.19**	
2	Luca Bianchin	ITA	1:55.09	
3	Stefaan Maene	BEL	1:55.68	
7	Adam Ruckwood	GBR	1:56.91	BR

100m Breaststroke
1	Philip Rogers	AUS	**59.56**
2	Ron Dekker	HOL	59.95
3	Seth Vanneerden	USA	1:00.08
4	Nick Gillingham	GBR	1:00.29

200m Breaststroke
1	Nick Gillingham	GBR	**2:07.91**	ER
2	Philip Rogers	AUS	2:08.32	
3	Eric Wunderlich	USA	2:08.49	

100m Butterfly
1	Milos Milosevic	CRO	**52.79**
2	Mark Henderson	USA	52.92
3	Rafal Szukala	POL	52.94

200m Butterfly
1	Franck Esposito	FRA	**1:55.42**
2	Christian Keller	GER	1:55.75
3	Chris-Carol Bremer	GER	1:56.86

200m Individual Medley
1	Christian Keller	GER	**1:56.80**	
2	Fraser Walker	GBR	1:58.35	BR
3	Curtis Myden	CAN	1:59.27	
8	Nick Gillingham	GBR	2:02.84	

400m Individual Medley
1	Curtis Myden	CAN	**4:10.41**
2	Segei Mariniux	MLD	4:11.96
3	Petteri Lehtinen	FIN	4:12.33

4 x 100m Freestyle
1	Brazil	**3:12.11**	WR
2	USA	3:12.68	
3	Russia	3:15.56	

4 x 200m Freestyle
1	Sweden	**7:05.92**
2	Germany	7:08.63
3	Brazil	7:09.38

4 x 100m Medley
1	USA	**3:32.57**	WR
2	Spain	3:36.92	
3	Great Britain	3:37.27	BR

WOMEN

50m Freestyle
1	Jingyi Le	CHN	**24.23**	WR
2	Angel Martino	USA	24.93	
3	Linda Olofsson	SWE	25.21	

100m Freestyle
1	Jingyi Le	CHN	**53.01**	WR
2	Angel Martino	USA	53.39	
3	Karen Pickering	GBR	54.39	WR

200m Freestyle
1	Karen Pickering	GBR	**1:56.25**	WR
2	Susan O'Neill	AUS	1:57.16	
3	Bin Lu	CHN	1:57.71	

400m Freestyle
1	Janet Evans	USA	**4:05.64**
2	Trina Jackson	USA	4:07.49
3	Julie Majer	AUS	4:07.91

800m Freestyle
1	Janet Evans	USA	**8:22.43**
2	Julie Majer	AUS	8:26.46
3	Trina Jackson	USA	8:27.50

100m Backstroke
1	Angel Martino	USA	**58.50**	WR
2	Cihong He	CHN	1:00.13	
3	Elli Overton	AUS	1:00.18	

200m Backstroke
1	Cihong He	CHN	**2:06.09**	WR
2	Yuanyuan Jia	CHN	2:07.95	
3	Cathleen Rund	GER	2:09.59	
6	Joanne Deakins	GBR	2:09.99	
8	Kathy Osher	GBR	2:10.80	

100m Breaststroke
1	Guohong Dai	CHN	**1:06.58**	WR
2	Linley Frame	AUS	1:07.65	
3	Samantha Riley	AUS	1:07.77	

200m Breaststoke
1	Guohong Dai	CHN	**2:21.99**	WR
2	Hitomi Maehara	JPN	2:24.45	
3	Samantha Riley	AUS	2:24.75	

100m Butterfly
1	Susan O'Neill	AUS	**59.19**
2	Limin Liu	CHN	59.24
3	Kristie Krueger	USA	59.53

200m Butterfly
1	Limin Liu	CHN	**2:08.51**
2	Susan O'Neill	AUS	2:09.08
3	Petria Thomas	AUS	2:09.40

200m Individual Medley
1	Allison Wagner	USA	**2:07.79**	WR
2	Guohong Dai	CHN	2:09.21	
3	Elli Overton	AUS	2:10.51	

400m Individual Medley
1	Guohong Dai	CHN	**4:29.00**	WR
2	Allison Wagner	USA	4:31.76	
3	Julie Majer	AUS	4:37.50	

4 x 100m Freestyle

1	China	3:35.97	WR
2	Sweden	3:39.41	
3	USA	3:40.40	

4 x 200m Freestyle

1	China	7:52.45	WR
2	Australia	7:56.52	
3	USA	8:02.99	

4 x 100m Medley

1	China	3:57.73	WR
2	Australia	4:00.17	
3	USA	4:01.30	

World Cup

Final Classification after 7 meets

MEN

Sprint Freestyle (50, 100, 200m)

1	**Alexander Popov**	**RUS**	**110 pts**
2	Raimundas Maz'lis	LTU	95
3	Vladimir Pyshnenko	RUS	78

Distance Freestyle (400, 800m)

1	**Evgeni Sadovyi**	**RUS**	**78 pts**
2	Steffen Zesner	GER	72
2	Jorg Hoffmann	GER	72

Backstroke (50, 100, 200m)

1	**Vladimir Selkov**	**RUS**	**98 pts**
2	Alexander Popov	RUS	96
3	Martin Harris	GBR	90

Breaststroke (50, 100, 200m)

1	**Ron Dekker**	**HOL**	**91 pts**
2	Nick Gillingham	GBR	81
3	Alex Dzhaburiya	UKR	78

Butterfly (50, 100, 200m)

1	**Denis Pankretov**	**RUS**	**98 pts**
2	Mark Foster	GBR	82
3	Luis Laera	ITA	78

Individual Medley (100, 200, 400m)

1	**Christian Keller**	**GER**	**104 pts**
2	Daniel Karlsson	SWE	68
3	Robert Seibt	GER	67

WOMEN

Sprint Freestyle (50, 100, 200m)

1	**Jingyi Le**	**CHN**	**101 pts**
2	Fran. van Almsick	GER	78
3	Martina Moravcova	SVK	63

Distance Freestyle (400, 800m)

1	**Dagmar Hase**	**GER**	**98 pts**
2	Malin Nilsson	SWE	65
3	Kerstin Kielgass	GER	62

Backstroke (50, 100, 200m)

1	**Xiuyu Bai**	**CHN**	**95 pts**
2	Lorenza Vigarani	ITA	81
3	Nina Zhivanevskaya	RUS	77

Breaststroke (50, 100, 200m)

1	**Guohong Dai**	**CHN**	**104 pts**
2	Brigitte Becue	BEL	85
3	Hanna Jaitner	SWE	67

Butterfly (50, 100, 200m)

1	**Mette Jacobsen**	**DEN**	**99 pts**
2	Jessica Amey	CAN	55
3	Limin Liu	CHN	49

Individual Medley (100, 200, 400m)

1	**Guohong Dai**	**CHN**	**79 pts**
2	Britta Vestergaard	DEN	78
3	Marianne Limpert	CAN	70

European Sprint Championships

Gateshead   Nov, 1993

MEN

50m Backstroke

1	**Pat Hermanspann**	**GER**	**25.76**

50m Breaststroke

1	**Vassily Ivanov**	**RUS**	**27.82**

50m Butterfly

1	**Carlos Sanchez**	**ESP**	**24.04**

50m Freestyle

1	**Joakim Holmquist**	**SWE**	**22.26**

100m Individual Medley

1	**Ron Dekker**	**HOL**	**55.77**

4x50m Backstroke

1	**Germany**	**1:44.97**
2	Great Britain	1:48.28

4 x 50m Breaststroke

1	**Germany**	**1:55.53**
2	Great Britain	1:58.24

4 x 50m Butterfly

1	**Sweden**	**1:36.53**
3	Great Britain	1:40.27

4 x 50m Freestyle

1	**Sweden**	**1:28.80**
4	Great Britain	1:33.30

4 x 50m Medley

1	**Sweden**	**1:39.54**

WOMEN

50m Backstroke

1	**Sandra Volker**	**GER**	**28.26**	**WB**
6	Alex Bennett	GBR	30.01	

50m Breaststroke

1	**Sylvia Gerasch**	**GER**	**31.57**
2	Karen Rake	GBR	31.89

50m Butterfly

1	**Louise Karlsson**	**SWE**	**27.49**

50m Freestyle

1	**Sandra Volker**	**GER**	**25.55**

100m Individual Medley

1	**Louise Karlsson**	**SWE**	**1:01.45**
4	Susan Rolph	GBR	1:04.20
6	Helen Slatter	GBR	1:06.09

4 x 50m Backstroke

1	**Germany**	**2:01.15**
2	Great Britain	2:02.45

4 x 50m Breaststroke

1	**Great Britain**	**2:11.28**
2	Germany	2:11.34

4 x 50m Butterfly

1	**Germany**	**1:53.06**
2	Great Britain	1:55.62

4 x 50m Freestyle

1	**Sweden**	**1:41.27**
3	Great Britain	1:46.04

4 x 50m Medley

1	**Germany**	**1:53.26**
3	Great Britain	1:57.13

National Championships
Crystal Palace   July 28-31

MEN

50m Backstroke

1	Martin Harris	Whitham Forest	26.18
2	Neil Willey	Barnet Copthall	26.75
3	Simon Handley	Bristol	27.30

100m Backstroke

1	Martin Harris	Whitham Forest	55.73	BR
2	Adam Ruckwood	Birmingham	57.10	
3	Matthew O'Connor	Leeds	57.31	

200m Backstroke

1	Adam Ruckwood	Leeds	2:02.49
2	Martin Harris	Whitham Forest	2:03.71
3	Matthew O'Connor	Leeds	2:03.72

50m Breaststroke

1	Gavin Brettell	Birmingham	29.60
2	Peter McGinty	Beckenham	29.81
3	James Parrack	Leeds	29.83

100m Breaststroke

1	James Parrack	Leeds	1:03.48
2	Gavin Brettell	Birmingham	1:04.05
3	Alex Clapper	Coventry	1:04.14

200m Breaststroke

1	Alex Clapper	Coventry	2:17.74
2	Andrew Ayers	Swansea	2:20.07
3	Max Belcourt	Wycombe	2:22.54

50m Butterfly

1	Mike Fibbins	Barnet Copthall	25.15
2	Janko Gojkovic	Sheffield	25.25
3	Simon Handley	Bristol	25.53

100m Butterfly

1	Janko Gojkovic	Sheffield	55.80
2	Stephen Mavin	Peterborough	56.45
3	Timothy Hart	Thurrock	56.63

200m Butterfly

1	James Hickman	Stockport Metro	2:02.24
2	Stephen Parry	Liverpool	2:02.32
3	David Russell	Portsmouth N'sea	2:07.44

50m Freestyle

1	Mike Fibbins	Barnet Copthall	23.33
2	Alan Rapley	Sheffield	23.54
3	Martin Carl	Redbridge	23.78

100m Freestyle

1	Nicholas Shackell	Millfield	51.49
2	Mike Fibbins	Barnet Copthall	51.69
3	Alan Rapley	Sheffield	51.78

200m Freestyle

1	James Salter	Birmingham	1:52.61
2	Steven Mellor	Satellite	1:53.05
3	Andrew Clayton	Leeds	1:53.05

400m Freestyle

1	Steven Mellor	Satellite	3:57.72
2	Graeme Smith	Stockport Metro	3:59.67
3	Paul Bavister	Coventry	3:59.68

1500m Freestyle

1	Ian Wilson	Leeds	15:19.70
2	Graeme Smith	Stockport Metro	15:28.41
3	Marc Clements	Portsmouth N'sea	16:01.65

200m Individual Medley

1	David Warren	Leeds	2:06.42
2	Grant Robins	Portsmouth N'sea	2:06.64
3	James Hickman	Stockport Metro	2:07.51

400m Individual Medley

1	David Warren	Leeds	4:27.86
2	Grant Robins	Portsmouth Northsea	4:28.41
3	Paul Bavister	Coventry	4:32.33

4 x 200m Freestyle Team

1	Leeds	7:47.83
2	Warrington Warriors	8:04.24
3	Sheffield	8:04.26

4 x 100m Medley Team

1	Leeds	3:49.22	BR (club)
2	Portsmouth Northsea	3:57.07	
3	Beckenham	3:59.62	

WOMEN

50m Backstroke

1	Kathy Osher	Barnet Copthall	30.48
2	Zoe Cray	Ipswich	31.02
3	Lauren Stent	Barnet Copthall	31.04

100m Backstroke

1	Emma Tattam	Portsmouth N'sea	1:03.82
2	Kathy Osher	Barnet Copthall	1:04.42
3	Helen Slatter	Warrington W	1:04.66

200m Backstroke

1	Kathy Osher	Barnet Copthall	2:16.38
2	Emma Tattam	Portsmouth N'sea	2:16.39
3	Joanne Deakins	Coventry	2:16.85

50m Breaststroke

1	Lorraine Coombes	Ealing	33.59
2	Karen Rake	Maxwell Chipping	33.72
3	Jaime King	Tigersharks	33.74

100m Breaststroke

1	Marie Hardiman	Birmingham	1:11.87
2	Nicole Thornley	Salford	1:12.15
3	Lorraine Coombes	Ealing	1:12.50

200m Breaststroke

1	Marie Hardiman	Birmingham	2:30.63	BR
2	Nicole Thornley	Salford	2:34.85	
3	Helen Gorman	Nova Centurion	2:36.42	

50m Butterfly

1	Susan Rolph	Newcastle	28.84
2	Teresa Dray	Portsmouth Northsea	29.02
3	Samantha Greenep	Ferndown	29.03

100m Butterfly

1	Samantha Greenep	Ferndown	1:03.27
2	Nicola Goodwin	Nova Centurion	1:03.62
3	Helen Jepson	Leeds	1:03.63

200m Butterfly

1	Helen Slatter	Warrington W	2:15.75
2	Helen Jepson	Leeds	2:16.92
3	Alex Bennett	Nova Centurion	2:17.89

50m Freestyle

1	Susan Rolph	Newcastle	26.41
2	Karen Pickering	Ipswich	26.67
3	Carrie Wilmott	Barnet Copthall	27.39

100m Freestyle

1	Susan Rolph	Newcastle	56.74
2	Karen Pickering	Ipswich	56.83
3	Alex Bennett	Nova Centurion	57.70

200m Freestyle

1	Karen Pickering	Ipswich	2:02.59
2	Alex Bennett	Nova Centurion	2:03.51
3	Claire Huddart	Leeds	2:03.71

400m Freestyle

1	Sarah Hardcastle	Bracknell	4:13.37
2	Katie Goddard	Portsmouth N'sea	4:19.20
3	Alex Bennett	Nova Centurion	4:19.97

800m Freestyle

1	Susan Colling	Derwentside	8:56.13
2	Katie Goddard	Portsmouth N'sea	9:05.37
3	Paula Wood	Hillingdon	9:05.37

200m Individual Medley

1	Susan Rolph	Newcastle	2:18.02
2	Lucy Findley	Wycombe	2:20.08
3	Dawn Palmer	Killerwhales	2:22.33

400m Individual Medley

1	Helen Slatter	Warrington W	4:52.15
2	Victoria Hale	Swansea	4:57.95
3	Dawn Palmer	Killerwhales	4:58.24

4 x 200m Freestyle Team

1	Portsmouth Northsea	8:36.86
2	Leeds	8:44.02
3	Nova Centurion	8:44.80

4 x 100m Medley Team

1	Portsmouth Northsea	4:21.79
2	Nova Centurion	4:27.29
3	Leeds	4:30.89

GB Club Team Championships

Men's winners are shown first, women's winners second, for each event

50m Freestyle

1 A Ruckwood	Birm'ham	24.79
1 N Goodwin	Nova Cent.	27.64

100m Freestyle

1 A Clayton	Leeds	53.38
1 S Rolph	Newcastle	59.14

200m Freestyle

1 A Clayton	Leeds	1:55.64
1 A Bennett	Nova Cent.	2:05.11

400m Freestyle

1 G Smith	Stockport	4:03.00
1 S Hardcastle	Bracknell	4:16.60

800m Freestyle (Women)

1 S Hardcastle	Bracknell	8:44.93

1500m Freestyle (Men)

1 G Smith	Stockport	15:26.74

100m Backstroke

1 A Ruckwood	Birm'ham	58.10
1 E Tattam	Portsm'th	1:05.93

200m Backstroke

1 A Ruckwood	Birm'ham	2:04.14
1 J Deakins	Coventry	2:18.48

100m Breaststroke

1 N Gillingham	Birm'ham	1:05.43
1 L Rogers	Millfield	1:14.44

200m Breaststroke

1 N Gillingham	Birm'ham	2:20.34
1 M Hardiman	Birm'ham	2:36.86

100m Butterfly

1 D Warren	Leeds	57.79
1 N Goodwin	Nova Cent.	1:03.77

200m Butterfly

1 J Hickman	Stockport	2:05.18
1 H Slatter	Warr'ton	2:18.25

200m Individual Medley

1 C Jones	Cardiff	2:08.84
1 H Slatter	Warr'ton	2:20.66

400m Individual Medley

1 C Jones	Cardiff	4:35.98
1 S Hardcastle	Bracknell	4:54.06

4 x 100m Medley Team

1 Birmingham		3:58.76
1 Portsmouth Northsea		4:24.29

4 x 100m Freestyle Team

1 Leeds		3:37.11
1 Nova Centurion		3:59.54

National Winter Championships

Men's winners are shown first, women's winners second, for each event

50m Freestyle

1 N Metcalfe	Leeds	23.71
1 K Pickering	Ipswich	25.99

100m Freestyle

1 A Clayton	Leeds	51.30
1 K Pickering	Ipswich	56.06

200m Freestyle

1 A Clayton	Leeds	1:49.17
1 S Hardcastle	Bracknell	2:00.08

400m Freestyle

1 A Clayton	Leeds	3:49.75
1 S Hardcastle	Bracknell	4:07.06

800m Freestyle (Women)

1 S Hardcastle	Bracknell	8:23.96

1500m Freestyle (Men)

1 G Smith	Stockport	15:12.20

50m Backstroke

1 N Willey	Barnet C	25.95
1 K Osher	Barnet C	29.62

100m Backstroke

1 M Harris	Waltham	54.26
1 K Osher	Barnet C	1:02.08

200m Backstroke

1 A Ruckwood	Birm'ham	1:57.22
1 K Osher	Barnet C	2:11.71

50m Breaststroke

1 A Clapper	Coventry	29.52
1 K Rake	Maxwell	32.72

100m Breaststroke

1 A Clapper	Coventry	1:03.05
1 J King	Tigersh'ks	1:10.06

200m Breaststroke

1 A Clapper	Coventry	2:14.85
1 J King	Tigersh'ks	2:30.00

50m Butterfly

1 M Foster	Barnet C	24.98
1 A Bennett	Nova Cent.	28.84

100m Butterfly

1 J Hickman	Stockport	55.55
1 S Greenep	Ferndown	1:02.48

200m Butterfly

1 J Hickman	Stockport	1:57.21
1 H Slatter	Warr'ton	2:15.59

200m Individual Medley

1 J Hickman	Stockport	2:02.11
1 S Hardcastle	Bracknell	2:16.39

400m Individual Medley

1 G Robins	Portsm'th	4:19.28
1 S Hardcastle	Bracknell	4:44.02

4 x 100m Freestyle Team

1 Leeds	3:24.68
1 Nova Centurion	3:53.94

4 x 200m Freestyle Team

1 Leeds	7:27.46
1 Nova Centurion	8:25.87

4 x 100m Medley Team

1 Birmingham	3:48.19
1 Nova Centurion	4:17.72

National Diving Championships

MEN

1m Springboard

1 A Ali (Sheffield)	328.40

3m Springboard

1 R Morgan (Sheffield)	589.55

Platform

1 R Morgan (Sheffield)	564.00

WOMEN

1m Springboard

1 V Stenning (Southend)	229.80

3m Springboard

1 O Clark (Southend)	444.25

10m Platform

1 H Allen (Sheffield)	346.80

Table Tennis

European Championships
Birmingham   Mar25-Apr 4

Men's Team

Group A		Group B	
Sweden 2	Belgium 4	England 4	Hungary 0
Poland 1	Sweden 4	Austria 0	Greece 4
Germany 4	Czech R 0	France 4	Greece 2
Sweden 4	Czech R 0	England 4	Greece 3
Germany 4	Poland 1	Russia 0	France 4
Holland 4	Czech R 3	Russia 2	England 4
Belgium 3	Holland 4	Austria 3	Hungary 4
Germany 4	Holland 1	France 4	Austria 0
Germany 4	Belgium 2	Russia 3	Hungary 4
Poland 4	Holland 0	England 2	Austria 4
Czech R 2	Belgium 4	Russia 4	Austria 3
Poland 1	Belgium 4	France 4	England 0
Poland 4	Czech R 0	Hungary 2	France 4
Holland 2	Sweden 4	Russia 4	Greece 3
Germany 2	Sweden 4	Greece 3	Hungary 4

Group A: 1. Sweden 9pts, 2. Germany 9, 3. Belgium 8, 4. Poland 7, 5. Holland 7, 6. Czech Rep. 5
Group B: 1. France 10pts, 2. England 8, 3. Hungary 8, 4. Russia 7, 5. Greece 6, 6. Austria 6
Semi-finals
England 1 Sweden 4
France 4 Germany 3
3rd/4th Play-off
England 2 Germany 4
Final
Sweden 3 France 4

Women's Team

Group A		Group B	
Sweden 1	Romania 4	France 4	Holland 3
Belgium 0	Germany 4	Hungary 4	Slovakia 0
Russia 4	Belgium 0	England 4	Slovakia 1
Romania 4	Belgium 0	Holland 4	Slovakia 1
Croatia 1	Russia 4	Italy 4	England 3
Romania 4	Croatia 0	Holland 2	Italy 4
Germany 4	Sweden 2	France 0	Hungary 4
Russia 4	Germany 2	England 4	Hungary 2
Croatia 1	Sweden 4	France 2	Italy 4
Belgium 2	Croatia 4	Italy 4	Slovakia 1
Sweden 4	Belgium 1	Hungary 4	Italy 0
Sweden 1	Russia 4	England 4	Holland 1
Germany 4	Romania 1	France 2	England 4
Croatia 0	Germany 4	Holland 2	Hungary 4
Romania 0	Russia 4	Slovakia 1	France 4

Group A: 1. Russia 10pts, 2. Germany 9, 3. Romania 8, 4. Sweden 7, 5. Croatia 6, 6. Belgium 5
Group B: 1. Hungary 9pts, 2. England 9, 3. Italy 9, 4. France 7, 5. Holland 6, 6. Slovakia 5
Semi-finals
England 1 Russia 4
Germany 4 Hungary 0
3rd/4th Play-off
England 0 Hungary 4
Final
Russia 4 Germany 1

Men's Individual
Singles Semi-finals
Jean-Michel Saive BEL bt Patrick Chila FRA 21-12, 21-15, 21-8
Jan-Ove Waldner SWE bt Zoran Primorac CRO 21-18, 24-26, 17-21, 21-19, 21-16
Singles Final
Jean-Michel Saive bt Jan-Ove Waldner 21-23, 21-10, 21-17, 21-16

Doubles Final
Calin Creanga/Zoran Kalinic GRE/INP bt Jean-Michel Saive/ Zoran Primorac BEL/CRO 21-17, 25-23

Women's Individual
Singles Semi-finals
Marie Svensson SWE bt Jie Schöpp GER 16-21, 21-14, 21-18, 21-17
Gerdie Keen HOL bt Nicole Struse GER 22-20, 21-16, 19-21, 16-21, 22-20
Singles Final
Marie Svensson bt Gerdie Keen 21-12, 21-14, 21-18

Doubles Final
Csilla Batorfi/Kriztina Toth HUN bt Elena Timina/Irina Palina RUS 21-17, 21-9

Mixed Doubles Final
Primorac/Batorfi bt Creanga/Badescu 21-16, 21-13

World Cup
Guangzhou   Aug 19-22
Quarter-finals
Zoran Primorac CRO bt Chen Xinhua ENG 21-17, 21-19
Peter Karlsson SWE bt Ding Yi AUT 21-13, 21-11
Wang Tao CHN bt Jean-Michel Saive BEL 21-12, 21-18
Johnny Huang CAN bt Ma Wenge CHN 21-12, 21-7
Semi-finals
Zoran Primorac bt Peter Karlsson 10-21, 21-19, 21-19, 21-23, 21-13
Wang Tao bt Johnny Huang 21-13, 21-15, 21-8
3rd/4th Play-off
Johnny Huang bt Peter Karlsson 16-21, 21-17, 21-19
Final
Zoran Primorac bt Wang Tao 21-19, 16-21, 21-18, 18-21, 21-18

European Nations Cup
Bayreuth   Jan 14 15

Group A	Group B
Poland 3 Germany 2	Sweden 3 England 0
Germany 3 Czech R. 1	Sweden 3 Austria 0
Germany 3 Belgium 1	Sweden 3 France 2
Belgium 3 Czech R. 0	France 3 Austria 2
Belgium 3 Poland 0	France 3 England 1
Czech R. 3 Poland 1	Austria 3 England 2

Semi-finals
Sweden 3 Belgium 1
France 3 Germany 0
Final
Sweden 3 France 2

European League Play Offs

MEN
Semi-final (1st Leg) *Liege* *Dec 14*
Belgium 4   England 2
Semi-final (2nd Leg) *Mansfield* *Feb 15*
England 4   Belgium 3

WOMEN
Final (1st Leg) *Crewe* *Feb 17*
England 1   Germany 4
Final (2nd Leg) *Stuttgart* *Feb 22*
Germany 5   England 0

Other Tournaments

SWEDISH OPEN *Karlskrona* *Nov 24-28, 1993*
Men's Singles
Andrzej Grubba POL bt Chen Xinhua ENG 15-21, 21-18, 21-12, 19-21, 21-18
Women's Singles
Csilla Batorfi HUN bt Wang Chen CHN 17-21, 21-8, 19-21, 21-19, 21-10
Men's Doubles
Lin Zhigang/Lin Guoliang CHN bt Fetzner/Rosskopf GER 21-19, 19-21, 21-7
Women's Doubles
Li Ju/Wu Na CHN bt Kim Book Sik/Park Hae Jung KOR 21-19, 21-17

EUROPE TOP 12 *Arezzo* *Feb 4-6*
Men's Singles
Jean-Michel Saive BEL bt Jan-Ove Waldner SWE 17-21, 21-10, 21-19, 15-21, 21-18
Women's Singles
Jie Schöpp GER bt Otiltia Badescu ROM 21-17, 17-21, 22-20, 21-15

ASIA TOP 8 *Huangshi City* *Nov 1-3, 1993*
Men's Singles
Wang Tao CHN bt Lee Chul Seng KOR 13-21, 21-15, 23-21, 21-14
Women's Singles
Deng Yaping CHN bt Chai Po Wa HKG 21-13, 21-17, 21-18

DEUTSCHLAND CUP *Trier* *May 21-22*
Men's Singles
Ma Wenge CHN bt Chen Xinhua ENG 21-12, 21-13, 21-18
Women's Singles
Zörner Tian CHN bt He Qianhong CHN 16-21, 21-12, 21-18, 22-20

CHINA GRAND PRIX *Dailian City* *June 3-5*
Men's Singles
Wang Tao CHN bt Kong Linghui CHN 21-15, 22-20, 21-17
Women's Singles
Liu Wei CHN bt Chan Tan Lui HKG 21-11, 21-18, 21-17

US OPEN *Annaheim* *June 30-July 4*
Men's Singles
Kong Linghui CHN bt Liu Guoliang CHN 21-9, 21-13, 21-17
Women's Singles
Gao Jun USA bt Amy Feng USA 21-16, 21-10, 21-14
Men's Doubles
Liu Guoliang/Li Zhigang CHN bt Chatelain/Legout FRA 21-16, 21-16

Women's Doubles
Park Kyung Ae/Lee Mi Ok KOR bt Chen Jing/Chen Chiu-Tan TPE 21-16, 21-19
Mixed Doubles
Fim Young Jin/Park Kyung Ae KOR bt Lee Sang Joon/Kim Min Kyu KOR 2-10, 17-21, 21-16

Domestic Events

English National Championships
Kings Lynn *Mar 5-6*
MEN
Quarter-finals
X Chen bt A Eden 21-12, 21-6, 21-11
M Syed bt G Solder 21-6, 21-17, 21-7
A Cooke bt S Andrew 21-15, 21-14, 21-10
N Mason bt C Prean 21-16, 15-21, 21-16, 21-17
Semi-finals
Chen bt Syed 15-21, 21-14, 14-21, 21-14, 21-15
Cooke bt Mason 21-15, 21-18, 21-15
Final
Chen bt Cooke 21-12, 21-13, 18-21, 21-8

Doubles Final
S Andrew/N Mason bt J Holland/A Cooke 21-16, 21-13

WOMEN
Quarter-finals
L Lomas bt L Radford 21-11, 21-16, 21-4
S Marling bt K Goodall 22-20, 21-15, 18-21, 19-21, 21-19
A Gordon bt F Mommessin 21-10, 21-18, 13-21, 18-21, 21-19
A Holt bt N Deaton 21-14, 20-22, 21-13, 21-13
Semi-finals
Lomas bt Marling 21-7, 21-10, 21-12
Holt bt Gordon 22-20, 14-21, 21-14, 21-14
Final
Lomas bt Holt 21-17, 21-17, 22-20, 21-19

Doubles Final
L Lomas/F Mommessin bt K Goodall/A Holt 19-21, 22-20, 21-10

Mixed Doubles Final
S Andrew/F Mommessin bt A Perry/S Marling 21-19, 21-9

British Leagues
MEN

Premier Division	P	W	D	L	SF	SA	Pts
BFL Grove	14	14	0	0	185	11	28
Team Peniel I	14	11	1	2	128	68	23
Sedgefield District I	14	7	3	4	101	95	17
DML Launceston I	14	6	0	8	82	114	12
Horsham Angels	14	5	1	8	85	111	11
Policy Plus St Neots	14	5	1	8	83	113	11
Vymura International I	14	2	1	11	65	131	5
Bathwick Tyres	14	2	1	11	55	141	5

Division 1 (North)	P	W	D	L	SF	SA	Pts
BFL Grove II	14	13	0	1	86	26	26
Olton & West Warwicks	14	11	2	1	86	26	24
Sedgefield District II	14	7	4	3	69	43	18
R M Lincoln	14	6	2	6	57	55	14
City of Sunderland	14	6	1	7	60	52	13
Bribar Humberside	14	2	4	8	35	77	8
British Gas CMK	14	2	3	9	40	72	7
Cheltenham Saracens	14	1	0	13	15	97	2

Division 1 (South)	P	W	D	L	SF	SA	Pts
BFL Grove III	12	8	1	3	58	38	17
Bribar Colley Toyota I	12	6	4	2	60	36	16
OLOP I	12	6	4	2	53	43	15
Edison T T C	12	5	3	4	46	50	13
BSG Brentwood I	12	4	1	7	43	53	9
G S Larkhall	12	2	4	6	41	55	8
Rejects I	12	2	2	8	35	61	6

Leading Averages (Premier)

	P	W	L	Ave %
Desmond Douglas (BFL)	39	39	0	100.00
Alan Cooke (BFL)	30	30	0	100.00
Eugueni Brainin (BFL)	36	35	1	97.22
Chris Oldfield (BFL)	30	28	2	93.33
Steve Ward (BFL)	27	24	3	89.89

WOMEN

Premier Division	P	W	D	L	SF	SA	Pts
BFL Grove I	10	10	0	0	57	3	20
Hull Sandhill I	10	8	0	2	40	20	16
S Kesteven Sovereigns I	10	6	0	4	31	29	12
Hull Sandhill II	10	3	1	6	21	39	7
Graham Spicer	10	1	1	8	13	47	3
Welsh Ladies	10	0	2	8	18	42	2

Division 1	P	W	D	L	SF	SA	Pts
BFL Grove II	10	9	1	0	45	15	19
Horsham Angels	10	5	3	2	37	23	13
City of Milton Keynes	10	5	2	3	30	30	12
Amity Generation	10	3	3	4	30	30	9
S Kesteven Sovreigns II	10	2	2	6	22	38	6
Bayer Bradford	10	0	1	9	16	44	1

Leading Averages (Premier)

	P	W	L	Ave %
Lisa Lomas (BFL)	16	16	0	100.00
Andrea holt (BFL)	12	12	0	100.00
Nicola Deaton (BFL)	6	6	0	100.00
Elena Timina (BFL)	14	13	1	92.85
Helen Tower (BFL)	12	10	2	83.33

County Championship

Premier Division	P	W	D	L	SF	SA	Pts
Essex	7	6	1	0	51	19	13
Derbyshire	7	4	1	2	36	34	9
Middlesex	7	4	0	3	36	34	8
Lancashire	7	2	3	2	35	35	7
Staffordshire	7	3	1	3	33	37	7
Devon	7	1	3	3	32	38	5
Sussex	7	1	2	4	30	40	4
Surrey	7	1	1	5	27	43	3

EPSON World Rankings

As at April 22 1994

MEN

1	Jean-Michel Saive	BEL	2021
2	Jan-Ove Waldner	SWE	2003
3	Ma Wenge	CHN	1985
4	Tao Wang	CHN	1982
5	Kim Taek Soo	KOR	1973
6	Zoran Primorac	CRO	1931
7	Jean-Philippe Gatien	FRA	1928
8	Peter Karlsson	SWE	1911
9	Li Gun Sang	KOR	1908
10	Andrzej Grubba	POL	1898
11	Jörgen Persson	SWE	1896
12	Jörg Rosskopf	GER	1869
13	Johnny Huang	CAN	1864
14	Chen Xinhua	ENG	1863
15	Liu Guoliang	CHN	1842
27	Carl Prean	ENG	1694
55	Alan Cooke	ENG	1577
80	Matthew Syed	ENG	1475

WOMEN

1	Deng Yaping	CHN	2258
2	Qiao Hong	CHN	2126
3	Gao Jun	CHN	1995
4	Chen Zihe	CHN	1992
5	Chai Po Wa	HKG	1977
6	Chen Jing	TPE	1972
7	Li Bun Hui	KOR	1949
8	Wang Chen	CHN	1945
9	Yu Sun Bok	KOR	1928
10	Tang Weiyi	CHN	1927
11	Liu Wei	CHN	1918
12	Jing Jun Hong	SIN	1911
13	Zhang Qin	CHN	1905
14	Geng Lijuan	CAN	1903
15	Zheng Yuan	CHN	1894
50	Lisa Lomas	ENG	1649
86	Alison Gordon	ENG	1483
90	Andrea Holt	ENG	1467

Tennis

So Martina's gone and even the Duchess of Kent, who ministered to Jana Novotna after last year's final, was not persuasive enough to make her stay another year. Shame, really. It took too long for Navratilova to get loved. This year, the passions of the crowd were with her and the women's competition was the high spot of The Championship. Passion in the men's game (for us Brits) lasted only until Guy Forget dismantled Jeremy Bates' game. The final was without emotion. Sampras walloped Ivanisevic. From Wimbledon to Wimbledon, the American won four of five grand slam events, losing only to Jim Courier in the quarter-finals of the French Open and while he may continue to find clay resistant to his charms, grass just wilts. Unless they do lift the net two feet, chain his back foot to the service line or string the rackets with window putty, Sampras really could compile a Wimbledon record that makes Navratilova's look moderate. Think of something quick, eh?

Andre Agassi may not be to everyone's taste; like Pat Cash in his heyday, he plays to the crowd just a little *too* much. Yet Agassi does offer an alternative. Having had to learn a different kind of game because he isn't twenty-foot tall, his tennis is imaginative. Not quite McEnroe imaginative or Rosewall imaginative, but not bad. Agassi had a spirited Wimbledon before losing to Todd Martin, and then went on to a sensational US Open. Unseeded, Agassi beat four seeds along the way to the title. Chang, Muster, Martin (sweet revenge) and Stich all fell to the whiplash forehand. Maybe there's a God after all.

Steffi Graf had a perfect start to the year, winning the Australian Open, her fifteenth grand slam title. As Graf is still only 25, it is a wonderful record of achievement. It offered her little by way of compensation for the rest of her year, though. The three-time winner of the French Open lost in the semi-final and two weeks later was unceremoniously dumped out of Wimbledon (a five-time winner) in the first round by Lori McNeil. Conchita Martínez took that title, but it was Arantxa Sanchez-Vicario's year. The Spaniard upset everybody by winning the 1989 French Open, but for four years won nothing else - except a few million dollars. This summer, though, the French and US titles finally gave the CV a touch of class.

Sanchez Vicario, though, is 23 and that, by Hingis standards, is over the hill and halfway up the next one. Martina Hingis (I'll leave you to guess what the parents were thinking) is the 14 year old prodigy who won junior Wimbledon in June and turned professional after her birthday at the end of September. Outrage everywhere, but it's worth recalling that Graf turned pro at 13 and Sanchez Vicario at a mature 14 and a half.

British tennis could do with a Hingis. Bates at Wimbledon was one of the few high points and it's comforting that Mark Petchey sits adjacent to Bates in the world's top 100. Neither, however, will like to be reminded of the fact that British teams have seven times won the Davis Cup. Defeat by Romania in July (and yes, they both lost crucial matches) condemned British tennis to the Davis Cup equivalent of the Beazer Homes League. British women were invisible, yet we leave you with this thought. At Wimbledon, Clare Wood lost in the first round of the singles, double and mixed doubles (without winning a set) and came way with £5,550 prize money. For less than three hours on court she earned over £1,800 pounds an hour. Even at the serious rates we get for compiling this book we're impressed

QUOTES

"It got to the point where I would have offered Sue Barker and Ann Jones wild cards - **George Hendon, tournament director at Brighton as players pulled out of the 1993 championship. Sadly, it happened in 1994 too.**

"Nein" - **Michael Stich, when asked if he received any good luck messages before the Davis Cup final against Australia.**

"A dream creation, whose eyes radiate like diamonds, whose hair shines like silk" - **Günther Parsche, who stabbed Monica Seles on court in April 1993, talking about Steffi Graf.**

"You guys need some serious help with the laws in Germany if that's all you can give someone who stabs a person" - **Martina Navratilova, on the two-year suspended sentence handed out to Parsche.**

"I've been at the twilight of my career longer than most people have had their careers" - **Martina Navratilova.**

"I like to be a good example, but I was too disappointed to care. I have never done that before and I never will again" - **Navratilova again, who smashed her racket then dumped it in a courtside bin after losing to Miriam Oremans in the first round of the French Open.**

"I don't know. I didn't go with him...'" - **Navratilova at Wimbledon, when asked about Boris Becker's 'toilet break'.**

"Smile a lot and enjoy it while it lasts, but it's hard to enjoy it when they start to take pictures through your bedroom window" - **Navratilova's advice to Mary Pierce.**

"I *am* normal" - **Lindsay Davenport, at Wimbledon, when asked by a journalist, "if she had a great fear of being normal".**

"You are chicken-shit, that's what you are" - **Wayne Ferreira to Wimbledon umpire, Harkan Roos. He was fined £660.**

"Maybe it was a bit like watching cricket" - **Pete Sampras, responding to criticism that his Stella Artois final against Todd Martin was boring.**

"One of the most boring finals in history" - **Fred Perry, on Sampras against Ivanisevic at Wimbledon. Seems everyone's got it in for Sampras.**

"In hindsight, maybe we made a mistake" - **Brian Tobin, International Tennis Federation president, on the decision to lower the miniumum age to 13 years and 11 months in order to allow Capriati to play on the professional circuit.**

"The next time a 14 year old girl turns pro, they ought to shoot the parents, hang the coach and send the WTA staff into exile in the Russian army" - **Richard Williams, who advises Venus Williams, a 14-year-old prodigy from California, touted to become the next phenomenon on the women's (or should it be the girls') tour.**

Tennis

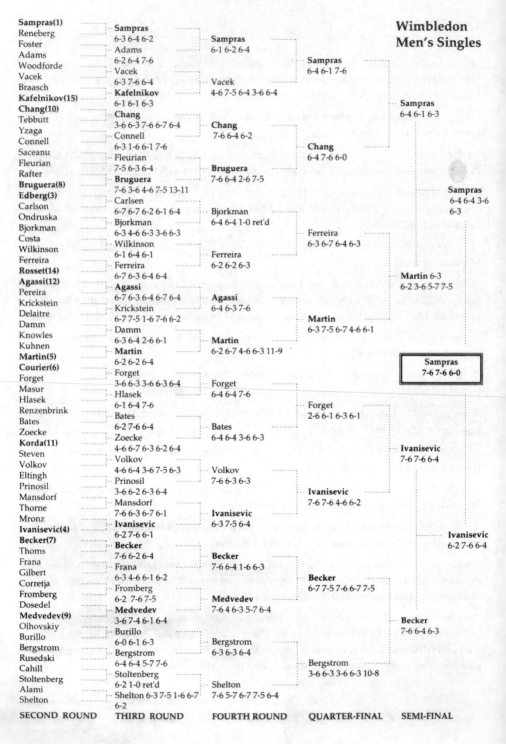

Wimbledon Men's Singles

SECOND ROUND

Sampras(1) — **Sampras** 6-3 6-4 6-2
Reneberg
Foster — Adams 6-2 6-4 7-6
Adams
Woodforde — Vacek 6-3 7-6 6-4
Vacek
Braasch — **Kafelnikov** 6-1 6-1 6-3
Kafelnikov(15)
Chang(10) — **Chang** 3-6 6-3 7-6 6-7 6-4
Tebbutt
Yzaga — Connell 6-3 1-6 6-1 7-6
Connell
Saceanu — Fleurian 7-5 6-3 6-4
Fleurian
Rafter — **Bruguera** 7-6 3-6 4-6 7-5 13-11
Bruguera(8)
Edberg(3) — Carlsen 6-7 6-7 6-2 6-1 6-4
Carlson
Ondruska — Bjorkman 6-3 4-6 6-3 3-6 6-3
Bjorkman
Costa — Wilkinson 6-1 6-4 6-1
Wilkinson
Ferreira — Ferreira 6-7 6-3 6-4 6-4
Rosset(14)
Agassi(12) — **Agassi** 6-7 6-3 6-4 6-7 6-4
Pereira
Krickstein — Krickstein 6-7 7-5 1-6 7-6 6-2
Delaitre
Damm — Damm 6-3 6-4 2-6 6-1
Knowles
Kuhnen — **Martin** 6-2 6-2 6-4
Martin(5)
Courier(6) — Forget 3-6 6-3 3-6 6-3 6-4
Forget
Masur — Hlasek 6-1 6-4 7-6
Hlasek
Renzenbrink — Bates 6-2 7-6 6-4
Bates
Zoecke — Zoecke 4-6 6-7 6-3 6-2 6-4
Korda(11)
Steven — Volkov 4-6 6-4 3-6 7-5 6-3
Volkov
Eltingh — Prinosil 3-6 6-2 6-3 6-4
Prinosil
Mansdorf — Mansdorf 7-6 6-3 6-7 6-1
Thorne
Mronz — **Ivanisevic** 6-2 7-6 6-1
Ivanisevic(4)
Becker(7) — **Becker** 7-6 6-2 6-4
Thoms
Frana — Frana 6-3 4-6 6-1 6-2
Gilbert
Corretja — Fromberg 6-2 7-6 7-5
Fromberg
Dosedel — **Medvedev** 3-6 7-4 6-1 6-4
Medvedev(9)
Olhovskiy — Burillo 6-0 6-1 6-3
Burillo
Bergstrom — Bergstrom 6-4 6-4 5-7 7-6
Rusedski
Cahill — Stoltenberg 6-2 1-0 ret'd
Stoltenberg
Alami — Shelton 6-3 7-5 1-6 6-7 6-2
Shelton

THIRD ROUND

Sampras 6-1 6-2 6-4
Vacek 4-6 7-5 6-4 3-6 6-4
Chang 7-6 6-4 6-2
Bruguera 7-6 6-4 2-6 7-5
Bjorkman 6-4 6-4 1-0 ret'd
Ferreira 6-2 6-2 6-3
Agassi 6-4 6-3 7-6
Martin 6-2 6-7 4-6 6-3 11-9
Forget 6-4 6-4 7-6
Bates 6-4 6-4 3-6 6-3
Volkov 7-6 6-3 6-3
Ivanisevic 6-3 7-5 6-4
Becker 7-6 6-4 1-6 6-3
Medvedev 7-6 4 6-3 5-7 6-4
Bergstrom 6-3 6-3 6-4
Shelton 7-6 5-7 6-7 7-5 6-4

FOURTH ROUND

Sampras 6-4 6-1 7-6
Chang 6-4 7-6 6-0
Ferreira 6-3 6-7 6-4 6-3
Martin 6-3 7-5 6-7 4-6 6-1
Forget 2-6 6-1 6-3 6-1
Ivanisevic 7-6 7-6 4-6 6-2
Becker 6-7 7-5 7-6 6-7 7-5
Bergstrom 3-6 6-3 3-6 6-3 10-8

QUARTER-FINAL

Sampras 6-4 6-1 6-3
Martin 6-3 6-2 3-6 5-7 7-5
Ivanisevic 7-6 7-6 6-4
Becker 7-6 6-4 6-3

SEMI-FINAL

Sampras 6-4 6-4 3-6 6-3
Ivanisevic 6-2 7-6 6-4

FINAL

Sampras 7-6 7-6 6-0

SECOND ROUND   THIRD ROUND   FOURTH ROUND   QUARTER-FINAL   SEMI-FINAL

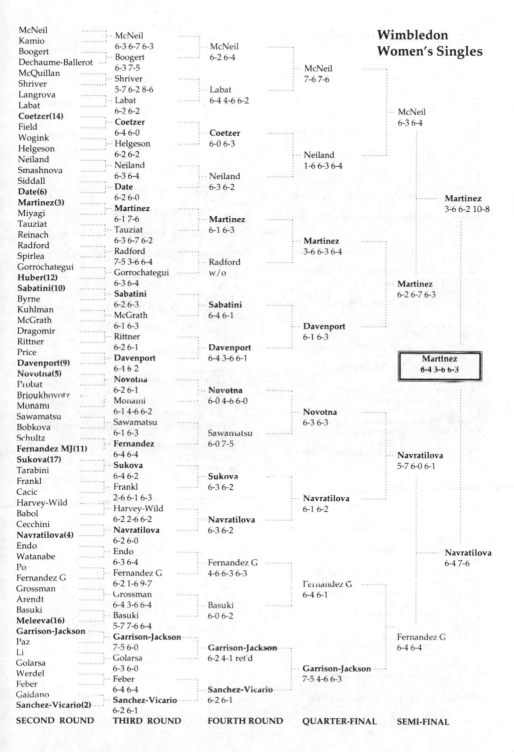

Wimbledon
Women's Singles

McNeil	McNeil				
Kamio	6-3 6-7 6-3	McNeil			
Boogert	Boogert	6-2 6-4			
Dechaume-Ballerot	6-3 7-5		McNeil		
McQuillan	Shriver		7-6 7-6		
Shriver	5-7 6-2 8-6	Labat			
Langrova	Labat	6-4 4-6 6-2		McNeil	
Labat	6-2 6-2			6-3 6-4	
Coetzer(14)	Coetzer				
Field	6-4 6-0	Coetzer			
Wogink	Helgeson	6-0 6-3			
Helgeson	6-2 6-2		Neiland		
Neiland	Neiland		1-6 6-3 6-4		
Smashnova	6-3 6-4	Neiland			
Siddall	Date	6-3 6-2			Martinez
Date(6)	6-2 6-0				3-6 6-2 10-8
Martinez(3)	Martinez				
Miyagi	6-1 7-6	Martinez			
Tauziat	Tauziat	6-1 6-3			
Reinach	6-3 6-7 6-2		Martinez		
Radford	Radford		3-6 6-3 6-4		
Spirlea	7-5 3-6 6-4	Radford			
Gorrochategui	Gorrochategui	w/o		Martinez	
Huber(12)	6-3 6-4			6-2 6-7 6-3	
Sabatini(10)	Sabatini				
Byrne	6-2 6-3	Sabatini			
Kuhlman	McGrath	6-4 6-1			
McGrath	6-1 6-3		Davenport		
Dragomir	Rittner		6-1 6-3		
Rittner	6-2 6-1	Davenport			
Price	Davenport	6-4 3-6 6-1			Martinez
Davenport(9)	6-4 6 2				6-4 3-6 6-3
Novotna(5)	Novotna				
Probat	6-2 6-1	Novotna			
Brioukhovotz	Monami	6-0 4-6 6-0			
Monami	6-1 4-6 6-2		Novotna		
Sawamatsu	Sawamatsu		6-3 6-3		
Bobkova	6-1 6-3	Sawamatsu			
Schultz	Fernandez	6-0 7-5		Navratilova	
Fernandez MJ(11)	6-4 6-4			5-7 6-0 6-1	
Sukova(17)	Sukova				
Tarabini	6-4 6-2	Sukova			
Frankl	Frankl	6-3 6-2			
Cacic	2-6 6-1 6-3		Navratilova		
Harvey-Wild	Harvey-Wild		6-1 6-2		
Babol	6-2 2-6 6-2	Navratilova			
Cecchini	Navratilova	6-3 6-2			Navratilova
Navratilova(4)	6-2 6-0				6-4 7-6
Endo	Endo				
Watanabe	6-3 6-4	Fernandez G			
Po	Fernandez G	4-6 6-3 6-3			
Fernandez G	6-2 1-6 9-7		Fernandez G		
Grossman	Grossman		6-4 6-1		
Arendt	6-4 3-6 6-4	Basuki			
Basuki	Basuki	6-0 6-2		Fernandez G	
Meleeva(16)	5-7 7-6 6-4			6-4 6-4	
Garrison-Jackson	Garrison-Jackson				
Paz	7-5 6-0	Garrison-Jackson			
Li	Golarsa	6-2 4-1 ret'd			
Golarsa	6-3 6-0		Garrison-Jackson		
Werdel	Feber		7-5 4-6 6-3		
Feber	6-4 6-4	Sanchez-Vicario			
Gaidano	Sanchez-Vicario	6-2 6-1			
Sanchez-Vicario(2)	6-2 6-1				

Martinez
6-4 3-6 6-3

SECOND ROUND	THIRD ROUND	FOURTH ROUND	QUARTER-FINAL	SEMI-FINAL

The Championships

Wimbledon   June 20 - Jul 3
MEN'S DOUBLES
Selected results from rounds 1-3; complete results from quarter finals. Seedings in brackets.
1st Round
Ferreira RSA/Stich GER(2) bt Cowan/Richardson GBR
4-6 6-4 6-3 6-4
Bates GBR/Van Rensburg RSA bt Garnett/Middleton
USA 7-6 6-1 6-4
Montana/Pugh USA bt Foster/Maclagan GBR
6-4 6-4 7-6
Masur AUS/Pate USA bt Hand/Wilkinson GBR
7-6 7-5 3-6 6-4
Henman/Petchey GBR bt Devries/Johnson USA
7-6 6-3 7-6
Bailey GBR/Rusedski CAN bt Hlasek SUI/Vacek CZE
6-4 6-3 7-6
2nd Round
Kruger/Ondruska RSA bt Bates/Van Rensburg
2-6 6-3 7-5 7-5
Goeliner GER/Kafelnikov RUS(14) bt Henman/Petchey
2-6 6-7 6-4 6-4 6-4
Quarter-finals
Ferreira/Stich(14) bt Barnard/Haygarth
6-3 7-5 6-2
Woodbridge/Woodforde(5) bt Eltingh/Haarhuis(3)
4-6 7-6 6-2 6-7 9-7
Goellner/Kafelnikov(14) bt Nijssen/Suk(6)
6-4 6-7 6-4 3-6 6-4
Connell/Galbraith(2) bt Bale/Steven
7-6 7-6 6-2
Semi-finals
Woodbridge/Woodforde(5) bt Ferreira/Stich(14)
6-2 7-6 6-2
Connell/Galbraith(2) bt Goellner/Kafelnikov(14)
4-6 6-3 6-4 6-2
Final
Woodbridge/Woodforde(5) bt Connell/Galbraith(2)
7-6 6-3 6-1

WOMEN'S DOUBLES
1st Round
Jaggard AUS/Werdel USA bt Durie GBR/Field AUS
6-2 7-6
Siddall/Wainwright GBR bt Benjamin USA/Dragomir
ROM 6-2 4-6 7-5
Golarsa ITA/Vis NED(16) bt Taylor/Ward GBR
6-2 7-6
Drichuia NED/Muric CRO bt Coorengel HOL/Smith
GBR 6-2 5-7 7-5
Hetherington CAN/Stafford USA(15) bt
Pullin/Woodroffe GBR 6-3 6-7 7-5
Novotna CZE/Sanchez-Vicario ESP(2) bt Lake/Wood
GBR 6-1 6-1
2nd Round
Halard/Tauziat FRA(12) bt Siddall/Wainwright
7-5 6-2
Quarter-finals
G Fernandez/Zvereva(1) bt Harvey-Wild/Rubin
6-1 4-6 6-0
Bollegraf/Navratilova(4) bt Drichuia/Muric
6-4 6-2

Arendt/Radford bt Medvedeva/Neiland(7)
2-6 6-3 6-3
Novotna/Sanchez-Vicario(2) bt Shriver/Smylie(5)
6-2 6-4
Semi-finals
Fernandez/Zvereva(1) bt Bollegraf/Navratilova(4)
6-4 6-4
Novotna/Sanchez-Vicario(2) bt Arendt/Radford
4-6 7-5 6-3
Final
Fernandez/Zvereva(1) bt Novotna/Sanchez-Vicario(2)
6-4 6-1

MIXED DOUBLES
1st Round
Bailey GBR/ Sanchez-Vicario ESP bt Bauer/Collins USA
6-3 7-6
Bates/Durie GBR bt Cannon/Stafford USA
6-3 6-3
Hand/Lake GBR bt Norval RSA/Vis NED(14)
6-4 1-6 6-3
Ruah VEN/Labat ARG bt Petchey/Wood GBR
7-6 7-5
Garat ARG/Monami BEL bt Foster/Taylor GBR
6-3 6-3
2nd Round
Connell CAN/Davenport USA (6) bt Bailey/Sanchez-
Vicario 3-6 6-3 6-4
Middleton/McNeil USA bt Bates/Durie
2-6 6-4 6-4
Ruah/Labat bt Hand/Lake
6-3 7-6
Quarter-finals
Connell CAN/Davenport USA (6) bt Fitzgerald/Smylie
AUS (11) 6-3 7-6
Woodbridge AUS/Sukova CZE (4) bt Olhovskiy
RUS/Neiland LAT (7) 6-2 6-4
Middleton/McNeil USA bt Ruah VEN/Labat ARG
6-3 6-2
Black ZIM/Shriver USA bt Woodforde AUS/McGrath
USA (5) 7-6 3-6 7-5
Semi-finals
Woodbridge/Sukova (4) bt Connell/Davenport (6)
6-2 6-4
Middleton/McNeil bt Black/Shriver (2)
6-3 7-6
Final
Woodbridge/Sukova bt Middleton/McNeil 3-6 7-5 6-3

BOY'S SINGLES
Semi-finals
Philippoussis AUS (3) bt Delgado GBR 6-3 6-1
Humphries USA (11) bt Schalken NED 6-4 7-6
Final
Humphries (11) bt Philippoussis (3) 7-6 3-6 6-4

GIRL'S SINGLES
Semi-finals
Hingis SUI (8) bt Castera FRA (11) 3-6 6-4 6-1
Jeon KOR (5) bt Nemsakova (6) 6-4 6-1
Final
Hingis (8) bt Jeon (5) 7-5 6-4

Australian Open

Melbourne   *Jan 17-30*

MEN'S DOUBLES

Selected results from rounds 1-3; complete results from quarter-finals. Seedings in brackets.

1st Round

Kratzmann/Kratzmann AUS bt Connell CAN/Galbraith USA (1) 6-7 6-4 6-4

Johnson/Sullivan USA bt Melville USA/ Mueller RSA (8) 6-3 6-4

Martin/Shelton USA bt Mc Enroe/Reneberg USA (6) 7-6 4-6 15-13

DeBeer/De Jager RSA bt Ferreira RSA/Sanchez ESP (16) 6-4 7-6

2nd Round

Kratzmann/Kratzmann bt Siemerink/Vacek CZE 6-4 7-5

Damm/Novacek CZE bt Pearce/Randall USA (15) 6-3 6-2

Lareau/Nestor CAN bt Casal/Sanchez ESP (11) 6-4 6-4

Apell/Bjorkman SWE bt Jensen/Jensen USA (5) 6-7 6-3 8-6

3rd Round

Damm/Novacek bt Kratzmann/Kratzmann 6-2 6-4

Apell/Bjorkman bt Holm/Jarryd SWE (12) 7-6 6-3

Quarter-finals

Damm/Novacek bt Flach/Leach USA (10) 6-4 4-6 6-4 6-3

Eltingh/Haarhuis HOL (3) bt Lareau/Nestor 6-4 7-5 3-6 4-6 7-5

Apell/Bjorkmann bt Woodbridge/Woodforde AUS (4) 6-4 6-2 6-4

Black ZIM/Stark USA (2) bt Nijssen HOL/Suk CZE (7) 6-3 6-4 6-4

Semi-finals

Eltingh/Haarhuis (3) bt Damm/Novacek 6-1 6-4 6-2

Black/Stark (2) bt Apell/Bjorkman 6-1 6-4 6-4

Final

Eltingh/Harhuis (3) bt Black/Stark (2) 6-7 6-3 6-4 6-3

WOMEN'S DOUBLES

1st Round

Lake/Wood GBR bt De lone/De lone USA 6-1 3-6 7-5

2nd Round

Fernandez USA/Zvereva BLR (1) bt Lake/Wood 6-1 6-2

Arendt USA/Radford AUS bt Adams/Rinaldi-Stunkel USA (8) 6-2 6-3

3rd Round

Bollegraf HOL/Graham USA (10) bt Martinez ESP/Neiland LAT (5) 6-3 6-4

Grossman USA/Richardson NZL(14) bt Mal.-Fragniere BUL/Sukova CZE (4) 6-1 6-4

Quarter-finals

Fernandez/Zvereva (1) bt Bollegraf/Graham (10) 6-1 6-3

Shriver USA/Smylie AUS (3) bt Hetherington CAN/Stafford USA (16) 6-3 6-2

Fendick/McGrath USA (7) bt Grossman/Richardson (14) 6-2 6-0

Novatna CZE/Sanchez-Vicario ESP bt Fernandez/Garrison-Jackson USA (6) 6-4 6-4

Semi-final

Fernandez/Zvereva (1) bt Shriver/Smylie 6-3 6-3

Fendick/McGrath bt Novotna/Sanchez-Vicario 6-3 7-5

Final

Fernandez/Zvereva (1) bt Fendick/McGrath (7) 6-3 4-6 6-4

MIXED DOUBLES

1st Round

Randall USA/Hetherington CAN bt Eltingh HOL/Zvereva BLR (3) 5-7 7-6 7-5

2nd Round

Stolle AUS/M Fernandez USA bt Galbraith/Rinaldi-Stunkel USA(5) 6-3 7-5

Quarter-finals

Woodbridge AUS/Sukova(1) CZE bt Stolle/M Fernandez 6-4 3-6 6-3

Sanchez/Sanchez-Vicario ESP (8) bt Woodforde/Stubbs AUS (4) 6-4 6-2

Haarhuis HOL/Medvedeva UKR (7) bt Randall/Hetherington 7-6 6-3

Olhovskiy RUS/Neiland LAT (6) bt Suk CZE/G Fernandez USA (2) 6-2 2-6 6-2

Semi-finals

Woodbridge/Sukova (1) bt Sanchez/Sanchez-Vicario (8) 6-3 6-4

Olhovskiy/Neiland (6) bt Haarhuis/Medvedeva (7) 6-1 1-0 ret'd

Final

Olhovskiy/Neiland (6) bt Woodbridge/Sukova (1) 7-5 6-7 6-2

BOY'S SINGLES

1st Round

Delgado GBR (9) bt Kur POL 6-1 6-4

2nd Round

Belobrajdic AUS bt Delgado (9) 6-4 6-1

Semi-final

Ellwood AUS (1) bt Humphries USA (7) 6-1 6-2

Ilie AUS (5) bt Goldstein USA (10)

Final

Ellwood (1) bt Ilie (5) 5-7 6-3 6-3

GIRL'S SINGLES

1st Round

Jelfs GBR (14) bt Kaiwai NZL 7-6 6-0

2nd Round

Jelfs (14) bt Kubota JPN 6-1 6-2

3rd Round

Basting (6) bt Jelfs (14) 6-1 6-3

Semi-finals

Schett AUT (1) bt Ellwood AUS (3) 5-7 6-4 7-5

Musgrave AUS (11) bt Drake-Brockman AUS (4) 6-2 7-6

Final

Musgrave (11) bt Schett (1) 4-6 6-4 6-2

Tennis

Australian Open Men's Singles

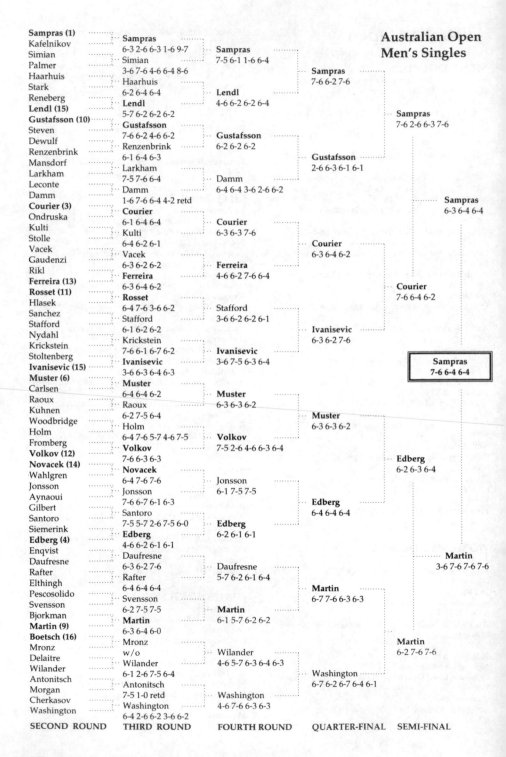

SECOND ROUND

Sampras (1)
Kafelnikov
Simian
Palmer
Haarhuis
Stark
Reneberg
Lendl (15)
Gustafsson (10)
Steven
Dewulf
Renzenbrink
Mansdorf
Larkham
Leconte
Damm
Courier (3)
Ondruska
Kulti
Stolle
Vacek
Gaudenzi
Rikl
Ferreira (13)
Rosset (11)
Hlasek
Sanchez
Stafford
Nydahl
Krickstein
Stoltenberg
Ivanisevic (15)
Muster (6)
Carlsen
Raoux
Kuhnen
Woodbridge
Holm
Fromberg
Volkov (12)
Novacek (14)
Wahlgren
Jonsson
Aynaoui
Gilbert
Santoro
Siemerink
Edberg (4)
Enqvist
Daufresne
Rafter
Elthingh
Pescosolido
Svensson
Bjorkman
Martin (9)
Boetsch (16)
Mronz
Delaitre
Wilander
Antonitsch
Morgan
Cherkasov
Washington

THIRD ROUND

Sampras 6-3 2-6 6-3 1-6 9-7
Simian 3-6 7-6 4-6 6-4 8-6
Haarhuis 6-2 6-4 6-4
Lendl 5-7 6-2 6-2 6-2
Gustafsson 7-6 6-2 4-6 6-2
Renzenbrink 6-1 6-4 6-3
Larkham 7-5 7-6 6-4
Damm 1-6 7-6 6-4 4-2 retd
Courier 6-1 6-4 6-4
Kulti 6-4 6-2 6-1
Vacek 6-3 6-2 6-2
Ferreira 6-3 6-4 6-2
Rosset 6-4 7-6 3-6 6-2
Stafford 6-1 6-2 6-2
Krickstein 7-6 6-1 6-7 6-2
Ivanisevic 3-6 6-3 6-4 6-3
Muster 6-4 6-4 6-2
Raoux 6-2 7-5 6-4
Holm 6-4 7-6 5-7 4-6 7-5
Volkov 7-6 6-3 6-3
Novacek 6-4 7-6 7-6
Jonsson 7-6 6-7 6-1 6-3
Santoro 7-5 5-7 2-6 7-5 6-0
Edberg 4-6 6-2 6-1 6-1
Daufresne 6-3 6-2 7-6
Rafter 6-4 6-4 6-4
Svensson 6-2 7-5 7-5
Martin 6-3 6-4 6-0
Mronz w/o
Wilander 6-1 2-6 7-5 6-4
Antonitsch 7-5 1-0 retd
Washington 6-4 2-6 6-2 3-6 6-2

FOURTH ROUND

Sampras 7-5 6-1 1-6 6-4
Lendl 4-6 6-2 6-2 6-4
Gustafsson 6-2 6-2 6-2
Damm 6-4 6-4 3-6 2-6 6-2
Courier 6-3 6-3 7-6
Ferreira 4-6 6-2 7-6 6-4
Stafford 3-6 6-2 6-2 6-1
Ivanisevic 3-6 7-5 6-3 6-4
Muster 6-3 6-3 6-2
Volkov 7-5 2-6 4-6 6-3 6-4
Jonsson 6-1 7-5 7-5
Edberg 6-2 6-1 6-1
Daufresne 5-7 6-2 6-1 6-4
Martin 6-1 5-7 6-2 6-2
Wilander 4-6 5-7 6-3 6-4 6-3
Washington 4-6 7-6 6-3 6-3

QUARTER-FINAL

Sampras 7-6 6-2 7-6
Gustafsson 2-6 6-3 6-1 6-1
Courier 6-3 6-4 6-2
Ivanisevic 6-3 6-2 7-6
Muster 6-3 6-3 6-2
Edberg 6-4 6-4 6-4
Martin 6-7 7-6 6-3 6-3
Washington 6-7 6-2 6-7 6-4 6-1

SEMI-FINAL

Sampras 7-6 2-6 6-3 7-6
Courier 7-6 6-4 6-2
Edberg 6-2 6-3 6-4
Martin 6-2 7-6 7-6

Sampras 6-3 6-4 6-4
Martin 3-6 7-6 7-6 7-6

Sampras 7-6 6-4 6-4

SECOND ROUND   THIRD ROUND   FOURTH ROUND   QUARTER-FINAL   SEMI-FINAL

Australian Women's Singles

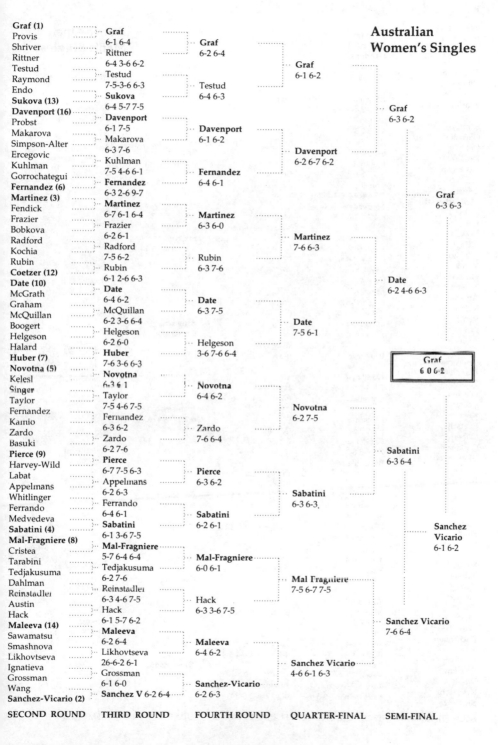

Graf (1)				
Provis	Graf 6-1 6-4			
Shriver		Graf 6-2 6-4		
Rittner	Rittner 6-4 3-6 6-2			
Testud			Graf 6-1 6-2	
Raymond	Testud 7-5-3-6 6-3			
Endo		Testud 6-4 6-3		
Sukova (13)	Sukova 6-4 5-7 7-5			Graf 6-3 6-2
Davenport (16)	Davenport 6-1 7-5			
Probst		Davenport 6-1 6-2		
Makarova	Makarova 6-3 7-6			
Simpson-Alter			Davenport 6-2 6-7 6-2	
Ercegovic	Kuhlman 7-5 4-6 6-1			
Kuhlman		Fernandez 6-4 6-1		
Gorrochategui	Fernandez 6-3 2-6 9-7			Graf 6-3 6-3
Fernandez (6)				
Martinez (3)	Martinez 6-7 6-1 6-4			
Fendick		Martinez 6-3 6-0		
Frazier	Frazier 6-2 6-1			
Bobkova			Martinez 7-6 6-3	
Radford	Radford 7-5 6-2			
Kochia		Rubin 6-3 7-6		
Rubin	Rubin 6-1-2-6 6-3			Date 6-2 4-6 6-3
Coetzer (12)				
Date (10)	Date 6-4 6-2			
McGrath		Date 6-3 7-5		
Graham	McQuillan 6-2 3-6 6-4			
McQuillan			Date 7-5 6-1	
Boogert	Helgeson 6-2 6-0			
Helgeson		Helgeson 3-6 7-6 6-4		
Halard	Huber 7-6 3-6 6-3			
Huber (7)				Graf 6 0 6 2
Novotna (5)	Novotna 6-3 6 1			
Kelesl		Novotna 6-4 6-2		
Singer	Taylor 7-5 4-6 7-5			
Taylor			Novotna 6-2 7-5	
Fernandez	Fernandez 6-3 6-2			
Kamio		Zardo 7-6 6-4		
Zardo	Zardo 6-2 7-6			Sabatini 6-3 6-4
Basuki				
Pierce (9)	Pierce 6-7 7-5 6-3			
Harvey-Wild		Pierce 6-3 6-2		
Labat	Appelmans 6-2 6-3			
Appelmans			Sabatini 6-3 6-3	
Whitlinger	Ferrando 6-4 6-1			
Ferrando		Sabatini 6-2 6-1		
Medvedeva	Sabatini 6-1 3-6 7-5			Sanchez Vicario 6-1 6-2
Sabatini (4)				
Mal-Fragniere (8)	Mal-Fragniere 5-7 6-4 6-4			
Cristea		Mal-Fragniere 6-0 6-1		
Tarabini	Tedjakusuma 6-2 7-6			
Tedjakusuma			Mal Fragniere 7-5 6-7 7-5	
Dahlman	Reinstadler 6-3 4-6 7-5			
Reinstadler		Hack 6-3 3-6 7-5		
Austin	Hack 6-1 5-7 6-2			Sanchez Vicario 7-6 6-4
Hack				
Maleeva (14)	Maleeva 6-2 6-4			
Sawamatsu		Maleeva 6-4 6-2		
Smashnova	Likhovtseva 2-6-6-2 6-1			
Likhovtseva			Sanchez Vicario 4-6 6-1 6-3	
Ignatieva	Grossman 6-1 6-0			
Grossman		Sanchez-Vicario 6-2 6-3		
Wang	Sanchez V 6-2 6-4			
Sanchez-Vicario (2)				

SECOND ROUND   **THIRD ROUND**   **FOURTH ROUND**   **QUARTER-FINAL**   **SEMI-FINAL**

343

Tennis

French Open
Men's Singles

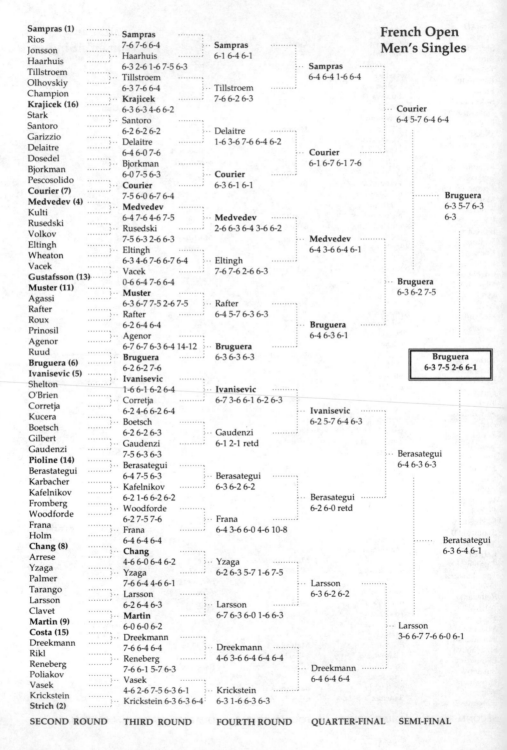

First round entrants / Second round

Player	Second Round	Third Round	Fourth Round	Quarter-Final	Semi-Final	Final
Sampras (1)	**Sampras** 7-6 7-6 6-4	**Sampras** 6-1 6-4 6-1	**Sampras** 6-4 6-4 1-6 6-4	**Courier** 6-4 5-7 6-4 6-4	**Bruguera** 6-3 5-7 6-3 6-3	**Bruguera** 6-3 7-5 2-6 6-1
Rios						
Jonsson	Haarhuis 6-3 2-6 1-6 7-5 6-3					
Haarhuis						
Tillstroem	**Tillstroem** 6-3 7-6 6-4	Tillstroem 7-6 6-2 6-3				
Olhovskiy						
Champion	**Krajicek** 6-3 6-3 4-6 6-2					
Krajicek (16)						
Stark	Santoro 6-2 6-2 6-2	Delaitre 1-6 3-6 7-6 6-4 6-2	**Courier** 6-1 6-7 6-1 7-6			
Santoro						
Garizzio	Delaitre 6-4 6-0 7-6					
Delaitre						
Dosedel	Bjorkman 6-0 7-5 6-3	**Courier** 6-3 6-1 6-1				
Bjorkman						
Pescosolido	**Courier** 7-5 6-0 6-7 6-4					
Courier (7)						
Medvedev (4)	**Medvedev** 6-4 7-6 4-6 7-5	**Medvedev** 2-6 6-3 6-4 3-6 6-2	**Medvedev** 6-4 3-6 6-4 6-1	**Bruguera** 6-3 6-2 7-5		
Kulti						
Rusedski	Rusedski 7-5 6-3 2-6 6-3					
Volkov						
Eltingh	Eltingh 6-3 4-6 7-6 6-7 6-4	Eltingh 7-6 7-6 2-6 6-3				
Wheaton						
Vacek	Vacek 0-6 6-4 7-6 6-4					
Gustafsson (13)						
Muster (11)	**Muster** 6-3 6-7 7-5 2-6 7-5	Rafter 6-4 5-7 6-3 6-3	**Bruguera** 6-4 6-3 6-1			
Agassi						
Rafter	Rafter 6-2 6-4 6-4					
Roux						
Prinosil	Agenor 6-7 6-7 6-3 6-4 14-12	**Bruguera** 6-3 6-3 6-3				
Agenor						
Ruud	**Bruguera** 6-2 6-2 7-6					
Bruguera (6)						
Ivanisevic (5)	**Ivanisevic** 1-6 6-1 6-2 6-4	**Ivanisevic** 6-7 3-6 6-1 6-2 6-3	**Ivanisevic** 6-2 5-7 6-4 6-3	**Berasategui** 6-4 6-3 6-3	**Beratstategui** 6-3 6-4 6-1	
Shelton						
O'Brien	Corretja 6-2 4-6 6-2 6-4					
Corretja						
Kucera	Boetsch 6-2 6-2 6-3	Gaudenzi 6-1 2-1 retd				
Boetsch						
Gilbert	Gaudenzi 7-5 6-3 6-3					
Gaudenzi						
Pioline (14)	Berastategui 6-4 7-5 6-3	Berastategui 6-3 6-2 6-2	**Berasategui** 6-2 6-0 retd			
Berastategui						
Karbacher	Kafelnikov 6-2 1-6 6-2 6-2					
Kafelnikov						
Fromberg	Woodforde 6-2 7-5 7-6	Frana 6-4 3-6 6-0 4-6 10-8				
Woodforde						
Frana	Frana 6-4 6-4 6-4					
Holm						
Chang (8)	**Chang** 4-6 6-0 6-4 6-2	Yzaga 6-2 6-3 5-7 1-6 7-5	Larsson 6-3 6-2 6-2			
Arrese						
Yzaga	Yzaga 7-6 6-4 4-6 6-1					
Palmer						
Tarango	Larsson 6-2 6-4 6-3	Larsson 6-7 6-3 6-0 1-6 6-3				
Larsson						
Clavet	**Martin** 6-0 6-0 6-2					
Martin (9)						
Costa (15)	Dreekmann 7-6 6-4 6-4	Dreekmann 4-6 3-6 6-4 6-4 6-4	Dreekmann 6-4 6-4 6-4	Larsson 3-6 6-7 7-6 6-0 6-1		
Dreekmann						
Rikl	Reneberg 7-6 6-1 5-7 6-3					
Reneberg						
Poliakov	Vasek 4-6 2-6 7-5 6-3 6-1	Krickstein 6-3 1-6 6-3 6-3				
Vasek						
Krickstein	Krickstein 6-3 6-3 6-4					
Strich (2)						

SECOND ROUND · THIRD ROUND · FOURTH ROUND · QUARTER-FINAL · SEMI-FINAL

344

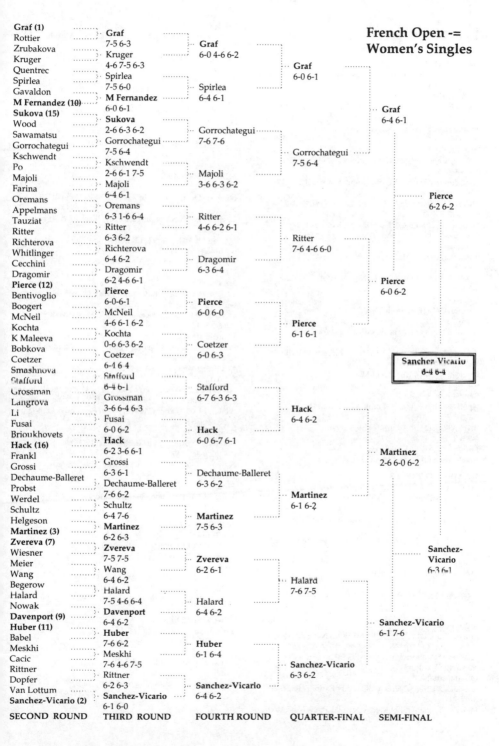

French Open -=
Women's Singles

Graf (1)	Graf				
Rottier	7-5 6-3	Graf			
Zrubakova	Kruger	6-0 4-6 6-2			
Kruger	4-6 7-5 6-3		Graf		
Quentrec	Spirlea		6-0 6-1		
Spirlea	7-5 6-0	Spirlea			
Gavaldon	M Fernandez	6-4 6-1		Graf	
M Fernandez (10)	6-0 6-1			6-4 6-1	
Sukova (15)	Sukova				
Wood	2-6 6-3 6-2	Gorrochategui			
Sawamatsu	Gorrochategui	7-6 7-6			
Gorrochategui	7-5 6-4		Gorrochategui		
Kschwendt	Kschwendt		7-5 6-4		
Po	2-6 6-1 7-5	Majoli			Pierce
Majoli	Majoli	3-6 6-3 6-2			6-2 6-2
Farina	6-4 6-1				
Oremans	Oremans				
Appelmans	6-3 1-6 6-4	Ritter			
Tauziat	Ritter	4-6 6-2 6-1			
Ritter	6-3 6-2		Ritter		
Richterova	Richterova		7-6 4-6 6-0		
Whitlinger	6-4 6-2	Dragomir			
Cecchini	Dragomir	6-3 6-4		Pierce	
Dragomir	6-2 4-6 6-1			6-0 6-2	
Pierce (12)	Pierce				
Bentivoglio	6-0 6-1	Pierce			
Boogert	McNeil	6-0 6-0			
McNeil	4-6 6-1 6-2		Pierce		
Kochta	Kochta		6-1 6-1		
K Maleeva	0-6 6-3 6-2	Coetzer			
Bobkova	Coetzer	6-0 6-3			Sanchez Vicario
Coetzer	6-4 6-4				6-4 6-4
Smashnova	Stafford				
Stafford	6-4 6-1	Stafford			
Grossman	Grossman	6-7 6-3 6-3			
Langrova	3-6 6-4 6-3		Hack		
Li	Fusai		6-4 6-2		
Fusai	6-0 6-2	Hack			
Brioukhovets	Hack	6-0 6-7 6-1		Martinez	
Hack (16)	6-2 3-6 6-1			2-6 6-0 6-2	
Frankl	Grossi				
Grossi	6-3 6-1	Dechaume-Balleret			
Dechaume-Balleret	Dechaume-Balleret	6-3 6-2			
Probst	7-6 6-2		Martinez		
Werdel	Schultz		6-1 6-2		
Schultz	6-4 7-6	Martinez			
Helgeson	Martinez	7-5 6-3			Sanchez-Vicario
Martinez (3)	6-2 6-3				6-3 6-1
Zvereva (7)	Zvereva				
Wiesner	7-5 7-5	Zvereva			
Meier	Wang	6-2 6-1			
Wang	6-4 6-2		Halard		
Begerow	Halard		7-6 7-5		
Halard	7-5 4-6 6-4	Halard			
Nowak	Davenport	6-4 6-2		Sanchez-Vicario	
Davenport (9)	6-4 6-2			6-1 7-6	
Huber (11)	Huber				
Babel	7-6 6-2	Huber			
Meskhi	Meskhi	6-1 6-4			
Cacic	7-6 4-6 7-5		Sanchez-Vicario		
Rittner	Rittner		6-3 6-2		
Dopfer	6-2 6-3	Sanchez-Vicario			
Van Lottum	Sanchez-Vicario	6-4 6-2			
Sanchez-Vicario (2)	6-1 6-0				

SECOND ROUND	THIRD ROUND	FOURTH ROUND	QUARTER-FINAL	SEMI-FINAL

French Open

Paris   May 23-June 5
MEN'S DOUBLES
Selected results from rounds 1-3: complete results from quarter
-finals. Seedings in brackets.
1st Round
Casal/E Sanchez ESP bt Davids NED/Norval RSA (9)
6-4 6-4
Kulti/Larsson SWE bt K Flach/Melville USA (16)
6-4 6-4
2nd Round
Gilbert/Raoux FRA bt Kafelnikov RUS/Rikl CZE (11)
6-4 6-4
Annacone/D Flach USA bt Damm/Novacek CZE (14)
4-6 6-3 6-4
Masur AUS/Pate USA bt Holm/Jarryd SWE (7)
6-7 7-6 7-5
Fleurian/Simian FRA bt Goellner/J Sanchez (10)
6-4 3-6 6-3
3rd Round
Casal/Sanchez bt McEnroe/Reneberg USA (8)
6-3 7-6
Apell/Bjorkman SWE (12) bt Nijssen HOL/Suk CZE (5)
6-3 6-1
Quarter-final
Connell CAN/Galbraith USA (1) bt Casal/Sanchez
7-6 5-7 6-3
Apell/Bjorkman (12) bt Woodbridge/Woodforde AUS
(4) 3-6 6-3 10-8
Adams AUS/Olhovskiy RUS (6) bt Eltingh/Haarhuis
HOL (3) 6-4 6-4
Black ZIM/Stark USA (2) bt Masur/Pate
6-4 6-3
Semi-final
Apell/Bjorkman (12) bt Connell-Galbraith (1)
6-7 6-3 7-5
Black/Stark (2) bt Adams/Olhovskiy (6)
6-3 6-3
Final
Black/Stark (2) bt Apell-Bjorkman (12) 6-4 7-6

WOMEN'S DOUBLES
1st Round
Dechaume-Balleret FRA/Labat ARG bt Lake/Wood GBR
6-2 6-1
Farina ITA/Helgeson USA bt Adams USA/Sukova CZE
(6) 6-4 0-6 6-3
Boogert/Muns-Jagerman HOL bt Hetherington CAN/
Stafford USA (13) 3-6 7-5 6-3
2nd Round
Probst/Singer GER bt Golarsa ITA/Paz ARG (14)
6-2 7-5
Maniokova RUS/Meskhi GEO bt Shriver/Smylie USA
(5)
6-4 6-3
3rd Round
Halard/Tauziat (15) bt Bollegraf HOL/Navratilova USA
(4) 2-6 7-6 6-3
Coetzer RSA/Gorrochategui ARG (9) bt Fendick/
McGrath (3) 6-1 6-3
Quarter-finals
Fernandez USA /Zvereva BLS (1) bt Farina/Helgeson
6-3 6-2
Halard/Tauziat (15) bt Medvedeva UKR/Neiland LAT

(10) 6-2 4-6 6-4
Coetzer/Gorrochategui (9) bt Maniokova/Meskhi
7-5 6-3
Davenport/Raymond USA (11) bt Provis AUS/Reinach
RSA 6-1 6-0
Semi-finals
Fernandez/Zvereva (1) bt Halard/Tauziat (15)
4-6 6-2 6-4
Davenport/Raymond (11) bt Coetzer/Gorrochategui (9)
7-6 6-7 6-4
Final
Fernandez/Zvereva (1) bt Davenport/Raymond (11)
6-2 6-2

MIXED DOUBLES
2nd Round
Boogert/Oosting HOL bt Zvereva BLR/Connell CAN (1)
6-2 7-6
Coetzer/Bale RSA bt Shriver USA/Black ZIM (4)
6-3 2-6 6-2
McNeil USA/Lozano MEX bt Bollegraf/Nijssen HOL (6)
6-2 6-4
Radford AUS/Pugh USA bt Adams/Adams USA (9)
6-1 7-5
3rd Round
Boogert/Oosting bt Raymond/Leach USA (10)
6-4 6-4
Coetzer/Bale bt Gorrochategui ARG/J Sanchez ESP(12)
1-6 6-2 6-4
Quarter-final
Boogert/Oosting bt Hetherington CAN/Galbraith USA
(8) 3-6 7-5 6-2
McGrath/Melville USA (14) bt Coetzer/Bale
6-4 6-4
Sukova CZE/Woodbridge AUS (3) bt Medvedeva UKR/
Haarhuis HOL (11) 7-5 5-7 6-2
Neiland LAT/Olhovskiy RUS (7) bt Fernandez USA/Suk
CZE (2) 7-5 6-3
Semi-final
Boogert/Oosting bt McGrath/Melville (14)
0-6 6-2 6-3
Neiland/Olhovskiy (7) bt Sukova/Woodbridge (3)
7-6 6-2
Final
Boogert/Oosting bt Neiland/Olhovskiy (7) 7-5 3-6 7-5

BOY'S SINGLES
1st Round
Mutis FRA bt Milligan GBR 6-4 6-2
Delgado GBE Roddick USA 7-6 6-3
2nd Round
Sabau ROM bt Delgado GBR 4-6 6-3 6-4
Final
Diaz ESP bt Galimberti ITA 6-3 7-6

GIRL'S SINGLES
1st Round
Sidot FRA bt Jelfs GBR 2-6 6-4 8-6
3rd Round
Cenkova CZE bt Miller GBR 6-0 6-1
Final
Hingus SUI bt Jeyaseelan 6-3 6-1

U S Open

New York   Aug 29-Sep 11

MEN'S DOUBLES

Selected results from rounds 1-3: complete results from quarter-finals. Seedings in brackets.

1st Round

Kulti/Larsson SWE bt Oosting HOL/Vacek CZE (15) 6-2, 6-7, 6-3

Jensen/Jensen USA bt Melville USA/Norval RSA (10) 6-2, 7-6

Bale RSA/Steven NZL bt Apell/Bjorkman SWE (6) 2-6, 7-5, 6-3

Annacone/Cannon USA bt Holm/Jarryd SWE (11) 7-6, 2-6, 6-1

Bergh SWE/Kiel USA bt Kafelnikov RUS/Rikl CZE (9) 6-4, 6-4

Jones/Lucena USA bt Connell CAN/Galbraith USA (2) 6-4, 6-4

2nd Round

De Jager/Stafford RSA bt Casal/Sanchez ESP (13) 6-2, 6-4

3rd Round

Kulti/Larsson bt Black ZIM/Stark USA (1) 6-1, 6-3

Woodbridge/Woodforde AUS bt O'Brien USA/Stolle AUS (14) 6-4, 6-4

Quarter-finals

Kulti/Larsson bt McEnroe/Palmer USA 6-4, 6-4

Woodbridge/Woodforde AUS (4) bt Damm/Novacek CZE (12) 6-2, 0-6, 7-6

Eltingh/Haarhuis HOL (3) bt Adams AUS/Olhovskiy RUS (5) 7-6, 5-7, 7-6

Knowles BAH/Ferreira RSA(16) bt Nijssen HOL/Suk CZE (8) 6-3, 6-4

Semi-finals

Woodbridge/Woodforde AUS bt Kulti/Larsson 6-3, 7-6

Eltingh/Haarhuis bt Knowles/Ferreira 6-3, 7-5

Final

Eltingh/Haarhuis bt Woodbridge/Woodforde 6-3, 7-6

WOMEN'S DOUBLES

1st Round

Jaggard-Lai AUS/Simpson-Alter CAN bt Halard/Tauziat FRA (9) 6-2, 4-6, 6-0

Bradtke/Reinach RSA bt Hetherington CAN/Stafford USA (14) 4-6, 6-1, 6-4

2nd Round

Hakami/Scott USA bt Cecchini ITA/Tarabini ARG (15) 4-6, 6-3, 6-4

K Maleeva BUL/White USA bt Basuki INA/Miyagi JPN (11) 7-6, 2-6, 6-4

3rd Round

Maleeva/White bt Shriver USA/Smylie AUS (4) 6-1, 6-4

Neiland LAT/Sabatini ARG (10) bt Coetzer RSA/Gorrochatequi ARG (7) 6-2, 6-1

Fendick/McGrath USA (3) bt Golarsa ITA/Vis HOL (16) 6-1, 6-4

Davenport/Raymond USA (5) bt Martinez ESP/Medvedeva UKR (12) 6-4, 6-3

Novotna CZE/Sanchez Vicario ESP (2) bt Arendt USA/Radford AUS (13) 7-6, 6-1

Quarter-finals

Fernandez USA/Zvereva BLS (1) bt Adams USA/Bollegraf HOL (6) 6-2, 6-2

Maleeva/White bt Bradtke/Reinach 6-3, 6-1

Neiland/Sabatini bt Fendick/McGrath 1-6, 7-6, 6-4

Novotna/Sanchez Vicario bt Davenport/Raymond 6-2, 6-4

Semi-finals

Maleeva/White bt Fernandez/Zvereva 7-6, 1-6, 6-3

Novotna/Sanchez Vicario bt Neiland/Sabatini 7-6, 6-2

Final

Novotna/Sanchez Vicario bt Maleeva/White 6-3, 6-3

MIXED DOUBLES

1st Round

McQuillan/MacPherson AUS bt Smylie/Fitzgerald AUS (7) 4-6, 6-3, 6-4

Pierce FRA/M Jensen USA bt Raymond/Leach USA (6)

2nd Round

M Fernadez USA/Stolle AUS bt Neiland LAT/Olhovskiy RUS (4) 7-5, 6-3

Quarter-finals

Novotna CZE/Woodbridge AUS (1) bt McQuillan/MacPherson 6-3, 7-5

G FernandezUSA/Suk CZE (3) bt Pierce/Jensen 6-3, 6-4

Hetherington CAN/De Jager RSA bt Fernandez/Stolle 6-4, 6-2

Reinach RSA/Galbraith AUS (8) bt McGrath USA/Woodforde AUS (2) 6-4, 3-6, 6-3

Semi-finals

Novotna/Woodforde bt Fernandez/Suk 7-5, 6-4

Reinach/Galbraith bt Hetherington/De Jager 7-6, 6-7, 6-1

Final

Reinach/Galbraith bt Novotna/Woodbridge 7-5, 6-4

BOY'S FINAL

Nicolas Kiefer GER bt Luke Milligan GBR 6-0, 6-1

Semi-finals

Sjeng Schalken HOL (4) bt Frederico Browne ARG (1) 6-4, 7-5

Mehdi Tahiri MAR (9) bt Nicolas Lapentti ECU(5)6-4, 6-0

Final

Schalken bt Tahiri 6-2, 7-6

GIRL'S FINAL

1st Round

Ludmila Varmuzova SMR (13) bt Megan Miller GBR 6-3, 6-0

Stephanie Halsell USA (7) bt Joanne Moore GBR 6-2, 7-6

Elizabeth Jelfs GBR bt Romana Tedjakusuma INA (5) 3-6, 6-1, 6-4

Cristina Moros USA bt Ekaterina Roubanova GBR 6-3, 6-4

Semi-finals

Martina Hingis SUI (1) bt Yvette Basting (15) 4-6, 6-3, 6-3

Meilen Tu USA (4) bt Kim De Weille HOL (8) 7-5, 6-4

Final

Tu bt Hingis 6-2, 6-4

US Open
Men's Singles

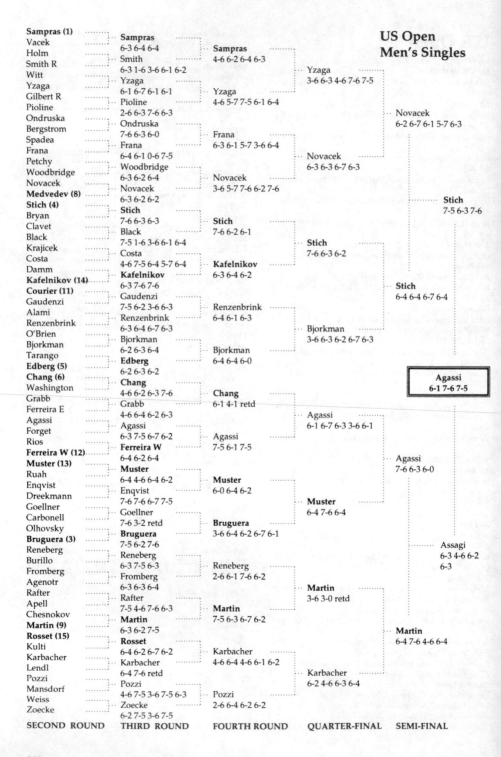

| SECOND ROUND | THIRD ROUND | FOURTH ROUND | QUARTER-FINAL | SEMI-FINAL |

Sampras (1)
Vacek
Holm
Smith R
Witt
Yzaga
Gilbert R
Pioline
Ondruska
Bergstrom
Spadea
Frana
Petchy
Woodbridge
Novacek
Medvedev (8)
Stich (4)
Bryan
Clavet
Black
Krajicek
Costa
Damm
Kafelnikov (14)
Courier (11)
Gaudenzi
Alami
Renzenbrink
O'Brien
Bjorkman
Tarango
Edberg (5)
Chang (6)
Washington
Grabb
Ferreira E
Agassi
Forget
Rios
Ferreira W (12)
Muster (13)
Ruah
Enqvist
Dreekmann
Goellner
Carbonell
Olhovsky
Bruguera (3)
Reneberg
Burillo
Fromberg
Agenotr
Rafter
Apell
Chesnokov
Martin (9)
Rosset (15)
Kulti
Karbacher
Lendl
Pozzi
Mansdorf
Weiss
Zoecke

Sampras
6-3 6-4 6-4
Smith
6-3 1-6 3-6 6-1 6-2
Yzaga
6-1 6-7 6-1 6-1
Pioline
2-6 6-3 7-6 6-3
Ondruska
7-6 6-3 6-0
Frana
6-4 6-1 0-6 7-5
Woodbridge
6-3 6-2 6-4
Novacek
6-3 6-2 6-2
Stich
7-6 6-3 6-3
Black
7-5 1-6 3-6 6-1 6-4
Costa
4-6 7-5 6-4 5-7 6-4
Kafelnikov
6-3 7-6 7-6
Gaudenzi
7-5 6-2 3-6 6-3
Renzenbrink
6-3 6-4 6-7 6-3
Bjorkman
6-2 6-3 6-4
Edberg
6-2 6-3 6-2
Chang
4-6 6-2 6-3 7-6
Grabb
4-6 6-4 6-2 6-3
Agassi
6-3 7-5 6-7 6-2
Ferreira W
6-4 6-2 6-4
Muster
6-4 4-6 6-4 6-2
Enqvist
7-6 7-6 6-7 7-5
Goellner
7-6 3-2 retd
Bruguera
7-5 6-2 7-6
Reneberg
6-3 7-5 6-3
Fromberg
6-3 6-3 6-4
Rafter
7-5 4-6 7-6 6-3
Martin
6-3 6-2 7-5
Rosset
6-4 6-2 6-7 6-2
Karbacher
6-4 7-6 retd
Pozzi
4-6 7-5 3-6 7-5 6-3
Zoecke
6-2 7-5 3-6 7-5

Sampras
4-6 6-2 6-4 6-3
Yzaga
4-6 5-7 7-5 6-1 6-4
Frana
6-3 6-1 5-7 3-6 6-4
Novacek
3-6 5-7 7-6 6-2 7-6
Stich
7-6 6-2 6-1
Kafelnikov
6-3 6-4 6-2
Renzenbrink
6-4 6-1 6-3
Bjorkman
6-4 6-4 6-0
Chang
6-1 4-1 retd
Agassi
7-5 6-1 7-5
Muster
6-0 6-4 6-2
Bruguera
3-6 6-4 6-2 6-7 6-1
Reneberg
2-6 6-1 7-6 6-2
Martin
7-5 6-3 6-7 6-2
Karbacher
4-6 6-4 4-6 6-1 6-2
Pozzi
2-6 6-4 6-2 6-2

Yzaga
3-6 6-3 4-6 7-6 7-5
Novacek
6-3 6-3 6-7 6-3
Stich
7-6 6-3 6-2
Bjorkman
3-6 6-3 6-2 6-7 6-3
Agassi
6-1 6-7 6-3 3-6 6-1
Muster
6-4 7-6 6-4
Martin
3-6 3-0 retd
Karbacher
6-2 4-6 6-3 6-4

Novacek
6-2 6-7 6-1 5-7 6-3
Stich
6-4 6-4 6-7 6-4
Agassi
7-6 6-3 6-0
Martin
6-4 7-6 4-6 6-4

Stich
7-5 6-3 7-6
Assagi
6-3 4-6 6-2 6-3

**Agassi
6-1 7-6 7-5**

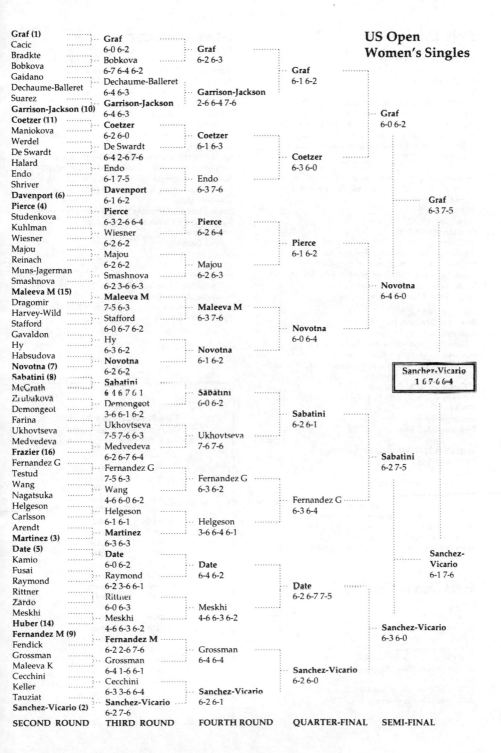

US Open
Women's Singles

SECOND ROUND

Graf (1)
Cacic
Bradkte
Bobkova
Gaidano
Dechaume-Balleret
Suarez
Garrison-Jackson (10)
Coetzer (11)
Maniokova
Werdel
De Swardt
Halard
Endo
Shriver
Davenport (6)
Pierce (4)
Studenkova
Kuhlman
Wiesner
Majou
Reinach
Muns-Jagerman
Smashnova
Maleeva M (15)
Dragomir
Harvey-Wild
Stafford
Gavaldon
Hy
Habsudova
Novotna (7)
Sabatini (8)
McGrath
Zrubakova
Demongeot
Farina
Ukhovtseva
Medvedeva
Frazier (16)
Fernandez G
Testud
Wang
Nagatsuka
Helgeson
Carlsson
Arendt
Martinez (3)
Date (5)
Kamio
Fusai
Raymond
Rittner
Zardo
Meskhi
Huber (14)
Fernandez M (9)
Fendick
Grossman
Maleeva K
Cecchini
Keller
Tauziat
Sanchez-Vicario (2)

THIRD ROUND

Graf 6-0 6-2
Bobkova 6-7 6-4 6-2
Dechaume-Balleret 6-4 6-3
Garrison-Jackson 6-4 6-3
Coetzer 6-2 6-0
De Swardt 6-4 2-6 7-6
Endo 6-1 7-5
Davenport 6-1 6-2
Pierce 6-3 2-6 6-4
Wiesner 6-2 6-2
Majou 6-2 6-2
Smashnova 6-2 3-6 6-3
Maleeva M 7-5 6-3
Stafford 6-0 6-7 6-2
Hy 6-3 6-2
Novotna 6-2 6-2
Sabatini 6 1 6 7 6 1
Demongeot 3-6 6-1 6-2
Ukhovtseva 7-5 7-6 6-3
Medvedeva 6-2 6-7 6-4
Fernandez G 7-5 6-3
Wang 4-6 6-0 6-2
Helgeson 6-1 6-1
Martinez 6-3 6-3
Date 6-0 6-2
Raymond 6-2 3-6 6-1
Rittner 6-0 6-3
Meskhi 4-6 6-3 6-2
Fernandez M 6-2 2-6 7-6
Grossman 6-4 1-6 6-1
Cecchini 6-3 3-6 6-4
Sanchez-Vicario 6-2 7-6

FOURTH ROUND

Graf 6-2 6-3
Garrison-Jackson 2-6 6-4 7-6
Coetzer 6-1 6-3
Endo 6-3 7-6
Pierce 6-2 6-4
Majou 6-2 6-3
Maleeva M 6-3 7-6
Novotna 6-1 6-2
Sabatini 6-0 6-2
Ukhovtseva 7-6 7-6
Fernandez G 6-3 6-2
Helgeson 3-6 6-4 6-1
Date 6-4 6-2
Meskhi 4-6 6-3 6-2
Grossman 6-4 6-4
Sanchez-Vicario 6-2 6-1

QUARTER-FINAL

Graf 6-1 6-2
Coetzer 6-3 6-0
Pierce 6-1 6-2
Novotna 6-0 6-4
Sabatini 6-2 6-1
Fernandez G 6-3 6-4
Date 6-2 6-7 7-5
Sanchez-Vicario 6-2 6-0

SEMI-FINAL

Graf 6-0 6-2
Novotna 6-4 6-0
Sabatini 6-2 7-5
Sanchez-Vicario 6-3 6-0

Graf 6-3 7-5
Sanchez-Vicario 6-1 7-6

Sanchez-Vicario
1 6-7 6-6-4

1994 Davis Cup
World Group
Seeded 1=Germany & USA
FIRST ROUND
Mar 25-27
USA bt India (Delhi) 5-0, Netherlands bt Belgium (Eindhoven) 5-0, Sweden bt Denmark (Lund) 5-0, France bt Hungary (Besancon) 4-1, Czech Rep. bt Israel (Tel Aviv) 4-1, Russia bt Australia (St Petersburg) 4-1, Spain bt Italy (Madrid) 4-1, Germany bt Austria (Graz) 3-2
SECOND ROUND
July 15-17
USA bt Netherlands (Rotterdam) 3-2, Sweden bt France (Cannes)3-2 ; Russia bt Czech Rep. (St Petersburg) 3-2 ; Germany bt Spain (Halle) 3-2
SEMI-FINALS
Gothenberg   Sep 23-25
Sweden bt USA 3-2
Swedish names first
S Edberg lost to T Martin 2-6 6-2 4-6 3-6
M Larson lost to P Sampras 7-6 4-6 2-6 6-7
Apell/Bjorkman bt Palmer/Stark 6-4 6-4 3-6 6-2
S Edberg bt P Sampras 6-3 retd
M Larson bt T Martin 5-7 6-2 6-2 6-4

Hamburg   Sep 23-25
Russia bt Germany 4-1
Russian names first
Y Kafelnikov bt B Karbacher 7-6 6-1 2-6 6-4
A Volkov bt M Stich 7-5 1-6 7-6 6-4
Kafelnikov/Olhovsky bt Stich/Braasch 6-4 7-6 3-6 6-7 10-8
Y Kafelnikov bt M Stich 7-5 6-3
A Vokov lost to B Karbacher 4-6 1-6
FINAL
Sweden v Russia
To be played Dec 2-4

Euro/African Zone Group 1
PLAY-OFF TIE
Manchester   July 15-17
Romania bt Great Britain 3-2
British names first
Jeremy Bates lost to Razvan Sabau 0-6 3-6 7-6 6-2 6-2
Mark Petchey lost to Andrey Pavel 3-6 6-3 6-4 6-2
Bates/Henman bt Cosac/Pascariu 6-2 6-7 5-7 6-2 6-1
Jeremy Bates bt Andrey Pavel 6-3 7-6 6-2
Mark Petchey lost to Ravan Sabau 5-7 6-4 6-7 6-3 6-2
Great Britain are relegated

1993 Davis Cup

FINAL
Düsseldorf   Dec 3-5
Germany bt Australia 4-1
German names first
M Stich bt J Stoltenberg 6-7 6-3 6-1 4-6 6-3
M-K Göllner lost to R Fromberg 3-6 5-7 7-6
Stich/Kuhnen bt Woodbridge/Woodforde 7-6 4-6 6-3 7-6
M Stich bt R Fromberg 6-4 6-2 6-2
M-K Göllner bt J Stoltenberg 6-1 6-7 7-6

FEDERATION CUP
First Round
Spain 3 Chile 0; Argentina 3 Cuba 0; Sweden 2 Belgium 1;
Japan 2 China 1; Germany 3 Colombia 0;
Slovakia 2 Finland 1; South Africa 3 Paraguay 0;
Netherlands 2 Belarus 1; Bulgaria 2 Croatia 1;
Indonesia 2 Chinese Taipei 1; Italy 2 Denmark 1;
France 3 Korea 0; Austria 2 Poland 1;
Australia 2 Latvia 1;
Canada 3 Switzerland 0; USA 3 Czech Republic 0
Second Round
Spain 3 Argentina 0; Japan 3 Sweden 0;
Germany 2 Slovakia 1; South Africa 2 Netherlands 1;
Bulgaria 3 Indonesia 0; France 3 Italy 0;
Austria 2 Australia 1; USA 3 Canada 0
Quarter Finals
Spain 3 Japan 0; Germany 3 South Africa 0; France 2 Bulgaria 1; USA 3 Austria 0
Semi Finals
Spain 2 Germany 1
USA 3 France 0
Final
Spain 3 USA 0
C Martinez bt M J Fernandez 6-2 6-2
A Sanchez Vicario bt L Davenport 6-2 6-1
Martinez/Sanchez Vicario bt G Fernandez/M J Fernandez 6-3 6-4.

The Navratilova Years
Since 1973, Navratilova has been an ever-present at Wimbledon. Her singles record speaks for itself

1994	Finalist
1993	Semi-finalist
1992	Semi-finalist
1991	Quarter-finalist
1990	**Winner**
1989	Finalist
1988	Finalist
1987	**Winner**
1986	**Winner**
1985	**Winner**
1984	**Winner**
1983	**Winner**
1982	**Winner**
1981	Semi-finalist
1980	Semi-finalist
1979	**Winner**
1978	**Winner**
1977	Quarter-finalist
1976	Semi-finalist
1975	Quarter-finalist
1974	3rd round
1973	1st round

ATP Tour 1993-94 (Men's Events)

Date	Tournament	Singles Final		Doubles Final		Prize Money
Sep 27 Oct 3	Salem Open Kuala Lumpar (I)	**Chang** Svensson	6-0 6-4	**Eltingh/Haarhuis** Bjorkman/Wahlgren	7-5 4-6 7-6	$300,000
Sep 27 Oct 3	Campionati Intl Palermo (Cl)	**Muster** Bruguera	7-6 7-5	**Casal/E Sanchez** Garat/Lozano	6-3 6-3	$315,000
Sep 28 Oct 3	Swiss Indoor Basel (HI)	**Stich** Edberg	6-4 6-7 6-3 6-2	**Black/Stark** Pearce/Randall	3-6 7-5 6-3	$800,000
Oct 4 Oct 9	Kronenbourg Cup Athens (Cl)	**Arrese** Berasategui	6-4 3-6 6-3	**De La Pena/Lozano** Deppe/Sullivan	3-6 6-1 6-2	$200,000
Oct 4 Oct 10	Aust Indoor Champs Sydney (HI)	**Yzaga** Korda	6-4 4-6 7-6 7-6	**McEnroe/Reneberg** Mronz/Rehman	6-3 7-5	$1,000,000
Oct 4 Oct 10	Toulouse GP Toulouse (H)	**Boetsch** Pioline	7-6 3-6 6-3	**Black/Stark** Prinosil/Riglewski	7-5 7-6	$400,000
Oct 11 Oct 17	Seiko Super Tennis Tokyo (I)	**Lendl** Martin	6-4 6-4	**Connell/Galbraith** L Jensen/M Jensen	6-3 6-4	$1,000,000
Oct 11 Oct 17	Riklis Open Tel Aviv(H)	**Pescosolido** Mansdorf	7-6 7-5	**Casal/E Sanchez** Bauer/Rikl	6-4 6-4	$200,000
Oct 11 Oct 17	GP Alto Adige Bolzano (CI)	**Stark** Pioline	6-3 6-2	**Davids/Norval** Adams/Olhovskiy	6-3 6-2	$315,000
Oct 18 Oct 24	Lyon GP Lyon (CI)	**Sampras** Pioline	7-6 1-6 7-5	**Muller/Visser** De Jager/Undruska	6-3 7-6	$600,000
Oct 18 Oct 24	CA Tennis Trophy Vienna (CI)	**Ivanisevic** Muster	4-6 6-4 6-4 7-6	**Black/Stark** Bauer/Prinosil	6-3 7-6	$325,000
Oct 18 Oct 24	Salem Open Bejing (CI)	**Chang** Rusedski	7-6 6-7 6-4	**Annacone/D Flach** Eltingh/Haarhuis	7-6 6-3	$300,000
Oct 25 Oct 31	Stockholm Open Stockholm (CI)	**Stich** Ivanisevic	4-6 7-6 7-6 6-2	**Woodbridge/Woodforde** Muller/Visser	6-1 3-6 6-2	$1,650,000
Oct 25 Oct 31	Hellmann's Cup Santiago (CI)	**Frana** E Sanchez	7-5 3-6 6-3	**Bauer/Rikl** Allgardh/Devening	7-6 6-4	$200,000
Nov 1 Nov 7	Paris Open Paris (CI)	**Ivanisevic** Medvedev	6-4 6-2 7-6	**Black/Stark** Nussen/Suk	4-6 7-5 6-2	$2,165,000
Nov 1 Nov 7	Sul American Open Sao Paulo (Cl)	**Berasategui** Dosedel	6-4 6-3	**Casal/E Sanchez** Albano/Frana	4-6 7-6 6-4	$200,000
Nov 8 Nov 14	EC Championship Antwerp (Cl)	**Sampras** Gustafsson	6-1 6-4	**Connell/Galbraith** Ferreria/J Sanchez	6-3 7-6	$1,110,000
Nov 8 Nov 14	Kremlin Cup Moscow (CI)	**Rosset** Kuhnen	6-4 6-3	**Eltingh/Haarhuis** Apell/Bjorkman	6-1 ret'd	$350,000
Nov 8 Nov 14	Topper S A Open Buenos Aires (CI)	**Costa** Berasategui	3-6 6-1 6-4	**Carbonell/Costa** Casal/E Sanchez	6-4 6-4	$300,000
Nov 16 Nov 21	World Champs Frankfurt (C)	**Stich** Sampras	7-6 2-6 7-6 6-2			$2,750,000

Nov 24 Nov 28	Standard Tour D Cha Johannesburg (HI)			**Eltingh/Haarhuis** Woodbridge/Woodforde	7-6 7-6 6-4		$1,200,000
Jan 3 Jan 9	Qatar Open Doha (HO)	**Edberg** Haarhuis	6-3 6-2	**Delaitre/Simian** Cannon/Talbot	6-3 6-3		$500,000
Jan 3 Jan 9	Hawaii Open Oahu (HO)	**Ferreira** Reneberg	6-4 6-7 6-1	**Nijssen/Suk** O'Brien/Stark	6-4 6-4		$288,750
Jan 3 Jan 9	Pura Milk Champ. Adelaide (HO)	**Kafelnikov** Volkov	6-4 6-3	**Kratzmann/Kratzmann** Adams/Black	6-4 6-3		$288,750
Jan 10 Jan 16	Peters NSW Open Sydney (HO)	**Sampras** Lendl	7-6 6-4	**Cahill/Stolle** Kratzmann/Warder	6-1 7-6		$288,750
Jan 10 Jan 16	Sony Indonesian Open, Jakarta (HO)	**Chang** Rikl	6-3 6-3	**Borwick/Bjorkman** Lozano/Pugh	6-4 6-1		$288,750
Jan 10 Jan 16	Benson & Hedges Op Auckland (HO)	**Gustafsson** P McEnroe	6-4 6-0	**P McEnroe/Palmer** Connell/Galbraith	6-2 4-6 6-4		$288,750
Jan 17 Jan 30	**Australian Open** Melbourne (HO)	**Sampras** Martin	7-6 6-4 6-4	**Eltingh/Haarhuis** Black/Stark	6-7 6-3 6-4 6-3		$A3,580,000
Jan 31 Feb 6	Dubai Tennis Open Dubai (HO)	**Gustafsson** Bruguera	6-4 6-2	**Woodbridge/Woodforde** Cahill/Fitzgerald	6-7 6-4 6-2		$1,013,750
Jan 31 Feb 6	Open 13 Marseille (CI)	**Rosset** Boetsch	7-6 7-6	**Siemerink/Vacek** Damm/Kafelnikov	6-7 6-4 6-1		$513,750
Jan 31 Feb 6	Volvo Tennis San Jose (HI)	**Furlan** Chang	3-6 6-2 7-5	**Leach/Palmer** Black/Stark	4-6 6-4 6-4		$288,750
Feb 7 Feb 13	Muratti Time Indoor Milan(CI)	**Becker** Korda	6-2 3-6 6-3	**Nijssen/Suk** Davids/Norval	4-6 7-6 7-6		$688,750
Feb 7 Feb13	Kroger St Jude In't Memphis (HO)	**Martin** Gilbert	6-4 7-5	**Black/Stark** Grabb/Palmer	7-6 6-4		$675,000
Feb 14 Feb 20	Eurocard Open Stuttgart (CI)	**Edberg** Ivanisevic	4-6 6-4 6-2 6-2	**Adams/Olhovskiy** Connell/Galbraith	6-7 6-4 7-6		$2,125,000
Feb 14 Feb 20	Comcast US Indoor Philadelphia (HI)	**Chang** Haarhuis	6-3 6-2	**Eltingh/Haarhuis** Grabb/Palmer	6-3 6-4		$588,750
Feb 21 Feb 27	ABN/AMRO Tour't Rotterdam (CI)	**Stich** W Ferreira	4-6 6-3 6-0	**Bates/Bjorkman** Eltingh/Haarhuis	6-4 6-1		$575,000
Feb 21 Feb 27	Nuveen Champs Scottsdale (HO)	**Agassi** Mattar	6-4 6-3	**Apell/K Flach** O'Brien/Stolle	6-0 6-4		$288,750
Feb 21 Feb 27	Mexican Open Mexico City (CL)	**Muster** Jabali	6-3 6-1	**Montana/Shelton** L Jensen/M Jensen	6-3 6-4		$300,000
Feb 28 Mar 6	Newsweek Cup Indian Wells (HO)	**Sampras** Korda	4-6 6-3 3-6 6-3 6-2	**Connell/Galbraith** Black/Stark	7-5 6-3		$1,470,000
Feb 28 Mar 6	Copenhagen Open Copenhagen (CI)	**Kafelnikov** Vacek	6-3 7-5	**Damm/Steven** Prinosil/Riglewski	6-3 6-4		$188,750
Mar 7 Mar 13	Zaragoza Open Zaragoza (CI)	**Larsson** Rehmann	6-4 6-4	**Holm/Jarryd** Damm/Novacek	7-5 6-2		$150,000
Mar 11 Mar 20	Lipton Champs Key Biscayne (HO)	**Sampras** Agassi	5-7 7-3 6-3	**Eltingh/Haarhuis** Knowles/Palmer	7-6 7-6		$1,625,000

Date	Tournament	Winner (Singles)	Score	Winners (Doubles)	Score	Prize
Mar 14 Mar 20	GP Hassan II Casablanca (Cl)	**Furlan** Alami	6-2 6-2	**Adams/Oosting** Brandi/Mordegan	6-3 6-4	$188,750
Mar 28 Apr 3	Salem Open Osaka (HO)	**Sampras** L Roux	6-2 6-2	**Damm/Stolle** Adams/Olhovskiy	6-4 6-4	$625,000
Mar 28 Apr 3	Estoril Open Estoril (Cl)	**C Costa** Medvedev	4-6 7-5 6-4	**Brandi/Mordegan** Krajicek/Oosting	w/o	$500,000
Mar 28 Apr 3	Standard Bank Open Sun City (HO)	**Zoecke** Dreckmann	6-4 6-1	**Barnard/Haygarth** Ferreira/Stafford	6-3 7-5	$288,750
Apr 4 Apr 10	Trofco Conde d Godo Barcelona (Cl)	**Krajicek** C Costa	6-4 7-6 6-2	**Kafelnikov/Rikl** Courier/J Sanchez	5-7 6-1 6-4	$775,000
Apr 4 Apr 10	Japan Open Tokyo (HO)	**Sampras** Chang	6-4 6-2	**Holm/Jarryd** Lareau/P McEnroe	7-6 6-1	$935,000
Apr 11 Apr 17	Philips Open Nice (Cl)	**Berasategui** Courier	6-4 6-2	**J Sanchez/Woodforde** Davids/Norval	7-5 6-3	$288,750
Apr 11 Apr 17	Salem Open Hong Kong (HO)	**Chang** Rafter	6-1 6-3	**Grabb/Steven** Bjorkman/Rafter	w/o	$295,000
Apr 11 Apr 17	Eddleman Champs Birmingham(Cl)	**Stoltenberg** Markus	6-3 6-4	**Reneberg/Van Rensburg** MacPhie/Witt	2-6 6-3 6-2	$288,750
Apr 18 Apr 24	Monte Carlo Open Monte Carlo (Cl)	**Medvedev** Bruguera	7-5 6-1 6-3	**Kulti/Larsson** Kafelnikov/Vacek	3-6 7-6 6-4	$1,470,000
Apr 18 Apr 24	Korean Open Seoul (HO)	**Bates** Renzenbrink	6-4 6-7 6-3	**Simian/Thorne** Kinnear/Lareau	6-4 3-6 7-5	$188,750
Apr 25 May 1	Trofco Groupo Zeta Madrid (Cl)	**Muster** Bruguera	6-2 3-6 6-4 7-5	**Bergh/Oosting** Fleurian/Hlasek	6-3 6-4	$775,000
Apr 25 May 1	BMW Open Munich (Cl)	**Stich** Korda	6-2 2-6 6-3	**Kafelnikov/Rikld** Becker/Korda	7-6 7-5	$400,000
Apr 25 May 1	AT & T Challenge Atlanta (Cl)	**Chang** Martin	6-7 7-6 6-0	**Palmer/Reneberg** Montana/Pugh	4-6 7-6 6-4	$288,750
May 2 May 8	German Open Hamburg (Cl)	**Medvedev** Kafelnikov	6-4 6-4 3-6 6-3	**Melville/Norval** Holm/Jarryd	6-3 6-4	$1,470,000
May 2 May 8	Clay Court Classic Pinehurst (Cl)	**Palmer** Martin	6-4 7-6	**Woodbridge/Woodforde** Reneberg/Palmer	6-2 3-6 6-3	$250,000
May 9 May 15	Italian Open Rome (Cl)	**Sampras** Becker	6-1 6-2 6-2	**Kafelnikov/Rikl** Ferreira/J Sanchez	6-1 7-5	$1,750,000
May 9 May 15	Red Clay Champs. Coral Springs (Cl)	**Mattar** Morgan	6-4 3-6 6-3	**Bale/Steven** Flach/Simian	6-3 7-5	$215,000
May 16 May 22	Peugeot Team Chps Dusseldorf (Cl) *World Team Cup* GER v ESP	**Stich** Bruguera **Costa** Karbacher	2-6 6-4 6-3 6-2 4-6 6-0	**Kuhnen/Stich** Costa/Carboneil	7-5 4-6 6-4	$1,500,000
May 16 May 22	Intl di Risparmio Bologna (Cl)	**J Sanchez** Berasategui	7-6 4-6 6-3	**Fitzgerald/Rafter** Flegl/Florent	6-3 6-3	$288,750
May 23 June 5	**French Open** Paris (Cl)	**Bruguera** Berasategui	6-3 7-5 2-6 6-1	**Black/Stark** Apell/Bjorkman	6-4 7-5	FF24,494,800

Date	Tournament	Singles	Score	Doubles	Score	Prize
June 6 June 12	Stella Artois London (G)	**Martin** Sampras	7-6 7-6	**Apell/Bjorkman** Woodbridge/Woodforde	3-6 7-6 6-4	$600,000
June 6 June 12	Firenze International Firenze, Italy (Cl)	**Filippini** Fromberg	3-6 6-3 6-3	**Ireland/Thorne** Broad/Van Emburgh	7-6 6-3	$288,750
June 6 June 12	Continental Champs. Rosmalen, Holl. (G)	**Krajicek** Braasch	6-3 6-4	**Noteboom/Wibier** Nargiso/Nyborg	6-3 1-6 7-6	$288,750
June 13 June 19	Gerry Weber Open Halle, Germany	**Stich** Larsson	6-4 4-6 6-3	**Delaitre/Forget** Leconte/Muller	6-4 6-7 6-4	$500,000
June 13 June 19	Raiffeisen GP St Polten, Austria (Cl)	**Muster** Carbonell	4-6 6-2 6-4	**Flegl/Florent** Malik/Tarango	3-6 6-1 6-4	$300,000
June 13 June 19	Manchester Open Manchester (G)	**Rafter** W Ferreira	7-6 7-6	**Leach/Visser** Davis/Kronemann	6-4 4-6 7-6	$290,000
June 20 July 3	**The Championships** Wimbledon	**Sampras** Ivanisevic	7-6 7-6 6-0	**Woodbridge/Woodforde** Connell/Galbraith	7-6 6-3 6-1	$4,024,971
July 4 July 10	Radio Swiss Open Gstaad (Cl)	**Bruguera** Forget	3-6 7-5 6-2 6-1	**Casal/E Sanchez** Oosting/Vacek	7-6 6-4	$450,000
July 4 July 10	Swedish Open Bastad	**Karbacher** Skoff	6-4 6-3	**Apell/Bjorkman** Kulti/Tillstrom	6-2 6-3	$288,750
July 4 July 10	Hall of Fame Champs. Newport, RI (G)	**Wheaton** Woodbridge	6-4 3-6 7-6	**Antonitsch/Rusedski** Kinnear/Wheaton	6-4 3-6 6-4	$215,000
July 18 July 24	Mercedes Cup Stuttgart (Cl)	**Berasategui** Gaudenzi	7-5 6-3 7-6	**Melville/Norval** Eltingh/Haarhuis	7-6 7-5	$915,000
July 18 July 24	Legg Mason Classic Washington, DC (HO)	**Edberg** Stoltenberg	6-4 6-2	**Connell/Galbraith** Bjorkman/Illasek	6-4 4-6 6-3	$525,000
July 25 July 31	Canadian Open Toronto (HO)	**Agassi** Stoltenberg	6-4 6-4	**Black/Stark** P McEnroe/Palmer	6-4 6-4	$1,470,000
July 25 July 31	Dutch Open Iliversum (Cl)	**Novacek** Fromberg	7-5 6-4 7-6	**Orsanic/Siemerink** Adams/Olhovskiy	6-4 6-2	$275,000
Aug 1 Aug 7	EA Generali Open Kitzbühel (Cl)	**Ivanisevic** Santoro	6-2 4-6 4-6 6-3 6-2	**Adams/Olhovskiy** Casal/E Sanchez	6-7 6-3 7-5	$375,000
Aug 1 Aug 7	Czech Open Prague (Cl)	**Bruguera** Medvedev	6-3 6-4	**Novacek/Wilander** Krupa/Vizner	w/o	$340,000
Aug 1 Aug 7	Los Angeles Open Los Angeles (HO)	**Becker** Woodforde	6-2 6-2	**Fitzgerald/Woodforde** Davis/MacPhie	4-6 6-2 6-0	$288,750
Aug 8 Aug 14	ATP Championship Cincinnati (HO)	**Chang** Edberg	6-2 7-5	**O'Brien/Stolle** W Ferreira/Kratzmann	6-7 6-3 6-2	$1,470,000
Aug 8 Aug 14	San Marino Internat. San Marino	**C Costa** Gross	6-1 6-3	**Broad/Van Emburgh** Arrese/Furlan	6-4 7-6	$275,000
Aug 15 Aug 21	Volvo International New Haven, Ct (HO)	**Becker** Rosset	6-3 7-5	**Connell/Galbraith** Eltingh/Haarhuis	6-4 7-6	$915,000
Aug 15 Aug 21	RCA Championships Indianapolis (HO)	**W Ferreira** Delaitre	6-2 6-1	**Woodbridge/Woodforde** Grabb/Reneberg	6-3 6-4	$915,000
Aug 22 Aug 28	Croatian Open Umag	**Berasategui** Kucera	6-2 6-4	**Perez/Roig** Kucera/Wekesa	6-2 6-4	$375,000

Aug 22	OTB International	**Eltingh**	6-3 6-4	Apell/Bjorkman	6-4 7-6	$288,750
Aug 28	Schenectady,NY(HO)	C Adams		Eltingh/Haarhuis		
Aug 22	Hamlet Cup	**Kafelnikov**	5-7 6-1 6-2	Delaitre/Forget	6-4 7-6	$288,750
Aug 28	Long Island, NY(HO)	Pioline		Florent/Petchey		
Aug 29	US Open	**Agassi**	6-1 7-6 7-5	Eltingh/Haarhuis	6-3 7-6	$4,100,800
Sept 11	Flushing M'ws (HO)	Stich		Woodbridge/Woodforde		
Sept 12	Romanian Open	**Davin**	6-2 6-4	Arthurs/Youl	6-4 6-4	$525,000
Sept 18	Bucharest (Cl)	Ivanisevic		Arrese/Conde		
Sept 12	GP Passing Shot	**W Ferreira**	6-0 7-5	Delaitre/Forget	6-2 2-6 7-5	$375,000
Sept 18	Bordeaux (HO)	Tarango		Nargiso/Roux		
Sept 12	Colombia W'ld Series	**Pereira**	6-3 3-6 6-4	Knowles/Nestor	6-4 7-6	$288,750
Sept 18	Bogota	Hadad		Jensen/Jensen		

IBM/ATP Tour Singles Ranking

As at 10th October

1	Pete Sampras	4884	35	Arnuad Boetsch	930	69	Karol Kucera	648
2	Goran Ivanisevic	3125	36	Richey Reneberg	929	70	Chuck Adams	645
3	Michael Stich	3092	37	David Wheaton	892	71	Brad Gilbert	642
4	Sergi Bruguera	2727	38	Jared Palmer	892	72	Stefano Pescosolido	641
5	Stefan Edberg	2642	39	Aaron Krickstein	877	73	Amos Mansdorf	623
6	Boris Becker	2577	40	Mark Woodforde	875	74	Jordi Arrese	609
7	Todd Martin	2477	41	Javier Sanchez	871	75	Hendrik Dreekman	608
8	Alberto Berasategui	2361	42	Renzo Furlan	870	76	Martin Damm	605
9	Michael Chang	2277	43	Gilbert Schaller	848	77	Byron Black	603
10	Andre Agassi	2132	44	Alexander Volkov	843	78	Jeff Tarango	597
11	Andrey Medvedev	2041	45	Jonathan Stark	835	79	Henri Leconte	587
12	Yevgeny Kafelnikov	1992	46	Anrey Chesnokov	834	80	Andrey Olhovsky	568
13	Wayne Ferreira	1976	47	Karsten Braasch	824	81	Jörn Renzenbrink	561
14	Jim Courier	1760	48	Horst Skoff	802	82	Alex O'Brien	556
15	Thomas Muster	1611	49	Alberto Costa	800	83	Jan Apell	550
16	Marc Rosset	1424	50	Ronald Agenor	788	84	Jean-Philippe Fleurian	550
17	Magnus Gustafsson	1415	51	Olivier Delaitre	783	85	Marc Goellner	550
18	Petr Korda	1347	52	Richard Fromberg	778	86	Nicklas Kulti	549
19	Richard Krajicek	1319	53	Guy Forget	770	87	Osdcar Martinez	544
20	Carlos Costa	1294	54	Fabrice Santoro	754	88	Fernando Meligeni	535
21	Jason Stoltenberg	1278	55	Jonas Bjorkman	748	89	Jim Grabb	533
22	Patrick Rafter	1247	56	Thomas Enqvist	740	90	Guillaume Raoux	532
23	Andrea Gaudenzi	1110	57	Greg Rusedski	740	91	Luiz Matter	528
24	Alex Corretja	1106	58	Daniel Vacek	723	92	**Jeremy Bates**	**528**
25	Malivai Washington	1101	59	Markus Zoecke	705	93	**Mark Petchey**	**524**
26	Slava Dosedel	1081	60	Franco Davin	699	94	Javier Frana	512
27	Magnus Larrson	1066	61	Jacob Hlasek	686	95	Lionel Roux	511
28	Bernd Karbacher	1065	62	Thomans Carbonell	685	96	Oliver Gross	503
29	Ivan Landl	1054	63	David Rikl	685	97	Younes El Aynaoui	499
30	Jaime Yzaga	1038	64	Marcelo Filippini	683	98	Lars Jonsson	484
31	Paul Haarhuis	1035	65	Henrik Holm	678	99	Vince Spadea	470
32	Cedric Pioline	1031	66	Emilio Sanchez	666	100	Karim Alani	470
33	Karel Novacek	1029	67	Francisco Clavet	665			
34	Jacco Eltingh	977	68	Patrick McEnroe	648			

Kraft/WTA Tour 1993-94 (Women's Events)

Date	Tournament	Singles Final	Doubles Final		Prize Money
Sep 28 Oct 3	Sapporo Open Mokomanai (I)	L Harvey-Wild 6-4 6-3 Spirlea	Basuki/Miyagi Kamio/N Kijimuta	6-4 6-2	$100,000
Sep 27 Oct 3	Volkswagen Cup Leipzig (I)	S Graf 6-2 6-0 J Novotna	G Fernandez/Zvereva Neiland/Novotna	6-3 6-2	$375,000
Oct 4 Oct 10	Barilla Indoors Zurich (CI)	M Maleeva-F. 6-3 7-6 MNavratilova	Garrison J./Navratilova G Fernandez/Zvereva	6-3 5-7 6-3	$750,000
Oct 5 Oct 10	P & G Taiwan Open Taipei (H)	S Wang 6-1 7-6 L Harvey-Wild	Basuki/Miyagi Faull/Radford	6-4 6-2	$100,000
Oct 11 Oct 17	Porsche Grand Prix Filderstadt (I)	M Pierce 6-3 6-3 N Zvereva	G Fernandez/Zvereva Fendick/Navratilova	7-6 6-4	$375,000
Oct 11 Oct 17	Languedoc Rou. Open Montpellier (I)	E Likhovtseva 6-3 6-4 D Monami	McGrath/Porwik Husarova/Monami	3-6 6-2 7-6	$100,000
Oct 19 Oct 24	Autoglass Classic Brighton (I)	J Novotna 6-2 6-4 A Huber	Golarsa/Medvedeva Huber/Neiland	6-3 1-6 6-4	$375,000
Oct 18 Oct 24	Budapest Open Budapest (I)	Z Garrison J. 7-5 6-2 S Appelmans	Gorrochategui/Vis Cecchini/Tarabini	6-1 6-3	$150,000
Oct 25 Oct 31	Nokia Grand Prix Essen (I)	N Medvedeva 6-7 7-5 6-4 C Martinez	Sanchez Vicario/Sukova Probst/Singer	6-2 6-2	$375,000
Oct 25 Oct 31	Bancesa Classic Curitiba, Brazil (Cl)	S Hack 6-2 6-0 F Labat	Hack/Martinek Chabalgoity/Vieira	6-2 7-6	$100,000
Nov 1 Nov 7	Bank of West Classic Oakland (I)	M Navratilova 6-2 7-6 Z Garrison J.	Fendick/McGrath Coetzer/Gorrochategui	6-2 6-0	$375,000
Nov 1 Nov 7	Bell Challenge Quebec City (I)	N Tauziat 6-4 6-1 K Maleeva	Adams/Bollegraf K Maleeva/Tauziat	6-4 6-4	$150,000
Nov 8 Nov 14	Virginia Slims Philadelphia (I)	C Martinez 6-3 6-3 S Graf	Adams/Bollegraf Martinez/Neiland	6-2 4-6 7-6	$750,000
Nov 15 Nov 21	Virginia Slims New York (I)	S Graf 6-1 6-4 3-6 A Sanchez Vicario 6-1	G Fernandez/Zvereva Neiland/Novotna	6-3 7-5	$3,708,500
Jan 3 Jan 9	Danone Hardc.Chps Brisbane (H)	L Davenport 6-1 2-6 6-3 F Labat	Golarsa/Medvedeva Byrne/McQuillan	6-3 6-1	$150,000
Jan 10 Jan 15	Tasmanian Open Hobart (H)	M Endo 6-1 6-7 6-4 R McQuillan	Harvey-Wild/Rubin Byrne/McQuillan	7-5 4-6 7-6	$100,000
Jan 10 Jan 16	Peters NSW Open Sydney (H)	K Date 6-4 6-2 M J Fernandez	Fendick/McGrath Novotna/Sanchez Vicario	6-2 6-3	$300,000
Feb 1 Feb 6	Toray Pan Pacific Op. Tokyo (H)	S Graf 6-2 6-4 M Navratilova	Shriver/Smylie Bollegraf/Navratilova	6-3 3-6 7-6	$750,000
Jan 31 Feb 6	Amway Classic Auckland (H)	G Helgeson 7-6 6-3 I Gorrochategui	Hy/Paz Byrne/Richardson	6-4 7-6	$100,000
Jan 17 Jan 30	Australian Open Melbourne (HO)	Steffi Graf 6-0 6-2 A Sanchez Vicario	G Fernandez/Zvereva Fendick/McGrath	6-3 4-6 6-4	$2,426,000

Dates	Tournament	Singles	Score	Doubles	Score	Prize
Feb 7 Feb 13	Virginia Slims Chicago (I)	N Zvereva C Rubin	6-3 7-5	G Fernandez/Zvereva Bollegraf/Navratilova	6-3 3-6 6-4	$400,000
Feb 7 Feb 13	EA Generali Linz (I)	S Appelmans M Babel	6-1 4-6 7-6	Maniokova/Meskhi Carlsson/Schneider	6-2 6-2	$150,000
Feb 8 Feb 13	Asia Open Osaka (CI)	M Maleeva-F. I Majoli	6-1 4-6 7-5	Neiland/Stubbs Shriver/Smylie	6-4 6-7	$150,000
Feb 15 Feb 20	Open Gaz de France Paris (I)	M Navratilova J Halard	7-5 6-3	Appelmans/Courtois Pierce/Temesvari	6-4 6-4	$400,000
Feb 14 Feb 20	IGA Tennis Classic Oklahoma (I)	M McGrath B Schultz	7-6 7-6	Fendick/McGrath Adams/Bollegraf	7-6 6-2	$150,000
Feb 14 Feb 20	Nokia Open Bejing (I)	Y Basuki K Nagatsuka	6-4 6-2	Chen/Li Guse/Lake	6-0 6-2	$100,000
Feb 21 Feb 27	Evert Cup Indian Wells (H)	S Graf A Coetzer	6-0 6-4	Davenport/Raymond Bollegraf/Sukova	6-2 6-4	$400,000
Feb 28 Mar 6	Virginia Slims Delray Beach (H)	S Graf A Sanchez Vicario	6-3 7-5	Novotna/Sanchez Vicario Bollegraf/Sukova	6-2 6-0	$400,000
Mar 11 Mar 20	Lipton Champ'ship Key Biscayne (H)	S Graf N Zvereva	4-6 6-1 6-2	G Fernandez/Zvereva Fendick/McGrath	6-3 6-1	$1,000,000
Mar 21 Mar 27	Virginia Slims Houston (Cl)	S Hack M Pierce	7-5 6-4	Bollegraf/Navratilova Adams/Garrison Jackson	6-4 6-2	$400,000
Mar 24 Mar 27	Light n' Lively Dbls Wesley Chapel (Cl)			Novotna/Sanchez Vicario G Fernandez/Zvereva	6-2 7-5	$175,000
Mar 28 Apr 3	Family Circle Cup Hilton Head Isl (Cl)	C Martinez N Zvereva	6-4 6-0	McNeil/SanchezVicario G Fernandez/Zvereva	6-4 4-1 ret'd	$750,000
Apr 4 Apr 10	Bausch & Lomb Ch. Amelia Island (Cl)	A Sanchez Vic. G Sabatini	6-1 6-4	Neiland/Sanchez Vicario Coetzer/Gorrochategui	6-2 6-7 6-4	$400,000
Apr 4 Apr 10	Japan Open Ariake Forest Park	K Date A Frazier	7-5 6-0	Donoshiro/Sugiyama Basuki/Miyagi	6-4 6-1	$150,000
Apr 11 Apr 17	Volvo Women's Open Pattaya City (H)	S Appelmans P Fendick	6-7 7-6 6-2	Fendick/McGrath Basuki/Miyagi	7-6 3-6 6-3	$100,000
Apr 19 Apr 24	In't Champs of Spain Barcelona (Cl)	A Sanchez Vic. I Majoli	6-0 6-2	Neiland/Sanchez Vicario Halard/Tauziat	6-2 6-4	$400,000
Apr 18 Apr 24	Singapore Tennis Cla. Kallang (H)	N Sawamatsu F Labat	7-5 7-5	Fendick/McGrath Arendt/Radford	6-4 6-1	$100,000
Apr 25 May 1	Citizen Cup Hamburg (Cl)	A Sanchez Vic. S Graf	4-6 7-6 7-6	Novotna/Sanchez Vicario Maniokova/Meskhi	6 3 6 2	$400,000
Apr 25 May 1	Ilva Trophy Taranto (Cl)	J Halard I Spirlea	6-2 6-3	Spirlea/van Lottum Cecchini/Demongeot	6-3 2-6 6-1	$100,000
Apr 25 May 1	Danamon Open Jakarta (O)	Y Basuki F Labat	6-4 3-6 7-6	Arendt/Radford Guse/Strnadova	6-2 6-2	$100,000
May 9 May 15	German Open Berlin (Cl)	S Graf B Schultz	7-6 6-4	G Fernandez/Zvereva Novotna/Sanchez Vicario	6-3 7-6	$750,000
May 10 May 15	BVV Prague Open Prague (Cl)	A Coetzer A Carlsson	6-1 7-6	Coetzer/Harvey-Wild Boogert/Golarsa	6-4 3-6 6-2	$100,000

May 16 May 21	Eurocard Open Lucerne (Cl)	**L Davenport** L Raymond	7-6 6-4	**Doubles cancelled due to rain**		$150,000
May 16 May 22	Strasbourg Inter'nal Strasbourg (Cl)	**M J Fernandez** G Sabatini	2-6 6-4 6-0	**McNeil/Stubbs** Tarabini/Vis	6-3 3-6 6-2	$150,000
May 23 June 5	**French Open** Paris (Cl)	**A Sanchez Vic.** M Pierce	6-4 6-4	**G Fernandez/Zvereva** Davenport/Raymond	6-2 6-2	$3,561,928
June 6 June 12	DFS Classic Birmingham (G)	**L McNeil** Z Garrison Jackson	6-2 6-2	**Garrison J/Neiland** Barclay/K Guse	6-4 6-4	$150,000
June 13 June 18	Volkswagen Cup Eastbourne (G)	**M McGrath** L Harvey-Wild	6-2 6-4	**G Fernandez/Zvereva** Gorrochategui/Sukova	6-7 6-4 6-3	$400,000
June 20 July 3	**Wimbledon** London (G)	**C Martínez** M Navratilova	6-4 3-6 6-3	**G Fernandez/Zvereva** Novotna/Sanchez Vicario	6-4 6-1	$3,361,848
July 5 July 10	Torneo International Palermo, Sicily	**I Spirlea** B Schultz	6-4 1-6 7-6	**Dragomir/Garrone** Canepa/Casoni	6-1 6-0	$100,000
July 25 July 31	Acura US Hardcourts Vermont, USA	**C Martínez** A Sanchez Vicario	4-6 6-3 6-4	**Shriver/Smylie** Martínez/Sanchez Vicario	7-6 2-6 7-5	$400,000
July 25 July 31	Styrian Open Styria, Austria	**A Huber** J Wiesner	6-3 6-3	**CecchiniTarabini** Fusai/Habsudova	7-5 7-5	$100,000
Aug 1 Aug 7	Toshibia Classic San Diego	**S Graf** A Sanchez Vicario	6-2 6-1	**Novotna/Sanchez Vicario** Helgeson/McQuillan	6-3 6-3	$400,000
Aug 8 Aug 14	Virginia Slims LA Manhattan Beach, CA	**A Frazier** A Grossman	6-1 6-3	**Halard/Tauziat** Novotna/Raymond	6-1 0-6 6-1	$400,000
Aug 15 Aug 21	Canadian Open Montreal	**A Sanchez V** S Graf	7-5 1-6 7-6	**McGrath/Sanchez Vicario** Shriver/Smylie	2-6 6-2 6-4	$750,000
Aug 22 Aug 28	OTB International New York	**J Wiesner** L Neiland	7-5 3-6 6-4	**McGrath/Neiland** Shriver/Smylie	6-2 6-2	$150,000
Aug 29 Sep 11	**US Open** Flushing Meadow	**A Sanchez V** Graf	1-6 7-6 6-4	**Novotna/Sanchez Vicario** K Maleeva/White	6-3 6-3	$3,900,000
Sep 26 Oct 2	Volkswagen Cup Leipzig, Germany	**J Novotna** M Pierce	7-5 6-1	**Fendick/McGrath** Bollegraf/Neiland	6-4 6-4	$375,000

Prize Money
Year to Date - Jan 1 to Oct 10

$

1	Arantxa Sanchez Vicario	2,054,665		16	Larisa Neiland	302,112
2	Steffi Graf	1,461,890		17	Julie Halard	276,273
3	Conchita Martínez	1,055,692		18	Sabine Hack	264,296
4	Natalia Zvereva	719,942		19	Iva Majoli	242,152
5	Jana Novotna	651,119		20	Helena Sukova	234,830
6	Gigi Fernandez	590,050		21	Brenda Schultz	232,746
7	Martina Navratilova	564,582		22	Amy Frazier	222,742
8	Mary Pierce	512,114		23	Petty Fendick	214,879
9	Gabriela Sabatini	425,070		24	Zina Garrison Jackson	208,283
10	Lindsay Davenport	391,120		25	Ann Grossman	205,692
11	Meredith McGrath	340,867		26	Ginger Helgeson	196,658
12	Magdalena Maleeva	324,347		27	Lisa Raymond	193,503
13	Kimiko Date	323,904		28	Pam Shriver	191,932
14	Lori McNeil	319,946		29	Manon Bollegraf	190,934
15	Amanda Coetzer	307,741		30	Ines Gorrochategui	186,971

Virginia Slims Rankings
As at Oct 10

SINGLES
1 Steffi Graf
2 Arantxa Sanchez Vicario
3 Conchita Martínez
4 Jana Novotna
5 Martina Navratilova
6 Mary Pierce
7 Natalia Zvereva
8 Lindsay Davenport
9 Gabriela Sabatini
10 Kimiko Date

DOUBLES
1 Natalia Zvereva
2 Gigi Fernandez
3 Arantxa Sanchez Vicario
4 Jana Novotna
5 Meredith McGrath
6 Martina Navratilova
7 Patty Fendick
8 Manon Bollegraf
9 Larisa Neiland
10 Pam Shriver

Career Prize Money
As at Oct 10

1	Martina Navratilova	19,997,227
2	Steffi Graf	14,615,990
3	Chris Evert	8,896,195
4	Gabriela Sabatini	7,439,422
5	Arantxa Sanchez Vicario	7,429,016
6	Monica Seles	7,408,981
7	Pam Shriver	5,264,057
8	Helena Sukova	5,233,436
9	Zina Garrison Jackson	4,221,656
10	Jana Novotna	4,205,422
11	Natalia Zvereva	3,940,931
12	Conchita Martínez	3,486,832
13	Hana Mandlikova	3,340,959
14	Manuela Maleeva-Fragniere	3,244,811
15	Gigi Fernandez	3,132,702
16	Mary Joe Fernandez	3,049,213
17	Wendy Turnbull	2,769,024
18	Lori McNeil	2,688,278
19	Larisa Neiland	2,399,551
20	Claudia Kohde-Kilsch	2,225,837

Reebok Tour, UK
Oct 1993-Sept 1993

GRAVES T & LC, SHEFFIELD
Oct 26-29
Men's Final
Miles Maclagan (W Sco) bt Danny Sapsford (Berks) 7-5 7-6
Women's Final
E Nortje bt Lizzie Jelfs (Oxon) 7-5 6-3

COLWYN BAY
Nov 11-14
Men's Final
Laurence Matthews (Hants) bt Daniel Sanders (Som) 6-2 6-3

PORTSMOUTH
Nov 18-21
Men's Final
Nick Weal (Hants) bt Andrew Richardson (Lincs) 3-6 6-2 7-6

WREXHAM
Nov 18-Dec 4
Men's Final
Laurence Matthews (Hants) bt Danny Sapsford (Som) 1-6 6-2 6-3
Women's Final
Caroline Hunt (Dor't) bt Mair Hughes (Wales)7-5 1-6 6-3

NOTTINGHAM
Dec 2-12
Men's Final
Laurence Matthews (Hants) bt Dylan Williams (Middx) 6-2 6-2
Women's Final
N Egorova bt Emily Bond (Glos) 6-1 6-0

CORBY ITC
Dec 15-19
Men's Final
Jeffroy Hunter (Surrey) bt Laurence Matthews (Hants) 7-6 7-5
Women's Final
G Coorengel bt Karen Cross (Devon) 6-4 4-6 6-4

COVENTRY
Dec 21-23
Men's Final
Paul Hand (Berks) bt Jeffrey Hunter (Surrey) 6-3 7-5
Women's Final
Karen Cross (Devon) bt G Coorengel 7-5 6-1

SWANSEA
Jan 6-9
Men's Final
M Barnard bt Danny Sapsford (Surrey) 3-6 6-1 6-0
Women's Final
Karen Cross (Devon) bt G Coorengel 6-2 6-2

DELTA TC, SWINDON
Jan 13-16
Men's Final
Jeremy Bates (Surrey) bt Ross Matheson (W Sco) 7-6 6-4
Women's Final
G Coorengel bt Kaye Hand (Berks) 7-5 6-2

WIGAN
Jan 20-23
Men's Final
G Muller bt Nick Fulwood (Derbys) 6-4 7-5
Women's Final
Alison Smith bt S Parkhomenko (RUS) 7-6 6-2

Tennis

TELFORD INTERNATIONAL CENTRE
Jan 24-28
Men's Final
Laurence Matthews (Hants) bt Ross Matheson (W Sco)
6-1 6-4
Women's Final
S Parkhomenko (RUS) bt N Egorova 6-3 3-2 retd

SURREY T & CC
Feb 28 -Mar 4
Women's Final
Kaye Hand (Berks) bt Caroline Herbert (Herts) 2-6 7-6 7-6

LINCOLN INDOOR
Mar 7-11
Women's Final
Caroline Herbert (Herts) bt Karen Cross (Devon) 7-5 2-2
retd

WIRRAL TENNIS CENTRE
Mar 28-Apr 2
Men's Final
Jamie Delgado (Warks) bt Nick Baglin (Cheshire) 7-6 3-6
6-3
Women's Final
Anne Simpkin (Leics) bt S Parkhomenko (RUS)
3-6 6-1 6-4

PUMA SUNDERLAND
Apr 6-9
Men's Final
James Fox (Lincs) bt Nick Baglin (Cheshire) 6-4 6-7 6-4
Women's Final
Kaye Hand (Berks) bt Lucie Ahl (Devon) 7-6 6-0

WESTSIDE LTC
Apr 11-17
Men's Final
Paul Hand (Berks) bt Nick Weal (Hants) 7-6 6-2
Women's Final
Lucie Ahl (Devon) bt Kaye Hand (Berks) 6-3 7-5

ROYAL BERKS
Apr 20-23
Men's Final
Graham Hobbs (Dorset) bt M Birch 5-7 6-4 7-6
Women's Final
Emily Bond (Glos) bt D Kristofova 6-3 2-3 retd

EDGBASTON ARCHERY
Apr 27-30
Men's Final
Gregg Saffery (Berks) bt Mark Blincow (N'hants) 6-1 6-4
Women's Final
Karen Cross (Devon) bt Tina Croson (Derbys) 6-1 6-4

FREELANCE LTC, SOUTHSEA
June 16-19
Men's Final
Chris Wilkinson (Hants) bt Paul Hand (Berks) 6-0 3-6 6-1
Women's Final
Lucie Ahl (Devon) bt E Nortje 6-3 2-6 6-2

BRIDGEND LTC
June 23-26
Men's Final
Nick Fulwood (Derbys) bt Sean Cole (Surrey) 6-4 6-4
Women's Final
Lucie Ahl (Devon) bt Caroline Herbert (Herts) 6-0 6-1

FELIXSTOWE
July 4-9
Men's Final
Gregg Saffery (Berks) bt Nick Fulwood (Derbys) 6-3 7-6
Women's Final
Samantha Smith (Essex) bt N Dechy 7-6 3-6 6-3

EAST GLOS LTC, CHELTENHAM
June 27-July 1
Men's Final
Gary Henderson (Yorks) bt Thomas Hand (Devon) 6-3
3-6 6-3
Women's Final
Kaye Hand (Berks) bt Julie Sinkins (Wales) 6-7 6-3 6-1

FRINTON
July 11-16
Men's Final
Laurence Matthews (Hants) bt G Steenkamp 6-3 6-7 8-6
Women's Final
T Morton-Rogers bt N Dechy 6-4 6-0

ILKLEY
July 18-23
Men's Final
Gary Henderson (Yorks) bt Nick Fulwood (Derbys)
6-2 6-1
Women's Final
S Parkhomenko (RUS) bt G Coorengel 6-4 6-3

British Men at Wimbledon
*Below are the players who have reached the fourth
round or better at Wimbledon since 1946*

1946	Tony Mottram	4th rd
1948	Tony Mottram	Q-final
1951	Tony Mottram	4th rd
1954	Mike Davis	4th rd
1957	Billy Knight	4th rd
	Bobby Wilson	4th rd
1958	Bobby Wilson	Q-final
1959	Bobby Wilson	Q-final
1961	Mike Sangster	S-final
1962	Alan Mills	4th rd
1963	Bobby Wilson	Q-final
1964	Billy Knight	Q-final
1966	Bobby Wilson	4th rd
1967	Roger Taylor	S-final
1968	Mark Cox	4th rd
1969	Bobby Wilson	4th rd
1970	Roger Taylor	S-final
1973	Roger Taylor	S-final
1975	Graham Stilwell	4th rd
1977	Mark Cox	4th rd
1979	Mark Cox	4th rd
1982	Buster Mottram	4th rd
1992	Jeremy Bates	4th rd
1993	Andrew Foster	4th rd
1994	Jeremy Bates	4th rd

Tenpin Bowling

AMF World Cup
Johannesburg, South Africa   Nov 7-14, 1993
Men: after 48 games

1	Tomas Leandersson SWE	(135 bonus)	9935
2	Rainer Puisis GER	(140)	9803
3	Paeng Nepomuceno PHI	(85)	9744
4	Erwin Groen HOL	(100)	9666
5	Jack Guay CAN	(80)	9658

Stepladder Final

Jack Guay bt Erwin Groen	237-207
Paeng Nepomuceno bt Jack Guay	196-180
Rainer Puisis bt Paeng Nepomuceno	227-174

Championship Game
Rainer Puisis bt Tomas Leandersson   258-184

Women: after 42 games

1	Rosalind Greiner HOL	(115 bonus)	8385
2	Arianne Cerdena PHI	(50)	8225
3	Stacy Manley USA	(55)	8190
4	Pauline Smith GBR	(95)	8079
5	Lotta Lundin SWE	(155)	8024

Stepladder Final

Pauline Smith bt Lotta Lundin	237-202
Pauline Smith bt Stacy Manley	223-182
Pauline Smith bt Arianne Cerdena	210-183

Championship Game
Pauline Smith bt Rosalind Greiner   178-177

Brunswick Memorial World Open
Swindon Super Bowl   July 16-17
Men

1	**George Patel**	**4881 (218 average)**
2	Chris Buck	4490 (202)
3	Lol Ellis	4433 (202)

Women

1	**Gemma Burden**	**3007 (192 average)**
2	Carol Callow	3000 (192)
3	Pauline Smith	2999 (193)

FIQ European Cup
Vienna, Austria   Apr 7-10
Men
1 **Juoko Kuossari FIN**
2 Mats Svensson SWE
3 Tore Torgersen NOR
4 Geoff Buck GBR
Women
1 **Asa Larsson SWE**
2 Pauline Smith GBR
3 Anniemiek Boogaart HOL
10 Judy Howlett GBR

BTBA UK Championships
Solar Bowl, Ipswich   May 15

Men	Pins	Avge	Prize
1 **Lesley Miranda**	**1829**	**216**	**£500**
2 Ron Oldfield	1810	216	£250
3 Steve Gomersall	1785	208	£100
4 Richard Hood	1726	208	
5 Paul Armitage	1707	203	
Women			
1 **Gemma Burden**	**2021**	**235**	**£500**
2 Pauline Smith	1786	209	£250
3 Kim Oakley	1738	204	£100
4 Judy Howlett	1562	185	
5 Gina Wardle	1534	184	

Inter County Finals 1993
Solar Bowl, Norwich   Nov 13-14

Men	W	L	Pins
1 **Dorset**	**14**	**4**	**8694**
2 Sussex	12	6	9060
3 Buckinghamshire	11	7	8329
Women			
1 **Yorkshire**	**14**	**4**	**8297**
2 Buckinghamshire	14	4	8158
3 County Durha,m	12	6	8122

Welsh Open
Cardiff Super Bowl   Feb 26-27
Men's Final
Kevin Hills bt Geoff Buck   234-205
Women's Final
Pauline Smith bt Gina Wardle 202-185

AIB Irish Open
Stillorgan Bowl, Dublin   1993
Men's Final
Geoff Buck bt Lol Ellis   179-151
Women's Final
Pauline Smith bt Kimberley Oakley   203-170

Trampolining

World Cup Final
Frankfurt, Germany   Nov 13, 1993

Men's Individual

1 Fabrice Schwertz	FRA	38.10
2 Martin Kuicka	GER	37.50
3 Fabrice Hennique	FRA	37.40

Women's Individual

1 Andrea Holmes	ENG	37.20
2 Anna Dogonadze	GEO	36.70
2 Susan Challis	ENG	36.70
8 Lorna Craig	SCO	31.30

Men's Synchronised

1 Morozov/Kasak	BLS	47.60
2 Buhotzev/Tjabus	UKR	46.80
3 Schwertz/Hennique	FRA	46.60
5 Murray/Linney	SCO	42.20

Women's Synchronised

1 Dogonadze/Khoperia	GEO	45.80
2 Roewe/Ludwig	GER	45.00
3 Karpenkova/Pisheiko	BLS	44.50

World Cup Series
Frankfurt, Germany   Mar 5

Men's Individual

1 Fabrice Hennique	FRA	37.40
4 Paul Smyth	ENG	36.00

Women's Individual

1 Tatiana Lushina	RUS	37.00
2 Andrea Holmes	ENG	36.40
11 Sue Challis	ENG	30.30

Men's Synchronised

1 Kypri/Smyth	ENG	46.40

Women's Synchronised

1 Haikova/Vachnikova	CZE	44.30
2 Challis/Holmes	ENG	43.60

European Championships
Sursee, Switzerland   Oct 14-16, 1993

Men's Individual

1 Fabrice Schwertz	FRA	38.70
2 Dmitrij Poliarush	BLS	38.30
3 Anders Christiansen	DEN	38.10
7 Theo Kypri	ENG	30.40

Women's Individual

1 Sue Challis	ENG	37.30
2 Anna Dogonadze	GEO	36.50
2 Rusudan Khoperia	GEO	36.50
10 Andrea Holmes	ENG	22.70

Men's Synchronised

1 Ledstrup/Dalsten	DEN	46.40
2 Kubicka/Kemmer	GER	45.20
3 Villafuerte/Villafuerte	HOL	45.10
6 Porter/Kypri	ENG	42.90
7 Linney/Murray	SCO	42.10

Women's Synchronised

1 Tsiguleva/Movchan	UKR	46.70
2 Dogonadze/Khoperia	GEO	46.30
3 Challis/Holmes	ENG	45.20

Men's Individual Team

1 Belarus	193.70
2 France	190.60
3 Germany	189.40

Women's Individual

1 Germany	189.90
2 Ukraine	189.40
3 Belarus	188.10
3 Great Britain	188.10

British Championships
Gillingham   July 8-10

Men's Overall

1 T Kypri	London	103.90
2 P Smyth	London	103.80
3 D Herring	Gateshead	102.00

Women's Overall

1 A Holmes	Dunstable	101.30
2 L Lyon	Liverpool	98.00
3 C Wright	Edgbarrow	95.80

Triathlon

European Olympic Distance Championships
Eichstaett, Germany   *July 2*

Men

1 Simon Lessing (GBR)	**1:50.38**
2 Ralf Eggert (GER)	1:52.34
3 Rainer Mueller (GER)	1:53.37
34 Mark Edmunds (GBR)	1:59.45
36 Craig Ball (GBR)	2:00.11
46 Julian Jenkinson (GBR)	2:01.35
53 Iain Hamilton (GBR)	2:02.30

Women

1 Sonja Krolic (GER)	**2:02.51**
2 Sabine Westoff (GER)	2:05.23
3 Isabelle Mouthon (FRA)	2:05.58
25 Helen Cawthorne (GBR)	2:14.46
39 Fiona Lothian (GBR)	2:19.25

Men's Team		Women's Team	
1 Germany	5:40.31	Germany	6:16.07
2 France	5:46.38	Denmark	6:28.58
3 Holland	5:47.46	France	6:30.27
7 Great Britain	5:50.34		
8		Great Britain	6:47.45

ITU World Series
Final Standings 1993

MEN

1 B Beven (AUS)	**440 pts**
2 M Stewart (AUS)	370
3 B Braun (USA)	368

WOMEN

1 J-A Ritchie (CAN)	**465 pts**
2 C Montgomery (CAN)	460
3 M Jones (AUS)	400

Long Distance World Championships
Nice, France   *June 25*

MEN

1 R Barel (HOL)	**5:59.47**
2 L Leder (GER)	6:00.18
3 Y Cordier (FRA)	6:03.09

WOMEN

1 I Mouthon (FRA)	**6:41.50**
2 K Smyers (USA)	6:57.21
3 L Reuze (USA)	7:01.17

Hawaiian Ironman Championships
Kailua-Kona, Hawaii

Men

1 M Allen (USA)	**8:07.45**
2 P Kiuru (FIN)	8:14.27
3 W Dittrich (GER)	8:20.13

Women

1 P Newby-Fraser (ZIM)	**8:58.23**
2 E Baker (NZL)	9:08.04
3 S Latshaw (USA)	9:20.40

European Duathlon Championships
Vuokatti, Finland   *May 21-22*

Men

1 Urs Dellsperger (SUI)	**2:37.14**
2 Norman Stadler (GER)	2:38.44
3 Tibor Lehmann (HUN)	2:40.07

Women

1 Dolorita Gerber (SUI)	**2:57.44**
2 Irma Heeren (HOL)	2:58.03
3 Melissa Watson (GBR)	3:00.12
6 Helen Cawthorne (GBR)	3:07.35
16 Ros Dunnington (GBR)	3:33.35

British Championships

OLYMPIC DISTANCE
Wakefield   *Aug 20-21*

Men

1 Steve Burton (Barnet)	**2:01.15**
2 Tim Stewart (Woking)	2:02.14
3 R Hobson (Southampton)	2:02.40

Women

1 Ali Hollington (Bath)	**2:18.02**
2 Helen Cawthorne (Nottm)	2:21.00
3 A Emerson (Spain)	2:23.12

SPRINT DISTANCE
Market Bosworth   *May 8*

Men		Women	
1 Robin Brew	55.42	Helen Cawthorne	1:04.31
2 Steve Burton	56.57	Loretta Sollars	1:04.56
3 Craig Ball	57.14	Ali Hollington	1:05.34

Junior Men		Junior Women	
1 Benjamin Price	58.34	Jessica Harrison	1:07.07
2 Alastair Johnson	59.09	Christine Johnson	1:07.27
3 Alex Herbert	59.54	Melanie Sears	1:09.38

DUATHLON
Chertsey   *Apr 24*

Men		Women	
1 Richard Allen	1:16.38	Helen Cawthorne	1:27.47
2 Craig Ball	1:17.26	Melissa Watson	1:28.28
3 Steve Burton	1:17.52	Kate Burge	1:32.33

Junior Men		Junior Women	
1 Richard Allen	1:16.38	Jessica Harrison	1:35.23
2 Russell Herbert	1:20.16	Kelly Newark	1:39.44
3 Mo Abed	1:20.37	Melanie Sears	1:41.17

Volleyball

World Grand Champions Cup
Osaka, Japan   Nov, 1993
Men's Team
1. Cuba, 2. China, 3. Russia
Women's Team
1. Italy, 2. Brazil, 3. Cuba

GB International Matches

HOLLAND TOUR
Feb 14
Great Britain 1 Alcom Capelle 3
Feb 15
Great Britain 0 Autodrop 3
Feb 16
Great Britain 3 TDK Brevok 0
Feb 17
Great Britain 1 Piet Zoomers 3

DENMARK IN BRITAIN
Dewsbury   Apr 8
Great Britain 3 Denmark 1
Huddersfield   Apr 9
Great Britain 0 Denmark 3

Royal Bank of Scotland National Leagues
MEN
Division 1

		P	W	L	SF	SA	Pts
1	Mizuno Lewisham	14	14	0	42	5	28
2	Polonia Ealing	14	9	5	31	21	18
3	Newcastle Staffs	14	9	5	30	24	18
4	Reebok Liverpool City	14	8	6	30	28	16
5	Tooting Aquila	14	7	7	29	26	14
6	Wessex	14	5	9	23	33	10
7	Whitefield Sportset	14	3	11	14	36	6
8	KLEA Leeds	14	1	13	14	40	2

Division 2

		P	W	L	SF	SA	Pts
1	Malory II Lewisham	22	19	3	59	23	38
2	Coventry Riga	22	18	4	60	27	36
3	Stockport	22	14	8	55	33	28
4	Man Utd Salford	22	14	8	55	33	28
5	Speedwell	22	12	10	44	45	24
6	Sheffield Wednesday	22	11	11	51	46	22
7	Essex Estonians	22	10	12	42	44	20
8	Gateshead Armitage	22	9	13	39	47	18
9	Thames Valley Jets	22	8	14	34	51	16
10	London Lynx	22	6	16	31	57	12
11	Dynamo London	22	6	16	29	54	12
12	Trent FM Rockets	22	1	21	19	65	2

WOMEN
Division 1

		P	W	L	SF	SA	Pts
1	Woolwich Brixton	13	11	2	35	14	22
2	Sale	13	9	4	34	16	18
3	Britannia Music City	13	8	5	32	20	16
4	Dynamo London	13	5	8	18	29	10

1	KLEA Leeds	13	10	3	32	20	20
2	Ashcombe Gilford	13	6	7	18	28	12
3	Wessex	13	2	11	15	35	4
4	Purbrook	13	1	12	15	37	2

Women's Division 2

		P	W	L	SF	SA	Pts
1	Birmingham Ladies	18	14	4	48	24	28
2	London Lynx	18	13	5	41	27	26
3	Reebok Liverpool City	18	12	6	44	26	24
4	Dynamo London II	18	11	7	42	31	22
5	Team Knights	18	10	8	43	34	20
6	Trent FM Rockets	18	9	9	38	35	18
7	Sheffield Wednesday	18	8	10	36	41	16
8	Man Utd Salford	18	7	11	36	41	14
9	Polonia Ladies	18	6	12	23	44	12
10	Portsmouth College	18	0	18	6	54	0

Royal Bank of Scotland Cup
MEN
Winners: Mizuno Malory Lewisham
Runners-up: Tooting Aquila
WOMEN
Winners: Britannia Music City
Runners-up: Sale

EVA Cup
MEN
Winners: Mayfield Portsmouth
Runners-up: Horfield
WOMEN
Winners: Loughborough
Runners-up: Essex Estonian

Scottish Leagues
Division One - Men

		P	W	L	SF	SA	Pts
1	Su Ragazzi	18	17	1	52	11	52
2	West Coast	18	16	2	52	9	50
3	Jets	18	14	4	46	19	46
4	Coatbridge	18	12	6	46	19	46
5	Dundee	18	8	10	28	37	34
6	Paisley	18	7	11	27	38	32
7	MCA Cardinals	18	5	13	24	40	26
8	Team Fife	18	4	14	22	44	26
9	Team Blantyre	18	4	14	15	49	25
10	TB MacKay Pentland	18	3	15	15	49	24

Division One - Women

		P	W	L	SF	SA	Pts
1	MCA Powerhouse C	16	15	1	47	7	46
2	Jets	16	13	3	42	13	42
3	Team Components	16	13	3	42	14	42
4	Hazlehead	16	10	6	34	24	36
5	News Ayrshire Kyle	16	7	9	25	32	30
6	Grangeburn Coaches	16	6	10	22	33	28
7	Pentland NUVOC	16	5	11	23	36	26
8	Paisley	16	3	13	12	41	22
9	Team Blantyre	16	0	16	1	48	12

Water Sports

Water Skiing

World Junior Championships
Lake Cajititlan, Mexico   Aug 9

Team

1 USA	7884.7
2 Great Britain	7621.2
3 France	7279.9

Men

1 J Javier	ARG	2866.8
2 G Hatzis	GRE	2522.1
3 T Asher	GBR	2517.0
4 P Price	GBR	2439.6

Women

1 B Hunt	USA	2922.2
2 M Toms	GBR	2621.9

European U21 Championships
Lake Avigliana, Turin   Aug 1

Men's Slalom: D Ganzukoff (FRA) 2.25 at 11m
Women's Slalom: N Huntridge (GBR) 3 at 12m
Men's Tricks: O Deviatovski (BLS) 8,110pts
Women's Tricks: E Milakova (RUS) 5,940 pts
Men's Jump: J Seels GBR 54.01m
Women's Jump: N Huntridge (GBR) 41.00m
Men's Overall: J Seels (GBR) 2,475.3pts
Women's Overall: M Mosti (ITA) 3,052.4pts
TEAM: Great Britain 7,693.6pts

British Championships
Holme Pierrepont   July 15-17

Men

1 J Fisher	2,678.8
2 J Steels	2,666.9
3 M Southam	2,428.7

Women

1 P Roberts	3,000.0
2 N Huntridge	2,458.2
3 S Blake	2,239.0

Carlsberg Export Masters
Reading   May 28-29

Men's Overall

1 C Perez	FRA	2,202 pts
2 J Seels	GBR	1,934
3 M Southam	GBR	1,792

Women's Overall

1 P Roberts	GBR	2,436 pts
2 O Gubarenko	RUS	2,382
3 N Rumiantseva	RUS	2,357

Surfing

European Championships
Thurso, Scotland   Oct 9

	Kneeboard	Longboard
1	K Osmond (JER)	A Gazzo (FRA)
2	P Alonso (FRA)	N Creavy (JER)
3	B Cromie (IRL)	C Griffiths (WAL)

Masters	Seniors
1 C Bright (WAL)	A Fernandez
2 G Robinson (IRL)	C French (WAL)
3 M Findlay (SCO)	E Graciet (FRA)

Bodyboard (Men)	Bodyboard (Women)
1 K Ulgade	L Cutts (WAL)
2 N Capdeville (FRA)	D Gomes (POR)
3 G Faria (POR)	I Bissiere (FRA)

Open (Men)	Open (Women)
1 D Pitier (FRA)	E Joly (FRA)
2 V Giraud (FRA)	A-G Hoaran (FRA)
3 R Winter (ENG)	E Burberry (ENG)

Team: France

Water Polo

World Championships
Rome Sep 1-11

MEN
Final: Italy 10   Spain 5
3rd/4th Place Play-off: Russia 14 Croatia 13
Final Classification: 1. Italy; 2. Spain; 3. Russia; 4. Croatia; 5. Hungary; 6. USA; 7. Greece; 8. Holland; 9. Germany; 10. Australia; 11. Cuba; 12. Kazakhstan; 13. Romania; 14. Canada; 15. South Africa; 16 New Zealand.
WOMEN
Final: Hungary 7   Holland 5
3rd/4th Place Play-off: Italy 14   United States 9
Final Classification: 1. Hungary; 2. Holland; 3. Italy; 4. USA; 5. Canada; 6. Australia; 7. Russia; 8. Germany; 9. Brazil; 10. New Zealand; 11. France; 12. Kazakhstan

Windsurfing

IMCO Olympic Class National Championships
Dale, Pembrokeshire   Aug 2

Men's Lightweight:	H Plumb	3.5 pts
Men's Heavyweight:	R Dannenburg	23.7
Women's Champion:	P Way	23.0

Octopush

World Championships
Rouen, France

	Men	Women
1	Australia	Australia
2	South Africa	South Africa
3	United States of America	Great Britain

UK National Championships

	Men	Women
1	Leeds Beaver Wetsuits	Yorkshire
2	West Wickham	Sirens
3	Southport	

UK Nautilus League
1 West Wickham
2 Southsea
3 Northampton

Dragon Boat Racing
National Championships - Final
Nottingham   Oct 9-10, 1993
Open 500m
1 **Kingston Royals**   **2:06.54**
2 Woodmill Canoe Club 2:07.31
3 Colenorton   2:09.26

Open 250m
1 **Woodmill Canoe Club**   **1:04.82**
2 Hartlepool Powermen 1:05.34
3 Colenorton   1:06.07

Women 500m *(Aggregate time over 3 races)*
1 **Kingston Royals**   **7:24.56**
2 Dawn Raiders   8:01.30
3 Amathus   8:03.33

Women *(Aggregate time over 3 races)*
1 **Kingston Royals**   **3:33.95**
2 Amathus   3:49.86
3 Dawn Raiders   3:56.47

London International
Albert Docks   Oct 3, 1993
500m
1 **Berlin Wann See**   **2:13.24**
2 Colenorton   2:17.15
3 BA Hurricanes   2:22.85

250m
1 **Berlin Wann See**   **1:05.68**
2 BA Hurricanes   1:10.51
3 Schwerin Mysteri   1:23.25

500m Relay
1 **England (Colenorton/BA Hurr.)**   **4:35.97**
2 Germany (Berlin/Schwerin)   5:01.35

European Rafting Championships
River Oetz, Solden, Austria July 26-28
RACE 1 *(Head to Head)*
Semi Finals
Holland bt Germany by 1.66s
Ireland bt Great Britain by 3.17s
3rd/4th Play Off
Germany bt Great Britain by 1.11s
Final
Holland bt Ireland by 2.28s

RACE 2 *(Slalom)*
Run 1
1 Germany   1:15.79
2 Austria   1:19.91
3 Holland   1:21.66 *(incl 5s pen)*
8 Ireland   1:33.85 *(incl 10s pen)*
11 G Britain 1:37.58 *(incl 15s pen)*

Run 2
1 Germany   2:37.79 *(incl 5s pen)*
2 Holland   2:48.83 *(incl 10s pen)*
3 Czech Rep. 2:55.89 *(incl 5s pen)*
8 G Britain 3:13.10 *(incl 15s pen)*
11 Ireland   4:03.65 *(incl 65s pen)*

RACE 3 *(Triple Headers)*
Semi Final A
1 Austria   3:22.31 *(incl 4pt pen)*
2 Switzerland 3:23.32
3 Sweden   2:05.50

Semi Final B
1 Germany   3:11.46
2 Finland   3:22.71
3 Ireland   3:24.71

Semi Final C
1 Holland   3:08.30
2 Slovenia 3:09.60
3 G Britain 3:15.27

Final
1 Germany   3:09.62
2 Holland   3:12.12
3 Austria   3:20.09

OVERALL POINTS STANDINGS

		R1	R2	R3	Tot
1	**Germany**	15	25	50	90
2	Holland	25	20	40	85
3	Austria	11	7	26 *	44
4	Slovenia	10	12	24 *	42
5	Ireland	20	5	16	41
6	Finland	7	9	22	38
7	Sweden	8	10	18	36
8	G Britain	12	8	14	34
9	Switzerland	9	4	20	33
10	Czech Rep.	5	15	12	32
11	Spain	6	11	8	25
12	France	2 *	6	2	14
13	Belgium	4	3	6	13
14	Portugal	3	2	4	9

* awarded a yellow card penalty

Weightlifting

World Championships

Melbourne, Australia   *Nov 12-21 1993*
MEN

54kg

			BW	Snatch	Cl+Jk	Ttl
1	Ivan Ivanov	BUL	53.70	120.0	157.5	277.5

59kg

1	Nikolai Peshalov	BUL	58.96	137.5	167.5	305.0

64kg

1	Naim Suleymanoglu	TUR	63.61	145.0	177.5	322.5

70kg

1	Yoto Yotov	BUL	69.64	155.0	187.5	342.5

76kg

1	Altym Orazdurdiev	TKM	75.71	167.5	202.5	370.0
16	Tony Morgan	GBR	75.04	127.5	155.0	282.5

83kg

1	Pyrros Dimas	GRE	82.46	175.0	202.5	377.5
-	Andrew Callard	GBR	82.95	132.5	-	-

91kg

1	Ivan Tchakarov	BUL	90.84	185.0	222.5	407.5

99kg

1	Victor Tregubov	RUS	97.76	185.0	222.5	407.5

108kg

1	Timur Taimazov	UKR	106.45	195.0	225.0	420.0

+108kg

1	Ronnie Weller	GER	123.19	200.0	242.5	442.5

WOMEN

48kg

1	Nan-Mei Chu	TPE	45.48	67.5	85.0	152.5

50kg

1	Liu Xiuhua	CHN	49.44	77.5	110.0	187.5

54kg

1	Chen Xiaomin	CHN	53.94	90.0	110.0	200.0

59kg

1	Caiyan Sun	CHN	58.03	97.5	120.0	217.5
12	Dianne Greenidge	GBR	57.94	70.0	87.5	157.5

64kg

1	Li Hongyun	CHN	62.11	102.5	117.5	220.0
7	Jeanette Rose	GBR	63.64	80.0	100.0	180.0

70kg

1	Milena Trendafilova	BUL	69.68	100.0	120.0	220.0

76kg

1	Ju Hua	CHN	72.50	105.0	125.0	230.0

83kg

1	Shu-Chih Chen	TPE	82.32	102.5	127.5	230.0

+83kg

1	Yajuan Li	CHN	125.07	105.0	155.0	260.0
6	Myrtle Augee	GBR	96.93	85.0	107.5	192.

European Championships

Sokolov, Czech Republic   *May 2-8*
MEN

54kg

			BW	Snatch	Cl+Jk	Ttl
1	Halil Mutlu	TUR	53.95	122.5	155.0	277.5

59kg

1	Nikolai Peshalov	BUL	58.95	135.0	162.5	297.5

64kg

1	Naim Suleymanoglu	TUR	64.00	145.5	180.0	325.5
15	Benjamin Devonshire	GBR	62.95	105.0	130.0	235.0

70kg

1	Yoto Yotov	BUL	69.75	152.5	192.5	345.0
14	Stewart Cruikshank	GBR	70.00	125.0	160.0	285.0

76kg

1	Rouslan Savtchenko	UKR	75.60	160.0	195.0	355.0

83kg

1	Vadim Bazham	UKR	82.65	172.5	205.0	377.5
14	Stephen Ward	GBR	82.50	137.5	177.5	315.0

91kg

1	Alexei Petrov	RUS	90.00	185.0	227.5	412.5

99kg

1	Sergei Syrtsov	RUS	98.65	190.0	225.0	415.0

108kg

1	Timur Taimazov	UKR	107.70	195.0	235.0	430.0
11	Giles Greenwood	GBR	106.60	152.5	182.5	335.0

+108kg

1	Andrei Chemerkin	RUS	148.20	200.0	250.0	450.0

EEC Championships

St Pol Sur Mer, France   *Mar 25-27*
MEN

54kg

			BW	Snatch	Cl+Jk	Ttl
1	Yakovous Polanidis	GRE	53.85	110.0	137.5	247.5

59kg

1	Marco Spanehl	GER	58.70	117.5	152.5	270.0

64kg

1	Valerios Leonidis	GRE	63.70	135.0	165.0	300.0

70kg

1	Francois Demeure	BEL	68.90	135.0	170.0	305.0

76kg

1	Ingo Steinhofel	GER	75.95	150.0	180.0	330.0

83kg

1	Lars Betker	GER	81.40	150.0	190.0	340.0

91kg

1	Odisseas Dimas	GRE	90.65	157.5	192.5	350.0

99kg

1	Igor Sadikov	GER	94.30	157.5	200.0	357.5

108kg

1	Thomas Schweizer	GER	107.25	165.0	195.0	360.0

+108kg

1	Ronnie Weller	GER	124.45	190.0	202.5	392.5

WOMEN

46kg

			BW	Snatch	Cl+Jk	Ttl
1	Blanca Fernandez	ESP	45.20	55.0	72.5	127.5

50kg

1	Anna Strobou	GRE	49.80	67.5	82.5	150.0

54kg

1	Constantina Misirli	GRE	53.70	67.5	87.5	155.0

59kg

1	Maria Christoforidi	GRE	58.80	87.5	100.0	187.5

64kg

1	Yvon. Van der Stoep	HOL	63.10	75.0	97.5	172.5

70kg

1	Stephanie Utsch	GER	66.00	87.5	110.0	197.5

76kg

1	Chr'tiane Marie Elise	FRA	72.95	77.5	97.5	175.0

83kg

1	Monique Riesterer	GER	78.60	95.0	115.0	210.0

+83kg

1	Myrtle Augee	GBR	96.45	90.0	120.0	210.0

Wrestling

World Championships

Winners only
FREESTYLE
Istanbul, Turkey   Aug 24-28
Light Flyweight (48kg)
Alexis Vila   CUB
Flyweight (52kg)
Valentin Jordanov   BUL
Bantamweight (57kg)
Alejandro Puerto   CUB
Featherweight (62kg)
Magomed Azizov   RUS
Lightweight (68kg)
Alexander Leipold   GER
Welterweight (74kg)
Turan Ceylan   TUR
Middleweight (82kg)
Lukman Shabrailov   MLD
Light Heavyweight (90kg)
Rasul Khadem Azghadi   IRN
Heavyweight (100kg)
Aravet Sabeyev   GER
Super Heavyweight (130kg)
Mahmut Demir   TUR

GRECO-ROMAN STYLE
Tampere, Finland   Sep 8-11
Light Flyweight (48kg)
Wilber Sanchez   CUB
Flyweight (52kg)
Alfred Ter-Mkrytschan   GER
Bantamweight (57kg)
Yury Melnitchenko   KZK
Featherweight (62kg)
Sergey Martinov   RUS
Lightweight (68kg)
Islam Dugutyev   RUS
Welterweight (74kg)
Mnatasakan Iskandarian   RUS
Middleweight (82kg)
Thomas Zander   GER
Light Heavyweight (90kg)
Gogi Koguashvili   RUS
Heavyweight (100kg)
Andrzey Wronski   POL
Super Heavyweight (130kg)
Aleksandr Karelin   RUS

WOMEN
Sofia, Bulgaria   Aug 6-7
Light Flyweight (44kg)
Shoko Yoshimura   JPN
Flyweight (47kg)
Misho Kamibajashi   JPN
Bantamweight (50kg)
Miyo Yamamoto   JPN
Featherweight (53kg)
Akemi Kawasaki   JPN

Lightweight (57kg)
Line Johansen   NOR
Welterweight (61kg)
Nikola Hartmann   AUT
Middleweight (65kg)
Yaoi Urano   JPN
Light Heavyweight (70kg)
Christine Nordhagen   CAN
Heavyweight (75kg)
Mitsuko Funakoshi   JPN

World Cup
Greco-Roman Style
Heinola, Finland   Nov 6-7, 1993
1 Russia   8 pts
2 Finland   6
Freestyle
Edmonton, Canada   Mar 24-26
1 United States   10
2 Iran   8

European Championships

Winners only
FREESTYLE
Rome, Italy   Apr 6-10
Light Flyweight (48kg)
Armen Mkrtysian   ARM
Flyweight (52kg)
Namik Abdullayev   AZE
Bantamweight (57kg)
Anusyavan Sakyan   ARM
Featherweight (62kg)
Muhar Demiregen   TUR
Lightweight (68kg)
Vadim Bogiyev   RUS
Welterweight (74kg)
Nazir Gadziyanov   RUS
Middleweight (82kg)
Rustem Kelesayev   RUS
Light Heavyweight (90kg)
Soslan Frayev   RUS
Heavyweight (100kg)
Marek Garmulewicz   POL
Super Heavyweight (130kg)
Mirab Valiyev   UKR
GRECO-ROMAN STYLE
Athens, Greece   Apr 15-17
Light Flyweight (48kg)
Zafar Guliyev   RUS
Flyweight (52kg)
Arsen Nazaryan   ARM
Bantamweight (57kg)
Seref Eroglu   TUR
Featherweight (62kg)
Grigoriy Kamusyenko   UKR
Lightweight (68kg)
Attila Repka   HUN
Welterweight (74kg)

Erol Koyuncu   TUR
Middleweight (82kg)
Thomas Zander   GER
Light Heavyweight (90kg)
Vyacheslav Oleynik   UKR
Heavyweight (100kg)
Andrzej Wronski   POL
Super Heavyweight (130kg)
Aleksandr Karelin   RUS

British Champions'ps
Lancing, W Sussex   May 7
Flyweight (52kg)
A Hutchinson (Leigh)
Bantamweight (57kg)
D Rigby (Bolton)
Featherweight (62kg)
J Melling (Leigh)
Lightweight (68kg)
B Aspen (Bolton)
Welterweight (74kg)
C McNeil (Milngavie)
Middleweight (82kg)
G K Kooner (Birmingham)
Light Heavyweight (90kg)
G English (E Kilbride)
Heavyweight (100kg)
N Loban (Hendon Police)
Super Heavyweight (130kg)
A Singh (Birmingham)
Women's 53kg
A Broadbent (Manchester Y)
Women's 57kg
T Williams (W London)

English Open
Eccles   Mar 12
Flyweight (52kg)
O Navarro (W London)
Bantamweight (57kg)
D Rigby (Bolton)
Featherweight (62kg)
P Morris (Bolton)
Lightweight (68kg)
B Aspen (Bolton)
Welterweight (74kg)
S Rigby (Bolton)
Middleweight (82kg)
S Morley (Wirksworth)
Light Heavyweight (90kg)
J Mossford (Manchester YMCA)
Heavyweight (100kg)
N Loban (Hendon Police)
Super Heavyweight (130kg)
A Singh (Birmingham)
Women's 53kg
A Broadbent (Manchester Y.)
Women's 57kg
T Williams (Met. Police)

Yachting

Whitbread Round The World Race 1993-94

Sept 25, 1993-June 3, 1994

FINAL RESULTS

IOR Maxi Class	Days	Hrs	Min	Sec
1 New Zealand Endeavour	120	5	9	23
2 Merit Cup	121	2	50	47
3 La Poste	123	22	54	58
4 Uruguay Natural	144	20	17	44

Whitbread 60 Class	Days	Hrs	Min	Sec
1 Yamaha	120	14	55	00
2 Intrum Justitia	121	5	26	26
3 Galicia 93 Pescanova	122	6	12	23
4 Winston	122	9	32	9
5 Tokio	128	16	19	48
6 Brooksfield	130	4	29	27
7 Hetman Sahaidachny	135	23	17	52
8 Reebok	137	21	3	17
9 Heineken	138	16	30	51
10 Odessa	158	4	34	40

IRYU World Sailing Championship

La Rochelle, France   July 26-Aug 7

LASER CLASS
Single Men

1 Francesco Bruni	ITA	40
2 Robert Scheidt	BRA	50
3 Alfonso Domingos	POR	62
4 Eivind Melleby	NOR	64
5 Santiago Lange	ARG	70
10 Mark Littlejohn	GBR	98

ENZA, skippered by Robin Knox-Johnston and Peter Blake, broke the world record for a round the world voyage when it crossed the finish off the coast of Brittany on 1st April. The 92 foot catamaran took 74 days, 22 hours, 17 minutes and 22 seconds to complete the 27,000 nautical miles and claim the Jules Verne Trophy. Knox-Johnston, who in 1966 became the first man to sail non-stop single handed around the world, beat the previous record held by Bruno Peyron, the French captain of the Commodore Explorer. Averaging 14.5 knots, the yacht with her eight-man crew of New Zealanders and Britons smashed the record by more than four days.

Single Women

1 Kristine Roug	DEN	16
2 Danielle Brennan	USA	24
3 Dorte Jensen	DEN	30
4 Gayl Harrhy	NZL	44
5 Alexandra Verbeek	HOL	46

470 CLASS
Double Men

1 John Merricks/Ian Walker	GBR	34
2 Kan Yamada/Seiji Saito	JPN	49
3 Paolo Cian/Marco Scotto	ITA	50
4 Marcus Westerlind/Henrik Wallin	SWE	59
5 Fabrice Knipping/Phil. Gasparini	FRA	62
6 Andrew Richards/Ian Park	GBR	66

Double Women

1 Teresa Zabell/Begonia Dufresne	ESP	19
2 Ruslana Taran/Natalya Hapanovich	UKR	36
3 Peggy Hardwiger/Christina Pinnow	GER	44
4 Laura Leon/Viviane Mainemare	ESP	46
5 Ines Bohn/Sabine Rohatzsch	GER	48

HOBIE CLASS
Multihull Open

1 Enrique Figueroa/Carla Malatrasi	PUR	13
2 Blaine Dodds/Steve Arnold	RSA	35
3 Shaun Ferry/Lewis Alison	RSA	39
4 Claudio Cardoso/Fred. Monteiro	BRA	39
5 Walter Myers/Mark Santorelli	USA	55

Multihull Women

1 Kerry Ireland/Vicki Tanner	AUS	12
2 Belinda Klaase/Margot Brache	RSA	26
3 Lisa Holman/Judith Herald	RSA	34
4 Sue Korzeniewski/Laura Geremia	USA	41
5 Gael Mercier/Caroline Maby	FRA	45

J24 CLASS
Keelboat Men

1 Sweden 2	36
2 Sweden 4	41
3 South Africa 2	46
4 Spain 1	46
5 Italy 2	53
8 Great Britain 1	63

Keelboat Women

1 France 1	6
2 Norway 1	21
3 Sweden 1	24
4 Sweden 4	25
5 Holland 2	28

Europe Class World Championships
La Rochelle, France   July 15

Women's Single Handed

1 Kristine Roug	DEN	100
2 Tine Moberg Parker	CAN	99
3 Margriet Matthysse	HOL	98

470 Class World Championships
Helsinki, Finland   Aug 25
Men's Double Handed

1	Ben Kouwenhoven/Jan Kouwenhoven	HOL	100
2	Kenji Nakamura/Masato Takaki	JPN	99
3	Markus Westerlind/Henrik Wallin	SWE	98
5	John Merricks/Ian Walker	GBR	96

Women's Double Handed

1	Ines Bohn/Sabine Rohatzsch	GER	100
2	Susanne Bauckholt M./Katrin Adlkofer	GER	99
3	Peggy Hardwiger/Christina Pinnow	GER	98

Laser Class World Championships
Wakayama   Aug 28

1	Nickolas Burfoot	NZL	100
2	Pascal Lacoste	FRA	99
3	Serge Kats	HOL	98
9	Richard Stenhouse	GBR	92

Tornado Class World Championship
Bastad   Aug 13

1	Fernando Leon/Jose Ballester	ESP	100
2	Helge Sach/Christian Sach	GER	99
3	Mitch Booth/Peter Kremsl	AUS	98

Star Class World Championship
San Diego, USA   Sept 16

1	Ross MacDonald/Eric Jespersen	CAN	100
2	Alan Adler/Rodrigo Meireles	BRA	99
3	Torben Grael/Marcelo Ferreira	BRA	98

Soling World Championship
July 8

1	Doreste/Valaides/Galmes	ESP	100
2	Bank/Nielsen/Jacobsen	DEN	99
3	Madrigali/Barton/Massey	USA	98

Finn Gold Cup
Tallinn, Estonia   Aug 21

1	Fredrik Loof	SWE	100
2	Hank Lammens	CAN	99
3	José van der Ploeg	ESP	98

IRYU World Boardsailing Championships
Gimli, Canada   Sept 3
Men

1	Aaron McIntosh	NZL	100
2	Bruce Kendall	NZL	99
3	Andrea Zimali	ITA	98

Women

1	Maud Herbert	FRA	100
2	Ke Li	CHN	99
3	Natasha Sturges	AUS	98

IRYU Nautica World Youth Sailing Championships
Marathon, Greece   July 19
Boy's Laser (Single Handed)

1	Daniel Slater	NZL	30
2	Ben Ainslie	GBR	30
3	Philipp Buchert	GER	57

Girl's Laser (Single Handed)

1	Shelley Hesson	NZL	39
2	Doris Wetzel	GER	42
3	Sara Ahlen	SWE	54

Boy's Laser 2 (Double Handed)

1	David Amirs/PJ Buhler	USA	47
2	Rodrigo Amado/Leonardo Santos	BRA	47
3	Justin Steel/Christian Stevens	AUS	50
5	Spencer Murray/Paul Kamean	GBR	55

Girl's Laser 2 (Double Handed)

1	Storm Nuttal/Sally Cuthbert	GBR	38
2	Briohny Hooper/Amanda Miller	AUS	40
3	Susie Wood/Jennifer Cheyne	NZL	46

Boy's Mistral (Board)

1	Amir Lebinson	ISR	23
2	Stephane Jaouen	FRA	49
3	Pawel Gardasiewick	POL	52
7	Dean Tomlinson	GBR	83

Girl's Mistral (Board)

1	Amelie Lux	GER	25
2	Agata Pokorowska	POL	32
3	Justine Gardahaut	FRA	38
15	B French-Greenslade	GBR	150

NAUTICA CUP

1	New Zealand	408
2	Australia	357
3	Germany	344
4	Great Britain	339

Extras

Cricket - Women

PREMIER LEAGUE FINAL
Meir Heath, Staffs   *Sep 17*
Wakefield   113-9 (P Lovell 3-16)
Redoubtables   114-3 (J Brittin 55*)
Redoubtables won by 7 wckts

NATIONAL PLATE COMPETITION
Westminster College, Oxford   Sep 3
Dukesmead   151-3 (C Ward 86)
Northern Marches   111-9 (L McLeod 38,
                          A Belonogoff 4-23)

NATIONAL CLUB KNOCK-OUT
Christchurch College, Oxford   Sep 3
Shepparton   118-6 (N Sheriff 37)
Newark & Sherwood 118-2 (E Donnison 59)

Croquet

WORLD CHAMPIONSHIP
Carden Park Aug 13-17
Quarter-finals
R Fulford (ENG) bt R Bamford (RSA) +26tp, +26tp, +5tp
A Westerby (NZL) bt M Taylor (AUS) +25tp, +7tpo
S Cornish (ENG) bt M Kobett (AUS) -26tp, +26tp, +17
C Clarke (ENG) bt C Irwin (ENG) -25tp, +26tp, +11tpo
Semi-finals
C Clarke bt S Cornish -26tp, +8tpo, +26, -25, +13tpo
R Fulford bt A Westerby +17tp, -17tp, +26tp, +20qp
Final
R Fulford bt C Clarke +12tpo, +12tp, +18tp, +13

Greyhound Racing

DAILY MIRROR/SPORTING LIFE
GREYHOUND DERBY
Wimbledon June 25
1 **Moral Standards**   **9/4F**
2 Ayr Flyer   3/1

Money Winners 1993

	Greyhound	Trainer	£
1	Ringa Hustle	Tony Meek	41,100
2	Heavenly Lady	Linda Mullins	22,255
3	I'm His	Eric Jordan	20,900
4	New Level	Harry Williams	20,100
5	Just Right Kyle	Charlie Lister	18,780
6	Galleydown Boy	John Copplestone	14,070
7	Magical Piper	Linda Mullins	13,980
8	Pearls Girls	Sam Sykes	13,335
9	Killenahg Dream	Charllie Lister	12,690
10	Stylefield Law	Natalie Savva	11,670

The British sled dog championship at Aberfoyle, Strathclyde had to be called off in January - because of arctic conditions. Apparently, there was ice on the track. That would have upset the average Siberian husky, I'll warrant......

If you like ice hockey, but can't skate. Table ice hockey is the answer. No, you don't have to climb on the table with dusters on your shoes. It's like table football, but more sophisticated. It's not too big in Britain, but it's huge in Scandinavia where ten of thousands play. They are good, too. According to Theodore Wood, one of the few addicts in Britain, "One of their top players came over last year and none of us could score against him, even when he played with one eye shut and took off his goalie" Doesn't sound much fun to us.

One result you might have missed; Ty Murray claimed his sixth all-round champion cowboy title at the National Western Rodeo in January. Just thought you'd like to know.

One result we haven't got is the World Elephant Polo Championship. It is held in Nepal in December and we are still trying to find out who won last year. Drop us a postcard.....

This story wasn't published on April 1st, so we assume it's true. Koji Harada, a 5ft 2in novice sumo wrestler had a six-inch silicone implant inserted in his skull in order to reach the sport's minimum height requirement of 5ft 8in. Apparently, the governing body came to an understanding that he could stay in sumo if he had the implant removed. Second thoughts, we don't believe a word of it.

The toughest race in the world and the most utterly ridiculous is organised by Billy Wilson at Tettenhall in the West Midlands. You run through bogs, rivers, pits that were once used for dipping cattle, along rope frames, among bramble bushes, through tyres and over hayricks. It's eight miles long, takes hours and if the weather's been bad, you can be wading muddy water chest-high. You get a horse brass if you finish and over 1000 people regularly start the race. And it's all to raise money for the donkeys, sheep, goats and Vietnamese pot-bellied pigs that Wilson keeps at his Tettenhall sanctuary.

Winter Olympics

History might correct the balance, but the Lillehammer Games was the Olympics where Nancy Kerrigan met Tonya Harding. If the International Olympic Committee itself had taken a baton to Nancy's knee on January 6th at Detroit, it could have created no more publicity. The story built steadily as the conspiratorial elements unfolded. So much detail, in fact, that when the Games opened on February 12th, it came as something of a relief. Even then, there were more media in attendance at Nancy Kerrigan's press conference that day, than there were at the opening ceremony.

Harding played her part in the drama magnificently. So well that it was difficult to know whether it was a performance or the real thing. She was, at turns, aggrieved, hurt, humble, injured, but above all petulant. She was sustained by one possibility; that she could actually win the figure skating title. This gave substance to the drama (though the script always looked to be going Nancy's way). However, when even that option evaporated, Harding played her last throw with such melodrama, that even rows of hardened old hacks were opened mouthed with disbelief - or was it admiration?

By the time the competition reached the free programme, Harding, languishing in tenth position, had no chance of a victory. To make it worse, Kerrigan, who always seemed to be in white, was in the lead. Harding knew that after this parting shot, the choices were limited to a court appearance in Oregon and wrestling in Japan. Unlike Kerrigan, she hadn't been able to sell the film script. Harding, in purple of course, took an eternity to come on to the ice. There were just seconds left on the clock. She arrived, fiddling with her boot, and barely a minute into her programme pulled out of a triple Lutz with a look of anguish that Chaplin himself would have applauded.

The referee, Britta Lindgren was impressed; her sympathy flooded in Harding's direction. When she was shown the offending boot and the recalcitrant lace, that simply wouldn't tie up properly, she was so moved as to offer her a second chance. Harding took it, but it was all too late. But by now we all knew it was for real and not a performance. A seasoned actor would have bowed out tearfully, turning the sympathy her way. It was an opportunity lost for, in no time at all, Kerrigan had skated and been dethroned, in every sense. The orphan from Ukraine, Oksana Baiul, took gold. Kerrigan smiled tightly on the podium, then griped backstage, complaining about the marks. The made-for-TV film kept the fairy-tale ending, but Kerrigan knew the difference between fact and fiction. Just.

The Kerrigan-Harding affair ensured that CBS enjoyed the Games. The American TV company had paid a mammoth $295m for the rights and came away with a handsome profit. In America, the Lillehammer Games with Dan Jansen, Tommy Moe, Bonnie Blair and a hundred other good stories probably ranked higher in interest than any summer Games. In Britain, too, with 23.95 million people tuned in for Torvill and Dean (*see front of book*), the Games was an undoubted hit. Nicky Gooch's speed-skating bronze also meant that Britain could claim a post-war best equalling performance with two medals, both bronzes, and eight top ten placings; four of which came from the bobsleigh teams, one from skater Steven Cousins and another from freestyle skier Richard Cobbing.

QUOTES

"We heard that one or two young guys grilled sausages on the flame one night.....they must have had spears 20 metres long, I suppose." - **Security guards at Olympia Park, where the flame sat atop a 20 metre tower.**

"We have nothing against little bells or musical instruments, but fans with heavy cowbells will have to hand them over to security agents" - **Security guards again.**

"Squashed elk means massive delays" - **Norwegian State Railways trying to explain the problems caused by elks, weighing as much as 1500lb, running on to the line. An average of 500 are killed each year.**

"The Olympic Games have created a kind of cultural apartheid between the local residents and the Olympic people with their yuppie attitudes" - **Thor Heyerdahl's son, Thor junior, who boycotted the Games his father opened.**

"I had no choice. I had to host the Olympics" - **Mrs Lilly Hammer, from the town of Ulvik, near Bergen, explaining that as the IOC president mispronounced the name of the Olympic venue to sound like hers, then she had to hold her own Games. Her husband was helping her. His name is Odd. Odd Hammer.**

"I may not be the normal figure skating image that everyone wants me to be, but I'm my own person. I may be a little rough around the edges, but overall I think I'm a good person" - **Tonya Harding on herself.**

"Tonya was made to be a pro-wrestler. She's about as tough as they come" - **Takashi Matsunaga, chairman of the All-Japan Wrestling Association, who offered $2m to Harding to take up the sport.**

"I'd just like to say that I'm really sorry that I interfered" - **Harding's apology in court**

"There's substantial evidence of prior knowledge" - **Oregon deputy district attorney Norm Frink on Harding. The ice skater received a fine of $100,000, three years probation and 500 hours of community service after a plea bargain that allowed her to plead guilty to the hindering the prosecution rather than involvement in the actual attack on Kerrigan.**

"We didn't want to be criticised. We didn't want to upset people by doing anything risque" - **Christopher Dean, explaining their new dance programme.**

"Chubby-cheeked and bloated, wearing far too much make-up and in an ill fitting costume, she looks like a London housewife attending the wedding of one of her children" - **Jean Christophe Papillon, correspondent of *Le Figaro*, on Jayne Torvill.**

"They did a kind of jump going over the head. For this fault, they lost marks because it is something that is not allowed under our new rules..." - **Hans Kutchera, referee for the Olympic ice dance competition.**

"We like to think the audience were our judges" - **Dean, after a rapturous reception to their free dance, but marks that earned only the bronze medal.**

ALPINE SKIING
MEN

DOWNHILL
Kvitfjell   *Feb 13*
Dist: 3035m   *Drop: 838m*   *Snow: Hard*   *Temp: -16° C*

			Time	Diff	Pts
1	Tommy Moe	USA	1:45.75	0.00	0.00
2	Kjetil Andre Aamodt	NOR	1:45.79	0.04	0.46
3	Edward Podivinsky	CAN	1:45.87	0.12	1.37

Also

26	Graham Bell	GBR	1:47.39	1.64	18.77
28	Martin Bell	GBR	1:47.49	1.74	19.91

SUPER-G
Kvitfjell   *Feb 17*
Dist: 2574m   *Drop: 641m*   *Snow: Hard*

			Time	Diff	Pts
1	Markus Wasmeier	GER	1:32.53	0.00	0.00
2	Tommy Moe	USA	1:32.61	0.08	0.80
3	Kjetil Andre Aamodt	NOR	1:32.93	0.40	3.98

Spencer Pession and Graham Bell (both GBR) did not finish

GIANT SLALOM
Hafjell   *Feb 23*   *Drop: 467m*   *Snow: Hard*

			1st run	2nd run	Total
1	Markus Wasmeier	GER	1:28.71	1:23.75	2:52.46
2	Urs Kaelin	SUI	1:28.70	1:23.78	2:52.48
3	Christian Mayer	AUT	1:28.34	1:24.24	2:52.58

Also

31	Spencer Pession	GBR	1:33.94	1:28.68	3:02.62

William Gaylord (GBR) disqualified on second run (gate 63)

SLALOM
Hafjell   *Feb 27*   *Drop: 227m*   *Snow: Hard*

			1st run	2nd run	Total
1	Thomas Stangassinger	AUT	1:01.00	1:01.02	2:02.02
2	Alberto Tomba	ITA	1:02.84	59.33	2:02.17
3	Jure Kosir	SLO	1:02.55	59.98	2:02.53

William Gaylord (GBR) did not finish first run

COMBINED
Downhill - Kvitfjell, Feb 14
Dist: 2829m   *Drop: 770*   *Snow: Hard*
Slalom(2 runs) - Hafjell, Feb 25
Drop: 195m   *Snow: Hard*

			D'hill(pos)	Slalom(pos)	Total
1	Lasse Kjus	NOR	1:36.95(1)	1:40.58(7)	3:17.53
2	Kjetil A. Aamodt	NOR	1:37.49(6)	1:41.06(9)	3:18.55
3	H. C. Str. Nilsen	NOR	1:39.05(21)	1:40.09(4)	3:19.14

William Gaylord (GBR) did not finish downhill, Graham Bell (GBR) did not start slalom

WOMEN

DOWNHILL
Kvitfjell   *Feb 19*
Dist: 2641m   *Drop: 708m*   *Snow: Hard*

			Time	Diff	Pts
1	Katja Seizinger	GER	1:35.93	0.00	0.00
2	Picabo Street	USA	1:36.59	0.66	8.32
3	Isolde Kostner	ITA	1:36.85	0.92	11.60

SUPER-G
Kvitfjell   *Feb 15*
Dist: 2035m   *Drop: 527m*   *Snow: Hard*

			Time	Diff	Pts
1	Diann Roffe	USA	1:22.15	0.00	0.00
2	Svetlana Gladischeva	RUS	1:22.44	0.29	3.25
3	Isolde Kostner	ITA	1:22.45	0.30	3.36

GIANT SLALOM
Hafjell   *Feb 24*   *Drop: 387m*   *Snow: Hard*

			1st run	2nd run	Total
1	Deborah Compagnoni	ITA	1:20.37	1:10.60	2:30.97
2	Martina Ertl	GER	1:21.34	1:10.85	2:32.19
3	Vreni Schneider	SUI	1:21.29	1:11.68	2:32.97

Emma Carrick-Anderson (GBR) did not finish first run

SLALOM
Hafjell   *Feb 26*   *Drop: 195m*   *Snow: Hard*

			1st run	2nd run	Total
1	Vreni Schneider	SUI	59.68	56.33	1:56.01
2	Elfriede Eder	AUT	59.54	56.81	1:56.35
3	Katja Koren	SLO	59.00	57.61	1:56.61

Clare de Pourtales and Emma Carrick-Anderson (both GBR) did not finish first runs.

COMBINED
Downhill - Kvitfjell, Feb 20
Dist: 2418m   *Drop: 641m*   *Snow: Hard*
Slalom(2 runs) - Hafjell, Feb 21
Drop: 166m   *Snow: Hard*

			D'hill(pos)	Slalom(pos)	Total
1	Pernilla Wiberg	SWE	1:28.70(5)	1:36.46(2)	3:05.16
2	Vreni Schneider	SUI	1:28.91(7)	1:36.38(1)	3:05.29
3	Alenka Dovzan	SLO	1:28.67(4)	1:37.97(3)	3:06.64

Germany's Katja Seizinger led after the downhill element, but failed to finish the first slalom run.

MEDAL TABLE

	G	S	B	Total
Russia	11	8	4	23
Norway	10	11	5	26
Germany	9	7	8	24
Italy	7	5	8	20
United States	6	5	2	13
Korea	4	1	1	6
Canada	3	6	4	13
Switzerland	3	4	2	9
Austria	2	3	4	9
Sweden	2	1	0	3
Japan	1	2	2	5
Kazakhstan	1	2	0	3
Ukraine	1	0	1	2
Uzbekistan	1	0	0	1
Belarus	0	2	0	2
Finland	0	1	5	6
France	0	1	4	5
Holland	0	1	3	4
China	0	1	2	3
Slovenia	0	0	3	3
Great Britain	0	0	2	2
Australia	0	0	1	1

BIATHLON

All events held on the Birkebeineren course.
In the women's 15km and the men's 20km, for each missed
target one minute is added to the competitor's time. In the
other events, for each missed target the competitor has to ski a
penalty loop of approximately 150m.

MEN

10KM

Feb 23   Total climb: 404m   Snow: Fine   Temp: -12° C

			Penalties	Total
1	Sergei Tchepikov	RUS	0	28:07.0
2	Ricco Gross	GER	0	28:13.0
3	Sergei Tarasov	RUS	1	28:27.4
Also				
49	Ian Woods	GBR	2	31:58.3

20KM

Feb 20   Total climb: 743m   Snow: Fine   Temp: -17° C

			Time	Penalties	Total
1	Sergei Tarasov	RUS	54:25.3	3	57:25.3
2	Frank Luck	GER	54:28.7	3	57:28.7
3	Sven Fischer	GER	55:41.9	2	57:41.9
Also					
54	Ian Woods	GBR		3	1:03:44.0
54	Mike Dixon	GBR		1	1:03:44.0

4 x 7.5KM RELAY

Feb 26   Total climb(lap): 279m   Snow: Fine   Temp: -12° C

		Penalties	Total
1	Germany	0	1:30:22.1
	(Gross/Luck/Kirchner/Fischer)		
2	Russia	2	1:31:23.6
3	France	1	1:32:31.3

WOMEN

7.5KM

Feb 23   Total climb: 271m   Snow: Fine   Temp: -17° C

			Penalties	Total
1	Myriam Bedard	CAN	2	26:08.8
2	Svetlana Paramygina	BLS	2	26:09.9
3	Valentyna Tserbe	UKR	0	26:10.0

15KM

Feb 18   Total climb: 504m   Snow: Fine   Temp: -14° C

			Time	Penalties	Total
1	Myriam Bedard	CAN	50:06.6	2	52:06.6
2	Anne Briand	FRA	49:53.3	3	52:53.3
3	Ursula Disl	GER	50:15.3	3	53:15.3

Each miss adds one minute to the competitor's time.

4 x 7.5KM RELAY

Feb 25   Total climb: 279m   Snow: Fine   Temp: -15° C

		Penalties	Total
1	Russia	0	1:47:19.5
	(Talanova/Snytina/Noskova/Reztsova)		
2	Germany	6	1:51:16.5
3	France	1	1:52:28.3

BOBSLEIGH

The Hunderfossen course is 1365m long and descends 107m.
There are six right curves and ten left. The air temperature for
the first run of the two-man bob, was a numbing -16° C.

TWO-MAN

Feb 19-20 (two runs each day)

		1st	2nd	3rd	4th	Total
1	Switzerland-1	52.33	52.91	52.72	52.85	3:30.81
	(Gustav Weder/Donat Acklin)					
2	Switzerland-2	52.38	52.76	52.79	52.93	3:30.86
3	Italy-1	52.61	52.80	52.69	52.91	3:31.01
Also						
6	Great Britain-1	52.77	53.15	52.99	53.24	3:32.15
	(Mark Tout/Lennox Paul)					
10	Great Britain-2	52.86	53.30	53.21	53.46	3:32.83
	(Sean Olsson/Paul Field)					

FOUR-MAN

Feb 26-27 (two runs each day)

		1st	2nd	3rd	4th	Total
1	Germany-2	51.67	51.88	52.07	52.16	3:27.78
	(Czudaj/Brannasch/Hampel/Szelig)					
2	Switzerland-1	51.80	51.87	52.04	52.13	3:27.84
3	Germany-1	51.82	51.91	52.14	52.14	3:28.01
Also						
5	Great Britain-1	52.03	52.24	52.14	52.46	3:28.87
	(Tout/Farrell/Wing/Paul)					
8	Great Britain-2	52.23	52.45	52.26	52.47	3:29.41
	(Olsson/Herbert/Ward/Field)					

CROSS-COUNTRY SKIING

All events held on the Birkebeineren course

MEN

10KM CLASSICAL

Feb 17
Total climb: 413m   Snow: Fine   Temp: -12° C

			Time	FIS	WC
1	Bjørn Dæhlie	NOR	24:20.1	0.00	100
2	Vladimir Smirnov	KZK	24:38.3	6.73	80
3	Marco Albarello	ITA	24:42.3	8.21	60

10KM C + 15KM F PURSUIT

Feb 19
Total climb: 630m   Snow: Fine   Temp: -4° C

			5km/10km	Total
1	Bjørn Dæhlile	NOR	24:20/35:48.8	1:00:08.8
2	Vladimir Smirnov	KZK	24:38/36:00.0	1:00:38.0
3	Silvio Fauner	ITA	25:08/36:40.0	1:01:48.6

30KM FREESTYLE

Feb 14
Total climb: 1136m   Snow: Fine   Temp: -18° C

			Time	FIS	WC
1	Thomas Alsgaard	NOR	1:12:26.4	0.00	100
2	Bjørn Dæhlie	NOR	1:13:13.6	5.86	80
3	Mika Myllylae	FIN	1:14:14.5	13.43	60

50KM CLASSICAL
Feb 27

Total climb: 1787m   Snow: Fine   Temp: -12° C

			Time	FIS	WC
1	Vladimir Smirnov	KZK	2:07:20.3	0.00	100
2	Mika Myllylae	FIN	2:08:41.9	5.87	80
3	Sture Sivertsen	NOR	2:08:49.0	6.39	60

4 x 10KM RELAY
Feb 22

Total climb: 398m   Snow: Fine   Temp: -10° C

		Lap1	Lap2	Lap3	Lap4	Total
1	Italy	26:13.0	25:53.9	24:59.1	24:09.0	1:41:15.0
	(De Zolt/Albarello/Vanzetta/Fauner)					
2	Norway	26:03.2	26:04.2	24:59.2	24:08.8	1:41:15.4
3	Finland	26:03.6	26:04.4	24:57.5	25:10.1	1:42:15.6

WOMEN

5KM CLASSICAL
Feb 15

Total climb: 199m   Snow: Fine   Temp: -12° C

			Time	FIS	WC
1	Ljubov Egorova	RUS	14:08.8	0.00	100
2	Manuela Di Centa	ITA	14:28.3	12.41	80
3	Marja-L. Kirvesniemi	FIN	14:36.0	17.30	60

5KM C + 10KM F PURSUIT
Feb 17

Total climb: 420m   Snow: Fine   Temp: -10° C

			5km/10km	Total
1	Ljubov Egorova	RUS	14:08/27:30.1	41:38.1
2	Manuela Di Centa	ITA	14:28/27:18.4	41:46.4
3	Stefania Belmondo	ITA	15:04/27:17.1	42:21.1

15KM FREESTYLE
Feb 13

Total climb: 563m   Snow: Fresh   Temp: -19° C

			Time	FIS	WC
1	Manuela Di Centa	ITA	39:44.5	0.00	100
2	Ljubov Egorova	RUS	41:03.0	17.78	80
3	Nina Gavriluk	RUS	41:10.4	19.45	60

30KM CLASSICAL
Feb 24

Total climb: 1064m   Snow: Fine   Temp: -4° C

			Time	FIS	WC
1	Manuela Di Centa	ITA	1:25:41.6	0.00	100
2	Marit Wold	NOR	1:25:57.8	1.73	80
3	Marja-L. Kirvesniemi	FIN	1:26:13.6	3.42	60

4 x 5KM RELAY
Feb 21

Total climb: 210m/lap   Snow: Fine   Temp: -13° C

		Lap1	Lap2	Lap3	Lap4	Total
1	Russia	15:05.4	14:47.4	13:58.7	13:21.0	57:12.5
	(Vaelbe/Lazutina/Gavriluk/Egorova)					
2	Norway	15:13.4	14:31.6	14:05.5	13:52.1	57:42.6
3	Italy	15:58.6	14:29.2	14:38.0	13:36.8	58:42.7

FREESTYLE SKIING
WOMEN
MOGULS
Feb 16

			Turns/Air/Time	/Total
1	Stine Lise Hattestad	NOR	14.00/6.25/29.51	25.97
2	Elizabeth McIntyre	USA	14.20/6.05/29.83	25.89
3	Elizaveta Kojevnikova	RUS	14.10/5.85/29.00	25.81

Jill Curry (GBR) did not start through injury

AERIALS
Feb 24

			Jump1	Jump2	Total Pts
1	Lina Tcherjazova	UZB	92.92	73.92	166.84
2	Marie Lindgren	SWE	81.78	84.10	165.88
3	Hilde Synnøve Lid	NOR	76.41	87.72	164.13

Jill Curry (GBR) finished 21st in the elimination round

MEN
MOGULS
Feb 16

			Turns/Air/Time	/Total
1	Jean-Luc Brassard	CAN	15.00/6.85/24.53	27.24
2	Sergei Shoupletsov	RUS	14.50/6.90/24.21	26.90
3	Edgar Grospiron	FRA	13.90/6.90/23.19	26.64

Hugh Hutchison (GBR) finished 25th in the elimination round and did not qualify for the final rounds

AERIALS
Feb 24

			Jump1	Jump2	Total Pts
1	Andreas Schönbaechler	SUI	113.19	121.48	234.67
2	Philippe Laroche	CAN	110.58	118.05	228.63
3	Lloyd Langlois	CAN	111.47	110.97	222.44
Also					
10	Richard Cobbing	GBR	102.22	94.36	196.58

ICE HOCKEY

Matches played in the Håkons Hall, Lillehammer or the Cavern Hall at Gjøvik. Where matches are still level after extra time, the result is decided by penalty shots

GROUP A

12/2	FIN v TCH	3-1	(2-1, 1-0, 0-0)
	RUS v NOR	5-1	(2-1, 1-0, 2-0)
	AUT v GER	3-4	(1-1, 0-0, 2-3)
14/2	GER v NOR	2-1	(1-0, 1-1, 0-0)
	TCH v AUT	7-3	(2-2, 4-1, 1-0)
	RUS v FIN	0-5	(0-1, 0-4, 0-0)
16/2	AUT v RUS	1-9	(0-1, 1-7, 0-1)
	TCH v GER	1-0	(0-0, 0-0, 1-0)
	NOR v FIN	0-4	(0-1, 0-2, 0-1)
18/2	GER v RUS	4-2	(2-0, 1-1, 1-1)
	FIN v AUT	6-2	(1-0, 2-1, 3-1)
	TCH v NOR	4-1	(3-0, 0-0, 1-1)
20/2	RUS v TCH	4-3	(2-2, 2-0, 0-1)
	GER v FIN	1-7	(0-3, 0-2, 1-2)
	NOR v AUT	2-4	(1-1, 1-1, 0-2)

GROUP A TABLE

		P	W	D	L	Gls	Pts
1	Finland	5	5	0	0	25-4	10
2	Germany	5	3	0	2	11-14	6
3	Czech Republic	5	3	0	2	16-11	6
4	Russia	5	3	0	2	20-14	6
5	Austria	5	1	0	4	13-28	2
6	Norway	5	0	0	5	5-19	0

GROUP B

13/2	SWE v SVK	4-4	(2-1, 0-2, 2-1)
	ITA v CAN	2-7	(1-2, 0-4, 1-1)
	FRA v USA	4-4	(1-1, 0-0, 2-2)
15/2	SWE v ITA	4-1	(1-0, 1-1, 2-0)
	USA v SVK	3-3	(1-1, 0-1, 2-1)
	CAN v FRA	3-1	(1-0, 2-0, 0-1)
17/2	SVK v ITA	10-4	(6-2, 3-1, 1-1)
	FRA v SWE	1-7	(0-3, 1-2, 0-2)
	CAN v USA	3-3	(1-0, 1-2, 1-1)
19/2	CAN v SVK	1-3	(1-1, 0-1, 0-1)
	ITA v FRA	7-3	(2-1, 3-2, 2-0)
	USA v SWE	4-6	(1-2, 0-2, 3-2)
21/2	SWE v CAN	2-3	(1-1, 1-2, 0-0)
	SVK v FRA	6-2	(4-1, 2-0, 0-1)
	USA v ITA	7-1	(5-1, 1-0, 1-0)

GROUP B TABLE

		P	W	D	L	Gls	Pts
1	Slovakia	5	3	2	0	26-14	8
2	Canada	5	3	1	1	17-11	7
3	Sweden	5	3	1	1	23-13	7
4	United States	5	1	3	1	21-17	5
5	Italy	5	1	0	4	15-31	2
6	France	5	0	1	4	11-27	1

MATCHES FOR POSITIONS 9-12

22/2	AUT v FRA	4-5	(2-2, 0-1, 2-1, 0-0, Pens)
	ITA v NOR	6-3	(3-2, 1-1, 2-0)

MATCH FOR POSITIONS 11-12

24/2	NOR v AUT	3-1	(1-0, 1-0, 1-1)

MATCH FOR POSITIONS 9-10

24/2	FRA v ITA	2-3	(1-1, 1-0, 0-2)

With two metres of snow arriving in the week before the Games and two weeks of sunshine during it, the Norwegians could not complain about the weather. But then Norwegians don't complain about the weather, anyway. On the final night of the Games, with temperatures dropping to **minus** 23 C, 15,000 Norwegians slept under canvas on the Birkebeineren, the wooded cross-country skiing course three miles above the town, in anticipation of the following day's 50 kilometre freestyle skiing event.

QUARTER FINALS

23/2	CAN v TCH	3-2	(0-1, 1-1, 1-0, 1-0)
	FIN v USA	6-1	(2-0, 2-1, 2-0)
	GER v SWE	0-3	(0-0, 0-1, 0-2)
	SVK v RUS	2-3	(2-1, 0-1, 0-0, 0-1)

MATCHES FOR POSITIONS 5-8

24/2	TCH v USA	5-3	(3-2, 1-0, 1-1)
	GER v SVK	5-6	(3-0, 0-3, 2-2, 0-1)

MATCH FOR POSITIONS 7-8

26/2	GER v USA	4-3	(1-1, 1-1, 2-1)

MATCH FOR POSITIONS 5-6

26/2	TCH v SVK	7-1	(4-1, 1-0, 2-0)

SEMI-FINALS

25/2	FIN v CAN	3-5	(0-0, 2-2, 1-3)
	RUS v SWE	3-4	(1-2, 0-1, 2-1)

MATCH FOR POSITIONS 3-4

26/2	RUS v FIN	0-4	(0-2, 0-2, 0-0)

FINAL

27/2	CAN v SWE	2-3	(0-1, 0-0, 2-1, 0-0, Pens)

FINAL POSITIONS

1	Sweden	7	Germany
2	Canada	8	United States
3	Finland	9	Italy
4	Russia	10	France
5	Czech Republic	11	Norway
6	Slovakia	12	Austria

Leading Scorers

			Gls	A1	A2	
1	Zigmund Palffy	SVK	3	3	4	10
2	Miroslav Satan	SVK	9	0	0	9
3	Peter Stasny	SVK	5	4	0	9
4	Håkan Loob	SWE	4	3	2	9
5	Gaetano Orlando	ITA	3	6	0	9
6	Patrik Juhlin	SWE	7	1	0	8

ICE SKATING

Positions in all events are determined, not by the judges' marks, but by the placings awarded. All marks count and the winner of a competition is the skater(s) who earns the most first places from the nine judges. Should skaters earn an equal number of first places, then the second places count.

PAIRS

There are two elements: the technical programme and the free-skating programme. The technical programme counts for a third of the marks (0.5, 1.0, 1.5,.....), the free counts for two-thirds (1.0, 2.0, 3.0,....)

			TP	FS	Pts
1	Ekaterina Gordeeva Sergei Grinkov	RUS	1	1	1.5
2	Natalya Mishkutenok Artur Dmitriev	RUS	2	2	3.0
3	Isabelle Brasseur Lloyd Eisler	CAN	3	3	4.5
Also					
15	Jacqueline Soames John Jenkins	GBR	16	15	23.0

ICE DANCING

There are four elements; two compulsory dances, an original dance and a free dance. Each compulsory dance counts for 10 % of the total (0.2, 0.4, 0.6...). The original counts for 30% (0.6, 1.2, 1.8...). The free dance 50% (1.0, 2.0, 3.0...).

			D1	D2	OD	FD	Pts
1	Oksana Gritschuk	RUS	2	1	3	1	3.4
	Yevgeny Platov						
2	Maya Usova	RUS	1	2	2	2	3.8
	Aleksandr Zhulin						
3	Jayne Torvill	GBR	3	3	1	3	4.8
	Christopher Dean						

D1 5.4, 5.5, 5.7, 5.6, 5.6, 5.6, 5.6, 5.5, 5.5
D2 5.6, 5.6, 5.8, 5.6, 5.6, 5.7, 5.6, 5.5, 5.3
OD 5.8, 5.8, 5.9, 5.8, 5.9, 5.9, 5.8, 5.8, 5.9 *(composition)*
    5.9, 5.9, 6.0, 5.9, 6.0, 5.9, 5.9, 5.9, 5.9 *(presentation)*
FD 5.8, 5.7, 5.9, 5.8, 5.7, 5.7, 5.7, 5.6, 5.7 *(Tech. merit)*
    5.8, 5.7, 5.9, 5.8, 5.7, 5.7, 5.7, 5.6, 5.7 *(Art. impress.)*

FIGURE SKATING

There are two disciplines; the technical programme and the free dance. The scoring is the same as in the Pairs competition.

MEN

			TP	FS	Pts
1	Alexey Urmanov	RUS	1	1	1.5
2	Elvis Stojko	CAN	2	2	3.0
3	Philippe Candeloro	FRA	3	5	6.5
Also					
9	Steven Cousins	GBR	7	9	12.5

WOMEN

			TP	FS	Pts
1	Oksana Baiul	UKR	2	1	2.0
2	Nancy Kerrigan	USA	1	2	2.5
3	Lu Chen	CHN	4	3	5.0
Also					
7	Katarina Witt	GER	6	8	11.0
8	Tonya Harding	USA	10	7	12.0
15	Charlene von Saher	GBR	13	16	22.5

LUGE

MEN

SINGLE
Feb 13-14 (two runs each day)

			Total
1	Georg Hackl	GER	3:21.571
	(50.296/50.560/50.224/50.491)		
2	Markus Prock	AUT	3:21.584
	(50.300/50.566/50.166/50.552)		
3	Armin Zoeggeler	ITA	3:21.833
	(50.441/50.601/50.365/50.426)		
Also			
26	Paul Hix	GBR	3:29.115
	(52.410/52.398/52.073/52.234)		

DOUBLE
Feb 18 (two runs)

		1st	2nd	Total
1	Italy	48.348	48.372	1:36.720
	(Kurt Brugger/Wilfried Huber)			
2	Italy	48.274	48.495	1:36.769
3	Germany	48.364	48.581	1:36.945

WOMEN

SINGLE
Feb 15-16 (two runs each day)

			Total
1	Gerda Weissensteiner	ITA	3:15.517
	(48.740/48.890/48.950/48.937)		
2	Susi Erdmann	GER	3:16.276
	(48.989/48.893/49.340/49.054)		
3	Andrea Tagwerker	AUT	3:16.652
	(48.961/49.157/49.277/49.257)		

NORDIC COMBINED

INDIVIDUAL
The competition consists of 2 x K90 jumps and a 15km cross-country race
Feb 18 (jumps)   Temp: -6° C
Feb 19 (x-country)   Snow: Fine   Temp: -11° C

			Jp Pts	15km Time
1	Fred Børre Lundberg	NOR	247.0	39:07.9
2	Takanori Kono	JPN	239.5	39:35.4
3	Bjarte Engen Vik	NOR	240.5	39:43.2

3 X 10KM RELAY

		Jp Pts	15km Time
1	Japan	733.5	1:22:51.8
	(Kono/Abe/Ogiwara)		
2	Norway	672.0	1:22:33.9
3	Switzerland	643.5	1:23:09.9

SKI JUMPING

Both competitions on the Lysgårdbakkene slope. Competitors take two jumps and are marked for distance and style. Shown below are the distances and the final points total only.

K90
Feb 25

			Distances	Total Pts
1	Espen Bredesen	NOR	100.5/104.0	282.0
2	Lasse Ottesen	NOR	102.5/ 98.0	268.0
3	Dieter Thoma	GER	98.5/102.5	260.5

K120
Feb 20

			Distances	Total Pts
1	Jens Weissflog	GER	129.5/133.0	274.5
2	Espen Bredesen	NOR	135.5/122.0	266.5
3	Andreas Goldberger	AUT	128.5/121.5	255.0

K120 TEAM

		Total Pts
1	Germany	970.1
	(Jaekle 117.0 & 124.0 /Duffner 119.5 & 108.0/ Thoma 126.0 & 128.5/Weissflog 131.0 & 135.5)	
2	Japan	956.9
3	Austria	918.9

SPEED SKATING
LONG TRACK
All events held in the Hamar Olympia (Viking Ship) Hall

WOMEN
500M
Feb 19

1	Bonnie Blair	USA	39.25
2	Susan Auch	CAN	39.61
3	Franziska Schenk	GER	39.70

1000M
Feb 23

1	Bonnie Blair	USA	1:18.74
2	Anke Baier	GER	1:20.12
3	Ye Qiaobo	CHN	1:20.22

1500M
Feb 21

1	Emese Hunyady	AUT	2:02.19
2	Svetlana Fedotkina	RUS	2:02.69
3	Gunda Niemann	GER	2:03.41

3000M
Feb 17

1	Svetlana Bazhanova	RUS	4:17.43
2	Emese Hunyady	AUT	4:18.14
3	Claudia Pechstein	GER	4:18.34

5000M
Feb 25

1	Claudia Pechstein	GER	7:14.37
2	Gunda Niemann	GER	7:14.88
3	Hiromi Yamamoto	JPN	7:19.68

MEN
500M
Feb 14

1	Aleksandr Golubev	RUS	36.33	OR
2	Sergei Klevchenya	RUS	36.39	
3	Manabu Horii	JPN	36.53	

1000M
Feb 18

1	Daniel Jansen	USA	1:12.43	WR
2	Igor Zhelezovsky	BLS	1:12.72	
3	Sergei Klevchenya	RUS	1:12.85	

1500M
Feb 16

1	Johann Olav Koss	NOR	1:51.29	WR
2	Rintje Ritsma	HOL	1:51.99	
3	Falko Zandstra	HOL	1:52.38	

5000M
Feb 13

1	Johann Olav Koss	NOR	6:34.96	WR
2	Kjell Storelid	NOR	6:42.68	
3	Rintje Ritsma	HOL	6:43.94	

10,000M
Feb 20

1	Johann Olav Koss	NOR	13:30.55	WR
2	Kjell Storelid	NOR	13:49.25	
3	Bart Veldkamp	HOL	13:56.73	

SHORT TRACK
All events held in the Hamar Olympic Amphitheatre

MEN
500M

A Final	1	Chae Ji-Hoon	KOR	43.45	OR
Feb 26	2	Mirko Wuillermin	ITA	43.47	
	3	Nicholas Gooch	GBR	43.68	
	4	Marc Gagnon	CAN	52.74	

Wilf O'Reilly (GBR) finished last in his first round heat in 46.41 and was eliminated

1000M

A Final	1	Kim Ki-Hoon	KOR	1:34.57	
Feb 22	2	Chae Ji-Hoon	KOR	1:34.92	
		Nicholas Gooch (GBR) disq			
		Derrick Campbell (CAN) did not finish			

Although finishing in the silver medal position, Gooch was disqualified for charging Campbell. As Campbell did not complete the course, the bronze medal was awarded to Marc Gagnon (CAN) who won the B Final. Wilf O'Reilly (GBR) finished third in his first round heat in 1:33.57 and was eliminated

5000M RELAY

A Final	1	Italy	7:11.74	OR
Feb 26	2	USA	7:13.37	
	3	Australia	7:13.68	
	4	Canada	7:20.40	

WOMEN
500M

A Final	1	Cathy Turner	USA	45.98	OR
Feb 24	2	Zhang Yanmei	CHN	46.44	
	3	Amy Peterson	USA	46.76	
	4	Won Hye-Kyung	KOR	47.60	

Debbie Palmer (GBR) finished last in 47.93 in the first round and was eliminated

1000M

A Final	1	Chun Lee-Kyung	KOR	1:36.87	OR
Feb 26	2	Nathalie Lambert	CAN	1:36.97	
	3	Kim So-Hee	KOR	1:37.09	
	4	Zhang Yanmei	CHN	1:37.80	
	5	Yang Yang	CHN	1:47.10	

Debbie Palmer (GBR) finished third in 1:44.72 in the first round and was eliminated

3000M Relay

A Final	1	Korea	4:26.64	OR
Feb 22	2	Canada	4:32.04	
	3	USA	4:39.34	
		China Disq		

The saddest story of the Games concerns the Norwegian cross-country skier Vegard Ulvang. In the Albertville Olympics in 1992, Ulvang had won three gold medals and he was hoping to repeat the triumph on his home territory. But in October, when the snows were already deep, Ulvang's brother disappeared while out skiing. The family knew he had died, but they could not search for the body until the snows melted. In May, they found the body and Ulvang could at last bury his brother.

Commonwealth Games

You have to be a romantic to believe in the Commonwealth Games, but there is nothing wrong with being a romantic. It is only that, as a romantic, your standards are higher. It is not just a question of running faster or jumping higher or going further. You have to play by the book. You have to respect your opponent. You have to love the occasion. In the context of modern sport, that is what the Commonwealth Games offers. There are no gold bars, no brown envelopes and the endorsement deals, if you win, might just stretch to a new Gore-Tex tracksuit.

You can lose the stars from a Commonwealth Games, survive the absence of Merlene Ottey, who palpably doesn't care for the event, or Roger Black, who after two years earning nothing probably couldn't afford the event, but lose the romance and the Games are imperilled. After Victoria, there is precious little romance left to play with. Almost every story that made front-page news concerned drugs. Paul Edwards, Diane Modahl and Horace Dove-Edwin, all fell foul of the tester, although only one of them actually at the Games. Dove-Edwin, the 100m silver medallist from Sierra Leone, was quickly established as a folk hero.

The *Daily Telegraph*, in particular, sung his praises. What they didn't and couldn't know until a few days later is that Dove-Edwin was making systematic use of steroids to achieve that performance. It's little wonder that the backlash is often over-the-top, the media themselves feel as if they have been hoodwinked. Perversely, the taking of drugs in sport - while deserving of censure - has become a crime rating somewhere between genocide and patricide in terms of column inches. When Solomon Wariso is headline news for taking (probably accidentally) pseudoephedrine, we've got something out of proportion.

The sting, though, is in the financial tail. Like every other major event, the existence of the Games relies on the support of sponsors and too many negative stories doesn't encourage them. They should be safe enough for the next Games, though. They are in Kuala Lumpur and nobody, but nobody takes drugs into Malaysia - even in their urine.

There was no doubting the performer of the Victoria Games; Kieren Perkins of Australia. We are grateful to Craig Lord of *The Times*, who pointed out that each 100m of Perkins record-breaking 1500m swim averaged out as the same time, 58.6, that Johnny Weissmuller swam to take the world 100m record in 1922. Tarzan, where are you now? The statistics are even more compelling when you consider that Perkins' first 200m was covered in the same time that Mark Spitz took to win the Olympic title at that distance in 1972.

The Australian swimming team won 24 gold medals, it's best-ever tally in the pool, took ten of the 13 cycling titles and generally dominated the Games. The final Australian tally of 87 gold medals was, by far, that nation's best ever. Scotland and Wales fared reasonably well, and England didn't. We haven't been able to discover the last time that England won fewer gold medals than 31, but it was a while back. Even in athletics, usually England's most fertile hunting-ground, they won gold in just nine of the 42 events. Kenya put that into perspective; they won five track golds with third and fourth-string runners, having decided, for political reasons, to leave every single one of their top athletes out of the team.

ATHLETICS
University of Victoria, Centennial Stadium   *Aug 22-28*

Men

100m	1	Linford Christie	ENG	9.91
(+1.9)	2	Michael Green	JAM	10.05
	3	Frankie Fredericks	NAM	10.06

Dove-Edwin of Sierra Leone finished 2nd in the final, but was disq after a positive drugs test

200m	1	Frankie Fredericks	NAM	19.97
(+1.5)	2	John Regis	ENG	20.25
	3	Daniel Effiong	NGR	20.40
400m	1	Charles Gitonga	KEN	45.00
	2	Du'aine Ladejo	ENG	45.11
	3	Sunday Bada	NGR	45.45
800m	1	Patrick Konchellah	KEN	1:45.18
	2	Hezekiel Sepeng	RSA	1:45.76
	3	Savieri Ngidhi	ZIM	1:46.06
1500m	1	Reuben Chesang	KEN	3:36.70
	2	Kevin Sullivan	CAN	3:36.78
	3	John Mayock	ENG	3:37.22
5000m	1	Rob Denmark	ENG	13:23.00
	2	Philemon Hanneck	ZIM	13:23.20
	3	John Nuttall	ENG	13:23.54
10,000m	1	Lameck Aguta	KEN	28:38.22
	2	Tendai Chimusasa	ZIM	28:47.72
	3	Fackson Nkandu	ZAM	28:51.72
Marathn	1	Steve Moneghetti	AUS	2:11:49
	2	Sean Quilty	AUS	2:14:57
	3	Mark Hudspith	ENG	2:15:11
3000msc	1	Johnstone Kipkoech	KEN	8:14.72
	2	Gideon Chirchir	KEN	8:15.25
	3	Graeme Fell	CAN	8:23.28
110mh	1	Colin Jackson	WAL	13.08
(+1.6)	2	Tony Jarrett	ENG	13.22
	3	Paul Gray	WAL	13.54
400mh	1	Samuel Matete	ZAM	48.67
	2	Gideon Biwott	KEN	49.43
	3	Barnabus Kinyor	KEN	49.50
HJ	1	Tim Forsyth	AUS	2.32m
	2	Steve Smith	ENG	2.32m
	3	Geoff Parsons	SCO	2.31m

Forsyth won after a jump-off

PV	1	Neil Winter	WAL	5.40m
	2	Curtis Heywood	CAN	5.30m
	3	James Miller	AUS	5.30m
LJ	1	Obinna Eregbu	NGR	8.05m
(+2.2)	2	David Culbert	AUS	8.00m
	3	Ian James	CAN	7.93m
TJ	1	Julian Golley	ENG	17.03m
(+0.9)	2	Jon Edwards	ENG	17.00m
	3	Brian Wellman	BER	17.00m
Shot	1	Matt Simson	ENG	19.49m
	2	Courtney Ireland	NZL	19.38m
	3	Chima Ugwu	NGR	19.26m
Discus	1	Werner Reiterer	AUS	62.76m
	2	Adewale Olukoju	NGR	62.46m
	3	Robert Weir	ENG	60.86m
HT	1	Sean Carlin	AUS	73.48m
	2	Paul Head	ENG	70.18m
	3	Peter Vivian	ENG	69.80m
JT	1	Steve Backley	ENG	82.74m
	2	Mick Hill	ENG	81.84m
	3	Gavin Lovegrove	NZL	80.42m
Decthln	1	Michael Smith	CAN	8326pts

(11.00/6.94m/16.22m/1.98m/48.85/14.82/
48.62m/5.10m/67.98m/4:47.38)

	2	Peter Winter	AUS	8074pts
	3	Simon Shirley	ENG	7980pts
30kmw	1	Nick A'Hern	AUS	2:07:53
	2	Tim Berrett	CAN	2:08:22
	3	Scott Nelson	NZL	2:09:10
4x100m	1	Canada		38.39

(Bailey, Gilbert, Chambers-J, Surin)

	2	Australia		38.88
	3	England		39.39

(John, Box, Goedluck, Williams)
Christie, Regis and Jarrett all absent

4 x 400m	1	England		3:02.14

(McKenzie, Crampton, Patrick, Ladejo)

	2	Jamaica		3:02.32
	3	Trinidad & Tobago		3:02.78

Women

100m	1	Mary Onyali	NGR	11.06
(-0.2)	2	Christy Opara-Thompson	NGR	11.22
	3	Paula Thomas	ENG	11.23
200m	1	Cathy Freeman	AUS	22.25
(+1.3)	2	Mary Onyali	NGR	22.35
	3	Melinda Gainsford	AUS	22.68
400m	1	Cathy Freeman	AUS	50.38
	2	Fatima Yusuf	NGR	50.53
	3	Sandie Richards	JAM	50.59
800m	1	Inez Turner	JAM	2:01.74
	2	Charmaine Crooks	CAN	2:02.35
	3	Gladys Wamuyu	KEN	2:03.12
1500m	1	Kelly Holmes	ENG	4:08.86
	2	Paula Schnurr	CAN	4:09.65
	3	Gwen Griffiths	RSA	4:10.16
3000m	1	Angela Chalmers	CAN	8:32.17
	2	Robyn Meagher	CAN	8:45.59
	3	Alison Wyeth	ENG	8:47.98
10,000m	1	Yvonne Murray	SCO	31:56.97
	2	Elana Meyer	RSA	32:06.02
	3	Jane Omoro	KEN	32:13.01
Marathn	1	Carole Rouillard	CAN	2:30:41
	2	Lizanne Bussieres	CAN	2:31:07
	3	Yvonne Danson	ENG	2:32:24
100mh	1	Michelle Freeman	JAM	13.12
(-2.0)	2	Jackie Agyepong	ENG	13.14
	3	Samantha Farquharson	ENG	13.38
400mh	1	Sally Gunnell	ENG	54.51
	2	Deon Hemmings	JAM	55.11
	3	Debbie Ann Parris	JAM	55.25
HJ	1	Alison Inverarity	AUS	1.94m
	2	Charmaine Weavers	RSA	1.94m
	3	Debbie Marti	ENG	1.91m
LJ	1	Nicole Boegman	AUS	6.82m
(+2.4)	2	Yinka Idowu	ENG	6.73m
	3	Christy Opara-Thompson	NGR	6.72m
SP	1	Judy Oakes	ENG	18.16m
	2	Myrtle Augee	ENG	17.64m
	3	Lisa Vizaniari	AUS	16.61m
DT	1	Daniela Costian	AUS	63.72m
	2	Beatrice Faumuina	NZL	57.12m
	3	Maria Etzebeth	RSA	55.74m

JT	1	Louise McPaul	AUS	63.76m
	2	Kirsten Hellier	NZL	60.40m
	3	Sharon Gibson	ENG	58.20m
Heptath	1	Denise Lewis	ENG	6325pts
		(13.66/1.74m/13.22m/25.11/6.44m/53.68m/ 2:17.60)		
	2	Jane Flemming	AUS	6317pts
	3	Catherine Bond-Mills	CAN	6193pts
10km	1	Kerry Junna-Saxby	AUS	44:25
	2	Anne Manning	AUS	44:37
	3	Janice McCaffrey	CAN	44:54
4x100m	1	Nigeria		42.99
		(Idehen, Tombiri, Opara-T, Onyali)		
	2	Australia		43.43
	3	England		43.46
		(Douglas, McLeod, Jacobs, Thomas)		
4x400m	1	England		3:27.06
		(Smith, Goddard, Keough, Gunnell)		
	2	Jamaica		3:27.63
	3	Canada		3:32.52

BADMINTON

MEN
Singles: Rashid Sidek MAL bt Ewe Hock Ong MAL 15-6, 15-4
Doubles: Cheah/Soo MAL bt Archer/Hunt ENG 15-10, 15-9
WOMEN
Singles: Lisa Campbell AUS bt Si-an Deng CAN 11-2, 11-5
Doubles: Wright/Muggeridge ENG bt Clark/Bradbury ENG 15-9, 15-11
MIXED
Doubles: Hunt/Clark ENG bt Archer/Bradbury ENG 15-11, 15-4
Team: England bt Malaysia 3-2

BOXING
Light-fly (48kg)
H Ramadhani KEN bt V Kasote ZAM 26-10 on points
Fly (51kg)
P Shepherd SCO bt D Karanja KEN 20-9 on points
Bantam (54kg)
R Peden AUS bt S Oliver ENG 20-18 on points
Feather (57kg)
C Patton CAN bt J Cook WAL 22-7 on points
Light (60kg)
M Strange CAN bt M Renaghan NIR 18-11 on points
Light-welter (63.5kg)
P Richardson ENG bt M Winters NIR 20-17 on points
Welter (67kg)
N Sinclair NIR bt A Eromosele NGR 25-16 on points
Light-middle (71kg)
J Webb NIR bt R Gasio WSA 10-4 on points
Middle (75kg)
R Donaldson CAN bt R Ojemaye NGR 26-13 on points
Light-heavy (81kg)
D Brown CAN bt J Wilson SCO after referee stopped contest 2:27 into first round
Heavy (91kg)
O Ahmed KEN bt S Gallinger CAN 23-3 on points
Super-Heavy (+91kg)
D Dokiwari NGR bt M Anyim KEN 13-9 on points

CYCLING
MEN
Sprint: Gary Neiwand AUS bt Curt Harnett CAN (Ride 1: 11.399, Ride 2: 11.488)
Individual Road Race: 1. Mark Rendell NZL 4:46.07.91, 2. Brian Fowler NZL 4:48.09.76, 3. Willem Engelbrecht RSA 4:48.10.23
1000m Time Trial: 1. Shane Kelly AUS 1:05.386 *CR*, 2. Darryn Hill AUS 1:05.632, 3. T O'Shannessey AUS 1:06.789
4000m Individual Pursuit: 1. Bradley McGee AUS 4:31.371 *CR*, 2. Shaun Wallace ENG 4:34.662, 3. Stuart O'Grady AUS 4:35.203
10 Mile: 1. Stuart O'Grady AUS 18:50.520 *CR*, 2. Glenn McLeay NZL, 3. Brian Walton CAN
40km Points Race: 1. Brett Aitken AUS (38), 2. Stuart O'Grady AUS (37), 3. Dean Woods AUS (23)
Team Time Trial: 1. Australia *(Dennis/ Vogels/ Anderson/ McDonald)* 1:53.19.13, 2. England *(Illingworth/ Jennings/ Lillistone/ Longbottom)* 1:56.40.76, 3. New Zealand 1:56.52.82
4000m Team Pursuit: 1. Australia *(Aitken/ McGee/ O'Grady/ O'Shannessey)* 4:10.485 *CR*, 2. England *(Doyle/ Hayles/ Newton/ Steel)*, 3. New Zealand 4:22.425
WOMEN
Sprint: Tanya Dubnicoff CAN bt Michelle Ferris AUS (Ride 1: 12.129, Ride 2: 12.164)
Individual Road Race: 1. Kathryn Watt AUS 2:48.04.73, Linda Jackson CAN 2:48.34.75, 3. Alison Sydor CAN 2:50.17.45
3000m Individual Pursuit: 1. Kathryn Watt AUS 3:48.522 *CR*, 2. Sarah Ulmer NZL 3:50.953, 3. Jacqueline Nelson NZL 3:55.241
25km Points Race: 1. Yvonne McGregor ENG (35), 2. Jacqueline Nelson NZL (32), 3. Sally Hodge WAL (28)
Team Time Trial: 1. Australia *(Nolan/ Reardon/ Victor/ Watt)* 1:04.03.20, 2. Canada 1:04.18.92, 3. England *(Johnson/ Lawrence/ McGregor/ Freeman)* 1:06:32.85

GYMNASTICS
ARTISTIC
MEN
Team: 1. Canada 164.700, 2. Australia 164.500, 3. England 162.375
All Round: 1. Neil Thomas ENG 55.950, 2. Brennon Dowrick AUS 55.525, 3. Peter Hogan AUS 54.950
Vault: 1. Bret Hudson AUS 9.375, 2. Kristan Burley CAN 9.312, 3. Neil Thomas ENG 9.306
Floor: 1. Neil Thomas 9.662, 2. Kristan Burley 9.437, 3. Alan Nolet CAN 9.150
Parallel Bars: 1. Peter Hogan AUS 9.400, 2. Kristan Burley CAN 9.350, 3. Brennon Dowrick AUS 9.250
Pommel Horse: 1. Brennon Dowrick 9.425, 2. Nathan Kingston 9.400, 3. Richard Ikeda CAN 9.225
Rings: 1. Lee McDermott ENG 9.475, 2. Peter Hogan AUS 9.275, 3. Brennon Dowrick AUS 9.150
High Bar: 1. Alan Nolet CAN 9.512, 2. Richard Ikeda CAN 9.500, 3. Nathan Kingston AUS 9.325
WOMEN
Team: 1. England 114.225, 2. Canada 113.650, 3. Australia

113.625

All Round: 1. Stella Umeh CAN 38.400, 2. Rebecca Stoyel AUS 38.037, 3. Zita Lusack ENG 37.725

Floor: 1. Annika Reeder ENG 9.750, 2. Jackie Brady ENG 9.662, 3. Lisa Simes CAN 9.550

Beam: 1. Salli Wills AUS 9.075, 2. Zita Lusack ENG 8.987, 3. Ruth Moniz AUS 8.900

Asymmetric Bars: 1. Rebecca Stoyel AUS 9.525, 2. Stella Umeh CAN 9.450, 3. Sarah Thompson NZL 9.337

Vault: 1. Stella Umeh CAN 9.556, 2. Sonia Lawrence WAL 9.543, 3. Lisa Simes CAN 9.506

Rhythmic

Team: 1. Canada 106.900, 2. Australia 105.300, 3. England 103.300

All Round: 1. Kasumi Takahashi AUS 36.850, 2. Camille Martens CAN 36.600, 3. Debbie Southwick ENG 36.350

Hoop: 1. Kasumi Takahashi AUS 9.300, 2. Lindsay Richards CAN 9.050, 3. Alcha McKenzie ENG 8.900

Ball: 1. Kasumi Takahashi AUS 9.200, 2. Camille Martens CAN 9.000, 3. Gretchen McLennan CAN 8.800

Clubs: 1. Kasumi Takahashi AUS 9.400, 2. Camille Martens CAN 9.150, 3. Leigh Marning AUS 9.000

Ribbon: 1. Kasumi Takahashi AUS 9.200, 2. Camille Martens CAN 9.050, 3. Gretchen McLennan CAN 9.000

LAWN BOWLS

MEN

Singles: Scotland bt England 25-20

Pairs: Australia bt Wales 18-14

Fours: South Africa bt Australia 21-18

Visually Impaired Singles: Scotland bt Australia 21-18

WOMEN

Singles: Northern Ireland bt Wales 25-17

Pairs: Scotland bt South Africa 32-18

Fours: South Africa bt Papua New Guinea 24-17

Visually Impaired Singles: New Zealand bt Wales 21-6

SHOOTING

MEN

Air Rifle: 1. Chris Hector ENG 685 CR, 2. J Senecal CAN 683, 3. Nigel Wallace ENG 680 **Pairs** 1. Canada 1166, 2. England 1161, 3. Scotland 1145

Running Target: 1. Bryan Wilson AUS 657.9 CR, 2. Mark Bedlington CAN 656.0, 3. Paul Carmine NZL 650.7 **Pairs** 1. Canada 1088, 2. Australia 1088, 3. New Zealand 1079

SB Rifle Prone: 1. Stephen Petterson NZL 698.4 CR, 2. James Cornish ENG, 3. Michel Dion CAN **Pairs** 1. New Zealand 1181, 2. Sri Lanka 1177, 3. Australia 1176

SB Rifle 3 Position: 1. Michel Dion CAN 1,234.2 CR, 2. Wayne Sorensen CAN 1228.7, 3. Alister Allan SCO 1,224.8 **Pairs** 1. Canada 2300, 2. Scotland 2271, 3. England 2259

Air Pistol: Jean-Pierre Huot CAN 672.4 CR, 2. Jaspal Rana IND 670.7, 3. Gregory Yelavich NZL 668.5 **Pairs** 1. Australia 1137, 2. Canada 1135, 3. India 1133

Free Pistol: 1. Michael Gault ENG 654.1 CR, 2. Phillip Adams AUS 647.0, 3. Bengt Sandstrom AUS 642.5 **Pairs** 1. Australia 1104, 2. New Zealand 1094, 3. England 1082

Rapid Fire Pistol: 1. Michael Jay WAL 98.2, 2. Robert Dowling AUS 93.4, 3. Patrick Murray AUS 96.1 **Pairs** 1. Australia 1148, 2. Wales 1142, 3. Guernsey 1131

Centre Fire Pistol: 1. Jaspal Rana IND 581, 2. Michael Gault ENG 581, 3. Gregory Yelavich NZL 575 **Pairs** 1. India 1168, 2. Australia 1149, 3. Canada 1148

WOMEN

Air Rifle: 1. Fani Theofanous CYP 488.7, 2. K Wickremasinghe SRI 488.5, Sharon Bowes CAN 488.4 **Pairs** 1. Sri Lanka 771, 2. England 771, 3. Canada 766

SB Rifle 3 Position: 1. Sharon Bowes CAN 666.4, 2. Roopa Unikrishnan IND 662.5, 3. Christina Ashcroft CAN 661.6 **Pairs** 1. Canada 1143, 2. England 1132, 3. India 1110

SB Rifle Prone 1. Sharon Bowes CAN 574, 2. Lindsay Volpin ENG 572, 3. Christina Ashcroft CAN 570 **Pairs** 1. Australia 1160, 2. Scotland 1158, 3. Canada 1158

Air Pistol: 1. Helen Smith CAN 474.2, 2. Annette Woodward AUS 466.1, 3. Sharon Cozzarin CAN 465.8 **Pairs** 1. Australia 747, 2. New Zealand 745, 3. England 744

Sport Pistol: 1. Christine Trefry AUS 679.4, 2. Margaret Thomas ENG 675.0, 3. Annette Woodward AUS 674.0 **Pairs** 1. Australia 1134, 2. Canada 1132, 3. England 1129.

OPEN

FB Rifle: 1. David Calvert NIR 398 CR, 2. Geoffrey Smith NZL 398, 3. Glynn Barnett ENG 397 **Pairs** 1. Australia 593, 2. England 588, 3. N Ireland 584

Skeet: 1. Ian Hale AUS 144 CR, 2. Christos Kourtellas CYP 143, 3. Andrew Austin ENG 143 **Pairs** 1. Cyprus 189, 2. New Zealand 186, 3. Scotland 186

Trap: 1. Mansher Singh IND 141, 2. George Leary CAN 140, 3. Andreas Anglou CYP 137 **Pairs** 1. N Ireland 188, 2. Canada 187, 3. England 186

SWIMMING

MEN

50m Freestyle		
1 Mark Foster	ENG	23.12
2 Darren Lange	AUS	23.13
3 Peter Williams	RSA	23.16
100m Freestyle		
1 Stephen Clarke	CAN	50.21
2 Christopher Fydler	AUS	50.51
3 Andrew Baildon	AUS	50.71
200m Freestyle		
1 Kieren Perkins	AUS	1:49.31 CR
2 Trent Bray	NZL	1:49.47
3 Danyon Loader	NZL	1:49.53
400m Freestyle		
1 Kieren Perkins	AUS	3:45.77 CR
2 Danyon Loader	NZL	3:49.65
3 Daniel Kowalski	AUS	3:50.41
1500m Freestyle		
1 Kieren Perkins	AUS	14:41.66 WR
2 Daniel Kowalski	AUS	14:53.61
3 Glen Housman	AUS	15:02.59
100m Backstroke		
1 Martin Harris	ENG	55.77 CR
2 Steven Dewick	AUS	56.09
3 Adam Ruckwood	ENG	56.52
200m Backstroke		
1 Adam Ruckwood	ENG	2:00.79 CR
2 Kevin Draxinger	CAN	2:02.19
3 Scott Miller	AUS	2:02.43

100m Breaststroke

1	Philip Rogers	AUS	1:02.62
2	Nick Gillingham	ENG	1:02.65
3	Jon Cleveland	CAN	1:03.20

200m Breaststroke

1	Nick Gillingham	ENG	2:12.54 CR
2	Philip Rogers	AUS	2:13.56
3	Jon Cleveland	CAN	2:14.91

100m Butterfly

1	Scott Miller	AUS	54.39
2	Stephen Clarke	CAN	54.45
3	Adam Pine	AUS	54.76

200m Butterfly

1	Danyon Loader	NZL	1:59.54
2	Scott Miller	AUS	1:59.70
3	James Hickman	ENG	2:00.87

4x100m Freestyle

1	Australia		3:20.89

(Lange/Baildon/Sheehan/Fydler)

2	New Zealand		3:21.79
3	England		

(Shackell/Foster/Clayton/Fibbins)

4x200m Freestyle

1	Australia		7:20.80 CR

(Housman/Dunn/Roberts/Perkins)

2	New Zealand		7:21.67
3	England		7:26.19

(Clayton/Mellor/Shackell/Salter)

4x100m Medley

1	Australia		3:40.41 CR

(Dewick/Rogers/Miller/Fydler)

2	Canada		3:43.25
3	England		3:43.72

(Harris/Gillingham/Hickman/Shackell)

100m Freestyle - S9 category

1	Andrew Haley	CAN	1:03.07
2	Brendan Burkett	AUS	1:03.75
3	Sean Tretheway	NZL	1:05.30

WOMEN

50m Freestyle

1	Karen van Wirdum	AUS	25.90
2	Andrea Nugent	CAN	26.24
3	Shannon Shakespeare	CAN	26.27

100m Freestyle

1	Karen Pickering	ENG	56.20 CR
2	Karen van Wirdum	AUS	56.42
3	Marianne Limpert	CAN	56.54

200m Freestyle

1	Susan O'Neill	AUS	2:00.86
2	Nicole Stevenson	AUS	2:01.34
3	Karen Pickering	ENG	2:01.50

400m Freestyle

1	Hayley Lewis	AUS	4:12.56
2	Stacey Gartrell	AUS	4:13.06
3	Sarah Hardcastle	ENG	4:13.29

800m Freestyle

1	Stacey Gartrell	AUS	8:30.18
2	Hayley Lewis	AUS	8:30.72
3	Nikki Dryden	CAN	8:37.70

100m Backstroke

1	Nicole Stevenson	AUS	1:02.68
2	Ellie Overton	AUS	1:02.90
3	Kathy Osher	ENG	1:03.27

100m Breaststroke

1	Samantha Riley	AUS	1:08.02 CR
2	Rebecca Brown	AUS	1:09.40
3	Penelope Heyns	RSA	1:09.86

200m Breaststroke

1	Samantha Riley	AUS	2:25.53 CR
2	Rebecca Brown	AUS	2:30.24
3	Lisa Flood	CAN	2:31.85

100m Butterfly

1	Petria Thomas	AUS	1:00.21 CR
2	Susan O'Neill	AUS	1:00.24
3	Ellie Overton	AUS	1:01.88

200m Butterfly

1	Susan O'Neill	AUS	2:09.96 CR
2	Hayley Lewis	AUS	2:12.21
3	Julie Majer	AUS	2:12.43

200m Individual Medley

1	Ellie Overton	AUS	2:15.59 CR
2	Marianne Limpert	CAN	2:15.97
3	Nancy Sweetnam	CAN	2:16.67

400m Individual Medley

1	Ellie Overton	AUS	4:44.01
2	Nancy Sweetnam	CAN	4:46.20
3	Hayley Lewis	AUS	4:46.62

4x100m Freestyle

1	England		3:46.23 CR

(Rolph/Bennett/Huddart/Pickering)

2	Australia		3:46.73
3	Canada		3:47.25

4x200m Freestyle

1	Australia		8:08.06 CR

(Windsor/Stevenson/Lewis/O'Neill)

2	England		8:09.62

(Hardcastle/Huddart/Bennett/Pickering)

3	Canada		8:14.97

4x100m Medley

1	Australia		4:07.89 CR

(Stevenson/Rily/Thomas/van Wirdum)

2	England		4:12.83

(Osher/Hardiman/Bennett/Pickering)

3	Canada		4:14.04

100m Freestyle - S9 category

1	Melissa Carlton	AUS	1:09.61 CR
2	Claire Bishop	ENG	1:11.00
3	Kelly Barnes	AUS	1:11.03

SYNCHRONISED SWIMMING

Solo

1	Lisa Alexander	CAN	189.4835
2	Kerry Shacklock	ENG	183.9717
3	Celeste Ferraris	AUS	172.6626

Duet

1	Alexander/Woodley	CAN	188.0894
2	Shacklock/Vakil	ENG	182.6803
3	Downes/Ferraris	AUS	167.1646

DIVING

MEN

1m Springboard

1	Jason Napper	CAN	364.080
2	Michael Murphy	AUS	363.180
3	Evan Stewart	ZIM	357.780

3m Springboard

1	Michael Murphy	AUS	671.760
2	Evan Stewart	ZIM	625.860

10m Platform

1	Michael Murphy	AUS	614.700
2	Robert Morgan	WAL	585.960

3 Claude Villeneuve	CAN	581.220

WOMEN

1m Springboard

1 Annie Pelletier	CAN	279.660
2 Jodie Rogers	AUS	252.720
3 Mary Depiero	CAN	245.340

3m Springboard

1 Annie Pelletier	CAN	529.860
2 Paige Gordon	CAN	529.080
3 Jodie Rogers	AUS	474.810

10m Platform

1 Anne Montminy	CAN	428.580
2 Paige Gordon	CAN	414.360
3 Myriam Boileau	CAN	411.210

WEIGHTLIFTING

UNDER 54KG

Snatch: 1. M Veerasamy IND 105.0, 2. B Adisekhar IND 105.0, 3. F Lagace CAN 105.0 **Clean & Jerk:** 1. Adisekhar 132.5, 2. M Guntali MAL 130.0, 3. Veerasamy 127.5
Overall: 1. Adisekhar 237.5, 2. Veerasamy 232.5, 3. Lagace 227.5

UNDER 59KG

Snatch: 1. M Stephen NAU 115.0, 2. R Chandrasekharan IND 110.0, 3. D Aumais CAN 107.5 **Clean & Jerk:** 1. Stephen 147.5, 2. Chandrasekharan 145.0, 3. B Devonshire ENG 132.5
Overall: 1. Stephen 262.5, 2. Chandrasekharan 255.0, 3. Aumais 237.5

UNDER 64KG

Snatch: 1. N Ogbodu NGR 125.0, 2. S Marinov AUS 125.0, 3. O Toby NGR 120.0 **Clean & Jerk:** 1. O Toby 152.5, 2. S Marinov 152.5, N Ogbodu 150.0
Overall: 1. Marinov 277.5, 2. Ogbodu 275.0, 3. Toby 272.5

UNDER 70KG

Snatch: 1. L Riliwan NGR 132.5, 2. S Cruikshank ENG 132.5, 3. M Oluwa NGR 130.0 **Clean & Jerk:** 1. Oluwa 165.0, 2. S Rai IND 165.0, 3. Cruikshank 160.0
Overall: 1. Oluwa 295.0, 2. Rai 292.5, 3. Cruikshank 292.5

UNDER 76KG

Snatch: 1. D Morgan WAL 147.5 CR, 2. S Tremblay CAN 145.0, 3. D Brown AUS 142.5 **Clean & Jerk:** 1. Brown 182.5, 2. Morgan 180.0, 3. Tremblay 172.5
Overall: 1. Morgan 327.5, 2. Brown 325.0, 3. Tremblay 317.5

UNDER 83KG

Snatch: 1. K Kounev AUS 152.5, 2. S Ward ENG 147.5, 3. J D Corbett CAN 147.5 **Clean & Jerk:** 1. Kounev 200.0, 2. Ward 187.5, 3. Corbett 182.5
Overall: 1. Kounev 352.5, 2. Ward 335.0, 3. Corbett 330.0

UNDER 91KG

Snatch: 1. H Goodman AUS 162.5, 2. P May ENG 155.0, 3. C Okoth KEN 120.0 **Clean & Jerk:** 1. Goodman 200.0 CR, 2. May 190.0, 3. Okoth 120.0
Overall: 1. Goodman 362.5, 2. May 345.0, 3. Okoth 240.0

UNDER 99KG

Snatch: 1. C Onyezie NGR 155.0, 2. A Saxton AUS 155.0, 3. P Christou AUS 152.5 **Clean & Jerk:** 1. A Callard ENG 197.5, Saxton 192.5, 3. Onyezie 190.0
Overall: 1. Callard 347.5, 2. Saxton 347.5, 3. Onyezie 345.0

UNDER 108KG

Snatch: 1. Nicu Vlad AUS 185.0 CR, 2. I Chika NGR 160.0, 3. G Hives WAL 130.0 **Clean & Jerk:** 1. Vlad 220.0, 2. Chika 200.0, 3. Hives 160.0
Overall: 1. Vlad 405.0, 2. Chika 360.0, 3. Hives 290.0

OVER 108KG

Snatch: 1. S Kettner AUS 165.0, 2. S Botev AUS 160.0, 3. V Edem NGR 155.0 **Clean & Jerk:** 1. Botev 200.0, 2. Kettner 195.0, 3. V Edem 190.00
Overall: 1. Botev 360.00, 2. Kettner 360.00, 3. Edem 345.0

WRESTLING

48kg: Jacob Isaac NGR bt Paul Ragusa CAN
52kg: Selwyn Tam CAN bt Andrew Hutchinson ENG
57kg: Robert Dawson CAN bt Ashok Kumar IND
62kg: Marty Calder CAN bt John Melling ENG
68kg: Chris Wilson CAN bt Ibo Oziti NGR
74kg: David Hohl CAN bt Rienold Ozoline AUS
82kg: Justin Abdou CAN bt Randhir Singh IND
90kg: Scott Bianco CAN bt Kodei Victor NGR
100kg: Greg Edgelow CAN bt Noel Loban ENG
130kg: Andrew Borodow CAN bt Bidei Jackson NGR

MEDAL TABLE

	G	S	B	Total
Australia	87	52	43	182
Canada	40	42	46	128
England	31	45	49	125
Nigeria	11	13	13	37
Kenya	7	4	8	19
India	6	11	7	24
Scotland	6	3	11	20
New Zealand	5	16	20	41
Wales	5	8	6	19
Northern Ireland	5	2	3	10
Nauru	3	0	0	3
South Africa	2	4	5	11
Jamaica	2	4	2	8
Malaysia	2	3	2	7
Cyprus	2	1	2	5
Sri Lanka	1	2	0	3
Zambia	1	1	2	4
Namibia	1	0	1	2
Zimbabwe	0	3	3	6
Papua New Guinea	0	1	0	1
Western Samoa	0	1	0	1
Hong Kong	0	0	4	4
Pakistan	0	0	3	3
Trinidad-Tobago	0	0	2	2
Uganda	0	0	2	2
Bermuda	0	0	1	1
Botswana	0	0	1	1
Ghana	0	0	1	1
Guernsey	0	0	1	1
Norfolk Island	0	0	1	1
Seychelles	0	0	1	1
Tanzania	0	0	1	1
Tonga	0	0	1	1

Goodwill Games

ARCHERY *July 31*
Men Gennadi Mitrofanov RUS
Women Kim Hyo-Jung KOR

ATHLETICS *July 24-29*
Men 100m: Dennis Mitchell USA 10.07 (-1.9); 200m: Michael Johnson USA 20.10 (+0.6), 3rd John Regis 20.31; 400m: Quincy Watts USA 45.21; 800m: Andrey Loginov RUS 1:46.65; Mile: Noureddine Morceli ALG 3:48.67; 5000m: Moses Kiptanui KEN 13:10.77, 3rd Jon Brown; 10,000m: Hammou Boutayeb MAR 28:10.89; 3000mSC: Marc Davis USA 8:14.31; 110mH: Colin Jackson GBR 13.29 (-1.9), 2nd Tony Jarrett GBR 13.33; 400mH: Derrick Adkins USA 47.86; PV: Igor Trandenkov RUS 5.90m; HJ: Javier Sotomayor CUB 2.40m; LJ: Mike Powell USA 8.45; TJ: Kenny Harrison USA 17.43m; SP: C.J.Hunter USA 20.35m; DT: Dimitri Shevchenko RUS 64.68m; HT: Lance Deal USA 80.20m; JT: Andrey Shevchuk RUS 82.90m; Dec: Dan O'Brien USA 8715 (10.49/7.81m/15.70m/2.20m/47.73/13.81/48.10m/4.90m /62.20m/5:10.94); 4x100m: USA/Santa Monica (Marsh, Burrell, Jefferson, Lewis); 4x400m: USA (Mills, Valmon, Rouser, Johson) 2:59.42

Women 100m: Gwen Torrence USA 10.95 (-0.5); 200m: Gwen Torrence USA 22.09 (-0.7); 400m: Jearl Miles USA 50.60; 800m: Maria Mutola MOZ 1:57.63; 1500m: Yekaterina Pokopayeva RUS 4:04.92; 3000m: Yelena Romanova RUS 8:41.06; 5000m: Yelena Romanova RUS 15:28.69; 10,000m: Tecla Lorupe KEN 31:52.39; 200mSC: Plusnikova RUS 6:11.84 *WB*; 100mH: Brigita Bukovec SLO 12.83 (+3.8); 400mH: Sally Gunnell GBR 53.51; PV: Sun Caiyun CHN 4.00m; HJ: Silvia Costa CUB 1.95m; LJ: Heike Drechsler GER 7.12 (+1.0); SP: Sui Xinmei CHN 20.15m; DT: Eloina Echevarria CUB 64.84m; JT: Trine Hattestad NOR 65.74; Hept: Jackie Joyner-Kersee USA 6606 (12.77w/1.84m/14.01m/23.68/6.96m/42.64m/2:26.76); 10kmW: Olimpiada Ivanova RUS 42:30.31; 4x100m: USA (Taplin, Young, Collins, Torrence) 42.98; 4x400m: USA (Kaiser-Brown, Malone, Miles, Collins) 3:22.27

BASKETBALL *July 23-28*
Men 1. Puerto Rico, 2. Italy, 3. United States
Women 1. United States, 2. France, 3. China

BOXING *July 23-30*
48kg 1. Mañuel Mantilla CUB, 2. Choi Yoon-Wook (KOR), 3. Albert Guardado USA, 3. Eric Morel USA
51kg 1. Waldemar Font CUB, 2. Carlos Navarro USA, 3. Roman Podoprigora RUS, 3. Kismatulla Akhmetov UZB
54kg 1. Vladislav Ivanov RUS, 2. Enrique Carrion CUB, 3. Timophey Skribin MDA, 3. Raimkul Malakhbekov RUS
57kg 1. Ramazi Palyani RUS, 2. Joel Casamayor CUB, 3. Dzhivoanni Dzhungato ITA, 3. Claude Chinon FRA
60kg 1. Paata Gvasalia RUS, 2. Heiko Hinz GER,

3. Larry Nicholson USA, 3. Bruno Wartelle FRA
63.5 kg 1. Hector Vincent CUB, 2. Nurham Suleymanoglu TUR, 3. Oleg Saitev RUS, 3. Nordine Mouchi FRA
67kg 1. Juan Hernandez CUB, 2. Aleksandr Shkalikov RUS, 3. Daniel Santos PUR, 3. Hans Janssen HOL
71kg 1. Sergey Karaayev.RUS, 2. Juan Lemus CUB, 3. Orhan Delibas HOL, 3. Dirk Dzemski GER
75kg 1. Ariel Hernandez CUB, 2. Sahne Swartz USA, 3. Stephen Beets USA, 4. Aleksandr Lebzyak RUS
81kg 1. Benjamin McDowell USA, 2. Dihosvany Vega CUB, 3. Dmitri Lynyshov BLS, 3. Yusuf Ozturk TUR
91kg 1. Felix Savon CUB, 2. Sergey Mochalov RUS, 3. Samilsan Sinan TUR, 3. Peer Müller GER
+91kg 1. Aleksai Lezin RUS, 2. Lance Whitaker USA, 3. Eric Fuhrmann GER, 3. Edward Mahone USA

CANOEING *Aug 3-4*
Men C1-500m: Knut Holmann NOR; C2-500m: Andrey Kabanov/Pavel Konovalov RUS; C1-1000m: Ivans Klementjevs POL; C2-1000m: Christian Fredericksen/Bob Dokkedal DEN; K1-500m: Aleksandr Kostoglod RUS; K2-500m: Anatoli Tishchenko/Oleg Goroby RUS; K1-1000m: Knut Holmann NOR; K2-1000m: Anatoli Tishchenko/Oleg Goroby RUS

Women K1-500m: Anna Olsson SWE; K2-500m: Irina Vaag/Olga Tishchenko RUS

CYCLING *July 30-31*
Men 125km individual road race: Vyacheslav Dzhavanyan RUS

Women 44km criterium: Brooke Blackwelder USA

DIVING *Aug 2-7*
Men 1m Springboard: Chen Sheng CHN 397.008
3m Springboard: Dmitri Sautin RUS 653.16
10m Platform: Vladimir Timoshinin RUS 599.01

Women 1m Springboard: Chen Lixia CHN 270.36
3m Springboard: Vera Ilyina RUS 524,64
10m Platform: Xiong Min CHN 429.27

FIGURE SKATING *Aug 3-7*
Men Final: Aleksei Urmanov RUS 1.5; Technical: Aleksei Urmanov 0.5; Free Skate: Aleksei Urmanov 1.0
Women Final: Surya Bonaly FRA 2.5; Technical: Surya Bonaly 0.5; Free Skate: Michelle Kwan USA 1.0
Pairs Final: Natalya Mishkutyonok/Artur Dmitriyev RUS 1.5; Technical: Natalya Mishkutyonok/Artur Dmitriyev 0.5; Free Skate: Natalya Mishkutyonok/Artur Dmitriyev 1.0
Ice Dance Final: Irina Romanova/Igor Yaroshenko UKR 1.0; Compulsory Dance: Yelena Grushina/Ruslan Goncharov UKR 0.2; Original Dance: Irina Lobacheva/Ilya Averbukh RUS 0.4

GYMNASTICS *July 24-29*

Men Team: Russia 171.400; All-around: Aleksei Nemov RUS 57.875; Individual Apparatus - Horizontal Bars: Aleksei Voropayev RUS 9.750, Parallel Bars: Yevgeni Shabayev RUS 9.725, Vault: Grigori Misyutin UKR 9.550, Pommel Horse: Aleksei Nemov RUS 9.700, Floor: Aleksei Nemov RUS 9.750, Rings: Dan Burinca ROM 9.800

Women Team: Russia 117.375; All-around: Dina Kochetkova RUS 39.325; Individual Apparatus - Floor: Shannon Miller USA 9.937, Asymmetric Bars: Svetlana Khorkina RUS 9.862, Vault: Lilya Paodkopyeva UKR 9.831, Beam: Shannon Miller USA 9.875

Mixed Ukraine/Belarus 95.712

HANDBALL *July 24-27*
Final (Men) France beat Russia 22-20

JUDO *July 24-26*
MEN
60kg Kim Hyuk KOR beat Yasuo Otoguro JPN
65kg Vladimir Drachko RUS beat Vsevolod Velenity LAT
71kg Chung Hoon KOR beat Thomas Schleicher AUT
78kg Yoon Dong-Sik KOR bt Yasuhiro Nakashima JPN
86kg Tagir Abdulayev RUS bt Fernando Gonzalez ESP
95kg Betlef Knorrek GER beat Leonid Svirid BLS
+95kg Yoshiharu Makishi bt Indrek Pertelson EST

WOMEN
61kg Jung Sung-Sook KOR beat Aneta Arak POL
72kg Ulla Werbrouk BEL beat Kim Mi-Jung KOR

RHYTHMIC GYMNASTICS *Aug 2*
All-around: Amina Zaripova RUS 39 000; Individual Apparatus - Hoop: Amina Zaripova RUS 9.775, Ball: Amina Zaripova RUS 9.800, Ribbon: Yekaterina Serebryanskaya UKR 9.775, Clubs: Yekaterina Serebryanskaya UKR 9.750

ROWING *Aug 6-7*
Men Eights (500m): Russia 1:18.58; Eights (1000m): USA 2:25.96; Single Sculls (500m): Jason Gailes USA 1:39.13; Single Sculls (1000m): Vladimir Sokolov RUS
Women Eights (500m): China 1:29.61; Eights (1000m): Belarus; Single Sculls (500m): Ruth Davidson USA 1:51.79; Single Sculls (1000m): Yekterina Khodotovich BLS

SHORT TRACK SPEEDSKATING *Aug 2*
Men 500m: Maurizio Carnino ITA; 1000m Mark Gagnon CAN
Women 500m: Isabella Charest CAN; 1000m: Marinella Canclini ITA

SWIMMING *July 23-24*
MEN
50m Freestyle: Alexander Popov RUS 22.55
100m Freestyle: Alexander Popov RUS 50.58
200m Freestyle: Dan Kanner USA 1:52.15
100m Breaststroke: Andrei Korneyev RUS 1:03.89
200m Breaststroke: Andrei Ivanov RUS 2:15.81
100m Backstroke: Martin Zubero ESP 56.41
200m Backstroke: Martin Zubero ESP 2:00.60
100m Butterfly: Denis Pankratov RUS 54.39
200m Butterfly: Melvin Stewart USA 1:58.46
4x100m Medley Relay: Russia 3:45.91

WOMEN
50m Freestyle: Angel Martino USA 26.05
100m Freestyle: Angel Martino USA 56.02
200m Freestyle: Claudia Poll CRC 1:59.72
100m Breaststroke: Ren Ying CHN 1:11.18
200m Breaststroke: Ren Ying CHN 2:33.45
100m Backstroke: Bai Yinyn CHN 1:02.19
200m Backstroke: BJ Bedford USA 2:14.24
100m Butterfly: Hong Shu CHN 1:00.76
200m Butterfly: Michelle Griglione USA 2:14.25
4x100m Medley Relay: China 4:13.60

SYNCHRONISED SWIMMING *July 31*
Solo Olga Sedakova RUS 197.200
Duet Becky Dyroen-Lancer/Jill Sudduth USA 197.880

TAEKWONDO *July 27-28*
MEN
64kg Lee Jun Hee KOR beat Clay Barber USA
76kg Kim Kyoung-Hun KOR bt Roman Korotkov RUS
+83kg Kim Joeng-Kyu KOR beat David Fraser GBR

WOMEN
55kg Kelly Thorpe USA beat Kim Mi-Sun KOR
65kg Kim Mi-Young KOR beat Angela Mitchell CAN
+70kg Choo Soo-Yeon KOR beat Natalya Ivanova RUS

TRIATHLON *July 28*
Men Simon Lessing GBR 1:55.32
Women Isabelle Mouthon FRA 2:09.34.8

VOLLEYBALL *Aug 30-July 5*
Men (Beach) Jan Kvalheim/Bjorn Maaseide NOR
Women (Beach) Karolyn Kirby/Liz Masakayen USA
(Indoor) Russia beat USA 3-0

WATER POLO *July 26-30*
Final Russia beat Germany 11-9

WEIGHTLIFTING *July 23*
99kg Snatch: Sergei Syrtsov RUS 191.0 *(WR)*, Clean & Jerk: Syrtsov 227.5 *(WR)*, Overall: Syrtsov 417.5 *(WR)*
108kg Snatch: Vadim Stasenko RUS 182.5, Clean & Jerk: Stasenko 215.0, Overall: Stasenko 397.5
+108kg Snatch: Andrei Chemerkin RUS 201.0 *(WR)*, Clean & Jerk: Chemerkin 250.5 *(WR)*, Overall: Chemerkin 450.0 *(WR)*

WRESTLING   *July 29-31*

FREESTYLE
48kg Vugar Orudzhyyev RUS beat Viktor Yefteni UKR
52kg Zeke Jones USA beat John Ali Khosrownejad IRN
57kg Ismail Zurnaci TUR bt Bagaudin Umakhanov RUS
62kg Magomed Azizov RUS beat Carlos Castillo CUB
68kg Townsend Saunders USA beat Vadim Bogeev RUS
74kg Nasyr Gadzhikhanov RUS bt David Schultz USA
82kg Rasul Katinovasov RUS beat Ibrahim Alkan TUR
90kg Makharbek Khadartsev RUS bt Melvin Douglas USA
100kg David Musulbes RUS beat Mark Kerr USA
130kg Zara Turmanidze GEO beat Andrei Shumilin RUS

YACHTING   *Aug 2-5*

MEN
Finn Craig Monk NZL
Mistral Murray McCaig CAN
WOMEN
Europe Ausling Bowman IRL
Mistral Lisa Neuberger ISV

Water isn't normally a problem at St Petersburg, lying as it does rather close to the Baltic Sea. It was, though, at the Goodwill Games nothing but trouble. First of all nobody wanted to use the swimming pool because the water was so murky. A filtration problem was the cause and the Swedish team withdrew rather than risk the discoloured water. American swimmer, Mel Stewart, reckoned he had to slow down before each turn because he couldn't see the wall early enough - it was that bad. The answer, in fact, was staring them in the face. Or, to be more geographically precise - just round the corner at the Yubileiny Palace where the ice skating was due to take place. It couldn't because the ice wouldn't freeze. The freezing was taking 2-3 hours a layer instead of 20 minutes, which meant the rink would be ready for the next Goodwill Game, but not this one. What more sensible than to switch the swimming there?

Such a remedy would still not have solved the problem of the journalist in the media v Goodwill v St Petersburg race that was held during the Games. They have these sort of events at major championships (usually on the rest day) and the journalists normally wheel out a few ex-Olympic champions that have gone into the business, but are still putting in 100 lengths a day and could stay with Kieren Perkins for the first five lengths. Not on this occasion they didn't. One short for the relay, they asked for volunteers and one duly stepped forward. Nobody thought to ask him if he could swim. Halfway down the pool, spectators started to raise doubts about whether the aforementioned journalist **could** swim. Three-quarters of the way down, the paramedics made their own decision, rescuing the journalist and ferrying him immediately to hospital. We understand the journalist later insisted that he didn't need saving, but by all accounts not since Lassie was a regular on Saturday morning pictures has anyone seen a swimming stroke like it.

Obituary

Jim Aitchison, cricketer   First capped against All-India in 1946, Aitchison was one of Scotland's finest cricketers and his total of 3,669 international runs remains a Scottish record. Aitchison died in February at Glasgow, aged 73.

Rex Alston, broadcaster   Alston commentated on more than 100 Tests for the BBC as well as reporting from four Olympics and covering rugby union and tennis events. After reaching retirement age in 1961, he continued to work as a freelance. In 1985, *The Times* prematurely printed his obituary. Alston complained that it was both early and incomplete. He died in September, aged 93.

Danny Blanchflower, footballer and football writer   Born in Belfast, Blanchflower began his playing career with Glentoran before being signed by Barnsley in 1949. From the Yorkshire club he moved to Aston Villa, then signed for Tottenham in 1954, when the manager Arthur Rowe paid a club record of £30,000 for the elegant wing-half. Blanchflower's career truly blossomed at Spurs and he led the north Londoners to the League and FA Cup double in 1961, with a team that remains the benchmark for quality football. That team added the European Cup Winners' Cup the next season and its captain, Blanchflower, also accumulated 56 Northern Ireland caps. His post-playing career included a brief spell of management with Northern Ireland and an even briefer spell at Chelsea. It was as a journalist that Blanchflower retained his connection with the game he loved, plying his sportwriting trade almost as eloquently as he played the game itself. Throughout his life, Blanchflower cherished his independence,he refused to appear on *This is Your Life*, and was one of the great romantics of the game. He died on December 9th, aged 67.

Sam Burns, boxing promoter and bookmaker   Originally a journalist with *The Sporting Life*, Burns moved into boxing promotion as he found sportswriting "too slow". Burns formed a partnership with Jack Solomons and together they staged most of the big fights of the forties and fifties. Their partnership also embraced a bookmaking business, while on his own account, Burns managed boxers like Terry Downes, Bobby Neill and Chris Finnegan. It was when Downes turned down a fight that the Burns/Solomons partnership foundered. Burns then joined William Hill, before setting up a chain of betting shops with Downes which was later bought by William Hill. As a result, Burns became managing director of the major bookmaking concern from 1972 to 1981. He died on April 25th, aged 74.

Sir Matt Busby, footballer and football manager   Brought up in miners' village of Old Orbiston, near Bellshill, Busby was destined to become a footballer of no mean ability, a manager without peer. For a brief while, Busby earned his living as a miner in the Lanarkshire pits, but while playing for Denny Hibernians was spotted by Manchester City scouts and moved to Maine Road. An attacking wing-half, Busby might have been criticised for his defensive technique, but it did not hamper his progress and he played regularly for both City and Scotland. Busby became manager of Manchester United in February 1945, but did not have to leave Maine Road as the Old Trafford ground was still being rebuilt following war damage and United temporarily moved across the city. Busby's first team included Johnny Carey, Jimmy Delaney, Stan Pearson and Jack Rowley and together they gave the club its first post-war success, lifting the 1948 FA Cup with a 4-2 defeat of Blackpool.That team added the League title in 1952, but it was not to be the most heralded of of United teams. That epithet belonged to the youthful squad that succeeded them. A team which would never realise its potential. Eight of that team - the Busby Babes - died on a freezing day at Munich airport in 1958 along with three officials, eight journalists, two crew and two other passengers. Busby, himself, was on the critical list for several days. That spring, United still reached the FA Cup final but it was to take Busby some years more to find a new magic. Busby's team of the sixties was memorable for its three biggest stars; the wantonly talented George Best, the lissom Denis Law and Bobby Charlton, who remains perhaps the best known British footballer of all time. That team of all talents took the FA Cup once, the League title twice and crowned Busby's career with a European Cup victory in 1968, becoming the first English club to carry off that trophy. Busby retired at the end of that season and the same year collected a knighthood. He remained an integral part of the United set-up, first as a director and then club president and he lived long enough to see another team created in the image of those he managed; to see football played with panache at Old Trafford again. Busby died from a heart attack on Jan 20th, he was 84.

Peter Cranmer, rugby union player and cricketer   Cranmer played in the centre for the England team in the thirties, gaining 16 international caps. He was also a notable cricketer who played 166 matches for Warwickshire from 1934 to 1954. He died on May 29th, aged 79.

John Curry OBE, figure skater   Curry's youthful ambition was to be a dancer, but through his father's insistence that it was no career for a man, he turned his talents to ice skating. The balletic quality remained, however, and as his career progressed, distinguished him from the pack. Curry's finest year was in the season of 1975-76 when he carried all before him. Ironically, in December 1975, he almost lost his British title to Robin Cousins, who was destined to succeed him as Olympic champion. He scraped through that competition, but had no problem with the rest of the season, taking the European and World titles and the Olympic crown at Innsbruck. After his Olympic triumph, Curry turned professional and diversified into dancing and stage-acting. Open about his homosexuality since 1976, Curry was diagnosed HIV positive in 1987 and died, from Aids, on April 15th. He was 44.

Elfed Ellis, football administrator   Ellis, president of the Welsh Football Association, died on January 7th, aged 69.

Jack Finch, footballer   Finch played 295 games for Fulham, scoring 51 times. He died on November 15th 1993, aged 84.

Alastair Gauld, tennis administrator   For 20 years, from 1974 on, Gauld was chief steward of the All England Lawn Tennis Club. He died on July 7th, aged 79.

Geof Gleeson, judo player and coach   Gleeson was the first Briton to win a medal in the European Championships, when he took silver in 1951 and later became the first British National Coach, establishing the coaching scheme in judo that became a model for other sports. He wrote 12 books on judo and was great believer in the holistic approach to sport. Gleeson died on February 4th, aged 67.

Duncan Hamilton, racing driver The highpoint of Hamilton's racing career was his victory in the 1953 Le Mans 24-hour race. The following year they finished second and Hamilton continued to race until 1959 when, saddened by the death of his friend Mike Hawthorn, he decided to retire. Hamilton died on May 13th, aged 74.

Johnny Hancocks, footballer Hancocks, only a small man, had an explosive shot for a right winger and scored 158 times in 343 League games for Wolves. He played in the Cup winning team of 1949 and won a League championship medal five years later. Hancocks was three times capped by England. He died, in February, aged 75.

Dame Marea Hartman, athletics administrator Hartman began her involvement in athletics as a sprinter with Spartan Ladies AC and began her long career as an administrator when she became honorary treasurer of the Women's Amateur Athletic Association in 1950. For the next forty years, the redoubtable Hartman was the pivotal force in British women's athletics. She was the British women's team manager for a 20 year period that coincided with the Olympic successes of Mary Rand, Ann Packer and Mary Peters. At times, she ran the offices of the Association, in Victoria, single-handedly. She was, for many years, chairwoman of the IAAF's Women's Commission and was feted by Japanese administrators who loved her brusque, but warm manner. Hartman, as most people in athletics knew, was never afraid to enjoy herself. She was awarded the MBE in 1967, the CBE in 1978. In the 1994 New Year's list, she became Dame Marea. She died, of cancer, on August 29th, aged 74.

Terry Hibbitt, footballer In 1966, Hibbitt scored with his first kick in his first league match. It was not, though, as a goalscorer that he became best known. Transferred from his first club, Leeds United, to Newcastle for £30,000 in 1971, he combined his deft talents with the thunderous skills of Malcolm Macdonald. Their partnership took Newcastle to the Cup Final in 1974 and Hibbitt to the verge of international honours. The call never came though as Hibbitt moved on to Birmingham, under Sir Alf Ramsay, and back to Newcastle before retiring from the game with a knee injury. He made a brief comeback with Gateshead in 1986, while working as a newsagent in Newcastle. He died of cancer on August 4th, aged 46.

John Hill, football spectator Hill, a dedicated Welsh supporter, lost his life when a distress rocket was fired into the crowd at the end of the World Cup qualifier between Wales and Romania on November 17th, 1993. Hill was 67.

Jim Holton, footballer Born in Strathclyde, centre-half Holton became a cult figure in the Manchester United team of the seventies. "Six foot two, eyes of blue, big Jim Holton's after you" was the chant of the United supporters. He made 15 appearances for Scotland and played for Sunderland and Coventry before ending his career at Sheffield Wednesday after almost 250 League games. He died on October 4th 1993, aged 42

Innes Ireland, racing driver Although he won the Lotus works team its first grand prix victory, in 1961, Ireland's place in the team was soon given to a young Jim Clark and the buccaneering Ireland never quite made it to the top rank of British drivers. Ireland retired from racing in 1966 and in his later years was president of the British Racing Drivers' Club. He died on October 23rd, 1993, aged 63.

David Jermy, racehorse trainer A former amateur jockey, Jermy had held a trainer's licence for 20 years. Jermy died of a cerebral haemorrhage on December 1st 1993, aged 53.

Brian Johnston OBE MC, cricket commentator Johnston's career in broadcasting began with a chance meeting, during the war, with Wynford Vaughan-Thomas and Stewart MacPherson who were reporting on the Allied advance for the BBC. Johnston, who served with distinction enough to be awarded the Military Cross, joined the BBC when the war was over, having previously worked in the family coffee business. He began broadcasting in January 1946 on the programme *In Town Tonight* and in the fifties gained a considerable reputation as the presenter of *Down Your Way*. Johnston hosted that programme 733 times, retiring then so as not to surpass the number hosted by his predecessor, Franklin Engelman. Johnston was also part of the commentary team for state weddings and funerals, but it is as a cricket commentator that he will be best remembered. Johnston spent 24 years with the BBC TV Test team before being asked to make way for someone younger. He immediately settled into an even more comfortable niche on radio with the Test Match Special team. His variety of genial schoolboy humour, his relish of the pun, his verbal gaffes richly embellished the commentary. As David Coleman has been attributed with every athletics gaffe (whether he actually said it or not) so the same happened with Johnston. He may not actually have said, "The batsman's Holding, the bowler's Willey", nor that he was watching, "Afaq to Knight at the Nursery End", but it was the same vein that he richly mined. Johnston died, from a heart attack, on January 5th. He was 81.

Len Julians, footballer Julians played for Leyton Orient, Arsenal, Nottingham Forest and Millwall. A free-scoring centre-forward, he was instrumental in Millwall's rise from the fourth to the second division in the mid-sixties. He died on December 17th 1993, aged 60.

Ridley Lamb, trainer and jockey The pinnacle of Lamb's career came in the 1987 Cheltenham Gold Cup, when he rode The Thinker to victory in a snowstorm. Lamb's first winner came when he was just 15 and he had ridden 547 winners when he retired to become a trainer. He drowned, following a car crash on July 25th, aged 39.

Mark Lees, rowing administrator Lees was the Amateur Rowing Association's international performance director from 1991-92. Last year, the Mark Lees Foundation was established to help international rowers. Lees died, aged 38, on June 14.

Jimmy McAlinden, footballer Capped four times for Northern Ireland, McAlinden was part of the Portsmouth Cup winning team of 1949. He died, aged 75, in December 1993.

Jimmy Meadows, footballer and manager Capped once for England, Meadows' playing career ended when he was injured playing for Manchester City in the 1956 Cup final. He had managerial spells at Stockport, Bolton, Blackpool and Bury. He died in January, aged 63.

Harry Miller, journalist Miller spent most of his career at the *Daily Mirror* where he established himself as one of Britain's most respected sportswriters. His final years were spent at the *Mail on Sunday* as deputy sports editor. He died, 27th December 1993, aged 56.

Rob Mitchell, motorcyclist Mitchell, from Aberdeen, was a former Scottish 600cc Supersport champion. He died after crashing in practice at the Isle of Man on June 2nd.

Mitchell, who was 33, thus became the 163rd rider to have been killed on the course since the first IOM TT was raced in 1907.

Ron Nicholls, cricketer Nicholls, who played 534 times for Gloucester, scored 23,607 runs in his career as an opening batsman. He partnered Martin Young, in 1962, to a first wicket county record stand of 395. Nicholls also played as a goalkeeper for Bristol Rovers, Bristol City and Cardiff City. He died in July, aged 60.

Tom Pearce OBE, cricketer In a 22 year career with Essex, Pearce scored 22 centuries and captained the county. He served as a Test selector in 1949 and 1950 and was also a county-class rugby union footballer. Pearce died on April 10th, aged 88.

Simon Prior, motorcyclist Yoshi Kumagaya and passenger, Prior, crashed during the German Sidecar Grand Prix at Hockenheim on June 12th. Prior died on June 14th, he was 40.

Arthur Rowe, footballer and manager Rowe initially joined Tottenham as an amateur in 1922. He went on to captain the team and played once at centre-half for his country. However, it was as a manager that he flourished, taking over the reins at White Hart Lane in 1949. He lead them out of Division Two the following year and, a season after, took them to the First Division title. Rowe introduced a style of football that became known as "push and run", in which he emphasised the importance of the players making space off the ball. Rowe finished with Spurs in 1955, suffering a nervous breakdown because of the pressures of the job. Rowe went on to manage Crystal Palace for a couple of years in the sixties and scouted for Leyton Orient before he retired. He died in November 1993, aged 85.

Alex Scott, racehorse trainer Scott began his career as an assistant to the Ripon-based trainer Peter Calvert. In 1986, he joined Dick Hern as number two to the then Queen's trainer. Scott set up his own yard in 1989, with the backing of two of the Maktoum brothers, and enjoyed considerable success in a very short time, winning the 1991 Irish Oaks with Possessive Dancer and the Breeders' Cup Sprint with Sheikh Albadou the same year. Scott was shot dead at his Cheveley Estate on September 30. He was 34.

Winnie Shaw, tennis player Shaw dominated the pre-war tennis scene in Scotland, as a singles player and in doubles with Donald MacPhail. The talent ran in the family and her daughter Winnie Wooldridge, who died two years ago from a brain tumour, was also a top player. Shaw died in hospital at Skelmorlie in February, she was 83.

Charlie Smirke, jockey Although he rode four Derby winners in a career that spanned 36 years, Smirke had a turbulent racing history. Apprenticed at 13, he rode his first winner at 15 yet was constantly at odds with both his trainers and the administrators of the sport. In 1928, he was banned when his mount Welcome Gift, an odds-on favourite, refused to start. The stewards not only withdrew his licence, but warned him off, which meant he could not attend any race meeting. Eventually, in 1933, Smirke's licence was restored and within a year he had landed his first Derby on Windsor Lad. Two years later, he won his second Derby on Mahmoud, winning in a time that has yet to be bettered, and in 1952 won on Tulyar. His final Derby victory came in his last season, 1958, when he won on Sir Victor Sassoon's Hard Ridden. He died on December 20th, aged 87.

Anne Smith, middle-distance runner   Anne Rosemary Smith became the first official holder of the world mile record when she ran 4 minutes and 37 seconds on the Polytechnic Harriers ground at Chiswick in June, 1967. Smith, who was coached by Gordon Pirie during part of her career, reached the final of the 800m at the Tokyo Olympics in 1964, finishing eighth behind Ann Packer. When Pirie emigrated to New Zealand, Smith followed him out and ran for her adopted country in the 1970 Commonwealth Games in Edinburgh. She returned to Britain in 1986 and took a post teaching at Queen's College, London. Smith collapsed and died from a cerebral haemorrhage on August 31st, aged 52.

Bradley Stone, boxer   Stone died after his fight for the British super-bantamweight championship against Richie Wenton was stopped in the tenth round at York Hall in Bethnal Green. Stone, from Canning Town, died on April 28th. He was 23.

Patrick Sullivan, journalist   Sullivan was, for 15 years, the bowls writer for *The Guardian* and also edited *World Bowls*. He died on January 7th, aged 61.

Cliff Temple, athletics writer and coach   Although best known as the Sunday Times athletics writer, a post he held for 25 years, Temple had also flirted with comedy writing in his early days. His gentle wit continued to percolate through his journalism and he was generally regarded as one of the finest athletics writers of his generation. Under the shadow of a divorce and threats from a British Athletics official, Andy Norman, Temple committed suicide in January. He was 46.

Roy Trigg, horseman   Trigg rode over 100 winners at point-to-point racing before moving on to produce show horses. He died in August, aged 79.

Arthur Turner, footballer and manager   Turner had a prolific League career, playing over 500 times for Stoke City, Southport and Crewe Alexandra. As a manager, he presided over Oxford United's extraordinary rise from the Southern League to the Second Division, in the early sixties with a team that cost £14,500. He died on January 12th, aged 85.

Roy Vernon, footballer   Vernon was a creative inside-forward who was also a very capable goalscorer. He began his career in 1955 at Blackburn, where he made 131 League appearances, scoring 49 goals. Moving on to Everton, Vernon was instrumental in bringing the League title to Goodison Park after a gap of 35 years. In 176 games for the Merseyside club, Vernon scored 101 goals. His final League club was Stoke City, where he spent three years under the stewardship of Tony Waddington before retiring. Vernon, earned 32 Welsh caps. He died in December 1993, aged 56.

Tony Waddington, football manager   Waddington had been a wing-half at Crewe, but it was when manager of Stoke City that his imagination took flight. He first revived the club with his purchase of the 46 year old Stanley Matthews and throughout his 17 year stay signed players that were no less committed to stylish football. Denis Violett, Sammy McIlroy, George Eastham, Peter Shilton, Gordon Banks and Alan Hudson all joined the Waddington ranks and if Stoke could only count a single League Cup final victory during Waddington's term, the club was none the poorer for it. Waddington resigned in 1977. He died on January 29th, aged 69.

Frances Waghorn, figure skater   Waghorn was runner-up for the British title in 1969 and represented her country at the European Championships in 1968 and the Winter Olympic Games at Grenoble in the same year. She died of cancer on January 5th, aged 43.

Corinna Williams, water-skier   At 18, Williams was already junior British and European champion and, competing against seniors, finished 12th in last year's World Championships. Williams died in December, aged 18.

Steve Wood, jockey   Wood, the stable jockey to David Chapman's Stillington stable, died when his mount, Kalar, stumbled and fell in a flat race at Lingfield on 6th May. Wood, who was 26, was the first flat race jockey to be killed on the racecourse since 1981.

Billy Wright, CBE, footballer   William Ambrose Wright was born in Ironbridge, Staffs and was turned away from Molineux the first time he went for a trial because the manager, Major Buckley, thought he was too small. Wright never was the conventional size for a centre-half, standing barely 5 feet 9 inches, but during his career reached heights that few other international footballers have attained. He finally joined Wolves in 1938 on a £2 a week salary and made his debut for the club in 1939 against Notts County. The war intervened and he did not win his first England cap until 1946, when England met Belgium. Within two years, Wright became captain of the national side and remained so for a record 90 internationals. In all, he won 105 England caps, a record at that time, and surpassed only since by Charlton, Moore and Shilton. Wright was also instrumental in the fortune of Wolves and, in 1949, took them to victory in the FA Cup and, in the fifties, led the team to three league titles. Wright briefly flirted with league management, holding down the Arsenal job from 1962-1966, but admitted that he was "too emotional to be a manager". He moved instead into television and became controller of sport with Central TV before retiring on his 65th birthday. Wright, who married Joy of the Beverley sisters, died of cancer on September 3rd, aged 70.

OVERSEAS

Ray Arcel, USA, boxing trainer   During a career that dated back to the 1920s, Arcel coached numerous champions, including Ezzard Charles, Jim Braddock, Tony Zale, Roberto Duran and Larry Holmes. He died in New York in March, aged 94.

Robert Bobin, France, athlete and administrator   Bobin was his country's top triple jumper during the post-war years. For 15 years, from 1953, he was the technical director of his sport and eventually became president of the French Athletic Federation in 1987. He was elected to the IAAF council in 1991 and was rewarded for his services to his nation's sport with the Legion d'Honneur. He died on February 10th, aged 73.

Julius Boros, USA, golfer   Boros was twice winner of the US Open, in 1952 and 1963 and helped to launch the Seniors' tour in 1980. He died on May 28th, aged 74.

Jean Borotra, France, tennis player   Borotra was the leading member of a quartet of French players, know as the four Musketeers, who kept the Davis Cup in French hands for five years, from 1927-32. Borotra himself revelled in the soubriquet of "The Bounding Basque". He won Wimbledon in 1924 and 1926, the French Open in 1924 and 1931 and in 1928 completed the hattrick of titles - the singles, doubles and mixed doubles - at the Australian Open. Borotra continued to play Davis Cup tennis until he was 48 and at Wimbledon, where he participated in 224 matches, until he was 65. He died in July, aged 95.

Luigi Chinetti, Italy, racing driver Chinetti three times won the Le Mans 24-hour race in his friend Enzo Ferrari's sports cars and was largely responsible for that company's sales success. Chinetti astutely kept the US Ferrari dealership until 1977. He died in Connecticut, in August, aged 93.

Jack Cowie, New Zealand, cricketer Cowie toured England with the 1937 and 1949 New Zealand teams. He died on June 3rd.

Marie Dollinger, Germany, athlete Dollinger was the most versatile of athletes. She finished fourth in the 1936 Olympic 100m in Berlin, but five years earlier had run an unofficial world record of 2:16.8 for 800m - an event that was not deemed acceptable for women in the Olympics until 33 years later. Dollinger died on August 10th, aged 83.

Andrés Escobar, Columbia, footballer Escobar played 55 times for his country as a defender. It was in the penultimate of those matches, against the United States in the World Cup, that Escobar scored the own goal that could well have cost him his life. The loss to the USA eliminated Columbia from the championship and, when Escobar returned to his native country, he was shot dead by assailants outside El Indio restaurant in Medellín. Escobar, who had spent the last four years playing for the Young Boys club in Switzerland, died on July 2nd. He was 26.

Joe French, Australia, rugby union player and administrator French was associated with Australian rugby for sixty years; as a player, coach and administrator. In 1988, he was made president of the Australian Rugby Union. He died of cancer, in December 1993, aged 78

Ivan Fuqua, USA, sprinter Fuqua was a member of the gold medal winning 4 x 400m relay team at the Berlin Olympics in 1932. He died on January 14th, aged 84.

Vitas Gerulaitis, USA, tennis player Geralaitis was one of the most flamboyant players on the tennis circuit. A Lithuanian immigrant's son, he reached number three in the world in 1979 and when he retired had won 27 singles and nine doubles championships. His solitary Gand Slam title came in December 1977 when he won the Australian Open, but he was runner-up in both the American and French Opens and twice reached the semi-final at Wimbledon. In the eighties, Gerulaitis admitted an addiction to cocaine but later overcame the habit and began a new career as a TV commentator. Gerulaitis died on September 18, apparently from carbon monoxide poisoning. He was 40.

Reinaldo Gorno, Argentina, marathon runner Gorno's finest hour came in the 1952 Olympics when he took the silver in the marathon behind Czechoslovakia's Emil Zátopek. He was shot by thieves at the sports complex where he worked and, despite five operations, died from the injuries on April 10th, aged 75.

Lew Hoad, Australia, tennis player Born in Sydney in 1934, Hoad was to become one of the most inspirational post-war tennis champions. The Australian won Wimbledon in successive years, 1956-57, in the latter year overwhelming his compatriot Ashley Cooper 6-2,

6-1, 6-2. In the previous year, Hoad had only been deprived of the grand slam of tennis titles when he lost in the final of the US Open to another Australian, Ken Rosewall. As well as his singles successes, Hoad also won eight doubles titles to make a total of 13 grand slam titles, and was a member of three successful Davis Cup teams before moving on to the Jack Kramer's professional circus. He later said that: "I was only sorry in a way that I had to turn pro - but you cannot eat silver cups, can you?" After the sport became open, Hoad returned, on the verge of retirement, to play at Wimbledon in 1968, 1970 and 1972. When his playing days were over, he established a tennis school in Spain. Hoad contracted leukaemia and died, in Spain on July 3rd, from a heart attack. He was 59.

Bosco Jancovic, Bosnia, footballer Jancovic won five caps for Yugoslavia before a two-year stay at Middlesborough from 1979. He died in October 1993, from cancer, aged 42.

Ulrike Maier, Austria, skier...Maier had been in Austria's World Cup squad since 1985 and her career had been highlighted with Super-G wins in the World Championships in 1989 and 1991. In 1989, she gave birth to a daughter, Melanie, and was the only mother competing on the international skiing circuit. Maier died after crashing beside a timing post on the Kandahar course at Garmisch-Partenkirchen. She was 26.

Antonio Martin, Spain, cyclist Voted most promising rider in the 1993 Tour de France in which he placed 12th, Martin was killed by a lorry on February 11 while racing . He was 23.

Jack Metcalfe, Australia, athlete Metcalfe was an versatile athlete who competed for his country at triple jump, high jump, long jump and javelin. Later in his career, he added another event, when he took up the shot. His finest hour came in 1935, when he broke the world record for the triple jump in Sydney for a leap of 15.78m. He died in January, aged 81.

Ira Murchison, USA, sprinter Only 5ft 2inches tall, Murchison was the shortest ever world record holder for the 100m. He died on March 28th from bone cancer. He was 61.

Simon Robert Naali, Tanzania, marathon runner Simon Robert was the best known of a family of three marathon running brothers. His marathon wins included Stockholm in 1990 and Rouen last year. He was injured after being struck by a vehicle whilst training and died three days later, on August 12th. He was 28.

Luis Ocaña, Spain, cyclist Ocaña led Eddy Merckx in the 1971 Tour de France before crashing when the race was his. Two years later, he came back to win the race, reaching Paris with a lead of more than 15 minutes over his nearest rival, and interrupting the five-year reign of Merckx. Ocaña died in May. He was 49.

Lord Porritt, New Zealand, sprinter The fame of Arthur Porritt was somewhat diminished when the film Chariots of Fire rewrote history and named the third man in the 1924 100m as Watson. It was, in fact, Porritt who took the bronze behind Britain's Harold Abrahams and American Jackson Scholz. Porritt was only sent to the Games at Paris because he was studying at Oxford. He became a surgeon to the royal family and subsequently governer-general of New Zealand and every year at 7pm on July 7th, the time of the Olympic final, he would dine with Abrahams, until the latter died in 1978. Porrit died in January, aged 93.

Puig-Albert, France, rugby league player Puig-Albert played full-back for France in 47 internationals and his tally of 18 goals in 18 kicks, achieved in the 1951 Test series against Australia, has never been bettered. Puig-Albert, whose devotion to smoking earned him the nomenclature of "pipette", died following a long battle against cancer. He was 69.

Roland Ratzenberger, Austria, racing driver Ratzenberger came to Formula One racing relatively late in life. Japanese Touring Car champion in 1990 and 1991, he was 31 years old and practising for only his third F1 Grand Prix when he spun off into a wall and was killed at Imola on April 30th.

Norman Read, New Zealand, walker Read was a surprise winner of the 50km walk at the 1956 Olympics in Melbourne. An Englishman by birth, he emigrated to New Zealand. He died on May 22, aged 62.

Michel Sansen, rally driver Sansen, a Belgian born painter, tried for six years to finish the tortuous Paris-Dakar rally. He died on January 5th in the Mauritanian capital Nouakchott when his ageing BMW motorbike collided with a local car. He was 58.

Herbert Schade, Germany, athlete Third in the 1952 Olympic 5000m, behind Emil Zátopek, Schade died in March, aged 71.

Bert Schoofs, Holland, table tennis player Schoofs was the national champion in 1970 and represented Holland on more than 100 occasions and went on to become the national coach. He died on October 19th, 1993, aged 48.

Ayrton Senna, Brazil, racing driver Senna won the British Formula Ford championship at his first attempt in 1981 and, the following year, dominated the European FF2000 series. In 1983, he won the British Formula Three championship and, with the Toleman team, moved into Formula One in the succeeding season. Senna, a deeply religious man, had a fiercely competitive approach to racing that did not always endear him to his fellow drivers. However, that commitment, allied with a wealth of talent, brought success and in 1985 with the Lotus-Renault team he duly won his first grand prix. There were 40 more to follow and three world titles, and an ongoing feud with Alain Prost. Senna, who had signed a two year contract with the Williams-Renault team, had warned at the beginning of this season that there would be problems with the new specifications that precluded the computer controlled suspension systems and the anti-lock brakes. It was a disturbingly prophetic pronouncement. In practice for the San Marino Grand Prix, Roland Ratzenberger died, the first F1 driver to be killed at a racetrack for 12 years. Barely more than 24 hours later, on lap seven of the actual race, Senna's car slid sideways into a concrete wall at 165mph and the Brazilian died from the injuries he sustained. In Brazil, the country went into mourning, with flags flown at half-mast and official engagements cancelled. An estimated 150,000 people filed past the coffin in São Paulo. Senna died on May 1st and was 34..

Jack Sharkey, USA, boxer Sharkey was heavyweight champion of the world for 12 months in 1932-3, but his most famous bout was a non-title fight against Jack Dempsey in 1927. Starkey dominated the fight, but Dempsey won after two palpably low blows, in the seventh round. Fifty-six years later, in 1983, when told of Dempsey's death, Starkey is purported to have remarked: "I finally beat the son-of-a-bitch, didn't I?". Starkey died in August, aged 91.

Dr George Sheehan, USA, athlete and writer   A miler in his college days, Sheehan took up running again in his forties and, at 50, set an age best of 4:47 for the mile. He became best known for his writing on the philosophy of running. Sheehan died of prostate cancer on November 1. He was 74.

Helen Stephens, USA, athlete   In the 1935 American national championships, Stephens won the shot putt, the 200m, beating the world record, the standing long jump, also breaking the world record, and wrapped up her championships by winning the 50 yard dash, this time only equalling the world record. In the Berlin Olympics, the following year, Stephens comfortably won the 100m and was invited by Hitler to spend a weekend in Berchtesgaden. Stephens declined. When she retired, after only two and a half years of competition, she was undefeated in running events. Stephens died in January, aged 75.

Hugh Tayfield, South Africa, cricketer   Hugh Joseph Tayfield began his cricket as a leg-spinner, but the chnage to off-spin brought him immediate success. He represented Natal when just 17 and duly became his country's leading exponent of spin bowling. In 1957, Tayfield returned his best test figures when he bowled England out and single-handedly won the fourth Test at Johannesburg, returning figures of 9 for 113. Tayfield also recorded figures of 7 for 23 in 8.4 overs in his first series, against Australia in 1949-50 and, in his career, claimed 170 Test wickets at 25.91 runs apiece. His strike rate of 4.6 wickets per Test remains the best of any post-war spinner. Tayfield married five times and died on February 24th, aged 65.

Wesley Leon Thomas, Grenada, cricketer   Thomas, a fast medium bowler and hard hitting batsmen, played for the Windward Islands and as a professional with Blaydon in the Tynedale Senior League, where he hit 11,621 runs, including a top score of 215 not out and took 855 wickets, including a best of 10-27. He died of liver cancer on February 1st, aged 29.

Frantisek Tokar, Slovakia, table tennis player   Tokar won the world men's doubles championships in 1949 with his compatriot Ivan Andreadis and was part of the 'Golden Era' of Czechoslovak table tennis. He became honorary president of the Slovak Table Tennis Association. Tokar died on 26th October, 1993, aged 68.

Vilmos Varju, Hungary, athlete   Twice European shot putt champion outdoors and once indoors, Varju's national record of 20.45m, set in 1971, still stands. Varju died on February 17th, aged 56.

Elsworth Vines, USA, tennis player   Vines won the 1932 Wimbledon title in one of the most one-sided finals ever. He beat Bunny Austin 6-4, 6-2, 6-0, but it was his only victory in tennis' most prestigious championship. He won the US title at Forest Hills in 1931, but switched to the professional ranks in 1933 and, for the next five years, was the world professional champion. When he retired from tennnis in 1940, Vines took up professional golf and played on the PGA tour for the next 15 years, though never winning a tournament. Vines died on March 17th of kidney disease, aged 82.

1995 Calendar

The calendar is arranged by date within sport. We have tried to be as accurate as possible, but all dates are subject to change.

AMERICAN FOOTBALL

Jan 7	AFC & NFC Divisional Playoffs	
Jan 8	AFC & NFC Divisional Playoffs	
Jan 15	AFC & NFC Championship Games	
Jan 29	Super Bowl XXIX	Joe Robbie Stadium, Miami
Feb 5	AFC-NFC Pro Bowl	Honolulu, Hawaii
July 7	Eurobowl Final	Stuttgart, Germany

ANGLING

July 1	National Championships, Division One	Gloucester Canal
July 15	NC, Division Two	Grand Union, Milton Keynes
Aug 12	NC, Ladies	Bridgewater Canal

ARCHERY

Mar 19	British Indoor Championships	NIA, Birmingham
Mar 23-26	World Indoor Championships	NIA, Birmingham
June 10-11	UK Masters Championships	Lilleshall
June 28-30	Grand National Archery Meeting	Lilleshall
Aug 12-13	Outdoor Target Championships	Beacon Park, Lichfield
Dec 16-17	Compound Indoor Championships	NIA, Birmingham

ASSOCIATION FOOTBALL

Jan 7	FA Cup 3rd Round	
Jan 7	Tennents Scottish Cup 2nd Round	
Jan 11	Coca-Cola Cup 5th Round	
Jan 28	FA Cup 4th Round	
Jan 28	Tennents Scottish Cup 3rd Round	
Feb 12	Coca-Cola Cup Semi-final 1st Leg	
Feb 18	FA Cup 5th Round	
Feb 18	Tennents Scottish Cup 4th Round	
Feb 18	FA Cup Round 5	
Feb 22	Coca-Cola Semi-Final 2nd Leg	
Mar 11	Tennents Scottish Cup 5th Round	
Mar 11	FA Cup Round 6	
Apr 2	Coca-Cola Cup Final	Wembley
Apr 8	Tennents Scottish Cup Semi-final	
Apr 8	FA Cup Semi Finals	
Apr 9	FA Cup Semi-Finals	
Apr 23	Football League Trophy Final	Wembley
Apr 30	FA Women's Challenge Cup Final	
May 3	UEFA Cup Final 1st Leg	
May 5	Tennents Scottish Cup Final	
May 10	European Cup Winners' Cup Final	
May 13	FA Challenge Vase Final	Wembley
May 14	FA Challenge Trophy Final	Wembley
May 14	Play-offs Semi Finals First Leg	
May 17	UEFA Cup Final 2nd Leg	
May 17	Play-offs Semi Finals Second Leg	
May 20	FA Cup Final	Wembley
May 24	European Champion Clubs' Cup Final	
May 27	Play-offs Third Division Final	Wembley
May 28	Play-offs Second Division Final	Wembley
May 29	Play-offs First Division Final	Wembley
June 5-18	FIFA Women's World Championships	Sweden

ATHLETICS

Mar 10-12	IAAF World Indoor Championships	Barcelona
Mar 25	World Cross Country Championships	Durham, England
Apr 2	London Marathon	London
Apr 9	IAAF World Marathon Cup	Greece
Apr 17	Boston Marathon	Boston

Apr 23	**Rotterdam Marathon**	Rotterdam
Apr 29-30	**IAAF World Cup of Race Walking**	Beijing, China
May 14	**New York Games Grand Prix I**	New York, USA
May 21	**São Paulo Grand Prix I**	São Paulo, Brazil
May 27	**Bruce Jenner Classic Grand Prix I**	San Jose, USA
May 30	**Comrades Marathon 90km**	Pietermaritzburg to Durban
Jun 7	**Golden Gala Grand Prix I**	Rome, Italy
June 18-19	**European Cup 1st & 2nd leagues**	
June 24-25	**European Cup Super League**	Villeneuve d'Ascq.
July 1-2	**European Cup of Combined Events**	Lage, Germany
July 3	**Meeting BNP Grand Prix I**	Paris, France
July 5	**Athletissima Grand Prix I**	Lausanne, Switzerland
July 7	**BAF Meeting Grand Prix I**	London
July 11	**DN Galan Grand Prix I**	Stockholm, Sweden
July 13	**Nikaïa-Mobil Grand Prix I**	Nice, France
July 15-16	**National Championships and WC Trials**	Birmingham
July 21	**Mobil Bislett Grand Prix I**	Oslo, Norway
July 25	**Gatorade Herculis Grand Prix I**	Monte Carlo, Monaco
July 27-30	**European Junior Championships**	Nyiregyhaza, Hungary
Aug 4-13	**IAAF World Championships**	Gothenburg, Sweden
Aug 16	**Weltklasse Grand Prix I**	Zürich, Switzerland
Aug 20	**Weltklasse Grand Prix I**	Cologne, Germany
Aug 25	**Memorial Ivo Van Damme Grand Prix I**	Brussels, Belgium
Sep 1	**ISTAF '95**	Berlin, Germany
Sep 9	**Grand Prix Final**	Monte Carlo, Monaco
Oct 1	**World Half Marathon Championships**	Belfort, France
Nov 12	**New York Marathon**	New York

BADMINTON

Feb 17-19	**Friends Provident Badminton Grand Slam**	Wimbledon
Mar 14-18	**Yonex All England Championships**	Birmingham, GB
Apr 1-2	**Friends Provident Badminton Grand Slam**	Portsmouth, GB
May 6-7	**Friends Provident Badminton Grand Slam**	Lancaster, GB
May 17-28	**World Championships & Sudirman Cup**	Lausanne, Switzerland
Aug 14-18	**Olympic Test Tournament**	Atlanta, USA
Nov 22-26	**Scottish Open**	
Dec 13-17	**World Grand Prix Finals**	

BASEBALL

Oct	**World Series**	USA

BASKETBALL

Jan 22	**League Trophy Final**	NIA, Birmingham
Mar 5	**National Cup Final**	Sheffield Arena
Mar 8 & 15	**Final of European Cup 'Radivoj Korac'**	
Mar 8 & 15	**Final of European Cup 'Liliana Ronchetti'**	
Mar 14	**Final of European Cup for Men's Clubs**	Istanbul, Turkey
Mar 22-23	**Finals of European Clubs Cup (Women)**	Como, Italy
Apr 11-13	**European Championships for Men's Clubs (Finals)**	Zaragoza, Spain
Apr 9-11	**European Men's Championships**	Paris
Apr 27	**NBA Playoffs start**	
Apr 29-30	**National Championships Final**	Wembley Arena, GB
June 7-18	**European Championship for Women - finals**	Brno, Czech Republic
June 21-July 2	**European Championship for Men - finals**	Athens, Greece
Oct 19-21	**McDonalds Open**	

BILLIARDS

Apr 3-9	**Strachan UK Professional Championship**	
Oct	**World Championships**	

BOBSLEIGH

Jan 16-22	**British Championships**	Igls, Austria
Feb 7 - 19	**World Championships**	Winterberg, Germany

BOWLS

Feb 26	**Churchill World Singles Final (Indoor)**	
Mar 15	**British Isles International Series (I)**	Rushcliffe
Apr 1-9	**Manchester Unity Finals (I)**	Melton & District IBC

July 3-7	British Isles Championships (Outdoor)	Wales
Aug 20-Sep 1	Sanatogen EBA Singles Championship (O)	Worthing
Sep 2	Middleton Cup (O)	Worthing

BOXING
| Apr 12 | ABA Finals | NIA, Birmingham |

CANOEING
June 25	World Cup Slalom	Prague
July 2	World Cup Slalom	Tacen, Slovenia
July 9	World Cup Slalom	Mezzana, Italy
Aug 6	World Cup Slalom	Ocoee, USA
Aug 13	World Cup Slalom	Minden, Canada
Aug 25-Sep 3	World Championships - Slalom	Nottingham
Aug 26-28	World Championships - Wildwater Racing	Bala, N Wales

CRICKET
Jan 1-5	Australia v England 3rd Test	Sydney
Jan 7	England v Zimbabwe B&H World Series	Brisbane
Jan 8	Australia v Australia A B&H WS	Brisbane
Jan 10	Australia v England B&H WS	Melbourne
Jan 12	Australia A v England B&H WS	Sydney
Jan 15	1st Final B&H WS	Sydney
Jan 17	2nd Final B&H WS	Melbourne
Jan 19	3rd Final B&H WS	Melbourne
Jan 21-2	England v Victoria	Bendigo
Jan 26-30	Australia v England 4th Test	Adelaide
Feb 3-7	Australia v England 5th Test	Perth
May 24	England v West Indies 1st One-day	Trent Bridge
May 26	England v West Indies 2nd One-day	The Oval
May 28	England v West Indies 3rd One-day	Lord's
May 30	Benson & Hedges Cup Quarter-finals	
June 8-12	England v West Indies 1st Test	Headingley
June 13	Benson & Hedges Cup Semi-finals	
June 22-26	England v West Indies 2nd Test	Lord's
June 27	Nat West Trophy 1st Round	
July 6-10	England v West Indies 3rd Test	Edgbaston
July 11 or 12	Nat West Trophy 2nd Round	
July 15	Benson & Hedges Cup Final	Lord's
July 27-31	England v West Indies 4th Test	Old Trafford
Aug 1	Nat West Bank Trophy Quarter-finals	
Aug 10-14	England v West Indies 5th Test	Trent Bridge
Aug 15	Nat West Bank Trophy Semi-finals	
Aug 24-28	England v West Indies 6th Test	The Oval
Sept 2	Nat West Trophy Final	Lord's

CURLING
| Apr 8-16 | World Championship | Brandon, Canada |
| Dec 3-9 | European Championship | Grindelwald, Switzerland |

CYCLING
Jan 29	Cyclo-cross World Championship	Eschenbach, Switzerland
Mar 18	Milan-San Remo (World Cup-race 1)	Italy
Apr 2	Tour de Flanders (World Cup-race 2)	Belgium
Apr 9	Paris-Roubaix (World Cup-race 3)	France
Apr 16	Liege-Bastogne-Liege (World Cup-race 4)	Belgium
Apr 22	Amstel Gold (World Cup-race 5)	Holland
May 1	Henninger-Turin (World Cup-race 6)	Germany-Italy
May 13-June 4	Giro d'Italia	Italy
July 1-23	Tour de France	France
Aug 8	Leeds International (World Cup-race 7)	Leeds
Aug 12	San Sebastian Classic (World Cup-race 8)	Spain
Aug 20	Zürich Classic (World Cup-race 9)	Switzerland
Sep 2-2	Vuelta a España	Spain
Sep 18-24	Mountain Bike World Championships	Kirchzarten, Germany
Sep 26-30	World Track Championships	Bogotá, Colombia
Oct 4	World Time Trial Championship	Tunja, Colombia

Oct 7	**World Professional Road Race Champ-men**	Djitama, Colombia
Oct 8	**World Road Race Champs-women and amateur**	Djitama, Colombia
Oct 21	**Tour of Lombardy**	Italy

DARTS

Dec 27-Jan2	**WDC World Championship**	Purfleet
Jan 1-8	**Embassy World Professional Championships**	Lakeside CC, Surrey

EQUESTRIANISM

Mar 23-26	**The Toggi National Championships**	Stoneleigh, Warwickshire
May 4-7	**Badminton Three-day Event**	Badminton
May 10-14	**Royal Windsor Horse Show**	Windsor Park, Berkshire
May 18-21	**Hickstead Nations Cup Meeting**	Hickstead, W Sussex
May 25-28	**Windsor Three-day Event**	Windsor
June 8-11	**Bramham Three-day Event**	Bramham
July 3-6	**The Royal Show**	Stoneleigh, Warwickshire
July 6-9	**Royal International Horse Show**	Hickstead, W Sussex
Aug 12-13	**Gatcombe Park Three-day Event**	Gatcombe Park
Aug 24-27	**Pairs' Driving World Championships**	Poznan, Poland
Aug 25-28	**Blair Castle Three-day Event**	Blair Castle
Aug 25-28	**The Silk Cut Hickstead Derby**	Hickstead, W Sussex
Aug 31-Sep 3	**Burghley Three-day Event**	Burghley
Sep 14-17	**Blenheim Three-day Event**	Blenheim
Sep 21-24	**Osberton Three-day Event**	Osberton
Sep 26-Oct 1	**Horse of the Year Show**	Wembley Arena
Sep 28-Oct 1	**Tweseldown Three-day Event**	Tweseldown
Dec 14-18	**Olympia Horse Show**	The Grand Hall, Olympia, London

FENCING

Jan 28	**British Epee Championships**	
Mar 4-5	**Men's Epee Grade International Competition**	
Mar 18	**British Sabre Championships - MS, WS & Teams**	
Apr 22	**Ipswich Cup - Womens Epee**	Ipswich
May 6	**British Women's Foil Championships**	
May 6	**British Men's Foil Championships**	

GOLF

Mar 23-26	**The Players' Championship (US Tour)**	
Apr 6-9	**US Masters**	Augusta National
June 15-18	**US Open**	Shinacock Hills, Southampton, New York
July 20-23	**Open Golf Championship**	Old Course, St Andrews, Scotland
Aug 10-13	**US PGA Championship**	Riviera CC, Pacific Palisades, Ca.
Sep 22-24	**Ryder Cup**	Oakhill Golf Club, Rochester, New York
Nov 9-12	**World Cup**	

GREYHOUND RACING

June 24	**Greyhound Derby Final**	Wimbledon

GYMNASTICS

June 16-18	**European Cup Final**	Rome, Italy
June 24-25	**European Rhythmic Cup Final**	Telford, Staffs
July 6-9	**11th European Rhythmic Championship**	Prague, Czech Republic
Sep 19-24	**XIXth World Championships**	Vienna, Austria
Oct 1-10	**XXXI World Championships combination**	Sabae, Japan
Nov 14-18	**Pre Olympics**	Atlanta, USA
Dec 1-3	**European Championships Team Final**	Charleroi, Belgium

HANDBALL

Apr 15-16	**English Open Championship (women)**	
May 6	**British Cup Final**	
May 21-22	**English Open Championship (men)**	
Apr 13-17	**European Cup Winners' Cup**	

HOCKEY

Feb 17-19	**European Indoor Club Championships**	Crystal Palace
Apr 30	**HA Cup/Trophy Finals Day**	Milton Keynes
May 20-21	**County Championships Finals**	
June 2-5	**European Club Championships**	

HORSE RACING

Mar 14	Smurfit Champion Hurdle	Cheltenham
Mar 16	Tote Cheltenham Gold Cup	Cheltenham
Apr 8	Martell Grand National	Aintree
Apr 29	Whitbread Gold Cup	Sandown
May 6	Madagans 2000 Guineas	Newmarket
May 7	Madagans 1000 Guineas	Newmarket
June 9	The Vodafone Oaks	Epsom
June 10	The Vodafone Derby	Epsom
June 20-23	Royal Ascot Meeting	
July 8	Coral-Eclipse Stakes	Sandown Park
July 22	King George VI and Queen Elizabeth Stakes	Ascot
July 25-29	Goodwood Meeting	
Aug 15-17	York Meeting	
Sep 9	Teleconnection St Leger Stakes	Doncaster
Sep 24	Queen Elizabeth II Stakes	Ascot
Oct 14	Dubai Champion Stakes	Newmarket
Nov 11	Mackeson Gold Cup	Cheltenham
Nov 25	Hennessey Cognac Gold Cup	Newbury
Dec 26	King George VI Tripleprint	Kempton

ICE HOCKEY

Jan 28	Centenary International: England v Scotland	
Mar 30-Apr 9	Premier/1st Division Play-offs	
Apr 9-23	World Championships (Pool B)	Bratislava, Slovakia
Apr 12	Stanley Cup starts	USA
Apr 16	Wembley Championships Final	Wembley Arena, London

ICE SKATING

Jan 30-Feb 5	European Figure Skating Championships	Dortmund, Germany
Mar 7-12	World Figure Championship	Birmingham, Great Britain

JUDO

Apr 8	British Open Championships	National Indoor Arena, Birmingham
May 11-14	European Senior Championships	National Indoor Arena, Birmingham
Sep 28-Oct 1	World Championships	Makuari, Japan
Oct 21-22	European Team Championships	Bratislava, Slovakia

KARATE

Mar 11-12	English Championships	Crystal Palace
May 5-7	EKU Senior Championships	Helsinki, Finland

KORFBALL

Jan 7-8	European Korfball Championship (indoor)	Debreen, Hungary
Nov 5-12	World Championship	New Delhi, India

LACROSSE

Apr 1	Wales v England, Women	
Apr 8	Scotland v Wales, Women	
Apr 23	England v Scotland, Women	

MODERN PENTATHLON

May 22-28	European Championship (Men)	Rome, Italy
June 15-18	European Championship (Women)	Berlin, Germany
July 25-30	World Championships (Men & Women)	Basle, Switzerland
Aug 11-12	World Cup Final (Men & Women)	Atlanta, USA

MOTOR CYCLING

Mar 26	Australian Grand Prix	Eastern Creek, Queensland, Australia
Apr 2	Malaysian GP	Shah Alam
Apr 23	Japanese GP	Suzuka
May 7	Spanish GP	Jerez
May 21	German GP	Nurburgring
May 28	GB Superbike Round	Donington
May 29-June 9	Isle of Man TT races	
June 11	Italian GP	Mugello
June 24	Dutch GP	Assen
July 9	French GP	Le Mans

July 23	**British GP**	Donington
Aug 6	**American GP**	
Aug 6	**GB Superbike Round**	Brands Hatch
Aug 20	**Czech Republic GP**	Brno
Sep 17	**Argentinian GP**	Buenos Aires
Sep 24	**Brazilian GP**	Rio de Janeiro
Oct 8	**European GP**	Catalunya, Spain

MOTOR RACING
No Grand Prix dates available at time of going to press

Jan 21-27	**Monte Carlo Rally**	
Feb 9-12	**Swedish Rally (World Championship event)**	
Mar 5	**Indy Car World Series**	Miami, USA
Mar 6-11	**Portuguese Rally (WC)**	
Mar 19	**Indy Car World Series**	Surfers' Paradise, Australia
Apr 2	**Indy Car World Series**	Phoenix, USA
Apr 9	**Indy Car World Series**	Long Beach, USA
Apr 23	**Indy Car World Series**	Nazareth, Pa., USA
May 2-6	**Corsican Rally (WC)**	
May 28	**Indy Car World Series**	Indianapolis, USA
June 4	**Indy Car World Series**	Milwaukee, USA
June 11	**Indy Car World Series**	Detroit, USA
June 25	**Indy Car World Series**	Portland, USA
July 9	**Indy Car World Series**	Road America, USA
July 16	**British Grand Prix**	Silverstone
July 16	**Indy Car World Series**	Toronto, Canada
July 23	**Indy Car World Series**	Cleveland, USA
July 27-30	**New Zealand Rally (WC)**	
July 30	**Indy Car World Series**	Michigan, USA
Aug 13	**Indy Car World Series**	Mid-Ohio, USA
Aug 20	**Indy Car World Series**	New Hampshire, USA
Sept 3	**Indy Car World Series**	Vancouver, Canada
Sept 10	**Indy Car World Series**	Laguna Seca, USA
Sep 15-18	**Australian Rally (WC)**	
Oct 22-25	**Catalunyan Rally (WC)**	Spain
Nov 19-22	**RAC Rally (WC)**	UK

MULTI-SPORTS EVENTS

July 9-14	**European Youth Olympic Days**	Bath
Aug	**Pan-American Games**	Argentina
Aug 23-Sept 3	**Universiade (World Student Games)**	Fukuoka, Japan

NETBALL

Apr 8-9	**Inter County Championship**	
Apr 23	**National Clubs finals**	
July 15-29	**World Championship**	Birmingham

ORIENTEERING

Feb 25	**British Night Championships**	Blackwood, Basingstoke, England
Mar 18-19	**British Orienteering Championships**	North Wales

RACKETBALL

Mar 24-26	**National Singles Championships**	Bromley, England
Nov 24-26	**National Doubles Championships**	Bromsgrove, England

REAL TENNIS/RACKETS

May 1-7	**Professional Singles Championship - Real Tennis**	Holyport
May 6	**Queen's Club Cup - Rackets**	Queen's

ROWING

Mar 25	**Head of the River**	Mortlake to Putney, River Thames
Apr 1	**The Boat Race**	Putney to Mortlake, River Thames
June 17-18	**French International Regatta**	Paris
June 28-July 2	**Henley Regatta**	Henley, River Thames
July 7-9	**Lucerne Regatta**	Lucerne, Switzerland
July 13-16	**National Championships**	Holme Pierrepont, Nottingham
Aug 20-27	**World Championships**	Tampere, Finland

RUGBY LEAGUE

Jan 28	Regal Trophy Final	
Feb 1	Wales v England	
Feb 15	England v France	
Mar 4	France v Great Britain	
Mar 4	France v Wales	
Apr 29	Silk Cut Challenge Cup	Wembley
May 21	Stones Bitter Premiership	Old Trafford
Oct 7-28	World Cup	England & Wales (final at Wembley)

RUGBY UNION

Jan 21	Five Nations: France v Wales	Parc des Princes, Paris
Jan 21	Five Nations: Ireland v England	Landsdowne Road, Dublin
Jan 21	Scotland v Canada	Murrayfield, Edinburgh
Feb 4	Five Nations: Scotland v Ireland	Murrayfield, Edinburgh
Feb 4	Five Nations: England v France	Twickenham, Middlesex
Feb 18	Five Nations: Wales v England	The National Stadium, Cardiff
Feb 18	Five Nations: France v Scotland	Parc des Princes, Paris
Feb 19	England A v Italy	Gloucester
Mar 4	Five Nations: Ireland v France	Lansdowne Road, Dublin
Mar 4	Five Nations: Scotland v Wales	Murrayfield, Edinburgh
Mar 18	Five Nations: England v Scotland	Twickenham, Middlesex
Mar 18	Five Nations: Wales v Ireland	The National Stadium, Cardiff
Apr 22	CIS Insurance County Championship Final	Twickenham, Middlesex
May 6	The Pilkington Cup Final	Twickenham, Middlesex
May 6	SWALEC Cup Final	Cardiff
May 13	The Save & Prosper Middlesex Seven-a-side Finals	Twickenham, Middlesex
May 25-24 June	World Cup	South Africa (final in Johannesburg)

SKIING

Apr 2-7	British Junior Championships	Tignes, France
Jan 7-8	Garmisch-Partenkirchen Alpine World Cup	Germany
Jan 14-15	Kitzbühel Alpine World Cup	Austria
Jan 30-Feb 12	World Championships	Sierra Nevada, Spain
Mar 15-19	Alpine World Cup Final	Bormio, Italy
Mar 25-26	Nordic Combination World Cup final	Sapporo, Japan
	Cross-country World Cup final event	
Mar 26	Ski Jumping World Cup final event	Oberstdorf, Germany
Mar 26-Apr 1	British Senior Championships	Tignes, France

SNOOKER

Jan 22-29	Regal Welsh	Newport Centre
Feb 5-12	Benson & Hedges Masters	Wembley Conference Centre
Feb 13-19	International Open	Bournemouth International Centre
Mar 10-18	Kloster Thailand Open	Bangkok
Mar 21-26	Benson & Hedges Irish Masters	Goffs Complex, County Kildare
Apr 1-9	British Open	Plymouth Pavilions
Apr 14-30	Embassy World Championship	Crucible Theatre, Sheffield
May 2-5	World Ladies Snooker Championship	

SPEED SKATING

Jan 6-8	European Long Track Championships	Heerenveen, Netherlands
Feb 11-12	World Long Track Championships - Men	Baselga di Pine, Italy
Mar 4-5	World Long Track Championships - Women	Savalen, Norway
Mar 17-19	World Short Track Championships	Hamar, Norway

SQUASH

Jan 12-17	National Championships	
Apr 1-10	British Open Championships	
Apr 27-30	European Team Championships	Netherlands
June 25-July 2	World Open - Women	Hong Kong
Nov 6-12	World Open - Men	Limassol, Cyprus
Nov 13-19	World Team Championships - Men	Cairo, Egypt

SWIMMING & DIVING

Jan 13-15	British Grand Prix	Gloucester
Feb 10-11	FINA World Cup	Sheffield
Feb 24-26	British Grand Prix	Leeds

Mar 24-26	British Grand Prix	Crystal Palace
Apr 14-16	European Diving Cup	Strasbourg, France
Apr 15-16	Eight Nations	Edinburgh
May 27-29	British Grand Prix	Cardiff
June 21-23	Scottish Open Championships	Edinburgh
July 20-24	ASA Long Course Championships	Coventry
July 29-30	Five Nations Meeting	Germany
Aug 3-5	FINA Synchronised Swimming World Cup	Atlanta, USA
Aug 17-27	European Swimming Championships	Vienna, Austria
Sep 12-17	FINA Diving World Cup	Atlanta, USA
Nov 17-19	British Grand Prix	Leicester
Nov 30-Dec 4	FINA Short Course Championships	Rio de Janeiro, Brazil
Dec 14-17	ASA Short Course Championships	Leicester

TABLE TENNIS

Jan 5-8	English Open	Thornaby Pavilion, Stockton-on-Tees
Jan 13-15	European Nations Cup	Germany
Jan 21-22	European Women's Team Cup	Germany
Feb 3-5	Europe Top 12	Dijon, France
May 1-14	World Championships	Tianjin, China
Aug 10-13	World Team Cup	Atlanta, USA

TENNIS

Jan 16-29	Australian Open	Melbourne
Apr 28-30	Davis Cup, Euro-African II, round 1 (GB)	
May 19-June 11	French Open	Paris
June 5-10	Stella Artois Championships	Queens Club, London
June 19-24	Direct Line Men's Championships	Manchester
June 19-24	Direct Line Women's Championships	Eastbourne
June 26-July 9	Wimbledon Championships	Wimbledon
Aug 8-Sep 10	US Open	New York
Oct 17-22	Women's Tour Event	Brighton
Nov 25-26	Federation Cup final	
Dec 1-3	Davis Cup final	

TENPIN BOWLING

Mar 11-26	BTBA National Championships	Superbowl 2000, Rotterdam
July 9-16	World Championships	Reno, USA
Nov 15-17	British Open	AMF Bowl, Nottingham

VOLLEYBALL

Apr 9	EVA Cup	

WATER POLO

Sep 12-17	FINA Water Polo World Cup	Atlanta

YACHTING

Jan 7-15	Finn Gold Cup	Melbourne, Australia
Jan 27-Feb 4	Europe World Championship	North Shore City, New Zealand
Feb 1-5	Miami Olympic Classes Regatta	Miami, USA
Mar 10-12	Spring OCR	Savannah, USA
Mar 27-Apr 1	Anzio OCR	Italy
Apr 9-21	Citizen Cup/Louis Vuiton Cup	San Diego, USA
Apr 22-29	Semaine Olympique Français	Hyères, France
May 6-May 13	Americas Cup	San Diego, USA
May 22-28	Spa OCR	Belgium
June 5-14	Laser World Championship	Tenerife, Canary Islands
June 14-17	Eurolympics	Hayling Island
June 21-25	Kiel Regatta	Germany
July 29-Aug 6	Pre-Olympics	Savannah, USA
Aug 11-18	Soling and Tornado World Championships	Kingston, Canada
Aug 13-19	470 World Championship	Toronto, Canada
Aug 29-Sep 9	British Olympic Trials	Weymouth
Sep 6-17	Star World Championship	Laredo, Spain
Sep 29-Oct 8	Imco World Championship	Port Elizabeth, South Africa

Sports Federations

AMERICAN FOOTBALL
British American Football
Association
22A Market Place, Still Lane,
Boston, Lincs PE21 6EH
Tel: 0205 363522
Fax: 0205 358139

ANGLING
National Federation of Anglers
Halliday House, Egginton Junction,
Nr Hilton, Derbyshire DE1 1PG
Tel: 0283 734735
Fax: 0283 734799

ARCHERY
Grand National Archery Society
National Agricultural Centre
Seventh Street, Stoneleigh Park
Kenilworth, Warwickshire CV8 2LG
Tel: 0203 696631
Fax: 0203 419662

ASSOCIATION FOOTBALL
The Football Association
16 Lancaster Gate, London W2 3LW
Tel: 071 262 4542
Fax: 071 402 0486

The Football League Ltd
319 Clifton Drive South
Lytham St Annes, Lancs FY8 1 JG
Tel: 0253 729421
Fax: 0253 724786

Football Association of Wales
3 Westgate Street, Cardiff CF1 1DD
Tel: 0222 372325
Fax: 0222 343961

Scottish Football Association
6 Park Gardens, Glasgow G3 7YF
Tel: 041 332 6372
Fax: 041 332 7559

Womens Football Association
9 Wyllyotts Place
Potters Bar, Herts EN6 2JD
Tel: 0707 651840
Fax: 0707 644190

ATHLETICS
British Athletic Federation
Edgbaston House
3 Duchess Place, Hagley Road
Edgbaston, Birmingham B16 8NM
Tel: 021 440 5000
Fax: 021 440 0555

BADMINTON
Badminton Association of England
National Badminton Centre
Bradwell Road, Loughton Lodge
Milton Keynes MK8 9LA
Tel: 0908 568822
Fax: 0908 566922

BALLOONING
British Ballon and Airship Club
Forde Abbey Farm House
Chard, Somerset TA20 4LP
Tel: 021 6434050 or 0460 20880

BASEBALL
British Baseball Federation
66 Belvedere Road,
Hessle, North Humberside
Tel: 0482 643551
Fax: 0482 643551

BASKETBALL
English Basketball Association
48 Bradford Road, Stanningley
Pudsey, W.Yorkshire LS28 6DF
Tel: 0532 361166
Fax: 0532 361022

BILLIARDS AND SNOOKER
World Ladies Billiards and Snooker
Association
3 Felsted Avenue, Wisbech
Cambs PE13 3SL
Tel: 0945 589589
Fax: 0945 589589

World Professional Billiards and
Snooker Association
27 Oakfield Road
Clifton, Bristol BS8 2AT
Tel: 0272 744491
Fax: 0272 744931

BOBSLEIGH
British Bobsleigh Association
Springfield House, Woodstock
Road
Coulsdon, Surrey CR5 3HS
Tel: 0737 555152
Fax: 0737 556832

BOWLS
English Bowling Association
Lyndhurst Road
Worthing, W.Sussex BN11 2AZ
Tel: 0903 820222
Fax: 0903 820444

BOXING
Amateur Boxing Association
Crystal Palace National Sports
Centre
London SE19 2BB
Tel: 071 778 0935

British Boxing Board of Control
Jack Petersen House
52A Borough High Street, London
SE1 1XW
Tel: 071 403 5879
Fax: 071 378 6670

CANOEING
British Canoe Union
John Dudderidge House
Adbolton Lane, West Bridgford
Nottingham NG2 5AS
Tel: 0602 821100
Fax: 0602 821797

CRICKET
Test and County Cricket Board
Lord's Cricket Ground
London NW8 8QN
Tel: 071 286 4405

Womens Cricket Association
41 St Michaels Lane
Headingley, Leeds LS6 3BR
Tel: 0532 742398

CROQUET
The Croquet Association
Hurlingham Club
Ranelagh Gardens
London SW6 3PR
Tel: 071 736 3148
Fax: 071 736 3148

CURLING
English Curling Association
66 Preston Old Road
Freckleston, Preston PR4 1PD
Tel: 0772 634154

CYCLING
British Cycling Federation
36 Rockingham Road
Kettering, Northants NN16 8HG
Tel: 0536 412211
Fax: 0536 412142

DARTS
British Darts Organisation
2 Pages Lane
Muswell Hill, London N10 1PS
Tel: 081 883 5544
Fax: 081 883 0109

EQUESTRIAN
British Equestrian Federation
British Equestrian Centre
Stoneleigh Park, Kenilworth
Warwickshire CV8 2LR
Terl: 0203 696697
Fax: 0203 696484

FENCING
Amateur Fencing Association
1 Barons Gate, 33-35 Rothschild Rd
London W4 5HT
Tel: 081 742 3032
Fax: 081 742 3033

GLIDING
British Gliding Association
Kimberley House
47 Vaughan Way, Leicester LE1 4SE
Tel: 0533 531051
Fax: 0533 515939

GOLF
Professional Golfers' Association
The Belfry, Wishaw
Sutton Coldfield, W Mids B76 9PT
Tel: 0675 470333

Womens Professional Golfers'
European Tour
The Tytherington Club
Dorchester Way, Tytherington
Macclesfield, Cheshire SK10 2JP
Tel: 0625 611444

GREYHOUND RACING
National Greyhound Racing Club
24-28 Oval Road
London NW1 7DA
Tel: 071 267 9256
Fax: 071 482 1023

GYMNASTICS
British Amateur Gymnastics Assoc
Registered Office, Ford Hall
Lilleshall National Sports Centre
Newport, Salop TF10 9NB
Tel: 0952 820330
Fax: 0952 820326

HANDBALL
British Handball Association
60 Church Street
Radcliffe, Manchester M26 8SQ
Tel: 061 7249656
Fax: 061 7249656

HANG GLIDING
British Hang Gliding and
Paragliding Association
The Old School Room
Loughborough Road
Leicester LE4 5PJ
Tel. 0533 611322
Fax: 0533 611323

HOCKEY
All England Womens Hockey
Association
51 High Street
Shrewsbury SY1 1ST
Tel: 0743 233572
Fax: 0743 233583

The Hockey Association
Norfolk House
102 Saxon Gate West
Milton Keynes MK9 2EP
Tel: 0908 241100
Fax: 0908 241106

**BRITISH HORSERACING
BOARD**
42 Portman Square
London W1H 0EN
Tel: 071 396 0011
Fax: 071 935 3626

ICE HOCKEY
British Ice Hockey Association
Second Floor Suite
517 Christchurch Road
Boscombe
Bournemouth BH1 4AG
Tel: 0202 303946
Fax: 0202 398005

JUDO
British Judo Association
7A Rutland Street
Leicester LE1 1RB
Tel: 0533 559669

LACROSSE
All England Womens Lacrosse Ass
4 Western Court
Bromley Street, Digbeth
Birmingham B9 4AN
Tel: 021 773 4422
Fax: 021 753 0042

English Lacrosse Union
Winton House, Winton Road
Bowdon, Altrincham
Cheshire WA14 2PB
Tel: 061 928 9600

LAWN TENNIS
All England Lawn Tennis &
Croquet Club
Church Road
Wimbledon, London SW19 5AE
Tel: 081 944 1066
Fax: 081 947 8752

Lawn Tennis Association
The Queens Club
Barons Court, West Kensington
London W14 9EG
Tel: 071 381 7000
Fax: 071 381 5965

MARTIAL ARTS
British Kendo Association
172 Watling Street,
Bridgtown, Cannock
Staffs WS11 3BD
Tel: 0543 466334
Fax: 0543 505882

British Taekwondo Council
Eastney
58 Wiltshire Lane, Pinner
Middx HA5 2LU
Tel: 081 429 0878
Fax: 081 866 4151

English Karate Governing Body
12 Princes Avenue
Woodford Green, Essex IG8 0LN
Tel: 081 599 0711

MODERN PENTATHLON
Modern Pentathlon Association of
Great Britain
8 The Commons
Shaftesbury, Dorset SP7 8JU
Tel: 0747 855833
Fax: 0747 855593

MOTOR CYCLING
Auto-Cycle Union, ACU House
Wood Street, Rugby
Warwickshire CV21 2YX
Tel: 0788 540519
Fax: 0788 573585

MOTOR SPORTS
British Automobile Racing Club
Thruxton Racing Circuit
Thruxton, Andover
Hants SP11 8PN
Tel: 0264 772607
Fax: 0264 773794

RAC Motor Sports Association Ltd
Motor Sports House
Riverside Park, Colnbrook
Slough SL3 0HG
Tel: 0753 681736
Fax: 0753 682938

NETBALL
All England Netball Association
Netball House
9 Paynes Park
Hitchen, Herts SG5 1EH
Tel: 0462 442344
Fax: 0462 442343

ORIENTEERING
British Orienteering Federation
Riversdale, Dale Road North
Darley Dale, Matlock
Derbyshire DE4 2HX
Tel: 0629 734042
Fax: 0629 733769

POLO
Hurlingham Polo Association
Winterlake, Kirtlington
Oxford OX5 3HG
Tel: 0869 350044
Fax: 0869 350625

POOL
English Pool Association
44 Jones House
Penkridge Street, Walsall WS2 8JX
Tel: 0922 35587

RACKETS
Tennis and Rackets Association
c/o The Queens Club
Palliser Road, West Kensington
London W14 9EQ
Tel: 071 386 3448

ROWING
Amateur Rowing Association
The Priory, 6 Lower Mall
Hammersmith, London W6 9DJ
Tel: 081 741 5314
Fax: 081 741 4658

RUGBY LEAGUE
The Rugby Football League
180 Chapeltown Road, Leeds LS7
4HT
Tel: 0532 624637
Fax: 0532 623386

RUGBY UNION
The Rugby Football Union
Rugby Road
Twickenham, Middx TW1 1DZ
Tel: 081 892 8161
Fax: 081 892 9816

Irish Rugby Football Union
62 Lansdowne Road
Ballsbridge, Dublin
Tel: 010 3531 668 4601

Scottish Rugby Union
7/9 Roseburn Street
Edinburgh EH12 5PJ
Tel: 031 3372346

Welsh Rugby Union
PO Box 22, Cardiff CF1 1JL
Tel: 0222 390111

Womens Rugby Football Union
Meadow House, Springfield Farm
Shipston-on-Stour
Warwickshire CV36 4HQ
Tel: 0703 453371 Ext. 4348

SHOOTING
National Rifle Association
Bisley Camp, Brookwood
Woking, Surrey GU24 0PB
Tel: 0483 797777
Fax: 0483 797285

SKATING
National Ice Skating Association of
UK Ltd
15-27 Gee Street, London EC1V 3RE
Tel: 071 2533824
Fax: 071 4902589

SKIING
British Ski Federation
258 Main Street
East Calder, Livingston
West Lothian EH53 0EE
Tel: 0506 884343
Fax: 0506 882952

SPEEDWAY
Speedway Control Board Ltd
ACU Headquarters, Wood Street
Rugby, Warwickshire CV21 2YX
Tel: 0788 540096

SQUASH
Squash Rackets Association
PO Box 1106
London W3 0TD
Tel: 081 746 1616
Fax: 081 746 0580

SWIMMING
Amateur Swimming Association
Harold Fern House, Derby Square
Loughborough, Leics LE11 0AL
Tel: 0509 230431
Fax: 0509 610720

TABLE TENNIS
English Table Tennis Association
Queensbury House, Havelock Road
Hastings, E.Sussex TN34 1HF
Tel: 0424 722525
Fax: 0424 422103

TENPIN BOWLING
British Tenpin Bowling Association
114 Balfour Road
Ilford, Essex IG1 4JD
Tel: 081 478 1745
Fax: 081 514 3665

TRAMPOLINING
British Trampoline Federation Ltd
146 College Road
Harrow, Middx HA1 1BH
Tel: 081 863 7278
Fax: 081 861 2591

TRIATHLON
British Triathlon Association
Dover Leisure Centre, Townhall
Street
Dover, Kent CT16 1LN
Tel: 0304 202565

TUG-OF-WAR
Tug-of-War Association
57 Lynton Road
Chesham, Bucks HP5 2BT
Tel: 0494 783057

VOLLEYBALL
British Volleyball Federation
27 South Road, West Bridgford
Nottingham NG2 7AG
Tel: 0602 816324
Fax: 0602 455429

WATER SKIING
British Water Ski Federation
390 City Road, London, EC1V 2QA
Tel: 071 833 2855
Fax: 071 837 5879

WEIGHTLIFTING
British Amateur Weight Lifters
Association
3 Iffley Turn
Oxford OX4 4DU
Tel: 0865 778319
Fax: 0865 249281

WRESTLING
British Amateur Wrestling
Association
41 Great Clowes Street, Salford
Greater Manchester M7 9RQ
Tel: 061 832 9209
Fax: 061 833 1120

YACHTING
Royal Yachting Association
RYA House, Romsey Road
Eastleigh, Hants SO5 4YA
Tel: 0703 629962
Fax: 0703 629924